LATIN
AMERICAN
WRITERS

LATIN AMERICAN WRITERS

Carlos A. Solé

EDITOR IN CHIEF

Maria Isabel Abreu

ASSOCIATE EDITOR

VOLUME III

CHARLES SCRIBNER'S SONS • NEW YORK

Charles Scribner's Sons
MACMILLAN PUBLISHING COMPANY
866 Third Avenue, New York, N.Y. 10022

Collier Macmillan Canada, Inc.

Library of Congress Catalog Card Number: 88–35481

PRINTED IN THE UNITED STATES OF AMERICA

printing number
3 4 5 6 7 8 9 10

Library of Congress Cataloging-in-Publication Data

Latin American writers / Carlos A. Solé, editor in chief,
Maria Isabel Abreu, associate editor.
p.   cm.
Includes bibliographies and index.
ISBN 0-684-18463-X (Set)
ISBN 0-684-18597-0 (Volume I)
ISBN 0-684-18598-9 (Volume II)
ISBN 0-684-18599-7 (Volume III)
1. Latin American literature—History and criticism. 2. Authors,
Latin American—Biography. I. Solé, Carlos A.   II. Abreu, Maria
Isabel.
PQ7081.A1L37   1989
860'.9'98—dc19
[B]   88-35481
                                                CIP

The paper in this book meets the guidelines for permanence and
durability of the Committee on Production Guidelines for Book Longevity
of the Council on Library Resources.

Acknowledgment is gratefully made to those publishers and individuals who permitted the use of the following materials in copyright.

"Pablo Neruda"

Excerpts from *Extravagaria* by Pablo Neruda. Copyright © 1958 by Editorial Losada, S.A. Translated by George D. Schade. Reproduced by arrangement with Farrar, Straus and Giroux, Inc. Excerpt from *Extravagaria* by Pablo Neruda. Translation copyright © 1974 by Alastair Reid. Reproduced by arrangement with Farrar, Straus and Giruoux, Inc. Excerpts from *The Heights of Macchu Picchu* by Pablo Neruda. Copyright © 1947 by Pablo Neruda. Translated by George D. Schade. Reproduced by arrangement with Farrar, Straus and Giroux, Inc. Excerpts from *Memoirs* by Pablo Neruda. Copyright © 1974 by The Estate of Pablo Neruda. Translated by George D. Schade. Reproduced by arrangement with Farrar, Straus and Giroux, Inc.

CONTENTS

VOLUME III

LATIN
AMERICAN
WRITERS

Xavier Villaurrutia

(1903–1950)

Merlin H. Forster

Xavier Villaurrutia y González was born 27 March 1903 in Mexico City, and with the exception of the 1935–1936 academic year, which he spent in the United States as a fellow of the Rockefeller Foundation, he lived, wrote, and died (on 25 December 1950) in that city. During the 1920's and 1930's he was part of the group of close friends now known as the Contemporáneos, and by the time of his death in 1950 he was widely regarded as one of Mexico's leading artistic and intellectual figures.

Villaurrutia's public life was active and varied. He took a prominent part in the theatrical world of Mexico City, taught classes at the National University, lectured frequently in the capital and in provincial cities, and was an important figure in the publication of literary journals and a regular participant in *tertulias* (literary roundtables). On the other hand, his private life was, as one friend has called it, a shadowy region of contradictory dimensions. A person of strong but well-controlled emotions, Villaurrutia cultivated both warm friendships and bitter enmities. He never married, preferring to live in the family home in Colonia Roma while at the same time maintaining a studio apartment in the downtown section of the city. He was cultured and widely read, but at the same time had a passion for popular music and dance that led him to write romantic song lyrics, which were published anonymously. Intensely rational and intellectual in most aspects of his life, Villaurrutia was also superstitious and beset by phobias. A friend recalls, for example, that he once called off a planned trip to France because of something that he took as a bad omen, and his fear of being buried alive was well known.

Villaurrutia was feared for his caustic wit and esteemed for his amazing verbal inventiveness. Many anecdotes reveal this facet of his personality. For example, the short stature of Alfredo Gómez de la Vega, a leading actor of the day, is the target in these mocking lines circulated privately by Villaurrutia:

> La lluvia siempre acongoja
> a don Alfredo. ¿Por qué?
> Porque si Alfredo se moja,
> por poco que Alfredo encoja,
> el público ya no lo ve.

The rain always gives Don Alfredo fits. Why?
Because if Alfredo gets wet,
no matter how little he shrinks,
the audience won't be able to see him.

The following epigram celebrates the imposing busts and bustles of Doña Virginia Fábregas and Doña

Prudencia Grifel, two grandes dames of the Mexican theater:

> Tanto han llegado a engordar
> que bien podremos decir
> Virginia tarda en entrar
> lo que Prudencia en salir.

The two have become so large
that we can be certain in saying
that Virginia takes as long to come on stage
as Prudencia does to go off.

Fundamentally, however, Xavier Villaurrutia the man was synonymous with Xavier Villaurrutia the writer, whose complexities were only partially expressed by humor and verbal facility. The definitive 1966 edition of his works, *Obras*, runs to somewhat more than a thousand pages and includes several collections of poems, fifteen plays, a short novel, and an extensive series of essays and notes written on many topics over his entire career. His essays brought him renown as a critic of art, literature, and the cinema, and his plays often received considerable public attention. Villaurrutia enjoyed this acclaim and took pleasure in twitting those less successful than he. As an example, this epigram reminds Rodolfo Usigli, with whom he shared experiences at the Yale Drama School from 1935 to 1936, that Usigli's experimental historical play *Corona de sombra* (Crown of Shadow, 1947) was a failure even before it opened:

> El fracaso de Carlota
> a Rodolfo lo incomoda
> y hace de bilis derroche.
> Usigli, no dés la nota.
> Eres el autor de moda
> —que nunca llega a la noche.

Carlota's failure
really bothers Rodolfo
and wastes a lot of good bile.
Don't whine, Usigli.
You're the fashionable author
—who never gets to opening night.

In spite of his success and importance in other genres, Villaurrutia considered himself to be prima-rily a poet, and it is in his verses that the most genuine expression of his complex personality can be found. His poetry is not voluminous, however, and is limited to three principal collections plus some very early poems and a few compositions published posthumously. His poems barely exceed one hundred in number and are contained in the first ninety pages of *Obras*, but despite its brevity, Villaurrutia's poetic work is unusually rich in imagery, expressing in powerful fashion a unique and anguished subterranean world.

Villaurrutia's first collection is *Reflejos* (Reflections), a gathering of thirty-four short pieces that appeared in 1926. These poems are vividly sensorial: a face reflected on the surface of a pool, a still life, landscapes seen through an open window, the shaded intricacies of a formal garden. Metrical form is never conventional, and the poems take a free-flowing shape that is simple but controlled. Imagery is often surprising (for example, a peach having "the skin of a fifteen-year-old"), and profundity of meaning is to be found beneath the limpid surface of the poetry, as in these lines from "Interior":

> El aire que vuelve de un viaje,
> lleno de dorado calor,
> se hiela en un marco para ser espejo
> y cuadro de comedor.
> (*Obras*, 1966, p. 30)

The air that has returned from its journey,
filled with golden warmth,
is frozen within a frame in order to be a mirror
and a dining room picture.

Nostalgia de la muerte (Nostalgia of Death, 1938), Villaurrutia's most important collection, evolved over almost two decades. A radical departure from previous work was evident as early as 1928, when the poet's singular "nocturnes" and "nostalgias" began appearing in literary journals. These texts were reprinted, together with other pieces, in the first edition of *Nostalgia de la muerte*. A number of subsequent "nocturnes," "nostalgias," and *décimas* (ten-line poems), which again were published separately as pamphlets or in literary journals, were added to the definitive edition (1946), which contains a total of twenty-three compositions of varying length.

Special note should be taken of the ten-stanza "Décima muerte" (Tenth Death), perhaps Villaurrutia's most significant poem on the theme of death, which also appeared in 1941.

Nostalgia de la muerte is a much more somber collection of poems than *Reflejos*. Youthful enthusiasms have vanished, and the reflected multiplicity of the world has been reduced to a single aspect: dark, silent, and often bitter. Both themes and imagery open inwardly toward nocturnal galleries, in which the poet's persona can be aware only of death, isolation, and obsessive self-reflection. Poetic forms are similarly self-conscious and often include alliterations and wordplay. The best example comes from "Nocturno en que nada se oye" (Nocturne in Which Nothing Can Be Heard): "y mi voz que madura / y mi voz quemadura / y mi bosque madura" (and my voice matures / and my searing voice / and my forest matures). These lines from "Nocturno Solo" (Solitary Nocturne) convey the insistent complexity of this collection:

> Soledad, aburrimiento,
> vano silencia profundo,
> líquida sombra en que me hundo,
> vacío del pensamiento.
> Y ni siquiera el acento
> de una voz indefinible
> que llegue hasta el imposible
> rincón de un mar infinito
> a iluminar con su grito
> este naufragio invisible.
> (*Obras*, 1966, pp. 50–51)

Solitude, boredom,
vain and profound silence,
liquid shadow in which I submerge myself,
empty of thought.
And without even the hint
of an indefinable voice
that might reach the impossible
corner of an infinite sea
to illuminate with its scream
this invisible shipwrecked state.

Villaurrutia's third major collection, *Canto a la primavera y otros poemas* (Song to Spring and Other Poems), appeared in 1948. The ten poems of the collection all deal with the anguish of unrealized love

and as such are the poet's most concentrated expression of this major theme. In technique and imagery these compositions tend to be less complex than those of earlier collections, and metrical forms are in general more traditional. *Canto a la primavera* contains three stanzas of "Décimas de nuestro amor" (*Décimas* to Our Love), Villaurrutia's most ambitious love poem (the final ten-stanza version appeared posthumously in 1951). Once again, as in "Décima muerte," each ten-line *décima* makes use of an intensified personification, here not the figure of death but rather the figure of the absent lover. The qualities of this collection are perhaps best expressed, however, in a poem like "Soneto de la granada" (Sonnet to a Pomegranate). Its carefully turned phrases and images circumscribe within the sonnet form the mysteries of Villaurrutia's world and at the same time show the impossibility of their being communicated completely. The quatrains are as follows:

> Es mi amor como el oscuro
> panal de sombra encarnada,
> que la hermética granada
> labra en su cóncavo muro.
>
> Silenciosamente apuro
> mi sed, mi sed no saciada,
> y la guardo congelada
> para un alivio futuro.
> (*Obras*, 1966, p. 78)

My love is like the dark
honeycomb of deep red shadow
which the hermetic pomegranate
produces within its concave walls.

I silently purify
and set aside my thirst, my thirst which is never
 quenched,
and hold it in a frozen state
for a future refreshing.

Villaurrutia devoted a great deal of his energy to the revival of the theater in Mexico. In 1928 he and several of his closest friends founded Teatro Ulises, a small experimental group that had as its goal the creation of new actors and an up-to-date repertory. Successful in several salon-type presentations, the group failed completely in its attempt to organize a

1928–1929 winter season at the Fábregas Theater. In 1932 Villaurrutia and many of the same friends formed Teatro Orientación, which enjoyed a bit more success. There was a 1933–1934 season and, in 1938, a briefer series, in which an ambitious number of foreign and original Mexican works were produced. As Frank Dauster has pointed out, Villaurrutia played a major role in these experimental theater movements: he directed, made a number of the translations, selected many of the plays, and wrote and produced two of his own works. In addition, he attempted to school himself in the theater outside Mexico, as can be seen from his year of study (1935–1936) at the Yale Drama School, which he attended with the support of a Rockefeller Foundation fellowship.

Villaurrutia's own dramatic writings began in the early 1930's and were expanded considerably in the 1940's. More than a third of the second edition of his complete works is devoted to his theatrical creations. Fifteen separate pieces are collected, ranging from experimental one-act plays to three-act plays for the commercial theater and including a movie script and an opera libretto. His plays are intelligent and well constructed and illustrate a concern with middle-class social patterns in Mexico. Octavio Paz observes that the plays are often more significant for what they do not express than for what they do and also that they are perhaps more literary than theatrical in quality.

The first major grouping of his plays was made by Villaurrutia himself, when in 1943 he published five short pieces under the title *Autos profanos* (Worldly Allegories). Written in the 1930's, and in several cases produced in Teatro Orientación and published separately, these plays are not daringly avant-garde. Rather they are spare in setting, highly conceptual in the interplay of dialogue and characters, and carefully worked in their use of humor and language—all qualities that can be observed in Villaurrutia's poetry as well. Perhaps the best of the five is "El ausente" (The Absent One), subtitled "Mito en un acto" (Myth in One Act), which was written in 1937, published in the journal *Tierra nueva* in 1942, and not produced until 1951. The absence and brief return of the husband Pedro sets up a ménage à trois in which Fernanda, the wife, confronts her rival, the unnamed Woman. The exchanges between the characters are controlled and verbal, with the rather maternal wife at one extreme, the almost diabolical mistress at the other, and the silent Pedro between the two. The result is as might be expected: the Woman leaves, Pedro follows silently, and Fernanda is obliged to create for herself the "myth" of her husband as he once was.

Villaurrutia wrote and saw produced six three-act plays. The first of these was *Invitación a la muerte* (Invitation to Death), a contemporary adaptation of William Shakespeare's *Hamlet* that was completed in 1940, published in *El hijo pródigo* in 1943, and staged with mediocre success in 1947. Alberto, the owner of a funeral agency, is so distraught over the disappearance of his father and has such suspicion as to the supposed infidelities of his mother that he is incapable of action and exists only in a kind of living death. There are many resonances of the Shakespearean model in Villaurrutia's play, but the central focus is changed; *Invitación a la muerte* is not a play about revenge, but rather an almost existential examination of a tortured personality. Indeed, as Frank Dauster has observed, the play has many of the same obsessive themes and images that dominate Villaurrutia's poetry.

The remaining five full-length plays were written for the commercial theater of Mexico City. In the space of some three years, Villaurrutia wrote and produced very successfully three plays in the comedy-of-manners tradition, all of which use as a setting middle-class Mexican family life: in 1941 *La hiedra* (The Ivy), a commentary on impossible love modeled to a certain extent on Jean Racine's *Phèdre* (1677); in 1942 *La mujer legítima* (The Legitimate Wife), which dramatizes the rivalry between wife and mistress; in 1944 *El yerro candente* (The Burning Error), which examines a conflict in rightful paternity. These plays are realistic treatments of conventional themes, thus representing a major departure from the playwright's previous patterns. One can understand why some critics complained during these years about Villaurrutia's surrender to commercial success. His last two plays were a brilliant and humorous comedy staged in 1947 under the title of *El pobre Barba Azul* (Poor Bluebeard) and *Juego peligroso* (Dangerous Game), a rather melodramatic commentary on infidelity produced in 1950 and first published in the 1953 collection of Villaurrutia's poetry and theater.

Villaurrutia's prose writings occupy more than a third of the second edition of his collected works and show a remarkable breadth of literary and cultural interests. His prose fiction pieces, included in his collected works as "Prosas varias," are not numerous. The most significant is *Dama de corazones* (Queen of Hearts), a novelette written in 1925–1926 and published separately in 1928, which shares many similarities with Villaurrutia's poetry and early one-act plays. Julio, a young Mexican studying at Harvard, has returned to his aunt's house in Mexico City for a visit. He is immediately aware of the differing personalities of his two cousins, Aurora and Susana, the one warm and outgoing and the other deliberate and controlled, as if they were the two opposed images of the Queen of Hearts playing card. Julio is attracted and repelled by both girls, and even imagines himself suspended between them in a deathlike state. The aunt dies during his visit, however, and Julio must return to his studies without making a decision. Modeled on the experiments of Benjamín Jarnés and Jean Giraudoux in Europe, this novelette made its contribution to the renovation in Mexican prose fiction that was undertaken in the 1920's and 1930's by Villaurrutia and other members of the Contemporáneos group.

Villaurrutia was also a recognized critic, who lectured frequently and whose reviews and notes appeared in a number of newspapers and journals over more than twenty years. A number of these texts were collected in 1940 as *Textos y pretextos* (Texts and Pretexts), and a number of others are grouped in *Obras* as "Juicios y prejuicios" (Judgments and Prejudices), a title which Villaurrutia himself had selected before his death. Octavio Paz remarks on the impeccable taste and the profound and wide-ranging cultural background that illuminate Villaurrutia's critical expositions but observes that he is more a commentator than an essayist. His principal contributions as a critic are to be found, perhaps, in his many writings on art, the theater, and the movies (Luis Leal concludes that Villaurrutia brought commentary on the cinema to a level it had never before

attained in Mexico), and in his notes, lectures, and comments on Mexican literature. Deserving of special mention are his 1924 lecture on Mexican poetry, published separately as *La poesía de los jóvenes de México* (The Young Poets of Mexico), the 1931 and 1940 collections of the poetry of Sor Juana Inés de la Cruz which he edited and annotated, the short commentaries on Mexican writers collected under the title "Seis personajes" (Six Personalities) in *Textos y pretextos*, and his lecture entitled "Introducción a la poesía méxicana" (Introduction to Mexican Poetry; included in *Obras*, pp. 764–772). His best piece of literary criticism, without doubt, is "El león y la virgen" (The Lion and the Virgin), a superb study that became the introduction to a 1942 edition of Ramón López Velarde's poetry.

In spite of his importance for modern Mexican letters, Xavier Villaurrutia is not one of the names most frequently cited in the current resurgence of interest in Latin American literature. Few of his works have been translated, and consequently he is virtually unknown outside the Spanish-speaking world. Nonetheless, his wit, his breadth of culture, and his unique literary creations make him a writer of substantial proportion, a contributor alongside such better-known figures as Vicente Huidobro, Jorge Luis Borges, César Vallejo, and Pablo Neruda to the shaping of literary expression in Latin America during the twentieth century.

SELECTED BIBLIOGRAPHY

Editions

Poetry

Reflejos. Mexico City, 1926.
Nostalgia de la muerte. Buenos Aires, 1938. 2nd ed. Mexico City, 1946.
Décima muerte y otros poemas no coleccionados. Mexico City, 1941.
Canto a la primavera y otros poemas. Mexico City, 1948.

Plays

La hiedra. Mexico City, 1941.
"El ausente." *Tierra nueva* 3/13–14:35–50 (1942).
Autos profanos. Mexico City, 1943.

Invitación a la muerte. El hijo pródigo 1/6:355–363 (1943); 2/7:41–50 (1943); 2/8:100–101 (1943). 2nd ed. Mexico City, 1948.

La mujer legítima. Mexico City, 1943.

El yerro candente. Mexico City, 1945.

El pobre Barba Azul. Mexico City, 1948.

Prose Narrative

Dama de corazones. Mexico City, 1928.

Essays

La poesía de los jóvenes de México. Mexico City, 1924.

Textos y pretextos. Mexico City, 1940. Includes "El león y la virgen."

Collected Works

Antología. With a prologue and selection of texts by Octavio Paz. Mexico City, 1980.

Cartas de Villaurrutia a Novo: 1935–1936. Mexico City, 1966.

Crítica cinematográfica. With a prologue, notes, and selection of texts by Miguel Capistrán. Mexico City, 1970.

Nostalgia de la muerte: Poemas y teatro. Mexico City, 1984.

Obras. With a prologue by Alí Chumacero; compilation of texts by Miguel Capistrán, Alí Chumacero, and Luis Mario Schneider; and a bibliography by Luis Mario Schneider. 2nd ed. Mexico City, 1966.

Poesía y teatro completos. With a prologue by Alí Chumacero. Mexico City, 1953. Includes *Juego peligroso.*

Biographical and Critical Studies

Aub, Max. "Poesía encrucijada: A propósito de la poesía de Xavier Villaurrutia." *Revista de la Universidad de México* 30/8–9:28–33 (1976).

Cypess, Sandra M. "The Influence of the French Theater in the Plays of Xavier Villaurrutia." *Latin American Theater Review* 3/1:9–15 (1969).

Dauster, Frank. "La poesía de Xavier Villaurrutia." *Revista iberoamericana* 18:345–359 (September 1953).

———. "El teatro de Xavier Villaurrutia." *Estaciones* 1/4: 479–487 (1956).

———. *Xavier Villaurrutia.* New York, 1971.

Echavarren Welker, Roberto. "Nocturno y cuerpo en 'Nocturno miedo' de Xavier Villaurrutia." *Escritura* 5/10:323–333 (1980).

Forster, Merlin H. "La fecha de nacimiento de Xavier Villaurrutia." *Revista iberoamericana* 33/63:131–132 (1967).

———. *Fire and Ice: The Poetry of Xavier Villaurrutia.* Chapel Hill, N.C., 1976.

Leal, Luis. "Xavier Villaurrutia, crítico." *Estaciones* 4/13: 3–14 (1959).

Leiva, Raúl. "Xavier Villaurrutia." In *Imagen de la poesía méxicana contemporánea.* Mexico City, 1959. Pp. 151–163.

Martínez, José Luis. "Con Xavier Villaurrutia." *Tierra nueva* 1/2:74–81 (1940).

Moretta, Eugene. *La poesía de Xavier Villaurrutia.* Mexico City, 1976.

———. "Villaurrutia y Gorostiza: Hacia una visión amplia de los poetas 'Contemporáneos.'" *Cuadernos americanos* 224:71–115 (May–June 1979).

Nandino, Elías. "La poesía de Xavier Villaurrutia." *Estaciones* 1/4:460–468 (1956).

Novo, Salvador. "Xavier Villaurrutia, epigramático." *Novedades* (México en la cultura). 12 December 1965. P. 2.

Paz, Octavio. *Xavier Villaurrutia en persona y en obra.* Mexico City, 1978.

Rodríguez Chicharro, César. "Disemia y paronomasia en la poesía de Xavier Villaurrutia." *La palabra y el hombre* (April–June 1964):249–260.

Segovia, Tomás. "Xavier Villaurrutia." *Revista mexicana de literatura* 16–18:49–63 (1960).

Shaw, Donald. "Pasión y verdad en el teatro de Villaurrutia." *Revista iberoamericana* 28/54:337–346 (1962).

Xirau, Ramón. "Presencia de una ausencia." In *Tres poetas de la soledad.* Mexico City, 1955.

Eduardo Mallea

(1903–1982)

Myron I. Lichtblau

Born in Bahía Blanca, 14 August 1903, Eduardo Mallea was a writer of profound psychological insight who probed man's inner feelings and emotions in an impersonal and uncaring society. Anticipating the post–World War II existential novels of Jean-Paul Sartre, Mallea wrote in the 1930's of man's anguish and alienation, in a volume of stories entitled *La ciudad junto al río inmóvil* (The City on the Motionless River, 1936) and in the essay *Historia de una pasión argentina* (History of an Argentine Passion, 1937). Mallea is at his best when analyzing unhappy, frustrated men and women who live out their lives in isolation and unfulfillment. Few writers in Hispanic America have so consistently portrayed the lack of communication among men. Most of his characters are sullen, closed, unresponsive, and cynical about the world around them. They are souls whose withdrawal and emotional mutism are the signs of their distress. His women are harsh and distant, cold, indifferent to the men who love them and the people who care about them, and as Mallea himself said, "alone in their aloneness." Mallea's characters seek to find themselves, to understand themselves and the sets of values they live by, whether it be in the dynamic capital, as in the case of Avesquin in "Sumersión" (Submersion), in the conservative provinces, as with the Ricart family in *La torre* (The Tower, 1951) and *Las águilas* (The Eagles, 1943), or in the coastal city of Bahía Blanca, with the tragic marriage of Agata Cruz in *Todo verdor perecerá* (All Green Shall Perish, 1941).

Early in his career, in the 1920's, Mallea came under the influence of the European avant-garde writers. It was the period of various "isms" (creationism, dadaism, ultraism, cubism) and the height of postmodernist poetry, as seen in the works of Jorge Luis Borges, Arturo Capdevila, and Enrique Banks. Mallea wrote no poetry, but his first work, *Cuentos para una inglesa desesperada* (Stories for a Desperate Englishwoman, 1926), is a collection of short stories that reveals his fine aesthetic sensitivity and linguistic subtlety. Weak in structure and development, the narratives are lyrical expressions of delicate moods and emotions.

Mallea's first important work and the one that catapulted him to national fame, *History of an Argentine Passion*, is at once his spiritual autobiography and a depiction of Argentina in the 1930's. A seminal work that presents Mallea's intellectual and philosophical ideology, this book-length essay contains many of the themes he subsequently used in his fiction. The most important of these is the theme of the two Argentinas—the visible and the invisible.

Around this metaphorical concept Mallea built a good part of his fictional world, in such novels as *La bahía de silencio* (*The Bay of Silence*, 1940), *Fiesta en noviembre* (*Fiesta in November*, 1938), and *Chaves* (*Chaves*, 1953). For Mallea, the visible Argentina is the false, pretentious, utilitarian exterior of the nation that is manifest in its political and economic systems, its government and society, and above all in the day-to-day life of millions of Argentines. The visible Argentina is the veneer, the show that hides and deforms the true nation. The invisible Argentina is the authentic country, its soul and essence evident in its traditional values and beliefs. The invisible Argentina is the legacy of its founding fathers and its potential greatness.

Some critics feel that the best of Mallea is in *History of an Argentine Passion* and that the abstract quality of many of his fictional characters is the result of his creating an expository, almost essayistic format for his novels. There is some truth to his judgment, but Mallea is a far more creative and imaginative novelist than what appears from a superficial examination of his works. It is true that there is a minimum of external action in his fiction; it is almost static, motionless, introspective, the conflicts and problems issuing from within the emotional disquietude of the characters and their attempts to resolve those conflicts through their own limited resources. Instead of responding to traditional action in the form of a sequential narrative, the reader reacts to the inner states of mind of the characters, as they try to reconcile reason and emotion, will and feeling, tradition and moral change.

Argentine writers of the generation preceding Mallea's, novelists like Ricardo Güiraldes, graphically captured the meaning and spirit of the land. Mallea undertook the task of capturing the spirit of man and his fundamental worth, of man not necessarily in conflict with nature or his environment, but in a deeper conflict with himself and his emotions and thoughts. Rather than pay homage to the South American scene and react to its awesome presence, Mallea paid homage to man, and man's struggles and anguish became the source from which he drew his narrative material. Mallea's fiction became more universal in theme than that of any other Argentine novelist, but he never ceased to reflect an Argentine

society that he felt was rapidly moving away from its values and ideals.

Mallea's whole life was his literature. He attended law school but soon found that his true vocation lay in the world of letters. In 1921, when he was only eighteen, he worked with a group of young writers to found the *Revista de América* (Review of America), a magazine that appears in his novel *The Bay of Silence* under the name *Basta* (Enough). He soon contributed articles and essays to other journals and newspapers, and in 1934 began a fifty-year association with *Sur* (South), one of the most influential literary magazines in Hispanic America. Of great significance, too, in Mallea's career was his association with the prestigious Buenos Aires newspaper *La Nación*, especially his editorship of its literary supplement for over twenty years, from 1934 to 1955.

During trips to Europe in 1928 and 1934, Mallea broadened his literary acquaintanceship and nurtured his longing for new intellectual and cultural experiences. In 1955, he was Argentina's delegate to UNESCO in Paris, and the following year, he traveled to New Delhi to represent his country at the UNESCO meeting. Mallea received many honors and prizes, among them the coveted First National Prize of Letters (1945), the Grand Prize of Honor of the Argentine Association of Writers (1946), and the Grand National Prize of the Arts (1970). He died in Buenos Aires on 12 November 1982.

Mallea's first novel, published in 1938, is perhaps the most representative of his work. *Fiesta in November* was written as a protest against Nazi brutality and the execution of the poet Federico García Lorca in 1936 by Spanish nationalist forces. The narration of a frivolous, lavish party that forms the nucleus of the work is interrupted six times by the italicized interpolated account of a young idealist's murder by authorities of some unnamed totalitarian state. Few words are exchanged as the officials force their way into the young man's house and execute him, under a cloak of anonymity and mystery. Although no thematic relationship exists between the party and the atrocity, the juxtaposition of the carefree loquaciousness of the guests and the mute Kafkaesque atmosphere of the murder is ironic in its contrast and tragically dramatic. And within the principal narration, as another counterpoise to the artificial congeniality of the gathering, the reader senses the taut restraint of the Rague sisters, the mutual silence and distance between them.

The Bay of Silence, Mallea's longest and most ambitious novel, is perhaps the work that best illustrates the author's concept of the two Argentinas. The novel relates the story of Mallea's literary generation—its values, hopes, and aspirations symbolic of the invisible Argentina, while the forces thwarting these young idealists represent the visible Argentina. The torment and disillusion of the protagonist Martín Tregua, as he views his misguided Argentina, form the motif of the novel and spell out its real meaning. The evolution of Tregua's thoughts and emotions is channeled into three thematically distinct sections. In the first, we see the awakening of Tregua's brooding concern and frustration over the materialistic and culturally insensitive Argentina that defiantly bares its head, while the genuine essence of the country lies dormant. The second part of the novel shifts to several European cities—Wimbledon, London, Paris, Como, Brussels—and serves as an interlude during which Tregua reexamines his cultural values. Although he feels exhilarated by the great wealth of European civilizations, he returns to Argentina with more confidence in its future and a deeper love for its traditions. In the third section, disappointment and defeat surround Tregua and his companions, yet they never despair; at the close of the novel, the protagonist utters an eloquent profession of faith, of determination to march ahead to an eventual triumph.

Mallea conceived of *The Bay of Silence* as an intimate and cathartic narration in the first person, a particularly suitable mode because of its autobiographical nature and its intensity of emotion and vividness of recollection. But Mallea enhanced the effectiveness of this personal narration by having Tregua address his story not to an anonymous reader but to one very important person in his private world, the woman he secretly esteems as his inspiration and ideal, despite the lack of personal contact with her. Yet this woman's role is far more than an ingenious device, for Tregua's life is inextricably tied up with hers and is narrated much more meaningfully with studied reference to it. His story is told not only *to* her, but in direct relation to the effect she made on

his life. To such an extent does Tregua present his autobiography against the background of this woman, the Señora de Cárdenas, that her own personal tragedy slowly unwinds through interpolations in the main thread of narration. Although this intercalated story occupies but a minute portion of *The Bay of Silence,* a sense of its communion with that of the protagonist pervades the work. Mallea assigns symbolic values to the members of the Cárdenas family. The Señora represents the potential greatness of an unfulfilled Argentina, the true worth of the invisible Argentina struggling to be noticed, while her husband represents the arrogant and shallow visible nation. And while her young son, dead at an early age, incarnates hopeful dreams of betterment cruelly crushed, her older child is the living spirit of a future Argentina impatient to cast off its old cloak and assume a more worthy existence.

The theme of the frustrated writer appears many years later in *Simbad* (Sinbad, 1957), in which the protagonist Fernando Fe resembles Tregua in his idealism and sensitivity. Fernando is a young dramatist who aspires to create a lasting work of literature; to that end, he conceives the novel he calls "Simbad," in which the legendary sailor on his eighth voyage finally finds the promised land of happiness. Simbad's destination symbolizes the ideal goal that we all seek, after overcoming the hardships of life. The narrative structure of *Simbad* is especially interesting. The novel is divided into four sections, which retrospectively trace the protagonist's thirty-eight years of life. Placed before each section are the parts of another, briefer narrative, set in the present time, in which Fernando anxiously awaits the return of his wife, who has just left him. Mallea skillfully juxtaposes Fernando's anguish and pain in the present with his emotional distress in the past.

In *All Green Shall Perish,* the novel many critics consider his masterpiece, Mallea shows that he is an artist fully conscious of the relationship between structure and language. The protagonist, Agata Cruz, is as bitter and hostile a woman as Mallea ever created. Her husband Nicanor is her harsh, silent counterpart in a marriage barren of love and communication. When he succumbs to pneumonia, Agata is left alone with her suffering and despair. After a brief, unhappy affair, Agata returns to her hometown, as if to take refuge in the past and rid herself of the painful present. But she cannot run from herself and ends as a half-deranged, pitiful woman, derided by neighborhood toughs. The solitary figure of Agata Cruz is masterfully reflected in the physical environment. Bahía Blanca, a region of desolation and aridness, austere and sparsely populated, serves as a powerful symbol of Agata and Nicanor. The deep psychological penetration achieved in *All Green Shall Perish* is enhanced by a wealth of metaphors, similes, and all manner of comparative associations that form an important part of the narrative.

Mutism appears as a recurring emotional state in many of Mallea's works. More than the sheer incapacity for verbalization of thoughts and sentiments, it implies a person's rejection of the reality surrounding him and a denial of his position and significance within the context of that reality. In *The Bay of Silence*, mutism applies to the emotional disposition of several characters but is most deeply rooted in Tregua's girlfriend Gloria Bambil, who incarnates the essence of silent retreat into one's own ungenerous self. The haughty, stolid presence of the aristocratic mansion that gives its name to the novel *Las águilas* is a symbol of moral decadence and warped social values. The imposing but austere house, built as a monument to the fortune amassed by a French immigrant, becomes a mute witness to the dissipation of noble ideals in favor of ostentation, spiritual want, and material opportunism. The remote, desolate location of the mansion is likewise symbolic of the loneliness and barrenness of many of its occupants. In *La ciudad junto al río inmovil*, the capital city is seen as severe and inhospitable amid its bustle and superficial glitter. Within its walls, silent, sorrowful people who have not yet reached their capabilities, who are struggling to know themselves, walk the streets in empty solitude, charged with bitterness and resentment, somehow seeking relief in an attitude of mutism. In "La angustia" (The Anguish), for example, the neglected childhood of Ana Borel carries over into her adult life in the form of indifference to her husband and sullen taciturnity toward her employer.

The case of mutism in the story "Conversación" ("Conversation") is ironical, since the heart of the work is a dialogue in a bar between a man and his wife. They are bored not only with each other but also with themselves and their tedious lives. Their conversation is mechanical, uneasy, strained to the point of near hostility. At the close of the story, the husband despairingly suggests they go home, for there is no other place to go. And the wife's rejoinder ("Let's go home. What else is there to do?") seems to sum up the aridness and insufficiency of their relationship.

It is in the novel *Chaves* that the concept of mutism is brought out most vigorously and creatively. In this short work, more than in any other, mutism becomes the very core of Mallea's psychological analysis of character. It is exemplified in the behavior of a sawmill worker whose naturally morose and withdrawn nature is accentuated by a series of personal disappointments and tragedies. His silence and evasiveness infuriate his fellow workers, who look upon his strange ways as a sign of rancor or of an attitude of superiority. Chaves refuses to utter more than a few syllables. After the death of his young daughter, his withdrawal worsens and he speaks only to his wife, for she alone inspires in him the love and confidence he needs to overcome his reticence. In the final scene, when Chaves encounters hostile workers, the foreman of the group asks sympathetically: "Are you never going to tell them what they want you to tell them? . . . Something. Aren't you ever going to say anything to them? Never going to converse, to speak?" Chaves responds with a stoic "No."

Around the statement "The soul has three enemies: the world, the devil, and the flesh," Mallea constructed one of his most depressing novels of domestic discord and individual anguish. *Los enemigos del alma* (The Enemies of the Soul, 1950) is a relentlessly gloomy portrait of the Guillén family, especially of the three siblings who lost their parents during adolescence and grew up in constant rebellion against traditional values and mores. Within the musty walls of the old family estate, Villa Rita, hatreds, resentments, jealousies, and moral depravity have exacted their toll on the lives of Mario, cynical, egotistical, and licentious; Cora, fickle, promiscuous, and indifferent to everything except her own pleasure; and Debora, bitter, disdainful, and resentful of the happiness of others. In the symbolism of *Los enemigos del alma,* Mario represents the World, Debora the Devil, and Cora the Flesh, but the novel is too diffuse and multifocused for this symbolic representation to sustain its full artistic effect on the reader. The climax of the novel occurs when Debora, a prisoner of her own frustrations as a middle-aged spinster, sets fire to the patriarchal home as a final act of self-destruction. She perishes, but Mario and Cora survive. The metaphor of the evil home being consumed in flames, along with the perpetrator of evil, is clear and striking.

Another fine example of Mallea's psychological probing into man's emotional behavior is *Triste piel del universo* (Sad Skin of the Universe, 1971), which takes place entirely in New Delhi. Mallea had visited the city in the mid-1950's and came away deeply impressed with its charm and beauty. The journalist Adhemar Ribas, in India gathering material for a book on religious sanctuaries and native customs, establishes a close friendship with Mr. Boona and his wife, Loanda. The loss of Adhemar's wife, Mara, some months earlier has left him depressed and lonely, but his association with the Boonas provides a measure of comfort. The major conflict occurs when Adhemar falls in love with Loanda, yet feels he would be betraying Mara's memory by pursuing this adulterous relationship. The fact that the locale is India leaves no particular impression on the reader. Mallea is essentially not a writer who uses environmental description as a prime component of his fiction. The portrayal of India is mostly an intellectual one that nicely frames the narrative but only on occasion envelops it.

In *En la creciente oscuridad* (In the Growing Darkness, 1973), matrimonial estrangement and emotional solitude lead to a desire for vengeance on the one hand, and a strange case of murder on the other. Riguroso Barboza incarnates alienation and the absence of communication but is also capable of violence when his equally reticent spouse Silvia runs off with his best friend. Curiously, Barboza had invited his erstwhile companion to spend some days at his home to kindle a spark of life in Silvia and break the monotony and emptiness of their existence. When he finally locates the lovers, Barboza is about to fulfill his mission of avenging his wife's unfaithfulness. But ironically he himself becomes the victim, as the sister of his wife's lover, after several enigmatic encounters with Barboza, plunges a dagger into his heart as an ultimate act of derangement brought about by frustration and reclusion.

Mallea is as skilled in the short story as he is in the novel, employing similar narrative techniques and devices. His short stories—like his novels—are conceived as vehicles for the transmission of emotional and mental states. Many of his longer stories, for instance "Los otros mundos" (The Other Worlds), strike the reader more as condensed novels than as traditional narratives of isolated and intense moments in the lives of the characters. The short stories included in a single volume are generally united by a common theme or idea, as in *La sala de espera* (The Waiting Room, 1953). In this collection of seven untitled stories, each of the protagonists sits in a railroad station late at night, awaiting the train for Buenos Aires. Each traveler is oblivious of the others, unaware of their existence, yet for the moment their lives are united spatially and temporally. There is no communication among them, but they are bound by the same set of circumstances—the anxious wait for the delayed train and the necessary but unwilling acceptance of their uncomfortable position. The clock on the wall is as mute as the passengers, although it constitutes a kind of common point of reference. Within each traveler's uneasy silence, however, there is a story of anguish and suffering, a tale of the events and circumstances that have led to his or her presence at the station. The comparison with Thornton Wilder's *The Bridge of San Luis Rey* (1927) quickly comes to mind, but in that novel one physical catastrophe destroys several lives, while in Mallea's work the tragedy lies within each person.

Several of the stories in *La sala de espera* involve characters who exhibit the same sort of taciturn and impassive behavior present in *La ciudad junto al río inmóvil.* One of the passengers, a frivolous but vulnerable woman, decides that her dull marriage to a reticent and apathetic husband may be more suitable than her many affairs. After her last lover abandons her, she slowly walks to the train she hopes will take her to the comfort of her husband's loyalty. The protagonist of another story, unable to tolerate the mute austerity of his overbearing wife, leaves her and wanders into the railroad station, with no particular destination in mind. One of the best stories presents an interesting juxtaposition of two searches that represent central moments in Cormorán's life. The search for his sister forms the outside limits of the narration: it starts with his lament that he has been looking for her for seven years and ends with his presence at the station, still looking, having traversed many miles. The other search, less extensive spatially but just as intense emotionally, is Cormorán's search for his wife and her lover through the shabby dock section of Buenos Aires. When Cormorán finally finds the lover's apartment, empty, his strongest emotion is not hatred or violence, but revulsion. He flees the site of his wife's unfaithfulness and for weeks wanders the city in silence. At this point, his deep feeling for his sister, who married for love beneath her social status, becomes the only positive force in his life.

In another story of *La sala de espera* that probes subtle emotional forces, the playwright-narrator Francisco Díaz makes the reader aware of the changing relationship between himself and his friend, the self-styled critic Claudio Murillo. Timid and lacking self-confidence, the narrator feels privileged to be in the company of the sophisticated and brash Claudio, a physician by profession, whose appraisal of Díaz' theatrical works has had a profound influence on his career. Claudio's criticism is at times overly candid, but Díaz accepts it because of his emotional dependence on his mentor. But then a change occurs. Claudio becomes resentful when Díaz marries Ema, and his criticism turns caustic and cruel. Although the narrator seems happy as a devoted husband, he considers himself a failure as a dramatist; on one occasion, after seeing Henrik Ibsen's *A Doll's House,* he feels his artistic insignificance even more. His wife's death shortly thereafter contributes to the tragedy of his aloneness. An interesting feature of this narration is the development of a kind of play within a play, as Díaz gives the reader a detailed account of the opening of his latest work.

Díaz feels the need to lose himself in the anonymous metropolis. After having launched his play to its destiny, he wants to fulfill certain acts of humility but, unable to execute his will, decides that the next best thing to do would be to walk through the poor neighborhoods and dissolve into the multitudes.

Díaz' play is a failure, and Claudio, now more estranged from him than ever, rejoices in his defeat. In a kind of surrealistic image, Díaz catches Claudio's diabolical smile as the two meet backstage. Beside himself with anger, Díaz almost chokes Claudio but desists, blaming himself for his play's failure, realizing he can never relinquish responsibility for his own life. Back home, he burns his papers and tries to run from himself, but he carries his suffering deep within himself as he travels aimlessly from town to town on trains filled with people oblivious to his plight. As he waits in the train station, he is overwhelmed by the theme of a great hate, the theme of himself.

Around the central motif of the obsessive desire for possession, Mallea wrote the three stories in the volume *Posesión* (Possession, 1958). In the first story, which bears the title of the volume, the theme is the overwhelming need to dominate the will of another person. At a party in London, Videla by chance meets his former lover, whom he once controlled and who now is an elegant, self-possessed, assertive woman eagerly sought by many admirers. The contrast between the woman Videla knew and subjected to his whims and the woman he sees now in all her confidence and feminine triumph is too great for him to bear, and he quietly leaves the gathering. In "Los zapatos" (The Shoes), the theme is the fanatical desire on the part of an office worker to purchase a pair of costly shoes he sees in a store window each day on his way to work. The satisfaction of this desire brings with it unforeseen changes in his life, including, ironically, his forced retirement to a life of leisure and tranquillity. Finally, in "Ceilan" (Ceylon), the motivating drive is the desire to form a lasting relationship with another person, to identify emotionally with another human being. In a Parisian cafe, Díaz strikes up an acquaintance with a woman who at first seems capable of fulfilling his desire, but whose vivid remembrance of her lover's recent suicide precludes her interest in another man.

In *La barca de hielo* (The Ice Ship, 1967), a group of nine separate narratives is tied together by the participation of a common narrator, the same Adhemar Ribas, son of a middle-class family in rural southern Argentina. A good part of the first story, "Violencia" (Violence), treats of the taciturn and petulant younger brother Nicanor, for whom

Adhemar feels a particularly deep affection. Nicanor is certainly not an original creation in Mallea's repertory of characters. What is novel is that the reader perceives his aberration and reacts to it through the anguish he causes another person, Adhemar. Nicanor's offensively silent behavior is broken only when he plays chess with his father, an activity that at least gives evidence of some form of personal communication. Nicanor's introvertedness masks an extreme emotional struggle, which one day reaches its limits of stress when he tries to assault the daughter of one of the region's wealthiest families. Blinded by fraternal love, Adhemar defends Nicanor but finds that his brother is incapable of offering any explanation or feeling any remorse.

In another story in *La barca del hielo,* "El olvido sobre Padre" (Father's Forgetfulness), the close relationship between Adhemar and his father is poignantly drawn and analyzed. For many years after his wife's death, Ribas senior has refused to speak of her to his family. Now that her image has become dim with the passing of time, he begins to reminisce in an attempt to capture her being once again. Indeed, the act of remembering (a form of communication) is the principal element of the narration. Memory serves to soothe him, to enable him to function within his loneliness. But this inner tranquillity soon becomes bitter frustration as he feels that his powers of recollection are waning and that each day he loses an important piece of his past.

La penúltima puerta (The Penultimate Door, 1969) is a series of three interrelated but independent narratives, with one central figure serving as the only unifying element. Adhemar Ribas is again the omnipresent narrator; in this work, he is a star reporter residing at the Imperial Hotel in New Delhi. From this vantage point, he proceeds to relate three stories of loneliness, frustrated love, incommunicability, and emotional anguish. The first story narrates Adhemar's past affair with a married woman in Buenos Aires, culminating in her suicide; the second narrative tells of Adhemar's platonic, almost spiritual relationship in Amsterdam with an eighteen-year-old girl; in the third, Adhemar is the confidant of a South African man named Denskel, whose tragic marriage is revealed through several cruelly candid letters sent him by his wife. In this last narrative, Adhemar as

narrator is not the central figure in the story that unfolds, but his presence is vitally felt as he reacts to Denskel's plight. What is more, the course of Denskel's unhappy life obliges Adhemar to reflect more somberly on his own goals and purposes.

Mallea's prose style merits comment because of its distinctiveness. His style reveals two different modes: a dense, heavy, psychologically oriented style, laden with a literary and academic lexicon and characterized by an abstractness that results from his thought process; and a lyrical, rhythmical style, frequently exalted and impassioned, spontaneously moving and charged with emotion. Although antithetical, both prose styles are suitable for the penetrating analysis of character so important in Mallea's fiction. Mallea can reach heights of poetic inspiration or can descend into a morass of tangled abstruseness and wordiness. He can write beautiful and moving prose, and he can languish in long paragraphs that are flat, dry, and cumbersome. At his worst, Mallea is unable to free himself from his web of complex thoughts; at his best, he can show perfection of form and word. He can please with his descriptive power or tire the reader with excessive verbalization of philosophical concepts.

Mallea's style is expansive rather than succinct; he protracts the expression of his thoughts and elaborates endlessly to describe emotions and feelings. Instead of using a single word to capture exact meaning, Mallea uses a plethora of synonymous words, groups of similar words, and all sorts of associative and repetitive devices that cumulatively approach the desired meaning. At times, Mallea's style can show ingenious linguistic play to reflect the intensity and subtlety of his intellectual and emotional world. His prose gropes for new and sometimes daring ways of verbal expression; yet the prime function of his language is never linguistic cleverness but the transmission of thought and sentiment in the most effective way possible. Few of his contemporaries have achieved such harmony of theme and style.

Mallea was never a popular novelist nor a commercially successful one in the way that his compatriots Hugo Wast and Manuel Gálvez were. His fiction is too intellectual and at times too abstract to attract a wide audience. But for almost five decades Mallea was one of the most important novelists not only in

Argentina but throughout Spanish America. Fiction in Hispanic America came of age with the regionalistic novels of the 1920's and the proletarian, politicized works of the 1930's and 1940's. And while Mallea's works contain some of these elements, they essentially represent a counterpoise to this *criollista*, telluric orientation. Mallea gave Hispanic America its novel of ideas, of universal values and human emotions in conflict, and he did it with great artistry and aesthetic sensitivity.

SELECTED BIBLIOGRAPHY

First Editions

Fiction

Cuentos para una inglesa desesperada. Buenos Aires, 1926.
La ciudad junto al río inmóvil. Buenos Aires, 1936.
Fiesta en noviembre. Buenos Aires, 1938.
La bahía de silencio. Buenos Aires, 1940.
Todo verdor perecerá. Buenos Aires, 1941.
Las águilas. Buenos Aires, 1943.
Los enemigos del alma. Buenos Aires, 1950.
La torre. Buenos Aires, 1951.
Chaves. Buenos Aires, 1953.
La sala de espera. Buenos Aires, 1953.
Simbad. Buenos Aires, 1957.
Posesión. Buenos Aires, 1958.
La barca de hielo. Buenos Aires, 1967.
La penúltima puerta. Buenos Aires, 1969.
Triste piel del universo. Buenos Aires, 1971.
En la creciente oscuridad. Buenos Aires, 1973.

Plays

El gajo de enebro. Buenos Aires, 1957.
La representación de los aficionados. Buenos Aires, 1962.

Essays

Conocimiento y expresión de la Argentina. Buenos Aires, 1935.
Nocturno europeo. Buenos Aires, 1935.
Historia de una pasión argentina. Buenos Aires, 1937.
Notas de un novelista. Buenos Aires, 1954.

Collected Works

Obras completas. 2 vols. Buenos Aires, 1961–1965.

Later Editions

Chaves. Edited by Bernard Gicovate and Alice Gicovate. Englewood Cliffs, N.J., 1971.
"La razón humana." In *Voces hispanoamericanas*, edited by Peter G. Earle. New York, 1966. Pp. 176–177.
Todo verdor perecerá. Edited and with an introduction in English by D. L. Shaw. Oxford, 1968.

Translations

All Green Shall Perish and Other Novellas and Stories. Translated by John B. Hughes et al. New York, 1966. Includes *Fiesta in November* and *Chaves.*
The Bay of Silence. Translated by Stuart E. Grummon. New York, 1944.
"Conversation." Translated by Hugo Manning. In *Spanish-American Literature in Translation 2*, edited by Willis Knapp Jones. New York, 1963. Pp. 295–302.
History of an Argentine Passion. Translated, annotated, and with an introduction by Myron I. Lichtblau. Pittsburgh, Pa., 1983.

Biographical and Critical Studies

Anderson Imbert, Enrique. "Eduardo Mallea y la guerra interior." *Boletín de la Academia Argentina de Letras* 47:229–233 (1982).
Carrero del Mármol, Elena. "Gálvez y Mallea: Imágenes de la Argentina." *Duquesne Hispanic Review* 2/3:179–190 (1963).
Chapman, Arnold. "Sherwood Anderson and Eduardo Mallea." *PMLA* 49/1:35–45 (1954).
_____. "Terms of Spiritual Isolation in Eduardo Mallea." *Modern Language Forum* 37/1–2:21–27 (1952).
Cohen, Howard. "Critical Approaches to Eduardo Mallea." *Revista de estudios hispánicos* 14/3:129–144 (1980).
Crow, John A. "Man Trapped by Tension." *Saturday Review*, 27 May 1967. Pp. 32–33.
Dudgeon, Patrick. *Eduardo Mallea: A Personal Study of His Work.* Buenos Aires, 1949.
Flint, J. M. "A Basic Concept in the Ideology of Eduardo Mallea." *Ibero* 3:341–347 (1971).
Foster, David W. "Eduardo Mallea and the Dilemma of the Prophetic Observer." In his *Currents in the Contemporary Argentine Novel.* Columbia, Mo., 1975. Pp. 46–69.
Hughes, John B. "Arte y sentido ritual de los cuentos y novelas cortas de Eduardo Mallea." *Revista de la Universidad de Buenos Aires* 5/2:192–212 (1960).

Lewald, H. Ernest. *Eduardo Mallea.* New York, 1977.

Lichtblau, Myron I. *El arte estilístico de Eduardo Mallea.* Buenos Aires, 1967.

———, ed. *Mallea ante la crítica.* Miami, 1985.

Peterson, Fred. "Notes on Mallea's Definition of Argentina." *Hispania* 45:621–624 (1962).

———. "The Relationship of Narrative Technique to Theme in Eduardo Mallea's *Posesión.*" *Books Abroad* 38:361–366 (1964).

Pintor, Genaro. *Eduardo Mallea: Novelista.* Río Piedras, Puerto Rico, 1976.

Polt, John H. R. *The Writings of Eduardo Mallea.* Berkeley, Calif., 1959.

———. "Algunos símbolos de Eduardo Mallea: Mallea y Hawthorne." *Revista hispánica moderna* 26/1–2:96–101 (1960).

Rivelli, Carmen. *Eduardo Mallea: La continuidad temática de su obra.* New York, 1969.

Rodríguez Monegal, Emir. "Eduardo Mallea." In his *Narradores de ésta América.* Montevideo, 1969. Pp. 249–269.

Roggiano, Alfredo A. "Eduardo Mallea." In *Diccionario de la literatura latinoamericana. Argentina.* Washington, D.C., 1961. Pp. 319–323.

Shaw, Donald. "Narrative Technique in Mallea's *La bahía de silencio.*" *Symposium* 20/1:50–55 (1966).

Topete, José M. "Eduardo Mallea y el laberinto de la agonía." *Revista iberoamericana* 39:117–149 (1955).

Villordo, Oscar H. *Genio y figura de Eduardo Mallea.* Buenos Aires, 1973.

Zum Felde, Alberto. "Eduardo Mallea." In his *Ídice crítico de la literatura hispanoamericana 2: La narrativa.* Mexico City, 1959, Pp. 435–446.

José Marín Cañas

(1904–1980)

Ramón L. Acevedo

Novelist, journalist, and short-story writer, José Marín Cañas is a Costa Rican author whose name is established beyond his country's frontiers as one of the best writers in Central America and as an important Latin American novelist. Marín was born in San José, Costa Rica in 1904. His father and mother were immigrants from southern Spain. After finishing secondary school in Costa Rica, he lived in Spain, where he studied civil engineering at the Academia de Artillería de Segovia, a military school. After three years of study, he had to return to San José without his degree because of his family's difficult economic situation. He had experienced Spain's political and cultural atmosphere in the 1920's, a very active decade when writers such as Miguel de Unamuno, Antonio Machado, and Azorín (José Martínez Ruiz) from the Generation of 1898 dominated the scene while avant-garde movements such as *ultraismo* forwarded radical innovations.

Back in San José, Marín had to work as retailer, violin player, and journalist to earn a living. He became acquainted with life in poor sectors of the city and with marginal bohemian types whom he later included as characters in his fiction. San José was a small town where simple life prevailed, although it had slowly started to grow.

National Costa Rican literature had begun with the turn of the century and was characterized by a strong realist and *costumbrista* tendency. To depict local customs and popular ways of life was the principal intention of writers like Joaquín García Monge, Manuel González Zeledón, and Aquileo Echeverría. Marín initially followed this tendency but soon gave it new and wider dimensions by delving more deeply into the human condition and extending his scope beyond Costa Rican reality.

Journalism was essential in his early career and throughout his life. Like many Latin American authors, he learned to write as a journalist, and most of his writings, including his fiction, were first published in small local newspapers, most frequently in *La Hora*, which he founded and directed himself, and in *Diario de Costa Rica*. As a writer of chronicles and articles, he compensated for a lack of sophisticated financial and technical resources by using his fertile imagination. In his best works he succeeds in going beyond the limitations of superficial journalism without losing its dramatic, direct, and spontaneous character.

Marín first became known as a creative writer with the publication in 1929 of *Lágrimas de acero* (Tears of Steel), a novel based on his life as a student in Spain; he became firmly established with *Los bígardos del ron* (The Drunken Vagabonds, 1929), a collection of short stories and sketches about the sad and often tragic lives of marginal people, especially poor frustrated artists, in Costa Rica. In 1929 he also published a short theatrical sketch, *Como tú* (Like You). Two years later, in his second novel, *Tú, la imposible* (You, the Impossible One), he tried, without much success, to combine experimental avant-garde techniques with a sentimental love story. His first international success was *El infierno verde* (The Green Inferno, 1935), a novel about the Chaco War between Bolivia and Paraguay. Seven years later he published *Pedro Arnáez,* considered by many his best work.

During the last four decades of his life, Marín dedicated himself mainly to journalism and his cattle ranch. He had written *Pueblo macho* (Macho People, 1937), in which he wrote about the tragic realities that led to the Spanish civil war, and during the 1970's collections of his articles, essays, and chronicles appeared: *Tierra de conejos: Por caminos, pueblos y tumbas de España* (Land of Rabbits: Through Roads, Towns, and Tombs of Spain, 1971), *Ensayos* (Essays, 1972), and *Realidad e imaginación* (Reality and Imagination, 1974).

In spite of his frank exposition of his polemical literary and political opinions, Marín was a respected and admired public figure in his own country. He became a member of the Academia Costarricense de la Lengua in 1950 and taught journalism at the University of Costa Rica. His two most important novels, *El infierno verde* and *Pedro Arnáez,* have been frequently reprinted in Spain and Costa Rica. He died in 1980, and today he is considered one of the principal novelists of Latin American regionalism.

With the exception of *Los bígardos del ron,* Marín's early works have little intrinsic value as literature; because of experimental techniques that he had not mastered, they are complicated and confusing. His style was too close to that of his Spanish models and he had not developed the ability to create convincing characters and to evoke social and natural environments.

Marín was inspired by the sad and difficult life of the poor in San José. The sketches and short stories of *Los bígardos del ron* are centered on characters who struggle for life but at heart feel defeated and seek refuge in alcohol. The author is sensitive to their finer feelings and their bitter, justified complaint against life's injustices. Action is reduced to a minimum in his texts, although there are always anecdotes that sustain the narratives and complete the portraits of human types. Some representative characters are two beggars, a married couple, brutalized by bad rum; a man in jail who longs to see his small son; and an orphan child abused by his stepfather.

Above all, the types that interest the author are poor, frustrated artists who try to maintain their dignity even when they are close to being beggars. Behind their frustration there is usually a sad sentimental story: the loss of a son, memories of love, or an impossible, obsessive love for a woman of the upper class. His artists, living in an insensible, materialistic society, also suffer a lack of recognition. These are those like Don Facundo, a clarinet player who offers a magnificent dinner in a restaurant to a bootblack who has not even had breakfast, although he knows that he does not have the money to pay and will go to jail. Another sad character is Eduardo, a poor writer who longs to win a literary prize that goes instead to a rich friend who writes as a hobby. A talented journalist quits journalism after writing a chronicle about the violent death of a singer he loved; a poet suffers because his poor, badly dressed appearance does not correspond to the beauty of his writings—he cannot declare himself to the woman he secretly loves; a young novelist sacrifices himself in order to write and publish a long novel nobody reads; a composer tries to repay with waltzes the alms he receives from the ladies, in order not to feel that he is begging.

A pessimistic view of life and a deep feeling for simple tragedies and the dignity of man, even when he is down, are typical themes in Marín's best writings. The style of *Los bígardos del ron,* in spite of abundant imagery and sophisticated vocabulary, and the narrative techniques, to which dialogue and dramatic rendering of action are very important, anticipate his two best novels.

One of the short stories included in *Los bígardos del ron,* "Rota la ternura" (Tenderness Shattered), has been included in many anthologies of Costa Rican and Central American short stories. Marín has provided a careful structuring of plot and a convincing presentation of the main character and his violent natural surroundings. The story is of a man who escapes from prison in order to see his only son and then discovers that the child is not really his. The unexpected but logical ending closes the story perfectly.

Coto, a story first published in *La Hora* in 1934, demonstrates that Marín had learned much from journalism and was prepared for *El infierno verde*. *Coto* is not properly fiction but the chronicle of an incident in the brief war, motivated by a territorial dispute, between Costa Rica and Panama (1921). A friend gave Marín some details, and he imagined the rest. The incident is narrated from the point of view of an anonymous Costa Rican soldier who experiences it as his first encounter with the enemy. A simple, dynamic style, a fast pace, and the subjective narration account for its success. It also reveals Marín's attraction to the theme of war and the pathos of men facing violence and death.

The genesis of *El infierno verde* is very similar to that of *Coto*. Marín had never been in Bolivia or Paraguay; nevertheless, he wrote one of the best novels about the Chaco War (1932–1935). Based on some photographs and books on the two countries, plus the reports he received for his newspaper, Marín produced an "autobiographical" account of the war supposedly written by a Paraguayan soldier. The narrative was reproduced as factual in *La Hora* and later published as a novel in Spain. The hoax was so successful that practically everybody, including literary critics, believed that it was an authentic document, or at least a novel, written by a Paraguayan who had witnessed the war. Praises nearly ceased when the truth was known, but this work is an excellent novel and a literary success, not only for its deep human interest, but also because of its effective modern narrative techniques and the expressionistic lyricism of its style.

The novel has no definite plot. It is simply a kind of diary written by an educated and sensible lawyer from Asunción who has joined the army and narrates his experiences from the beginning of the war until he gets lost in the arid Chaco desert and awaits imminent death. He takes part in some important battles, is wounded, recovers in a military hospital, and goes back to the front where he finds that Nitsuga, a Guarani Indian who has protected him, is dead. He deserts with a young soldier, who dies of thirst and exhaustion, and is left alone in the desert.

In spite of magnificent descriptions of action on the war front, what is really important is the protagonist's inner experience, his nightmare vision of the war, a war against an anguished enemy like himself, against nature, and against his own conscience. Even when he is close to madness, the author manages to convince us that he can be an efficient observer and that he can record naturally his own process of brutalization, his loneliness, his horror of death, and his eroding identity. The most important secondary character, Nitsuga, represents the mystery and force of the native Indian race.

The novel's effectiveness is based on the creation of atmosphere. In this sense, it is one of the best examples of early Latin American expressionism. Atmosphere is evoked by fragmented rendering of action, with flashbacks and narrative ellipses that culminate in the protagonist's chaotic stream of consciousness while he is in the hospital. Visionary and expressionist imagery, lyric tension, and fast pace characterize Marín's style and result in a somber, hallucinatory, but poetic atmosphere.

Marin considered *Pedro Arnáez* his best novel, perhaps because it presents Central American realities. The story of a simple man from the lower class, it reflects the political, social, and existential crisis between the world wars. The narrator, a Costa Rican doctor who by chance is close to Arnáez at three key moments when he faces death, reconstructs his life and their three personal encounters: on a banana plantation, after Arnáez loses his father; in San José, where he loses his wife; and in El Salvador, during the Indian rebellion and massacre of 1932, during which more than thirty thousand peasants were killed by the army. His son is wounded and Arnáez is captured and sentenced to death, although we never know if he is killed.

The novel is structured as a search for meaning in a chaotic and cruel world marked by a profound crisis of traditional values. This search leads both protagonist and narrator toward a painful confrontation with death, suffering, injustice, forces of good and evil, self-identity, and the mysteries of life. According to the narrator, Arnáez may have finally found himself by returning to essential Christian values. Slow pacing, direct style, and close detailed description, interrupted by dramatic scenes, predominate in this novel.

Marín's later works are journalistic. *Tierra de conejos* subjectively renders his experience of traveling through Spain, to which he returns after forty years. *Ensayos* is a collection about such varied themes as praise of poverty, the defense of Latin America's narrative boom, and his experience as a hospital patient. His strong personality is present in everything he writes.

As is the case with other important Central American authors, there has not been much critical writing on Marín's works. Aside from small articles and brief commentaries on Marín in survey texts of Latin American and Costa Rican literature, *El infierno verde* has aroused interest as a novel about the Chaco War and has been partially analyzed by critics such as María de Villarino and Willis Knapp Jones. *La novela centroamericana* (The Central American Novel), by Ramón L. Acevedo, contains relatively complete analyses of Marín's most important novels.

SELECTED BIBLIOGRAPHY

First Editions

Novels and Short Stories

Los bígardos del ron. San José, 1929.
Lágrimas de acero. Madrid, 1929.
Tú, la imposible. Madrid, 1931.
El infierno verde: La guerra del Chaco. Madrid, 1935.
Pedro Arnáez. San José, 1942.

Plays

Como tú. San José, 1929.

Chronicles, Essays, and Articles

Coto. San José, 1935.
Pueblo macho: Ensayo sobre la realidad española. San José, 1937.
Tierra de conejos: Por caminos, pueblos y tumbas de España. Salamanca, Spain, 1971.
Ensayos. San José, 1972.
Realidad e imaginación. San José, 1974.

Biographical and Critical Studies

Acevedo, Ramón L. "El sentido humano del criollismo costarricense." In his *La novela centroamericana.* Río Piedras, Puerto Rico, 1982. Pp. 397–425.

Bonilla, Abelardo. "José Marín Cañas." In his *Historia de la literatura costarricense.* 3rd ed. San José, 1981. Pp. 317–319.

Chase, Alfonso. "José Marín Cañas y *Pedro Arnáez.*" *La República* (San José), 19 January 1969. P. 13.

De Villarino, María. "La novela de la guerra chaqueña." *Sur* 8/42:58–66 (1938).

Jones, Willis Knapp. "Literature of the Chaco War." *Hispania* 21/1:33–46 (1938).

Agustín Yáñez

(1904–1980)

Stella T. Clark

"Village of women in black. Hither and yon, at night, at dawn, throughout the flow of morning, under the baking sun, at dusk, they come and go, strong, bright, dull and suffering. Old crones, matrons, maidens, girls in church atria and lonely streets. They can be spotted in shops and, rarely—very rarely—glimpsed through furtively open doors."

This passage is from Agustín Yáñez' famous introductory essay to his novel *Al filo del agua* (*The Edge of the Storm*, 1947). A writer who has earned a high place in Mexican letters, Yáñez published this novel at a time when the development of contemporary fiction was at an adolescent stage in Mexico, drawing attention to a predominance of form over theme. The use of avant-garde techniques, such as stream of consciousness, counterpoint, interior monologue, and time distortion, to re-create a tense and hermetic village in the state of Jalisco established the novel as a landmark. The revolution of 1910 had been the subject of Mexican fiction since the 1920's, as writers tried to analyze and comprehend that cataclysmic movement. Yáñez' contribution was not only his description of a society at the edge of violent change but also his transformation of a Mexican story into a depiction of the human condition in time of stress. The novel's success stems from its combination of a powerful theme, a carefully conceived structure, and a highly metaphorical, evocative language.

The Edge of the Storm also marked a turning point in Yáñez' career. As did many Mexican intellectuals of his generation, the writer possessed qualities of both artist and statesman. His work, moreover, was a reflection of the times, in that it represented the conflict, which many Mexican writers experienced, of loyalties to his hometown and the big metropolis. Born into a family of laborers on 4 May 1904 in Guadalajara, Yáñez was brought up in a very conservative environment that, although part of the provincial city, had the characteristics of a village. His early works focus on the idyllic aspects of small town life, in which traditional customs and values prevail.

Yáñez first took a law degree and later trained as a teacher of literature. In the early 1930's he received a master of philosophy degree from the University of Mexico, where he was later appointed professor of literary theory. It was during his career as a critic and educator that Yáñez shifted his writing toward the novel. As a young man he had been a member of several literary circles in Guadalajara and had been a frequent contributor to journals such as *Bandera de provincias* (The Province Banner). Although the essays and the translations of foreign literature in

Bandera reflected an interest in avant-garde currents and in writers such as James Joyce, Yáñez' early writings show very little influence of experimental fiction. His collections of short prose pieces, many of which he wrote over a fifteen-year period, focus on provincial Mexican life and are traditional in structure and style. The autobiographical themes evolve around the rites of passage of a typical youth of central Mexico. Best known are those that comprise the short-story collection *Flor de juegos antiguos* (Bouquet of Childhood Games, 1942) and the novellas collected as *Archipiélago de mujeres* (Archipelago of Women, 1943), each a series of episodes in the lives of young males awakening to their sexuality and experiencing first love.

At this time Yáñez also produced works in a genre that he called the "poetic essay"—writings that he described as "experiments in lyric prose." In these short and rhythmic pieces, the best known of which are *Espejismo de Juchitán* (Juchitan Mirage, 1940) and *Días de Bali* (Bali Sojourn, 1964), Yáñez sought to re-create personal experiences through poetic language. The lushness of such places as Juchitán, in the Mexican southern state of Oaxaca, and the island of Bali provided a rich contrast to Yáñez' austere native region and inspired vivid, evocative pieces of prose poetry that display his virtuosity with the Spanish language. Their vibrant imagery and polished structure served to establish Yáñez' reputation as a master stylist.

The "poetic essays" inspired *The Edge of the Storm*, Yáñez' first full-length novel. As he experimented with the "Acto preparatorio" (overture), Yáñez re-created the atmosphere of a small Jalisco town much as he had described Juchitán before. Under the influence of John Dos Passos' *Manhattan Transfer* (1925), Yáñez established contrapuntal characters who embodied the "women in black dress," as well as the town's collective fears and desires so vividly evoked in the overture. With the additional inspiration of French composer Gabriel Fauré's *Requiem*, Yáñez succeeded in creating a powerful work reminiscent of William Faulkner's repressive small-town world. Evoking the psychological effects of a system ruled by the Catholic church, as well as by tradition and the fear of change, Yáñez makes the reader feel vividly the anguish experienced by those who cannot escape their fate because of external forces or their own sense of guilt.

The novel was so well received after its publication that it gave Yáñez immediate recognition and placed him in a gallery with such illustrious Mexican literary figures as Mariano Azuela, Alfonso Reyes, Ramón López Velarde, and Manuel Gutiérrez Nájera. *The Edge of the Storm* also paved the way for the landmark experimental novels that followed and that have given Mexican literature a place in world letters. These include Juan Rulfo's *Pedro Páramo* (1955) and Carlos Fuentes' *La muerte de Artemio Cruz* (*The Death of Artemio Cruz*, 1962).

Almost concurrently with his success as a novelist, Yáñez turned his career toward politics, diplomacy, and cultural affairs. He served as governor of his native state of Jalisco from 1953 to 1959. Subsequently, and until his death in 1980, he continued to perform many important political and diplomatic roles, from that of ambassador to Argentina to his most prestigious one as secretary of public education from 1964 to 1970. During this time *The Edge of the Storm* became required reading in Mexican public schools.

At this busy stage of his public life, encouraged by his success as a literary figure, Yáñez returned to the project he had begun with *The Edge of the Storm*: the attempt to portray Mexican life in all its facets. He abandoned such subjects as the intimate and personal conflicts of youth in favor of those with a clear social and political commitment. The novels written after the long pause that followed *The Edge of the Storm* are fictionalizations of Yáñez' ideology and convey various themes of social protest. Either as indictments of Mexican postrevolutionary society or of outdated repressive systems, they fall into two categories. First are the rural novels, *La tierra pródiga* (The Fertile Land, 1960) and *Las tierras flacas* (The Lean Lands, 1962). The others have an urban setting and include *La creación* (The Creation, 1959) and *Ojerosa y pintada* (Hollow-eyed and Made-up, 1960). Although none were of the quality or received the recognition of *The Edge of the Storm*, the novels as a collection add up to a panoramic view of Mexican reality and display Yáñez' artistic versatility.

The imagery-laden *Tierra pródiga* portrays the lives of several caciques (rural bosses) who fight for control of virgin lands on the Mexican west coast. As a variation on the recurring Latin American theme of civilization versus primitivism, the novel conveys a message of the triumph of progress over chaos. The land as an instrument of power, another traditional Latin American theme, is the basis for the struggle among the characters. Through his comparison of the modern exploiter to the conquistadors, the author shows that the earth yields fruit when it is cherished and destroys when abused. The protagonist, symbolically called El Amarillo (Mr. Yellow), overcomes his six rivals but loses out to the engineer who develops the land. The ultimate message is optimistic, however: although the struggle for power is ongoing and will never die, reason will control barbarism and order will prevail.

The tropical setting provided Yáñez the opportunity to use in *La tierra pródiga* a rich, baroque style reminiscent of his poetic essays. Its descriptions of nature were some of Yáñez' personal favorites; he selected one for a recorded reading of his most representative work. Moreover, the structure of the novel continues his use of the techniques of counterpoint and shifting point of view seen in *The Edge of the Storm*. The humorous vein that appears in Yáñez' earlier works returns in the characterizations of the caciques, who embody the *macho* as described by Octavio Paz in his famous work *El laberinto de la soledad* (*The Labyrinth of Solitude*, 1950). An episode shows El Amarillo and his men taking a tractor across a river on a raft. When it capsizes and the men fall into the water, the raging boss takes out his revolver, points it at the men and says: "If one of you drowns, I'll kill him!" Yáñez seems to make the point that the cacique, with all his faults, is inherent to Mexican life and must be accepted.

The Lean Lands continues the rural theme but shifts the setting to an austere region characterized by dour, superstitious people. In this novel, Yáñez focuses on the strong folkloric vein in the legends and proverbs of the inhabitants of the central plains. The author shows how the caciques were mythicized through the story of Don Epifanio, who haunts the region after his death. The novel clearly echoes Rulfo's *Pedro Páramo*, but Yáñez makes the character humorous through the use of hyperbole. The feudal lord of Yáñez's novel, whose children are sadistic replicas of

their father, is a benevolent and sympathetic being rather than a social menace. Yáñez achieves this characterization by having Don Epifanio speak primarily in proverbs, a device that makes him seem an exaggerated version of the typical rural inhabitant. The novelist also counterposes the earthly boss with the folk healer Matiana, who represents the obscure powers of superstition and the fear of the unknown.

A third theme is that of progress, which appears as a sewing machine, a symbol of a force that neither the cacique nor the sorceress can control. As in *La tierra pródiga*, Yáñez shows that progress is inevitable, that enlightenment will prevail over obscurantism, and that civilization will overcome ignorance.

The urban novels, published during the same period, take place in Mexico City and incorporate real settings and characters. *Ojerosa y pintada*, whose title comes from a poem by López Velarde, makes reference to the fast-paced capital city, which is "hollow-eyed" from insomnia and wears the heavy makeup of the fallen city woman. Yáñez, despite the time he spent in the city, still felt that it corrupted those transplanted from the provinces. Not forgetting his roots, he never accepted the values adopted by the postrevolutionary exiles to Mexico City.

The framework of *Ojerosa y pintada* spans twenty-four hours during which a taxi driver must drive his cab because the relief driver is ill. Beginning with a birth and ending with a death, the novel portrays a cross section of urban life, from the poor waif to the corrupt politician, from the rich society woman to the humble, working-class family. The traditional, episodic structure gives voice to social commentary. Placed in the center of the novel is an interlude with a character who describes the city sewers as the underbelly of civilization. Yáñez, perhaps inspired by the murals of his compatriot artists, created a panorama of the city that presented a "dance of death" theme. As Azuela had done earlier, Yáñez reminds us that society was headed for a downfall after the Revolution. Despite the caricature and flat characterizations that result from a panorama, Yáñez effectively conveys his message of hope and despair.

Ojerosa y pintada succeeded because of the vivid picture of everyday life that Yáñez was able to create. *La creación*, on the other hand, although it conveys a similar message, is one of his weakest efforts. The main characters, from *The Edge of the Storm*, are transplanted to the city after the Revolution. Gabriel, the runaway bellringer, is an artist who has returned from Europe; Victoria, the "city woman" who had driven the men mad in the repressed village, is his benefactor. In contrast to the sculptural countenance she displayed in the earlier work, she is confined to a wheelchair. María, married to a politician who is also a village native, is a persistent hindrance to Gabriel's creativity.

This novel brings home the fact that in Yáñez' style, the symbiosis between atmosphere and character development is vital. The impact that resulted, in *The Edge of the Storm*, from the characters' interaction with their milieu is diminished as they become absorbed in the busy artistic life of the city. As he turned his vivid characters into abstract representations of the creative act, Yáñez eliminated the strong impact they had had on the reader as forces in the earlier book. The structure, arranged as a symphony in four movements, fails to communicate the message and appears contrived. The predominance of form over character development becomes an obstacle to the theme, since Gabriel's conflict remains superficial and cannot be shared. A dream in which the Muses appear to the artist is, as one critic aptly stated, "overly worked out" and adds little to our understanding of Gabriel.

The last novel to appear was *Las vueltas del tiempo* (As Time Marches On, 1973). This work, also related to *The Edge of the Storm* in that it revives its characters, was written much earlier, but because of its controversial political nature, it was published only after Yáñez left his important government post. By that time, however, the novel was of little interest because its political attacks were no longer inflammatory and because structurally it lacked innovation. By 1973 the Latin American novel was beyond the revolutionary moment known as the boom, and in Mexico the new-wave novel called *la novela de la onda* had reached its peak. The student movements and the Tlatelolco massacre of 1968 replaced the Revolution as the most important literary Mexican theme.

Notwithstanding some failed efforts in his literary production, Yáñez remains an important Latin American writer. His panoramic sense of Mexican life, his strong social commitment, his stylistic talent, and his role in the culture and politics of his country make him a revered and versatile figure in Mexico, and one who was instrumental in the country's struggle to come into the twentieth century. Yáñez' statue in Guadalajara, the streets and buildings that bear his name in various Mexican cities, and the reissuing of his works remind us that Agustín Yáñez is an integral part of Mexico's present as well as of its past.

SELECTED BIBLIOGRAPHY

First Editions

Fiction

Flor de juegos antiguos. Guadalajara, Mexico, 1942.
Archipiélago de mujeres. Mexico City, 1943.
Pasión y convalecencia. Mexico City, 1943.
Ésta es mala suerte. Mexico City, 1945.
Melibea, Isolda y Alda en tierras cálidas. Buenos Aires, 1946.
Al filo del agua. Mexico City, 1947.
La creación. Mexico City, 1959.
Ojerosa y pintada. Mexico City, 1960.
La tierra pródiga. Mexico City, 1960.
Las tierras flacas. Mexico City, 1962.
Las vueltas del tiempo. Mexico City, 1973.

Essays

Espejismo de Juchitán. Mexico City, 1940.
Genio y figuras de Guadalajara. Mexico City, 1941.
El contenido social de la literatura iberoamericana. Mexico City, 1944.
Fichas mexicanas. Mexico City, 1945.
Yahualica. Mexico City, 1946.
Don Justo Sierra: Su vida, sus ideas y sus obras. Mexico City, 1950.
Discursos por Jalisco. Mexico City, 1958.
Días de Bali. Mexico City, 1964.
Por tierras de Nueva Galicia. Mexico City, 1975.
Santa Anna: Espectro de una sociedad. Mexico City, 1982.

Translations

The Edge of the Storm. Translated by Ethel Brinton. Austin, Tex., 1963.
The Lean Lands. Translated by Ethel Brinton. Austin, Tex., 1968.

Biographical and Critical Studies

Arango, Manuel Antonio. "Aspectos sexuales y sicológicos en el 'Acto preparatorio' en la novela *Al filo del agua* de Agustín Yáñez." *Cuadernos americanos* 37/215: 173–181 (1978).

Brushwood, John S. *Mexico in Its Novel.* Austin, Tex., 1966.

———. "The Lyric Style of Agustín Yáñez." *Symposium* 26/1:5–14 (1972).

Camp, Roderic. "An Intellectual in Mexican Politics: The Case of Agustín Yáñez." *Mester* 12/1–2:3–17 (1983). This issue of *Mester* is dedicated to Yáñez.

Carballo, Emmanuel. *Diecinueve protagonistas de la literatura mexicana del siglo XX.* Mexico City, 1965. Pp. 283–324.

Clark, Stella T. "El estilo y sus efectos en la prosa de Agustín Yáñez." Ph.D. diss., University of Kansas, 1971.

———. "Efectos estilísticos en el ensayo poético de Agustín Yáñez." *Explicación de textos literarios* 4/1:75–81 (1975–1976).

Connolly, Eileen M. "La centralidad del protagonista en *Al filo del agua.*" *Revista iberoamericana* 32/62:275–280 (1966).

Dellapiane, Angela B. "Releyendo *Al filo del agua.*" *Cuadernos americanos* 34/201:182–206 (1975).

Doudoroff, Michael J. "Tensions and Triangles in *Al filo del agua.*" *Hispania* 57/1:1–12 (1974).

Durand, Frank. "The Apocalyptic Vision of *Al filo del agua.*" *Symposium* 25/4:333–346 (1971).

Evans, Gilbert. "El mundo novelístico de Agustín Yáñez." Ph.D. diss., Yale University, 1965.

Fernández, Magali. *Rómulo Gallegos y Agustín Yáñez.* New York, 1972.

Flasher, John J. *México contemporáneo en las novelas de Agustín Yáñez.* Mexico City, 1969.

Giacoman, Helmy F., ed. *Homenaje a Agustín Yáñez: Variaciones interpretativas en torno a su obra.* Long Island City, N.Y., 1973.

Graham, Barbara. "Social and Stylistic Realities in the Fiction of Agustín Yáñez." Ph.D. diss., University of Miami, 1969.

Haddad, Elaine. "Agustín Yáñez: From Intuition to Intellectualism." Ph.D. diss., University of Wisconsin, 1962.

———. "The Structure of *Al filo del agua.*" *Hispania* 47/3:522–529 (1964).

Hancock, Joel, and Ned Davison. "*Al filo del agua* Revisited: A Computer-Aided Analysis of Theme and Rhythm in the 'Acto preparatorio'." *Chasqui* 8/1: 23–42 (1978).

Martínez, José Luis. "La formación literaria de Agustín Yáñez y *Al filo del agua.*" *Mester* 12/1–2:26–40 (1983).

Menton, Seymour. "Asturias, Carpentier y Yáñez: Paralelismos y divergencias." *Revista iberoamericana* 35/67:31–52 (1969).

Merrell, Floyd F. "Sacred-Secular Complementarity in *Al filo del agua* and *Pedro Páramo*: An Inquiry into Mythmaking." Ph.D. diss., University of New Mexico, 1973.

O'Neill, Samuel J. "Interior Monologue in *Al filo del agua.*" *Hispania* 51/3:447–456 (1968).

Rangel Guerra, Alfonso. *Agustín Yáñez.* Mexico City, 1969.

Schade, George D. "Augury in *Al filo del agua.*" *Texas Studies in Literature and Language* 2/1:78–87 (1960).

Skirius, John. "The Cycles of History and Memory: *Las vueltas del tiempo*, a Novel by Agustín Yáñez." *Mester* 12/1–2:78–100 (1983).

Sommers, Joseph. *After the Storm: Landmarks of the Modern Mexican Novel.* Albuquerque, N.Mex., 1968.

Souza, Raymond D. "Two Early Works of Agustín Yáñez." *Romance Notes* 11:522–525 (1970).

Torres, Otto Ricardo. "El léxico en *Al filo del agua.*" *Thesaurus* 30/2:346–358 (1975).

Van Conant, Linda M. *Agustín Yáñez: Intérprete de la novela mexicana moderna.* Mexico City, 1969.

Walker, John L. "Time in the Novels of Agustín Yáñez." Ph.D. diss., University of California, 1971.

———. "Timelessness Through Memory in the Novels of Agustín Yáñez." *Hispania* 57/3:445–451 (1974).

Young, Richard A. "Perspectivas autobiográficas en *Flor de juegos antiguos* de Agustín Yáñez." *Abside* 40/3: 247–269 (1976).

Pablo Neruda

(1904–1973)

George D. Schade

Pablo Neruda was the most frequently discussed Latin American poet of his time. Today, years after his death, his eventful life still evokes great interest, and his works arouse great admiration. Whatever defects critics may find in his vast and steady outpouring of verse, Neruda remains the indisputable master of twentieth-century Spanish, as well as Spanish-American, poetry. His international reputation continues to swell, going far beyond Hispanic boundaries; he is a major poet to reckon with in any language. Near the end of his life, Neruda's poetic genius, apparent to readers everywhere, was recognized by Nobel judges as they awarded him the prize for literature in 1971.

Neruda's verse, from the earliest tomes published in the 1920's to the posthumous volumes of 1974— about fifty books in just over fifty years—is notable not only for its prodigious quantity, but also for its consistently high aesthetic quality. There are so many Nerudas, so many different styles of writing, that it is not easy to break down his work and analyze it. He began with an apprenticeship to modernism that he cast off almost immediately; then came the bittersweet, realistic love poems that brought him fame when he was barely twenty. Next he produced the *Residencia en la tierra* (*Residence on Earth*) series: ferocious, world-weary, often hermetic poetry that

dazzled most critics. This work was followed by a style that indulged in prophecy, in which political propaganda seemed at times to overshadow poetic inspiration, though this style at its best characterized the masterful "Alturas de Macchu Picchu" ("The Heights of Macchu Picchu," published in book form in 1947), a beautiful and moving hymn to Latin America, especially its Indian origins.

In the 1950's Neruda, in his volumes of odes, turned to a simple style filled with lyricism and the rich throb of everyday life and things. In the last decade of his life, he published a series of autobiographical books, with many nostalgic glances at his past. As one critic has shrewdly observed, Neruda did not go looking for new styles of writing so much as he sloughed off old ones, like a lizard discarding its skin. Perhaps that explains in part why this Chilean poet has provoked such a variety of critical reactions, from grudging admiration to idolatry, and why he strikes a responsive chord in most readers.

Neruda's autobiography, *Confieso que he vivido: Memorias* (I Confess I Have Lived: Memoirs, 1974; translated as *Memoirs*), came out shortly after his death and is written from the perspective of an immensely successful poet looking back over his life. Although this book helps to explain the man and his works, perhaps the real interior biography can be pieced together only by studying Neruda's poetry. At one point Neruda declares, "If you ask what my poetry is, I must confess that I don't know; but if you'll ask my poetry, it will tell you who I am" (quoted in Hernán Loyola, ed., *Antología esencial*, p. 7).

Neruda's poems are filled with his hopes and desires, his innermost feelings of joy and sadness, rage and despair. Much critical work has been published on Neruda: the bibliography grows apace, and there now exist a number of worthy book-length studies, scholarly articles, and interviews containing pertinent and useful information. In addition, Neruda's memoirs house a rich lode of personal reminiscences. These varied sources yield a plentiful harvest: a full-length portrait, in some depth, of the man and his prolific outpouring of works.

Neftalí Eliecer Ricardo Reyes Basoalto—Neruda's real name, which he officially changed as soon as he could, in 1920, to the more euphonious Pablo Neruda—was born on 12 July 1904 in Parral, a small wine-producing town in the central valley of southern Chile. Neruda came from sturdy peasant stock of mixed Spanish and Indian heritage. His father was from a large and impoverished family of landholders, and his mother was a schoolteacher who died of tuberculosis scarcely a month after his birth. His father soon remarried a kind, gentle woman, who raised Neruda with the same loving care she lavished on her own children, Neruda's half sister and half brother.

In 1906, when Neruda was still a small child, his father set out to make a better living, as a railroad conductor, moving his family much farther south to the frontier city of Temuco. There Neruda grew up, in a thickly forested country that was almost constantly drenched by rain. The images of wood and water this land evoked in the sensitive child recurred later, obsessively, in his poetry. As a child, Neruda liked to wander about in the woods, and he came to admire the Indians of that area, who were trying to preserve the remains of their culture. He also loved reading and in section 1 of his memoirs confessed, "I gobbled up everything, indiscriminately, like an ostrich." He was precocious in writing, too, and penned his first poems as a young boy. His father was always stern with his son and, from the beginning,

frowned on his poetic leanings. In these early years, Neruda did meet a kindred spirit, Gabriela Mistral, who later would also be awarded a Nobel Prize for literature. For several years Mistral held a post in Temuco as principal of the girls' high school. She recognized Neruda's talent, encouraged him to write poems, and loaned him books.

When he finished his secondary studies in Temuco in 1921, Neruda decided to strike out on his own and go to Santiago, Chile's big city, ostensibly to continue his studies in order to become a French teacher. However, this move proved to be the first in a series of radical changes he would make in his life, usually involving trips and moves to far-off places. In Santiago, Neruda led a bohemian existence, barely eking out a subsistence. He never finished his studies at the university but was happy with his new friends, most of them poets and some very extravagant in their behavior. Neruda's rather turbulent love life, involving many women over the course of his life, began during these student years in Santiago. Chiefly memorable at this time was his affair with the mysterious girl in the beret (identified many years later as Albertina Azócar), whom he immortalized in some of the poems of his celebrated *Veinte poemas de amor y una canción desesperada* (*Twenty Love Poems and a Song of Despair*, 1924).

Twenty Love Poems, Neruda's first major book, brought him acclaim at age twenty. Even earlier, however, in 1921 his "Canción de la fiesta" (Fiesta Song) had won first prize in the Spring Festival of the Students' Federation in Santiago, and in 1923 his first volume of poems, *Crepusculario* (Twilight Book), appeared, much influenced by the modernist mode of theme and style. Neruda soon cast off the romantic and modernist trappings of these adolescent poems, although echoes of them remain in *Twenty Love Poems*. In this collection, Neruda adhered to certain traditional verse forms and meters, but the content and tone of the poetry had changed. These poems are voluptuous, and both joyous and sad, written in a style of remarkable simplicity and sincerity that appeals to readers of all ages, especially young lovers.

Two years later, in 1926, Neruda published two works of little resonance: *Anillos* (Rings), prose pieces written in collaboration with his friend Tomás Lago, and a short novel, *El habitante y su esperanza* (The Inhabitant and His Hope). The same year, his poetic work exhibited a new phase, reflected in the almost tortured turn taken in the verses of his next book, *Tentativa del hombre infinito* (Venture of Infinite Man). Here he plunged into the vanguard stream, where for many conventional critics real poetry seemed to disintegrate—all run on together, with no punctuation or capital letters, the meaning often floating off into obscurity. This book was a challenge, a slap at traditional patterns of rhyme, meter, and stanza, a far cry from *Twenty Love Poems*, which all readers could understand and appreciate. Here Neruda seemingly broke with tradition in both form and content, and expressed his doubts and anguish about mankind through an obscure interior monologue. Nonetheless, a careful analysis of this long poem reveals that it does hang together, following the model of such hermetic and extensive voyage poems as Arthur Rimbaud's *Le bateau ivre* (*The Drunken Boat*, 1898) and Charles Baudelaire's "Le voyage" ("The Voyage," 1861). Because of the difficulty of reading *Tentativa*, this book has not received the attention Neruda expected or that it probably merits. What is important is that it serves, with its innovative language, style, and highly charged lyricism, as a link between the two masterpieces *Twenty Love Poems* and *Residence on Earth*.

By this time Neruda had long since given up on his studies, and his father had stopped sending his meager monthly allowance. Despite the popularity of *Twenty Love Poems*, Neruda had problems making ends meet and soon became despondent. Restless and adventuresome, in 1927 he obtained an appointment as Chilean consul to Rangoon in faraway Burma and, together with a close friend, set out on the long journey to the Far East. He traveled first across the Andes to Buenos Aires, and from there embarked for Europe, stopping off in Lisbon, then Madrid and Paris. From the port of Marseilles, he took another boat to the Orient, where he stayed for five years.

Though some of the poetry of the first volume of *Residence* was composed between 1925 and 1927, before Neruda left Chile, most of these anguished poems were written while he was serving abroad as consul, first in Burma, later in Ceylon and Java. Almost totally isolated from Occidentals in Rangoon,

where there were no Spanish speakers, Neruda suffered in the tropical heat and had money problems. He was ill-paid, and sometimes the checks were delayed for months. For Neruda, the Orient became a mixture of chaos, poverty, and oppression, though his own personal solitude and feelings of despair were uppermost in his mind. During these years he wrote some of his gloomiest poems. Poetry served him as an escape, but not into beauty, as it had with modernists like Rubén Darío.

Sex also distracted him, and he carried on a torrid romance with a native Burmese girl with an English name, Josie Bliss. She moved in with him and soon showed herself to be of an extremely jealous nature, threatening to kill him with her carving knife if he should betray her. In 1928 Neruda was appointed to the Chilean consulship in Colombo, which he accepted with alacrity to escape from Josie's clutches, and without her knowledge, he set sail for Ceylon. Josie followed him there, where their second and final break took place. Neruda recounts the chief details of this tempestuous affair and the remorse he felt afterwards not only in his memoirs; he also leaves an impressive testimony of it in several poems of *Residence*, such as "Tango del viudo" ("Widower's Tango").

In Ceylon, Neruda continued to be plagued by solitude and loneliness. In 1930 he was transferred to another Far East post, Batavia in the Dutch East Indies. There he fell in love with a Dutch girl, Maria Antonieta Hagenaar, and married her. From the start this marriage was a failure, for the two young people had little in common. Neruda's wife knew no Spanish and showed scant interest in poetry or in the life of the intellect. After a year's stay as consul in Singapore, Neruda returned to Chile in 1932 with his new wife and no money. The couple journeyed by train to Temuco, where Neruda's father received them coolly.

Despite marital problems and constant monetary setbacks, the decade of the 1930's was of great significance for Neruda. During these years the formidable volumes of *Residence on Earth* made their appearance, and his life and poetry were indelibly marked by a four-year stay in Spain. During this decade he separated from Maria Hagenaar and began his long and tender affair with the Argentine painter

Delia del Carril, with whom he lived until the early 1950's.

At this time Neruda was unable to live on what his poetry brought in, so again he took on consular jobs, whose bureaucratic nature he despised: first in Buenos Aires in 1933, then in Spain in 1934. While in Buenos Aires, he became fast friends with the gifted Spanish poet Federico García Lorca, who was visiting the Argentine capital. Shortly after he moved to Spain in 1934, Neruda's only child was born. But the girl, Malva Marina, was always frail and died in Holland in 1942.

For the most part these years in Spain were a triumph for Neruda. Spain seemed to be waiting for him; after so many years of struggle and material hardship, he found almost unqualified success beyond the boundaries of his native land. He became a leader among the young Spanish poets and intellectuals. García Lorca introduced him at a poetry reading in Madrid, where he was acclaimed. The second edition of *Residence on Earth* (1925–1935), in two volumes, was published in Madrid in 1935, the first edition in one volume having come out two years earlier in Chile. A group of Spanish poets, with Neruda as editor, brought out several numbers of a new poetry journal called *Caballo verde para la poesía* (Green Horse for Poetry). All of these Spaniards—García Lorca, Rafael Alberti, Luis Cernuda, Miguel Hernández—admired Neruda's work tremendously and became his staunch friends. The only holdout was the skeptical, acid-tongued Juan Ramón Jiménez, who never really seemed to appreciate Neruda's volcanic poetry. Jiménez suggested that Neruda was "a great bad poet."

Neruda's happy days in Madrid were colored by sadness toward the end with the onset of the civil war, which raged there between 1936 and 1939. While Neruda's poetry had a powerful influence on his Spanish contemporaries, he was influenced in turn by his politically active friends. Alberti and Hernández, involved in the Communist party, helped persuade Neruda to their cause. Neruda threw himself into the political struggle with all his force, aiding the leftists against the fascist groups while he continued writing poetry. *España en el corazón* (Spain in My Heart), printed in 1937 by the soldiers of the Republic, expresses the poet's deep sympathy for his Spanish comrades. This long poem was later included in the third of his *Residence* volumes. Neruda eventually lost his consular post in Madrid because of his partisan stand, but when he returned to Chile in 1937, he continued the political battle there, traveling around the country, giving lectures and poetry readings, defending Republican Spain. He put these words into action in 1939, when as special consul in Paris he supervised the emigration to Chile of thousands of Spanish emigrés who had fled to France after the victory of Francisco Franco.

Neruda returned to Chile in 1940, but he was soon off to Mexico, where he had been named consul general by the Chilean government. He spent three years in Mexico City, fascinated by much that he found there, especially the muralist painters who dominated the cultural scene. Neruda declares in section 7 of his memoirs that Mexico was "repressed, violent, and nationalistic, wrapped in its Pre-Columbian courtesy," but at the same time he found it magical and mysterious. From Mexico he could survey the whole American continent to the south, and though he was still passionately interested in what was happening in Europe, he now became more concerned with his own roots in Hispanoamerica.

On his return to Chile in 1943, Neruda traveled by land part of the way, stopping off in Peru to see some extraordinary Indian ruins. There we find the genesis of one of his greatest poems, "The Heights of Macchu Picchu." Neruda recalls in section 8 of his memoirs how he responded to the sight of this great Incan city:

> I felt infinitely tiny in the center of that navel of stone; navel of a world uninhabited, proud and eminent, to which in some way I belonged. I felt that my own hands had worked there in some far-off epoch, digging grooves and smoothing away cliffs. I felt Chilean, Peruvian, American. I had found in those difficult heights, among those glorious ruins, a profession of faith for the continuation of my song.

Indeed, the song continued splendidly, though at times in a somewhat unruly fashion, in Neruda's next important book, *Canto general* (General Song, 1950). In the years between his return to Chile in 1943 and the appearance of *Canto general*, Neruda's life continued to be fraught with excitement and adventure. He was elected as a senator in 1945, and he officially joined the Chilean Communist party, to which he maintained allegiance for the rest of his life. In 1947, however, he quarreled with the leftist Chilean president Gabriel González Videla, who had become conservative while in office. González Videla's government outlawed the Communist party, and Neruda's arrest was ordered. The poet had to go into hiding, and he moved about from one Chilean town and city to another to escape detection. Much of *Canto general* was composed while he was being pursued, a situation reflected in the indignation that colors the book's form, tone, and language. In 1949, with his manuscript safely in hand, he managed to cross the Andes in southern Chile by horseback to take refuge in Argentina.

From 1934 until the early 1950's, Neruda's faithful and constant companion was Delia del Carril. Delia was almost twenty years older than Neruda, a strong-minded, lively, and attractive woman who helped him in many ways. They had met and spent their first years together in Madrid, where, according to Neruda, they were both as poor as church mice, though she came from a rich, landholding, Argentine family. Later, they were in a much better economic situation in Chile, where on any given day in Santiago twenty people or more would show up or be invited for dinner at their home. During the difficult days of Neruda's persecution as a communist in Chile, Delia also accompanied him, hiding for almost a year in a fisherman's shanty in Valparaiso, trying to keep up his flagging spirits. Unlike Neruda's first wife, Delia was intelligent and intellectual. She admired his poetry and served him as proofreader and critic. When he finally separated from her after eighteen years, it was because he had fallen in love with another woman, Matilde Urrutia, a Chilean. Matilde, who was a good deal younger than Neruda, became his last wife, and the inspiration for many books of poetry during the final two decades of his life.

The first of these volumes was published in Italy in 1952 as *Los versos del capitán* (*The Captain's Verses*)— anonymously, because Neruda did not wish to wound Delia. Later the truth emerged, and he acknowledged authorship of these poems. The joy and sheer exuberance of living during the first years with Matilde, in the 1950's, are attested to by Neruda in a series of sprightly books initiated by *Odas elementales* (*Elemen-*

tary Odes, 1954). These volumes mark another important change in Neruda's style of writing and surprised everyone with their unusual simplicity and their praise of such unpoetic things of daily life as onions, lemons, socks, and spoons. They also evoked disappointment from critics who preferred his former baroque hermeticism and from those who thought that all his poetry should reflect a strong social commitment.

From 1952 on Neruda was more or less settled in Chile, where he established several houses, one in Valparaiso, another in Santiago, and the most famous, where he spent much of his time, on Isla Negra, a peninsula facing the sea near the port of Valparaiso. Here he indulged in his weakness for collecting bric-a-brac (seashells, figureheads, and the like) and books. He was happy to stay at home for a change, content with his success and now treated with great respect in his native land and abroad. But his voyages to all parts of the globe continued. Just before his return to Chile, he had traveled in 1951 throughout Europe, the Soviet Union, and Asia, especially to Communist China, making friends everywhere and meeting important people, heads of state among them. In 1953 he received the Stalin Peace Prize. In 1965 Oxford University in England recognized him with an honorary degree, and in 1966 he spoke to the PEN Club in New York.

After the series of odes, Neruda's poetry continued to evolve and change, and a number of significant volumes appeared with astonishing regularity, particularly in his last years, as though he knew the end was near. *Estravagario* (*Extravagaria,* 1958), a book of "vagaries," marked still another change in Neruda's style. It is a combining of past styles, a book born of memories but also a response to ideas of the present. Beginning with the opening poem, set in unusual typography, this work was unexpected. While in some of Neruda's previous volumes his posture as writer of the people was clearly flaunted, in *Extravagaria* the poet turned inward. Solemnity has departed; conversation, individualism, and even a note of frivolity reign in this miscellaneous text filled with poems of substance. By now Neruda no longer needed to accept diplomatic jobs to make a living. His poetry brought in enough money that he could devote full time to it. Despite his frequent journeys, he now reveled in the tranquillity of his island retreat. His collections of poetry reflected this change, becoming generally more personal and contemplative.

A steady stream of books poured forth from the poet's untiring pen, among them *Cien sonetos de amor* (One Hundred Love Sonnets, 1959), in which Neruda reverted to traditional verse form to express his love for Matilde, and *Las piedras de Chile* (The Stones of Chile, 1961), a collection extolling the virtues and charms of the rock formations around Isla Negra. Neruda reached another high point with the five autobiographical volumes published under the broad title *Memorial de Isla Negra* (*Isla Negra: A Notebook*, 1964). At sixty years old, Neruda looked back nostalgically over his life in these testimonial books. After starting with his early childhood memories in Temuco, "where the rain is born," he recalled early affairs of the heart, the opiate days spent in the Far East and with Josie Bliss, and his enduring love for Chile—all cast in the warm glow of memory and reminiscence. At this time he also began to work on his prose memoirs, parts of which he published in a Brazilian journal in 1962.

Neruda also tried his hand at writing a theatrical piece, *Fulgor y muerte de Joaquín Murieta* (*Splendor and Death of Joaquín Murieta*, 1967). And he continued to publish important books of poems, like *Las manos del día* (The Hands of Day, 1968) and *Aún* (*Still Another Day*, 1969). The poet's prolific writing during these years did not diminish his interest in politics; indeed, in 1969 and 1970 he again became involved in the campaign for the Chilean presidency as the official Communist candidate. Later, however, he renounced his candidacy in order to support the other chief leftist candidate from the Socialist party, his friend Salvador Allende. When Allende won the election, Neruda again accepted a diplomatic post, this time as ambassador to France. While living in Paris, he received the Nobel Prize for literature in 1971, the crowning achievement of his long career devoted to poetry. But he was now suffering from cancer and in 1972 returned for the last time to Chile, where he worked feverishly on various books of verse as well as his memoirs in prose. He died on 23 September 1973 in Santiago, at the age of sixty-nine, a few days after a military coup overthrew the Allende government.

Eight slender books of poetry as well as his admirable prose autobiography came out within a year after his death. In addition to the themes we are accustomed to in Neruda's work, in these volumes the poet comes face to face with his own imminent demise, giving a somber tone to some of the poems. But many others pulse with life and the exuberance of living; only death could still Neruda's vibrant song, his extraordinary production of poems full of heart at the core.

In this century of slogans, everything must be labeled. In this respect the critics have had a field day with the many-sided Neruda, who slips off one skin to take on another. We can divide his work into general categories for analysis, as two critics, Manuel Durán and Margery Safir, have aptly done: the nature poet, the public poet, the erotic poet, and the personal poet, lumping together volumes from distinct eras in his career under each of these headings. Or we can turn to other critics like René de Costa, who discusses his major works as cycles: love poetry, the vanguard experiment, hermeticism, epic poetry, plain lyricism, and conversational poetry. Perhaps the latter method provides the best sense of order; however, an exhaustive analysis of all of Neruda's significant works is beyond the scope of this article.

Some poets write poems, and others write books. Neruda is a poet who undoubtedly wrote books. With the exception of some of his earliest adolescent verse, written while he was still searching for his true voice, his books contain a sense of unity and seem to develop within a cycle. As one of his most perspicacious critics, Emir Rodríguez Monegal, remarked, "Neruda seems to start from a single conception or internal impulse that postulates from the beginning the form of the new book. With him it is always a question of a concrete book to be produced: a discovery through verse of the total shape of the book" (*Review 74*, p. 6).

Of Neruda's multitudinous achievements, few have compared in immediate popularity and continuing success with his first significant book, *Twenty Love Poems and a Song of Despair*. This slender work has been translated into many languages and has sold over two million copies in Spanish since it was first published in 1924, a feat seldom achieved by a book of poetry in any language. *Twenty Love Poems* reveals in the main part of its title its central theme, the love for women, and imparts in the second part, *A Song of Despair*, its melancholy uniformity of tone. Neruda's love for women in these poems is overwhelmingly physical. Woman is not the idealized beloved we find in Petrarch or Garcilaso de la Vega. She is a concrete reality based especially on the love Neruda felt for two women, one whom he knew during his days in Temuco, the other a classmate at the university in Santiago. In the poems themselves these two young women remain unidentified. Thirty years later Neruda referred to them rather cryptically in an interview as Marisol and Marisombra, and only when some of his purloined letters were published posthumously in 1974 was the main inspiration of these poems, the passionate Santiago girl in the beret, revealed to be Albertina Azócar, the sister of his close friend Rubén Azócar.

What matters most, of course, is not exactly who these young women were but how they inspired the poet. In *Twenty Love Poems* Neruda obsessively describes the beloved's body, and in Poem 1 through Poem 20 he encounters woman through the act of love. But the speaker in these poems is alone, recalling the moments of passion he shared with his beloved. The woman is absent and remote; consequently, the sincerity of the emotion seems more poignant. Neruda conveys this first, young love with great force and persuasiveness. We feel the awakening of erotic passion, the trembling and astonishment, the desire for possession, the tenderness, and finally the loneliness that follows.

Twenty Love Poems was daring in its frankness in the eyes of many readers of that era. Though the poems lost their shock value long ago, they still remain impressive in their sincerity; they emerge from deeply felt emotions. As Neruda later observed to his friend and commentator Margarita Aguirre, "I have never uttered insincere words of love. I could not have written a single line that departed from the truth" (*Las vidas de Pablo Neruda*, p. 113). Books of erotic poetry tend to be short, as is this one, for the tension involved from the beginning is great and cannot be sustained too long. After a climax the poet sinks into melancholy and solitude. In such poetry we usually find particular elements: passion, sensuality,

reproaches, the absence of the beloved, and consequent loneliness. Neruda succeeds in using the right proportions of these ingredients in *Twenty Love Poems*, creating a mixture of elements that goes a long way toward explaining their immense popularity. Passion dominates in the book and is especially strong at the start, but little by little shadows present themselves along with the light, and in the end, darkness seems to take over. A song of despair closes the collection.

The form in *Twenty Love Poems* is significant, too. It represented a change from the earlier modernist insistence on sculptured form in Spanish-American poetry, but it was not a real break with tradition; that would come with Neruda's next books. Each of these love poems is slightly different in form from the rest, but we find a predominance of fourteen-syllable alexandrines, fixed and unfixed strophe patterns with stanzas of only one line occurring regularly, a mixture of consonance and assonance, and often a suppression of rhyme. Here, content takes precedence over form, which seems to have become subservient to the unity of theme and the poet's unabashed sincerity. This book affects readers with its sincerity and its intensity. Though contemporary readers are no longer shocked by the sexuality in these poems, we are moved by the intimacy of the emotions.

Each decade in Neruda's poetic career seemed to produce a major work. If the 1920's were marked by *Twenty Love Poems*, the 1930's clearly were devoted to his distinguished *Residence on Earth* volumes. While the composition of these three books spanned two decades (the first two volumes the years 1925 to 1935, and *Tercera residencia* [*Third Residence*], 1935 to 1945), most of these poems were published during the 1930's, and their main impact was felt then. With these books, Neruda became internationally acclaimed as the great poet of the Spanish language. In them, he furnished a new diction and a new style of writing for Spanish poetry. In his masterful hands poetry became voluble, fierce, volcanic. It unleashed forces seemingly not seen or heard before. In the *Residence* books, antipoetical imagery abounds, metaphors are heaped one upon another, and obscurity sometimes prevails.

Neruda expressed in the *Residence* cycle the oppressive loneliness and the feelings of acute depression that consumed him during the years he spent in the Far East, when most of these poems were written. All the hostility, aggressiveness, and repugnance he felt toward mankind and the world, especially the so-called civilized world, break forth and spew out in this poetry. He visualizes man as adrift in an unfriendly and indifferent world, and rebels against this, sometimes declaiming in halting but harsh tones, at other times ranting and raving.

Amado Alonso, the first important critic to publish a major book on Neruda, analyzes at some length many poems in *Residence*. He stresses the Chilean's extraordinarily bleak world vision, noting how he makes inordinate use of the ugly and the hideous to describe the way things are. In the *Residence* books, life seems to be incessantly dying, the physical world crumbles around us, death has us in its grasp. Alonso captured the anguished essence of these books, in which Neruda's verses are "filled with images of deformity, dispossession and destruction" (*Review 74*, p. 18). Ashes and dust are mentioned most frequently; the first words of the opening poem are "Como cenizas" ("Like Ashes"). The perpetual disintegration of life is unquestionably the main theme of the first volume of *Residence*, in which the headlong rush toward death is aptly rendered in the title of the opening poem, "Galope muerto" ("Dead Gallop").

The disintegration at work in nature affects the human scene as well. Sex, for instance, is treated in various poems as sordid and degrading, a far cry from the erotic hymns of *Twenty Love Poems*. A good example of this murky sex can be found in "Caballero solo" ("Gentleman Without Company"), where Neruda provides a long enumeration of sexual encounters lacking in love. The poem closes with the poet hemmed in by all these elements of humanity as in a thick forest.

> . . . *respiratorio y enredado*
> *con grandes flores como bocas*
> *y dentaduras*
> *y negras raíces en forma de*
> *uñas y zapatos.*

> . . . tangled and breathing
> with enormous mouthlike flowers
> and dentures

and black roots shaped like
fingernails and shoes.

Nature here has taken on a grotesquely human form.

A deformed, crumbling, frightful urban landscape is the vision that obtains in most of the *Residence* cycle. One of the best poems to illustrate the poet's despair and exhaustion with this disintegration is the often-anthologized "Walking Around," with its title in English. Here Neruda's anguish and self-doubts spill over, and the external world, full of man-made products that he finds repellent, is unfeeling, alien, and hostile. Neruda conveys his spiritual malaise and repugnance in memorable lines that often contain sharp and violent imagery. As Durán and Safir observe, "The vision is overwhelming, it is quite literally mind-blowing for the poet, and for his readers" (*Earth Tones*, p. 45). For example:

> *Sucede que me canso de ser hombre.*
> . . . .
> *Y me empuja a ciertos rincones, a ciertas*
> *casas húmedas,*
> *a hospitales donde los huesos salen por la*
> *ventana,*
> *a ciertas zapaterías con olor a vinagre,*
> *a calles espantosas como grietas.*

> *Hay pájaros de color de azufre y horribles*
> *intestinos*
> *colgando de las puertas de las casas que odio,*
> *hay dentaduras olvidadas en una cafetera,*
> *hay espejos*
> *que debieran haber llorado de vergüenza y*
> *espanto,*
> . . . .
> *Yo paseo . . .*
> . . . .
> *. . . patios donde hay ropas colgadas de un*
> *alambre:*
> *calzoncillos, toallas y camisas que lloran*
> *lentas lágrimas sucias.*

> I'm sick and tired of being a man.
> . . . .
> I'm shoved into corners, certain damp
> houses,
> hospitals where bones stick out the
> windows,
> shoeshops smelling of vinegar,
> and ghastly streets all split and cracked.

There are sulphur-colored birds and
    horrible intestines
hanging from the doors of the houses I
    loathe,
there are dentures forgotten in a coffeepot,
and mirrors
that must have wept with shame and fear,
. . . .
I pass by . . .
patios with clothing on a wire:
undershorts, towels and shirts shedding
    slow, dirt-streaked tears.

Certain themes are repeated compulsively in the *Residence* volumes, such as the forces of destruction at work, the mind's questioning anguish, and sexual arousal and activity without personal feeling. A deeply negative world vision prevails. Neruda often described the chaos he sensed around him by using a technique of enumeration. Following the example of Walt Whitman, a poet he revered, Neruda strung together long catalogs of disparate elements and disjointed metaphors to express his dismay and repugnance at what he felt was happening in the natural world. Like Picasso during his cubist period in the 1930's, Neruda tended to present distorted images, giving a grotesque yet powerful effect to this collection. The existential anguish and pessimism of the *Residence* volumes are attenuated, albeit slightly, in the section of the second book called "Tres cantos materiales" ("Three Material Songs"), in which the poet sings the praises of earthly things: wood, celery, and wine. These three poems prefigure the optimism, exuberance, and joy in simple matter and objects that predominate in his odic volumes, which were published twenty years later.

Neruda's third *Residence* book continued in the same vein as the previous two but with a shift in emphasis. From the troubles of the world in general Neruda moved his camera to focus sharply on Spain, torn asunder by the throes of its savage civil war. In this way, the poet voiced not his individual concerns and suffering but spoke out collectively for all mankind. The most compelling poem in this book, "Espania en el corazón," is long, running to 800 lines, and expresses the profound tragedy of the Spanish people. Since it was so different from his earlier work, Neruda felt obliged to suggest what he

was about in one section of the poem, aptly subtitled "Explico algunas cosas" (I Explain a Few Things). This poem commences in a conversational, almost colloquial tone, but ends in a chilling scream, repeated several times, "Venid a ver la sangre por las calles!" (Come and see the blood in the streets!) These stark verses manifest Neruda's moral outrage just as his two earlier *Residence* volumes had done.

From the 1930's on, Neruda's work contained a strong element devoted to themes of social justice. After he joined the Communist party and was himself a fugitive fleeing from the police in Chile during the 1940's, this social commitment became obsessive at times and is particularly noteworthy in his next major work, *Canto general*, composed during the 1940's and published in 1950. *Canto general* was Neruda's longest and most ambitious book; usually printed in two volumes, it extends to about 500 pages, containing fifteen sections and more than 300 individual poems. Despite its prodigious length and the fact that quite a few of its poems are marred by an insistent note of political propaganda, this collection includes one of Neruda's greatest poems, "The Heights of Macchu Picchu."

Neruda divided *Canto general* into sections called cantos, like Dante's *Divine Comedy* or Ezra Pound's *Cantos*. The book gets off to an appropriately epic start with its opening poem, "Amor América" (Love, America), a beautiful hymn to Latin America, and continues splendidly in the same vein with the second canto, "The Heights of Macchu Picchu." There follow cantos dedicated to the *conquistadores* and the liberators of America, and various ones to Chile. Each canto is organized on a chronological basis: for example, the list of heroes in canto 4 begins with Mexico's Aztec emperor Cuauhtemoc and comes up to the present time. Likewise, canto 5, devoted to "La arena traicionada" ("The Land Betrayed"), starts with a harangue against Dr. Rodríguez de Francia, one of the first nineteenth-century Latin American dictators, and closes with the poet's *bête noire*, the Chilean president González Videla. The second five cantos deal almost exclusively with Chile, and the last five with the poet's everyday experiences with his people.

Rodríguez Monegal rightly called this book rich and complex, yet poor and simplistic. Probably Neruda tried to accomplish too much here; as a result, the book does not come off as neatly or as successfully as his other major works. The critics have generally been in two camps about *Canto general*, either praising it too highly (those who agreed with Neruda's politics) or dismissing it too lightly (those who disagreed with his communist ideas and propaganda). Today we can stand back and judge it more fairly. Most will admire the book's grand proportions and the audacity of its conception, though some may continue to carp at them. Though Neruda's politics passionately color the entire volume, few would disagree that he remains a great poet, here unfolding his powers as the epic bard of Latin America. This is especially evident in the second canto.

"The Heights of Macchu Picchu" was first published by itself in 1947, and since then has been printed separately in various bilingual editions and translations, though it obviously belongs within the epic scope of *Canto general*. As de Costa observed, this is the text that in the large context of the complete work authenticates the poet's voice and authorizes him to speak for the hemisphere. The poet especially achieves this effect in the latter parts of the second canto, particularly in the final section, in which he exhorts all the peoples of Latin America to join him, telling them that he speaks for them and through their mouths. His final, tremendously affecting exhortation is "Hablad por mis palabras y mi sangre" (Speak through my speech and through my blood!).

Though "The Heights of Macchu Picchu" does not belong among Neruda's hermetic poetry, it still must be counted as fairly complex. However, with careful analysis, the poem can be read and understood. From section 8 on, we are constantly aware of the poet speaking to his people. Neruda experiments here with form, as he does in section 9, which is an impressive, verbless enumeration running to forty-three lines, describing the shape of the towering Macchu Picchu ruins. The poet's fertile imagination produces a stunning array of metaphors: "geometría final" (final geometry), "témpano entre las ráfagas labrado" (iceberg carved by squalls), "arquitectura de águilas perdidas" (architecture of lost eagles), and "dentadura nevada" (snowswept teeth).

In *Canto general* Neruda mythified Latin America,

and his exploration of cultural identity found an echo in the work of other contemporary Latin American writers, such as Octavio Paz in Mexico. In order to attain this collective cultural discovery, the Chilean probed the past, especially the glorious Incan past, in "The Heights of Macchu Picchu." He also chronicled other facets of Latin America's past (colonial times and the heroes of the independence era), drawing on two main wellsprings, history and myth. His language in this book, though it becomes baroque at times, tends to be direct, discursive, factual, and referential. Neruda attempted to convey a great many things simultaneously in this diverse and rambling volume: world genesis, geography, chronicle, satire, political harangue, autobiography, and prophecy. As Saúl Yurkievich observed, all this requires "a structure which is open, multiform, polytonal, prone to mixtures, superimpositions and repetitions" (Yurkievich, "Mito e historia: dos generadores del *Canto general*," in *Pablo Neruda*, edited by Emir Rodríguez Monegal and Enrico Mario Santí, p. 201).

Canto general commences with an earthly cosmogony, "La lámpara en la tierra" ("The Lamp on Earth") and concludes with an aquatic one, "El gran océano" ("The Great Ocean"). In between, many poems recall the day of origin. But Neruda felt that the world had gone astray from the mythological Edenic model. It had become denaturalized by the abuse and rapacity of powerful human groups and by social injustice. Neruda stuck to his proletariat commitment. He wanted his poetry to pass from myth to history, from nostalgic evocation to combat, from individual alienation to collective militancy, from solitude to solidarity. Such proposals are rife in *Canto general*, and they add to or detract from the book's power, depending on the reader's reaction to them. In the last cantos, the poet endeavored with an autobiographical slant to join myth and history, to bind the visionary and the militant.

The decade of the 1950's brought forth another radical change in Neruda's poetry, in which he turned from the prophetic tones and the epic flavor of *Canto general* to the simplicity and joy in elemental things expressed in his four volumes of odes. In *Elementary Odes, Nuevas odas elementales* (New Elementary Odes, 1956), *Tercer libro de odas* (Third Book of Odes, 1957), and *Navegaciones y regresos*

(Voyages and Homecomings, 1959), Neruda paid special homage to things, inanimate objects as well as living things. And all of them, frequently humble in nature, spring to life under the poet's magic touch. If we ransack Neruda's earlier work, we come across examples of his fascination with simple things, such as the poems to wood and celery in *Residence,* but in the odic cycle this quality predominates.

Brimming over with optimism and vitality, his odes display an elegant simplicity in form, with their very abbreviated lines, and in content, with their typical concentration on one object. The odes sing the praises of all kinds of things: animals, birds, flowers, fruits, and vegetables; tools, such as scissors and spoons; trucks and trains; books and typography. Neruda also included a few odes to abstractions, such as time, joy, love, happiness, and envy, and a very few were dedicated to specific people. The tone of these poems is generally light, and many of them seem to be a mixture of the calculated and the impromptu. Herein lies much of their undeniable charm, as though the poet had dashed them off in a moment of divine inspiration.

This multivolume series of poems constitutes another cycle, like the *Residence* volumes and *Canto general.* Some readers were surprised at the content and form of the odes. They seem unorthodox or unpoetic to the unsophisticated; their audaciously short lines, often only one or two syllables long, raised some eyebrows, too. But the critics were soon won over by their substance as well as their format. Delicately suspended on the page, they are attractive to look at in their short, broken-line typographical disarray, as well as satisfying in what they have to say to us.

Neruda used a technique in the odes that Durán and Safir call a spiraling pattern. His point of departure is small, almost insignificant, and the reader wonders what can be done artistically with an artichoke or onion, with the human liver, or with a truck. But Neruda manages to create an emotional link with the object. A fine example is his ode to the lowly onion, which assumes an almost unbelievable splendor and grace in his praises:

> cebolla,
> luminosa redoma
> pétalo a pétalo

se formó tu hermosura,
escamas de cristal te acrecentaron
y en el secreto de la tierra oscura
se redondeó tu vientre de rocío.
. . . .
Estrella de los pobres,
hada madrina,
envuelta
en delicado
papel, sales del suelo,
. . . .
y vive la fragrancia de la tierra
en tu naturaleza cristalina.

Onion,
luminous phial,
petal by petal
your beauty was formed,
crystal scales you sprouted
and in the secret of the dark earth
your glistening belly grew round
. . . .
Star of the poor
fairy godmother
wrapped
in delicate
paper, you emerge from the ground,
. . . .
and the fragrance of the earth lives on
in your crystalline essence.

Neruda apprehended the value and the dignity of the concrete world, which he celebrated in his odes. He was aware that our lives are immersed in the concrete, even the trivial. He knew, too, that what is significant often comes to us wrapped up in the multitudinous details of the quotidian and that these concrete things have a dignity, for they exist and are omnipresent. His "Oda a las tijeras" (Ode to Scissors) is a good example of how things are bound to man, how we are influenced in our daily lives by ordinary things. Scissors play a part in our lives from birth to death:

> Unas tijeras olvidadas
> cortaron en tu ombligo
> el hilo
> de la madre
> y te entregaron para siempre
> tu separada parte de
> existencia:

otras, no necesariamente
oscuras,
cortarán algún día
tu traje difunto.

Some forgotten scissors
cut your navel,
the thread
of your mother
and gave you forever
your own existence:
others, not necessarily
obscure,
will some day cut
your shroud when dead.

The buoyant quality of Neruda's odes is infectious. He regards things and objects, animals and plants, people, too, especially women, with joy and exuberance. Now and again he may turn critical; he does so bitingly in his "Oda a la crítica" (Ode to Criticism). But his mood is generally happy here, and his appetite for life and for living things seems unquenchable. Gleams of humor and flashes of wit light up these odes, and philosophical moments recur. Because Neruda seemed to be searching for metaphysical answers in the concrete, we find him placing much significance on objects and things. The brilliant craftsman of the earlier volumes is at work in the books of odes with an unfaltering command of his tools. Despite their fragile look upon the page, Neruda's odes are full of vigor. The best of them, like the best of his poems in other collections, have strength and body, the power to delight our imagination and to move us.

In the midst of the volumes of odes, which came out in a seemingly unending stream in the 1950's, Neruda surprised his readers again in 1958 with a very different book called *Extravagaria*, a word he coined to suggest a collection of extravagant things. For many critics *Extravagaria* is Neruda's most personal book. It is also one of his major works. Neruda himself would have agreed with this appraisal, for he described it in the following way in section 11 of his *Memoirs*:

Of all my books, *Extravagaria* is not one that sings the most, but rather the one that skips about the best. Its dancing poems skip over distinction, respect, mutual protection, establishments, and obligations, in order to sponsor reverent disrespect. Because of its irreverence, it is my most personal book. Because of its range, it achieves transcendence within my poetry. For my taste, it is a momentous book, with the tang of salt the truth always has.

Neruda's summing up of *Extravagaria* gives us an excellent idea of the book's individualistic and irreverent tone, even its willful frivolity. Here he did not ask, as he did in the odes, that his poems be practical or utilitarian. Gone is the solemnity regarding himself and his work that is found in *Canto general*. Everything in *Extravagaria* seems to be taken lightly, including the poet himself. He can even shrug off literature with a drollness that is refreshing. Poetry is no longer on its pedestal.

The untitled opening poem of *Extravagaria* sets the stage with its unusual typography and word spacing, as well as its mishmash of images joining the logical and the absurd. The poem presents a kind of intellectual puzzle or game. Indeed, games and play abound in the book, along with an emphasis on humor. Neruda seemed to want to entertain us, which he does with great success. Those searching for echoes from his earlier books will find them here. The stress on the personal goes back, some say, to *Twenty Love Poems*; a certain hermetic quality at times recalls the *Residence* cycle; the exuberance of the odes is sometimes present; the episodic narrative creeps in here and there, and we can even find traces of politics. But as Neruda tells us in his memoirs, all is irreverent here. We are in the realm of mockeries of establishments and authoritative forces, even such poetic forces as Neruda himself.

Behind the apparent jumble of poems in the collection, we can discern a sequence of themes that are related and give unity to the book. These broad themes, as Rodríguez Monegal has indicated, are life and death; a return to the past, which is ever more recurrent and strongly evoked from now on in his work; the poet's dreams; love, which overcomes all obstacles and to which the poet returns as his only firm conviction in a shifting world; and finally, one's worst enemy, oneself, that is, Pablo Neruda. Another recurring theme in *Extravagaria* is Neruda's rejection of any kind of categorization. Thus we find a poem entitled "Demasiados nombres" ("Too Many

Names"), in which the poet belabors the abundance and the meaning of names:

> Se enreda el lunes con el martes
> y la semana con el año:
> . . . .
> y todos los nombres del día
> los borra el agua de la noche.
>
> Nadie puede llamarse Pedro,
> ninguna es Rosa ni María,
> todos somos polvo o arena,
> todos somos lluvia en la lluvia.

Mondays are meshed with Tuesdays
and the week with the whole year:
. . . .
and all the names of the day
are washed out by the waters of night.

No one can claim the name of Peter,
nobody is Rose or Marie,
all of us are dust or sand,
all of us are rain in the rain.

Extravagaria is full of such ingratiating, unexpected poems, most of them quite short, many couched in colloquial, conversational language. Occasional narrative poems crop up, such as the brief and fanciful "Fábula de la sirena y los borrachos" ("Fable of the Mermaid and the Drunks"):

> Todos estos señores estaban dentro
> cuando ella entró completamente
>   desnuda
> ellos habían bebido y comenzaron
>   a escupirla
> ella no entendía nada recién
>   salía del río
> era una sirena que se había
>   extraviado.

All these gentlemen were there inside
when she entered, utterly naked.
They had been drinking, and began
   to spit at her.
Recently come from the river, she
   understood nothing.
She was a mermaid who had lost
   her way.
              (Translated by Alastair Reid)

Extravagaria comes off as an extremely individualistic, personal book, especially when we compare it with other volumes in which Neruda postures publicly as a writer of the people. The style is often what has been called antipoetry. The closing poem, "Testamento de otoño" ("Autumn Testament"), is Neruda's last will, an appropriate way to wind up this extraordinary book. In "Autumn Testament," the longest poem in the volume, Neruda speaks of the changes in himself and in his work. He shares with us his joys and sorrows, and then in the middle of the poem addresses his beloved Matilde ecstatically:

> . . . aquí te dejo
> lo que tuve y lo que no tuve,
> lo que soy y lo que no soy.
> . . . .
>
> eres para mí suculenta
> como una panadería,
> es de tierra tu corazón
> pero tus manos son celestes.

. . . I leave you here
what I had and did not have,
what I am and what I'm not
. . . .

you are as succulent for me
as a bakery full of bread,
your heart is made of earth
but your hands are celestial.

After several pages of final instructions and farewells, the poet ends the book confirming his faith in poetry.

Neruda's phenomenal capacity for turning out poetry became more apparent during the last fifteen years of his life. Between *Extravagaria* in 1958 and his death in 1973, he produced nineteen books. If we add to this total the eight slender volumes of posthumous verse, published in 1973 and 1974, plus his prose memoirs, published in 1974, we have a large body of work still to examine. Though at times we may detect an irregular pulse in the heartbeat of these later books, their quality generally remains high, for the same verbal legerdemain Neruda displayed all along is present in them. *Extravagaria*, with its eclectic tone and wide-ranging variety of themes, set the pattern for some of the books to follow, but others concentrate on one theme, such as *Arte de pájaros* (*Art of Birds*, 1966) or *Las piedras de Chile*. The latter volume, handsomely illustrated in the original edition with photographs by Neruda's friend Antonio Quintana, is devoted to the rocky formations of Chile, especially the stones the poet spies from his island home. On almost every page of this book we can get a whiff of the sea. The stones take on whimsical forms, often those of animals, in the poet's imagination; we encounter poems to a bull, a lion, three little ducks, and an ancient turtle. Neruda describes the world-weary turtle:

> De tan vieja se fue
> poniendo dura, . . . cerró
> los ojos que tanto
> mar, cielo, tiempo y tierra desafiaron,
> y se durmió
> entre las otras piedras.

> she was so old
> she hardened.
> she closed
> her eyes
> that had defied
> so much
> sea and sky, time and terrain
> and fell fast asleep
> among the other
> stones.

Neruda's love for his native Chile, a recurring theme in his work, sprang forth anew in this book. He examined the national landscape and found it strewn with all kinds of rock: the lofty Andean peaks, the calcinated stone of the northern desert region, and the boulders along the coast. As we read the pages of this most engaging volume, we marvel again at the poet's singular inventiveness, his ability to poetize earthly elements and make them come alive.

The most ambitious book Neruda published after *Extravagaria* is doubtless his autobiographical *Isla Negra: A Notebook*. The poet had just turned sixty and decided, in his words, to celebrate the occasion with a long nostalgic look backward. *Isla Negra* came out first in five separate volumes, which together form what we may consider another cycle in his poetry. In these volumes, the author explored a world he knew very intimately—himself. Of course, many

of Neruda's earlier works dealt in passing or at some length with his life. Here the autobiographical element dominates the entire collection, exclusively so in the first three books. What we find throughout *Isla Negra* is a multiple vision—a technique the poet has often used—shifting between the lyric and the narrative. The poet reconstructs his memories, which recall significant moments of his life, illustrating their importance through the use of telling detail, sharply caught sensation, and brief anecdotes.

Book 1, *Donde nace la lluvia* (*Where the Rain Is Born*), is a tremulous elegy to his childhood and early adolescence spent in Temuco. The twenty poems in this volume evoke with great tenderness the people and things he knew and loved there, and chart his awakening to life's experiences: his first glimpse of the sea as a child, his first sexual encounter as a small boy, school, books, his early fascination with poetry. The first poem celebrates his birth, and the last his arrival in Santiago and the bleak boardinghouse on Maruri Street where he first lodged in the city. Book 2, *La luna en el laberinto* (*Moon in the Labyrinth*), presents two main themes, his early loves and his voyages, particularly to the Orient. The third volume, *El fuego cruel* (*Cruel Fire*), stresses themes of political consciousness that took hold of Neruda during the Spanish civil war but also includes love poems (to Josie Bliss).

The last two books of this autobiographical series, *El cazador de raíces* (*The Hunter After Roots*) and *Sonata crítica* (*Critical Sonata*), furnish us with a splendid portrait of the mature Neruda. While in the first three books we catch glimpses of the Nerudas of the past, lovingly recreated and evaluated by the present-day poet, in the last two tomes we encounter a sort of permanent, unchanging Neruda in the different periods of his life, what one critic has called an accumulative poet, reflecting the experience amassed throughout his life and through all his poetic visions. The strong meditative and autobiographical strands in *Isla Negra* are fittingly combined in the long closing poem dedicated to his last and greatest love, Matilde Urrutia.

The personal note continues unabated in succeeding Neruda collections, like *Una casa en la arena* (*A House in the Sand*, 1966), a mixture of prose and poetry focusing on the sea, sand, rocks, and plants at

Isla Negra and also on the poet's personal involvement in the building of his home there. In 1967 *La barcarola* (La Barcarole) appeared, a volume of more complex poetry filled with further personal reminiscence. This is one of Neruda's most introspective and difficult books, in which we hurtle from one theme to another without apparent transition. Still, there are connecting threads, such as his love for Matilde and descriptions of places, like Paris, where they were together. The dominant note of introspection appears forcefully also in *Las manos del día* and *Still Another Day*. *Fin del mundo* (World's End, 1969) is in a different vein, that of Neruda's public poetry. Nevertheless, though this volume is full of despairing comments on the state of the world, the poet returns time and again to the theme of himself. He confesses in a little poem called "Siempre Yo" (Always Myself):

> Yo que quería hablar
> del siglo
> adentro de esta enredadera,
> que es mi siempre libro
> naciente,
> por todas partes me encontré
> y se me escapaban los hechos.
> . . . .
> volvía a hablar de mi persona
> y lo que me parece peor
> es que me pintaba a mí mismo
> pintado un acontecimiento

I who wanted to speak of the century
we are all wrapped up in,
within my book still being born,
everywhere I found myself
while events escaped me.
. . . .
over and over I spoke of myself
and what is worse
I painted myself
on top of each event.

Among Neruda's most interesting last books are *Las piedras del cielo* (The Stones of the Sky, 1970) and *Geografía infructuosa* (Barren Terrain, 1972).

Posthumously, Losada, his publishers in Buenos Aires, issued a cluster of poetic volumes that Neruda had finished, including in 1973 *El mar y las campanas*
(The Sea and the Bells) and *La rosa separada* (*The Separate Rose*)—inspired by a trip to Easter Island, Chile's possession in the Pacific far from the mainland—and in 1974 *Jardín de invierno* (*Winter Garden*), *El corazón amarillo* (The Yellow Heart), and *Libro de las preguntas* (The Book of Riddles). The repeated themes of fifty years of poetry are found in these last works: love and nature, the poet and his public, politics, and his beloved, as well as an additional note contrasting regenerative nature with man's waning days. The poet knew he was ill and that his death might not be far off. But Neruda knew too that he was part of the natural cycle, in which to die is also to be born or reborn.

Neruda's final major work was his prose autobiography, of which he first published fragments in 1962 in a Brazilian journal, and on which he continued to work during the last decade of his life. These *Memoirs*, which came out posthumously in 1974, are prefaced with an explanatory note that tells us much about him and his poetic methods:

These memoirs are intermittent and at times forgetful, for that's the way life is. . . . Many of my memories have faded away as I evoke them, have turned into dust like crystal irrevocably shattered. . . . The usual author of memoirs may well have lived less intensely than I, but he took more snapshots and pleases us with an abundance of detail. The poet, on the other hand, gives a gallery of ghosts shaken by fire and the darkness of his times. Perhaps I did not live in myself; perhaps I lived the life of others. The pages of these memoirs are like a forest or vineyards in the fall, they give forth yellow leaves and grapes ready to live again in the sacred wine. This is a life made up of other lives, for a poet has many lives.

With this disarmingly poetic and sincere confession at the outset of the book, Neruda gives us some idea of how he went about writing his memoirs. Later on in the beginning of section 4, when trying to recall events that took place in the Orient in 1929, he admits the difficulty he found in reconstructing them: "I shall recover these images without chronology, just like the waves that come and go." Neruda, unlike many other writers, did not stick to a strict chronological sequence in organizing his memoirs. However, he did begin with brief childhood reminiscences and followed the calendar more or less, zigzagging back and forth at will when he remembered something interesting or worthwhile to relate.

The *Memoirs* are divided into twelve *cuadernos*, (notebooks, or sections) that take the place of chapters; they vary in length considerably, although most are about thirty-five pages. Their titles provide an idea of the contents of each one: "El joven provinciano" ("The Country Boy"), "Perdido en la ciudad" ("Lost in the City"), "Los caminos del mundo" ("The Roads of the World"), "La soledad luminosa" ("Luminous Solitude"), "España en el corazón" ("Spain in My Heart"), and "La patria en tinieblas" ("My Country in Darkness"). In addition, these confessions are bound together by a series of reiterated motifs that lend unity to the book's structure. One of the most significant of these is the erotic element—the women in his life— from individual sexual encounters in exotic places to his undying love for Matilde Urrutia. Another strand that knits the volume together is geography, or the voyage. Besides these motifs, the memoirs also contain brief descriptive passages—set in italics and interlarded throughout the volume—which impart a particularly strong poetic atmosphere. For example, the first notebook commences with one called "El bosque chileno" ("The Chilean Forest"), a two-page hymn to the wooded region where Neruda passed his childhood, where he started to walk and "to sing through the world."

These memoirs are spiced with humor and amusing anecdotes. We see in them the acute pleasure Neruda took in people, animals, and houses; his passion for collecting things like seashells; his strong interest in politics; his love of the good life; his fondness for women and nature, for land, sea, and sky. Neruda's autobiography is full of the same magic poetry as his major poetic works.

Among Latin American writers, Neruda stands out as a giant. His poetry, translated into many languages, is admired everywhere. He was famous throughout his lifetime, and his reputation still waxes strong. His appeal and his themes are universal. We find mirrored in his work all the excitement of the outer world as well as the crises of his inner world. The warm current of life courses through his poetry and moves us. His poems are sometimes an intellectual and, most often, an emotional treat. He is a charismatic poet who satisfies on more than one level.

SELECTED BIBLIOGRAPHY

First Editions

Poetry

Crepusculario. Santiago, 1923.

Veinte poemas de amor y una canción desesperada. Santiago, 1924.

Tentativa del hombre infinito. Santiago, 1926.

El hondero entusiasta, 1923–1924. Santiago, 1933.

Residencia en la tierra (1925–1931). Santiago, 1933.

Residencia en la tierra (1925–1935). 2 vols. Madrid, 1935.

España en el corazón. Santiago, 1937.

Alturas de Macchu Picchu. Santiago, 1947.

Tercera residencia (1935–1945). Buenos Aires, 1947.

Canto general. Mexico City, 1950.

Los versos del capitán. Naples, 1952.

Odas elementales. Buenos Aires, 1954.

Las uvas y el viento. Santiago, 1954.

Nuevas odas elementales. Buenos Aires, 1956.

Tercer libro de odas. Buenos Aires, 1957.

Estravagario. Buenos Aires, 1958.

Cien sonetos de amor. Santiago, 1959.

Navegaciones y regresos. Buenos Aires, 1959.

Canción de gesta. Havana, 1960.

Cantos ceremoniales. Buenos Aires, 1961.

Las piedras de Chile. Buenos Aires, 1961.

Plenos poderes. Buenos Aires, 1962.

Memorial de Isla Negra. 5 vols. Buenos Aires, 1964.
    1. *Donde nace la lluvia.* 2. *La luna en el laberinto.* 3. *El fuego cruel.* 4. *El cazador de raíces.* 5. *Sonata crítica.*

Una casa en la arena. Barcelona, 1966.

Arte de pájaros. Santiago, 1966.

La barcarola. Buenos Aires, 1967.

Las manos del día. Buenos Aires, 1968.

Aún. Santiago, 1969.

Fin del mundo. Buenos Aires, 1969.

La espada encendida. Buenos Aires, 1970.

Las piedras del cielo. Buenos Aires, 1970.

Geografía infructuosa. Buenos Aires, 1972.

Incitación al nixonicidio y alabanza de la revolución chilena. Santiago, 1973.

El mar y las campanas. Buenos Aires, 1973.

La rosa separada. Buenos Aires, 1973.

El corazón amarillo. Buenos Aires, 1974.

Defectos escogidos. Buenos Aires, 1974.

Elegía. Buenos Aires, 1974.

Jardín de invierno. Buenos Aires, 1974.

Libro de las preguntas. Buenos Aires, 1974.

2.000. Buenos Aires, 1974.

Plays

Fulgor y muerte de Joaquín Murieta: Bandido chileno injusticiado en California el 23 de julio de 1853. Santiago, 1967.

Prose

Anillos. Written in collaboration with Tomás Lago. Santiago, 1926.

El habitante y su esperanza. Santiago, 1926.

Viajes: Al corazón de Quevedo y por las costas del mundo. Santiago, 1947.

Comiendo en Hungría. Written in collaboration with Miguel Angel Asturias. Budapest and Barcelona, 1969.

Cartas de amor de Pablo Neruda. Edited by Sergio Fernández Larraín. Madrid, 1974.

Confieso que he vivido: Memorias. Buenos Aires, 1974.

Para nacer he nacido. Edited by Matilde Neruda and Miguel Otero Silva. Barcelona, 1978.

Collected Works

Antología esencial. Edited by Hernán Loyola. Buenos Aires, 1971.

Obras completas. Buenos Aires, 1957. 3rd ed., 2 vols., 1968. 4th ed., 3 vols., 1973.

Obras escogidas. Edited by Francisco Coloane. 2 vols. Santiago, 1972.

Obra poética. 10 vols. Santiago, 1947–1948.

Translations

Art of Birds. Translated by Jack Schmitt. Austin, Texas, 1985.

The Captain's Verses. Translated by Donald D. Walsh. New York, 1972.

The Early Poems. Translated by David Ossman and Carlos B. Hagen. New York, 1969.

The Elementary Odes of Pablo Neruda. Translated by Carlos Lozano. New York, 1961.

Extravagaria. Translated by Alastair Reid. New York, 1974.

Fully Empowered. Translated by Alastair Reid. New York, 1975.

The Heights of Macchu Picchu. Translated by Nathaniel Tarn. London, 1966. New York, 1967.

Incitement to Nixonicide and Praise for the Chilean Revolution. Translated by Steve Kowit. Austin, Texas, 1979.

Isla Negra: A Notebook. Translated by Alastair Reid. New York, 1981.

Let the Rail Splitter Awake and Other Poems. Translated by Joseph M. Bernstein et al. New York, 1950.

Memoirs. Translated by Hardie St. Martin. New York, 1977.

Neruda and Vallejo: Selected Poems. Edited by Robert Bly. Translated by Robert Bly, John Knoepfle, and James Wright. Boston, 1971.

A New Decade (Poems: 1958–1967). Translated by Ben Belitt and Alastair Reid. New York, 1969.

New Poems: 1968–1970. Translated by Ben Belitt. New York, 1972.

Pablo Neruda: A Basic Anthology. Edited by Robert Pring-Mill. Oxford, 1975.

Residence on Earth. Translated by Clayton Eshleman. San Francisco, 1962.

———. Translated by Donald D. Walsh. New York, 1973.

Residence on Earth and Other Poems. Translated by Ángel Flores. Norfolk, Conn., 1946.

Selected Poems. Edited by Nathaniel Tarn. Translated by Anthony Kerrigan, W. S. Merwin, Alastair Reid, and Nathaniel Tarn. New York, 1972.

Selected Poems of Pablo Neruda. Translated by Ben Belitt. New York, 1961.

The Separate Rose. Translated by William O'Daly. Port Townsend, Wash., 1985.

Splendor and Death of Joaquín Murieta. Translated by Ben Belitt. New York, 1972.

Still Another Day. Translated by William O'Daly. Port Townsend, Wash., 1984.

Twenty Love Poems and a Song of Despair. Translated by W. S. Merwin. London, 1969. New York, 1976.

Twenty Poems. Translated by Robert Bly and James Wright. Madison, Wis., 1967.

We Are Many. Translated by Alastair Reid. New York, 1968.

Winter Garden. Translated by William O'Daly. Port Townsend, Wash., 1987.

Biographical and Critical Studies

Aguirre, Margarita. *Genio y figura de Pablo Neruda.* Buenos Aires, 1964.

———. *Las vidas de Pablo Neruda.* Santiago, 1967.

Alazraki, Jaime. *Poética y poesía de Pablo Neruda.* New York, 1965.

Alegría, Fernando. *Las fronteras del realismo.* Santiago, 1962.

Alonso, Amado. *Poesía y estilo de Pablo Neruda.* Buenos Aires, 1940.

Becco, Jorge Horacio. *Pablo Neruda: Bibliografía.* Buenos Aires, 1975.

Camacho Guizado, Eduardo. *Pablo Neruda: Naturaleza, historia y poética.* Madrid, 1978.

Carrillo Herrera, Gastón. "La lengua poética de Pablo Neruda: Análisis de *Alturas de Macchu Picchu.*" *Boletín* del *Instituto de Filología de la Universidad de Chile* 21:293–332 (1970).

Concha, Jaime. *Tres estudios sobre Pablo Neruda.* Palma de Mallorca, Spain, 1974.

Costa, René de. *The Poetry of Pablo Neruda.* Cambridge, Mass., and London, 1979.

Durán, Manuel, and Margery Safir. *Earth Tones. The Poetry of Pablo Neruda.* Bloomington, Indiana, 1981.

Ellis, Keith. "Change and Constancy in Pablo Neruda's Poetic Practice." *Romanische Forschungen* 84:1–17 (1972).

Felstiner, John. *Translating Neruda: The Way to Macchu Picchu.* Stanford, Calif., 1980.

Figueroa, Esperanza. "Pablo Neruda en inglés." *Revista iberoamericana* 39/82–83:301–347 (1973).

Flores, Ángel, ed. *Aproximaciones a Pablo Neruda.* Barcelona, 1974.

González Cruz, Luis F. *Memorial de Isla Negra: Integración de la visión poética de Pablo Neruda.* Miami, 1972.

Loveluck, Juan, et al. *Simposio Pablo Neruda: Actas.* New York, 1975.

Loyola, Hernán. *Ser y morir en Pablo Neruda, 1918–1945.* Santiago, 1967.

Lozada, Alfredo. *El monismo agónico de Pablo Neruda: Estructura, significado y filiación de "Residencia en la tierra."* Mexico City, 1971.

Monguió, Luis. "Kingdom of This Earth: The Poetry of Pablo Neruda." *Latin American Literary Review* 1/1: 13–24 (1972).

Montes, Hugo. *Para leer a Neruda.* Buenos Aires, 1974.

Review 74. No. 11, *Focus on "Residence on Earth"* (Spring 1974).

Riess, F. T. *The Word and the Stone.* London, 1972.

Rodman, Selden. *South America of the Poets.* New York, 1970.

Rodríguez Monegal, Emir. *El viajero inmóvil.* Buenos Aires, 1966.

———, and Enrico Mario Santí, eds. *Pablo Neruda.* Madrid, 1980.

Salmon, Russell, and Julia Lesage. "Stones and Birds: Consistency and Change in the Poetry of Pablo Neruda." *Hispania* 60/2:224–241 (1977).

Santí, Enrico Mario. *Pablo Neruda: The Poetics of Prophecy.* Ithaca, N.Y., and London, 1982.

Schade, George D. "Sight, Sense, and Sound: Seaweed, Onions, and Oranges: Notes on Translating Neruda." *Symposium* 38/2:159–173 (1984).

Vial, Sara. *Neruda en Valparaíso.* Valparaiso, 1983.

Wood, Michael. "The Poetry of Neruda." *New York Review of Books* 21:8–12 (3 October 1974).

Yurkievich, Saúl. *Fundadores de la nueva poesía hispanoamericana.* Barcelona, 1971.

Alejo Carpentier

(1904–1980)

Klaus Müller-Bergh

Alejo F. Carpentier y Valmont spent his childhood on a country estate near the village of El Cotorro, just outside Havana, where he was born on 26 December 1904. As a child, he suffered from asthma, and when at the age of ten his attacks worsened, his parents took him to the country east of the capital, first to El Lucero, a farm near San Francisco de Paula, and later to Loma de Tierra, between El Cotorro and San José de las Lajas. Friends and playmates there became his inspiration for characters in his first novel, ¡Écue-Yamba-Ó! (Praised Be God!, in the Afro-Cuban ñáñigo dialect), published in 1933. Other memories of this time—doing chores on the farm, horseback riding, swimming, raising chickens and geese—also appear in the rural setting of the last scenes of El reino de este mundo (The Kingdom of This World, 1949).

Carpentier grew up in a family of immigrants who had arrived in Cuba in 1902, one year after the establishment of the new constitution. He learned French at home and Spanish in the warm, tropical environment that surrounded him. His father, Jorge Julian Carpentier, a French architect, was fascinated by the Spanish-speaking world. He designed numerous buildings in Havana, such as the Tallapiedra Electric Plant, which today houses the Instituto Superior de Arte, a school of fine arts, the Trust Company, and the Old Country Club. His mother, Catalina (Lina) Valmont, was born in Novgorod, on the Volkhov River, near its outlet from Lake Ilmen. It was a Russian city in the Byzantine tradition, exemplified by the famous Cathedral of Saint Sofia, founded in 1045, which may well have inspired the name of the principal character in El siglo de las luces (Explosion in a Cathedral, 1962). Esteban, the other main character of the novel, who shares many of the author's traits as well as much of his Weltanschauung, is named after Carpentier's patron saint, Stephen, the first martyr of the Catholic church. Carpentier's mother studied medicine in Switzerland, then taught French and Spanish. She had a literary bent, an artistic inclination that probably came from the Valmont bloodline. Carpentier's love for music and architecture, like his knowledge of French and Spanish literature—especially the novels of Pío Baroja—tastes in part inherited, would be important factors in his later work.

After completing his primary education at the Colegio Mimó in Havana, he went to school at the Candler College in Havana, and at the Lycée Jeanson de Sailly. This French schooling probably took place in 1914, during his stay in Paris, when the family lived with his paternal grandparents, Julian and Gabriela Carpentier. Carpentier also visited his maternal grandparents, Valdemar and Eudoxia Blado-brasof Valmont, in Baku, the capital of Azerbaijan in Soviet Transcaucasia. Experiences from life in this industrial oil-refining town, whose proletariat played a decisive role in the revolutions of 1905 and 1917, surfaced years later, transformed by Carpentier's art, in *La consagración de la primavera* (The Rites of Spring, 1978). All of this is well summarized by the Cuban critic Salvador Bueno. Carpentier, he said, was uprooted in his youth, adding a French education to a Cuban background that combined:

> . . . Western European, Hispanic and African elements in a rich mixture of the surrounding environment. At home, conversations and books evoked echoes of European cultures, the Breton and the Slavic in fruitful conjunction. Outside on the street and throughout the city, among his budding friendships, amid casual conversation, he learned the singular blend of colonial Spanish and transplanted African traditions that ultimately make up our particularly Cuban diction. The future narrator incorporates everything and feeds his spirit on all.
>
> (Bueno, pp. 153–179)

This fertile mixture and these privileged circumstances nourished a keen intelligence and a prodigious memory, from which sprang Carpentier's creative work and the will to harmonize, synthesize, and unify the diverse elements in his own Cuban and Latin American world.

Carpentier studied musical theory in Paris and became in his own words "an acceptable pianist," albeit admitting that his "theoretical training is much more self-taught: attendance of concert rehearsals and living with musicians." He believed that "every writer should be familiar with a parallel art form because it enriches his spiritual world." Carpentier owed a great deal to the environment in which he was brought up, and music played a fundamental role in his life. He became an important musicologist and, in the course of a long artistic career, collaborated with the Brazilian composer Heitor Villa-Lobos, the Cuban composers Alejandro García Caturla and Amadeo Roldán, as well as with Marius François Gaillard, Darius Milhaud, and Edgar Varese. Carpentier wrote the famous study *La música en Cuba* (Music in Cuba, 1946).

In the early 1920's, Carpentier began his studies in architecture at the University of Havana, and he took up journalism in 1921. He published his first literary pieces as a columnist. He wrote summaries of well-known books in a section entitled "Obras famosas" (Famous Works) in the daily newspaper *La Discusión*, headquartered in the old mansion occupied today by Havana's Museum of Colonial Art. Carpentier's first article was "Pasión y muerte de Miguel Servet por Pompei Gener" (The Passion and Death of Miguel Servet by Pompei Gener). It was published in *La Discusión* on 23 November 1922. The same year, Carpentier abandoned his university career "for exclusively personal reasons," because there was no more money to finance his education. He dedicated himself completely to journalism and, in 1923 and 1924, contributed music and theater reviews to *La Discusión*, *El Heraldo de Cuba*, and *Chic*. "El sacrificio: Historieta fantástica" (The Sacrifice: A Fantastic Tale) first appeared in May 1923 in *Chic*, on whose staff Juan Marinello also worked. Later that year, on 20 December, Carpentier published "El milagro—leyenda" (The Miracle—a Legend) in Havana's *El Universal*. These are escapist tales, in the *modernista* fashion, the Spanish-American equivalent of the French Parnassianism or symbolism, or of English Pre-Rafaelism; exotic North Sea settings, the coasts of Greenland, and the Nola, Italy, of the second century serve as background for Viking pirates and Italian saints.

During his formative years, the outlines of Carpentier's artistic personality became more sharply defined. He explored the picturesque neighborhoods of Old Havana, discovering the singular charm of its colonial architecture. These indelible impressions later reappeared as the locale and the characters of his native city reflected in many short stories and novels. "Viaje a la semilla" ("Journey Back to the Source," 1944), *El acoso* (Manhunt, 1956), *Explosion in a Cathedral*, *La ciudad de las columnas* (The City of Columns, 1970), *Concierto barroco* (Baroque Concert, 1974), *La consagración de la primavera*, and *El recurso del método* (Reasons of State, 1974) all reveal the changing face of the Cuban capital through space and time. Of greater importance is the fact that, during the 1920's, the young writer took part in the intellectual movements and the political restlessness of his peers and spiritually identified himself with the Cuban avant-garde of his generation. In *La música en Cuba*, Carpentier insists that the Grupo Minorista (the Minority Group), which he joined early on, is not fundamentally a political movement:

> Encouraged by the aborted revolution of "Veterans and Patriots" (1923), a coup d'etat . . . without cohesion, direction, or concrete ideology, some writers and young artists caught up in the movement . . . got the habit of getting together frequently, to preserve a camaraderie born in more troubled days. The "Grupo Minorista" was born in this fashion, without manifestos or cliques, like a gathering of men interested in the same things. Without pretending to create a movement, the "minorismo" very soon became a state of mind. Thanks to it we organized exhibitions, concerts, and lecture series, published pamphlets, established contacts with American and European intellectuals who represented a new way of thinking and seeing. Needless to say that in this period we discovered Picasso, Joyce, Stravinsky, "Los seis" [The Six] and the *Esprit Nouveau* and all "-isms." Books printed without capital letters circulated from person to person. It was the time of the "vanguardia," the avant-garde, far-fetched metaphors and reviews with titles such as *Espiral, Proa, Vertice, Helice*, etc. [Spiral, Bow, Vortex, Helix]. Moreover, in those years all the youth of the continent had caught the same fever.
>
> (p. 235)

The Afro-Cuban or neo-African black element discovered by Caribbean artists during the 1920's and 1930's, and hailed as their own heritage, was possibly one of the most important ideological aesthetic components of the Latin American avant-garde movement. In *La música en Cuba*, Carpentier would later add:

> For the very reason that it offended the sensibilities of old-fashioned intellectuals, we gleefully went to ñáñigo initiation rites, the secret black fetishist cults similar to voodoo, and praised the dance of the "diablito," the small, ritual dancing devil. Thus was born the Afro-Cuban mode that provided subject matter for poems, novels, folkloric and sociological studies for more than ten years. Often it tended to remain at a superficial, local color level, the black man under sun-drenched palm trees; nevertheless it also constituted a necessary first step to understand better certain poetic, musical, ethnic, and social factors that have contributed to and

given a special character to the "criollo," the creole, the quintessence of Cuba.

> (p. 236)

Carpentier worked with Amadeo Roldán on four librettos for scores of Cuban ballets and choreographic poems, inspired by the European success of Manuel de Falla's *El sombrero de tres picos* (*The Three-Cornered Hat*, 1919) and Igor Stravinsky's *Le sacre du printemps* (*The Rites of Spring*, 1912). In the novel *La consagración de la primavera*, the work of the Russian composer was transformed into the leitmotif of the Cuban author, an emblem of his youth and his artistic and revolutionary ideals. At night, after his work at the Fausto Theater, Roldán would meet Carpentier at the café Las Columnas, where they would collaborate on projects. In 1927 they hit upon the idea of *La rebambaramba* (1927), a "colonial ballet in two scenes," based on romantic etchings by Mialhe that portray masked actors for the Feast of the Epiphany, the Día de Reyes (The Day of the Three Wise Men), before the old church of Saint Francis in the Havana of the 1830's. "El milagro de Anaquillé" ("The Miracle of Anaquillé") was written in 1927 and published in the *Revista cubana* ten years later. It is a "choreographic Afro-Cuban Mystery in One Act" about initiation ceremonies, with staging by Hurtado de Mendoza and music by Roldán. It evokes country scenes, thatched palm huts, and cane fields in the shadow of the sugar mill. Carpentier also elaborated, but never published, two choreographic poems, "Mata cangrejo" (Kill the Land Crab) and "Azúcar" (Sugar), in which he attempted "a dynamic representation of the frightening life of the sugar mill, the rhythm of cane cutting, the labor of men, and the blind movement of the machines" ("The Miracle of Anaquillé," p. 56). In early 1927, the author, together with Jorge Mañach, Juan Marinello, Francisco Ichaso, and Martín Casanovas formed the group Los Cinco (The Five), which played an active role in establishing the *Revista de avance*. Between 15 March 1927 and 15 September 1930, the intellectual review became a prominent voice of the avant-garde and the movement's main organ of expression in Cuba.

In 1927, Carpentier was persecuted for political reasons and charged in a so-called communist trial. After spending forty days in the Prado jail, the novelist sought exile, during which his experiences with the movement called *vanguardismo* began to bear fruit. Between 1 and 9 August 1927, he wrote the first draft of *¡Écue-Yamba-Ó!*, an Afro-Cuban story. In a prologue to a 1979 edition of the novel, the author confessed that "the prison scenes ('Bars [a] [b] [c]') are those I observed in the days I wrote the first draft . . . slightly altered, although substantially expanded in a 1933 version." Luckily Carpentier was released on bail, and the Seventh Congress of the Latin Press, which met in Havana on 15 and 16 March 1928, gave him the opportunity to flee the oppressive regime of Gerardo Machado. Carpentier met Robert Desnos, the representative of the Buenos Aires newspaper *La Razón*, who helped him use the event to flee the island by providing him with his own French passport.

After his arrival in Paris, the Cuban novelist earned his living as a correspondent for Parisian and Cuban magazines, and as a sound-effect specialist for advertising firms and radio programs. Under the guidance of Desnos, Carpentier plunged into the surrealist movement that, together with the Cuban avant-garde, would powerfully influence his writing. Probably in July 1928, André Breton invited him to participate in the publication of the magazine *La revolution surrealiste*. Through Breton he met Louis Aragon, Tristan Tzara, Paul Éluard, Georges Sadoul, Benjamin Péret, and the painters Giorgio De Chirico, Yves Tanguy, and Pablo Picasso. Carpentier, however, did not hesitate to distance himself from the review and Breton's disciples. He even participated in the writing of *Un cadavre* (A Cadaver), a vitriolic pamphlet that led to the famous breach in the orthodox surrealist lines championed by Desnos. *Un cadavre*, as well as another account of a fistfight in a literary café by Carpentier ("El escándalo de Maldoror" [The Maldoror Scandal], *Carteles*, 20 April 1930), and the squabbles it precipitated, are important because they reveal Carpentier's ambivalence regarding surrealism at the time. In addition, they explain the evolution of his aesthetic ideas and help place him in relation to his future work. In the prologue to *The Kingdom of This World*, he claims to have shed, once and for all, the dependency on orthodox surrealism and affirms his own theory of the "marvel of the real in America." Nevertheless, later

in the 1930's, Carpentier did write two surrealist short stories: the unpublished tale "El estudiante" (The Student), the manuscript of which is in the National Library of Cuba, and "Histoire de lunes" ("Tale of Moons"), which appeared in the pages of the *Cahiers du sud* in December 1933.

The Maison de la Culture, a French cultural organization backing the cause of the Spanish Republic whose director was Louis Aragon, sponsored the Second International Congress of Writers Against Fascism and in Defense of Culture. The event, organized by Spain's Ministry of Instruction and the Alliance of Anti-Fascist Writers, to be held in Paris, Barcelona, Valencia, and Madrid, in 1937 was beseiged by the armies of Generalísimo Francisco Franco. Carpentier was part of the Cuban delegation, which included Juan Marinello, Nicolás Guillén, Félix Pita Rodríguez, and Leonardo Fernández Sánchez. In *Confieso que he vivido: Memorias* (Memoirs, 1974) Pablo Neruda described how he, Delia del Carril, José Mancisidor, Carlos Pellicer, and Claude Aveline traveled together from the French capital. Carpentier made the Paris–Valencia–Madrid journey at the end of June, accompanied by César Vallejo, André Malraux, Octavio Paz, Paz' bride Elena Garro, Marinello, and Pita Rodríguez. The atmosphere of war in the republican zone, the propaganda posters, the militia, the antiaircraft guns, the air raids, the blackouts, and the International Brigades, as well as the sessions of the Congress, form the experiences that surfaced forty years later, filtered by memory, in the first and second parts of *La consagración de la primavera*.

Possibly the last of Carpentier's French projects, before he returned to Cuba in May 1939, was the "radiophonic fresco" of Paul Claudel's *Le livre de Christophe Colomb* (The Book of Christopher Columbus, 1933). Jean-Louis Barrault starred in the first performance of the adaptation, broadcast by Radio Luxembourg in 1935. This subject matter would find definitive form in the second part of "La mano" ("The Hand") of *El arpa y la sombra* (*The Harp and the Shadow*, 1979), finished on 10 September 1978, a year and a half before Carpentier's death in Paris. In his last novel, the author's characterization of the discoverer of America is complex, multifaceted, and contradictory in its presentation of a visionary genius and a poet of action. Although Carpentier's Columbus is full of new ideas, he possesses especially that human weakness associated with the cardinal sin of avarice: blinded by gold, he is greedy for easy wealth. In addition, the Cuban writer incorporates into his book many allegorical figures, as well as other elements of Claudel's lyrical drama, such as fantastic and supernatural characters. Claudel may, in fact, be a direct source, since he and Pierre Mabille are the first authors who specifically alerted Carpentier to the distinct artistic possibilities of the Columbian theme and literature directly related to the marvelous.

Carpentier's stay in Paris from 1929 to 1939 enriched his intellectual world and oriented him to new mediums of expression. By honing and refining his sensibilities, he managed to distance himself from the provincial manifestations of Afro-Cubanism and orthodox surrealism with which he severed relations by signing *Un cadavre*. Much like the hero of his novel *Los pasos perdidos* (*The Lost Steps*, 1953), Carpentier departed from Europe with relief mingled with vexation just before World War II.

At the end of 1943, accompanied by his wife, Lilia, and a French friend, the actor Louis Jouvet, Carpentier took a trip to Haiti, where he traveled along the coastal region, through the north, and to the central plain. He visited the ruins of the palace of Sans-Souci, the fortress La Ferrière, Cap Haitien, and the ancient palace of Paulina Bonaparte. The Cuban novelist also met the French cultural attaché in Port-au-Prince, the doctor and writer Pierre Mabille, whom he had known while living in Paris. On his return to Cuba, Carpentier began *The Kingdom of This World*, an imaginative re-creation of Haiti's violent past and the troubled reign of Henri Christophe. The novel was not published until May 1949 because the author undertook another project. After his first youthful effort, *¡Écue-Yamba-Ó!*, he had not completed much fiction, although he had always kept busy as a journalist and researcher in archives and libraries. Since the documents, newspapers, colonial pamphlets, and old records of Havana and Santiago, Cuba, proved to be a great source for unpublished musicological material, he wrote *La música en Cuba*. The obsessive examination of roots and identity that characterizes this excellent study, commissioned by

the Centro de Cultura Económica de México, one of the largest editorial houses in Latin America, coincided with similar goals set by José Lezama Lima for the distinguished Cuban review *Orígenes*. *La música en Cuba* is closely related to several pieces of fiction by Carpentier: "Oficio de tinieblas" ("Tenebrae," the offices of devotion performed on the last three days of Holy Week to commemorate the sufferings and death of Christ), published in 1944; *The Kingdom of This World*; "El camino de Santiago" ("The Road to Santiago"), the first chapters of which were published in *El Nacional* (Caracas) in 1954; and "Semejante a la noche" ("Like the Night"), first published in *Orígenes* in 1952.

This literary context, combining search of identity with minute historical research and Mabille's *Le miroir du merveilleux* (The Mirror of the Marvelous, Paris, 1940 and 1962), may well have been the catalytic agent that triggers, accelerates, and eventually produces definitive style. Ultimately it led to the conception of stories like "Journey Back to the Source" published in 1944, in a limited edition of one hundred copies; "Tenebrae"; and "Like the Night." The first story soon became a part of many anthologies of Hispanic-American short fiction. The second, barely known until 1968, is distinguished by a subtle perception of Cuba's colonial past as well as for the author's particular refinement; Carpentier was one of the few Spanish-American writers of his generation who had a keen concern for the writer's craft. "Journey Back to the Source," "The Road to Santiago," and "Like the Night" are included in the collection *Guerra del tiempo* (*The War of Time*, 1958). The three tales merit attention because they reveal early stages of the techniques and themes that would develop in Carpentier's later works.

In 1945, his friend Carlos E. Frias asked Carpentier to found a radio station in Venezuela. The author traveled to Caracas on 21 August of that year, where he became part of the intellectual community until 1959. In March 1948, he put the final touches on *The Kingdom of This World* and finished a study entitled *Tristán e Isolda en tierra firme: Reflexiones al margen de una representación wagneriana* (Tristan and Isolde on the Mainland: Reflections at the Side of a Wagnerian Performance, 1949). In *The Kingdom of This World*, Carpentier evokes the bloody chapters of Haitian history, in which, as Salvador Bueno notes, "the refined rational world of eighteenth-century French Enlightenment collides with the powerful, instinctive natural impulses of the magical Afro-American world" (Bueno, p. 168). The inclination toward magical realism apparent in "Journey Back to the Source" climaxes in the Haitian tale, in the prologue to which the author unmercifully attacks Breton through his idol, Isidore Ducasse, the nineteenth-century Count of Lautréamont. The orthodox surrealist group and some of the principal leaders of the movement fare no better when Carpentier defines his theory of "the marvel of the real in America."

The marked attention to detail in *The Kingdom of This World* maintains the essential truth of the narrated historic events. Yet Bueno rejects the label of "historical novel" and prefers instead "legendary chronicle" of the Haitian past, possibly because many important historical incidents are omitted or never explained in the work. Along with the fictional characters Lenormand de Mezy and Ti Noel, master and slave, figures who personify two colliding worlds, we find true-to-life characters, such as the witch doctor Mackandal, the Jamaican leader Bouckman, the king Henri Christophe, his wife María Luisa, the princesses Ametista and Atenais, the French confessor Cornejo Breille, General Leclerc, Paulina Bonaparte, her black masseur Solimán, as well as the Cuban composer Esteban Salas, who also appears in *La música en Cuba*. Carpentier's text does not so much as mention directly the most important figure of Haiti's independence, Toussaint L'Ouverture, the father of the Haitian nation. Other historical figures such as Jean Jacques Dessalines, General Clairveaux, and the mulatto president Alexandre Pétion, a friend of Simón Bolívar, do not appear either.

Thus, in the final analysis, the emphasis of *The Kingdom of This World* does not seem to lie on empiric fact or on proven historical accuracy, but instead on the exotic, haunting spell of legend, the selective revelation of strange and incongruous events that amaze the reader with an aura of the bizarre. Nevertheless, the fictional characters have real elements, and the real characters have fictional overtones. The master Lenormand de Mezy bears the same name as that of the northern plantation where the first slave rebellion broke out. The black masseur Solimán

might or might not have massaged the figure of the famous marble statue of his former mistress in Rome's Villa Borghese: Paulina Bonaparte relaxing as Venus, by the Italian sculptor Antonio Canova (1757–1822). In any case, as Carpentier engagingly assures us in *The Harp and the Shadow*, "if it could, it surely would or should have happened this way." As the Chilean critic Fernando Alegría concludes in "Alejo Carpentier: Realismo Mágico" (*Humanitas* 1/1:356 [1960]), the singular contribution of *The Kingdom of This World*

> consists of the placement of elements and in the focus and distance with which they are presented to the reader. . . . By selecting the episodes, introducing the characters . . . in a climactic moment of their incredible adventures, by ordering the objects and the setting in a form that heightens their incongruence and poetic absurdity, history takes on an air of madness in Carpentier's hand, a frenzied, nightmarish quality, a richness of associations that touches our senses as quickly as our intellect.

Here it might be well to consider what this work has in common with Mabille's *Le miroir du merveilleux*. Mabille's anthology, prefaced by André Breton, is a collection of hermetic, esoteric, fantastic, magical, imaginary literature of the marvelous and the bizarre, loosely strung together by the author's commentaries. The selections include representative samples from distinct cultural traditions separate in space and time. They range from works of classical antiquity such as Apuleius' *Golden Ass* or Ovid's *Metamorphoses* to Lewis Carroll's *Alice's Adventures in Wonderland* (1865) and twentieth-century works such as Franz Kafka's *Ein Landarzt* (*The Country Doctor*, 1919) and Breton's autobiographical novel *Nadja* (1928). There are also anonymous examples from the Bible, as well as from folklore, myths, and fairy tales of different cultures and historical periods. Mabille's anthology also illustrates the related concepts of the marvelous, convulsive beauty, and mad love, which are central to the surrealist aesthetic, and is organized around motifs such as the creation, the destruction of the world, across the elements, across death, the struggle of the hero against death, the myth of the Resurrection, the voyage of the marvelous, predestination, and the quest of the Holy Grail. These elements may also constitute the various stages of the itinerary through which Carpentier's hero passes in *The Lost Steps*, a wonderful journey to the sources of the Orinoco and of life itself.

It is evident that Mabille's *Le miroir du merveilleux* profoundly influenced the Cuban novelist, who also contributed to the volume. In addition he later took a number of the central ideas and developed them further in "Journey Back to the Source," "Tenebrae," *The Kingdom of This World*, *The Lost Steps*, "Los advertidos" ("The Chosen," which first appeared as "Les elus" in the French version of *Guerra del tiempo* in 1967, with the dateline 1965), "El derecho de asilo" ("Right of Sanctuary," which first appeared with "The Chosen"), and possibly even in the epigraph of *Alice's Adventures in Wonderland* that introduces *La consagración de la primavera*. Carpentier's contribution to Mabille's anthology consists of two translations of magical Aztec texts previously unpublished in French: "Incantation for Defeating One's Enemies" and "Incantation for Netting Birds," taken from Hernando Ruiz de Alarco's *Tratado de supersticiones* (A Treatise on Superstitions, 1629). Some of the central themes the Cuban writer derived from Mabille and later incorporated into his own writing, particularly *The Kingdom of This World*, are fragments of the second canto of *Les chants de maldoror* (1868–1870), by Ducasse, Alfred Jarry's "Prolégomènes de Hadernablou," from *Les Minutes de Sable Memorial* (1894), Matthew Gregory Lewis' *Ambrosio, or The Monk* (1796), which includes "Le Miroir magique" (The Magic Mirror), from which Mabille derived the title of his own anthology.

In the prologue of *The Kingdom of This World*, Carpentier directly or indirectly takes potshots at all of the precursors of surrealism and protosurrealist heroes, decrying their bag of trite, shopworn tricks. He particularly deplores the codes of the fantastic in the domain of literature, learned by rote and mindlessly applied by Salvador Dali, De Chirico, Tanguy, Max Ernst, and André Masson, Breton's followers, in fabricating art and fiction. The Cuban novelist then contrasts the authentic with the artificial, faith with disbelief, the marvelous with the fantastic. In short, he compares the contrived search of reflexive, rationalist Europe with the living faith of the American continent, where marvels and prodigies are still alive. In fact, Carpentier postulates that his revelation is an

exclusive privilege not only of Haiti, but of America as a whole, and concludes with the rhetorical question "Indeed, what is the history of America if not a chronicle of the 'Marvel of the Real'?"

Even the novelist's dominant thesis that the marvelous is omnipresent, a distinctive mark of American reality, may be implicit in *Le miroir du merveilleux*. Mabille includes two selections dealing with zombies from W. B. Seabrook's *The Magic Island* (1929): "Les mortes esclaves d'Haiti," the undead slaves of Haiti, and as voodoo initiation ritual, "Ceremonie d'initiation vaudou." In *The Kingdom of This World*, Carpentier used a similar episode, the sacrifice of a black pig by the followers of Bouckman, Jean François, Biassou, and Jeannot, in the Bois Caiman, the night of 15 August 1791. In that climactic scene, two hundred delegates of voodoo sects from the Northern Plain seal a revolutionary pact by drinking the lukewarm blood of the slaughtered animal. In *Le miroir du merveilleux*, Mabille even features as one of his final examples, in the section called "The Creation of Man," a prodigious South American creation myth from the Mayan *Popol Vuh* (Book of Counsel). The sacred book of the Maya-Quiché people of Guatemala plays a fundamental role in *The Lost Steps*, since the nameless hero reads the work in chapter 6, the entry of 20 October.

Carpentier also uses an epigraph from the *Popol Vuh* to introduce chapter 4, only to end it with a Judeo-Christian counterpart, the words from the creation myth in the Book of Genesis. Mabille's "The Destruction of the World" and "The Creation" may well be the two opposite poles around which Carpentier structured *The Lost Steps*. The hero's voyage into the Orinoco jungle is actually a journey back to the sources, to Genesis, the origins of art, music, and thought, the beginning of history, man, the world, time itself. As Roberto González Echevarría has pointed out in the edition he edited, the six chapters "have the form of the week of Genesis and thus concretely announce the existence of a seventh chapter-day, the fabulous Sunday of fiction. The new Latin American novel is written in that Sunday foretold by Carpentier" (p. 53).

If creation myths and foundational texts such as the *Book of Manou*, "Menes et Minos," the *Kalevala*, and other gnostic, anthropological, and African versions are a prominent part of *Le miroir du merveilleux*, so is the apocalypse. Imminent cosmic cataclysm, flood, earthquake, hurricane, and fire, as well as catastrophe by war and revolution, figure prominently in Carpentier's aesthetic, in *¡Écue-Yamba-Ó!*, "Tenebrae," *Explosion in a Cathedral*, "The Chosen," "Right of Sanctuary," *Reasons of State*, and *The Harp and the Shadow*. The apocalyptic vision in *The Lost Steps* is particularly apt because it criticizes modern, rootless, cosmopolitan society, in line with Oswald Spengler's ideas of decadence in *The Decline of the West* (1918–1922), as well as with all of the negative assessments of European culture obsessively voiced by the surrealists between World Wars I and II. *The Lost Steps* also incorporates a primitive version of the flood found in petroglyphs of the Venezuelan aborigines on the high rocks in the jungle above the Orinoco.

The sketch of universal deluge and rebirth that appears briefly in *The Lost Steps* is developed fully in the short story "The Chosen." As occurs so often in Carpentier's fiction, his multiple sources are real as well as textual. It is very likely the author actually saw petroglyphs during his voyage up the Orinoco, although he also read about them and saw their photographs in Alain Gheerbrant's *Des hommes qu'on appelle sauvages* (Men Who Are Called Savages, 1952) and *L'expedition orénoque amazone* (published in English as *Journey to the Far Amazon*, 1952). In fact Carpentier wrote about these books in articles for *El Nacional*—"El gran libro de la selva" (The Great Book of the Jungle and "Los hombres llamados salvajes" (The Men Who are Called Savages)—in May 1952. However, it is probable that the direct literary source of the deluge story in *The Lost Steps* and in "The Chosen," as well as the ideas of a common denominator between the Venzuelan Indian and the Greek myths and the Noah story of the Bible is El Inca Garcilaso de la Vega's *Royal Commentaries*, (1609;1616) and *Le miroir du merveilleux*. Mabille actually includes Ovid's version of man's origin from the *Metamorphoses*, the fable of Pyrrha and Deucalion, who rode out the flood in a boat that stopped on Mount Parnassus and then repopulated the earth. Mabille also mentions another Noah, from the deluge story of the epic of Gilgamesh. Carpentier incorporates the Greek and the Mesopotamian legends in

"The Chosen," to which he adds three Noahs from other cultures. All of this is done in order to fashion his own relativistic, ethnocentric, ironic tale of man after the Fall, from a South American perspective; the main figure is Amalivaca, the cultural hero of the Venezuelan Indians.

Many other parallels can be drawn between Mabille's and Carpentier's works. The French surrealist had already posited modern man's fragmented condition; alienated from collective life, the individual is a cog in the mechanical civilization of our time. Enslaved by the production process and the consumer society of which he is a part, the individual leads an existence ruled by the machine and the rhythms of the factory. Mabille expressed his nightmarish vision of labor in the following words: "Suddenly, like a dreaded blow, the howl of a siren rends the air. . . . The mad rush to the doors . . . and a thousand workers are spit out on the street: men, women, children return to their homes after work. Their tired bodies trembling in the darkness of night" (Mabille, pp. 123–124).

In the first chapter of *The Lost Steps*, the composer-hero slaves away in the sound studios of the advertising world. His demeaning job has dulled his senses and stifled his creativity. The negative view of progressive twentieth-century urban life permeates the novel. Carpentier's conception is broad and personal, anguished and introspective, in that it describes a harried professional who has lost control of his existence, an expatriate seeking his identity among the masses of a foreign city, an uprooted individual caught in artificial life cycles that subject him to anomie and future shock. The Cuban author elaborated on the barren lives in the "tentacular cities" of our time in the article "Presencia de la naturaleza" (The Presence of Nature), published in *El Nacional* on 23 August 1952. This view, as well as modern man's condition in *The Lost Steps*, actually corresponds to a reelaboration of elements present in Mabille, who had already pinpointed the dilemma of the creative artist and the romantic individual in his own book. However, it would be foolish to dismiss *The Lost Steps* as a derivative work.

Carpentier's novels and short fiction progressively expand the locale of fantasy and erudition in space and time, in order to form a complex, coherent world in his own image and likeness. These works, ironic and multifaceted, contradictory and pessimistic, include *The War of Time*, *Explosion in a Cathedral*, *Reasons of State*, *Concierto barroco*, *The Harp and the Shadow*, and *La aprendiz de bruja* (The Sorcerer's Apprentice, 1983). Carpentier emphasizes and develops the American component of his fiction, and extends its repertory of prodigious characteristics. The possible exceptions are *Manhunt*, an overwritten stylistic tour de force about the assassination of a terrorist in a Havana concert hall, and *La consagración de la primavera*, the most autobiographical of his novels.

Explosion in a Cathedral continued Carpentier's tendency toward a progressively broader locale and a more universal view of American reality. It is the logical outcome of an evolution from the imaginative reconstruction of relatively local neo-African elements in Cuba, to neighboring Haiti in *The Kingdom of This World*, to the discovery of prototypes, cities, villages, and remote corners of the continent in *The Lost Steps*. *Explosion in a Cathedral* is a complete "Caribbean symphony," in which the resonant themes of the French Revolution reecho in the luminous, tropical Antilles. Although this process had already begun in *The Kingdom of This World*, with some scenes taking place in Santiago, Cuba, and Rome, the setting is infinitely more vast in *Explosion in a Cathedral*: Havana–Santo Domingo, Paris and the lower Pyrenees, Guadeloupe, Cayenne, Paramaribo, and again Havana, Cayenne, and Madrid.

The final decade of the eighteenth century was an extraordinary moment in the history of the Old World, and it was no less so in the New, where the incipient Creole consciousness, gradually developed during the colonial period, crystallized. Although the Spanish title, *El siglo de las luces*, literally "The Century of Lights," alludes to the whole century, the events of the novel take place between 1789 and 1808, dates suggested by the fall of the Bastille and the uprising of the Spanish populace on 2 May against Napoleon's forces occupying Madrid. This undoubtedly amounts to an intentional irony, because the Age of Enlightenment, characterized by the worship of reason, ends with one of the bloodiest periods of terror and strife in Western history. On the cover of the manuscript, held in Havana's National Library, the author jotted down a brief explanation of his title: "El siglo de las luces fue el teatro de una gigantesca lucha entre lo temporal y lo absoluto" (The Enlightenment was the theater of a giant struggle between the temporal and the absolute [order]). The work contains frequent references to natural disasters and violent upheavals, symbolic of the destruction of the established order.

"Explosion in a Cathedral," a painting by the Neapolitan artist Monsú Desiderio, opens and closes the novel with its "apocalyptic immobilization of catastrophe" and surfaces constantly as an allusion to the end of an era. The hurricane that hits the old mansion in the first chapter is also an omen placing the main characters "in the doorway of a period of transformations." Later, the conflagration in Port-au-Prince, the plague that scourges Havana, and the Spanish War of Independence against Napoleon, which ends the book, continue the theme of calamity and collapse. The vast apocalyptic panorama ends with a Goya-like final scene in varying hues of scarlet, coral, and crimson red, symbolic of the revolution, the passions unleashed by the conflict, and the bloodshed that conclude the novel.

The technique of color gradations reaches its highest intensity in *Concierto barroco*. The narrative structure of the novella is based on chromatic systems of different hues, symbolic of specific qualities, the ultimate development of a colorist technique already suggested in *Explosion in a Cathedral*. The desire to transcend and dominate time may explain the evident color and pictorial sensibility as an eternal search for continuity, stability, and permanence, which attempts to secure a crumbling world threatened by continuous change, through the imposed order of artistic creation. The view of a universe menaced by destruction also characterizes avant-garde poets such as Pablo Neruda in *Residencia en la tierra* (Residence on Earth, 1933) and Jorge Carrera Andrade in "Morada terrestre" (Earthly Abode). The story of *Concierto barroco* is structured on different chromatic systems; eight chapters are painted in symbolic colors, or hues, each correlating with a spiritual significance.

The first chapter opens and closes with a silvery tour de force, the words "de plata" (of silver), a metal and an emblem of Mexico's viceroyal wealth. This gives way to a yellow hue, symbolic of the fever epidemic that scourges Havana in the second chapter. A virtual absence of color in the third stresses the pervasive grayness of a bleak, intellectually and culturally barren Madrid. The Venetian episodes of the fourth chapter initially evoke a diffuse, pastel-hued seascape in the manner of Rosâlba Carriera or J.M.W. Turner, later replaced by a dizzy wave of brilliant colors in the midst of festive Mardi Gras scenes. In order to stress by explicit contrast the resounding exaltation of a concerto grosso orchestrated in a convent, the fifth chapter reverts to traditional color symbolism, probably derived from a painting by Tintoretto. It also relies heavily on the interplay of light and shadow, taken from Rembrandt's chiaroscuro technique, in accordance with the dark interiors of the nocturnal episode. It is no coincidence that the scenes from the sixth chapter, which takes place in the twentieth century, are tinged in a chromatic system that closely resembles photography, the graphic medium that best characterizes our time. The predominant use of black and white, colors at opposite ends of the chromatic scale, fixes a series of spectral, dehumanized images that seem like glossy prints on high-contrast paper.

The preoccupation with the visual and the systematic use of color are essential constants of Carpentier's style. At times they achieve a realistic effect; often they follow the traditional symbolic patterns of Hispanic culture and bring about sustained colorist allegory by means of the insistent accumulation of new, static expressive hues. While the beginning of this technique, closely related to states of mind, goes back to the short story "Tenebrae," in *Concierto barroco*, these mechanisms show the great subtlety and intensity that characterize Carpentier's later period, in which the colorist tendencies of his fiction, as well as other neo-baroque techniques, are carried to their ultimate conclusions.

The Spanish title *El recurso del método (Reasons of State)* amounts to a play on words that echoes René Descartes' famous *Discours de la méthode pour bien conduire sa raison et chercher la verité dans les sciences* (*Discourse on the Method of Rightly Conducting Reason, and Seeking Truth in the Sciences*, 1637). On the jacket of the first edition of the novel, the author discusses the context and the American circumstances neces-

sary to understand the work's broad implications. Carpentier explains how a nineteenth-century Paraguayan dictator:

> . . . Doctor Francia (1766–1840), transcending his own adventure, installed among us a method of government whose infinitely multiplied resorts are those that continue to be pursued today in the political life of many Latin American nations. Hence the title 'el recurso del método' [the recourse of the method] given to a work that takes place in a country of the American continent, a geographical summa, the least Cartesian of all possible worlds.

If, to paraphrase Cervantes' words, Carpentier's novel alternates between Paris and a "nation of Latin America, the name of which he has no desire to recall," the chronological time frame in which the events of this imaginary republic happen falls between the summer of 1913 and the end of the 1920's. Two historical references that rigorously enclose the beginning and the end of the story are the reports of German mobilization movements in the French newspapers of 2 August 1914, following the assassination of the Austro-Hungarian crown prince in Sarajevo on 28 June, and the First Worldwide Conference Against Colonial Imperialist Policies, lead by Henri Barbusse, held in Brussels on 10 February 1927.

In addition to the apparent, precise chronology, the careful reader will easily perceive that the novel has another, less obvious, historical and imaginative dimension. Carpentier assures us that the novel's plot ". . . extends over a fifteen-year period clearly defined in the history of this century, although the character, by his omnipresence on the continent, transcends his own chronology, by simultaneously placing himself *before* and *after* the era in which the author sets him." For instance, a considerable part of the novel's Cuban historical background centers around Gerardo Machado, president of Cuba from 1925 to 1933, but the full range of the story, its fictionalization and inclusion in *Reasons of State*, is much more complex. The figures of the First Magistrate and his family—his wife Hermenegilda, his sons Radamés and Marco Antonio, and his daughter Ofelia—exceed the time frame of the Machado era. One of Carpentier's characters ironically confesses:

Gerardo Machado greatly resembled the man who had been our First Magistrate, in physical appearance, political posturing and methods; however he was different, in that he lacked breeding and sophistication, and did not build temples to Minerva as his close contemporary, Guatemala's Estrada Cabrera [1857–1923] did, nor was he frenchified as many dictators and illustrious tyrants of the continent had been.

(*El recurso del método*, p. 327)

The informed reader will find in the characters of the novel surprising parallels with various Latin American dictators: Mexico's Porfirio Diaz, Venezuela's Antonio Guzmán Blanco, Cipriano Castro, and Juan Vicente Gómez, Santo Domingo's Rafael Leonidas Trujillo Molina, and Argentina's Eva Duarte de Perón. For as Carpentier stated, the story of the life and times of his illustrious tyrant "is truly a montage of elements that characterize Latin American dictatorships past and present, faithfully integrated into the robot picture, so that everyone familiar with our history may point out where they came from." Just as in *Manhunt*, another novel that recycles episodes from the Machado era, the specific historical references in *Reasons of State* are easily documented. The author's intention was to avoid limiting himself to a narrow chronology, and his observations on the factual base and its fictionalization do not exclude or exhaust other possible textual interpretations.

The Spanish title *La consagración de la primavera* (The Rites of Spring) has multiple meanings. First, there is the symbolic value for Carpentier and other members of the Spanish-American avant-garde in Chile, Cuba, and Mexico: the title specifically refers to Stravinsky's ballet, whose opening bars serve as an epigraph for the novel. The Russian composer's work is the last of three ballets written for Sergey Diaghilev, the impresario and founder of the Ballet Russe. The ballet shone for its innovative orchestration and strong rhythmic patterns, as well as for the refined yet primitive theme that celebrates irrational, instinctive forces of nature; it captured the artistic imagination of its time. Secondly, from a personal point of view, *La consagración de la primavera* is also "the portrait of the artist as a young man," the awakening of Carpentier's artistic and professional conscience. This is why the novel corresponds to memoirs of the heroic

stage of Cuban *minorismo* and French surrealism in the 1920's and 1930's when, for Ernest Hemingway as well as for the Cuban author, Paris was "a moveable feast." Finally, from a fictional and ideological perspective, the title assumes an exemplary, didactic value, a play on words that implies an ideal that gives direction and meaning to life: a synthesis of art, reform, and revolution as well as the hope of reaching the uncertain wonderland of the future. The march toward this goal progresses through the steady steps of the main character, Vera, the prima ballerina, who opens and closes the novel with her daily routine, an effort closely bound to beat and rhythm, scores and space: "—1 . . . 2 . . . 3 . . . —watching the ground— aaand 2 aaand 3. . . . "

Thus *la consagración de la prima Vera* in Spanish also means the dedication, the attention and care, of the *prima* (first ballerina but also cousin), Vera, a kin to whom Carpentier feels spiritually and ideologically attached. The artist's craft is presented as a path of perfection "toward that light, the edge of the footlights—beacon and goal," the Faustian ideal of securing salvation by our daily effort. The choir of angels in act 5 of *Faust* states: "The noble member of the spirit world is saved from evil, he who strives and ever strives, him we can redeem." Carpentier was interested in the human desire to achieve plenitude, a Utopian state where all paradoxes, dualism, and conflicts are resolved, and the eternal human yearning for a fuller, more beautiful existence is satisfied.

The considerable international acclaim Carpentier's work received in the 1950's and 1960's was recognized officially by Germany, Spain, France, England, Italy, Rumania, Russia, Mexico, and Venezuela during the 1970's. On 4 April 1978, the novelist delivered "Cervantes en el alba de hoy" (Cervantes in Today's Dawn), his speech in acceptance of the Miguel de Cervantes Saavedra Prize, at Alcalá de Henares, a university town near Madrid. It is fitting that the same distinction was also conferred at Cervantes' birthplace upon the Argentine Jorge Luis Borges, for he and Carpentier were the two most imaginative Latin American writers of their generation, instrumental in changing prose fiction in the Spanish language of their time.

Carpentier died in Paris on 24 April 1980. The Cuban people mourned him officially in a state funeral held at the foot of the José Martí Monument, in Havana's main square, the Plaza de la Revolución. On 24 May 1982, the Centro de Promoción Cultural Alejo Carpentier (the Alejo Carpentier Center for Cultural Advancement) opened near the cathedral and the Bodeguita del Medio, one of Hemingway's favorite watering holes in Old Havana. The restored colonial residence that houses the center, as well as the Cuban author's memorabilia, is the beautiful eighteenth-century mansion of the main characters in *Explosion in a Cathedral*:

> The carriage heeled over to take the corner . . . and stopped in front of the nail-studded door, from whose knocker hung a black bow. The entrance way, the vestibule and the patio, were carpeted with jasmine, tuberoses, white carnations, and immortelles fallen from wreaths and bouquets. . . . Crossing the patio, the trunks of two palm trees rose among the malangas, like columns foreign to the rest of the architecture, and their soaring fronds merged into the darkness of imminent night.
>
> (chap. 1, scene 1)

SELECTED BIBLIOGRAPHY

First Editions

Poetry, Fiction, and Musical Works

Dos poemas afro-cubanos. With music by Alejandro García Caturla. Paris, 1930. Contains "Mari-Sabel" and "Juego santo."
Poèmes des Antilles: Neuf chants sur des textes d'Alejo Carpentier. Music by Marius François Gaillard. Paris, 1931.
"Blue." Paris, n.d. A poem set to music by Marius François Gaillard.
¡Écue-Yamba-Ó!: Historia afrocubana. Madrid, 1933.
"Liturgia." In *Antología de poesía negra hispanoamericana*, edited by Emilio Ballagas. Madrid, 1935. Pp. 65–67.
"Un ballet afrocubano: El milagro de Anaquillé." *Revista cubana* 8/22–24:145–154 (1937).
"Canción." In *Órbita de la poesía afrocubana 1928–1937*, edited by Ramón Guirao. Havana, 1938. Pp. 80–81.
"Oficio de tinieblas." *Orígenes* 1/4:32–38 (1944).
Viaje a la semilla. Havana, 1944. Limited edition of 100 copies.
El reino de este mundo (relato). Mexico City, 1949.
Los pasos perdidos. Mexico City, 1953.
El acoso. Buenos Aires, 1956.
Guerra del tiempo: Tres relatos y una novela: "El camino de Santiago," "Viaje a la semilla," "Semejante a la noche," y El acoso. Mexico City, 1958.
El siglo de las luces. Mexico City, 1962.
"El año '59." *Casa de las Américas* 4/62:45–50 (1964). Part of an unfinished trilogy.
"Le droit d'asile." In *Guerre du temps.* Paris, 1967. Short story dated "La Havane, 6 Mai 1965."
"Les elus." In *Guerre du temps.* Paris, 1967. The story, dated "La Havane, 13 Juin 1965," was translated with the stories of *Guerra del tiempo*, by René Durand. *Guerre du temps* differs from *Guerra del tiempo* in that it omits *El acoso* of the 1958 Mexican edition and includes "Les elus" ("Los advertidos") and "Le droit d'asile" ("El derecho de asilo").
"Los advertidos." In *Guerra del tiempo.* Barcelona, 1971. First Spanish edition of "Les elus."
Concierto barroco. Mexico City, 1974.
El recurso del método. Mexico City, 1974.
La consagración de la primavera. Mexico City, 1978.
El arpa y la sombra. Mexico City, 1979.

Nonfiction

La música en Cuba. Mexico City, 1946.
Tristán e Isolde en tierra firme: Reflexiones al margen de una representación wagneriana. Caracas, 1949.
Tientos y diferencias. Mexico City, 1964.
Literatura y conciencia política en América Latina. Madrid, 1969.
La ciudad de las columnas. Barcelona, 1970.
La novela latinoamericana en vísperas de un nuevo siglo y otros ensayos. Mexico City, 1981.
Alejo Carpentier: Ensayos. Havana, 1984. The most complete edition of his essays.

Journalistic Works

Letra y solfa. Edited and with a prologue and notes by Aléxis Márquez Rodríguez. Caracas, 1975. Contains columns written for Caracas' daily newspaper *El Nacional* from 1945 to 1961.
Crónicas. 2 vols. Havana, 1976. Contains articles written for Havana's *Carteles* and *Social.*

Collected Works

Cuentos completos. Barcelona, 1979.
Obras completas. 8 vols. Mexico City, 1983.

Translations

Explosion in a Cathedral. Translated by John Sturrock. Boston, 1963.

"The Fugitives." Translated by Hardie St. Martin. In *Doors and Mirrors: Fiction and Poetry from Spanish America, 1920–1970,* selected and edited by Hortense Carpentier and Janet Brof. New York, 1972. Pp. 156–166.

The Harp and the Shadow. Translated by Mete a Benjamin and Jean Stubbs. *Granma Weekly Review* (January 1980:7–8).

The Kingdom of This World. Translated by Harriet de Onís. New York, 1957.

The Lost Steps. Translated by Harriet de Onís. New York, 1956. 2nd ed., with an introduction by J. B. Priestly, 1967.

Manhunt. Translated by Harriet de Onís. In *Noonday 2,* edited by Cecil Hemley and Dwight W. Webb. New York, 1959. Pp. 109–180.

"The Miracle of Anaquillé: An Afro-Cuban Ballet." Translated and annotated by Kathleen Ross. *Latin American Literary Review* 8/16:55–62 (1980).

Reasons of State. Translated by Frances Partridge. New York, 1976.

"Return to the Seed." Translated by Zoila Nelken. In *Short Stories of Latin America,* edited by Arturo Torres Rioseco. New York, 1963. Pp. 95–110. Also in *From the Green Antilles,* edited by Barbara Howes. New York, 1966. Pp. 286–297.

"Tale of Moons." Translated and annotated by José Piedra. *Latin American Literary Review* 8/16:63–86 (1980).

The War of Time. Translated by Frances Partridge. London and New York, 1970.

Biographical and Critical Studies

Arias, Salvador, ed. *Recopilación de textos sobre Alejo Carpentier.* Havana, 1977.

Bueno, Salvador. "Alejo Carpentier, novelista antillano y universal." In *La letra como testigo.* Santa Clara, Cuba, 1957.

Chao, Ramón. *Palabras en el tiempo de Alejo Carpentier.* Barcelona, 1984.

Chiampi, Irlemar. *El realismo maravilloso.* Caracas, 1983.

Duran Lucio, Juan. *Lectura histórica de la novela: El recurso del método de Alejo Carpentier.* San José, Costa Rica, 1982.

González Echevarría, Roberto. *Alejo Carpentier: The Pilgrim at Home.* Ithaca, N.Y., 1977.

_____, ed. *Los pasos perdidos,* by Alejo Carpentier. Madrid, 1985.

González, Eduardo G. "'Viaje a la semilla' y *El siglo de las luces:* Conjugación de dos textos." *Revista iberoamericana* 41/92–93:423–443 (1975).

Janney, Frank. *Alejo Carpentier and His Early Works.* London, 1981.

Müller-Bergh, Klaus. "Sentido y color de *Concierto barroco.*" *Revista iberoamericana* 41/92–93:445–464 (1975).

_____. "Texto y contexto de *El recurso del método:* Vida y hechos de un tirano ilustrado." In *Historia y ficción en la narrativa hispanoamericana.* Caracas, 1984. Pp. 209–219.

_____. "Paul Claudel and Alejo Carpentier's *El arpa y la sombra:* An Intertextual Approach." In *Comparative Literature Studies,* University Park, Pa. Fall 1986.

_____, ed. *Asedios a Carpentier: Once ensayos críticos sobre el novelista cubano.* Santiago, Chile, 1972.

Sánchez, Modesto G. "El fondo histórico de *El acoso.*" *Revista iberoamericana* 41/92–93:397–422 (1975).

Shaw, Donald. *Alejo Carpentier.* Boston, 1985.

Weber, Frances Wyers. "*El acoso,* Alejo Carpentier's War on Time." *PMLA* 78:440–448 (1963). A Spanish version is included in *Asedios a Carpentier* (above), Klaus Müller-Bergh, ed., pp. 147–164.

Bibliographies

González Echevarría, Roberto, and Klaus Müller-Bergh. *Alejo Carpentier: Bibliographical Guide/Guía bibliográfica.* Westport, Conn., 1983.

García Carranza, Aracéli. *Biobibliografía de Alejo Carpentier.* Havana, 1984.

Rodolfo Usigli

(1905–1979)

Ramón Layera

One of Rodolfo Usigli's most famous lines, "A people without drama is a people without truth," best characterizes both his penchant for dramatic effect and the uncompromising nature of his commitment to the establishment and development of a national theater in Mexico. As a much-published and successfully performed dramatist, as a drama historian, and as a teacher and indefatigable advocate of dramatic activity, Usigli sought to modernize the Mexican stage, to raise the aesthetic consciousness of the public, and to examine national symbols and historical events as the basis for a critical understanding of Mexico's cultural identity. During a life dedicated to these goals, Usigli created a theater company, wrote theater reviews and reports for newspapers and magazines, wrote histories of Mexican drama and a manual of dramatic composition, translated French, British, and American plays for radio and stage, was one of the first professors of theater and dramatic theory at Mexico's National University, and wrote Mexico's (if not Latin America's) best-known and most-performed drama classics. His multifaceted contribution has earned him the descriptions "Playwright of the Mexican Revolution" and, more fittingly, "Apostle of Mexican drama."

The intensity of Usigli's commitment to the creation of a national theater and the poignant quality of his interpretation of Mexican history and culture are especially significant in view of the facts that Usigli's parents were European émigrés and that his work in the Mexican diplomatic service took him outside the country for a number of years. The validity of his interpretation of Mexico's past and the accuracy of his dramatic representation of contemporary society and values, however, has been consistently viewed as most authentic; in addition to receiving the national prize for literature in 1972, he has been universally acclaimed and recognized as Mexico's foremost and most representative playwright.

Rodolfo Usigli was born on 17 November 1905 to Alberto Usigli and Carlota Wainer, both recent immigrants to prerevolutionary Mexico. His father, an Italian citizen born in the port city of Alexandria in Northern Africa, died when Rodolfo was too young to remember. His Polish-born mother, a strong-willed but sensitive woman of Austro-Hungarian descent was, as he acknowledges in his writings and clearly demonstrates in numerous female characters, the most beneficial and strongest influence Usigli had during his formative years; widowed almost at the start of the violent and chaotic phase of the Revolution, she raised four children under very difficult circumstances. Rodolfo grew up as the lower-middle-class child of an embattled but ambitious neighborhood shopkeeper and cleaning woman, who could barely make ends meet but was still able to speak Polish, German, and fluent French to her children and to instill in them the desire to aspire higher and to engage in artistic and intellectual pursuits.

The message did not go unheeded by the young Usigli. Although legally blind until the age of three, permanently troubled by eye and ear defects, and forced to work at an early age, Usigli cultivated an active interest in puppets and theatrical activities, read voraciously any book in sight, and taught himself English and French. One of Mexico's most erudite and sophisticated intellects was unable to finish his secondary school education; he attended two years of adult education evening courses, offered primarily to workers and the poor, without attempting anything resembling a college education. Usigli was a tenacious and naturally gifted man who did not allow physical and socioeconomic limitations to hinder his purpose in life. It is said that his lack of social status and formal education kept him from belonging to the Teatro de Ulises (founded in 1928) and the Teatro de Orientación (founded in 1932)—those organized intellectual and artistic circles that brought together other major pioneering figures, such as Celestino Gorostiza, Salvador Novo, Gilberto Owen, and Xavier Villaurrutia.

In a literary diary of the period 1925 to 1933, Usigli records the details of his apprenticeship as an artist, including his increasing involvement in other literary circles and cultural activities. Aside from the chaos and the destruction that occurred during the period 1910 to 1917, these were crucial years in Usigli's life and in the history of Mexican literature and the arts. With the appointment, in 1920, of José Vasconcelos as Minister of Education, Mexico entered a period of radical and long-lasting educational reform. The availability of public funds, as never before, permitted throughout the country the construction of schools and libraries and the establishment of publishing houses, fine arts academies, and teacher-training programs. This was the period when Mexican artists started painting the monumental murals that glorify Mexico's indigenous past, and when musicians, dancers, and filmmakers began to develop their expressions of cultural nationalism.

During the early 1930's, as part of a carefully designed plan of action, Usigli started to write plays and to train himself for a career as a dramatist. His earliest attempts were not successful; the Mexican theater was not ready to deal with controversial contemporary subjects or to indulge in the kind of experimentation Usigli offered. Motivated by his identification with the liberal ideas and combative style of his idol, George Bernard Shaw, Usigli attempted to discuss current issues and personalities in his plays, a practice that had little precedent in Mexican political circles, much less on the stage. The military phase of the Revolution had barely come to an end, and the conditions for a free and open dialogue on public issues were yet to be created. By 1933 his considerable self-acquired learning and reputation as a scholar had earned him a position on the faculty at the National University and an administrative job in the Ministry of Education, where he undertook to create a radio program that broadcast dramatic classics from around the world. During the academic year 1935–1936, he received, along with the distinguished poet and dramatist Xavier Villaurrutia, a Rockefeller scholarship to study drama direction and composition at Yale University.

Upon his return to his country, Usigli taught in the university, worked as an administrator for the Institute of Fine Arts, and wrote some of his major plays, including his world-renowned *El gesticulador* (The Impostor, written in 1937, premiered in 1947). His efforts continued to meet with considerable rejection by fellow dramatists and critics. Usigli's career as an artist and intellectual was far from established, even though he had written well over sixteen plays, a literary diary, a collection of poems, a variety of play reviews, and prologues and essays on Mexican drama, as well as having produced some of the best Spanish translations of T. S. Eliot's poetry. His concentration on current sociopolitical subjects was not acceptable to a theater establishment then preoccupied with formal experimentation and more cosmopolitan and universal themes; moreover, his pioneering and highly realistic treatment of the nascent Mexican middle class did not appeal to a self-conscious public.

As a result, in part, of financial and family difficulties but mostly because of his inability to make even a modest impact on the theatrical scene, Usigli decided to join the diplomatic service and leave the country. His first assignment was in France. Actually, his stay there, from 1944 to 1946, proved a very valuable experience: it reinforced his lifelong fascination with French literature and culture, and enabled him to see Europe firsthand, to meet contemporary artists and intellectuals, and to travel twice to London to see George Bernard Shaw in person. Their contact and the Anglo-Irish dramatist's familiarity with Usigli's work stimulated the much-quoted remark by Shaw: "If you ever need an Irish certificate of vocation as a dramatic poet I will sign it. . . . Mexico can starve you; but it cannot deny your genius." His interviews with Henri René Lenormand, T. S. Eliot, and Jean Cocteau and, especially, his visits with Shaw had an enormous impact on Usigli's personal development as an artist; they are described in *Conversaciones y encuentros* (Conversations and Encounters, 1974), a book of interviews and autobiographical commentary that includes as well meetings with and vignettes about André Breton, Bruno Traven, Elmer Rice, Clifford Odets, and Paul Muni.

Usigli's eventual return to Mexico entailed both the promise of artistic triumph and the reality of continued failure. *El gesticulador* enjoyed a phenomenal popular success when it was premiered in 1947 but at the same time was the object of the most vicious attacks. Viewed by some as the play that signaled the beginning of Mexico's modern drama and considered by others as an ill-disguised attack against Mexican values and traditions, especially against the Revolution and the party in power, the play ran for two immensely successful weeks until it was removed from the stage under pressure from unionized workers and the government. Subsequent attempts at putting his plays on the stage were also affected by Usigli's legendary, idiosyncratic ability to engage in diatribe in newspaper articles as well as in some of his plays. His highly polemic choice of subject matter brought him enormous popular success with two plays, *El niño y la niebla* (The Child and the Mist, premiered in 1951) and *Jano es una muchacha* (Janus is a Girl, premiered in 1952).

After a few years of fleeting success and more disappointments, Usigli was again forced to leave the country, probably for political reasons, this time on a more permanent basis. Suffering a fate usually re-

served for intractable military generals, Usigli was sent, in 1956, to "diplomatic exile," first to Lebanon, then to Norway. He did return to Mexico periodically and was able to keep up with literary and artistic events there. He finished several plays, including *Corona de fuego* (Crown of Fire, premiered in 1961), the third work of his famous *Corona* (Crown) trilogy, which he finished in Beirut in 1960, but, on the whole, his separation from the Mexican theatrical scene had an adverse artistic and personal effect.

By the time Usigli returned to Mexico in the early 1970's, the younger dramatists, some of whom had been his students and disciples, had capitalized on the innovations and the work of the previous generation and had, in fact, superseded the old masters. Usigli's concept of drama was outmoded and his creative energy almost spent. Aside from producing some painfully bitter yet touching poems dedicated to old age, Usigli wrote drama that had very little impact. In his last two plays, he spoke against youth and reform. In spite of the continued success of some of his earlier plays and official recognition of his contributions to the theater movement and a whole generation of dramatists, his last years were characterized by loneliness and relative dissatisfaction. When he died on 18 June 1979, Usigli was experiencing, as he had throughout his professional career, both a certain degree of misunderstanding and the incipient recognition of the true impact he had had on Mexican drama.

To gain a clear understanding of Usigli's aesthetics and to appreciate the nature and extension of his contribution to modern Mexican drama, one has to take into account both the artist as an individual and the social and historical milieu in which he developed his ideas. This is generally true of Mexican writers and artists who lived through the Mexican Revolution, but it is especially true of individuals, like Usigli, who saw themselves as innovators and as both the subjects and agents of change. The history of twentieth-century Mexican painting, cinema, dance, music, and the other areas touched by the new reformist spirit instigated by the Revolution is peopled by individuals and groups who understood their mission to be one of recovery and interpretation of the past, of reshaping and recreating Mexican values and institutions, and of laying the foundations for a new, proudly nationalist and populist culture.

As a student and interpreter of literary traditions, Usigli looked toward Europe and classical antiquity. He declared a strong preference for French literature and art, with Jean Racine and Jean-Baptiste Molière as his favorites. He also read the Greek and Roman classics carefully and critically, showing greater affinity for the Greek tragedians. In the German tradition, G.W.F. Hegel, Arthur Schopenhauer, and J. W. von Goethe provided literary and philosophical bases for his view of Mexican history and society. English literature offered the Shakespearean canon, as well as the ideological and comedic example of Shaw's drama and social ideals. But his interests and areas of expertise were not only in past literary traditions. He read and translated contemporary European and American authors, showing a clear interest in American psychological drama, in Pirandellian dramatic theories, and in T. S. Eliot's poetry and drama, especially the latter's concept of poetic drama. He exhibited some reticence toward German expressionist theater, and he was mildly, albeit skeptically, curious about both agitprop drama and the postwar theater of the absurd.

Usigli had a strong pedagogical motivation and an exemplary dedication to teaching and scholarly work in the field of dramatic art. He had suffered from a lack of educational opportunities and was familiar with the unavailability of teaching materials and research tools for the study of Mexican drama. In 1937 he taught courses in dramatic theory and composition that are considered to be the beginning of the School of Drama at the College of Philosophy and Letters at the National University. He taught at the School of Drama between 1946 and 1956 and served as director. He also wrote a monograph on Juan Ruiz de Alarcón (the great Mexican dramatist of the Spanish Golden Age), authoritative literary histories of Mexican drama, and manuals of dramatic theory and composition for his students at the university. He even made, in 1940, an unsuccessful but important attempt to establish his own repertory theater company, the Teatro de Medianoche (Midnight Theater), where he pioneered the use of paintings as stage scenery and of movable mechanical stage settings, as well as the elimination of the prompter. These innovative practices continued the earlier efforts of the Teatro de Ulises and Teatro de Orientación groups. Later these procedures became commonly accepted by Mexican playwrights who went on to establish private drama academies and university drama departments.

Usigli's didactic inclinations and scholarly interests are reflected in the now-legendary prefaces and epilogues that he attached to most of his plays. In them Usigli explained his artistic motives, his thematic and stylistic choices, his literary models and influences, his views on life, literature, and society, and even the failures and successes that accompanied the stage production of his plays. Viewed by some as a literary affectation (a presumptuous self-identification with Shaw) and a clear demonstration of Usigli's creative shortcomings (the inability to exhaust a theme, a situation, or a character portrayal within the natural confines of a play) but seen by others as some of the best attempts at expository prose writing in Mexican literature, his prefaces and epilogues remain as some of the best sources for the study of both Usiglian and Mexican drama and a necessity for beginning students of Mexican drama. In addition to the didactic and scholarly aspects of his intellectual personality, Usigli had a far richer and more complex artistic dimension. He wrote poetry and a single detective novel, *Ensayo de un crimen* (Trial Run for a Murder, published in 1944 and made into a movie by Luis Buñuel in 1955).

Yet it is in his numerous plays that one finds the complete breadth of Usigli's artistic ability. His plays are, in fact, a compendium of the great themes and preoccupations of most Mexican artists and writers of the postrevolutionary period. They contain the great myths of the Mexican people, and major historical events are presented as a synthesis of Mexico's cultural development. Usigli provides a new protagonist for the Mexican stage: the developing middle class, with its furniture, its dress and speech, its petty cares, its uncertainty, its pretentiousness. His drama is concerned with the relationship between the individual and the state, the function of art, and the role of the artist and the intellectual in public affairs, as well as with the role of women in a patriarchal society in transition, the interplay of traditional and changing values, and the conflict between generations, social classes, and political groups. Usigli's drama is meant to be a public space for readers and spectators in which the great issues of the moment are discussed in direct, realistic, plain language. It is small wonder then that several of his plays either created a major public commotion when they were first performed and became overnight commercial successes, or had to wait several decades before they could even appear in print.

El niño y la niebla, for example, a probing drama of congenital insanity, was a commercial success when it was premiered in 1951; an absolute first in Mexican theatrical history, the play had an eight-month run with 450 uninterrupted performances. Its popular, mass appeal was the result of the play's emotionally charged, naturalistic portrayal of a wife's hatred for her husband that leads to their child's attempted murder of his father and subsequent suicide. *Jano es una muchacha,* on the other hand, was equally popular when it was first produced in 1952, but like *El gesticulador* it was attacked for its polemic choice of subject matter. The play's daring and critical analysis of Mexico's sexual mores and of society's hypocritical views on sex and prostitution was far from accepted by the establishment but it most certainly contributed to the drama's success at the box office.

The detailed and accurate presentation of familiar, everyday experiences, historical events, and easily recognizable Mexican types depicted in Usigli's plays have led many to identify Usigli with the more conventional and superficial aspects of dramatic realism. More observant students of his works have pointed out that Usigli's dramaturgy is a careful blend of traditional and innovative methods of dramatic composition. In his plays, Usigli does not achieve verisimilitude through the more naive and traditional means of photographic realism; instead, he uses what has been termed a "poetry of selective realism." He borrows basic characters and situations, central cultural myths, and historical events from the apparently pointless chaos of everyday experiences or the formless mass of historical detail. He then transforms them into meaningful and complex dramatic wholes. His works are unlike other contemporary artistic expressions, such as the novel of the Mexican Revolution, which evokes epic and panoramic images of battlefields and of peasants and soldiers on the march,

or the muralist tradition, with its schematic, larger-than-life representations of oppressors and oppressed. Usigli's overall dramatic production tends to be structurally more compact, stylistically more direct, more urban in setting, more issue-oriented in thematic content, and decidedly closer to the reality of the average middle-class Mexican.

Far from being quaint and picturesque comedies of manners or vignettes of Mexican family life, most of Usigli's plays manage to convey a good measure of verifiable reality, a sense of immediacy, and a credible atmosphere of true-to-life drama. In keeping with the Aristotelian, Ibsenian, and Shavian roots of his conception of drama as a faithful reflection of life and the communication of ideas, his plays are artistically contrived and carefully thought-out vehicles for Usigli's liberal ideas for social and political reform. More than thinly veiled social or political diatribes, like some of his Shavian models, however, Usigli's comedies are truly well-made plays that purposefully aim to raise the social and aesthetic consciousness of the Mexican public and to deepen their understanding of their personal moral dilemmas. Some of his more accomplished plays are so true to life and so disturbingly accurate in their depiction of basic human weaknesses that they indeed make truly universal statements on human nature.

Usigli's total dramatic production—over forty comedies, tragedies, farces, historical plays, and dramas of ideas—can be grouped in three major categories, according to their thematic content: social and political satires, dramas of psychological realism, and historical dramas in a Mexican context. These three major categories include his best-known and most successful plays and exclude only several minor light comedies and dramatic classroom exercises (like *El apóstol* [The Apostle], written in 1931, with ill-disguised autobiographical overtones and, perhaps, an oblique reference to Vasconcelos; *Quatre chemins,* also called *Quatre chemins quatre* [Four Roads, written in 1932 entirely in French]; and *Alcestes* [written in 1936, based on Molière's *Le misanthrope*]).

His earliest attempts at political satire were described by Usigli as "impolitical" comedies, underscoring both their manifest irreverence and their fictional character. Linked by their subject matter and their admitted Shavian origin, these "three impolitical comedies" deal with different aspects of Mexico's contemporary political life, in particular, with the still tense and uncertain atmosphere that existed during President Lázaro Cárdenas' administration from 1934 to 1940. In *Noche de estío* (Summer Night, written 1933 to 1935, premiered in 1950) Usigli used three actual historical incidents to conceive an imaginary, albeit improbable coup d'état. In *El Presidente y el Ideal* (The President and the Ideal, written in 1935), again based on the tense rivalry between Cárdenas and the current strongman, General Plutarco Elías Calles, Usigli experiments with a series of dramatic vignettes and highly stylized character abstractions attributable, no doubt, to his obvious fascination with German expressionist drama. The third impolitical comedy and the earliest manifestation of Usigli's treatment of corruption in government is his *Estado de secreto* (State of Secret, written in 1935, premiered in 1936). Still in a satirical and highly political vein, he wrote between 1934 and 1936 *La última puerta* (The Last Door), a highly experimental, absurdist treatment of Mexican bureaucracy, and *Un día de éstos* (One of These Days, written in 1953, premiered in 1954), a very provocative and nationalistic treatment of the question of self-determination and national sovereignty for dependent countries like Mexico.

It is in *El gesticulador* that Usigli achieves his ultimate goal of going beyond strict political satire and the denunciation of national vices. In this, his classic play, the author produces a truly Mexican drama capable of both criticizing and capturing the essence of Mexican political values and institutions. Much to Usigli's credit, *El gesticulador* does far more than just encapsulate Mexico's classic struggle for political decency and institutional stability. The play is more than standard social or political commentary, although on the surface it may seem a realistic and faithful representation of Mexican customs and traditions. His play is, in fact, a highly sophisticated examination of the moral choices that confront the individual both in personal and in public matters. In addition, *El gesticulador* articulates Usigli's metatheatrical concept of life, his basic belief that Mexican public and private life are experiences guided and controlled by dramatic principles that dictate that people in real life, like the characters in a play, have

to engage in false, inauthentic behavior to achieve personal and public goals.

César Rubio, the protagonist of *El gesticulador*, is an erstwhile idealist but now failed and morally confused professor of Mexican history who tries to improve his lot by deceitfully taking advantage of his knowledge and familiarity with the official historical record. With the help of gullible and corrupt politicians, he assumes the identity of a legendary general and is summarily elevated to the highest rank within the official revolutionary party. The next step is to rule the nation, except that he is confronted by the ruling strongman, another imposter who lives by an even greater lie. Usigli's very pessimistic and critical view of Mexico's political culture is embodied in the ultimate triumph of one lie over another, the people's need to believe in any kind of political messiah, and the values and institutions that allow the promotion of bogus leaders and the propagation of hollow myths, the very substance of this play.

Partly because political and social satire elicited a mixed response but mostly because of his interest in psychoanalysis and his reading of authors such as Stendhal, Fyodor Dostoyevski, August Strindberg, and Henrik Ibsen, who stressed the importance of heredity and the environment in the formation of personal character, Usigli turned to the study of human psychology in his drama. Convinced that he could attract a larger audience with a good dose of psychological intrigue and melodrama, he wrote a series of comedies and closet dramas dealing with abnormal psychology and problematic middle-class family relations. This period includes, among others, *El niño y la niebla*, on abnormal child psychology; *Aquas estancadas* (Stagnant Waters, written in 1938, premiered in 1952), on the exorcism of guilt and the search for lost youth; *Otra primavera* (Another Springtime, written 1937 to 1938, premiered in 1945), on the struggle between love and insanity; and *Jano es una muchacha*, on sex and hypocrisy. These works to a large extent helped establish Usigli's reputation as a successful and popular dramatist.

In spite of their commercial success and their popular appeal, however, the plays of psychological realism were only a prelude to Usigli's greater and more lasting artistic plan, the *Corona* trilogy. These three plays, *Corona de fuego*, *Corona de luz* (Crown of

Light, written 1945 to 1963) and *Corona de sombra* (*Crown of Shadows*, written in 1943, premiered in 1947) are Usigli's most ambitious attempt to produce a truly autonomous New World drama in a Mexican context. He meant them to be comparable in literary significance and cultural impact to the classical and European national dramas. In this trilogy, his most scholarly and artistically ambitious project, Usigli aimed to create a dramatic synthesis of Mexico's cultural past, a vast, panoramic representation and interpretation of Mexico's greatest myths and most central historical figures and events. They were meant to be, in his theoretical and ideological scheme, a dramatic crystallization of those national images and symbols that had served the Mexican people in the gradual formation of their national cultural identity.

Using what he described as an "antihistorical" method of dramatic composition ("remembering with the help of the imagination"), he freely selected those "superlative myths" that had occupied the Mexican popular imagination, arbitrarily combining them with the official version of history to produce his own interpretation of both. In the case of *Corona de fuego*, which centers on the clash between the Spaniards and the Aztecs at the time of the conquest, he turns Hernán Cortés and Cuauhtémoc into tragic victims of their respective public roles as conquistador and last Aztec emperor. Through an act of daring historical imagination, he translates a squalid record of greed, betrayal, and violent confrontation into a hauntingly poetic, ritualized representation of the ultimate contest between two peoples poised to do battle but also destined to become the basis of the new Mexican race. What for others has traditionally been a story of genocide, oppression, and destruction, in Usigli's play becomes the productive fusion of two cultures and the beginning of a new nation. Malinche, Cortés' Indian interpreter and lover, the female companion who had previously been viewed as the symbol of either violation or betrayal, becomes in Usigli's dramatic interpretation the bridge that links the races, the original mother of all Mexicans.

Crown of Light, also an interpretive treatment of the early period of the conquest, deals with the next stage in the pacification of the Aztec people through the establishment of the Catholic church in the New World. The story is that of the so-called miracle of the Virgin of Guadalupe. The protagonists, an anachronistic but interesting group of bishops, chroniclers, monks, friars, and Indian believers, argue the factual and imaginary details of the event. Rather than taking sides, Usigli devises a clever and imaginative alternative that allows for both historical plausibility and religious dogma. Furthermore, his interpretation touches on the larger question of the nature of faith when he suggests that the only possible miracle is the newly acquired faith of the indigenous population who, feeling abandoned by their own gods, identify with and accept the dark-complexioned Virgin as their new divinity.

In his dramatic version of the miracle, we find not only the expected and equivocal role of the church authorities along with the unquestioning, childlike devotion of peasants and Indians, but also a series of cleverly designed and humanly possible incidents, including scenes with a Spanish nun who is prone to pious hallucinations and an exceptional gardener who is capable of growing flowers in the most unlikely places. The result is a magically poetic and ideologically provocative interpretation of an otherwise prosaic historical phenomenon; the play becomes a truly imaginative verbal space in which the secular and political motives of both the Spanish Crown and the Roman Catholic church, as well as the needs of a defeated and spiritually orphaned people, are artfully reconciled.

Crown of Shadows, the third piece in the trilogy and, according to many, Usigli's best work (along with *El gesticulador*), is yet another artistic treatment of a crucial moment in Mexico's historical past, this time during the struggle to remain a sovereign republic in the face of a French attempt to restore the monarchy in the New World. The story is that of Carlotta and Maximilian, the Hapsburg monarchs who were persuaded, by the Catholic church and some conservative Mexican exiles, to come to Mexico as that country's new emperors, under the sponsorship of Napoleon III. In close agreement with the historical record, Usigli's version shows them losing their short-lived empire and Maximilian being executed, because of their folly and ambition but mostly because of the Mexican people's courageous response under the able leadership of Benito Juárez. Fascinated by the romantic appeal of Carlotta and Maximilian's tragic destiny, Usigli presents first the touching details of their love and the fairy-tale quality of their imperial court, but he also concentrates largely on Carlotta's less than altruistic personality and on her lifelong insanity after Maximilian's death in 1867 (she lived until 1927).

The real substance of Crown of Shadows is derived from the political implications of Maximilian's execution and the end of the French invasion of Mexico. Usigli pictures Maximilian as a latent democrat who secretly identifies with the liberal cause and almost willingly sacrifices his dream and his life in order to save Mexico and Juárez from those who conspire against them from Europe and from within. Maximilian's actions work against Carlotta's personal and ill-fated designs.

According to Usigli, just as the creation of a new race represents in Corona de fuego a form of "material sovereignty" and the establishment of an indigenous church in Crown of Light represents the beginning of a "spiritual sovereignty," so the victory of democratic, republican ideals over European monarchic aspirations in Crown of Shadows represents the final accomplishment of "political sovereignty" for the people of Mexico. Grandiose as this may seem, Usigli's artistic vision contains the basic characteristic ingredients prevalent in all of Mexican literature and art.

Usigli's Coronas, like his social and political satires and his drama of psychological realism, as well as his scholarly and expository works and numerous other writings not discussed here, constitute the multifaceted expression of a truly Mexican artistic vision, a clearly remarkable intellectual and artistic achievement, and the embodiment of a lifelong passion and dedication to dramatic art. Usigli's remark "Either drama or nothing" was more than just a personal motto; it was clearly a statement of faith. Mexico boasts today one of the most vital and distinguished theater movements in the Hispanic world, an achievement that would not have been possible without the significant contribution of Rodolfo Usigli, "Playwright of the Mexican Revolution" and "Apostle of Mexican drama."

SELECTED BIBLIOGRAPHY

First Editions

Plays

El apóstol. Resumen 35–38 (13, 20, 27 January 1930; 3 February 1931). Mexico City.
Medio tono. Mexico City, 1938.
La crítica de "La mujer no hace milagros." Letras de México 13:5–9 (15 January 1940, 14 February 1940). Mexico City.
Corona de sombra. Cuadernos americanos. Mexico City, 1943.
El gesticulador. El Hijo Pródigo. Mexico City, 1943.
La familia cena en casa. El Hijo Pródigo 21, 22, 23 (December 1944; January–February 1945). Mexico City.
La última puerta. Hoy. Mexico City, 1948.
La mujer no hace milagros. América. Mexico City, 1949.
Sueño de día. América 59:167–194 (February 1949). Mexico City.
El niño y la niebla. Novedades. Mexico City, 1950.
Los fugitivos. Novedades. Mexico City, 1951.
La función de despedida. Novedades. Mexico City, 1951.
Aguas estancadas. Novedades. Mexico City, 1952.
Jano es una muchacha. Mexico City, 1952.
Mientras amemos. Panoramas. Mexico City, 1956.
Otra primavera. Mexico City, 1956.
Vacaciones II. Novedades. Mexico City, 1956.
Un día de éstos . . . . Mexico City, 1957.
La exposición. Cuadernos americanos. Mexico City, 1960.
Vacaciones I. Tercera antología de obras en un acto. Mexico City, 1960.
Corona de luz. Mexico City, 1965.
Carta de amor. Revista de la Universidad de Mexico. Mexico City, 1968.
El gran circo del mundo. Cuadernos americanos. Mexico City, 1969.
Los viejos. Mexico City, 1971.
¡Buenos días, señor Presidente! Mexico City, 1972.

Poetry

Conversación desesperada: Poemas. Mexico City, 1938.
Sonetos del tiempo y de la muerte. Mexico City, 1954.

Novel and Prose Narrative

Ensayo de un crímen. Mexico City, 1944.
Obliteración. Mexico City, 1973.

Essays

México en el teatro. Mexico City, 1932.

Caminos del teatro en México. Mexico City, 1933. Also as a long prologue to *Bibliografía del teatro en Mexico*, by Francisco Monterde García Icazbalceta. Mexico City, 1934. Pp. vii–lxxx.

Itinerario del autor dramático. Mexico City, 1940.

Juan Ruiz de Alarcón en el tiempo. Mexico City, 1967.

Anatomía del teatro. Mexico City, 1967.

Memoirs

Voces: Diario de trabajo (1932–1933). Mexico City, 1967.

Conversaciones y encuentros. Mexico City, 1974.

Translations by Usigli

There exist many unpublished Spanish translations of European and American drama classics by Rodolfo Usigli that were used in the 1930's and 1940's as radio scripts or as playscripts for university and Institute of Fine Arts drama productions.

Walt Whitman constructor para América [Babette Deutsch]. Mexico City, 1942.

La llave de cristal [Dashiel Hammet]. Mexico City, 1942.

La casa de té la luna de agosto [John Patrick]. Mexico City, 1957.

Historia de Vasco [Georges Schéhadé]. Mexico City, 1959.

La condición humana [André Malraux]. Mexico City, 1971.

Mexico, tierra india [Jacques Soustelle]. Mexico City, 1971.

Collected Works

Usigli wrote several plays that were not published in book form until they appeared in *Teatro completo*.

Corona de sombra, Corona de fuego, Corona de luz. Mexico City, 1973.

Un navío cargado de . . . , El testamento y el viudo, y El encuentro. Three comedies. Mexico City, 1966.

Teatro completo 1: Falso drama, 4 Chemins 4, Alcestes, Noche de estío, El Presidente y el Ideal, Estado de secreto. 2: Vacaciones I, Dios, Batidillo y la mujer, Las madres, La diadema, Corona de fuego. 3: Un navío cargado de . . . , El testamento y el viudo, El encuentro, El caso Flores, and prologues and epilogues. Mexico City, 1963–1979.

Tiempo y memoria en conversación desesperada. Edited by José Emilio Pacheco. Mexico City, 1981.

Tres comedias inéditas. Mexico City, 1967.

Later Editions

Corona de fuego. Edited by Rex Edward Ballinger. Indianapolis, Ind., 1972.

Corona de luz. Mexico City, 1965.

Corona de luz. Edited by Rex Edward Ballinger. New York, 1967.

Corona de sombra. Edited by Rex Edward Ballinger. New York, 1961.

La función de despedida. Mexico City, 1952.

El gesticulador. Edited by Rex Edward Ballinger. Englewood Cliffs, N.J., 1963.

El niño y la niebla. Edited by Rex Edward Ballinger. Boston, 1965.

Los viejos. Mexico City, 1971.

Translations

Although *El gesticulador* is one of the most extensively used foreign language texts in American universities, there is no published English translation.

Another Springtime. Translated by Wayne Wolfe. London and New York, 1961.

Crown of Shadows. Translated by William F. Stirling. London, 1947.

The Great Middle Class. Translated by Edna Furness. *Poet Lore* 63:156–232 (1966).

Mexico in the Theater. Translated by Wilder P. Scott. University, Miss., 1976.

Two Plays: Crown of Light, One of These Days . . . . Translated by Thomas Bledsoe. Carbondale, Ill., 1971.

Biographical and Critical Studies

Beardsell, Peter R. "Insanity and Poetic Justice in Usigli's *Corona de sombra*." *Latin American Theatre Review* 10/1:5–14 (1976).

———. "Usigli and the Search for Tragedy: *Corona de fuego*." In *Hispanic Studies in Honour of Frank Pierce*, edited by John England. Sheffield, England, 1980. Pp. 1–15.

Beck, Vera F. "La fuerza motriz, en la obra dramática de Rodolfo Usigli." *Revista iberoamericana* 18/36:369–383 (1953).

Di Puccio, Denise M. "Metatheatrical Histories in *Corona de luz*." *Latin American Theatre Review* 20/1:29–36 (1986).

Finch, Mark S. "Rodolfo Usigli's *Corona de sombra, Corona de fuego, Corona de luz*: The Mythopoesis of Antihistory." *Romance Notes* 22/2:151–154 (1981).

García Lora, José. "Rodolfo Usigli 'esperó a Godot' dieciséis años antes que Samuel Beckett." *Papeles de son armadans* 90/269–270:129–147 (1978).

Gates, Eunice G. "Usigli as Seen in His Prefaces and Epilogues." *Hispania* 37/4:432–439 (1954).

Kronik, John W. "Usigli's *El gesticulador* and the Fiction of Truth." *Latin American Theatre Review* 11/1:5–16 (1977).

Labinger, Andrea G. "Age, Alienation and the Artist in Usigli's *Los viejos.*" *Latin American Theatre Review* 14/2:41–47 (1981).

Larsen, Catherine. "No conoces el precio de las palabras: Language and Meaning in Usigli's *El gesticulador.*" *Latin American Theatre Review* 20/1:21–28 (1986).

Layera, Ramón. "Mecanismos de fabulación y mitificación de la historia en las 'comedias impolíticas' y las *Coronas* de Rodolfo Usigli." *Latin American Theatre Review* 18/2:49–55 (1985).

———. "*Conversaciones y encuentros:* Prolegómenos para la autobiografía de Rodolfo Usigli." In *De la crónica a la nueva narrativa: Coloquio sobre la literatura mexicana,* edited by Merlin H. Forster and Julio Ortega. Mexico City, 1986. Pp. 151–160.

Lomelí, Francisco A. "Los mitos de la mexicanidad en la trilogía de Rodolfo Usigli." *Cuadernos hispanoamericanos* 333:466–477 (1978).

Martínez Peñaloza, Porfirio. "Sobre el poeta Rodolfo Usigli." *Ábside* 39/4:429–436 (1975).

Merritt Matteson, Marianna. "On the Function of the Imposter in the Plays of Rodolfo Usigli." *Selecta* 2:120–123 (1981).

———. "Usigli's *Obliteración:* An Intimate Inferno." *Selecta* 3:127–133 (1982).

Monterde, Francisco. "Juárez, Maximiliano y Carlota en las obras de los dramaturgos mexicanos." *Cuadernos americanos* 136/5:231–240 (1964).

Perri, Dennis. "The Artistic Unity of *Corona de sombra.*" *Latin American Theatre Review* 15/1:13–19 (1981).

Petersen, Gerald W. "El mundo circular de Rodolfo Usigli." *Explicación de textos literarios* 6/1:105–108 (1977–1978).

Ragle, Gordon. "Rodolfo Usigli and His Mexican Scene." *Hispania* 46/2:307–311 (1963).

Rodríguez, Roberto R. "La función de la imaginación en las *Coronas* de Rodolfo Usigli." *Latin American Theatre Review* 10/2:37–44 (1977).

Rodríguez-Seda, Asela. "Las últimas obras de Rodolfo Usigli: Efebocracia o gerontocracia." *Latin American Theatre Review* 8/1:45–48 (1974).

Savage, Vance R. "Rodolfo Usigli's Idea of Mexican Theater." *Latin American Theatre Review* 4/2:13–20 (1971).

Schanzer, George O. "Usigli, Calderón and the Revolution." *Kentucky Romance Quarterly* 26/2:189–201 (1979).

Scott, Wilder P. "Rodolfo Usigli and Contemporary Dramatic Theory." *Romance Notes* 11/3:526–530 (1970).

———. "Toward an Usigli Bibliography (1931–1971)." *Latin American Theatre Review* 6/1:53–63 (1972).

———. "French Literature and the Theater of Rodolfo Usigli." *Romance Notes* 16/1:228–231 (1974).

———. "Rodolfo Usigli's *4 Chemin 4:* The Quest for a Title." *Language Quarterly* (Tampa, Fla.) 12/3–4:51–52 (1974).

Shaw, Donald L. "Dramatic Technique in Usigli's *El gesticulador.*" *Theatre Research International* 1:125–133 (Glasgow, 1976).

Tilles, Solomon H. "Rodolfo Usigli's Concept of Dramatic Art." *Latin American Theatre Review* 3/2:31–38 (1970).

Zalacaín, Daniel, and Esther P. Mocega González. "El ciclo vital heroico en *El gesticulador.*" *Language Quarterly* (Tampa, Fla.) 22/3–4:35–38 (1984).

Érico Veríssimo

(1905–1975)

Claude L. Hulet

Érico Veríssimo, perhaps Brazil's most ardent student of the novel genre, belonged to the second generation of modernism, a literary current that gained recognition in the early 1930's and continued to produce in volume for some thirty years. His acquaintance with the novels of the past was only surpassed by his knowledge of the literature of his Western-world contemporaries. He studied their languages and techniques, and he often experimented with themes, setting, and structure; nevertheless he remained faithful to his philosophy, to his language, and to the importance of the story. Although Veríssimo also published several collections of short stories and ten children's books, he was especially known as a novelist, authoring twelve books in that genre. To his credit, too, are four travel books (two on the United States and one each on Mexico and Israel) plus an outline history of Brazilian literature that he wrote in English, based on a course he gave in California.

Veríssimo was born on 17 December 1905 in the interior city of Cruz Alta, Rio Grande do Sul. His education was interrupted during high school owing to the separation of his parents and by the subsequent need to work. He disliked his jobs as a clerk in a store and in a bank, and as part owner of a pharmacy, and having seen one of his short stories published in the state capital, Porto Alegre, he decided to follow a literary career. He found employment first as secretary of the *Revista do Globo* (Review of the World) magazine, and later, for several years, as the editor. At the same time, he did a number of fine translations from English-language literature for the Globo publishing house and launched into writing the novels, short stories, and travel books on which his fame rests.

In 1941 Veríssimo spent three months in the United States at the invitation of the Department of State, and on his return to Brazil published *Gato Preto em Campo de Neve* (Black Cat in the Snowfield, 1941), a humorous account of his observations while traveling across the United States. Two years later the Department of State invited him to give a course at an American university, and he chose the University of California at Berkeley. At the end of the 1944 school year, Mills College in Oakland, California, invited him to give a course on Brazilian history and literature in its summer session, and conferred on him an honorary Ph.D. Drawing on this teaching experience, Veríssimo published *Brazilian Literature* (1945), the only book he wrote directly in English. He stayed in the United States with his family until September 1946, spending several months in Los Angeles and giving lectures in a number of states. That year saw the appearance of a sequel to his first travel book, *A Volta do Gato Preto* (The Return of the Black Cat), and the following year he began to write *O Tempo e o Vento* (*Time and the Wind*, 1949–1962), whose first volume, *O Continente*, would appear in 1949 to excellent sales and a warm reception by the critics.

In 1953 Veríssimo received an invitation to become director of the cultural division of the Pan American Union in Washington, D.C., where he remained for three years. He gave numerous conferences in the United States and participated in conferences, symposia, and roundtables in various countries. Touring Mexico when on vacation in 1955, he was inspired to write *México, História de uma Viagem* (*Mexico*, 1957). In 1959, accompanied by his wife and son, he visited Portugal, Spain, Italy, France, Germany, Holland, and England. In March of 1961 Veríssimo suffered a heart attack. Although ever after in delicate health, he traveled frequently between his home in Porto Alegre and his daughter's home in the United States; continued to write and correct proofs; and made trips to Greece, Italy, and France. In 1966 he and his wife took a trip to Israel at the invitation of the Israeli government, a voyage he described in *Israel em Abril* (*Israel in April*, 1970). In 1972 Veríssimo's forty years of literary activity were celebrated in Brazil on a national scale. Érico Veríssimo died at his home in Porto Alegre on 28 November 1975. He was survived by his wife, Mafalda, his daughter, Clarissa, and his son, Luís Fernando, a well-known prose writer.

The first Brazilian writer to live by his pen, Veríssimo could have boasted many other firsts as well if it had been in his nature to do so. For example, he was the first in his country to gain best-seller status as well as the first to attempt the truly modern, urban novel, emphasizing the role of the then small but developing Brazilian middle class and employing an innovatively clear, easy, and supple language whose vocabulary, syntax, and tone are representative of cultured members of that socioeconomic group. He was also the first to make effective use of the point-counterpoint novel; to place the principal setting of some of his novels entirely outside his country's borders; to write a unique, multivolumed novel portraying the dogged, largely silent, unheroic and unsung role the people themselves played over two centuries in the development of his region of southern Brazil;

and to publish an existentialist-type novel with surrealistic overtones. Noteworthy, too, is the fact that he was one of the first authors of children's literature in Brazil. Veríssimo, characteristically, was the only Brazilian novelist to dare to challenge the Brazilian dictatorship stemming from the 1964 coup d'état, by publishing the novel *Incidente em Antares* (Incident in Antares, 1972), openly satirizing the regime.

The main thrust of Veríssimo's works exalts love of humanity, and his lofty message stresses brotherhood, justice, and peace, along with the importance of work. By accepting the title of simple storyteller gratuitously given him by certain critics perhaps envious of his success, Veríssimo, knowingly or not, gave the public an image of himself that shifted attention from his ideological position. His ideology, mere background early on, came increasingly to the forefront of his work following the 1964 military coup in Brazil and the United States' entry into the war in Vietnam.

The long list of Veríssimo's novels testifies to his versatility. Often different in structure, in locale, or in subject, even his novels set in Brazil proclaim the universality of his characters, settings, plots, conflicts, stories, and language. Although he used time and space shifts, Veríssimo created his fictive world straightforwardly, without deforming it. He did not emphasize local color, *costumbrismo* (depiction of regional customs), folklore, tradition, or the exotic to gain reader empathy, nor did he use a backward perspective portraying the centuries-old, inherited problems of man in relation to the land or the injustice of the underlying rural institutions, at that time a common subject of novels of the northeast of Brazil. As the years went by, he depended less on scene and more on drama, and the amplitude of his plots and settings and the scope of his themes became gradually more encompassing.

The youthful Veríssimo was enamored of the plastic arts, but he left painting with colors for painting with words, which may account for his fiction's strong visual element. Clearly evident are his sharp grasp of the material world and his ability to choose the proper angle and setting to advantageously present his characters and their problems, which readers see evoked and framed in scenes that unfold as in a film. His perspective is that of the first person without the first person showing through. Veríssimo "sees" the universe he creates and he communicates its details around a story line so cogent and convincing that the reader receives a full, mimetic impression of thoughts and events and becomes absorbed in the characters' problems and conflicts. The ambience per se, the intricacies of the human mind, the psychological development of the characters, and complex philosophies are all subordinate to the narrative.

Just as Veríssimo's humanistic and ideological concerns, often communicated through symbols and embodied in characters, govern his themes, music, one of his passions, is often found in his works in the form of allusions and symphonic structures, features that first became especially apparent in *Música ao Longe* (Music in the Distance, 1935). Veríssimo focused on the average reader with whom his relationship is direct, intimate, uncomplicated, and conversational—the characteristics of a born storyteller, which he superbly was. The dialogue, used sparingly in his early novels, takes on an increasingly important role beginning with *O Tempo e o Vento.*

In their search for the lyrical in reality, the novelists of Brazil's second modernist generation, to which Veríssimo belonged, at first preferred the short novel, or novelette, and emphasized one character, one perspective, and a limited space and time. Veríssimo's initial fictional effort, the novelette *Clarissa* (Clarissa, 1933), an immediate success, is brief and memorialist, thus coinciding with that modernist tendency. It emphasizes nostalgic reminiscences bathed in the suffused luminescence of pictorial impressionism. (Although *Fantoches* [Puppets, 1932], a collection of short stories, was really his first book to appear in print, the first edition was largely destroyed in a warehouse fire and the book only gained significant distribution years later in a second edition.)

Although the short story and the novelette gave Veríssimo entry into prose fiction writing, beginning with *Música ao Longe,* he quickly adopted the novel, with its multiple physical and chronological planes and perspectives, as his preferred genre. He focused on the urban scene and immediately became a best-selling novelist. Other novels, *Caminhos Cruzados* (Crossroads, 1935); *Um Lugar ao Sol* (A Place in the Sun, 1936); *Olhai os Lírios do Campo* (*Consider the Lilies of the Field: A Novel by Érico Veríssimo,* 1938), and *O Resto É Silêncio* (*The Rest Is Silence,* 1943), followed in rapid succession, each one by way of an experiment in Veríssimo's continuing search for a better fictive medium. Collage, counterpoint, cuts, flashbacks, montage, parallel plots, simultaneity, telescoping, the diary, and the documentary are only a few of the devices he used in his broad, cosmopolitan view of the world.

Significantly, Porto Alegre, the setting in these early novels, is a city that at least up through the 1950's was probably the most atypical and the most modern of Brazil's urban centers, having more the air of a small American city. Brazil was on the way to becoming an urban society, and the capital of Rio Grande do Sul was in the vanguard. Sensing the significance of that transitional atmosphere and realizing that life in the city, not Brazil's mainly agricultural past, held the key to the country's future, Veríssimo presented a whole array of the implications of contemporary life in the city, such as political, economic, and social injustice and hindrances to self-realization. Racism, bossism, and other forms of oppression, the lopsided distribution of wealth, and inadequate health services and educational opportunities form the background to the role played by psychological conflicts and such human foibles as unbridled ambition, selfishness, and greed. He was almost alone in that perspective. The newness and appropriateness of the themes treated, along with their universal applicability, can be pointed to as strong contributing reasons for these novels' immediate appeal, both in Brazil and in translation into English.

Veríssimo gives the reader a dense, coherent view of the hustle-bustle and stridency of modern life in his early novels; he was not simply a reporter or producer of documentaries. He was genuinely interested in people, sympathized honestly and unaffectedly with his fellowman, and created plausible and memorable characters who tend to be symbols representing social positions, attitudes, and interests. He lets them work out their own destinies in accordance with their personalities and attributes, and through them situations and scenes that make the all-important story evolve. Since readers were by definition principally urbanites, they easily identified with the middle-class characters.

Independent of mind, a democratic socialist and a pacifist, Veríssimo was more universally oriented than many of his more dogmatic contemporaries. There are no extremes, no exaggerations, no radicalization of positions in him. His belief in humanity and his abhorrence of authoritarianism and violence, whether physical or moral, set him apart. His ideal was to see man as an independent-thinking individual pursuing goals common to and in voluntary concert with his fellowmen. Such a world would be characterized by cooperation, mutual assistance, and concern for others. There everyone would have a right to a place in the sun, as the title of one of his novels suggests.

The three-year period during which Veríssimo was the director of the letters and science division of the Pan American Union in Washington, D.C. (1953–1956), was a particularly prolific time for him, for it was then that he wrote several of his most ambitious novels. He continued to show his superb control of novelistic techniques, versatility of treatment, and universality of theme, but he no longer limited himself to the local urban scene that had hitherto held his attention. In these later novels, he raised his sights to encompass momentous historic developments at home and abroad. In *Time and the Wind*, Veríssimo demonstrated his broad yet penetrating view of the dramatic history of his home state of Rio Grande do Sul. On this wide, panoramic, and imaginative screen developed in three hefty volumes (the third of which itself has three parts), Veríssimo follows the vicissitudes of two families. He presents in human terms the development of Rio Grande do Sul (and indirectly of Brazil itself) from the nebulous mists of the mythical past and its history from the founding of the society of that state in the middle of the eighteenth century up to the dictatorship of Getúlio Vargas in the first half of the twentieth century. The area's bellicose history and its distinctly telluric origins are essentially symbolic and in no way represent the principal thrust of this monumental work, in which Veríssimo depicts the evolution of the present-day, urban middle class, along with the whole gamut of inherent issues. Volume 1, *O Continente* (The Continent), appeared in 1949 and vol-

ume 2, *O Retrato* (The Portrait), in 1951; the first two books of volume 3, *O Arquipélago* (The Archipelago), were published in 1961 and the third, the following year. Veríssimo interrupted the fifteen-year period during which he wrote the multivolumed *Time and the Wind* to publish *Noite* (Night, 1954), an existentialist novelette with surrealistic overtones reminiscent of a type then in vogue in France.

Veríssimo's Washington, D.C., experience probably provided stimulation and material for his *O Senhor Embaixador* (His Excellency the Ambassador, 1965). It must be remembered, however, that his sensitivity to the broader picture was already apparent; concerned about the implications of the intromission of the two armed fascist giants, Germany and Italy, into Spain, he placed one of his early novels, *Saga* (Saga, 1940), in the time of the Spanish civil war. His literary contemporaries still were engrossed in purely local matters. *His Excellency the Ambassador* is a long novel with a fast-moving story depicting the rise and fall of a mythical and presumably Caribbean-area dictator; it offers an incisive contrastive analysis of Spanish-American, Brazilian, and American philosophies and customs, along with a keen insight into the ramifications of Western Hemisphere politics. The far-off conflict in Vietnam also gave him incentive to write *O Prisioneiro* (The Prisoner, 1967), a powerful novel against war and racism, from an even more forceful, humanitarian viewpoint than his earlier *Saga*.

In 1972, in direct defiance of the censorship laws, which he always courageously condemned, Veríssimo published his last novel, *Incidente am Antares*, a highly symbolical work strongly satirizing the military dictatorship. Veríssimo began publishing his autobiography, *Solo de Clarineta: Memórias* (Clarinet Solo: Memories), in 1973, but publication was interrupted by his death. The second volume came out posthumously, in 1976.

SELECTED BIBLIOGRAPHY

Editions

Short Stories

Fantoches. Porto Alegre, Brazil, 1932. Facsimile edition, with author's comments and drawings, commemorating Veríssimo's forty years of literary activity, Lisbon, 1973.

As Mãos do meu Filho. Porto Alegre, Brazil, 1935.

Novels

Clarissa. Porto Alegre, 1933.
Caminhos Cruzados. Porto Alegre, Brazil, 1935.
Música ao Longe. Porto Alegre, Brazil, 1935.
Um Lugar ao Sol. Porto Alegre, Brazil, 1936.
Olhai os Lírios do Campo. Porto Alegre, Brazil, 1938.
Saga. Porto Alegre, Brazil, 1940.
O Resto É Silêncio. Porto Alegre, Brazil, 1943.
O Tempo e o Vento 1: O Continente. Porto Alegre, Brazil, 1949.
O Tempo e o Vento 2: O Retrato. Porto Alegre, Brazil, 1951.
Noite. Rio de Janeiro. 1954.
O Tempo e o Vento 3, Books 1 and 2: O Arquipélago. Porto Alegre, Brazil, 1961.
O Tempo e o Vento 3, Book 3: O Arquipélago. Porto Alegre, Brazil, 1962.
O Senhor Embaixador. Porto Alegre, Brazil, 1965.
O Prisioneiro. Porto Alegre, Brazil, 1967.
Incidente em Antares. Porto Alegre, Brazil, 1972.

Children's Literature

As Aventuras do Avião Vermelho. Porto Alegre, Brazil, 1937.
As Aventuras de Tibicuera, Que São Também as Aventuras do Brasil. Porto Alegre, Brazil, 1937.
Rosamaria no Castelo Encantado. Porto Alegre, Brazil, 1937.
Os Três Porquinhos Pobres. Porto Alegre, Brazil, 1937.
O Urso com Música na Barriga. Porto Alegre, Brazil, 1938.
Aventuras no Mundo da Higiene. Porto Alegre, Brazil, 1939.
Outra Vez os Três Porquinhos. Porto Alegre, Brazil, 1939.
Viagem à Aurora do Mundo. Porto Alegre, Brazil, 1939.
A Vida do Elefante Basílio. Porto Alegre, Brazil, 1939.
A Vida de Joana d'Arc. Porto Alegre, Brazil, 1944.

Travel

Gato Preto em Campo de Neve. Porto Alegre, Brazil, 1941.
A Volta do Gato Preto. Porto Alegre, Brazil, 1946.
México, História de uma Viagem. Porto Alegre, Brazil, 1957.
Israel em Abril. Porto Alegre, Brazil, 1970.

Nonfiction

Brazilian Literature: An Outline. New York, 1945.

Memoirs

Solo de Clarineta: Memórias. 2 vols. Porto Alegre, Brazil, 1973–1976.

Collected Works

Ficção Completa. 5 vols. Rio de Janeiro, 1966.

Translations

Consider the Lilies of the Field: A Novel by Érico Veríssimo. Translated by Jean Neel Karnoff. New York, 1947.
Crossroads. Translated by L. C. Kaplan. New York, 1943.
His Excellency the Ambassador. Translated by Linton Lomas Barrett and Marie McDavid Barrett. New York, 1967.
Mexico. Translated by Linton Lomas Barrett. New York, 1960.
Night. Translated by Linton Lomas Barrett. New York, 1956.
The Rest Is Silence. Translated by L. C. Kaplan. New York, 1946.
Time and the Wind. Translated by Linton Lomas Barrett. New York, 1951.

Biographical and Critical Studies

Adonias, Filho. In O Romance Brasileiro de 30. Rio de Janeiro, 1969. Pp. 147–155.
Amado, Jorge. "Érico Veríssimo pelo Mundo Afora." In Vida Literária de Érico Veríssimo, edited by Flávio Loureiro Chaves. Porto Alegre, Brazil, 1972. Pp. 29–34.
Andrade, Jorge de. "O Galho da Nespereira." In O Contador de Histórias: Quarenta Anos de Vida Literária de Érico Veríssimo, edited by Flávio Loureiro Chaves. Porto Alegre, Brazil, 1972.
Ayala, Walmir. "Minha Infância com Érico." In Vida Literária de Érico Veríssimo, edited by Flávio Loureiro Chaves. Porto Alegre, Brazil, 1972. Pp. 26–28.
Barrett, Linton Lomas. "Érico Veríssimo and the Creation of Novelistic Character." Hispania 29/3:321–338 (1947).
——. "Érico Veríssimo's Idea of the Novel: Theory and Practice." Hispania 34/1:30–40 (1951).
Cândido, Antônio. "Érico Veríssimo de Trinta a Setenta." In O Contador de Histórias: Quarenta Anos de Vida Literária de Érico Veríssimo, edited by Flávio Loureiro Chaves. Porto Alegre, Brazil, 1972. Pp. 40–51.
César, Guilhermino. "O Romance Social de Érico Veríssimo." In O Contador de Histórias: Quarenta Anos de Vida Literária de Érico Veríssimo, edited by Flávio

Loureiro Chaves. Porto Alegre, Brazil, 1972. Pp. 71–85.

Chagas, Wilson. *Mundo Velho sem Porteiras: Ensaio Sobre a Obra de Érico Veríssimo.* Porto Alegre, Brazil, 1985.

Chaves, Flávio Loureiro. "Érico Veríssimo e o Mundo das Personagens." In *Contador de Histórias: Quarenta Anos de Vida Literária de Érico Veríssimo,* edited by Flávio Loureiro Chaves. Porto Alegre, Brazil, 1972. Pp. 71–85.

———. "A Crônica em Decadência." In *Música ao Longe,* by Érico Veríssimo. 3rd ed. Porto Alegre, Brazil, 1973.

———. "O Realismo da Vida Presente." In *Um Lugar ao Sol,* by Érico Veríssimo. 3rd ed. Porto Alegre, Brazil, 1973.

———. "Releitura de Clarissa." In *Clarissa,* by Érico Veríssimo. 4th ed. Porto Alegre, Brazil, 1973.

———. "O Romance de Tônio Santiago." In *O Resto É Silêncio,* by Érico Veríssimo. Porto Alegre, Brazil, 1974.

———. "A Narrativa da Solidão." In *Noite,* by Érico Veríssimo. 3rd ed. Porto Alegre, Brazil, 1975.

———. "Um Depoimento Humanista." In *Saga,* by Érico Veríssimo. 8th ed. Porto Alegre, Brazil, 1976.

———. *Érico Veríssimo, Realismo e Sociedade.* Porto Alegre, Brazil, 1976. With a bibliography on pp. 159–185.

Filipouski, Ana Mariza Ribeiro, and Regina Zilberman. *Érico Veríssimo e a Literatura Infantil.* Porto Alegre, Brazil, 1978.

Foster, Merlin H. "Structure and Meaning in Érico Veríssimo's *Noite.*" *Hispania* 45/4:712–716 (1962).

Furlan, Oswaldo Antônio. *Estética e Crítica Social em "Incidente em Antares."* Porto Alegre, Brazil, 1977.

Gomes, Duílio. "Érico Veríssimo Quarenta Anos Depois." *Minas Gerais, Literary Supplement.* 14 April 1973.

Lima, Alceu Amoroso (Tristão de Athayde). "Érico Veríssimo e o Antimachismo." In *O Contador de Histórias: Quarenta Anos de Vida Literária de Érico Veríssimo,* edited by Flávio Loureiro Chaves. Porto Alegre, Brazil, 1972. Pp. 86–102.

Lins, Álvaro. *Os Mortos de Sobrecasaca.* Rio de Janeiro, 1963. Pp. 220–229.

Lucas, Fábio. "O Romance de Érico Veríssimo e o Mundo Oferecido." In *O Contador de Histórias: Quarenta Anos de Vida Literária de Érico Veríssimo,* edited by Flávio Loureiro Chaves. Porto Alegre, Brazil, 1972. Pp. 144–157.

Maciel, Carlos Alberto Antunes. *Richesse et evolution du vocabulaire d'Erico Veríssimo (1905–1975).* Porto Alegre, Brazil, 1986.

Martins, Wilson. *O Modernismo.* In *Ficção Completa 1,* by Érico Veríssimo. Rio de Janeiro, 1966. Pp. 20–23.

Mazzara, Richard A. "Paralelos Luso-Brasileiros: Eça e Érico." *Luso-Brasilian Review* 1/2:63–73 (1964).

———. "Structure and Verisimilitude in the Novels of Érico Veríssimo." *PMLA* 80/4:451–458 (1965).

Olinto, Antônio. "A História em Estado de Pureza." In *Ficção Completa,* by Érico Veríssimo. Rio de Janeiro, 1966. Pp. 13–20.

———. "Érico Veríssimo." In *A Literatura no Brasil 5,* edited by Afrânio Coutinho. Rio de Janeiro, 1968–1971.

Patai, Daphne. "Veríssimo e Huxley: Um Ensaio de Análise Comparada." *Minas Gerais, Literary Supplement.* 26 January and 2, 9, and 16 February 1974.

Pompermayer, Malori José. *Érico Veríssimo e o Problema de Deus.* Porto Alegre, Brazil, 1968.

Zilberman, Regina. *A Literatura no Rio Grande do Sul.* Porto Alegre, Brazil, 1982. Pp. 156–165.

Enrique A. Laguerre

(1906–   )

Rosario Ferré

Enrique A. Laguerre is one of Puerto Rico's most renowned novelists; he is also well known as a newspaper columnist and the author of numerous short stories, essays, poems, and one theatrical drama. His novels are studied at high school and university levels and have been published in numerous editions. *La llamarada* (The Blaze, 1935) is in its twenty-eighth printing, and *La resaca* (The Undertow, 1949) in its fifteenth. Two of his novels, *El laberinto* (*The Labyrinth*, 1959) and *Los amos benévolos* (*Benevolent Masters*, 1976), have been translated into English, and *La llamarada,* as of early 1988, was soon to be published in that language. Laguerre's works have been the object of intense critical discussion in Puerto Rico for the past fifty years and have been commented upon by such prestigious literary figures as José Enrique Pedreira, Concha Meléndez, Francisco Arrivi, Margot Arce de Vázquez, Anita Arroyo, María Teresa Babín, and many others. In the international arena, his works have been discussed by Juan Bosch, Tomás Navarro Tomás, and Concha Castroviejo.

Laguerre, born 3 May 1906, came from a family of coffee plantation owners from the vicinity of Moca, a small town in the western part of Puerto Rico. Growing up in this environment contributed to the powerful way that nature influenced his novels, and the countryside of his childhood afforded him with many of their characters, which are made up of humble country folk. He had to walk some four kilometers each day in order to attend a rural schoolhouse; he later attended high school in the coastal city of Aguadilla, where he began to write short pieces and took a course in teaching. Shortly afterward he embarked on what would be a lifelong career in teaching, first at the elementary and later at the university level. In 1941 he obtained his master's degree in education from the University of Puerto Rico. His thesis on that occasion, *La poesía modernista en Puerto Rico* (Modernist Poetry in Puerto Rico), published in 1969, remains today the most complete and extensive study written about the modernist poets of the island. In 1951 he acquired his doctorate at Columbia University in New York.

Laguerre's effort to follow carefully the social and historical changes of the island as a writer of fiction and newspaper correspondent was encompassing and persistent. For several years, beginning in 1952, he had a radio program, "Puntos de partida" (Points of Departure), in which he commented on the events of the times, and which he later published as a book of essays titled *Pulso de Puerto Rico* (Pulse of Puerto Rico), in 1956. He was also director of the magazine *Presente,* together with Ciro Alegría, the Peruvian novelist, who was at the time a visiting professor at the University of Puerto Rico. He was a contributor to the famed *Puerto Rico Ilustrado* and codirector of *Palique*, both prestigious literary publications of the island during the first half of the century, and he contributed the column "Hojas libres" (Free Pages) to the newspaper *El Mundo* for more than twenty-five years. In 1955 he was elected to the Puerto Rican Academy of the Spanish Language and joined the directorship of the Institute of Puerto Rican Culture.

Although untiringly versatile as a writer, it is as a novelist that Laguerre has made an undisputed place for himself in Puerto Rican literature. He has published eleven novels and, as of early 1988, was at work on a twelfth, which makes him the most productive Puerto Rican writer to date. His works, originally identified with the regional novel of the land, have evinced a surprising resiliency to the changing aspects of Puerto Rican reality. Laguerre was initially identified with the Generation of 1930, which became active after the demise of modernism and the vanguardist "isms" of the postwar period. His generation can be established as that born between 1895 and 1910, which also included Tomás Blanco, Emilio S. Belaval, Alfredo Collado Martell, Vicente Géigel Polanco, Samuel R. Quiñones, and José Enrique Pedreira. These writers were preoccupied by the search for the Puerto Rican self, the "what we are" and "who we are" which also claimed the attention of the Spanish writers of the Generation of '98. As a novelist of the 1930's, however, Laguerre was also profoundly influenced by such Latin American novelists as Rómulo Gallegos, José Eustasio Rivera, and Ricardo Güiraldes, who cultivated the regional novel of the land and whose characters struggle to find their true selves through an identification with nature. Pedreira was the first to point out *La llamarada*'s kinship with the novel of the land and he called it the sister of Rivera's *La vorágine* (*The Vortex*, 1924), Gallegos' *Doña Bárbara* (1929), and Güiraldes' *Don Segundo Sombra* (*Shadows on the Pampas*, 1926).

As in the novels of these writers, the social and political aspects are of supreme importance in Laguerre's first novels, although he adds to them a new element: the psychological development of character. Laguerre himself has confessed that he is an inveter-

ate reader of Fyodor Dostoyevsky, Charles Dickens, and William Makepeace Thackeray, from whom he probably derived his taste for psychological speculation. In a sense, his greatest contribution to the Puerto Rican novel rests on his ability to combine the social and historical chronicle with a profound analysis of the weaknesses and strengths of the Puerto Rican personality as they are reflected in the actions of his characters, and this joining of diverse elements can be said to be the unifying theme of his oeuvre. Because of the wide focus of his narrative point of view, Laguerre can be considered the inheritor of the tradition of Manuel Zeno Gandía, Puerto Rico's best novelist from the end of the nineteenth century and the beginning of the twentieth. Zeno Gandía also wrote a cycle of novels in which he portrayed the ailments of Puerto Rican social reality, and which he titled *Crónicas de un mundo enfermo* (Chronicles of a Diseased World), and he was the author of the first naturalist novel published in Latin America, *La charca* (The Pond, 1894), to which Laguerre wrote an excellent prologue in the Venezuelan edition of Biblioteca Ayacucho (volume 55). Laguerre's and Zeno Gandía's tradition has been continued by such Puerto Rican writers as Pedro Juan Soto, José Luis González, Emilio Díaz Valcárcel, and Luis Rafael Sánchez, who also evinced a social concern in their novels, although the works of these writers (as is also Laguerre's case) cannot be considered to be purely social and differ greatly among themselves.

Because of his youth at the publication of his first novel, *La llamarada*, in 1935, as well as his long productive life-span, Laguerre has been able to give testimony in his work to more than fifty years of Puerto Rican history. During this half century the society of the island underwent profound changes, from an agrarian economy still rooted in Spanish traditions and beliefs, to a modern, industrialized society, with a whole new set of values attuned to the American way of life. In his novels, Laguerre has persistently described the collective and individual problems that this transformation has brought about in the Puerto Rican people. If in his early novels the preoccupation with the conflicts of land is foremost, as in *La llamarada, Solar Montoya* (Montoya Plantation, 1941), and *Los dedos de la Mano* (The Fingers of the Hand, 1951), which describe the sugarcane, coffee, and tobacco plantations, respectively, in those written after 1950 Laguerre focused on the urban social problems brought about by the modernization of the island. As examples of some of the transcendental events which Laguerre has witnessed, and which he describes in his novels, one can mention that, in 1953, there were forty-five sugar mills on the island and today there are only five; the coffee and tobacco industries have practically disappeared; the massive emigration of the Puerto Rican people persists, although at a more moderate rate than previously; and the growing economic dependence of the island on foreign markets is an undeniable fact.

Laguerre's narrative has also demonstrated a surprising resiliency as to style, and if his early novels are identified with a realism tinged with psychologism, his later novels have given testimony of an awareness of the changes in novelistic techniques undergone by the contemporary Latin American novel. *Benevolent Masters* is, in this respect, his most ambitious novel. It includes elements of *real maravilloso*, the real that seems marvelous, and defies easy classification. As Estelle Irizarry, Laguerre's most dedicated scholar and author of various books of literary criticism about his oeuvre, has pointed out, *Benevolent Masters* can be read as a mystery novel or an existential, psychological, sociohistorical, or picaresque novel, depending on the aspect one wishes to emphasize. In spite of his new narrative techniques, however, Laguerre's style has remained basically simple and direct, appealing both to the intellectual and to the common reader.

Another valuable aspect of Laguerre's novels is his ability to reproduce the changing speech of the differing historical epochs and environments he describes. The language he employs is in fact the most valuable testimony to the radical social transformations of Puerto Rico during the last fifty years. Through it he constantly rescues the past and makes it possible for Puerto Ricans of the present to get to know the inner fabric of their evolution as a people: the world of the sugarcane plantation, as well as that of the coffee and tobacco plantations (*La llamarada, Solar Montoya,* and *Los dedos de la mano*); the world of the street gangs in the slums of Puerta de Tierra in the 1930's and 1940's in *El 30 de febrero* (The 30th of February, 1943); of the Puerto Rican immigrants in

the Bronx in *La ceiba en el tiesto* (The Ceiba in the Flower Pot, 1956); of San Juan's socially prestigious new bourgeoisie, the suburban elite of Green Plains, in *Cauce sin río* (River Bed Without a River, 1962) and *El fuego y su aire* (Fire and Its Air, 1970); of San Juan's political dignitaries and leaders in *Benevolent Masters*; and of the inhabitants of a small coastal fishing village who emigrate to Las Troneras, the slum near a U.S. military base (Ramey Field, Aguadilla), where a booming economy is tainted by social ills, in *Infiernos privados* (Private Hells, 1986).

In spite of his impressive production, Laguerre's best loved and most often quoted novel remains *La llamarada*. In 1937, Pedreira called it the best Puerto Rican novel written up to then, with the exception of Zeno Gandía's *La charca*, and Concha Meléndez pointed out its similarity to *The Vortex* in the transformation of Juan Antonio Borrás from an idealistic youth recently graduated from the university into a cynical, ambitious sugarcane overseer. Like Arturo Cova of *The Vortex*, Juan Antonio is the victim of the abusive system of exploitation of the land (sugar takes the place of the rubber in *The Vortex*), as he falls prey to the bestiality that permeates the plantation's inferno. Borrás is in fact the first of a series of such characters to appear in later novels (Victor H. R. Sandeau in *Cauce sin río*; Miguel S. Valencia in *Benevolent Masters*), and he personifies the weaknesses which Laguerre considers endemic to some Puerto Ricans in his indecisiveness, his inability to act according to his conscience, his selling out to corporation interests, and his betrayal of the burgeoning labor movement. The novel is a direct indictment of the social ills provoked by absentee landlords, monoculture, and inhuman exploitation of the cane worker. One of the most memorable passages of the novel, in chapter 2, describes Ventura Rondón, a cane worker, falling into one of the ditches of the Hacienda Palmares, a victim of illness and exhaustion, at Juan Antonio Borrás' feet.

I stood petrified looking at that vanquished face, with a terrible fear shaking all the fibers of my being. What a face! It was a dry, yellow face, with the indelible marks of anemia and arthritis, it was the face of despair, fallen amidst the cutting leaves of the cane. It was a face that came from a nightmare, it became larger and larger, filling all the landscape, showing itself behind every bud of green blade. It was the face of a suffering martyr which persecuted me obstinately to the utmost hiding place of my soul.

Solar Montoya, Laguerre's second novel, differs from *La llamarada* in that it is more of an elegy of the bygone world of the coffee plantations than a chronicle of social ills. The coffee plantation is, in contrast to the sugarcane Central of *La llamarada,* owned by Puerto Rican farmers, and the novel relates its economic ruin as a consequence of the loss of international markets after Puerto Rico became a part of the United States, as well as of damage from hurricanes and general disinterest and lack of subsidies on the part of the island's government. In contrast to the "green hell" of the cane fields, the mountain coffee plantations are described as a lost arcadia in a series of genre scenes of *costumbrista* (folkloric) style that may remind the reader of the works of Don Miguel Pou, a Puerto Rican painter of the 1930's and 1940's. The description of the old hacienda house in chapter 1, for example, is quite colorful:

> There was a feeling of solitude and seclusion about El Retiro. The two-storied house, built with native wood and a zinc ceiling, was on a hill. Its balcony smiled upon the green woods, bathed by a light as yellow as that of budding pumpkin flowers. . . . As it was reaping time, there was a lot of activity amidst the peasants, who came and went diligently in front of it. . . . They would spread the coffee grains upon the glacis, near the peeling wheel. They perspired and went barefoot, working in their undershirts. . . . From the nearby coffee groves one could hear them singing old ballads, and every now and then a sad *¡ay, le, lo, le con le, lo, lay!* would pierce the air.

Other genre scenes include vivid descriptions of the cockfight; *la fiesta del acabe,* the feast which celebrates the end of the coffee harvest; and the feasts of Holy Week and *La candelaria,* or Candlemas. As in *La llamarada* and other novels, Laguerre bemoans in *Solar Montoya* the loss of national customs and rites, as well as of the economic independence which he believes would have been the result of a productive system of agriculture. In the coffee plantations, as in the sugar haciendas and fishing villages of the coast, the farmers and fishermen also cultivated their own

vegetable patches and raised their own livestock, so that the food consumed was locally produced. In later novels this was to change drastically, as the migration to the cities and suburbs imposed upon the inhabitants new habits of conspicuous consumption of imported goods.

The principal character of *Solar Montoya,* Gonzalo Mora, in contrast to Juan Antonio Borrás, is a courageous, determined young man, who after having emigrated to the United States returns to the coffee plantation of his friend Don Alonso Montoya and tries to save it. Other characters, Rodrigo and Paco Pérez, embody the virtues of the *jíbaro* (mountain farmer), who lives in harmony with nature and respects its fertile cycles. Paco Pérez, for example, who already has five children, rejoices at the arrival of a sixth, because "children are the wealth of the poor."

> Paco Pérez was untiring, with a heart that clung to the earth with the tenacity of the purslane vine. His knife at his belt and machete in hand, he kept coming and going through the farm. He never wasted anything; he would feed the animals with what humans couldn't eat. The pigs always had their food: palm fronds, the new bananas which had fallen from the tree, breadfruits, fruits . . . he made good use of everything.
>
> (chapter 3, p. 79)

In *La resaca,* second only to *La llamarada* in popularity among Laguerre's novels, he treats the theme of political intervention, situating the narrative in the nineteenth century, when Puerto Rico was under Spanish colonial rule. Dolorito Montojo, the protagonist, is the popular hero who rebels against the oppression of the Spanish owners of the Hacienda Santa Rita. In the opening scene, when he is just an eleven-year-old boy, he courageously defies Balbino Pasamonte, the overseer, who is about to torture a pregnant black slave because she has stolen some codfish, biting his hand and snatching the whip away from him. Dolorito also belongs to a gallery of characters who appear time and again in Laguerre's novels, the fugitives who have challenged absolute power: that of a tyrannical father, as does Gonzalo Mora in *Solar Montoya;* of an orphan asylum's director, as does Teófilo Sampedro in *El 30 de febrero;* or of the Spanish Guardia Civil, as does Dolorito

Montojo in *La resaca*. Other characters, such as those in *La ceiba en el tiesto* and *The Labyrinth*, which take place mainly in New York, are seen as tragically fleeing the narrow geographical limits of the island as well as the political and economic dependence which are in part the result of its geographical conformation. Of all of these, Dolorito Montojo is the only one who refuses to submit, either to absolute authority or to a sense of national inferiority.

The last novels of Laguerre all deal with the problems of alienation and emigration, which are seen as intrinsically related. In *Cauce sin río*, Victor H. R. Sandeau recalls his birth in Sanetién, a sugarcane hacienda near San Germán, and his emigration to the capital, where he became a lawyer and made a fortune by the sale of arable lands for urbanization and industrial development purposes. Sandeau has been "uprooted" (a particular form of alienation) from the nourishing humus of his native soil, and his life has become an empty, meaningless round of social activities which threaten to drive him mad. It is only after his decision to return to Sanetién that he recovers his sanity. Laguerre makes a point of the fact that Sandeau is not proposing a return to the past or to more rudimentary forms of existence. "I have no objection to civilization," Sandeau claims. "I object to the fact that civilization should step on what permits us to breath in the first place. . . . My hope is that tradition should be the sap of progress."

In similar fashion, in *Benevolent Masters* Miguel Valencia is an alien in his own homeland. Like Sandeau, he belongs to the prosperous urban bourgeoisie; he is a successful lawyer who has struck it rich from land speculation, prefers exotic foods and exotic foreign beauties to local girls, and recognizes "that persistent tendency of mine to emigrate far from my own traditions." Emigration is only the eventual physical enactment of this alienation in situ from the "homeland" that many members of the urban Puerto Rican bourgeoisie are seen to suffer. Laguerre underlines the dangerous aspect of this alienation, when Miguel observes "that the same thing happens to many of the emigrants as to the lemmings, who, when they swim into the open seas, swim desperately until they die." Another example of the suicide Laguerre sees as implicit in emigration is Lenny Chang, a young man raised in New York and trans-planted to Puerto Rico who is really an alien in both places. As Estelle Irizarry has pointed out, the main theme of these novels is man's selfishness and ambition, which alienate him from himself as well as from future generations when he destroys his traditions and his natural resources.

Although these later novels manifest a surprising diversity of urban themes and locations, which vary from the elegant urbanized Green Plains, with its circles of influential politicians and "dignitaries" of San Juan, and the luxury condominiums of the coastal cities, to the tragic slums inhabited by those who have emigrated to the mainland, the presence (or absence) of nature continues to be of persistent importance. Thus, although these novels cannot technically be called classical regional novels of the land in the sense that *La llamarada* and *Solar Montoya* can be so classified, the sense of homeland remains a constant physical material reality in them, as well as a mythical one, which forms the nurturing subsoil of the Puerto Rican identity, determining its virtues and strengths as well as its weaknesses. As Octavio Paz has said in *Posdata* (Postscript, 1970), "geographies can also possess a symbolic nature: the physical spaces are resolved in geometric archetypes which become symbol-emitting forms. Plains, valleys, and mountains: the accidents of the landscape become significative as soon as they are inserted within a historical process." Viewed from this perspective, Laguerre's eleven novels "of the land" evince a surprisingly coherent weltanschauung and must therefore be valued to their full extent as an autonomous world in a profound artistic as well as a political and social sense.

SELECTED BIBLIOGRAPHY

First Editions

Novels

La llamarada. Aguadilla, Puerto Rico, 1935.
Solar Montoya. San Juan, 1941.
El 30 de febrero. San Juan, 1943.
La resaca. San Juan, 1949.
Los dedos de la mano. San Juan, 1951.

La ceiba en el tiesto. San Juan, 1956.
El laberinto. New York, 1959.
Cauce sin río. Madrid, 1962.
El fuego y su aire. Buenos Aires, 1970.
Los amos benévolos. Río Piedras, Puerto Rico, 1976.
Infiernos privados. Río Piedras, Puerto Rico, 1986.

Play

La resentida. Barcelona, 1960.

Essays

Pulso de Puerto Rico: 1952–1954. San Juan, 1956.
La poesía modernista en Puerto Rico. San Juan, 1969.
Polos de la cultura iberoamericana. Boston, 1977.

Collections, Prologues

Antología de cuentos puertorriqueños. Prologue and selection by Enrique A. Laguerre. Mexico City, 1954.
La charca, by Manuel Zeno Gandía. Edited and with a prologue and chronology by Enrique A. Laguerre. Caracas, 1980.
Cuentos españoles. Selection and notes by Enrique A. Laguerre. Mexico City, 1953.
El jíbaro de Puerto Rico: Símbolo y figura. Selected by Enrique A. Laguerre and Esther Melón. Sharon, Conn., 1968.

Complete Works

Obras completas. 3 vols. San Juan, 1962–64.

Translations

Benevolent Masters. Translated by Gino Parisi. With an introduction and notes by Estelle Irizarry. Maplewood, N.J., 1986.
The Labyrinth. Translated by William Rose. New York, 1960. Reprinted with an introduction and bibliography by Estelle Irizarry. Maplewood, N.J., 1984.

Biographical and Critical Studies

Books

Casanova Sánchez, Olga. *La crítica social en la obra novelística de Enrique A. Laguerre.* Río Piedras, Puerto Rico, 1975.
García Cabrera, Manuel. *Laguerre y sus polos de la cultura iberoamericana.* San Juan, 1978.

Irizarry, Estelle. *Enrique A. Laguerre.* Boston, 1982.
_____. *"La llamarada," clásico puertorriqueño: Realidad y ficción.* Río Piedras, Puerto Rico, 1985.
Monserrate Gámiz, María del Carmen. *Enrique A. Laguerre y "Los amos benévolos."* San Juan, 1987.
Morfi, Angelina. *Enrique A. Laguerre y su obra "La resaca"; cumbre en su arte de novelar.* San Juan, 1964.
Rosa-Nieves, Cesáreo. *Cañas al sol en "La llamarada."* Humacao, Puerto Rico, 1938.
Umpierre, Luz María. *Ideología y novela en Puerto Rico.* Madrid, 1983.
Zayas Micheli, Luis O. *Lo universal en Enrique A. Laguerre: Estudio de conjunto de su obra.* Río Piedras, Puerto Rico, 1974.

Essays and Articles

Arce de Vázquez, Margot, y Mariana Robles de Cardona, eds. "Enrique A. Laguerre, notas biográfico críticas." In *Lecturas portorriqueñas: Prosas.* Sharon, Conn., 1966. Pp. 283–284.
Arroyo, Anita. "La novela en Puerto Rico." *Revista del Instituto de Cultura Puertorriqueña* 8/28:48–54 (1965).
_____. *"El fuego y su aire."* El Caribe (Santo Domingo, Dominican Republic), 30 August 1975. P. 4.
Babín, María Teresa. "Landmarks in Contemporary Puerto Rican Letters." *The Americas* 14:255 (1958).
Beauchamp, José Juan. "Enrique A. Laguerre." In *Imagen del puertorriqueño en la novela.* Río Piedras, Puerto Rico, 1976, Pp. 71–159.
Bosch, Juan. "Cañas y letras en las Islas." *El mundo* (San Juan), 2 June 1940. P. 17.
Braschi, Wilfredo. "Enrique A. Laguerre, *La resentida.*" *Treinta años de teatro en Puerto Rico* 11/1:98–99 (1955).
_____. "Laguerre, el I.C.P. y una 'telenovela.'" *El mundo* (San Juan), 16 October 1978. P. 7A.
Cabrera, Francisco Manrique. "Notas sobre la novela puertorriqueña en los últimos 25 años." *Asomante* 11/1:24–28 (1955).
Cadilla, Carmen Alicia. "El paisaje en Enrique A. Laguerre." *Puerto Rico ilustrado,* 24 August 1935. P. 22.
Campos, Jorge. "Amor a la tierra y crítica social: Una novela de Enrique A. Laguerre." *Insula* 17/190:11 (1962).
Castroviejo, Concha. *"Cauce sin río."* Informaciones (Madrid), 7 July 1962. P. 6.
Cherubini, Arnaldo. "La narrativa sociale di Enrique Laguerre." *Ausonia* 31/5–6:70–78 (1977).
Cuevas, Clara. "Laguerre: Un autor habla de sus obras, de

su vida, de sus inquietudes." *Puerto Rico ilustrado*, 3 June 1973. Pp. 12–13.

Díaz Alfaro, Abelardo. "*El laberinto*, obra de Laguerre, se incorpora a la literatura universal." *El mundo* (San Juan), 21 November 1959. P. 2 (Sunday supplement).

Friedenberg, Daniel M. "Caribbean Labyrinth." *The New Republic*, 16 January 1961. Pp. 17–18. Reprinted in *La Voz* (New York), January 1961. Pp. 11–12.

González Díaz, José Emilio. "Breve comentario sobre *La resaca.*" *Puerto Rico ilustrado*, 9 September 1950. P. 8.

_____. "*Los amos benévolos.*" *Rojo, claridad* (supplement), 18–24 March 1977. P. 13.

González, José Luis. "*Los dedos de la mano.*" *Album literario puertorriqueño* 515:36–37 (1954).

Guiness, Gerald. "*Los amos benévolos* by Enrique A. Laguerre." *San Juan Star*, 20 March 1977. P. 11 (Sunday supplement).

Hartman, Mary Elizabeth. "Conflicts in Puerto Rico as Portrayed in the Novels of Enrique Laguerre" (unpublished monograph). Syracuse University (N.Y.), December 1964.

Hawes, Oliver. "*El 30 de febrero.*" *Books Abroad* 19:285 (Summer 1945).

Hill, Marnesba D., and Harold B. Schleifer. "Enrique A. Laguerre." In *Puerto Rican Authors: A Bibliographic Handbook*. Metuchen, N.J., 1974. Pp. 130–132.

Maldonado Denis, Manuel. "De Enrique A. Laguerre: *Cauce sin río.*" *El mundo* (San Juan), 21 January 1963. P. 21.

Marqués, René. "*La ceiba en el tiesto*, La novela de Laguerre en nuestra literatura actual." *El mundo* (San Juan), 19 May 1956. P. 20. 26 May 1956. P. 24.

Meléndez, Concha. "De Enrique A. Laguerre, *La llamarada.*" *Brújula* 1/3–4:119 (1935) and 2/7–8:270 (1936).

_____. "El llamado de la montaña; Apuntes sobre la novela de Enrique A. Laguerre." In her *Signos de Iberoamérica*. Mexico City, 1936. Pp. 119–124. Reprinted in *Obras completas* 1. San Juan, 1970. Pp. 397–404.

_____. Prologue to *Solar Montoya*, by Enrique A. Laguerre. San Juan, 1941. Pp. 5–8. Reprinted in *Alma latina* (San Juan) 16/428:14, 34–35 (1944).

_____. "Visita a la *Capilla Alfonsina* y *El fuego y su aire.*" *Sin nombre* (San Juan) 2/2:7–12 (1971).

Montaner, Carlos Alberto. "Enrique A. Laguerre." *Angela Luisa* 2/19:48–49 (1968).

Navarro Tomás, Tomás. "Novela y realidad del cafetal." *El mundo* (San Juan), 27 March 1958. P. 6.

Pedreira, Antonio S. "*La llamada*: Gran novela puertorriqueña." *El mundo* (San Juan), 11 August 1935. P. 7. Reprinted in *Aclaraciones y crítica*. Río Piedras, Puerto Rico, 1969, Pp. 165–169.

_____. Prologue to *La llamada*, by Enrique A. Laguerre. 2nd ed. San Juan, 1939. Pp. i–xii. Reprinted in Laguerre, *Obras completas* 1 (1962). Pp. 19–25.

Pérez Diego, Ismael. "El novelista Laguerre." *Novedades* (Mexico City), 23 April 1952. P. 4.

Picó, Rafael. "El hombre y el medio en las dos obras puertorriqueñas de Pedreira, *Insularismo* y Laguerre, *La llamada.*" *Caribe* (Río Piedras, Puerto Rico) 1/1: 33–35, 43 (1941).

Quintana, José. "Enrique A. Laguerre en la narrativa sudamericana." *Hojas del lunes* (Las Palmas, Canary Islands), 4 September 1972 and 18 September 1972.

Quintero, Luisa A. "Habla una novelista puertorriqueño." *Ecos de Nueva York*, 29 August 1954. Pp. 32–33, 47–48.

Sayers, R. S. "*La ceiba en el tiesto.*" *Revista hispánica moderna* 24/1:63 (1958).

Soravilla, Lesbia. "Entrevista con Laguerre: Señala a Cervantes, Dostoievsky, Kafka, Camus, Arthur Miller como sus escritores predilectos." *El mundo* (San Juan), 2 August 1962. P. 7.

Valenzuela, Víctor M. "*El laberinto.*" *La voz* (New York), 4/2:21 (1960).

Vientós Gastón, Nilita. "Enrique A. Laguerre, *La llamarada.*" *Ateneo puertorriqueño.* 1/4:310–312 (1935).

_____. "Indice cultural. El segundo festival de teatro puertorriqueño." *El mundo* (San Juan), 4 April 1959. P. 25.

Zayas Micheli, Luís Osvaldo. "El fuego y su aire, síntesis del novelar de Enrique A. Laguerre." *Anales de literatura hispanoamericana* (Madrid) 1:252–280 (1972).

_____. "La estrutura mítica de *La resaca.*" *Horizontes* (Ponce, Puerto Rico) 29/38:27–44 (1976).

_____. "El pensamiento mítico en *Los amos benévolos.*" *Horizontes* (Ponce, Puerto Rico) 29/38: 63–66 (1976). Reprinted as "Laguerre: *Los amos benévolos.*" *El Mundo* (San Juan), 11 September 1977. P. 13C.

Arturo Uslar Pietri

(1906–   )

Martin S. Stabb

Arturo Uslar Pietri exemplifies the tradition in Latin America of dedication to things of the spirit along with involvement in practical matters. Novelist, essayist, and short story writer, Uslar Pietri has served his country, Venezuela, in a variety of diplomatic posts, as head of several cabinet ministries, as an educator, as a senator, and as a presidential candidate. Not surprisingly, much of his literary activity has been closely linked to his active public life and to his deep-seated interest in his nation's history, identity, and destiny.

The son of General Arturo Uslar and Helena Pietri, Uslar Pietri was born in Caracas on 16 May 1906. After preparatory education in private schools, he enrolled in 1923 in the Central University of Venezuela, where he earned a doctorate in political science in 1929. He immediately entered the diplomatic corps and was sent to Paris, a fortunate assignment for a young man of Uslar Pietri's literary bent. While in France, he shared an apartment with two other Spanish-Americans destined to become literary celebrities: the brilliant young Cuban Alejo Carpentier and Guatemala's future Nobel laureate, Miguel Ángel Asturias. After his return from Europe in 1934, Uslar began a university teaching career, which he pursued intermittently through his early and middle years.

In 1939 he was named minister of education, followed a few years later by his appointments as minister of finance (1941) and minister of the interior (1942). When the government under which Uslar was serving was overthrown by a coup in 1945, he left the country for several years' residence in Canada and the United States. During 1947 he taught at Columbia University as visiting professor of Spanish-American literature. On returning to Venezuela in 1950, he combined university teaching with activities in journalism. He reentered the political arena in 1959 as an independent senator representing Caracas in the National Congress. He was an unsuccessful candidate for the Venezuelan presidency in 1963; however, in part as a result of political realignments after the campaign, he became secretary general of a fairly important opposition party, the Frente Nacional Democrático (National Democratic Front). Under the aegis of this conservative but democratic party, Uslar again served as senator from 1964 to 1969. After one term, he withdrew from active politics to devote himself to writing, teaching, and related pursuits.

Uslar Pietri's literary work covers a broad spectrum. He began publishing short stories as early as 1924, but his first book-length work, *Barrabás y otros relatos* (Barabbas and Other Tales), appeared in 1928, a year before he left the university. In 1931, during his European sojurn, when he was still in his mid-twenties, he published his first and unquestionably most-celebrated novel, *Las lanzas coloradas (The Red Lances)*. Not only has this work gone through several Spanish editions, but it has been translated into French, German, and English—a noteworthy endorsement for any Latin American book of that time. His second collection of short stories, *Red* (The Net), appeared in 1936 and contains perhaps his best work in the genre. A second historical novel, *El camino de El Dorado* (The Road to El Dorado), was published in 1947. During approximately the same period, Uslar Pietri produced a number of essay collections, the most important of which are *Letras y hombres de Venezuela* (Men and Letters of Venezuela, 1948) and *Las nubes* (Clouds, 1951). Another major volume of short stories, *Treinta hombres y sus sombras* (Thirty Men and Their Shadows), was published in 1949. These titles represent only a small portion of Uslar Pietri's abundant production over the years.

In more recent decades, he has enhanced the solid recognition gained earlier as a writer of fiction by producing an important corpus of essays, centering on such basic themes as the nature of New World culture, Venezuelan national identity, and political ideology. Representative of these aspects of his work are the collections *Valores humanos* (Human Values, 1955), *En busca del nuevo mundo* (In Search of the New World, 1969), and *Fantasmas de dos mundos* (Ghosts of Two Worlds, 1979).

It would be difficult to find a writer whose literary production has been more closely tied to the historical and political realities of his nation. Thus, to appreciate the work of Uslar Pietri, especially his novels, certain basic facts of Venezuelan history and culture must be considered. Most striking among these has been the almost constant presence, except for the last several decades, of what has become a Latin American stereotype: the *hombre de hierro* (man of iron), the strong man, the hero on horseback. Whether it was the dashing, romantic figure of the Liberator, Simón Bolívar of the Independence period, the rough-and-ready plainsman José Antonio Páez of the mid-nineteenth century, the colossally vain but sophisticated Antonio Guzmán Blanco of the 1870's and 1880's, or the self-styled epitome of

"democratic Cesarism," Juan Vicente Gómez, who ruled from 1908 to 1935, Venezuelan politics have been characterized by violence, dictatorship, and repression.

Uslar Pietri, himself the son of a general, grew to manhood under the regime of Gómez. As a student in the 1920's, he appears to have been on the fringe of activities directed against the dictator, though at the time his revolutionary spirit took a literary rather than political course; and when he entered the diplomatic service in 1929, it was as an appointee of the Gómez regime. Yet, like many other intellectuals of his country, Uslar Pietri apparently had ambiguous attitudes toward dictatorship in general and Gómez in particular. His views on the subject appear in a number of his essays. Good examples can be found in the chapter "La constitución y el refranero" (The Constitution and Folk Sayings) in *Las nubes* and in his essay "Ideólogos y guerrilleros" (Ideologues and Guerrillas) in the collection *Del hacer y deshacer de Venezuela* (On the Making and Unmaking of Venezuela, 1962). Briefly, Uslar Pietri has been very much aware of the vast gulf separating those democratic aspirations that he and others clearly cherish and the contrasting sociohistorical realities that, until recently, have worked against their attainment. He pinpoints the problem nicely in "La constitución y el refranero":

> Our written constitutions were liberal; our actual constitution was never anything but autocratic; our written constitutions affirmed the existence of juridical institutions; our actual constitution rested on the fact of individual command and personal connections; our written constitutions would proclaim a democratic republic; our actual constitution established the unchallenged authority of the boss.

Many of these issues—tradition versus change, high-sounding principles versus harsh realities, the charismatic leader on a charging stallion versus the common folk—shape Uslar Pietri's fictive world. Nowhere is this better seen than in *The Red Lances*. Set in the Venezuelan countryside during the wars of independence from 1811 to 1821, the story is centered on the lives and exploits of several characters rather than on a single protagonist. Chief among these are Presentación Campos, a brutal mixed-breed man who finds in the conflict a convenient opportunity to rise from his position as a lowly ranch overseer to that of a military hero; Fernando Fonta, a cultured, indecisive upper-class landowner who finally casts his lot with the revolutionary forces; and General Boves, an authentic historical figure, commandant of the feared cavalry unit whose lances have become red with the blood of their enemies. The novel's plot is not tightly structured: rather, Uslar Pietri presents a loosely woven tapestry of chaos, gory violence, and ideological as well as military confusion. Virtually all the characters meet a tragic fate at the story's conclusion. Campos and Fonta both die in the fighting, the latter's sister is brutally raped, and Fonta's friend, the idealistic young Englishman Captain David, perishes in his romantic dedication to South American independence.

In terms of Spanish-American literary history, *The Red Lances* is fairly typical of many novels of the 1920's and 1930's, known variously as "novels of the land" or "novels of national interpretation." Like his compatriot and contemporary Rómulo Gallegos, the Mexican master of narrative Mariano Azuela, and the Indianist novelists of the Andean region, Uslar Pietri has sought to illuminate his country's essence and character by means of fiction. In attempting this, he has often slighted certain qualities of the novelist's art. Thus characters tend to be superficially presented as stereotypes rather than fleshed-out human beings; well-wrought narrative structure is ignored for an episodic or cinematic approach; and dialogue tends to reflect the fragmented speech of roughhewn country folk. In general, Hispanic novels of this kind are open to critical attack as being overly picturesque, superficial, and frequently disorganized.

While *The Red Lances* has some of these defects, it also has qualities that distinguish it from many lesser works of the period. For one thing, the author has deliberately avoided simplistic equations between political position and social class: the poor, uneducated Campos becomes a royalist leader, while the wealthy landholder, Fonta, embraces the revolutionary cause. The fact that many of those involved in the struggle have no clear notion of the issues or ideologies involved and no real understanding of why they are fighting gives the novel a ring of truth. Also to Uslar Pietri's credit is the sheer power and dra-

matic force of many passages in the book; the battle scenes especially exemplify his skill at blood-and-guts description.

On balance, *The Red Lances* compares quite favorably with any of the novels produced in Spanish America before the recent crop of internationally acclaimed masterpieces of the "new narrative." Several critics liken it to Azuela's *Los de abajo* (*The Underdogs*, 1915), perhaps the greatest novel of the Mexican Revolution and a work similar in technique and perspective. Others, in praising the poetic richness of Uslar Pietri's prose, have linked him to the *modernista* movement of the turn of the century. Present-day readers of Spanish-American fiction, conditioned by the pyrotechnics of writers such as Julio Cortázar, Carlos Fuentes, and Gabriel García Márquez, may find *The Red Lances*, with its omniscient third-person narrator and linear presentation of time, rather out of fashion; nonetheless, in the context of its period and in consideration of what the author set out to accomplish, it is a notable achievement.

Several of Uslar Pietri's other novels have gained recognition, but of a lesser order. *El camino de El Dorado* is a very readable account of the exploits of the conquistador Lope de Aguirre; two novels under the rubric *El laberinto de la fortuna* (The Labyrinth of a Fortune, 1962, 1964) deal with politics, especially the era of the dictator Gómez; his most recent novel, *Oficio de difuntos* (The Duty Toward the Deceased, 1976), is a novelized biography of two Hispanic dictators whose careers strongly resemble those of Venezuela's Gómez and Cipriano Castro. Although this last novel has not attracted a great deal of attention, the critic C. D. Hamilton notes approvingly that Uslar Pietri has used a nonlinear time frame and other modern novelistic devices in producing a truly contemporary work. Most scholars seem to agree, however, that after *The Red Lances*, it is as a writer of short stories rather than novels that Uslar Pietri has made his most important contributions to Spanish-American letters.

His first effort in this genre, *Barrabás y otros relatos*, is the work of a very young man experimenting with the prevailing literary styles of the period: *modernismo* (Spanish America's somewhat self-consciously "arty" blend of symbolism, decadence, and other exotic elements); surrealism, then the newest vogue of the European vanguard; and, in some of the stories, a generous dose of traditional Hispanic realism. In terms of Venezuelan literature, the better stories of this collection—"El ensalmo" (The Spell) and "La voz" ("The Voice")—clearly break new ground in departing from the typical reliance on long descriptions of local color. As Domingo Miliani, a critic of Uslar Pietri's short stories, observes at the end of chapter 5 in *Uslar Pietri: Renovador del cuento venezolano,* "They contributed, within Venezuelan narrative, to give greater weight to the subjective world of humans and to limit ambience to its true position: that of the space needed to develop a specific action."

The second volume of stories, *Red,* contains some of Uslar Pietri's most celebrated and most widely anthologized short fiction. What makes several stories of this collection so impressive is the way in which the maturing writer combines the most effective technical resources available at the time with a realistic, though not sentimentally picturesque, rendering of genuine human beings. The story that best illustrates these qualities is unquestionably "La lluvia" ("The Rain"). The setting and background situation are deceptively typical: an aging *campesino* (farmer) and his wife are struggling through a drought, desperately awaiting the first rains of the wet season. One day, under rather mysterious circumstances, a young boy wanders onto their land. The childless, lonely couple takes in the lad, even though he is strangely uncommunicative regarding his origins and name. Oddly, they begin calling him Cacique (Chief), after a long-lost pet dog. Uslar Pietri deliberately creates an atmosphere of strangeness about the child and his relationship with the couple. After a while, the previously barren existence of the two is seen to change: they begin to show more affection toward each other and life takes on more interest. The drought continues, though ever so slowly clouds begin to gather over the distant hills. As the story concludes, the first drops of life-giving rain begin to fall, and Cacique mysteriously vanishes.

A résumé of "The Rain" seems to emphasize the obvious symbolism and hardly does justice to the skill and artistry with which Uslar Pietri constructs this tale. Indeed, critics have called the story a minor

masterpiece of Spanish-American short fiction; moreover, they have found in it an early example of Hispanic magical realism, a literary current that has figured prominently in the work of such masters as Carpentier and Gárcia Márquez. This story, more than any other work of Uslar Pietri, places him in the vanguard of prose writers of his day and links him to the most innovative authors. In subsequent short story collections, he continued to exploit the literary possibilities of magical realism, but these more recent efforts have failed to attract the critical attention of his earlier work.

Uslar Pietri was still publishing an occasional piece in a Caracas newspaper in the mid-1980's, but it appears safe to say that his status as one of Venezuela's major writers of fiction rests upon works produced earlier, such as *The Red Lances* and *Red.* It would be an exaggeration to claim that his name figures among the internationally recognized writers of the continent, men like Borges, Fuentes, or the Noble laureates Pablo Neruda and García Márquez. However, among those Latin Americans who have made a significant contribution to their country's literature while also pursuing active careers in public service, the name of Uslar Pietri will continue to rank high.

SELECTED BIBLIOGRAPHY

First Editions

Short Stories

Barrabás y otros relatos. Caracas, 1928.
Red. Caracas, 1936.
Treinta hombres y sus sombras. Buenos Aires, 1949.
Pasos y pasajeros. Madrid, 1966.
Los ganadores. Barcelona, 1980.

Novels and Novelized Biography

Las lanzas coloradas. Madrid, 1931.
El camino de El Dorado. Buenos Aires, 1947.
El laberinto de fortuna: Un retrato en la geografía. Buenos Aires, 1962.

El laberinto de fortuna: Estación de máscaras. Buenos Aires, 1964.
Oficio de difuntos. Barcelona, 1976.
La isla de Róbinson. Barcelona, Caracas, and Mexico City, 1981.

Plays

Teatro. Caracas and Madrid, 1958. Includes *El día de Antero Albán, La Tebaida, El diós invisible,* and *La fuga de Miranda.*
Chúo Gil y las tejedoras. Caracas, 1960.

Essays

Letras y hombres de Venezuela. Mexico City, 1948.
De una y otra Venezuela. Caracas, 1950.
Las nubes. Caracas, 1951.
Tierra venezolana. Caracas, 1953.
Breve historia de la novela hispanoamericana. Caracas, 1954.
El otoño en Europa. Caracas, 1954.
Valores humanos. Caracas, 1955.
La ciudad de nadie. Buenos Aires, 1960.
Del hacer y deshacer de Venezuela. Caracas, 1962.
En busca del nuevo mundo. Mexico City, 1969.
El globo de colores. Caracas, 1975.
Fantasmas de dos mundos. Barcelona, 1979.
Bolívar hoy. Caracas, 1983.

Collected Works

La lluvia y otros cuentos. Santiago, Chile, 1967.
Obras selectas. Caracas and Madrid, 1977.
Tiempo de contar. Caracas and Madrid, 1954.
Treinta cuentos. Caracas, 1983.
Veinticinco ensayos. Caracas, 1969.

Translations

"The Drum Dance." Translated by G. Alfred Mayer. In *The Eye of the Heart: Short Stories from Latin America,* edited by Barbara Howes. Indianapolis and New York, 1973. Pp. 169–176.
"Ignis Fatuus." Translated by Harriet de Onís. In *The Golden Land: An Anthology of Latin American Folklore in Literature.* New York, 1948. Pp. 291–297.
"The Rain." Translated by Seymour Menton. In *The Spanish American Short Story: A Critical Anthology.* Berkeley, Calif., Los Angeles, and London, 1980. Pp. 327–341.
The Red Lances. Translated by Harriet de Onís. With an introduction by Federico de Onís. New York, 1963.

"The Voice." Translated by W. E. Colford. In *Classic Tales from Spanish America.* Great Neck, N.Y., 1962. Pp. 118–126.

Biographical and Critical Studies

Alonso, María Rosa. "¿Por qué ya no se cultiva la poesía épica? Un aspecto de *Las lanzas coloradas* de Uslar Pietri." *Cultura universitaria* 47:114–119 (1955).
_____. "El cuento y la novela de Uslar Pietri." *Insula* 24/272–273:26 (1969).
Ballesteros, David. "Arturo Uslar Pietri, Renovador de la conciencia nacional." Ph.D. diss., University of Southern California, 1968.
Brushwood, John S. *The Spanish American Novel.* Austin, Tex., and London, 1975. Pp. 88–91.
Callan, Richard. "La estructura arquetípica de 'La lluvia' de Uslar Pietri." *Cuadernos americanos* 193/2:204–212 (1974).
Campos, Jorge. "Las novelas de Uslar Pietri." *Insula* 17/15:188–189 (1962).
_____. "Nueva novela de Uslar Pietri: *Estación de máscaras.*" *Insula* 20/227:11 (1965).
Cluff, Russell M. "El realismo mágico en los cuentos de Uslar Pietri." *Cuadernos americanos* 204/1:208–224 (1976).
Coll, Edna. *Indice informativo de la novela hispanoamericana* 3. San Juan, 1978. Pp. 296–312.
Dougherty, R. M. *The Essays of Arturo Uslar Pietri.* University Microfilms. Ann Arbor, Mich., 1971.
Englekirk, John E. "Sobre autores del cuento moderno venezolano." *Revista iberoamericana* 4/7:183–187 (1941).
Gnutzmann, Rita. "Sobre la función del comienzo en la novela: Un análisis de las novelas *Las lanzas coloradas* y *El reino de este mundo,* a través de sus comienzos." *Cuadernos hispanoamericanos* 302:416–431 (1975).
Hamilton, Carlos D. "Arturo Uslar Pietra, novelista contemporáneo." *Cuadernos americanos* 242/3:209–227 (1982).
Leal, Luis. *Historia del cuento hispanoamericano.* 2nd ed. Mexico City, 1971. Pp. 85–86.
Miliani, Domingo. *Uslar Pietri: Renovador del cuento venezolano.* Caracas, 1969.
Osorio Tejada, Nelson. "El primer libro de Uslar Pietri y la vanguardia literaria de los años veinte." *Revista de crítica literaria latinoamericana* 9:135–139 (1979).
Parra, Teresita J. "Visión histórica en la obra de Arturo Uslar Pietri." Ph.D. diss., University of Virginia, 1979.

Picón Salas, Mariano. *Comprensión de Venezuela.* Caracas and Madrid, 1955. Pp. 579–587.

Szichman, Mario. *Uslar.* Caracas, 1975.

Vivas, José Luis. *La cuentística de Arturo Uslar Pietri.* Caracas, 1963.

Yates, Donald A. "Chaos Was the Order of the Day." *Saturday Review,* 12 October 1963. P. 41.

Zum Felde, Alberto. *Indice crítico de la literatura hispanoamericana 2: La narrativa.* Mexico City, 1959. Pp. 494–495.

Jorge Icaza

(1906–1978)

Manuel Corrales Pascual

Jorge Icaza Coronel, first an actor in the theater, later the author of dramatic works that he presented himself, and finally a novelist and a writer of short stories, was born in Quito, Ecuador, on 10 July 1906. While he was still a small boy his father died and his mother remarried. Icaza's stepfather, a militant Liberal party politician, was persecuted by governments opposed to his ideas, and the family was forced to take refuge on the landed estate of Don Enrique Coronel, a maternal uncle of young Jorge.

In a newspaper interview in June 1970, Jorge Icaza alluded to that period of his youth:

> On that enormous estate and at that age, when impressions are indelible, I was very close to the Indians. . . . Everything belonged to "Master Enrique." In my childish innocence, I was amazed at the fabulous power that guy had. Everything belonged to him, while "his" Indians, the people who worked for him from sunup to sundown, had nothing, were dying of hunger, and, on top of that, were whipped, kicked around, and humiliated. I saw it with my own eyes!
>
> (*Vistazo* [Guayaquil], p. 100)

This episode from his childhood perhaps influenced his writing. But political rather than personal events had a greater influence. Eleven years before Icaza's birth, on 5 June 1895, Eloy Alfaro, a Liberal

strongman, seized power, ending a long period of Conservative party governments in Ecuador. Under Alfaro, political power in Ecuador was no longer disputed between several parties or opposing ideological tendencies but rather between factions of the same liberal ideology. The guidance given to Ecuador by the Liberals largely determined the nation's course during the first half of the twentieth century, especially in the areas of education and culture.

Ángel F. Rojas, author of the most complete history of the Ecuadorian novel, tells us this with regard to the country's cultural life: "The period comprising the second stage of the Ecuadorian novel lasted thirty years. It began with the political transformation of 5 June of the previously mentioned year [1895] and concluded with the military coup of June 1925."

Three years before the debut of Icaza's first dramatic work, the three-act play *El intruso* (The Intruder, 1928), on 19 July 1925, a military coup ended the tyranny of the bankers of Guayaquil, Ecuador's most important commercial city, who surreptitiously—but with everyone's knowledge—pulled the strings of national politics. The coup opened the way, however, for a new oligarchy which dominated Ecuador until it was in turn overthrown by the revolution of 28 May 1944. Between those two dates (1925 and 1944), Icaza produced most of his work and, of course, his best-known novel, *Huasipungo* (*The Villagers*, 1934). These tumultuous years in the political and social life of the country (between 1925 and 1944 there were more than twenty acting presidents) were those of the blossoming of Ecuadorian literature, particularly in narrative form. It was precisely during these years that the famous Generation of 1930, to which Icaza belongs, reached its apogee.

Icaza's work, like that of other writers of his generation, is eminently realistic and social. This fundamental characteristic of the times arose from a momentous event a few years before the revolution of 9 June 1925: the bloody repression of the people in Guayaquil on 15 November 1922. This act, which became the subject of the novel *Las cruces sobre el agua* (Crosses Upon the Water, 1946) by Joaquín Gallegos Lara, heralded the breakdown of the oligarchical and hermetic ruling order. One must add that there were even defectors, opposed to the oppressive and unjust order, in the ranks of the ruling Liberals. In 1923 the Liberal party assembly that met in Quito to designate its candidate for the presidency of the republic designed a program of great social content. And in May 1926 the Socialist party of Ecuador was founded.

Icaza and those of his literary generation entered upon the new path with furious enthusiasm. The literature they produced was a social literature—criticism of society, a denouncement of the great defects, injustices, and wretchedness of that society.

The death of Icaza's mother in 1924, shortly after that of his stepfather, forced him to drop out of the Central University of Quito and abandon his hopes for a medical career. Instead he became an actor, met his future wife—Marina Moncayo, Ecuador's most gifted actress—and wrote half a dozen comedies. After a play he presented was suppressed in 1932 and he was fired from his position as a provincial treasury clerk, he began writing fiction. Icaza later owned a bookstore in Quito, was director of the National Library, and served in other government posts, including ambassador to the Soviet Union. He died on 26 May 1978.

The first edition of *Barro de la sierra* (Mountain Clay), containing Icaza's first stories, appeared in 1933; his first novel, *The Villagers*, in 1934. The

stories in *Barro de la sierra* exhibit a curious and determinant characteristic; they contain the seeds of the worldview and the thematic, formal, and characterological concerns of almost all the rest of Icaza's narratives.

Between 1933 and 1972, Icaza published seven novels and several collections of stories, and he left an unfinished rough draft of an eighth novel. The narrative form is, then, the type of poetic language he found most appropriate for his self-expression and the repository of his poetic and human message.

It is noteworthy that the same form was chosen by the other writers of his generation. In 1930 a group of very young writers from Guayaquil, some of them virtually adolescents, added a new twist to a realist-naturalist literary style that had grown stale. José de la Cuadra, Demetrio Aguilera Malta, Enrique Gil Gilbert, Joaquín Gallegos Lara, and Alfredo Pareja Diezcanseco (the "five of them as close as the fingers of a fist") were the initiators. Though geographically distant, these writers were closely accompanied spiritually by Jorge Icaza in Quito and Ángel F. Rojas in Loja, the southernmost province of Ecuador.

In 1930, a book of stories signed by Aguilera Malta, Gallegos Lara, and Gil Gilbert was published. Entitled *Los que se van* (Those Who Are Leaving), it carried the significant subtitle "Stories of the *mestizo* [mixed white and Indian ancestry] and country people." This book came to represent the generation's manifesto and the point of departure for Ecuadorian literature for almost thirty years. The general characteristics of the Ecuadorian narrative of this generation were social realism rooted in the soil, denunciations of social evils, standard indigenism (especially in Icaza's early works), and the presence of stereotyped characters and situations.

The language underwent violent alterations to which the small number of readers, who belonged to the bourgeoisie, were unaccustomed. In some cases the vocabulary reflected popular and rural speech in the folkloric manner of the genre (such as the stories in *Los que se van*); in others, as in the case of Jorge Icaza, syntax itself was smashed by the rocky, violent language of the narrative.

Although Icaza in his last novel, *Atropado* (Trapped, 1972), tried with some success to go beyond these general characteristics, as did Aguilera

Malta and Pareja Diezcanseco in their last works, the shadow of the Generation of 1930 hovered over Ecuadorian narrative until well into the 1960's, when a new group of young poets and writers tried to break with what had been achieved by this prolific group.

The narrative work of Jorge Icaza, seen as a whole and in its historical milieu, resembles a pilgrimage in search of the proper invocation of theme and tone, of language and the world. The first stammerings of *Barro de la sierra*, the simple schematic character of *The Villagers*, slowly increase in complexity until they arrive at the most that Icaza could give of himself as a narrator: *El chulla Romero y Flores* (The Social Climber Romero y Flores, 1958).

Icaza has been relegated—perhaps a bit precipitously—to the area of literary Indianism. If we allow his first short stories, *The Villagers*, and certain thematic lines from the rest of his narrative to guide us, it is evident that Icaza rightfully belongs to Indianist literature. But does this exhaust the author's poetic world? I believe that the Indian is not the only, nor even the main, theme of Icaza's novels. If, for example, an anthropologist were to search Icaza's works for the configuration of the world as experienced by Ecuador's Indians—in the anthropological sense—he would frankly come away disappointed. Icaza's stories really reveal very little of the Indian's worldview. Agustín Cueva, in *Jorge Icaza*, tells us that Icaza dedicated around three-fourths of his work to the trauma of the *mestizo*, not that of the Indian. And Theodore A. Sackett, after an exhaustive analysis of *The Villagers* in *El arte en la novelística de Jorge Icaza*, states that "in more than half the novel, the novelistic interest centers not on a collective or individual Indian protagonist, but on the large landowner Pereira and his problems."

The narrative of Icaza is not, then, the emergence of the cultural identity of the Indian, but the molding of a sociological reality masterfully described by the Peruvian José María Arguedas: "But the literature called Indianist is not, nor could it be, a narrative confined to the Indian; rather, it embraces the entire social context to which the Indian belongs." This narrative describes the Indian in terms of the *señor*, that is, the creole, who controls the economy and occupies the highest social sphere, and in terms of the *mestizo*, an individual of intermediate social and cultural level who is almost always at the service of the *señor* but is sometimes allied with the indigenous population.

In reality, the reflections and quotations offered here speak of what Tomás G. Escajadillo has called "orthodox Indianism," as established by stories that speak more of a social structure than of the characters' intimate thoughts. In brief, one can say that Icaza's first short stories and first novel fit loosely into the category of orthodox Indianism. But with his second novel begins the aforementioned pilgrimage, whose driving force is one persistent question: Who are we? The author does not, of course, abandon the perspective of a social structure based on injustice, oppression, and misery. But that structure, which was originally the author's greatest concern, slowly gives way to the description of the central, internal life experiences of the characters.

On the other hand, beginning with the second novel, the *mestizo* characters, the *cholos*, begin to occupy more and more narrative space—though the Indian characters do not disappear altogether—until in *El chulla Romero y Flores* the *mestizo* character is individualized. Or at least the *mestizo* character acquires the greatest degree of individuation that the author is able to give him. That character is the urban *mestizo* popularly known as the *chulla*—middle class, with ambitions to rise to higher status.

It is impossible here to offer an exhaustive analysis of the cerebral ingredients of Icaza's narrative. But a leitmotiv should be mentioned whose importance cannot, of course, be measured, unless it be in connection with the structural whole of the works that followed *The Villagers*. This leitmotiv can be defined as the *mestizos'* rejection of all things Indian, and even all things related to the Indian. And since they are a racial mixture of Indian and white blood, they try to eliminate, or at least hide, the Indian ingredients of their own being. This leitmotiv is of clear importance with regard to the problem of cultural identity in Ecuador, since the *mestizo* of Icaza's works represents a majority of the Ecuadorian population. The narrator has perceived a problematic trait of the population's consciousness of itself and has depicted it with indisputable vividness in these works. But that trait identifies the characters in a culturally negative way; that is, the characters deny and reject an element of their own being. The rejected element lies in their Indian roots, racial as well as cultural. And this negation of something undeniable, this earnest desire to eliminate something which represents a central part of the characters' being, comes to represent a fundamental element of the trauma, of the tragedy of Icaza's characters. Cueva says with regard to this:

> In the narrative of Icaza the *mestizo* is manifested essentially as the point of subjective crystallization of all the social contradictions. Trapped between two "races," two cultures, two structural urgencies, and even two historical epochs, his configuration is one of rending or uprooting rather than fusion. As Icaza said, an interior monologue does not really develop within the *mestizo* soul, but rather a dialogue between two irreconcilable worlds.

Clearly one again encounters "uprootedness" as the identifying element of the Ecuadorian cultural identity, but this uprootedness is quite different from that which was given form during the modernist period. In modernism it emerged in the series of foreign ingredients which shaped the modernists' poetic manner. Mario Benedetti, the Uruguayan writer, describes Latin American modernism in these words:

> Modernism has classical, romantic, and autochthonous elements: it has Spanish, French, English, and other more exotic resonances. But by not being exclusively any of these things, it is typically Latin American, since the modernists were perhaps the first to see that one possible way of finding one's roots at this juncture of jumbled paths consisted of defining uprootedness.
>
> (p. 354)

In Icaza's narrative, uprootedness is of another type. The problem is at the heart of each of his novels, as the constitutive tragedy of the character himself: the character is the one uprooted. He is, as Icaza says of the *chulla*, "an exile of two opposing races . . . of a people that venerates what it hates and hides what it loves."

It remains to be determined whether the Ecuadorian novel resolved that internal contradiction, whether it presented the characters in a process of finding the roots of their identity. I can state that

Icaza's novel did not achieve this. It is true that at the end of *El chulla Romero y Flores* he presents the protagonist as one who has proposed "to love and to respect equally in remembrance his ancestral spirits . . ." But Icaza never wrote a novel in which this actually occurred, nor did any other narrative writer of Icaza's generation. The task of inquiring into Ecuadorian cultural identity and giving it poetic form was passed on to others.

Translated from the Spanish by Philip Donley

SELECTED BIBLIOGRAPHY

First Editions

Novels

Huasipungo. Quito, 1934.
En las calles. Quito, 1935. This work received the First National Prize for 1935.
Cholos. Quito, 1937.
Media vida deslumbrados. Quito, 1942.
Huairapamushcas. Quito, 1948.
El chulla Romero y Flores. Quito, 1958.
Atrapados. 3 vols. Buenos Aires, 1972.

Short Stories

Barro de la sierra. Quito, 1933. Contains "Cachorros," "Sed," "Éxodo," "Interpretación," "Mala pata," and "Desorientación." The author did not authorize later editions of the last three stories.
Seis relatos. Quito, 1952. Contains "Barranca grande," "Mama Pacha," "El nuevo San Jorge," "Contrabando," "Rumbo al sur," and "Cholo ashco."

Collected Works

Obras escogidas. Edited by F. Ferrándiz Alborz. Mexico City, 1961. Contains *Huasipungo, En las calles, Huairapamushcas, El chulla Romero y Flores,* and eight stories.
Relatos. Buenos Aires, 1969. Contains "En la casa chola," "Cachorros," "Sed," "Éxodo," "Barranca grande," "Mama Pacha," "El nuevo San Jorge," "Contrabando," "Rumbo al sur," "Cholo ashco."

Later Editions

Cholos. Quito, 1983.
El chulla Romero y Flores. With an introduction by Hernán Rodríguez Castelo. Guayaquil-Quito, n. d.
El chulla Romero y Flores. Quito, 1983.
Huasipungo. Quito, 1983.
En las calles. Quito, 1985.

Translations

The Villagers. Translated by Philip Dulsey, with an introduction by Bernard M. Dulsey and a prologue by J. Cary Davis. Carbondale, Ill., 1964.

Biographical and Critical Studies

Alarcón, Jorge N. "Jorge Icaza y su creación literaria." Ph.D. diss., University of New Mexico, 1970.
Albán Gómez, Ernesto. "Presente y futuro de *Huasipungo.*" *Mundo nuevo* 49:30–39 (1970).
Benedetti, Mario. "Temas y problemas." In *América latina en su literatura,* edited by César Fernández Moreno. Mexico City and Paris, 1972.
Carrión, Benjamín. *El nuevo relato ecuatoriano. Crítica y antología.* 2nd ed., rev. Quito, 1958. Pp. 114–122.
Corrales Pascual, Manuel. "El chulla quiteño en *El chulla Romero y Flores.*" *Mensajero* (Quito):21–22 (March 1973).

———. *Jorge Icaza: Frontera del relato indigenista.* Quito, 1974.
———. "Relato indigenista e identidad cultural." Cultural supplement of *El Comercio* (Quito), 6 March 1983. Pp. 4. 13 March 1983. Pp. 6–7.
Cueva, Agustín. *Jorge Icaza.* Buenos Aires, 1968.
———. "En pos de la historicidad perdida (Contribución al debate sobre la literatura indigenista del Ecuador)." *Revista de crítica literaria latinoamericana* 4/7–8:23–38 (1978).
Garro, J. Eugenio. "Jorge Icaza: Vida y obra." *Revista hispánica moderna* 13:193–235 (1947).
González Poyatos, José. "*Huasipungo y Atrapados.*" *Literatura Icaciana.* Quito, 1977. Pp. 61–73.
Ojeda, Enrique. *Cuatro obras de Jorge Icaza.* Quito, 1961.
Pareja Diezcanseco, Alfredo. "Consideraciones sobre el hecho literario ecuatoriano." *Revista de la Casa de la Cultura Ecuatoriana* 1:127–145 (1948).
Ribadeneira, Edmundo. *La moderna novela ecuatoriana.* Quito, 1958. Pp. 60–72.
Rojas, Ángel F. *La novela ecuatoriana.* Mexico City, 1948.
Sackett, Theodore Alan. *El arte en la novelística de Jorge Icaza.* Quito, 1974.
Tijerina, Servando G. "A Study of Jorge Icaza as Literary Figure and as a Social Reformer." M.A. thesis, Columbia University, 1964.
Vetrano, Anthony J. *La problemática psico-social y su correlación lingüística en las novelas de Jorge Icaza.* Miami, 1974.

João Guimarães Rosa

(1908–1967)

Eduardo F. Coutinho

One of the most distinguished writers of twentieth-century Brazilian literature, João Guimarães Rosa was born in Cordisburgo, Minas Gerais, on 27 June 1908. He spent his childhood in this small town of the backlands—the area that would constitute the setting for the majority of his stories. He was educated in Belo Horizonte, where he received his degree as a medical doctor in 1930. By this time, he had already published several short stories in the magazine *O Cruzeiro* (The Cross), in Rio de Janeiro, and had won four prizes. From 1931 to 1934, Guimarães Rosa worked as a physician in Itaguara, Minas Gerais, and participated as a volunteer in the Revolution of 1932. This period, though not very productive in literary terms, was extremely important for his later career as a writer. He declared (in *Diálogo com América Lotina*, by Günter Lorenz, p. 323): "As a physician, I came to know the mystical greatness of suffering; as a rebel, the value of consciousness; and as a soldier, the importance of the proximity of death."

The year 1934 marked an important point in Guimarães Rosa's professional life, for that was when he entered the Ministry of Foreign Affairs and began his career as a diplomat. From that moment on, he also dedicated himself more and more to literature. In 1936 he won the poetry award of the Brazilian Academy of Letters with his volume "Magma," which he never published. The following year, he wrote *Sagarana* (Sagarana), a collection of short stories, and submitted it to another contest, winning second place.

In 1938, Guimarães Rosa was sent to Hamburg, Germany, as a consul. During Hitler's persecution, he helped several Jews to leave the country. In 1942, he was interned for a few months in Baden-Baden, together with other Brazilian intellectuals. He was then transferred to Bogotá, where he rewrote *Sagarana*. When the book was published in 1946, it met with tremendous success, winning a prize from the Society Felipe d'Oliveira.

For Guimarães Rosa, the years following the publication of *Sagarana* were marked by his intense activity as a diplomat both in Brazil and abroad. Although he did a great deal of literary work during this period, the result would not be made known until 1956. That year, he published, within a space of four months, two major works: the collection of novellas *Corpo de Baile* (Corps de Ballet) and the novel *Grande Sertão: Veredas* (translated as *The Devil to Pay in the Backlands*). The success he had achieved with *Sagarana* (already in its fourth reprinting) was confirmed, and Guimarães Rosa's respectability as a writer of high quality was definitely established. Serious studies

1069

of his works began to appear, and he won four more literary awards, the last of them conferred upon his works as a whole by the Brazilian Academy of Letters. In 1961, *Sagarana* was published in Portugal, and three of his novellas from *Corpo de Baile* were translated into French and published by Editions du Seuil.

Guimarães Rosa's next book came out in 1962 with the title *Primeiras Estórias* (translated as *The Third Bank of the River and Other Stories*). This collection of very short stories repeated the success of his previous works. The following year, he was unanimously elected to the Brazilian Academy of Letters. By 1965, the writer was very well known abroad. Several of his books had been translated into French, Italian, English, and German, and had been successfully reprinted. *The Devil to Pay in the Backlands,* for instance, had three reprintings in Germany. In Brazil, he began to gain the interest of filmmakers who presented the first cinematic versions of his works. *The Devil to Pay in the Backlands* was filmed in 1965 and "A hora e vez de Augusto Matraga" ("Augusto Matraga's Hour and Turn") in 1966. Films were later made of *Sagarana, a Duel* (1973) and *Noites do Sertão* (Backlands' Nights, 1984).

The year 1967 started out very well for Guimarães Rosa. He was sent to Mexico to represent Brazil in the First Latin American Congress of Writers, and soon after his return, he published *Tutaméia* (Tutaméia). This collection consisted of even shorter stories and, in spite of its hermetic nature, enjoyed the same success as his previous books. In November, after a very unusual delay of more than four years, he finally assumed his position at the Brazilian Academy of Letters. On 19 November, only three days after the ceremony, which he had feared as if with some kind of magical instinct, he died of a heart attack while writing at home in his study.

Two posthumous works, *Estas Estórias* (These Stories) and *Ave, Palavra* (Hail, Word), were published in 1969 and 1970, respectively. They are collections of short stories, some that had never before been published and others that had never been gathered into book form. The only exception, in *Estas Estórias*, was the journalistic piece *Com o Vaqueiro Mariano* (With the Cowboy Mariano), published originally in 1947 in the newspaper *Correio da Manhã*

(The Morning Post, Rio de Janeiro) and reprinted in a limited edition as a book in 1952. Two other works made available posthumously to the public are the speech he gave when he took office at the Brazilian Academy of Letters, included in the volume *Em Memória de João Guimarães Rosa* (In Memory of João Guimarães Rosa, 1968), and his letters to the Italian translator of *The Devil to Pay in the Backlands,* published under the title of *J. Guimarães Rosa: Correspondência com o Tradutor Italiano* (J. Guimarães Rosa: Correspondence with the Italian Translator, 1972).

Guimarães Rosa was married twice. He had two daughters from his first marriage, Agnes and Vilma, the latter also a writer. Most of his books are dedicated to his second wife, Aracy Moebius de Carvalho.

Works

Guimarães Rosa is usually classified by critics as belonging to the third generation of the modernist movement in Brazil, a generation often characterized by its preoccupation with the means of literary expression. Yet he took this preoccupation to such an extreme that he effected throughout his works a real revolution of narrative language that stands out as a landmark in twentieth-century Brazilian prose fiction.

At the time he wrote his first narratives (the short stories of *Sagarana*), the novel of protest was predominant in Brazil; it found a fertile ground in the 1930's, particularly among the northeastern writers. This type of fiction, respectable as it may be, presented a problem: the use of conventional language, worn out by stereotyped formulas. Since the authors were primarily concerned with unmasking their country's social, political, and economic reality, they did not give much attention to the role of language in their works and sometimes failed to express in a vivid and dynamic manner their views of the world.

Aware of the insufficient importance attributed to language by the writers of the previous generation and basing his work on the belief that literature is above all language, Guimarães Rosa set himself the task of breaking with the automatic character that language had assumed in their works. He thus revitalized writing on every one of its levels: words, which had lost their primitive energy and acquired new fixed meanings associated with one specific context (for example, the words "jungle" or "backlands" in the regionalist novel); expressions, which had become vague and weakened, clouded with connotations that concealed their original strength; and finally, syntax, which had abandoned its infinite possibilities and had limited itself to ready-made sentences and clichés.

In spite of the great number and radical character of some of Guimarães Rosa's linguistic innovations, the process of revitalization effected by him does not imply the creation of a new language. It is true that he frequently violated the grammar rules of Portuguese and that as a result some of his works are rather hermetic, but at no time did he disregard the structure of the language nor did he attempt to cross the barriers it imposes. What he did was to exploit its potentialities and restore its poetic character.

Besides, Guimarães Rosa's process of revitalization is not limited simply to language in the strict sense of the word. Rather, it is extended to narrative discourse as a whole, an element also worn out in the novels of the 1930's. The author tried to break with the excessive linearity and causal coherence of the narrative; he searched for new technical devices that would be better suited to express the dynamic and multifaceted reality of his time and place.

The procedures employed by Guimarães Rosa for the revitalization of literary language, in both its stricter and wider senses, are many and varied, to the point of taking the author into considerable experimentation. Yet at no moment did he either fall into pure verbal Luddism or indulge in innovations for their own sake. His preoccupation with form is not an alienating attitude but, on the contrary, a conscious political enterprise based on the premise that in order to express a revolutionary view of the world, it is necessary to begin by revolutionizing the means of expressing that view.

For Guimarães Rosa, the language of a people is intimately connected with their way of thinking, with their view of the world. Thus, if an author wishes to alter this world view, to free his readers from their old categories of thought, he must start by changing the language that reflects the thought. The writers of the 1930's are considered revolutionary because they criticized and denounced the Brazilian reality of their time. But because they used a language of the establishment in order to attain their aim, their protest, though direct and vehement, lost a great deal of its strength. Guimarães Rosa, by rejecting the crystallized forms of traditional narrative language and by restoring its poetic character, cast criticism on the society of which this language is a manifestation.

Guimarães Rosa is a regionalist writer in the sense that he uses the backlands as the setting of his stories and the inhabitants of that area as his characters. He departs, however, from traditional regionalism in one fundamental aspect—the emphasis on man as the pivotal element of his fictional world. In the traditional regionalist narrative, the landscape occupies the core of the work, and man is relegated to a secondary level, as a mere representative of the region (he is the *gaucho* [cowboy] or the backlands man, for example). In Guimarães Rosa's prose, man holds the center of interest, and the landscape is seen through him. The landscape is no longer depicted in terms of its typical or specific elements alone but is presented as a multifaceted reality. Thus the backlands of Guimarães Rosa's narratives are a close literary recreation of a specific area of Brazil, in both its physical and sociocultural aspects; but they are also, and perhaps most especially, the representation of a human, existential region, present and alive within the minds of his characters—a region that can be seen as a microcosm of the world.

For Guimarães Rosa, regional and universal elements, far from being in opposition, complement each other as two sides of the same coin. The regional character can never be fully represented if it is not depicted with some measure of universality, yet it constitutes an indispensable element for attaining universality. It is not by denying its regional nature, but only by assuming it, that Brazilian prose fiction can find its identity and enter the realm of Western literature as a whole.

This wider regionalist perspective is not, however, an isolated phenomenon in Guimarães Rosa's works. On the contrary, it is part of a general conception of reality as something multiple and constantly changing which can only be fully represented in artistic terms if this is done in an all-encompassing manner, or, in other words, in a way that tries to express it both in its dynamics and in as many of its facets as possible. The world of Guimarães Rosa's narratives is never static, nor is it ever built up on one level only. The myth and fantasy of the characters, for example, are as much a part of it as their rational consciousness, and these elements are all treated in a similar manner by the author.

Myth and fantasy, as well as other levels of reality that transcend Western logic, are present in Guimarães Rosa's narratives in many forms: superstition and premonitions, belief in apparitions, devotion to healers and fortune-tellers, mysticism and religious fear, such as the terror of the devil, and a wonder about mystery and the unknown. These elements are integral parts of the mentality of the backlands man and can by no means be omitted, for, as the author himself affirmed (in Lorenz, *ibid.*, p. 350), in order to understand the Brazilian way of life, it is important to learn that knowledge is different from logic. Yet he was aware of the fact that the Brazilian consciousness also has a logical side, and he never completely abandoned a rationalistic perspective. What he does in his stories is to put into check the tyranny of rationalism, to condemn its supremacy over the other levels of reality—hence his affinity with those characters who do not approach life from a purely logical point of view (aged people, children, madmen, artists, and sorcerers). Yet he never rejects rationalism as one among other possibilities to explain the facts and events of life. In this sense, Guimarães Rosa remains on the borderline. He questions traditional realism but does not adopt the perspective of either fantastic or magical realism. This aspect distinguishes his works from those of the other great contemporary Latin American writers of fiction, especially in the Spanish-speaking countries.

Guimarães Rosa's conception of art is one of the elements most responsible for his inclusion in the third generation of Brazilian modernism. For Guimarães Rosa, a literary piece has its own reality, which cannot be subordinated to that of the outside world; yet it is set into a dialectical relationship with the world. The work is not a copy, a faithful reproduction of external things and events, but a representation, a transposition of such a reality into

an invented structure. As such it must never lose track completely of that which has served as its point of departure.

Guimarães Rosa employed a number of devices in his works to express his consciousness of their fictional character, ranging from a simple interruption of the narrative for a brief comment about his own technique to the insertion of a longer theoretical discussion of the craft of fiction. However, the very elements of his narratives—his characters, the space in which they move, and the type of language they speak—are enough to illustrate the issue. Guimarães Rosa's language, for example, is an aesthetic creation composed of the fusion of elements deriving from experience and observation with others entirely invented at the moment of expression. It has a regionalist component proper to the area in the backlands that forms the setting of his stories, but it does not constitute an accurate reproduction of any specific dialect spoken in Brazil. It is rather the amalgamation of the various dialects existing in the country plus contributions from foreign languages (including classical Greek and Latin) and from the author's capacity for inventing words and expressions.

This hybrid language—which, though not corresponding exactly to any actual reality, very well reflects the backlands man's way of speaking—is not a mere stylistic trait of Guimarães Rosa's prose. It can also be said to constitute a metaphor for his entire oeuvre, whose major feature is the synthesis of elements traditionally seen as opposed. In his narratives, imagination, rather than being opposed to "realism," is the essential condition of a more vital realism. In the same way, aestheticism, or formal concern, constitutes the proper way to express the writer's reality, and regionalism, or the particular, is an indispensable element for attaining the universal. Guimarães Rosa's works are at the same time regional and universal, mimetic and self-conscious, "realist" and "antirealist." It is precisely this plural, globalizing status that best characterizes it.

The fusion of apparent opposites that confers upon Guimarães Rosa's fiction its synthetic character is not an exclusive trait of his narratives; it can also be found in the works of other writers of the 1945 generation (for example, Adonias Pilho and João Cabral de Melo Neto, the latter a poet). Yet

Guimarães Rosa excels in this sense and creates a kind of fiction in which things and events are never absolute or exclusive but rather always revealed through a wide spectrum of possibilities, all with the same chances of being actualized. In his works, Guimarães Rosa does not affirm in a definitive manner. Instead, he raises problems: his language is one of questioning, a language that is created at the very moment of expression. And in this fluid, ephemeral universe, the reader is constantly urged to make choices, thus becoming a coparticipant in the creative process. Guimarães Rosa's fiction is, in short, of an "open" kind; it is par excellence an art of its century—an art of synthesis and relativity—and at the same time a perfect representative of the author's country, a land that can be clearly understood only when seen as a great melting pot of cultures.

When *Sagarana* came out in 1946, the critics were so impressed with the novelties it contained that a great number of studies followed its publication, and Guimarães Rosa immediately conquered a vast reading public. The majority of these studies have dealt especially with two aspects of the work: the issue of language and narrative discourse, and the treatment given to regionalism.

Sagarana is a collection of nine stories, each of which constitutes an independent narrative, with its own characters and plot. Yet the world view present in them is so uniform that they form a block, a kind of multicolored mosaic. They are the physical, psychological, and sociological portrait of a particular area of the Brazilian backlands, its cultural habits and idiosyncrasies recreated through art.

In *Sagarana*, the region is presented in all its rawness and concreteness. It is depicted in terms of its physical and geographical aspects, such as its fauna, flora, climate, and hydrography, as well as the customs of its people and their social and economic system. In spite of the massive presence of these elements and the faithful and detailed manner with which they are often described, the book transcends regionalism in the strict sense of the term. The region encountered in its pages is less a specific geographical reality than a microcosm of the world. It is a mysterious, unlimited area where man lives in a constant search for meaning. And the characters of

its tales, rather than particular types, are men of all times and places, living with their contradictions and experiencing situations that are the representation of everyone's daily life, especially in its moments of extreme tension.

Lalino Salãthiel in "A Volta do Marido Pródigo" ("The Return of the Prodigal Husband") and Nhô [Mister] Augusto Matraga in "A Hora e Vez de Augusto Matraga" ("Augusto Matraga's Hour and Turn"), as well as the characters in "Duelo" ("Duel"), "Sarapalha" (translated as "The Straw-spinners"), "Minha Gente" ("Mine Own People"), "São Marcos" (translated as "Woodland Witchery"), and "Corpo Fechado" (translated as "Bulletproof"), are certainly typical inhabitants of the Brazilian backlands. The characters confront a series of problems extremely significant in that area—malaria ("The Straw-spinners"), witchcraft ("Woodland Witchery"), superstition and banditry ("Bulletproof"), vengeance ("Duel"), machismo ("The Return of the Prodigal Husband"), and social exploitation and religious fervor ("Augusto Matraga's Hour and Turn"). Yet they are also universal human beings, whose conflicts are not exclusive to the region where they live, but common to all men at all times and places (for example, Matraga's conflict between good and evil).

In this universe, where nature is not merely a setting but the living expression of the collective character of its inhabitants, man is not always the protagonist of the story. This position is at times occupied by animals, as in "O Burrinho Pedrês" (translated as "The Little Dust-brown Donkey") and "Conversa de Bois" ("Conversation Among Oxen"). When that happens, the animals are not presented as pure mirror images of men, as in fables or apologues. In Guimarães Rosa's texts, they are real animals, with an acute intuitive knowledge ("The Little Dust-brown Donkey"), and the narrative is totally presented from their perspective (for example, "Conversation Among Oxen," in which the oxen express their thoughts about men and life, building up a sort of philosophical theory of mankind).

Even in the narratives in which the protagonists are animals, the focus is never on the description of local color, nor is the author concerned about the verisimilitude of the episodes. The region of Guimarães Rosa is a region of art, a universe created in language. He is, above all, a great storyteller, for whom truth is present in narration, not in the events themselves, and one of his greatest achievements is to restore the old technique of narrating stories. His plots are never linear but always interrupted by a series of embedded tales, and narrating for him is a vital necessity.

When Guimarães Rosa entitled his book *Sagarana*, a word formed with the Germanic root *saga* and the Tupi Indian suffix *-rana*, he defined his position toward language. This hybrid word, composed of elements from languages that have no connection, indicated his break with conventionality and proclaimed his adherence to a concept of aesthetic freedom. Henceforth, he would use the elements that seemed most appropriate to transmit his world view, regardless of whether they were considered grammatical or corresponded to any actual reality. This program was not only put into practice in his narrative, but was also frequently made explicit, as in "Woodland Witchery," in which he exposes, in a highly poetic way, his theory of the revitalization of literary language.

Language for Guimarães Rosa is not simply a literary experience; it is instead identified with action. The word for him has the weight of an act and often determines in his narratives the destiny of his characters. In "The Straw-spinners," it is the naive confession of a feeling that causes the rupture of the protagonists' old friendship and condemns them to solitude; in "Duel," it is the oath made to a man at the moment of his death that generates the murder of one of the main characters; and in "Woodland Witchery," it is the words of a prayer that reveal to the protagonist the secret of his misfortune, saving him at the end. The word in Guimarães Rosa's narratives is endowed with power.

With the publication of *Corpo de Baile* in 1956, Guimarães Rosa temporarily abandoned the short story genre and presented a series of seven novellas. The first printing of this book came out in two heavy volumes, but from the third printing on, it was redivided into three, with the original title transformed into a subtitle. The three titles are *Manuelzão e Miguilim* (Manuelzão and Miguilim, 1964), *No*

Urubuquaquá, no Pinhém (In Urubuquaquá, in Pinhém, 1965), and *Noites do Sertão* (Backlands' Nights, 1965).

In *Corpo de Baile*, the elements that form the universe of *Sagarana* are present again and widely developed; the author takes his linguistic and structural innovations much further. The subjects of these stories are the same as the previous ones, but their themes are of a greater variety and are more deeply explored. Man's existential conflicts acquire a larger dimension here, and reality is viewed from a wider perspective. In these narratives, myth and fantasy play a relevant role, and reason is frequently with those who question the established order.

The backlands in *Corpo de Baile*, as in *Sagarana*, is a double, ambiguous region; its inhabitants are men divided between a logical-rational and a mythical-sacred world. Yet the importance of intuition is so much stressed in Guimarães Rosa's novellas that myth seems at times to dominate the author's world view. It is present in all of its forms in man's attitude toward life, and it often constitutes the only way of approaching the mystery of existence. Besides, there is a whole population of predominantly intuitive beings in the book, and these characters are in many cases the focal point of attention.

In this universe, where intuition plays a decisive role in the apprehension of reality, childhood is very well represented, and it is not by chance that the first narrative of *Corpo de Baile* is centered upon the figure of an eight-year-old boy. Although the story deals with the child's process of growth and constantly points to the changes that take hold of him, his world view is present throughout the entire narrative and is often contrasted with that of the adults. Whereas the latter are in general predominantly rationalistic and have, as a consequence, a limiting view of the world, the child is imaginative and wise, closer to the immediacy of things.

The author's empathy for the child is also extended to all other characters who, by not placing reason above everything in their lives, are marginalized by the everyday world of adults. Among these characters, aged people play an important role (for example, the wise old lady of "A Estória de Lélio e Lina" [The Story of Lelio and Lina] and the couple Manuelzão and Joana Xaviel of "Uma Estória de Amor" [A Love

JOÃO GUIMARÃES ROSA

Story]), but the gallery would not be complete without the deranged men, criminals, sorcerers, and popular artists so abundant in Guimarães Rosa's novellas. In "O Recado do Morro" (A Message from the Hill), these people form a special group of great significance. This tale, in which a man is saved from murder after listening to a mysterious message transmitted by a chain of intuitive beings, can be seen as a real apology for antirationalistic thought.

If myth and intuition are at the core of Guimarães Rosa's novellas, emotion also constitutes one of their basic elements. *Corpo de Baile* is a symphony, a repository of feelings and sensations; emotional conflict is at the heart of several of the narratives. In "Buriti" (The Buriti Palm Tree), it is in passion and carnal love that the tension of the story resides, and in "Dão-Lalalão" (Ding-Ling-a-Ling), all the motivations for action are founded on jealousy and insecurity. Love is a pervading theme, present in each tale in a different form. Again, preference rests with those who question the status quo and transcend common sense. Emotion is for Guimarães Rosa a total, almost sacred state. It is aesthetic experience at its utmost, for art is identified with life. Hence the meaning of the cowboy Grivo's quest in the story "Cara-de-Bronze" (The Bronze Face): the girl for whom he desperately searches is poetry in its full sense.

Guimarães Rosa's linguistic and structural experiments, initiated in *Sagarana*, are greatly expanded in *Corpo de Baile*. One of the aspects most developed is the fusion of elements traditionally considered incompatible, such as those that characterize prose as opposed to poetry or that distinguish one literary genre from another. This kind of separation was never accepted by the author, who saw it as an absurd limitation. His prose is filled with traits usually considered proper to poetry, such as onomatopoeia, alliteration, rhyme, and rhythm: the poetic devices are so much exploited in *Corpo de Baile* (such as in "Uma Estória de Amor") that, in the third printing of the book, he came to the point of defining his narratives as poems. The mixture of genres reaches an extreme point in the novella "Cara-de-Bronze," which fuses the structure of a narrative, a poem, a drama, and even a filmscript.

Here again, as in *Sagarana*, Guimarães Rosa's theoretical preoccupations are made explicit in the

text of his stories, and language frequently constitutes a significant element of the narrative's thematic structure. It is in the words of an embedded story that the protagonist of "Uma Estória de Amor" can find the clue for his peace of mind, and through the words of a popular song that the hero of "O Recado do Morro" can recognize the trap that has been prepared to swallow him. Finally, it is upon language itself, or upon poetry and its relationship with life, that the story of "Cara-de-Bronze" is centered.

Guimarães Rosa's only novel, *The Devil to Pay in the Backlands*, is not only the author's masterpiece and a synthesis of all he has written; it is also one of the greatest works of twentieth-century Brazilian literature. It has had a large number of reprintings and translations, and is one of the most widely studied novels in Brazil.

Breaking completely with traditional regionalism, Guimarães Rosa presents the story of a backlands man, Riobaldo, who is at the same time a typical representative of his native region and a common man of his century; tormented by doubt and insecurity, he searches desperately for the meaning of existence. The narrative consists of the report Riobaldo makes to an urban citizen traveling through the backlands. He describes his former life as a *jagunço* (in Brazilian Portuguese, a member of a group of outlaws, inhabitants of the backlands, who formed a sort of bodyguard to defend either their own interests or those of the landowners who supported them). Yet the tale is not the mere narration of past facts and events. The protagonist had once been led to contract a pact with the devil in order to obtain victory in war; having achieved his aim, he is dominated by the guilty feeling that he has sold his soul. Since the devil never appears to him as a concrete entity, however, he cannot be sure of the latter's existence. He therefore decides to narrate his life for the purpose of clearing up his doubt and finding, if possible (it is not by chance that he chooses as interlocutor a predominantly rationalistic person), some relief for his conscience. He does not come up with any definite answer for his question. The best conclusion he can draw is that relativity is the only possible way of approaching reality.

Although Riobaldo's report is given in one extended narration, without even a division into chapters, it is constructed around two basic lines, or levels. The levels are associated with two different moments in the protagonist's life and are marked by two distinct attitudes on his part. One consists of a past time during which he experiences the facts narrated, marked above all by his action in the backlands. The other centers around the present time and is characterized by a speculative attitude in which he reports those past events and experiences them again in the act of narrating.

The first line, the past, corresponds to the story that Riobaldo sets out to tell, that is, the story of his life as a *jagunço*. It is composed of those episodes that occur at that time. Since these episodes are of two distinct kinds, it is possible to distinguish the presence of two sublines. An objective one is formed by the succession of external facts and events with which the protagonist is involved in the backlands, that is, his battles and struggles. A subjective one is constituted by the inner conflicts he has at that time. These two sublines differ in the nature of their component episodes and conflicts, and in the aim pursued by the protagonist in each of them: in the former, that which is sought is the equilibrium of the *jagunço*'s world; in the latter it is Riobaldo's personal happiness. They are nevertheless very similar in their structure. They conclude by merging into a single climax.

The second line, the time of narration, is composed of the protagonist's experiences at the very moment in which he reports his life to his interlocutor. It involves speculations about those facts or events and his attempt to organize them into narrative terms. Here again, there can be distinguished the presence of two sublines. One is basically speculative; the other, critical and metalinguistic. In the former, Riobaldo is preoccupied with deciphering those things he could not understand until then and dissipating the doubt that continues to torment him. In the latter, he is concerned with his own way of narrating those things, with finding a suitable expressive means to reconstruct them in his narration. These two sublines differ fundamentally from those of the past in that they exist only in the act of narration. But since they are interwoven with the former ones,

they imply the existence of an isomorphic relationship in the book between art and life.

This relationship, one of the most important in the novel, is indicated also by several of its themes, among which is that of a search, present from beginning to end. Riobaldo is a man in a constant state of uncertainty, and he makes use of narration to accomplish his search. But this process can be effected only if he finds a new type of language adequate to express his state, a language that inquires more than it affirms. As a result, there occurs an identification between living and narrating, and his quest is represented through the search for a new expression. In other words, the protagonist accomplishes his investigation by means of looking for a new expression and neutralizes the opposition between art and life. This is the meaning of the parallel construction that recurs as a leitmotif: "Living is very dangerous," and "narrating is very, very difficult."

The Third Bank of the River and Other Stories (*Primeiras Estórias*) marked Guimarães Rosa's return to the short story. Yet there is a difference between the kind of stories in this volume and those that formed *Sagarana*. In the title in Portuguese, *estórias* is a neologism, based on the English word "stories." It is used in opposition to the *conto*, the traditional name of the genre. By employing this term, preceded by the ordinal *primeiras* (first), the author made clear a distinction between this book and *Sagarana*. The new stories are much more condensed and are characterized by a sharper philosophical tone. They are of a more lyrical sort and freer from traditional plot structure.

Although the book is composed of twenty-one different stories, their themes are so similar that the book's unity is even greater than that of *Sagarana*. The stories are sketches of backlands life, based on varied subjects, but Guimarães Rosa's preoccupation with man's relationship with the world is so significant in all of them that it can be said to constitute their central element. Reality is presented in several distinct perspectives, and the characters are always focused on in their dynamic multiplicity, but the motivations that set them to act have the same basis in most cases: to decipher the mystery of life and the meaning of human existence.

In this universe, where life is seen as mystery and perplexity and where relativity constitutes the only possible way of approaching reality, rationalism and common sense are called into question more vehemently than ever before in this writer's works. Hence many stories center upon a child's world view or are based on the issue of madness, here revealed as a deeper or sometimes more lucid way of facing life. The children of *The Third Bank of the River* are special, superior beings, endowed with a sensibility that the adults can never possess. Its madmen are prophets who can see beyond appearance and who have commanded people's respect, ironically, on account of their wisdom.

The importance of the world view of children is evidenced by the depiction of their sensibility in the first and last narratives, in which a little boy experiences the conflict of good and evil in two different and extreme moments of his life, but it is in "A Menina de Lá" ("The Girl from Beyond") and "Partida do Audaz Navegante" (translated as "The Aldacious Navigator") that the contrast between the child's and the adult's world is definitely established. The former is the story of a strange and lonely little girl who is thought to have become a miracle worker. The latter presents the case of a girl who sees things that, however logical, are not perceived by anyone else. "Pirlimpsiquice" (translated as "Hocus Psychocus"), is the story of a group of boys who create a theater piece parallel to the one they are expected to play, and in "Nenhum, Nenhuma" (translated as "No Man, No Woman"), the narration is filtered through the memory of a boy.

Several of the narratives of *The Third Bank of the River* are based on the issue of madness, and in all of them, the one-sided perspective usually adopted in those cases is replaced by the elimination of any sort of barrier between madness and sanity. Thus, in "A Banfazeja" (translated as "A Woman of Good Works"), a madwoman who has murdered her husband is revealed as a sensible person whose feelings demand respect. The old madman of "Tarantão, Meu Patrão" ("Tantarum, My Boss"), who undertakes a real crusade in order to kill his doctor, is highly appreciated by those he meets along the way. In "Darandina" (translated as "Much Ado"), the episode of a madman hanging at the top of a palm tree drives an entire population to question their system of values. In "Sorôco, Sua Mãe, Sua Filha" ("Sorôco, His Mother, His Daughter"), the song of two madwomen at the moment of their departure to the sanitorium is the only true element of communication among the inhabitants of the town.

But if madness is frequently treated in the book in an explicit manner, in other stories it is merely suggested and confused with simple absurdity. Such is the case of the old man who divides his property among his servants with no explanation to the daughters he sincerely loves ("Nada e a Nossa Condição" ["Nothingness and the Human Condition"]) and of the suspicious foreigner who gives beer to his horse ("O Cavalo que Bebia Cerveja" ["The Horse That Drank Beer"]). The most intriguing story in this respect is that of a man who abandons all he owns, to live for the rest of his life on a canoe going up and down the same part of a river ("A Terceira Margem do Rio" ["The Third Bank of the River"]). This story, a jewel of narrative technique, is fundamental for the understanding of Guimarães Rosa's works. On the one hand, it can be said to be one of his sharpest criticisms of the supremacy of rationalistic thought; on the other, it never transcends the limits of rationalism. The situation presented in the narrative can in no way be explained in rationalistic terms, but it remains outside the realm of the marvelous or magical, for the protagonist's basic needs for survival (food and clothing) are supplied by his family.

This view of life as mystery and perplexity is also a basic theme in other stories of the book, especially in those more obviously marked by a philosophical preoccupation: "Fatalidade" (translated as "My Friend the Fatalist"), "Seqüência" (translated as "Cause and Effect"), "Luas-de-Mel" ("Honeymoons"), "Um Moço Muito Branco" ("A Young Man, Gleaming White"), "Substância" ("Substance"), and "O Espelho" ("The Mirror"). In all these cases, man is moved by a desire to understand the world, but the facets of reality are so many and the moment so ephemeral that all he can grasp is sheer relativity. This is the meaning of the *salto mortale* (somersault) to which the protagonist of "The Mirror," one of the densest and most essaylike stories of the book, refers after the experience he undertakes in order to face himself the way he actually is.

In *The Third Bank,* Guimarães Rosa's concern with language reaches a previously unattained stage of elaboration. The innovations the author introduces in both language and narrative discourse are innumerable and at times extremely sophisticated; his theorization on the subject is present in several of the stories. The aspects that the author most develops are the use of discourse to characterize his children's world view ("The Girl from Beyond" and "The Aldacious Navigator"), and the device of using language as the very theme of the narrative as in "Famigerado" ("Notorious"), in which the whole story consists of the exploitation of the meaning of a word.

Tutaméia, the last book published during Guimarães Rosa's lifetime, is a collection of stories that are even shorter than those of *The Third Bank of the River* and still more marked by a philosophical tone. They are a series of episodes, of circumstances or situations, with practically no plot or sequence, and no commitment to any sort of rationalism. They are quick flashes, miniatures of life.

Although this type of story is a novelty in Guimarães Rosa's works, the great innovation brought about by this book does not lie in the stories themselves, but in the fact that the author presents therein his own conception of art. *Tutaméia* is divided into four parts, each of which is preceded by a preface, a true literary essay, in which the author discusses some of the major aspects of his aesthetic conception. The subjects of the parts are the opposition between "history" and "story" and the notion of inner coherence in the work of art, the creation and use of neologisms, the relationship between the work and the world of its author, and the problems of aesthetic creation. The stories of each section are to a great extent a demonstration of the theories developed in the prefaces.

The first preface begins with the opposition between "story" and "history." The story, the author thinks, must be different from history, for whereas the latter is the narration of facts that are supposed to have taken place, the former is pure invention, a creation that has a logic entirely its own. The story is akin to the anecdote in the sense that it requires originality and questions the limits of logic. However, not every kind of anecdote serves this purpose. The author sketches a classification of anecdotes and concludes that the "anecdote of abstraction" is the one that best defines the story, because it contains a great deal of nonsense. Guimarães Rosa makes clear that it is on this level, not on that of common sense, that he reaches his poetic realization.

The second preface deals more specifically with one very important aspect of the author's language: the creation of neologisms. Guimarães Rosa defends the right to create words and affirms that this is a common trait in the language of the unprivileged social classes in the backlands. The average educated man lives in a pragmatic society, dominated by materialistic preoccupations, and he does not feel the need to increase the expressiveness of his language. His mind is prejudiced by the concepts he has acquired throughout the process of his education, and he limits himself to ready-made ideas, not bothering much about expressing the movements of his soul. The uncultivated man, on the other hand, has not yet been under the influence of the pragmatic society. His language is composed of a poor and simple vocabulary, and his mind is not dominated by the concepts and relationships of Western logic. His view of the world is basically intuitive, and he feels as an imperative the creation of words. Yet the necessity of producing neologisms is not exclusive to this man. The poet, as well, is a highly intuitive being, and he must venture into this task every time the forms of his language are insufficient to express his world view.

The third preface is composed of a series of anecdotes about drunkards who try to escape from the drama of their existence by transforming into fantasy the problems of everyday life. In this preface, the opposition between reality and unreality is eliminated, and everything becomes a matter of point of view. That which is traditionally considered real is revealed as being mere appearance, and fantasy—here represented by drunkeness—is what brings consciousness to man. The mystery of life lies in the hidden side of things, and it is necessary to go beyond the external facades represented by common sense. Guimarães Rosa does this by making use of nonsense, by representing the world from the perspective of a drunkard. The nonsense brings into question the nature of objective reality and opens a path toward the search for "suprasense." This third preface makes it clear that the traditional structure of language and narrative logic do no more than represent the external side of things; hence the search for a new expression that characterizes the writer's works.

The fourth preface, which deals with the problem of the creative act, is a sort of conclusion to the preceding ones. Guimarães Rosa questions the antithetical tendencies that have concerned him throughout the creation of his works and concludes that a literary piece must be a synthesis of these oppositions. The world is full of contrasts and contradictions, and the work of art must reflect through its structure the vital conflicts of man. The author defends the right to shake the established order, which supports apparent reality, and once again denies the objective value of words, by stating that everything acquires new sense when language goes beyond this barrier. Doubt is for him a first step to aesthetic creation, because it opens a door to a deeper reality that cannot be explained in rational terms. Guimarães Rosa confesses that his life has always been affected by strange occurrences (dreams, premonitions, coincidences, and intuitions) and affirms that these manifestations have been most evident on the level of art and creation. For Guimarães Rosa, the work of art is often born in a sort of dream state that lies beyond the domain of reason. He explains how he has conceived some of his stories and concludes by recalling a novel that he could never finish because he caught the illness of his protagonist.

Guimarães Rosa's two posthumous fictional works, *Estas Estórias* and *Ave, Palavra,* are collections of stories written at different moments of the author's life and prepared by him to be printed as books. *Estas Estórias* is composed of eight stories in the manner of *Sagarana,* plus the journalistic piece *Com o Vaquiero Mariano.* Of the eight stories, four had never been published, three had come out in the periodical *Senhor* (from 1960 to 1962), and one was part of a collective book entitled *Os Sete Pecados Capitais* (The Seven Capital Sins, 1964). The unpublished stories had been reviewed several times by the author but had not yet reached their final form.

Ave, Palavra is a collection of fifty-four literary pieces defined by the author as a miscellany. It includes poetry, short stories, lyrical essays, poetic reportings, maxims, travel notes, and fragments of a diary, most of them published in Brazilian journals and periodicals from 1947 to 1967. It also includes five brief essays, added at the end by the editor, that were not intended to form part of the book, but were to be published as a separate volume under the title "Jardins e Riachinhos" (Gardens and Little Streams).

SELECTED BIBLIOGRAPHY

Editions

Sagarana. Rio de Janeiro, 1946.
Com o Vaqueiro Mariano. Niterói, Brazil, 1952.
Corpo de Baile. Rio de Janeiro, 1956. Later divided into *Manuelzão e Miguilim* (Rio de Janeiro, 1964), *No Urubuquaquá, no Pinhém* (Rio de Janeiro, 1965), and *Noites do Sertão* (Rio de Janeiro, 1965).
Grande Sertão: Veredas. Rio de Janeiro, 1956.
Primeiras Estórias. Rio de Janeiro, 1962.
O Mistério dos M M M. Edited by João Condé. Rio de Janeiro, 1962. A novel written in collaboration with Viriato Correia, Dinah Silveira de Queiroz, et al.
Os Sete Pecados Capitais. Novellas by Guimarães Rosa, Oto Lara Resende, Carlos Heitor Cony, et al. Rio de Janeiro, 1964.
Tutaméia (Terceiras Estórias). Rio de Janeiro, 1967.
Estas Estórias. Rio de Janeiro, 1969. Posthumous edition.
Ave, Palavra. Rio de Janeiro, 1970. Posthumous edition.
J. Guimarães Rosa: Correspondência com o Tradutor Italiano. São Paulo, 1972. Posthumous edition.
Sagarana Emotiva: Cartas de João Guimarães Rosa a Paulo Dantas. São Paulo, 1975. Posthumous edition.

Translations

The Devil to Pay in the Backlands. Translated by James L. Taylor and Harriet de Onís. New York, 1963.
Sagarana: A Cycle of Stories. Translated by Harriet de Onís. New York, 1966.
The Third Bank of the River and Other Stories. Translated by Barbara Shelby. New York, 1968.

Biographical and Critical Studies

Adonias Filho et al. *Guimarães Rosa.* Lisbon, 1969.
Brasil, Francisco Assis. *Guimarães Rosa.* Rio de Janeiro, 1969.

Bruyas, Jean-Paul. "Técnicas, Estruturas e Visão em *Grande Sertão: Veredas.*" *Revista do Instituto de Estudos Brasileiros* (São Paulo) 18:75–92 (1976).

Campos, Augusto de. "Um Lance de 'Dês' do *Grande Sertão*. *Revista do Livro* (Rio de Janeiro) 4/16:9–27 (1959).

Candido, Antonio. "O Homem dos Avessos." In *Tese e Antítese*. São Paulo, 1964. Pp. 119–140.

Castro, Nei Leandro de. *Universo e Vocabulário do "Grande Sertão."* Rio de Janeiro, 1970.

César, Guilhermino, et al. *João Guimarães Rosa.* Porto Alegre, Brazil, 1969.

Chaves, Flávio Loureiro. "Perfil de Riobaldo." In *Ficção Latino-americana.* Porto Alegre, Brazil, 1973. Pp. 109–132.

Coelho, Nelly Novaes, and Ivana Versiani. *Guimarães Rosa: Dois Estudos.* São Paulo, 1975.

Coutinho, Eduardo de Faria. *The Process of Revitalization of the Language and Narrative Structure in the Fiction of João Guimarães Rosa and Julio Cortázar.* Valencia, Spain, 1980.

———, ed. *Guimarães Rosa.* Coleção "Fortuna Crítica," vol. 6. Rio de Janeiro, 1983.

Dacanal, José Hildebrando. "A Epopéia Riobaldiana." In *Nova Narrativa Épica no Brasil.* Porto Alegre, Brazil, 1973. Pp. 7–108.

Daniel, Mary L. *João Guimarães Rosa: Travessia Literária.* Rio de Janeiro, 1968.

Diálogo. (São Paulo) 8 (1957).

Doyle, Plínio. *Bibliografia de e sobre Guimarães Rosa.* Rio de Janeiro, 1968. Also in *Em Memória de João Guimarães Rosa.*

Em Memória de João Guimarães Rosa. Rio de Janeiro, 1968.

O Estado de São Paulo 13/604 (30 November 1968). Literary supplement.

Galvão, Walnice Nogueira. *As Formas do Falso.* São Paulo, 1972.

Garbuglio, José Carlos. *O Mundo Movente de Guimarães Rosa.* São Paulo, 1972.

Jornal de Letras (Rio de Janeiro) 19/211–212 (1967).

Lima Filho, Luiz Costa. "O Mundo em Perspectiva: Guimarães Rosa." *Tempo Brasileiro* 6:67–83 (1963).

Lisboa, Henriqueta, et al. *Guimarães Rosa.* Belo Horizonte, Brazil, 1966.

Lorenz, Günter. "Diálogo con Guimarães Rosa." *Mundo nuevo* 45:27–47 (1970). Later included in *Diálogo com America Latina.* Translated by Fredy S. Rodrigues and Rosemary C. Abilio. São Paulo, 1973. Pp. 315–356.

Marques, Oswaldino. "Canto e Plumagem das Palavras." In *Ensaios Escolhidos.* Rio de Janeiro, 1968. Pp. 77–148.

Minas Gerais (Belo Horizonte, Brazil) 25 November 1967; 23 November 1968; 23 and 30 March 1974; and 6 April 1974. Literary supplement.

Nunes, Benedito. "Guimarães Rosa." *O Dorso do Tigre.* São Paulo, 1969. Pp. 143–212.

Oliveira, Franklin de. "Guimarães Rosa." In *A Literatura no Brasil 5,* edited by Afrânio Coutinho. 2nd ed. Rio de Janeiro, 1970. Pp. 402–448.

Pérez, Renard. "Guimarães Rosa." In *Escritores Brasileiros Contemporâneos.* Rio de Janeiro, 1960. Pp. 177–188.

Portella, Eduardo. "A Estória cont(r)a a História." *Jornal do Brasil* (Rio de Janeiro), 30 December 1967.

Proença, M. Calvalcânti. *Trilhas no "Grande Sertão."* Rio de Janeiro, 1958.

Revista de cultura brasileña (Madrid) 6/21 (1967).

Rodríguez Monegal, Emir. "En busca de Guimarães Rosa." *Mundo nuevo* 20:4–24 (1968).

Rónai, Paulo, ed. *Seleta de João Guimarães Rosa.* Rio de Janeiro, 1973.

Schüler, Donaldo. "O Épico em *Grande Sertão: Veredas.*" In *João Guimarães Rosa,* by Guilhermino César et al. Porto Alegre, Brazil, 1969. Pp. 47–76.

Schwarz, Roberto. "*Grande-sertão* e *Dr. Faustus.*" In *A Sereia e o Desconfiado: Ensaios Críticos.* Rio de Janeiro, 1965. Pp. 28–36.

Vincent, Jon S. *João Guimarães Rosa.* Boston, 1978.

Visão (Rio de Janeiro) 29/23 (1966).

Xisto, Pedro, Augusto de Campos, and Harolde de Campos. *Guimarães Rosa em Três Dimensões.* São Paulo, 1970.

Emilio Ballagas

(1908–1954)

Argyll Pryor Rice

When Emilio Ballagas sent a copy of his *Sabor eterno* (Eternal Taste, 1939) to Juan Ramón Jiménez, the Spanish poet responded with a letter revealing the esteem in which he held Ballagas' work: "You are without doubt the poet of that poetry which is intimately human and which flows from its beginnings to its end through the depths of the man, of the man himself, prisoner of time and space; poetry always of its own epoch, without the extravagance and abandon that disfigures and lessens in others their greatest beauty" (Rice, p. 131). Jiménez has captured the unifying characteristic of the Ballagas oeuvre, for his poetry does indeed run through the depths of the man. Poetry is the essence of the poet; poet and poetry are inseparable; creator and creation are one.

Ballagas spoke of the art of poetry as "life within life." When commenting upon his poem "Nocturno y elegía" (Nocturne and Elegy), he recognized the essential unity between himself and his poetry: "To change a line would not only disfigure the poem but would disfigure me as well. It is clear that I cannot be different from my own substance, and the poem is the substance of the poet" (Ballagas, 1939, p. 9).

Even as a boy, Ballagas sensed poetry in his surroundings. He was born on 7 November 1908 in Camagüey, a colonial city situated in the central part of Cuba. The towers of churches such as La Merced, La Soledad, and San Francisco rise high over the flat-roofed houses and the narrow, twisted streets. The young Emilio wrote affectionately of his home: the patio, the mockingbirds, the "little orange tree, weak and elegant like an effeminate adolescent." He reacted to the brilliant sunlight and intense colors of hibiscus and bougainvillea, to the cries of street vendors, to the rhythms of the bongo, to the fragrant jasmine and the pungent spikenard, to the taste of the guanabana, mango, and mammee. The intensity of his early perceptions would later find expression in his poetry.

While still an adolescent, Ballagas wrote both prose and poetry, some of which was published. In "El mágico prodigioso" (The Prodigious Magician, 1938), he recalled this period of his life when he spoke of "the seriousness of the fifteen-year-old." Although his father could not afford to send him to the University of Havana, Ballagas' pen succeeded in opening the doors to that old and respected institution. In 1926, during his last year of study at the secondary school in Camagüey, he won first place in a contest with his essay on José Martí, and the prize was a fellowship to the university. Throughout his life, Ballagas continued to write critical articles and essays. His poetic impulse, clearly evident in his poetry, manifests itself in his prose style as well.

Although the form and images of many of his early poems are classical, the young poet's contact with the avant-garde is apparent in his metaphoric and occasionally typographic experimentation. Ballagas was a student at the university when the principal organ of vanguardism, the *revista de avance* (1927–1930), was being published in Havana. This publication brought together several contemporary trends in poetry: postmodernism, avant-gardism, pure poetry, black poetry, and sociopolitical poetry. Ballagas' celebrated Afro-Cuban poem "Elegía de María Belén Chacón" (Elegy for María Belén Chacón) was first published in the August 1930 issue of the *revista de avance*. Although Ballagas occasionally introduces avant-garde images to achieve striking effects, he found his voice in the medium of pure poetry. His poetic vision was far more closely related to the sensibilities of the Spanish poets of the Generation of '27 and the Cuban poet Mariano Brull than to the audacity of the avant-garde.

Ballagas' first book, *Júbilo y fuga* (Jubilation and Flight), was published in 1931, two years before he received the degree of doctor of pedagogy from the University of Havana, and it was immediately recognized as a significant contribution to contemporary Cuban poetry. A fine example of "pure poetry," the book is representative of the first of three phases of Ballagas' creative work. In 1937, he characterized this first stage as one of "jubilant realization and of intellectual gymnastics," the period of "the joyful mysteries" of his verse.

From the dichotomy of the title *Júbilo y fuga* flow the two currents that now distinguish themselves from one another, now merge in fleeting joy or joyous flight. Jubilation takes numerous forms that are always personal. We glimpse it in the arcane region of the poetic experience, and we witness it in the inception of the Adamic world of the poet. In the initial poem of the book, "Víspera" (On the Eve), joy exists in the prenatal state in which poet and poetry lie, in the perfect union of the embryo. Outside of time and thus not dominated by it, the poet's vision of time is whole, intact, unfragmented. His very inspiration sleeps in its oneness, enveloped in the clarity of preexistence. One senses the presence of the creative force—consisting of unseen, transparent pulsations—in the moment before it enters into the

confines of the word. It is poetry in its virgin state prior to its union with the material. Ballagas thus poetizes the region of pure poetry as understood by Henri Bremond.

Still another form that jubilation takes is the use of words to generate sensuous delight. In the poem "Sentidos" (Senses), all five senses are present, although only sight and touch are explicitly mentioned. Unusual synesthetic effects, however, succeed in blending with sight and touch the gustatory, auditory, and olfactory delights. The eagerness of the poet for union with the senses leaves the impression not of death, but of metempsychosis to the senses themselves. The desired ecstasy is not that of passion. It is rather the jubilation associated with the innocence of childhood. This paradisaic quality pervades the poetry of *Júbilo y fuga*.

Jorge Mañach describes Ballagas' first book as "ultra-individualistic." As he stated in a review in the newspaper *El País*, "What is characteristic of this poetry is not what it reveals, but what it conceals: it is not the meaning that it unfolds, but the meaning that it encloses and often hides." In renouncing well-trodden paths, Ballagas proceeds to create a unique Edenic world.

Ballagas was known for his Afro-Cuban poetry even prior to the publication of *Júbilo y fuga*. His *Cuaderno de poesía negra* (Notebook of Black Poetry) was published in 1934, soon after he had been named professor of literature and rhetoric at the Normal School in Santa Clara, Cuba, a position he held until 1946. Besides the *Cuaderno*, he published numerous essays and articles, and two important anthologies: *Antología de poesía negra hispanoamericana* (Anthology of Black Hispanic-American Poetry, 1935) and *Mapa de la poesía negra americana* (Map of Black American Poetry, 1946). In 1946, he received the degree of doctor of philosophy and letters and published his thesis, "Situación de la poesía afroamericana" (The State of Afro-American Poetry) in the *Revista cubana*. Here his approach is not only literary and linguistic, but historical, ethnographic, and sociological as well. The quality of Ballagas' own Afro-Cuban poems compensates for their limited number; we have only two *divertissements*, as Cintio Vitier calls them, and fifteen poems, twelve of which are included in the *Cuaderno*.

Like *Júbilo y fuga*, Ballagas' Afro-Cuban poetry belongs to his first period, and the *Cuaderno* has certain qualities in common with that work. If we were to characterize them in a single word, it would be "jubilation": Edenic, sensorial, and verbal. The differences, however, are notable, and the essence of these lies in the distance that exists between the abstract Eden of *Júbilo y fuga* and the terrestrial locus of the *Cuaderno*. Ballagas created in *Júbilo y fuga* his own extratemporal, extraspatial world, where the five senses awaken in all their pristine joy. The world of the *Cuaderno* also possesses the ingenuous quality of the primitive, but such a world, overflowing with passionate rhythmic life, is far removed from abstraction.

Although Ballagas was not black, the quality of his Afro-Cuban poetry was second only to that of Nicolás Guillén. He was able to identify himself with black culture to such an extent that his senses were keenly attuned to the rhythms of the bongo and to the movements of the dance. In his poem "Rumba," he captures the beat of the bongo in the accented *o* at the end of seven of the fifteen lines. The passionate intensity of the dance is evident in the cyclonic movements of the body of the female dancer. During the rumba, the navel, "vortex of a cyclone," becomes a single eye fixed upon *Changó*. The last line of the poem thus unites rhythm and movement with a strong reference to the black experience of the *Changó*, the climactic moment in voodoo ritual.

Many of Ballagas' Afro-Cuban poems capture brief scenes from the daily life of the blacks. The call of a fruit vendor, for example, resounds through the streets and appeals to the reader's auditory, olfactory, and gustatory senses. The lilting cry is repeated rhythmically throughout the poem, and the senses joyfully lose themselves in its mellow resonances.

When presenting life situations, Ballagas often focuses upon the simple, universal emotions of his characters. In a lullaby, one perceives the tenderness of a mother's love for her baby. Her affection is expressed in terms of sweets and tropical fruits and by her addressing the little one in a series of Afro-Cuban variants for a small child: *chiviricoqui*, *chiviricocó*, *chiviricoquito*. These words of endearment are immediately associated with the vocabulary of black Cubans. Several poems, including the lullaby, are written in the Afro-Cuban dialect, a device that imbues the scenes with intimacy and authenticity.

Although Ballagas was not a poet of social protest, the concern and compassion that he felt for his black compatriots are apparent nonetheless. His "Elegía de María Belén Chacón," a poem that Ballagas confesses to favor above all others in his *Cuaderno*, exhibits his empathy with the black experience. The narration of the death from overwork of the laundress María Belén Chacón is brief. We observe the gracefulness of her undulating walk as she carries her weighty basket of clothes between Camagüey and Santiago. We soon learn, however, that the beauty of her movements will never again be seen in dancing the rumba and that it was ironing, not sorcery, that "burned [her] lung." The true cause of the death of María Belén is clearly indicated, without direct accusation, as the economic conditions oppressing the blacks. The lament for her death begins when the poet asks that no one dance, that Andrés cease playing his guitar, and that the Chinese who fashion maracas leave off their noisy work. The poet then whispers his prayer of supplication to the Virgin in the *sotto voce* of a parenthesis. After the personal expression of erotic nostalgia, the poem ends, like the traditional *villancicos*, or ballads, with a slight variation of the rhythmic refrain with which the elegy began.

In his article "Poesía negra liberada" (Liberated Black Poetry, 1937), Ballagas writes that black poetry must present not the superficial aspects of Afro-Cuban culture, but the most profound traits of the Afro-Cuban character. Miguel de Unamuno, in a letter to Nicolás Guillén, wrote, "You speak of . . . 'Cuban color.' We shall ultimately attain human color that is universal, total." Like Unamuno, Ballagas foresaw the day when art, like humanity, would be free from prejudice and labels that attempt to destroy the beautiful sphere of creation. Certainly, his Afro-Cuban poetry is of such distinguished quality that it forms an integral part not only of his total work, but of the great body of poetry that Unamuno had called poetry of "human color . . . universal, total."

The years Ballagas spent in Havana at the university were productive, and his creative work was accorded substantial recognition not only by Jiménez and the more significant Cuban critics, but by the eminent Mexican man of letters, Alfonso Reyes. Professional success, however, was often accompanied by periods of anguish.

In 1934, Ballagas was named director of the Normal School in Santa Clara, but if he derived any satisfaction from the appointment, the polemics concerning his poetry must have taken it from him. When Gustavo E. Urrutia, in the newspaper *Diario de la Marina,* unjustly accused Ballagas of plagiarism, Rafael Suárez Solís came to his rescue and, from his column in the newspaper *Ahora,* successfully defended the young poet. In an article published in 1959, Samuel Feijóo remembers Ballagas' reaction to the charge leveled against him: "He was easily hurt. The attack on his poetry, the petty intrigue, the gossip, the offensive, accusing little tongues—all of this brought him great unhappiness."

Ballagas recalled that as a twelve-year-old boy he was small and slender, and at twenty-three he evidently had the same fragile build. Those who knew him spoke of his boyishness, his delicate manners, his accentuated timidity, his quiet reserve, his elegant appearance, and his soft voice. All who described him spoke of his eyes, "soft and tranquil," eyes in which "one might glimpse his profoundly mystic soul," eyes that seemed to seek compassion, "but were slow to solicit it and were content with the hidden path of their interior landscapes."

Ballagas was obviously a sensitive young man, highly vulnerable in his personal relationships. The seeds of impending anguish are evident in some of his early poems. Amorous disillusionment became complicated by the severity of his Catholic conscience, which scourged him without respite. His tragedy, then, was twofold: he suffered because of both unfulfilled or terminated relationships and unresolved inner conflicts. His own moral judgments struggled against sentiments and instincts that he found natural.

The years 1932–1935 represent a period of transition in his creative work. Without relinquishing the first stage of "jubilant realization" that Ballagas called the "mysterious joys" of his verse, he began moving toward a second stage, a somber region that he called "a stage of anguish," known intimately by him as the "sorrowful mysteries" of his poetry. The poems of this transitional period were destined to form "Blancolvido" (White Forgetfulness), the first section of his

next major work, *Sabor eterno.* The first edition, however, was withdrawn by the poet, and a second appeared immediately. In this second edition, he omitted the poems of "Blancolvido," the greater part of which were more closely related to the period of jubilant intellectualism than they were to the anguished tone of the other poems in the volume. His tragic personal experiences and subsequent inner conflicts had intensified, and with them arose the need for a mode of expression more appropriate to the anguish he felt. Ballagas therefore distanced himself from pure poetry and embraced the neoromantic mode.

The only emotional respite Ballagas was to experience during this period occurred between September 1937 and January 1938. The secretary of education granted him a fellowship to undertake research on the American manuscripts written in many Indian languages that had been collected at the Bibliothèque Nationale in Paris. Leaving behind the routine work of the Normal School and the provincialism of Santa Clara, Ballagas immersed himself in the cultural atmosphere of Paris. There he had the opportunity to mingle with other writers, such as Nicolás Guillén, Juan Marinello, Octavio Paz, León Felipe, José Bergamín, Manuel Altolaguirre, Ventura García Calderón, Gregorio Martínez Sierra, Tristán Tzara, and Pierre Flouquet. He also expanded his cultural horizons by frequenting the theaters and art galleries, by attending the soirees of Argentinita and of Robert Desnos, and by spending evenings at the Opéra with friends, among them the composer Silvestre Revueltas.

Ballagas' reaction to Paris was similar to the one he had had during his first months in Havana: "Writing, writing a great deal, for the pleasure of writing, for myself, for a few or for those who may wish to read me," Ballagas said in a 1937 letter to Manuel de Zayas. He had never been able to reconcile himself to being a teacher in the provinces. Preparing classes and correcting "piles of papers" absorbed time he would have preferred to dedicate to poetry. The conflict between Ballagas-professor and Ballagas-poet was intensified by his stay in Paris, as he exclaimed to Manuel de Zayas: "What am I to do! . . . I am a poet; I would be a poet even if I were not to write poetry." It would seem that this is "the moment" and "the outcry" in the life of Ballagas to which Unamuno refers when he writes, in the "Prólogo" to *Tres novelas ejemplares*, that a man reveals himself, indeed "bares the soul of his soul" to us "in a moment, in a phrase, in an outcry."

Financial problems forced Ballagas to leave Paris, the city in which his creative spirit had enjoyed an exalted sense of liberation. Upon his return to teaching at the Normal School, he again encountered the oppressive situations of the past, and he writes in "El mágico prodigioso," "Never as now have I experienced so great a need for silence." In the epilogue to the second edition of *Júbilo y fuga* (1939), Ballagas refers to the years 1931–1939 as "eight years intensely lived." *Sabor eterno* represents the poetization of that intensity of life, and it is in the poems of this book that Ballagas speaks with the deepest and most resonant part of his voice. The centrifugal force of *Júbilo y fuga* now gives way to the centripetal one of *Sabor eterno*. With his own hands, the poet breaks the dike that has contained the dark waters of his turbulent life. The emotion overflows in forms that are often consciously irregular.

It is from the poem "Canción" (Song) that the title of *Sabor eterno* derives. Representing eternal poetry, eternal taste embodies all the disparate songs that poets from time immemorial have sung. In "Canción," Ballagas sees himself as a link in that endless creative chain that has sung the "eternal" song that is "always different, always the same."

Of the twelve poems following "Canción," "Elegía sin nombre" (Elegy Without Name) is the focal point. The poem was published separately in 1936, and among the poet's personal copies of that first edition is one whose margins Ballagas filled with observations concerning images and influences. Among the marginalia are the names of poets such as Homer, Hesiod, Sappho, Theognis, Aeschylus, and Shakespeare, specifically as author of *A Midsummer Night's Dream*. Although Ballagas skillfully mingled literary and personal experiences, the personal takes precedence over the literary.

"Elegía sin nombre" narrates with poignancy an ill-fated love affair, and it is divided thematically, if not structurally, into three parts: the poet prior to his meeting with the beloved, the meeting and consummation in reality, and his disillusionment, sublimated

in poetry. During the scene of consummated love, the elegiac motif insinuates itself in the form of restless waves that have brought the lover to the poet and that are destined to carry the lover away. In a moment of meditation, the poet contemplates the mutable character of the lover, but it is the disastrous emotional result of the affair that Ballagas prefers to poetize. José Martí has said, "In the language of emotion, as in the Greek ode, one hears the wave break, and the one that responds, and then the echo." The breaking of the anguished emotional wave of "Elegía" finds its inevitable reply in the hand of destiny that separates Ballagas from his lover. The echo is heard when the poet renounces the beloved, according him eternal life in poetry.

"Elegía sin nombre" is the central poem of *Sabor eterno*, and except for "Canción," each poem in the book gives expression to some emotion inherent in this elegy. The last stanza of the poem consists of a single verse that links the poet to the Spanish mystic tradition. In the first edition of the elegy, the verse appears alone on a single page, and the enforced meditative pause prepares us for the resolution of the poem. The poet, unsuccessful in earthly love, is sustained by finding refuge in the life of the spirit. It is in this final verse that we glimpse a foreshadowing of the last stage of the Ballagas oeuvre, in which the poet is increasingly concerned with "all that is beyond silence."

The major part of the poetry of Ballagas' last period, that written between 1940 and his death in Havana on 11 September 1954, appears in three works: *Nuestra Señora del Mar* (Our Lady of the Sea, 1943); *Cielo en rehenes* (Heaven in Hostage), awarded the National Prize for Poetry in 1951 and published posthumously in 1955 by Cintio Vitier; and the *Décimas por el júbilo martiano* (Décimas for the Martí Jubilee, 1953), awarded the José Martí Centenary Prize. The spiritual crisis that Ballagas was experiencing determined both the thematic material to which he was drawn and his new mode of expression. Traditional themes concerning the Virgen de la Caridad (the Virgin of Charity) and the "apostle" José Martí, as well as other themes distinctively Cuban, led Ballagas to abandon neoromanticism in favor of traditional forms: the sonnet, the *décima*, and the shorter five-line stanza known as the *lira*. The *décima* was well suited to *Nuestra Señora del Mar* and to the *Décimas por el júbilo martiano*, as it is the Cuban equivalent of the Spanish *romance*, or ballad form. In both works, the form contributes to the intimate tone, a characteristic unmistakably Ballaguean.

In 1947, Ballagas married Antonia López y Villa-verde, and he dedicated the *Décimas* to their young son Manolo, whom he called "my true work and all my treasure." The poem consists of twenty *décimas* in which Ballagas converses intimately with the Apos-tle, as Martí is called with affectionate reverence by the Cubans. It is evident from the biblical images in the poem that Ballagas is stressing the Christ-like qualities of Martí.

In *Nuestra Señora del Mar*, Ballagas approaches the world of the Cuban peasant, or *guajiro*, both in form and in content. Without abandoning the popular tradition, Ballagas omits many superstitious elements in order to isolate what he calls "the luminous popular religiousness." Together with popular and biblical influences, there is a marked literary influence of the poems *Noche oscura* and the *Cántico espiritual* by Saint John of the Cross. The reappearance of Cuban themes in the last phase of Ballagas' work does not imply that he relinquished subjective expression. His approach was rather to elevate his inner struggle to a spiritual plane.

When in 1937 Ballagas described his first phase as the "mysterious joys" of his verse and the period of *Elegía sin nombre* as that of the "anguished mysteries" of his poetry, he ended by saying humbly, "In this rosary of my work I don't expect a coming of the 'glorious mysteries'" ("La poesía en mí," pp. 160–161). From the darkness of the "anguished mysteries" of his poetry, he had lamented his "eye that did not glimpse its heaven." When in 1951 he was in the midst of the unexpected moment of the "glorious mysteries," his eye sought its heaven, and glimpsed it, and contemplated it in the three phases of *Cielo en rehenes:* "Cielo gozoso" (Joyous Heaven), "Cielo sombrío" (Somber Heaven), and "Cielo invocado" (Invocation to Heaven). The first phase celebrates earthly manifestations of heaven that we hold hostage as proof of the existence of absolute Beauty yet to be seen. The intimations of heaven are to be understood, however, not only as joyful but also as tragic. Ballagas moves from the somber manifestations of

heaven into the third phase, which serves as his personal devotional and concludes the canticle *Cielo en rehenes*. The innocent hymn to joy and flight of his first book is transformed into elegy, and elegy into a spiritual epithalamium. Ultimately "touching heaven with his brow," Emilio Ballagas thus sanctifies both the final canticle and his own life, in which creation and creator are one.

SELECTED BIBLIOGRAPHY

Editions

Poetry

Júbilo y fuga. Havana, 1931.
Cuaderno de poesía negra. Santa Clara, Cuba, 1934.
Antología de poesía negra hispanoamericana. Madrid, 1935.
Elegía sin nombre. Havana, 1936.
Nocturno y elegía. Havana, 1938.
Júbilo y fuga. 2nd ed. Havana, 1939.
Sabor eterno. Havana, 1939.
Nuestra Señora del Mar. Havana, 1943.
Mapa de la poesía negra americana. Buenos Aires, 1946.
Décimas por el júbilo martiano en el centenario del apóstol José Martí. Havana, 1953.
Obra poética de Emilio Ballagas. With an introduction by Cintio Vitier. Havana, 1955. Posthumous edition. Contains *Cielo en rehenes*.

Prose

"José Martí." *Revista martiniana* 6/1 (1926).
"Los movimientos literarios de vanguardia." *Cuadernos de la Universidad del Aire* (Havana), 1 July 1933. Pp. 97–104.
"Pasión y muerte del futurismo." *Revista cubana* 1/1: 91–111. (1935).
"La poesía en mí." *Revista cubana* 9/26:158–161 (1937).
"Poesía negra liberada." *Universidad* 4/18:5–6 (1937).
"El mágico prodigioso." *Grafos* (1938).
"Sergio Lifar, el hombre del espacio." *Revista lyceum* 3/9 and 10:3–18 (1938).
"Sobre *Nocturno y elegía*." *Varona* (1939). Pp. 9–10, 28.
"A un doble destino lírico." Preface to *Canción cruzada*, by

Acacia and Aída Hernández Jiménez. Havana, 1940. Pp. 7–13.

La herencia viva de Tagore. Havana, 1941.

"Poesía negra española." *Carteles* 22/9:30 (1941).

"Poda y espiga de lo negro." In *Mapa de la poesía negra americana.* Buenos Aires, 1946. Pp. 7–13.

"Situación de la poesía afroamericana." *Revista cubana* 21:5–60 (1946).

"La poesía nueva." *Cuadernos de la Universidad del Aire,* September 1949. Pp. 51–61.

"Poesía afrocubana." *Revista de la Biblioteca Nacional de Cuba.* 2/4:6–18 (1951).

"La fábula de la serpiente." *Diario de la Marina,* 16 August 1952. P. 4.

Translations by Ballagas

Ballagas' translations from English and French may be found in the following publications:

Ballagas, Emilio, ed. *Mapa de la poesía negra americana.* Buenos Aires, 1946.

———. "Ronsard, ni más ni menos." *Revista lyceum* 7/ 28:5–22 (1951).

Biographical and Critical Studies

Augier, Ángel. Preface to *Orbita de Emilio Ballagas.* Havana, 1965. Pp. 7–18.

Biaín, P. Ignacio. "El alma cristiana de Emilio Ballagas." *Semanario católico* 2014–2015:24–26 (1954).

De la Torre, Rogelio. *La obra poética de Emilio Ballagas.* Miami, 1977.

Feijóo, Samuel. *Azar de lecturas: Crítica.* Santa Clara, Cuba, 1961. Pp. 194–203, 224–225.

Fernández de la Vega, Oscar. "Piedra-Bueno y Ballagas: Recuerdo y homenaje." *El Mundo* (20 September 1959) and *Excelsior* (23 September 1959).

Fernández de la Vega, Oscar, and Alberto N. Pamies. *Iniciación a la poesía afro-americana.* Miami, 1973. Pp. 32–87. Introductory essay and reprints "Situación de la poesía afroamericana" and "Poesía afrocubana."

Fernández Retamar, Roberto. *La poesía contemporánea en Cuba (1927–1953).* Havana, 1954. Pp. 39–43, 54–56.

García de Caturla, Othón. *"Júbilo y fuga:* Poemas angélicos." *El País* (15 February 1932).

Linares Pérez, Marta. *La poesía pura en Cuba y su evolución.* Preface by José Olivio Jiménez. Madrid, 1975. Pp. 83–121.

López, César. "El respeto a la palabra bella." *Revolución* (11 September 1964).

Lunes de revolución 26 (14 September 1959). Articles by Samuel Feijóo, Pablo Armando Fernández, Roberto Fernández Retamar, José Lezama Lima, Virgilio Piñera, and Loló de la Torriente.

Mañach, Jorge. "Ballagas: *Júbilo y fuga."* *El País* (March 1932). In two parts.

Marinello, Juan. *Poética: Ensayos en entusiasmo.* Madrid, 1933. Pp. 49–61, 99–143.

Nandino, Elías. "Estudio y pequeña antología poética de Emilio Ballagas." *Estaciones* 1/2:202–237 (1956).

Pallás, Rosa. *La poesía de Emilio Ballagas.* Madrid, 1973.

Paz, Octavio. "Sabor eterno." *Taller* 2/10:52–53 (1940).

Piñera, Virgilio. "Ballagas en persona." *Ciclón* 1/5:41–50 (1955).

Rice, Argyll Pryor. *Emilio Ballagas: Poeta o poesía.* Mexico City, 1966.

Soler, Clara. "Colaboraciones: Margen infantil a *Júbilo y fuga."* El Mundo (28 February 1932).

Suadíaz, Luis. "Emilio Ballagas, el poeta." *Revolución* (11 September 1964).

Suárez Solís, Rafael. Articles in *Ahora* from 11 December 1934 to 1 January 1935.

Urrutia, Gustavo E. Articles in *Diario de la Marina* from 9 December 1934 to 3 January 1935.

Vitier, Cintio. *Lo cubano en la poesía.* Havana, 1958. Pp. 329–338, 353–354.

———. "La poesía de Emilio Ballagas." In *Obra poética de Emilio Ballagas.* Havana, 1955. Pp. v–xli.

Juan Carlos Onetti

(1909–   )

Hugo J. Verani

Although Juan Carlos Onetti began publishing in 1933, he attracted scant critical attention outside of his native Uruguay until the mid-1960's, when the increased interest in Latin American fiction stimulated by the extraordinary literary creativity of the writers of that decade prompted a reevaluation of the generation of writers that had preceded it. Until then, to read Onetti's works had been a privilege of a small circle of friends; his books were published in limited editions and sold poorly.

Born in Montevideo on 1 July 1909, he lived for two long periods (1930–1934 and 1941–1955) in Buenos Aires, where he published most of his works in relative obscurity. A high-school dropout, married four times, he worked at odd jobs (doorman, waiter, soccer ticket vendor, salesman of tires and adding machines, grain inspector), until becoming a writer for various periodicals and for the Reuters news agency in Buenos Aires and Montevideo, and, finally, director of Municipal Libraries in his native city. In 1974, he was imprisoned by the military dictatorship of Uruguay for participating in a jury that awarded a literary prize to a short story considered pornographic and subversive by the government. His forced exile to Madrid in 1975 brought him visibility and unprecedented critical support. He has gained a long-deserved international recognition through the many new editions of his books published in Spain, new translations, particularly into French and Italian, but also into English, and the granting of the prestigious Cervantes Prize (1980). The genuine excellence of his narrative art and his indispensable role as an originator of the contemporary Latin American novel have been acknowledged by critics and younger writers alike.

Onetti was the first literary director of the weekly *Marcha* (Forward), the respected journal that, from its founding in 1939 until its closure in 1974, voiced the unrest of progressive circles in Uruguay. In "La piedra en el charco" (Ripples in the Pool), the weekly column he wrote between 1939 and 1941 under the pseudonym Periquito el Aguador (Petey Wet Blanket), Onetti posed the problem of the stagnation of Uruguayan letters and insisted on the need for renewals in language and in narrative technique. Caustic statements that invite polemic, the articles aimed to disconcert a conformist, sterile environment, dominated by the epigones of regionalism. Conscious of the limitations of a narrative that in the 1940's still reflected outmoded aesthetic trends, Onetti defined the context of his own generation through his experience as a reader.

In the few critical notes he wrote between 1939 and 1941, collected in *Réquiem por Faulkner y otros artículos* (Requiem for Faulkner and Other Articles, 1975), Onetti, stirred by the fervor of a new relationship with literature, formulated his radical challenge to tradition in a kind of extended literary manifesto that is also a self-affirmation. In these writings, Onetti began the struggle against the mediocrity of the narrative writing of that time, chained as it was to a stagnant rhetoric; he condemned the writers' lack of precision and dedication, insisting on the need to internalize the story and achieve new forms while remaining faithful to human values; he outlined his artistic credo, the basic premises of his narrative art, which he put into practice in his first works of indisputable value: *El pozo (The Pit,* 1939), "Un sueño realizado" ("A Dream Come True," 1941), and *Tierra de nadie* (No Man's Land, 1941). Onetti constantly emphasized the writer's need to assume his vocation as an exclusive activity, a way of life requiring from the creator a total surrender to literature.

The Pit, Onetti's first novel (or novella), is the finest example of his early work. At the same time, it marks a turning point in the style and technique of Latin American narrative; it transcends the regional and the close identification with social types, distinctive traits of Latin American fiction up to that point. The multiplicity of narrative planes, the complex temporal ordering of inner experience, the use of elusive free associations, and the lyrical narrative mode all anticipate the mature Onetti. The narrator is also pure Onetti: a man cut off from human contact, on the edge of despair, who seeks to give meaning to his life through the invention of a fantasy world in the image of his own unfulfilled dreams.

The search for an affective bond constitutes the unifying motif of *The Pit* and of Onetti's subsequent literary production. The pattern that was repeated in his works was made up of several elements: The protagonist is aware of his precarious situation and of his alienation from his human and social surroundings. Remembering his failed attempts to communicate, he faces his incapacity to establish an affective bond. The way out for Onetti's characters is in rebuilding the world, inventing it anew; through creativity, they find the path that leads toward salvation, and yet finally, they return to isolation and total alienation.

In *The Pit,* the interaction of two narrative levels—the life of Eladio Linacero, confined to a room in a boarding house, writing his memoirs, and his projection into his imagination, into inner time—is arranged to give the impression of simultaneity. The deliberate fragmentation of the literary discourse and the superposition of objective and subjective realities (fantasies, desires, recollections, dreams), are attempts to arrest time and, most important, to create a purely verbal universe where there is no need to account for factual experience.

Onetti's narrative evolves from the dualism of reality and fantasy: the radical solitude of the outsider lost in an inhospitable city, unable to find a reason for his sordid life, condemned to invent stories in which his dreams of friendship, love, and power are fulfilled. Situations change, but the novelistic design remains unaltered. With Onetti, narrative becomes a search for self-affirmation that ends in the fragmentation of the self, in a plurality of masks, farces, and mock representation, in an ambiguous probing that frees a multiplicity of disquieting inferences. The representation of a degrading way of living—the consciousness of marginality, the uselessness of effort, the impossibility of love, the inevitability of failure—repeatedly points up the futility of life. To write, to invent, and to dream, however, are artistic answers to the misfortunes of living.

In the ambitious and complex novel *La vida breve (A Brief Life,* 1950), Onetti's masterpiece, the principle that gives artistic continuity to his narrative work is most evident, namely, the conception of literature as an undertaking of the imagination, as an act of inventing one's own reality.

The affirmation of faith in the creative powers of language is a distinguishing feature of the contemporary Latin American novel. Octavio Paz, among others, points out in "Littérature de fondation" that the most important works in contemporary Spanish-American literature are essentially imaginative ones in which the writer attempts the invention or foundation of a world ("Littérature de fondation," *Les lettres nouvelles* 16:5–12 [1961]). This observation confirms Jorge Luis Borges' preeminence, for one of the guiding principles of his short stories is the endless configuration of fictitious universes. But in Gabriel García Márquez' *Cien años de soledad (One Hundred Years of Solitude,* 1967), as in Julio Cortázar's

Rayuela (*Hopscotch,* 1963) and in other novels in which verbal exploration of reality is even more extreme (such as Carlos Fuentes' *Cambio de piel* [*A Change of Skin,* 1967] and José Donoso's *El obsceno pájaro de la noche* [*The Obscene Bird of Night,* 1970]), the authors also attempt to restore language to its original power of creation, to turn the novel into a basically literary experience. Such a literary approach consists of making the very act of creating a novel the subject of narration. The reader of twentieth-century literature is often confronted with a narrative in which several realities are superimposed to create what Marina Mizzau has called "a reality that is continually belied as such and established as fiction" (*La novela experimental,* Caracas, 1969. P. 75).

In *A Brief Life,* the main narrator, Brausen, introduces second and even third orders of reality that modify the initial conditions. The novel is an interweaving of three contiguous stories—Brausen's life, and his gradual evolution into Arce and then into Díaz Grey. The converging development and final fusion of the narrator's triple spatial and mental extension exemplify the prevalent structural principle of Onetti's literary creation. Brausen founds a world (the mythical town of Santa María); he imagines two other ways of life, and these two simultaneous fantasies begin to acquire autonomy, to become independent of their creator, finally displacing the fiction that gave them form. Ultimately, therefore, these worlds are reflected as one literary reality imposing itself upon another.

A novel in the making and a narrator in the process of creating his own reality are sources of complexity and, sometimes, difficulty for the reader accustomed to traditional fiction. As if reflected in a set of facing mirrors, reality branches off into variations of the original story. The novel renews itself endlessly in exploratory reiterations. Each successive episode of *A Brief Life* introduces a variation of the basic conflict, duplicating the preceding fiction in a perpetual symmetry that intensifies Brausen's helplessness and nullifies every effort to shape his own destiny: "Nothing is interrupted, nothing ends; although the nearsighted might be misled with changes of circumstance and character" (*Obras completas,* p. 289).

The novel becomes a stage, and each character plays a part, participating in the absurd, never-ending game of life. The conception of life as a play, the poetics of fiction-within-fiction, and the progressive disintegration of Brausen's personality are the coordinates that give unity to the narrative sequences of *A Brief Life.* By means of his interior duplication and his use of masks, Brausen imposes upon himself an end that alters his passive and routine existence. The act of creation becomes the only reason for being, the mechanism that justifies his life.

A Brief Life is also an example of what is called a novel-within-a-novel. One story serves as the initial phase for the creation of another world, a completely relative one that exists only in the mind of the narrator-protagonist. The ambiguity of *A Brief Life* results from the confrontation of the reality created by the author and the reality created by the narrator's imagination. The fictitious setting of Santa María as well as the characters begin to free themselves from Brausen's influence, displacing him as the generator of fiction.

As Leon Livingstone has studied in a broader context, the technique of fiction-within-fiction and the interior duplication of characters become symbolic statements ("Interior Duplication and the Problem of Form in the Modern Spanish Novel," *Publication of the Modern Language Association* 73:399–406 [1958]). By introducing doubt about the validity of the distinction between the real and the fictional in a universe whose component parts are interchangeable, an author creates a disconcerting perplexity in the mind of the reader.

A Brief Life reflects a conception of existence as a network of brief episodes or stages. For Brausen, life is a series of "little suicides," of "deaths and resurrections," a world in which the transitory quality of life precludes any attempt at human communication or any possibility of establishing an affective bond. For him, invention is the only way to self-realization, the only chance to give meaning to this life or to justify his existence. The world appears as a continuous invention of possible existences, which, once accepted, must be continued until exhausted, until the end of the imagined life is reached and a new variation, a new brief life, begins. The characters are aware that they are playing a part and, having accepted the convention, are obliged to live by its rules. One of the essential tenets of Onetti's narrative art is that life is a farce, a lie, a never-ending game. This idea, sketched by Onetti in his early short stories, emerges some thirty years later as the guiding motif of *El astillero* (*The Shipyard*, 1961).

The inexhaustible game of creation persists throughout *A Brief Life* and culminates in self-creation. Brausen projects the image of his creator, and through the emergence of Onetti as a character in his own novel, we perceive the root of all existence as an act of spiritual creation, an act of love. Brausen gives life to other characters and satisfies his creative urge by incorporating his own creator into the fiction. It is a way of declaring his freedom and of affirming the "real" existence of his imagined world, of postulating the independent destiny of his own creative effort.

A Brief Life has no narrative thread, in the traditional sense of the term; instead, it introduces a series of cyclical mutations of a single image. Onetti does not emphasize the mimetic quality of narrative. The aim of his fiction is not to reflect an existent reality, a factual order, but, on the contrary, to create an essentially fabulated reality invested with mythic significance.

The final two chapters place parallel scenes in a contrapuntal relationship and, in the process, suspend reality. Both chapters remain inconclusive. Onetti himself affirms that *A Brief Life* is an "open" book, and certainly it is a forerunner of Cortázar's *Hopscotch* and Guillermo Cabrera Infante's *Tres tristes tigres* (*Three Trapped Tigers*, 1967)—the two most representative open novels in Spanish-American literature. Thematic tensions are left unresolved, since a definite anecdotal resolution is not forthcoming, and internal relationships remain potent, open to new stimuli. The ending of the novel coincides with the last day of the carnival season, and the relationship between carnivalesque make-believe and existence itself is disconcerting. Life appears transformed into a masquerade, but behind each mask or costume there are only the various transformations of the self, the dissolution of the self into a plurality of masks, the representation of one role after another.

Onetti was extremely productive during the 1950's. Two short novels serve as good examples of his achievement as a storyteller, as a master of the craft of fiction. *Los adioses* (The Farewells, 1954) and *Una tumba sin nombre* (A Nameless Tomb, 1959) clearly reveal distinctive qualities of Onetti's vision: the elusiveness of reality, the impossibility of arriving at the truth of a situation, and the undermining of objective reality.

Los adioses is a masterpiece of the use of ambiguity as an aesthetic principle, of the problematic nature of reading a story. A former athlete goes to a sanatorium in the mountains to be cured or to await death; he is observed by a witness-narrator, a lonely shopkeeper, who guides the reader into a believable version of the athlete's last days. The novel is an example of the relativity of truth; the ambiguity is not incidental but deliberate. The narrator bases his story on his observation and on conflicting reports of other people; he observes, conjectures, speculates, and withholds information. He imagines an erotic relationship between the athlete and the two women who visit him regularly, constructing a story out of few details and much imagination. Dazzled with his role as a storyteller, the narrator invents a story that is readily accepted by the reader for its apparent objectivity, a story in which truth is just one of the casualties. Its major impact comes from the tension between reliable and unreliable narrating, from the impossibility of establishing the boundary between reality and imagination.

The multiplicity of perspectives is most evident in *Una tumba sin nombre*. Divergent points of view are used to tell the story of Rita, a maid exploited as a prostitute, and her funeral in Santa María. The different versions of the same event—all potentially objective, but all emanations of the characters' fantasies—and the telling of "deliberate lies" underlie the endless proliferations of the story. The novel is a further move away from the possibility of capturing truth; it is impossible to determine the exact nature of the story of Rita. Each narrator tells a conflicting version, and these are progressively modified throughout the novel. Elaborating unreliable testimonies of supposedly true events, Onetti underscores that narrating is an exaltation of the powers of imagination, rather than a transcription of reality. On closing the novel, Díaz Grey, the main narrator—frequently Onetti's characters reappear in several novels—does not clear up the ambiguities. On the contrary, he feels pleased to highlight the collective effort to construct a story as the only consolation to the misfortunes of life: "All that matters is that on finishing writing the story I felt at peace, sure of having achieved the most that can be expected from this kind of task: I had accepted a challenge, I had converted into a victory at least one of the daily defeats" (*Obras completas*, p. 1,046).

La cara de la desgracia (The Face of Misfortune, 1960) is another example of Onetti's technical control and stylistic maturity. The story is seemingly simple: a man anguished by his brother's recent suicide accepts the accusation that he has murdered a young, deaf bicyclist at a beach resort, after seducing her, yet he has apparently not committed the murder. The deliberate ambiguity that characterizes Onetti's best work marks this novel. The narrator writes with full knowledge of events but consciously undermines reality; contradictory attitudes are left to the reader to decipher. What the narrator is trying to communicate (a feeling of guilt for his brother's death) is disclosed not directly but through multiple poetic suggestions. The prose possesses many formal attributes associated with poetry: the recurrence of symbolic imagery and allusions, the many symmetries and parallelisms, the appeal to the senses, and the persuasive silence of the characters combine to create a distinctive reality, to reinforce the ambiguity of a situation that demands not logical but poetic apprehension. Through poetic suggestion, the reader becomes aware of the disquieting connotations of living in a world inhabited by misfortune.

Santa María is a fictional provincial town on the banks of the River Plate, a kind of Yoknapatawpha County (William Faulkner is Onetti's favorite writer) that was created by Brausen in *A Brief Life*. The saga of this mythical city reaches its highest elaboration as an unifying center of Onetti's fiction in two other works of the 1960's, *Juntacadáveres* (Corpsegatherer, 1964) and its sequel, *The Shipyard*. Although *Juntacadáveres* was published later, its narrative events are completed in *The Shipyard*.

The title *Juntacadáveres* is an allusion to the protagonist's proclivity to collect aging whores, that is, corpses. In the novel, Onetti narrates two stories. One of them tells the founding of the "perfect brothel," Larsen's dream. For Onetti all activities, no matter how humble or degraded, enrich life, if guided by the zeal for perfection. For Larsen the founding of a brothel is his best answer to life; it is an artist's victory, in the sense that what matters is not the product but the reaffirmation of the creative act as an end in itself. Onetti shares Faulkner's idea of art, as stated in the American's novel *Mosquitoes* (1927): "Art means anything consciously done well, to my notion. Living, or building a good lawn mower, or playing poker" (p. 183). Larsen is forced to abandon his goal; condemned by a self-righteous society as a corrupter of public decency, he is expelled for owning a brothel. His efforts to raise himself above the ordinary in a sordid world are attempts at self-fulfillment. The other story narrates the passionate life of Julita, a demented widow who refuses to accept her husband's death by making his younger brother her lover. Larsen and Julita cling to dreams, but both fail; he is exiled, she commits suicide. Their subversive endeavors to evade the values of a bourgeois society through the fantasies of perfect brothels and idealized relationships are inevitably doomed to failure. Both stories are intertwined and project a typically Onettian vision of the world: the illusory search for perfection and the inability to attain love in a sordid environment in which men and women exist outside conventional boundaries.

With *The Shipyard*, Onetti's art reaches a synthesis; the mastery he exhibits in this novel is unsurpassed in his other works. It is a major work, unfortunately poorly translated into English. Beginning with *The Pit*, Onetti had constructed a narrative universe whose evolution leads, naturally, to a progressive and irreversible disintegration. The static descriptions reduce all actions to mock appearances or semblances of activities. *The Shipyard* is a disturbing metaphor of the gratuity of living in a world built upon senseless illusions. After five years of exile, Larsen returns to Santa María, his lost paradise. He is defeated by old age and skepticism, and in search of a new motivation for living. Determined to assume a responsibility, to accept an indefinite challenge or commitment to avoid facing the oppressive emptiness of his life, Larsen makes the rehabilitation of a ruined shipyard his chief preoccupation. The farce feeds the illusion that he is living with dignity and gives some value to an otherwise meaningless existence. In Onetti's world, everything is condemned to failure, but there is an imperative to persist in searching for a refuge from degradation. The farce, the game, is the only means for an outsider to bring dignity to his marginal existence.

The parody of normal activities is a common device of contemporary literature, employed by such diverse writers as Franz Kafka, Samuel Beckett, and Vladimir Nabokov. For Onetti, parody is the best way to question a society that rejects individuals who do not conform with its categories. It underlines the pathos of marginal men desperately trying to assert their dignity.

Not knowing which way to turn, Larsen invents a series of responsibilities to mitigate a palpable desolation; he accepts the comedy of work, activity, and prosperity, faithfully looking after a ruined shipyard, needing to believe in something. The absurd hope of restoring the shipyard justifies his life. Any activity is acceptable for Larsen; he only looks for an opportunity to assert his identity. He becomes the general manager of Petrus' shipyard, a long-abandoned business, where he routinely pretends to labor furiously, in order to postpone the truth of his insignificance: "Besides this farce which he had literally accepted as employment, there was nothing but winter, old age, nowhere to go, even the possibility of death" (Obras completas, p. 1,105). Larsen works in earnest, reading heaps of old files, stained by rain, taking inventory in empty rooms, writing reports or estimates for the repair of nonexistent ships. He sits under a riddled tin roof, among layers of rust and filth, weeds growing around everything; he breathes the perennially damp air that reeks of latrines, deceit, and icy desolation. Larsen's empty ritual becomes a way to survive, a compensatory self-delusion to reduce the feeling of humiliation. The deliberate game imposes an order, bringing to an imperfect world a provisional perfection; it requires an unconditional plunge into make-believe until the end of the game, until another futile cycle begins.

With Larsen, Onetti stretches to its limit the disintegration of the identity of the self, the jump into otherness. In a world of hostility, desolation, and contempt, he assumes a different role in each of the four places where the novel develops (a shipyard, the city of Santa María, a gazebo, and a shack), as if

time had stood still and he relived, simultaneously, the elusive dream goals of his entire life. Fragile masks invade the empty present. In "The shipyard," he plays the game of power and domination; in "Santa María," he presumes that he still maintains the lost prestige as head of the brothel; in "The gazebo," he attempts an impossible communication with Petrus' demented daughter, modeled on his nostalgia for lost youth, on romantic ideals; in "The shack," he attempts to assert his existence with a new beginning, a last chance at domestic happiness. The cumulative effect of Larsen's interior duplication multiplies his defeat and lends the story its deepest sense of desolation.

The futility that pervades the novel is revealed by its structure. The circularity of the narrative is suggested by the progression of the settings; they maintain the illusion of a flux, of a continuous movement, as if they were closing circles that progressively compress space, trapping Larsen and depriving him of identity entirely, until all hopes to continue are abolished. The novel ends with a typically Onettian rejection of objective knowledge: alternative versions of the same event are given. Larsen either dies of pneumonia or heads north on a boat. Throughout the novel, the narrators undermine external reality; they propose multiple hypotheses and subsequently question or contradict their words, creating a conflictive tension, a suspension of judgment about what actually happened. The deliberately ambiguous ending discredits factual reality, revealing the uncertain nature of reading a novel in which everything is ambivalent and conjectural, in other words, in which everything is an aesthetic experience.

The Shipyard has become an allegory of contemporary society in Uruguay; it is not symbolic, but it is in many ways prophetic. Onetti always subordinates concrete social conflicts to essentially ambiguous situations in alternate and imaginary worlds; he is primarily concerned with subjective individual experiences. However, his narrative parallels the growing decay and breakdown of Uruguayan society. Although there is no direct correspondence between literature and society, The Shipyard is unquestionably a testimony to the historical period in which it was written; it reveals a deep nonconformity with a marginal existence, with a life touched by an uncontainable moral, spiritual, physical, social, and economic degradation.

Onetti's production in the 1970's and 1980's diminished considerably. Only *Dejemos hablar al viento* (Let the Wind Speak, 1979), a title borrowed from Ezra Pound, deserves attention, mainly because it is the book that closes the saga of Santa María. The city burns, consumed by a purifying fire, the ironic cleansing schemed by Medina, the chief of police. The novel is the logical consequence of Onetti's narrative, a self-conscious and parodic reelaboration of the literary conventions of his own fiction. It belongs to a long tradition of literature whose main preoccupation is literature. Beginning with *A Brief Life*, textual self-reference has been commonplace in Onetti's narrative; the rewriting of fiction in order to deliberately expose the artifice of fiction, a major device from *Juntacadáveres* on, is taken to its limit in *Dejemos hablar al viento*. There is a conscious effort to flaunt the constitutive processes of fiction, to write a text that never ceases to allude to its textual condition. The novel reabsorbs and rewrites stories already told and presupposes a reader familiar with the author's tales since the publication of *The Pit* in 1939.

In *Dejemos hablar al viento*, the self-referential modes of writing include the lexical, syntactical, semantic, and structural. Literal quotes from previous works, allusion to earlier situations, the rewriting of plots, and the use of well-known phrases and stylistic tics establish metaphorical associations among different characters and stories, a kinship that is based on parody. The main intertextuality consists in the reformulation of the exemplary model of Onetti's narrative, the founding book, *A Brief Life*. The intercalation of fragments of previous works and the rewriting of plots is deliberate, highlighting the artifice of a self-conscious discourse and ending by subverting the idea of the literary work as a self-sufficient whole. It opens new fictive dimensions in a story where everything is literature, as if Onetti were searching for total self-referentiality.

Onetti's tendency to transport the reader to the realm of the character's fantasy world is at the center of his vision as a writer. Toward the end of *Dejemos hablar al viento*, the management of artifice is deliberately parodic. We are reminded once again of the hide-and-seek games self-conscious novelists play.

Onetti is depicted in the novel, but in the version given almost forty years earlier by Brausen in *A Brief Life*, as the amiable and indifferent clerk who rented him an office in a publicity agency. He is now the judge of Santa María, called upon to investigate a murder and a suicide. This self-representation as a character in his own fiction is an attempt to call attention to the artifice of literature, to convey to the reader the sense that everything is fiction.

Onetti's narrative art is a response to the necessity of justifying existence, of overcoming the limitations of the human condition. Far from being a gratuitous aesthetic game, his work draws its narrative material from the empirical world and, above all, from subjective experiences. But Onetti's narrative universe arises as a fictitious entity distinguished by the projection of his own inner search into the sphere of the imaginary, the sphere of pure invention. "A novel should be integral," says Onetti, and the dominant aspect of his work is indeed the masterly integration of narrative strata—the intimate fusion of content and form, a synthesis that is essential to all art—because it conjoins the inquiry into man's destiny ("I only want to express man's adventure, the senselessness of life" [*Reporter* 25:27 (1961)]) and the need to create a parallel and imaginary world that dominates Onetti's entire work: "I believe that literature is art, a sacred thing. Accordingly, never a means but always an end in itself" (*Acción*, 24 October 1963, p. 19).

SELECTED BIBLIOGRAPHY

First Editions

Prose Narratives

El pozo. Montevideo, 1939.
Tierra de nadie. Buenos Aires, 1941.
Para ésta noche. Buenos Aires, 1943.
La vida breve. Buenos Aires, 1950.
Un sueño realizado y otros cuentos. Montevideo, 1951.
Los adioses. Buenos Aires, 1954.
Una tumba sin nombre. Montevideo, 1959. Reprinted as *Para una tumbe sin nombre.* Montevideo, 1967.
La cara de la desgracia. Montevideo, 1960.
El astillero. Buenos Aires, 1961.

El infierno tan temido. Montevideo, 1962. Short stories.

Tan triste como ella. Montevideo, 1963.

Juntacadáveres. Montevideo, 1964.

Jacob y el otro. Un sueño realizado y otros cuentos. Montevideo, 1965.

Tres novelas. Montevideo, 1967.

La muerte y la niña. Buenos Aires, 1973.

Réquiem por Faulkner y otros artículos. Montevideo, 1975.

Dejemos hablar al viento. Barcelona, 1979.

Presencia y otros cuentos. Madrid, 1986.

Cuando entonces. Madrid, 1987.

Collected Works

Cuentos. Buenos Aires, 1971.

Cuentos completos. Buenos Aires, 1967. Twelve short stories.

Cuentos completos. Caracas, 1968. Ten short stories.

Cuentos completos. Buenos Aires, 1974. Edited by Jorge Ruffinelli.

Novelas cortas completas. Caracas, 1968.

La novia robada y otros cuentos. Montevideo, 1968.

Obras completas. Mexico City, 1970.

Tan triste como ella y otros cuentos. Barcelona, 1976. With a prologue by Joaquín Marco.

Tiempo de abrazar y los cuentos de 1933 a 1950. Montevideo, 1974. Edited by Jorge Ruffinelli.

Translations

A Brief Life. Translated by Hortense Carpentier. New York, 1976.

"Dreaded Hell." Translated by Jean Franco. In *Latin American Writing Today,* edited by J. M. Cohen. Baltimore, 1967. Pp. 34–48.

"A Dream Come True." Translated by Inés de Torres Kinnell. In *Doors and Mirrors,* edited by Hortense Carpentier and Janet Brof. New York, 1972. Pp. 190–203. Also in *The Borzoi Anthology of Latin American Literature,* edited by Emir Rodríguez Monegal. New York, 1976. Pp. 566–576.

"Esbjerg, On the Coast." Translated by Zulema Seligson. *Fiction* 4/3:8–10 (1976).

"Jacob and the Other." Translated by Izaak A. Langnas. In *Prize Stories from Latin America.* New York, 1963. Pp. 307–345. Also in *The Eye of the Heart,* edited by Barbara Howes. New York, 1973. Pp. 267–312.

"Onettiana: Selections from 'Ripples in the Pool' and Other Writings." Edited by Hugo J. Verani; translated by Peter Egelston. *Review* 29:21–25 (1981).

The Pit. Translated by Hugo J. Verani. *Review* 29:26–34 (1981).

The Shipyard. Translated by Rachel Caffyn. New York, 1968.

"Welcome, Bob." Translated by Hanna Edwards. *Odyssey Review* 3/2:192–199 (1963). Also translated by Donald Shaw. In *Short Stories in Spanish,* edited by Jean Franco. Baltimore, 1966. Pp. 83–101. Also translated by Hardie St. Martin. In *Contemporary Latin American Short Stories,* edited by Pat McNees Mancini. Greenwich, Conn., 1974. Pp. 355–364.

Biograpical and Critical Studies

Adams, Michael Ian. *Three Authors of Alienation.* Austin, Tex., 1975. Pp. 37–80.

Aínsa, Fernando. *Las trampas de Onetti.* Montevideo, 1970.

Benedetti, Mario. "Juan Carlos Onetti y la aventura del hombre." In *Literatura uraguayan siglo viente.* Montevideo, 1963. Pp. 76–95.

Brotherston, Gordon. "Survival in the Sullied City." In *The Emergence of the Latin American Novel.* Cambridge, England, 1977. Pp. 60–70.

Concha, Jaime. "Conciencia y subjetivadad en *El pozo.*" *Estudios filológicos de la Universidad Austral de Chile* 5:197–228 (1969).

Cuadernos hispanoamericanos 292–294 (1974). Special issue on Onetti.

Deredita, John. "The Shorter Works of Juan Carlos Onetti." *Studies in Short Fiction* 8/1:112–122 (1971).

Giacoman, Helmy F., ed. *Homenaje a Juan Carlos Onetti.* Long Island City, N.Y., 1974.

Gibbs, Beverly J. "Ambiguity in Onetti's *El astillero.*" *Hispania* 56:260–269 (1973).

Hancock, Joel C. "Psychopathic Point of View: Juan Carlos Onetti's *Los adioses.*" *Latin American Literary Review* 2/3:19–29 (1973).

Jones, Yvonne Perier. *The Formal Expression of Meaning in Juan Carlos Onetti's Narrative Art.* Cuernavaca, Mexico, 1971.

Kadir, Djelal. *Juan Carlos Onetti.* Boston, 1977.

―――, ed. *Review* 16:4–33 (1975), Focus on *A Brief Life.*

Kulin, Katalin. "Reasons and Characteristics of Faulkner's Influence on Juan Carlos Onetti, Juan Rulfo and Gabriel García Márquez." In *Proceedings of the Seventh Congress of the International Comparative Literature Association.* Stuttgart, 1979. Pp. 277–280.

Ludmer, Josefina. *Onetti: Los procesos de construcción del relato.* Buenos Aires, 1977.

Millington, Mark. *Reading Onetti: Language, Narrative and the Subject.* Liverpool, England, 1985.

Prego, Omar, and María Angélica Petit. *Juan Carlos Onetti, o La salvación por la escritura.* Madrid, 1981.

Puccini, Dario. "Vida y muerte como representación en 'Un sueño realizado' de Onetti." *Hispanamérica* 38: 19–26 (1984).

Rama, Ángel. "Origen de un novelista y de una generación literaria." In Onetti's *El pozo,* Montevideo, 1965. Pp. 57–110.

Rodríguez Monegal, Emir. "Onetti o el descubrimiento de la ciudad." In *Narradores de esta América 2.* Buenos Aires, 1974. Pp. 99–129.

Ruffinelli, Jorge. "Onetti antes de Onetti." In Onetti's *Tiempo de abrazar y los cuentos de 1933 a 1950.* Montevideo, 1974. Pp. xi–liv.

_____, ed. *Onetti.* Montevideo, 1973.

Terry, Arthur. "Onetti and the Meaning of Fiction: Notes on *La muerte y la niña.*" In *Contemporary Latin American Fiction,* edited by Salvador Bacarisse. Edinburgh, 1980. Pp. 54–72.

Texto crítico 6/18–19 (1980). Special issue on Onetti.

Verani, Hugo J. "Juan Carlos Onetti." In *Narrativa y crítica de nuestra América,* edited by Joaquín Roy. Madrid, 1978. Pp. 161–197.

_____. *Onetti: El ritual de la impostura.* Caracas, 1981.

_____, ed. *Juan Carlos Onetti.* Madrid, 1987.

Ciro Alegría

(1909–1967)

Antonio Urrello

Ciro Alegría was born of *mestizo* (mixed European and American Indian ancestry) and Irish stock, on 4 November 1909 in Sartimbamba, Huamachuco, in northern Peru, where his family owned a small estate, Marcabal Grande, on the banks of the Marañón River. His father, José Alegría Lynch, occasionally wrote articles for the newspapers of Trujillo, the capital city of the state of La Libertad; in 1935 he wrote a short review of his son's first novel, *La serpiente de oro* (*The Golden Serpent*). Alegría's childhood, spent mostly in northern Peru, was marked by his having as his first-grade teacher the great poet César Vallejo. When he finished primary school, he went to live for a time on the family estate with his grandfather; it was there that he experienced the reality of Peruvian society through contact with the lives of the Indians and *cholos* (half-breeds) of the region.

Once he had finished his secondary education, Alegría began to contribute to the newspaper *El Norte*. At the same time he published some poems and short stories in the literary magazines of Trujillo and began his political participation in the ranks of the Alianza Popular Revolucionaria Americana (APRA), a political party under the leadership of Víctor Raúl Haya de la Torre, and for some time under the parallel influence of José Carlos Mariá-tegui, the founder of the Peruvian Communist party. The APRA advocated reforms in the socioeconomic structures of Peru that maintained a large part of the population, especially its Indian majority, in a state of servitude.

Because of Alegría's militancy and participation in the APRA campaigns, he was arrested in 1931 and sentenced to ten years in prison. In 1932 and 1933 he was freed, reimprisoned after new political activity, and freed again, only to be arrested in 1934 and exiled to Chile, where he endured hardship and grave illness but also became famous as a writer. He won the literary prize of the Nascimiento Publishing Company in 1935 for *The Golden Serpent*. In 1936, gravely ill with tuberculosis, he was interned in San José de Maipo Sanatorium, where during his recuperation he completed his second novel, *Los perros hambrientos* (The Hungry Dogs, 1939), which received a prize from another Chilean publishing company, Editoral Zig-Zag, in 1938. His third novel, the one that would make him famous, *El mundo es ancho y ajeno* (*Broad and Alien Is the World*, 1941), won a prize from Farrar and Rinehart of New York the year it was published. That same year he moved to the United States, where he lived until 1949, working as a journalist and a professor of Spanish-American Literature at Columbia University. In 1949 he moved to Puerto Rico to take a post as a professor, and four years later he took up residence in Cuba, staying in Havana long enough to witness the first stages of the Cuban Revolution. In 1957, the year he married Dora Varona, after twenty-three years of exile, Alegría returned to his native Peru, where he joined the ranks of the Acción Democrática party, a rival of the APRA. He was elected and served as a deputy in the new ranks. Alegría died in 1967.

After receiving the prize from Farrar and Rinehart, Alegría wrote articles, short stories, poems, screenplays, and children's stories but did not produce a major novel, though we know of projected novels such as *Lázaro* (Lazarus, published in its unfinished version in 1973) and "El dilema de Krause" (The Dilemma of Krause). In 1963 appeared *Duelo de caballeros* (Duel of Gentlemen), a collection of stories including some that had been previously published, such as "La ofrenda de piedra" (Stone Offering) and "Calixto Garmendia." Posthumously two books of a very different nature were published: *Gabriela Mistral íntima* (An Intimate Portrait of Gabriela Mistral, 1969) and *La revolución cubana: Un testimonio personal* (The Cuban Revolution: A Personal Testimony, 1973).

The appearance of the works of the essayist Mariátegui was of prime importance to both the political and artistic activities of Peruvian society. During the dictatorship of Augusto B. Leguía y Salcedo, Mariátegui tried to find a way to escape the imperialistic expansion of the world powers as well as to liquidate the remnants of the obsolete feudal oligarchy. Mariátegui, by proposing a socialist solution for the Peruvian economy, inevitably had to face the problems of the Indian population. The solution he proposed was intimately tied to the restitution of the land and of the tools of production to the indigenous communities. The work that Mariátegui proposed for the Peruvian intellectuals was central to the vindication of the Indian majority, and when it came to the literature that portrayed the original inhabitants of Peru, he would reject the idealized approach and the exotic and ornamental framework in which the Indians were presented. His new approach proposed that the natives be depicted within the dynamic of their social context and that their problems be

examined in order to find better alternatives to their exploited condition.

Historically, strong manifestations of this tendency existed from the days of Father Bartolomé de Las Casas. This approach led to two great pioneer works, *Comentarios reales que tratan del origen de los Incas* (*Royal Commentaries of the Incas*, 1609) by the Inca Garcilaso de la Vega and *Primera nueva crónica y buen gobierno* (The New Chronicle and Good Guide, 1936) by Huamán Poma de Ayala. Other works include *Celajes de sierra* (Highland Skies, 1934) and the study *Nuestra comunidad indígena* (Our Indian Community, 1924) by Hilderando Pozo and narratives such as *El padre Horan* (Father Horan, 1918) by Narciso Arestegui, *La trinidad del indio* (The Indian Trinity, 1885) by José Torres Lara, and *Aves sin nido* (*Birds Without a Nest*, 1889) by Clorinda Matto de Turner. However the emphasis on the socioeconomic solution to the problem, as well as the intensity of its approach, would be attained only through the intellectual leadership of Mariátegui in *Amauta* and by the contributors to this very important journal. According to most critics, the works of Alegría, especially *Broad and Alien Is the World*, follow this approach.

The Golden Serpent is a novel of telluric unity that shows the very close relationship between nature and man represented by a series of *cuadros* (scenes) that have as their principal subject the relationship between the omnipresent Marañón River and the population that lives along its shores. The duality of survival and death shows itself to be permanently positive and negative; the power of the river offers not only life and abundance but also death and destruction to the men who inhabit its banks. Only the jungle, where life also is destroyed or multiplies, is the river's rival in determining the destiny of men. The destructive role of nature, the river, and the jungle is clear, especially in the case of the drowning of a group of raftmen, but its protective nature is also evident. For example, Don Osvaldo Martínez de Calderón arrives from Lima with the desire to change the environment and the people, but he comes to a tragic end when the forces of nature eventually destroy him.

Structurally the novel is a fairly loose amalgamation of tales that has as its original nucleus the short story "La balsa"—rejected, according to the author, once by a newspaper in Buenos Aires and a second time as a novella with the title "Marañón" before winning an award in its final version. To the central plot of old Matías and his sons, El Roge and Arturo, other material is added, such as legends, fables, and numerous tales. Many have no direct connection with the central material, but some serve to deepen and enlarge it.

Despite the weakness and the trial and error of these first narrative ventures, and given the variety of material that the author tries to integrate and the weak presence of a narrator who only asserts himself in the final pages, the novel nonetheless offers the reader some glimpses of future promise.

Los perros hambrientos is a novel whose central components are a few sheep dogs and a girl who guard the flock. The dogs—Wanka, Zambo, Güeso, Pellejo, and others—act like human beings: they love, hate, suffer, fight, survive, and die. The reader cannot help but react to them and their tribulations: the disappearance of Güeso, the death of Tinto at the hands of Rafles, and the cruel death by dynamite of Máuser.

The process of personification that began in *The Golden Serpent* is accentuated in *Los perros hambrientos*. Man and beast fight to survive under the same iron fist of the landowner and the system that shamelessly supports their exploitation, all of this in the midst of a terrible drought. Paradoxically, the loyal friend of man turns into his enemy, rebelling and devouring the sheep under their care. The reader encounters intensely violent and crude scenes, such as the death of the boy Damián, the vengeance of Culebrón, and the assault of the shepherds.

Again Alegría employs the technique of amalgamation, using stories both short and extensive; but some of these are independent narrative units joined solely by the tenuous device of a hidden narrator, seriously weakening the narrative continuity. Nevertheless, at times Alegría is capable of powerful effects in constructing extensive pictures of tragic events whose most salient features are injustice and suffering; only when they are assembled in one scene do they acquire their full impact. Often with a restraint in expressing its point, at times with a pathetic voice that dramatizes the author's love for the land and justifies bloody rebellion to defend it, almost always anchored in a realistic framework charged with a strong sense of protest, this novel contains the worst and the best of *indigenismo* (nativism). Also, according to the majority of the critics, the development of this approach, which seeks solutions to the "Indian problem" as well as the acknowledgment of cultural contributions of the natives, reaches its peak in the writing of Alegría in *Broad and Alien Is the World* and José Maria Argüedas in *Los ríos profundos* (*Deep Rivers*, 1958).

Broad and Alien Is the World is the work that won fame for Alegría and made him one of the best-known Spanish-American novelists in the 1940's and 1950's. The novel was reprinted constantly from 1941 to 1983, remaining popular even during the boom period of approximately 1950 to 1980. The narrative begins with a detailed description of the life of the natives of the community of Rumi. This ancient community is threatened by the greed and cruelty of the landowner Don Alvaro Amenábar y Roldán. The Indians are dispossessed of their land in an unjust and illegal manner, and are guided by their leader, Rosendo Maqui, to other less fertile and less productive lands, preferring to maintain their human dignity rather than risk enslavement. The initiation period in the new community is very long and painful, and because of this some of its members abandon Yanañahui in search of another way of life. Again Don Alvaro succeeds in dispossessing the new community. This time under the command of another leader, Benito Castro, the Indians rise and in a bloody and cruel battle are defeated by the army led by Amenábar.

The novel for the most part employs a simple narration, linear and direct, though it does include examples of interior monologues, such as that of Valencio. The work is enriched by means of integrating legendary, historical, and epic aspects. Two temporal dimensions flow together, the legendary and the historical. Through the symbolic memories of Maqui, the past of the Inca culture gathers strength within the novel. The historical dimension is achieved through the introduction of documented facts from Peruvian history, from the colonial period to the 1930's. The spatial dimension encompasses various distinct layers of the Peruvian world, acquiring in this fashion an epic quality.

Both the community of Rumi and that of Yanañahui represent, within the Indian conception, the center of the world, from which various paths branch out. In this way, through the personal histories of various members of the community, the reader discovers and gets to know distinct spaces of the novel and the narrated world at the same time. Benito Castro discovers the city, Augusto Maqui the Peruvian jungle, Amadeo Illas the plantations of coca, Calixto Páucar the mines, and Valencio and Casiana the Andean pastures. The central idea of the novel has been summed up succinctly by the critic Tomás G. Escajadillo: "The community is the only habitable place." This postulate explains and determines the novel's structure. The community is the only place where the Indian can live with joy and dignity, while the rest of the world is "broad and alien." Alegría contrasts life in the outside world with that in the community: the town of Muncha, the center of individualism, darkness, and egotism, with the community of Rumi, where solidarity, companionship, and sharing are the rules to live by. The same contrast is presented through the histories of various characters in diverse and multiple regions of the country. In other words, the contrast is found at both the individual and communal levels, and structurally it gives unity to the novel.

The narration of the dispossessions of the community's lands divides the novel into two narrative cycles. The first is made up of eight chapters and ends with the culmination of the first dispossession, when the community members leave for other lands. The second cycle begins in chapter 9 with the description of life in the new community and lasts until the uprising of the community in chapter 24. The narration of these two cycles is interrupted by various tales that slow down the development of the action, in spite of the fact that all of the tales are more or less tied to the central conflict of the novel, the dispossession of the native communal lands. In *Broad and Alien Is the World* the main narrator is omniscient. He adopts a concrete and deliberate position: he narrates what is substantial and significant and tries not to leave loose ends or unresolved mysteries. In order not to overload the development of the novel, the narrator makes use of fragmentary information, as in a jigsaw puzzle. This narrative technique builds suspense in the story, capturing the reader's interest, since the omniscient narrator tells only what the

reader does not yet know. The narrator adopts both third-person narration, in recounting the flow of Rosendo's memory or telling the life of Fiero Vásquez, and first-person plural narration, adopting the "we" with multiple functions. The two points of view come together in an epic approach.

The characters of the novel can also be placed in two groups, the oppressors and the oppressed. The oppressor's group is represented by Don Alvaro Amenábar y Roldán, lord of the hacienda Umay, and his acolytes, the priest Don Gervasio Mestas, the clerk Iñíguez, and the justice of the peace. Also in this group are weak and greedy men, such as Bismarck Ruiz and the *caporales* (administrators). This group is ruled by selfishness, ambition, and money; all else is secondary to them. Alegría creates some prototypes and seems to preserve all of his creative energy in order to depict an Indian who is not good just because he is an Indian and has a humble attitude, but because he is raised in a developed culture and in a rich historical past. Alegría presents, through the epic and legendary world of the novel, characters with their own styles of life. In the community of Rumi, the Indians enjoy a dignified and peaceful existence working the land. Each member of the community has a specific function within it, living in harmony with nature and other human beings. The destruction of the community highlights the inhumanity of its enemies.

SELECTED BIBLIOGRAPHY

First Editions

Prose Narratives

La serpiente de oro. Santiago, Chile, 1935.
Los perros hambrientos. Santiago, Chile, 1939.
El mundo es ancho y ajeno. Santiago, Chile, 1941.
Duelo de caballeros. Lima, 1963.
Lázaro. Edited by Dora Varona. Buenos Aires, 1973. Unfinished novel.

Nonfiction

Gabriela Mistral íntima. Lima, 1969.
La revolución cubana: Un testimonio personal. Lima, 1973.

Memoirs

Mucha suerte con harto palo. Edited and with a prologue and notes by Dora Varona. Buenos Aires, 1976.

Collected Works

La ofrenda de piedra. Edited by Dora Varona. Lima, 1969.
Sueño y verdad de América. Edited by Dora Varona. Lima, 1969.

Translations

Broad and Alien Is the World. Translated by Harriet de Onís. New York, 1941.
The Golden Serpent. Translated by Harriet de Onís. New York, 1943.

Biographical and Critical Studies

Bonneville, Henry. "Mort et résurrection de Ciro Alegría." *Bulletin hispanique* 70:122–133 (1968).

_____. "L'indigenisme littereraire andin." *Les langues neolatines* 157:1–58 (1961).

Bunte, Hans. *Ciro Alegría y su obra dentro de la evolución literaria hispano americana.* Lima, 1961.

Callan, Richard J. "The Artistic Personality of Demetrio Sumallacta." *Hispania* 45:419–421 (1962).

Collantes de Terán, Juan. "Teoría y esquema en las narraciones de Ciro Alegría." *Estudios americanos* 17/90–91:119–140 (1959).

Cornejo Polar, Antonio. "La estructura del acontecimiento de *Los perros hambrientos.*" In *Ciro Alegría: Trayectoria y mensaje,* edited by Dora Varona. Lima, 1972.

_____. Prologue, notes, and chronology in *El mundo es ancho y ajeno,* by Ciro Alegría. Caracas, 1978.

_____. "La imagen del mundo en *La serpiente de oro.*" *Revista de crítica literaria latinoamericana* 1/2:51–62 (1975).

Corvalán, Octavio. "Ciro Alegría." In *El postmodernismo.* New York, 1961. Pp. 126–134.

Dávila Andrade, César. "Ciro Alegría y su alto y ancho mundo." *Revista nacional de cultura* 29/180:45–48 (1967).

Durand, Luis. "Algunos aspectos de la literatura peruana, hasta Ciro Alegría." *Atenea* 19/210:278–308 (1942).

Endres, Valerie. "The Role of Animals in *El mundo es ancho y ajeno.*" *Hispania* 48/1:67–69 (1965).

Escajadillo, Tomás G. *Alegría y "El mundo es ancho y ajeno."* Lima, 1983.

Escobar, Alberto. "Ciro Alegría's Worlds." *Américas* 15/2:7–10 (1963).

Férreira, João Francisco. *O Indio no Romance de Ciro Alegría.* Porto Alegre, Brazil, 1957.

Galaos, José Antonio. "La tierra y el indio en la obra de Ciro Alegría." *Cuadernos hispanoamericanos* 48/144:387–395 (1961).

Guillermo, Edenia, and Juana Amelia Hernández. "*El mundo es ancho y ajeno.*" In *Quince novelas hispanoamericanas.* Long Island City, N.Y., 1971. Pp. 77–83.

Jozef, Bella. "Dimensión temporal en *El mundo es ancho y ajeno* de Ciro Alegría." In *Libro de homenaje a Luis Alberto Sánchez.* Lima, 1967. Pp. 249–257.

Lazo, Raimundo. "Ciro Alegría." In *La novela andina: Pasado y futuro.* Mexico City, 1971. Pp. 57–69.

Leon Hazera, Lydia de. "*La serpiente de oro.*" In *La novela de la selva hispanoamericana.* Bogotá, 1971. Pp. 173–182.

Lorenz, Günter. "Ciro Alegría." In *Diálogo con Latinoamérica.* Santiago, Chile, 1972. Pp. 213–234.

McGourn, Francis T. "The Priest in *El mundo es ancho y ajeno.*" *Romance Notes* 9/2:224–230 (1968).

Mate, Hubert E. "Social Aspects of Novels by López y Fuentes and Ciro Alegría." *Hispania* 39/3:287–292 (1956).

Onís, Harriet de. "Afterword." In *The Golden Serpent,* by Ciro Alegría. Paperback ed. 1963. Pp. 183–190.

Rodríguez Monegal, Emir. "Hipótesis sobre Ciro Alegría." In *Narradores de esta América 1.* Montevideo, 1969. Pp. 166–174.

Rojas Guardia, Pablo. "Ciro Alegría o el mundo es ancho y ajeno." In *La realidad mágica.* Caracas, 1969. Pp. 59–63.

Sánchez, Luis Alberto. "Notas sobre Ciro Alegría." *Lotería* 136:7–10 (1967).

Spell, Jefferson Rea. "Ciro Alegría, *Criollista* of Peru." In *Contemporary Spanish-American Fiction.* Chapel Hill, N.C., 1944. Pp. 253–268.

Tamayo Vargas, Augusto. "Ciro Alegría, José María Arguedas y la generacion del 30." In *La novela iberoamericana contemporanea: XIII congreso internacional de literatura iberoamericana.* Caracas, 1968. Pp. 125–136.

Tocilovac, Goran. *La comunidad indígena y Ciro Alegría.* Lima, 1975.

Urdanivia Bertarelli, Eduardo. "Para una nueva lectura de Ciro Alegría." *Revista de crítica literaria latinoamericana* 4/7–8:175–181 (1978).

Varona, Dora. *Ciro Alegría: Trayectoria y mensaje.* Lima, 1972.

Vázquez Amaral, José. "Ciro Alegría: *Broad and Alien Is the World.* The Indian in Literature." In *The Contemporary Latin American Narrative.* New York, 1970. Pp. 64–80.

Vilariño de Oliveri, Matilde. *La novelística de Ciro Alegría.* Rev. and enlarged ed. Río Piedras, Puerto Rico, 1980.

Wade, Gerald E., and William H. Archer. "The *Indianista* Novel Since 1889." *Hispania* 33/3:211–220 (1950).

Enrique Anderson Imbert

(1910–   )

Fernando Rosemberg

Enrique Anderson Imbert, born on 12 February 1910 in Córdoba, Argentina, is one of the purest, sharpest writers that country has produced. With integrity and passion, Anderson Imbert has dedicated his life to literature, in the form of teaching, literary criticism, and artistic creation; in each area, he has demonstrated brilliance, depth, and rigor.

Anderson Imbert attended the University of Buenos Aires, where he studied under Amado Alonso and Pedro Henríquez Ureña. He taught at the principal Argentine universities before emigrating to the United States in 1946. He was a professor at the University of Michigan and Harvard University, retiring from the latter in 1980 with the title professor emeritus. Since then he has served as vice-president of the Argentine Academy of Letters.

At an early age, Anderson Imbert dedicated himself to journalism and began to publish essays that reveal a surprising maturity and continue to hold interest and value. In 1940, he abandoned journalism to devote himself to a university career, beginning his work in the fields of literary criticism, theory, and history. In 1942, Anderson Imbert published *Tres novelas de Payró, con pícaros en tres miras* (Three Novels by Payró, with Picaros in the Cross Fire), a study in which the stylistic method—which tries to capture the unique expressivity of a work or an author—was applied for the first time to the analysis of a work by an Argentine writer. In 1948, he published his doctoral thesis, *El arte de la prosa en Juan Montalvo* (The Art of Prose in Juan Montalvo), and in 1954, *Estudios sobre escritores de América* (Studies on Writers of America). Some notable qualities of the author are displayed in these works: discipline, wisdom, sensitivity, and a clean, precise prose style that vibrates and sparkles with similes, images, and metaphors.

Anderson Imbert's subsequent books place him decisively among the most qualified critics and specialists in Latin American literature. A few of his most important works are *Historia de la literatura hispanoamericana* (Spanish-American Literature: A History, 1954–1961), which as of 1984 had gone through nine editions, *La originalidad de Rubén Darío* (The Originality of Rubén Darío, 1967), *Genio y figura de Sarmiento* (Genius and Figure of Sarmiento, 1967), *Estudios sobre letras hispánicas* (Studies on Hispanic Letters, 1974), *La crítica literaria y sus métodos* (Literary Criticism and Its Methods, 1979), *Teoría y técnica del cuento* (Theory and Technique of the Short Story, 1979), and *La prosa: Modalidades y usos* (Prose: Manners and Uses, 1984).

Anderson Imbert's three novels and seven collections of short stories place the author among the most relevant Latin American narrators. Inherent in his works are such key ingredients as fantasy and reality, vitality and imagination. Although the excellence of his writing never wanes, among his most significant titles are the novel *Vigilia* (Awake, 1934), for its dazzling poetic richness; *La locura juega al ajedrez* (Insanity Plays Chess, 1971), his best collection of short stories; and the short story "El Grimorio" (the name of a reputedly magical book from the Middle Ages), the finest single example of his narrative skill.

The first version of *Vigilia* appeared in 1934, the second and definitive version in 1963. The novel takes place in the region of La Plata, Argentina, in 1926 and recounts the adventures of a gang of five adolescents. Each of them has peculiar personal traits, represented in stereotypical form. The differentiations are elaborated for aesthetic effect rather than for psychological motivation. The book is a deliberate and sustained poetic exercise, resulting in a poetic novel that demonstrates not only verbal virtuosity but a lyricism capable of transforming reality. The only character developed in any depth is Beltrán, the protagonist and the axis around whom the tale revolves. The novel unfolds almost exclusively from this character's perspective, either indirectly, through the author's third-person narrative, or directly, by way of interior monologue. Beltrán's diary and the introspective analysis of the author reveal his literary and spiritual anxieties. He experiences the crisis of adolescence with great intensity and suffers his first amorous defeat. Within his hypersensitive and impassioned soul, this failure acquires the proportions of total disaster. In confusion and spiritual darkness, in the midst of despair, Beltrán's passion and very existence are extinguished.

The style of the diary is similar to that of the novel as a whole. Metaphors abound throughout, expressionistic metaphors such as: "A window, boarded over with planks, moaned of its blindness from the corner"; "Beltrán pushed forward, hammering his footsteps, while Basilio followed behind, unnailing them"; "The lye-whitened houses slumbered on their sides, one on top of the other. Some garbage cans told jokes among themselves. In the foreground, an illuminated window kept a vigil, without blinking." An extraordinary range of impressionistic metaphors are to be found as well:

As he advanced across the pavement of the plaza, the stars took refuge behind the cathedral; and the cathedral leaned forward, threatening to fall over like a playing card. Crossing the night sky, an owl suddenly appeared, whose white wings inscribed, as though on a blackboard, a line of unknown meaning—immediately erased by the tail feathers. The towers of the cathedral approached in disorder, in the darkness.

In addition to the poetic style, there are other similarities between the diary of the protagonist and the novel itself. The diary is almost void of real episodes; in it, everything is self-transformed. Likewise, the novel does not contain many concrete events: the descriptive sluggishness of narration subdues the action and stretches it into images and living pictures, into an analysis of sentiments and impressions, into lyrical effusion. Moreover, everything is transfigured by the novel's emotional intensity, its metaphors and transpositions, its dislocated and hallucinatory images.

This parallelism between the intimate diary and the novel suggests yet another correspondence, one that exists between the author and the protagonist. As the diary corresponds to the novel as a whole, the protagonist corresponds to the author. Consequently, the reflections of Beltrán concerning his diary and literature in general are, in reality, the reflections of the author concerning his own novel. Anderson Imbert discussed this device in one of his critical studies, *Qué es la prosa*, referring to the poetic novel: "What the protagonist-poet attempts to do is to present moments of supreme beauty. These moments are as fleeting as the exploits of the hero; but it is *he* who chooses them, *he* who unites them. In this way, the lyric miniature becomes a poem in prose" (p. 55).

There are beautiful poems in *Vigilia*. The finest examples—those that best reveal the aesthetic resources of the author and those in which a certain verbal splendor achieves a plasticity difficult to improve upon—are without a doubt the descriptive poems: the procession of the girls in the forest, the interior of the bordello, shown in slow motion and with the density of a nightmare. It is possible to see the illuminating effects of Miguel Ángel Asturias, Gabriel Miró, and Jules Renard throughout these pages; the extent of the influence of these authors on Anderson Imbert could be the topic of endless debate. Yet these same pages, based on their particular approach to feeling and understanding the world, can as easily be grouped with the work of writers to whom no specific influence can be attributed. Anderson Imbert himself, through his protagonist, recognizes that his work contains traces of James Joyce, Marcel Proust, Jules Renard. Yet these traces represent a natural and even inevitable assimilation of literary processes, which capture, each in their own way, the multiple and hidden aspects of reality.

Because of its literary resources (in particular metaphors and artistic transpositions), its underlying theme (a novel that reflects upon itself), and its aesthetic and lyrical motifs, *Vigilia* is one of the purest expressions of the poetic novel, and as a result of its stylistic force, assortment of images, and emotional intensity, it is one of the most brilliant examples of Argentine literature.

La locura juega al ajedrez brings together fourteen stories and an appendix consisting of very brief narrations, the majority of them fantastic. The work that opens the book, "Qué voy a hacer yo con una guitarra" (What Am I Going to Do with a Guitar?), has a fictitious protagonist, Ángel Wyndham, meet a historical figure, the Argentine writer Macedonio Fernández, portrayed here as a decrepit old man, only weeks before his death. Their chance encounter and an ensuing conversation that touches upon a host of literary themes gradually evolves into a repetition of an earlier meeting, in 1901, some twenty years before the birth of Wyndham. At that time, he had appeared in the form of an angel before the then unknown Dr. Fernández, to reveal to him his literary vocation and the original traits that would later convert him into a writer of the avant-garde. This story, agile and precise, demands a careful reading to capture its fine combination of intelligence and fantasy.

The following short story, "Viento norte" (North Wind), changes its color like a chameleon: it is fantastic and at the same time it is not. An engraving artist sketches the face of the man who will later become his murderer. Shortly afterward, the artist encounters a monument maker in the act of engraving his name onto a gravestone; an argument quickly ensues, after which the premonition is carried out. "Los Dióscuros" (The Dioscuri) differs greatly from

the preceding two stories: it contains neither fantastic nor libertine elements; it envisions an ironic and rough realism that contrasts the tender with the sordid. The present and the past alternate ably and fluidly: the past, full of the happiness of home life and filial tenderness; the present, a hospital room where a father expires after a death agony far too prolonged. The story's brutal conclusion possesses a cruelty and a bitterness rarely demonstrated by the author.

"Manuscrito anónimo sobre un vals triste" (Anonymous Manuscript on a Sad Waltz) is a historic, almost hallucinatory portrait of great plastic strength, which utilizes for its final effect a sudden change in the point of view. One of the characters, the only survivor of an attack and subsequent slaughter after a night of revelry, reveals himself to be the narrator. "El nigromante, el teólogo y el caballero fantasma" (The Necromancer, the Theologian and the Phantom Knight) contains a hidden trap for careless readers. It is not truly a fantastic tale; rather it is a disguised parody of a fantastic tale. "Museo de cicatrices" (Museum of Scars) portrays an old-time *guapo de comité* (henchman) whom the narrator believes to be the reincarnation of a brave warrior who fought in the nation's civil wars one hundred years earlier. "Ovidio lo contó de otra manera" (Ovid Told It Differently) exposes a conjugal crisis. Realistic yet subtly stylized, it fuses strength and lyricism with extraordinary efficacy. The story unfolds in two scenes possessing an almost dramatic structure, based on a dialogue constructed with precision and verisimilitude. Characters, situations, and mood are solidly depicted with economy of expression.

"'Murder'" is an especially revealing story, as it shows the manner in which Anderson Imbert plays with the nature and significance of his fictions. It begins with testimony concerning the violent character of southerners from the United States; after executing a sharp pirouette, the story concludes as an obvious caricature of a detective story. "Sólo un instante, un instante solo" (Only an Instant, One Single Instant) clearly shows two characteristics often encountered in the narrations of the author: literature, as a theme in and of itself, and the difficulty of establishing borders between reality and fantasy. This story is not realistic, nor is it fantastic or strange.

Nonetheless, the final result is realistic. With first-hand knowledge and imagination, the author reconstructs the unique and almost magical moment in which Ricardo Güiraldes feels compelled to write his memorable novel *Don Segundo Sombra.*

"Pejesapo" (Angler) tells the story of an annihilating, erotic relationship, a variation on the vampire theme. Caustic, audacious, even crude in certain dialogues and situations, "Pejesapo" is among the best short stories of the collection because of the self-assuredness, the precision, and the variation with which it is developed. "Esta bestia feroz que . . ." (This Wild Beast That . . .) elaborates the theme of the *runa-uturunco,* the man-tiger of the legends of northern Argentina. In this account, the protagonist is a cultivated man who does not believe in folkloric fantasies. The anecdote is realistic until almost the end, but the last paragraph cautiously insinuates a fantastic metamorphosis: the narrator, confronting the young and desirable teacher of the village, advances upon her decisively, as he feels an increasing hunger and as his teeth and facial hair begin to grow—in short, he is turning into the *runa-uturunco.*

"Glaciar" (Glacier) reveals the profound poet in Anderson Imbert. Prose sections of varied tones—nostalgic evocation, dramatic parlance, lyric effusion—create what is, in effect, a beautiful love poem, as intensely melancholy as an elegy. "Amistad" (Friendship) contains light fantastic ingredients, as well as a strong dose of erudition. The protagonist, an author, tells his audience a story in which another protagonist relates a popular legend. This legend permits the first protagonist to rationally discuss the origins of literature. The tale thus constitutes a learned analysis of the short story genre. The story "La locura juega al ajedrez" is one of Anderson Imbert's most complete and suggestive tales. One man creates another by the efforts of his thinking. The first is named White, the second Black. They pursue a carnivorous and chaotic game of chess in which all the rules are broken and in which ultimately no one knows who is who and there is complete confusion between the good and the bad. To classify "La locura juega al ajedrez" as a fantastic short story is to say nothing at all, for this tale defies facile classification. The work might be described more accurately as allegory, that is, a metaphoric representation of the human condition, with all its contradictions and duplications. Even when seen in this light, the story allows diverse readings: philosophical, psychological, political, and social aspects may each be emphasized.

Overall, the collection *La locura juega al ajedrez* reveals in compressed form what the entire narrative work of the author demonstrates: an artistic excellence that frequently reaches the highest levels to be obtained in short fiction and a diversity that makes it extremely difficult to classify these works, despite the author's self-proclaimed adherence to antirealism and the judgments of critics who would label him a "pure artist." According to one study, Anderson Imbert's very diversity impeded, for some time, the just recognition that his fiction enjoys today. For many readers, this diversity constitutes one of his greatest attractions: the knowledge that a surprise may always leap from his pen.

"El grimorio" is the piece that gives its name to a volume of short stories published in 1961 and translated in 1966 as *The Other Side of the Mirror.* The story consists of a strange adventure experienced by one Professor Rabinovich, a specialist in ancient history. Having finished his university course, he finds himself drained, on the verge of a nervous collapse. He decides to utilize his vacation for the purpose of physical recovery, planning to rest in the mountains of Córdoba. On the way to the train station, Rabinovich discovers a used-book store that he has never seen. He enters, and his attention is captured by a loose-leaf manuscript, written in an unknown language, whose handwriting resembles his own. Suddenly the first lines, which simultaneously promise and warn, become comprehensible.

> Reader, traveling companion, whither will you accompany me? The greater your effort to read me, the greater you will come to understand this story, yours as well as mine. But you will never complete it! Though you were to read unceasingly, you will die before finishing this book. It is well for you to understand this ahead of time: You hold in your hands the Book of No Ending. It is my life.

In fact, the book recounts the life of the legendary Wandering Jew. Rabinovich's curiosity overwhelms him; he abandons his plans to rest, buys the book, and returns to his house to read it. The reading demands a total and uninterrupted denial of self. The last page again refers to the warning of the first and fulfills its prophecy of being a book that never ends. Rabinovich, exhausted and intoxicated from coffee and Benzedrine, collapses.

> Before losing consciousness, he believed that he, Rabinovich, was the Wandering Jew, reading his own book; with his eyes he miraculously wrote it and read it at the same time; and it was *he,* in the final analysis, who was the protagonist, like in a detective novel—too perfect for someone to have been able to have conceived it—in which the assassin turns out to have been the reader himself.

This brief synopsis does not do justice to the richness and vivacity of this story. The identification of the protagonist with the Wandering Jew is not the only theme. There is something more: an image of human existence, of the eternal inquietude of man. The story's principal technical virtue resides in the dexterity with which it incorporates impassioned, erudite material into the narration. For that purpose, the author brings two essential elements into play: a harmonic interweaving of protagonist and supportive materials, and a confident manipulation of varying perspectives, or points of view. The overall coordination of these techniques serves to maintain the unity of the narration. Without it, the story might lose its strict identity, dissolving instead into an ambiguous short story/essay. This magnificent tale, however, explodes into dramatic climax, following a constantly accelerating rhythm of narration, one embellished with poetic and at times playful notes.

Poetry is constantly awake in the prose of Anderson Imbert, whatever his themes may be. Such an attitude toward literature not only derives from a spirit kept constantly fresh; it also reveals this author's terror of all undue solemnity.

Translated from the Spanish by David H. Nagel

SELECTED BIBLIOGRAPHY

First Editions

Essays and Critical Studies

Tres novelas de Payró, con pícaros en tres miras. Tucumán, Argentina, 1942.

Ibsen y su tiempo. La Plata, Argentina, 1946.
El arte de la prosa en Juan Montalvo. Mexico City, 1948.
Estudios sobre escritores de América. Buenos Aires, 1954.
Historia de la literatura hispanoamericana. 2 vols. Mexico City, 1954–1961; 9th ed., 1984.
Qué es la prosa. Buenos Aires, 1958.
Genio y figura de Sarmiento. Buenos Aires, 1967.
La originalidad de Rubén Darío. Buenos Aires, 1967.
Una aventura amorosa de Sarmiento. Buenos Aires, 1968.
La flecha en el aire. Buenos Aires, 1972.
Estudios sobre letras hispánicas. Mexico City, 1974.
El realismo mágico y otros ensayos. Caracas, 1976.
Las comedias de Bernard Shaw. Mexico City, 1977.
Los primeros cuentos del mundo. Buenos Aires, 1977.
La crítica literaria y sus métodos. Mexico City, 1979.
Teoría y técnica del cuento. Buenos Aires, 1979.
La crítica literaria: Sus métodos y problemas. Madrid, 1984.
La prosa: Modalidades y usos. Buenos Aires, 1984.
Nuevos estudios sobre letras hispanicas. Buenos Aires, 1986.

Short Stories and Novels

El grimorio. Buenos Aires, 1961.
Vigilia. Fuga. Buenos Aires, 1963.
El gato de Cheshire. Buenos Aires, 1965.
La sandía y otros cuentos. Buenos Aires, 1969.
La locura juega al ajedrez. Mexico City, 1971.
La botella de Klein. Buenos Aires, 1975.
Victoria. Buenos Aires, 1977.
Dos mujeres y un Julián. Buenos Aires, 1981.

Anthologies

Los duendes deterministas y otros cuentos. Englewood Cliffs, N.J., 1965.
Cuentos en miniatura. Caracas, 1976.
El leve Pedro. Madrid, 1976.
El milagro y otros cuentos. Buenos Aires, 1985.

Translations

"*Awake: An English Translation of Enrique Anderson Imbert's novel Vigilia.*" Translated by Mary H. Lusky. Ph.D. diss., Columbia University, 1977.
Cage with Only One Side [*El gato de Cheshire*]. Translated by Isabel Reade. Reno, Nev., 1967.
Fugue. Translated by Esther Whitmarsh Phillips. Lawrence, Kans., 1967.
The Other Side of the Mirror [*El grimorio*]. Translated by Isabel Reade. Carbondale, Ill., 1966.
Spanish-American Literature: A History. 2 vols. Translated by John V. Falconieri. 2nd ed. Detroit, Mich., 1969.

Biographical and Critical Studies

Ainsa Amigues, Fernando. "Lo imaginario y lo fantástico: Enrique Anderson Imbert." In *Río de la Plata.* Paris, 1984.

Andrade, Renée. "El tema de la dualidad a través de *La locura juega al ajedrez.*" *Alba de América* (California) 2/2–3 (1984).

Avellaneda, Andrés. "Enrique Anderson Imbert: Refutación y práctica del compromiso." In *El habla de la ideología.* Buenos Aires, 1983. Pp. 170–207.

Azzario, Esther A. "La dialéctica creadora de Enrique Anderson Imbert en *La locura juega al ajedrez* y *La botella de Klein.*" *Revista de estudios hispánicos* 16/3:443–452 (1982).

Baker, Armand F. "La visión del mundo en los cuentos de Enrique Anderson Imbert." *Revista iberoamericana* 42/96–97:497–516 (1976).

Blanco Amores de Pagella, Angela. "El cuento en Enrique Anderson Imbert." *La Prensa* (Buenos Aires), 29 June 1980.

Campos, Jorge. "Los cuentos de Anderson Imbert." *Insula* 31/358:11 (1976).

Falconieri, John V. "Introducción." In *Los duendes deterministas y otros cuentos,* by Enrique Anderson Imbert. Englewood Cliffs, N.J., 1965.

Ghiano, Juan Carlos. "Discurso de bienvenida." *Boletín de la Academia Argentina de Letras* 54/171–174:13–22 (1979).

Giacoman, Helmy F., ed. *Homenaje a Enrique Anderson Imbert: Variaciones interpretativas en torno a su obra.* Long Island City, N.Y., 1973.

Lojo de Beuter, María Rosa. "Estudio preliminar." In *El milagro y otros cuentos.* Buenos Aires, 1984.

Lusky, Mary. Introduction to "*Awake:* An English Translation of Enrique Anderson Imbert's Novel *Vigilia.*" Ph.D. diss., Columbia University, 1977.

———. "The Function of Fantasy: Creativity and Isolation as Related Themes in the Fiction of Enrique Anderson Imbert." *Latin American Literary Review* 7/14:28–39 (1979).

Murphy, Allen Forrest, Jr. "Reality and Fantasy in the Creative Literature of Enrique Anderson Imbert." Ph.D. diss., Ohio State University, 1972.

Rosemberg, Fernando. "*Vigilia,* novela lírica." *La Prensa* (Buenos Aires), 3 June 1979.

Zapata, Celia. "En torno al realismo mágico: *Vigilia—Fuga* de Enrique Anderson Imbert." In *Ensayos hispanoamericanos.* Buenos Aires, 1978.

Zárate, Armando. "Anderson Imbert: Odisea y curiosidades de la escritura." *La Prensa* (Buenos Aires), 24 May 1981.

María Luisa Bombal

(1910–1980)

Fernando Alegría

In 1934, María Luisa Bombal published a short novel, entitled *La última niebla* (*The Final Mist*), that revolutionized the narrative art of Chilean women authors. It was her first attempt at writing fiction, and major critics in Argentina, where the novel was published, welcomed it as a great innovative effort. However, many years passed before critics in her native country of Chile fully realized what Bombal had accomplished.

Bombal was born on 8 June 1910, in the Chilean seaside resort of Viña del Mar, near Valparaiso, where her upper middle-class family lived in a comfortable and cultured environment. Her father, Martín Bombal Videla, died when she was twelve, and her mother, Blanca D'Anthes Precht, decided to move with her to Paris. María Luisa attended school at Notre Dame de l'Assomption and at the Lycée La Bruyère. She completed her baccalaureate, with a major in Latin. She then enrolled at the Sorbonne, where she studied literature and philosophy. Her dissertation dealt with the works of Prosper Mérimée. At age fifteen, she wrote a play that was generously praised by the Argentine novelist Ricardo Güiraldes. Referring to those formative years, María Luisa described herself as an avid reader. In an interview with Alfonso Calderón, she said, "My literary life began under the influence of Andersen. Then I discovered *Victoria* by Knut Hamsun, and Goethe's *Werther*, a book about impossible love that, in time, would lose its significance for me due to its rhetorical tightness. I also read Selma Lagerlöf and other Nordic writers, seduced by their mixture of dreams and tragedy, mist and temptations."

She wanted to write, but other artistic disciplines had, at the time, a stronger appeal for her. She studied violin with Jacques Thibaud. Then she joined Théâtre de l'Atelier and took acting lessons with Charles Dullin in a group that included Jean Louis Barrault. What is most important about her experience in France is that Bombal was a witness to the development of the literary avant-garde at a time when key figures of Latin American art and literature were already working in Paris—writers such as Vicente Huidobro, Alejo Carpentier, and Miguel Ángel Asturias, and painters such as Diego Rivera and (Roberto) Matta.

In 1931, Bombal returned to Chile and lived at Los Molles, a country property owned by her family in southern Chile, near the Malleco River. These were times of deep political commotion in her native country. The Chilean navy—sailors and petty officers—rebelled in 1931 against the government in a revolutionary movement that, indirectly, resulted a few months later in the establishment of a socialist

1111

republic, which lasted scarcely two weeks. A de facto junta took power and ruled the country for three months. Bombal left Chile in 1933 and settled in Buenos Aires. She soon realized that, in contrast to the political turbulence she had left behind, Argentina was experiencing what amounted to a cultural renaissance. Powerful young writers had gathered around Jorge Luis Borges and Victoria Ocampo, contributing their work to Ocampo's new journal, *Sur*. In Buenos Aires, Bombal lived in the house of Chilean Consul Pablo Neruda, and through him she met Federico García Lorca and other famous literary figures. Neruda was instrumental in inducing her to work with a sense of discipline. According to Bombal, they worked together in the kitchen, sharing a large table; they showed each other their production and engaged in serious discussions.

In 1934, Bombal married the Argentine painter Jorge Larcos. By that year, she had finished the manuscript of *The Final Mist*. The book was published in a limited edition by Oliverio Girondo under the seal of Ediciones Colombo and included three short stories: "El árbol" ("The Tree"), "Islas nuevas" ("New Islands"), and "Lo secreto" ("The Unknown"). Practically no one remembers this edition anymore. In 1935, Ocampo brought out what amounts to the official first edition of the novel and these stories.

Bombal's husband died, and in 1940 she moved to the United States. In New York she met Count Raphael de Saint Phalle and married him; they had a daughter, Brigitte. Bombal led a productive and exciting literary life in the United States. Her novellas were published in English translation. Bombal rewrote *La última niebla* in English as *House of Mist* and motion picture rights were sold to Paramount Pictures. In 1970, her second husband died, and she returned to Chile.

The publication of *The Final Mist* had surprised everyone in Argentina. The book was totally alien to the traditions of Chilean regionalism, strongly and sometimes brilliantly sustained by the likes of Mariano Latorre, Eduardo Barrios, and Fernando Santiván. It showed no relation to the slow-moving, solidly documented, dramatically inclined type of fiction written by Marta Brunet and her disciples. Bombal's brief novel had a mysterious and poetic aura

about it, a conciseness and adroitness in its fast-moving descriptions, and at the same time a self-conscious ambiguity of language that certainly did not derive from Spanish peninsular novels. Bombal's roots were of a different and distant world. Had she read the works of Virginia Woolf? Most critics answer in the affirmative. Yet if one considers the facts carefully, it is rather improbable that she had. There is no record of her having read Woolf while living in France. Ocampo, who introduced Woolf's works in Argentina, did not begin to publish them in *Sur* until December 1935, and her edition of *A Room of One's Own* came out in 1936. It is possible, of course, that earlier Bombal may have read something by Woolf, either in Europe or in Argentina, and that she had an understanding, however superficial, of the experimental nature of Woolf's work.

Bombal was never a feminist in the current sense of the word. She never joined any movement, political or social, devoted to arguing for women's rights. Gabriela Mistral, who was militantly involved in feminist campaigns, never associated with Bombal and had no literary influence on her. Bombal was not a fighter, but rather an outsider. She never editorialized about anything. She lived in a Chilean bourgeois society heavily dominated by class distinctions and the interplay between machismo and matriarchy and felt deeply hurt by it; she wrote about it with irony, pity, and disillusionment, covering all with a delicate veil of sophistication that almost succeeds in concealing her painful scars. A few lines in her second novel, *La amortajada* (*The Shrouded Woman*, 1938) reveal Bombal's basic feeling about the position of women:

> Why, why is a woman's nature such that a man must always be the center of her life?
>
> Men succeed in applying their passion to other things. But women's destiny is to brood over a love pain in an orderly house, surrounded by an unfinished tapestry.
>
> (p. 142)

In *The Final Mist*, Bombal writes about the state of alienation of both a woman and a man living under the unwritten terms of a fraudulent matrimonial pact. There is no real love between the two, only the acceptance of a situation that, in the high society to which they belong, must be kept under wraps. The man is a widower, haunted by the memory of his first wife. The woman is an artificial figure destined to preside over their stately home in a remote country estate in southern Chile. It is the man who dictates the rules of the game; she submits for social convenience. This state of alienation is the cause of her hysterical neurosis, which includes moments of strong hallucination. He reacts with a cold indifference that is at the same time cruel and morbid. Abandoning themselves to cynical sensuality, they indulge in a sexual relationship that the narrator describes as shameful and perverse.

In a state of hallucination, she finds a lover. Her encounters with him are always lost in a setting of thick mist and darkness. She appears to be in extreme agitation, feverish, unconscious. A series of brutal happenings awakens her from her dream: A servant's child drowns in a pond in which she bathes naked; Regina, her intimate friend, who is thought to live in blessed happiness, having everything that the heroine lacks, commits suicide; suicide tempts her also; suddenly, she recognizes the real face of her husband in its sinister ugliness. Then her lover dies in a mysterious way. We learn that the lover was a blind man who lived in an old house, in which he falls to his death.

The Final Mist is a moving tale of love, mystery, illusion, and disillusion. The reader is left with the impression that the whole episode involving the lover has been the result of a painfully sweet, sad hallucination. But then uncertainty enters in. Perhaps the love affair was real. There were letters written; there was a tree, a street, a garden; there were stairs—secret signs of a real world now dead in the mist that disappeared. This haunting feeling of ambiguity is so masterfully sustained by the narrator that the reader never comes to a clear understanding of the episode. Here lies the power and fascination of Bombal's narrative. One is never aware that the narrator is manipulating the characters and the development of the story. The literary elements flow effortlessly, everything falls into place smoothly, no time is lost in needless descriptions or explanations. Bombal keeps tight control of language and silences.

Amado Alonso, the eminent Spanish critic who lived for years in exile in Buenos Aires, was quick to salute and celebrate Bombal's novel as a masterpiece,

in an article in the journal *Nosotros* (We) in 1936; it was used as a prologue in the first Chilean edition (1941) and in modern editions of the book. After praising her use of language and sure instinct in sketching characters and situations, Alonso emphasizes the "fantastic nature" of Bombal's story: He takes it for granted that the love affair with the blind man has been imagined by the narrator. He says, "Everything that happens in this novel happens within the mind and the heart of a woman who dreams and fantasizes" (*La última niebla*, 2nd ed., Santiago, Chile, 1941, p. 11).

Unintentionally perhaps, in his analysis Alonso has ignored one of the most important factors in Bombal's narrative style: the element of poetic ambiguity. However, he recognizes that Bombal's instinct to discard all that is superfluous in her descriptions is the result of her "poetic conception and sense of structure." He adds, "Once the dreamer has adopted the autobiographical form to attain total identification with the life narrated, she experiences the fearful conflict between dream and reality, somewhat in the manner of Don Quixote in his adventure in the Montecinos cave. Both remember as real that which has been a dream" (pp. 21–22).

In his observations, Alonso pays tribute to Bombal for her admirable fusion of reality and unreality. What is difficult to accept in his analysis, still venerated by some critics, is the assumption that Bombal is the kind of writer she is because she is an extremely sensitive, fantasizing woman. He says, "Hers is the creation and expression of a manner typically feminine and at the same time originally personal in her expression of emotion and sentimental life. . . . It is a primal emotion, born out of the primary impulses of a woman" (p. 25).

The narrator, according to Alonso, is possessed by a passion that cannot find an object, a passion that is like "stagnant water" that becomes more and more poisoned by its own fermentation. This, he adds, symbolizes all the strength and weakness of the novel: "If women live for emotions of the soul, and men for the creations and realizations of the spirit, this narrator has a totally feminine temperament" (p. 27).

Aside from the fact that this assertion smacks of sexism, Alonso seems to be suggesting a feminist reading of *The Final Mist*, something that women critics are practicing today based on entirely different premises. Their point of reference is the social reality in which Latin American women are condemned to live, a reality full of injustices and abusive conventions. Bombal was twenty-one years old when she left Europe with the intention of living in Chile. At that time, Chilean women did not have the right to vote, could not open bank accounts in their own names, needed their husbands' permission to leave the country. No women were seen at the meetings of the Chilean Society of Writers. Among the members of the Society, there was a manifest dislike for Gabriela Mistral, who was identified as a perennial suffragette and laughed at because of her mannish appearance. Bombal was not one to run away from difficulties or to sulk in isolation. She went to Argentina because she was aware of the avant-garde literary movement growing there and because she wanted to be near Neruda.

The feeling of alienation and the ambiguity permeating her novel are forms of protest against society. But, on a deeper level, they are also the expression of a rupture between a woman and the reality in which she is meant to discover the meaning in her life. Lucía Guerra-Cunningham has made particularly lucid observations about this subject. Analyzing Bombal's first novel, she says, "Originated in the basic stratum of the narrative mode, ambiguity in *The Final Mist* is mainly the result of two phenomena: (a) absence of specificity regarding the surrounding reality and the objective temporal element, and (b) elimination of rational and exact limits between the oniric experience, dreaming, and objective reality" (p. 70).

Guerra-Cunningham suggests that ambiguity and subjectivity are connected to a "typical" avant-garde vision of reality. This can be accepted, but not her inference that Bombal's narrative discourse is related to an avant-garde style. A brief comparison between Neruda's *El habitante y su esperanza* (The Inhabitant's Hope, 1926) and Bombal's novel reveals the intrinsic difference that separates a poetic surrealistic narrative from an intuitive psychological one.

The narrator of Bombal's fiction experiences reality as the failure of an overwhelming aspiration to sexual fulfillment. Hers is the defeat of a passion that fails to identify, and thus to possess, its object. Bombal

named Werther as one of the obsessions of her youth: The romantic inevitability of her character's tragedy is akin to the desperation of Goethe's hero.

It would seem that the natural assurance with which the narrator simply, although equivocally, tells her tale owes much to music, that is, to a movement of cadences that surrounds her intimate world and that leads her to fuse dream and reality.

Bombal deftly handles symbols and leitmotiv, playing on certain words and phrases, like playing notes on a musical instrument, to evoke ancient sounds and meanings, ancestral connotations. The reader may recognize, for instance, allusions to Christianity and Druidism in the use of *agua* (water) and *árbol* (tree).

The Final Mist is a moving tale of love, mystery, illusion and disillusion. It is said that Paramount Pictures bought the movie rights to the novel because of its title (*House of Mist*) and the ambiguity of its subject matter (unsubstantiated adultery), but the story was never filmed.

In 1938, Ocampo published the first edition of *The Shrouded Woman* under the Sur imprint. The world of passions, which in *The Final Mist* came out as a secret well of undefined feelings of hurt and desperation, of presentiments and divinations, becomes, in *The Shrouded Woman*, a vibrant discovery of the heroine's senses, an experience of deep suffering in body and soul, expressed in a language of innumerable tones and echoes, surprising for its preciseness and sense of timing.

The couple—Bombal's eternal couple—is no longer the creation of a dream; these are real people who marry and expect to make a lasting union out of an obvious mismatch. She has had an affair and an abortion and is still secretly in love with the man who abandoned her. The young husband, very much in love, doesn't know her secret but senses that she loves someone else. Irked by her rejections, he takes her back to her parents. Then the old game begins. Slowly, painfully at first, she begins to miss the physical power and the considerate tenderness of her husband. She thinks she is discovering a new form of love, a mature understanding and appreciation of the man she has abandoned. She decides to come back, but her husband is no longer the devoted lover. He is still kind and patient, but now sexually indifferent to her. From that point on, they become the couple of

The Final Mist, joined by a shameful and tacit agreement, silently hating each other. With time, even hate disappears, because hate inadvertently has become routine, habit, indifference.

Why did Bombal resort to a metaphor—a dead woman witnessing her own funeral—to give form to the retelling of the old fable so familiar to her? Is it possible that the affair of passion was no longer the real object of her story, but death itself and, as a tour de force, a surrealistic vision of the world beyond? The shrouded woman is a corpse who desperately holds on to life. The narrative device reminds the reader of André Maurois' fantastic tale *Le peseur d'âmes* (The Man Who Weighed Souls, 1931). The woman's last bit of life—a suspended fragment of consciousness—is slowly leaving her body and soon will disappear completely. From the brink of another world, she takes a last look at relatives and friends, people she loved, people she hated, people she observes with detachment now. She becomes the supreme ominiscient narrator. Her voice will be heard beyond the limits of time and over the constraints imposed by conventional feelings. An eye and an ear give testimony: they have memory but no moral commitment.

The shrouded woman's testimony is built on sensory perceptions. She evocatively narrates her awakening to sexual impulses in terms of pure physical sensitivity:

> Then, one night came the revelation.
>
> It was as if from the center of her entrails had risen a boiling, slow chill, growing with every caress, embracing her with rings to the root of her hair, grasping her throat, stopping her breathing, shaking her body until, exhausted and faint, she found herself abandoned in the crumpled bed.
>
> Pleasure! So that was pleasure! That trembling, that immense flap of wings and that falling together into a common shame!
>
> (p. 134)

Her description of how, as an adolescent, she became aware of being pregnant is another example of this sensuous writing:

> What day was it? I can't remember the precise moment when this sweet tiredness began. I imagined that Spring made me languish, a Spring still hidden under the winter soil, breathing already, wet and perfumed through the half closed pores of the earth. I recall. I felt lazy, without wanting anything, body and spirit indifferent, as if already satiated through passion and pain. I thought it was some kind of truce, I abandoned myself to it. . . . I didn't know why the landscape, things, all became an object of distraction, a placidly sensual pleasure: the dark and wavy mass of forest immobile in the horizon, like a monstrous wave at the point of crashing down, the doves' flight, coming and going, leaving shadowy traces on the open book resting upon my knees
>
> (pp. 105–106)

The effectiveness of Bombal's narrative art in this novel depends on the balance between two essential factors: the time frame in which events find an untransferable place, and the structure that, through the use of language, lends that frame the necessary consistency and permanence. Timing is essential in this kind of narrative, and Bombal handles it masterfully. The structure is based on a counterpoint between the first-person and the third-person speakers. The speaking voice slides from one person to the other, without transition or interruption; characters talk in soliloquies, yielding almost absentmindedly to the voice of the shrouded woman's conscience. The impression given to the reader is that of a choir cleverly orchestrated. Again, Bombal's narratives are like musical scores, or perhaps echoes of sounds and voices that at one time had a musical structure. "The Tree" is another good example.

It is difficult to say how conscious Bombal was of manipulating language. At times one notices her deliberate choice of an adjective over a noun, of one verbal form over another. There is never accumulation of words or hesitancy of any kind. That is why we have the feeling that the narrative moves along like a dance in which gestures and attitudes do not admit breaks or indecisions.

The Shrouded Woman begins with the words of an unnamed narrator who avoids the intrusion of the voice and consciousness of the dead woman. Then the shrouded woman's voice takes over. The lead goes back to the narrator for about four pages, and then the dead woman takes over for three pages. This alternation goes on for a while until suddenly we hear a third voice: that of Fernando, the rejected lover.

The narrator helps him along and eventually takes control, until a priest's voice provides important information. At the end, the narrator's voice becomes dominant and, in a grandiose solo, describes the definitive fall into death. The final words have a subdued tone, like that of oboes and strings, a meditative, philosophic fading out: "She had experienced the death of the living. Now she wanted a total immersion, a second death: the death of the dead ones."

I have mentioned "The Tree" in connection with musical influence on Bombal's composition. This short story may well be the quintessence of Bombal's narrative art, an art that caught critics by surprise, as if it had come before its time, strong and fragile, mature from the very beginning and, in its innocence, also a little puerile. In "The Tree," Bombal's basic theme, that of solitude and unmanageable nostalgia, appears in its most dramatic and poignant force. We learn that the solitude of the woman in love without a lover is the other face of a more painful and lasting one: the mythical solitude of the woman-tree, the mother of all, and that her discovery of her hidden roots leads into the majestic, helpless, and sad entrance to the labyrinth of death.

Bombal's art is, in essence, the art of her personal solitude and the power to conjure in her stories the shadows of persons who appear and disappear like leaves in the forest of her childhood and her youth.

Bombal wrote other short stories, including "Trenzas" ("Braids"), "The Unknown," "New Islands," "La historia de María Griselda" (María Griselda's Story), and "La maja y el ruiseñor" (The Maja and the Nightingale).

These stories add little, if anything, to her literary reputation. They seem to reflect her impatience before the vast silence that had begun to engulf her. Some of them were written in her brilliant Argentine period. "María Griselda" and "New Islands" are, in my opinion, the best. Borges praised them, with reason, because there is mystery, fatalism, and fantasy in them, as well as strong traces of Emily Brontë.

Bombal is, like Neruda, a poet of strong atavistic, telluric roots. Intrinsic elements in their creations are the woods, forests, and rains of southern Chile. (See, as an example, a description of the Malleco River in "María Griselda".) Bombal seemed to write from the depths of a remote world that marked her from childhood: a world of gigantic trees, of dazzling climbing plants, and undercurrents.

Her narrative world is a closed one. She had only one story to tell; she told it profoundly and beautifully, then remained silent. She wrote about one woman, one man, and one solitude. The anguish and the hope are the same in all of her stories. The poetic projections of her voice never lost their somber resonance.

It is a tribute to her greatness as a novelist that new generations continue to read and venerate her in spite of the silence and isolation that surrounded her at the end of her life. Many writers, young and old, demanded that the Chilean National Prize of Literature be awarded to her. She never received it.

María Luisa Bombal died on 6 May 1980.

SELECTED BIBLIOGRAPHY

Editions

Prose Narratives

La última niebla. Buenos Aires, 1934. Santiago, Chile, 1941.
La amortajada. Buenos Aires, 1938.

Memoirs

"La maja y el ruiseñor." In *El niño que fue.* Santiago, Chile, 1975. Pp. 15–35.

Collected Works

La última niebla, La amortajada. Barcelona, 1984. Includes "El árbol," "Trenzas," "Lo secreto," "Las islas nuevas," and "La historia de María Griselda."

Translations

House of Mist. Written in English by María Luisa Bombal. New York, 1947.
New Islands and Other Stories. Translated by Richard and Lucia Cunningham. New York, 1982. Includes *The Final Mist,* "The Tree," "Braids," "The Unknown," and "New Islands."
The Shrouded Woman. New York, 1948.

Biographical and Critical Studies

Adams, M. Ian. "María Luisa Bombal: Alienation and the Poetic Image." In *Three Authors of Alienation*. Austin, Tex., 1975. Pp. 15–35.

Agosin, Marjorie. *Los desterrados del paraíso: Protagonistas en la narrativa de María Luisa Bombal.* New York, 1983.

Allen, Martha E. "Dos estilos de novela: Marta Brunet y María Luisa Bombal." *Revista iberoamericana* 18/35:63–91 (1952).

Alone [Hernán Díaz Arrieta]. *Historia personal de la literatura chilena.* Santiago, 1954. P. 234.

Alonso, Amado. "Aparición de una novelista." *Nosotros* 1/3:241–256 (1936).

Blanco, Marta. "La implacable Bombal y sus bondades." *Paula* 204:29 October 1975. Pp. 29–31.

Borges, Jorge Luis. "La amortajada." *Sur* 47:80–81 (1938).

Brown, Catherine Meredith. "Haunted Hacienda." *Saturday Review of Literature*, 3 May 1947. P. 22.

Calderón, Alfonso. "María Luisa Bombal: Los poderes de la niebla." *Ercilla* 5:8 September 1976. Pp. 39–42.

Campbell, Margaret V. "The Vaporous World of María Luisa Bombal." *Hispania* 44/3:415–419, (1961).

Correa, Carlos René. "María Luisa Bombal." *Atenea* 19/199:17–22 (1942).

Debicki, Andrew P. "Structure, Imagery and Experience in María Luisa Bombal's 'The Tree.'" *Studies in Short Fiction* 8:123–129 (1971).

Geel, María Carolina. "María Luisa Bombal." In *Siete escritoras chilenas*. Santiago, Chile, 1953. Pp. 33–43.

Goic, Cedomil. "La última niebla." In *La novela chilena:*

Los mitos degradados. Santiago, Chile, 1968. Pp. 144–162.

Guerra-Cunningham, Lucía. *La narrativa de María Luisa Bombal: Una visión de la existencia femenina.* Madrid, 1980.

Leal, Luis. *Historia del cuento hispanoamericano.* Mexico City, 1966. Pp. 125–126.

Montes, Hugo, and Julio Orlandi. *Historia de la literatura chilena.* Santiago, Chile, 1955.

Natella, Arthur A. "El mundo literario de María Luisa Bombal." In *Cinco aproximaciones a la narrativa hispanoamericana*. Madrid, 1977. Pp. 133–159.

Nelson, Esther W. "The Space of Longing: *La última niebla.*" *The American Hispanist* 3/21:7–11 (1977).

Santana, Francisco. *La nueva generación de prosistas chilenos.* Santiago, Chile, 1949. P. 45.

Torres Ríoseco, Arturo. "El estilo en las novelas de María Luisa Bombal." In *Ensayos sobre literatura latinoamericana*. Mexico City, 1958. Pp. 179–190.

Valdivieso, Mercedes. "Social Denunciation in the Language of 'El árbol.'" *Latin American Literary Review* 4/9:70–76 (1976).

Valenzuela, Víctor M. *Grandes escritoras hispanoamericanas: Poetisas y novelistas.* Bethlehem, Pa., 1974. Pp. 108–109.

Vial, Sara. "María Luisa Bombal: Nuestra abeja de fuego." In *La historia de María Griselda*. Quillota, Chile, 1976. Pp. 57–89.

Vidal, Hernán. *María Luisa Bombal: Le feminidad enajenada.* Barcelona, 1976.

Rachel de Queiroz

(1910–)

Fred P. Ellison

Born on 17 November 1910 in Fortaleza, in the Brazilian state of Ceará, Rachel de Queiroz has for years divided her time between her family ranch at Quixadá and her home as a journalist and writer in Rio de Janeiro, nearly fifteen hundred miles to the south. In 1964, she was her country's representative to the United Nations and in 1977 was the first woman to be elected to the Brazilian Academy of Letters. She and the Bahian novelist Jorge Amado are the two surviving members of a celebrated group of writers from northeastern Brazil who devoted themselves to the novel of social criticism now called "the novel of the 1930's in the Northeast." Deriving from a nineteenth-century form of the regionalist "novel of the Northeast," the novel written by Queiroz and her group falls within the second, or consolidating, phase of the modernist movement, which had its origin in São Paulo in the early 1920's and whose effects could be observed in the articles of the critic Joaquim Inojosa in Recife, Pernambuco, by the mid-1920's (Teles, p. 48).

Although its narrative forms and techniques did not evolve much beyond nineteenth-century models, modernism influenced novelists to abandon older, more rhetorical expression in favor of a new stylistic synthesis much closer to popular speech. An important precursor was the novel A Bagaceira (Trash,

1928), by José Américo de Almeida, a political leader as well as a novelist, who was also influenced by the São Paulo modernists. Published in 1933, Gilberto Freyre's monumental study of the Brazilian family and patriarchal society, Casa Grande e Senzala (The Masters and the Slaves), did much to create interest in northeastern literature and culture.

Queiroz' O Quinze (The Year Fifteen) initiated the new northeastern novel, in 1930. Like Trash, it belongs to the traditional "drought literature" of that corner of Brazil, but in its integration of language and theme it goes beyond Américo's work. Queiroz was too young to remember much about the events, but her family had experienced cyclic drought firsthand in the very bad year of 1915, in the arid backlands around Quixadá, some one hundred miles south of Fortaleza. Fifteen years later, she produced a short, well-written novel that avoided the clichés of earlier drought literature; it won the immediate acclaim of critics in Rio and São Paulo, who were taken with its artistry; they were astonished that a work of such maturity of conception and stylistic innovation could come from a writer only twenty years old. A partial explanation lies in the fact that Queiroz comes from a family that includes as a forebear the romantic novelist José de Alencar and that taught her early the joy of books and the cultivation of writing.

O Quinze tells two stories: one is about the young schoolmistress Conceição and her ill-fated love for her cousin Vicente, a rancher. Conceição eventually rejects Vicente, suspecting (perhaps unfairly) that he, under the patriarchal system that expected relative sexual freedom for men and rigorous chastity for women, has had a casual sexual encounter with the daughter of a ranch hand. In the other story, simultaneous and interleaved with chapters of the love story, the cattle herder Chico Bento and his family are forced to abandon everything and flee to the coast. Their journey costs the life of one of Bento's children. Finally, the family reaches a refugee camp in Fortaleza, where Conceição befriends Chico and agrees to adopt one of the remaining children—she decides that marriage to Vicente and having a family of her own are unthinkable. The drought itself contributes to the tone of the blighted romance. However, the two plots are not as well integrated as they might be, and there are some minor defects in this first novel.

Nonetheless, Queiroz was successful in inventing an "oral style" that is fresh, authentic, and lyrical. From the first, her objective was, as she said in *O Caçador de Tatu* (The Armadillo Hunter, 1967) "to achieve a literary language that will be as close as possible to the spoken language, that is, to what is original and spontaneous as well as rich and expressive in the spoken language. And this spoken language can be the speech of the Northeasterner or the slang of the person from Rio, can be any Brazilian's speech that my ears hear and appreciate" (p. 25).

Displaying some of the stylistic features of its predecessor, her second novel, *João Miguel* (John Michael, 1932), again employs the narrative mode of the omniscient author. Social injustice is satirized through irony and implication. The prisoner João Miguel, downtrodden but self-respecting, is in jail for a murder committed in a drunken brawl. He waits for his case to come to trial and is eventually freed. Freedom is a major theme. The reader meets his friends and acquaintances, a cross section of *sertanejos*, or backlands people, especially women, who are in jail as criminals or as relatives or concubines of the prisoners. It is said that her fellow novelist Graciliano Ramos, the hard-bitten realist and perhaps the most distinguished of all the Northeastern-

ers, preferred *João Miguel* among all of Queiroz' work written during his lifetime.

Queiroz waited five years before publishing her third novel, *Caminho de Pedras* (Rocky Road, 1937), which followed the stylistic lines laid down in the two preceding novels. From 1931 to 1933, she had been active as a communist in her home state, and, in 1937, though she had quit the party, she spent some months in jail as a result of the detention of leftist intellectuals by the government of Getulio Dornelles Vargas (van Steen, pp. 186–187). Her book reflects some of these experiences, artistically and imaginatively transformed. Discovering in leftist politics "the possibilities of freedom," the protagonist Noemi asserts her independence. In the same spirit, she leaves João Jacques, her husband, whom she no longer loves, in favor of Roberto, a communist organizer from Rio. This move brings her almost universal opprobrium, all the more devastating because of the death of her child. At the novel's close, she is pregnant with Roberto's child. Noemi's action is not a challenge to society but rather a step toward her own liberation as an individual.

Queiroz' fourth novel, *As Três Marias* (*The Three Marias*, 1939), is about the education of northeastern girls and young women (with implications for all of patriarchal Brazil). Sex and love are principal themes. In the early 1920's, Queiroz attended the boarding school in Fortaleza that is depicted here. An innovation in this novel is Queiroz' subtle and discerning first-person narration through the character Maria Augusta (Guta), a thoughtful, retrospective view that allows a better psychological understanding of the central character. Some of the novel's space is given over to Guta's first serious love affair, with the Jewish refugee Isaac in Rio de Janeiro. This liaison has a tragic outcome, as do, for a variety of reasons, so many of the schoolgirls' lives chronicled in *The Three Marias*.

In the early 1940's, Queiroz moved with her husband to the Ilha do Governador, an island in Rio's Guanabara Bay. She devoted herself to journalism, including political articles. She wrote *crônicas* (short, often lyrical prose pieces, flexible in form and theme), which were published weekly in Rio in the popular magazine *O Cruzeiro*. She has since become known as one of the creators of this very Brazilian subgenre. Her first book of *crônicas* was *A Donzela e a Moura Torta* (The Damsel and the Cross-eyed Mooress, 1948), which was followed, over the years, by five similar collections. In 1950, she published in serial form in the pages of *O Cruzeiro* her fifth novel, *O Galo de Ouro* (The Golden Cock). Unlike her other novels, its setting is exclusively Rio de Janeiro and the Ilha do Governador, and it introduces a variety of lower-middle-class and proletarian types, many of Afro-Brazilian extraction. The story is ostensibly about Mariano, who ekes out a living sometimes as a seller of numbers in Rio's illegal *jogo do bicho*, a form of gambling, and sometimes as a smalltime cockfighter. However, the novel's real interest lies in the perceptive characterizations of the three women in Mariano's life: Percília, who dies tragically; then Nazaré, who leaves him and their children; and finally Loura, the motherly spouse to whom he ultimately turns. Each dominates the well-meaning but pusillanimous Mariano. The novel is enhanced by the subtle satire of folk religion, notably of spiritualism, as it shapes the lives and determines the plot of *O Galo de Ouro*. Queiroz was dissatisfied with the serially published first version. For the 1985 edition, she completely revised the language, clearly for the better.

In 1975, at age sixty-five, Queiroz published her most recent novel, *Dôra, Doralina*. Because of its artistic elaboration and maturity, many critics consider it the high point of her work thus far. The northeastern setting of its opening and closing sections, its mode of narration, and its insight into the psychology of the narrator, Maria das Dores (shortened to the names Dôra or Doralina), reflect continuity with her earlier work. In her conversation with Edla van Steen, Queiroz called Dôra "the most complex" of all her female characters (p. 190). *Dôra, Doralina* is divided into three books. The first book concerns Dôra's life on the ranch and her marriage to Laurindo. The circumstances of his death suggest murder by Delmiro, Dôra's strange, self-appointed "bodyguard," who was with her when they discovered that her mother, Senhora, had been having an affair with Laurindo. The second book is about Dôra's breaking away (at age twenty-five) from Senhora's "captivity" and the social conformity she demanded, to live her life on the road—which stretches over

much of northern and central Brazil—as an actress and singer with Brandini's Comic Arts Company. The third book centers on Dôra's profound love for Asmodeu, "the Commander," a riverboat captain and smuggler named for a demon—and with something of the devil in him; they live together for some years in Rio. After his death, Dôra sadly goes back alone to the family ranch in Ceará, which is hers following the death of Senhora. The novel is Dôra's re-creation, as a wise and experienced older woman, of the circular journey that has been her life.

In *Dôra, Doralina*, one senses the author's desire to embrace the whole of Brazil, to incorporate into her literary language varieties of Brazilian Portuguese from areas other than her native Ceará, and, above all, to write about a heroine with whom readers throughout Brazil could identify. Present-day feminist critics find Queiroz particularly interesting, despite her lack of enthusiasm for some of their claims: "Nowadays, in our world, it seems to me that the demands are more individual than *sexual*, that is, the demands of the feminine sex. I am a great believer in the individual" (van Steen, p. 190). In a recent study of the "problematic heroines" in Queiroz' novels, Joanna Courteau seems to catch the spirit of Queiroz' own affirmation when she says that her "heroines always remain profoundly human individuals with a problematic, which while being universal remains at the same time uniquely their own."

Queiroz has written two plays in which women figure prominently, and which are based on the time-honored northeastern themes of banditry and religious fanaticism. *Lampião* (premiered in 1953) has been criticized for its handling of the motivation of Maria Bonita. Why has she left husband and children to follow the violent and predatory bandit Lampião (an actual historical figure)? To attribute her behavior merely to "fate" strains our credulity. Though *Lampião* has value as a sociological symbol of violence, he has no redeeming qualities of character, and his death and that of Maria Bonita at the hands of likewise violent and brutal militiamen in the final tableau fail to move us.

Far better in its construction is *A Beata Maria do Egito* (Blessed Mary of Egypt, 1958), which has been acclaimed by critics, who like its greater unity, intensity, and clarity. The setting is a backlands jail in Ceará where Blessed Mary has been incarcerated as a dangerous religious fanatic; the young woman is named for a Catholic saint of Egypt said to have bartered her body to a boatman for a ride across a river in order to continue on a religious pilgrimmage. Queiroz revives the old legend: the police lieutenant falls in love with Blessed Mary and spends the night in her cell. She rejects his offer of marriage, precipitates his death at the hands of his corporal, and continues on her way to aid Father Cícero, a priest famed for his sedition against the government. The unities of time, place, and action focus our attention upon the woman's ambiguous spirituality, set against the lieutenant's romantic passion. In the clash between the representatives of authority and the fanatical country woman, there are echoes of Euclides da Cunha's early-twentieth-century classic *Os Sertões* (*Rebellion in the Backlands*, 1902).

In a career as a writer and journalist that now extends over sixty years, Queiroz has won a permanent place in Brazilian literature. From her beginnings as one of the creators of the "novel of the Northeast" in the 1930's, with an inimitable colloquial literary style, she has also come to be appreciated for her plays and her hundreds of *crônicas*, as well as for her literary translations. She has been especially successful in the creation of characters who reflect her deep understanding of the situation of women, in the society not only of the Northeast but of all Brazil. Many of her personal qualities also characterize her work: above all, her honesty, her simplicity and directness, her sense of humor, her warmth and generosity toward others, and her democratic concern for the individual.

SELECTED BIBLIOGRAPHY

First Editions

Novels

O Quinze. Fortaleza, Brazil, 1930.
João Miguel. Rio de Janeiro, 1932.
Caminho de Pedras. Rio de Janeiro, 1937.
As Três Marias. Rio de Janeiro, 1939.
Dôra, Doralina. Rio de Janeiro, 1975.

Short Prose Pieces (Crônicas)

A Donzela e a Moura Torta. Rio de Janeiro, 1948.
100 Crônicas Escolhidas. Rio de Janeiro, 1958.
O Brasileiro Perplexo. Rio de Janeiro, 1963.
O Caçador de Tatu. Rio de Janeiro, 1967.
As Menininhas e Outras Crônicas. Rio de Janeiro, 1976.
O Jogador de Sinuca e Mais Historinhas. Rio de Janeiro, 1980.

Plays

Lampião: Drama em 5 Quadros. Rio de Janeiro, 1953.
A Beata Maria do Egito: Peça em 3 Atos e 4 Quadros. Rio de Janeiro, 1958.

Later Editions

Individual Works

Caminho de Pedras. Rio de Janeiro, 1976.
O Galo de Ouro. Rio de Janeiro, 1985.
João Miguel. Rio de Janeiro, 1978.
O Quinze. 16th ed. Rio de Janeiro, 1973. Reprints laudatory poem by Manuel Bandeira, drawings by Poty, and critical articles by Adonias Filho and others.
As Três Marias. Rio de Janeiro, 1977. With an introductory study by José Aderaldo Castello.

Collected Works

Quatro Romances. Rio de Janeiro, 1960. Contains *O Quinze*, *João Miguel*, *Caminho de Pedras*, and *As Três Marias*.
Seleta de Rachel de Queiroz. Rio de Janeiro, 1973. With notes and critical study by Renato Cordeiro Gomes.
Três Romances. Rio de Janeiro, 1948. Contains *O Quinze*, *João Miguel*, and *Caminho de Pedras*.

Translations

Dôra, Doralina. Translated by Dorothy Scott Loos. New York, 1984.
Metonymy; or, the Husband's Revenge. In *Modern Brazilian Short Stories*. Translated and with an introduction by William L. Grossman. Berkeley, Calif., 1967. Pp. 27–32.
The Three Marias. Translated and with an introduction by Fred P. Ellison. Austin, Tex., 1963. Paperback reprint, 1985.

Biographical and Critical Studies

Adonias Filho. "Um Drama da Terra." In *Modernos Ficcionistas Brasileiros*. Rio de Janeiro, 1958. Pp. 221–228.

―――. "Rachel de Queiroz." In *O Romance Brasileiro de 30*. Rio de Janeiro, 1969. Pp. 83–93.

―――. "O romance *O Quinze*. In *Modernos Ficcionistas Brasileiros*. 2nd ser. Rio de Janeiro, 1965. Pp. 19–24.

Almeida, José Maurício Gomes de. "O Regionalismo Nordestino de 30." In *A Tradição Regionalista no Romance Brasileiro*. Rio de Janeiro, 1981. Pp. 161–263.

Andrade, Mário de. *"As Três Marias."* In *O Empalhador de Passarinho*. São Paulo, n.d. Pp. 103–106.

Athayde, Tristão de. "Rachel." In *Meio Século de Presença Literária*. Rio de Janeiro, 1969. Pp. 110–114.

Bosi, Alfredo. "Rachel de Queiroz." In *História Concisa da Literatura Brasileira*. 2nd ed. São Paulo, 1977. Pp. 444–445.

Bruno, Haroldo. *Rachel de Queiroz: Crítica, Biografia, Bibliografia, Depoimento, Seleção de Textos, Iconografia*. São Paulo, 1977.

Carelli, Mario. "Un roman épurée: *Dôra, Doralina* de Rachel de Queiroz." *Les langues néo-latines* 76.1/240:83–90 (1982).

Castello, José Aderaldo. "Rachel de Queiroz e o Romance do Nordeste." *Anhembi* 30/89:349–352 (1958).

Castro, Sílvio. "Rachel de Queiroz e o Chamado Romance Nordestino." *Revista do Livro* 6/23–24:107–120 (1961).

Courteau, Joanna. "A Beata Maria do Egito: Anatomy of Tyranny." *Chasqui* 13/2 and 3:3–12 (1984).

―――. "The Problematic Heroine in the Novels of Rachel de Queiroz." *Luso-Brazilian Review* 22/2:123–144 (1985).

Coutinho, Afrânio. "Rachel de Queiroz." In *A Literatura no Brasil 5*. 2nd ed. Rio de Janeiro, 1970. Pp. 219–220.

Delos, Katherine. *"Dôra, Doralina."* *Chasqui* 5/3:77–78 (1976).

Ellison, Fred P. "Rachel de Queiroz." In *Brazil's New Novel: Four Northeastern Masters*. Berkeley and Los Angeles, 1954. Pp. 135–154.

―――. "Social Symbols in Some Recent Brazilian Literature." *The Texas Quarterly* 3/3:112–126 (1960).

Hulet, Claude L. "*A Beata Maria do Egito*: Uma Nova Tragédia por Rachel de Queiroz." In Instituto Internacional de Literatura Iberoamericana. *Memoria del XI Congreso*. Austin and San Antonio, Tex., 1963. Pp. 135–141.

―――. "Rachel de Queiroz." In *Brazilian Literature 3*. Washington, D.C., 1975. Pp. 320–321.

Lima, Herman. "Rachel de Queiroz a Precursora." Introduction to *O Caçador de Tatu*, by Rachel de Queiroz. Rio de Janeiro, 1967. Pp. xix–xxx.

Mimoso-Ruiz, D. "L'Invitation au voyage dans le roman *Dôra, Doralina*." *Les langues néo-latines* 76.3/242:21–41 (1982).

Monteiro, Adolfo Casais. "Rachel de Queiroz." In *O Romance (Teoria e Crítica)*. Rio de Janeiro, 1964. Pp. 223–229.

Montenegro, J. Braga. "Três Romances e Algumas Crônicas" and "João Miguel, Romance?" In *Correio Retardado*. Fortaleza, Brazil, 1966. Pp. 94–98, 180–186.

Nunes, Cassiano. "Análise do Romance Nordestino." In *A Experiência Brasileira*. São Paulo, 1964. Pp. 49–64.

Perez, Renard. "Rachel de Queiroz." In *Escritores Brasileiros Contemporâneos*. Rio de Janeiro, 1960. Pp. 331–346.

Portella, Eduardo, ed. *O Romance de 30 no Nordeste*. Fortaleza, Brazil, 1983.

Queiroz, Rachel de. "Eu Sou Mesmo uma Contadora de Histórias." *Leia* 8/86:12–13 (1985). Interview.

Rónai, Paulo. "Rachel de Queiroz ou a Complexa Naturalidade." *Revista Brasileira de Cultura* 3/10:85–91 (1971).

Schade, George D. "Three Contemporary Brazilian Novels." *Hispania* 39/4:391–396 (1956).

Steen, Edla van. "Rachel de Queiroz." In *Viver e escrever 1*. Porto Alegre, Brazil, 1981. Pp. 179–193.

Teles, Gilberto Mendonça. "A Crítica e o Romance de 30 no Nordeste." In *O Romance de 30 no Nordeste*, edited by Eduardo Portella. Fortaleza, Brazil, 1983. Pp. 39–132.

Woodbridge, Benjamin M., Jr. "The Art of Rachel de Queiroz." *Hispania* 40/2:144–148 (1957).

José Lezama Lima

(1910–1976)

Irlemar Chiampi

Until the 1960's José Lezama Lima was hardly known outside Cuba. With the publication in 1966 of his first novel, *Paradiso* (the English translation carries the same title), he achieved international prominence. The book caused scandal because of the bold descriptions of his characters' erotic activities, admiration for his overflowing erudition, and puzzlement in the face of his obscure, sometimes unintelligible language. These initial reactions soon gave way to acknowledgment of Lezama Lima's aesthetic innovations, which he had been patiently inscribing in puzzling and unclassifiable poems and essays over a period of thirty years. Understandably, Lezama Lima became known as a "difficult" writer, the guardian of arcane poetic secrets, in the modern tradition that includes Arthur Rimbaud and the Comte de Lautréamont, Stéphane Mallarmé and Ezra Pound, James Joyce and Marcel Proust.

Born into a bourgeois creole family on 19 December 1910, Lezama Lima received a law degree in Havana but hardly worked as a lawyer. His poetic vocation had already been revealed in a splendid poem, "Muerte de Narciso" (Death of Narcissus), which he wrote at age twenty-one, and in his multiple activities promoting culture as an editor of literary magazines (*Verbum*, *Espuela de Plata*, *Nadie parecía*, and *Orígenes*). Around the last one, which

was published from 1944 to 1956 and became in its time the best medium to spread texts and modern ideas in the Hispanic world, Lezama Lima assembled a group of talented poets, such as Cintio Vitier, Eliseo Diego, Ángel Gaztelu, and Fina García Marruz, among others; painters and sculptors, such as Amelia Peláez, René Portocarrero, Mariano Rodríguez, and Alfredo Lozano; musicians, such as José Ardévol and Julián Orbón; and philosophers, such as María Zambrano and Guy Pérez Cisneros.

The *origeneists* were not so much a movement as a literary or artistic school. With them Lezama Lima created what he called "a state of poetic competition." Without manifestos or programs, they shared Catholicism and intellectualism, in a philosophical and critical perspective rooted in Neoplatonism and aiming at fusing faith and reason. Their discreet vocation to life in isolation reflected their disillusionment over the dictatorship of Fulgencio Batista, a feeling materialized in their scorn for the official culture as well as self-exile in their own country. In their works they assumed a mystic and philosophical position, similar to the post-avant-garde transcendentalism of the 1940's and 1950's in Hispanic America.

Lezama Lima naturally embodied the ethical awareness and artistic ideal of that group of rare poets. An untiring conversationalist, this huge and asthmatic creole, always smoking a cigar, charismatically officiated as the leading wizard of the sect, projecting the secret Cubanness that the *origeneists* pursued alongside history.

In 1959, with the victory of the Cuban revolution, Lezama Lima joined forces with the new ideals announced by the Sierra Maestra guerrillas. Using his poetic vision, he celebrated the revolution as opening an "imaginary era" that offered "infinite possibilities" and in which "all negative conjurors have been beheaded." In 1960 he was named director of the Literature and Publications Department of the National Council of Culture, and in 1961 he was one the vice-presidents of the National Union of Cuban Writers and Artists.

Ironically, the fight for literary power and the intergenerational antagonism of the new regime's cultural politics eventually turned Lezama Lima into a scapegoat for mistakes of the past. Along with the other *origeneists*, he was the target of a series of attacks and accusations of escapism in his works, and he was unfairly identified with the ideology of Batista's regime, to which the *origeneists* offered a form of opposition. Although Lezama Lima never took the stand of a dissenter nor intended to live in exile, he was ignored until the international success of *Paradiso* partially changed the situation. He could not, however, adapt to the new regime's cultural program and remained solitary to the end.

Misunderstanding seems to have been the common denominator of the situations that made him both a political and a literary case. Never did he surrender to clear messages, social solutions, or recipes for historical action. Lezama Lima's commitment to the great issues of art, history, and culture always materialized aside from ideological fashions, that is, it was always carried out as a hypostasis of poetry, in which the poetic act is the only and absolute cognitive means.

Lezama Lima's works, whether in prose or in verse, form a coherent and organic whole, centered on his devotion to difficulty. One of his most exact postulates is "only what is difficult is stimulating," with which he invites us to the aesthetic experience with verbal obscurity. Never a precious, empty luxury, this experience is rather a profound compromise with remote things, mysterious beings, and mythical events. His five books of poetry obsessively deal with the theme of the invisible world, understood as a transcendence of subjective emotion, historic happening, or simple material reality.

In Lezama Lima's poetry the invisible comprehends the original space, the time of gods and archetypes. In his first three books—*Muerte de Narciso* (Death of Narcissus, 1937), *Enemigo rumor* (Enemy Rumor, 1941), and *Aventuras sigilosas* (Secret Adventures, 1945)—the tone of the poems is reminiscent of beginnings. They celebrate motives from Greek fables and Catholic and esoteric traditions; they make incursions into the fields of sex and sin (man's fall) or treat the theme of a primeval island, the symbol of the creation beginning. One of the most beautiful poems from this phase, "Noche insular: Jardines invisibles" (Insular Night: Invisible Gardens), invokes the world of Genesis within an image of the mythological island as a vast placental night.

> La misma pequeñez de la luz
> adivina lo más lejanos rostros.
> La luz vendrá mansa y trenzando
> el aire con el agua apenas recordada.
> (Enemigo rumor)

The same smallness of light
guesses the farthest faces
Light will come meek interweaving
the air with the water slightly remembered.

In Lezama Lima's conception, the world of Genesis is not a place of harmony and perfection but a nocturnal magma of undifferentiated forms perceived in their proliferation and metamorphosis, as in "Una oscura pradera me convida" (A Dark Meadow Invites Me).

> Allí se ven, ilustres restos,
> cien cabezas, cornetas, mil funciones
> abren su cielo, su girasol callando.
> (Enemigo rumor)

There illustrious remains can be seen,
a hundred heads, trumpets, a thousand functions
open their sky, the sunflower silencing.

The language that inscribes this strange landscape is remarkably baroque, but its aestheticism differs from the one of "Muerte de Narciso." In this poem, the particular manner of the baroque, the gongoristic style, is willfully used by Lezama Lima and made notorious in its striking metaphors, the preciosities of vocabulary (or cultisms), as well as in the latinized syntax, with its dislocated word order. But from *Enemigo rumor* on, Lezama Lima "Americanizes" his baroque style, giving liveliness and eroticism to the network of metaphors, woven with unpredictable analogies, ellipses, and hyperbole, and magic sound effects, consisting of echoes and resonances that simulate music and breathing.

Lezama Lima's baroque Americanness attempts to magnetize sound with meaning, making the poem a living, significant body, dynamized by the sensuality of its images. This type of mystic apprehension of invisible unity through the senses was rightly named *Eros relacionable* (relatable Eros) by Lezama Lima. In this way, his poetry invites us to have an aesthetic experience free from the understanding of meaning, leading us through the enchanting movement of signs toward the whole, which rationality cannot communicate. Gods and fables, myths and origins are not therefore inscribed as the consequence of the representational power of the words, but are represented as simultaneous with them. Perhaps it is correct to say that his poetry carries with it, as Martin Heidegger said about Friedrich Hölderlin, the linguistic foundation of beings: in this poetic operation the verbal act is given back its primitive naming power, through which things substantialize before us, during the very happening of the poem.

From *La fijeza* (Fixity, 1949) onward, Lezama Lima gave his poems a significant turn. This book—which Octavio Paz has considered the inaugural landmark of a "new avant-garde," one that started to look into language in Hispanic America, taking it as "a destiny and choice"—emphasizes the author's concern for the poetic phenomenon. Without abandoning formal obscurity, the theme of his poetry is now poetry itself. In a central poem, "Rapsodia para el mulo" (Rhapsody for the Mule), the poet's duty, to pursue "potencia oscura" (obscure potency), is allegorized in the animal's obstinate, blind march toward an abyss. Like the poet at his work, the mule suffers and resists, by its firm stepping, to advance "en lo oscuro con sus quatro signos" (in the dark with its four signs), until its destiny is fulfilled.

*Con sus ojos sentados y acuosos,
al fin el mulo árboles encaja en todo abismo.*

With its sedate and watery eyes,
at last the mule fits trees into the whole abyss.

Lezama Lima elaborated in his essays the self-reflective or metapoetic aspect of his poetry, which from *La fijeza* to *Dador* (Giver, 1960) had moved from allegory to the clearly conceptual. Like Mallarmé, T. S. Eliot, Paul Valéry, and Jorge Luis Borges, he used criticism and theory in his prose writings to speak indirectly of his own poetic practice. It is useless, however, to expect obvious explanations from his exuberantly erudite essays, which Lezama Lima wrote as a poet, using the baroque and obscure style of his poems. Between 1937 and 1968, he published more than one hundred essays in four volumes, the core of which forms what he called a "poetic system of the world." It is, generally speaking, a theory of image and culture that, brought together, contains his concept of poetry.

The seminal text, which irradiates its fundamental concepts to the others, is "Las imágenes posibles" (The Possible Images), dated 1948 and included first in *Analecta del reloj* (Analecta of the Clock, 1953) and later in *Introducción a los vasos órficos* (Introduction to the Orphic Vases, 1971). The image is taken "as an absolute, the image that recognizes itself as image, the image as the last possible history." A key notion justifies the preeminence of the image to reach the total knowledge: The world—space and time—is a meaningless heap because it has lost the memory of the primeval form; it is, he says, "a breakage with no mnemosyne of what existed before." To overcome such breakage, to fill again the gap is the function of poetry ("knowledge of salvation," he would say), which therefore becomes the only possibility for rescuing the forgotten essential form.

Images are the media to achieve the "progressive apprehension" of authentic beings and, as such, they are semblances that try the impossible. This awareness of the utopia of the poetic act, whose face in writing is verbal ambiguity, is summarized in a paradoxical, but exact, formulation: "The network of images forms the image." In other words, the resemblances woven by the images, in trying to reach the

One and Universal Essence, make a figuration of it. This does not destroy the function of poetic imagination, since this, when concocting a lie, promotes truth free from any and all rational verification.

The claim that the poetic falsity of the image is a different kind of truth comes from the eighteenth-century Neapolitan philosopher Giambattista Vico, recently rediscovered by philosophers of language. Other of Lezama Lima's concepts align with phenomenology or with the Platonic doctrine of ideas, handed down by the theological writings of medieval philosophers; Blaise Pascal and Pythagoras echo here and there. It is difficult to determine with any precision which current of Western thought Lezama Lima embraces. Plural and multiform, the Lezamic manner ("Lezamic" has become an adjective that indicates a whole critical category in Latin America) reinvented Americanness through the appropriation of texts that are devoured and resynthesized so as to shine in a new form.

From the presuppositions of the theory of image, Lezama Lima derived a theory of cultures—a kind of outline of a poetic history of both Eastern and Western civilization—that he called mankind's "imaginary eras." These are made up of long periods of time or archetypal situations that are consolidated in an expressive synthesis through images. To identify such situations, he focuses on myths, fables, rites, concepts of sexuality—in short, significant facts that could be projected beyond geographic limits and historic times.

It was only in 1958 that Lezama Lima managed to formulate this theory in the essay "Las eras imaginarias" (The Imaginary Eras), which appeared in *La cantidad hechizada* (The Bewitched Quantity, 1970). Later on, in essays collected in the same book, he demonstrated his proposition in the analysis of Greek, Egyptian, and Chinese myths, respectively, with "Introducción a los vasos órficos" (Introduction to the Orphic Vases, 1961), "Las eras imaginarias: Los egipcios" (The Imaginary Eras: The Egyptians, 1961), and "Las eras imaginarias: La biblioteca como dragón" (The Imaginary Eras: The Library as Dragon, 1965). He could not complete his proposed concept with other examples from other peoples. However, his theory of 1958 was advanced by the most spectacular of his poetic stories, *La expresión americana*

(The American Expression, 1957). Here four centuries of life and art—from the heroes of the pre-Columbian cosmogenies, through the conflicts of colonization, through the *mestizo* baroque artists, through the romantic rebels of the era of independence, to the popular creole poets—illustrate in a large synthesis how the New World men (including the North Americans, mentioned in the last chapter) outlined their image in history. In this, all of us are characters who, magnetized by the physical space of the continents, are building a new imaginary era for mankind.

It is understandable why *Paradiso* brought fame to its author and impact to its readers. This book, a real summa of Lezama Lima's previous labor, is both a condensation and an expansion of the essayist's complex thinking and of the obsessions of his poetry, now recorded in a narrative structure. "*Paradiso*," he announced, "will allow a new, correct penetration into my previous works." However, if *Paradiso* actually mirrors the road traveled before, the recasting doubles the obscurity of previous poems and prose writings.

The story told in *Paradiso* follows the development of the child José Cemí from the age of five to the age of twenty; he grows up incorporating several influences on his imagination, until he achieves full acquisition of poetic knowledge of the world. In this novel about personality formation, like works by Joyce or Proust, the first part (chapters 1 through 7) narrates life inside a Havana family—parents, sisters, servants, relatives, friends, and neighbors—whose behavior, gestures, characteristics, and manners of speech are seized by the protagonist child; the second part (8–11) shows his adolescence and his sexual dilemmas, mainly the result of his contacts with Fronesis and Foción; the last part (12–14) narrates how Cemí approaches Oppiano Licario—the magus of language, the clairvoyant and eccentric Icarus—who introduces him to the magical rhythm of poetry. When Licario dies, Cemí is ready to reproduce his master's lesson.

Paradiso is the dramatization of the image theory, in which the process of "progressive apprehension" of the Essence is incarnated in the action of a novel. But the novel also includes a theory of Cuban (and, by extension, American) culture, recorded in the perception of flavors and smells, cultural rites, historic facts from the republican period, and the humor and cunning of the creole characters. Paradiso is a mythical island, the locus of love and nostalgia, of invisible gardens that echo Lezama Lima's verses. This monumental novel is also an intellectual and poetic autobiography, recognizable in the course of José Cemí's formation as well as in the mask of the vertiginous and obscure Oppiano Licario.

Lezama Lima's poetic adventure is his most remarkable contribution to the letters of Latin America. As a poet, essayist, and novelist he took the risk proper to the greatest creative ambition by using the unmeasurable as his own measure. Without surrendering to literary fashions or ideological conventions, he brought to the decisive period of the 1950's and 1960's the mark of his essential Americanness, whose aesthetic profile results from the combination of different traditions, a passion for knowledge, and voracious reading. In spite of being recognized now as a great writer, on a par with Borges and Paz, his works urgently need critical and annotated editions to provide a definite exegesis for the future. Until that happens, we may enjoy, in the oddity of Lezama Lima's language, the challenging and mysterious art of his poetry.

SELECTED BIBLIOGRAPHY

Editions

Poetry

Muerte de Narciso. Havana, 1937.
Enemigo rumor. Havana, 1941.
Aventuras sigilosas. Havana, 1945.
La fijeza. Havana, 1949.
Dador. Havana, 1960.
Fragmentos a su imán. Havana, 1977; Mexico City, 1978. Posthumous.

Prose

"Invocación para desorejarse." Orígenes 5/20:22–23 (1948).
Analecta del reloj. Havana, 1953.
La expresión americana. Havana, 1957.
Tratados en La Habana. Havana, 1958.
Paradiso. Havana, 1966.
La cantidad hechizada. Havana, 1970.
Oppiano Licario. Havana and Mexico City, 1977. Continuation of Paradiso. Posthumous.

Letters

Cartas (1939–1976). Edited and with an introduction by Eloísa Lezama Lima. Madrid, 1979.

Collected Works

Antología de la poesía cubana. 3 vols. Havana, 1965. With an introduction.
Obras completas. With an introduction by Cintio Vitier. 2 vols. Mexico City, 1975–1977.
Órbita de José Lezama Lima. Edited by Armando Alvarez Bravo. Havana, 1966. With interviews with the author and a selection of his texts.
Poesía completa. Havana, 1970; Barcelona, 1975.
El reino de la imagen. Edited and with an introduction by Julio Ortega. Caracas, 1981. A very useful edition with a good selection of Lezama Lima's works.

Later Editions

Cangrejos, golondrinas. Buenos Aires, 1977. Contains "Autorretrato poético" and all of Lezama Lima's short stories.
La cantidad hechizada. Madrid, 1974. This volume and the one above reproduce the contents of the first edition of La cantidad hechizada.
Las eras imaginarias. Madrid, 1971.
La expresión americana. Santiago, Chile, 1969; Madrid, 1969.
Introducción a los vasos órficos. Barcelona, 1971. Twelve theoretical essays.
Paradiso. Buenos Aires, 1968; 2 vols., Lima, 1968; Mexico City, 1968; Madrid, 1974; Madrid, 1980.
Tratados en La Habana. Buenos Aires, 1969; Santiago, Chile, 1970; Barcelona, 1971.

Translations

Paradiso. Translated by Gregory Rabassa. New York and London, 1974.

Biographical and Critical Studies

Junco Fazzolari, Margarita. Paradiso y el sistema poético de Lezama Lima. Buenos Aires, 1979.

Ortega, Julio. "La biblioteca de José Cemí." *Revista iberoamericana* 41/92–93:509–521 (1975).

Pérez Firmat, Gustavo. "Descent into *Paradiso*: A Study of Heaven and Homosexuality." *Hispania* 59/2:247–257 (1976).

Review 74: "Focus on *Paradiso*." Fall 1974.

Rodríguez Monegal, Emir. "*Paradiso*: Una silogística del sobresalto." *Revista iberoamericana* 41/92–93:523–533 (1975).

Santí, Enrico Mario. "Párridiso." *Modern Languages Notes* 94/2:343–365 (1979).

Sarduy, Severo. "Dispersión/falsas notas. Homenaje a Lezama." *Mundo nuevo* (Paris) 24:5–17 (1968).

Simon, Pedro, ed. *Recopilación de textos sobre Lezama Lima.* Havana, 1968.

Souza, Raymond D. "The Sensorial World of Lezama Lima." In *Major Cuban Novelists: Innovation and Tradition.* Columbia, Mo., 1976. Pp. 53–79.

———. *The Poetic Fiction of José Lezama Lima.* Columbia, Mo., 1983.

Sucre, Guillermo. "Lezama Lima: El logos de la imaginación." *Revista iberoamericana* 41:92–93:493–508 (1975).

Ulloa, Justo C. "De involución a evolución: La transformación órfica de Cemí en *Paradiso* de Lezama." In *The Interpretation of Hispanic Texts: Current Trends in Methodology,* edited by L. E. Davis and I. Tarán. New York, 1976. Pp. 48–60.

———, ed. *José Lezama Lima. Textos críticos.* Miami, 1979.

Vitier, Cintio. "Crecida de la ambición creadora. La poesía de José Lezama Lima y el intento de una teleología insular." In *Lo cubano en la poesía.* Havana, 1970. Pp. 436–468.

Vizcaíno, Cristina, and Eugenio Suárez Galbán, eds. *Coloquio internacional sobre la obra de José Lezama Lima.* 2 vols. Madrid, 1984.

José María Arguedas

(1911–1969)

Julio Ortega

Possibly the greatest Peruvian novelist of the twentieth century, José María Arguedas is not only a great narrator with a powerful and bold voice, but also an author whose combination of traditional and modern values is characteristic of the artistic revolution in Latin America. Arguedas' understanding of the language and culture of both the Spanish and the Quechua Indians and his persistent efforts to develop an interaction between fiction and anthropological analysis make him a distinctive writer. Functioning outside of existing conventions and literary models, he was an intellectual who, in the same tradition as José Carlos Mariategui, viewed his own awareness as integral to the social and cultural evolution of his country. His suicide, on the other hand, throws a tragic light on his life and work, and although it neither supports nor contradicts them, in his last writing it underlines the profoundly autobiographical nature of all his fiction.

José María Arguedas was born on 18 January 1911, in Andahuaylas, the capital of the province of the same name, in the state of Apurímac, a predominantly Quechua region in the southern range of Peru. His father was a lawyer from Cuzco, whose occupation required him to travel frequently. His mother died when he was not yet three years old. When his father remarried in 1917, José went to live with his stepmother in the town of San Juan de Lucanas. Arguedas later recalled that while his father was away from home he was the victim of the cruelty of his stepmother and her sons and that he fled from them and was protected by the Indians of the community. Through his contact with the natives he not only learned Quechua but was also introduced to their ethical communal values, which had a profound and abiding effect over him. The feelings of desertion and abandonment that dominated his childhood were compensated by the feelings of love and compassion among the Indians—an experience that shaped his cultural and social vision of Peru.

In 1923, according to the author, he accompanied his father on several trips by horse through the sierras of his country. His father died in 1931. Arguedas lived in Abancay, the capital of Apurímac, between 1924 and 1925, and his experience as a student there forms the basis for his great novel *Los ríos profundos* (*Deep Rivers*, 1958). His studies in various locations, including San Juan, Puquio, Ica, and Huancayo, as well as Abancay (where he concluded primary school), attest to the erratic and uncertain circumstances of his life with a traveling father, which is depicted in *Deep Rivers*. In 1931 Arguedas entered the Universidad Nacional Mayor de San Marcos in Lima, and the following year he began working in the post office there, remaining until 1937. In that year he was imprisoned for having protested against Francisco Franco's aggression against the Spanish Republic; he remained a prisoner for almost a year, an experience on which he later elaborated in his novel *El sexto* (The Sixth, 1961), named after the notorious prison in Lima. In 1939 he traveled to Sicuani, Cuzco, where he taught Spanish and geography at the Colegio Nacional Mateo Pumacahua; that same year he married. In 1940 he made his first trip outside of Peru, to Mexico. He suffered a nervous breakdown in 1943. Arguedas worked as a high school Spanish teacher until he returned to the university in 1946 to complete his studies in anthropology, a task he finished in 1948. He traveled to La Paz in 1950 and to Chile in 1951. In 1953 he was named director of ethnic studies at the National Museum of History in Lima.

Gradually, Arguedas' literary and folkloric work became recognized as a new intellectual and artistic vision of the country, and his importance as a writer continued to grow. It was only in the decade of the 1960's, however, after the publication of *Deep Rivers*, that Arguedas reaped full recognition for his artistic talent, both in Peru and abroad. Ironically, that recognition came as his health was waning. At the beginning of that decade, Arguedas had been named director of the Casa de la Cultura, and later a professor at San Marcos and director of the Museum of Anthropology. He was invited to international conferences, and his work began to be translated. Then, in 1966, he attempted suicide, with an overdose of barbiturates; he was saved after several days of treatment and hospitalization and seemed to experience a remarkable recovery, even marrying for the second time, after divorcing his first wife. But on 28 November 1969 he shot himself and died shortly after, on 2 December. "I am retiring now because I feel that somehow I no longer possess the energy and illumination to continue working, that is, to justify life," he wrote in a letter sent to the dean of the Universidad Agraria where he was a professor. A year earlier, in a Lima magazine, Arguedas had announced his position: "I am now once again at the doors of suicide. Because, anew, I feel incapable of fighting well, of working well. And because I do not desire, as I did in April of 1966, to become an inept, sickly person, a lamentable witness of events."

The literary beginnings of Arguedas are particularly interesting, forced as he was to choose between two important alternatives: to write in Spanish or in Quechua. He had begun to write stories as a reaction to the indigenous literature of the 1930's, which was superficial and external; written by authors with no real understanding of indigenous culture. At that time there existed no literature that communicated the depth of emotions and experiences of the indigenous world. Arguedas was exceptionally suited to initiate such a literature because of his bilingualism, but to write in Spanish seemed to violate his experience. On the other hand, he could not write in Quechua because there were no publications in that language and the majority of the Quechua people were illiterate. Arguedas has described the creation of a hybrid literary language, constructed from Spanish speech and Quechua syntax, a style that he spent great effort elaborating. This authentic poetic creation ultimately became a futuristic language, one that all Peruvians would have spoken had they been bilingual or, said in another way, the written Spanish that the natives would have evolved from their own language.

This sole reflection poses Arguedas as a modern narrator in spite of the fact that his chosen theme is traditional rural life. Language is the determining instrument of his works, and their textual drama reveals his poetic and critical disposition. He is a realistic writer because he shows the inside of a forgotten world, but he is also a poetic one, because language is the cultural material with which he gives imaginative shape to his experience. In this sense, Arguedas is an extremely complex writer, not only because of the interior roughness of works based on antagonistic experiences and oppositions, ever present in multi-ethnic Peru, but also because they reflect in part the very nature of Peruvian culture, its indigenous and Spanish alliances, its unequal breeds, its syncretism, in short, its overwhelming indigenous character. The work of Arguedas corresponds to an unofficial cultural project, that is, to the incorporation of Western cultures according to indigenous cultural guidelines. It is in this way that the traditional may become modern without being negated. It is instead affirmed as an alternative art.

Arguedas' literary beginnings were rooted in an

atmosphere dominated by discussions about Hispanism and the indigenous, in the context of the search for a more deeply rooted indigenousness, first articulated by José Carlos Mariategui, and the exploration of possibilities for a national literature. The debate was intense and passionate, although it developed on a narrowly defined intellectual level. Nevertheless, Arguedas is, at least in part, the refined product of the polemical ferment that existed in Peru toward the end of the 1920's, when the social and political experience of the international fiscal crisis inspired intellectuals to search for new modes of expression.

Arguedas' first book, *Agua* (Water, 1935), is a small collection of stories that reveal the most permanent aspects of his style, a style made dramatic by extreme events, by a rich and controlled subjectivity, along with a lyrical vision of the natural milieu, and by communication between man and nature. These stories are refreshing glimpses of indigenous communal life, in effect ethnic reports, but they also contain an element of intimate rebelliousness, a challenge to the traditional social order of Peru—a denunciation of social conditions, but effected through a series of dramatic and psychological situations that were something totally new in Peruvian literature at the time. "Agua," "Los escoleros" (The Students), and "Warma Kuyay" are also partly autobiographical, dealing with a *mestizo* boy (of mixed European and American Indian ancestry) who relates his experiences among the Indians, something he does with critical judgment in the retelling. This double perspective proved a permanent characteristic in Arguedas: the biography is in the action, in the fabula, while the criticism is found in the perspective of the narrator. Arguedas the author cannot separate himself from Arguedas the narrator in these stories, and in the end the author exits the primary plane and participates through his character, through the biography of the indigenous boy. In this technique another characteristic of Arguedas' fiction is revealed: the genres will not be fixed or sacred norms, but instead will become discursive spaces, very open and permeable, where several conflicting discourses coincide.

Yawar fiesta (Bloody Fiesta, 1941; published in English as *Yawar Fiesta*) was Arguedas' first novel. Although it is the most traditional one he wrote, it is also a powerful evocation of the indigenous world, as it uniquely exists in and around Lima. To *Diamantes y pedernales* (Diamonds and Flints, 1954), a short novel about communal life, Arguedas affixed an important prologue in which, with his habitual candor, he discusses the linguistic dramas of his writing. In the meantime he had published a series of works on folklore, beginning with a collection of Andean songs, *Canto kechwa* (Quechuan Song, 1938; translated in English in *The Singing Mountaineers*), that includes another important prologue, "Ensayo sobre la capacidad de creación artistica del pueblo indio y mestizo" (An Essay on the Creative Artistic Capacity of the Indian and Mestizo People; translated in English as "On Andean Fiestas and the Indian"). In collaboration with Francisco Izquierdo Rios, he also published a later compilation, *Mitos, leyendas, y cuentos peruanos* (Myths, Legends, and Short Stories from Peru, 1947), which masterfully conveys the richness of native tradition, both rural and urban. This collection anticipated one of Arguedas' later projects: to describe the cultural transformations of the migration from the mountains to the coast, from the traditional to the modern world. Finally, in 1949 he published *Canciones y cuentos del pueblo quechua* (Songs and Stories of the Quechua People; translated in English in *The Singing Mountaineers*) and *Cuentos mágico-realistas y canciones de fiestas tradicionales en el valle del Mantaro* (Magical-realist Stories and Songs from Traditional Celebrations in the Valley of Mantaro, 1953), still further examples of his efforts to preserve popular art. The designation "magical-realist" is interesting: it announces that Arguedas perceived as innate to the folkloric tale a literary categorization that had already begun to circulate among literary camps in Latin America during that epoch.

From its publication, *Deep Rivers*, Arguedas' great novel, was considered in this very light of magical realism. In the beginning, various critics insisted on the importance of the magical element, on the traditional pantheism, on the presence of nature as a fountain of regeneration. Later, the novel was read as the product of a realist aesthetic: a denunciation of injustice, an exact depiction of social conditions. And, in general, the novel was regarded as a revelation of the Andean world, the beginning of a modern neo-indigenism, and an end to the outdated picturesque treatment hitherto afforded all things native.

But actually Arguedas was also liberating himself from the traditional realist constrictions of the Hispanic American narrative of the 1920's and 1930's, and while his denunciation is more powerful and severe than anything in the work of his predecessors, his literary solution is different, that is, it is far richer in its narrative complexity. In one sense, Arguedas constructed a work parallel to that of Alejo Carpentier and Juan Rulfo; like them, he sought to transform native elements into a literature capable of standing as a self-sufficient art form. He also coincided with both in his need to freely utilize fiction to enlarge the Latin American cultural experience. Like them, he also represents a unique symbiosis of traditional and modern elements. On the other hand, *Deep Rivers* escapes all canonic classifications: it is a moving work born of an unfettered creative impulse, full of humanity and beauty.

The novel begins with the return of a father and son to Cuzco, now occupied by the Viejo (the Old One), a powerful and hated relative. This frustrated return to the patriarchal paradise ("My father's Cuzco . . . couldn't be this one") is an image that hovers over the conflict unleashed by the usurpation of setting and the substitution of sense. The original setting and sense have been exiled, and it is from this exile that the text will evolve as a radical revision of the models in dispute. It is the tale of the apprenticeship of a boy that will frame the acting out of this dispute.

As in Juan Rulfo's *Pedro Paramo* (1955), there is an underlying mythic scheme in the culpability of the Viejo: the distortion of the original space can be deduced through the distortion of the leader. The Viejo "cries out with a condemned voice" and "hoards the fruits of the garden, and lets them rot." The opposition between the two patriarchal figures (father/uncle) is mirrored in the same configuration in the setting: upon the Inca stone mural has been raised the white Spanish wall. The Viejo's house is "on the street of the Inca wall," and even the tree in the patio "is stooped with languid limbs." It is there that a crucial encounter with the "pongo" occurs ("an Indian who freely serves in the house of the master," we are informed by the "narrator-witness"). Ernesto, the "narrator-witness," had not been familiar with these two paradigmatic signs of communica-

tion before this visit to Cuzco. Although reproachfully converted into a public urinal, the Inca wall is restored through an act of communication; its carved stones are transformed in the perception of the child:

> I touched the stones with my hands; I followed the wavy, unpredictable line, like that of the rivers in which the large boulders are found. In the dark street, in the silence, the wall seemed alive, above the palm of my hand the juncture of the stones quivered where it had been touched.

This act of communication is initiated, then, as a ritual of recognition: the child transmutes the cultural material (an Inca monument) into the material of origin (the rivers of his youth). In this way the natural order is established as a finished model that not only implies "nature" or "landscape," but also reintegrates the subject with the natural world in a cultural model, which in turn will essentially be a communication model.

The other paradigm of communication appears in the figure of the Viejo's servant, to whom Ernesto attempts to speak. The humiliation that marks his role as servant negates his very humanity: "One could perceive the effort he made just to seem alive, the invisible weight that labored his breathing." After the communicative exultation the boy had experienced from touching the wall, he directs himself to the servant:

> I spoke to him in Quechua. He looked at me strangely.
> "Can he not speak?" I asked my father.
> "He doesn't dare," he replied. "In spite of the fact that he accompanies us to the kitchen."
> There had been no Indian servants in any of the many towns and villages that my father had visited.
> "*Tayta,*" I said to the Indian in Quechua. "Are you from Cuzco?"
> "*Mánan,*" he answered. "From the ranch."

The emitter here makes use of the common code (Quechua), but the receiver lacks a part in the communication, something that would distinguish him as a specific being: his role as a servant has excluded him from the speech act. And even when he responds, he defines himself through his association with an economic system, the ranch, which reflects his dominated nature. He is denied the use of speech in terms of distinctive communication: social stratification imposes a distortion on the act of communication, establishing among men a different speech practice, one that sanctions some and manipulates others. In *Deep Rivers* the complexity of this conflict and distortion supports the powerful denunciation of usurped speech.

Multiple communication (listening to the call of things, naming them, speaking to them, but also internalizing and discerning their meaning like a decoded alphabet) opens up a dual space, typically ambivalent. One space delineates fortune, the other suffering. Cuzco itself has a dual existence: it includes the signs of a fractured and dominated alphabet and the signs of the dominant code. "In no place does the human creature suffer more severely," it is concluded. The same constructions form part of the agonist and polar structure. In their reading of these cultural monuments, father and son read the cosmic discourse, both eschatological and moral; and this reading is made from a perspective that includes the lessons of the Andean world and the evidences of Hispanic culture, a perspective that we can call cultured but without deducing from it a homogenous culturization, the cross-breeding of both cultural sources. Instead it is a syncretic perspective that the child imparts derived from semantic fields present in the Andean origin.

Quechua in this novel is an authenticating element. It is evident that a Quechuan ontology (its character of a co-informative source along with Spanish, its sustaining reserve) is manifested in a typology of communication that corresponds to the first paradigm, or the model of natural communication. Being an oral language, and at the same time a socially rejected language, it occurs as a cultural unraveling: it reveals the original "natural being" of the speakers; and for that reason its expressive function is also appellative. In Quechua there is an "I" speaking that looks to communicate as a "we": in the act of its occurrence the ethnic identification of the speakers is manifested.

Quechua also fulfills other communicative functions. On one level it provides a distinct etymological, linguistic source; on a second level it multiplies the meaning of the discourse: the text adheres to the mediations of Quechua (in the dialogue and in the songs) not only as testimony to the native world, but also as self-expansion through bilingualism (the recourse of feedback).

This is, then, the original purpose conceived by Arguedas: to create a text about communication, to dramatize his social existence, to re-elaborate his latent identity, his possible plenitude; and, moreover, to create it with unequal materials relative to a situation of fractured communication, the stratification of communication, and social violence about speech and freedom. From the perspective of this critique, the novel generates its utopian postulate: a cultural, pluralist communication.

After *Deep Rivers*, Arguedas wrote *El sexto*, a description of prison life filled with pathos. After showing the violent humanity of the brutally sentenced men, he closes by offering a symbolic image of his country: the different representatives of the various cultural regions in Peru brought together in the prison, along with their political views and their profound divisions.

Todas las sangres (All the Races, 1964) is an ambitious novel, although limited by an obtrusive, final schematic. Here, Arguedas tries to depict the intimate separations of his country through the confrontation of two brothers: one, a traditional landowner who assumes a patriarchal role with the Indians; the other, a modern miner, who represents the country's dependence on foreign influence, on reckless modernization. Occupying a middle position between the brothers is Rendon Wilka, an everyday hero who leads his own band of followers. The novel contains passages of extraordinary beauty and expressive power, as on the first page where the father, an old property owner, curses his sons from the tower of a church in the public plaza. Also it is excellent in terms of the vivid social depiction of its characters; the impoverished man, the upper classes, the mixture of power and race are analyzed and represented by Arguedas with great conviction. It is, in effect, a novel of all the races in Peru, and, in this sense, a tragic vision of the racial conflicts that divide the country.

Amor mundo y todos los cuentos de José María Arguedas (Love World and Other Stories by José María Arguedas, 1967) introduces a disturbing variant, the traumatic perception of sex. More fiction with autobiographical dimensions, these stories seek to exorcise the violence of the erotic tale, demonstrating to what extent the traditional, rural perceptions affected Arguedas' world vision, where sex is a natural form of communal existence.

In his last years, Arguedas worked on a novel about the industrial port of Chimbote. He wanted to describe the life of the villagers who, upon immigrating to find work in the fish-harvesting industry, were culturally and socially transformed. But the transformation is actually that of modern Peru, so that the narrator and anthropologist participate jointly in this new account, although at times they do conflict. *El zorro de arriba y el zorro de abajo* (The Fox Above and the Fox Below, 1971) was the title finally given this posthumous book, left incomplete by the author, or completed in a tragic manner with his own suicide. In effect, the fictional portion of the narrative is connected through a series of "diaries" in which Arguedas realizes his struggle against suicide.

The book consists of three diaries and a "Final Entry?," in which the author establishes the final balance and decides in favor of his death. Between these diaries the author has composed, with great difficulty, a novel that must remain inconclusive. There is no fictional relation between the diaries and the novel itself: the relation is rather more internal. Arguedas wrote the diaries when depression or deep suffering prevented him from continuing with the novel. The first diary begins with the decision to kill himself, but it is evident that the decision is postponed by the novel that the author has begun. The second diary (February 1969) seems to indicate that the author has deferred his suicide because, in essence, he now possesses the novel, which is growing in spite of his enormous difficulties. At the end of this entry two lines announce that the author has been able to begin work again on his text.

The third diary (May 1969) declares that "asphyxiation" stops fiction, but depression does not reclaim the intention to commit suicide, but rather results in a recourse to trips: Arguedas wrote these pages, and the novel, traveling between Chimbote, Arequipa, Lima, and Chile. But, once again, a coda announces that the author has been able to return to his fiction. Nonetheless, the "Final Entry?" (August 1969)

comes to the following conclusion: "I have fought against death or at least believe to have fought against death valiantly, writing this flickering, complaining text"; the suicidal intention reappears, now apparently unavoidable. An epilogue, added by the editor, brings together the letters and final messages that reveal the meticulousness with which Arguedas attempted to organize events before shooting himself.

The novel, in effect, had become involved in a struggle with death, seeking a deferment and exorcism. Perhaps Arguedas knew that salvation for him was no longer possible, but having attempted it, in a hallucinated state, he endowed his novel with a passionate and desolate impulse.

The attempt to save himself through words is, in reality, the final preparation for death. From the perspective of his suicide ("this theme is the only one whose essence I feel and live"), and following the first diary, the novel opens with two chapters that introduce several characters within their environment. The second diary dwells on the enormous difficulty of describing the city and its chaos; and in a confession of impotence, Arguedas makes the statement that fear of his inflexible material is another reason for his suicide. But here the central paradox of the book is revealed: the diaries, directly assuming the effects of depression and failure, conjure the suicide because they represent the fall and the transition, the recuperation from each breakdown in the progress of the novel. It is upon resuming the text of the story that suicide returns, not as a mere theme, but as a metaphor for deterioration and the lonely frustration of writing.

In the end, the diaries abandon the author and he abandons the novel. The last confessions tell how the plots and the lives of the characters might have proceeded had the author continued to write. The questions and the doubts in the final chapter suggest that the author fully expected to find new energy to continue. Finally, all that remains is for the author to take his life so as not to deny his very existence: to die settling his accounts, confident in the destiny of his country and its people, and in the value of his own work.

In the third diary Arguedas finds renewed purpose; he says: "Perhaps it is because I have reached the most intricate part of the course of the lives that I pretend to relate and of those that my own intricacy, instead of finding the unlinking path, attempts to cover or hide." In the text are evident the two great difficulties that constitute the work: the complex existence (even more complex for Arguedas) of the urban people, and his own, personal situation. His speech must become other speeches: an unfolding continuity must exist between the fragments of autobiography and the expository chronicle. It is revealing that in response to the overwhelming distress of the situation that he experiences (a situation reflected in his trips as well as his confessions) Arguedas should oppose the almost ingenuous will to build coherence into the tale; not only have the characters been selected in an exemplary fashion, but the locale of an industrial port is defined and schematized as if the author wished to create for himself a complete and coherent account of the social hell that attracts him through its human ferment and that repels him through its dehumanization.

In spite of the attempted coherence of the story, the novel employs a delirious form of speech: the dialogues quickly generate a feverish intensity in which the narrator escapes the inapprehensible vital chaos of the city, the infernal labyrinth that resists reason. A discourse on the verge of deliverance marks the central occurrence of the work, as its reclamation and best poetic possibility. In the diaries this talk is prefigured by the fervor of the suicide, by the arbitrariness of summary judgments, by the need to reason freely and without conventions about the author's vital situation, following the discontinuous flow of events, the memory and ideas of hope and redemption.

The speech of delirium resurfaces in the center of the fictional text. This impulse toward vertigo also reveals how the author wanted to transgress the borders of fiction, to magnify it through questioning, through rational discourse, not only capturing social chaos but also attempting to let poetry say for itself what the narrated chronicle cannot say. Perhaps the author was searching for total comprehension through this discourse, a comprehension that would be critical, social, poetic, and also, to some extent, prophetic. The dialogues yield to the delirium, and at times conclude in a kind of character dance, with songs and new voices. One of the characters, Tarta,

is called "the poet," "the intellectual," but is depicted as a stutterer. More important is Mocada, a crazy man, who "prophesies" in the streets and markets while carrying a large cross.

Arguedas gives special attention to this character, who is taken from the countryside of Chimbote. The speech of a crazed person affords him the opportunity to approach the work and the city through a language that, in its delirium, is critical, like an accusation that is at the same time an insult. This discourse finds its echo in Esteban de la Cruz, a former miner who is already infected with death; the language of both characters brings forth the image of the city, setting the tone of the drama of those lives destroyed by the country's poverty. De la Cruz says:

> When the drunk speaks the truth, the real truth, with God as a witness, the police, the engineers, etc., say: "You're drunk, You're drunk; to prison you go, to hell." And they take you prisoner, and beat you. Screwed. The word of a drunk man, even though it is the real truth of the Savior's own heart, doesn't count.

This marginal speech, the language of the insane, the drunken, the condemned, converts the act of speech itself into a total protest, an extreme demand; in the preaching of Mocada this demand becomes imperative, the call of a badly wounded utterance.

The fox from above and the fox from below are figures in Huarochiri mythology; in the novel one represents the Sierra (highlands) and the other the Costa (coast). They converse at one point in the novel, and they also intervene in the narrative wearing the face of characters. But this mythic plane is never developed: it appears only as the possibility of a choral dialogue, of another suprarational discourse, between the two zones of Peru. On the last page Arguedas writes: "Within me are departing Peru, whose races will always be sucking juice from the earth to sustain those who live in our land, in which any man not shackled or diminished by egoism may live happily, all of the peoples." All of Arguedas' books speak to us of the happiness and the desolation that co-exist in that country: his work discovers for us a world composed of utopia and strife, fed by the dream of redemption through the practice of criticism.

Translated from the Spanish by Robert Reynolds

JOSÉ MARÍA ARGUEDAS

SELECTED BIBLIOGRAPHY

Editions

Agua. Lima, 1935.

Canto kechwa. Lima, 1938.

Yawar fiesta. Lima, 1941; rev. ed. 1958.

Mitos, leyendas, y cuentos peruanos. Lima, 1947.

Canciones y cuentos del pueblo quechua. Lima, 1949.

Cuentos mágico-realistas y canciones de fiestas tradicionales en el valle del Mantaro . . . Lima, 1953.

Diamantes y pedernales. Lima, 1954.

Los ríos profundos. Buenos Aires, 1958.

El sexto. Lima, 1961.

Todas las sangres. Buenos Aires, 1964.

Amor mundo y todos los cuentos de José María Arguedas. Lima, 1967.

El zorro de arriba y el zorro de abajo. Buenos Aires, 1971.

Formación de una cultura nacional indoamericana. Mexico City, 1975.

Señores e indios; Acerca de la cultura quechua. Montevideo, 1976.

Translations

Deep Rivers. Translated by Frances Barraclough. Austin, Tex., 1978.

The Singing Mountaineers. Translated by Ruth Stephan and Kate and Ángel Flores. Austin, Tex., 1957. Contains *Canto kechwa* and *Canciones y cuentos del pueblo quechua.*

Yawar Fiesta. Translated by Frances Barraclough. Austin, Tex., 1985.

Biographical and Critical Studies

Castro Klaren, Sara. *El mundo mágico de José María Arguedas.* Lima, 1973.

Cornejo Polar, Antonio. *Los universos narrativos de José María Arguedas.* Buenos Aires, 1973.

Escobar, Alberto. *Arguedas, o La utopía de la lengua.* Lima, 1984.

Lienhard, Martin. *Cultura popular andina y forma novelesca. Zorros y danzantes en la última novela de Arguedas.* Lima, 1981.

Marín, Gladys. *La experiencia americana de José María Arguedas.* Buenos Aires, 1973.

Merino de Zela, Mildred. "Vida y obra de José María Arguedas." *Revista peruana de cultura* 13–14:127–178 (1970).

Ortega, Julio. *Texto, comunicación y cultura en "Los ríos profundos."* Lima, 1982.

_____, ed. *Revista iberoamericana* 122 (1983). Special issue dedicated to Arguedas.

Rowe, William. "Bibliografía sobre José María Arguedas." *Revista peruana de cultura* 13–14:179–197 (1970).

_____. *Mito e ideologia en la obra de Arguedas.* Lima, 1979.

Urrelo, Antonio. *José María Arguedas: El nuevo rostro del indio.* Lima, 1974.

Ernesto Sábato

(1911–   )

Howard R. Cohen

Ernesto Sábato rejected his first loves, science and mathematics, in favor of a literary career. He was born on 24 June 1911 in Rojas, a small town about 160 miles from Buenos Aires. In 1937 he took a doctorate in physics. He continued his scientific education at the Massachusetts Institute of Technology in 1939 but returned to his country a year later to become a professor of theoretical physics until his resignation was forced by the Perón government in 1945. However, by this time he was writing for the literary magazine *Sur* and his scientific career was quickly becoming a thing of the past. His works reflect an obsession with the spiritual problems of modern man, his novels being a natural outgrowth of the themes he develops at length in his essays. The overriding theme in all of his works is that of finding, or perhaps giving, meaning to an existence that seems to have none. A note of profound despair is easily discernible, and indeed one must wait for the last part of Sábato's second novel, *Sobre héroes y tumbas* (*On Heroes and Tombs*, 1961) to find, if not a solution, at least a measure of hope with which to confront life's problems. Although not a prolific author, his contribution to River Plate literature is enormous; two of his three novels, *El túnel* (The Tunnel, 1948; published in English as *The Outsider*) and *On Heroes and Tombs*, are certainly among the most critically acclaimed in all of Latin American literature.

In 1945 Sábato published a slender volume of essays, *Uno y el universo* (One and the Universe). This work, which won the Premio Municipal (Municipal Prize), displays no philosophical system, nor does the author claim any. Sábato's observations on such diverse topics as education, history, and science and mathematics reflect one man's attempt to divest himself of an overreliance on science, a dependence that had served him well as a protective cloak during the earlier and quite difficult years of his life, and to turn his attention to his more irrational side and thus put himself more closely in touch with the tenebrous zone of the human situation. One theme that appears and reappears is the idea that an excessive reliance on science can only destroy the most valuable part of man, the part that defies calculation; art that is created through an adherence to scientific dictates and without regard for human emotions serves only to convert man into a thing.

While *Uno y el universo* received a generally favorable response from critics and the reading public, it was Sábato's first novel, *The Outsider*, that brought him international recognition. Because the final outcome of the plot is revealed in the first line, in which Juan Pablo Castel admits to the murder of

María Iribarne Hunter, the book's success lies in the author's adroit ability to sustain interest in the motivations of the assassin. This psychoanalytic method of probing the inner mind is replete with Freudian implications. The use of the first-person narrative provides the vehicle for the exclusion of external reality; indeed the reader sees everything through Castel's eyes and must constantly play the role of active participant in determining what constitutes reality. The characterization of Juan Pablo is penetrating, and the reader, while probably not really liking his overly rational approach to people and life, is nevertheless compelled to hear him out.

Juan Pablo's acting out of Sábato's existential concepts converts the novel into a Freudian case study. Life is a tale told by an idiot, devoid of essential meaning. Twentieth-century man is isolated and can merely confront an absurd and chaotic world, aware of the prospect of his own death looming in the distance. True communication and love are impossible. The novel is highly reminiscent of Camilio José Cela's *La familia de Pascual Duarte* (*The Family of Pascual Duarte*, 1942), inasmuch as Cela and Sábato focus on the inner workings of the mind in similar ways. *The Family of Pascual Duarte* was a *tremendista* novel (*tremendismo* has been defined as the search for a god of love), but what is found is a capricious and whimsical deity. Perhaps *The Outsider* is best viewed as sharing, with *The Family of Pascual Duarte*, that *tremendista* longing to find a god of love, and both discover a god who reigns over a universe that often seems unsympathetic and chaotic.

Of central importance in the novel, and a motif that has led to a myriad of critical interpretations, is the painting "Maternidad." At an exhibition of his paintings, Juan Pablo notices that María is observing the painting intently. He intuits that María has understood the symbolic significance of the work, and he is magnetically drawn to her. While the critics have focused their attention on the foreground, in which a mother watches a child at play, only María has noted the window scene in the upper left corner. This scene consists of nothing more than a woman looking out over the sea from a barren beach. Ángela Dellepiane, in her excellent book on Sábato, sees the painting as a symbol of the Jungian concept of "el choque de nacer" (the shock of childbirth); she

concludes that the sea symbolizes the amniotic fluid and that the relationship between Juan Pablo and María has oedipal overtones. Undoubtedly the scene in the painting was meant to show the essential aloneness of all human beings. Convinced that he has communicated his deepest feelings to María, he sets out to possess her at any cost.

Another key to a proper understanding of *The Outsider* is found in a sequence of three dreams. In the first dream, Castel finds himself in a house that is reminiscent of one from his childhood; the house reminds him of the awakening of sexuality. Several other people are present and are making fun of his naïveté. Upon awakening, he understands that the house in the dream is María. The dream gives us a glimpse of an insecure adolescent confronting a dangerous world. His desire is to return to the protectiveness of the womb (that is, the house of his youth that is María).

In the second dream, Castel is at a social gathering. He suddenly realizes that something is amiss and tries to extricate himself from the situation, but to no avail. His host transforms him into a monstrous bird. Castel hopes that his friends will arrive and free him from the spell of the enchanter; however, when they arrive, they take no note of his transformation. His feeble attempts at communication with others are now nothing more than the screeches of a bird that no one can possibly understand; his friends take no note of this malady, and he understands that the secret of his transformation will follow him to the tomb. At no place in the novel is Juan Pablo's inability to communicate better exemplified.

The third dream is but a brief fragment. Here Castel finds himself in a dark and lonely room. Hunter, one of María's lovers, and María are present, and the two appear to be scorning him. His belief that they are lovers is confirmed in his mind. His mental breakdown is at hand, and his spiritual isolation is complete. Through this dream trilogy, the reader is able to trace the progressively demented behavior pattern of the protagonist.

Harley Dean Oberhelman, in his highly recommended book *Ernesto Sábato*, sees *The Outsider* as a reflection of "the defeat of reason." Indeed Juan Pablo's ultimate defeat is caused by a strict adherence to reason in his quest for absolutes. He responds to

María with calculation rather than love and in so doing destroys any possibility of communication and interaction on a human level. His search places the novel squarely in the mainstream of existentialist literature. His quest for identity leads him to María and the belief that he had escaped his tunnel of isolation. However, his reliance on deductive logic rather than human emotion causes him to destroy the one person who he has believed might love and understand him. While such themes as oedipal involvement, jealousy, isolation from society, and inability to communicate may prove distasteful for some, the novel has achieved an enormous popularity that parallels its generally excellent critical reviews.

Sábato published *Hombres y engranajes* (Men and Gears) in 1951. The book attempts to define the most crushing problems that confront twentieth-century man. This is certainly Sábato's most succinct and possibly his best essay. It revolves around the central theme of man's attempt to find spiritual fulfillment in a overly rational and consumer-oriented environment. The work is best viewed as a lament for twentieth-century man, dehumanized by the almighty mechanized society. In Sábato's estimation, Big Brother has watched over man so closely that his life's blood has been drained. His thought closely parallels that of the Spanish novelist and member of the Generation of '98, Pío Baroja, who believed that science and technology had mushroomed to such an extent that man's power to control them for productive ends had been lost. Thus man has been systematized, regimented, and effectively transformed into a thing, or *hombre-cosa*. Romanticism, surrealism, and existentialism are man's outcries of anguish as he periodically attempts to redefine his rightful place in the universe. Although the vision of history presented here could be deemed pessimistic, Sábato is by no means ready to embrace Jean Paul Sartre's hopeless rejection of the existence of God. Even in the face of the catastrophe of history, man can erect that which is eternal; however, this will require that people work together toward a new social order and a new dignity.

In 1953, Sábato published *Heterodoxia* (Heterodoxy), followed in 1956 by the publication of two other essays, *El otro rostro del peronismo* (The Other Side of Peronism) and *El caso Sábato* (Sábato's Case).

Heterodoxia revolves around the concept of the dichotomy of the sexes; Sábato views the male arena as that of logic and reason, while a woman's element is more often that of the irrational and the intuitive. This work also contains valuable observations on the Argentine novel. Critical reviews of the work were mixed. The *El otro rostro del peronismo* and *El caso Sábato* are political in nature. In the first of these, Sábato treats resentments that have continually festered among the social classes of the nation. His call is for mutual respect between the Peronists and the anti-Peronists. The remedies proposed in *El caso Sábato* are those of a true patriot who criticizes his country out of a deep love and an abiding faith in its future potential. From a literary standpoint, the three works occupy a marginal position in Sábato's total production.

The year 1961 marked the publication of Sábato's finest work of fiction, *On Heroes and Tombs*. Although no single classification can do justice to this monumental and multifaceted work, it is primarily a psychological novel. Nevertheless, it would be manifestly unfair to categorize the novel as nothing more than a clinical case study. Throughout the book, Martín del Castillo attempts to unravel the puzzle of Alejandra Vidal Olmos' nature. However, an understanding of Alejandra requires an understanding of her father, Fernando; and of her relationship to him. For this reason, the third part of this baroque novel, the "Informe sobre ciegos" ("Report on the Blind"), is indispensable for properly understanding it. The powerful, instinctive, carnal drives of Fernando are prominent in Alejandra; the demons of Fernando's psyche are destined to haunt the spirit of his daughter. This is reflected in her twisted view of sex, occasioned to a large extent by the incestuous relationship with her father, a relationship that causes her to seek out the purifying heat of fire as the instrument of her eventual suicide. As in *The Outsider*, oedipal overtones are present throughout the novel. For his part, Martín's knowledge that his mother had attempted to abort him causes him to view her as a *madre cloaca*, or "mother-sewer." It should be born in mind that "woman" symbolizes Sábato's deepest mythological vision and is synonymous with the land and, therefore, Argentina itself. The analogy is clear: The Argentine motherland is deformed and in need of a spiritual reawakening. *On Heroes and Tombs* is also a national novel in which the history and geography of the country assume major importance. The author includes representative national types from the diverse groups that constitute the Argentine populace. Sábato's search for national and geographic unity is embodied in Lavalle's march, a motif that Sábato employs near the beginning as well as near the end of the novel; Argentina's past greatness (symbolized by the Olmos family as well as by Buenos Aires itself) has stagnated and lies twisted and dormant. But the spirit of her heroes (that is, Lavalle and his troops) continues to march in the north. Martín, infused with the spirit of the dead Alejandra, will journey south, at the close of the novel, to Patagonia, a cold and sterile region laden with possibilities for rebirth.

In many ways, this novel amplifies the themes found in the essays and in *The Outsider*. And as in the first novel, dreams are of central importance. Sábato continues to explore the irrational and often chaotic inner world of man. If the author offers no final solution for life's problems, nevertheless, through Martín's chance meeting with Hortensia Paz, a simple person with an abiding faith, Sábato suggests that life can be positive for those who reach out. Although, strictly speaking, *On Heroes and Tombs* has no ideology, the author seems to be saying once again that modern man has lost his way in the civilized and mechanized world, and that happiness can come only through a rediscovery of the self.

In 1963 Sábato published *El escritor y sus fantasmas* (The Writer and His Ghosts) and *Tango: Discusión y clave* (Tango: Discussion and Key). While the second of these two books is of lesser importance, the first is one of the most influential contemporary essays. In the first part of this work, Sábato responds to many questions that have been put to him over the years. This section is valuable not only for the author's view of his own work but also for his observations on literature in general. While Sábato does not reject gratuitous literature, such as that of Jorge Luis Borges, he does place it on a secondary plane. In this work, Sábato once again shows himself to be primarily an existentialist, while effectively reworking many of the themes found in *Hombres y engranajes*.

In his last novel, *Abaddón el exterminador*, (Abaddon the Exterminator, 1974), Sábato continues to explore the major themes of his earlier novels. Most of the main characters are once again present as themselves, and indeed Sábato becomes a character also. This offers the reader a poignant glimpse of a very vulnerable Sábato. The power of the author's pen has not deserted him: the novel has many fine moments. One of the most memorable revolves around the death of Ernesto ("Che") Guevara, another around the meeting of Sábato-character and Sábato-author. The attempt at communication and understanding between the two is unrealized. Sábato's comments on the nature of the creative process form another strong component of the work.

Sábato is clearly at his best when depicting man lost in an incomprehensible and seemingly meaningless universe, in which suffering is the only road to salvation. While *Abaddón el exterminador* is laudable in this regard, its plotless structure will undoubtedly disappoint many who will compare it unfavorably to *On Heroes and Tombs*, a novel that truly represents the culmination of the psychological novel in Latin America.

SELECTED BIBLIOGRAPHY

First Editions

Essays

Uno y el universo. Buenos Aires, 1945.
Hombres y engranajes: Reflexiones sobre el dinero, la razón y el derrumbe de nuestro tiempo. Buenos Aires, 1951.
Heterodoxia. Buenos Aires, 1953.
El otro rostro de peronismo: Carta abierta a Mario Amadeo. Buenos Aires, 1956.
El caso Sábato: Torturas y libertad de prensa. Carta abierta al Gral. Aramburu. Buenos Aires, 1956. A private publication.
Tango: Discusión y clave. Buenos Aires, 1963.
El escritor y sus fantasmas. Buenos Aires, 1963.
Tres aproximaciones a la literatura de nuestro tiempo: Robbe-Grillet, Borges, Sartre. Santiago, Chile, 1968.
La convulsión política y social de nuestro tiempo. Buenos Aires, 1969.

ERNESTO SÁBATO

Novels

El túnel. Buenos Aires, 1948.
Sobre héroes y tumbas. Buenos Aires, 1961.
Abaddón el exterminador. Buenos Aires, 1974.

Collected Works

Itinerario. Buenos Aires, 1969.
Obras de ficción. Buenos Aires, 1966. Contains El túnel and Sobre héroes y tumbas, as well as an excellent introduction to Sábato's life and work by Harley D. Oberhelman.

Translations

On Heroes and Tombs. Translated by Helen R. Lane. Boston, 1981.
The Outsider. Translated by Harriet de Onís. New York, 1950.

Biographical and Critical Studies

Acquaroni, J. L. "El concepto, mensaje artístico llevado a sus últimas consecuencias en la novela de la soledad y la destinación." Cuadernos hispanoamericanos 20/57:389–392 (1954).

Azancot, Leopoldo. "El escritor y sus fantasmas." Indice de artes y letras 17/186:31 (1964).

Brushwood, J. S. "Ernesto Sábato: Hombres y engranajes." Books Abroad 26/3:281–282 (1952).

Buonocore, Domingo. "El escritor y sus fantasmas, por Ernesto Sábato." Universidad (Santa Fé, Argentina) 58:416–417 (1964).

Canal Feijóo, Bernardo. "En torno a una 'novelle' de Ernesto Sábato." Escritura 3/7:98–101 (1949).

———. "Ernesto Sábato: Sobre héroes y tumbas." Sur 276:90–99 (1962).

Castellanos, Carmelina de. "Dos personajes de una novela argentina." Cuadernos hispanoamericanos 78/232:149–160 (1969).

Catania, Carlos. "El universo de Abaddón el exterminador." Cuadernos hispanoamericanos 391–393:498–516 (1983).

———. Sábato: Entre la idea y la sangre. San José, Costa Rica, 1973.

Dellepiane, Ángela B. Ernesto Sábato: El hombre y su obra. New York, 1968.

Fernández Suárez, Alvaro. "Ernesto Sábato: Hombres y engranajes." Sur 204:71–74 (1951).

———. "Ernesto Sábato: Heterodoxia." Sur 224:129–132 (1953).

Févre, F. B. "Sobre El escritor y sus fantasmas: Un libro de Ernesto Sábato." Criterio. Revista internacional de teología 37:690–692 (1964).

Giacoman, Helmy F., ed. Homenaje a Ernesto Sábato: Variaciones interpretativas en torno a su obra. New York, 1973.

Gibbs, Beverly J. "El túnel: Portrayal of Isolation." Hispania 48/3:429–436 (1965).

Goldschmidt, W., V. Massuh, and J. A. Vázquez. "En torno a Hombres y engranajes: Tres opiniones." Notas y estudios de filosofía (Tucumán, Argentina) 3/11:259–261 (1952).

Harris, Yvonne J. "Ernesto Sábato: El túnel." Books Abroad 26/2:185 (1952).

Lichtblau, M. I. "Interés estético en La familia de Pascual Duarte y en El túnel." Humanitas (Tucumán, Argentina) 7:247–255 (1966).

Lipp, Solomon. "Ernesto Sábato: Síntoma de una época." Journal of Inter-American Studies 8/1:142–155 (1966).

Ludmer, I. J. "Ernesto Sábato y un testimonio del fracaso." Boletín de las literaturas hispánicas (Santa Fé, Argentina) 5:83–100 (1963).

Oberhelman, Harley Dean. Ernesto Sábato. New York, 1970.

Olguín, Manuel. "Ernesto Sábato: Uno y el universo." Books Abroad 21/2:201–202 (1947).

Petersen, F. "Notas en torno a la publicación reciente de Ernesto Sábato." La torre (Río Piedras, Puerto Rico) 13/51:197–203 (1965).

———. "Sábato's El túnel: More Freud than Sartre." Hispania 50/2:271–276 (1967).

Prada Oropeza, Renato. "Texto, contexto e intertexto en Abaddón el exterminador." Cuadernos hispanoamericanos 391–393:517–525 (1983).

Wainerman, Luis. Sábato y el misterio de los ciegos. Buenos Aires, 1971.

Dinah Silveira de Queiroz

(1911–1982)

Dário M. de Castro Alves

In the course of a literary career that spanned forty-four years, Dinah Silveira de Queiroz wrote within a great many literary genres with rare skill and mastery, leaving her mark on modern Brazilian literature. Committed to good writing all her life, she produced prose fiction, psychological and historical novels, short stories, biography, books for children and teenagers, science fiction, plays, scholarly works on literature, newspaper columns, and radio commentaries. The novel, however, was her foremost field of endeavor. It was in this genre that she became a consummate artist of the written word, achieving a superlative style in the Portuguese language, of whose variety, richness, and profundity she had absolute command, employing it with meticulous correctness and great clarity.

Born in São Paulo on 9 November 1911, Dinah Silveira de Queiroz attended an elegant girls' school with her sister, Helena, who also became a fine writer known especially for her short stories and newspaper columns. Their father, Alarico Silveira, held high government positions, including chief of staff to the president of Brazil, and served as a civilian judge. He was also a writer, journalist, and lexicographer who completed extensive work on a Brazilian encyclopedia, the only published volume of which was hailed as a masterpiece. In 1929 Dinah married Marcelo de

Queiroz, a judge who shared her father's strong literary bent.

Dinah Silveira de Queiroz made her literary debut in 1939 with the novel *Floradas na Serra* (Blossomings on the Hill), to this day a best seller. The previous year, she had written a short story, "Pecado" ("Sin"), which had elicited the surprise and admiration of her father. The short story was deemed worthy of being translated into English and later won a prize from the magazine *Mademoiselle*, where it was published in August 1943 as part of a Latin American literary contest. At about the same time, Silveira de Queiroz wrote a novelette entitled *A Sereia Verde* (The Green Mermaid, 1941), published for the first time in *Revista do Brasil* (Review of Brazil), then headed by Otávio Tarquínio de Souza, a well-known historian. The piece soon caught the attention of the noted sociologist Gilberto Freyre, who referred to the author in a letter to the director of the magazine as a newcomer "who writes very well."

Floradas na Serra appeared in print in September 1939, at the onset of World War II. With the book, an instant critical and public success, Silveira de Queiroz was definitively launched as a writer. Sold out in less than a month, the first printing was followed by many others. The author had poured into the work much of her obsession with the subject of tuberculosis, an illness that, when she was a young child, had claimed the life of her mother, under circumstances that had left a lasting mark on her. *Floradas na Serra* won the Alcântara Machado Award of the São Paulo Academy of Letters in 1940 and has gone through numerous editions at Editora José Olympio, the firm that has published most of her works. The novel contrasts the world of the healthy with the world of the sick, hope with disappointment, and life with death. In one of her columns, after watching the movie based on Erich Segal's novel *Love Story* (1970), the author reported detecting similarities in matters of concept and content between the film and her book.

In 1942 *Floradas na Serra* was published in Buenos Aires under the title of *Cuando la sierra florece*. In 1955 the novel was made into a movie, directed by Luciano Salci and starring Cacilda Becker, a renowned Brazilian actress. It was also serialized for the radio and in comic strips. In 1982 it appeared as a twenty-two-episode series shown on São Paulo's TV Cultura. The series was then aired by television stations throughout Brazil.

Silveira de Queiroz published a second novel in 1949. *Margarida La Rocque: A Ilha dos Demônios* (Margarida La Rocque: The Isle of Demons), which differs dramatically from the author's first book according to novelist Renard Pérez:

> It is a strange work, in which the author pursues totally unexpected paths. With none of the youthful romanticism of *Floradas na Serra*, it is like a liberation. The story goes back in time to the era of the Great Discoveries and has quite another setting, for the author fetches her protagonist in France, only to cast her on a lost island with her lover and her maid. The novel tells the story of this threesome in conflict, caught up, as it were, in a nightmare. It is a tale that shows the depths of misery and degradation into which a human being can be hurled by jealousy and loneliness. As regards technique and style, the author achieves complete self-realization, turning out a book that is a beautiful literary achievement.
>
> (*Escritores Brasileiros Contemporâneos* 1, p. 120)

Margarida La Rocque, which was the author's favorite of her own works, is written in powerful, beautifully

articulated language with a slightly archaic flavor. In March 1978 the critic Ivan Junqueira wrote in the Rio de Janeiro newspaper *O Globo* that Silveira de Queiroz will always be remembered and celebrated for this extraordinary work.

> That which really shapes the plot and imbues the work with an eerie atmosphere, as well as making it into a masterpiece, is the language in which this unusual, poignant tale unfolds by twists and turns along its convoluted course, as the central character relates it to a silent listener, the counterpart of her own conscience, perhaps; for Margarida La Rocque's confession is but a monologue in the guise of a dialogue.

Junqueira goes on to say that in this book Silveira de Queiroz shows "unexcelled mastery, thus achieving that chiaroscuro quality, that shifting interplay of light and darkness indispensable to the fusing of the real and the unreal, the ordinary and the fantastic, the pagan and the Christian into a unique, seamless fiction mosaic." Many see in this novel, born of the author's own private suffering when it was being written, the precursor of fantastic realism. This was the view of Aguinaldo Silva, a renowned writer, critic, and author of scripts for television serials, who includes it among the ten greatest works in Brazilian literature. *Margarida La Rocque* has been published in Portugal and translated into French, Italian, Japanese, Korean, and Spanish. Colette referred to it as "Le meilleur démon de notre enfer" (The most real demon in our own hell).

In 1954, Silveira de Queiroz published *A Muralha* (*The Women of Brazil*), a historic novel on the grand scale, set against the background of the colonial period of the late seventeenth and early eighteenth centuries, as a Brazilian national consciousness was emerging. The first edition was preceded by its publication in serialized form in the weekly *O Cruzeiro* of Rio de Janeiro. It was serialized on radio and turned into a television series in 1969, running for more than one hundred episodes and starring great names in Brazilian cinema and television. The work was also published in the form of comic strips. It has been published in Portugal and translated and published in Japan, Argentina, Burma, Bangladesh, Pakistan, South Korea, and the United States. Adonias Filho writes in *Modernos Ficcionistas Brasileiros* that in *The Women of Brazil*

> Dinah Silveira de Queiroz recreates the landscape and the customs of the time, the *paulista* family as vigorous stock, the men's struggles in the jungle, the fighting over the gold the virgin land did not hide. In the center, as lord over life and death, stood the patriarch whose wish is law. Energetic women who would give birth to an entire people. On the lower rungs, Indians and slaves, priests and Jews, and adventurers on whose bones the edifice of a nation would rest. Within this circle of violence, despair, heroism, and betrayal, the drama in its more romantic-styled way unfolds, powerful and human, as the novelist weaves into her tale the history of her native land.

Silveira de Queiroz also wrote a children's book, *As Aventuras do Homem Vegetal* (The Adventures of the Vegetable Man, 1951), and *O Oitavo Dia* (The Eighth Day, 1956), a play on a biblical theme. In the play she creates a delicate fantasy on the dawning of passions after the creation of man. *As Noites do Morro do Encanto* (The Nights of the Enchanted Hill, 1957) is a collection of thirteen short stories that won the Afonso Arinos Award from the Brazilian Academy of Letters. In 1960 *Era Uma Vez uma Princesa* (Once upon a Time There Was a Princess) was published along with several novels by other authors. In 1966 it appeared separately as *A Princesa dos Escravos* (Princess of the Slaves). It is a children's book that tells the story of the daughter of Emperor Pedro II, Princess Isabel, who, on 13 May 1888, signed the so-called Golden Law, an instrument doing away with slavery in Brazil. Also in the same year, she wrote *Êles Herdarão a Terra* (They Will Inherit the Earth), a volume of short stories that made the author one of the leading precursors of science fiction in Brazil.

In 1961 Silveira de Queiroz' husband died and a year later she married Dário Moreira de Castro Alves. In 1963 she accompanied her husband on a diplomatic assignment in Moscow, where she wrote *Os Invasores* (The Invaders). In this historical work the author offers a fictional solution to the mysterious, still-unexplained death of Jean François Duclerc, a French corsair at the time of Louis XIV. The author portrays, in a moving miniature portrait, the Rio de Janeiro of the early eighteenth century, with its population of approximately twelve thousand people. Written originally as a play, strongly nationalist and stressing the role played by students in the fight against French invaders, the text was later reworked by the author into a novel, published in 1965. A few years later, while in Rome, where her husband had been posted, Silveira de Queiroz wrote *Verão dos Infiéis* (Summer of the Unfaithful, 1968), a novel about modern life in Rio de Janeiro. In June 1969 Paulo Ronai wrote in *O Estado de São Paulo* that:

> All through her book the author is able to take great advantage of the endless series of those things that motivate the *cariocas* [natives of Rio de Janeiro]. . . . The swift changes of focus, the interference of dream and drunkenness with everyday reality, and the interplay of shadow and light give the story a feverish, engrossing rhythm that imparts a rough and exotic beauty to the novel.

The story focuses on the city over a period of three days when it is being lashed by torrential summer rains. The situation brings to the fore familiar woes: flooding, tumbling houses, poignant scenes in the midst of catastrophe, political fights, interdenominational gatherings, street protests, and a family's dramatic search for their father. Silveira de Queiroz said that the inspiration for the novel came to her in a flash as she drove around the borough of Queens, in New York City, after listening to Pope Paul VI's address to the United Nations General Assembly. She found the first appearance of a Roman pope in the United Nations a deeply moving experience and was struck especially with the idea of the world searching for a father, a *papa*. She named the father of this work Domingus, meaning *Dominus*, or Lord (father). In February 1970 in the *Correio Braziliense* (Brazilian Post) the critic Fábio Lucas commented that the novel is a "dense, and modern work, in which the fate of the characters is played out at the whim of certain fixations of the contemporary world: sex, politics, gratuitousness, and solitude. This book has unquestionably secured for itself a major place in the writer's oeuvre."

In the course of her prolonged stay in Brasília, Brazil's new capital, where she lived from 1970 until

1979, Silveira de Queiroz wrote a book that thoroughly engaged her feelings, namely, an "autobiography" of Christ, in two volumes. The *Memorial do Cristo* (*Christ's Memorial*, 1974 and 1977) is a first-person narrative of the life of Christ, from the moment of divine conception in Mary's womb to his passion, death, and appearance to Mary Magdalene in the guise of an affable and candid gardener. The sublime Master tells his story in direct language that is sweet without being cloying, elevated, noble, and truly convincing in nature. Not once does the book deviate from the lofty style that is appropriate and germane, for the text is subtly and skillfully conceived, and finely polished. Pope Paul VI instructed his secretary of state to write a letter to the author and commend *Christ's Memorial*, pointing out the "well-honed pen" she used to honor Christ's memory.

While living in Lisbon, from 1979 through 1982, Silveira de Queiroz wrote a novel set in our time, whose action takes place in Portugal, Switzerland, Italy, and São Paulo. *Guida, Caríssima Guida* (Guida, Dearest Guida, 1981) was published in Portugal under the title *O Desfrute* (The Enjoyment). In this work the author tells the story of a beautiful and hedonistic woman driven by a determination to grow, to climb in life, and to dazzle, to the point of shedding motherhood; she pushes away her only son, for whom she shows a strange lack of affection. As she unraveled the thread of her terrifying story, Silveira de Queiroz kept at hand contemporary newspapers and magazines, weaving into the plot, as they occurred, international events such as kidnappings, earthquakes, elections, and scandals. Guida, the central character, even comes to the point of urging her son to commit incest in order to prove that she is not his mother. Throughout the book there runs a subtle element of ambiguity as to the legitimacy of Guida's husband, Marco, an issue the author cunningly preferred not to clarify completely.

Silveira de Queiroz's extensive output has frequently been the object of study and analysis. Bela Jozef compiled a series of critical surveys for inclusion in an anthology of her work published in 1974. Speakers in the academic world have offered critical appraisals of the writer's work. They include R. Magalhães Júnior's speech welcoming the author into the Brazilian Academy of Letters on 7 April 1981, Sérgio Corrêa da Costa's remarks as he was received into the same academy on 15 June 1984 to occupy the seat left vacant after Silveira de Queiroz' death, Nelson Carneiro's, as he was admitted to the Brasília Academy of Letters on 12 June 1984, and Jarbas Passarinho's as he saluted her at the same academy on 5 July 1971.

Other important critical appraisals include an article, prepared by Almeida Fischer for the acclaimed newspaper *O Estado de São Paulo* on 6 February 1983, entitled "O Humano e o Literário em Dinah Silveira de Queiroz" (The Human and the Literary in Dinah Silveira de Queiroz), as a posthumous homage; a speech delivered by Edilberto Coutinho on 24 October 1983 as he was sworn in as a member of the PEN Club of Brazil to occupy the seat left vacant by the author; the obituary in the leading newspaper *Folha de São Paulo* (Register of São Paulo) on 29 November 1982; the publication *Dinah Silveira de Queiroz, Cadeira Sete* (Dinah Silveira de Queiroz, Chair Seven), with photographs and numerous bibliographical references, issued by the state of São Paulo's Cultural Department in 1981 and containing articles by Antonio Soares Amora and Henrique L. Alves; and an anthology published in 1982 entitled *Dinah Silveira de Queiroz*, containing quotations from her works, with a critical and biographical introduction, edited by Nataniel Dantas, one of the author's former secretaries. Dalmo Juenon, also a former secretary, is currently preparing a book on her life and work. Malcolm Silverman has written an excellent, thorough essay included in a book on Brazilian writers. Danilo Gomes has published an interview with Silveira de Queiroz in a collection of interviews entitled *Escritores Brasileiros ao Vivo* (Brazilian Writers by Word of Mouth, 1979–1980).

Silveira de Queiroz spearheaded a movement to change the bylaws of the Brazilian Academy of Letters, which up to 1977 did not allow for the admission of women as members. The campaign she waged from 1970 through 1977 finally met with success. In 1980, when Rachel de Queiroz had already been admitted, Silveira de Queiroz submitted her candidacy and was elected. She also belonged to the following academic institutions: the Academy of Sciences of Lisbon; the Academies of Letters of

Brasília, Rio de Janeiro, São Paulo, and Espirito Santo; and the PEN Club of Brazil. Her short stories have been included in anthologies in many countries, including Brazil, Argentina, Israel, Italy, Japan, Norway, Portugal, the United States, Venezuela, Peru, and France.

For a period of almost forty years, Silveira de Queiroz wrote columns for newspapers and commentaries for the radio, producing over eleven thousand pieces of approximately one page each. An untiring worker, the author never stopped writing these short pieces, an occupation she dearly loved, particularly because of the opportunity it afforded for continuous dialogue and close contact with the public. Three volumes of these articles have been published. *O Quadrante* (1962) and *O Quadrante II* (1963) are collections that include her columns along with those of other authors, while *Café da Manhã* (Morning Coffee, 1969) is devoted solely to her writings.

Silveira de Queiroz used to say that she would stop writing only when she died. When very ill, she continued to dictate her daily pieces, until just three days before her death in São Paulo on 27 November 1982.

Translated from the Portuguese by João Moreira Coelho

SELECTED BIBLIOGRAPHY

First Editions

Novels and Short Stories

Floradas na Serra. Rio de Janeiro, 1939.
A Sereia Verde. Rio de Janeiro, 1941.
Margarida La Rocque. A Ilha dos Demônios. Rio de Janeiro, 1949.
A Muralha. Rio de Janeiro, 1954.
As Noites do Morro do Encanto. Rio de Janeiro, 1957.
Eles Herdarão a Terra. Rio de Janeiro, 1960.
O Mistério dos M.M.M. Detective story written in collaboration with other writers. Rio de Janeiro, 1962.
Os Invasores. Rio de Janeiro, 1965.
Verão dos Infiéis. Rio de Janeiro, 1968.
Comba Malina. Rio de Janeiro, 1969.
Os Dez Melhores Contos de Dinah. Brasília, 1981.
Guida, Caríssima Guida. Rio de Janeiro, 1981.

Plays

O Oitavo Dia. Rio de Janeiro, 1956.

Children's and Juvenile Literature

As Aventuras do Homem Vegetal. Rio de Janeiro, 1951.
Era Uma Vez uma Princesa. . . . São Paulo, 1960. Includes works by other writers. Published separately as *A Princesa dos Escravos.* Rio de Janeiro, 1966.
A Baía da Espuma e Outras Histórias. São Paulo, 1979.

Prose

O Quadrante. Rio de Janeiro, 1962. Contains selected columns by nine Brazilian writers.
O Quadrante II. Rio de Janeiro, 1963. Contains selected columns by nine Brazilian writers.
Café da Manhã. Rio de Janeiro, 1969. Selected columns and commentaries.
Eu Venho: Memorial do Cristo 1. Rio de Janeiro, 1974.
Eu, Jesus: Memorial do Cristo 2. Rio de Janeiro, 1977.

Translations by Silveira de Queiroz

O Navio Fantasma [*The Cruise of the Raider Wolf*, by Roy Alexander]. Rio de Janeiro, 1940.
Deuses de Barro [*Disputed Passage*, by Lloyd C. Douglas]. Rio de Janeiro, 1941.
Até um Dia Meu Capitão [*Quietly My Captain Waits*, by Evelyn Eaton]. Rio de Janeiro, 1942.
Razão e Sentimento [*Sense and Sensibility*, by Jane Austen]. Rio de Janeiro, 1944.
Santa Joana [*Saint Joan*, by George Bernard Shaw]. Rio de Janeiro, 1951.

Translations

Christ's Memorial. Translated by Isabel do Prado. London, 1978.
"Guidance." Translated and with an introduction by William L. Grossman. In *Modern Brazilian Short Stories.* Berkeley and Los Angeles, Calif., 1967. Pp. 100–106.
_____. Translated by William L. Grossman. In *Other Fires: Short Fiction by Latin American Women.* New York, 1986. Pp. 62–69.
"Tarciso." Translated by Hardie St. Martin. In *The Eye of the Heart*, edited by Barbara Howes. Indianapolis and New York, 1973. Pp. 235–252.
The Women of Brazil. Translated by Roberta King. New York, 1980.

Biographical and Critical Studies

Academia Brasileira de Letras—Dinah Silveira de Queiroz, Cadeira Sete. Texts by Antonio Soares Amora and Henrique L. Alves. São Paulo, 1981.

Adonias Filho. *Modernos Ficcionistas Brasileiros.* Rio de Janeiro, 1958.

Arroyo, Leonardo. "Dois Romances e Dois Mundos." *Folha de São Paulo,* 8 February 1940.

Athayde, Tristão de. "Romances Modernos." *Diario de São Paulo,* 8 February 1940.

Barroso, Haydée Jofre. "La Prodigiosa Fantasía de Dinah." *Histonium* (Buenos Aires), July 1969.

Boletim Cultural [das Bibliotecas Itinerantes] (Lisbon), May 1981. Pp. 37–39. On Brazilian female writers.

Campos, Siqueira. Speech in the House of Representatives of the Brazilian National Congress. *Diario do Congresso Nacional* (Brasília), 29 April 1977.

Carneiro, Nelson. *Nelson Carneiro na Academia Brasiliense de Letras.* Brasília, 1984.

Cavalcanti, Valdemar. "Dinah: Romance Novo." *O Jornal* (Rio de Janeiro), 24 March 1968.

Coelho, Jacinto do Prado, António Soares Amora, and Ernesto Guerra da Cal, eds. *Dicionário de Literatura.* Oporto, Portugal, 1969.

Costa, Sérgio Corrêa da. *Posse de Sérgio Corrêa da Costa na Academia Brasileira de Letras.* Rio de Janeiro, 1984.

Coutinho, Edilberto. *Uma Literatura sem Fronteiras.* Speech given to the PEN Club of Brasil. *Correio das Artes* (João Pessoa, Brazil), 8 January 1984.

Cunha, Fernando Whitaker da. "O Demônio da Ilha." *Jornal do Commércio* (Rio de Janeiro), 19 January 1961.

Dantas, Nataniel. "O Presente Repetido no Passado." *Estado de São Paulo,* 30 April 1972.

_____. "À Sombra de uma Memória Amiga." *Jornal de Brasília,* 5 December 1982.

_____. *Dinah Silveira de Queiroz.* Critical essay with selection of texts. São Paulo, 1982.

Damata, Gasparino. "Dinah entre *A Muralha* e o *Verão dos Infiéis.*" *Minas Gerais, Suplemento Literário,* 18 January 1969.

Dias, Maria Helena. "*Floradas na Serra:* Notas e Comentário sobre o Primeiro Romance de Dinah Silveira de Queiroz." *Gaidai Bibliotheca* (Review of the Kyoto University for Foreign Studies) 6 (1983).

Fischer, Almeida. "Dois Romances de Dinah." *Correio do Povo* (Porto Alegre, Brazil), 21 March 1970.

_____. "A Vida de Cristo por Ele Mesmo." *Estado de São Paulo, Suplemento Cultural,* 10 January 1978.

_____. *O Áspero Ofício.* 2nd series, Brasília, 1972; 5th series, Rio de Janeiro, 1983.

Gomes, Danilo. *Escritores Brasileiros ao Vivo.* Belo Horizonte, Brazil, 1979–1980.

Grande Enciclopédia Delta Larousse. Rio de Janeiro, 1970.

Jozef, Bella, ed. *Selecta de Dinah Silveira de Queiroz.* Rio de Janeiro, 1974. With an introduction, critical studies, and notes.

Junqueira, Ivan. "*Margarida La Rocque.*" *O Globo* (Rio de Janeiro), 26 March 1978.

_____. "*Os Evangelhos Segundo Dinah Silveira de Queiroz.*" *O Globo* (Rio de Janeiro), 14 January 1979.

Lins, Alvaro. In *Jornal de Crítica.* 2nd series, Rio de Janeiro, 1943. Pp. 185–191.

Lispector, Clarice. "A Indulgência mais Produtiva." *Jornal do Brasil* (Rio de Janeiro), 5 December 1970.

Litrento, Oliveiros. "Dinah Silveira de Queiroz." *Jornal do Comercio* (Rio de Janeiro), 5 December 1982.

Lucas, Fábio. "*A Muralha.*" *Diario Carioca* (Rio de Janeiro), 26 February 1956 and 4 March 1956.

Magalhães Júnior, Raimundo. *Discursos na Academia Brasileira de Letras.* Rio de Janeiro, 1981.

Maldonado, João C. "A Grande e Derradeira Viagem." *Tribuna Literária* (Petrópolis, Brazil), 19 December 1982.

Marques, Rodrigues. "Novos Rumos de Dinah." *Jornal do Brasil* (Rio de Janeiro), 15 March 1969.

Martinez, Carlos D. "Enfoque Feminista y Épico en La Muralla." *La Opinion* (Buenos Aires), 23 August 1978.

Martínez, Maria Teresa Leal de. *Dinah Silveira de Queiroz: An Innovator in Brazilian Literature.* Rice University Studies 64/1 (1978).

Martins, Wilson. "O Romance Histórico." *Estado de São Paulo,* 18 March 1954.

Mendes, Oscar. "Morre uma Escritora." *Estado de Minas* (Belo Horizonte, Brazil), 2 December 1982.

Montello, Josué. "Em Louvor de Dinah Silveira de Queiroz." *Manchete* (Rio de Janeiro), 12 November 1982.

Mourão, Ronaldo Rogério de Freitas. "Astronomia e Astronáutica—Uma Lembrança de Dinah." *Jornal do Brasil* (Rio de Janeiro), 4 December 1982.

Nunes, Cassiano. "Ambigüidade em *Margarida La Roque.*" *Correio Braziliense* (Brasília), 25 December 1970.

Olinto, Antonio. "40 Anos de Via Literária de Dinah." *O Globo* (Rio de Janeiro), 3 December 1982.

_____. "Dinah Amplia o Terreno da Ficção Científica." *O Globo* (Rio de Janeiro), 29 May 1969.

Peixoto, Silveira. In *Falam os Escritores* 2. Curitiba, Brazil, 1941. Pp. 181–188.

Pérez, Renard. In *Escritores Brasileiros Contemporâneos* 1. Rio de Janeiro, 1960. Pp. 113–126.

Queiroz, Rachel. "Dinah." *O Cruzeiro* (Rio de Janeiro), 4 February 1956.

_____. "*Verão dos Infiéis.*" *Diário de Aracaju,* 11 December 1968.

_____. "Saudades de Dinah." *Ultima Hora* (Rio de Janeiro), 13 December 1982.

Rego, José Lins do. "*Margarida La Rocque.*" *O Jornal* (Rio de Janeiro), 6 October 1948.

Ronai, Paulo. "Um Verão como Nenhum Outro." *Estado de São Paulo,* 14 June 1969.

Salema, Álvaro. "Dinah Silveira de Queiroz." *Colóquio Letras* Lisbon, (7 January 1983).

Silveira, Helena. "Dinah a Mágica do Verbo." *Folha de São Paulo,* 4 December 1982.

_____. *Paiságem e Memória.* São Paulo, 1983.

Silveira, Miroel. "O Oitavo Dia." *Diario de Notícias* (Rio de Janeiro), 26 January 1956.

Silverman, Malcolm. *Diversity in the Prose of Dinah Silveira de Queiroz.* Lisbon and San Diego, 1979.

Soares, Flavio de Macedo. "Verão dos Infiéis." *Correio da Manhã* (Rio de Janeiro), 10 November 1968.

Trigueiros, Luís Forjaz. "Dinah Silveira de Queiroz." *Ocidente, Revista Portuguesa da Cultura* (Lisbon), special issue (1982).

Jorge Amado

(1912–   )

Jon S. Vincent

Jorge Amado is Brazil's most energetic producer of best sellers, and outside of his country he is sure to be the one Brazilian writer known, if any are. In a society in which the designation "professional writer" is a contradiction in terms, he is one of a handful who lives by the pen, and after a career over fifty years long, a new Amado title is still an event eagerly awaited by his vast public.

Amado was born near the cacao port of Ilhéus, in the southern part of the state of Bahia, on 10 August 1912. His family was sufficiently affluent to send him to a Jesuit boarding school in the state capital of Salvador, where he demonstrated a precocious literary bent but very little interest in other subjects. He was guided to the Portuguese classics and, among others, to Charles Dickens, who remains a favorite of his. He ran away from school and stayed for several months with an uncle in the state of Sergipe, and later sat out a year on the family plantation. Returning to Salvador, he nominally studied but was in fact more attracted to the bohemian life-style of his contemporaries and the excitement generated by the Brazilian modernists, who were turning the intellectual establishment on its ear.

In 1930 Amado's father sent him to Rio de Janeiro, then Brazil's capital, where he entered law school and eventually earned a diploma he never bothered to pick up. He also wrote his first novel, *O País do Carnaval* (Carnival Country, 1931), which he managed to have published through the efforts of some friends. He was nineteen. During this period he also read the works of his contemporaries, notably the regionalists of the Northeast, some Russians (Fëdor Vasilievich Gladkov), and at least one American, Michael Gold, whose *Jews Without Money* (1930) is widely held to be a major influence on Amado and his friends.

Amado's second novel betrays none of the tentativeness of the first, and it is with *Cacau* (Cacao, 1933) that he first indicated that the search for answers, which was the essence of his first novel, was over. The answers were not likely to be pleasing to the neofascist government of Getúlio Vargas: in *Cacau*, Amado made clear his sympathies with the aims of the recently founded Brazilian Communist party. The book was immediately confiscated from bookstores around the country, and it was later returned to circulation only through the good offices of a member of the national cabinet. Amado's reputation, or notoriety, was no doubt enhanced by the hasty action of the police, and for many years he was the Brazilian writer most closely identified in the public mind as a communist. Although he claims not to have joined the party until 1945, when it experienced one of its brief periods of legality, his early works, though uneven in both quality and ideology, never make a secret of the author's sympathy with communism. Leftist politics among writers were no more unusual in Brazil in that era than they were in the United States, but whereas the New Deal provided sufficient liberalization to tarnish the attraction of the far left in the United States, the Vargas regime became increasingly authoritarian, with the result that Brazilian writers saw no alternative to the extreme left.

Amado wrote four more novels during the 1930's: *Suor* (*Slums*, 1934), *Jubiabá* (*Jubiabá*, 1935), *Mar Morto* (*Sea of Death*, 1936), and *Capitães da Areia* (Captains of the Sand, 1937). From 1935 on, his works are less the discursive treatises on oppression the first books were, and an element that becomes a lifelong trademark begins to appear as an essential ingredient: Brazilian popular culture. Amado began by using such folk artifacts as folk songs, circus posters, and folk remedies as themes or motifs, and gradually moved in the direction of employing them as part of narrative tone and texture. Other essentially folk-based themes are Carnival, a national catharsis, and the Afro-Brazilian religious ceremony of *candomblé*, which is most widely practiced in his very African home state. Amado was also one of the first Brazilian writers to employ in his populist fiction the vocabulary of spoken Brazilian Portuguese used by the lower levels of society. In addition, Amado became known not only as a political writer but also as a pornographer, though the term seems almost quaintly inappropriate today.

Whether it was because of the vaguely populist quality of the works, their political content, their sexual explicitness, or simply unpretentious, good storytelling, Amado became one of the most prominent members of the Generation of 1930 and one of the two best-selling novelists in the country. He was also a member of the National Liberation Alliance, an umbrella group of left-leaning and centrist politicians and military men that botched a coup in 1935. That membership and the political content of his works seems to have impressed the Vargas government much more than Amado's popularity as a writer—he was jailed for two months shortly after the 1935 attempt, and in 1937 the government staged a

public book burning in Salvador, where most of the books destroyed were Amado's. In 1938, shortly after Amado returned from a trip to various American countries, including the United States, where he met Michael Gold, the Brazilian government banned his books.

World War II did very little to better the plight of the Brazilian left, already in disarray, and Amado, a banned writer and a "subversive," fled to Argentina in 1941. There he wrote his infamous biography of the founder of the Brazilian Communist party, Luiz Carlos Prestes, *O Cavaleiro da Esperança* (The Knight of Hope, 1942). The next year, in Uruguay, he wrote *Terras do Sem Fim* (*The Violent Land*, 1943), a work that marks a new beginning in his fiction. He may have thought that the censors would recognize that fact when he returned to Brazil in 1942. They did not. He was immediately arrested, though the government decided not to keep him in jail but to restrict his activities to the city of Salvador. In 1944 he published a sequel, *São Jorge dos Ilhéus* (literally Saint George of the Islanders [Ilhéus is Brazil's principal cacao port in southern Bahia]). He was arrested again in 1945, just before the fall of the Vargas regime, possibly as a result of the sectarian tone of this latter work.

The new direction in these works appears at first to be mainly one of scope. *The Violent Land* is a much more complex narrative than, for example, *Cacau*, which in many ways is an elaboration of the earlier story. While *Cacau* focused on the fortunes of one man on one plantation, *The Violent Land* is an attempt to capture the epic proportions of a bloody struggle among landowners, speculators, and adventurers for control of the "brown gold," cacao. There are dozens of major characters and several interconnecting plot lines, and though much of the novel's effect and some of its conventions seem to be drawn from the American Western movie, the book is as engaging and absorbing as the best of that genre. It is also an unusual book for the early Amado in that a character's moral qualities cannot always be predicted on the basis of his social class—some of the best-drawn characters are landowners, a class Amado previously treated with undisguised contempt. The central narrative focus in *The Violent Land* is the struggle for control of the land. In *São Jorge dos Ilhéus*, the struggle is for control of money, which allows Amado to introduce the new theme of international imperialism. The two major classes portrayed are the imperialists and the communists, and because of the stereotypical treatment of these groups, conservative (mostly Roman Catholic) criticism of this work was especially virulent.

Vargas was ousted from office by a clique of the military in 1945, and the Communist party enjoyed its greatest moments during the brief period following the coup. Amado, at last officially a member of the party, ran on its ticket for the office of federal deputy (congressman) for the state of São Paulo. He was elected in 1945. In 1946 he published *Seara Vermelha* (Red Harvest), a title that indicates the book's political purposefulness. *Seara Vermelha* shares with the two previous novels a propensity for girth, but it does not possess their panoramic view and has the most politically intrusive narrator of the three books.

Amado's novels to this point have all been problem-oriented works. More specifically, they are works that focus on problems peculiar to Brazil, and it might be said that in each the problem is presented as an issue of the exploitation of one social group by another. The earlier works are about the exploitation of rural labor, the urban poor, blacks, and abandoned children. The two novels preceding *Seara Vermelha* demonstrate a sense of history; they are not just about the powerless but also about power. *Seara Vermelha* seems rather odd in this context, because while it is again a problem-oriented novel, it seems merely to address a potpourri of problems not previously examined. It seems to possess no organizing principle other than the identification of problems, many of which had already been dealt with by other Brazilian writers. It is also Amado's first work not to have as its locale his home state of Bahia, which places it at some remove from the rest of his work; at this point Amado was known at least in part as a novelist of place, the bard of Bahia.

Amado's biography of Prestes was not published in Brazil until the Communist party was legalized in 1945. It was further proof, if any was needed, that Amado intended to be Brazil's communist writer. But the party was declared illegal again within two years, and Amado left the country almost immediately. He lived in Paris for two years and attended various European writers' conferences, including some in Eastern Europe. He attended one conference in Poland as vice-president of the World Congress of Artists and Writers for Peace; and he traveled extensively in the Soviet Union, Hungary, Czechoslovakia, and Bulgaria. In 1950 he moved to Prague, where his daughter Paloma was born. From there he traveled to Albania, China, and Mongolia.

His travel memoir about his experiences behind the Iron Curtain, *O Mundo da Paz* (The World of Peace) was published in Brazil in 1951 and immediately seized. In 1951 Amado won the Stalin Peace Prize. He returned to Brazil in 1952, and in 1954 his trilogy *Os Subterrâneos da Liberdade* (The Freedom Underground) appeared. It was published simultaneously in Portuguese, French, Russian, German, Czech, and Polish. The trilogy has at least the superficial trappings of historical fiction, though the history in this case is not a very remote one: the story is a novelization of the most oppressive years of the Vargas period, 1937 to 1940. Ironically, Vargas, though ousted by the military in 1945, returned to power by popular election in 1950. He committed suicide in 1954.

Os Subterrâneos da Liberdade is Amado's longest work, and by far his most politically explicit. Historical figures such as Vargas (and others obviously based on real people) appear as minor characters, but the focus is largely on the fictitious revolutionaries who are the principal characters. The plot is rich in episodic detail, and one of the basic narrative devices is the presentation of events first from the perspective of an establishment character and later from the point of view of a communist. Episode, in fact, appears to be the principal ingredient of fabrication in all three volumes: characters seem not so much to develop as to insist on reappearing with precisely the same virtues and vices they initially possessed, and there is none of the lyric effusion or charming sense of place that often lightened the didactic ballast of earlier works. The book is probably best described as an experiment in the mechanics of plot elaboration.

Political events in the Soviet Union coincided with what many take to be a complete reversal in Amado's ideological position. With Stalin's death and the de-Stalinization campaign initiated with the "secret" report delivered by Nikita Khrushchev in

1956, there appeared to be signs of a thaw in the cold war between East and West, but the Hungarian revolt and the subsequent invasion of Hungary by Soviet troops seemed to doom that hope. Nine months after the release of the Khrushchev report, Amado joined other members of the Brazilian Communist party in a call for an open discussion of the strengths and weaknesses of socialist realism, with specific mention of the "cult of personality" that had been Stalin's trademark. But the ponderous machinery of the party apparatus moved slowly, if at all, toward such a debate, and many Brazilian intellectuals simply defected from the party. Though Amado was active in the call for discussion and reportedly even wrote a venomous attack on Soviet policy following the Hungarian invasion, he did not abandon the party for another six years, if in fact at all. But whatever his affiliation with the party, both his public persona and his novels underwent considerable change.

His next novel, *Gabriela, Cravo e Canela* (*Gabriela, Clove and Cinnamon*), was published in 1958. Bourgeois, Catholic, and unaffiliated critics, many of whom had steadfastly ignored the existence of his last few books, suddenly began writing reams about Amado. Many on the left either expressed dismay or pretended that his work from 1958 on simply did not exist; many leftists continue to ignore Amado's work after 1958. *Gabriela* won five national prizes in 1959 and within two years of issue was in its sixteenth printing. Sales of the novel surpassed those of any book of any kind in Brazil in the late 1950's, and it became a best seller even in Portugal, where previous to this time Amado's books had been banned.

Such popularity is evidently taken by leftists as proof that Amado had finally sold out and become a bourgeois writer no longer concerned with the downtrodden, and most of the attention they pay him is now limited to nostalgia-tinged rehashes of his earlier, ideologically correct works. Conservatives have generally accepted that popularity as proof that there is a "new" Amado, a gifted storyteller who has abandoned an alien and subversive ideology to take his proper place in bourgeois society. A substantial number of critics have, by a different route than the leftists, concluded that Amado has not only abandoned ideology but betrayed his gifts in order to produce a popular pseudoliterature whose only real

end is to make money for its author. Yet another faction identifies Amado's betrayal not simply as the production of slick fiction but as an appeal to prurient interest; they feel that the basic shift has been away from politics and toward pornography.

There is no denying that there is a qualitative difference between Amado's novels before and after *Gabriela*. Most critics, however, seem to have ignored the fact that Amado was an immensely popular writer before his "conversion" to capitalism, and, more important, the fact that the ingredients of the "new" Amado's fiction existed in some measure in all his early works. It is important to note that Amado was never a political thinker, and he claims not even to have made a systematic study of Marxism. Like many American writers of the 1930's, he used fiction as a way to unmask abuses in the system, and he is somewhat like John Steinbeck and John Dos Passos in that he does not expound a philosophy of political economy but merely expresses a political attitude in favor of social justice. Given Amado's circumstances, it is no surprise that, for him, Karl Marx seemed a better solution than Vargas, or that he was openly hostile to a government which capriciously held public burnings of even his less tendentious works, and which both banned his books and threw him in jail.

Ideologically, in fact, the principal difference between the earlier and the later works seems to be a diminished faith in the dictates of the Communist party and a diminished exploitation of its icons (Marx, Friedrich Engels, Prestes). Aside from the romantic characterizations of the party and its luminaries in the early works, the political attitude in all of Amado's work is identifiable as closer to anarchy than to any particular orthodoxy. The overriding social attitude in all of his fiction is one of hostility toward the hypocrisy of the bourgeoisie and a glorification of the cultural and spiritual qualities of the common people, a general posture that has several corollaries: Roman Catholicism, at least the official church, is viewed as negative, while *candomblé* and folk Catholicism are positive; sexual depravity is evil, but sexual activity (even in heroic proportions and including that with and by prostitutes) is good; political opportunism for gain is negative, but subversion can be good, and even fun; racial prejudice is evil, while miscegenation is good. At least two other elements found in some of the early works become increasingly important in the later ones. The first is Amado's lively and sometimes vicious sense of humor, which in the early works was used sparingly. The works from *Gabriela* on are all essentially comic. The second element is Amado's penchant for, and skill with, extremely convoluted plot construction, an art he first displayed fully in *Os Subterrâneos da Liberdade*. The recombination of these ingredients produces novels that, while fundamentally different in effect, share with their predecessors a complex of thematic and ethical preoccupations that remains basically unaltered in Amado's fiction.

Gabriela marks, then, a kind of great divide in Amado's work, but it is a divide considerably less great than many assume. Subtitled *Crônica de uma Cidade do Interior* (Chronicle of a Backwoods Town), the plot centers on the Syrian-born owner of a bar in Ilhéus and his desperate search for a cook and domestic servant. Gabriela is a destitute but gorgeous mulatto, a refugee of a northeastern drought, who arrives in Ilhéus propitiously and is hired by Nacib. They become lovers, and his middle-class morals finally impel him to insist on marriage. They do marry, but Gabriela, a sort of prototypical free spirit, fails to see the advantages of monogamy and is caught cheating. A truly civilized man, Nacib beats her but does not, as the unwritten law demands, kill her. He has the marriage annulled but eventually has to rehire her and, later, invite her back into his bed.

The plot is framed by another narrative concerning another infidelity, this the betrayal of a rich cacao planter by his wife. The planter behaves in a less civil but more conventional manner—he kills both his wife and the cuckolding dentist. In an unprecedented turn of events at the end of the story, he is sent to prison. The narrative is also fleshed out by numerous subplots concerning political bossism, power rivalries, and the notion of progress, exemplified by the complicated maneuvering by a young exporter to get the government to dredge the harbor for the benefit of the cacao business.

In some senses, *Gabriela* is a rewrite of a rewrite, because it merely elaborates the theme of *Cacau*, which was itself reelaborated in *The Violent Land* and *São Jorge dos Ilhéus*. But the focus and tone of *Gabriela* are different from all the other cacao-zone novels. Though in some senses a love story, it is still a novel about power and money, although the focus is less on power itself than on the social organization of a Brazilian boom town. And though there is social satire in the work, some of it biting, the tone is more tongue-in-cheek than declamatory. Those who criticize Amado for abandoning his crusade to unmask social evils should note that in some of the training for American Peace Corps volunteers bound for Brazil, *Gabriela* was used as a textbook—not only to teach the language, but as a handbook on the social organization and social control systems of rural Brazil. Those who consider Amado a bourgeois sellout should consider that *Gabriela* was a best seller in the Soviet Union, in twelve different Soviet languages.

Since the appearance of *Gabriela*, Amado has published a new novel on the average of once every three years. He has a contract with the New York publishing house of Alfred A. Knopf for almost immediate translation of his works into English and similar arrangements with publishers in a dozen other countries. (His works have been translated into no less than forty languages.) Since the release of *Gabriela*, he has traveled at least once in the Soviet Union and in China, and he has also visited the United States. He lives in a charming but unassuming house in the Bahian suburb of Rio Vermelho, which only occasionally serves as his place of work since it has become a tourist attraction. He has a vast network of friends, many of them artists and writers, and he has written much of his recent work while staying with friends in various parts of Brazil and Portugal. He has been a perennial Brazilian candidate for the Nobel Prize for literature, and in the process of becoming Brazil's most beloved, or at least most read, novelist, he has become a sort of national institution. His profile is so high that the government no longer dares interfere with the publication of his works or attempt to curb his frequent public pronouncements. During the peak of the military government's censorship campaign in the 1970's, while many younger and lesser-known writers were going into exile or seeing their works banned, Amado continued to publish novels that contained fairly scandalous references to the government, and he continued to state openly his opinions about the government's excesses.

Os Velhos Marinheiros (published in English as *Home Is the Sailor* and *The Two Deaths of Quincas Wateryell*, 1961) and *Os Pastores da Noite* (*Shepherds of the Night*, 1964) are minor novelties in Amado's fiction because they are not exactly novels. The first contains two narratives, one that might be called a novelette and another that probably is most accurately termed a long short story. *Shepherds* consists of three interconnected tales dealing with the same characters.

Home Is the Sailor is the story of Vasco Moscoso de Aragão, reputedly a retired sea captain but thought by some small minds to be a charlatan. The story unfolds by means of a clever narrative subterfuge—two narrators, with opposing points of view, recount two versions of events. A large ship, having lost its captain, docks in Bahia. Since there are no other licensed captains in the area, Vasco is pressed into service in a purely titular role to take the ship to Belém. When the ship reaches that port, in fine weather, Vasco inexplicably orders all the vessel's lines fastened, providing one narrator with proof that he is a fraud. That night, however, a terrible storm unexpectedly hits Belém. The only ship that rides out the storm untouched is Vasco's, giving the other narrator proof of Vasco's credibility.

In the story *The Two Deaths of Quincas Wateryell*, a similar dichotomy exists, except that a single narrator is attempting to ascertain the truth about the death of the main character. In this story, the narrator provides two contradictory versions of events, one plausible and one somewhat less so, and the reader must decide which to believe. The main character is Quincas Berro D'Água, formerly known as Joaquim Soares da Cunha. Once a pillar of Bahia's lower middle class, he simply drops out one day and becomes a vagrant, a drunk, and a womanizer. He dies in the squalor of the town's worst neighborhood, and his family decides to bury him quietly to avoid further embarrassment. But his vagrant friends think his death calls for a wake, and they arrive to salute their comrade, at which point he seemingly comes back to life and accompanies them to a party on a boat, from which he falls and drowns. Or perhaps he was dead all along. The fun of this story—it is a small masterpiece—is not in deciding which version to accept but in attending to the perverse narrator's

exposition of the odd circumstances surrounding this odd personage.

Shepherds of the Night also deals with vagabonds, gamblers, womanizers, and drunks. The first episode is a somewhat contrary little fable about the views these characters hold of such things as love and loyalty. The second is a magic-infused and highly complex story about what appears to be—but, of course, is not—an ordinary baptism. The final episode is the story of a group of urban squatters who invade public land on which to build their shanties; this part of the story reflects a real problem in Brazil and a topic made to order for Amado's sometimes ungenerous perspective on the activities of governments.

Dona Flor e Seus Dois Maridos (*Dona Flor and Her Two Husbands*, 1966) is a rich, detailed, roman à clef that has been Amado's biggest success since *Gabriela*. Like the story about Berro D'Água, it begins with the death of the protagonist, and an unlikely premise is the key ingredient in an essentially comic narrative. The story centers on Flor, the long-suffering wife of the city's most notorious bum. When Vadinho dies at the beginning of the book, it appears that Flor, now an attractive widow, will land a better man or at least one with better morals. She does in fact eventually marry an upstanding if insufferably dull pharmacist. But Vadinho keeps appearing to her, and his appearances become less and less spiritual and increasingly physical. In desperation, she has a *candomblé* ceremony performed to drive off Vadinho's lecherous spirit but finally reverses her decision when she realizes how much she needs him. In the end, since Vadinho remains invisible to the pharmacist, she is able to enjoy the company of both husbands.

A plot outline like this provides very little sense of the experience of reading the novel, since, as with most of Amado's novels, the pleasure of reading *Dona Flor* is a little like listening to a malicious gossip tell tales about the neighbors. In this case a lot of those neighbors are also real people, many of them Amado's friends and most of them portrayed as engaged in rather more sinister activities than is true in real life.

Tenda dos Milagres (*Tent of Miracles*, 1969) is Amado's first novel since *Jubiabá* to deal with the problem of race relations. In fact, because in *Jubiabá* race relations is a secondary theme, it might be said that this novel is his only work with race as a central theme. *Tent of Miracles* also has the most polemic tone of any of the later works, not surprising in a society in which the notion of racial harmony has become an important component of the national mythology of self. The story is about Pedro Archanjo, a self-taught scholar of folklore and race relations who has published several books. Unread for years, Archanjo's work is discovered by an American scholar who comes to visit the mulatto's birthplace, and suddenly all of Brazil becomes interested in the forgotten books. The story is principally about exploitation and hypocrisy—first that of the establishment during Archanjo's life, and second that of commercial enterprises, academics, and newspapers as the centennial of Archanjo's birth draws near.

Tereza Batista, Cansada de Guerra (*Tereza Batista, Home from the Wars*, 1972) is similar to *Gabriela* in that the heroine, another free spirit, is a transparent symbol of the Brazilian common people. Tereza's story starts when, at the age of thirteen, she is sold to an aging but vigorous sadist. She finally kills him and flees, and the rest of the tale recounts a long series of adventures and reversals: she becomes a concubine, falls in love with a married man, and finally turns to prostitution, in which profession she leads first a heroic struggle against a smallpox epidemic in the country's interior and later a prostitutes' strike in the city of Salvador. The five main episodes are told, all tongue in cheek, by a total of at least thirteen narrative voices (one of them Antônio de Castro Alves, the nineteenth-century abolitionist poet).

Tieta do Agreste, Pastora de Cabras (*Tieta, the Goat Girl*, 1977) is another whore-with-a-heart-of-gold story, this time about a goatherd who is driven out of the house by her father at a tender age because of her promiscuity. Tieta goes from the Bahian town of Agreste to São Paulo, where she becomes the mistress of a wealthy industrialist and owner of one of the city's finest bordellos. When her lover dies, she returns to Agreste and becomes a local saint—first for arranging to have electric power brought into the town, then for helping protect the hamlet from the depredations of a projected chemical plant.

Farda, Fardão, Camisola de Dormir (Uniform, Vestment, Nightgown, 1979) is another convoluted nar-

rative with numerous flashbacks, narrative reversals, and asides. The story begins with the death of a poet named Bruno, a member of the Brazilian Academy of Letters. His death opens a vacancy in the academy, and most of the story is about the various factions and the strategies they use to get a candidate elected. Most of the action is set in the 1940's, with a backdrop of World War II and Brazil's problems with a resident profascist population, sympathizers with European fascism (mostly of German and Italian descent) and also members of the Integralista party, a neofascist Brazilian movement. One candidate is a pro-Hitler colonel, whose candidacy is opposed by a liberal faction. The liberals find themselves in the position of having virtually to invent a candidate out of thin air, choosing as it turns out a moderately liberal general. Midway through the book the fascist unexpectedly dies, and the liberals have to scramble to get their increasingly arrogant candidate defeated. The odd title refers to the military uniforms of the candidates, the rather gaudy vestments worn by members of the academy, and a nightgown that is the title of an unfinished love poem left by the dead Bruno, whose story is recounted near the end of the book. The plot is loosely based on real events (the dictator Vargas was himself a member of the academy—Amado has been one since 1971), but again the structure of the plot is merely a framework on which Amado spins his yarns about love and lust and the pretensions of the bourgeoisie.

Tocaia Grande: A Face Obscura (Big Ambush: The Dark Side, 1984) has been another blockbuster bestseller of the magnitude of *Gabriela*. In it, Amado returns to the theme of the struggle for control of land in the cacao zone. In terms of chronology, the action of *Tocaia Grande* falls after that of *The Violent Land* and before that of *Gabriela*. The ambush of the title is a bloody massacre in which one landowner's gunslingers wipe out those of another. The head gunman on the winning side earns the surrounding land as a prize for his valor and determines to build a town on the site. The plot is the story of the growth of Tocaia Grande from an overnight stop for mule trains to something resembling a town. In the process of telling the story, Amado creates some of his most interesting and appealing characters. At the end of the book, another treachery takes place, and a double ambush puts an end to most of the main characters. The "dark side" of the story is that the press reports the events of the final ambush as just the opposite of what they were—only the folk poets (and Amado) know the truth.

Amado's visibility on the Brazilian literary scene has not diminished appreciably since the publication of *Gabriela*. Each of the eight novels published since has been a best seller, and some have set new records for sales. Amado has now sold so many books in Portuguese that it is unlikely that any writer could surpass him in this century. But that visibility has also made him a very large target, and many critics have been unable to resist the opportunity for easy sniping. Some of the criticism of his work is at least partly justifiable—Amado is neither a seeker of transcendent truths, nor a formal experimentalist, nor a consistent master of characterization. Since much of the fun of reading these works depends on finding out what happens to the various characters, and since much of what happens relies on highly elaborate and sometimes slightly implausible turns of events, his plots have at times been compared with those of the soap opera. But some of the criticism has been extreme, occasionally to the point of wrongheadedness.

Most critics agree that one of the charming features of Amado's fiction is the alternation between what seems to be traditional realism and passages of lyric or even magical evocation. The use of the two modes has given rise to the term "magical realism" in descriptions of his works. What some readers see as fantasy, others view as self-indulgence; and some critics have taken the position that such effusions are flaws in otherwise well-constructed tales, while some have gone to the extreme of disparaging the poetic passages for their historical inaccuracies. Amado has also been taken to task by those who look for inconsistencies in his treatment of certain themes, in an attempt to unmask his unconscious racism or sexism. This criticism may contain elements of truth, but some of these detractors take any reference to sex as sexist and any reference to blacks (by a white author) as racist. Some have used the soap opera comparison to describe Amado as a middlebrow writer, while others object to the moral dubiousness of his heroes and heroines or accuse him of being repetitious and predictable. None of these criticisms

stands up to serious examination, since they seem to presume things about the Brazilian reading public that are not true or are merely the result of an excess of primness.

Much of the negative criticism of Amado, in fact, overlooks the essential qualities of his fiction. He is, and wants to be, a populist writer, and his plots are thus not spiritual quests but sequences of minor triumphs and tragedies in the lives of his characters. Rather than philosophers or seers, his narrators are engaging blabbermouths who tell stories in a leisurely and digressive fashion that emphasizes narrative gusto over the expounding of any coherent philosophy. But contrary to what such characterizations might lead one to believe, Amado is anything but a simple spinner of yarns. His later novels are deceptively sophisticated fictions by a writer with a perfect ear for the right word, a flawless sense of dramatic and comic pace, and a keen sensibility for narrative pattern.

SELECTED BIBLIOGRAPHY

First Editions

Fiction

O País do Carnaval. Rio de Janeiro, 1931.
Cacau. Rio de Janeiro, 1933.
Suor. Rio de Janeiro, 1934.
Jubiabá. Rio de Janeiro, 1935.
Mar Morto. Rio de Janeiro, 1936.
Capitães da Areia. Rio de Janeiro, 1937.
Terras do Sem Fim. São Paulo, 1943.
São Jorge dos Ilhéus. São Paulo, 1944.
Seara Vermelha. São Paulo, 1946.
Os Subterrâneos da Liberdade. São Paulo, 1954.
Gabriela, Cravo e Canela. São Paulo, 1958.
Os Velhos Marinheiros. São Paulo, 1961.
Os Pastores da Noite. São Paulo, 1964.
Dona Flor e Seus Dois Maridos. São Paulo, 1966.
Tenda dos Milagres. São Paulo, 1969.
Tereza Batista, Cansada de Guerra. São Paulo, 1972.
Tieta do Agreste, Pastora de Cabras. Rio de Janeiro, 1977.
Farda, Fardão, Camisola de Dormir. Rio de Janeiro, 1979.
Tocaia Grande: A Face Obscura. Rio de Janeiro, 1984.

Other Writings

A Estrada do Mar. Estância, Brazil, 1938. Poetry.
ABC de Castro Alves. São Paulo, 1941. Biography.
O Cavaleiro da Esperança. Buenos Aires, 1942. Biography.
Bahia de Todos os Santos. São Paulo, 1945. Travel guide.
O Amor do Soldado. Rio de Janeiro, 1947. Play.
O Mundo da Paz. Rio de Janeiro, 1951. Travel memoir.
O Gato Malhado e a Andorinha Sinhá. Rio de Janeiro, 1976. Children's literature.

Translations

Dona Flor and Her Two Husbands. Translated by Harriet de Onís. New York, 1969.
Gabriela, Clove and Cinnamon. Translated by William L. Grossman and James L. Taylor. New York, 1962.
Home Is the Sailor. Translated by Harriet de Onís. New York, 1964.
Jubiabá. Translated by Margaret A. Neves. New York, 1984.
Sea of Death. Translated by Gregory Rabassa. New York, 1984.
Shepherds of the Night. Translated by Harriet de Onís. New York, 1966.
Showdown. Translated by Gregory Rabassa. New York, 1988.
Slums. Translated by Ann Martin. New York, 1938.
The Swallow and the Tomcat: A Love Story. Translated by Barbara Shelby Merello. New York, 1982.
Tent of Miracles. Translated by Barbara Shelby (Merello). New York, 1971.
Tereza Batista, Home from the Wars. Translated by Barbara Shelby (Merello). New York, 1975.
Tieta, the Goat Girl. Translated by Barbara Shelby Merello. New York, 1979.
The Two Deaths of Quincas Wateryell. Translated by Barbara Shelby (Merello). New York, 1965.
The Violent Land. Translated by Samuel Putnam. New York, 1945. Reprinted 1965.

Biographical and Critical Studies

Almeida, Alfredo Wagner Berno de. *Jorge Amado: Política e Literatura*. Rio de Janeiro, 1979.
Baden, Nancy T. "Jorge Amado: Storyteller of Bahia." Ph.D. diss., University of California, Los Angeles, 1971.
———. "The Significance of Names in Jorge Amado's *Gabriela, Cravo e Canela*." *Proceedings of the Pacific Coast Council on Latin American Studies* 3:87–94 (1974).
———. "Popular Poetry in the Novels of Jorge Amado." *Journal of Latin American Lore* 2/1:3–22 (1976).
Batista, Juarez da Gama. *Gabriela: Seu Cravo e Sua Canela*. Rio de Janeiro, 1964.
———. *Os Mistérios da Vida e os Mistérios de Dona Flor*. João Pessoa, Brazil, 1972.
———. *O Barroco e o Maravilhoso no Romance de Jorge Amado*. João Pessoa, Brazil, 1973.
———. *A Contraprova de Tereza, Favo-de-Mel*. João Pessoa, Brazil, 1973.
Bernard, Judith. "Narrative Focus in Jorge Amado's Story of Vasco Moscoso de Aragão." *Romance Notes* 8/1:14–17 (1966).
Bruno, Haroldo. "O Sentido da Terra na Obra de Jorge Amado." In *Estudos de Literatura Brasileira*. Rio de Janeiro, 1957. Pp. 121–134.
Chamberlain, Bobby J. "Humor: Vehicle for Social Commentary in the Novels of Jorge Amado." Ph.D. diss., University of California, Los Angeles, 1975.
———. "The *Malandro*, or Rogue Figure, in the Fiction of Jorge Amado." *Mester* 6:7–10 (1976).
———. "Double Perspective in Two Works of Jorge Amado." *Estudios iberoamericanos* 4:81–88 (1978).
Dimmick, Ralph Edward. "The Brazilian Literary Generation of 1930." *Hispania* 34/2:181–187 (1951).
Ellison, Fred P. *Brazil's New Novel*. Berkeley, California, 1954.
———. "Social Symbols in Some Recent Brazilian Literature." *Texas Quarterly* 3:112–125 (1960).
Hamilton, Russell G. "Afro-Brazilian Cults in the Novels of Jorge Amado." *Hispania* 50/2:242–252 (1967).
Jorge Amado: Documentos. Lisbon, 1964.
Jorge Amado, Povo e Terra: Quarenta Anos de Literatura. São Paulo, 1972.
Jorge Amado: Trinta Anos de Literatura. São Paulo, 1961.
Lima, Luís Costa. "Jorge Amado." In *A Literatura no Brasil* 5, edited by Afrânio Coutinho. 2nd ed. Rio de Janeiro, 1970. Pp. 304–326.
Martins, Wilson. "Jorge Amado." In *The Modernist Idea*. New York, 1970. Pp. 289–293.
Mazzara, Richard A. "Poetry and Progress in Jorge Amado's *Gabriela, Cravo e Canela*." *Hispania* 46/3:551–556 (1963).
Monteiro, Adolfo Casais. *O Romance*. Rio de Janeiro, 1964.
Olinto, Antônio. "The Negro Writer and the Negro Influence in Brazilian Literature." *African Forum* 2/4:5–19 (1967).
Perez, Renard. *Escritores Brasileiros Contemporâneos*. Rio de Janeiro, 1960.
Portella, Eduardo. *Dimensões I*. Rio de Janeiro, 1959.

———. *Dimensões II.* Rio de Janeiro, 1959.

———. *Dimensões III.* Rio de Janeiro, 1965.

Putnam, Samuel. "The Brazilian Social Novel, 1935–1940." *Inter-American Quarterly* 2:5–12 (1940).

Rabassa, Gregory. "The Five Faces of Love in Jorge Amado's Bahian Novels." *Revista de Letras,* 1963. Pp. 94–103.

Russo, David T. "Bahia, Macumba and Afro-Brazilian Culture in Jorge Amado's *Jubiabá.*" *Western Review* 6:53–58 (1969).

Schade, George D. "Three Contemporary Brazilian Novels." *Hispania* 39/4:391–396 (1956).

Silverman, Malcolm N. "An Examination of the Characters in Jorge Amado's *Ciclo da Comédia Baiana.*" Ph.D. diss., University of Illinois, Champaign-Urbana, 1971.

———. "Allegory in Two Works of Jorge Amado." *Romance Notes* 13/1:67–70 (1971).

———. "Moral Dilemma in Jorge Amado's *Dona Flor e Seus Dois Maridos.*" *Romance Notes* 13/2:243–249 (1971).

Táti, Miécio. *Estudos e Notas Críticas.* Rio de Janeiro, 1958.

———. *Jorge Amado: Vida e Obra.* Belo Horizonte, Brazil, 1961.

Tavares, Paulo. *Criaturas de Jorge Amado.* São Paulo, 1969.

Turner, Doris Jean. "The Poor and 'Social Symbolism': An Examination of Three Novels of Jorge Amado." Ph.D. diss., Saint Louis University, 1967.

Vincent, Jon S. "Jorge Amado: Politics and the Novel." Ph.D. diss., University of New Mexico, 1970.

———. "The Brazilian Novel: Some Paradoxes of Popularity." *Journal of Inter-American Studies and World Affairs* 14/2:183–199 (1972).

———. "Jorge Amado, Jorge Desprezado." *Luso-Brazilian Review.* 15 (supplementary issue):11–17 (1978).

Octavio Paz

(1914-   )

Alberto Ruy-Sánchez

Toward the end of the 1930's a new generation of Mexican writers emerged from the cultural milieu surrounding the magazine *Taller* (Workshop). These writers were conspicuous from the start, aggressively demonstrating a new sensibility and a new attitude toward literature and the world. Their principal difference from the preceding generation was their belief that poetic endeavors have a special place in various phases of history, being neither indifferent nor subordinate to it. Members of this generation were the direct inheritors of thirty years of avant-garde artistic production.

Gradually, through numerous books, this new sensibility gave shape to a large part of the Mexican literary culture for the following fifty years, opening a literary epoch that continues to this day. At the same time, the poets of this Mexican generation—together with their counterparts in other Latin American countries and in Spain—initiated the movement toward what eventually became the modern poetry of Hispanic America.

Among these young writers—none of whom had reached the age of thirty when the decade of the 1940's began—was Octavio Paz. He was exceptionally active, belligerent, and productive in his poetic creation and in other cultural endeavors. As time went on, it became increasingly evident that he was the protagonist of the literary epoch that this generation opened.

Octavio Paz was born in Mexico City on 31 March 1914. His father's family was proud of its Creole heritage, having settled in Mexico several generations before; his mother was of Andalusian stock. Paz's grandfather, Ireneo Paz, was a prominent liberal intellectual and a native of the state of Jalisco. He participated in the great historical events of his century. He served in the army that fought against Napoleon III and the French invasion of Mexico, reaching the rank of colonel. He was government secretary in the state of Sinaloa, and then participated in the movement that led Porfirio Díaz to the presidency of the country. He was a councilman in Mexico City and a representative in the Congreso de la Unión (Congress of the Union). And he was a writer, composing a biography of Porfirio Díaz, the historical novels *Doña Marina* (1883), *Amor y suplicio* (Love and Torture, 1873) and *Leyendas históricas de la Independencia* (Historical Legends of the Independence Movement), and the *costumbrista* novels *Amor de viejo* (Love in Old Age, 1882), *Las dos Antonias* (The Two Antonias, 1883), and *La piedra del sacrificio* (The Sacrificial Stone, 1871). (The *costumbrista* movement sought to record local culture in literature through the use of realistic detail.) He also wrote plays—*La bolsa o la vida* (Your Purse or Your Life, 1863), *Los héroes del día siguiente* (The Heroes of the Next Day, 1859), *La manzana de la discordia* (The Apple of Discord, 1871)—memoirs, and even a book of poems, *Cardos y violetas* (Thistles and Violets, 1892). Thanks to his grandfather's well-stocked library, Paz could read Benito Pérez Galdós and Lucio Apuleyo at a young age; later, he also read Lope de Vega, Pedro Calderón, Pedro Alarcón, Luis de Góngora, Francisco de Quevedo, and other authors. French fiction-writers and poets occupied a prominent place in the great library, as did the works of the Hispanic modernists who wrote at the turn of this century. Ireneo Paz was nearly ninety when he died, his eyes fixed on the clock in anticipation of his final hour. His ten-year-old grandson witnessed this event and relived it much later in the poem "Elegía interrumpida" ("Interrupted Elegy"; English translation in *Early Poems*, p. 72), first published in the section "Puerta condenada" (Condemned Door) in *Libertad bajo palabra* (Freedom on Parole, 1949). In this poem Paz recounts the deaths in his house, staring death in the face but at the same time examining death within himself.

Paz' father, Octavio Paz Solórzano, was an active political journalist. He worked with the revolutionary Emiliano Zapata, writing his biography and serving as his representative in Mexico during Zapata's exile in the United States. Paz Solórzano was also one of the initiators of agrarian reform in Mexico. While his only son was still young, the elder Paz was run over and killed by a train. Octavio Paz writes of his father's death in the poem "Pasado en claro" (Clean Copy, translated into English as "A Draft of Shadows"), in which he says that "La muerte es madre de las formas," ("death is the mother of forms") and that "los años y los muertos y las sílabas, / [son] cuentos distintos de la misma cuenta" ("years and the dead and the syllables / [are] different accounts from the same account").* The key elements of Paz' background, then, were an impoverished family, a very intense intellectual inheritance, and a house full of cracks, pictures of deceased

relatives, and books. The two generations of intellectuals that preceded his were not solely scholars or creators: they were also people of social passion and of action. It is not surprising then that Paz has shown great sensitivity to social problems in Mexico since his youth and that he participated in the student movements of the time. After completing his secondary school studies, he attended the Escuela Preparatoria Nacional (National Preparatory School). The school was on the site of the seventeenth-century Jesuit college San Ildefonso. Some four decades later, he composed his important poem "Nocturno de San Ildefonso" ("San Ildefonso Nocturne," first published in the collection *Vuelta*, 1976; English translation in *CP*, p. 410), which invokes the Mexico he knew in the early 1930's. During his years at this school, he became personally acquainted with the most important poets of the preceding generation and immersed himself in the poetry of his time. Carlos Pellicer, José Gorostiza, and Samuel Ramos were his teachers. Jorge Cuesta and Xavier Villaurrutia met him and thought well of him. He was introduced to the world of Spanish poetry through Gerardo Diego's renowned anthology and to that of Mexican poetry through Cuesta's anthology. In collaboration with Salvador Toscano, José Alvarado, Rafael López Malo, and Arnulfo Martínez Lavalle, he founded and edited his first magazine, *Barandal* (Balustrade). This journal, published during 1931–1932, served as a vehicle for announcing their generation as the new literary avant-garde. In 1933–1934 he edited his second magazine, *Cuadernos del Valle de México* (Notebooks from the Valley of Mexico), featuring the same group of writers, who used the journal to formulate arguments for progressing beyond "pure poetry."

In 1937, when he was twenty-three, Paz decided to leave his home and his law studies and to abandon Mexico City. He spent several months in Yucatán, in the southeast of the country, where he and some of his friends founded a progressive school for workers. This was the era of the populist government of Lázaro Cárdenas, of agrarian reform, and of the great mobilizations of the masses. The miserable lives of the Mayan peasants, who were bound to the cultivation of henequen, made a deep impression on him and led him to write the first version of his poem "Entre la piedra y la flor" (Between Stone and Flower, first

*Translated by Eliot Weinberger, in *The Collected Poems of Octavio Paz*, 1987, p. 455. This work will be further referred to as *CP*.

published in 1941; completely redone in 1976 and published in *Vuelta* 1/9:12–14 [1977]). In this poem he contrasts the simple, ritualistic life of the peasants with the abstract international monetary system that suffocated their existence without their even suspecting it. But aside from expressing the author's fundamental sociopolitical observations, this poem—in its first version—is an intense re-creation of life. It contains a profound truth that transcends the political intentions that motivate it. Though the author considered the poem a failure, or at least an unsatisfactory achievement (even after he rewrote it several times), it shows clearly Paz' poetic inclinations during that period. "Entre la piedra y la flor" was not as much of a "social poem" as another that Paz published in 1936. *¡No pasarán!* (They Shall Not Pass) was written in response to the Spanish civil war in a rhetorical style that he later rejected completely. Profits from the poem were donated to the Frente Popular Español (Popular Spanish Front) in Mexico.

Both of these poems are in clear contrast with the poems contained in his first two books, *Luna silvestre* (Savage Moon, 1933), and *Raíz del hombre* (The Root of Man, 1937). In *Luna silvestre*, Paz shows his obvious intent to unite intellectual rigor with lyricism. Love and eroticism—important themes in this and all of his subsequent poetry—occupy primary positions in these two volumes.

While *¡No pasarán!* was considered a highly rhetorical work, *Raíz del hombre* was recognized as being of the quality expected from a young poet of great talent. The critic and poet Jorge Cuesta was the first to comment on Octavio Paz and this book. In the 1 February 1937 issue of the biweekly *Letras de México* (Mexican Letters) he wrote:

What I noticed about Octavio Paz in his youth was the decisiveness and willpower with which he was able to reveal his penetration into the all-consuming essence of an object. . . . And I was waiting for a book, like *Raíz del hombre*, the poetry of which would confirm the influence of some destiny over him. Now I am certain that Octavio Paz has a future. He will not be able to liberate himself from that future nor from what he has made manifest to us. The voices of López Velarde, Carlos Pellicer, Xavier Villaurrutia, and Pablo Neruda resonate unmistakably in Paz's poems . . . [and] the fact that they

are being heard through Octavio Paz assures them of the richest and most certain future they could possibly have.

During his stay in Yucatán, one of the most important archaeological zones in Mexico, Paz discovered treasures of the country's prehistoric past and briefly entertained the thought of becoming an archaeologist. His feeling of fascination—love, horror, impassioned curiosity—for the ancient world of Mexico plays a fundamental role in his poetic work and in his essays. His subsequent writing on pre-Columbian Mexico—and especially on its art—is invaluable, even for specialists in the subject.

While in Yucatán he received an invitation to attend the Second International Congress of Antifascist Writers in Republican Spain. This invitation was of great importance, for many of the world's most prominent writers would be at the conference. Participants from Mexico were, for the most part, artists who were members of the Communist party and especially of the Liga de Escritores y Artistas Revolucionarios (League of Revolutionary Writers and Artists). Paz did not belong to the league, for he did not agree with its aesthetic orthodoxy of socialist realism and proletarian art. He was one of only two poets invited who were Communist sympathizers but not party members; the other was Pellicer. Among the conference organizers were Rafael Alberti and Neruda. Alberti was personally acquainted with Paz; Neruda had already read *Raíz del hombre* and, as he later recounted in his memoirs, was one of the first readers who enthusiastically appreciated the talent of the young Mexican poet.

First in Paris and then in Spain, the twenty-three-year-old Paz talked with writers he had never imagined meeting. Among these were Neruda himself, Louis Aragón, César Vallejo, André Malraux, Stephen Spender, Jorge Guillén, Julien Benda, Tristán Tzara, Vicente Huidobro, Miguel Hernández, and Luis Cernuda. In Valencia he met the young Spanish poets who edited the magazine *Hora de España* and who were later exiled to Mexico. This first contact with Europe was of seminal importance in his life for several reasons. First, it led to the publication in Valencia of a new collection of his poems, *Bajo tu clara sombra y otros poemas sobre España* (In Your Illustrious Shadow and Other Poems About Spain,

1937). The volume contained an introduction by the Spanish poet and editor Manuel Altolaguirre. Secondly, he felt the onset of political doubts that in the long run led him to confront his more "committed" friends and caused him to defend a writer's need to be independent. Finally, he lived for a short time with the reality of a people in the throes of civil war, a reality quite distant from the image of the war presented in his own poems; this too was a very hard lesson. He returned from Spain convinced that there were indeed causes in the world to fight for, contrary to what his friends believed, the poets of the previous generation—the generation of the magazine *Contemporáneos* (Contemporaries), in particular Villaurrutia. The question that was already troubling him before his trip to Spain became even more pressing after his return: How was he to write poetry that was not alienated from history—poetry that wasn't simply "pure" and detached—but that wasn't limited by the aesthetic dogmas of his time? His poetic and editorial labors of the following years yielded his first answers to this central question of his generation.

From 1938 to 1941 the focal point of this inquiry and of the new sensibility it provoked was the magazine *Taller*. Paz' editorial role—alongside that of Rafael Solana (the magazine's founder), Efraín Huerta, and Alberto Quintero Álvarez—was significant. Paz' essay "Razón de ser" (Reason for Being), which appeared in the second issue (April 1939) exemplified the ways in which the magazine both differed from and was similar to *Contemporáneos*. Writers of the earlier magazine espoused the idea of pure poetic rigor, in the manner of Paul Valéry or Juan Ramón Jiménez. In his manifesto Paz acknowledged the artistic merits of his predecessors and their creative assimilation of a new modernity, which Paz and the poets of *Taller* had inherited, but he lamented the sense of hopelessness in their artistic revolution. The skepticism of the contributors to *Contemporáneos* is understandable, for they formed the first generation of writers after the Mexican Revolution. They could not believe that violence would produce utopian improvements in the lives of men. The new generation could. "They are the postwar generation," stated Paz. "We live before the next great hecatomb; they lived after one." Several

decades later he wrote in his essay "Antevíspera" (Before the Eve):

> Although it is impossible for me to summarize in a sentence what separated us from our predecessors, it appears that the greatest difference lay in the fact that our consciousness of the time in which we lived was more vital and, if not clearer, definitely deeper and more complete. Time asked us a question we had to respond to if we didn't want to lose face and our souls as well. Our place in history filled us with anguish.

In the poetry of this generation, and especially of Paz, the response assumed a shape that became more and more definite but no less rich and variable: the modern city, with its ruins and promises, was the motivation behind the efflorescence of a poetry that both faced history head-on and stood within it. A new space had been introduced into the poetic landscape of Mexico and Latin America, and with time this space only grew larger.

Several years later, Paz became aware that poets in other countries had already found answers to the question about the felicitous marriage of poetry and history. On one hand there was surrealism, with its combined powers of rebellion and expression. On the other was the peculiar solution of T. S. Eliot and Ezra Pound, which introduced prosaic and historic elements into poetry, making them poetic. Both answers served as experiences through which Paz enriched the vitality of his own work. What is evident in Paz' work of that era is the desire—which in his case is almost the same as saying the project—simultaneously to situate himself in the poetic tradition of the Spanish language and to break with that tradition. He was eager to discover how—in what new costume or metamorphosis—the profound and varied destiny of man manifested itself, for he did not see this sense of destiny in the poetry of his predecessors. In one of his *Conversaciones* (Conversations) produced in 1984 for Mexican television Paz said:

> For us destiny adopts the shape of history. . . . Never has the destiny of men—the fact that we are mortal, that we are going to die, that we are capable of love, that we are born, work, and make things—been presented in the form of a historical conflict. And this is what exists in the city of the twentieth century. And this is what I did

not find in the poetry of my teachers and the poetry I tried to write.

After the fourth issue of *Taller*, Paz was named sole editor of the magazine, and several young Spanish exiles whom he had met in Spain were added to the staff. They were Juan Gil-Albert, Ramón Gaya, Antonio Sánchez Barbudo, Lorenzo Varela, and José Herrera Petere. Seven more issues were published before the magazine folded. His arguments with the leftist authors became more intense. Leon Trotsky was assassinated during that era, and the pact between Adolf Hitler and Joseph Stalin separated Paz even further from his Communist friends. Paz became acquainted with Víctor Serge, Jean Malaquais, and Benjamin Péret, well-known Marxist dissidents of those years, who helped him give new meaning to his concept of political criticism. In 1942 he published another volume of poetry, *A la orilla del mundo* (At the Edge of the World), which reprints some old poems alongside the new ones. Guided by the epigram of Quevedo—"Nothing disillusions me; the world has enchanted me"—Paz explored the narrow limits between vigil and the kind of sensory dream that is the poetic experience of this book.

He collaborated in 1943 in the founding of the magazine *El hijo pródigo* (The Prodigal Son); editorial responsibilities for the magazine were assigned to Octavio G. Barreda. In August of that year, Paz' essay "Poesía de soledad y poesía de comunión" (Poetry of Solitude and Poetry of Communion, later included in *Las peras del olmo*, 1957) was published in the magazine. In this essay, which can be viewed as a kind of manifesto, he writes of the fate of the modern poet, who is obligated to write not outside of society—which does not tolerate him—but within it and against it. The poet's challenge is to achieve a rigorous authenticity, "to unite consciousness and innocence, experience and expression, acts and the words that reveal them." This yearning evokes man radically alone in the multitudes of the city, which question him with their silence. But it is also a yearning that prefigures the experience Paz had a few years hence with surrealism: a vital force that could be described in part as a mysterious union of consciousness and innocence and the word that becomes action.

Toward the end of 1943 Paz left Mexico to begin ten years of life abroad. He spent two years in the United States, the first year supported by a Guggenheim Fellowship; the following year he held various jobs. While in the United States, he became familiar with that country's poetry. He lived for a while in San Francisco, and then in New York, where he studied the work of the Mexican poet José Juan Tablada, recently deceased in that city. At the invitation of Columbia University, he delivered a paper in homage to Tablada. This was the first modern essay on a man who was not much appreciated in Mexico at the time. Both Alfonso Reyes and Villaurrutia, for example, viewed him with disdain, and Paz' essay, "Estela para José Juan Tablada" (In Memory of José Juan Tablada, published on 1 October 1945 in *Letras de México*), initiated the reevaluation of his work. On more than one subsequent occasion, Paz similarly upset the established values of Mexican literary history and helped shape the character of Mexico's modern culture. At the same time, Tablada influenced Paz' poetry; Paz became part of his tradition. And it was Tablada's writings that provoked Paz' curiosity about the literatures and cultures of the Orient, a curiosity that later became a passion. In contrast with those who saw Tablada as an author who was affected and too literary, Paz finds him offering an invitation to life, adventure, and travel. Significantly, the poet ends his eulogy in New York with these words:

> [Tablada] invites us to open our eyes, to know how to abandon the city of our birth and the verse that has become a bad habit; he invites us to look for new skies and new loves. All is marching toward itself, he tells us. And now we know: in order to return to ourselves, we have to sally forth and take risks.

In his paper, Paz describes his own need to find a way out, and what his own path would be.

In 1945 a friend of his father suggested he join Mexico's diplomatic corps. He ended up spending the next twenty-three years of his life in diplomatic service. Thanks to José Gorostiza, who worked in the foreign ministry, Paz was assigned to the Mexican embassy in Paris, where he was given a minor post. Paris proved to be a very stimulating cultural environment for Paz. Among the friends he made was the Greek philosopher and historian Kostas Papaioannou (1925–1951), who was living in exile. There was no better source than he, the clear-thinking and erudite Marxist, for up-to-date information on the realities of the socialist countries and their concentration camps in the postwar years. There was no better guide than he to the art of ancient Greece and Byzantium and to contemporary music and art. Papaioannou became one of the most important historians and critics of totalitarianism as well as one of Paz' best friends during his years in Paris. Paz' *El ogro filantrópico* (*The Philanthropic Ogre*, 1979), a book of critical essays on history and politics, was dedicated to this Greek philosopher.

In Paris he also began to see Benjamin Péret again and through him was able to participate in various activities and publications of the surrealists. In time he became friends with André Breton and at long last began his passionate and enduring relationship with surrealism. Many years later, in *Corriente alterna* (*Alternating Current*, 1967), he acknowledged: "Many times I write as though I were having a silent conversation with Breton: objections, answers, agreement, disagreement, homage, all these things at once" (Lane trans., p. 53). Paz did not see surrealism as an aesthetic school or an artistic style, but as "a secret focus of poetic passion in our vile times," a subversion of sensibilities, a radical movement to liberate art, eroticism, morality, and politics. It was for him, above all, a vital adventure. While adopting elements of surrealist poetics in his poems, Paz renounced the dogma of automatic writing and abandonment of content. It was precisely content—vital contemporary history personalized with everyday detail—that Paz had learned to incorporate into a poem from his reading of Eliot and Pound.

During the late 1940's Paz' poetic work reached its maturity. In 1949 he published his first major book, *Libertad bajo palabra* (Freedom on Parole). The following year he wrote the essay on the nature of the Mexican people that quickly became a classic: *El laberinto de la soledad* (*The Labyrinth of Solitude*, 1950). And the next year another important book, written in a prose-poetry that reflected his new aesthetic formulations, *¿Águila o sol?* (*Eagle or Sun?*), came out.

Three books in three years: all important to his work and to the literature of his language.

Libertad bajo palabra is a new vision of an earlier poetry, a rewriting under new exigencies. But above all, it is something radically new. The entire book presents itself as an avant-garde work at a time when the avant-garde is in rapid decline and has become mired in academicism. By contrast, Paz champions a critical avant-garde, an avant-garde that can free itself from stereotype. The poems of this collection express a new and vital attitude that Paz shared, without knowing it, with other Latin American authors of the same period. At the start of the 1950's, José Lezama Lima, Enrique Molina, Emilio Adolfo Westphalen, Nicanor Parra, Álvaro Mutis, Gonzalo Rojas, and Paz were defining the poetry of contemporary Hispanic America. Their poetry shared a characteristic that Paz later described in *Los hijos del limo* (*Children of the Mire*, 1974) as a way of living in language:

> The issue was not to invent, as in 1920, but to explore. The territory that attracted these poets was neither outside nor within. It was that space where interior meets exterior: the zone of language. Their preoccupation was not aesthetic; for those young writers language was a contradiction: it was simultaneously destiny and choice; something given and something we make; something that makes us.

In one of the most important poems in *Libertad bajo palabra*, "Himno entre ruinas" ("Hymn Among the Ruins," English translation published in *Early Poems*, p. 95), a new artistic form appears, a form that Paz would explore in greater depth in the future: simultaneity. Paz' process of showing two parallel actions at the same time became the new form of the poetics of modernity in the Spanish language. He creatively translated into Spanish what Guillaume Apollinaire and Blaise Cendrars had discovered in French poetry and Pound and Eliot in English poetry. In 1960 and 1968 *Libertad bajo palabra* saw new editions that each significantly transformed the book, converting it into a revision of Paz' poetic work between 1935 and 1957.

Although Paz had found a way to make poetry into history, there remained a more explicit formulation of his historical preoccupations that would fit only into the essay. *The Labyrinth of Solitude* is the answer to two basic questions: What does it mean to be Mexican in the twentieth century? What does Mexico mean in this period? The word "solitude" has a predominantly historical meaning in this book: to be alone in time, in history. Further, Paz regards solitude as a state that is the fate of all men and all nations. Written in the prose of a poet, the book is a lucid analysis of the most profound rites of the contemporary Mexican, that is, of the Mexican who lives in different historical periods simultaneously. For the author, the discipline of history is a kind of knowledge that lies midway between science and poetry. In *The Labyrinth of Solitude* Paz passionately penetrates the fog shrouding the Mexican identity and provides succeeding generations with words for describing this identity.

All of Paz' poetic efforts up to this time are focused in *Eagle or Sun?*, a series of prose poems. None of his earlier writings exhibits, as this book does, the conception of the poet who is literally made by language. Each poem in the book is an exploration of worlds and underworlds that are external and internal, personal and Mexican, and worldly. "Trabajos del poeta" ("The Poet's Work") and "Arenas movedizas" ("Shifting Sands") are titles of two sections of *Eagle or Sun?*, a book with all the sensibilities of surrealism. In fact, one of the poems in this book, "Mariposa de obsidiana" ("Obsidian Butterfly"), was Paz' first contribution to a surrealist publication, Breton's *Almanach surréaliste du demi-siècle*, in 1950.

Paz spent most of 1952 traveling in Japan and India, which made a deep impression on his subsequent work. His visit to Japan intensified the literary seduction that had started when he first read Tablada, the poet who introduced haiku to the literature of the Spanish language. In 1955 Paz collaborated with a Japanese friend, Eikichi Hayashiya, in the preparation of the first Western-language version of Bashō Matsuo's poems *Sendas de Oku* (published in 1957; translated into English by Earl Miner as *The Narrow Road Through the Provinces*, 1966). He also wrote several articles on Oriental art and literature. Later, between 1962 and 1968, Paz lived in India, and in 1969 he published a book of poems written in the Orient, *Ladera este* (*Eastern Slope*, English translation in CP, pp. 163–331). This book contains two sec-

tions he wrote in India, Afghanistan, and Ceylon: "Hacia el comienzo" ("Toward the Beginning") and "Blanco" ("White"). In 1971 he and the French poet Jacques Roubaud, the Italian Edoardo Sanguinetti, and the Englishman Charles Tomlinson collaborated on a poem in four languages and four voices, *Renga* (*Renga*, 1972). This poem was a re-creation and transformation of the Japanese tradition of *renga* (a collective poem), which developed between the ninth and fifteenth centuries. His long prose poem, *El mono gramático* (*The Monkey Grammarian*, 1974), refers repeatedly to India and specifically to the Galta Road in Rajasthan.

Paz lived in Mexico between 1952 and 1958, still in the employ of the foreign ministry. Following his return to his homeland, he became one of the most active forces in Mexican culture, introducing writers from abroad and showing Mexican painters and writers in a new light. He had obvious influence on *La revista mexicana de literatura* (The Mexican Review of Literature), which was edited in its early years by Carlos Fuentes and Emmanuel Carballo. In 1955 he founded the experimental theater group *Poesía en voz alta* (Poetry Out Loud) in collaboration with several other artists. During its existence, this group was recognized for its avant-garde stage productions. In 1956 he published his only play, *La hija de Rappaccini* (*Rappaccini's Daughter*, English translation in Chantikian, ed., *Octavio Paz*, pp. 34–65), a work in one act based on a story by Nathaniel Hawthorne. The play was produced that year under the direction of Héctor Mendoza.

The year 1956 saw the publication of another important book of poetics by Paz, *El arco y la lira* (*The Bow and the Lyre*), which continued the exploration into the nature of poetry begun almost fifteen years before in his essay "Poesía de soledad y poesía de comunión." From the outset the author rejected the contention that this book was a theoretical tract, preferring to characterize it as testimony to an encounter with several poems. According to Paz—who follows Heraclitus in using this image—poetic man simultaneously shares in the nature of the lyre, which locates him in the world with its song, and of the bow, which impels him beyond himself. The first edition of the book, which is divided into three sections, addresses these questions: Is there a poetic statement that cannot be reduced to any other statement? What do poems say? How is the poetic statement communicated? The first question points to an examination of the elements of a poem itself: language, rhythm, verse and prose, and imagery. The second leads us into the world of poetic revelation, of inspiration, and of the trip we take to "the other shore" in order to have the poetic experience. In addressing the third question, Paz again shows his preoccupation with the relationship between history and poetry—with the ways in which the irreducible poetic act introduces itself into the world. Once again, Paz concludes that poetry should not sing to history but *be* history. Once again he conceives of the poetic experience as a return to oneself, to one's most profound and authentic desires. And once again he affirms that solitude continues to be the dominant note in the poetry of today. This essay displays erudition and originality in its interpretation of the passionate adventure of contemporary poetry. The author concludes by leaving open the questions he raised in the beginning, asking himself if answers for them even exist. In fact, Paz leaves a path open for his future work as an essayist. A strong and wide current of thought sweeps through all of his books of literary essays; this is true in particular of *Children of the Mire*, which in certain ways can be seen as an extension of *The Bow and the Lyre*.

In the second edition of *The Bow and the Lyre* (1967), the original epilogue is replaced by an essay titled "Los signos en rotación" (Signs in Rotation). This essay presents a new poetic manifesto, arguing that modern poetry is not "poetic poetry," as had been maintained before by the poets of the older generation, but rather that the most elevated form of poetry currently consists in the negation of poetry, in the criticism of language and of the poetic experience itself. It is the sign of our times: the reading of a poem lies in the poem itself, but this reading should never be fixed or closed. Furthermore, poetry should not be invention, but discovery of others, of the otherness that surrounds us. Hence, poetry is the mysterious and authentic search for a here and a now. The theme of poetry and revolution, of poetry and society, is revised and placed again in parentheses— identifying it as a sort of intrusion. According to Paz, the mission of the poet had previously been seen as

giving a purer meaning to the words of the tribe; today the poet's task is to question that meaning. At the same time, poetry is an attempt to reunite elements that have been pulled apart.

Paz' activity as literary critic and essayist has been enormous. *Las peras del olmo* (Pears from the Elm Tree, 1957) was his first volume of relatively miscellaneous literary essays. It was followed in 1965 by *Cuadrivio* (Quadrivium), in 1966 by *Puertas al campo* (Gateway to the Field), by *Alternating Current* in 1967, and by *Los signos en rotación y otros ensayos* (Signs in Rotation and Other Essays) in 1971. *El signo y el garabato* (The Sign and the Scribble) appeared in 1973, *In/Mediaciones* (Im/Mediations) in 1979, *Sombras de obras* (Shadows of Works) in 1983, and *Hombres en su siglo* (Men in Their Century) in 1984.

Interspersed among these were other collections that focused on a single theme. *Claude Lévi-Strauss; o, El nuevo festín de Esopo* (Claude Lévi-Strauss; or, Aesop's New Festival, translated into English as *Claude Lévi-Strauss: An Introduction*) came out in 1967. Two years later *Conjunciones y disyunciones* (*Conjunctions and Disjunctions*) was published. In 1971 *Traducción: Literatura y literalidad* (Translation: Literature and Literalness) appeared, in 1973 *Apariencia desnuda: La obra de Marcel Duchamp* (*Marcel Duchamp: Appearance Stripped Bare*), and in 1974 *La búsqueda del comienzo* (Search for the Beginning) and *Children of the Mire*. *Xavier Villaurrutia en persona y en obra* (Xavier Villaurrutia in Person and in His Work) was published in 1978, and in 1982 the by now already indispensable volume of literary history *Sor Juana Inés de la Cruz; o, Las trampas de la fe*. *Sor Juana* is both a study of the times in which the sixteenth-century Mexican nun and poet lived and an audacious and very complete reflection upon her life and work.

On occasion Paz has given interviews, which are no less important than his essays because of the careful attention he gives to them. Two noteworthy collections of his interviews are *Solo a dos voces* (A Solo for Two Voices, 1973) and *Pasión crítica* (A Critical Passion, 1985). *Solo a dos voces* is an interview with Julián Ríos; *Pasión crítica*, which was edited by Hugo J. Verani and is the more important volume, includes the interview with Ríos.

In all of these books one sees Paz' intense dedication to cultural journalism, a moderate amount of his reminiscing about writers he knew in earlier times, and studies of writers whose works have become classics of Spanish-language literature and literature in other languages. These collections contain fundamental ideas: that modernity in art is a tradition, a tradition made up of ruptures; that the decline of the avant-garde becomes plausible when one realizes the impossibility of believing in linear and progressive time; and that the modern is in a state of crisis, which leads to the dissolution of the notion of the future and of change as well. Paz anticipated by at least fifteen years all the concerns that are now subsumed under the label "postmodern."

Paz' exploration of modernity and the directions of its development has centered on literature—especially poetry—and on other forms of art, with particular emphasis on painting. As an art critic, Paz opened up Mexico to modernity, not only by informing the country about what was happening in the world, but also by helping people understand the work of modern Mexican painters. Before long pre-Columbian art was being seen in a new light, because Paz had passed through surrealism and therefore was able to appreciate—and inculcate appreciation of—"the primitive" as an authentic and remarkable art form. He also threw himself into the debates of the most irritated nationalists, defending Rufino Tamayo's art against its detractors.

Paz lived in Paris again from 1959 to 1962, after which he was named ambassador to India. He stayed in India until 1968. That year, after the massacre of students at the Plaza de Tres Culturas on 2 October, he resigned his diplomatic post and spoke out against his government in the international press, causing tremendous public outrage. A short time later he wrote *Posdata* (Postscript, 1970), a critical and self-critical update of *The Labyrinth of Solitude*. It was a criticism of the government and even more deeply a criticism and interpretation of the history of Mexico, with all its recent errors and horrors: a "Crítica de la pirámide" ("Critique of the Pyramid") and of the idols within ourselves.

Paz' ideas have been echoed elsewhere in Latin America and on occasion have provoked considerable debate. In 1979, nearly ten years after the publication of *Posdata*, he published a thick volume of historical and political criticism, *El ogro filantrópico* (*The Philanthropic Ogre*). The title points to the principal characteristics of the Mexican state. The first section of the book, "El presente y sus pasados" ("The Present and Its Pasts"), contains essays on Mexico that continue the analyses of *The Labyrinth of Solitude* and *Posdata*; the second section returns to the history of Mexico; the third discusses totalitarianism and eroticism; and the final section is a set of essays on intellectuals and power. Dissent, says Paz, is the nobility and honor of our time.

Tiempo nublado (Clouded Time, translated as *One Earth, Four or Five Worlds*, 1983) brings together essays on international politics and on the crises caused by the imperial democracy of the United States and by the Russian bureaucracy; it gives particular attention to the nature of the relationship between the United States and Latin America. In all his political essays Paz affirms the need for the modern intellectual and critic to be independent of political parties or "sciences of truth." He describes his work in political analysis as the inquisitive passion of a writer, of a poet who gives testimony about his times outside of his poetry. A large number of his literary and political articles were originally published in the cultural magazines he edited during the 1970's and 1980's. These were *Plural*, which he edited from 1971 to 1976, and *Vuelta* (Return), which he has edited since 1976.

But no less important than his role as witness to his time has been his role as champion of poetry. He has read, commented on, and supported the work of many young poets. In collaboration with three Mexican poets—Alí Chumacero, Homero Aridjis, and José Emilio Pacheco—Paz edited and wrote the introduction to an anthology of modern Mexican poetry that is a classic in its genre: *Poesía en movimiento: México 1915–1966* (*New Poetry of Mexico*, 1966). He had already edited and written the introduction and notes for another anthology of Mexican poetry in 1950. Commissioned by UNESCO, this anthology was translated from the French into several languages; the English translation, published in 1958, was by an Irishman who was not well known at the time, Samuel Beckett.

Paz has been a passionate and tireless translator.

He has developed theories of translation and, most importantly, has made many foreign poets known to Mexicans, including the Portuguese Fernando Pessoa (1888–1935). He has collaborated on the translation of Chinese, Japanese, and Swedish writers. His book *Versiones y diversiones* (Versions and Diversions, 1974) is a compilation of a large portion of his translation work up to that date.

During his stay in Mexico in the 1950's and after he wrote *Eagle or Sun?*, Paz' poetic work became ever more innovative and experimental. His poetic adventures were opening new pathways for young poets as well, poets who always followed in his steps. In 1954 he published *Semillas para un himno* (Seeds for a Hymn), and in 1957 the long poem *Piedra de sol* (*Sun Stone*), the culmination of a poetic search. This circular poem is simultaneously about love and about the crimes of history. It is about a meeting with the beloved when the world is in ruins, and when the sun opens minds like stones and makes life spring forth from them. In 1958 *La estación violenta* (The Violent Season) was published; it included *Sun Stone*. In 1960 *La estacion violenta* was itself included in the new edition of *Libertad bajo palabra*.

Paz' poems written between 1958 and 1961 and collected in 1962 in the volume *Salamandra* (Salamander) are fervent examples of a poetry that—as Paz had already noted—lives and grows: it creates and re-creates itself through critical self-reflection. The same volume contains short and equally fervent poems on erotic encounters.

In 1967 the poem *Blanco* ("White") (English translation in *CP*, 309–331) came out in a limited first edition, well suited to the poem's experimental form. The poem is printed on a single folded sheet that on being unfolded produces the text, as space itself becomes text. The intention is for the reading act to become a ritual, a trip with several possible routes. The three parallel columns, each written in a different script, offer at least six combinations or possibilities for reading.

The following year, in 1968, his experimentation with spaces and the art of combinations reached its culmination when he published *Discos visuales* (Visual Disks) in collaboration with the painter Vicente Rojo. The year before he had experimented with the Apollinairean calligram and the concrete poetry of Tablada in his *Topoemas* ("Topoems," published in 1971; English translation in *CP*, pp. 333–339).

In the majority of poems included in *Eastern Slope*—where "White" is presented in linear form—the poetic process reaches an immense calm, as if the whirlwind of innovation were now working more deeply inside Paz than before, and as if silence had transformed everything. Then comes the singular experience of *The Monkey Grammarian*, written in 1970. Aside from the beauty of its intense prose, the book again synthesizes Paz' poetic efforts of various years. In this volume writing is simply movement, and as we travel down the Galta Road, it gradually fades away before us, leaving us in our own hands, defenseless before ourselves. Several times we find our bearings, only to become lost again. Are we the Way? Or is everything that distracts us the Way? The book advances in a spiral, and in the end poetry is seen as the convergence of all points and an act that at the same time is a body. A poem writes itself as it is read: both actions coincide and in the process both reconcile themselves and liberate themselves from one another.

The book *Vuelta* ("Return," 1976; English translation in *CP*, pp. 341–429) contains poetry written between 1969 and 1975. These are the poems of a homecoming, of a return not only from the geographical Orient, but also from the Orient of poetry into which the poet had penetrated. Memory reveals a "Paisaje inmemorial" ("Immemorial Landscape"). But it is not the exploration of memory but of poetry that creates and re-creates disturbed worlds as the poetry is made and makes itself, as it is spoken and speaks, and as it is read and reads itself. One sees Paz' friends and Mexico City of the 1930's; one hears the quiet breath of his "Jardines errantes" ("Nomadic Gardens"). His long poem of this period is *Pasado en claro* (The Past Illuminated, 1975; translated as *A Draft of Shadows*). In this poem the poet invokes the past and yields himself to possession by the past. A new grammar of the world takes form, and as the poet proceeds, he recognizes, among all the references to the past lives of others, references to himself. A large house looms up from his infancy, in decay, and inhabited by ghosts. "Mis palabras, / al hablar de la casa, se agrietan" ("My words, / speaking of the house, split apart," *CP*, p. 449), says Paz. "En mi casa los muertos eran más que los vivos. . . . Mientras la casa se desmoronaba / yo crecía. Fui (soy) yerba, maleza / entre escombros anónimos." ("In my house there were more dead than living. . . . As the house crumbled, I grew / I was (I am) grass, / weeds in anonymous trash," *CP*, p. 451). And the poem's conclusion conforms to the pattern we have already seen elsewhere in his poetry: action, poem, and poet making themselves and being made, as the boundaries between them dissolve.

> *pasos dentro de mí, oídos con los ojos,*
> *el murmullo es mental, yo soy mis pasos,*
> *oigo las voces que yo pienso,*
> *las voces que me piensan al pensarlas.*
> *Soy la sombra que arrojan mis palabras.*

> footsteps within me, heard with my eyes,
> the murmur is in the mind, I am my footsteps,
> I hear the voice that I think,
> the voices that think me as I think them.
> I am the shadow my words cast.
> (CP, p. 465)

In 1976 a new edition of all his poetry written between 1935 and 1975 was published under the title *Poesía* (Poetry). In 1987 he published *Árbol adentro* (*A Tree Within*, English translation in *CP*, pp. 594–635). In this book the erotic tendency of his poetry forcefully manifests itself, confirming that his poetics is an "erotic treatise" in the sense that it is a search for the other, for the "otherness" he desires, and an encounter with it on the tactile surface of the poem. In *A Tree Within* everything—the trees rustling their leaves, for example—becomes language for speaking with the beloved, and things are signs that lovers impregnate each other with.

The year 1987 also saw the publication in three volumes of Paz's writings on Mexico. The first volume, *El peregrino en su patria* (The Pilgrim in his Fatherland), unites a broad selection of the articles he wrote on the politics and history of Mexico. The second volume, *Generaciones y semblanzas* (Generations and Biographical Sketches), contains articles on literature and Mexican writers. The third, *Los privilegios de la vista* (Privileges of View), is the most unusual: it presents a rich collection of essays on Mexican art never brought together before, including articles on pre-Columbian art, art of the nineteenth century, contemporary artists, and certain aspects of muralism. The three volumes were published under the title, *México en la obra de Octavio Paz* (Mexico in the Work of Octavio Paz). Later, a series of twelve programs on the books was aired over Mexican television. Paz has worked with Mexican television in the past, contributing such cultural programs as *Conversaciones con Octavio Paz* (Conversations with Octavio Paz), produced in 1984, and a series on Ezra Pound, aired in 1986.

Among the numerous awards that Paz has received are the Premio Miguel de Cervantes (Miguel de Cervantes Prize), awarded in Madrid in 1981; the Jerusalem Literature Prize, 1977; the German booksellers' Peace Prize, 1984; and El Premio Nacional de Letras (The National Prize in Letters), awarded in Mexico in 1977. In 1963 he won the International Poetry Prize in Brussels; he was awarded the Oslo Poetry Prize in 1985, the Premio Menéndez Pelayo (Menéndez Pelayo Prize) of Spain in 1987, the Premio Ollin Yoliztli (Ollin Yoliztli Prize) of Mexico in 1980, and the Neustadt Literature Prize of the University of Oklahoma in 1982. In addition he has received honorary doctorates from Boston University (1973), the University of Mexico (1978), Harvard (1980), and New York University (1984).

Octavio Paz' work as poet, essayist, political polemicist, editor, translator, and active champion of culture during his career of fifty years has opened the doors of modernity to the Spanish language. It has also built bridges to the literatures of other languages and of other times and showed how to apply criticism to creation and creation to criticism.

Translated from the Spanish by S. G. Stauss

SELECTED BIBLIOGRAPHY

Editions

Poetry

Luna silvestre. Mexico City, 1933.
¡No pasarán! Mexico City, 1936.
Bajo tu clara sombra y otros poemas sobre España. With an

introductory note by Manuel Altolaguirre. Valencia, Spain, 1937.

Raíz del hombre. Mexico City, 1937.

Entre la piedra y la flor. Mexico City, 1941.

A la orilla del mundo. Mexico City, 1942.

Libertad bajo palabra. Mexico City, 1949. 2nd ed. expanded (1935–1957), 1960.

Semillas para un himno. Mexico City, 1954.

Piedra de sol. Mexico City, 1957.

La estación violenta. Mexico City, 1958.

Salamandra 1958–1961. Mexico City, 1962.

Viento entero. Delhi, India, 1965.

Blanco. Mexico City, 1967.

Discos visuales. Four poems printed in four paper disks, with art by Vicente Rojo. Mexico City, 1968.

La centena: Poemas 1935–1968. Barcelona, 1969.

Ladera este (1962–1968). Mexico City, 1969.

Topoemas. Mexico City, 1971.

Renga. In collaboration with Jacques Roubaud (French part of the poem), Edoardo Sanguinetti (Italian part of the poem), and Charles Tomlinson (English part of the poem). Mexico City, 1972.

Pasado en claro. Mexico City, 1975.

Vuelta. Barcelona, 1976.

Hijos del aire/Airborn. In collaboration with Charles Tomlinson. Mexico City, 1979.

Poemas (1935–1975). Barcelona, 1979.

Prueba del nueve. Mexico City, 1985.

Árbol adentro (1976–1987). Barcelona, 1987.

Poetical Prose

¿Águila o sol? Mexico City, 1951.

El mono gramático. Barcelona, 1974.

Plays

La hija de Rappaccini. In *Revista mexicana de literatura* (Mexico City) 2/7:3–26 (1956). One-act play.

Essays

El laberinto de la soledad. Mexico City, 1950.

El arco y la lira: El poema, la revelación poética, poesía e historia. Mexico City, 1956.

Las peras del olmo. Mexico City, 1957.

Cuadrivio. Mexico City, 1965.

Los signos en rotación. Buenos Aires, 1965.

Puertas al campo. Mexico City, 1966.

Claude Lévi-Strauss; o, El nuevo festín de Esopo. Mexico City, 1967.

Corriente alterna. Mexico City, 1967.

Marcel Duchamp; o, El castillo de la pureza. Mexico City, 1968.

Conjunciones y disyunciones. Mexico City, 1969.

México: La última década. Austin, Tex., 1969.

Posdata. Mexico City, 1970.

Las cosas en su sitio: Sobre la literatura española del siglo XX. In collaboration with Juan Marichal. Mexico City, 1971.

Los signos en rotación y otros ensayos. Introduced and selected by Carlos Fuentes. Madrid, 1971.

Traducción: Literatura y literalidad. Barcelona, 1971.

Apariencia desnuda: La obra de Marcel Duchamp. Mexico City, 1973.

El signo y el garabato. Mexico City, 1973.

Solo a dos voces. An interview with Julián Ríos. Barcelona, 1973.

La búsqueda del comienzo. Madrid, 1974.

Los hijos del limo: Del romanticismo a la vanguardia. Barcelona, 1974.

Teatro de signos/Transparencias. Edited by Julián Ríos. Madrid, 1974.

Xavier Villaurrutia en persona y en obra. Mexico City, 1978.

In/Mediaciones. Barcelona, 1979.

México en la obra de Octavio Paz. Edited and with an introduction by Luis Mario Schneider. Mexico City, 1979.

El ogro filantrópico: Historia y politica, 1971–1978. Barcelona, 1979.

Sor Juana Inés de la Cruz; o, Las trampas de la fe. Mexico City and Barcelona, 1982.

Sombras de obras. Barcelona, 1983.

Tiempo nublado. Barcelona, 1983.

Hombres en su siglo y otros ensayos. Barcelona, 1984.

Pasión crítica: Conversaciones con Octavio Paz. Selected, introduced, and with notes by Hugo J. Verani. Barcelona, 1985.

México en la obra de Octavio Paz 1: El peregrino en su patria: Historia y política de México. 2: Generaciones y semblanzas: Escritores y letras de México. 3: Los privilegios de la vista: Arte de México. Edited by Luis Mario Schneider and Octavio Paz. Mexico City, 1987.

Primeras páginas. Edited and with an introduction by Enrico Mario Santi. Barcelona, (forthcoming).

Translations and Editions by Paz

Laurel: Antología de la poesía moderna en lengua española. Edited by Xavier Villaurrutia, Emilio Prados, Juan Gil-Albert, and Octavio Paz. Mexico City, 1941.

Anthologie de la poésie mexicaine. Edited and introduced by Octavio Paz, with a note by Paul Claudel. Paris, 1952.

Bashō, Matsuo. *Sendas de Oku*. Translated by Eikichi Hayashiya and Octavio Paz, with an introduction by Octavio Paz. Mexico City, 1957.

Anthology of Mexican Poetry. Edited and introduced by Octavio Paz, with a note by C. M. Bowra, and translated into English by Samuel Beckett. Bloomington, Ind., 1958.

Pessoa, Fernando. *Antología*. Selected, translated, and introduced by Octavio Paz. Mexico City, 1962.

Poésia en movimiento: México 1915–1966. Edited by Octavio Paz, Alí Chumacero, Homero Aridjis, and José Emilio Pacheco. Mexico City, 1966.

New Poetry of Mexico. Edited by Octavio Paz, Alí Chumacero, Homero Aridjis, José Emilio Pacheco, and Mark Strand. New York, 1970. English version of *Poesía en movimiento*.

Versiones y diversiones. Poems translated by Octavio Paz from French, English, Portuguese, Swedish, Chinese, and Japanese. Mexico City, 1974.

Translations

Poetry

Airborn/Hijos del aire. In collaboration with Charles Tomlinson. London, 1981.

Blanco. Translated by Eliot Weinberger. With "Illuminations" by Adja Yunkers. New York, 1974.

The Collected Poems of Octavio Paz: 1957–1987. Edited and translated by Eliot Weinberger. With additional translations by Elizabeth Bishop, Paul Blackburn, Lysander Kemp, Denise Levertov, John Frederick Nims, Mark Strand, and Charles Tomlinson. New York, 1987.

Configurations. Various translators. New York and London, 1971.

A Draft of Shadows and Other Poems. Edited and translated by Eliot Weinberger (with additional translations by Mark Strand and Elizabeth Bishop). New York, 1979.

Early Poems: 1935–1955. Various translators. New York, 1973. Bloomington, Ind., 1974.

The Four Poplars. Translated by Eliot Weinberger. With artwork by Antonio Frasconi. New York, 1985.

Homage and Desecrations. Translated by Eliot Weinberger. With artwork by Richard Mock. New York, 1987.

Obsidian Butterfly. Translated by Eliot Weinberger. With artwork by Brian Nissen. Barcelona, 1983.

Piedra de Sol/The Sun Stone. Translated by Donald Gardner. York, England, 1969.

Renga: A Chain of Poems. Translated by Charles Tomlinson. Poem in four voices by Jacques Roubaud, Edoardo Sanguinetti, Charles Tomlinson, and Octavio Paz. New York, 1972.

Selected Poems. Translated by Muriel Rukeyser. Bloomington, Ind., 1963.

Selected Poems. Edited by Charles Tomlinson. Various translators. London, 1979.

Selected Poems. Edited and with an introduction by Eliot Weinberger. Various translators. New York, 1984.

Sun Stone. Translated by Muriel Rukeyser. London and New York, 1962, 1963.

Sun-Stone. Translated by Peter Miller. Toronto, 1963.

3 Notations/Rotations. With graphic art by Toshihiro Katayama. Cambridge, Mass., 1974.

Poetical Prose

¿Águila o sol?/Eagle or Sun? Translated by Eliot Weinberger. New York, 1970. A new version by Eliot Weinberger is published as *Eagle or Sun?* New York, 1976.

The Monkey Grammarian. Translated by Helen Lane. New York, 1981.

Plays

Rappaccini's Daughter. Translated by Harry Haskell. In *Octavio Paz: Homage to the Poet*. Edited by Kosrof Chantikian. San Francisco, Calif., 1980. Pp. 34–65.

Essays

Alternating Current. Translated by Helen Lane. New York, 1973.

The Bow and the Lyre: The Poem, the Poetic Revelation, Poetry and History. Translated by Ruth L. C. Simms. Austin, Tex., 1973.

Children of the Mire: Modern Poetry from Romanticism to the Avant-Garde. Translated by Rachel Phillips. Cambridge, Mass., 1974.

Claude Lévi-Strauss: An Introduction. Translated by J. S. Bernstein and Maxine Bernstein. Ithaca, N.Y., 1970.

Conjunctions and Disjunctions. Translated by Helen Lane. New York, 1974.

Convergences: Essays on Art and Literature. Translated by Helen Lane. New York, 1987.

The Labyrinth of Solitude. Translated by Lysander Kemp. New York, 1961.

The Labyrinth of Solitude; The Other Mexico; Return to the Labyrinth of Solitude; Mexico and the United States; The Philanthropic Ogre. Translated by Lysander Kemp, Yara Milos, and Rachel Phillips. Belash, N.Y., 1985.

Marcel Duchamp: Appearance Stripped Bare. Translated by Rachel Phillips and Donald Gardner. N. Y., 1978.

Marcel Duchamp; or, The Castle of Purity. Translated by Donald Gardner. New York and London, 1970.

One Earth, Four or Five Worlds: Reflections on Contemporary History. Translated by Helen Lane. New York, 1985. Translation of *Tiempo nublado.*

On Poets and Others. Translated by Michael Schmidt. New York, 1986.

The Other Mexico: Critique of the Pyramid. Translated by Lysander Kemp. New York, 1972.

The Siren and the Seashell, and Other Essays on Poets and Poetry. Translated by Lysander Kemp and Margaret Sayers Peden. Austin, Tex., 1976.

Sor Juana. Translated by Margaret Sayers Peden. Cambridge, Mass., 1988.

Biographical and Critical Studies

Céa, Claire. *Octavio Paz.* Paris, 1965.

Chantikian, Kosrof, ed. *Octavio Paz: Homage to the Poet.* San Francisco, Calif., 1980.

Cuadernos hispanoamericanos 343–345 (1979). Homage to Octavio Paz.

Fein, John M. *Toward Octavio Paz: A Reading of his Major Poems, 1957–1976.* Lexington, Ky., 1986.

Flores, Ángel, ed. *Aproximaciones a Octavio Paz.* Mexico City, 1974.

Gimferrer, Pere. *Lectures de Octavio Paz.* Barcelona, 1980.

_____, ed. *Octavio Paz.* Madrid, 1982.

Gradiva (Paris) 6–7 (1975). Homage to Octavio Paz.

Ivask, Ivar, ed. *The Perpetual Present: The Poetry and Prose of Octavio Paz.* Norman, Okla., 1973.

Lemaître, Monique. *Octavio Paz: Poesía y poética.* Mexico City, 1976.

Magis, Carlos H. *La poesía hermética de Octavio Paz.* Mexico City, 1978.

Martinez Torrón, Diego. *Variables poéticas de Octavio Paz.* Madrid, 1979.

Peña labra 38 (1980–81). Homage to Octavio Paz.

Perdigó, Luisa M. *La estética de Octavio Paz.* Madrid, 1975.

Phillips, Rachel. *The Poetic Modes of Octavio Paz.* London, 1972.

Review 6 (1972). Homage to Octavio Paz.

Revista iberoamericana 37:74 (1971). Homage to Octavio Paz.

Rodriguez Padrón, Jorge. *Octavio Paz.* Madrid, 1975.

Roggiano, Alfredo, ed. *Octavio Paz.* Madrid, 1979.

Rojas Guzmán, Eusebio. *Reinvención de la palabra: La obra poética de Octavio Paz.* Mexico City, 1979.

Sucre, Guillermo, et al. *Acerca de Octavio Paz.* Montevideo, 1974.

Tizzoni, Julia L. M. *La palabra, el amor y el tiempo en Octavio Paz.* Paraná, Argentina, 1973.

Valencia, Juan, and Edward Coughlin, eds. *Homenaje a Octavio Paz.* Mexico City, 1976.

Wilson, Jason. *Octavio Paz: A Study of his Poetics.* Cambridge, England, 1979.

Xirau, Ramón. *Octavio Paz: El sentido de la palabra.* Mexico City, 1970.

Bibliography

Verani, Hugo J. *Octavio Paz: Bibliografía critica.* Mexico City, 1983.

Julio Cortázar

(1914–1984)

Evelyn Picon Garfield

Julio Cortázar was born on 26 August 1914 in Brussels, Belgium, where his Argentine parents, Julio José and Maria Herminia (Descotte) Cortázar, were on business. When he was four years old, the family returned to establish permanent residence in Banfield, a suburb of Buenos Aires. By then he had already acquired the distinctive guttural French r, which he never lost. Many years later the critics would erroneously attribute that pronunciation to his long residency in Paris. When he was still very young, Cortázar and the family were abandoned by his father; his mother and aunt raised him and his sister.

Cortázar earned a degree as a primary and secondary school teacher (1935), but before finishing his first year of studies at the University of Buenos Aires, he left to take a position as a high school teacher, which he held until 1944. From 1944 to 1945 he taught literature at the University of Cuyo in the province of Mendoza, where he was imprisoned for a short period for participating in anti-Perón demonstrations.

In 1946 he returned to Buenos Aires, where he worked as the manager of Cámara Argentina del Libro (the Argentine Publishing Association). After passing examinations in languages and law, he worked as a public translator from 1948 to 1951. As

we shall see, several of his fictional protagonists are translators. In 1951 he was awarded a scholarship by the French government to study in Paris; he left Argentina the same month Bestiario (Bestiary, whose stories are included in the English-language collection entitled End of the Game), his first collection of short stories, was published. The rest of his life was spent in Paris, where he began working as a translator for UNESCO in 1952. He also translated into Spanish such authors as Louisa May Alcott, Daniel Defoe, G. K. Chesterton, André Gide, John Keats, Edgar Allan Poe, and Marguerite Yourcenar. Cortázar married the Argentine translator Aurora Bernárdez in 1953.

Cortázar thrived in France. In 1974 he was awarded the Prix Médicis (Étranger) for his fourth novel, Libro de Manuel (A Manual for Manuel, 1973); the prize money he donated to an organization that aids the families of political prisoners in Chile. In 1976 he received the Grand Aigle d'Or de la Ville de Nice for his entire work to date. Without relinquishing his Argentine citizenship, he acquired French citizenship in 1981. He returned to Argentina for several short visits; he also visited Cuba (1961) and Nicaragua (1983), maintaining ties with and political commitments to the socialist regimes of those countries. In 1975 he participated as a member of the

Second Russell Tribunal investigating violations of human rights in such Latin American countries as Brazil, Chile, Uruguay, Bolivia, and Paraguay. After 1960 he also visited the United States on several occasions, lecturing as a distinguished writer at universities from coast to coast. He died of leukemia in Paris on 12 February 1984.

Cortázar's international fame is evidenced by the widespread translation of most of his major works into other languages, including Bulgarian, Czech, Dutch, English, French, German, Italian, Japanese, Latvian, Lithuanian, Swedish, and Turkish. He is the author of ten collections of short stories, five novels, four collections of poetry, and about ten books (depending on how they are classified) of miscellanea and essays. Although *Presencia* (Presence, 1938; published under the pseudonym Julio Denís), his first publication, was a collection of poems (a genre he was to cultivate again in his later years), Cortázar is best known and has been most influential for his short stories and his second novel, *Rayuela* (1963), which was translated into English by Gregory Rabassa as *Hopscotch* in 1966 (it won the National Book Award for translation).

Cortázar had always preferred French and English literature to Spanish. As a young man he was particularly attracted to French surrealism and recognized its influence on his work; he once stated in a letter that "it undeniably constituted the most intensive motivating force of all or nearly all of my books, something which can't please me enough." In his later years he was fascinated by books on psychology, psychoanalysis, and anthropology. Among his hobbies were photography, watching boxing, playing jazz trumpet, and listening to jazz. We shall see how he incorporated these hobbies into his writings. He also dabbled in making "surrealist objects," such as the tiny, compartmentalized chest, filled with stones and snail shells and whose door had a knob made of a compass, that rested atop the desk in his summer house in the hills of Saignon, in the south of France.

Cortázar considered himself to be the only one of his generation in Argentina to employ the techniques and themes of both of the schools of writing that dominated Buenos Aires during the period between 1920 and 1940: the Florida group, with its European type of intellectualism, polished style, and universal themes, best represented by Jorge Luis Borges; and the Boedo group, with its realistic urban scenes, commonplace themes, and unkempt style, best represented by Roberto Arlt. One can see Cortázar in part as a product of both groups, for most of his characters speak the typically Argentine Spanish of several different social classes; yet his fiction has a universal appeal, dealing with searches for self-identity, the fantastic that lurks beyond everyday reality, and man's relationship to other men and to society.

In 1962, after publishing several collections of short stories, Cortázar wrote the article "Algunos aspectos del cuento" (Some Aspects of the Short Story) for the literary magazine *Casa de las Américas* (Havana). Here he defined the short story as "a mysterious brother to poetry" in which fantasy opposes the false realism ruled by reason. For him the fantastic represents an alteration in the laws that supposedly regulate an ordered reality based on the Western notion of logic. As in the works of Alfred Jarry, one of the French writers whom Cortázar admired, the exceptions are just as important as the rules for a full understanding of the hidden and perhaps ignored realities that surround us.

With his short stories Cortázar first gains our confidence, putting us at ease by creating a normal setting and conventional characters in familiar situations. But very shortly we find ourselves trapped by some strange, even nightmarish, turn of events that threatens the routine. This fantastic, illogical dimension infiltrates and subverts the routine reality, allowing both reader and writer to experience a shared exception to the rule.

Cortázar likened the short story to a photograph. Unlike the novel or the movie, which provide abundant detail and a complete, well-rounded plot, the short story (like a photograph) limits its scope to a single frame, a fragment of reality, which forces the reader-observer to supply the missing pieces. As he stated in "Algunos aspectos del cuento," it is a "fabulous opening of the minute onto the gigantic, of that which is individual and circumscribed onto the very essence of the human condition."

In "Del cuento breve y sus alrededores" ("On the Short Story and Its Environs"), an article collected in *Ultimo Round* (Last Round) in 1969 (and that appears in the English collection entitled *Around the Day in Eighty Worlds*), Cortázar explained how writing the short story served as an exorcism for him, the only possible way of "casting off invading creatures." Such imaginary and real beasts appear in his first collection of short stories. They often represent repressed instincts, phobias, and obsessions that Cortázar alluded to when explaining the genesis of some of these tales. For example, in "Carta a una señorita en Paris" ("Letter to a Young Lady in Paris"), the author worked out a recurring nausea he had felt as the result of extreme stress while studying for exams to become a public translator in Buenos Aires.

In that story, a translator moves into the Buenos Aires apartment of a friend, Andrea, who has gone to Paris. The translator is one of many characters in Cortázar's short stories who are ordinary people, such as a bank employee, a nurse, a brother and sister; the settings are equally commonplace, such as a house or an apartment; and the characters' routines are innocuous, like knitting, working, or playing games. But every time the protagonist returns from work and rides up in the elevator to his friend's apartment, he vomits up a live bunny. The birth is described in endearing, not at all repugnant, terms:

> When I feel that I'm going to bring up a rabbit, I put two fingers in my mouth like an open pincer, and I wait to feel the lukewarm fluff rise in my throat like the effervescence in a sal hepatica. It's all swift and clean, passes in the briefest instant. I remove the fingers from my mouth and in them, held fast by the ears, a small white rabbit. The bunny appears to be content, a perfectly normal bunny only very tiny, small as a chocolate rabbit, only it's white and very thoroughly a rabbit.
>
> (*Blow-Up and Other Stories*, p. 37)*

Although this fantastic episode is wholly accepted by the protagonist as normally possible and has happened to him before, the situation becomes somewhat alarming due to the frequency with which the bunnies are "born," the manner in which he must

*In most cases, translations of excerpts from Cortázar's works that appear in this article are taken from the English-language versions of Cortázar's writings that appear in the bibliography. Where no published translations exist, translations in this article are the work of its author.

secretly care for them so the maid doesn't find out, and the destruction of the neat, orderly apartment as the rabbits grow. The tender acceptance of the fantastic becomes a cause of anxiety. At the end, the letter the protagonist is writing to Andrea indicates that the rabbits (now numbering eleven, both beautiful and terrifying) will dominate him until the next morning. At that time no one will even notice them splattered on the sidewalk below the balcony because everyone will be too busy cleaning up the "other body" before the students walk by on their way to school. The fictitious translator succumbs to the concrete invasion of these self-generated beasts, whereas Cortázar assures us that he was exorcised of his nausea by writing this story.

In this very first collection, Cortázar exhibits a constant of his worldview that coincides with that of the surrealists: the so-called real, concrete world is only one side of a coin whose other face is the fantastic, the repressed, the hidden, the taboo, the oneiric. Like the surrealists, Cortázar ventures upon the darker, ignored, and repressed side of man: his obsessions (like Salvador Dali and Max Ernst), his desires (like André Breton and Paul Éluard), the communicating vessels between dream and wakefulness (like René Magritte and Paul Delvaux). He and such surrealists did not consider those things to be pathological or abnormal; instead, they served as an exciting key or bridge to a dimension of existence that was necessary for one to live in full contact with the entire world. With a work as early as the "dramatic poem" *Los reyes* (The Kings, 1949), Cortázar adapted and altered the myth of the Minotaur —half bull, half man—using him as a sympathetic character to symbolize his acceptance of man's basic dichotomy. (*Minotaure* was the name of a leading French surrealist magazine.)

This man/beast dichotomy can be found in *Bestiario*. Here Cortázar represents the mind as a house teeming with unknown invaders in "Cefalea" or inhabited by a family and a roaming tiger in "Bestiary"; he treats man's hostility toward his fellowman in "Omnibus"; and he uncovers parallel worlds and lives—real and mysterious—that seem to intersect and penetrate each other in "La lejana" ("The Distances"). Since this last theme is of particular importance in later works, a lengthier description of "The Distances" (an English translation of which appears in *Blow-Up and Other Stories*) is in order.

Diary entries chronicle the recurrent visions that a young woman in Buenos Aires has of a beggar woman in Budapest. That other world is revealed to her in a game of anagrams when she comes upon this phrase: "Alina Reyes, *es la reina y* . . . That one's so nice because it opens a path, because it does not close. Because the queen and . . . *la reina y*. . . ." From this first story collection to major novels like *Hopscotch* games always play an important role in Cortázar's works. Like rites of passage, games lead to zones of authentic reality, often hidden by humdrum daily routine.

Alina seems to experience the beggar's hardships, her suffering; she feels how the cold, wet snow enters the poor woman's shoes. At once repulsed and attracted, she yearns to meet her, to understand her and, since Alina is the queen in the anagram, to save her from misery. On her honeymoon, Alina travels to Budapest. At that point the diary ends, and an omniscient narrator describes the meeting and decisive embrace between the two women on a bridge. It is the beggar woman who is victorious; Alina is subsumed into the beggar's body, and she observes herself through the beggar woman's eyes as the shell of her former self walks away. Alina first intuited the existence of her "double" by means of a word game that served as a catalyst to dreams in which she shared the woman's misery. Finally that communication resulted in a transmigration of one being into another.

In succeeding volumes, Cortázar continued to deal with the theme of otherness in stories like "Axolotl," "La noche boca arriba" ("The Night Face Up"), and "El otro cielo" ("The Other Heaven"). In almost all cases, the dreamlike, mysterious, or dangerous zone into which the characters venture or that includes their so-called normal lives is victorious over the more realistic zone from which they emerge like moths drawn to a flame.

In his second collection, *Final del juego* (End of the Game, 1956), he adds two important elements to his short-story repertoire: a character portrayal independent of any intrusion of the fantastic, as in "Torito," and eroticism, in a story such as "El río" (The River).

"Torito," which has received little critical attention, is about an aged, hospitalized boxer who reminisces in a monologue about his past glories. The boxer's nickname conveys Cortázar's sympathetic homage to that sport, for "Torito" is the diminutive and endearing form for "little bull." And the author tries faithfully to imitate a speech pattern dotted with colloquial Argentine expressions. In his next collection of short stories, *Las armas secretas* (Secret Weapons, 1959), Cortázar once again uses this type of character portrayal in a story about a jazz musician. Based on the life of the black saxophone player Charlie "Bird" Parker, "El perseguidor" ("The Pursuer") was only the beginning of this tendency, which would evolve even more fully in later collections.

The second new element in *Final del juego*, eroticism, is emphasized more in the novels *Hopscotch* and *A Manual for Manuel*, as well as in his collage-books *La vuelta al día en ochenta mundos* (*Around the Day in Eighty Worlds*, 1967) and *Ultimo Round*. This theme is usually accompanied by sadism and violence in such stories as "El río," "Las Ménades" (The Maenads), and "El ídolo de las Cícladas" ("The Idol of the Cyclades"). In *Cortázar por Cortázar* (Garfield, 1978), he explained his interest in the subject: "Evidently the sadistic component of my eroticism is very strong. It follows then that one notices it in the erotic scenes of my works." Eroticism and sexuality, both heterosexual and homosexual, form an integral part of his fiction.

Let us return now to that third collection, *Las armas secretas*, where Cortázar for the first time begins to deal with the problems of the creative process as both theme and mode of expression. The dichotomy between artist and critic appears in "The Pursuer" in the characters of Johnny, the anguished jazz musician, and his analytical critic, Bruno. Johnny's perceptions of time are enriched when he plays jazz; he feels a great compression of time in the few minutes of a "take" and compares this phenomenon to a minute-and-a-half subway ride, in which he experiences fifteen minutes of thoughts and feelings. These escapes from time into music are in keeping with his disdain for wristwatch time, routine schedules, and traditional life-styles. He tries to explain to Bruno how he sees holes in daily existence, sensing that there must be something more authentic to life.

Johnny is the perfect character for Cortázar, who in much of his writing rails against similar conventions and establishes fictitious situations to escape to other, often parallel, worlds. Bruno, though, sees Johnny more analytically, both as a creative genius whom he envies and as a poor bastard addicted to alcohol and drugs. Not being a creator himself, the critic Bruno cannot give up the security of his way of life for Johnny's dangerous and anguished talent and experiences. He writes Johnny's biography, comparing his music to a communion with God, a concept Johnny soundly rejects. Despite Bruno's cautious coldness and his comparison of Johnny to a "hunter with no arms or legs," he admits, and in so doing explains the story's title, that ". . . Johnny was no victim, not persecuted as everyone thought, as I'd even insisted upon in my biography of him. . . . Johnny pursues and is not pursued, that all the things happening in his life are the hunter's disasters, not the accidents of the harassed animal" (*Blow-Up and Other Stories*, p. 196).

"Las babas del diablo" ("Blow-Up"), another story from the third collection, was the basis for Michelangelo-Antonioni's film *Blow-Up* (1966). For the first time Cortázar begins to manipulate the narrative voice in order to depict how difficult it is to express problematic situations and hidden realities, suddenly and painfully uncovered. Such is the case of the protagonist Roberto Michel, a French-Chilean translator in Paris who snaps a photograph of an older woman talking to an adolescent; later, while obsessively contemplating the enlargement he has made of the photograph, he realizes his mistaken interpretation. The woman is not, as he supposed, trying to seduce the boy for herself; she is acting as a go-between for a man awaiting them in a nearby car. Michel identifies with the boy, and so the story becomes difficult to tell, as one can see from this opening passage:

> It'll never be known how this has to be told, in the first person or in the second, using the third person plural or continually inventing modes that will serve for nothing. If one might say: I will see the moon rose, or: we hurt me at the back of my eyes, and especially: you the blond woman was the clouds that race before my your his our yours their faces. What the hell.
>
> (p. 100)

Throughout the story, the narrator distances himself from the situation by switching from the first-person to the third-person perspective, from which he observes himself as if he were the boy's double. He also constantly reflects on his choice of words—"Right now (what a word, *now*, what a dumb lie) . . ." —and in so doing calls into question the reality he is describing and how it is perceived and commented upon. Time and again he brings himself back into character and his apartment from which he writes the story while gazing through a window, noticing the birds or clouds passing by. This multi-perspectival narrative stance appears in many of Cortázar's major works, such as *Hopscotch*, and in other short stories. Another example is "La señorita Cora" ("Nurse Cora"), also about an adolescent, in which the peripatetic first-person narrative skillfully travels, without warning or identification, from one character to another, even within the same sentence, creating a gallery of voices.

Reality is rarely what it seems to be on the surface. Although Michel helped the boy escape from a seductive woman when he snapped the photograph, it is not until his obsessive gaze at the blowup on his wall causes it to become a movie—replaying the episode in which the elderly homosexual man in the car enters the picture—that Michel is able to help the boy escape again, this time from the real seducer.

Exposing the false face of surface reality is a constant in many of Cortázar's short stories, where the reverse of the coin is not always the fantastically inexplicable—vomiting up bunnies—but also the unpleasant or the overlooked dimensions of the very reality we behold. Into this category fall the lives of exceptional characters—"not-always-repugnant monsters," according to Michel—whom Cortázar usually portrays sympathetically: jazz musicians, insane people, homosexuals and lesbians, and his own creations, called *cronopios*.

These cronopios appear in the collection *Historias de cronopios y de famas* (*Cronopios and Famas*, 1962), his first work comprising a potpourri of anecdotes written at different times and in a variety of places. It was not conceived as a unified book. *Cronopios and Famas* marks a transitional moment in the evolution of Cortázar's work. Standing between his early fiction and *Hopscotch*, it includes a substantially new ingredient—an imaginatively playful sense of humor used as an antidote to absurd existence.

Divided into four sections, *Cronopios and Famas* is Cortázar's most overtly surrealistic book, for it challenges the reader to transform everyday reality, coaxing it to yield unexpected marvels. Beyond his already established interest in the surrealistic communicating vessels of the conscious/subconscious, the acceptable/the taboo, and reason/instinct—that is, the real and surreal—Cortázar now shows us how to mold life to our desires, how to make humdrum existence exciting. In the section "Manual de Instrucciones" ("The Instruction Manual"), he rethinks common emotions and actions—crying, singing, being afraid, climbing stairs, and winding a watch—and uncommon ones—dissecting a ground owl or killing ants in Rome. The effect of such detailed, humorous descriptions is similar to that of surrealist ready-mades like Man Ray's object *Cadeau* (Gift, 1921), a flatiron with tacks. Both works of art force us to think about our blind, daily use of common, practical objects that the artist and writer transform into useless or dangerous ones.

The section "Ocupaciones raras" ("Unusual Occupations") reads like a series of dadaist or surrealist "happenings," with the visual provocation and spontaneity of illogical events that reflect an absurd world and man's precarious condition in it: a family invades a wake and takes over amid hypocritical friends and relatives; another family takes over the post office, dispensing balloons and shots of vodka with veal cutlets and stamps; while still another happily erects gallows in front of its house one Sunday afternoon.

The especially playful section "Cronopios and Famas" lends its name to this small and unique volume. Here, the leaders and bosses (called *famas*) are authoritarian and businesslike; the bureaucrats immersed in trivial details who wish they could be *famas* are called *esperanzas;* and the *cronopios* are the rather self-centered beings who are intuitive, impractical, artistic, and spontaneous. Cortázar first used the term *cronopio* in his 1952 article about a concert Louis Armstrong gave in Paris; he dubbed the jazz musician "Super-Cronopio." He then conceived of these amorphous microbes floating in the air, attributed human characteristics to them, and began writing anecdotes about their lives.

Particularly charming is the anecdote about the *cronopio* who sees a *fama* carefully winding a wall clock, and decides to invent his own. At home he hangs a wild artichoke on the wall and uses the leaves to indicate the hours, plucking them off, one at a time from left to right, when he wants to know the hour. Upon reaching the artichoke heart, "time cannot be measured," and so he contentedly removes it from the wall; eats it smothered in oil, vinegar, and salt; and puts another artichoke clock in its place. The *cronopio* has invented a surrealistic object much like Meret Oppenheim's *Object* (1936), a fur-covered cup, saucer, and spoon, liberating an ordinary object from its practical and traditional function.

The critics initially categorized *Cronopios and Famas* as a frivolous work; but now it is considered integral to Cortázar's need to reinstate elements of play, humor, fantasy, and desire in the lives of serious, repressed and civilized adults. This magical and free world of a child-man transforms the commonplace into an adventure, albeit sometimes hostile, as demonstrated by the anecdote about the family that erects the gallows in its front yard. In later novels and stories Cortázar continued to seek adventure in the commonplace. In "La autopista del sur" ("The Southern Thruway"), for example, an ordinary traffic jam on a major highway south of Paris lasts for months, stretching beyond the initial heat of August into the colder seasons. The passengers in the cars establish a certain routine and become inhabitants of the highway. Caused by pure chance, the exceptional situation becomes exaggerated and then reverts to the rule. Unlike characters in stories written before this one, collected in *Todos los fuegos el fuego* (All Fires the Fire and Other Stories, 1966), these people glimpse the extraordinary but do not succumb to it; they transform it into the ordinary. Routine is victorious.

Cortázar wrote four more collections of short stories and another volume of anecdotes, *Un tal Lucas* (A Certain Lucas, 1979), in the same vein as *Cronopios and Famas* but without its flair. In these works two new elements—politics and a greater emphasis on interpersonal relationships—are of major significance. His first overtly political fiction was the short story "Reunión" ("Meeting") in *All Fires the Fire*. The political theme continued with other stories, such as

"Segunda vez" ("Second Time Around"), "Apoca-lipsis de Solentiname" ("Apocalypse at Solenti-name"), "La noche de Mantequilla" ("Butterball's Night"), and "Alguien que anda por ahí" ("Someone Walking Around") in *Alguien que anda por ahí* (1977; published in English as *A Change of Light and Other Stories*). These stories concern revolution and coun-terrevolution, foreign intervention, massacres, perse-cutions, and torture in Latin America, as do the novel *A Manual for Manuel* and such nonfiction works as *Literatura en la revolución y revolución en la literatura* (Literature in Revolution and Revolution in Literature, 1970), *Fantomas contra los vampiros multi-nacionales: Una utopía realizable* (Fantomas Takes on the Multinational Vampires: An Attainable Utopia, 1975), *Nicaragua tan violentamente dulce* (Nicaragua, So Violently Sweet, 1983), and *Argentina: Años de alambradas culturales* (Argentina: Years of Cultural Barbed-Wire, 1984).

The second new element was Cortázar's growing interest in his characters' interpersonal relationships. Before *A Change of Light and Other Stories*, character doubles communicated with each other across space and time in such fantastic stories as "The Distances," "All Fires the Fire," and "The Night Face Up," or in games and chance encounters in such stories as "Blow-Up" and "The Southern Thruway." These characters were usually dominated by a "figure" and inexplicable forces beyond their control. The term *figure* was expressed in Cortázar's first novel, *Los premios* (The Winners, 1960), and explored much more profoundly in his third novel, *62: Modelo para armar* (62: A Model Kit, 1968). It refers to the notion that we are like stars in a constellation about which we are ignorant, as are, for example, Alina and the beggar woman in "The Distances," or the motorcycle accident victim and the sixteenth-century Indian in "The Night Face Up." Although the author does not abandon this type of story, in *A Change of Light and Other Stories* he adds a significant new twist to characterization. The solitary figure faced with a particular situation that he or she never fully com-prehends, as is Madame Francinet in "Los buenos servicios" ("At Your Service"), or faced with an anguished search for a more authentic reality, as is Johnny in "The Pursuer," is now joined in the best stories of this collection by two equally important

protagonists in relationships of complicity and an atmosphere of mutual helplessness. With previous stories such as "Letter to a Young Lady in Paris" or "The Southern Thruway," the description of daily minutiae usually seduced the reader, who ended up accepting the stories' fantastic or unusual resolution anchored in the character's *situation*. In this volume the descriptions urge the reader to identify with the characters themselves so that the eventual realistic outcome of the story is even more devastating.

This new focus is further enhanced by Cortázar's customary stylistic consciousness because he broadens the narrative base of his fiction to reflect this new, mutual concern. In stories like "Blow-Up," the protagonist shifted his narrative stance to reflect his own individual state of mind. Now, the narrative point of view and choice of verb forms reflect neutrality or both characters' equally weighted dilem-mas. For example in "Vientos alisios" ("Trade Winds") an abundance of nonreferential verb forms such as the reflexive, the gerund, and the infinitive, relate both Vera and Mauricio's thoughts and emo-tions. In "Usted se tendió a tu lado" (*You* Lie Down by *Your* Side), the narrator alternately addresses both a mother and her son with the two Spanish forms for the word *you*, the formal *Usted* and the familiar *tú*, respectively, thus being equally attentive to the problematic relationship of one to the other, from both sides of the coin, without choosing sides. This dual mode of expressing what in English is one word would be lost in translation. (In fact, when the volume of stories was translated into English, this story was omitted.) But in that unique short story, familiar themes of adolescence, eroticism, and social taboos are dealt with by an omniscient narrator who enjoys a degree of intimacy with both of his charac-ters and a concern for their problems. If this story had been written earlier in Cortázar's career, it would probably have been told from the standpoint of the adolescent boy.

Although certain figures and searches are common to Cortázar's short stories and novels, he has always differentiated the genres, depicting the novel as the more dangerous of the two because of the liberties it permits and the risk of carelessness. He maintained that he identified with particular characters in his three novels: Horacio Oliveira in *Hopscotch*, Juan in

62: A Model Kit, and Andrés in *A Manual for Manuel.*
All seek a new way of life and love and a more just
social order, and they all fail at their attempts
without ever losing hope.

Cortázar's first novel, *The Winners,* is a thriller
about a cross section of Argentine society, winners of
a lottery whose prize is a cruise on a ship, the
Malcolm. The large cast of characters includes some
wealthy people, some lower-class families, a homosexual, middle-class schoolteachers, a divorced
mother and her son, a dentist and his lover, and an
adolescent boy. Each social class represented is characterized by its own manner of speech, ranging from
the literary esoteric to low-class jargon. Aboard ship
the characters react in different ways when threatened by a mystery: the crew speaks a strange language; they are denied knowledge of the itinerary; the
boat's doctor is unavailable despite official pronouncements that typhus has broken out; and they
are forbidden access to the stern of the ship. The
novel is also about men in search of the unknown
(the stern) and about the complacency and indifference of a society that lives in the present without
forging its own destiny. Certain passengers blindly
accept the official explanation of an epidemic, while
others decide to seek a route to the stern and an
explanation for the secrecy surrounding the journey
of a ship that has never lifted anchor.

As with most of his novels, Cortázar undertakes
some experimental structuring; in this case there is a
series of nine poetic monologues that reflect one
character's views of the situation. These italicized,
analogical passages with their free-flowing associations clearly break with the novelistic form and
conversational prose of most of the book. The monologues are those of Persio, a proofreader who is a sort
of psychic, groping to discern the meaning behind
the "figure" comprising the individuals aboard the
Malcolm. The poetic and sometimes surrealistic
monologues serve as a commentary on Argentine
society's fearful acceptance of a false order, and as a
criticism of noninvolvement when personal interest
does not seem to be at stake.

Man's search for a center and Cortázar's revolutionary approach to the novel genre were perhaps
only partially realized in *The Winners.* But they reach
maturity with *Hopscotch,* the novel that definitively

established Cortázar internationally as one of the
most important twentieth-century Latin American
writers.

Hopscotch is divided into three sections: "Del lado
de allá" ("From the Other Side"), "Del lado de acá"
("From This Side"), and "De otros lados" ("From
Diverse Sides"). At the beginning of the novel,
Cortázar offers a "Tablero de dirección" ("Table of
Instructions") for reading the novel and suggests that
Hopscotch consists of many books, but two books
above all. He invites us to choose between, first, a
traditional reading of chapters 1 through 56 (the first
two sections) and, second, a more unconventional
reading that begins with chapter 73 and proceeds in
hopscotch fashion through a sequence of at least 153
brief chapters.

The traditional reading revolves around Horacio
Oliveira, an unemployed Argentine intellectual in
his forties, living first in Paris and then in Buenos
Aires around 1950. He and his bohemian friends—a
Russian, a North American couple, two Frenchmen,
a Chinese, and a Spaniard—form a group, called the
Serpent Club, that spends hours discussing art, literature, music, and philosophy, and listening to jazz
records in smoke-filled rooms. The novel, however,
focuses on Oliveira's persistent and anguished self-
analysis and questioning of his every thought, emotion, word, and action. As a product of Western
civilization, he is constantly rationalizing, drowning
in a well of dialectic possibilities. Like a good
cronopio, Oliveira is aware of the absurdity of daily life
but is not yet sure of how to contend with it, and he
searches without experiencing the typical *cronopio's*
joy, feeling alone and condemned to "bovine conformity, the cheap and dirty joy of work, and sweat of
the brow and paid vacations."

Whenever possible he immerses himself in situations that force him to confront the absurd world. By
"touching bottom" and facing the absurd with its own
equally absurd weapons, he feels that he will stop
intellectualizing and manage to experience a more
authentic existence. Some of the most memorable
episodes in the novel describe such absurd encounters: Oliveira wallowing drunk under the bridge with
the ragpicking *clocharde;* his coaxing his wife, Talita,
out onto two planks precariously stretched between
building windows, three flights up from the street,

just to bring him some leaves to brew maté; or Oliveira attending Berthe Trepat's concert. Madame Trepat is a grotesque pianist whose terrible performance drives the audience of twenty, with the exception of Oliveira, from the auditorium. He even ends up accompanying her home in the rain, congratulating her enthusiastically and comforting her for the audience's indifference and ingratitude. Although Oliveira is repulsed by the old woman, his disgust turns momentarily to joy at this absurdly laughable circumstance. For a few moments he frees himself of his analytical, unfeeling self, touches bottom, and leaps out toward "the other."

The novel begins with Oliveira asking himself, "Would I find La Maga?" She is his lover, a Uruguayan woman living in Paris with her baby, Rocamadour. Unlike Oliveira, she is spontaneous and intuitive, uninterested in abstract reasoning and free of the limitations of the anguished dialectic that confounds him. Oliveira is perfectly aware of the difference between them:

> There are metaphysical rivers, she swims in them like that swallow swimming in the air, spinning madly around a belfry, letting herself drop so that she can rise up all the better with the swoop. I describe and define and desire those rivers, but she swims in them. And she doesn't know it any more than the swallow. . . . Oh, let me come in, let me see some day the way your eyes see.
>
> (ch. 21)

Dissatisfied with his routine, self-centered life based on logic, Oliveira seeks out unusual experiences and unconventional reactions, all the while envying La Maga's unfettered existence. At times these reactions result in black humor. For example, one day during a meeting of the Serpent Club, in a dark room, amid the sounds of music and metaphysical discussion, Oliveira approaches the baby Rocamadour and discovers he is dead. Rather than crying or shouting, he chooses to ignore the fact and wait for the others to discover the tragedy. In contrast to Oliveira's seemingly callous reaction, La Maga shortly thereafter writes a farewell letter to her dead baby that is one of the most tender chapters in the novel:

> BABY Rocamadour, baby, baby. Rocamadour.

> By now I know you're like a mirror, Rocamadour, sleeping or looking at your feet. Here I am holding a mirror and thinking that it's you. But don't you believe it, I'm writing to you because you don't know how to read. If you did know I wouldn't be writing to you or I'd be writing about important things. . . . Now I can only write to you in the mirror, sometimes I have to dry my finger because it gets wet with tears. . . . I've got my toes curled all the way under and I'm going to split open my shoes if I don't take them off, and I love you so much, Rocamadour, baby Rocamadour, little garlic-clove, I love you so much, sugar-nose, sapling, toy pony . . .
>
> (ch. 32)

Oliveira leaves Paris and returns to Argentina in the two sections of the traditionally read novel. Although La Maga physically disappears in Paris, she remains present in Oliveira's mind, as does his desire to rid himself of the trappings of Western civilization. In Buenos Aires, his relationships with an old friend, Traveler—who, ironically, has never journeyed far from home—and with his wife, Talita, are the material for most of his soul-searching. The three form a certain "figure." Traveler becomes a complementary double for Oliveira, for he is an Argentine without intellectual and existential anguish, at home in his own territory; Talita replaces La Maga as an attraction, becoming her double. The three work in a circus and then in a sanatorium for the insane, where the last chapters of the second section take place. Oliveira has barricaded himself in a room and set out obstacles to trap Traveler: pans of water and ball bearings on the floor, string crisscrossed from wall to wall, forming a kind of spiderweb. Perched on the windowsill, he leans dangerously far out, watching his friends Talita and Traveler below in the yard near a hopscotch design, and thinking about how easy it would be to let himself fall out onto the game board drawn on the ground. With this open ending, the author never tells us whether or not Oliveira commits suicide or goes crazy, although the careful reader of the second version of the book will discover the following statement in chapter 104: that life is "a *commentary* of something else we cannot reach, which is there within reach of the leap we will not take."

In the more unconventional, hopscotchlike reading of the novel, the "Table of Instructions" guides us through all but one of the fifty-six chapters in the first two sections and all of the chapters in the third section, "From Diverse Sides," subtitled "Capítulos prescindibles" ("Expendable Chapters"). In this reading, these "expendable" chapters are interspersed randomly within the chronological sequence of the first fifty-six chapters of the book. The reader, who must piece together the collage of chapters, is aided by the author's introductory instructions and numbers at the end of each chapter, telling him where to "jump" next. In this way Cortázar exacts our participation in constructing the second reading of a novel that ends in a perpetual open-ended deadlock, alternating between chapters 58 and 131. *Hopscotch* thus becomes a double—and even multiple—novel, with at least two objectives involving a search for authenticity: to tell the story of man's self-analysis and search for an Absolute, and to reevaluate the traditional novelistic structure, carrying out its destruction and planning for its revival.

The goal of Oliviera's search is represented in various symbols: an Absolute, a Center, a "kibbutz of desire," a hopscotch game:

Hopscotch is played with a pebble that you move with the tip of your toe. The things you need: a sidewalk, a pebble, a toe, and a pretty chalk drawing, preferably in colors. On top is Heaven, on the bottom is Earth, it's very hard to get the pebble up to Heaven, you almost always miscalculate and the stone goes off the drawing. But little by little you start to get the knack of how to jump over the different squares (spiral hopscotch, rectangular hopscotch, fantasy hopscotch, not played very often) and then one day you learn how to leave Earth and make the pebble climb up into Heaven. . . . [T]he worst part of it is that precisely at that moment, when practically no one has learned how to make the pebble climb up into Heaven, childhood is over all of a sudden and you're into novels, into the anguish of the senseless divine trajectory, into the speculation about another Heaven that you have to learn to reach too.

(ch. 36)

In Cortázar's native Argentina and in his adopted France, the game of hopscotch has sections for Heaven and Earth at opposite ends of the design. He had always been fascinated by labyrinths, such as the Tibetan mandala with its many compartments used

for spiritual exercises and meditation, and the children's game, which he maintains also stems from religious origins. The Heaven that Oliveira aims for is not the Christian Heaven, but an Absolute attainable in one's lifetime, for on the sidewalk game board, Heaven is on the same level as Earth. Furthermore, Oliveira explains to La Maga that Heaven, or the Absolute, is "that moment in which something attains its maximum depth, its maximum reach, its maximum sense, and becomes completely uninteresting." Once possessed, the Absolute ceases to be the Absolute, that is, the total encounter between self and surrounding circumstance achieved without benefit of dialectical reason. He sees it as both collective and individual: a kibbutz of desire.

Through "brink" situations, absurd adventures, and "happenings," Oliveira glimpses the Center. These episodes, such as the one with Madame Trepat, are usually characterized by a mixture of pathos and humor. For Oliveira, like his creator Cortázar, has a capacity for laughing at himself and for pulling the reader's leg. And it is precisely this capacity that saves Cortázar and his characters from falling into existential anguish. Humor in all its forms is visible in this novel, in gags, jokes, farce, and fantasy. It is grotesque, ironic, and black. Oliveira's optimism lies precisely in his search, the road, the voyage, the stone aimed at Heaven. Far from destroying logical man, Oliveira seeks a fusion of opposites, of reason and desire, a union he glimpses in the novel's brink episodes. In an interview, Cortázar maintained that Oliveira could not commit suicide by jumping out the window onto the hopscotch design. *Hopscotch*, he said, as recorded in *Cortázar por Cortázar* (1978 ed.), is essentially an optimistic book:

No, no, he doesn't jump. One doesn't know for sure: but he doesn't jump, no, no. I'm sure he doesn't jump. . . . Oliveira doesn't commit suicide. But I couldn't say that. It would have destroyed the book. The idea is that there you, or any other reader, have to decide. . . . Of course it's an optimistic book.

(pp. 24–25)

Obviously *Hopscotch* has a limited audience, one with patience and a willingness to play the rules of the game that is the novel itself, or more precisely the antinovel, for the "expendable" chapters tend to break the novelistic progression of the plot as they comment on the actions and thoughts of the protagonist from other perspectives.

It is precisely in the third section that Cortázar's spokesman, Morelli, exposes us to the theory of the antinovel. Morelli, an old man, is a famous author, one read by the bohemians; his manuscript notes on the antinovel are discovered while he is in the hospital recovering from a car accident. It is Morelli who proposes to make the reader an accomplice in the creative process, challenging us to juggle the chapters in a second reading of *Hopscotch*. The third section of the book becomes, in part, a diary of the emerging novel, a heterogenous collection of notes, meditations, and excerpts from books and periodicals, some only a few lines or paragraphs long, that echo or contrast with the original fifty-six chapters.

The concept of the antinovel—the fragmented, polysemous literary structure—was in the air in the early 1960's, when *Hopscotch* was published. In Paris, for example, Raymond Queneau's *Cente mille milliards de poèmes* (One Hundred Trillion Poems, 1961) and Marc Saporta's *Composition no. 1* (1962) were published. The former is a book of poems; each page has strips of verse that can be lifted to uncover other verses for that poem. This facilitates a multiple reading of each poem, transformed at will by the reader. The latter is a long novel with unbound and unnumbered pages, which is to be read in multiple ways by shuffling the pages like cards. Such structures have been dubbed "open works" by the critic Umberto Eco, since they require active physical and mental involvement and offer multiple levels of interpretation.

Hopscotch can also be seen as a natural consequence of the dissolution of the novelistic form in Spanish America. This phenomenon began in the late nineteenth century with modernist novels like *De sobremesa* (After Dinner, 1925; written 1887–1896), by the Colombian José Asunción Silva, and *Sin rumbo* (Aimlessly, 1885), by the Argentine Eugenio Cambaceres, in which very brief chapters quickly transport the reader from one setting to another. By the early 1920's and 1930's Spanish-American vanguard poets such as the Chileans Vicente Huidobro and Pablo Neruda and the Peruvian César Vallejo were revolutionizing, desacralizing, and prosifying poetry. During the same period, these two Chileans and such writers as the Argentine Macedonio Fernández, the Mexican Arqueles Vela, and the Ecuadorian Pablo Palacio, were writing disjointed, fragmented, and often brief novels with little novelistic plotting and much self-reflection on the bankruptcy of the novel's traditional form. *Hopscotch* and its innovative structure are related to these antecedents.

Cortázar not only challenges the traditional novelistic structure but also revolutionizes the conventional modes of expression, aiming at a revival of language and its liberation from habitual molds. With short stories such as "Blow-Up," Cortázar aims to destroy literary rhetoric and false, hollow, and outmoded forms. His expression is heterogenous: lyrical, comic, mystic, esoteric, ironic, inventive. He masters erotic descriptions and desacralizes, using richly varied imagery, as the following passage demonstrates: "A pureness as of coitus between crocodiles, not the pureness of oh Mary my mother with dirty feet; a pureness of a slate roof with doves who naturally shit on the heads of ladies wild with rage and radishes, a pureness of . . ." (*Hopscotch*, ch. 18). His characters play with words, engage in word games like "seesaw-questions" or "the cemetery" (which refers to the dictionary and its dead words), and invent languages such as La Maga's Gliglish, which is based on sounds and neologisms. The erotic intention of the following Gliglish passage, though nonsensical, is quite clear:

"Tell me how Ossip makes love," Oliveira whispered, putting his lips hard against La Maga's. "The blood is rushing to my head, I can't do this much longer, it's frightening."

"He does it very well," La Maga said, biting his lip. "Much better than you and much longer."

"But does he retilate your murt? Don't lie to me. Does he really retilate it?"

"A lot. Everywhere, sometimes too much. It's a wonderful feeling."

"And does he make you put your plinnies in between his arguts?"

"Yes, and then we trewst our porcies until he says he's had enough, and I can't take it any more either, and we have to hurry up, you understand. But you wouldn't understand that, you always stay in the smallest gumphy."

(ch. 20)

In addition to inventing language, Cortázar makes unusual orthographic changes based on phonics, joins words in strings to emphasize their vulgarity, and inserts random lines from a novel by Benito Pérez Galdós, a famous nineteenth-century Spanish novelist. The last is to emphasize and criticize the outmoded ideas and style of the traditional novel that La Maga is reading.

It is in that very passage that Oliveira senses he and La Maga are like flies buzzing around a room, motes of dust floating aimlessly in the air, or colored glass pieces falling in and out of place in a kaleidoscope, "forming an absurd pattern." From this perception and Morelli's comments in expendable chapter 62, Cortázar posits his next novel, 62: A Model Kit, in which characters interact as if compelled by some force greater than themselves. As Persio perceived in The Winners, characters in a novel do not understand the figure they form, nor do they know how to control it. Unlike Oliveira, who plays a game in order to save himself from reasoned reality, the characters in 62: A Model Kit, are played with like chess pieces. The novel becomes a vertiginous juxtaposition of the protagonist's experiences in two different, although related, territories called the Zone and the City: the former is a meeting place of the group (similar to the bohemian Serpent Club in Hopscotch), while the City has no geographic limitations, only high sidewalks and a hotel with labyrinthine rooms.

The novel's protagonist is actually a group of characters; these deliberately sketchy images and echoes of one another perceive a subliminal level of reality and intuit associations that reveal what life is all about. The analogical associations, in constant metamorphosis as if in a dream or an hallucination, explain the achronological order of episodes, their free associations across time and space, and the utilization of hermetic symbols. The opening scene gives a clear example of how events reverberating in the mind of a character initiate a chain of associations.

Juan, an Argentine interpreter living in Paris, is seated in the Polidor restaurant facing a wall of mirrors when he overhears a customer asking for a château saignant. The phrase refers to châteaubriand saignant, a "rare steak." Those words remind Juan of a series of coincidences: a book he just bought by Michel Butor in which he found a description of

Niagara Falls by another Frenchman, Châteaubriand, the author of Atala; and of a related phrase, château sanglant, the "bloody castle." Free-associating from this last phrase, other images occur to him: the countess, Frau Marta; Transylvania, the birthplace of vampire tales; and the similar-sounding word Sylvaner, the name of the drink he has just ordered. Word associations, like Alina Reyes' anagram in "The Distances," open up onto mysteriously disturbing worlds. This particular association exposes us to the novel's Gothic episodes about Vienna and the Basilisken Haus, with its legends of the Blood Countess Erzebet Bathori, who bled and tortured girls in her castle, and bathed in their blood. More associations occur to Juan and are borne out in the novel's plot, in which desire without love, ill-fated relationships among characters, and pseudovampirism all play a part.

Some five years later, Cortázar turned away from this type of novel to his most politically committed work of fiction, A Manual for Manuel. This mixture of fact and fiction, humor and eroticism, concerns itself with political conditions in Latin America. He wrote the novel in order to expose the systematic torture of political prisoners in those countries, and since his other books had been best-sellers throughout Latin America, he hoped that this novel would enjoy wide circulation and influence. In part to avert censorship in this region, he did not write a political treatise expressing his socialist vision for Latin America. Instead he chose a bizarre mixture of fantasy and fact: the plot is imaginary but the news articles inserted in the text are factual. The novel's protagonist, Andrés, is like Cortázar the product of two worlds—middle-class comfort and socialist commitment—and Cortázar seems to be saying that a blind adherence to either might deny the individual freedom that he always valued.

A Manual for Manuel is about the kidnapping of a Latin American diplomat by a group of strange guerrillas in Paris. It has two narrators: one of the group's members, jokingly referred to as "you know who," who takes notes on the assault plans, and Andrés, who is indecisive about joining the group and uncovers the plot of the novel by reading those notes. The articles that interrupt the plot are from actual French and Latin American newspapers and appear in the novel in reduced print. These articles concern individual protests against societal pressures that usurp personal liberties and exact conformity: the torture of political prisoners in such countries as Brazil, Argentina, and Uruguay; guerrilla activities in Latin America and Europe; and such taboos as homosexuality. The articles are being collected for two members of the group, Susana and Patricio, who are making a scrapbook for their baby boy, Manuel. They aim to educate him—along with the reader—in protest, change, and revolution in Latin American societies.

The group, as international as the cast of *Hopscotch* and *62: A Model Kit*, incites unrest in middle-class neighborhoods with miniprovocations that are a strange mixture of guerrilla activity and pranks designed to disturb bourgeois sensibilities. Apart from these sallies and the more important kidnapping, the social commitment seems to be consistently undermined by Andrés' erotic preoccupations and adventures and by the strange undertakings of another very colorful member of the group: Lonstein, an Argentine Jew, washes dead bodies in the morgue and speaks an imaginative language combining musical rhythms and sounds, Argentine slang (called "lunfardo"), and neologisms based on French (*femucha* = "woman") and English (*kidnapeados*). Thus *A Manual for Manuel* becomes the author's assertion of his adherence to socialist revolution but also his statement that he will not sacrifice personal freedom of expression—erotic rites, aesthetic predilections, humor, and imagination—to any ideology.

Nevertheless, Cortázar devotes twelve of the final seventeen pages to two factual excerpts: the testimony of political prisoners in a press conference of the Forum for Human Rights denouncing cases of torture in Argentina; and a section from *Conversations with Americans* (1970), testimony taken by the lawyer Mark Lane from thirty-two Vietnam veterans who attested to the torture for which they were trained and commended during that war. These texts run down the pages in two parallel columns and end with a shocking statistical table from the United States Department of Defense (1969), which shows, by country, numbers of Latin American military personnel trained in the United States. The author is suggesting that the United States aids oppressive regimes in their programs of torture by training their police.

Cortázar's other works—poetry and miscellanea—have been studied less than his novels and short stories. However, it is important to emphasize that they share a certain unified vision. Cortázar's poems often inventively referred to by him as *pameos*, *meopas*, and *prosemas* (three neologisms) rather than *poemas*, can take fairly traditional or nontraditional forms. Some of these poems were written as tangos and have been set to music. The unique volume *Fantomas contra los vampiros multinacionales* is written in part like a comic book, while the lengthy prose poem *Prosa del observatorio* (Prose from the Observatory, 1972) combines text and photographs.

In *Prosa del observatorio*, Cortázar addresses two issues basic to much of his writing: how one confronts and acquires information about the unknown and how such knowledge heads one to further investigation or to a complacent, passive satisfaction. The first photograph, taken like all the others by Cortázar in 1968 during a visit to Jai Singh's observatories in Jaipur and Delhi, compels the reader's eye to move up along a stone staircase to a door engulfed in darkness. Cortázar urges us up those steps to the place where the eighteenth-century Indian astronomer-sultan sought to discover the vast unknown skies. The author juxtaposes the seas and skies, comingling contemporary research on eels undertaken by French Academy of Sciences professor Maurice Fontaine with Jai Singh's conjuring of the unmapped constellations. Once again we see the figures taking shape, the analogies being established: the "golden galaxy" of stars in the heavens/the "black galaxy" of eels in the sea. As with Oliveira's Absolute that ceases to exist once obtained, Jai Singh questions the cosmos, aware that the only truth is the relative one of constant mutability: ". . . damned if the answer matters to him, Jai Singh knows that thirst quenched by water will return to torment him, Jai Singh knows that only by being water will he quench his thirst."

As in his previous books, Cortázar's inquiry in *Prosa del observatorio* transcends factual reality, emphasizing exceptional states and states of becoming. It is an interstitial inquiry, a peering through the crevices, that reflects the searches of Cortázar's greatest fictional characters, such as Oliveira and Johnny.

Cortázar derides science for wrapping us up in enumerations and classifications that inform us but also stunt our curiosity, our will to adventure, our openness to what lies beyond our reach, to cosmic revelations and historic revolutions.

Those two inextricable planes—revelations and revolutions—of Cortázar's Möbius strip, "where reconciliation is possible, where anverse and reverse will cease to tear each other to shreds," are enhanced by the erotic imagery that describes the sultan's exploration of the heavenly harem of stars, his "redheaded night" with which he carries on an "interminable, slow copulation" as he peers out from the curved, marble observatories. As in *Hopscotch* and *A Manual for Manuel*, eroticism plays a principal role in the concept of revelation and revolution, for to Cortázar rebellion is both sexual and political, a liberation of society as a collectivity and also of the individual's desires. He explains his concept of revolutionary man in *Literatura en la revolución y revolución en la literatura*: "Authentic reality is much more than the 'sociohistoric and political context.' I am reality and . . . all of the Latin American population . . . man and men, each man and all men, agonizing man, man in the historic spiral, *homo sapiens* and *homo faber* and *homo ludens*, eroticism and social responsibility" (*Literatura*, p. 65). In *Prosa del observatorio*, one can glimpse Cortázar's socialist politics but also his desire for some sort of accord in the troubled world of multiple crises. His Möbius strip harmonizes opposites, symbolized by the correspondence between stars and eels; it is a middle road, a reconciliation of sorts, as abstract as Oliveira's Absolute or his kibbutz of desire. But it speaks to those who, like Jai Singh, dare to peer into the darkness, to confound antiquated traditions as well as doctrinaire political programs in a great

> leap that leaves science and politics behind on the level of dandruff, of flags, of language, of a chained sex. . . . Here what I call eels or stars is not crazy; there is nothing more material and dialectic and tangible than the pure image that does not tie itself to the eye, that seeks beyond to understand better, to fight against the rampant material of closure, of nations against nations and blocks against blocks.
>
> (*Prosa del observatorio*, pp. 71–73)

Experimentation, the coopting of artistic forms, and above all a collage-reality infuse Cortázar's fiction and such miscellaneous writings as *Around the Day in Eighty Worlds* and *Ultimo Round*. Both serve as biographical collages of anecdotes, essays, memories, daily experiences, poems, quotations, and reflections about diverse subjects that fascinate the author; both are interspersed with photographs, engravings, and drawings. The titles reflect Cortázar's preferences: the first based on his affection for his namesake, Jules Verne, whose books he read voraciously as a child, and the second on boxing. The pages of both books are populated by his favorites: surrealists Raymond Roussel, Marcel Duchamp, Antonin Artaud, Ernst, Salvador Dalí, Delvaux, Man Ray; writers William Shakespeare and John Keats; jazz musicians Louis Armstrong, Thelonious Monk, and Clifford Brown; the insane painter Adolf Wölfi; the strange Juan Esteban Fassio, who invented a machine to read *Hopscotch*; and Jack the Ripper. Also evident are his fascination with mystery, murderers, and victimization, his obsessions with hands and his fear of being buried alive, his "figures" and ideas about the fantastic short story, even the genesis of "Torito" and some words about the antinovel theories expressed by the character Morelli in *Hopscotch*. The title page of *Around the Day in Eighty Worlds* sports a drawing of an aquarium filled with odd beasts—a bird-fish, a horse-fish, a cow-fish—a miniature trunk, a horseshoe, and a Jules Verne–style of balloon, all inviting us to jump in and swim about in the adventures of his eighty worlds. One of the book's more interesting poems is "La hoguera donde arde una" ("The Fire Where Burns a"), in which Cortázar uses incomplete verse lines. He maintains that he is only imitating daily conversation in which we often fail to complete sentences, but nevertheless understand each other. Here are a few lines from the beginning of that poem:

> *Fue el primero en acusarme de*
> *Sin pruebas y quizá doliéndole, pero había los que*
> *Ya se sabe en un pueblo perdido entre*
> *El tiempo pesa inmóvil y sólo cada*
> *Gentes que viven de telarañas, de lentas*
> *Acaso tienen corazón pero cuando hablan es*
> *¿De qué podía acusarme si solamente habíamos*
> *Imposible que el mero despecho, después de aquella*

(Tal vez la luna llena, la noche en que me llevó hasta
Morder en el amor no es tan extraño cuando se ha
(1969 ed., p. 157)

He was the first to accuse me of
Without proof and perhaps with regret and yet there
   were those who
Everyone knows that in a town hidden among
Time holds still and only every
People obsessed with trifles, with slow
They may have hearts but when they speak it is
What can they accuse me of, if only we had
Surely not just spite, after that
(Maybe the full moon, the night when he took me to
In love a bite is not so strange, especially when one has
(p. 109)

His second collage-book, *Ultimo Round,* is even more unusual in format. Cortázar has cut the volume into two uneven sections, labeled "ground floor" and "first floor." Both of these collage-books read like the "expendable" chapters of *Hopscotch* written by a true collage-personality: all of his beliefs, games, theories, and predilections reach out in brief impressions, both literal and visual, to jab at the reader like a boxer sparring with his partner. Structural and stylistic playfulness in his fiction always saved Julio Cortázar from the crushing seriousness of the world he tried to influence through his writings up to the very end of his life. In those final years, that humor was still to be found in his poetry and in the collage travelogue he wrote in collaboration with his companion Carol Dunlop, who died shortly before Cortázar. The very title of the book, published in 1983, echoes the persistence of Jules Verne's essence, still very much alive in Cortázar's life and works: *Los autonoautas de la cosmopista. Un viaje atemporal Paris–Marsella* (The Autonauts of the Cosmothruway. A Timeless Journey from Paris to Marseille).

SELECTED BIBLIOGRAPHY

Editions

Novels, Poetry, Prose Narratives

Presencia. (Published under pseud. Julio Denís.) Buenos Aires, 1938.

Los reyes. Buenos Aires, 1949.
Bestiario. Buenos Aires, 1951.
Final del juego. Mexico City, 1956.
Las armas secretas. Buenos Aires, 1959.
Los premios. Buenos Aires, 1960.
Historias de cronopios y de famas. Buenos Aires, 1962.
Rayuela. Buenos Aires, 1963.
Todos los fuegos el fuego. Buenos Aires, 1966.
La vuelta al día en ochenta mundos. Mexico City, 1967; 5th ed., 1969.
62: Modelo para armar. Buenos Aires, 1968.
Ultimo Round. Mexico City, 1969.
Viaje alrededor de una mesa. Buenos Aires, 1970.
Literatura en la revolución y revolución en la literatura. In collaboration with Oscar Collazos and Mario Vargas Llosa. Mexico City, 1970.
Pameos y meopas. Barcelona, 1971.
Prosa del observatorio. Barcelona, 1972.
Libro de Manuel. Buenos Aires, 1973.
Convergencias. Divergencias. Incidencias. Barcelona, 1973.
Octaedro. Buenos Aires, 1974.
Fantomas contra los vampiros multinacionales: Una utopía realizable. Mexico City, 1975.
Alguien que anda por ahí. Madrid, 1977.
Un tal Lucas. Buenos Aires, 1979.
Queremos tanto a Glenda y otros relatos. Mexico City, 1980.
Deshoras. Madrid, 1982.
Los autonautas de la cosmopista. Un viaje atemporal Paris–Marsella. In collaboration with Carol Dunlop. Barcelona, 1983.
Cuaderno de bitácora de "Rayuela." In collaboration with Ana María Barrenechea. Buenos Aires, 1983.
Nicaragua tan violentamente dulce. Managua, Nicaragua, 1983.
Argentina: Años de alambradas culturales. Barcelona, 1984.
Pameos, meopas y prosemas. Barcelona, 1984.
Salvo el crepúsculo. Buenos Aires, 1984.
El examen. Buenos Aires, 1986.

Translations

Alechinsky Country. New York, 1968.
All Fires the Fire and Other Stories. Translated by Suzanne Jill Levine. New York, 1973. Stories from *Todos los fuegos el fuego.*
Around the Day in Eighty Worlds. Translated by Thomas Christensen. San Francisco, 1986. Contains selections from *La vuelta al día en ochenta mundos* and *Ultimo Round.*

Blow-Up and Other Stories. Translated by Paul Blackburn. New York, 1967. Originally published in English as *End of the Game and Other Stories*.

A Certain Lucas. Translated by Gregory Rabassa. New York, 1984.

A Change of Light and Other Stories. Translated by Gregory Rabassa. New York, 1980. Contains stories from *Alguien que anda por ahí* and *Octaedro*.

Cronopios and Famas. Translated by Paul Blackburn. New York, 1969.

End of the Game and Other Stories. Translated by Paul Blackburn. New York, 1963, 1967. Contains stories from *Bestiario*, *Las armas secretas*, and *Final del juego*.

Hopscotch. Translated by Gregory Rabassa. New York, 1966.

A Manual for Manuel. Translated by Gregory Rabassa. New York, 1978.

62: A Model Kit. Translated by Gregory Rabassa. New York, 1972.

We Love Glenda So Much and Other Tales. Translated by Gregory Rabassa. New York, 1983. Contains stories from *Queremos tanto a Glenda y otros relatos* and *Alguien que anda por ahí*.

The Winners. Translated by Elaine Kerrigan. New York, 1965.

Biographical and Critical Studies

Alazraki, Jaime. *En busca del unicornio: Los cuentos de Julio Cortázar*. Madrid, 1983.

_____, and Ivar Ivask, eds. *The Final Island: The Fiction of Julio Cortázar*. Norman, Okla., 1978.

Amestoy, Lida Aronne. *Cortázar: La novela mandala*. Buenos Aires, 1972.

Amícola, José. *Sobre Cortázar*. Buenos Aires, 1969.

Boldy, Steven. *The Novels of Julio Cortázar*. New York, 1980.

Books Abroad 50/3 (1976). Issue devoted to Cortázar.

Bottone, Mireya. "Bibliografía de Cortázar." *Boletín de literaturas hispánicas* 6:93–96 (1966).

Brody, Robert. *Julio Cortázar*. "*Rayuela*." London, 1976.

Burgos, Fernando, ed. *Los ochenta mundos de Cortázar: Ensayos*. Madrid, 1987.

Carter, E. Dale, ed. *Otro Round: Ensayos sobre la obra de Julio Cortázar*. Sacramento, Calif., 1988.

Casa de las Américas. (Havana) 25/145–146 (July-October 1984). Issue devoted to Cortázar.

Cohen, Keith. "Cortázar and the Apparatus of Writing." *Contemporary Literature* 25/1:15–27 (1984).

Cuadernos hispanoamericanos 364–366 (1980).

Curutchet, Juan Carlos. *Julio Cortázar o la crítica de la razón pragmática*. Madrid, 1972.

D'Haen, Theodor Luis. *Text to Reader: A Communicative Approach to Fowles, Barth, Cortázar, and Boon*. Amsterdam, 1983.

Escamilla Molina, Roberto. *Julio Cortázar, Visión de conjunto*. Mexico City, 1970.

García Canclini, Néstor. *Cortázar: Una antropología poética*. Buenos Aires, 1968.

Garfield, Evelyn Picon. "The Exquisite Cadaver of Surrealism." *Review 72* (Center for Inter-American Relations) 7:18–21 (1972). Issue includes a "Focus" on Cortázar.

_____. *¿Es Julio Cortázar un surrealista?* Madrid, 1975.

_____. *Julio Cortázar*. New York, 1975.

_____. "*Octaedro*: Eight Phases of Despair." *Books Abroad* 50/3:576–589 (1976).

_____. "*Usted* tiende la mano a *tu* prójimo: *Alguien que anda por ahí* de Julio Cortázar." *Revista iberoamericana* 44/102–103:89–98 (1978).

_____. *Cortázar por Cortázar*. Veracruz, Mexico, 1978, 1981; Montevideo, 1988.

_____. "Julio Cortázar's Redheaded Night: Notes on Ordering the Universe in *Prosa del observatorio*." *Review of Contemporary Fiction* 3/3:71–77 (1983).

_____. "Modelo moderno para armar." In *Otro Round: Ensayos sobre la obra de Julio Cortázar*, edited by E. Dale Carter. Sacramento, Calif., 1988. Pp. 139–155.

Giacoman, Helmy F., ed. *Homenaje a Julio Cortázar*. Long Island City, N.Y., 1972.

González Bermejo, Ernesto. *Conversaciones con Cortázar*. Barcelona, 1978.

Gyurko, Lanin A. "Alienation and the Absurd in Two Stories by Cortázar." *Kentucky Romance Quarterly* 21/1:43–58 (1974).

_____. "Destructive and Ironically Redemptive Fantasy in Cortázar." *Hispania* 56/4:988–999 (1973).

INTI, Revista de literatura hispánica 10–11 (1979–1980).

Jitrik, Noé, et al. *La vuelta a Cortázar en nueve ensayos*. Buenos Aires, 1968.

Lagmanovich, David, ed. *Estudios sobre los cuentos de Julio Cortázar*. Barcelona, 1975.

Lastra, Pedro, ed. *Julio Cortázar*. Madrid, 1981.

MacAdam, Alfred J. *El indivíduo y el otro: Critica a los oventos de Julio Cortázar*. Buenos Aires and New York, 1971.

Masiello, Francine. "Grotesques in Cortázar's Fiction: Toward a Mode of Signification." *Kentucky Romance Quarterly* 29/1:61–73 (1982).

Paley de Francescato, Marta. "Juguemos a la crítica mientras Cortázar está." *Texto crítico* 3/7:116–122 (1977).

Rein, Mercedes. *Julio Cortázar: El escritor y sus máscaras.* Montevideo, 1969.

Review of Contemporary Fiction 3/3 (1983). Half of this issue is devoted to Cortázar.

Revista iberoamericana. 39/84–85 (1973).

Roy, Joaquín. *Julio Cortázar ante su sociedad.* Barcelona, 1974.

Sola, Graciela de. *Julio Cortázar y el hombre nuevo.* Buenos Aires, 1968.

Sosnowski, Saúl. *Julio Cortázar; una búsqueda mítica.* Buenos Aires, 1973.

Stabb, Martin S. "Not Text but Texture: Cortázar and the New Essay." *Hispanic Review* 52/1:19–40 (1984).

Zamora, Lois Parkinson. "European Intertextuality in Vargas Llosa and Cortázar." *Comparative Literature Studies* 19/1:21–38 (1982).

Bibliographies

Foster, David William. Bibliography in *The Twentieth-Century Spanish-American Novel: A Bibliographic Guide.* Metuchen, N.J., 1975. Pp. 64–75.

Mundo Lo, Sara de. *Julio Cortázar. His Works and His Critics: A Bibliography.* Urbana, Ill., 1985. The most complete bibliography to date.

Paley de Francescato, Marta. "Bibliografía de y sobre Julio Cortázar." *Revista iberoamericana* 39/84–85:697–726 (1973).

Reyzabal, Maria Victoria. "Bibliografía de y sobre Cortázar." *Cuadernos hispanoamericanos* 364–366:647–667 (1980).

Yurkievich, Gladis. "Bibliografía de Cortázar." In *Conversaciones con Cortázar,* by Ernesto González Bermejo. Barcelona, 1978.

Nicanor Parra

(1914–   )

Antonio Skármeta

Nicanor Parra was born in San Fabián, near Chillán, in southern Chile on 5 September 1914. His father was a schoolteacher; his mother came from a peasant family. Parra's sister, Violeta Parra, is an internationally known poet, composer, and singer, and his nephew and niece, Ángel Parra and Isabel Parra, are composers and authorities in the study of Latin American folklore. Parra began his study of physics and mathematics in his native Chile and completed his work in the United States (at Brown University, 1943–1945) and England (at Oxford, 1949–1951). During his residence in the United States and England he became acquainted with movements in English and American verse that rejected the rarified language of poetry for that of everyday life. Over the course of his life, Parra has conducted further travels, going to Western Europe, Japan, and the Soviet Union. For many years he has served as professor of theoretical physics in the University of Chile's Department of Physical Sciences and Mathematics.

Parra's winning of Chile's National Prize for Literature in 1969 confirmed the place of his innovative and controversial work. In *Hojas de Parra* (Pages from Parra, 1985), he took a brief look back at the award: "I have four defects that my Dulcinea will never forgive," he wrote. "I am old, worn out, Communist, and the winner of the National Prize for Literature. My family would forgive the first three, but not the fourth." In the 1960's Parra's poetry caught the attention of readers in the United States and was published in American magazines in translations by Lawrence Ferlinghetti, Allen Ginsberg, Miller Williams, and others. The beats found in Parra's treatment of the middle-class world a straightforwardly sarcastic tone with which they could readily identify.

Parra's second book, *Poemas y antipoemas* (*Poems and Antipoems*), published in 1954 and today considered a pivotal work in Chilean verse, clearly defines his approach to poetry. The originality of his work involves the concept of a poetic voice heard outside poetry's "lyrical" tones and nobly separated from the poetic creation itself. This voice, or "character," rejects obscure, surrealistic images and heavy-handed emotionalism, declaring itself instead for a kind of verse that is clear and natural. In "La montaña rusa" (Roller Coaster) from *Versos de salón* (Salon Verse, 1962), Parra writes,

> Durante medio siglo
> La poesía fue
> El paraíso del tonto solemne.
> Haste que vine yo
> Y me instalé con mi montaña rusa.

For half a century
Poetry was
The paradise of the solemn fool.
Until I came along
And set up my roller coaster.

In *Hojas de Parra* the poet adds that "antipoetry seeks poetry, not eloquence," a statement that confirms Parra's attempt to establish a tone that is truly his own, and therefore in conflict with tradition. Parra writes in *Poesía política* (Political Poetry, 1983):

Arte poética
la misma de siempre
escribir efectivamente como se habla
lo demás
dejaría de ser literatura
(p.181)

The art of poetry
is the same as always:
to write effectively, as one speaks
anything else
would cease to be literature

In a number of texts Parra tries to define his idea of space and perspective, turning this search for a definition into a theme, just as his contemporary, Julio Cortázar, incorporated his search for the theory of the novel into his creation of *Rayuela* (*Hopscotch*, 1963). An ironic desire to find a "middle ground" and to use common sense, which usually ends up being more absurd than the absurd, stands out in Parra's poems: we see a fondness for the day to day, the conventional, and especially for the cliché. When he speaks ironically through clichés and charges them with poetic tension, the poet has a twofold objective. On the one hand, he reveals the dullness of the psychology and philosophy of the masses, while, on the other, he calls into play an innocence that enables him to demythologize what is ordinarily taken as sacred, as in these lines from "Padre nuestro" (Our Father, translated as "Lord's Prayer"):

Padre nuestro que estás en el cielo
Lleno de toda clase de problemas
Con el ceño fruncido
Como si fueras un hombre vulgar y corriente
No piense más en nosotros

Comprendemos que sufres
Porque no puedes arreglar las cosas.

Sabemos que el Demonio no te deja tranquilo
Desconstruyendo lo que tú construyes.

El se ríe de ti
Pero nosotros lloramos contigo:
No te preocupes de sus risas diabólicas.

Padre nuestro que estás donde estás
Rodeado de ángeles desleales
Sinceramente: no sufras más por nosotros
Tienes que darte cuenta
De que los dioses no son infalibles
Y que nosotros perdonamos todo.
(*Obra gruesa*, p. 171)

Our father who art in heaven
burdened with all kinds of problems
with your brow furrowed
as if you were a common, ordinary man
don't worry about us anymore.

We understand that you suffer
because you can't fix everything.

We know that the devil won't leave you in peace,
tearing down what you have erected.

He is laughing at you, but we weep with you:
pay no attention to his fiendish laughter.

Our father who art
surrounded by unfaithful angels
sincerely: suffer no more on our account
you must realize
that the gods are not infallible
and that we can forgive anything.

Searching for a tone, Parra resorts to narration, to prosaic manners of expression, and to theatrical devices—the masking of the poet behind the voices of his poems, making it impossible to conclude with any legitimacy that his personal sympathies lie with the ethics, philosophy, or political opinions espoused by those voices. When we read poetry, we often try to go behind the images expressed in the poem to discover the poet himself. A method for reading Parra, however, would demand that Parra's poetry be read like theater: his poems consist of voices that give speeches. For instance, because Parra's work has such an intense relation to daily existence, it is frequently interpreted politically. Such an interpretation leads to attributing to the poet ideological stances that instead should be attributed to the voices in the poems.

Certainly, biographical factors and Parra's personal opinions color his speakers' provocative texts, but the poetry's diversity and contradictions make it impossible to pigeonhole the poet into the rigid categories of political theory. If his stance must be defined, it should perhaps be seen as anarchistic. An example of Parra's willingness to take a shot at anyone is *Artefactos* (Gadgets, 1972), which irritated readers of varying and contradictory sectors:

> USA
> Donde la libertad
> es una estatua
> (Poesía polí-
> tica, p. 87)

> USA
> Where
> liberty
> is a statue

is countered with

> La realidad
> no cabe en un zapato chino
> menos aún en un bototo ruso
> (p. 88)

> Reality
> cannot be contained in a Chinese shoe
> much less in a Russian boot

From the time that *Poems and Antipoems*, his second book, was published, Parra's work and person have engendered controversy. The following piece of criticism (about *Versos de salón*) by Prudencio Salvatierra, a Capuchin priest, which appeared in Chile's conservative *Diario Ilustrado* on 15 November 1964, became famous:

Can a work like this, with neither head nor tail, that exudes poison and rottenness, madness and satanism, be released to the public? They have asked me if this book is immoral. I would say not; it is too dirty to be immoral. A garbage can is not immoral, no matter how many times we walk around it trying to figure out what's inside.

On the other hand, the great Pablo Neruda celebrated the book's appearance by saying, "This poetry is as delightful as the gilded tint of early morning or fruit ripened to perfection in the shadows."

Certainly the critical attention directed toward Parra did its utmost to eviscerate the "anti" from the antipoems. The critics were not defeated by the whimsical, anarchic game with which Parra intended to deceive and confound the theoreticians, whom he saw as poised, ready to employ their critical scalpels:

> Qué es la antipoesía:
> Un temporal en una taza de té?
> Una mancha de nieve en una roca? . . .
> Un ataúd a gas de parafina?
> Una capilla ardiente sin difunto?

> Marque con una cruz
> La definición que considere correcta.
> (from "Test," in *Obra gruesa*,
> pp. 184–185)

> What is antipoetry:
> A tempest in a teapot?
> A snowy stain on a rock? . . .
> A coffin of paraffin gas?
> A funeral chapel without the corpse?

> Indicate with a mark
> The definition you consider correct.

Years after these early efforts to define the antipoem, it seems appropriate to attempt again to determine their scope. To start with, the antipoem represents a form of poetry scant in metaphor. Parra describes the "sublime" images of Hispanic modernist poetry as "megametaphors." The antipoem is a text springing from a group of only vaguely identifiable speakers whose reduction to the single poetic voice of traditional poetry would be impossible. Antipoetry frequently utilizes elements borrowed from street language and shows a preference for stock phrases, clichés, and other standardized forms of expression such as legal parlance, the language of newspaper editorials, the stylized speeches given at festivities or solemn events, funeral announcements, and political jargon. Although the antipoem employs spoken language as it is really used, the language is made to serve situations that take it out of its usual context. This inappropriate combination of images with language that does not suit them achieves the humor, an effect which seems to well up from the soul, that predominates in Parra's work. It also succeeds in distancing the reader's emotions.

Certain philosophical constants in Parra's poetry should be added to the basic characteristics enumerated above. For example, the contemporary world and existence in general are perceived as devoid of foundation; the chaos we hold as reality clings to no set values, levels all differentiation in the world, and consequently disrupts the logic of the poem. Man is wasted motion, and death shadows his every step. Apparent also is an anarchist criticism of society and the structures, whether creative or religious, that society has devised for itself to deform and misinterpret reality, creativity, and spontaneity. The antipoem is therefore an anguished, yet comic, exaltation of the insignificance and freedom of the individual.

Another notable characteristic of Parra's texts is the rejection of sentimentality. Refusing to accept the notion that the poem is a vessel to be filled with feeling and emotion, Parra's speakers adopt a language that is distant, almost descriptive, and that keeps emotion in check. To point to this distance is not to deny the presence of a subtle emotionality that breathes life into his poems; rather, one must see how this emotionality operates within boundaries imposed by rationality and irony. "Hay un día feliz" (Oh Happy Day, 1954), a poem similar in its workings to traditional verse, provides an example of this aspect of Parra's work. The poet returns to his native village, and his emotional turmoil while there gives rise to meditations that eventually lead him to pour out his feelings:

> ¡Buena cosa, Dios mío!; nunca sabe
> Uno apreciar la dicha verdadera,
> Cuando la imaginamos más lejana
> Es justamente cuando está más cerca.
> Ay de mí, ¡ay de mí!, algo me dice
> Que la vida no es más que una quimera;
> Una ilusión, un sueño sin orillas,
> Una pequeña nube pasajera.

> Vamos por partes, no sé bien qué digo,
> La emoción se me sube a la cabeza.
> (Obra gruesa, p. 21)

My God, what a good thing! One never knows
How to appreciate true happiness;
It is when we imagine it farthest
That it is nearest.
What can I do? Something tells me
That life is no more than a fantasy;
An illusion, a shoreless dream,
A fleeting little cloud.
We just wander around—what am I saying?
Emotion is rushing to my head.

Since *Poems and Antipoems* Parra's work has been characterized by a renewed search for stark poetic forms congruent with the view of the world that he earlier formed.

One strain of popular Chilean poetry is versified, humorous, and eager to celebrate the language of the peasant; this poetry embodies a philosophy of life that exalts wine, friendship, and sex. These motifs appear throughout Parra's work, but they find their purest expression in *La cueca larga* (The Long Cueca [a native Chilean dance], 1958) and are again given considerable attention in *Hojas de Parra*. The second section of *Hojas* brings into play a decrease in Parra's expressive inhibitions that allows him to transform violence and cynicism into verse. The naive grace of the peasant is made into something brutal and is described with a dry amorality, as in "La venganza del minero" (The Miner's Revenge). The miner in the poem murders his wife to avenge himself for her infidelity. The ballad is reminiscent of Federico García Lorca's "La casada infiel" (The Unfaithful Wife), except that its common, crude expressions (which are lifted spontaneously out of the tortured psyche of the miner, who does not hestitate to comply with the blind code of macho honor) shock us because they are presented as fine poetry. In the genre's brief history, this is antipoetry at its most radical.

Hojas de Parra represents the perfection of the poet's abilities and is one of the most exciting efforts in contemporary Latin American poetry. With brazenness and wit, diverse lines of Parra's talent converge in this book. Its melancholic meditations and farcical musings on death are notable achievements; the emotion that these passages generate is not neutralized even by the cynical and self-deceiving language they use. They are the most dramatic texts that Parra has written and achieve their impact by establishing a conflict between the seriousness of their theme and the almost bewitching joy with which they are written. The best example of this artistic triumph lies in the section in which Parra confronts both the idea of individual death, with which he is obsessed, and the general funereal tone established by the dictatorship in Chile, where murder has become another resource for maintaining the regime; see, for instance, the first of "Los 4 sonetos del Apocalipsis" (The Four Sonnets of the Apocalypse).

Other of the book's high points depend on Parra's use of texts that are not his own. The antipoet introduces other writers' poems, which he "knows by heart," and through their adaptation succeeds in meshing his own poetry with that of popular tradition. A translation of Hamlet's soliloquy achieves an unexpected colloquiality and a highly contemporary tone through Parra's inventive introduction of stock phrases and verbs from everyday speech to scale down the lofty concepts of the Shakespearean passage.

In two books of 1977 and 1979, *Sermones y prédicas del Cristo de Elqui* and *Nuevos sermones y prédicas del Cristo de Elqui* (published together in translation as *Sermons and Homilies of the Christ of Elqui*) Parra utilizes a figure from Chilean folklore and history—a preacher named Domingo Zárate Vega, who was active during the first half of the twentieth century—to create a mask for mixing political criticism with a dizzying repertoire of meditations and bits of advice on topics ranging from religion to hygiene. The tension between the solemn tone of the speaker and the absurdity of what he is saying produces humor. This comic element acquires more force when, exploiting an obvious anachronism to its fullest extent, the poet uses the figure of Christ to make pronouncements on themes directly related to Chile's current domination by a military dictatorship. The combined effect of these books is the fluid transmission of an absurd concept of existence. Statements in the texts contradict each other; one affirmation cancels out another. The very language of the poems becomes a vehicle of meaninglessness. They speak in parody of the necessity of establishing hierarchies and values in a world that essentially has neither.

In 1986, at the age of seventy-two, Parra introduced a new concern into his life and work: the defense of humankind against environmental pollution, the dread nuclear apocalypse, and, in general, all modes of industrial exploitation that upset the world's ecological equilibrium. In short, ecology is now leading Parra to write *ecopoems*. This development is a fitting coup de grace for a turbulent poet unable to find comfort in a natural world dominated by human brutality. Parra's new attitude imposes limits on the bitter skepticism he has expressed elsewhere. To write in defense of the environment implies the recognition that human life must continue. Parra's solidarity with nature, a loyalty that is not linked to a particular ideology, also allows him to plant himself more forcefully in an anarchic center from which he can attack the world's holders of nuclear weapons. The poet had already written his "Defensa del árbol" ("Defense of the Tree," from *Poems and Antipoems*) in 1954:

> Porqué te entregas a esa piedra
> Niño de ojos almendrados
> Con el impuro pensamiento
> De derramarla contra el árbol.
> Quien no hace nunca daño a nadie
> No se merece tan mal trato.
> Ya sea sauce pensativo
> Ya melancólico naranjo
> Debe ser siempre por el hombre
> Bien distinguido y respetado:
> Niño perverso que lo hiera
> Hiere a su padre y a su hermano.
>   (*Obra gruesa*, p. 15)

Child with almond-shaped eyes
Why are you giving into that rock
And thinking the impure thought
Of hurling it at the tree?
Someone who never harms anybody
Doesn't deserve such ill treatment.
Whether a pensive willow
Or a melancholy orange tree
It should always be highly honored
And well respected by man:
Oh perverse child who would consider wounding it
Go wound your father or your brother instead.

By 1985, the implacable antipoet had come full circle and encountered again the poet of his youth. But now the anguished tenderness of his early days has become a plea:

> Ya no pedimos pan
> techo
> ni abrigo
> nos conformamos con un poco de aire
> EXCELENCIA!
> > (Poesía política, p. 156)

> We no longer ask for bread
> a roof
> or a coat
> we will settle for a little air
> YOUR EXCELLENCY!

Translated from the Spanish by Theodore Parks

SELECTED BIBLIOGRAPHY

First Editions

Poetry

Cancionero sin nombre. Santiago, Chile, 1937.
Poemas y antipoemas. Santiago, Chile, 1954.
La cueca larga. Santiago, Chile, 1958.
Versos de salón. Santiago, Chile, 1962.
Canciones rusas. Santiago, Chile, 1967.
Artefactos. Santiago, Chile, 1972.
Tarjetas postales. Santiago, Chile, 1972.
Sermones y prédicas del Cristo de Elqui. Santiago, Chile, 1977.
Nuevos sermones y prédicas del Cristo de Elqui. Valparaíso, Chile, 1979.
Hojas de Parra. Santiago, Chile, 1985.

Collected Works

Obra gruesa. Santiago, Chile, 1969. Includes all works listed above except Cancionero sin nombre, plus a collection of poems entitled "La camisa fuerte." Ends with the sections "Otros poemas" and "Tres poemas," which consist of twenty-five texts not previously published in book form.
Poesía política. Santiago, Chile, 1983. An anthology that includes some unpublished poems.

Translations

Antipoems. Translated by Jorge Elliot. San Francisco, Calif., 1960. Reprinted 1973.

Antipoems: New and Selected. Edited by David Unger; translated by Lawrence Ferlinghetti and others. New York, 1985.
Emergency Poems. Translated by Miller Williams. New York, 1972. Bilingual edition.
Poems and Antipoems. Edited by Miller Williams; translated by Fernando Alegría and others. New York, 1967. Bilingual edition.
Sermons and Homilies of the Christ of Elqui. Translated by Sandra Reyes. Forward by Miller Williams. Columbia, Mo., 1984.

Biographical and Critical Studies

Aguirre, Margarita, and Juan Agustín Palazuelos. "Nicanor Parra, antipoeta." Prologue to Nicanor Parra, La cueca larga y otros poemas. Buenos Aires, 1964. Pp. 5–14.
Alegría, Fernando. "Parra anti-Parra." In his Literatura y revolución. Mexico City, 1971.
Benedetti, Mario. "Nicanor Parra descubre y mortifica su realidad." In Letras del continente mestizo. Montevideo, 1974.
Cortínez, Carlos. "Sermones y prédicas del Cristo de Elqui." Revista chilena de literatura 24:137–143 (1984).
Goić, Cedomil. "La antipoesía de Nicanor Parra." Los libros 9:6–7 (1970).
Gottlieb, Marlene. La poesía de Nicanor Parra: "No se termina nunca de nacer." Madrid, 1978.
Grossman, Edith. "The Technique of Antipoetry." Review (Center for Inter American Relations) Winter 1971/ Spring 1972:72–83.
_____. The Antipoetry of Nicanor Parra. New York, 1975.
Ibañez Langlois, José Miguel. In Poesía chilena e hispano-americana actual. Santiago, Chile, 1975. Pp. 256–290.
Lerzundi, Patricio. "In Defense of Antipoetry, An Interview with Nicanor Parra." Review (Center for Inter-American Relations) Winter 1971/Spring 1972: 65–71.
Rodríguez Fernández, Mario. "Nicanor Parra, destructor de mitos." In Nicanor Parra y la poesía de lo cotidiano, edited by Hugo Montes and Mario Rodríguez Fernández. Santiago, Chile, 1970.
Rodríguez Monegal, Emir. "Meetings with Nicanor Parra." Review (Center for Inter-American Relations) Fall 1972:48–54.
Schopf, Federico. "La escritura de la semejanza en Nicanor Parra." Revista chilena de literatura 2–3:42–132 (1970).
_____. "Introducción a la antipoesía." Prologue to Nicanor Parra, Poemas y antipoemas. Santiago, Chile, 1970.
Yamal, Ricardo. Sistema y visión de la poesía de Nicanor Parra. Valencia, 1985.

Adolfo Bioy Casares

(1914–   )

Mireya Camurati

One of the most significant events in contemporary literature has been the emergence of Latin American writers to world prominence. Particularly in the 1950's and 1960's a group of authors created what their European and North American counterparts considered to be masterpieces of fiction. Critics examining the development of the so-called new Latin American narrative turn their attention to such early works as Adolfo Bioy Casares' 1940 novel, *La invención de Morel* (*The Invention of Morel*). The plot of this book, which Jorge Luis Borges did not hesitate to qualify as perfect, involves original themes presented with creative techniques. These are applied with amazing skill, especially considering the author's youth. At the time Bioy Casares was twenty-five years old, but this is not to suggest that he was an inexperienced writer. He had already published *Prólogo* (Prologue; miscellanea, 1929); *Diecisiete disparos contra lo porvenir* (Seventeen Shots at the Future; short stories, 1933); *Caos* (Chaos; short stories, 1934); *La nueva tormenta o La vida de Juan Ruteno* (The New Storm or The Life of Juan Ruteno; novel, 1935); *La estatua casera* (The House Statue; miscellanea, 1936); and *Luis Greve, muerto* (Luis Greve, Deceased; short stories, 1937). There were an equal number of texts from this period that Bioy Casares left unfinished or unpublished. He aban-

doned these works because he considered them to be failures. Even if we agree with such a negative evaluation, these rejected pieces nonetheless demonstrate the author's early and firm commitment to dedicate himself to writing.

In Bioy Casares' case, his family and social standing made it easier for him to reach his goals. He was born into an upper-class family in Buenos Aires on 15 September 1914, the son of Adolfo Bioy and Marta Casares.

In interviews and autobiographical notes, Bioy Casares recalls that, as a small child, his mother told him stories about animals that left their burrows, ran into all sorts of dangers and, finally, returned to safety. He notes that this idea of a refuge and the risks and threats that lurk outside has always appealed to him. He also remembers his father reciting poems and fables to him. As a youth, Bioy Casares' father had intended to write novels and comedies. This plan never materialized, but near the end of his life he wrote two books of memoirs. As Bioy Casares speculates, his father's frustrated aspirations—in addition to love for his son—could explain the encouragement he received in his early literary endeavors. This could be why his father financed the publication of *Prólogo*, his first book.

The only child of attentive, well-educated, and

wealthy parents, Bioy Casares grew up in an environment in which he was free to develop his talents and interests. At the age of ten he traveled to Europe with his family, and at fifteen he visited the United States. He enjoyed sports, played rugby, tennis, and soccer; and he boxed. He has always loved the movies. When he had trouble learning algebra in school, his parents sought the help of an elderly professor who introduced him to the pleasures of mathematics and reasoning. In 1933 he studied at the University of Buenos Aires, first in the School of Law and then in the Faculty of Philosophy and Letters. He became dissatisfied with academia and withdrew in 1935.

Bioy Casares noted such autobiographical details in a "Chronology," published by the Center for Inter-American Relations. Its style is a mixture of seriousness and calculated humor. Although some of the facts might appear superficial or anecdotal, most are actually relevant to Bioy Casares' work. For example, he mentions his early attraction to the supernatural and the fantastic. And he notes that almost since childhood he had a propensity for falling in love with his cousins and girls in his neighborhood, and later, with movie stars and chorus girls. Such infatuations, incipient and necessarily frustrated, later insinuate themselves into the personalities and actions of some of his fictitious characters.

As a young man, Bioy became familiar with country life and work. His father owned a ranch in the town of Pardo in the province of Buenos Aires, where the family spent several months each year. According to the "Chronology," in 1935 Bioy convinced his father to let him administer the ranch, located a few hours from Buenos Aires. While working there he increased his knowledge of the countryside and its people.

Lists of the books read by Bioy Casares are recorded in the "Chronology." In the beginning this was a heterogeneous collection ranging from the classics to contemporary works and popular magazines that published tango lyrics. Later his reading became more selective and broadened to include works of philosophy, aesthetics, and science, along with keeping up with contemporary literature and rereading the classics.

In 1932 Bioy recorded, "At Victoria Ocampo's house in San Isidro, I meet Jorge Luis Borges." This entry marks two milestones in his life and work. First, it notes his relationship with Victoria Ocampo (1891–1979), who for more than half a century was one of the most influential figures in Argentine cultural life. A writer and critic in her own right, she also had both the financial resources and wisdom to use her fortune to invite the most famous writers and intellectuals to Buenos Aires. She founded and directed *Sur*, which was, from 1931 until its regular publication ceased in 1970, one of the leading literary journals in the Hispanic world. Through this journal and its adjoining publishing house it was possible to know about the principal contemporary authors and read their works in Spanish. Bioy records that he was a member of the so-called "group of *Sur*" from its earliest years. In 1940 Bioy married Silvina Ocampo, Victoria's sister, an excellent poet and short story writer. Silvina Ocampo and Bioy Casares collaborated on a detective novel, *Los que aman, odian* (Those Who Love, Hate, 1946).

The second important event in the 1932 entry was the meeting with Borges, which marked the beginning of a literary relationship and strong friendship that lasted until Borges' death in 1986. Borges was fifteen years older than Bioy Casares, but the age difference did not seem to have been an obstacle either socially or in their collaborative writings. Each claimed to be an admirer of the other and grateful for the benefits of their friendship.

For *The Invention of Morel*, Bioy Casares was awarded the First Municipal Prize for Literature of the City of Buenos Aires in 1941. After this the entries in the "Chronology" are basically about his literary works. *The Invention of Morel* was followed by five novels: *Plan de evasión* (A Plan for Escape, 1945); *El sueño de los héroes* (The Dream of Heroes, 1954); *Diario de la guerra del cerdo* (Diary of the War of the Pig, 1969); *Dormir al sol* (Asleep in the Sun, 1973); and *La aventura de un fotógrafo en La Plata* (The Adventure of a Photographer in La Plata, 1985).

Bioy Casares also wrote a number of short stories that were published in several collections: *La trama celeste* (The Celestial Plot, 1948); *Historia prodigiosa* (Prodigious Story, 1956); *Guirnalda con amores* (Garland with Love, 1959); *El lado de la sombra* (The Shadowy Side, 1962); *El gran Serafín* (The Great Seraphim, 1967); *Historias de amor* (Love Stories,

1972); *Historias fantásticas* (Fantastic Stories, 1972); *El héroe de las mujeres* (The Women's Hero, 1978); and *Historias desaforadas* (Outrageous Stories, 1986).

In addition, Bioy Casares wrote *La otra aventura* (The Other Adventure, a collection of articles and essays, 1968); "Siete soñadores" (Seven Dreamers, 1968), a one-act comedy; *Memoria sobre la pampa y los gauchos* (Memories of the Pampa and the Gauchos, 1970), a study of the Argentine countryside and its inhabitants; and *Breve diccionario del argentino exquisito* (Brief Dictionary of the Vain Argentine, 1978), notes on mannerisms and idiosyncrasies of the language spoken in Argentina in recent decades. Collaborative works with Borges and with Silvina Ocampo complete Bioy Casares' literary production through 1986.

The Invention of Morel was published with a prologue by Borges, which has reached a level of popularity and importance in Spanish-American literary criticism equal to that of the novel itself. Borges rejected the psychological and realistic novel, favoring the adventure story, the novel of "reasoned imagination." He proposed a narrative that is a "verbal artifice," a work of pure fiction that does not tolerate any superfluous elements. In this sense, Borges considered Bioy Casares' novel exemplary.

The Invention of Morel is the story of a fugitive running from justice who arrives on an apparently uninhabited island. But he soon encounters a number of people, among them a woman, Faustine, and Morel, a bearded tennis player who is always with her. The protagonist struggles to survive the tides that flood his part of the island, to find food, and to avoid being discovered by the other inhabitants. However, he falls in love with Faustine and wants to be near her. In the meantime, strange things are happening: no one seems to see him or to be aware of his presence; once in a while the people repeat the same words or gestures they had used before; and they disappear as suddenly as they appear. As Borges notes, the "fantastic but not supernatural" explanation is that they and their setting are just images formed by Morel's "invention." This consists of machines, activated by the tides, that film, tape record, and then project the complete presence of people and things. The invention captures not only the visual and auditory, but is capable of reconsti-

tuting a complete reality, with olfactory, thermal, gustatory, and tactile sensations. The protagonist, carried away by his love for Faustine, decides to insert himself into the sequence of projected images. Faced with impending death, he hopes to be able to remain eternally at the side of his beloved.

The themes of the novel are both important and appealing: the creation of beings and objects by machine; the refutation of time and the quest for immortality; the fortunes and misfortunes of love. The fundamental value of this work, though, rests on its compositional techniques, especially on the interplay of narrative levels and points of view.

The novel begins with the protagonist-narrator explaining that what we are reading is the journal in which he recorded the strange events that occurred on the island. Every so often there are footnotes written by "the editor," who usually contradicts or criticizes what the protagonist is saying and, in one instance, what Morel is saying. Also there is a manuscript by Morel that includes an explanation of his invention, as transcribed by the protagonist-narrator. Thus, the reader has three sources of information, or three narrative voices, none of them reliable. The first is the voice of the protagonist who has given more than enough reasons for distrust. We know, by his own admission, that he is a fugitive who has been convicted, although perhaps unjustly. He recognizes that he might appear deceitful but, what is more serious, he speaks of sickness, hallucinations, and madness. Also, he declares himself to be a writer, though this may be only to impress his beloved Faustine. The last introduces the possibility that the protagonist's text is not a diary at all, but his own literary fiction.

The voice of the editor, although sporadic, plays an important role in the structure of the novel. Most of the time he objects to the protagonist's notations with hostility. Sometimes he exceeds his role as editor, appearing to be interested only in demonstrating his knowledge or in giving his interpretations of events. Finally, there is Morel, whose text is evaluated by the protagonist as "a repugnant and disorderly discourse." The fugitive sees Morel as a murderer or a madman, but these negative judgments may be based on jealousy because Morel is his rival for Faustine. Therefore, each narrative voice is trying to discredit the others. In this regard, the novel is similar to a detective story because it presents bits of information or clues to help interpret a mystery. In some ways the reader is invited to participate in the investigation.

The novel's title offers a variety of meanings. It might refer to the invention of the machine that creates images; the invention of the character of Morel in the fugitive-writer's text; or the creation of a phantasmal reality by Morel's machine: a week in the life of a group of people living on an island that will repeat itself forever. Above all, this is the invention of Bioy Casares. This novel is fiction within fiction, a calculated interplay of narrators and characters, verbal repetitions that evoke temporal repetitions, all in order to construct a text that is self-affirming in its autonomous reality as pure literary artifice.

A Plan for Escape, published five years later, has thematic and technical similarities to *The Invention of Morel*. Again, the principal action takes place on an island, Devil's Island, near the coast of French Guiana. It seems that some relatives of the protagonist, the naval lieutenant Enrique Nevers, used their influence to have him assigned to this penal colony to punish him for an alleged crime that had damaged the family's good name and fortune. They also want to separate him from his fiancée, Irene. Disgusted and suspicious, Nevers arrives at Cayenne, French Guiama's main town; and what he finds there increases his fears. The governor, Pedro Castel, has moved to Devil's Island, where he is living with his secretary and three prisoners. He has left strict orders that Nevers may not go to the island. The first time Nevers catches a glimpse of Castel, he sees him being followed by a herd of animals. Nevers feels like a prisoner himself, threatened by unknown dangers. Nevers soon decides to find a way out of this situation and return to France and Irene. He thinks about his "plan for escape." At the same time, he is intrigued by the governor's strange activities on the island and wants to learn more. At the tragic and bloody end, Nevers finds the explanation for the mystery in a letter the governor has left for him. Apparently, Castel had discovered a way to modify the mechanisms of perception using surgical techniques. After operating on the convicts, he had put them in special cells, where the location of walls and the arrange-

ments of colors and mirrors gave these men the impression that they were free. Thus, the governor had offered his prisoners a way out, a plan for escape.

The subject of sensory perception is presented through quotations from and allusions to various authors. For example, there are almost literal transcriptions of paragraphs from "The Stream of Thought," a chapter in William James' *The Principles of Psychology* (1890). And although it is not mentioned, it is possible that Sir Francis Galton's *Inquiries into Human Faculty and Its Development* (1883), a book that had deeply impressed Bioy Casares, influenced some of the ideas in this novel. Literary quotations related to the sensory perception experiments are from William Blake, Arthur Rimbaud (the first line of the sonnet "Voyelles" ["Vowels"]), Charles Baudelaire's "Correspondances," and René Ghil. On a more general level, there is allusion to *The Island of Doctor Moreau* (1896) by H. G. Wells. All this material is skillfully organized—in the same manner as clues in a mystery—leaving the reader with an impression of ambiguity.

As with *The Invention of Morel*, the structure of *A Plan for Escape* is based on the interplay of narrative voices. The first belongs to Antoine Brissac, who copies some letters from his nephew Enrique and another nephew, Xavier Brissac, as well as Castel's "Instructions" to Nevers. At other points, the uncle comments on letters or gives his own interpretations of the people and events; he frequently assumes the position of omniscient narrator. The reader is thus given different versions of the story, but not enough information to judge which one is most reliable.

Bioy Casares' ability to compose precise and complex narrative structures is also apparent in the stories in *The Celestial Plot*, especially "El otro laberinto" ("The Other Labyrinth") and "El perjurio de la nieve" ("The Perjury of the Snow"). The latter employs the literary device of the framed narrative. One character-narrator, Alfonso Berger Cárdenas, writes the frame—introduction and the final comments—to an "Account" of events as recorded by another character-narrator, Juan Luis Villafañe. Berger Cárdenas signs his texts with his initials, A.B.C., which are also Adolfo Bioy Casares' initials. In this way, Bioy Casares seems to be playing with a quite common confusion when readers identify the narrator with the author. This insinuation of the author into his work is not a new technique; here it effectively contributes to discredit the narrators by blurring the lines that separate a real person (Adolfo Bioy Casares) from a fictitious character (Alfonso Berger Cárdenas). The framed narrative is not a new device either; traditionally it serves to define the limits between one narration and the other. In "The Perjury of the Snow," though, the two narrations combine and interpenetrate. In the frame, A.B.C. describes and judges Villafañe and the other main character, Carlos Oribe. In the "Account," Villafañe talks about Oribe and A.B.C., and then A.B.C. tells Villafañe what Oribe had said. A.B.C. is both a narrator of the frame and a character in the framed narration. Thus, the reader receives multiple versions of the events, biased or incomplete versions that are questionable. "The Perjury of the Snow" shares some characteristics with mystery fiction, in which a detective has to reveal the plan that the criminal has executed, and also he has to consider differing explanations from other characters involved in the intrigue. Actually, the work can be classified as a detective story for it satisfies two fundamental requirements of the genre: the investigation of a mystery, generally a crime; and the presence of an investigator. There is, in fact, more than one mystery and more than one investigator in "The Perjury of the Snow." This short story, which Bioy Casares started writing in 1932, was first published in book format in 1944. In addition to its intrinsic literary merits, it is also one of the earliest detective stories in Latin American literature.

The Dream of Heroes, perhaps Bioy Casares' best novel, appeared in 1954. Here the setting is not a remote island, but the most familiar parts of the city of Buenos Aires. This is not to say that the story always develops in a realistic atmosphere. On the contrary, the central theme revolves around a dream, or a state of mind that is being remembered as magnificent and to which a man tries to return.

At the beginning of the story, a young mechanic named Emilio Gauna wins some money gambling at the races. He decides to spend it in the company of his friends and the so-called "doctor" Valerga, a man they admire for his reported courage. It is the carnival season of 1927, and Emilio and his companions go off on a three-day spree that includes bars, masquerades, and brothels. The last night, at a ball, Emilio has a brief encounter with a masked woman. They part, and in a confused way he believes he remembers a knife duel with Valerga. Later, he awakes in an unfamiliar place in the middle of a park.

The central part of the novel includes episodes in Emilio's life during the following three years: his relationship with Serafín Taboada, a strange person who is a combination philosopher and clairvoyant; his love for and marriage to Clara, Taboada's daughter, who happens to be the mysterious masked woman from the ball; and above all, his growing obsession with the three days in 1927. In 1930 Emilio again wins at the races, and in the last part of the novel he tries to relive the events of 1927—in spite of Taboada's and Clara's attempts to persuade him to abandon his plan. The story ends with Emilio ready to face death in a knife fight with Valerga. Emilio is happy because he discovers that he is not a coward, and he understands the meaning of the dream (or memory) of the mysterious adventure that has haunted him for so long.

The novel's plot and narrative structure are built around the subjects of dreams, premonitions, and the interconnection of past, present, and future. The adventures of Emilio and his friends at the carnival of 1927 take only one chapter (5), while those of the 1930 carnival involve eighteen (38–55). The events at the beginning of the book are presented in a confused and incomplete manner, as if they were mixed up with a dream, while the events at the end of the book are well developed and detailed. The idea that dreams may anticipate the future raises a troublesome question: is it not possible then to alter, to control the future? With such a question one enters the field of metaphysics and even theology with the dispute between determinism and free will. Perhaps Bioy Casares found some suggestions about this in John William Dunne's *An Experiment with Time* (1927), a text he read in 1939. Dunne was a minor British writer whose ideas attracted the attention of such men of letters as H. G. Wells and J. B. Priestley. According to Bioy Casares, Dunne had considerable influence on his fiction and that of Borges.

The image of a young man sacrificing himself while trying to demonstrate his courage also appears in

"Homenaje a Francisco Almeyra" (Homage to Francisco Almeyra), a short story published in 1954 and later included in the collection *Historia prodigiosa*.

As with all of Bioy Casares' works, the theme of love in *The Dream of Heroes* is central. In this case, the focus is on the weakness of the lover unable to protect the beloved and with the failure to avoid degradation in a conflict of values.

Bioy Casares' next novel is *Diary of the War of the Pig*. The war referred to in the title is generational, between children and parents. The young people attack and try to exterminate the old. This work presents the most extreme examples of Bioy Casares' dark and grotesque humor. Frequently the old men appear as laughable and pathetic figures who humiliate themselves to avoid being discovered. The protagonist, Isidoro Vidal, and his companion Nélida exemplify a love relationship between an older man and a younger woman. Similar relationships are depicted in several stories in the collection *Historios desaforadas*, for example, "Planes para una fuga al Carmelo" (Plans for an Escape to Carmelo) or "El relojero de Fausto" (Faust's Clockmaker).

Many of Bioy Casares' stories portray a certain resentment and fear of old age. In modern versions of the ancient Faust legend, characters resort to physicians, charlatans, and even more or less benign devils to avoid or reverse the deterioration that comes with age. Usually the latent or manifest motive for this is love, the desire to obtain and preserve it throughout life. But the majority of these brave lovers are unable to understand their feelings or to really know the person they love. This is what happens to Lucio Bordenave, the protagonist in *Asleep in the Sun* (1973). Lucio is married to Diana, an ill-humored shrew who is apparently neurotic. With the hope that she might be cured, Lucio commits her to the Institute of Reger Samaniego, a half-philanthropic, half-mad doctor. Diana returns home as a kind and gentle woman, thanks to a series of "transplants" of bodies and souls. But then Lucio misses the old Diana and tries desperately to get her back.

The complexity of love is a predominant theme in all of Bioy Casares' stories, as some of his collections demonstrate from their titles: *Guirnalda con amores* and *Historias de amor*; and suggested in the volume entitled *El héroe de las mujeres*.

Humor is ever present in Bioy Casares' work. Generally, it is a veiled humor expressed through irony, witty sayings, or light mockery. If satirical, as are the entries in *Breve diccionario del argentino exquisito*, the humor becomes heavy and even grotesque. Such are the works Bioy Casares and Borges wrote in collaboration, where a nonsensical and bold humor functions as a sharp instrument for criticism. A good example is the multifaceted parody *Chronicles of Bustos Domecq*, which makes fun of artistic eccentricities, ridicules critics and their work, and even parodies language itself.

La aventura de un fotógrafo en La Plata (1985) includes many features and subjects characteristic of Bioy Casares' work. Some are dealt with minimally, such as dreams, the mystery of a possible crime, and humor. Other elements are placed in the center of the plot. This is true of the idea of a machine: in this case a simple camera that captures and composes reality. The paradoxes and inconsistencies of love are also central in this novel. The themes and the plot are presented in a controlled manner, in a light tone that gives with levity what in other stories was administered with intensity.

In the later works it is possible to discern a pattern in the evolution of Bioy Casares' narrative style: a trend toward an eloquent and essential simplicity that can be observed on different levels. In his characterizations, there is a change from the strange to the more average individuals with whom readers can relate more easily. In his settings, there is a change from exotic and distant islands to the well-known landscapes of both the province and city of Buenos Aires. In his plots, there is a change from the complicated (at times overloaded) structures of early works to more streamlined stories. This does not suggest a scarcity of literary resources, but rather a process of distillation of the most relevant elements. Above all, Bioy Casares' narratives continue to be well-told stories supported by structures that are calculated to the minutest detail. At the same time, one of the evidences of great virtuosity in Bioy's work is, precisely, that he does not leave traces of his skills.

The protagonist in *La aventura de un fotógrafo en La Plata* subordinates every other activity or feeling to the practice of his profession. He wonders if "a photographer is a man who looks at things in order to take a picture of them; or better yet, a man who looking at things sees where a good picture is" (chapter 19). It might be argued that the photographer trying to compose his pictures is comparable to the writer trying to organize his narratives. Both adopt a particular point of view, arrange their materials, characterize their human subjects, and plan the sequence of scenes. The difference is that the instrument with which the writer determines and expresses the images—language—is infinitely more complex and much more subtle than the most sophisticated camera.

In this story, the power of the protagonist's vocation manifests itself constantly, and it seems that the only way he observes the outside world is through the lens of his camera. Looking at Bioy Casares' lifelong commitment to literature and his pure joy of writing, one feels confident to venture a comparison between the author and the character in this novel.

Bioy Casares' books have been translated into several languages, and he has received numerous prizes and distinctions. Modest by nature and not in need of material rewards for his writings, Bioy Casares has never been interested in any kind of self-promotion. This may account for his works frequently not getting the recognition they deserve. Another reason might be his close personal and professional relationship with Borges, a monumental figure who usually attracted all the attention. Such overshadowing may have occurred, in spite of the fact that Borges often commented on the fallacy of assuming that because he was older he was always the master. According to Borges, he learned from Bioy Casares more than he taught his younger friend.

The growing interest of readers and critics in Adolfo Bioy Casares' writings, as demonstrated by the increasing volume of scholarly studies and the reprints of his works in Spanish and in translation, indicates that this author is assuming a deserved position of literary prominence.

SELECTED BIBLIOGRAPHY

First Editions

Novels

La invención de Morel. Buenos Aires, 1940.
Plan de evasión. Buenos Aires, 1945.

El sueño de los héroes. Buenos Aires, 1954.
Diario de la guerra del cerdo. Buenos Aires, 1969.
Dormir al sol. Buenos Aires, 1973.
La aventura de un fotógrafo en La Plata. Buenos Aires, 1985.

Collections of Short Stories

La trama celeste. Buenos Aires, 1948.
Historia prodigiosa. Mexico City, 1956.
Guirnalda con amores. Buenos Aires, 1959.
El lado de la sombra. Buenos Aires, 1962.
El gran Serafín. Buenos Aires, 1967.
Historias de amor. Buenos Aires, 1972.
Historias fantásticas. Buenos Aires, 1972.
El héroe de las mujeres. Buenos Aires, 1978.
Historias desaforadas. Buenos Aires, 1986.

Essays and Miscellaneous Prose

La otra aventura. Buenos Aires, 1968.
Memoria sobre la pampa y los gauchos. Buenos Aires, 1970.
Breve diccionario del argentino exquisito. Buenos Aires, 1978.

Plays

"Siete soñadores: Tragicomedia en un acto." In Sur 314:21–35 (1968).

Works in Collaboration

With Jorge Luis Borges

Seis problemas para don Isidro Parodi. (Published under pseud. H. Bustos Domecq.) Buenos Aires, 1942.
Dos fantasías memorables. (Published under pseud. H. Bustos Domecq.) Buenos Aires, 1946.
Un modelo para la muerte. (Published under pseud. B. Suárez Lynch.) Buenos Aires, 1946.
Los orilleros y El paraíso de los creyentes. Buenos Aires, 1955.
Crónicas de Bustos Domecq. Buenos Aires, 1967.
Nuevos cuentos de Bustos Domecq. Buenos Aires, 1977.

With Silvina Ocampo

Los que aman, odian. Buenos Aires, 1946.

Translations

Asleep in the Sun. Translated by Suzanne Jill Levine. New York, 1978.
Chronicles of Bustos Domecq. By Jorge Luis Borges and Adolfo Bioy Casares. Translated by Norman Thomas Di Giovanni. New York, 1976.
Diary of the War of the Pig. Translated by Gregory Woodruff and Donald A. Yates. New York, 1972.

The Dream of Heroes. Translated by Diana Thorold. London, 1987.

The Invention of Morel and Other Stories from "La trama celeste." Translated by Ruth L. C. Simms. Austin, Tex., 1964.

The Perjury of the Snow. Translated by Ruth L. C. Simms. New York, 1964.

A Plan for Escape. Translated by Suzanne Jill Levine. New York, 1975.

Six Problems for Don Isidro Parodi. By Jorge Luis Borges and Adolfo Bioy Casares. Translated by Norman Thomas Di Giovanni. New York, 1981.

Biographical and Critical Studies

Adams, Robert M. "No Escaping Evasion." *Review* (Center for Inter-American Relations) 15:50–54 (1975).

Bastos, María Luisa. "Habla popular/Discurso unificador: *El sueño de los héroes* de Adolfo Bioy Casares." *Revista iberoamericana* 125:753–766 (1983).

Bioy Casares, Adolfo. "Chronology." *Review* (Center for Inter-American Relations) 15:35–39 (1975).

Camurati, Mireya. "Bioy Casares y el lenguaje de los argentinos." *Revista iberoamericana* 123–124:419–432 (1983).

_____. "El texto misceláneo: *Guirnalda con amores* de Adolfo Bioy Casares." In *Actas del Octavo Congreso de la Asociación Internacional de Hispanistas. Providence, Rhode Island (22–27 agosto 1983)* 1, edited by A. David Kossoff, José Amor y Vázquez, Ruth H. Kossoff, and Geoffrey W. Ribbans. Madrid, 1986. Pp. 309–315.

Gallagher, David. "The Novels and Short Stories of Adolfo Bioy Casares." *Bulletin of Hispanic Studies* 52/3:247–266 (1975).

Kovacci, Ofelia. *Adolfo Bioy Casares.* Buenos Aires, 1963.

Levine, Suzanne Jill. *Guía de Adolfo Bioy Casares.* Madrid, 1982.

MacAdam, Alfred J. *Modern Latin American Narratives: The Dreams of Reason.* Chapters 3 and 4. Chicago, 1977.

Manguel, Alberto. "Estudio preliminar y Notas." In *Plan de evasión* by Adolfo Bioy Casares. Buenos Aires, 1974.

Matas, Julio. "Adolfo Bioy Casares o la aventura de narrar." In *La cuestión del género literario: Casos de las letras hispánicas.* Madrid, 1979.

Meehan, Thomas C. "Estructura y tema de *El sueño de los héroes* por Adolfo Bioy Casares." *Kentucky Romance Quarterly* 20/1:31–58 (1973).

_____. "Temporal Simultaneity and the Theme of Time Travel in a Fantastic Story by Adolfo Bioy Casares." *Kentucky Romance Quarterly* 30/2:167–185 (1983).

Paley de Francescato, Martha. "Adolfo Bioy Casares [entrevista]." *Hispamérica* 9:75–81 (1975).

Pezzoni, Enrique. "Prólogo." In *Adversos milagros* by Adolfo Bioy Casares. Caracas, 1969. Pp. 7–17.

_____. "Adolfo Bioy Casares." In *Enciclopedia de la literatura argentina.* Buenos Aires, 1970.

Rivera, Jorge B. "Lo arquetípico en la narrativa argentina del 40." In *Nueva novela latinoamericana II: La narrativa argentina actual,* edited by Jorge Lafforgue. Buenos Aires, 1972. Pp. 174–204.

Rodríguez Monegal, Emir. "The Invention of Bioy Casares." *Review* (Center for Inter-American Relations) 15:41–44 (1975).

Snook, Margaret L. "The Narrator as Creator and Critic in *The Invention of Morel.*" *Latin American Literary Review* 7/14:45–51 (1979).

Tamargo, María Isabel. *La narrativa de Bioy Casares: El texto como escritura-lectura.* Madrid, 1983.

Torres Fierro, Danubio. "Las utopías pesimistas de Adolfo Bioy Casares." *Plural* 55:47–53 (1976).

Villordo, Oscar Hermes. *Genio y figura de Adolfo Bioy Casares.* Buenos Aires, 1983.

Weinberger, Deborah. "Problems in Perception." *Review* (Center for Inter-American Relations) 15:45–49 (1975).

Augusto Roa Bastos

(1917–   )

Juan Manuel Marcos

The most representative author of the Paraguayan neobaroque period is Augusto Roa Bastos, whose oeuvre has inspired an international bibliography that easily exceeds that of all the other Paraguayan writers combined. He was born in Asunción on 13 June 1917, spent his childhood in the provincial city of Iturbe, moved to Buenos Aires in 1947 and to Toulouse, France, in 1975. Roa Bastos has worked for the most part as a scriptwriter and university professor. He was allowed to visit Paraguay in the 1970's, but after being expelled in 1982 he was forced to remain in exile. In his several volumes of short stories and especially in his two novels, *Hijo de hombre* (*Son of Man*, 1960) and *Yo el Supremo* (*I the Supreme*, 1974), Roa Bastos explores the Paraguayan social unconscious, revealing not only its poetic myths but also remythifying its most noble and profound values in favor of a utopian, revolutionary project: the collective resurrection of Paraguay as a coherent community.

Asunción, founded in 1537, was the historical capital of the River Plate area (Argentina, Paraguay, and Uruguay). During the colonial period, the social regime of the *encomienda* (Indian servitude) was established. At least fifteen massive Indian insurrections occurred in Paraguay between 1537 and 1559; they continued until 1660, when a well-organized resistance movement suffered cruel repression in Arecayá. During the seventeenth century, several *comuneros* (autonomistic) movements, led by Asunción's creoles, who benefited from the *encomienda* system, came into conflict with the Jesuits, who had developed a solid program of Indian colonization in their settlements.

Colonial Paraguay produced a number of major literary figures—Alvar Núñez Cabeza de Vaca, Martín del Barco Centenera, and Félix de Azara among them. The most important work of Paraguayan colonial literature, and certainly an antecedent of Roa Bastos' writing, is *Anales del descubrimiento, población y conquista del Río de la Plata* (Annals of the Discovery, Settling, and Conquest of the River Plate), a chronical composed in 1612 by Ruy Díaz de Guzmán, the grandson of a Spanish captain and a Guarani Indian. Guzmán does not follow Renaissance models or Thomistic political theology; he is one of the first New World writers who felt and wrote as an American and not as a European. *Anales* is not only an objective account of River Plate geography and sixteenth-century political history; it is also a chronicle that documents a search for original expression with regard to both style and ideas, themes and discourse. Guzmán's "dragons" and "giants" (somewhat like Roa Bastos' fantastic concepts of time and space) are not medieval hyperboles, but rather mythical descriptions of American nature by an observer who considered himself a part of that environment. Guzmán shows a deep respect for the Indians whose insurrections and courage he admired and whose language, Guarani, he knew and employed in his writing. He was not really the founder of River Plate historiography—as many scholars from Paraguay, Argentina, and Uruguay say—because he did not have an academic background and did not write a systematic document according to colonial ideology. But Guzmán is the authentic father of Paraguayan and River Plate fiction, the founder of an imaginative practice conceived as a remythification of democratic values based on the quest for American expression and thought.

When the Jesuits were expelled from Paraguay and the rest of the Spanish Empire in 1767, such universities as Córdoba in Argentina, where Francisco Suárez' ideology was flourishing, were transferred to the Franciscans. But the followers of Saint Francis could not restore scholasticism. Suárez' theology survived along with that of Sir Isaac Newton, René Descartes, and Pierre Gassendi, which had also been introduced by the Jesuits. In addition, it is well documented that most of Córdoba's students read Voltaire and Jean Jacques Rousseau much more avidly than Thomas Aquinas.

Paraguayan and Jesuit traditions and Córdoba's subversive intellectual atmosphere produced one of the most radical figures of modern history and certainly the first successful Latin American statesman: José Gaspar de Francia (1766–1840), the protagonist of Roa Bastos' masterpiece, *I the Supreme*. Francia played a major role in Paraguay's revolution of 1811. Elected supreme dictator by a free congress of one thousand delegates in 1814, he ruled the country until his death in 1840. He eliminated all oligarchic and ecclesiastical privileges and confiscated the church's properties.

Francia was succeeded by Carlos Antonio López and then Francisco Solano López. Both men maintained many of Francia's policies—a state capitalistic economy, an independent and anti-imperialistic foreign policy, a popular program with regard to elementary education and income distribution, and a strong national defense. Paraguay became one of the most prosperous and democratic Latin American countries, with excellent prospects of exerting a revolutionary influence in South America against any neocolonial ambitions. But England manipulated and financed the oligarchic governments of Brazil, Argentina, and Uruguay and had them sign a secret Triple Alliance war treaty against Paraguay in London in 1865. After five years of war, the devastated country lost a major part of its national territory and almost all its adult male population.

The postwar years were dominated by anti-López Paraguayans who had created in Buenos Aires the "Paraguayan Legion" and had helped the Alliance against their own country. In *Son of Man*, Roa Bastos denounces that under Legion governments, Paraguay's state capitalism and democratic social institutions were dismantled; the economy was put under control of Anglo-Argentine companies; the country contracted a ruinous foreign debt with London (the Lópezes had never owed a penny); the railroad was sold to a British agency; and enormous extensions of state-owned land were undersold to foreign private capitalists, who created, among other things, the pathetic peasant exploitation of the *yerbales* (maté tea plantations).

The most important precursor of Roa Bastos is the Spanish-born essayist Rafael Barrett, one of the most original and profound thinkers of his or any time in Latin America, who was born in Torrelavega (Santander), studied humanities and mathematics at Paris and Madrid, and moved to Buenos Aires in 1903 and to Asunción the following year. Barrett founded a revolutionary weekly in 1908 and gave a number of lectures for the workers. A very prolific writer, Barrett is the author of such essay collections as *Lo que son los yerbales* (What the Yerbales Are Like, 1910) and his posthumous *El dolor paraguayo* (The Suffering of Paraguay, 1911). He was the initiator of almost every progressive idea or technique in Paraguayan contemporary prose and thought: the revindication of the Guarani language and Paraguayan bilingualism, native folklore, mythical herbs, and popular music; "magic realism"; countercultural satire; the "intrahistorical" revision of the past as a universe of poetic symbols in the collective memory; women's liberation; psychiatric reform; social or "engaged" literature; ecological defense; pedagogical revolution; children's rights; the theory of capitalist alienation; the theory of capital as accumulated human work; land reform; worker's rights; the first critical revision of the war of the Triple Alliance as neocolonial genocide; the condemnation of torture as well as military coups d'état as repressive practices; the well-documented denunciation of peasant exploitation in the *yerbales* as a part of the pillage of the Third World; impressionistic description borrowed from painting and cinema; a critical defense of heterodox Marxism; the conception of socialism as an international movement; the search for a Paraguayan national identity; self-criticism of petit-bourgeois intellectuals; and the practice of writing as a courageous moral act. All of these elements play a crucial role in the complex ideology and aesthetics of Roa Bastos.

In 1912, after eliminating the nightmare of the reign of militarism, the Radicals (a moderate, middle-class party) achieved a democratic, peaceful, and prosperous period. Paraguayan exports benefited as a consequence of World War I; the country enjoyed an atmosphere of optimism, fueled by honest public administrators, and the general respect for civil authority, which was also instilled at the new military school. Human rights were respected, and an independent yet stable foreign policy secured nonalignment and dignity. No Paraguayan presidents had had, or would ever again enjoy, more international prestige than did the Radicals Eligio Ayala, Eusebio Ayala, and Marshall José Félix Estigarribia. In Solano López' centenary celebration, President Eligio Ayala publicly honored his memory, burying once and for all the Legion anathema. The Radicals reformed elementary and higher education, expanded national defense, increased exports, favored political dialogue and democratic participation, and organized a solid, national front of morale to respond to the United States–backed occupation of the Chaco region by Bolivia in 1932, which caused a long and intense armed conflict. Paraguay won the war under the presidency of Eusebio Ayala in 1935 and kept the territory in dispute. The Chaco war is the theme of the major chapters of *Son of Man*.

During this period, another important precursor of Roa Bastos, the novelist Gabriel Casaccia, combined the provincial atmosphere of the novel of the land, the psychosociological analysis of the regionalistic essay, and the "scandalous" uninhibited discourse of that period's poetry to create a fascinating, Kafka-esque microcosmos. His influence is remarkably evident in Roa Bastos' first short-story collection, *El trueno entre las hojas* (Thunder Among the Leaves, 1953). Casaccia's psychological realism opened the door of international criticism on Paraguayan narrative form. He focused on the obscure and profound individual psychology of Paraguayans toward formulating an image of their collective unconscious.

President Estigarribia died in September 1940 in a plane crash. The Radicals collapsed with him, and rightist militarism has held power ever since. General Alfredo Stroessner inaugurated in 1954 the longest presidential tenure in Paraguayan history. Paraguay expanded its economy, increased its public services, and modernized its communications at the expense of human rights, national morale, and international prestige. Almost all of the important neobaroque Paraguayan writing has been produced in exile, including that of Hérib Campos Cervera, Elvio Romero, Rubén Bareiro-Saguier, Rodrigo Díaz Pérez, and, of course, Roa Bastos. In most recent short stories—for example, the collections *El baldío* (The Vacant Lot, 1966) and *Moriencia* (Slaughter, 1969)—Roa Bastos assumes a lucid transparency not only to describe his private feelings of solitude but also to embody poetically the desolation and frustration of his generation and to denounce in an unmistakably critical way both interior and exterior exiles. Only a few Latin Americans, and certainly none from Paraguay, have ever brought more worldwide literary recognition to their countries than has Roa Bastos. The fact that this man, who never practiced any sectarian political activism, must reside far from his own land and people is the most overwhelming evidence of the moral decadence of this period in Paraguay. It is also a pathetic demonstration of the values of a regime that, as of this writing, has lasted more than three decades and that has reached its lowest point in proclaiming silence to be a subversive activity.

Roa Bastos portrays a Christian metaphoric system in *Son of Man* in accordance with the neobaroque concept of magic realism. In *I the Supreme*, however, he anticipates many post-boom techniques—for example, the carnivalization of historical discourse, transtextualization, and parody—that would flourish in the late 1970's and 1980's. The neobaroque period brought worldwide visibility to Latin American literature, which then became possibly the most popular literature on the international market. Not surprisingly, this literature, based on cultural authenticity and extremely elaborated craftsmanship, and representing a major Third World revolution, was voraciously read abroad. However, this period cannot be reduced to a single ideology. The neobaroque style displays a very complex system of metaphors, some of which are evidently oligarchic. This is the case with Jorge Luis Borges, for example, who conceives the intellectual as an impotent minotaur isolated in a labyrinth not only of words or books but above all of threatening social forces that he neither controls nor understands. Other neobaroque writers, like Roa Bastos, stand for the opposite symbolism; they understand Latin American society and think its problems can be solved by political action to which every honest intellectual should be intensely committed, not necessarily through sectarian activism but—as Miguel de Cervantes showed us—through an ironic, critical subversion of the status quo. A number of neobaroque writers oscillate between the "minotauric" and "cervantian" positions. In the manner of Pablo Neruda, Roa Bastos adapted a system of metaphors based on pantheistic mineral, botanical, and zoological images to symbolize the people's mythical alchemy, through which they recover freedom as well as their ancestral fatherland. Following the example of Juan Rulfo and João Guimaraes Rosa, Roa Bastos has also combined myth with a highly metaphorical style to describe abuse and violence and to introduce a meticulous codification of Spanish prose based in part on Guarani oral traditions.

The influence of Roa Bastos can be perceived not only in the work of foreign post-boom writers such as Mempo Giardinelli, Isabel Allende, Eraclio Zepeda, Antonio Skármeta, Saúl Ibargoyen, and Luisa Valenzuela, but also in the new generation of Paraguayan authors.

SELECTED BIBLIOGRAPHY

First Editions

El trueno entre las hojas. Buenos Aires, 1953.
Hijo de hombre. Buenos Aires, 1960.
El baldío. Buenos Aires, 1966.
Moriencia. Caracas, 1969.
Yo el supremo. Buenos Aires, 1974.

Translations

I the Supreme. Translated by Helen Lane. New York, 1986.
Son of Man. Translated by Rachel Caffyn. London, 1965.

Biographical and Critical Studies

Aldana, Adelfo León. La cuentística de Augusto Roa Bastos. Montevideo, 1975.
Andreu, Jean L. "El hombre y el agua en la obra de Augusto Roa Bastos." Revista iberoamericana 46/110–111:97–121 (1980).
Antúnez de Dendia, Rosalba. Augusto Roa Bastos: Una interpretación de su primera etapa narrativa. Bonn, West Germany, 1983.
Bareiro Saguier, Rubén. "Estratos de la lengua guaraní en la escritura de Augusto Roa Bastos." Estudios paraguayos 10/2:53–66 (1982).
Barthelemy, Françoise. "Augusto Roa Bastos: De l'auteur unique a l'auteur collectif." Critique 363–364:814–830 (1977).
Benedetti, Mario. "El recurso del supremo patriarca." Casa de las Américas 17/98:12–23 (1976).
Bravo, Víctor. "Yo el supremo: De la novela de la dictadura al discurso del poder." Revista de literatura hispanoamericana 16–17:111–133 (1979).
Comentarios sobre "Yo el supremo." Asunción, 1975.
Cruz-Luis, Adolfo. "Dimensión histórica de Yo el supremo." Casa de las Américas 16/95:118–127 (1976).
Da Rosa, Doris C. "Yo el Supremo" and Augusto Roa Bastos' Search for the Future of Paraguay." Discurso literario 1/2:169–176 (1984).
Ezquerro, Milagros. Prologue to her critical edition of Yo el supremo. Madrid, 1983. Pp. 11–89.
Ferrer Agüero, Luis María. El universo narrativo de Augusto Roa Bastos. Madrid, 1981.
Foster, David William. Augusto Roa Bastos. Boston, 1978.
Franco, Jean. "Narrador, autor, superestrella: La narrativa latinoamericana en la época de cultura de masas." Revista iberoamericana 47/114–115:129–148 (1981).
Giacoman, Helmy F., ed. Homenaje a Augusto Roa Bastos. Long Island City, N.Y., 1973.
Keefe Ugalde, Sharon. "La reestructuración de la dicotomía latinoamericana civilización-barbarie en las obras de Roa Bastos." Eco 266:202–215 (1983).
Kohut, Karl. "Augusto Roa Bastos." In Escribir en París. Frankfurt, 1983. Pp. 233–263.

Krysinski, Wladimir. "Un référent complexe: Le dictateur vu par Alejo Carpentier, Miguel Angel Asturias, Gabriel García Márquez et Augusto Roa Bastos." In *Carrefours de signes: Essais sur le roman moderne.* La Haye, 1981. Pp. 377–444.

Leenhardt, Jacques, et al. *Litterature latino-américaine d'aujourd'hui.* Paris, 1980.

Lienhard, Martin. "Apuntes sobre los desdoblamientos, la mitología americana y la escritura en *Yo el Supremo.*" *Hispamérica* 7/19:3–12 (1978).

Lorenz, Günter W. "Augusto Roa Bastos." In *Dialog mit Lateinamerika.* Tübingen, West Germany, 1970.

Marcos, Juan Manuel. *Roa Bastos, precursor del post-boom.* Mexico City, 1983.

_____, ed. *Actas del Coloquio Internacional sobre la obra de Augusto Roa Bastos.* Madrid, 1986.

Martin, Gerald M. "*Yo el supremo:* The Dictator and His Script." In *Contemporary Latin American Fiction,* edited by S. Bacarisse. Edinburgh, 1980. Pp. 73–87.

Méndez-Faith, Teresa. "Reflexiones en torno a textos-contextos paraguayos: Rescate de una realidad camuflada." *Discurso literario* 1/1:37–48 (1983).

Miliani, Domingo. "El dictador: Objeto narrativo en *Yo el supremo.*" *Revista de crítica literaria latinoamericana* 2/4:103–119 (1976).

Morley, Mónica D. "Sobre el discurso cultural americano; su vigencia y elaboración en los textos de Roa Bastos." *Discurso literario* 1/2:257–266 (1984).

Pacheco, Carlos. "La intertextualidad y el compilador: Nuevas claves para una lectura de la polifonía en *Yo el supremo.*" *Revista de crítica literaria latinoamericana* 10/19:47–72 (1984).

Rama, Angel. *Los dictadores latinoamericanos.* Mexico City, 1976.

Schrader, Ludwig, ed. *Augusto Roa Bastos, Actas del Coloquio Franco-Alemán.* Tübingen, West Germany, 1984.

Seminario sobre "Yo el supremo" de Augusto Roa Bastos. Poitiers, France, 1976.

Textos sobre el texto: Segundo seminario sobre "Yo el supremo" de Augusto Roa Bastos. Poitiers, France, 1980.

Turton, Peter. "*Yo el supremo:* Una verdadera revolución novelesca." *Texto crítico* 5/12:10–60 (1979).

Valdés, Edgar. "Literatura paraguaya y realidad nacional." *Criterio* 2/2:8–14 (1977).

Vila Barnés, Gladys. *Significado y coherencia del universo narrativo de Augusto Roa Bastos.* Madrid, 1984.

Juan Rulfo

(1918–1986)

Luis Leal

The reputation of Juan Rulfo in the annals of contemporary Latin American fiction is well assured, although his publications are few: a collection of short stories, *El llano en llamas* (*The Burning Plain*), in 1953; a novel, *Pedro Páramo*, in 1955; a novelette, *El gallo de oro* (The Golden Cock), in 1980; a few film scripts and critical essays; and a collection of his own photographs, *Juan Rulfo: Homenaje nacional (Inframundo: The Mexico of Juan Rulfo)*, also in 1980. No study of the development of the Latin American short story or the novel, however, would be complete without a consideration of Rulfo's fiction, since he introduced during the 1950's, with his first two slender volumes, a narrative mode new in Spanish-American literature, which was to influence the development not only of Mexican literature but also that of the other Spanish-speaking countries as well.

Rarely does a writer publish two successful first books within the short span of two years, as was the case with Rulfo. His collection of short stories became an instant success, and although his novel, due to its complex structure, was not well received when it first appeared in 1955, it was later recognized by critics as a work of extraordinary merit, worthy of detailed analysis, not only for its original structure but also for its poetic style and dramatic plot.

Although many years passed before another work by Rulfo appeared, the fame that the two early volumes gave him has not diminished. On the contrary, studies dedicated to his fiction, which now number several books and hundreds of articles, continue to appear, and his works have been translated into the principal languages of the world. No less important are the awards he received, including the Premio Nacional de Letras in Mexico City in 1970, and the Premio Príncipe de Asturias in Madrid in 1983. The Mexican Institute of Fine Arts (Instituto Nacional de Bellas Artes, INBA) presented an homage in his honor in 1980 and published a collection of one hundred of his best photographs, for Rulfo was also an accomplished photographer. The same year the Fondo de Cultura Económica edited deluxe editions of his works.

Recognition did not come easily to Rulfo, whose early years were plagued with disappointments and even misfortune. He was born on 16 May 1918, in Apulco, a small community near the town of Sayula in the state of Jalisco in central Mexico. His ancestors had come from northern Spain during the latter part of the eighteenth century and had settled in Nueva Galicia, as the region of which Jalisco was the center was called during the colonial period. There his father, Juan Nepomuceno Pérez, and his mother,

María Vizcaíno Arias, were born. He himself explained why he bears the surname Rulfo:

My name is Juan Nepomuceno Carlos Pérez Rulfo Vizcaíno. . . . My father was called Juan Nepomuceno, my paternal [maternal] grandfather was Carlos Vizcaíno; the name Rulfo I have because of Juan del Rulfo, a "caribe" adventurer, so called because he served under José María Calleja, alias "El Caribe," who had a daughter called María Rulfo Navarro, who married my paternal grandfather, José María Jiménez. This Juan del Rulfo arrived in Mexico toward the end of the eighteenth century.

(Roffé, 1973, pp. 29–30)

In the year Rulfo was born the country was still in turmoil as a result of the revolution that Francisco I. Madero had started in 1910. Although Madero had been elected president and the fighting had stopped, he was assassinated in 1913 and the armed struggle was renewed and did not end until 1920, the year Álvaro Obregón was elected president for a four-year term. It was perhaps with the purpose of obtaining greater security that Rulfo's family moved soon after his birth to the city of San Gabriel, not far from his birthplace:

I went to elementary school in San Gabriel, that is my world. I lived there until I was ten. It is one of those towns that have lost even their name. Now it is called Venustiano Carranza. There I and my brothers lived with my grandmother—a descendant of the Arias, probably from Andalucía.

(ibid., p. 46)

In San Gabriel people told the young boy stories about ghosts, about wars, about crimes. And there, at that early age, he learned the art of the popular storyteller, an art that he was later to utilize to great advantage in his own stories, some of which take place in San Gabriel, as does his novel *Pedro Páramo*.

Rulfo was in San Gabriel when the *Cristero* revolt broke out in 1926, a religious war that was the aftermath of the revolution of 1910. As a child he experienced some of the events of this war, which left a permanent impression on him. Speaking of that struggle Rulfo has said that it was

an internal war that broke out . . . against the federal government. There was a decree that enforced an article of the Revolution [Constitution] according to which priests were forbidden to mix in politics and the churches became the property of the state, as they are today. A set number of priests was assigned to each village, in accordance with its population. Of course, people protested.

(Harss, p. 252)

Before making the above statement he had published the short story "La noche que lo dejaron solo" ("The Night They Left Him Behind"), dealing with that conflict as seen from the perspective of a young boy who accompanies his two uncles, helping them to bring arms to the *cristeros*, as the rebels fighting the federal government were called due to their war cry, ¡Viva Cristo Rey! (Long Live Christ the King!). As is characteristic in Rulfo's fiction, the story ends tragically, with the two uncles killed by the *federales*. The boy is mysteriously saved, as he inexplicably falls asleep on the way and is left behind. This tragic sense of life that pervades Rulfo's fiction is probably derived from the fact that his father was assassinated when Juan was only seven years old. Some critics have said that his father was killed by a peon. Rulfo has stated that "they killed him while he was fleeing . . . and my uncle was also assassinated" (Roffé, p. 31).

After his mother died of a heart attack in 1927, Rulfo and his two brothers lived with their grandmother until they were sent to Guadalajara in 1928, to be placed in the Luis Silva School for orphan children, where he was to remain until 1932. "When the *cristeros* ran us out of there I arrived in Guadalajara. I was already an orphan. For thirteen pesos a month they registered me in the Orfanatorio Silva, a kind of correctional school" (Cortés Tamayo, 1959, p. 4). Before leaving San Gabriel, however, he had begun to develop an interest in reading, since the town's priest had left his private library with his grandmother for safe keeping while he was away with the *cristeros*.

Upon completing his secondary education Rulfo registered at the University of Guadalajara but was unable to remain because a student strike was declared. "The strike began the same day I entered together with a cousin, a Vizcaíno, and lasted about a year and a half. Because of that I went to Mexico

City to continue my studies" (Roffé, p. 47). That year was 1934, when Lázaro Cárdenas was elected president of the republic for a six-year term.

In Mexico City Rulfo attended the national university for a short time, with the financial aid of an uncle. Soon, however, he had to seek employment, for his relative stopped the meager allowance he received. These were difficult times for Rulfo, who by that time had decided to give up the study of law, a career he had chosen because his grandfather had been a lawyer, "and someone had to use his books. But much time had passed, and I had forgotten a great deal. I was unable to pass the qualifying exam to which we were submitted. Thus I had to go to work. I left school because I was not interested in the study of law" (ibid., pp. 49–50). In 1935 he began to work as an immigration agent with the department of the interior, first in Mexico City, then in Tampico, from where he was sent to Guadalajara.

Having decided by this time to be a writer, he read extensively, especially European fiction. He told the poet José Emilio Pacheco, in a later interview, that he had chosen the writing of fiction because what is important in a writer is his imaginative power. "I have read Sillanpää, Björson, Ian Mail, Haupmann, and the early Hamsun. In them I found the basis of my literary faith" (Pacheco, 1959, p. 3). While working at immigration in Mexico City he met the short story writer and novelist Efrén Hernández, who encouraged him to write a novel. His first effort as a fiction writer was El Hijo del Desaliento (Son of Affliction), a novel he destroyed because he considered it mediocre. The manuscript, according to the author, dealt with the theme of solitude:

> I had to be a writer. The novel that I wrote soon after I arrived in Mexico City, dealing with solitude . . . contained biographical materials, events that had actually happened to me, but applied to another personage. . . . But I did not like it. I don't think I saved any of it. It seems that a periodical, many years ago, published a fragment as a short story. As for the rest, I threw it away. It was a rather conventional novel, very high-strung, in which I tried to express certain solitary feelings
>
> (Roffé, p. 52)

The story was published in the Revista mexicana de literatura in 1959 under the title "Un pedazo de noche" (A Night's Fragment), and is dated January 1940. It was reprinted in his Antología personal (1978) and is considered Rulfo's earliest known writing. Although it was intended to be part of a longer work, it has the structure of a short story; however, it is difficult to know if changes were made by the author between the year it was written and the publishing date. It is the only one of his prose writings in which the action takes place in Mexico City, except for a short scene in the story "Paso del Norte," which was eliminated in the 1980 revised edition. "Un pedazo de noche" contains traces of style and technique that Rulfo was to develop later in his most famous stories. Noticeable are the aura of vagueness that surrounds the characters and objects and the prevailing indecisiveness of the people in the world that Rulfo creates. Equally important is the tendency, perfected in later stories and novels, of personifying the emotions, as when Pilar, the prostitute-protagonist, says that "fear is the thing that fears solitude the most, according to what I know" (Antología personal, p. 144). Also of importance is the distance that Rulfo establishes between himself and his characters, a form of self-effacement that allows the characters to tell the reader about themselves. Pilar reveals her profession by saying, "One night a man approached me. That was not important, for that is why I was there, to be sought by men" (p. 144). Claudio, the other important person in the story, tells about his life in a conversation with Pilar. Even the child he carries in his arms becomes a person. Pilar says of him, "I kept looking at the baby, who kept on squirming in his arms. His eyes were those of grown-up people, full of malice and bad intentions. He seemed to be the reflection of our vices . . ." (p. 145).

It was not until 1945 that Rulfo published his first short story with the help of his friend Efrén Hernández, who was a member of the group of writers who published the periodical América. It was there that the story "La vida no es muy seria sus cosas" (Life Is Not Very Serious About Things) appeared but was forgotten until 1978 when it was included in his Antología personal. It cannot compare with two of his other stories published the same year in Guadalajara in the literary review Pan, "Nos han dado la tierra" ("They Gave Us the Land") and "Macario," both included in The Burning Plain and highly praised by critics. Although "La vida no es muy seria" is not so rich in stylistic devices as "Un pedazo de noche," it is in this story that the theme of death, a constant in Rulfo's fiction, appears for the first time. Present also is the recurrent element of irony: the mother's tragedy is the result of her preoccupation with the life of her unborn child.

About the same time that he was busy publishing his first story, Rulfo associated himself with two writers from Guadalajara, the fabulist Juan José Arreola and the critic Antonio Alatorre. Together they published the short-lived but first-rate literary periodical *Pan*. The second number, which appeared in July 1945, contains Rulfo's short story "They Gave Us the Land," and the sixth number, November 1945, has the story "Macario." They are his first significant works, for they show a remarkable improvement in the writing of his short fiction.

"They Gave Us the Land" deals with a social reform introduced by the revolutionary governments, the distribution of land to the *campesinos* (farmers). By 1940 land distribution in Mexico had reached 63 million acres. By the year the story was published, however, the distribution had declined considerably, and the land distributed was not always suitable for cultivation. In the story a group of poor farmers are to receive land from the government officials. Soon they realize that they are not to receive the good land near the river but a dry, hard lot that not even a sharp plow can penetrate. They finally give up hope of ever having any land and go to the town by the river protesting that the revolution has not been for the farmer; during the fighting at least they had horses and rifles, while now they have nothing. The plight of the farmers is made more intense by the description of the desolate land in the plains of southern Jalisco, the first description by Rulfo of his native region, the *llano grande* (great plain). The oppressive nature of the *llano* is described with images that cut deeply into the nature of the people through metaphorical associations. Their taciturn nature is expressed with these words by the narrator, one of the peons in search of the promised land: "If you start a conversation here the words get hot in your mouth with the heat from the outside and they dry on your tongue until they take your breath away" (Tezontle ed., p. 12). And as for the land they have received, he makes this observation: "Yes, they have given us this land. And in this hot grill they want us to sow some seeds, to see if something grows. But nothing will come up here. Not even buzzards" (*ibid.*, p. 15). The social protest in the story is not stated explicitly but by the actions and conversations of the characters themselves. This technique is effective, for the reader gets an excellent picture of the failure of the revolution in treating the problem of land reform. Important also is the story's mythical structure of death and resurrection. The journey of the *campesinos* through the *llano* is like a journey through hell, while their arrival at the community by the river is symbolic of their resurrection. This element, combined with the sociopolitical nature of the subject, gives the story, as in all of Rulfo's fiction, a universal character.

The second *Pan* story, "Macario," was selected by the author as the lead story for the collection *The Burning Plain*, except for the last (1980) edition, where "They Gave Us the Land" has been placed first. "Macario" is doubtless one of Rulfo's best pieces of short fiction, not only because of its new technique—new in Latin American fiction—but also because of the treatment of the subject matter, characterization, and style. Using the technique William Faulkner employed in *The Sound and the Fury* (1929), wherein Benjy describes the world from the perspective of a mentally retarded person, Rulfo allows Macario, a boy of limited intelligence, to express his fear of being punished by his godmother if he lets the frogs disturb her sleep.

> I'm sitting here next to the sewer opening waiting for the frogs to come out. Last night, at supper time, they made a lot of noise and did not stop croaking until dawn. My godmother also says that the frogs' uproar scared her sleep away. And now she wants to sleep well. That's why she ordered me to sit here, near the sewer, with a board in my hand to squash every frog that comes out to jump around.
> (*ibid.*, p. 81)

During his night watch, Macario reconstructs in his mind his relationship with his godmother and the people of the community, all of whom, except for the servant Felipa, who feeds him with her own milk, torment him. In this story, within a limited space and a limited time, Rulfo has created a rich unity of impression from a very simple plot.

In 1947, the year he married Clara Aparicio, with whom he had four children, Rulfo accepted a position in the publicity department of Goodrich-Euzkadi, a position he held until 1954, that is, one year after publishing his collection of stories. In 1952 he had received a fellowship from the Centro Mexicano de Escritores, which helped him to complete the manuscript of *The Burning Plain*, published in 1953 by the prestigious Fondo de Cultura Económica. The book became an immediate success, and as a result the fellowship from the Centro was extended for another year in order to allow him to complete the novel he was writing, pages of which he had read at the literary sessions of the Centro. In 1983 its executive director, Felipe Beraza, recalled how Rulfo "brought the first drafts of *Pedro Páramo* to the critique sessions at the Center" (Fishman, p. 29).

The first edition of *The Burning Plain* contained fifteen stories, six of which had already been published in periodicals: "Macario," "They Gave Us the Land," "La cuesta de las comadres" ("The Hill of the *Comadres*"), "Talpa," "El llano en llamas" ("The Burning Plain"), and "¡Diles que no me maten!" ("Tell Them Not to Kill Me"). The rest appeared for the first time: "Es que somos muy pobres" ("Because We Are Very Poor"), "El hombre" ("The Man"), "En la madrugada" ("At Daybreak"), "Luvina," "La noche que lo dejaron solo" ("The Night They Left Him Behind"), "Acuérdate" ("Remember"), "No oyes ladrar los perros" ("No Dogs Bark"), "Paso del Norte," and "Anacleto Morones." There is no appreciable difference between the published and unpublished stories, either in technique or style. The two stories "El día del derrumbe" ("The Day of the Landslide") and "La herencia de Matilde Arcángel" ("Matilde Arcángel") were added to the second revised edition of 1970, and one, "Paso del Norte," was eliminated. Asked why he took out that particular story, Rulfo replied that it had been the editor's decision, but that he did not mind since he considered it to be flawed:

It had two transitions difficult to unite: the moment when the man goes to look for work as a *bracero* [farmhand] in the United States and when he returns. There is an internal theme that is not well elaborated,

that is not even worked out. I would like to have worked on that story more.

("Juan Rulfo examina . . . ," 1976, p. 309)

Actually, the story has three transitions, the third being when the protagonist goes to Mexico City to earn money to pay the unscrupulous agent (the *coyote*) to transport him across the border without documents. This episode had been eliminated from the latest version of the story but was reinserted in the most recent edition, that of 1980.

The year 1955 saw the appearance of the novel *Pedro Páramo*, considered to be Rulfo's best work. The public was by then aware of its forthcoming publication, as two of its fragments had appeared in periodicals the year before; one, "Un cuento" (A Tale), was published in the January–March issue of *Las letras patrias*, with a notation saying that it was a chapter of the unpublished novel "Una estrella junto a la luna" (A Star Near the Moon); and the other, "Los murmullos" (The Murmurs), in the *Revista de la universidad de México*, as a fragment of a novel by that name. When it was finally published by the Fondo de Cultura Económica, the title selected was *Pedro Páramo*, the name of the protagonist. The action takes place in San Gabriel, the town where Rulfo had passed his early years, although in the novel it is called Comala, which is much more appropriate, since it helps to create the image of the furnacelike atmosphere that prevails in the town. Rulfo explains it this way:

The name does not exist, no. The town of Comala is a progressive, fertile town. But the derivation of *comal*—a *comal* is an earthenware utensil that is placed over the embers for the purpose of heating the tortillas—, and the heat in that town was what gave me the idea of the name Comala: the place over the embers."

(Roffé, p. 61)

Gabriel García Márquez has said in *El olor de la guayaba* (*The Fragrance of Guava*) that he wrote *Cien años de soledad* (*One Hundred Years of Solitude*, 1967) in less than two years, but that he spent fifteen or sixteen years thinking about the book before he sat down at the typewriter. The same thing happened to Rulfo, who said that *Pedro Páramo* was planned about ten years before the actual writing of the book:

Although the idea was with me, I had not written a single page. And then something happened that gave me the key to unravel that thread that was still woolly. It was my going back to the town where I had lived thirty years earlier, and I found it abandoned. It is a town I had known, of about seven to eight thousand inhabitants. When I arrived there were only 150 persons there. . . . The doors were locked up. The people had left.

(*ibid.*, pp. 60–61)

The novel is the result of a desire to bring the town back to life; it lives again in the imagination of the personages. The town San Gabriel appears under its own name in the story "At Daybreak" and under the name of Luvina in the story of that name. It is not of great importance that these two towns and the Comala of *Pedro Páramo* should be associated with San Gabriel inasmuch as the towns are not realistically described and could be one of many similar small towns in Mexico.

It has been pointed out that the story "Luvina" can be considered "the strongest evidence available regarding the gestation of the ambience of *Pedro Páramo*, and perhaps it could be stated that it contains the germ from which the novel grew" (Estrada, p. 117). While it is true that the ambience in both stories is similar, the plots differ. In "Luvina" a teacher who has lived in that ghost town for some years tells about his life there to another teacher who is on his way to replace him. He remembers Luvina as a desolate place, more like a dead town than a community where human beings can live. The few inhabitants living there have remained in order to guard their dead. Luvina, located at the top of a hill, is covered with gray dust that is blown in by a constant wind. That black wind "scratches as if he had nails; one can hear him morning and afternoon, hour after hour, without rest, scratching the walls, tearing off the plaster, digging with his pointed shovel under the doors until you feel him stirring inside you, as if trying to shake the moorings of your bones" (Tezontle ed., p. 126). Luvina is, indeed, a sad place. "I would say it is the place where sadness nests, where smiling is unknown" (p. 128). The teacher finally says, "San Juan Luvina. The name sounded to me like the name of heaven. But the place is purgatory. A dying place where there is no one to

bark at silence, for even the dogs have died" (pp. 135–136).

In Luvina there are still a few people living there. In Comala, Rulfo has extended the realm of death to include all the inhabitants, even the narrator, Juan Preciado, Pedro Páramo's son, who is recalling his experiences from the grave. He had gone to Comala in search of his father, who had abandoned him and his mother after having appropriated her land and properties. When Juan Preciado arrives in Comala he finds a dead town, but its people, although dead, are capable of remembering and reliving their tragic lives from the grave. The town had died when Pedro Páramo, the local overlord and owner of all lands surrounding it, decided to punish the townspeople for holding a fiesta instead of mourning the death of his beloved Susana San Juan. In *Pedro Páramo*, as he had done earlier in "Luvina," Rulfo creates a magic atmosphere by combining realistic and fantastic elements and motifs. As the novel unfolds, the reader passes from the real to the unreal, from the objective to the subjective, to the phantasmagoric. The author has said that the village is the central character. But above it and its inhabitants stands the figure of Pedro Páramo, the *cacique* (political boss) of Comala, whose life is reconstructed from three perspectives: that of his son Juan Preciado (who bears his mother's name), that of the omniscient narrator, and that of the inhabitants of the town. This technique helps the author to give his antihero depth and complexity and at the same time engages the attention of the reader, who must assemble the parts to get the full portrait.

Although there are many Latin American novels dealing with the *cacique*, so prevalent in Latin American society, the best characterization to be found is Rulfo's Pedro Páramo because he has all the characteristics that define a *cacique*: he operates behind the scenes, never in public; he is despotic, greedy, cruel, shrewd, and, of course, macho, an indispensable qualification. In Rulfo's fiction the *cacique* is also found in the short story "At Daybreak." Don Justo, in that story, could be considered the precursor of Pedro Páramo. However, Pedro Páramo is the fictitious character that has become the prototype in Latin American fiction. His life, unlike that of Don Justo, unfolds from his youth in poverty until he becomes the most powerful person in Comala: his marriage of convenience to Dolores Preciado, his great love for Susana San Juan, his defense of his properties from the revolutionaries by bribery and deceit, his troubles with his dissolute and violent son Miguel, his control of the local priest, and finally his death at the hands of his illegitimate son Abundio, who hated him. As for the origin of this *cacique*, Rulfo has said:

> I do not know from where the personage Pedro Páramo came. I never met a person like that. I do not consider it easy to classify him. I believe he is a *cacique*. *Caciques* are plentiful in Mexico. But their attitudes, their acts, are medals with which the people decorate them. I mean, I do not know if there ever was a *cacique* who made his own revolution to defend himself from the Revolution. But he can be classified by other means: he is, for example, never generous; on the contrary, he is an evildoer. He forms, with others, part of a consciousness, a way of thinking, a mentality that most likely does exist.
>
> (Roffé, p. 65)

The Latin American *cacique* often becomes a dictator, a character common in the novel of that region. Some of the most famous novelists have written about them, from the Guatemalan Miguel Ángel Asturias to the Colombian Gabriel García Márquez, both Nobel Prize winners. The difference between a *cacique* and a dictator is to be found in the domain they rule. The *cacique* dominates a town or at the most a county, while the dictator governs a country. The *cacique* is a local figure, while the dictator attains national and often international stature. Some of Latin America's greatest dictators began life as simple *caciques*. The psychology of both, however, is the same. Under favorable circumstances Pedro Páramo could have ruled the entire country instead of the town of Comala.

The year 1955 was an eventful one for Rulfo. In addition to his novel, the film "Talpa," based on his short story of that name, was released. It was directed by Alfredo B. Cravenna. Rulfo also published two additional short stories, "The Day of the Landslide" and "Matilde Arcángel." That year also saw the birth of his third child, Juan Pablo.

The short story "The Day of the Landslide" is of interest because there Rulfo makes use, for the first

and only time, of political satire to ridicule the inflated, vulgar politician who deceives the people for his own gain. In this case it is a governor who visits a small town to survey the damage done by an earthquake. What he and his entourage eat and drink turns out to be much more costly than the damage done by the earthquake. The townspeople laugh at his table manners, but are overpowered by his rhetoric. They "were breaking their necks to see the governor and commenting how he had eaten the turkey and if he had sucked on the bones and how fast he was scooping up the tortillas one after another and spreading them with guacamole . . . and he so quiet, so serious, wiping his hands on his socks . . ." (Tezontle ed., p. 177). The governor's after-dinner speech is a masterful parody of the empty talk characteristic of the politician who uses the rhetoric of the revolution to cover up the prevailing inefficiency and lack of ideas. The people became entranced with the speaker's oratorical ability: "The great moment came when he began to speak. We were so moved at hearing him talk that we got goose pimples all over" (*ibid.*, p. 179).

After the appearance of those two stories in 1955, Rulfo stopped publishing for reasons unknown. Since then his works have attained universal recognition. The German translation of *Pedro Páramo* appeared in 1958, and the English and French in 1959. In that year he returned to Guadalajara with his family where he remained until 1962, and then went back to Mexico City where he began to work for the Instituto Nacional Indigenista. During those years he also wrote several film scripts and announced that he was to publish a new novel, "La cordillera" (The Packtrain), which never appeared, although short excerpts were published in periodicals, and some critics have analyzed its content and style. Rulfo himself said that the novel dealt with the history of a town in central Mexico during the colonial period that he wanted to bring to life through the experiences of a family, not unlike what he had done for San Gabriel. On 13 March 1974 Rulfo, in a dialogue with the students of the Universidad Central de Venezuela, said that he had written many pages of a work he called "La cordillera," but that he had problems with it and had therefore decided to destroy the manuscript. ("Juan Rulfo examina . . . ," p. 316).

El gallo de oro (The Golden Cock), as it appeared in book form in 1980, is not a film script but a novelette of eighty pages. The narrative technique is that of a work to be read, since there is an omniscient narrator who describes the landscape, makes comments about the characters, and passes judgment on them. As in the film, folkloric elements predominate. The protagonist, Dionisio Pinzón, is a cockfighter and later a gambler, and his wife Bernarda is a carnival singer. The story deals with the adventures of these two in their travels from town to town in central Mexico to take part in the activities of the carnivals. When Dionisio becomes a gambler, his wife brings him luck; when she dies, he loses all his properties. Although the novelette lacks depth, it is characteristic of Rulfo's fiction: the world is that of his native region, the tone is tragic, and his technique of characterization is similar to that found in his other works. The protagonist, Dionisio, represents the best treatment done of a popular Mexican folk character, the cockfighter.

Another of Rulfo's scripts, "El despojo" (The Plunder), is very much like some of his short stories. It is a stark tale of the plight of an Indian, Pedro, his wife Petra, and their child, who are persecuted by the local *cacique*, Don Celerino. Of interest in the script is the technique used by Rulfo in freezing the character while the action continues. Most likely Rulfo was influenced by the short story "An Occurrence at Owl Creek Bridge" by Ambrose Bierce, which was made into a movie for television. As in Bierce's story, the actions of Pedro continue after he has been killed by Don Celerino. The viewer does not know that he is dead until the end of the film, when it is revealed that the action had taken place in the mind of the character before he died. The same technique was used by Jorge Luis Borges in his story "El milagro secreto" ("The Secret Miracle"). Unlike Borges, Rulfo takes advantage of the Indian's plight to denounce the *cacique* system prevalent in rural Mexico to this day.

In addition to his fiction, Juan Rulfo published a number of articles on literary criticism and gave numerous interviews in which he expressed his views about writers and writing, especially the novelist and the novel. From these materials Reina Roffé assembled a unique "autobiography" of Rulfo and published it under the title *Autobiografía armada* (A Reconstructed Autobiography). Although it is well known that Rulfo never published an autobiography, the account of his life as given by the excerpts collected by Roffé are so ingeniously organized that it gives the impression of having been written by Rulfo himself.

One of the most important lectures given by Rulfo was the one he delivered in 1965 at the Instituto de Ciencias y Artes de Chiapas in which he revealed his preferences for certain writers and certain books. In another lecture, or rather discussion with the students at the Universidad Central de Venezuela in Caracas, he spoke about his life, work, and favorite authors. When he was admitted to the Mexican Academy of Letters in 1980, Rulfo spoke about the poet José Gorostiza, whose chair he then occupied; but as a critic he gave preference to the novel, a genre with which he was very well acquainted. Rulfo wrote, and expressed his ideas in interviews, about the Mexican, Latin American, Anglo-American, and European novels.

As a means of placing Rulfo's own fiction within the context of the Mexican novel, it is of interest to see how he himself viewed it. According to him, the Mexican novel did not obtain originality until the period of the Revolution. For him, novels written before that time belong more to Spanish (peninsular) than to Mexican literature. The first novel, *El Periquillo Sarniento (The Itching Parrot)*, published in Mexico City in 1816 by José Joaquín Fernández de Lizardi, belongs, according to Rulfo, to the Spanish picaresque tradition. Although he did not elaborate on this statement, it may be assumed that he was referring to the form—the picaresque—a Spanish narrative form with a long tradition, and not its content, which is certainly Mexican. The depiction of the antihero, the boy Periquillo in the Mexico City of the late eighteenth century, the language, the scenery, the nationalistic sentiment, the landscape, are all thoroughly Mexican. The novelist Agustín Yáñez, Rulfo's contemporary, has observed that Lizardi's protagonist, Periquillo Sarniento, is as Mexican as Babbitt is American. Fernández de Lizardi, of course, has been credited with the creation of Mexican *costumbrismo* (regional writing). However, and this was Rulfo's idea, the creation of a national novel in Mexico—which had been proposed by Ignacio

Manuel Altamirano as early as 1868—did not take place until Mariano Azuela, Martín Luis Guzmán, Rafael Muñoz, José Rubén Romero, and others wrote novels depicting the revolution of 1910. Rulfo has stated that "the great Mexican novel began with the Revolution. It can be stated that at that time it reached its greatest moments" (Avilés, p. 1).

Besides Azuela, Guzmán, and Muñoz, Rulfo praised other novelists of the Revolution, among them the precursor Heriberto Frías, the author of *Tomóchic* (1896), a novel considered to be the first in which there is a protest against the repressive Porfirio Díaz government; he also praised Gregorio López y Fuentes, the author of *Tierra* (Land), one of the few novels about Emiliano Zapata and his revolutionary struggle in southern Mexico; and Cipriano Campos Alatorre, from the state of Jalisco, the author of another *zapatista* novel, *Los fusilados* (The Executed). With the works of these writers, Rulfo believed, Mexican literature saw the birth of the contemporary novel, which was to reach its high point with the works of Agustín Yáñez, the author of the epoch-making novel *Al filo del agua* (The Edge of the Storm), published in 1947. Eight years later Rulfo himself was to write *Pedro Páramo*, which changed the route that Mexican narrative was to take after 1955.

Rulfo's appreciation of the novel of the Revolution is opposed to that of other Mexican critics, among them Octavio Paz and Carlos Fuentes. For Paz, who began to criticize that novel in the forties, the Revolution as subject matter had forced the writers to reduce Mexican reality to acts of violence, and had therefore "mutilated novelistic reality, the only one that counts for the novelist. . . . All the novels of the Revolution are nothing but reports and chronicles" (Paz, 1973, p. 93). However, Paz has praised Rulfo very highly: "Juan Rulfo is the only Mexican novelist to have provided us an image—rather than a mere description—of our physical surroundings. Like Lawrence and Lowry, what he has given us is not photographic documentation or an impressionistic painting; he has incarnated his intuitions and his personal obsessions in stone, in dust, in desert sand. His vision of this world is really a vision of *another world*" (Paz, 1973, pp. 15–16).

Another critic and famous novelist, Carlos Fuentes, criticized the novels of the Revolution for their lack of perspective, their testimonial technique, their "documental ballast," and in general their lack of depth in the depiction of characters and the interpretation of events. He gives those novelists credit, however, for having introduced "an original note in the Spanish-American novel: they introduce ambiguity" (*La nueva novela hispanoamericana*, 1969, p. 15). The technique of the novels of the Revolution, according to Fuentes, was put to rest in 1955 by Rulfo with his *Pedro Páramo*, who "was able to proceed with the mythification of the situations, the characters, and the speech of the Mexican countryside, closing forever, with a golden key, the documental technique of the [novel] of the Revolution" (*ibid.*, p. 16).

The novelist Agustín Yáñez concurs with Paz and Fuentes in considering *Pedro Páramo* a deeply Mexican work. His appreciation of the novel, however, is not based on the imagery, but on the use of the Spanish language: "Rulfo transforms colloquial language and gives it an aesthetic category. . . . This has been his triumph; this his path of magical realism open to the future of our letters, of our aesthetic expression, comparable only to that of our great painters" (Yáñez, p. 22). Rulfo, a few years earlier, had reviewed another of Yáñez's novels, *La tierra pródiga* (The Prodigal Land), having called it "one of the great works of fiction in Mexican literature" (*El Nacional*, 8 November 1964). Of his contemporaries, Rulfo acclaimed the novels of Vicente Leñero, Carlos Fuentes, Salvador Elizondo, Fernando del Paso, Rosario Castellanos, and Elena Garro. The younger generation of novelists, however, did not receive much of his attention, in writing at least, although he read their works, and often helped them with the art of the novel in the sessions held at the Centro de Escritores Mexicanos, with which he was associated since the 1950's.

The novels of Latin American, Anglo-American, and European writers were the frequent subject of Rulfo's criticism. Of the Latin Americans he expressed preference for the novels of the Brazilians and the two Nobel Prize winners Miguel Ángel Asturias and Gabriel García Márquez. Important from the standpoint of Rulfo's appreciation of other novelists have been his remarks about American and European authors. For him, the great American novelists are William Faulkner and John Steinbeck, two other Nobel Prize recipients. He also mentioned J. D. Salinger, William Styron, Norman Mailer, Truman Capote, John Updike, Jack Kerouac, and Joseph Heller. Of this group, he considers Heller one of the best North American writers. In general, however, he believed that the new American novel has not surpassed those of William Faulkner.

As has been stated, the European novelists he preferred are those of the Nordic countries, although he spoke well of the Italians, believing that Vasco Pratolini, with his novel *Cronache di poveri amanti* (*A Tale of Poor Lovers*, translated in 1949), advanced European narrative fiction considerably. On the other hand, he was frank about his dislike of the French antinovelists. He said that "to write anti-novels is, precisely, to avoid all thinking in order to concentrate on seeing and describing what is being observed" ("Situación . . . ," p. 116).

The above statement confirms Rulfo's theory of the novel, as observed in his own works. For Octavio Paz, Rulfo did not simply describe what he observed, but tried to give a sense of reality by presenting—by means of verbal images, often poetic—that reality as it impinges on the consciousness of the characters. It is a reality that is ever changing: "The air changes the colors of everything," says Dolores in *Pedro Páramo*. Paz's observation was confirmed by Rulfo in a statement he made regarding the novel *La región más transparente* (*Where the Air Is Clear*) by Carlos Fuentes. In that statement Rulfo separated the novelists into two groups, those who try to give expression to the world they carry within them, and those who try to get hold of the world of others:

> There are novelists who select those aspects of reality that best fit their ideas or sentiments but who nevertheless leave a margin of independence between them and their materials. And there are others, like Fuentes, who take reality in its totality and transfer to it their own views, to a point where one does not know where objectivity begins and where the novelist begins.
>
> (Rebolledo, p. 3)

Rulfo's fiction, because of its tragic nature, has been used as an example of the cult of death and violence predominant in Mexican literature. It is true that in his narrative towns are dead, people are dead or waiting for death, or tied down to a place by their dead. This preoccupation with death and violence is the result of Rulfo's personal experiences while a boy and young man in his native province of Jalisco, during the years when revolution and civil war were prevalent. Violent death touched his relatives more than once. However, Rulfo stated that he did not want to continue to write or talk about death.

Death and violence are themes that give Rulfo's fiction a unity unmatched in Mexican literature. There are, of course, other elements that contribute to produce this unity, such as the fact that all the stories take place in his native region of central Mexico; that all the characters belong to the rural class, living in a society in transition between the feudal system inherited from colonial days and the modernization that the Revolution was trying to bring about; the style is always poetic, although never departing from the colloquial speech of the people of Jalisco; the style is elaborated to a literary level characterized by the avoidance of learned quotations, economy of expression, and the use of a vocabulary, rhythm, and syntax that are peculiarly Mexican. Above all, there is in Rulfo's fiction an ever-present tragic sense of life reflecting a violent, often primitive, world. At the same time, his use of a new narrative technique has given his novels and short stories an international status that no other Mexican fiction writer, with the possible exception of Carlos Fuentes, has attained.

In spite of the universal recognition that Rulfo attained, he studiously avoided taking advantage of that prestige to obtain material wealth. His personal modesty was well known. In an interview that took place in 1976 the interviewer made this statement to Rulfo: "Gabriel García Márquez said on a certain occasion that you are the writer who has had the greatest influence on his works." Rulfo answered: "I don't think so. Gabo [Gabriel] is one of those great writers who have found their form of expression: personal and well defined" (Vázquez, 1977, p. 19). Rulfo's answer revealed his modesty, for he himself found his own personal form of expression, which, in turn, influenced other great novelists.

Juan Rulfo died in Mexico City on 7 January 1986 at the age of sixty-seven.

SELECTED BIBLIOGRAPHY

First Editions

Prose Narratives and Novels

"La vida no es muy seria en sus cosas." *América* 40:35–36 (1945).

"Nos han dado la tierra." *Pan* 2: n. pag. (1945).

"Macario." *Pan* 6: n. pag. (1945).

"La cuesta de las comadres." *América* 55:31–38 (1948).

"Talpa." *América* 62:79–81 (1950).

"El llano en llamas." *América* 64:66–85 (1950).

"¡Diles que no me maten!" *América* 66:125–130 (1951).

El llano en llamas. Mexico City, 1953.

"Un cuento." *Las letras patrias* 1:104–108 (1954).

"Los murmullos." *Universidad de México* 8/10:6–7 (1954).

Pedro Páramo. Mexico City, 1955.

"La herencia de Matilde Arcángel." *Cuadernos médicos* 1/5:57–61 (1955).

"El día del derrumbe." *México en la cultura* 334:3,5 (14 August 1955).

"Un pedazo de noche (Fragmento)." *Revista mexicana de literatura* (Nueva Época) 3:7–14 (1959).

El gallo de oro y otros textos para cine. Mexico, 1980.

Essays and Other Prose Writings

Prólogo y Selección. *Noticias históricas de la vida y hechos de Nuño de Guzmán.* Guadalajara, Jalisco, 1962.

Review. *Tres cuentos* by Agustín Yáñez. *Bulletin* (Centro de Escritores Mexicanos) 11/4:4 (1964).

Review. *La ruta de la libertad* by Fernando Benítez. *Bulletin* (Centro de Escritores Mexicanos) 11/4:4 (1964).

Review. *Los palacios desiertos* by Luisa Josefina Hernández. *Books Abroad* 38:294 (1964).

Review. *La tierra pródiga* by Agustín Yáñez. *Revista mexicana de cultura.* Sunday literary supplement of *El nacional,* (Segunda Época) 919:6 (8 November 1964).

"Situación actual de la novela contemporánea." ICACH (Instituto de Ciencias y Artes de Chiapas, Tuxtla Gutiérrez) 15:111–122 (1965).

Discurso al recibir el Premio Nacional de Letras 1970. *El Día* (26 November 1970). P. 10.

"Juan Rulfo examina su narrativa." *Escritura* 2:305–317 (1976).

"Dos textos." *Texto crítico* 6/16–17:37–39 (1980).

"España en el corazón." *Unomasuno* (Mexico City). Reprinted in *La comunidad.* Sunday supplement of *La opinión* (Los Angeles, Calif.) 200:2,3 (20 May 1984).

Collected Works

Antología personal. With a prologue by Jorge Ruffinelli. Mexico City, 1978. Includes eight short stories from *El llano en llamas;* two selections from *Pedro Páramo;* "Un pedazo de noche," and "La vida no es muy seria en sus cosas."

Obras completas. Edited by Jorge Ruffinelli. Caracas, Venezuela, 1977.

Pedro Páramo y El llano en llamas. Barcelona, 1969. Includes "Un pedazo de noche," "El día del derrumbe," and "La herencia de Matilde Arcángel."

Pedro Páramo; El llano en llamas. With a prologue by Felipe Garrido. Mexico City, 1979.

Later Editions

El llano en llamas. Mexico City, 1959. Paperback edition.

El llano en llamas. Mexico City, 1970. Paperback edition. Contains two new stories, "El día del derrumbe" and "La herencia de Matilde Arcángel"; one story, "El Paso del Norte," is omitted.

El llano en llamas. Englewood Cliffs, N.J., 1973. School edition edited by Hugo Rodríguez Alcalá and Ray A. Verzasconi.

El llano en llamas. Mexico City, 1980. Paperback edition containing all the stories.

El llano en llamas. Mexico City, 1980. Tezontle edition illustrated by Juan Pablo Rulfo and with a photograph of the author by Rafael López Castro.

Pedro Páramo. Mexico City, 1964. Paperback edition.

Pedro Páramo. New York, 1970. School edition edited by Luis Leal.

Pedro Páramo. Mexico City, 1980. Tezontle edition illustrated by Juan Pablo Rulfo and with a photograph of the author by Rafael López Castro.

Pedro Páramo. Mexico City, 1984. An edition of 50,000 copies published conjunctively by the Fondo de Cultura Económica and the Secretaría de Educación Pública.

Translations

"Anacleto Morones." Translated by Anna West. *Chelsea Review* 6:47–59 (1960).

"Because We Are Very Poor." Translated by Lysander Kemp. In *Great Spanish Short Stories,* edited by Ángel Flores. New York, 1962. Pp. 300–304.

"Because We Are Very Poor." Translated by Henry Dyches. *Mexico Quarterly Review* 1/3:166–169 (1962).

The Burning Plain and Other Stories. Translated by George D. Schade. Austin, Tex., 1967.

The Burning Plain and Other Stories. Pan American paperback edition. 3rd ed. Austin, Tex., 1978. A reprint of Schade's translation.

"The Day of the Landslide." Translated by Hardie St. Martin. In *Doors and Mirrors. Fiction and Poetry from Spanish America, 1920–1970,* edited by Hortence Carpentier and Janet Brof. New York, 1972. Pp. 223–229.

"The Hill of the *Comadres.*" Translated by Lysander Kemp. *Atlantic* 213:102–105 (1964).

"Luvina." Translated by Joan and Boyd Carter. *Prairie Schooner* 31/4:300–306 (1957–1958). Reprinted in *Mexican Life* 34/3:11–12, 64 (1958).

"Macario." Translated by George Schade. *Texas Quarterly* 2/1:48–51, 52–55 (1958). Reprinted in *The Muse in Mexico,* edited by Thomas Cranfill. Austin, Tex., 1959. Pp. 48–51.

"Matilde Arcángel." Translated by Margaret Shedd. *Kenyon Review* 28/2:187–193 (1966).

"The Miraculous Child." Translated by Irene Nicholson. *Encounter* 5/3:13–19 (1959).

"The Night They Left Him Behind." Translated by Robert Cleland. *Mexican Life* 32/11:17–18 (1956).

"No Dogs Bark." Translated by George D. Schade. *Texas Quarterly* 2/1:52–55 (1959). Reprinted in *The Muse in Mexico,* edited by Thomas Cranfill. Austin, Tex., 1959. Pp. 52–55.

Pedro Páramo. Translated by Lysander Kemp. New York, 1959.

"Talpa." Translated by Robert Cleland. *Mexican Life* 33/1:62,64 (1957).

"Talpa." Translated by Darwin J. Flakoll and Claribel Alegría. In *New Voices of Spanish America.* Boston, 1962. Pp. 32–39.

"Talpa." Translated by J. A. Chapman. In *Short Stories in Spanish/Cuentos Hispánicos,* edited by Jean Franco. Harmondsworth, Middlesex, England, 1966. Pp. 167–187.

"Talpa." Translated by Pat M. Ness. In *Contemporary Latin American Short Stories,* edited by Pat M. Ness. Greenwich, Conn., 1974.

"Tell Them Not to Kill Me." Translated by Lysander Kemp. In *New World Writing* 14. New York, 1958. Pp. 116–122.

"They Gave Us the Land." Translated by Jean Franco. *Encounter* 25/3:15–17 (1965). Reprinted in *Latin American Writing Today,* edited by J. M. Cohen. Baltimore, 1967. Pp. 174–178.

Biographical and Critical Studies

Avilés, Alejandro. "Juan Rulfo opina sobre nuestra novela." *Diorama de la cultura.* Sunday supplement of *Excélsior* (8 June 1969).

Bell, Alan S. "Rulfo's *Pedro Páramo:* A Vision of Hope." *Modern Language Notes* 81:238–245 (1966).

Burton, Julianne. "Sexuality and the Mythic Dimension in Juan Rulfo's *Pedro Páramo.*" *Symposium* 28/3:228–247 (1974).

Cortés Tamayo, Ricardo. "Juan Rulfo." *Diorama de la Cultura.* Sunday supplement of *Excélsior* (31 May 1959).

Crow, John A. "*Pedro Páramo:* A Twentieth Century Dance of Death." In *Homenaje a Irving A. Leonard,* edited by Raquel Chang-Rodríguez and Donald A. Yates. East Lansing, Mich., 1977. Pp. 219–227.

Estrada, Ricardo. "Los indicios de *Pedro Páramo.*" *Universidad de San Carlos* (Guatemala City) 65:67–85 (1965).

Fishman, Lois R. "Searching for Juan Rulfo." *Américas* (Washington, D.C.) 36/1:28–33 (1984).

Foster, David William. "Rulfo, Juan." In *Mexican Literature: A Bibliography of Secondary Sources.* Metuchen, N.J., 1981. Pp. 306–323.

Freeman, George Ronald. *Paradise and Fall in Rulfo's ''Pedro Páramo'': Archetype and Structural Unity.* Mexico City, 1970.

Fuentes, Carlos. "Mugido, muerte y misterio: El mito de Rulfo." *Revista iberoamericana* 47 116–117:11–21 (1981).

Gordon, Donald K. *Los cuentos de Juan Rulfo.* Madrid, 1976.

Gyurko, Lanin A. "Rulfo's Aesthetic Nihilism: Narrative Antecedents of *Pedro Páramo.*" *Hispanic Review* 4:451–466 (1972).

Harss, Luis, and Barbara Dohmann. "Juan Rulfo, or the Souls of the Departed." In *Into the Mainstream.* New York, 1967. Pp. 246–275.

Homenaje a Juan Rulfo. Edited by Helmy F. Giacoman. New York, 1974.

Inframundo: El México de Juan Rulfo, edited by Frank Janney. New York, 1983. Collection of critical articles by Fernando Benítez, Carlos Fuentes, Gabriel García Márquez, Carlos Monsiváis, José Emilio Pacheco, and Elena Poniatowska, plus almost one hundred photographs by Rulfo. Reprint of *Juan Rulfo: Homenaje nacional.*

Inframundo: The Mexico of Juan Rulfo. Translated by Frank Janney. New York, 1983. Contains a poem by José

Emilio Pacheco and articles by Elena Poniatowska, Fernando Benítez, and Gabriel García Márquez; also the story "Luvina" and almost one hundred photographs by Rulfo.

Juan Rulfo: Homenaje nacional. Mexico City, 1980. Collection of articles and photographs by Rulfo. Deluxe edition.

Leal, Luis. *Juan Rulfo.* Twayne's World Authors Series no. 692. Boston, 1983.

Lioret, E. Kent. "Continuación de una Bibliografía de y sobre Juan Rulfo." *Revista iberoamericana* 40/89:693–705 (1974). Supplements Ramírez' bibliography below.

Merrell, Floyd. "Multiple Images of Death in the Final Scenes of *Pedro Páramo.*" *Chasqui* 6/1:31–41 (1976).

Pacheco, José Emilio. "Imágenes de Juan Rulfo." *México en la cultura.* Sunday supplement of *Novedades* (19 July 1959).

Paz, Octavio. *Alternating Current.* Translated by Helen R. Lane. New York, 1973.

Ramírez, Arthur. "Hacia una bibliografía de y sobre Juan Rulfo." *Revista iberoamericana* 40/86:135–171 (1974).

Rebolledo, Carlos. "Sigue la discusión sobre *La región más transparente.*" *Diorama de la cultura.* Sunday supplement of *Excélsior* (8 June 1958).

Rodríguez Alcalá, Hugo. *El arte de Juan Rulfo.* Mexico City, 1965.

Roffé, Reina, ed. *Juan Rulfo: Autobiografía armada.* Buenos Aires, 1973.

Ros, Arno. *Zur Theorie literarischen Erzählens. Mit einer Interpretation der "cuentos" von Juan Rulfo.* Frankfurt, 1972.

Sommers, Joseph. "Los muertos no tienen tiempo ni espacio (Un diálogo con Juan Rulfo)." In his *La narrativa de Juan Rulfo: Interpretaciones críticas.* Mexico City, 1974. Pp. 17–22.

Vázquez, Enrique. "Una entrevista con Juan Rulfo." *La Gaceta* (Mexico City) 7/82:18–19 (1977). Reprinted from *Somos* (24 December 1976).

Yáñez, Agustín. "Premio Nacional 1970." *Tiempo* (30 November 1970).

Juan José Arreola

(1918–   )

Russell M. Cluff and L. Howard Quackenbush

Juan José Arreola was born in Ciudad Guzmán (formerly Zapotlán el Grande) in the Mexican state of Jalisco on 21 September 1918. The fourth of fourteen children, Juan José was obliged to quit school at the age of eight to apprentice in various menial trades. Before leaving school, he achieved verbal facility by reciting poetry at religious festivals and gained what proved to be a lifelong devotion to the written word. Between the late 1920's and 1939 he began his literary career in Guadalajara by editing two short-lived literary journals, *Pan* and *Eos*. During this time he began to meet with local literati, the most important of whom was Juan Rulfo, who came to be considered Mexico's foremost short-story writer and one of its best novelists. While still in Guadalajara, Arreola published his first significant story, "Hizo el bien mientras vivió" (He Did Good While He Lived), a work that received considerable recognition from writers in Mexico City, thereby leading to the publication of two additional stories in a prestigious journal of the time in the nation's capital.

In 1939 Arreola began studying theater in Mexico City at the Palace of Fine Arts, where he rubbed shoulders with Rodolfo Usigli and Xavier Villaurrutia, two of Mexico's finest dramatists. In 1945 he received a fellowship to continue his studies in France, where he played secondary roles in the Comédie Française and acted in Alexandro Jodorowsky's film *Fando and Lis*. His stay in Paris was brief, since he developed a nervous disorder that inhibited his ability to cope with his new challenges. Returning to Mexico City in 1946, he was given an editorial position at Fondo de Cultura Económica, one of the country's most important publishing firms.

He returned to serious fiction writing and in 1949 published his first book, *Varia invención* (Various Inventions), a collection of short stories that over the years underwent several metamorphoses. The book's fourth edition includes his play *La hora de todos* (Moment of Truth). In 1952 Arreola published his most important prose work, *Confabulario* (Confabulary), a book of short stories of varying themes and styles, although almost all are of a satiric, humorous nature that has come to be recognized as his trademark. In 1962 these two books were combined under the title *Confabulario total*, published in the United States in 1964 as *Confabulario and Other Inventions*. His two other most important books are *La feria* (The Fair, 1963), his only novel, and *Palindroma* (Palindrome, 1971), a collection of short prose pieces accompanied by his best play, *Tercera llamada ¡tercera! o empezamos sin usted* (Last Call, Last Call! Or We'll Start Without You).

Arreola is almost completely self-taught. The two

1229

Mexican writers who most influenced him were Alfonso Reyes and Julio Torri. From the latter, he learned concision and wit; from the former, his works acquired fantasy and universal language and motifs. Arreola's production—especially in terms of the short story—surpasses that of his masters in both quantity and quality. From a historical perspective, Arreola is recognized for his central role in the establishment of a Mexican literature that goes beyond the purely national, that treats universal human truths and archetypes, and eschews in large part colloquial language and customs. While the author's works display a wide variety of genres, themes, and techniques, one can gain a fair appreciation of his total production by examining the subjects and themes of religiosity, the absurd, the materialism and commercialism of the United States, and the battle between the sexes.

Arreola's parents were deeply religious, and two uncles, an aunt, and other more distant relatives took religious vows. According to Yulan M. Washburn, Arreola considered his family's brand of Catholicism a "gloomy faith whose only assurances were those of sin, guilt, and certain retribution" (*Juan José Arreola* p. 6). His attitudes toward religion surfaced in many of his works. Perhaps Arreola's most famous story constructed on a biblical motif is "I'm Telling You the Truth" (a poor translation that loses the biblical flavor of the original: "En verdad os digo" would best be rendered as "Verily I say unto you"). This story is based on the New Testament axiom that it would be harder for a rich man to make his way into heaven than for a camel to pass through the eye of a needle. To create his satire, Arreola used another of his favorite targets, science. Arpad Niklaus, seeking to disassociate himself from "death-dealing scientists," turns the focus of his research toward the humanitarian goal of saving the souls of the rich. His plan is to entice the wealthy to finance his project of dismantling a camel and passing it "in a stream of electrons through a needle's eye." The trick will be to rematerialize the animal without having caused its death, thus undermining the biblical metaphor. The final irony is that the plan is foolproof: if the experiment succeeds, so do the rich; if it fails, the rich still achieve their goal, since the enormous expense of the experiment will have rendered them poor.

Another satire that underscores false religious presuppositions and fanaticism is "El silencio de Dios" ("God's Silence").[*] The work is divided into two parts: the first a letter to God from a guilt-ridden soul; the second God's answer—a silent one because God, "accustomed to managing more spacious things," finds mankind's language inadequate for true communication. The relationship between God and man inevitably translates into loneliness for the latter. The story is a fitting model for deistic existentialism in that God is presumed to exist but neither interferes with nor assists in mankind's affairs. The paradox of the work is double. First, while God admits that he cannot communicate with man, he is nevertheless willing to pass down "a few useful pointers." Second, while the protagonist is doomed to receive no response, the reader has the benefit of God's answer on the printed page. God sums up the human condition—from an existentialistic point of view—by espousing the following: that it would be preferable for human beings to see the world as He sees it, "like a grandiose experiment"; that man ought to seek religion only if it will give him repose; that we must be satisfied to take beauty to heart by enjoying our surrounding small cosmos; that each person must lose himself in an occupation that will leave him little free time—hence reinforcing the existentialistic tenet of "doing as a means of becoming," a metaphor for the notion that "existence precedes essence." Finally, God asserts that the only way to avoid loneliness is to seek the company of other souls but warns us not to forget that "each soul is especially constructed for solitude." The story, as with so many of Arreola's works, ends with a peculiar twist: first, God promises that, instead of signing his return letter, He will appear before this poor soul in an unmistakable manner in daylight, but He then reverses himself, saying: "For example—But no, you alone will have to discover how." Between this isolation imposed by God and the debilitating limits of his language, man's inescapable loneliness is reaffirmed.

As with most avant-garde writers, there is for Arreola but one small step between employing exis-

[*]Translations of material from "God's Silence," "Baby H. P.," "Announcement," and "The Rhinoceros" are by George D. Schade, from *Confabulario and Other Inventions*, published by The University of Texas Press in 1964.

tentialistic philosophies in a coherent fictional world and combining them with the literary strategies of the absurd. His particular brand of the absurd is nowhere more evident than in his best-known story, "El guardagujas" ("The Switchman"). Many teachers and critics fail to go beyond the surface level of the tale, seeing it as a simple satire that ridicules human institutions by using the railroad as a metaphor for society. Some situate the railroad company in Mexico, although the work provides no clues as to the setting. The careful reader will discover deeper levels of meaning that attain what we have called the absurd. Rather than a metaphor for a nationalistic, fumbling bureaucracy, the story conveys a more universal theme that depicts the journey of life as a frustrating, uncertain experience.

Science and technology are favorite objects of ridicule for Arreola. In "Baby H.P." (1952; "H.P." for "horsepower"), he is not content merely to satirize the scientific temperament in the abstract. While creating a parody of the commercial language of the United States, he makes a frontal attack on that country's materialism and technocracy. The work's implied message is that modern technology is not a panacea for the world's human problems. While "Baby H. P." could be categorized as one of Arreola's hybridized "story-essays," in that there is no true story line, it does share with most of his fictional works a steady, sardonic tone and an ironic vision of the human condition. A seemingly boisterous narrator—as in a radio commercial—speaks directly to the "lady of the house," attempting to sell her a new mechanical gadget that, when fixed to her baby, will collect all the excess energy radiating from his/her busy little body. "The kicking of a nursing baby" declares our enterprising announcer, "during the twenty-four hours of the day, is now transformed, thanks to Baby H. P., into some useful seconds of electric blending or into fifteen minutes of radio music." He also assures his client that any rumors concerning possible dangers to the child are totally "irresponsible." The final sentences of the piece contain all the commercial rhetoric that the narrator can muster, and the parody is obvious: "Baby H. P. is available in good stores in different sizes, models, and prices. It is a modern, durable, trustworthy apparatus, and you can hook up extensions to all its parts. It carries the factory

guarantee of J. P. Mansfield & Sons of Atlanta, Illinois."

Almost a decade after writing "Baby H. P.," Arreola published another story using this hybrid invention, "Anuncio" ("Announcement," better translated as "commercial" or "advertisement"). The reproach of North American materialism persists, but the narrative voice now beats the drum for a more daring product: "Plastisex©" . . . "these attractive, hygienic creatures" . . . "the woman you have dreamed about all your life." The scientific acumen and commercial verbiage of the earlier work recur here, but "Announcement" guides us toward another of Arreola's basic preoccupations: Woman. While the overtones of the opening sentences clearly suggest a sexist attitude—and Arreola is regularly accused of being sexist—the ending is once again ironic in that it displays, in a tongue-in-cheek tone, an attitude that may or may not be sincere: "When the use of Plastisex© becomes popularized we will witness the birth of feminine genius, so long awaited. Women, freed then from their traditionally erotic obligations, will establish forever in their transitory beauty the pure reign of the spirit."

In an interview with Emmanuel Carballo, Arreola addressed the issue of sexism and all but apologized for having treated woman as he did in "Homenaje a Otto Weininger" ("Homage to Otto Weininger"), a cross between his false "biographies" and his better-known fables. The narrator is a mangy dog at the foot of a crumbling wall, scratching himself and lamenting: "Like a good romantic, I wasted my life pursuing a bitch." His love for her is unrequited, and his physical desires toward her have ended in frustration. His one concrete memento of her is the mange that causes him to scratch. He flies into a rage when "malicious creatures come to tell me that she is wandering about in this or that district . . . rapturously mating with huge dogs, much bigger than herself." At such moments he even contemplates suicide but always returns to his wall and his scratching. In defending himself, Arreola harks back to his earlier statement in "God's Silence" that "each soul is especially constructed for solitude." For him there can be no true companionship. He would have us believe that his true anger, following the philosophies of Weininger, is directed toward "a radical loneliness that sprang from the initial separation of that Platonic being who contained both man and woman in one biological mass" (Carballo, *El cuento mexicano* . . . , p. 69). Yet he openly admits that, for good or ill, it is woman upon whom he heaps that radical bitterness.

In several more typical stories, Arreola comes closer to shedding the mantle of sexism. While these stories begin by placing women in degrading postures, ironic endings rescue them. In "El rinoceronte" ("The Rhinoceros")—the story, not the fable—Eleanor, the timid female narrator, begins by saying, "For ten years I fought with a rhinoceros; I'm the divorced wife of Judge McBride. Joshua McBride possessed me for ten years with his imperious egoism. I knew his furious rages, his momentary tenderness, and, late at night, his insistent and ceremonious lust." In contrast to her degrading past with a dehumanized husband, the present for Eleanor is a moment of catharsis or at least of revenge. In the past, she withstood her husband's abuses in exchange for "the protection of a respectable man." At present, in solitude, she observes from the sidelines while Pamela, her successor, tames the erstwhile beast. Whereas McBride had always demanded of Eleanor great meals of roast beef and strong-smelling cheeses, (Patagras and Gorgonzola), neighbors now inform her that they have seen him devouring giant platters of salad and modest amounts of insipid cream cheese. Pamela also rations his pipe tobacco and whiskey and puts out his cigar when it is half smoked. Between vegetarian meals and her adroitness at handling head-on attacks (by grabbing his tail and hanging on while he clumsily spins in circles until exhausted), Pamela has not only subdued the beast, but now has him "devoutly listening to the Sunday services." This is what they tell Leonor, and she exults. Her favorite image, however, is of her own creation: "I especially like to imagine the rhinoceros late at night, in his slippers, his great shapeless body under his robe, knocking timidly and persistently on an obstinate door." Here, the victory is double: Pamela has tamed and molded her animallike husband to her own satisfaction; Eleanor, far from being jealous of the woman who presently controls her former husband, now enjoys watching the misery of this tame creature who once had tyrannized her life.

Another story that uses the same motif is "Una mujer amaestrada" ("A Tamed Woman"). In this case, the onlooker is a man. The other actors are a man, his dwarfed son who beats a drum, and a woman who, to the delight of most male spectators, obeys his every command. At first the narrator presumes that the man is in control, but soon he determines that he is suffering, that there is more between man and woman than meets the careless eye, since he notices tears rolling down the man's cheek. Finally, the narrator feels that he must become the woman's accomplice, perhaps even her savior. This situation coincides perfectly with Arreola's aforementioned defense, wherein he admitted that "all of us who dismember the feminine structure are wrong because we always return and kneel before it" (Carballo, *ibid.*). Such an admission of hypocrisy does not dismiss the case; Arreola's stand on the issue remains ambiguous to the end. Even in his latest collections he proves to be divided. The best example is *Palíndroma*, in which both poles are clearly represented: while "El himen en México" (The Hymen in Mexico) reproduces the degrading tone of "Homage to Otto Weininger," the play *Tercera llamada* portrays woman as spiritually superior to man.

In the mid-1950's, Arreola was stereotyped as a cosmopolitan writer who avoided Mexican themes and motifs. Even at that time the notion was not entirely true, and at present it is unthinkable. In 1952 Arreola wrote "Corrido" ("Ballad"), a story whose setting, subject, and theme are undeniably Mexican: a young girl goes to a plaza in Zapotlán to fetch water; two young men appear on the scene and fight over her, to the death; this misfortune brands the innocent girl for life, and she is never able to marry. The novel *The Fair* runs the entire gamut of particularly Mexican speech, including sixteenth-century regal proclamations, biblical quotations, folkloric refrains, and contemporary jokes, obscenities, and slang. Since the publication of *The Fair*, Arreola has never had to face the nationalist-cosmopolitan issue again.

The Fair won Arreola the Villaurrutia Prize but did not receive the critical acclaim his other books enjoyed. While the author's recognizable constants (satire, irony, humor, and the themes of religion and women,) are still at the forefront—together with the long-awaited nationalistic flavor—some readers consider its lack of novelistic structure a major drawback. In our opinion, this feature is responsible for much of the novel's artistic and cultural significance. Rather than a pointless, ragged mosaic, the work can be seen as a parody and, ultimately, a caricature of Agustín Yáñez' *Al filo del agua* (*The Edge of the Storm,* 1947). Both authors are from the state of Jalisco, and each novel is more the story of a town than of a particular protagonist. Among the important concerns shared by the citizens of both towns are their boredom, their sins, and their guilt.

Although he is most widely recognized for work in the narrative, Arreola has produced and published two plays. Since each was included in a volume of narrative, they tend to be overlooked as authentic theatrical expressions. In the case of *La hora de todos,* this avoidance may be more justified than it is for *Tercera llamada,* but in any case it is unfortunate that Arreola's theater has not received more attention. *La hora de todos* has all the earmarks of a prose writer's first attempt at writing serious theater; the problem is that the author tried to write a "serious" drama and produced a prosaic, plodding work based on overused and outdated stereotypes. Arreola is most adroit when he blends humor into his satire of ethics, human hypocrisy, and weakness. It is the humor that saves his prose pieces from becoming diatribes, and it is humor that is lacking in *La hora de todos.* Regardless, the work was acclaimed by the National Institute of Fine Arts as the best play written for the Mexican stage in 1953. The title refers to a final judgment of sorts and serves as a reminder that everyone is responsible for the consequences of his or her actions. The protagonist, Harrison Fish, is the archetypal Ugly American, a vice-ridden, bigoted, high-stakes business executive, devoid of conscience, who uses money to further his dominion. The stereotypes of North American society have long since lost their validity; they tend to date the play, blunting its transcendence and universal appeal. In spite of these drawbacks, Arreola tested a theatrical form in *La hora de todos* that he refined and polished in his second play. He wrote modern metatheater (audience-actor interplay, the destruction of the fourth wall, and foregrounding theatrical action as a substitute for reality) before that method was recognized or before

it became popular in Spanish-American literature and theater. Harras, the antagonist of the play, is the work's director as well as its author-creator. He talks to the audience, involving them in the process of the dramatic creation of this "reality." Harras sees himself as the conscience of his protagonist and the creator of each scene, aided by a loudspeaker that adds to his omniscience and gives precise details about the character's life when Fish is reluctant to do so.

When Arreola's second play, *Tercera llamada,* appeared, it was immediately apparent that, as a playwright, the author had corrected many of his previous mistakes. He continued to innovate in areas in which he had major strength as a writer, the areas of literary form and dramatic structure. *Tercera llamada* is one of the finest examples of theatrical creativity and innovation to appear in the Latin American theater. Its success arises from the union of two disparate and seemingly incongruous dramatic methods: the Latin American *auto* form (traditionally, a one-act religious play based on the struggle between good and evil, often with an allegorical interpretation and always containing some miraculous element), which had its beginnings in the medieval Spanish religious theater, and the ultramodern theatrical posture of the theater of the absurd. This unlikely combination is joined with Arreola's use of metatheatrical devices, which give the play depth of symbolism and aesthetic force. The themes surrounding Adam and Eve, the Temptation and the Fall, viewed from a contemporary perspective, give voice to common preoccupations, and Arreola laces them with satiric, raucous humor. Three of Arreola's most important motifs appear in this piece: religious parody, the conflict between the sexes, and the love triangle.

As suggested by the title of the book in which it appears, the palindrome is the predominant symbol for the play. In Spanish, Adam and Eve (*Adán y Eva*) if read backwards (*ave y nada*) means "bird and nothing." The palindrome ("Adán y Eva—ave y nada") conveys an inversion of the common perception of the first human couple. Instead of a blissful union, there is conflict: a disinterested husband neglects his wife, and a woman seeks fulfillment and companionship in a third party, Ángel. The latter is a binary being, a combination of light and darkness, holiness and evil, who reveals the side that suits the requirements of the moment. The internal structure reflects the symbolic extension of the reverse half of the palindrome (bird and nothing). Contrary to the common biblical view of Adam as the patriarch and axis of action, in this interpretation Eve is the central figure in the symbolic struggle between male and female, between free agency and conformism, and it is she who "spreads her wings" with the help of Ángel (acting in this case the part of Lucifer) and flies. It is Adam who, because of his inertia and lack of consciousness and volition, in an existentialistic sense, symbolizes nothingness and the human void.

Arreola adds to the chaotic, absurdist effect of the palindrome imagery a multifaceted metatheatrical level of meaning. There exists a human cognizance of a paradisiacal equivalent; the characters are both human and mythological. These players reveal their multiple levels of existence as biblical symbols, as characters in a play, as actors playing characters in a drama, and as spectators watching the actors of the play, who are themsleves. There is even a Director-character who addresses the audience and restages the production. Several plays within plays dramatize the interdependence of the many levels of interpretation. Arreola, in *Tercera llamada*, quickens our understanding of ourselves by touching the primordial threads of our consciousness.

In the 1950's Arreola edited two important literary series, *Cuadernos del unicornio* (The Unicorn's Notebooks) and *Los presentes* (Those Present), which served as an introductory forum for many of Mexico's best contemporary writers, among them Carlos Fuentes, José Emilio Pacheco, Sergio Pitol, Elena Poniatowska, and José de la Colina. He was also one of the early directors of the Centro Mexicano de Escritores (Mexican Writers Center), which provides support for promising young writers. Arreola's fertile imagination and his sense of form and humor have immortalized him as one of Mexico's foremost writers of prose.

SELECTED BIBLIOGRAPHY

First Editions

Varia invención. Mexico City, 1949.
Cinco cuentos. Mexico City, 1951.

Confabulario. Mexico City, 1952.
La hora de todos: Juguete cómico en un acto. Mexico City, 1954.
Confabulario y varia invención. Mexico City, 1955.
Punta de plata. Mexico City, 1958.
Bestiario. Mexico City, 1959.
Confabulario total. Mexico City, 1962.
La feria. Mexico City, 1963.
Lectura en voz alta. Mexico City, 1968.
Palindroma. Mexico City, 1971.
Mujeres, animales y fantasías mecánicas. Barcelona, 1972.
Letras vivas; Páginas de la literatura mexicana actual. Mexico City, 1972.
La palabra educación. Edited by Jorge Arturo Ojeda. Mexico City, 1973.
Y ahora, la mujer . . . Edited by Jorge Arturo Ojeda. Mexico City, 1975.
Inventario. Barcelona, Buenos Aires, and Mexico City, 1976.
Confabulario personal. Barcelona, 1979.

Later Editions

Antología de Juan José Arreola. Mexico City, 1969.
Bestiario. 5th rev. ed. Mexico City, 1981.
Confabulario. 5th ed. Mexico City, 1971.
Confabulario total [1941–1961]. 3rd ed. Mexico City, 1962.
La feria. 6th ed. Mexico City, 1980.
La hora de todos. In *Curso Nacional de Teatro, Obras Premiadas 1954–1955.* Mexico City, 1955. Pp. 292–452.
Palindroma. 4th ed. Mexico City, 1980.
Varia invención. 4th ed. Mexico City, 1980.

Translations

Confabulario and Other Inventions. Translated by George D. Schade. Austin, Tex., 1964.
The Fair. Translated by John Upton. Austin, Tex., 1977.

Biographical and Critical Studies

Adoum, Jorge Enrique. "El realismo de la otra realidad." *América Latina en su literatura.* 2nd ed. Mexico City, 1974. Pp. 204–216.
Barrenechea, Ana M. "Elaboración de la 'circunstancia mexicana' en tres cuentos de Arreola." In *Textos hispanoamericanos: de Sarmiento a Sarduy.* Caracas, 1978. Pp. 235–246.
Benítez, Jorge. "J. J. Arreola: Las experiencias del paciente." *Mundo nuevo* 1/7: 27–37 (1974).

Bente, Thomas O. "'El guardagujas' de Juan José Arreola: ¿Sátira política o indagación metafísica?" *Cuadernos americanos* 31/6: 205–212 (1972).

Boyd, John P. "Imágenes de animales y la batalla entre los sexos en dos obras de Juan José Arreola." *Nueva narrativa hispanoamericana* 1/2: 73–77 (1971).

Brushwood, John S. *Mexico in its Novel: A Nation's Search for Identity.* Austin, Tex., 1966. Pp. 28–30, 51.

_____. *The Spanish American Novel: A Twentieth-Century Survey.* Austin, Tex., 1975. Pp. 260–261.

Carballo, Emmanuel. *Cuentistas mexicanos modernos.* 2 vols. Mexico City, 1956.

_____, ed. *El cuento mexicano del siglo XX.* Mexico City, 1964. Pp. 60–70, 71–72.

_____. "Arreola y Rulfo, cuentistas." *Revista de la Universidad de México* 8/7: 28–29, 32 (1954).

_____. "La narrativa mexicana de hoy." *Sur* 320: 1–14 (1969).

Castellanos, Rosario. "Tendencias de la narrativa mexicana contemporánea." In *El mar y sus pescaditos.* Mexico City, 1975. Pp. 136–151.

Chávarri, Raúl. "Arreola en su varia creación." *Cuadernos hispanoamericanos* (Paris) 242: 418–425 (1970).

Cheever, Leonard A. "The Little Girl and the Cat: 'Kafkaesque' Elements in Arreola's 'The Switchman.'" *American Hispanist* 4/34–35: 3–4 (1979).

Durán, Manuel. "El Premio Villaurrutia y la novela mexicana contemporánea." *La torre* 13/49: 233–238 (1965).

Foster, David William, and Virginia Ramos Foster, eds. *Modern Latin American Literature* 1. New York, 1975. Pp. 104–110.

Gilgen, Read G. "Absurdist Techniques in the Short Stories of J. J. Arreola." *Journal of Spanish Studies: Twentieth Century* 8/1-2: 67–77 (1980).

Glantz, Margo. "Juan José Arreola y los bestiarios." In *Latin American Fiction Today*, edited by Rose S. Minc. Montclair, N. J., 1980. Pp. 61–69.

González-Araúzo, Ángel. "Ida y vuelta al *Confabulario.*" *Revista iberoamericana* 34/65: 103–107 (1968).

Herz, Theda M. "Las fuentes cultas de la sátira del *Confabulario.*" *Hispanófila* 72: 31–49 (1981).

_____. "Continuity in Evolution: Juan José Arreola as Dramatist." *Latin American Theatre Review* 8/2: 14–26 (1975).

_____. "René Avilés Fabila in the Light of J. J. Arreola: A Study in Spiritual Affinity." *Journal of Spanish Studies: Twentieth Century* 7/2: 147–171 (1979).

Lagmanovich, David. "Estructura y efecto en 'La migala,' de Juan José Arreola." *Cuadernos hispanoamericanos* 320–321: 419–428 (1977).

Larson, Ross. *Fantasy and Imagination in the Mexican Narrative.* Tempe, Ariz., 1977.

_____. "La visión realista de J. J. Arreola." *Cuadernos americanos* 171/4: 226–232 (1970).

Leal, Luis. "Contemporary Mexican Literature: A Mirror of Social Change." *Arizona Quarterly* 18/3: 197–207 (1962).

_____. "The Mexican Short Story." *Arizona Quarterly* 12/1: 24–34 (1956).

_____. "The New Mexican Short Story." *Studies in Short Fiction* 8/1: 9–19 (1971).

Lewald, H. E. Review of *La feria* by Juan José Arreola. *Books Abroad.* 38/4: 412–413 (1964).

McMurray, George R. "Albert Camus' Concept of the Absurd and Juan José Arreola's 'The Switchman.'" *Latin American Literary Review* 6/11: 30–35 (1977).

_____. Review of *Palindroma* by Juan José Arreola. *Books Abroad* 46/4: 628 (1972).

Mason, Margaret L., and Yulan M. Washburn. "'Bestiario' in Contemporary Spanish-American Literature." *Revista de estudios hispánicos* 8/2: 189–209 (1974).

Menton, Seymour. "Juan José Arreola and the Twentieth-Century Short Story." *Hispania* 42/3: 295–308 (1959).

Merrell, Floyd. "*Los de abajo, La feria,* and the Notion of Space-Time Categories in the Narrative Text." *Hispanófila* 27/79: 77–91 (1983).

Newgord, Jerry. "Dos cuentos de Juan José Arreola." *Cuadernos hispanoamericanos* 336: 527–533 (1978).

Ocampo Gómez, Aurora M., and Ernesto Prado Verázquez, eds. *Diccionario de escritores mexicanos.* Mexico City, 1967. Pp. 22–24.

Ojeda, Jorge Arturo, ed. "La lucha con el ángel: Siete libros de Juan José Arreola." Introduction to *Antología de Juan José Arreola.* Mexico City, 1969. Pp. 7–128.

_____. "Teatro lúcido y didáctico." *Revista de bellas artes* 24: 57–62 (1968).

Ortega, José. "Ética y estética en algunos cuentos de *Confabulario.*" *Sin nombre* 13/3: 52–59 (1983).

Otero, José. "Religión, moral y existencia en tres cuentos de Juan José Arreola." *Cuadernos americanos* 234/1: 222–231 (1981).

Ramírez, Arthur, and Fern L. Ramírez. "Hacia una bibliografía de y sobre J. J. Arreola." *Revista iberoamericana* 45/108–109: 651–667 (1979).

Rosaldo, Renato. "A Decade of Mexican Literature, 1950–1960." *Arizona Quarterly* 16/4: 319–331 (1960).

Schwartz, Kessel. *A New History of Spanish American Fiction* 2. Coral Gables, Fla., 1971. Pp. 292–295.

Selva, Mauricio de la. "Autovivisección de Juan José Arreola." *Cuadernos americanos* 29/171: 69–118 (1970).

Sommers, Joseph. Review of *Confabulario and Other Inventions* by Juan José Arreola. *Hispania* 47/2: 394–395 (1955).

Trifilo, S. Samuel. "Mexican Theater Goes to Paris . . . And . . . A Polemic." *Hispania* 47/2: 335–337 (1964).

Washburn, Yulan M. "An Ancient Mold for Contemporary Casting: The Beast Book of Juan José Arreola." *Hispania* 56: 295–300 (1973). A special issue.

———. *Juan José Arreola.* Twayne World Authors series no. 693. Boston, 1983.

Xirau, Ramón. "Variety and Contrast: The New Literature." Translated by Juan M. Alonso. *Atlantic Monthly* 213/3: 142–145 (1964).

Yates, Donald A. "Caught in Our Logical Absurdities." Review of *Confabulario and Other Inventions* by Juan José Arreola. *Saturday Review,* 1 August 1964. P. 32.

René Marqués

(1919–1979)

Bonnie Hildebrand Reynolds

The Puerto Rican author René Marqués was a prolific writer whose energy never seemed to lessen. He wrote primarily essays, short stories, and plays, but also published two successful novels and, early in his career, one book of poetry. Many of his works have been translated into English and other languages, and his influence extends throughout the Hispanic world. Marqués was born on 4 October 1919 in Arecibo, Puerto Rico. While growing up, he spent time both in the town of Arecibo and on his grandparents' haciendas of San Isidro, near Lares, and Carrizales, near Hatillo. In 1942 he received a degree from the College of Agriculture and Mechanical Arts in the city of Mayagüez. Shortly afterward Marqués married Serena Velasco, with whom he had three children—two sons and a daughter—before his divorce in 1957. In 1946, having worked for two years for the Department of Agriculture, he went with his wife and two children to Madrid, where he studied literature and classical and contemporary Spanish theater for one year. While there, he wrote the play *El hombre y sus sueños* (The Man and His Dreams, premiered in 1973). When he returned to Puerto Rico in 1947, he went to work as a manager for Velasco Alonzo, Inc., in his native Arecibo.

That same year, he founded the small theater group Pro Arte de Arecibo and began publishing chronicles and literary reviews in the important San Juan newspaper *El Mundo* and literary criticism in the journal *Asomante*. He also wrote his play *El sol y los MacDonald* (The Sun and the MacDonalds, premiered in 1950). The following year, 1948, the Rockefeller Foundation awarded him a fellowship to study dramaturgy in the United States, which he postponed accepting for one year. He then moved to San Juan where he worked as a writer for the editorial staff of *El Diario de Puerto Rico*. He also reviewed books and theater productions during that period.

Marqués accepted the Rockefeller Fellowship in 1949 and went to New York City to study playwriting at Columbia University, taking additional courses at Erwin Piscator's Dramatic Workshop. During that time he wrote "Palm Sunday" in English as a class assignment. Before returning to San Juan in 1950, he toured experimental theaters at Yale University, Catholic University in Washington, D.C., and the Cleveland and Karamu playhouses in Cleveland. Upon his return to San Juan, he went to work as a writer for the Department of Public Instruction's Division of Community Education, serving as chief of the editorial division from 1953 to 1969.

He was also named secretary of the board of the Puerto Rican Atheneum (Ateneo Puertorriqueño), in which capacity he served for several years. In

1951, together with his longtime friend and colleague José M. Lacomba, he founded the Experimental Theater of the Atheneum, which has survived into the present as the theater division of the Atheneum. In 1950 his play *El sol y los MacDonald* was produced for the first time by Teatro Nuestro (Our Theater), which Marqués had founded the previous year.

The Puerto Rican premiere of his now-famous work *La carreta (The Oxcart)* in December 1953 (the play was produced in New York two months earlier than in San Juan) resulted in controversy and in Marqués leaving his post on the Atheneum's board. The troupe wanted to move the play from the Atheneum's small stage to the larger one in the Tapia Theater while retaining the name and support of the Experimental Theater. When the board denied permission, the group moved to the Tapia anyway, a move that brought Marqués the audience attention he had hoped for and opened the door to his future success as a playwright.

In 1954 Marqués was awarded a Guggenheim Fellowship but postponed acceptance of it until 1957, at which time he moved to New York, where he began writing his first novel, *La víspera del hombre* (The Eve of Man, 1959). In the meantime, he traveled to Madrid once again in 1954, this time for the Spanish premiere of *The Oxcart* as well as to meet his father's family. In 1955 he published his first collection of short stories, *Otro día nuestro* (Another Day of Ours). From then on, he produced many works of fiction, plays, and essays, for which he received numerous prizes (see bibliography).

In 1958 Marqués traveled to Mexico City as a member of the Puerto Rican delegation to the First Interamerican Biennial of Painting. Upon his return to San Juan, he began writing for the radio station WIPR. During that year, his essay "Pesimismo literario y optimiso político: Su coexistencia en el Puerto Rico actual" ("Literary Pessimism and Political Optimism: Their Coexistence in Contemporary Puerto Rico," 1959) received the Atheneum's first prize for essays. The following year, with Eleizer Curet Cuevas, he founded the Club del Libro de Puerto Rico (The Book Club of Puerto Rico).

During the years 1957–1958 he wrote what many consider to be his best dramatic works, *La muerte no entrará en palacio* (Death Will Not Enter the Palace), which for political reasons has never been produced, *Los soles truncos* (The Fanlights, premiered in 1959), and *Un niño azul para esa sombra* (A Blue Boy for That Shadow, premiered in 1959). From 1969 to 1976 he was professor of literature at the University of Puerto Rico. In 1976 he retired to a house he had had built on the banks of the Cubuy River, bordering on El Yunque rain forest, and lived there until his death on 22 March 1979. In 1970 he received the Diplo Trophy as the most outstanding author of the Puerto Rican Theater Festival. Only three days before his death, the Institute of Puerto Rican Culture awarded him the Diploma of Honor for his contribution to Puerto Rican culture. On 23 June 1979 he was posthumously awarded the HOLA Dramaturgy Award. His major dramas have been translated into several languages and produced in various countries. In addition, several short stories and the novel *La mirada* (The Look, 1975) have been translated into English.

When Marqués entered the Puerto Rican literary scene, he became part of a well-established tradition in both the essay and prose fiction. However, despite the fact that there was a fairly long history of theater in Puerto Rico, that genre was not nearly as well institutionalized as the other two. Possibly for that reason, Marqués made his greatest impact in the theater.

Marqués was associated with the Generation of the Forties (his own phrase) in the island's literature, which includes such well-known authors as José Luis González, Pedro Juan Soto, and Emilio Díaz Valcárcel. This generation continued the impulse of the previous generation, writers of the 1930's who had attempted the revalorization of Puerto Rican identity in the face of the traditional literary dependence on Spain and the encroaching presence of the United States in Puerto Rico's culture, economy, and politics. Nevertheless, Marqués' generation also added to this issue of cultural identity a thematic preoccupation with human existence in general and an affinity for the technical and stylistic innovations of the contemporary literatures of Europe and the United States.

Both technically and philosophically, Marqués' works reflect his interest in and knowledge of the most significant European and North American writers of the period—especially Luigi Pirandello, Anton Chekhov, Marcel Proust, Franz Kafka, Eugene O'Neill, and Tennessee Williams—and he was responsible for a technical renaissance in both the Puerto Rican short story and theater. Marqués also demonstrated an affinity for the existential philosophies of Albert Camus, Jean-Paul Sartre, and Martin Heidegger, and to the thought of the turn-of-the-century Spanish philosopher Miguel de Unamuno. Technical innovations and an existentialist philosophy form the basis of Marqués' expression of his strong commitment to the preservation of Puerto Rico's cultural identity, as well as to the establishment of its political autonomy. Throughout a writing career spanning more than two decades, Marqués refined and intensified the various techniques and focuses with which he began his literary career, always with the goal of expressing his personal commitment to the development of his beloved Puerto Rico's fullest potential.

Marqués was particularly concerned about what he believed to be the erosion of Puerto Rican cultural values as a result of the materialism imposed by the United States' presence and influence on the island. Another of his concerns was what he believed to be his countrymen's reluctance or failure to defend their cultural identity. He was also critical of the lack of freedom both of Puerto Rico as a nation and of Puerto Ricans as individuals, circumstances Marqués believed to be the result of the legal relationship to which Governor Luis Muñoz Marín agreed in 1952 when Puerto Rico became an *estado libre asociado* (free associated state) of the United States. This Spanish term is officially rendered into English as "commonwealth," in which relationship Puerto Rico enjoys a certain amount of autonomy while being greatly dependent on the United States both economically and politically.

René Marqués initiated his career as an essayist when he wrote a series of fifteen articles for the San Juan daily *El Mundo* about Spain while he was studying in that country in 1946–1947. Those articles, published between 4 August 1946 and 23 March 1947, treated various aspects of Spanish literature, especially theater. Only in the article published on 27 October 1946 did he talk about a non-Spanish topic—the theater in Puerto Rico—which was eventually to become his preferred subject. He continued to publish essays until 1975.

His essays fall mainly into three categories, the first of which is theater criticism, including discussions of his own works as well as those of other Puerto Rican dramatists. In 1947 the Institute of Puerto Rican Literature awarded him a journalism prize for his essay on Franciso Arrivi's drama *María Soledad*. He also published essays and reviews about the works of well-known foreign dramatists such as Pirandello, George Bernard Shaw, Rodolfo Usigli, O'Neill, and Williams. In addition, he wrote articles about the state of the art in Puerto Rican theater in which he was often critical of the lack of dedicated dramatists in his country, the lack of preparation and training for theater professionals, and the scarcity of theatrical facilities.

The second category of essays includes those written on other literary topics. He is especially remembered for his essay "El cuento puertorriqueño en la promoción del cuarenta" ("The Puerto Rican Short Story of the Forties Generation"), published in 1959 as a prologue to a collection of short stories by young authors to whom Marqués referred as the Generation of the Forties. The essay carefully relates the generation in question to past generations of Puerto Rican authors, especially the Generation of the Thirties, and in addition Marqués tried to impress upon young Puerto Ricans the importance of Spanish- and North American authors. The essay is important both for its contribution to the study of Puerto Rican letters and for our understanding of Marqués as a literary critic. Marqués' critical comments had a solidifying effect on this group of young authors (such as José Luis González, Pedro Juan Soto, and Emilio Díaz Valcárcel), many of whom have continued to publish successfully into the 1970's and 1980's. Furthermore, with this essay Marqués established his credentials as a literary critic by demonstrating his commanding knowledge of current literary trends.

A third category of essays, several of which proved to be very controversial to Puerto Rican readers, concerns the island's social, political, and cultural life. These essays express clearly and succinctly Marqués' views on the prevalent national issues of his day and communicate the personal philosophy that underlay his own works in prose fiction and drama. One of two especially enlightening essays in this category is "Literary Pessimism and Political Optimism." Marqués' essay examines the continuing pessimism among the island's intellectuals, despite the atmosphere of optimism on the political front, and concludes that he and his fellow writers perceived the underlying problem as the erosion of Puerto Rico's cultural and historical awareness, due in part to the imposition of the United States' culture and institutions on the island. A second part to his conclusion is that the writer has the moral and ethical obligation to make his public aware of hidden problems in the society and that in doing so a pessimistic author writes from an attitude of optimism that his work will help to correct his society's problems.

By far the most controversial of Marqués' essays is "El puertorriqueño dócil (literatura y realidad psicológica)" ("The Docile Puerto Rican: Literature and Psychological Reality," 1962), winner of the Atheneum's essay prize in 1960 and subsequently published in the Mexican literary journal *Cuadernos americanos*. Marqués uses the following definition of "docility," taken from Roque Barcia's *Gran diccionario de sinónimos castellanos* (Big Dictionary of Spanish Synonyms):

> Docility is lacking strength and even free will to resist what others demand, insinuate, or order; a certain propensity to obey, to follow the example, the opinion, the advice of others, which originates in one's own weakness, whether from ignorance, lack of confidence in one's own intelligence, knowledge, or strength.

The purpose of the essay is to explore and to prove the Puerto Rican's docility based on thematic evidence taken from Puerto Rican literature. Among other evidence, he cites such historical antecedents as the tendency of his countrymen to place authority in the hands of a central figure, whether in government or in professional or social organizations; the imposition of a matriarchal society on what was, prior to the United States' influence, a patriarchal one; and the acceptance of what Marqués calls *estadolibrismo* ("Unitedstatesism"), in which many persons, according to Marqués, attempt to "sweeten the medicine" by rationalizing defensively the political, eco-

nomic, and cultural dependence upon the United States. Whether one accepted his premises or not, this essay made a tremendous impact on the intellectuals of the island, and the term "docility" became nearly synonymous with René Marqués. The essay has been criticized not merely for its premises and conclusions but also for the fact that the author primarily used his own literary works as the basis of his evidence.

The value of this essay for the student of Hispanic literature in general and Marqués' works in particular lies in what it reveals about the author's personal philosophy and attitudes toward his own literary creations. As he states in the section "Nacionalismo y anexionismo: El impulso autodestructor" ("Nationalism and Annexationism: The Self-Destructive Impulse"):

> The writer's mission is always that of revealing, clarifying, illuminating. No phenomenon is so needy of revelation, clarification and illumination for the benefit of the poorly enlightened Puerto Rican man as the phenomenon of psychological annexationism. The writer should never stop picking up the glove that reality, with a sarcastic grimace, throws at his feet.

There is no doubt that Marqués saw his personal mission as one of inciting the "docile" Puerto Rican public into addressing the ills that he saw in his society. In other essays, he touched upon these same topics while giving attention to other subjects that concerned him: namely, the erosion of the Spanish language spoken in Puerto Rico and the loss of past cultural values.

Marqués also wrote both short stories and novels. With only two novels—*La víspera del hombre* and *La mirada*—published seventeen years apart, but with twenty-nine published short stories to his credit, he is better known for the latter. He published his first three stories at the age of twenty-one in May, June, and August of 1941 in the Puerto Rican literary journal *Alma latina*: "Crepúsculo" (Dusk), "En el campo no es lo mesmo" (It Isn't the Same in the Country), and "Sus ojos verdes" (Her Green Eyes).

Marqués' first major collection of stories appeared in 1955 under the title *Otro día nuestro* (Another Day of Ours), whose title story (published in translation as

"Give Us This Day") is still considered one of his major literary creations. Subsequent short stories appeared in the major literary journals of the island, *Asomante* (later *Sin nombre*) and *Revista del Instituto de Cultura Puertorriqueña*, as well as in anthologies.

Marqués published two more collections: *En una ciudad llamada San Juan* (In a City Named San Juan) in 1960, and *Inmersos en el silencio* (Immersed in Silence) in 1976. These two collections contain many new stories as well as the original stories of *Otro día nuestro*. In 1985 a previously unedited short story, "La venganza" (The Revenge), written in 1962, was published posthumously. A great many of Marqués' stories captured the Atheneum's coveted literary prizes, and the collection *En una ciudad llamada San Juan* earned him a prestigious award from the Cuban publishing house Casa de las Américas in 1962.

Thematically, his short stories reflect the philosophy Marqués expresses in his essays. He develops social and political themes by presenting characters terrorized by their own fear, often resulting in self-victimization and inaction. The author clearly espouses the political and cultural autonomy of his island as opposed to its official "commonwealth" status. He relates the more restricted social and political themes to the broader existential concerns of his characters, thus saving his literary creations from becoming political pamphlets. In most cases, historical and political circumstances cause his characters existential worries and emphasize their feelings of loneliness and helplessness and their thoughts of death; many stories end in murder, suicide, or resignation to one's plight. In fact, Marqués was the first Puerto Rican writer to treat the Ponce Massacre of 21 March 1937, when twenty-one people were killed by police during a march in support of the Nationalist leader Pedro Albizu Campos. In the story, "La muerte" ("Death," 1955) the protagonist is killed when he raises the Nationalist flag after the flag-bearer dies in the massacre. The political events serve more as a backdrop to the protagonist's inner thoughts about existence and death, however, and his decision to choose his own destiny by raising the flag merely coincides with the event of the massacre.

Another important theme of Marqués' narratives is time, conceived both as the historical past, which coexists with the present, and as a force in human events whose effect is nearly always negative or destructive. This theme is most clearly demonstrated in "Purificación en la Calle del Cristo" (Purification on Cristo Street). The protagonists, three sisters who have failed to face directly the changes in the world surrounding them, find that the passage of time has destroyed any possibility of their living in that world. They then make a final and definitive choice to "purify" themselves through the ritual of fire, destroying their house and themselves with it.

Technically, Marqués' fiction is characterized by a very strong ambience and characters who are an integral part of their surroundings. The ambience enhances the reader's perception of the characters' inner states and creates an aura of isolation. Whether the setting be the countryside, the sea, the city, or an interior space such as a house, a room, or a bar, it is almost always distinctively Puerto Rican. The characters' perceptions of their setting or space determine the development of their personalities to the point that they at times seem inseparable from their surroundings. One cannot, for instance, imagine the Burkhart sisters outside of their house on Cristo Street, nor can one imagine anyone from the surrounding world entering that house.

Stylistically, Marqués makes use of an implied interior monologue. Even though he writes in the third person, his readers enter directly into the thoughts and perceptions of his characters. Often flashbacks evoke the physical presence of persons from former times to make the past an integral part of the present. Dialogue is often part of a flashback appearing as memory. In any case, dialogue between characters frequently is limited to short, uncommunicative exchanges, in stark contrast to the deep feelings expressed in their interior thoughts. Language is both poetic, often with beautiful nature imagery, and starkly realistic in the dialogue itself. All of Marqués' fiction, especially his short stories, has a clear dramatic quality due to his ability to create a sense of conflict and anticipatory tension.

When Marqués proposed the idea of the Experimental Theater to the Atheneum's board of directors in 1951, he began a career that would immortalize him as an energizing force in the continuing development of Puerto Rican theater and as an undaunted defender of Puerto Rican culture. Marqués' dedication to the total freedom—both political and personal—of the Puerto Rican people is overwhelmingly obvious in the large majority of his dramatic works. Almost all of his characters suffer crises in which their way of life is threatened by some more powerful force, resulting in their struggle to maintain, find, or acknowledge their national and individual identity within a culture under great stress. As in his fiction, he relates the menacing power, directly or indirectly, of the materialistic consumer society that the United States' presence imposes on Puerto Rican life.

The resolution of these dramatic crises, whether negative or positive, communicates to the theatergoing public on two levels: it points to the injustice of the system portrayed, and it implies the individual's complicity in the maintenance of that unjust system by virtue of the fact that he/she neither overtly rejects nor accepts it. For example, the Burkhart sisters, unable to face the changing society, resolve their immediate crisis—the loss of the house and the youngest sister's death—by committing suicide. They do not, however, resolve the societal crisis at the heart of the play. Marqués' message to the Puerto Rican people, therefore, is a criticism in which he says that one must make some kind of a choice. Inaction always leads to disaster for his characters, just as he believed it would for his people.

The dynamics of his theatrical compositions depend on the particular ways in which he uses time and space to create dramatically the various crises. For example, he combines the elements of real stage space—the set, lights, colors, sounds, props—to create a virtual space whose architectural ambience is at the heart of the crisis dramatized. Each play's created space or set is a form of family living quarters that reflect the conscious or subconscious states of mind of the principal characters. These living quarters offer protection from outside threats and become self-created, escapist worlds that symbolize the self-condemnation of the individuals confined to them (for instance, the Burkhart's house). Such confinement prevents both physical freedom, related politically to Puerto Rico's status as a commonwealth of the United States, and personal freedom, related to the development of every human being's creative potential.

Time, in Marqués' plays, serves to heighten the urgency of the major conflicts, occasionally becoming a powerful villain. The longer the characters procrastinate, the more relentlessly time passes until it is transformed into an uncontrollable, life-destroying force. Time manifests itself in various ways in these dramatic works as the author translates temporal elements such as rhythm and tempo into dramatic devices integrated into the ambience of the virtual space. Marqués also often toys with his audience while he experiments with a particular play's linear movement. Frequently he avails himself of the cinematic flashback or creates a temporal universality in which past, present, and future coexist. In addition, history as a record of time plays a very important role in Marqués' dramatic creations, manifesting itself sometimes as an account of actual events and other times as fictionalized history. Whether real or invented, history always influences the present roles of the characters.

The particular crises are created or revealed when any of the spatial and temporal elements are integrated. In one of the early plays, El sol y los MacDonald, for instance, the past history of the MacDonald house coincides with that of the present generations: the bigotry and prejudice of past generations contribute to the incestuous crisis of the present, and only the youngest family member is able to escape. The others have waited too long and cannot now change. A similar relationship between space and time is evident in his other early plays: El hombre y sus sueños, "Palm Sunday," and "Los condenados" (The Condemned, 1982). The latter two works remain unpublished but have both been produced.

Comparable integrations of space and time in the later plays result in crises that always involve the characters' struggle between the fear of losing personal security and the desire for the freedom of dignity and self-respect. In Un niño azul para esa sombra and The Fanlights, past, present, and future coexist—in the first case in the innermost consciousness of the child protagonist, Michelín, and in the second, within the family home and interpersonal relationships of the three Burkhart sisters. In these two plays, a final forced confrontation with the limits of space and time effectuates the characters' suicide. However, the acts of suicide are themselves neutral, while the decisions finally to do something to combat the outside menace are heroic. The result of the choice made is not as important as finally taking some kind of stand. Both plays are based on earlier short stories: *Un niño azul para esa sombra* comes from a story by the same name as well as from "La sala" (The Living Room), and *The Fanlights* is developed from "Purificación en la Calle del Cristo."

The crises arising in *The Oxcart* and *Carnaval afuera, carnaval adentro* (Carnival Outside, Carnival Inside, premiered in 1962) correspond closely to the concept of rhythm within the created virtual space. In the first, the rhythm begins with a sense of the slow, peaceful life of the country, represented by the sound of the oxcart, and develops into the fragmented, nonrhythmic noise of city life, perhaps best represented by the jackhammer heard at the beginning of the third act. The disintegrating rhythm correlates to the breakdown of a family that has moved from the Puerto Rican countryside to New York City; its growing distance from the native culture; and finally Luis' death and Doña Gabriela's and Juanita's decision to return to their native land. The rhythm of *Carnaval afuera, carnaval adentro* reflects the chaos of Carnival juxtaposed with the tranquillity that the artist Angel advocates. This rhythmic conflict itself is mirrored in the characters' speeches and actions and in the stage set. For example, the first person to enter the stage is the maid Felícita, whose actions and nonsensical speech imitate the movement and sound of a train. Later, Angel's tranquillity is represented by violin music, quiet talk, and balletlike movements. The set portrays a colonial house whose best features are covered but not totally hidden by a trite, contemporary decor. The title likewise indicates that the conflict is spatial, with the "outside" being the actual Carnival in which participants are masked and the "inside" being the individual's disguising of his/her true motivations, resulting in hypocrisy. Both plays end in a death. In *The Oxcart* Luis is responsible for his own end because he stubbornly adheres to foreign ways. In *Carnaval afuera, carnaval adentro* the characters never give up their hypocrisy and in the end collectively assassinate Rosie, who represents their innocence.

The historical space of the past plays a key role in *La muerte no entrará en palacio* and *Mariana o el alba* (Mariana or the Dawn, premiered 1965). The first of these two plays dramatizes Governor Muñoz Marín's signing of the Commonwealth agreement, surrounding it with an aura of myth and immortality. The well-known events, however, are fictionalized as the famous and popular governor is murdered before he is able to sign the agreement and the murderer, who appears in the play's opening scene immortalized in the form of a statue to a hero, is his daughter. The play takes place on the terrace of the governor's mansion, a famous historic building called La Fortaleza (The Fortress) in present-day Puerto Rico and El Palacio in the play. The governor's movement toward signing the agreement gradually transforms the palace into a figurative prison, which those who live inside are afraid to leave. The governor's assassination in this famous space, before the agreement can be signed, leaves the audience to cope with Marqués' rewriting of history. In fact, Governor Muñoz Marín did sign the Commonwealth agreement in 1952, an event that created the political circumstances contemporary to the play's composition in 1956.

Mariana o el alba treats history in a slightly different way. The history re-created here is faithful in detail, but the historical space and events are unfamiliar to the audience (or were at the time of the play's writing). The play emphasizes the experience of time through waiting. First, the characters must wait for the unsuccessful revolution and Mariana's stillborn child. At play's end, the audience finds itself still waiting for the successful revolution. The spectators also are charged with initiating the unfulfilled revolution, since the play's heroes—being historical figures from the previous century—cannot. In this way, past, present, and future are actually fused into the virtual historical space created on the stage.

Marqués' last three plays, *Sacrificio en el Monte Moriah* (Sacrifice on Mount Moriah, premiered in 1970) and the unperformed twin plays *David y Jonatán/Tito y Berenice* (David and Jonathan/Tito and Berenice), treat space and time much differently, but the crises themselves follow a pattern comparable to that of the previous plays. The times and spaces dramatized are from a remote biblical past, and only the stories themselves are familiar. Marqués eliminates (or nearly so) the spatial and temporal limits that the stage would ordinarily impose. *Sacrificio en el Monte Moriah* presents the conflict of Abraham's thirst for material comforts and power at the cost of victimizing Sara and her son Isaac. The action shifts back and forth between a remote past and one even more remote to dramatize the motivation for Sara's final act of violence. The fourteen scenes shift between one stage space and another by the use of platforms and lights, creating the illusion of the fast-moving montage one usually expects from the cinema. This effect focuses the attention of the spectator more on the events dramatized than on the elements of real stage space and real time, making more explicit than ever the message that submitting to the materialistic values of a more powerful society leads to the violent destruction of humanistic values.

The same can be said of the twin plays *David y Jonatán* and *Tito y Berenice*, which the author requested be published and produced as one. The dynamic element of time in these plays, aside from a cinematic celerity like that of *Sacrificio en el Monte Moriah*, is the flashback. Events are presented in short impressionistic scenes with very few details, and the stage sets are for the most part simple to permit many rapid changes. The flashbacks provide the characters' motives that led to scenes previously portrayed and leave the spectator to fill in the missing details. Moreover, because both plays take place in biblical times and concern the Jewish people, time and space tie the works together. Structural parallels between the dramatized events and Puerto Rico's political and economic relationship to the United States imply the plays' relevance to the present world.

In view of the analogous patterns and themes in Marqués' works, it is appropriate to relate those patterns to his own circumstances. Marqués offers as an epigraph to his pantomime ballet, *Juan Bobo y la dama de occidente* (Juan Bobo and the Western Lady 1956), the following quotation from José Ortega y Gasset's *Meditaciones del Quijote* (*Meditations on Quixote*, 1914): "I am I and my circumstance, and if I don't save this, I don't save myself." This quotation expresses the essence of all Marqués' works. The confined spaces of his plays and the interior monologues of his fiction are analogous to his own living space on a small island between the Atlantic Ocean and the Caribbean Sea. While the seas might offer the unlimited freedom he advocates, the political relationship between Puerto Rico and the United States prevents the island's unique potential from developing fully. In a similar way, the materialism Marqués associates with the United States adversely affects both the people of his homeland and his characters.

Marqués' treatment of time in his theater and prose imitates the fusion of past and present that is so obvious in the juxtaposition of old and new buildings throughout Puerto Rico. Furthermore, the rhythms established in several of his works imitate that of the consumer society, which is portrayed as a threat to the survival of Puerto Rican culture. Marqués' handling of the passage of time—always the villain—suggests that while the people wait and fail to take a stand, time runs out so that any action comes too late.

René Marqués is one of the leading Puerto Rican writers of the twentieth century because of the boundless energy he dedicated to the intellectual history of his homeland. His expertly researched and well-developed essays touch on the issues most important to his fellow Puerto Ricans. He is further credited with unifying the authors of prose of his generation and rejuvenating the short story. In the theater, he continually worked to improve, refine, and develop the embryonic accomplishments of the previous generation. As a result of his insistence on better preparation and training for himself, he created a body of dramatic works that have influenced and helped to define dramaturgy in other parts of Hispanic America, including the Hispanic community within the country he saw as his principal antagonist, the United States. René Marqués, sincerely dedicated to the well-being of his people and of his land, was, and through his works continues to be, one of the great Latin American writers of the century.

SELECTED BIBLIOGRAPHY

Editions

Essays

"J.P. Sartre. *The Flies y No Exit.*" *Asomante* 3/4:88–91 (1947).

"Teatro puertorriqueño: *María Soledad.*" *El Mundo* 10:10, 17 (1947).

"T. Williams. *A Street Car Named Desire.*" *Asomante* 4/2:73–75 (1948).

"Usigli, Rodolfo—*Corona de sombra.*" *Asomante* 4/1: 97–100 (1948).

"Benavente, el hombre, el mito y la obra." *Asomante* 4/3:58–65 (1948).

"Usigli, Rodolfo—*El gesticulador.*" *Asomante* 4/3:71–73 (1948).

"J.P. Sartre. *Teatro.*" *Asomante* 5/2:96–98 (1949).

"T. Williams. *Summer and Smoke.*" *Asomante* 5/1:88–90 (1949).

"El existencialismo de T.S. Eliot." *Asomante* 6/3:92–102 (1950).

"Miller, Arthur—*Teatro.*" *Asomante* 7/3:75–82 (1951).

"Williams, Tennessee—*The Rose Tatoo.*" *Asomante* 8/1: 83–85 (1952).

"O'Neill, Eugene—*A Moon for the Misbegotten.*" *Asomante* 9/2:91–95 (1953).

"Notas" and "Autobiografía." In *Cuentos puertorriqueños de hoy,* an anthology selected and with a prologue and notes by Marqués. Mexico City, 1959. Pp. 97–107. 2nd ed. Río Piedras, Puerto Rico, 1968. 7th ed. 1981.

"Pesimismo literario y optimismo político: Su coexistencia en el Puerto Rico actual." *Cuadernos americanos* 18/3: 43–74 (1959). Essay Prize, Puerto Rican Atheneum, 1958.

"El puertorriqueño dócil (literatura y realidad psicológica)." *Cuadernos americanos* 21/1:144–195 (1962). Essay Prize, Puerto Rican Atheneum, 1960.

"El teatro de Ghelderode." *Asomante* 18/3:7–19 (1962).

"La función del escritor puertorriqueño en el momento actual." *Cuadernos americanos* 27/2:55–63 (1963).

"Las tres vertientes del problema del idioma." *El Mundo* 26:17 (1963).

Ensayos (1953–1966). Río Piedras, Puerto Rico, 1966. Rev. and aug. ed. 1972; published as *El puertorriqueño dócil y otros ensayos,* 1977.

"Luigi Pirandello: El hombre ante su espejo." *Asomante* 18/4:27–37 (1967).

"Memorias mínimas." *Puerto* 1:7–17 (1967).

Poetry

Peregrinación. Arecibo, Puerto Rico, 1944.

Novels and Short Stories

"Crepúsculo." *Alma latina* 11/285:59, 62 (1941).

"En el campo no es lo mismo." *Alma latina* 11/291:5, 20, 24, 54 (1941).

"Sus ojos verdes." *Alma latina* 16/298:10, 24, 58 (1941).

Otro día nuestro. With a prologue by Concha Meléndez. San Juan, 1955. Short stories. Includes "La Muerte" and "Otro día nuestro."

La víspera del hombre. Mexico City, 1959. 2nd ed. Río Piedras, Puerto Rico, 1970. 3rd ed. 1974.

En una ciudad llamada San Juan. Mexico City, 1960. Havana, 1962. 3rd ed., aug., Río Piedras, Puerto Rico, 1970. 4th ed., aug., 1974. 5th ed., aug., 1983. Short stories. Includes "Purificación en la Calle del Cristo."

La mirada. Río Piedras, Puerto Rico, 1975.

Inmersos en el silencio. Río Piedras, Puerto Rico, 1976. Short stories.

"La venganza." *Caribán* 1/3–4:1, 21, 22–24 (1985).

Plays

El hombre y sus sueños (Esbozo intrascendente para un drama trascendental). *Asomante* 4/2:58–72 (1948). Río Piedras, Puerto Rico, 1971.

La carreta. *Asomante* 7/4:67–87 (1951); 8/1:54–78 (1952); 8/3:66–92 (1952). San Juan, 1952. Río Piedras, Puerto Rico, 1961 (this edition is reprinted almost annually). Barcelona, 1962.

Juan Bobo y la dama de occidente. Pantomima puertorriqueña para un ballet occidental. Mexico City, 1956. 2nd ed. Río Piedras, Puerto Rico, 1971.

El sol y los MacDonald. *Asomante* 13/1:43–82 (1957).

La muerte no entrará en palacio. In *Teatro I.* Mexico City, 1959. In *El teatro hispanoamericano contemporáneo I,* edited by Carlos Solórzano. Mexico City, 1964.

Un niño azul para esa sombra. In *Teatro I.* Mexico City, 1959. First Prize, Atheneum, 1958. Award Puerto Rican Culture Institute, 1959. In *Teatro puertorriqueño. Tercer Festival. 1960.* San Juan, 1961. Pp. 17–127.

Los soles truncos. In *Teatro I.* Mexico City, 1959. Río Piedras, Puerto Rico, 1963. In *Teatro puertorriqueño. Noveno Festival. 1966.* San Juan, 1968. In *9 dramaturgos hispanoamericanos: Antología del teatro hispanoamericano del siglo XX,* edited by Frank Dauster, Leon Lyday, and George Woodyard. Ottawa, 1979. Pp. 11–62.

La casa sin reloj (Comedia antipoética en dos absurdos y un final razonable). In *Teatro puertorriqueño.* San Juan, 1960. Xalapa, Mexico, 1962.

El apartamiento. Encerrona en dos actos. In *Teatro puertorriqueño. Séptimo Festival.* San Juan, 1965. Pp. 247–277. Award, Atheneum, 1962. Also appears in *Three Contemporary Latin American Plays,* edited by Ruth S. Lamb. Waltham, Mass., 1971.

Mariana o el alba (*Drama histórico en tres actos y diez cuadros*). In *Teatro puertorriqueño. Octavo Festival*. San Juan, 1966. Pp. 503–728. Río Piedras, Puerto Rico, 1968.

Sacrificio en el Monte Moriah. Río Piedras, Puerto Rico, 1969.

David y Jonatán/Tito y Berenice (*Dos dramas de amor, poder y desamor*). Río Piedras, Puerto Rico, 1970.

Carnaval afuera, carnaval adentro (*carnavalada en tres pasos y varios golpes de tambor*). Río Piedras, Puerto Rico, 1971. Honorable Mention, Casa de las Américas, Havana, 1962.

Vía crucis del hombre puertorriqueño. Río Piedras, Puerto Rico, 1971.

Collected Plays

Teatro I (*Los soles truncos, Un niño azul para esa sombra, La muerte no entrará en palacio*). Mexico City, 1959. 2nd ed. Río Piedras, Puerto Rico, 1970.

Teatro II (*El hombre y sus sueños, El sol y los MacDonald*). Río Piedras, Puerto Rico, 1971.

Teatro III (*La casa sin reloj, El apartamiento*). Río Piedras, Puerto Rico, 1971.

Translations

"The Blue Kite." Translated by Eloise Roach. In *Americas*. Washington, D.C., 1965.

"Death." Translated by G. R. Coulthard. In *Short Story International*. New York, 1965. In *Caribbean Literature*. London, 1966.

The Docile Puerto Rican: Essays. Translated and with an introduction by Barbara Bockus Aponte. Philadelphia, 1976.

The Fanlights. Translated by Richard John Wiezell. In *The Modern Stage in Latin America: Six Plays*, edited by George W. Woodyard. New York, 1971.

"Give Us This Day." Translated by Catherine Randolph. In *New Voices of Hispanic America: An Anthology*, edited, translated, and with an introduction by Darwin J. Flakoll and Claribel Alegría. Boston, 1962.

The House of the Setting Suns. Translated by Willis Knapp Jones. In *Poet Lore* 59:99–131 (1965).

The Oxcart. Translated by Charles Pilditch. New York, 1969.

Biographical and Critical Studies

Dauster, Frank. "New Plays by René Marqués." *Hispania* 43/3:451–452 (1960).

————. "The Theater of René Marqués." *Symposium* 18/1:35–45 (1964).

Feeny, Thomas. "Woman's Triumph over Man in René Marqués's Theater." *Hispania* 65/2:187–193 (1982).

Holzapfel, Tamara. "The Theater of René Marqués: In Search of Identity and Form." In *Dramatists in Revolt: The New Latin American Theater*, edited by Leon F. Lyday and George W. Woodyard. Austin, Tex., 1976. Pp. 146–166.

Hortas, Carlos R. "René Marqués: *La mirada*: A Closer Look." *Latin American Literary Review* 8/16:196–212 (1980).

Lugo, Eunice. "*La víspera del hombre*: A Novel by René Marqués." In *Studies in Honor of M. G. Bernadette* (*Essays in Hispanic and Sephardic Culture*). New York, 1965. Pp. 245–270.

Lyday, Leon F., and George W. Woodyard. A *Bibliography of Latin American Theater Criticism: 1940–1970*. Austin, Tex., 1976.

Martin, Eleanor J. "*Calígula* and *La muerte no entrará en palacio*: A Study in Characterization." *Latin American Theatre Review* 9/2:21–30 (1976).

————. *René Marqués*. Boston, 1979.

Ortiz Griffin, Julia. "The Puerto Rican Woman in René Marqués' Drama." *Revista Chicano-Riqueña* 11/3–4:169–176 (1983).

Pilditch, Charles. *René Marqués: A Study of His Fiction*. New York, 1976.

Reynolds, Bonnie Hildebrand. "Coetaneity: A Sign of Crisis in *Un niño azul para esa sombra*." *Latin American Theatre Review* 17/1:37–45 (1983).

————. "*La carreta*: Virtual Space and Broken Rhythm." *Crítica hispánica* 7/1:75–83 (1985).

————. "The Multiples of Reality in *El apartamiento*." In *Selected Proceedings of the Mid-America Conference on Hispanic Literature*, edited by Luis T. González del Valle and Catherine Nickel. Lincoln, Neb., 1986. Pp. 93–101.

————. *Space, Time and Crisis: The Theatre of René Marqués*. York, S.C., 1988.

Rodríguez Ramos, Esther. "Aproximación a una bibliografía de René Marqués." *Sin nombre* 10/3:121–148 (1979).

Shaw, Donald L. "René Marqués' *La muerte no entrará en palacio*: An Analysis." *Latin American Theatre Review* 2/1:31–38 (1968).

Siemens, William L. "Assault on the Schizoid Wasteland: René Marqués' *El apartamiento*." *Latin American Theatre Review* 7/2:17–23 (1974).

João Cabral de Melo Neto

(1920–)

Richard Zenith

João Cabral de Melo Neto is often cited as the greatest poet of the so-called Generation of '45 in Brazil, though he might better be described as one who kept his distance from the group. Cabral shared the Generation of '45's criticism of modernism for having fallen into petty nationalism and formal sloppiness, but he faulted the new movement for its use of cheap devices, such as puns and gratuitous emotion, in lieu of disciplined composition. At its worst, the Generation of '45 was a nostalgic return to the highly refined "poetic" language of premodernist or even presymbolist days, and Cabral, who believed that poetry should be grounded in everyday reality, rejected as fantasy the group's celebration of the "sublime against the prosaic" (*Diário Carioca*, 21 December 1952).

The foundations of Cabral's poetic program were by that time already well established, but in succeeding decades his work took new and unexpected turns, thereby frustrating those critics who would categorize him and disappointing the literary schools that would claim him. In retrospect it is clear that in spite of some sudden shifts in style or theme, Cabral has consistently adhered to the rigor and logic of his basic ideology: to forge a vigorous poetry that needs no linguistic gimmicks or personal interferences to prop it up. Images and other poetic elements are reduced to their essential structural lines, which are then tightly organized into a "poem machine" that functions on its own with as little intrusion from the poet as possible.

Cabral's childhood provided the Brazilian themes and popular verse traditions that the poet would later merge with literary forms learned through his studies and travels. Born in Recife on 6 January 1920, João Cabral spent his early youth on the family's sugar plantations in the interior of Pernambuco. He was an avid reader, even as a young boy, and in the evenings the illiterate plantation workers would gather together to hear him recite *cordel* poems. These were narrative poems sold at the marketplace in pamphlets hanging from strings (hence the name *cordel*). Cabral would later use the cadences of these popular verses to describe, with ironic detachment, the often subhuman living conditions of northeast Brazil's sugarcane workers. In 1930 the family moved to Recife, where Cabral was deeply impressed by the Capibaribe River and the contrast between the majestic homes and the homeless people that lined different stretches of its banks.

João Cabral never went to college, but he was from a literary family—the poet Manuel Bandeira and the sociologist Gilberto Freyre were his cousins—and read modern French authors as an adolescent. He subsequently read authors in English and Spanish and also became interested in the visual arts. Stéphane Mallarmé, Paul Valéry, Francis Ponge, Carlos Drummond de Andrade, and Marianne Moore were among the poets he admired, and such painters as Piet Mondrian and Joan Miró were crucial to his aesthetic development, but Cabral has said that the architect Le Corbusier was the single greatest influence on his poetry.

Cabral moved to Rio de Janeiro in 1942 and married Stella Maria Barbosa in 1946. He joined Brazil's diplomatic service in 1945 and held numerous posts in Europe, Africa, and Latin America before being made an ambassador in 1972. He served as ambassador to various countries and retired to Rio de Janeiro in 1987. Of all the countries where Cabral has lived, Spain has left the deepest mark on his poetry. Besides using Spain for the setting of many of his poems, Cabral also has incorporated and reworked Spanish verse forms, particularly the medieval *cuaderna vía*, or "fourfold way," employed by the clerical poets.

All of these different influences, which in a mediocre poet might have resulted in a kind of pastiche, have led Cabral to a pure and strict verse that uses language to create landscapes rather than to announce them. Cabral's vision is architectural—poetry not as revelation but as construction—and while Valéry had already described the same vision in theory, few poets besides Cabral have succeeded in producing verses so rigorously limpid and at the same time tightly woven. Cabral's impersonal style has enabled him to document in the starkest terms, and without pamphleteering, his country's social problems. In recognition of his achievements, Cabral was elected to the Brazilian Academy of Letters in 1968.

João Cabral de Melo Neto was twenty-two years old when he published his first book of poems, *Pedra do Sono* (Stone of Sleep, 1942). In these short pieces the poet makes free and even playful associations of words, but the sometimes ethereal quality of the verses is brought down to earth by the plastic relief of their images. Cabral was still searching for his way, oscillating between a surrealistic preoccupation with the poetry latent in sleeping states and his desire for hard clarity, as in the last lines of "Poesia" (Poetry):

jardins de minha ausência
imensa e vegetal;
ó jardins de um céu
viciosamente frequentado:
onde o mistério maior
do sol da luz da saúde?

gardens of my vast
and vegetable absence;
o gardens of an enchanting,
addictive sky:
where is the larger mystery
of light, the sun, health?

O Engenheiro (The Engineer, 1945) largely abandons the intuitive technique and emotional suggestion of Cabral's first collection. No longer concerned with the expression of subjective states, here the poet makes verses with the logic of a builder. Never had a Brazilian poet propounded in such clear terms this poetry of construction, from which the adherents of the international movement known as concretism and succeeding vanguard figures would take their cues:

A luz, o sol, o ar livre
envolvem o sonho do engenheiro.
O engenheiro sonha coisas claras:
superfícies, tênis, um copo de água.

O lápis, o esquadro, o papel;
o desenho, o projeto, o número:
o engenheiro pensa o mundo justo,
mundo que nenhum véu encobre.

(Em certas tardes nós subíamos
ao edifício. A cidade diária,
como um jornal que todas liam,
ganhava um pulmão de cimento e vidro.)

A água, o vento, a claridade,
de um lado o rio, no alto as nuvens,
situavam na natureza o edifício
crescendo de suas forças simples.

Light, sun and the open air
surround the dream of the engineer.
The engineer dreams clear things:
surfaces, tennis courts, a glass of water.

A pencil, a T-square, paper;
designs, projects, numbers:
the engineer imagines the world correct,
a world that is never veiled.

(Sometimes we went up the building.
The daily city, like a newspaper
for all to read, was gaining
a lung of cement and glass.)

The water, the wind, the brightness,
the river on one side and the clouds on high
made a place in nature for the building,
growing by its own simple strength.

This title poem not only tells but also shows by its very form the aspiration and technique of the poet-engineer. His "dream" is not wishful, nor does it proceed from the imprecise world of the subconscious. The engineer's dream is thought itself, the projecting of definite ideas onto paper or into concrete. It is as if the engineer would by his labors show us a Platonic world of pure ideas—"a world that is never veiled"—existing not in the human mind but in the natural order of which man is only a part. The city, and the building within the city, have their places in nature alongside the clouds and the river. In this broad view of nature, man—the individual—is not given great importance, but mankind—the city—is exalted as its most original component.

The poet-engineer's building-poem gives a "lung" to the city and a perspective from which we can see the city as plainly as we read a newspaper. Finally the engineer stands back, allowing his construction to take its place in the world, to grow by its own force. True to the spirit of the poem, Cabral announces a new and radical poetic program without resorting to personal appeals or oratory. He applies his techniques—analogy, assonance, and the four-line stanza, all of which will become mainstays in his poetry—in such a way that the poem seems to carry itself forward.

The mechanics of poetic creation become the nearly exclusive theme of the trilogy published in 1947 under the title *Psicologia da Composição* (Psychology of Composition). The title work catalogs the difficulties and frustrations of poetic creation, while Cabral's virulent *Antiode* (Antiode) categorically re-

nounces lyrical poetry. The subtitle—*Contra a Poesia Dita Profunda* (Against So-called Profound Poetry)—stands as a fundamental tenet of João Cabral's ideology, and he wastes no time in removing poetry from its sacred standing:

> *Poesia, te escrevia*
> *flor! conhecendo*
> *que és fezes. Fezes*
> *como qualquer . . .*

> Poetry, I wrote you
> flower! knowing
> you are feces. Feces
> like any other . . .

Later the poet decides that he may again call poetry "flower," but with this difference:

> *Flor é a palavra*
> *flor, verso inscrito*
> *no verso, como as*
> *manhãs no tempo.*

> Flower is the word
> flower, verse
> inscribed in verse,
> as mornings in time.

"Flower" is no longer a metaphor, but is what it is: the word flower, with no more right to inclusion in the poem than "feces" or any other word.

Having purified his verse of the sublime and decorative language that occasionally encumbered *Pedra do Sono*, Cabral was ready to write about austere subjects with uncompromising diction. *O Cão sem Plumas* (The Dog Without Feathers, 1950) initiates a cycle of narrative poems that focus on the Capibaribe River and the poverty-stricken people who live on its shores. It is a common, unsophisticated man rather than a sociologist who speaks, and his unpretty, unpolished language reinforces the message of frank misery. The poetic tension that characterized *O Engenheiro* and *Psicologia da Composição* is less evident. Metaphors are introduced in the most commonplace manner, by "like" and "as," for here even poetry must yield to the urgency of the discourse. This is no sloppy art or poetic laziness; on the contrary, every prosaic element and even clichés have been deliberately placed. This is in keeping with Cabral's ambition: to achieve a poetry whose architecture perfectly and purposefully fits its thematic content, so that the two become indistinguishable.

João Cabral's communicative success reached its highest point in *Morte e Vida Severina* (*Death and Life of a Severino*, 1956), the most widely read and translated of all his works. A staged version of the dramatic poem (subtitled "Auto de Natal Pernambucano" [A Pernambuco Nativity Play]) won prizes in Brazil and France and brought international stature to Cabral. "*Somos muitos Severinos / iguais em tudo na vida*" (We are many Severinos / equal in everything in life), says the protagonist, a prototype of the northeastern migrant who journeys hopefully to Recife. He encounters exploitation and misery in the "rosório de vilas" (rosary of small towns) along the way but realizes in the end that human life, no matter how oppressed, still offers some hope for change.

The settings for the poems in *Paisagens com Figuras* (Landscapes with Figures, 1956) alternate between the poet's native Pernambuco and Spain, where he had been living since 1947. As with Cabral's destitute homeland, the arid Spanish countryside offered analogues for his harsh and exact poetry. Of all the bullfighters described in "Alguns Toureiros" (Toreadors), Cabral singled out

> o de nervos de madeira,
> de punhos secos de fibra,
> o da figura de lenha,
> lenha seca de caatinga,
>
> o que melhor calculava
> o fluido aceiro da vida,
> o que com mais precisão
> roçava a morte em sua fímbria,
>
> o que à tragédia deu número,
> à vertigem, geometria,
> decimais à emoção
> e ao susto, peso e medida.

> the one with wooden nerves,
> whose fists are dry and fibrous,
> with a figure like a stick,
> a piece of dried-out brush,

> the one who knew to calculate
> the steely fluid of life,
> who with the greatest precision
> brushed with death on the fringe,

> who gave a number to tragedy,
> decimals to feelings,
> to vertigo a geometry,
> and height and weight to fear.

Quaderna (Four Spot, 1960) documents Cabral's increasing awareness of the similarities between northeast Brazil and Spain. The poet's contact with Spain's dry, unyielding plateau and its discouraged inhabitants, still under the dictator Francisco Franco, seemed to sharpen his memories of the flatness and poverty of his homeland. This collection contains poems about women, rare in Cabral's work, poems about poetry itself, and poems about cemeteries. Common to all of these works is the poet's ever sparer diction, which seeks to communicate subjects in their most essential aspects. "Cemitério Pernambucano (Floresta do Navio)" (Cemetery in Pernambuco) satirizes political orators whose florid rhetoric contrasts dramatically with the

> . . . fôlha plana
> do Sertão, onde, desnuda,
> a vida não ora, fala,
> e com palavras agudas.

> . . . flat sheet
> of the backlands, where naked
> life does not make speeches
> but talks with short sharp words.

It is this language of the arid backlands of northeast Brazil that Cabral takes as his model, and the backlands, more than a geographical area, represent honest perception, "naked life."

The quatrain that characterized *Quaderna* returns to serve as a building block in *Serial* (Serial, 1961), while the poet steps further into the background. The first person singular is entirely absent from this collection, whose title suggests the series produced by constructivist artists and dodecaphonic composers. These sixteen series are not the anonymous output of an assembly line, but neither are they presented as the objects of a sublime art. Rather than invoking hidden meanings, Cabral strives to harmonize word and image, so that the poem reads like an objective document.

A Educação pela Pedra (Education by Stone, 1966) is Cabral's most audacious attempt to free his art from individualism. This collection of forty-eight two-part poems, formulated as if they were theorems, is as hard and didactic as the title promises, and one might expect that its fanatic symmetry would produce a tedious verse, but Cabral's ingenious facing off of key words, images, and entire poems achieves a masterful counterpoint such as few other poets have accomplished. In the title poem, Cabral expounds his belief that poetry is more work than inspiration:

> Una educação pela pedra: por lições;
> para aprender da pedra . . .
> captar sua voz inenfática, impessoal

> An education by stone: through lessons;
> to learn from the stone . . .
> to catch its level, impersonal voice

Only by exact and systematic operations does poetry attain the consistency and resilience of a stone.

Museu de Tudo (Museum of Everything, 1975), as the title suggests, focuses on a wide range of themes, styles, and geographical settings, whereas *A Escola das Facas* (The School of Knives, 1980) is set entirely in Pernambuco. The poems of this latter collection are still tightly and rigorously constructed, but they also have a lyric quality that, though never wholly absent despite the poet's own claims to the contrary, is now more accessible. The geography of Pernambuco is as barren as ever, the knives—and the poet's words—just as sharp, but the poetry seems to sing nevertheless.

Cabral's next book, *Auto do Frade* (The Friar, 1983), returns to the dramatic narrative style of *Death and Life of a Severino*. More accurately, both works can be regarded as plays written in verse. *Auto do Frade*, which has been dramatized for the stage, tells of the last day in the life of Frei Caneca, who was sentenced to death in 1825 for republican ideas and for his leadership in the Pernambuco revolutionary movement of the previous year.

The ninety poems in Cabral's *Agrestes* (Rough and Rude, 1985) constitute an autobiography of sorts. The book begins with poems about Pernambuco, particularly childhood remembrances of it, and ends with poems that talk about death in Cabral's customarily even, detached tone. In between there are poems about places the poet has lived—Spain, Africa, and Ecuador—and about writers and artists he admires. Cabral's quasi-autobiography is unusual in that whereas a traditional autobiography cites historical details, places, and other people in order to tell the author's personal story, Cabral tells about the people, places, and things he has known for their own sake. Like a scientist taking notes, he uses the first person to say "I observed" rather than "I felt." Some poets write to express the world inside them; Cabral writes poems in order to create a world. In "Homenagem Renovada a Marianne Moore" (Renewed Homage to Marianne Moore) he credits her for showing

> que a poesia não é de dentro,
> que é como casa, que é de fora;
> que embora se viva de dentro
> se há de construir, que é uma coisa
> que quem faz faz para fazer-se
> —muleta para a perna coxa.

> that poetry is not on the inside,
> but is a house in which to reside,
> and before one lives inside it
> it must be built—this something
> one makes to make oneself able,
> this crutch for the one who is lame.

In a verse-writing career that has spanned almost half a century, João Cabral has successfully built a durable house not only for himself, but also for readers from a wide range of cultures. Following the slow "education by stone" that couples patience with passion, he has achieved a poetry that on the one hand is veritable and verifiable art, and on the other hand makes a stirring and meaningful sociological statement. The poet himself has stayed in the background, like the engineer who from a distance regards his construction "growing by its own simple strength."

JOÃO CABRAL DE MELO NETO

SELECTED BIBLIOGRAPHY

Editions

Poetry

Pedra do Sono. Recife, Brazil, 1942.
Os Três Mal-amados. Rio de Janeiro, 1943.
O Engenheiro. Rio de Janeiro, 1945.
Psicologia da Composição. Barcelona, 1947.
O Cão sem Plumas. Barcelona, 1950; 2nd ed. Rio de Janeiro, 1984.
O Rio. São Paulo, 1954.
Duas Águas. Rio de Janeiro, 1956. Includes previously published works plus *Morte e Vida Severina*, *Paisagens com Figuras*, and *Uma Faca só Lâmina*.
Quaderna. Lisbon, 1960.
Dois Parlamentos. Madrid, 1961.
Terceira Feira. Rio de Janeiro, 1961. Includes *Quaderna*, *Dois Parlamentos*, and *Serial*.
A Educação pela Pedra. Rio de Janeiro, 1966.
Museu de Tudo. Rio de Janeiro, 1975; 2nd ed. 1976.
A Escola das Facas. Rio de Janeiro, 1980; 2nd ed. 1982.
Auto do Frade. Rio de Janeiro, 1983; 3rd ed. 1984.
Agrestes, Rio de Janeiro, 1985; 2nd ed. 1986.
Crime na Calle Relator. Rio de Janeiro, 1987.

Collected Poetry

Antologia Poética. Rio de Janeiro, 1966; 6th ed. 1986.
Os Melhores Poemas de João Cabral de Melo Neto. São Paulo, 1985.
Morte e Vida Severina e Outros Poemas em Voz Alta. Rio de Janeiro, 1966; 23rd ed. 1987.
Poesias Completas. Rio de Janeiro, 1968; 4th ed. 1986. Includes all poetry published through 1966.
Poesia Completa 1940–1980. Lisbon, 1986.
Poesia Crítica. Rio de Janeiro, 1982.

Essays

Considerações Sobre o Poeta Dormindo. Supplement to *Renovação.* Recife, Brazil, 1941.
Joan Miró. Barcelona, 1950; Rio de Janeiro, 1952.
"A Geração de 45." *Diário Carioca,* 23 November 1952. Sec. 3, p. 3; 30 November 1952. Sec. 3, p. 3; 7 December 1952. Sec. 3, p. 1; 21 December 1952. Sec. 3, p. 1.
"Poesia e Composição—A Inspiração e o Trabalho de Arte." In *Revista Brasileira de Poesia* 7. São Paulo, 1956. Reprinted in *Vanguarda Européia e Modernismo brasileiro,* edited by Gilberto Mendonça Teles. Petrópolis, Brazil, 1976.

Da Função Moderna da Poesia. São Paulo, 1957. Reprinted in *João Cabral de Melo Neto,* by Benedito Nunes. Petrópolis, Brazil, 1971.

Translations

Many translations of Cabral's poems have appeared in periodicals. The following list includes only translations found in books.
An Anthology of Twentieth-Century Brazilian Poetry. Edited by Elizabeth Bishop and Emanuel Brasil. Middletown, Conn., 1972.
The Borzoi Anthology of Latin American Literature 2. Edited by Emir Rodríguez Monegal. New York, 1977. Includes *O Cão sem Plumas,* translated by Thomas Colchie.
Latin American Writing Today. Edited by J. M. Cohen. London, 1967.
Modern Brazilian Poetry. Translated and edited by John Nist. Bloomington, Ind., 1962.
Poesia Brasileira Moderna: A Bilingual Anthology. Edited by José Neistein; translated by Manoel Cardozo. Washington, D.C., 1972.

Interviews

"A Arquitetura do Verso." *Veja,* 28 June 1972. Pp. 3–5.
Rodman, Selden. In *Tongues of Fallen Angels.* New York, 1974. Pp. 219–231.
"João Cabral, Nu e Cru." *Isto É,* 5 November 1980. Pp. 53–55.
Steen, Edla van. In *Viver & escrever.* São Paulo, 1981. Pp. 99–109.
"Entrevista de João Cabral de Melo Neto." In *João Cabral: A Poesia do Menos,* edited by Antonio Carlos Secchin. São Paulo, 1985. Pp. 219–307.

Biographical and Critical Studies

Barbosa, João Alexandre. *As Ilusões da Modernidade.* São Paulo, 1986.
———. *A Imitação da Forma.* São Paulo, 1975.
Buarque de Holanda, Sérgio. *Cobra de Vidro.* São Paulo, 1978. Pp. 167–180.
Campos, Haroldo de. "O Geômetra Engajado." In *Metalinguagem.* Petrópolis, Brazil, 1967. Pp. 67–78.
Carone, Modesto. *A Poética do Silêncio.* São Paulo, 1979.
Escorel, Lauro. *A Pedra e o Rio.* São Paulo, 1973.
Gullar, Ferreira. *Vanguarda e Subdesenvolvimento.* Rio de Janeiro, 1969. Pp. 72–81.

1252

Houaiss, Antônio. *Seis Poetas e um Problema.* Rio de Janeiro, 1960. Pp. 97–130.

Lima, Luís Costa. *A Metamorfose do Silêncio.* Rio de Janeiro, 1974. Pp. 73–128.

Merquior, José Guilherme. *A Astúcia da Mímese.* Rio de Janeiro, 1972. Pp. 69–172.

Nist, John. *The Modernist Movement in Brazil.* Austin, Tex., 1967. Pp. 179–183.

Nunes, Benedito. *João Cabral de Melo Neto.* Petrópolis, Brazil, 1971.

Peixoto, Marta. *Poesia com Coisas.* São Paulo, 1983.

Sampaio, Maria Lúcia Pinheiro. *Processos Retóricos na Obra de João Cabral de Melo Neto.* São Paulo, 1980.

Secchin, Antonio Carlos. *João Cabral: A Poesia do Menos.* São Paulo, 1985.

Senna, Marta de. *João Cabral: Tempo e Memória.* Rio de Janiero, 1980.

Soares, Angélica Maria Santos. *O Poema, Construção às Avessas.* Rio de Janiero, 1978.

Zagury, Eliane. *A Palavra e os Ecos.* Petrópolis, Brazil, 1971. Pp. 74–85, 102–115.

Mario Benedetti

(1920–   )

María Rosa Olivera Williams

Mario Benedetti was born on 14 September 1920 in Paso de los Toros, a town in the department of Tacuarembó, Uruguay. When he was four years old, his parents moved to the capital, Montevideo, and this city, with its European style and aspirations, shaped Benedetti and inspired his writing. Benedetti defined himself as *Montevideano*, and his literary work is essentially urban. In Uruguay, nearly half the population lives in Montevideo, yet, until the end of the 1930's, Uruguayan literature had been primarily rural. The prestige of *gaucho* and, later on, creole works (in which *gauchos* and rural men were seen nostalgically) kept the national literature essentially rural in character and subject matter. In 1939, Juan Carlos Onetti, the greatest Uruguayan novelist of the twentieth century, complained that Montevideo did not exist, that writers did not re-create the city in their works.

Benedetti's literary work shows the development of Uruguayans through two periods. The first provided a very critical and realistic portrait of their lives in Montevideo, and the second reflected their diaspora, which occurred as the result of the dictatorial military regime that governed Uruguay from 27 June 1973 until 1 March 1985. Beginning as a very localist literature that reflected the dreams and deceptions, the frustration and mediocrity, of the Uruguayan middle class, Benedetti's literary works have moved parallel with Uruguayan history and have linked the suffering of his countrymen to the suffering of the rest of Latin America.

Benedetti is a prolific writer who has worked within all genres: poetry, narratives (novels and short stories), essays, dramas, political articles, and polemical songs. His passion for the present, for everything that interests and worries Latin Americans, especially Uruguayans, suffuses his writing, colors it, and gives it colloquial and almost journalistic characteristics. Through his transformation into literature of middle-class myths and reactions to contemporary history, he has become the sagacious and sympathetic contemporary analyst of the Uruguayan.

His first book, a collection of poems entitled *La víspera indeleble* (The Ineffaceable Eve, 1945), was the product of a young writer who was learning his profession. Benedetti regretted its publication, and when in 1963 he started collecting his poetry in a volume entitled *Inventario* (Inventory), he did not include any of the poems of *La víspera indeleble*. Benedetti continued his development by publishing in many literary magazines, some of which he edited: *Marginalia* (1948), *Número* (1943–1955; 1966), and the literary section of the journal *Marcha* (1954; 1960). In 1948, he published a book of essays,

Peripecia y novela (Incident and Novel), which won the Premio del Ministerio de Instrucción Pública; in 1949, the short-story collection *Ésta mañana* (This Morning); in 1950, the volume of poetry *Sólo mientras tanto* (Only in the Meanwhile); and in 1951, *El último viaje y otros cuentos* (The Last Trip and Other Stories). All these books, which were written during Benedetti's literary initiation, were revised and published in later editions.

The short stories of *Ésta mañana* show Benedetti's literary preferences: William Faulkner, Marcel Proust (whom he admired especially), James Joyce, Virginia Woolf, and Juan Carlos Onetti. Onetti had already adopted and reformed the narrative strategies of the masters of Western literature, and his work became influential among the young writers of the Generation of '45. Stream of consciousness and the interior monologue are the predominant narrative techniques in *Ésta mañana*. The young Benedetti sought to surprise, to astonish his readers with his short narrations. Benedetti wrote in his book *Sobre artes y oficios: Ensayo* (On Arts and Professions: Essay, 1968) that "the effect of the short story is the surprise, the astonishment, the revelation" (p. 22). Powerful, sudden effect—impact—is for Benedetti one of the essential characteristics of the genre, even if the complex structure of the short stories of his first collection weakens the impact.

Nevertheless, as was noticed by one of the most sensible critics of Benedetti, Jorge Ruffinelli, this early book contained the themes that a few years later would make Benedetti a best-selling author. "El presupuesto" ("The Budget") presents the office world, with its ho-hum characters who dream of a salary raise that never arrives and with its worthless bureaucratic structure that traps public employees in a maze of papers and endless meetings. In "Ésta mañana" (This Morning), Uruguay and Montevideo are presented as the realms of the middle class, where people are divided into two groups: bosses and subordinates who envy and loathe their bosses but want to become bosses themselves. The negative effect of a routine life is explored in "Como siempre" (Like Always) and "Idilio" (Idyl). In this first book, Benedetti also focuses on the topics of death, love (its deterioration and destruction owing to the tedious life of the characters), fate, and time as a powerful force that human beings cannot hope to overcome.

Benedetti's first novel, *Quién de nosotros* (Who of Us, 1953), is a short work about a love triangle in which all the relationships end in frustration. In *Quién de nosotros*, Benedetti continued his mastering of the narrative techniques of Faulkner, Woolf, and Joyce. The story of the novel is narrated according to the different perspectives of its characters. Even when Benedetti's books reflect his apprenticeship, the gray tones of his literary world and the mediocrity of his characters did not correspond to the myth of Uruguay as the "Switzerland of America," where, in the words of a popular phrase of President Batlle's era, "nothing could disturb its calmness and security." Benedetti, like Onetti, foresaw the problems of the proud Uruguayan society. While the economic structure of the country experienced a financial crisis in 1955, signs of the weakening of the system had begun to appear in the late 1930's. Benedetti paid attention to those signs and portrayed them in the weaknesses of his characters.

In 1956, Benedetti published *Poemas de la oficina* (Office Poems), and with this book Uruguayan poetry changed. Benedetti introduced a new theme to poetry: life, or lack of life, in an office. This topic was considered antipoetic since there was thought to be nothing interesting in the monotonous routine of an office. Nevertheless, numbers, balances, inventories, accounts, salaries, budgets, ink stains, calendars, and telephone calls became the new language of poetry. The book was a success. It interpreted the bureaucratic middle class that constituted a large part of the population of Montevideo—the hydrocephalic head of the country. Benedetti himself had been an employee of the bureaucratic system, and he knew intimately the feelings of people who were intelligent and educated but whose lives deteriorated in an office, without hope for the future. The style of *Poemas de la oficina* is direct and colloquial, which makes the poetry very easy to read. As Ruffinelli noticed, this kind of poetry, which would become successful years later, was not popular in Latin America in 1956. It was the novelty of the book that assured its success.

Poemas de la oficina initiated Benedetti's period of literary maturity. The books that followed—the short stories *Montevideanos* (1959), the novel *La tregua* (*The Truce*, 1960), and the essays *El país de la cola de paja* (The Country with the Straw Tail, 1960)—made him the most-read Uruguayan author in his own country and abroad. The theme of *Poemas de la oficina* is developed in four genres, according to four different perspectives. Benedetti had found the topic he knew best: the world of the middle class to which he belonged. His characters are common people whose stories are or may be everybody's stories—although they take unexpected turns—and the style of his narrative and poetry is simple and clear. Benedetti's readings and literary preferences dissolved in a style that was coherent with his theme. His works became mature literature.

If in *Poemas de la oficina* Benedetti dealt with the bureaucratic sector of Montevideo, in the short stories *Montevideanos* he enlarged his social spectrum to include the entire middle class, in all its economic and social aspects. Benedetti succeeded in interpreting and representing the Uruguayan urban sector through an increasing understanding of his characters and a strong command of narrative techniques. Although he was still reading foreign literature when he wrote *Montevideanos*, he managed to develop his own style. Commenting on one of the best short stories of the collection, "Retrato de Elisa" (Portrait of Elisa), Benedetti said, "I do not know whether Enrique Amorim or Rodríguez Monegal said that he was surprised that being myself a reader and admirer of Henry James I had not developed that topic following Henry James' style" (Ruffinelli, *Palabras en orden*, pp. 221–222).

In all the books of his period of literary maturity, there is a moral and humane criticism of individuals who are motivated by mediocre goals, by envy, by inertia, by tediousness. Benedetti showed empathy for his characters, but at the same time he separated himself from them. He understood his characters' idiosyncracies—the idiosyncracies of Uruguayans in the 1950's—but he worried for the future of a country whose inhabitants had been anesthetized by old myths that no longer worked. In "Retrato de Elisa," Elisa Montes, who had fallen from her middle-class status into poverty, struggled until the end of her life (she was dying of cancer) to differentiate her extreme poverty from that of "the populace." She could do

nothing to stop her decline, but she was preoccupied with saving the illusory "nobility" of her class. Benedetti felt that another sort of cancer like the one that ate Elisa Montes was torturing and destroying the country. Nevertheless, there was no overt political or social criticism in the works of this period. The alienation of the Uruguayan was re-created through the psychology of Benedetti's characters.

The Truce and *El país de la cola de paja* are works of transition. Both the novel and the book of essays contain traces of political concern, even though they are not political works. The characters of *The Truce*— Santomé, who is about to turn fifty years old and whose only expectation is his retirement, and Avellaneda, the young woman who for a short time has given Santomé love, life, and hope—start thinking of the problems of their flattened and grayish country. They have progressive attitudes. They search for authenticity in a country of appearances. Avellaneda is not the woman-trophy in the office, the one wanted by the employees because she is the property of the boss, as women had been portrayed in Benedetti's previous works (an excellent example is "Familia Iriarte" ["The Iriartes"] from *Montevideanos*). She is instead a fellow employee as well as Santomé's companion, friend, partner, and lover. By 1957, the time of the novel, Uruguayans are becoming aware of the illness of their country, but it is still too early for changes to occur, and Avellaneda dies. The novel won the Municipal Prize for Literature and was later adapted for the theater and the cinema. Positive literary criticism was accompanied by a strong popular reception in all its versions. *The Truce* strengthened Benedetti's position as the reigning Uruguayan best-selling author of his time.

Although *El país de la cola de paja* and *The Truce* take different forms, they share an identical function: to show the moral crisis that Uruguay was suffering. If in the novel Benedetti did not take up the subject of politics, in the essays he wrote about the corruption of the political parties. Benedetti did not pretend to assume the role of a political scientist or sociologist. In the prologue of the first edition of *El país de la cola de paja* he acknowledged his limitations and said, "I do not want those limitations to make me feel like an accomplice of the great silence that surrounds the present moral crisis, which is undoubtedly the largest in our short history as a nation." Nevertheless, critics reacted negatively to the book. Silence had been very thick in Uruguay, and critics had become accomplices of the rhetoric of silence. But Uruguayans found in Benedetti's essays an expression of their feelings and thoughts, and this book became another best seller. (In one year, there were four reprintings.)

The year 1959 was a very important one for Benedetti. Two events made him become a "compromised" writer, a writer deeply interested in the political dimension of Uruguay and that of the rest of Latin America. These were the Cuban Revolution and his trip to the United States under a fellowship from the American Council of Education. The Cuban Revolution showed him that Uruguay was not isolated from the rest of Latin America and that Latin America had a new possibility for the solution of its problems. The trip to the United States, besides allowing him to know the great American theater— he received a fellowship because of the success of his play *Ida y vuelta* (Round Trip, written in 1955, presented in 1958, and published in 1963)—showed him poverty, social injustice, racism, and solitude. His American experience is reflected in the poem entitled "Cumpleaños en Manhattan" ("Birthday in Manhattan"), which appears in the book *Poemas del hoyporhoy* (Day to Day Poems, 1961). The poem was written in New York, where Benedetti turned thirty-nine years old. His time in the United States is also revealed in the short story "El resto es selva" (The Rest Is Jungle), in *Montevideanos*. Both works show the solitude of the protagonist in a world that he cannot penetrate. But his solitude is not an alienation. In the powerful country where different races and nationalities meet, the protagonist identifies with the marginal Latin Americans.

His third novel, *Gracias por el fuego* (Thank You for the Light, 1965), also re-creates some of Benedetti's experience in the United States. The novel opens with a group of Uruguayan tourists and Uruguayan residents of the United States meeting at a Hispanic restaurant in the Spanish section of New York City. Benedetti comments on the poverty, dirtiness, and inhuman conditions in which Hispanics live in New York. Nevertheless, the Uruguayans who are away from their country do not see the misery that surrounds them and admire the greatness

and excellence of the United States. While the Uruguayan myth for several decades had been that Uruguay was the "Switzerland of America," after the economic crisis of 1955, Uruguayans lost faith in their country and saw it as a crippling place where no one wanted to work. One of the women of the group says: "It is painful, but we must recognize that among us, the working class is the mob. Here it is different. Here the worker is a conscious man, who knows that his salary depends on the capital that gives him work, and thus he defends it" (p. 16).

The Uruguayan privileged class tried to blame the working class for the crisis of the country. In the novel, a tragedy (the Uruguayan floods of 1958) strikes these representatives of the privileged sector who feel guilty for their position, who cry for and pity their distant country. Although some critics thought that the chapter set in the United States did not add much to the main story of the novel, which takes place in Montevideo, it is important that the protagonist, Ramón Budiño, is one of the Uruguayans at the New York restaurant. After his return from the United States and after thinking of his country when he was abroad, Budiño needs to examine his guilt, which is the central problem in the story of his family. Budiño's drama—his frustrating struggle against his father, the powerful politician and businessman Edmundo Budiño, which ends in Ramón's suicide—cannot be a local existential story. The sociopolitical conditions of Uruguay that force Ramón to act are related to the rest of Latin America.

Ramón realizes that one cannot live according to one's principles and morality because "others"—the hegemonic sector, his father—dictate principles and morality. Ramón belongs to the generation who knew the apparently paradisal Uruguay in their childhood, and he admired his father as one of its creators. But at the same time he is aware that the creators of the old myth are the destroyers of the country. Ramón loves and hates his father. These feelings that he discovers should be read not as an Oedipus complex but as the frustrations of a group that does not know how to fight against the system that makes possible its well-being. Thus, Ramón's death is a positive act. Even when he could not destroy the system—he could not kill his father—he stopped supporting it. The younger generation, represented by Ramón's son Gustavo, will have to change the corrupted system.

Gracias por el fuego, like *The Truce* and *El país de la cola de paja*, presents a moral analysis of the problems of Uruguay. In each book, Benedetti enlarges the realm of his characters and moves from the psychological study of the characters into a social study of their world. Benedetti finished his third novel in 1963 and entered it in the annual literary competition sponsored by Seix Barral, the Barcelona publishers. Although the novel was one of the finalists in the competition, Spanish censorship did not allow its publication. The "localism" of the early Benedetti had vanished, and although he was and is one of the most conscientious Uruguayan writers in regard to his country, his literature reflects many, if not all, of the contemporary Hispanic societies. Two years later, *Gracias por el fuego* was published in Uruguay.

During the 1960's, Benedetti traveled extensively: to Santiago, Chile (1962), to Stockholm and Copenhagen (1963), to Havana (1966 and 1967), to Mexico (1967), and to Paris, where he stayed for almost a year (1966–1967). In 1968, Benedetti started going to Cuba and staying for long periods. He said that one social experience that was reflected in his literature was the Cuban Revolution, not the abstract concept of the revolution, but the two and a half years that he spent working on the island. In 1969, he visited Algeria.

In the 1960's, Benedetti published novels, short stories, plays, literary and political essays, and poetry. In the short stories of *La muerte y otras sorpresas* (Death and Other Surprises, 1968), Benedetti looks for new ways to express his themes, which have become more universal. *Inventario* compiles all of Benedetti's poetry since 1950 and has continued growing until the tenth edition of 1980, with eight new volumes added to the first edition.

In the 1970's, Benedetti began a very intensive political and literary life. By the end of the 1960's, Uruguay had been transformed from a country where "nothing could disturb its calmness and security" into a country where everything was in a state of unrest: the 1965 financial crash; the struggling of the Tupamaro guerrilla movement, and the increasing violence of police reaction; the systematic and violent repression of the demonstrations of the labor unions and mass manifestations against the government between 1967 and 1972; and finally the coup d'etat of 27 June 1973. In 1971, Benedetti became the leader of the "Movement of the Independents of 26 March," which integrated the union of left-leaning parties, "Frente Amplio" (Wide Front). His political speeches and articles, which had been published in the journal *Marcha*, were compiled in *Crónicas del 71* (Chronicles of '71), published in 1972. Benedetti opposed the government, which was becoming more and more repressive, not only with his writing, like the rest of the progressive intellectuals; he also participated directly in Uruguayan political life.

In 1971, Benedetti published *El cumpleaños de Juan Ángel* (Juan Ángel's Birthday). This novel in verse was his literary response to the sociopolitical situation in Uruguay. Benedetti said during an interview with Ruffinelli that Uruguay, within a very short period of time, was going through different historical periods; as a symbol of that rapid process, he synthesized in one day the entire life of a character. The day that summarizes the character's life is the day when Osvaldo Puente becomes Juan Ángel—in other words, when Osvaldo Puente, a member of the Uruguayan middle class, joins the Tupamaro movement. The thirty-five-year-old Juan Ángel narrates the story of his life from the age of eight. But the past is not narrated in the past tense. Each birthday, each period of the life of Osvaldo Puente/Juan Ángel, is seen in the present time, on top of which another present is superimposed. Therefore, the narrator, already converted into a revolutionary, can comment critically on his past. In one day that started at seven-fifty in the morning and ended at midnight, Osvaldo Puente/Juan Ángel lived twenty-seven years. On the morning of 27 August, Osvaldo turned eight years old and at twelve o'clock at night Juan Ángel became a thirty-five-year-old revolutionary penetrating into the underworld. The unity and integrity of this novel is reinforced by its poetic conception. Poetry, which can transform the past into a continued present, shows Juan Ángel as the result of Osvaldo Puente in a continuous state of change and growth.

After the coup d'etat of 1973, censorship, torture, death, *desaparecidos* (missing persons), and exile were the powerful weapons that the military regime consistently used to attack those who opposed its ideology. Benedetti joined the diaspora of Uruguayan intellectuals and went into exile. But not only did the man go into exile; so did the politician, the thinker, and the creator. His works and his name were banished from the country. Benedetti lived in Argentina, Peru, and Cuba for some time and then in Spain. If exile was the weapon that the military dictatorship used to silence those who opposed the system, Benedetti subverted that punishment by writing and publishing constantly. The banning of his books, which prevented Uruguayans from reading them, was partially invalidated, because Benedetti's work was almost completely republished in Mexico and he found new readers. Benedetti could not be read in Uruguay, but Uruguayan literature, thanks to Benedetti and other important writers in exile, was becoming known in other parts of the continent, as well as in Europe.

Benedetti's writing in exile had the important function of informing the rest of the world about what was happening in his country, from the vantage point of his painful personal and collective experiences. Spain offered Benedetti the advantage of publishing articles in El País, the most important Spanish newspaper, very soon after his arrival. This material was compiled in a volume entitled El desexilio y otras conjeturas (Desexilio and Other Conjectures, 1984). But Benedetti did not write only testimonial articles; he transformed historical, personal and collective events into literature. Thus, he enlarged his work in almost all the genres, even theater, a category that he appeared to have abandoned after 1955, the year he wrote Ida y vuelta. In 1979, the play Pedro y el capitán (Peter and the Captain) was published, and on the day of the book's presentation to the public and critics, 28 March 1979, the Uruguayan theater company in exile in Mexico, El Galpón, staged it. This play is the first work that deals directly with the theme of the Uruguayan military horror.

Benedetti's work in exile is best characterized by its hybrid nature. He was unable to divorce his testimonial writing from his fiction, as in his novel Primavera con una esquina rota (Spring with a Broken Corner, 1982). And his poetry and prose are strongly united, as in Geografías (Diverse Geography, 1984). The

fourteen sections into which Geografías is divided are made up of a poem and a short story. The poem has the function of a long epigraph. It contains the essence of the story that is developed in prose. If contemporary Western literature is characterized by the dissolution of generic definitions, Benedetti's last works show that not only the topic but the experience of exile is such a complex reality that its transformation into literature overflows the traditional divisions of literary genres.

Benedetti is the creator of a new Spanish word: desexilio. "Desexilio" is almost the antonym of exile—almost, because the opposite of exile is community. Benedetti knows that the exiled person who comes back home after the dismissal of the military regime does not integrate again into the old community. The country has been hurt, and its wounds will take time to heal. Furthermore, the returned exile is also a· different person with a new geography, a new language, new loves, and new nostalgias. In Primavera con una esquina rota and the volume of poetry La casa y el ladrillo (The House and the Brick, 1977), to mention only two books, Benedetti refers to the long and difficult process of reconstruction of Uruguayan culture. But exile has not been a negative force for Benedetti, and in 1986, after one year of democratic civilian government in Uruguay, he has built a cultural bridge between Spain and Uruguay. Benedetti has succeeded in showing Spain and Europe a new, a more complex and contemporary image of Latin America and Uruguay. Through his writings as well as through the works of other Latin American writers in exile, Spaniards feel a growing interest in Latin America, and especially in the problems of the Southern Cone countries. Benedetti is aware of the importance of keeping alive this interest. His desexilio is strengthening the literary and cultural link between Uruguay and Spain.

SELECTED BIBLIOGRAPHY

Editions

Poetry

La víspera indeleble. Montevideo, 1945.
Sólo mientras tanto. Montevideo, 1950. Included in the many editions of Inventario.

Poemas de la oficina. Montevideo, 1956. 3rd ed. under the title *Poemas de la oficina y otros expedientes.* Montevideo, 1969.

Poemas del hoyporhoy. Montevideo, 1961. Included in the many editions of *Inventario.*

Contra los puentes levadizos. Montevideo, 1966. Included in the many editions of *Inventario.*

Antología natural. Montevideo, 1967.

A ras de sueño. Montevideo, 1967. Included in the many editions of *Inventario.*

Letras de emergencia. Buenos Aires, 1973.

Poemas de otros. Buenos Aires, 1974. Included in the 11th ed. of *Inventario* (1980).

La casa y el ladrillo. Mexico City, 1977. Included in the 11th ed. of *Inventario* (1980).

Cotidianas. Mexico City, 1979. Included in the 11th ed. of *Inventario* (1980).

Viento del exilo. Mexico City, 1981.

Preguntas al azar. Madrid, 1986.

Novels

Quién de nosotros. Montevideo, 1953.

La tregua. Montevideo, 1960.

Gracias por el fuego. Montevideo, 1965.

El cumpleaños de Juan Ángel. Mexico City, 1971.

Primavera con una esquina rota. Madrid, 1982.

Short Stories

Ésta mañana. Montevideo, 1949. Enlarged ed. under the title *Esta mañana y otros cuentos.* Montevideo, 1967.

El último viaje y otros cuentos. Montevideo, 1951. The majority of the short stories in this volume were later compiled in *Esta mañana y otros cuentos* and in *Montevideanos.*

Montevideanos. Montevideo, 1959.

Datos para el viudo. Buenos Aires, 1967. This work is included in *La muerte y otras sorpresas.*

La muerte y otras sorpresas. Mexico City, 1968.

Con y sin nostalgia. Mexico City, 1977.

Geografías. Mexico City, 1984.

Essays

Peripecia y novela. Montevideo, 1948.

Marcel Proust y otros ensayos. Montevideo, 1951.

El país de la cola de paja. Montevideo, 1960.

Mejor es meneallo. Montevideo, 1961.

Literatura uruguaya siglo XX. Montevideo, 1963.

Genio y figura de José Enrique Rodó. Buenos Aires, 1966.

Letras del continente mestizo. Montevideo, 1967.

Sobre arte y oficios: ensayo. Montevideo, 1968.

Cuaderno cubano. Montevideo, 1969.

Crítica cómplice. Havana, 1971.

Los poetas comunicantes. Montevideo, 1972.

Crónicas del 71. Montevideo, 1972.

Terremoto y después. Montevideo, 1973.

El escritor latinoamericano y la revolución posible. Buenos Aires, 1974.

El recurso del supremo patriarca. Buenos Aires, 1974.

Hasta aquí. Buenos Aires, 1974.

Algunas formas subsidiarias de la penetración cultural. Mexico City, 1979.

El ejercicio del criterio. Mexico City, 1981.

El desexilio y otras conjeturas. Madrid, 1984.

Plays

Ustedes, par ejemplo. Montevideo, 1953.

El reportaje. Montevideo, 1958.

Ida y vuelta. Buenos Aires, 1963.

Pedro y el capitán. Mexico City, 1979.

Collected Works

Cuentos completos. Prologue by Jorge Ruffinelli. Santiago, Chile, 1970.

Inventario. 1st ed., Montevideo, 1963; 2nd ed., Montevideo, 1965; 3rd ed., Montevideo, 1967; 4th ed., Montevideo, 1970; 5th ed., Buenos Aires, 1974; 6th ed., Mexico City and Buenos Aires, 1978; 7th ed., Mexico City and Buenos Aires, 1978; 8th ed., Caracas, 1978 (published without Benedetti's authorization); 9th ed., Mexico City, 1979; 10th ed., Mexico City, 1980; 11th ed., Madrid, 1980; 12th ed., Madrid, 1981; 13th ed., Madrid, 1983; 14th ed., Madrid, 1984; 15th ed., Madrid, 1985; 16th ed., Madrid, 1986. Includes *Cotidianas, La casa y el ladrillo, Poemas de otros, Letras de emergencia, Quemar las naves, A ras de sueño, Contra los puentes levadizos, Próximo prójimo, Noción de patria, Poemas de hoyporhoy, Poemas de la oficina, Sólo mientras tanto.*

Todos los cuentos de Mario Benedetti. Havana, 1980. Includes *Ésta mañana, Montevideanos, La muerte y otras sorpresas, Con y sin nostalgia.*

Translations

"Birthday in Manhattan." Translated by Margaret Randall and Sergio Mondragón. *The Plumed Horn/El corno emplumado* (Mexico City) 3:112–119 (July 1962).

"The Budget." Translated by Gerald Brown. In *Short Stories in Spanish/Cuentos hispánicos,* edited by Jean Franco. Harmondsworth, 1966. Pp. 27–41.

"Gloria's Saturday." Translated by Darwin J. Flakoll and Claribel Alegría. In *New Voices of Hispanic America*. Boston, 1962. Pp. 121–127.

"The Iriartes." Translated by Jean Franco. In *Latin American Writing Today*, edited by J. M. Cohen. Harmondsworth, 1967.

"The Iriartes." Translated by Lynn Tricano and Suzanne Jill Levine. *Fiction* 5/1 (1976).

Juan Ángel's Birthday. Translated by David Arthur McMurray. Amherst, Mass., 1974.

The Truce. Translated by Benjamín Graham. New York, 1969.

Biographical and Critical Studies

Alegría, Fernando. "Mario Benedetti." In *Historia de la novela latinoamericana*. 3rd ed. Mexico City, 1966. Pp. 235–236.

Altamirano, Carlos. *Poesía del siglo XX: España e Hispanoamérica*. Buenos Aires, 1975. Pp. 65–88.

Barros, Daniel. "Tres poetas de hoy: Teillier, Benedetti y Gelman." In *Poesía sudamericana actual*, edited by Miguel Castellote. Madrid, 1972. Pp. 57–88.

Caballero, Agustín. *Antología del humor 1961–1962*. Madrid, 1962.

Campos, Julieta. "*La muerte y otras sopresas*." In *Oficio de leer*. Mexico City, 1971. Pp. 80–82.

Carrillo, Germán D. "La biopsia como técnica literaria de Mario Benedetti en *Gracias por el fuego*." *Cuadernos americanos* 177/4:217–233 (1971).

Cotelo, Rubén. *Narradores uruguayos*. Caracas, 1969. Pp. 201–202, 203–211.

Curutchet, Juan Carlos. "Los montevideanos de Mario Benedetti." *Cuadernos hispanoamericanos* 232: 141–148 (1969).

Englekirk, John E. *La narrativa uruguaya*. Berkeley and Los Angeles, 1967. Pp. 21, 121–123.

Fornet, Ambrosio. "Mario Benedetti y la revolución posible." *Revista de crítica literario latinoamericana* (Lima) 1/2:63–72 (1975).

―――, ed. *Recopilación de textos sobre Mario Benedetti*. Havana, 1976.

Foster, David William. "Una aproximación a la escritura metateatral de *Ida y vuelta* de Mario Benedetti." *Hispamérica* 7/19:13–25 (1978).

Franco, Jean. *The Modern Culture of Latin American: Society and the Artist*. New York, 1967. Pp. 208–209, 214–215.

―――. *La cultura moderna en América Latina*. Mexico City, 1971. Pp. 209–210, 218–219, 223–224, 235–236, 260.

Hayden, Rose Lee. *An Existential Focus on Some Novels of the River Plate*. East Lansing, Mich., 1973.

Kuehne, Alyce de. "Influencias de Pirandello y de Brecht en Mario Benedetti." *Hispania* 51/3:408–415 (1968).

Latchman, Ricardo. "*Montevideanos, por Mario Benedetti*" and "*La Tregua, por Mario Benedetti*." In *Carnet crítico: Ensayos*. Montevideo, 1962. Pp. 141–147, 148–152.

Leal, Luis. "Mario Benedetti." In *Breve historia de la literatura hispanoamericana*. New York, 1971. Pp. 354–355.

Legido, Juan Carlos. *El teatro uruguayo*. Montevideo, 1968.

Lewald, Ernest H. "The 1965 Literary Scene in Argentina and Uruguay." *Books Abroad* 40/2:145–148 (1966).

Liano, Dante. "Album de famila: La pequeña burguesía en la narrativa de Mario Benedetti." *Studi di letteratura ispano-americana* 13–14:199–212 (1983).

Mansour, Mónica. *Tuya, mía, de otros: La poesía coloquial de Mario Benedetti*. Mexico City, 1979.

Marún, Gioconda. "Análisis literario de *El cumpleaños de Juan Angel, de Mario Benedetti*." *Texto crítico* (Veracruz) 3/6:161–177 (1977).

Mathieu, Corina S. "Aspectos del mundo burgués de Mario Benedetti." In *Proceedings of the Pacific Northwest Conference of Foreign Languages* 25. Corvallis, Ore., 1979. Pp. 173–176.

Morelli, Gabrielle. "'El yo,' 'El otro' nella poesia sociale di Mario Benedetti." *Studi di letteratura ispano-americana* 13–14:213–242 (1983).

Rama, Angel. *La conciencia crítica*. Montevideo, 1968.

―――. "El escritor y su país." *Marcha* (Montevideo), 16 December 1960.

―――. "Del horizonte de uno al horizonte de todos." *Marcha* (Montevideo), 16 July 1965.

Real de Azúa, Carlos. "El voto que el alma denuncia." In *El Uruguay visto por los uruguayos* 26. Montevideo and Buenos Aires, 1968. Pp. 161–163.

Ricapito, Joseph V. "Sobre *La tregua* de Mario Benedetti." *Cuadernos hispanoamericanos* 331:143–151 (1978).

Rodríguez Monegal, Emir. "Las ficciones de un testigo implicado: Mario Benedetti." In *Narradores de ésta América*. Montevideo, 1961. Pp. 209–255.

Roggiano, Alfredo A. "Mario Benedetti." In *En éste aire de América*. Mexico City, 1966. Pp. 213–214.

Ruffinelli, Jorge. "Explorando caminos." *Marcha* (Montevideo) 19 September 1969.

―――. "Prologo" to *Cuentos completos* by Mario Benedetti. Santiago, Chile, 1970. Pp. 9–17.

―――, ed. *Mario Benedetti: Variaciones críticas*. Montevideo, 1973.

_____, ed. "La trinchera permanente." In *Palabras en orden*. 2nd ed. Jalapa, Mexico, 1985. Pp. 215–240.

_____, ed. "Mario Benedetti: Perfil literario." *Studi di letteratura ispano-americana* 13–14:103–111 (1983).

Spitaleri, Mario. "*Gracias por el fuego:* Estudios de variables temáticas." *Chasqui: Revista de literatura hispanoamericana* 2/1:31–44 (1972).

Valverde, José María. "Verso versus prosa: Dos casos en Hispanoamérica." *Revista canadiense de estudios hispánicos* 1/1:101–107 (1976).

Zeitz, Eileen M. "Los personajes de Benedetti: En busca de identidad y existencia." *Cuadernos hispanoamericanos* 297:635–644 (1975).

_____. "Entrevista a Mario Benedetti." *Hispania.* 63/2: 417–419 (1980).

Marco Denevi

(1922–   )

Donald A. Yates

Marco Denevi was born on 12 May 1922, in the Buenos Aires suburb of Sáenz Peña, the youngest of seven children. His father, Valerio Denevi, had immigrated to Argentina from Italy, and the Italian linguistic and cultural heritage would have a considerable bearing on the younger Denevi's formation. His early years were spent in tranquil surroundings that allowed him to indulge his reflective nature and to become an omnivorous reader. Denevi's formal schooling led to a degree in law, but he shied away from legal practice, securing instead a position as legal consultant with the Argentine National Postal Savings Bank.

This was the post he held when in 1955 his novel *Rosaura a las diez* (*Rosa at Ten O'Clock*) won the Premio Kraft, a literary prize offered for a new work by an Argentine writer. Denevi's astonishment was perhaps surpassed only by that of the Kraft judges, for he was absolutely unknown to the Buenos Aires literary world. As he himself confessed in the prologue to the first edition of the work: "[*Rosa at Ten O'Clock*] is my first book; its first paragraph, my first paragraph; the word with which it begins, my debut as a 'man of letters.'" The novel, which recounts in several narrative voices the circumstances surrounding the murder of a young woman in a shabby Buenos Aires hotel room, established the author's name immediately and became a best-selling book that has remained in print for three decades—indisputably one of the most popular works of Argentine fiction of this century. Denevi's principal literary model was the nineteenth-century English writer Wilkie Collins, author of *The Woman in White* (1860) and *The Moonstone* (1868), but there is a touch of Luigi Pirandello's influence as well in this extraordinarily compelling and suspenseful tale. The novel's structure and some specific details are clearly derivative, but Denevi demonstrated a control of his material uncommon in a fledgling writer, and several of the most memorable features of the work (the pathetic loneliness of the protagonist, Camilo Canegato, for example, or the subtle insinuation of a fantastic explanation of realistic events) were the product of Denevi's own creative genius.

While the book's reception was generally very favorable, there was some adverse criticism for the new author, to which Denevi conceded disproportionate importance. In a sense, he seemed to withdraw into himself. However, he was destined to experience continued success. In 1957 he wrote a satirical three-act play, *Los expedientes* (*The Dossiers*), which was performed by the Comedia Nacional at the prestigious Teatro Cervantes and subsequently won a National Literary Prize for drama.

Drawing on certain techniques of the theater of the absurd, the play denounces the dehumanizing effects of a huge, faceless bureaucracy. In the same year, Denevi collaborated in the adaptation of *Rosa at Ten O'Clock* for the screen, in a version that won more local prizes and, in 1958, was an Argentine entry at the Cannes Film Festival. Denevi accompanied the film to Europe on what has been his only trip away from the country of his birth.

In 1960 Denevi's novelette, *Ceremonia secreta* (*Secret Ceremony*, 1961), was selected from over 3,000 manuscripts as winner of the $5,000 first prize in a Latin American literary competition sponsored by the Spanish-language edition of *Life* magazine. As did *Rosa at Ten O'Clock*, this story deals with an almost magical experience of a solitary individual. This time it is Leonides Arrufat, an aged spinster who, mistaken by a mentally disturbed young woman for her dead mother, is drawn into the deranged woman's confused world of fear and violence, and of love and loyalty as well. In essence, it is a tale of implacable, ritualistic vengeance for an unspeakable crime against the human spirit. The prose of *Secret Ceremony* is richer and more suggestive than that of *Rosa at Ten O'Clock*, more poetic and less colloquial—none of which disguised Denevi's underlying purpose of recounting one more parable of loneliness.

For a brief period in the 1960's, Denevi continued to write for the theater. A one-act play, *El emperador de la China* (The Emperor of China) was presented to wide acclaim in Buenos Aires in 1960, and in 1962 Denevi staged a full-length drama entitled "El cuarto de la noche" (The Night Room). Its production convinced the author that he had no talent for the theater, and he subsequently destroyed all copies of the play.

During the decade following the publication of *Rosa at Ten O'Clock*, Denevi published a series of short stories, satirical and moralistic in nature, and told for the most part from an impersonal, objective narrative point of view. He also began fashioning dozens of brief prose pieces that dealt in a playful, revisionist manner with literary and historical themes. In these he proposed, for example, that Nero was not cruel or depraved, but only embarrassingly myopic, and that Don Quixote did not create his "Dulcinea," but rather that that proud village slat-

tern invented a gallant knight who performed deeds of bravery in her honor and a local fellow, who was somewhat taken with her, decided to assume that role. Characterized by wit, humor, and a freewheeling attitude toward what constitutes "reality," these short, lucidly expressed concepts were collected in a volume called *Falsificaciones* (Falsifications, 1966). There are some eighty pieces in all, their authorship in most cases ascribed to another writer, the result being a highly intellectualized anthology of apocrypha. These are, above all, entertaining games with ideas as the subject matter.

A short novel, *Un pequeño café* (A Small Café) appeared in 1966. Its protagonist, Adalberto Pascumo, is a humble employee of the Buenos Aires governmental bureaucracy who refers to himself as "a man without character." Denevi narrates in totally realistic detail Pascumo's love affair with a woman who believes him to be the chief of his section in the public records section instead of a lowly file clerk. Interwoven with Pascumo's idyll is the account of his surprising role in a general strike called by the employees of his bureaucratic backwater. In *Un pequeño café* Denevi once more proves himself to be a master of limpid, expressive prose and one of the most adept transcribers of colloquial Argentine Spanish.

In 1968 the author came to a major decision, one rarely reached by Latin American writers: he withdrew from his position with the Postal Savings Bank and set out to support himself solely from his writing. Around 1969 Denevi experienced a crisis in his professional life. He believed he had exhausted the capacity of his terse, witty "falsifications" to communicate his world view. In 1970 he brought out two volumes of short stories and "microtales," culled from his published and unpublished work in the years leading up to his reevaluation of his narrative techniques. *El emperador de la China y otros cuentos* (The Emperor of China and Other Stories) brings together his previously uncollected short stories from the 1960's, and *Parque de diversiones* (Amusement Park) is a kind of companion volume to *Falsificaciones*, consisting mainly of laconic, playful sketches that offer alternate versions of conventional attitudes and beliefs.

After 1970 Denevi tended to cultivate longer

narrative forms. *Los asesinos de los días de fiesta* (The Holiday Murderers, 1972) is a novel whose principal characters are the brothers and sisters of an amoral Buenos Aires family who pursue a criminal adventure in a mansion they invade and occupy in a fashionable suburb of that city. As is the case with Denevi's other novels, here one finds many neo-Gothic trappings, but the mood is now darker, unrelieved by the author's characteristic irony or by the appeal of a sympathetic or even pathetic figure.

The first collection of short stories from Denevi's "second" period, *Hierba del cielo* (Heaven's Herb), appeared in 1973. It contains nine tales that embody the modification of the author's focus. Present are many of his old themes—games, illusions, shifting identities, ironic destinies—as well as his typical concern for the requirements of a well-developed plot. However, the brittleness and objective tone of his earlier stories are replaced with a deep sense of sympathy, if not affection, for his characters. Life hands out bitter disappointments and cruel reverses, to be sure, but Denevi seems less inclined in these narratives to underline the wry consequences of this and more given to developing the emotional impact on his protagonists. *Hierba del cielo* is a showcase for Denevi's mature short-story art. "Viaje a Puerto Aventura" (Journey to Port Adventure), one of the pieces in this collection, is a model of meticulous narrative construction and an example of the author at his entrancing, story-telling best.

The linear simplicity and lucid style of much of Denevi's writing makes his work particularly accessible to young readers. In the mid 1970's a Buenos Aires publisher brought out two volumes of Denevi's miscellanea, in editions prepared for secondary students. *Salón de lectura* (Reading Room, 1974) and *Los locos y los cuerdos* (The Sane and the Insane, 1975) gathered uncollected prose, poetry, and drama together with some new material. Denevi's customary unpretentiousness is manifested in the latter book, where the representative selections of these three genres are grouped, respectively, under the headings "Cuentos y recuentos" (Tales and Retellings), "Ejercicios de escritura vertical" (Exercises in Vertical Writing), and "Teatro para leer" (Plays for Reading). In 1980 Denevi published a fable for children entitled *Robotobor*, recounting the experiences of a young

brother and sister with a domestic robot. The tale is narrated by the family cat and, perhaps predictably, makes a strong case for an existence uncomplicated by mechanized objects.

Since the transitional 1973 collection of stories, *Hierba del cielo*, Denevi has published four volumes destined for mature readers. *Reunión de desaparecidos* (Meeting of Missing Persons, 1977) is his most heterogeneous collection of stories and brief prose sketches. While there is much variety in theme and focus, the subjects of several of the stories are realistically drawn inhabitants of the great metropolis, Buenos Aires, that Denevi knows so intimately. With economy and precision, the author illuminates his characters and their crises. In the best of these, the reader feels that he has been led to the understanding of an entire human life in the space of a few dozen pages. In "Salvación de Yayá" (Salvation of Yayá), Denevi accurately depicts the Italo-Argentine temperament and idiom, while neatly characterizing the traditional relationship between the sexes in Argentina. *Reunión de desaparecidos* is a wise and insightful book that proves that when Denevi undertakes to infuse his short stories with the human substance of his novels, he has much to offer.

In 1979 Denevi brought out a revised and augmented edition of his *Parque de diversiones*, a volume thematically and technically akin to his *Falsificaciones*. Adopting a mildly apologetic tone, Denevi took this occasion to explain the long series of laconic, quintessential pieces that he had composed. He wrote for the jacket copy: "Incapable of articulating my critical ideas (concerning the world we live in) as an essayist might do, I fall back on the only resources at my disposal: the literary (or supposedly dramatic) confection, the minitale, the aphorism." It would seem that with this volume Denevi has ceased to cultivate this unusual literary subgenre, with which his name has been associated for so long.

In the third decade of his career as a writer, Denevi has given increasing attention to other pursuits. He has written extensively for Argentine television, and in 1981 his didactic and moralistic bent found a new path of expression. In that year he began writing, for the prominent Buenos Aires newspaper *La Nación*, a series of controversial journalistic columns that took the Argentine people severely to task for the distressing state in which the country found itself. Denevi created an alter ego, a person he called Ramón Civedé (an anagram of the letters of his own name) and sustained soul-searching dialogues with him in the pages of *La Nación*. The columns were widely quoted, praised, and refuted, and the author, never fond of the limelight, found himself a celebrity. For a writer who had never frequented professional authors' societies, who had assiduously avoided formal literary gatherings, and whose social life consisted mainly of intimate soirees in the homes of his close friends, this was a monumental step. The explanation may be that the events of the period from 1974 to 1982 in Argentina were too calamitous for Denevi to ignore: the death of Juan Perón, followed by the accession of Isabel Perón to the presidency of the nation, sixteen months of near anarchy, a military coup, and finally the disasterous war with Great Britain over the possession of the Falkland Islands. It was a period in Argentina's history when too many fell silent. Denevi was not to be counted among those numbers.

In 1982, perhaps in reaction to the pervasive mood of civil strife that gripped his country, Denevi published his most personal, introspective work, *Araminta, o El poder* (Araminta, or The Power). The volume is dedicated to the memory of his mother, and includes, together with the title story and a group of seven elegant prose sketches, four sensitive autobiographical essays. In the latter the author discusses openly and without intruding artifice, his life, his sentimental attachments, and the world of his creations. An uncharacteristic sense of nostalgia invades all of these delicately evocative pages. The seven brilliantly executed pieces gathered under the title of "Siete extrañas desapariciones" (Seven Strange Disappearances) relate with an imaginative vigor equal to that of Gabriel García Márquez the astonishing manner in which seven curious individuals vanish from the face of the earth. On the merit of these tales alone, Denevi could rightfully occupy a place alongside the most eminent contributors to Latin America's celebrated literary boom of the past four decades, a movement for which the author had previously professed no particular affinity.

Denevi's most recent work is *Manuel de historia* (Manuel of History, 1985), a novel that partakes even more generously of some of the typical "boom techniques," such as interior duplication and the fracturing of narrative and chronological perspectives. Adopting an admonitory posture, the author constructs a complex futuristic narrative that develops from the premise that before the end of the twentieth century Argentina is "internationalized" by a world council of nations and placed under the control of the United States, whose mandate is to "culturize" the hapless citizens of that floundering country. The novel is multifaceted and many-layered, but the message it delivers is abundantly clear: Argentines, become responsible, face up to your past and take charge of your present, or else. . . . The reader perceives a chorus of carefully orchestrated literary echoes—George Orwell, John Le Carré, and Jorge Luis Borges, among other authors whose styles are evoked in this, Denevi's most eclectic work.

Marco Denevi has come a long way since the appearance of *Rosa at Ten O'Clock,* demonstrating that he is an important chronicler of Argentine life, as well as one of Spanish America's most gifted narrators. He has a proven talent for freshness and innovation, and he has displayed the capacity to continue developing. It is surely safe to affirm that his work will be read and admired for many years to come.

SELECTED BIBLIOGRAPHY

Editions

Novels and Novelettes

Rosaura a las diez. Buenos Aires, 1955.
Ceremonia secreta. New York, 1961.
Un pequeño café. Buenos Aires, 1966.
Los asesinos de los días de fiesta. Buenos Aires, 1972.
Manuel de historia. Buenos Aires, 1985.

Short Stories and "Microtales"

Falsificaciones. Buenos Aires, 1966. Rev. and augmented 2nd ed. Buenos Aires, 1969.
El emperador de la China y otros cuentos. Buenos Aires, 1970.
Parque de diversiones. Buenos Aires, 1970. Rev. and augmented 2nd ed. Buenos Aires, 1979.

Hierba del cielo. Buenos Aires, 1973.
Salón de lectura. Buenos Aires, 1974.
Los locos y los cuerdos. Buenos Aires, 1975.
Reunión de desaparecidos. Buenos Aires, 1977.
Robotobor. Buenos Aires, 1980.
Araminta, o El poder. Buenos Aires, 1982.

Plays

Los expedientes. Buenos Aires, 1957.
El emperador de la China. Buenos Aires, 1960.

Collected Works

Antología precoz. Santiago, Chile, 1973.
Ceremonia secreta y otros cuentos. New York, 1965.
Obras completas. 4 vols. Buenos Aires, 1980–1984.
Páginas de Marco Denevi, seleccionadas por el autor. Buenos Aires, 1983.

Translations

Rosa at Ten O'Clock. Translated by Donald A. Yates. New York, 1964.
Secret Ceremony. Translated by Harriet de Onís. New York, 1961.

Biographical and Critical Studies

Becco, Horacio J. "Bibliografía." In *Los locos y los cuerdos,* by Marco Denevi. Buenos Aires, 1975. Pp. 153–157.
Carranza, José María. "La crítica social en las fábulas de Marco Denevi." *Revista iberoamercana* 38/80:477–494 (1972).
Denevi, Marco. "Reportaje a mí mismo." *Bibliograma* 44:5–6 (1973).
Feeny, Thomas. "The Influence of Wilkie Collins' *The Moonstone* on Marco Denevi's *Rosaura a las diez.*" *Rivista di letterature moderne e comparate* 31:225–229 (1978).
Grove, Ivonne R. *La realidad calidoscópica en la obra de Marco Denevi.* Mexico City, 1974.
Gyurko, Lanin A. "Romantic Illusion in Denevi's *Rosaura a las diez.*" *Ibero-romania* (Munich) 3:357–373 (1971).
Jofre Barroso, Haydée. "Marco Denevi: Descubrimiento del hombre y encuentro con el escritor." In *Obras completas 1,* by Marco Denevi. Buenos Aires, 1980. Pp. 7–37.
Merlo, Juan Carlos. "Nota preliminar." In *Páginas de Marco Denevi.* Buenos Aires, 1983. Pp. 11–35.
———. "Las 'falsificaciones' de Marco Denevi." In *Obras completas 4,* by Marco Denevi. Buenos Aires, 1984. Pp. 9–16.
Poletti, Syria. "El idioma de Marco Denevi." In *Obras completas 2,* by Marco Denevi. Buenos Aires, 1983. Pp. 19–25.
Ramos Escobar, José L. "*Ceremonia secreta:* Ritos." *Revista/Review interamericana* 10/1:19–26 (1980).
Yahni, Roberto. "Marco Denevi." In *Enciclopedia de la literatura argentina.* Buenos Aires, 1970. Pp. 184–185.
Yates, Donald A. "Marco Denevi: An Argentine Anomaly." *Kentucky Foreign Language Quarterly* 9/3:162–167 (1962).
———. "Introduction." In *Ceremonia secreta y otros cuentos,* edited by Donald A. Yates. New York, 1965. Pp. 1–4.
———. "Para una bibliografía de Marco Denevi." *Revista iberoamericana* 33/63:141–146 (1967).
———. "Un acercamiento a Marco Denevi." In *El cuento hispanoamericano ante la crítica,* by Enrique Pupo-Walker. Madrid, 1973. Pp. 223–234.

Lygia Fagundes Telles

(1923–   )

Fábio Lucas

Lygia Fagundes Telles was born on 19 April 1923 in São Paulo. When she was twenty-two, she published her first book, *Praia Viva* (Living Beach, 1944), a volume of short stories. Five years later, her second collection of short stories appeared under the title *O Cacto Vermelho* (The Red Cactus). It won the Alfonso Arinos Prize awarded by the Brazilian Academy of Letters. Some of her early works are still reprinted from time to time in modified form, but not the stories from those two volumes, which the author has effectively disowned.

Fagundes Telles tends to belittle her adolescence. "These days," she once commented, "a girl of fifteen smokes, drinks, reads Kafka, and has sex. She dares all. At that age, I was pure ignorance. And fear." Beginning with her earliest works, Fagundes Telles' characters are possessed by insecurity and fear. She was wrapped up in postwar existential philosophy with its built-in notion that everything is relative. And Fagundes Telles' prose is marked from the outset by an innovative rhythm of advances and retreats that reflects psychologies that are neither round nor square, but oblong.

Because of the period in which her first works were produced, Fagundes Telles has been included in the Generation of '45. That label has been attached to the Brazilian writers who emerged in the postwar period in open reaction against the abuses of exaggerated experimentalism that, under the generic designation of modernism, had taken root in the 1920's and 1930's. The postwar generation revived the sonnet, admitted to a taste for the neoclassical, and appreciated the strict formality of poetic composition. However, it was influenced, to a certain extent, by the literary innovations of the period. Fagundes Telles' prose fiction incorporates elements of expressionism and surrealism. Her style is colloquial and communicative, close to speech and receptive to the manifestations of the unconscious. Her earliest stories quickly brought her public recognition. But her ordeal by fire was her first novel, *Ciranda de Pedra* (published in English as *The Marble Dance*), first issued in 1954 and reprinted fifteen times by the mid-1980's.

Fagundes Telles brought to Brazilian literature thematic concerns that departed from the tradition of its prose fiction. The genre at that point had exhausted the possibilities of social realism, which claimed to provide a positivistic depiction of social evils, and of psychologism, which went to extremes in the protracted analysis of pathological mental states. In *The Marble Dance*, Fagundes Telles introduces a special tonality in her treatment of female psychology and employs a highly personal technique in her handling of dramatic narrative. Many of the idiosyncrasies that appeared in her first novel reappeared later as the author developed her fictional cosmos: constellations of myths, philosophical concepts, and fictional circumstances that turn up again and again, repeating themselves in different contexts and forming the writer's basic repertory.

In *The Marble Dance*, Fagundes Telles revealed to her readers one of her most striking characteristics: the convincing description of desires, which are made articulate but which the characters are unable to transform into pleasure. She inaugurated a kind of routine of frustration with a strong erotic content. Compulsions, both good and evil, inspire her characters with hope and provide them with an incentive to carry on.

Virgínia, the central character, is depicted within the family context that gives rise to her complexes. To her sisters—Bruna, big and dark-complexioned, and Otávia, with near-golden tresses—she projects hatred. Even greater is her hatred for her mother, Laura, a sick woman who has separated from her husband and lives with another man. Laura dies, and her lover commits suicide. Following a stay in a boarding house, Virgínia returns to her sisters and their father, although she knows that she is the daughter of her mother's lover. Her response to her increasing rejection complex remains the same: departure and travel.

The tragic damnation of Fagundes Telles' characters is tempered by the myth of the renewal of life: a renewal sometimes wished for, sometimes latent, but often present as the spur to survival. From a small episode in chapter 10 in which Virgínia saves the life of a dragonfly there arises the reflection that "more important than being born is being reborn." The pattern found in *The Marble Dance* of three sisters unsuccessfully attempting to achieve communication reappears in the writer's most recent novel, *As Meninas* (The Girls, 1973; published in English as *The Girl in the Photograph*).

In her second novel, *Verão no Aquário* (Summer in the Aquarium), published in 1963, the central character, Raíza, suffers from a rejection complex from the outset. In the play of opposition, she confronts her companion Marfa, but her main adversary is her mother, Patrícia. Never has the Electra complex been demonstrated so transparently as in the mental processes of the character who suspects that her rival in love is her own mother, a solitary, superior woman and a novelist.

It is clear from the obsessive manner in which the characters are impelled toward chaos or tragedy, dragging with them their terrible stigmas, that Fagundes Telles has been influenced, directly or indirectly, by modern psychology.

The earliest reference to Freud in Brazilian literature occurs in Mário de Andrade's expressionistic novel *Amar Verbo Intransitivo* (The Intransitive Verb, 1927; published in English as *Fraülein*). But Andrade accorded Freud a timid, respectful, bookish treatment. In contrast, Fagundes Telles treats psychoanalysis with levity. Marfa, a character in *Verão no Aquario*, speaks of it jestingly. Observing her friend Raíza's persistent care of her fingernails, Marfa advises her to visit a psychoanalyst. "It's best to start the treatment on account of a single detail," she says. "Do you understand? You go to him to find out why you spend so much time looking at your nails, and you end up finding out that when you were ten you wanted to strangle your mother with her hair ribbon" (chapter 4). The scene continues in a mordant tone. "The psychoanalyst will dig down to the root of your pain," Marfa says, with an unconscious play on words: Raíza's name is almost identical to *raiz*, the Portuguese word for "root."

Duplicity is a suitable theme for Fagundes Telles' fiction. It appears as part of the affective, existential, and operative inertia of many of her characters. Raíza refers to her own "undefinable viscous state." Laziness is the subject of a novela, *Gaby*, published in 1954. The narrative of *Verão no Aquário* revolves around a triangle of women: Raíza, Marfa, and Patrícia, the mother. The conflict between generations is uppermost, with the rivalry between mother and daughter left unresolved in an atmosphere of suffering and unfulfillment.

In Fagundes Telles' third novel, *The Girl in the Photograph*, the female triad is made up of three girls, three discontinuous psyches, living at the same boarding house: Lorena, Lia, and Ana Clara. Lorena possesses to a certain extent the emotional availability of Virgínia in the first novel. Written with maturity at a moment when Brazil was undergoing one of its most ferocious dictatorships, this novel is more colored than the others by political and social considerations. In a concession to realism, the author reproduced the horrifying torture of an innocent victim.

In *The Girl in the Photograph*, Fagundes Telles perfected her skill as a narrator, particularly in following the behavior of a mind affected by drugs, insecurity, and fear. In mapping the hazy borderline between sanity and madness, she called on her full strength as a writer of fiction. An admirable example is the passage in chapter 2 in which Ana Clara, in a scene of love and drugs with her lover, Max, emits outbursts from her unconscious that are cut short by the censorship imposed by her superego and by the unconvincing rationalization of her conscious mind. The narrative process is a curious one in which the memories of the two characters become intertwined. The dialogue is telescoped; elliptical phrases, suggestions, and unfinished statements are left suspended. An example is the conversation between Ana Clara and Max in chapter 4 in which a surrealistic dream landscape is described.

Fagundes Telles' dramatic intensity is occasionally interrupted by bits of humor and irony, as in chapter 5 in this monologue by Lorena: "If he doesn't come looking for me I shall hang myself. I'll be the first suicide to be made a saint," and this description: "When Ana Clara picks up a glass, she crooks her little finger, displaying the etiquette of a truck driver at a wedding reception." Aware that her fiction has nothing in common with that of the nineteenth century, in chapter 5 Fagundes Telles has Lorena remark about Lia, with whom the writer clearly enjoys a special rapport: "She goes on and on about how sick she is of nineteenth-century literature with all those characters running like trains on rails that carry them to their fate, whether good or bad. 'There are no rails!'"

Fagundes Telles' first book was a collection of short stories. These were not, as short stories often are, warm-up exercises in preparation for a first novel with its more complex narrative and more diffuse set of situations. On the contrary, they were the result of her choice of a genre in which she became one of the most acclaimed writers in Brazilian literature. The mythography projected in her novels can also be found in the stories. But the brevity of the narrative, the condensation of layers of meaning, and the preparation of the effect have been handled with a narrative technique particularly adapted to the genre.

Fagundes Telles has published twelve volumes of short stories, each possessed of its own unity, each depicting a given moment in the writer's appropriation of reality and the exercise of her inventive capacity. A difficulty in proposing a generic interpretation of Fagundes Telles' literary output is that some of the stories appear more than once, in modified forms. Some passages are expanded and others cut, but the essence remains.

In her stories, Fagundes Telles focuses on the conjunction of myth, magic, and mystery, together with a commitment to the real. These are combined to form a dense fictional whole, vibrant in its drama and loaded with surprises in its execution. The effect of the real combines with the effect of fantasy to produce an interplay of scenes, emotional intensities, and aesthetic values.

The author's evaluation of her own work may be observed in the number of times some of the stories have appeared in different collections. Three appear six times each: "A Caçada" (The Hunt), "As pérolas" (The Pearls), and "Venha Ver o Pôr do Sol" (Come and See the Sunset). Three others appear five times each: "Eu Era Mudo e Só" (I Was Dumb and Alone), "Natal na Barca" (Christmas Aboard the Ferry), and "O Encontro" (The Encounter). Eight other stories make four appearances each. There are thus fourteen stories altogether for which the author has indicated a strong preference. Nine of the fourteen appear in the collection entitled *Dez Contos Escolhidos* (Ten Selected Short Stories), published in 1984. Another collection was brought out in 1984 under the title *Os Melhores Contos* (The Best Short Stories). Of the sixteen stories in the book, eleven feature in the list of preferences. These two recent collections enable the reader to form an acquaintance with Fagundes Telles' narrative processes.

In 1958 Fagundes Telles published *Histórias de Desencontro* (Stories of Missed Encounter), a title that reflects the content of the stories. In her propensity for the natural and the instinctive the author emphasizes the chaotic, preoedipal world in an attempt to escape from the rules of society, which find predominant expression in paternal authority. Curiously, her male characters are not endowed with aspects of their own. They do not share the female characters' clearly marked delineations. They generally carry symbols of power, wealth, or status, designating their social functions, their roles. Their psychological outlines are not filled in with the richness of shading that the female characters receive.

While many writers explore the worlds of fantasy and marvel because they have exhausted certain forms of realism, some arrive in this region as the result of a natural spiritual inclination. Such is the case with Fagundes Telles. She brings great determination to her investigations of her characters' clashes with one another. She unveils the dramatic face of human weakness, barring the paths to redemption. And when the intensity of a situation overcomes the will to resist, the world is metamorphosed into mystery, the product of magic, the realm of enchantment. Her short story "A Caçada" is a true appeal to the imagination, a plunge into the unconscious, into a past that may feed as well upon individual biographies as upon the history of mankind. The creation of myths fulfills a more vital need in the work of Fagundes Telles than in that of most Brazilian writers of fiction. It is the channel through which she proclaims herself a writer.

Through semiological investigation, one can identify in the stories many signs of disenchantment with human beings in a general sense. Yet at bottom we always encounter a nostalgia for lost innocence, for paradise before the Fall or, rather, before the initiation of the civilizing process. Hence the permanent atmosphere of evocation that characterizes her best work. Afterward comes the denser meaning of this literary adventure: an orbital trajectory around the sacred, the discovery of the deepest laws of the cosmos, a pantheistic vision of sorcery and divination in which animate and inanimate beings alike are coded messages.

In *Misterios* (Mysteries, 1981), the author proves that modern literature has inherited the estate bequeathed by religion or, rather, by mysticism, inasmuch as, reading the stories, we recall "mystic states" experienced in solitude, beyond intellectual perception. Fagundes Telles subtly introduces details—ants, rats, birds, cats, fragments of dreams, volcanoes,

fingernails, fingers, hands, gestures—that wait to be made manifest, messages that cry out to be decoded.

The interplay of love and death is also handled with subtlety. The perfect states of love and innocence are portrayed as very perishable. The path to the realm of childhood, or the return to the past, is discovered amid the horror of expiation, as in "Noturno Amarelo" (Yellow Nocturne). Amorous encounters are presided over by the divine intoxication of death, in opposition to good intentions grounded on rational thought.

The ecstasy of being is thus precipitated to the level of death. It is at this limit that Fagundes Telles constructs the mosaic of her fantasies. The impulse to suicide shows through at several points. She constructs plots in which the natural is interlaced with the supernatural. To these thematic nuclei she adds subplots that ramify outward, proposing ambiguities, subtle psychological states, surprises of miscarried actions, and chasms of doubt. She prefers to employ the current of thought, the rotating drama of consciousness, making the reader the character's confidant in a flow of confession upon which are imprinted, in conscious speech, clear marks of the unconscious. The end product is the vast autonomy of the character, whose individuality is in conflict with social relationships and with the mystery of the world.

In *Seminário dos Ratos* (Rats' Seminars, 1977; published in English as *Tigrela and Other Stories*) the reader may study cases of affective ambivalence, as in the monologue of "Senhor Diretor" (The Director), interpolated by the experience of a walk. In "A Sauna" (The Sauna), the character reflects in these terms: "I can't be as clear as I'm asked to be. Is it possible to tell a fact clearly? Things should be told with display so that they don't seem petty." The narrative takes place on two levels at once as the character simultaneously experiences her past love life and her sauna. Symptomatically, she is the victim of an oversight: she goes barefoot because she has forgotten her slippers.

First-person narrative predominates in Fagundes Telles' work, as does the technique by which she establishes a free, indirect style with the purpose of bringing the character's consciousness closer to the reader's perception. In consequence, a confidential tone emanates from the text as its intrinsic nature, a natural property that flows with none of the rough, coarse features of early experiments in the renewal of prose fiction. There is no aggressive introduction of the extraordinary.

Fagundes Telles abstains from any attempt to impose rational order on characters and events. Desire is protean by nature, assuming diverse forms; its disguises lend eros a constant ambivalence. It will succumb at last to death alone, and the attraction of the abyss is well-known to many of the author's characters. The human being is as afraid of death as he is of the fulfillment of his desires—hence the fermentation of dreams and fantasies and, figuratively, artistic manifestation. According to Freud, the ghosts that aim at stimulating pleasure in the spectator have their home in unsatisfied desire. The writer's consciousness is known to be inhabited by a maker of images bursting with affectivity. And the public, in its turn, enjoys watching that which it forbids itself to do. The ghosts are there to correct a pleasureless reality.

Translated from the Portuguese by Brian Gould

SELECTED BIBLIOGRAPHY

First Editions

Short Stories

Praia Viva. São Paulo, 1944.
O Cacto Vermelho. São Paulo, 1949.
Gaby. In *Os Sete Pecados Capitais.* Rio de Janeiro, 1954.
Histórias do Desencontro. Rio De Janeiro, 1958.
Histórias Escolhidas. São Paulo, 1964.
O Jardim Selvagem. São Paulo, 1965.
"Trilogia da Confissão." In *Os Dezoito Melhores Contos do Brasil.* Rio de Janeiro, 1968.
Antes do Baile Verde. Rio de Janeiro, 1970.
Seleta. Edited by Nelly Novaes Coelho. Rio de Janeiro, 1971.

Seminário dos Ratos. Rio de Janeiro, 1977.
Filhos Pródigos. São Paulo, 1978.
A Disciplina do Amor. Rio de Janeiro, 1980.
Mistérios. Rio de Janeiro, 1981.
Dez Contos Escolhidos. São Paulo, 1984.
Os Melhores Contos de Lygia Fagundes Telles. São Paulo, 1984.

Novels

Ciranda de Pedra. Rio de Janeiro, 1954.
Verão no Aquário. São Paulo, 1963.
As Meninas. Rio de Janeiro, 1973.

Translations

The Girl in the Photograph. Translated by Margaret A. Neves. New York, 1982.
The Marble Dance. Translated by Margaret A. Neves. New York, 1986.
Tigrela and Other Stories. Translated by Margaret A. Neves. New York, 1986.

Biographical and Critical Studies

Gomes, Celuta Moreira. *Bibliografia do Conto Brasileiro.* 2 vols. Rio de Janeiro, 1968.
Hohlfeldt, Antônio. *Conto Brasileiro Contemporâneo.* Porto Alegre, Brazil, 1981.
Lopes, Óscar. *Crítica e Interpretação Literária.* Oporto, Portugal, 1972.
Lucas, Fábio. "Mistério e Magia: Contos de Lygia Fagundes Telles." In *A Face Visível.* Rio de Janeiro, 1973. Pp. 143–146.
_____. "O Conto no Brasil Moderno." In *O Livro do Seminário.* São Paulo, 1983. Pp. 103–164.
Magalhães Junior, Raimundo. *Panorama do Conto Brasileiro.* 10 vols. Rio de Janeiro, 1959–1961.
Malard, Letícia. *Escritos de Literatura Brasileira.* Belo Horizonte, Brazil, 1981.
Silva, Vera Maria Tietzmann. *A Metamorfose nos Contos de Lygia Fagundes Telles.* Rio de Janeiro, 1985.
Silverman, Malcolm. *Moderna Ficção Brasileira 2.* Rio de Janeiro, 1981.
Tufano, Douglas. *Estudos de Literatura Brasileira.* São Paulo, 1983.

José Donoso

(1924–   )

Cedomil Goic

José Donoso was born in Santiago, Chile, at 292 Avenida Holanda, in the suburb of Providencia, on 5 October 1924, the son of Dr. José Donoso and Alicia Yáñez. His father was a prestigious physician who belonged to a family of professionals related to landowners of central Chile. His mother was the niece of Don Eliodoro Yáñez, the founder of the newspaper *La Nación* and an outstanding figure in Chilean politics. She was also related to the novelist and storyteller María Flora Yáñez and to Alvaro Yáñez, the author of *Miltín* (Miltin, 1935), *Diez* (Ten, 1937), *Umbral* (Doorstep, 1977), and other narratives of the avant-garde.

From 1932 to 1942, Donoso studied at the Patrocinio de San José and the Grange School in Santiago. He attended the latter along with Luis Alberto Heiremans and Carlos Fuentes, whose father was the Mexican ambassador to Chile. In 1943, he quit school and went to work. During 1945 and 1946, he traveled to Magallanes and Patagonia, in the far south of Chile, worked on the sheep farms there, and then went to Buenos Aires, where he worked as a dockhand.

In 1947, he returned to Chile, finished high school, and began his studies in literature at the College of Philosophy and Educational Sciences of the University of Chile, in the old Pedagogical Institute, concentrating on English literature. In 1949, he was awarded a scholarship by the Doherty Foundation. From that year until 1951, he studied English literature at Princeton University, where he wrote in English his first short stories, "The Blue Woman" and "The Poisoned Pastries," published in *MSS*, a student literary magazine, in 1950 and 1951. In 1952, after traveling around the United States, Mexico, and Central America, he returned to Chile.

Donoso then began a period of increasingly creative activity, producing short stories, novelettes, and novels. During this stage, the reading public and the critics gradually recognized the originality and value of his work, although he made his living by teaching and through an increasing dedication to journalism. He taught at the Kent School and lectured on English literature at the Catholic University in Santiago. He took part in the Primeras Jornadas del Cuento (First Readings of the Chilean Short Story), organized by the writer Enrique Lafourcade in 1953. Lafourcade selected Donoso's story "China" (China) for his *Antología del nuevo cuento chileno* (Anthology of the New Chilean Short Story, 1954).

A year later, Donoso published his first book, *Veraneo y otros cuentos* (Summer Vacation and Other Stories, 1955), which won that year's Municipal Literary Prize. In 1956, he published *Dos cuentos*

(Two Short Stories) and, in 1957, his first novel, *Coronación* (*Coronation*). He spent the years 1958 to 1960 in Buenos Aires, returning to Chile in 1960. He began writing as a journalist for *Ercilla*, an important national weekly magazine for which he soon became a staff reporter, and was awarded the Chile-Italia Prize for excellence in journalism in 1960, the year he published his book of short stories *El charleston* (*Charleston and Other Stories*). In 1961, he married María Pilar Serrano, a Bolivian painter he had met in Buenos Aires. He began writing *El obsceno pájaro de la noche* (*The Obscene Bird of Night*, 1970) at the 1962 Writers Workshop at the University of Concepción. He then took part in the 1962 Writers' Congress in Concepción. During this period, he renewed his friendship with the Mexican novelist Carlos Fuentes. In 1964, Donoso traveled to Chichén Itzá, Mexico, on an invitation from the Third Symposium of the Interamerican Foundation for the Arts, and, in 1965, to New York, to be present at the publication of the English translation of *Coronation*. He returned to Mexico to write for the literary magazines *Siempre* (Always) and *Dialogos* (Dialogues). At Fuentes' home, he wrote the novels *El lugar sin límites* (*Hell Has No Limits*, 1966) and *Éste domingo* (*This Sunday*, 1966).

After 1965, Donoso matured as a writer, and his work was increasingly recognized. In 1962 he had won the William Faulkner Foundation Prize for the Latin American Novel, for *Coronation*. From 1965 to 1967, he was writer-in-residence at the University of Iowa's Writer's Workshop. He received a Guggenheim Fellowship in 1968 (and again in 1973), and during the late 1960's he lectured at numerous universities in the United States. In 1965, he completed five years of reporting for *Ercilla*; his collected short stories, *Los mejores cuentos de José Donoso* (The Best Stories of José Donoso) were also published that year. In 1967 he traveled to Portugal and Spain; while staying in Mallorca, he suffered a psychological depression. While teaching at Colorado State University at Fort Collins, he underwent emergency surgery, and because of morphine injections, experienced hallucinatory side effects. He returned to Mallorca and afterward settled in Barcelona. There he finished, after eight years of strenuous work, *The Obscene Bird of Night*. Under pressure by his literary

agent, Carmen Balcells, Donoso eliminated several chapters and wrote the final pages in one night. The novel, published in 1970, gave him a distinguished place among contemporary novelists. It had been chosen to win the 1970 Premio Biblioteca Breve, but that year the award was permanently suspended because of an internal crisis at the Spanish publishing company Seix Barral. Donoso settled down in the small village of Calaceite, in Teruel, where he lived in a seventeenth-century house and where he remained until 1982.

In 1971, his *Cuentos* (Short Stories) were compiled, and the following year, his *Historia personal del boom* (*The Boom in Spanish American Literature: A Personal History*, 1972) was published in Spain. In this book, Donoso scrutinizes with humor and grace Émir Rodríguez Monegal's discussion of the editorial boom of the new novel, as presented in *El boom de la novela latinoamericana* (The Boom of the Latin American Novel, 1972). With *Tres novelitas burguesas* (*Sacred Families: Three Novelas*, 1973), Donoso defined a new genre, the *novelita* (novelette), ironically representing a break in the practical, materialistic bourgeois way of life and its ordinarily recognized common sense—a fantastic break from the usual way of representing the world. In 1975, he taught at Princeton University. He taught at Darmouth College later in 1975 and attended a colloquium on his work at the Congress of the International Institute of Iberoamerican Literature in Philadelphia. In that same year, he wrote *Casa de campo* (*A House in the Country*, 1978) in Calaceite, adding for the first time a political note to his narrative production. In 1976, he returned for a few months to Chile, after a ten-year absence. His mother, who had been ill for some time, died in Santiago. Carlos Flores, a Chilean filmmaker, made a documentary entitled *José Donoso*, later distributed as a videocassette. Biographical information of interest accompanies the images and dialogues with fellow writers of his generation.

In 1978, *A House in the Country*, Donoso's second great novel, was published. The novel won the Premio de Critica (Critic's Prize) in Madrid. He later published the novels *La misteriosa desaparición de la marquesita de Loria* (The Mysterious Disappearance of the Nice Marquise of Loria, 1980), in which several popular narrative genres of the beginning of the century converge, and *El jardín de al lado* (The Neighbor's Garden, 1981), a novel about exile. He also published his only book of poems, *Poemas de un novelista* (Poems of a Novelist, 1981). In 1981, the Winthrop College Symposium on Major Writers met to study his work.

The following year, Donoso returned to live in Santiago. This stage in Donoso's life was characterized by his increased interest in Chile's social and cultural realities. He published his second collection of *novelitas*, *Cuatro para Delfina* (Four Stories for Delphina, 1982), following the genre begun with *Sacred Families*. In 1983, a dramatic version of *Suenos de mala muerte* (Miserable Dreams), one of the *novelitas*, was staged by the Ictus Theatre company in Santiago, and the dramatic text was published as a book in 1985. The same year, Donoso was detained by the police on the island of Chiloe, in southern Chile, during a political demonstration. In 1986, he attended the international book fair at Frankfurt, West Germany, to launch his novel *La desesperanza* (Hopelessness, 1986), afterward traveling to Madrid for the same purpose. In this well-received novel, Donoso for the first time makes direct reference to the political and social situation in Chile.

Donoso began to write at the age of twenty-five. His literary beginnings coincided with the first stirrings of the Generation of the 1950's, who began to publish between 1950 and 1965. These were the writers who participated in the Jornadas del Cuento, organized by Lafourcade, who collected their stories in two anthologies, *Antologia del nuevo cuento en Chile* (Anthology of the New Story in Chile, 1954) and *Cuentos de la generación del cincuenta* (Stories of the Generation of '50, 1959). The so-called Generation of '50 was, as a matter of fact, only a small group of writers—those participating in Lafourcade's Jornadas, and not all the writers of the generation. The group even lacked internal cohesiveness. Actually, there were dissidents within the group who broke with the organizer and did not want their stories collected in his anthologies or whose stories were rejected by him. The most important factor explaining their coming together was in fact their age, their generational proximity. The most telling fact regarding the literary production of the generation is that between 1950 and 1965 a new generation began to

publish. Members of this generation, besides Donoso, were Guillermo Blanco, Jorge Edwards, Jorge Guzman, Heiremans, Lafourcade, and Enrique Lihn. Over the years, they were awarded literary prizes and received the reading public's recognition. Donoso, undoubtedly the most outstanding figure among them, was the first to attain international recognition. His stature is comparable to that of his contemporaries Fuentes and Gabriel García Márquez of Colombia. Translation of his books into numerous languages, his prolonged visits to Latin American countries, and his protracted stay in Spain have contributed to the international scope of his literary reputation. In addition to being identified as a representative figure of Latin American literature, he is considered part of the literary "boom."

Donoso has contributed significantly to the discussion and clarification of this term in *The Boom in Spanish American Literature: A Personal History*. Following Rodríguez Monegal's idea of a literary "boom," Donoso presents the different layers or age groups that were part of the publishing phenomenon of the 1960's. He begins with the boom's *gratin* (kernel), composed of Donoso's own generational peers, the Mexican novelist Carlos Fuentes (1928–), the Colombian Nobel Prize winner Gabriel García Márquez (1928–), the older Argentine Julio Cortázar (1914–1984), and the comparatively young and very successful Peruvian novelist Mario Vargas Llosa (1936–), all of them favored by a widening, during the 1960's, of the European and North American markets to include the Latin American novel. After describing this fundamental layer of the boom's geology, Donoso further distinguishes the "proto-boom," or predecessors, namely, Alejo Carpentier, Juan Carlos Onetti, Juan Rulfo, Jorge Luis Borges, and José Lezama Lima, and the younger generation, or "junior boom," composed of Alfredo Bryce Echeñique, José Emilio Pacheco, Gustavo Saínz, Severo Sarduy, Antonio Skármeta, and other young writers.

Donoso tells the story of the boom with humor and ingenuity, describing both its central and marginal components. His book is a clever reflection on the external aspects of literature in general and the novel in particular from 1962, the year of the first Seix Barral Biblioteca Breve Prize, to 1971, when the dissident Cuban poet Herberto Padilla was arrested by

Fidel Castro's government, an event that seriously affected the political stand of Latin American writers and changed many views regarding the significance of the Cuban Revolution. The book, grounded on facts and on shared literary beliefs, is yet written from an intuitive point of view. Structured as a literary memoir, it is enriched with irony and skepticism. The expanded second edition adds two appendices, one written by María Pilar Serrano, that turn the book into a minor chronicle of the lives of contemporary Latin American writers. Serious scholars have used Donoso's classifications as their own when studying the "new" Latin American novel.

The dominant trait of Donoso's narrative style is the grotesque irrealism he has systematically practiced, which gives him a place of his own among the great contemporary Latin American novelists. Representations from the dark side of the imagination (forms of confinement, transformations, a descent into Hell) produce in Donoso's narrative a network of rich and complex connections. On the one hand, his narrative draws on classical and modern European works, popular and learned; on the other, it harks back to fundamental works of Latin American literary tradition and folklore. Charles Dickens, Henry James, James Joyce, Virginia Woolf, D. H. Lawrence, and William Faulkner constitute his closest affinities within English-language literature. The French writers Jean-Paul Sartre and Albert Camus have been of decisive importance for Donoso, as well as for other Latin-American writers of his generation. Claude Lévi-Strauss's *Tristes tropiques* (1955) had a revelatory effect on Donoso. Among Latin American writers, his work is very close to that of Uruguayan novelist Onetti.

Donoso's narrative style is characterized by the disintegration of the narrator, which he accomplishes through the creation of multiple narrative voices; the cancellation of the narrator's interpretive capacity and authority coincides with the assumption of a skeptical cognitive position or a dialogic intertwining of different narrative voices that share the same cognitive capacity. He has also practiced, like Borges, the deception of the narrator, canceling in a surprise ending the momentum gained up to that point. In this regard, Donoso has made use of several possibilities, such as the deception of the basic

narrator, in *El jardín de la lado,* who is replaced in the final chapter by a female narrator; the romantic irony of the nineteenth-century narrator in *Casa de campo;* and, in a parodic mood, the successful mixing of several narrative genres, especially the erotic novel and the mystery novel.

An English critic considered Donoso's first work, *Coronation,* a "vastly overfurnished novel. We have not seen anything like it since 1890." Local critics, similarly on the wrong track, thought that it was a response to the *neorrealismo* (neorealism) that was on the decline during the 1950's. The novel was in fact something else.

Coronation portrays three types of existence: inauthentic, as contrasted with authentic, existence; the existence of madness; and innocent existence. The middle-aged protagonist, Andres, lives an inauthentic existence, conducting his life according to a methodical and disciplined daily routine, symbolized by his collection of walking sticks, which he maintains at ten pieces, selling one when he acquires another and buying only to improve the quality of the collection. The security and stability with which he has planned his life become problematic when Andres' alienated and impersonal existence is invaded by a presence that bursts into his world and gradually begins to undermine its security.

Andres had long fantasized and idealized the world of inauthentic existence in a place he calls Omsk, a city in which everyone leads a life of routine. He was motivated to create this dreamworld when a glimpse of authentic consciousness filled him with anguish. All the insecurity of his existence finds its refuge in his harmless and recurrent dream. Omskians live the gregarious, undifferentiated forms of existence adopted by society, in which individuality and personality remain alienated. Omsk reflects the existence Andres has always led and now hesitates to abandon, because leaving it would entail the sacrifice of placidity and security.

Andres' gradual transformation at first takes on an ominous and dark form that does not make its way into his consciousness; we are introduced to it through the novel's objective narration. The arrival of the maid Estela establishes the motif that allows us to trace the process of change in Andres' psyche. The girl's modest aspect is presented, along with the first occurrence of the image that will dominate the narration: the vision of her pink palms at first fills Andres with disgust, which later turns into a feeling of ominous and brutal torment. While for Andres this feeling is still dark and intangible, his mad grandmother speaks out, with exact lucidity, on the significance of what is happening. The violence of the old woman unsettles her grandson, who considers her reasoning absurd and intolerable. The situation is intensified when the old woman orders Estela to wear a pink shawl, an image that repeats the motif of the palms. These images reappear as Andres' disturbed consciousness suffers a crisis and the full import of his overwhelming anguish becomes clear to him.

Andres has been contacted by a seller of antiques, who wants to show him a walking stick. At his house, Andres is confronted with the deformed and perverse sensuality of the antique dealer's wife, draped in her own pink shawl. The full epiphany in Andres' consciousness occurs when he leaves the antique dealer's house and the presence of the abominable woman. Only then does he realize that he desires Estela and accepts the existence of this desire. When he comes across the girl and her boyfriend, he discovers that what has attracted him to the girl has been true passion, more than just desire. Eventually Estela falsely yields to Andres for a moment. Then, when she uses his passion as part of a self-interested scheme, she pushes him headlong into self-annihilation.

Andres is thus propelled into the second form of existence: that of madness, which has been emblematized in the novel by his grandmother. Andres had noticed, first of all, her clairvoyance and, through her, the cognitive virtues of madness, which render one capable of understanding reality with perfect lucidity. He has also observed that she frequently speaks about death, without anguish. He has had a conversation with his doctor about the disorder of the universe and its congruence with the insanity and thoughtlessness that are part of anarchy, injustice, and the world's turmoil. When Andres finds that he has been deceived by Estela, he recognizes the absurdity and meaninglessness of everything and, at that point, enters the existence of madness: he will consciously and deliberately alienate himself in order to avoid the harrowing anguish of a fall he cannot endure. In this manner, inauthentic existence, briefly transformed into anguished authenticity, leads to another mode, in which he can escape the fear and trembling of authentic existence.

The third form of existence characterized in the novel is an unconsciousness that antecedes good and evil, and that may be called innocent existence. Full of precariousness and of extreme helplessness, its miserable situation is the manifestation of the merely vital, of the purely instinctive, blind, and spontaneous. At the same time, it is a form of existence capable of recognizing the deformation of personal dignity and even of experiencing evil as an ominous presence, although not clearly or distinctly. In *Coronation*, this form of existence essentially represents life, and the interplay of life and death shapes the represented world; this interrelationship is felt in every significant moment of the story, engendering the interdependence between the different modes of existence. From a slightly different perspective, members of the social classes are presented as projections of either decaying or life-giving realities. In Donoso's later novels, characters who belong to the higher class absorb life anxiously from the lower-class characters, who generously share with them their vitality.

Donoso began *The Obscene Bird of Night* in Chile and finished it in Spain. A sort of diary about the novel's composition, its planning stages, and the author's reflections is available in Donoso's "Note Books," numbers 37 to 47, at Princeton University's Firestone Library. The title, presented in its context in the novel's epigraph, is taken from a letter to William and Henry James from their father; it is an image that points to the dark side of the imagination. The world represented in the novel lends an animated existence to a grotesque reality: the persistent, indeterminate existence of a plurality of worlds that constantly affirm and deny their identities, giving rise to impersonation, masks, and disguise. Multiplying the number of worlds and tensions, and adding to them the blurred conscience of an elaborately structured narrator, the novelist unfolds, with his unequaled genius for the monstrous, for all that does violence to the common norm, his labyrinthine novel.

Donoso goes beyond the types of disintegrated narrators who exist in the novels of Onetti and Fuentes, offering us something markedly different. His narrator embodies the greatest complexity that a novel can propose, in that he is narrator-character-witness, presented through an extraordinary structure. Within the apparent unity of the narrator, each dimension takes on a totally novel character and a strangeness that subjectively conditions the objectivity of the narrated world. The disintegration of the narrator consists in the shapeless fluctuation of multiple identities—his substitution and participation in different personalities—and, at the same time, in a reductive movement, accompanied by a physical dwarfing, down to the level of the miniscule and contemptible. Upon the ambiguity of this double movement, the narrator bases his will to live and his will to self-annihilate. Two myths polarize this double tension: one, that of Oedipus; the other, that of the *imbunche,* a myth of the Indians of southern Chile, in which a victim is monstrously transformed by the closing of all the openings of the body.

The ambiguity of the narrator is presented, in one aspect, in the character of Humberto Peñaloza, author of the biography of the wealthy Don Jerónimo de Azcoitía and the intended chronicler of La Rinconada, an estate inhabited by a society—created by Don Jerónimo as a way to hide his deformed son, Boy—that shields abnormal beings from the ordinary context of life. The ambiguity of the narrator is also presented in Mudito, who narrates and hides manuscripts under his bed, as do his fellow inhabitants at the Casa de Ejercicios Espirituales de la Encarnación de la Chimba (House of Spiritual Exercises of the Incarnation at La Chimba), a retreat house dating from the eighteenth century that now offers asylum to elderly female servants and orphan girls, and serves as a storehouse for their personal junk and useless possessions. On two planes—that of the narrator as such and that of the narrator as characters—the tensions are overlapped. It is on this novel within a novel that part of the identity of the narrator is founded. On the one hand, Humberto Peñaloza's name is repeated 9,300 times in the one hundred volumes of the biography that are kept in the library of Don Jerónimo; on the other, the chronicle of La Rinconada is imagined and mentally conceived but

not written and, in a similarly unsatisfactory way, not perfected. Mudito's narration to Mother Benita and the entire narration in the second person, whose degree of immediacy, ensured by the constant address to the *usted* or to the *tu* (the formal and familiar forms of "you" in Spanish), fails to certify its reality, because no voice is proferred by the narrator. This expressive impotence characterizes the narrator in all his dimensions.

The ambiguous structure of the narrator is achieved in singular manner, beginning with his perspective, that is, his interpretation of reality, his peculiar point of view. This is the most characteristic aspect of the narrator and the one that appeals most vividly to the active and credulous participation of the reader, because it concerns a magical view of the world. This viewpoint establishes a cause-and-effect relation between distant but synchronic situations with unusual traits, presented with surprising efficacy in a series of repetitions, participations, and substitutions of demonological resonance. These devices describe a world in which reality is partly at a standstill (time has been suspended) and partly blurred, fluctuating, and indeterminate (the dislocation of time is absolute). Through this magical view, the novel expresses the ahistorical strangeness of the world: there is instability in every narrative sequence. With the transfiguration of the narrator, the narration controls and then loses its point of view, only to redefine it in a new context of discourse, exploiting at the same time the indicative possibilities of the personal pronouns of the first and second person.

The reader must constantly readjust to the narrator's fluctuating perspective, in order to harmonize it with the new "point of speech" (*punto de hablada,* in the Spanish philosopher José Ortega y Gasset's terminology). The disintegration of the narrator is thus governed by a pervading lack of determination. The identity, the personality of the narrator, his point of speech, his spatial-temporal positioning, are in constant fluctuation and contradiction. The narrator's own degree of knowledge is affected by this lack of determination, to the extent that he represents himself as impotent to grasp the real condition of what he observes or experiences, or the consistency of his own sphere of reality. To him, the real seems ambiguous, an uncertainty that lies somewhere between hallucination, dream, nightmare, magic, ritual, invention, and practical reality. Yet, at the same time, some constants are established in the crepuscular conscience of the narrator: the suspicion and even the conviction he has developed concerning the virtues of magic; the dark and unconscious impulses of the characters; the duplicity and disguises of the world; the compulsion for order and the determination of the self by the "Other"; the intolerance of the world for the foreign and the transformation of the latter into the monstrous and the obscene; the unendurable anguish of being a stranger in the world.

In his function as witness, the narrator defines his condition as that of voyeur. This voyeurism is used to interpret the power of the servants and the dispossessed. The narrator interprets his own power in terms of voyeurism and represents it magically. The narrator-witness projects the characteristics of the world in a sexual sense, with an explicit phallic symbolism, especially with the attribution of that sense to the eyes, which, magically, transmit their power to those who do not have it and who need a witness in order to perform adequately. The expression coincides with resentment and aggressiveness that are expressed in a sexually ambiguous way. This sense forms part of the magical situation in which the son of Don Jerónimo is conceived, that is, in the synchronism of a magical coupling that renders the impotent fertile from the dark side of the real. The magical participation is negatively experienced, in accordance with the loss of the narrator's identity.

The feeling of divestment, that is, the theft of his identity by his father, who reveals to Humberto the insignificance of his name and of his social extraction, motivates his identity crisis and the search for a face of his own. This search is represented in the fluctuating aspect of the transformations of the character, in whom the longing for a face of his own is confused with the longing or the demand for love, which takes on attributes of the Oedipus complex. When, toward the end, circumstances throw the witness into total annihilation, in a parallel to the myth of the *imbunche*, he still senses another presence. He then forgets his purpose of self-abandonment and desperately opens himself toward the presence he has perceived, "because there is someone out there waiting to tell me my name and I

want to hear it." But this possibility is denied, and his being is annihilated, perfectly, by a blind, terrible, and grotesque power.

As character, the narrator-witness embodies different identities of miserable beings who are either dispossessed or servants. These—the narrator included—are regarded not merely as inhabitants of a low and contemptible sector of the universe, but as a complementary part, intimately and dialectically linked to the owners. These two classes—servants and owners—support one another, each possessing its own order, governed by a legality that tolerates transgressions. The narrator-character is in charge of relating the different orders of the universe to each other. On his shoulders falls the demonic and unsatisfactory possibility of not belonging to any order and therefore the desire to belong to one of them: his condition is that of an ambiguity full of longing and anguish. His ubiquity is the expression of his sense of misplacement; it is also the expression of the loss of his face, of the insignificance of his name, and of the search for the mask that may be identified with his true face.

The story of Humberto Peñaloza unfolds in crucial stages. The first is the one in which the motherless child receives from his father the revelation of the insignificance of his name. This first deprivation has a profound influence on his subsequent existence. The second deprivation has to do with the wound inflicted on Humberto when he and Don Jerónimo escape a violent protest over a fraudulent election. Don Jerónimo appropriates that wound, staining his bandaged hand with Peñaloza's blood and showing himself as a wounded man in order to take political advantage of the situation. Humberto feels involved in Don Jerónimo's deceit, involved in his being, but at the same time, he is deprived of his own wound and of the meaning of its blood. The third deprivation entails his nightmarish sexual encounter with Inés. Under the direction of the witch Peta Ponce, the ritual of fertilization takes place, synchronized in the actions of two couples: the dark and the luminous. In that act, only power, only sexual potency, is accepted by Inés, who rejects and ignores the body and the identity of Humberto. His muteness originates in this denial, in Inés' rejection of his mouth.

Another series of deprivations takes place in the

monstrous world of La Rinconada. There the monsters who have gathered to build an isolated world, in which they have no experience except of themselves, nullify Humberto Peñaloza, whom they see as a stranger and as a monstrous being. Following the frenzied experience of a pierced ulcer and under the vague impression that he has undergone an operation that reduced his stomach by eighty percent, Humberto imagines that his entire body has been reduced by that proportion (a sensation in fact experienced by Donoso). The exchange of his organs for those of the monsters creates a confusion between his normality and the monstrous condition.

In the final series of deprivations, the papiermâché mask of a giant carnival figure (symbolizing the acquisition of power) is wrested away from him by neighborhood kids, who destroy it, signifying the end of his power. The phallic symbolism is evident, clear, and explicit in the text. In this series, Mudito is presented. A servant in the Casa de Ejercicios, he assists the three nuns who care for the elderly women and the orphan girls. His identification with the elderly women derives from this final deprivation. He identifies himself as one of the seven old ladies who await the miracle of their salvation, the son of the orphan Iris Mateluna. He is then identified with the miraculous child and finally emasculated by Inés in the frustrated repetition of the magical possession. Once the symbol of power and of the longing to be and to love is obliterated in this character, the reduction, the self-annihilation, and the myth of the *imbunche* are realized, making up a new order of existence, which, like every other order presented in the novel, finally breaks apart, giving way to the experience of anguish and mystery.

A House in the Country differs from Donoso's previous work in that this novel is a political allegory, a rich system of allusions to Chile's political life during the administration of Salvador Allende and the military coup of 1973. Nonetheless, the world represented in the novel is, as in the author's other works, essentially unreal, uncertain, and indeterminate—again a remarkable narration in which Donoso fills the rooms of the House with the products of his spectacular ability for the grotesque. With the configuration of space—upstairs/downstairs and inside/outside—as a backdrop, the central adventure of the allegory is the exploration and occupation of the House by the children, whose parents have left for the weekend (for them, the equivalent of a year). The absence of their repressive parents allows the children to invade forbidden and secret rooms and to explore them in ways that are both childlike and imitative of the adults' games. The children transgress prohibitions and dare to enter strange spaces, making contact with human sectors from which they are normally kept away and constantly violating the rules of the adult world. When the adults return, so do the limitations and repressions imposed in the past. Allegorical allusions to Chilean political events of the 1970's are easily identifiable, including the verbatim reproduction of some of Allende's political speeches, attributed by the narrator to the character Adriano.

The narrative proposes a vision of the social order similar to that of the Chilean historian Alberto Edwards in his book *La fronda aristocrática en Chile* (The Aristocratic Frond in Chile, 1928), which conceives all national political manifestations as the expression of one of two forces that dominate the Chilean aristocracy. The character Adriano, a dissident within a social group that contemptuously isolates him, is represented in the novel as a member of the aristocratic class, a trait shared by Allende. All in all, the representation of the world offers a view of reality that affirms the aristocratic bent of its perspective. The two antagonistic forces that have alternately governed and characterized Chilean political life—the one conservative, with the accent on traditional, intellectual, and historical values, and the other liberal, rebellious, adventurous, and innovative—are in this way confirmed in the narration. In spite of this, the novel constructs a world of prevailing unreality, of duplications, the use of trompe l'oeil regarding the painted figures on the ballroom fresco, and real figures that propose the grotesque ambiguity of real and pictorial representation. Doors and fences systematically point to what is shut away and forbidden. Upward and downward movement through the spaces of the House evokes the symbolism of the celestial and the infernal. The ambiguity of time—one weekend for the parents amounts to a year for the children—is a major factor in the deformation of the experience of reality. Its allegorical value sets clear bounds on the blend of seriousness and humor that affects the world view of this novel.

The narrator is at all times engaged in the commentary on the events he narrates and the text itself. A narrator's extensive, intrusive presence, under the guise of romantic irony, was a dominant trait of the nineteenth-century novel, constituting a control by the narrator-author over the narration that generally lessened the autonomy of the characters. Yet in this novel, rather than exhibiting control or romantic irony in the nineteenth-century sense, the intrusive narrator is part of a grotesque parody, a sustained act of humor. More important still, such a narrator does not make for an ostentatious, superior interpretive capacity or an exceptional conscience, as in the nineteenth-century novel. On the contrary, *A House in the Country* draws the image of a narrator-author who works in favor of uncertainty and self-irony; when he speaks directly to the reader, it is with the intention of undermining his confidence in an ordinary reading of the novel, of denying him the apparent advantages of an exact and unequivocal interpretation of the narration. A cognitive skepticism deprives the narrator's interpretive faculty of authority, making him a manifest parody of the nineteenth-century narrator.

The novel *La desesperanza* was written as a result of Donoso's immersion in the life of his country after his return there in 1982 following a protracted absence. The novel marks a clear change in the author's narrative, with a more than merely allusive rapprochement to present-day Chile. The context of the dictatorship, the repression and pauperization of society, the political indifference to daily outrage, the sclerosis of society, and the frustrated longing for social change—these motifs shape the background of the novel. The action transpires in Santiago, over the course of twenty-four hours. Within this period, two central events converge: the return to Chile of Manungo Vera, an internationally renowned popular singer, and the funeral of Matilde Urrutia, the widow of Pablo Neruda. The experience of one day and one night in Santiago are sufficient to introduce the singer to the extremes of life under the dictatorship: the curfew hours, the fear, the mechanisms of repres-

sion, torture, and death, and, above all, the sense of hopelessness in the lives of the people, who find no other alternative to their condition than that of the occasional protest or impotent act of violence. The funeral of Matilde Urrutia gives rise to negotiations over the establishment of the Pablo Neruda Foundation for the study of poetry, exposing the ways in which the ruling power and its beneficiaries take personal advantage of the situation. The funeral itself reveals the impossibility of engaging in any social act of importance without the ominous presence of repressive force.

Manungo Vera, moved by constant dreams and illusions about his native land, gives life to the profound urge for social transformation by means of his evocation of the story of El Caleuche, a traditional Chilean myth probably originating in the Dutch legend of the Ghost Ship. In the short time that has elapsed since his arrival, affected by his personal experience and that of his foreign-born son, he makes the decision to settle down in his country and to confront its harsh and desolate reality. Manungo Vera's decision stands out against the unbearable hopelessness as a positive sign, a universal call to change and transformation that reaches those who hold power, as well as those who remain indifferent to the cause of the dissident and the persecuted. This strange chronicle of a day in Santiago is thus exposed to partisan considerations and to an exacting analysis of the conduct of its characters, whose motives, in several instances, are weak and unconvincing. In the context of Donoso's works, this novel reveals a gradual displacement of the mythic dimension by that of everyday life, allusion and fictive representation giving way to the context of present-day reality. Myth is nevertheless still present as the most constantly reiterated aspect of the narrative discourse, the most important recurrent theme and the bearer of the dominant meaning of the narrative.

The short story was the narrative genre cultivated by Donoso in his first books: *Veraneo, Dos cuentos,* and *Charleston and Other Stories,* all of which are collected in the volume *Cuentos.* They represent an initial style that produced a good number of masterfully written tales. In them, everyday life and the magical or mysterious come together in an ambiguous convergence that is one of the main characteristics of the grotesque in Donoso. A further step, evident in their greater maturity and ambition, is taken with *Sacred Families* and *Cuatro para Delfina*. Donoso's original *novelitas* maintain the characteristics of his earlier works, but they are enhanced and perfected by his imaginative genius and his extraordinary narrative ability. Urban themes and complicated artistry alternate with simpler subjects and a persistent mixture of common experience and the strange, the mysterious, and the marvelous. Donoso's narrative artistry looks with one eye to Borges, although he is more verbose than the great Argentine innovator, and with the other eye to Cortázar. Donoso's style rejects the commentary or the theoretical stand characteristic of both Borges and Cortázar, who thereby provide interpretive help to the reader. More sensitive than intellectual, Donoso creates a unique and unmistakable narrative style. His work enjoys worldwide acclaim, and his renown excedes that of any living Chilean author. Experimenting with new ways of expression and of rapport and communication with the public, the novelist Donoso has tried two other literary genres: poetry and theater. He has staged the story *Sueños de mala muerte* (Miserable Dreams), from his volume *Cuatro para Delfina*. Recently published in book form, this dramatization makes evident the inherent dramatic tension of Donoso's narrative as a component of central importance in his work.

Suenos de mala muerte presents Donoso's usual grotesque style, mixing humor and death, and ordinary and extraordinary people, such as a fortune teller, a woman who is also a beggar, who plays a role that is somehow anticipatory and ominous. This character establishes the actual self-reflecting interpretation of the entire comedy: "hay que inventarse cada día para sobrevivir" (to survive you must reinvent yourself every day; act 1, scene 8). The beggar's sporadic appearances in the play, though incidental, are the certain indicator that the fortune of one of the characters is about to change. The beggar acts as the helper of the main character, who is in love with a woman who dreams of marrying a property owner, which the hero is not. The beggar reveals to him the existence of his family mausoleum, which he is entitled to and which qualifies him as a property owner. The woman's dream is finally fulfilled when

she marries him. Then, when happiness has apparently prevailed, the bride suffers an accident caused inadvertently by the presence of the beggar, and she suddenly dies. She is buried in one of the two remaining niches in the family mausoleum, which the couple had expected both to use when they died. However, the burial of a recently deceased aunt deprives the husband of the right to be buried in the remaining niche, frustrating his dream of being laid to rest next to his wife. People's thwarted illusions and frustrated dreams are the main theme of the comedy. The protagonist is supposed to reinvent his life, but it is clear that he will never be free of cruel frustrations. A realistic description of Chilean life is provided by the scenes of the picturesque, common life of a boarding house, but the atmosphere is altered by grotesque black humor.

Donoso's fictional narratives stand out as the most important part of his creative work. His novels *The Obscene Bird of Night* and *A House in the Country*, in particular, constitute the most valuable narratives of the contemporary period in Chile. They are also significant manifestations of the contemporary Spanish-American novel, standing alongside García Márquez' *Cien años de soledad* (*One Hundred Years of Solitude*, 1967) and Fuentes' *Terra nostra* (1975). Donoso's literary expression is distinctive and represents the dark side of the imagination, a grotesque re-creation of myth, folklore, psychology, and the fantastic. The mixed, peculiar voices of his narrative constitute the unmistakable feature of his style.

Translated from the Spanish by Nicolás Goic

SELECTED BIBLIOGRAPHY

First Editions

Novels and Short Stories

Veraneo y otros cuentos. Santiago, Chile, 1955.
Dos cuentos. Santiago, Chile, 1956.
Coronación. Santiago, Chile, 1957.
El charleston. Santiago, Chile, 1960.
Éste domingo. Santiago, Chile, 1966.

El lugar sin límites. Mexico City, 1966.
El obsceno pájaro de la noche. Barcelona, 1970.
Tres novelitas burguesas. Barcelona, 1973.
Casa de campo. Barcelona, 1978.
La misteriosa desaparición de la marquesita de Loria. Barcelona, 1980.
El jardín de al lado. Barcelona, 1981.
Cuatro para Delfina. Barcelona, 1982.
La desesperanza. Barcelona, 1986.

Essays, Poetry, and Theater

Historia personal del boom. Barcelona, 1972.
Poemas de un novelista. Santiago, Chile, 1981.
Sueños de mala muerte. Santiago, Chile, 1985.

Collected Works

Cuentos. Barcelona, 1971.
Los mejores cuentos de José Donoso. Santiago, Chile, 1965.

Translations

The Boom in Spanish American Literature: A Personal History. Translated by Gregory Kolovakos. With a foreword by Ronald Christ. New York, 1977.
Coronation. Translated by Jocasta Goodwin. New York, 1965.
Charleston and Other Stories. Translated by Andrée Conrad. Boston, 1977.
Hell Has No Limits. Translated by Hallie D. Taylor and Suzanne Jill Levine. In *Triple Cross. Carlos Fuentes: Holy Place, José Donoso: Hell Has No Limits, Severo Sarduy: From Cuba with a Song.* New York, 1972. Pp. 145–229.
A House in the Country. Translated by David Pritchard with Suzanne Jill Levine. New York, 1984.
The Obscene Bird of Night. Translated by Hardie St. Martin and Leonard Mades. New York, 1973.
Sacred Families: Three Novellas. Translated by Andrée Conrad. New York, 1977.
This Sunday. Translated by Lorraine O'Grady Freeman. New York, 1967.

Biographical and Critical Studies

Achúgar, Hugo. *Ideología y estructuras narrativas en José Donoso, 1950–1970.* Caracas, 1979.
Boorman, Joan Rea. *La estructura del narrador en la novela hispanoamericana contemporánea.* Madrid, 1976. Pp. 111–123.
Borinsky, Alicia. "Repeticiones y máscaras: *El obsceno pájaro de la noche.*" *Modern Language Notes* 88/2:281–294 (1973).
Castillo-Feliú, G. I., ed. *The Creative Process in the Works of José Donoso.* York, S.C., 1982.
Caviglia, John. "Tradition and Monstrosity in *El obsceno pájaro de la noche.*" PMLA 93/1:33–45 (1978).
Cornejo Polar, Antonio, ed. *José Donoso: La destrucción de un mundo.* Buenos Aires, 1975.
Donoso, Jose. "Chronology." *Review* 9:12–19 (1973).
Gertel, Zunilda. "Metamorphosis as Metaphor of the World." *Review* 9:20–23 (1973).
Goic, Cedomil. *La novela chilena: Los mitos degradados.* Santiago, Chile, 1968. Pp. 163–176, 211–214.
———. *Historia de la novela hispanoamericana.* Valparaiso, Chile, 1972. Pp. 260–270, 274.
Gutiérrez Mouat, Ricardo. *José Donoso: Impostura e impostación. La modelización lúdica y carnavalesca de una producción literaria.* Gaithersburg, Md., 1983.
Hasset, John J., Charles M. Tatum, and Kirsten Nigro. "Bio-bibliografía: José Donoso." *Chasqui* 2/1:15–30 (1972).
Iñigo Madrigal, Luis. "Alegoría, historia, novela a propósito de *Casa de campo.*" *Hispamérica* 9/25–26: 5–31 (1980).
Joset, Jacques. "El imposible *boom* de José Donoso." *Revista iberoamericana* 48/118–119: 91–101 (1982).
Lipski, John M. "Donoso's *Obscene Bird*: Novel and Anti-Novel." *Latin American Literary Review* 5/9:39–47 (1976).
MacAdam, Alfred J. *Modern Latin American Narratives: The Dreams of Reason.* Chicago, 1977. Pp. 110–118.
Magnarelli, Sharon. "From *El obsceno pájaro* to *Tres novelitas burguesas*: Development of a Semiotic Theory in the Works of Donoso." In *The Analysis of Literary Texts: Current Trends in Methodology,* edited by Randolph D. Pope, Ypsilanti, Mich., 1980. Pp. 224–235.
———. "The Baroque, the Picaresque, and *El obsceno pájaro de la noche.*" *Hispanic Journal* 2/2:81–93 (1981).
Martínez, Z. Nelly. "El carnaval, el diálogo y la novela polifónica." *Hispamérica* 6/17:3–21 (1977).
———. "Lo neobarroco en *El obsceno pájaro de la noche.*" In *El barroco en América.* Madrid, 1978. Pp. 635–642.
———. *El obsceno pájaro de la noche:* La productividad del texto." *Revista iberoamericana* 46/110–111:51–65 (1980).
———. "*Casa de campo* de José Donoso: Afán de descentralización y nostalgia de centro." *Hispanic Review* 50/4:439–448 (1982).
McMurray, George R. "La temática en los cuentos de José Donoso." *Nueva narrativa hispanoamericana* 1/2:133–138 (1971).

_____. "José Donoso: Bibliography-Addendum." *Chasqui* 3/2:23–44 (1974).

_____. *José Donoso.* Boston, 1979.

Medina Vidal, Jorge, et al. *Estudio sobre la novela "Éste domingo" de José Donoso.* Montevideo, 1978.

Montero, Oscar. "*El jardín de al lado:* La escritura y el fracaso del éxito." *Revista iberoamericana* 49/123–124: 449–467 (1983).

_____. "Writing on the Margin: José Donoso's Notebooks." *Dispositio* 24–26:237–243 (1984).

Neghme Echeverría, Lidia. "Tres novelitas burguesas y lo aleatorio de los eventos." *Revista lingua e literatura* (Sao Paulo) 7:157–174 (1978).

Nigro, Kirsten F. "From *Criollismo* to the Grotesque: Approaches to José Donoso." In *Tradition and Renewal: Essays on Twentieth-Century Latin American Literature and Culture,* edited by Merlin H. Foster. Urbana, Ill., 1975. Pp. 208–232.

Ocanto, Nancy. "Bio-bibliografía de José Donoso." *Actualidades* 2/2:191–215 (1977).

Promis, José. "El mundo infernal del novelista José Donoso." *Anales de la Universidad del Norte* 7:201–223 (1969).

_____. "La desintegración del orden en la novela de José Donoso." In *La novela hispanoamericana: Descubrimiento e invención de América,* edited by Cedomil Goic. Valparaiso, Chile, 1973. Pp. 209–238.

_____. *La novela chilena actual: Orígenes y desarrollo.* Buenos Aires, 1977.

Pujals, Josefina A. *El bosque indomado, donde chilla el obsceno pájaro de la noche: Un estudio sobre la novela de Donoso.* Miami, 1981.

Quinteros, Isis. "Artículos publicados por José Donoso en la revista *Ercilla.*" *Chasqui* 3/2:45–52 (1974).

_____. *José Donoso: Una insurrección contra la realidad.* Madrid, 1978.

Rodríguez Monegal, Émir. "The Novel as Happening: An Interview with José Donoso." Translated by Suzanne Jill Levine. *Review* 9:34–39 (1973).

Sarduy, Severo. "Writing/Transvestism." *Review* 9:31–33 (1973).

Solotorevsky, Myrna. *José Donoso: Incursiones en su producción novelesca.* Valparaiso, Chile, 1983.

Swanson, Philip. "Concerning the Criticism of the Work of José Donoso." *Revista interamericana de bibliografía* 33/3:355–365 (1983).

Tatum, Charles M. "*El obsceno pájaro de la noche:* The Demise of a Feudal Society." *Latin American Literary Review* 1/2:99–105 (1973).

Valdés, Adriana. "El "imbunche": Estudio de un motivo en *El obsceno pájaro de la noche.* In *José Donoso: La destrucción de un mundo,* edited by Antonio Cornejo Polar. Buenos Aires, 1975. Pp. 125–160.

Vidal, Hernán. *José Donoso: Surrealismo y rebelión de los instintos.* Barcelona, 1972.

Weber, Frances Wyers. "La dinámica de la alegoría: *El obsceno pájaro de la noche.*" *Hispamérica* 4/11–12: 23–31 (1975).

Emilio Carballido

(1925–   )

Jacqueline Eyring Bixler

Mexico's foremost living dramatist was born in Córdoba, Veracruz, on 22 May 1925. At the age of one, he moved with his mother to Mexico City, where he has spent the majority of his life. In 1939, he returned briefly to Córdoba and his father—a period, a setting, and adolescent experiences that would later resurface in his dramas and narratives. The separate and distinct life-styles of his parents provided the young Carballido a dual sense of identity with both the capital and the provinces that is visible in his equal use of both as settings. He decided early on to be a writer and by the age of twenty-three had already penned four plays. Two years later, his only son was born, his first full-length drama, *Rosalba y los Llaveros* (Rosalba and the Llaveros) opened the theatrical season at Mexico City's Palace of Fine Arts, and the dramatist traveled to New York on a Rockefeller fellowship in his first of many trips abroad.

In the years that followed, Carballido wrote almost continuously, producing scores of plays as well as short stories and novellas. His plays have won national and international recognition and drama awards, and many have been translated and staged abroad. Carballido himself has traveled extensively throughout Asia and Europe, the United States, and Latin America, where he is often invited to partici-

pate on juries and panels at theater festivals. As a result of his travels, he is highly familiar with contemporary world theater, a knowledge that is patent in his continual experimentation with diverse dramatic styles.

In addition to his literary career, Carballido has served in various administrative capacities, notably as director of cultural programs, professor of dramatic art, theater director, and editor of *Tramoya*, a theater journal he founded in 1975. In 1977, he resigned from all but the last duty in order to devote himself entirely to writing and promoting Mexican theater, which he has accomplished through his fostering of a group of young playwrights, whose works he has collected in a series of volumes titled *Teatro joven* (Young Theater).

Carballido's most significant contribution to Mexican culture has been his leadership among his own generation of post–World War II dramatists in the revitalization of the national theater. In the early 1950's, he and his contemporaries began renovating a theatrical tradition in which conventional realism and bourgeois comedies had run their course. Under the tutelage of maestro Rodolfo Usigli, these young dramatists succeeded in reconciling vanguardist tendencies with those of the realists. Retaining the distinctly Mexican setting of the latter and borrowing innovative techniques from their European counterparts, the playwrights tackled the basic existential problems facing modern man and produced a lasting theater at once Mexican and universal, traditional and bold.

Carballido is undoubtedly the most prolific and versatile of contemporary Latin American dramatists. Since 1948, he has written over one hundred dramatic works, including operas, film scripts, librettos, adaptations, and children's theater. His works traverse the gamut of dramatic styles, from macabre fantasy to strict provincial realism, from allegorical farce to plays of explicit social protest. Despite the structural, technical, and topical diversity of his theater, there are certain Carballido trademarks: the compassionate portrayal of characters, particularly women, from either the capital or the Veracruz provinces; the gentle humor present in even his most socially committed pieces; the distinctly Mexican setting and language; and the fusion of diverse dramatic styles and levels of reality within individual works.

While critics commonly emphasize the mixture of fantasy and reality as a prominent feature of his theater, his early plays pertain strictly to one or the other mode. His first published work, *La zona intermedia* (*The Intermediate Zone*, 1950), and a trilogy of one-act plays, *El lugar y la hora* (*The Time and the Place*), are entirely nonrealistic. The first, an existential *auto* (religious play), concerns a group of nonhumans brought to the Intermediate Zone for their final judgment. The trilogy is oneiric, often grotesque in nature, while its greater technical complexity reflects the playwright's interest in the expressive potential of nonverbal forms of communication such as dance, music, and lighting. (The date given for a dramatic work in the text of this essay refers the play's first performance.)

During the same period as these short pieces of fantasy, Carballido wrote four full-length plays that remain within the boundaries of the real world. The first and best known of these, *Rosalba y los Llaveros*, presents the disruptive visit, or rather intrusion, of the educated and city-bred Rosalba into the lives of her provincial, old-fashioned relatives, the result of which is a series of misunderstandings and confrontations. *La danza que sueña la tortuga* (The Dance of Which the

Turtle Dreams, 1955) follows a similar pattern of confusion and clarification involving the futile attempts of two spinsters to liberate themselves from their brother's overbearing, paternalistic "protection." *Felicidad* (Felicity, 1957) is the only one of the tetralogy not set in Carballido's native state. Here the psychological and thematic depth of the other three plays yields to caricature, melodrama, and a blatant moral when a pedantic professor tries to buy happiness. In *Las estatuas de marfil* (The Ivory Statues, 1960), the focus changes from family relationships to a group of theater people, who are actors in their personal as well as their professional lives. Through shifting perspectives and a metaphoric game in which the characters adopt and try to maintain rigid poses, Carballido reveals the hypocrisy of their feigned identities. Collectively, these four plays are representative of his ability to work within the realistic mode, to create well-structured, psychological studies of complex human relationships, and to express universal concerns within a local setting.

Carballido's interest in large provincial families later reappears in *Un vals sin fin sobre el planeta* (An Endless Waltz around the World, 1970) and *Fotografía en la playa* (Photo on the Beach, 1984). The first returns to the same family of *La danza que sueña la tortuga*, with the focus shifting from the old maids to an adolescent and his initiation into the adult world. The second captures in a static portrait a network of relationships among a family whose lives converge only on the surface. While these subsequent works share the tetralogy's focus on human relationships, they are psychologically more profound and technically more mature.

After several years of fluctuating between realism and the fantastic, Carballido began to combine the two veins, merging reality and nonreality to the point where they became indistinguishable from one another. Through semireal, ambivalent characters and symbolically rich images such as the web, the heart, the butterfly, and the rose, Carballido conveys the potential of man's imagination over his material existence. In each of these plays, the nonreal or fictitious world serves in some way to disclose hidden or unknown aspects of the characters' daily realities, thus suggesting that realism and the fantastic are complementary rather than opposite modes of perception. In his first attempt to commingle reality and fantasy, *La hebra de oro* (*The Golden Thread*, 1956), the world of two lonely old women soon merges with one of dreams and magic. Amid a spectacle of dance, pantomime, and music, a mysterious visitor leads the two women through a series of inner plays, which in turn lead to their own hidden truths. *El día que se soltaron los leones* (*The Day They Let the Lions Loose*, 1963) offers a stylized, farcical portrayal of the perpetual conflict between the forces of repression and man's desire to be free. Comic exaggeration and nonrealistic staging devices serve to underscore the absurdity of Mexico's social and political institutions. In *El relojero de Córdoba* (*The Clockmaker from Córdoba*, 1960), fiction and truth coalesce when a seventeenth-century clockmaker finds himself ensnared in a crime that oddly parallels a lie of his own design. The best known of these experiments with forms of nonreality is *Yo también hablo de la rosa* (*I Too Speak of the Rose*, 1966). A critic's delight, this complex and challenging piece offers opposing perspectives and interpretations of a seemingly simple train derailment. Structural fragmentation, multiple points of view, and the multivalent symbols of the heart and the rose all convey the enigmatic and multifaceted nature of reality.

In *Las cartas de Mozart* (*The Mozart Letters*, 1975) and *Orinoco* (1982), Carballido returns to the same basic formula. In the first, a ragged beggar proves the power of mind over matter by gradually metamorphosing into the young Mozart. Actual Mozart letters and music provide the background for this humorous recreation of middle-class life in a socially repressive, nineteenth-century Mexico City. In *Orinoco* the characters are two showgirl-cum-prostitutes, the setting a dilapidated cargo boat adrift on the Orinoco River. Despite an atmosphere of doom, the continual clash between Mina's fatalism and Fifí's poetic fantasies provides the standard touch of humor.

In a similar fashion, two plays based on ancient myth—*Teseo* (*Theseus*, 1962) and *Medusa* (1966)—produce tragicomic results when the most banal realities of modern man fuse with the magical legends of the ancient Greeks. With existential overtones, the once heroic prototypes lose their mythic stature and become as vulgar and common as their surroundings. In a more recent work, *En-Dor*, Carballido

merges once again the tragic and the comic, the real and the magical, when an embittered, wealthy widow appropriates the powers of vulgar spirits in a willful effort to control her rebellious daughter. While primarily concerned with the vanity and greed of the powerful, *En-Dor* provides comic relief in the form of a mischievous spirit whose truth-filled obscenities function as the voice of social consciousness.

Although the combination of distinct levels of reality and dramatic forms has been the most salient and repeated feature of Carballido's theater, he has also written comedies of a more traditional nature, such as *Te juro, Juana, que tengo ganas* (I Swear to You, Juana, I Want You, 1966) and *¡Silencio, pollos pelones, ya les van a echar su maíz!* (Quiet, You Damned Chickens, You'll Get Your Corn!, 1963). In the first, he pokes fun at nineteenth-century provincial mores with the shotgun marriage between a pubescent, tongue-tied poet and his forty-year-old teacher. In the second play, he relies on verbal humor and the sheer absurdity of the situation to transform a story of death, poverty, and arbitrary charity into a source of laughter. In yet another dark comedy, *Acapulco, los lunes* (Acapulco on Mondays, 1970), moral corruption proves necessary for the survival of those who must remain in Acapulco after all the tourists go home. *La rosa de dos aromas* (The Rose with Two Scents), written in 1986, makes fun of the traditional notions of *machismo* with its portrayal of two women on the path to liberation and self-fulfillment. Having discovered by chance that they have a common bed partner, wife and mistress concoct, in one of Carballido's wittiest dialogues, a hilarious scheme for vengeance and freedom.

While most of his plays fall into the broad category of bittersweet comedies, Carballido has on occasion written works devoid of humor. In *Conversación entre las ruinas* (Conversation among the Ruins, 1971), for example, two ill-fated, would-be lovers meet and discuss their past relationship amid the ashes of their memories. *Un pequeño día de ira* (A Short Day's Anger, 1966) also stands apart as a result of its overt political statement as well as its relative seriousness. The protagonist is a whole town, the catalyst the unpunished murder of a child, and the result a prophetic mass rebellion against corruption and injustice. These same themes predominate in the 1985 dramatic work *Ceremonia en el templo del tigre* (Ceremony in the Temple of the Tiger), wherein Carballido, inspired by the American invasion of Grenada, blends poetry, ancient Indian rites, and the social awakening of an adolescent in a setting of colonialism and rural feudalism.

Like many of his generation, Carballido is fascinated with his country's history, particularly that of the nineteenth century, and frequently bases his works on historical personages and events. *Almanaque de Juárez* (Juárez's Almanac, 1969) is an epic montage of the life and times of Indian president Benito Juárez, in which the dramatist draws parallels between social conditions reigning then and now. Inspired by the works of a nineteenth-century lithographer, Carballido also wrote a musical-theatrical revue called *José Guadalupe (Las glorias de Posada)* (The Glories of Posada). And in his longest and most spectacular work, *Tiempo de ladrones* (A Time of Thieves, 1984), he offers a series of melodramatic and highly amusing playlets, all based on the legendary bandit-hero Chucho el Roto.

In addition to these full-length works, Carballido has written scores of one-act plays, most of which comprise his anthology *D.F.* (the abbreviation for Distrito Federal, or Mexico City). Highly diverse in tone, each play offers a distinct slice of life in the capital. According to Carballido, the collection serves two basic purposes by offering his own personal vision of the metropolis in which he resides and by providing basic material for students of dramatic composition and novice actors.

First and foremost a dramatist, Carballido has also produced a considerable amount of prose, including several novellas and a collection of short stories titled *La caja vacía* (The Empty Box, 1962). The narrative style is, however, the only distinction between his prose and his drama, for the former displays several features characteristic of his theater: the frequent focus on the making and breaking of relationships among the members of large provincial families; the penetrating psychological study of these individuals; the division of each novella into short, episodic chapters similar to dramatic scenes; the predominance of dialogue over narrative description; and the dramatic building of suspense before the final revelation or awakening, shared by both the protagonist,

usually an adolescent male, and the reader. The concise, poetic, almost impressionistic style of his prose suggests the influence of fellow novelist Sergio Galindo as well as that of Agustín Yáñez, one of Carballido's earliest teachers. Because of the highly elliptical style of these works, what is not said often becomes more important than what is said, with the reader left to fill the gaps and resolve the ambiguities. The most widely known and structurally interesting of the short novels is *El norte* (The Norther, 1958), wherein chapters alternating between past and present portray simultaneously the formation and dissolution of a sexual relationship between the young protagonist and a mature, lonely widow.

Today, after forty years in the limelight of Mexican theater, Carballido shows no sign of slowing down. With a boundless energy, he continues to write one or two plays a year, travel widely, and foment the national theater in every way possible. By sharing his broad knowledge of the theater with the current generation of young playwrights, he is ensuring that the renaissance of Mexican theater will continue well into the future. His varied and limitless creative talents are apparent in the many works that he himself has contributed to this vital, cultural movement. With each new play, he discovers a different way of transforming Mexican reality into art and thus of providing a meaningful yet artistic representation of modern man. While fully aware of the social and economic inequities present in his society, Carballido never allows his protest to dominate his art, but rather subtly voices his concerns through such vehicles as farcical exaggeration, historical perspectives, and parallels between fiction and reality. By successfully adapting form to content and incorporating imaginative elements into his portrayal of daily life and human relationships, Carballido has achieved a lasting theater of universal transcendence, meaning, and appeal.

SELECTED BIBLIOGRAPHY

Editions

Prose Narratives And Novels

La veleta oxidada. Mexico City, 1956.
El norte. Xalapa, Mexico, 1958.

La caja vacía. Mexico City, 1962.
Las visitaciones del diablo. Mexico City, 1965.
El sol. Mexico City, 1970.
Los zapatos de fierro. Mexico City, 1983.
El tren que corría. Mexico City, 1984.

Dramatic Works

La zona intermedia. In *América* (Mexico City) 48:73–112 (1948).
La danza que sueña la tortuga. In *Teatro mexicano del siglo XX* vol. 3. Mexico City, 1956.
La hebra de oro. Mexico City, 1957.
El lugar y la hora. Mexico City, 1957. Trilogy containing the one-act plays *El amor muerto, El glaciar,* and *La bodega.*
D.F. Mexico City, 1957, 1962, 1973, 1978, 1984. The number of plays in these editions has grown from the original nine to twenty-six.
Las estatuas de marfil. In *Colección ficción 15* (1960).
Teseo. In *La palabra y el hombre* 6/24:651–673 (1962).
Rosalba y los Llaveros. In his *Teatro.* Mexico City, 1965.
El relojero de Córdoba. In his *Teatro.* Mexico City, 1965.
El día que se soltaron los leones. In his *Teatro.* Mexico City, 1965.
Medusa. In his *Teatro.* Mexico City 1965.
Yo también hablo de la rosa. Mexico City, 1970.
Te juro, Juana, que tengo ganas. Mexico City, 1970.
Almanaque de Juárez. Nuevo León, Mexico, 1972.
Felicidad. In *Textos del teatro de la Universidad de México* 27 (1972).
Las cartas de Mozart. In *La palabra y el hombre* (1974)
Acapulco, los lunes. In his *Tres obras.* Mexico City, 1978.
Un pequeño día de ira. In his *Tres obras.* Mexico City, 1978.
¡Silencio, pollos pelones, ya les van a echar su maíz! In his *Tres obras.* Mexico City, 1978.
Fotografía en la playa. In a three-play anthology, listed under the title *Te juro, Juana, que tengo ganas.* Mexico City, 1979.
Un vals sin fin sobre el planeta. In his *Tres comedias.* Mexico City, 1981.
Tiempo de ladrones: La historia de Chucho el Roto. Mexico City, 1983.
Orinoco. Mexico City, 1985.
Ceremonia en el templo del tigre. Mexico City, 1986.
La rosa de dos aromas. Mexico City, 1986.

Unpublished Dramatic Works

The date given refers to the year in which the play was written.
Los dos mundos de Alberta, 1947.

La sinfonía doméstica, 1958.
Conversación entre las ruinas, 1969.
José Guadalupe (Las glorias de Posada), 1976.
En-Dor, 1984.

Translations

The Day They Let the Lions Loose. Translated by William I. Oliver. In *Voices of Change in the Spanish American Theater,* edited by William I. Oliver. Austin, Tex., 1971. Pp. 1–46.
Goheen, Douglas-Scott. "An English Translation of Three Plays by Emilio Carballido: *Te juro, Juana, que tengo ganas, Medusa, ¡Silencio, pollos pelones, ya les van a echar su maíz!* with a Critical Analysis of His Work." Ph.D. diss. Univ. of Denver, 1974.
The Golden Thread and Other Plays by Emilio Carballido. Translated by Margaret Sayers Peden. Austin, Tex., 1970. Includes *The Mirror, The Time and the Place, The Golden Thread, The Intermediate Zone, The Clockmaker from Córdoba,* and *Theseus.*
I Too Speak of the Rose. Translated by William I. Oliver. In *The Modern Stage in Latin America: Six Plays,* edited by George W. Woodyard. New York, 1971.
The Norther. Translated by Margaret Sayers Peden. Austin, Tex., 1968.
Orinoco. Translated by Margaret Sayers Peden. *Latin American Literary Review* 12/23:51–83 (1983).

Critical Studies

Bixler, Jacqueline Eyring. "Emilio Carballido and the Epic Theatre: *Almanaque de Juárez.*" *Crítica hispánica* 2/1:13–28 (1980).
———. "Freedom and Fantasy: A Structural Approach to the Fantastic in Carballido's *Las cartas de Mozart.*" *Latin American Theatre Review* 14/1:15–23 (1980).
———. "Myth and Romance in Emilio Carballido's *Conversación entre las ruinas.*" *Hispanic Journal* 6/1:21–35 (1984).
———. "The Family Portrait: Dramatic Contextuality in Emilio Carballido's *Un vals sin fin sobre el planeta* and *Fotografía en la playa.*" *Chasqui* 14/1:66–85 (1984).
———. "A Theatre of Contradictions: The Recent Works of Emilio Carballido." *Latin American Theatre Review* 18/2:57–65 (1985).
Bravo-Elizondo, Pedro. "*Un pequeño día de ira:* La potencialidad subyacente." In *El teatro hispanoamericano de crítica social.* Madrid, 1975. Pp. 62–72.
Cypess, Sandra Messinger. "I, too, Speak: 'Female' Dis-

course in Carballido's Plays." *Latin American Theatre Review* 18/1:45–52 (1984).

Dauster, Frank. "El teatro de Emilio Carballido." In *Ensayos sobre teatro hispanoamericano*. Mexico City, 1975. Pp. 143–188.

Holzapfel, Tamara. "A Mexican Medusa." *Modern Drama* 12/3:231–237 (1969).

Kerr, Roy A. "La función de la Intermediaria en *Yo también hablo de la rosa*." *Latin American Theatre Review* 12/1:51–60 (1978).

López, Oswaldo A. "Crítica a las limitaciones del individuo [*El día que se soltaron los leones*]." *Explicación de textos literarios* 3:151–159 (1975).

———. "*Un pequeño día de ira*: Crítica de la realidad social en su conjunto." *Latin American Theatre Review* 9/1:29–35 (1975).

Montes Huidobro, Matías. "Zambullida en el *Orinoco* de Carballido." *Latin American Theatre Review* 15/2:13–25 (1982).

Peden, Margaret Sayers. *Emilio Carballido*. Twayne World Author Series no. 561. Boston, 1980.

———. "Emilio Carballido: Curriculum operum." *Texto crítico* 2/3:94–112 (1976).

———. "Emilio Carballido: *Fotografía en la playa*." *Texto crítico* 4/10:15–22 (1978).

———. "Greek Myth in Contemporary Mexican Theatre." *Modern Drama* 12/3:221–230 (1969).

———. "Theory and Practice in Artaud and Carballido." *Modern Drama* 11/2:132–142 (1968).

———. "Tres novelas de Carballido." *La palabra y el hombre* 43:563–579 (1967).

Petersen, Karen. "Existential Irony in Three Carballido Plays." *Latin American Theatre Review* 10/2:29–35 (1977).

Rufinelli, Jorge. "*El sol* de Carballido: Novela de la iniciación." *Texto crítico* 2/3:68–93 (1976).

Skinner, Eugene R. "Carballido: Temática y forma de tres autos." *Latin American Theatre Review* 3/1:37–47 (1969).

———. "The Theater of Emilio Carballido: Spinning a Web." In *Dramatists in Revolt*, edited by Leon F. Lyday and George W. Woodyard. Austin, Tex., 1976. Pp. 19–36.

Taylor, Diana. "Mad World, Mad Hope: Carbillado's *El día que se soltaron los leones*." *Latin American Theatre Review* 20/2:67–76 (1987).

Tilles, Solomon H. "La importancia de 'la palabra' en *Rosalba y los Llaveros*." *Latin American Theatre Review* 8/2:39–44 (1975).

Troiano, James J. "The Grotesque Tradition in *Medusa* by Emilio Carballido." *Inti: Revista de literatura hispánica* 5–6:151–156 (1977).

Vázquez Amaral, Mary. *El teatro de Emilio Carballido (1950–1965)*. Mexico City, 1974.

Vélez, Joseph F. "Una entrevista con Emilio Carballido." *Latin American Theatre Review* 7/1:17–24 (1973).

———. "Tres aspectos de *El relojero de Córdoba* de Emilio Carballido." *Explicación de textos literarios* 1–2:151–159 (1973).

Villacrés Stanton, Helena. "*El almanaque de Juárez* de Emilio Carballido y México en 1968." *Latin American Theatre Review* 12/2:3–12 (1979).

Rosario Castellanos

(1925–1974)

Maureen Ahern

In the writing of Rosario Castellanos gender, culture, and textuality meet in the genres of essay, poetry, prose, and theater. Born in Mexico City on 25 May 1925, she grew up on the family ranch near the Guatemalan border and later in Comitán, Chiapas. This was a region of century-old conflicts between the Tzotzil Indians and the landholding families, privileged for generations by class, race, and language. The death of her younger brother, who was her parents' favorite, sharpened their rejection of her and intensified her solitude—themes that dominate her early poetry and prose. In 1941, when the land reform program launched by President Lázaro Cárdenas stripped the Castellanos family of their properties, they moved to Mexico City to lead an urban life of limited means.

At the National University of Mexico, where Castellanos enrolled in the College of Philosophy and Letters, she joined the group of young Mexican and Central American writers who became known as the Generation of 1950. Most of her earliest writing was published in *América, revista antológica*, which was directed by their mentor, Efrén Hernández. The death of her parents within a month of each other in 1948 and the experience of reading José Gorostiza's vanguard poem "Muerte sin fin" ("Death Without End") resulted in the publication of her first two long poems, "Trayectoria del polvo" ("Trajectory of Dust," 1948) and "Apuntes para una declaración de fe" (Notes for a Declaration of Faith, 1948). It also brought her the freedom she sought to manage her own life and dedicate herself professionally to literature. In 1950 she received a master's degree in philosophy; her thesis, *Sobre cultura femenina* (On Feminine Culture), was an early manifestation of her lifelong concern with women's place in culture. At the end of 1951, after a year of postgraduate study at the University of Madrid, Castellanos returned to Mexico and went directly to Tuxtla Gutiérrez, Chiapas, to begin work as director of that state's cultural program.

Castellanos' first novel, *Balún-Canán* (published in English as *The Nine Guardians*), earned her the Mexican Critics' award for the best novel of 1957 and the Chiapas prize in 1958. In 1956, Castellanos had begun directing El Teatro Petul, the puppet theater for the National Indigenist Institute in San Cristóbal de las Casas. For two years the troupe traveled to remote areas of Chiapas, affording the young writer direct contact with the rich Indian cultures of her native region and the chance to write her second novel, *Oficio de tinieblas* (A Service of Darkness, 1962), which won major critical acclaim.

Rosario Castellanos married Ricardo Guerra, a

professor of philosophy at the University of Mexico, in January 1958. It was a difficult marriage that she soon came to perceive as a lonely failure. There were two miscarriages prior to the birth of her son, Gabriel Guerra Castellanos, in 1961, and eventually she obtained a divorce. The poems in *Lívida Luz* (Livid Light, 1960) and *Materia Memorable* (Memorable Matter, 1969) reflect those experiences of grief, solitude, and rejection.

From 1960 to 1966, Castellanos was press and information director for the National University of Mexico. In 1963 she began to write short essays for the weekly cultural supplements of several Mexico City newspapers, some of which were later published in her four collections of essays. For several years Castellanos held visiting professorships in Latin American literature at the Universities of Wisconsin, Indiana, and Colorado. Her stay in the United States coincided with the commemoration of the fiftieth anniversary of woman suffrage in that country and major demonstrations of the women's liberation movement, events that galvanized Castellanos' thinking. She returned to Mexico to accept a Chair of Comparative Literature at the National University.

The early 1970's marked the publication of Castellanos' short stories in *Álbum de familia* (Family Album, 1971), the essays in *Mujer que sabe latín* (Woman Who Knows Latin, 1973) and the compilation of her collected poems, *Poesía no eres tú* (You Are Not Poetry, 1972). In 1971, President Luis Echeverría Álvarez named her Mexican ambassador to Israel, where she also was a lecturer in Latin American literature at the Hebrew University in Jerusalem. Israeli colleagues and students responded warmly to her skillful representation of Mexican culture and art, and by all accounts she was a very successful diplomat. In Israel, Castellanos was free to develop her experimental play, *El eterno femenino* (*The Eternal Feminine*, 1975) and enjoy life with her son Gabriel. "That's why the accident that killed her was so absurd," her friend the Mexican author Elena Poniatowska wrote in the biography of Castellanos that she included in *¡Ay vida, no me mereces!* (Life, You Don't Deserve Me!, 1985). On August 7, 1974, Rosario Castellanos was electrocuted in her home in Tel Aviv when she turned on a lamp in her living room just after stepping out of the shower. Mexico paid tribute to her at a state funeral in Mexico City.

The hundreds of essays that Castellanos wrote for *Novedades*, *¡Siempre!*, *Excélsior*, and other Mexican periodicals during the period 1960 to 1974 constitute the point of entry to the development of her thought and writing because they can be read as intertexts for her poems, fiction, and plays. They are also aesthetic creations in their own right. In the essays collected in *Juicios sumarios* (Summary Arguments, 1966) Castellanos developed her ideas about cultural ideology and gender through exploration of the official silences that she found in her readings of Mexican culture, and in her analysis of the texts of her intellectual mentors, Simone de Beauvoir, Simone Weil, and Virginia Woolf. Their role in the development of her feminist ideology is evident in the numerous essays to and about them; Castellanos was particularly impressed by de Beauvoir's arguments that culture determines gender values and role, and that myths distort the images of women. Her reading of the diaries that Simone Weil wrote about her experiences as a factory worker helped Castellanos understand the relationships between the oppressed and their oppressors. Woolf's subtle but substantial presence in Castellanos' work is evident in the mixed modes of biography and literary analysis, the reader in the text, the imagery of the body to explore sexual differences, and a commitment to writing for and about women.

If Castellanos had learned from de Beauvoir that the study of a culture's myths was a way of decoding its attitudes toward women, "Otra vez Sor Juana" (Once Again Sor Juana, 1963) presents her own ideas on women as creatures of myth and silence in Mexico. In this essay, reprinted in *Juicios sumarios*, she wrote: "There are three figures in Mexican history that embody the most extreme and diverse possibilities of femininity. Each one of them represents a symbol, exercises a vast and profound influence on very wide sectors of the nation, and each arouses passionate reactions. These are the Virgin of Guadalupe, Malinche, and Sor Juana." From a historical perspective Castellanos considered conflicting national attitudes about the Virgin, "a woman who sublimates her condition in motherhood," and about

Malinche, "who incarnates sexuality in its most irrational aspect." Castellanos rejected the Freudian analysis of Sor Juana postulated by the German Hispanist Ludwig Pfandel, going on to point out the silences in Sor Juana's writing and experiences in a world ruled by masculine logic.

The archetypal figures of Malinche, the Virgin of Guadalupe, and Sor Juana provided Castellanos with a rich cluster of metaphors that she used to explore gender, sexuality, and inequality in Mexican life and art. In Castellanos' writing they become poems; paradigms or signs in her essays; and, finally, actors in a play. For Castellanos, the women of Mexico represent both a means of explaining and understanding the cultural myths of their country, and the focus of new literature. In her essay "La Mujer y su imagen" (Woman and Her Image, 1968), Castellanos used the discourse of scientific reporting as a caricature of the forces that have kept women outside of history, and created a series of intertextual mirrors that reflected the destructive stereotypes imposed upon women.

The diaries of a nineteenth-century forerunner, Fanny Calderón de la Barca, provided the point of departure for Castellanos' inquiry into women's lives within history. In "La mujer mexicana del siglo XIX" (The Nineteenth-Century Mexican Woman), the gripping colloquium of female voices that span 170 years of Mexican life detect silences that speak louder than words. "La liberación del amor" (The Liberation of Love) skillfully reverses male rhetoric to show how women become willing accomplices in their own degradation, while "La abnegación es una virtud loca" (Self-Denial is a Mad Virtue, 1971) demolishes traditional self-sacrifice as a viable ideal. Other major texts focus on Castellanos' own writing, women writers, language as an instrument of domination, and the relationships between Mexican women and their servants.

Poesía no eres tú contains Castellanos' poetry published from 1948 to 1969, as well as four unpublished collections written between 1968 and 1971. Three central concepts underlie all her verse: the search for her own voice, the exploration of otherness, and the reversal of myth imposed on female experience in Mexico. Her reading of the Bible and the works of the Chilean poet and Nobel Prize–winner Gabriela Mistral and the Spanish poet Jorge Guillén helped

Castellanos to develop her own style after the rhetorical blind alleys she met in her first poems. *Al pie de la letra* (Word for Word, 1959), *Lívida luz*, and *Materia memorable* illustrate what Castellanos, in *Mujer que sabe latín*, called the cardinal points of her verse: "humor, solemn meditation and contact with my carnal and historical roots. All bathed by that livid light of death that makes all matter memorable." The reconstruction of female experience in earlier long poems like "Lamentación de Dido" (Dido's Lament, 1957), "Judith" (1956), and "Salome" (1952), dramatized women of antiquity, In "Malinche," the speaking voice challenges the ethnic and gender stereotypes inherent in the Mexican national myth that has cast this woman as a symbol of betrayal. In "Monólogo de la extranjera" (Monologue of a Foreign Woman), Castellanos contended that if male myth has distorted the image of women, the language that encodes these myths alienates women.

Although many critics have viewed Castellanos' poems as expressions of an obsession with death, it is only one element of a much wider concept that permeates all her writing: the exploration of the "other." That other may be woman, indigenous culture, language, silence, or writing itself. In "Toma de consciencia" (Consciousness) the other transcends the self to become an awareness of community that enables her to define life in death, self in other, utterance in muteness. *"Yo soy un ancho patio, una gran casa abierta: / yo soy una memoria"* (I am a wide patio, a great open house: / a memory). Her concept of otherness transcends gender, becoming the passage to creativity itself.

> El otro. Con el otro
> la humanidad, el diálogo, la poesía, comienzan.

> The other. With the other
> humanity, dialogue, poetry, begin.

In her final four collections of verse, Castellanos abandoned the canon, and created poems from the voices of women speaking to women in the intimate *tú* (you). Their voices enunciate domestic or biographical events that serve as metaphors for larger social issues. The monologues of "Autorretrato" (Self Portrait) and "Lecciones de cosas" (Learning About

Things) dramatize the way women are socialized to be self-effacing and manipulative and to play roles that have little to do with their authentic selves. These devastating parodies reflect how subservience is internalized by its victims. The discourse of "Kinsey Report" is cast in the format of scientific inquiry, thereby enabling its victims of the double standard to "say the unsayable" about female sexuality in Mexico. "Pequeña crónica" (Brief Chronicle) uses the metaphor of menstrual flow to state that blood is the scribe of women's emotional history and the link between sexuality and textuality. "Se habla de Gabriel" (Speaking of Gabriel) uses the metaphor of pregnancy to link literary and biological creativity, an example of how the fusion of biography and domesticity became the mainsprings for some of Castellanos' most incisive writing. "Ninguneo" (Nobodying) uses a pun to analyze language and oppression, where the "we" of authoritarian utterance codifies a long tradition of discounting. Castellanos' view of how language has denied women access to power dovetails with the writings of the North American poet and essayist Adrienne Rich, and French feminists of the 1980's such as Luce Irigaray.

Another characteristic of Castellanos' poetry is her incorporation of a wide variety of signs from other texts to create new ones of her own. For example, one of her best poems, "Memorial de Tlatelolco" (Memorandum on Tlatelolco), takes on the format of a standard judicial report, the *memorial*, used throughout the Hispanic legal system. Thus, Castellanos' poem became the report that the Mexican government never issued about the massacre committed by troops who killed hundreds of civilians in an attempt to quell riots in Tlatelolco in 1968—an event that signified a profound social crisis in Mexico. In the text, the memory of the dead becomes the blood of the living, and as the poem draws to a powerful close, the personal "I" moves to the collective "we" of humankind.

Recuerdo, recordamos.

*Ésta es nuestra manera de ayudar que amanezca
sobre tantas conciencias mancilladas,
sobre un texto iracundo, sobre una reja abierta
sobre el rostro amparado tras la máscara.*

*Recuerdo, recordemos
hasta que la justicia se siente entre nosotros.*

I remember, we remember.

This is our way of helping dawn to break
upon so many stained consciences,
upon an irate text, upon an open grill,
upon the face shielded behind the mask.

I remember, we must remember
until justice be done among us.

Beyond the female images and voices in "Meditación en el umbral" (Meditation on the Brink), whose existence under patriarchal contraints led to suicide, silence, and self-denial, Castellanos searched for a way of realizing lives and writing for women that is beyond madness, muteness, or penance. According to Castellanos, literature, like women themselves, must find "another way" of representing female otherness. The closure of the poem turns toward the future, leaving negative history behind.

*Debe haber otro modo que no se llame Safo
ni Mesalina ni María Egipciaca
ni Magdalena ni Clemencia Isaura.*

Otro modo de ser humano y libre.

Otro modo de ser.

There must be another way that's not named Sappho
or Messalina or Mary of Egypt
or Magdalene or Clemence Isaure.

Another way to be human and free.

Another way to be.

Rosario Castellanos' poetic journey from self to otherness, the search for voices among silences, and the reversal of cultural myths are part of the larger paradigm that her writing represents in the evolution of feminine poetry in twentieth-century Latin America.

Upon her return to Chiapas in 1952, Castellanos reaffirmed her commitment to achieve a firsthand knowledge of the Chamula Indian culture. Her first novel, *The Nine Guardians*, drew on her early memories and the myth-shrouded world of the Tzotzil as seen through the eyes of a seven-year-old girl. Working with the Indigenist Institute allowed her direct contact "with the mentality, customs and hopes of the Indians." ("*Cartas a Elias Nandino*." *Revista de Bellas Artes* 18:21 [1974]). The short stories in *Ciudad real* (Royal City, 1960) grew out of those experiences, but the ideological paradigm that explained the relations of domination and oppression, Castellanos found in her reading of Simone Weil on "the attitude of the conquered toward the conquerors, the treatment of the weak by the powerful . . . the current of evil that runs from strong to weak, returning once again to the strong," she later declared in an interview in *Diecinueve protagonistas de la literatura mexicana del siglo XX* (Nineteen Protagonists of Twentieth-Century Mexican Literature). In Castellanos' story "El advenimiento del águila" ("The Eagle"), the conflicts between races are explored through the perversion of signs that are manipulated to oppress an Indian community. *Oficio de tinieblas* used the historical events of a Chamula uprising in San Cristóbal in 1867 that culminated in the crucifixion of one of the participants. Castellanos recast them into the struggle of her powerful protagonist Catalina Diaz Puiljlá, the Indian woman leader who used her powers as an *ilol* (priestess) to lead the rebellion of her people. The novel, which is still considered to be one of the best examples of neo-indigenist Latin American writing, signified a major break with the lurid picture-postcard prose that portrayed indigenous peoples as poetic victims who inhabited exotic worlds. *Los convidados de agosto* (The Guests of August, 1964) examined another neglected sector of Mexican society: the middle-class women of provincial Chiapas whose place, designated by tradition, was "under a man's hand." The short stories "Las amistades efímeras" (Fleeting Friendships) and "El viudo Román" (The Widower Román) examine the lives of women who are considered the "property" of their fathers and husbands and become objects of exchange to ensure continuity and control of a community. Castellanos' representation of women as signs of conflict, and their relationships to each other, were topics that had not been addressed by male writers or critics in Mexico.

The stories in *Álbum de familia* (1971) concentrate on the alienation of urban women and women's struggles to develop vocations. "Lección de cocina" (Cooking Lesson) demonstrates the author's superb command of feminine metaphors to create literature that is intrinsically feminine in speech act situation and message. The analogies that begin with the one that compares the female body to raw beefsteak transform Castellanos' vision of middle-class marriage in Mexico into a social catastrophe.

Castellanos' early one-act satire, *Tablero de damas* (A Chessboard of Women, 1952), allegedly based on Gabriela Mistral and her literary circle, is an acid view of women working against each other according to men's rules. In 1973, Castellanos wrote a three-act farce, *The Eternal Feminine*, that was published posthumously in 1975. Rafael López Miarnau directed and coproduced it in Mexico City in April 1976, with Emma Teresa Armendáriz playing fourteen different female characters. Reviews were mixed and when financial backing was withdrawn after a few weeks the play was forced to close. Set in a beauty salon in Mexico City, the play uses a hair dryer that enables the women who sit under it to dream of the past, present, or future. This device allowed Castellanos to dramatize episodes from Mexican history and myth and to shed light on the stereotypes—and women's collusion with them—that have oppressed Mexican women for centuries. In a prologue, Raúl Ortiz wrote, "Each character projects her present dimension at the same time that she incarnates the symbol of ancestral lies."

Kirsten Nigro has shown how Castellanos' "debunking" of Malinche, Sor Juana, the Empress Carlotta, Adelita, and other Mexican female figures in *El eterno femenino* infuses them with new literary and historical life on the stage, and in the minds of the audience. One of the most radical theatrical pieces ever staged in Mexico, *The Eternal Feminine* showcases Castellanos' brilliant use of ironic humor to demolish the myths that define women's experiences.

In the writing of Rosario Castellanos, women are the speakers and hearers, writers and readers, actors and audience. Woman as subject and as sign acquires critical as well as creative value. In the aesthetic space created by Rosario Castellanos, literature by and about women in Mexico comes into its own.

SELECTED BIBLIOGRAPHY

Editions

Poetry

Trayectoria del polvo. Mexico City, 1948.
Apuntes para una declaración de fe. Mexico City, 1948.
De la vigilia estéril. Mexico City, 1950.
Dos poemas. Mexico City, 1950.
Presentación al templo: Poemas (Madrid, 1951). Mexico City, 1952.
El rescate del mundo. Mexico City, 1952. 2nd ed. Chiapas, Mexico, 1952.
Poemas (1953–1955). Mexico City, 1957.
Salomé y Judith: Poemas dramáticos. Mexico City, 1959.
Al pie de la letra: Poemas. Xalapa, Mexico, 1959.
Lívida luz: Poemas. Mexico City, 1960.
Materia memorable. Mexico City, 1969.

Collected Poems

Medicación en el umbral: Antología poética. Mexico City, 1985.
Poesía no eres tú: Obra poética: 1948–1971. Mexico City, 1972. 2nd ed., 1975.

Novels and Prose Narratives

Balún-Canán. Mexico City, 1957.
Ciudad real: Cuentos. Xalapa, Mexico, 1960.
Oficio de tinieblas. Mexico City, 1962.
Los convidados de agosto. Mexico City, 1964.
Álbum de familia. Mexico City, 1971.

Collected Essays

Juicios sumarios: Ensayos. Xalapa, Mexico, 1966.
Juicios sumarios: Ensayos sobre literatura. 2 vols. Mexico City, 1984.
El mar y sus pescaditos. Mexico City, 1975.
Mujer que sabe latín. Mexico City, 1973. 2nd ed. 1978.
Sobre cultura femenina. Master's thesis, National University Mexico, 1950. Published by *América, revista antológica,* 1950.
El uso de la palabra. Prologue by José Emilio Pacheco, Mexico City, 1974.
For more than ninety uncollected essays, see bibliography in *Homenaje a Rosario Castellanos.*

Theater

"Tablero de damas: Pieza en un acto." *América, revista antológica* 68:185–224 (1952).
"Petul en la escuela abierta." In *Teatro Petul.* Mexico City, n.d. [1962]. Pp. 42–65.
El eterno femenino. Mexico City, 1975.

Translations

With the exception of her first novel, the writing of Rosario Castellanos received only occasional translation until the 1980's. For a complete record of her work in translation until 1979, see bibliography in *Homenaje a Rosario Castellanos.* The following compilations include only discrete editions, although Castellanos' work has been represented in most of the recent anthologies of writing by Latin American women in English translation.

Anthologies

A Rosario Castellanos Reader. Edited and with a critical introduction by Maureen Ahern. Translated by Maureen Ahern et al. Austin, Tex., 1988. Contains twenty-five poems, five short stories, twelve essays, and the complete text of *El eterno femenino.*

Poetry

Looking at the Mona Lisa. Translated by Maureen Ahern. Rivelin/Ecuatorial Latin American Series. Bradford, England, 1981.
Meditation on the Threshold. Translated and with an introduction by Julian Paley. Tempe, Ariz., 1988. A bilingual anthology.

Prose

The Nine Guardians. Translated by Irene Nicholson. London, 1958; New York, 1959.

Theater

Just Like a Woman. A translation of *El eterno femenino* by Virginia Marie Danielle Bouvier. Master's thesis, University of South Carolina, 1984. Act 2 of this translation was published in *Latin American Literary Review* 14/28:52–63 (1986).
The Eternal Feminine. Translated by Diane Marting and Betty Tyree Osiek. In *A Rosario Castellanos Reader.* The complete text of *El eterno femenino.*

Biographical and Critical Studies

This list is designed to acquaint the reader with the major critical studies of Castellanos' writing, with emphasis on more recent works available in English. Monographic studies and a few key critical studies in Spanish are included. For the major critical studies in Spanish, consult bibliographies listed below.

Ahern, Maureen. "A Critical Bibliography of and about the Works of Rosario Castellanos." In Ahern and Vásquez, *Homenaje a Rosario Castellanos.* Valencia, Spain, 1980. Pp. 121–174.

———. "A Select Bibliography of Rosario Castellanos Criticism." In *A Rosario Castellanos Reader.* Austin, Tex., 1988.

———. "Reading Rosario Castellanos: Contexts, Voices and Signs." In *A Rosario Castellanos Reader.*

———, and Mary Seale Vásquez, eds. *Homenaje a Rosario Castellanos.* Valencia, Spain, 1980.

Alarcón, Norma. "Rosario Castellanos' Feminist Poetics: Against The Sacrificial Contract." *DAI* 44:1466A (1983).

Allgood, Myralyn Frizelle. "Conflict and Counterpoint: A Study of Characters and Characterization in Rosario Castellanos' Indigenist Fiction." *DAI* 46:1958A (1986).

Anderson, Helene M. "Rosario Castellanos and the Structures of Power." In Doris Meyer and Margarite Fernández Olmos, eds. *Introductory Essays.* Vol. 1 of *Contemporary Women Authors of Latin America.* 2 vols. Brooklyn, N.Y., 1983. Pp. 22–32.

Baptiste, Victor N. *La obra poética de Rosario Castellanos.* Santiago, Chile, 1972.

de Bouchony, Claire Tron. "Women in the Work of Rosario Castellanos: A Struggle for Identity." *Cultures* 8/3:66–82 (1982).

Bouvier, Virginia M. Introduction to "Just Like a Woman" by Rosario Castellanos. *Latin American Literary Review* 14/28:47–51 (1986).

Calderón, Germaine. *El universo poético de Rosario Castellanos.* Mexico City, 1979.

Carballo, Emmanuel. "Rosario Castellanos. La historia de sus libros contada por ella misma." Interview in *Diecinueve protagonistas de la literatura mexicana del siglo XX.* Mexico City, 1965. Pp. 411–424.

Cossé, Rómulo. "El mundo creado en *Oficio de tinieblas* de Rosario Castellanos." In *Critica Latinoamericana: Propuestas y Ejercicios.* Xalapa, Mexico, 1982. Pp. 111–137.

Crumley de Perez, Laura Lee. "*Balún-Canán* y la construc-ción narrativa de una cosmovisión indígena." *Revista iberoamericana* 50:491–503 (1984).

Cypress, Sandra. "The Narrator as Girl in *Balún-Canán* by Rosario Castellanos." In J. Cruz Mendizábal, ed. *El niño en las literaturas hispánicas.* Bloomington, Ind., 1978. Pp. 71–78.

———. "*Balún-Canán*—A Model Demonstration of Discourse as Power." *Revista de estudios hispánicos* 19/3: 1–15 (1985).

Dauster, Frank. "Rosario Castellanos: The Search for a Voice." In *The Double Strand: Five Contemporary Mexican Poets.* Lexington, Ky. 1987. Pp. 134–162.

Dorward, Frances R. "The Function of Interiorization in *Oficio de Tinieblas.*" *Neophilologus* 69/3:374–385 (1985).

Fiscal, Maria Rosa. *La imagen de la mujer en la narrativa de Rosario Castellanos.* Mexico City, 1980.

Foster, David William. "Castellanos, Rosario." In "Bibliografía de indígenismo hispanoamericana." *Revista iberoamericana* 127:610–611 (1984).

Franco, Maria Estela. *Rosario Castellanos (1925–1974): Semblanza sicoanalitica.* Mexico City, 1985.

Garcia Flores, Margarita. "Rosario Castellanos: La lucidez como forma de vida." Interviews in *Cartas Marcadas.* Mexico City, 1979. Pp. 167–177.

Gómez Parham, Mary. "Intellectual Influences on the Works of Rosario Castellanos." *Foro Literario: Revista de Literatura y Lenguaje* (Montevideo) 7/12:34–40 (1984).

González, Alfonso. "La soledad y los patrones del dominio en la cuentística de Rosario Castellanos." In Ahern and Vásquez, *Homenaje.* Pp. 107–113.

Holm, Susan Fleming. "Defamiliarization in the Poetry of Rosario Castellanos." *Third Woman* 3/1–2:87–97 (1986).

Lindstrom, Naomi. "Rosario Castellanos: Pioneer of Feminist Criticism." In Ahern and Vásquez, *Homenaje.* Pp. 65–73.

———. "Women's Expression and Narrative Technique in Rosario Castellanos' In Darkness." *Modern Language Studies* 13/3:71–80 (1983).

Lorenz, Gunter W. "Rosario Castellanos." Interview in *Diálogo con Latinoamérica.* Santiago, Chile, 1972. Pp. 186–211.

Macdonald, Regina Harrison. "Rosario Castellanos: On Language." In Ahern and Vásquez, *Homenaje.* Pp. 41–64.

Miller, Beth. "The Poetry of Rosario Castellanos: Tone and Tenor." In Ahern and Vásquez, *Homenaje.* Pp. 75–83.

———. "Rosario Castellanos' Guests in August: Critical

Realism and the Provincial Middle Class." *Latin American Literary Review* 7/14:5–19 (1979).

———. *Rosario Castellanos: Una consciencia feminista en México.* Tuxtla Gutiérrez, Chiapas, Mexico, 1983.

Miller, Martha LaFollette. "A Semiotic Analysis of Three Poems by Rosario Castellanos." *Revista/Review Interamericana* 12/1:77–86 (1982).

Nigro, Kirsten F. "Rosario Castellanos's Debunking of the Eternal Feminine." *Journal of Spanish Studies: Twentieth Century* 8:89–102 (1980).

Nelson, Esther W. "Point of View in Selected Poems by Rosario Castellanos." *Revista/Review Interamericana* 12/1:56–64 (1982).

O'Quinn, Kathleen. "*Tablero de Damas* and *Álbum de Familia:* Farces on Women Writers." In Ahern and Vásquez, *Homenaje.* Pp. 99–105.

Ortiz, Raúl. "Presentación." Prologue to *El eterno femenino* by Rosario Castellanos. Mexico City, 1975. Pp. 7–17.

Paley de Francescato, Martha. "Transgresión y aperturas en las cuentas de Rosario Castellanos." In Ahern and Vásquez, *Homenaje.* Pp. 115–120.

Paley, Julian. Introduction to *Meditation on the Threshold* by Rosario Castellanos. Translated by Julian Paley. Tempe, Ariz., 1988.

Poniatowska, Elena. "Rosario Castellanos: Vida nada te debo!" In her ¡*Ay Vida, no me mereces!* Mexico City, 1985. Pp. 45–132.

Rebolledo, Tey Diana. "The Wind and the Tree: A Structural Analysis of the Poetry of Rosario Castellanos." *DAI* 40:5070A (1979).

Rivero, Eliana. "Visión social y feminista en la obra poética de Rosario Castellanos." In Ahern and Vásquez, *Homenaje.* Pp. 85–97.

———. "Paradigma de la poética femenina hispanoamericana y su evolución: Rosario Castellanos." In Merlin H. Forster, and Julio Ortega, eds. *De la crónica a la nueva narrativa mexicana: Coloquio sobre literatura mexicana.* Mexico City, 1986.

Rodriguez-Peralta, Phyllis. "Images of Women in Rosario Castellanos' Prose." *Latin American Literary Review* 6/11:68–80 (1977).

Scherr, Raquel Lorraine. "A Voice Against Silence: Feminist Poetics in the Early Works of Rosario Castellanos." Ph.D. diss., University of California, Berkeley, 1979.

Schlau, Stacey. "Conformity and Resistance to Enclosure: Female Voices in Rosario Castellanos' *Oficio de tinieblas.*" *Latin American Literary Review* 12/24:45–57 (1984).

Sommers, Joseph. "El ciclo de Chiapas: Nueva corriente literaria." *Cuadernos americanos* 2:246–261 (1964).

———. "Forma e ideologia en *Oficio de tinieblas* de Rosario Castellanos." *Revista de critica latinoamericana* 7/8:73–91 (1978).

Stoll, Anita K. "'Arthur Smith Salva Su Alma': Rosario Castellanos and Social Protest." *Critica hispánica* 7/2:141–147 (1985).

Vásquez, Mary Seale. "Rosario Castellanos, Image and Idea." In Ahern and Vásquez, *Homenaje.* Pp. 15–40.

Washington, Thomas. "The Narrative Works of Rosario Castellanos: In Search of History—Confrontations with Myth." Ph.D. diss., University of Minnesota, 1982.

Clarice Lispector

(1925–1977)

Alexandrino Severino

Although she was considered a difficult writer in her lifetime, Clarice Lispector today is highly regarded by fellow writers and the Brazilian public in general. Her novels and short stories have been adapted for the stage and made into films with much success. The more autobiographical, ethereal novels she wrote toward the end of her life, dealing with metaphysical issues and with death, have been sung by Brazil's best-known singers and rock-and-roll groups. Some have been choreographed for the modern dance. Lispector, who led an intensely private, solitary life, especially after her divorce in 1959, would never have imagined herself as such a fashionable writer. All her life she avoided publicity, refraining from taking part in the social activities that, in Brazil, are so essential to a writer.

For many years she was considered an outsider because of the unconventional quality of her fiction, strangely innovative then, though widely imitated now. And she seemed out of step with Brazilian sensibility, since the writers of the mid 1940's were preoccupied with social problems, especially the impoverished conditions of the peasants in the drought-ridden Brazilian Northeast.

Lispector, by contrast, offered a kind of introspective fiction that appeared excessively egotistical for a writer from a developing country. She attributed little or no value to Brazil's historical past and did not seem concerned with contemporary sociopolitical problems. She was mostly preoccupied in examining the self, independent of nationality, as it encountered and interpreted physical objects and outside events. The account of these existential or metaphysical speculations was transmitted in a style peculiarly her own; the rigid Portuguese syntax was made pliable in order to scrutinize realms of consciousness heretofore impervious to verbalization.

To write about Lispector is to recall a most extraordinary individual. I visited the Brazilian writer in her apartment in Copacabana three times in July 1971 and once in July 1976, a little more than a year before she died. What impressed me most was how the writer and the human being were one. She spoke at length about the perennial problems afflicting her most, which were the same as the unresolved issues treated in her fiction: the intricacies of love, the institution of marriage, the rearing of children, the writing craft, death, God, and others. Throughout our meeting, I noticed that she spoke as if she were one of her characters, dwelling on the problems that troubled her. It is interesting to note that in her future books she abandoned characterization altogether, speaking directly through the voice of an author-narrator, as she did during our meeting.

Lispector's beauty was also impressive. Tall and slender with sandy-blond hair and prominent cheekbones that highlighted her emerald-colored eyes, almond shaped and slightly slanted, she bespoke her Slavic ancestry. She sat straight up in a chair, hands folded on her lap, one cupped discreetly over the deformed fingers of the other. Lispector had been burned seriously in a 1967 fire in her apartment. She had almost lost her hand.

Lispector's well-defined accent, emphasizing her exotic appearance, was also notable. It was not a foreign accent, but rather a speech defect, which slightly deformed her diction. The charges of "non-Brazilianity" leveled against her, along with the rumor that she first wrote in another language before translating her texts into Portuguese, stemmed, no doubt, from her appearance and accent. But in fact, Lispector was brought up in an almost totally Portuguese-language environment and spoke no other languages.

Clarice Lispector was born on 10 December 1925, in Tchetchelnik, a small village in the Ukraine, where her parents stopped while on their way to the New World. (At the time, they did not know whether they would be going to Brazil or to the United States.) Two months later, the family—the parents, Clarice, and her two sisters, Tania and Elisa—arrived in Brazil. They settled in the Northeast, first in the state of Alagoas and later in Recife.

Life in Recife was pleasant, though darkened by her mother's illness. (Her mother had become an invalid after giving birth to Clarice.) Although the family was poor and her mother was seriously ill, Clarice had a happy, carefree childhood. Recalling those days, she told two interviewers: "I was such a happy child, I hid the pain I saw around me" (*Escrita* 3/27:20–24 [1978]). Clarice went to school, and in the afternoons she played on the street with neighborhood children from various social and racial backgrounds. Together with a friend, she made up stories even before she knew how to read and write. After she learned to do both, she read avidly. At first she thought books were born like animals. When she found out they were not, that people had actually written them, she wanted to write them too. When she was nine, her mother died; three years later the family moved to Rio de Janeiro, where Clarice

finished secondary school. She decided to study law, not necessarily to become a lawyer but because she was interested in criminal law and Brazil's penal system. While in law school, she worked as a reporter for several newspapers, among them *A Noite*.

In 1943 she married Mauro Gurgel Valente, a classmate from law school. After graduating the following year, they left to live abroad since Mauro was working for the Brazilian diplomatic service. Also in 1944 Lispector's first novel, *Perto do Coração Selvagem* (Close to the Savage Heart), was published through an arrangement with *A Noite*. The work was enthusiastically reviewed by the leading critics of the day. At eighteen, Lispector was already a successful author.

Lispector had started writing at the age of seven. The first stories she sent to the Recife newspapers were never published, probably because they had no plot. She read much throughout her adolescence. Since she did not have much money, she rented books from a local library. As soon as she found a job, she used her first paycheck to buy books. In a Rio de Janeiro bookstore, she came across Katherine Mansfield's *Bliss* (1920). She was awestruck. The New Zealander's style so accurately expressed the way Lispector felt that she remembers thinking: "This book is me" (Olga Borelli, *Clarice Lispector*, p. 66). Katherine Mansfield's stories helped to confirm the introspective stance she adopted with her own writing. Other influences Lispector acknowledged were Fyodor Dostoyevski; James Joyce; Herman Hesse, especially his novel *Steppenwolf* (1927); and Virginia Woolf, whose works she read when she was already a published writer.

Lispector's first novel, *Perto do Coração Selvagem*, descended upon Brazil like a meteorite, formidable and strange, radiantly brilliant, too powerful and too luminous to be ignored. It won the Fundação Graça Aranha prize. In spite of the prize, the critics' reactions were varied, mixing praise with incomprehension and wonder at this novel written by such a young person. Sérgio Milliet called it "the most serious attempt at an introspective novel yet written in Brazil," while Antônio Cândido hailed the novel as "an impressive attempt to take the awkward Portuguese language into regions of the mind as yet unexplored. . . ." One dissenting voice belonged to

Álvaro Lins, who while praising the thematic originality and the innovative technique, especially the manipulation of time, criticized the excessive solipsisms, the incompleteness of the plot, and the poetic language, which he considered inappropriate for fiction. Lins characterized the excessive presence of the author's personality in the novel as typical of feminine literature. While it is true that Lispector viewed the human condition from a subjective point of view and may therefore be called a feminine writer, she never wrote the kind of literature classified as "feminist."

Perto do Coração Selvagem recounts Joana's life as an adolescent and young woman and wife. The narrative is fragmented, thematically as well as structurally, in order to convey the effect outside events have on the protagonist. Scenes are presented without chronological sequence or binding commentary, and it is only at the end that, revealing a structural—but not a thematic—progression, the novel comes together in a final extensive monologue.

For this is not simply a story about marital infidelity. It is, rather, the story of a quest for personal identity, manifested in the examination of the subconscious and in the interpretation of the outside world imbedded therein. Joana yearns to discern an elemental universal force that would bind all things, spiritual as well as physical, in one common, harmonious whole. That force may be interpreted as God.

Throughout her fictional work, Lispector pursues this binding universal force. At first she does this through halfhearted attempts at conventional plotting and character delineation, but later she abandons all fictional pretense and engages in direct philosophical speculation, creating a literary text closer to the essay than the novel.

Accustomed to plot and character, Brazilian critics have always preferred Lispector's short stories to the novels. The author readily acknowledged this preference when she remarked: "I think I write short stories better, but only the novel gives me the exhaustive feeling of having said all that I wanted to say" (*Minas Gerais, Suplemento Literario*, 28 September 1968, pp. 8–9).

Lispector's first collection of short stories is *Laços de Família* (Family Ties, 1960). These stories explore, from multiple perspectives, the elemental life force, depicting people who deviate from it and those who embrace it. To deviate from the life force is to yearn after love, freedom, hope, all that is particularly human and unattainable. Such characters are abruptly made aware of the metaphysical insufficiency of life. They suffer anguish, inebriation, and nausea until they encounter the life force and gladly and consciously return to their roles as wives and mothers and to the drudgery of their daily existence, rendered meaningful by the experience. They have become aware that their routine, as unglamorous as it is, assures human survival and the continuation of the species. Lispector felt that animals—guided by primitive, basic instincts—are closer to the true essence of being than humans. Humans lose sight of life's basic goals through emotions and reveries. Several of her short stories have animals as their principal characters. One of the most famous stories from *Family Ties* is "Uma Galinha" ("A Chicken"), which treats the short, happy life of a Sunday-dinner chicken. Before noon, she escapes onto a rooftop, where "she looked so free"—yearning for freedom, like the women of many of the other stories. Finally caught, the chicken lays an egg. The whole family suddenly becomes concerned over the hen, taking the egg-laying as a sign of generous affection. "The chicken had become queen of the household. Everyone knew it except her." She continues wandering between the back porch and the kitchen. For a brief, glorious moment she had escaped, "silhouetted against the sky ready to annunciate." But chickens do not annunciate. "It was just a chicken's head, the same that had been designed in the beginning of time." Unlike humans, animals are content to attune themselves to the life force. In Lispector's view there is enough heroism in doing that.

A word must be said about Lispector's stories for children. She published three in this category, the most important being *O Mistério do Coelho Pensante* (The Mystery of the Thinking Rabbit, 1967) and *A Mulher Que Matou os Peixes* (The Woman Who Killed the Fish, 1968). Although they are primarily for children, these stories may be read by adults with a great deal of pleasure. In the first story, a rabbit is imprisoned in a cage covered by a steel lid. Threatening to escape if he does not get enough to eat, the rabbit does so time and again. Nobody knows how he does it. The mystery is alluring to children, but to adults the tale is an allegory for man's yearnings for freedom under duress. This story was published three years after the military takeover of the Brazilian government in 1964. *A Mulher Que Matou os Peixes* tells of a woman who is so distracted by household and other chores that she forgets to feed the fish and they die. The author-narrator apologizes to children everywhere for her transgression. It is a story of guilt and, on another level, it reflects world suffering caused by neglect and violence.

After *Perto do Coração Selvagem,* Lispector wrote *O Lustre* (The Chandelier, 1945), a novel that gave her great pleasure to write, and *A Cidade Sitiada* (The Besieged City, 1948). These two novels are not very different from the first one. The same female protagonist absorbs, transforms, and personalizes the physical world, creating patterns of unusual imagery. Lispector also uses the same literary techniques—manipulations of time and space and stream of consciousness. Since these two novels are narrated in the third person, free indirect discourse allows the author to speak through the mind of a character. This narrative technique is frequently used by Lispector.

In her fourth novel, *A Maçã no Escuro* (*The Apple in the Dark,* 1961), which many consider her best, Lispector is much more plot conscious than in her previous ones. Martim has committed a crime—the reader does not find out what it is until the last few pages of the book—for which he is not punished. He goes to find his true identity through self-awareness, on a farm, where he comes in contact with raw nature and performs the most menial tasks. He thinks life anew, and is able, finally, to return to the world of people and to atone for his crime.

As in earlier works, the mysteries of existence are tied to the instinctive life of animals. The simple contact with animals and other inert objects draws Martim close to the elemental life force common to all, man and beast. For Martim to find himself, he needs to observe and to partake in life's most rudimentary and crudest manifestations. The cows in the corral provide the clue. "They intimated their secret mystery as if they had already crossed the infinite length of their subjectivity, which no longer needs to be demonstrated."

In her next novel, *A Paixão Segundo G. H. (The* *Passion According to G. H.,* 1964), Lispector limits the action to a room where the narrator-protagonist, a woman known only by her initials, crushes a cockroach with the door of a wardrobe. As with Martim's experience among the cows in the corral, the protagonist seeks to understand the mystery of the universe by attempting to discover, through scrutiny and speculation, the life force manifested in both the cockroach's mutilated body and in the depths of her subconscious. The epiphanic moment occurs when the protagonist, in an attempt to fully partake of the life force materialized in the cockroach's entrails, eats them. Immediately spitting them out, she realizes, by the natural repulsion she feels, that it is not meant for a human to penetrate into the secret of being. Only animals do that:

> Within myself there opened with the slowness of locked doors, the wide life of silence, the same that existed in the immobile sun, the same that existed in the inert cockroach. And which would have been the same in me, had I the courage to abandon my feelings. Had I the courage to abandon hope.

Although *Água Viva* (White Water, 1973) carries the label "fiction," it is even less of a conventional novel than the others. The protagonist-narrator is not identified by name, and the plot takes the form of a letter she is writing to a former lover. The sentiments she uncovers and puts into words constitute the substance of the book.

Again the reader is presented with the pursuit of the life force, now called "neuter," a state that lies beyond the rational, and even beyond the imagination. The recognition of the ineffable state of neuter is transmitted through epiphany—the moment the narrator realizes that there is no distinction between masculine and feminine, the "I" and the "other," the "we" and the "them." There is just the "it" (as in the neuter pronoun in English).

In no other novel by Lispector is language so important. It is made to go beyond the realm of conceptual reflection—the other side of the "I"—in an attempt to apprehend and express the inexpressible, that is, the primary substance that permeates all beings and things. This is accomplished by fishing with words (as Lispector put it) and emphasizing the crude, the arid, the humus of the earth.

The next novel, *A Hora da Estrela* (*The Hour of the Star*, 1977), was her last. If *Água Viva* brings to mind my first visit with Lispector—she had just finished it that day, and the atmosphere was still charged with an intense creative process—I associate *The Hour of the Star* with my last visit, in July 1976. Lispector had just returned from Brasília, where she had received an important and financially generous prize, from the Fundação Cultural do Distrito Federal. When I mentioned that the year before another important writer had refused the money and the prize to protest the presence of the military in the government of Brazil, she startled me with her answer: "I wish I had refused it, too." Until then she had chosen to depict man's alienation from metaphysical fulfillment, not man's sociopolitical plight. Yet her answer reflected a new commitment, which was confirmed when she began to narrate the plot of her latest novel, whose pages were still spread over the dining-room table.

Macabea is a nineteen-year-old refugee from the Brazilian Northeast. Like so many others from that impoverished region, this antiheroine comes to São Paulo hoping to find a job. She is poor, inept as a secretary (since she is barely literate), and unloved. She is, nevertheless, irrepressible. From the arid desert of her spirit, scattered weeds begin to sprout. She hesitantly gropes for the answers to questions prompted by brief educational radio programs. But all is in vain. She visits a fortune-teller who tells her she is to come into a great deal of money by marrying a rich young foreigner. Stepping into the street after leaving the fortune-teller's house, she is run over by a car driven by a handsome young foreigner.

The Hour of the Star is a fitting tribute to the northeastern region where Lispector lived as a child. It is also a desperate call for action that would improve the conditions of that forlorn part of Brazil. "There is nothing I can do. . . . Why do I feel guilty? And trying to get some relief from the burden of having done nothing for this young woman?" the novel's narrator says.

Clarice Lispector died on 9 December 1977, two months after the publication of *The Hour of the Star* and one day before her fifty-second birthday. Writing, for this extraordinary woman, had been an intrinsic part of living; she wrote about the existential and metaphysical problems that troubled her most. In order to conceptualize the quest into the metaphysical (that is, the pursuit of God) or the probing into the subconscious (that is, the pursuit of the self), she resorted to such innovative literary techniques as stream of consciousness and the manipulation of time and space. Most important of all, she renovated the Portuguese language, creating new syntactical patterns with simple words and reaching realms of knowledge seldom before explored. Although she was not a feminist writer, many of her novels and short stories view the world from a feminine point of view. Others do not, since the protagonist is male. Clarice Lispector belongs to no time and to no place, though she was definitely a Brazilian by virtue of her upbringing in the most Brazilian of regions—the Northeast—and by her education. Through her exploration of existential and metaphysical issues, however, she is a universal writer, belonging to the world.

SELECTED BIBLIOGRAPHY

First Editions

Prose Narratives

Perto do Coração Selvagem. Rio de Janeiro, 1944.
O Lustre. Rio de Janeiro, 1946.
A Cidade Sitiada. Rio de Janeiro, 1949.
Laços de Família. São Paulo, 1960.
A Maçã no Escuro. Rio de Janeiro, 1961.
A Legião Estrangeira. Rio de Janeiro, 1964.
A Paixão Segundo G. H. Rio de Janeiro, 1964.
Uma Aprendizagem ou o Livro dos Prazeres. Rio de Janeiro, 1969.
Felicidade Clandestina: Contos. Rio de Janeiro, 1971.
Água Viva. Rio de Janeiro, 1973.
Onde Estivestes de Noite. Rio de Janeiro, 1974.
A Via Crucis do Corpo. Rio de Janeiro, 1974.
A Hora da Estrela. Rio de Janeiro, 1977.
Um Sopro de Vida. Rio de Janeiro, 1978.
A Bela e a Fera. Rio de Janeiro, 1979.

Children's Books

O Mistério do Coelho Pensante. Rio de Janeiro, 1967.
A Mulher Que Matou os Peixes. Rio de Janeiro, 1968.

Essays

Visão do Esplendor: Impressões Leves. Rio de Janeiro, 1975.
De Corpo Inteiro. Rio de Janeiro, 1975.
A Descoberta do Mundo. Rio de Janeiro, 1984.

Translations

The Apple in the Dark. Translated by Gregory Rabassa. New York, 1967. Reissued Austin, Tex., 1986.
An Apprenticeship; or, The Book of Delights. Translated by Richard A. Mazzara and Lorri A. Parris. Austin, Tex., 1986.
"Better Than to Burn." Translated by Alexis Levitin. In *Latin American Literature Today,* edited by Anne Fremantle. New York, 1977. Pp. 169–171.
Family Ties. Translated by Giovanni Pontiero. Austin, Tex., 1972.
The Foreign Legion. Translated by Giovanni Pontiero. Manchester, England, 1986.
The Hour of the Star. Translated by Giovanni Pontiero. Manchester, England, 1986.
"The Man Who Appeared." Translated by Alexis Levitin. In *Latin American Literature Today,* edited by Anne Fremantle. New York, 1977. Pp. 165–169.
"Marmosets." Translated by Elizabeth Bishop. In *The Eye of the Heart.* New York, 1973. Pp. 455–457.
The Passion According to G. H. Translated by Ronald W. Sousa. Minneapolis, Minn., 1988.
"The Smallest Woman in the World." Translated by Elizabeth Bishop. In *The Eye of the Heart.* New York, 1973. Pp. 447–454.
"Temptation." Translated by Elizabeth Lowe. *Inter-Muse* 1/1:91–92 (1976).

Biographical and Critical Studies

Borelli, Olga. *Clarice Lispector: Esboço para um Possível Retrato.* Rio de Janeiro, 1981.
Brasil, Assis. *Clarice Lispector: Ensaio.* Rio de Janeiro, 1969.
Bruno, Haroldo. "Água Viva, um Solilóquio de Clarice Lispector Sobre o Ser." *Estado de São Paulo, Suplemento Literario,* 3 February 1974. P. 1.
Bryan, C. D. B. "Afraid to Be Afraid." *New York Times Book Review,* 3 September 1967. Pp. 22–23.
Cândido, Antônio. "No Raiar de Clarice Lispector." In *Vários Escritos.* São Paulo, 1970. Pp. 125–131.
Cook, Bruce. "Women in the Web." *Review* (Center for Inter-American Relations) 73:65–66 (1973).
Coutinho, Afrânio. *An Introduction to Literature in Brazil.*

Translated by Gregory Rabassa. New York, 1969. P. 249.
Filho, Adonias. *Modernos Ficcionistas Brasileiros.* Series 2. Rio de Janeiro, 1965. Pp. 81–83.
Fitz, Earl E. "Clarice Lispector and the Lyrical Novel: A Re-examination of *A Maçã no Escuro.*" *Luso-Brazilian Review* 14/2:153–160 (1977).
———. "Clarice Lispector: The Nature and Form of the Lyrical Novel." *Dissertation Abstracts International* 37:7119 A (City University of New York, 1977).
———. "The Leitmotif of Darkness in Seven Novels by Clarice Lispector." *Chasqui: Revista de literatura latinoamericana* 7/2:18–28 (1978).
———. "The Rise of the New Novel in Latin America: A Lyrical Aesthetic." *Inter-Muse* 2:17–27 (1979).
———. "Freedom and Self-Realization: Feminist Characterization in the Fiction of Clarice Lispector." *Modern Language Studies* 10/3:51–61 (1980).
———. "Point of View in Clarice Lispector's *A Hora da Estrela.*" *Luso-Brazilian Review* 19/2:195–208 (1982).
———. *Clarice Lispector.* Boston, 1985.
Garcia, Frederick C. H. "Os Livros Infantis de Clarice Lispector." *Minas Gerais, Suplemento Literario,* 10 February 1979. Pp. 4–5.
Herman, Rita. "Existence in *Laços de Família.*" *Luso-Brazilian Review* 4/1:69–74 (1967).
Hill, Amariles Guimarães. "O Sistema Original de Clarice Lispector." *Tempo Brasileiro: Revista de Cultura* 48:59–71 (1977).
Jozef, Bella. "Clarice Lispector: La transgresión como acto de libertad." *Revista iberoamericana* 43/98–99:225–231 (1977).
Lima, Luiz Costa. *Lira e Antilira.* Rio de Janeiro, 1968.
———. *A Literatura no Brasil 5,* edited by Afrânio Coutinho. Rio de Janeiro, 1970. Pp. 449–472.
Lindstrom, Naomi. "Clarice Lispector: Articulating Women's Experience." *Chasqui: Revista de literatura latinoamericana.* 8/1:43–52 (1978).
———. "A Discourse Analysis of 'Preciosidade' by Clarice Lispector." *Luso-Brazilian Review* 19/2:187–194 (1982).
Lins, Osman. "O Tempo em *Feliz Aniversario.*" *Coloquio/Letras* 19:16–22 (1974).
"A Literatura, Segundo Clarice." *Minas Gerais, Suplemento Literario,* 28 September 1968. Pp. 8–9.
Lowe, Elizabeth Anne Schlomann. "The Passion According to Clarice Lispector." *Review* (Center for Inter-American Relations) 24:34–37 (1980).
———. *The City in Brazilian Literature.* Rutherford, N.J., 1982.
Lucas, Fábio. "Contemporary Brazilian Fiction: Guimarães

Rosa and Clarice Lispector." In *Contemporary Latin American Literature,* edited by Harvey L. Johnson and Philip B. Taylor. Houston, Tex., 1973. Pp. 60–66.

Milliet, Sérgio. "Com Veleidade a Crônica." In *Diário Crítico 2.* São Paulo, 1945. Pp. 27–32.

_____. *Diário Crítico 4.* São Paulo, 1945. Pp. 40–44.

_____. *Diário Crítico 7.* São Paulo, 1953. Pp. 33–44.

_____. *Diário Crítico 8.* São Paulo, 1955. Pp. 235–237.

Moisés, Massaud. "Clarice Lispector Contista." In *Temas Brasileiros.* São Paulo, 1964. Pp. 119–124.

_____. "The Contemporary Brazilian Novel." In *Fiction in Several Languages,* edited by Henri Peyre. Boston, 1969.

_____. "Clarice Lispector: Fiction and Cosmic Vision." Translated by Sara M. McCabe. *Studies in Short Fiction* 8/1:268–281 (1971).

Nunes, Benedito. "O Mundo Imaginário de Clarice Lispector." In *O Dorso do Tigre.* São Paulo, 1969. Pp. 93–139.

_____. *Leitura de Clarice Lispector.* São Paulo, 1973.

Nunes, Maria Luísa. "Narrative Modes in Clarice Lispector's *Laços de Família:* The Rendering of Consciousness." *Luso-Brazilian Review* 14/2:174–184 (1977).

Paes, José Paulo. "Clarice Lispector." In *Pequeno Dicionário de Literatura Brasileira.* 2nd ed., revised and enlarged by Massaud Moisés. São Paulo, 1980.

Patai, Daphne. "Clarice Lispector and the Clamor of the Ineffable." *Kentucky Romance Quarterly* 27/2:133–149 (1980).

Pontiero, Giovanni. "The Drama of Existence in *Laços de Família.*" *Studies in Short Fiction* 8/1:256–267 (1971).

_____. "Excerpts from the Chronicles of *The Foreign Legion.*" *Review* (Center for Inter-American Relations) 24:37–43 (1980).

Rabassa, Gregory. "La nueva narrativa en el Brasil." *Nueva narrativa hispanoamericana* 2/1:145–148 (1972).

Reis, Fernando G. "Quem tem Medo de Clarice Lispector." *Revista Civilização Brasileira* 4/17:225–234 (1968).

Rodríguez Monegal, Emir. *El boom de la novela latinoamericana.* Caracas, 1972. Pp. 27, 93.

Sá, Olga de. *A Escritura de Clarice Lispector.* Petrópolis, Brazil, 1979.

Sant'Anna, Affonso Romano de. *Análise Estrutural de Romances Brasileiros.* 3rd ed. Petrópolis, Brazil, 1975.

_____, and Marina Colassanti. "Dezembro sem Clarice." *Escrita* 27:20–24 (1977).

Schwartz, Roberto. *A Sereia e o Desconfiado.* Rio de Janeiro, 1965.

Severino, Alexandrino E. "Major Trends in the Development of the Brazilian Short Story." *Studies in Short Fiction* 8/1:199–208 (1971).

_____. "The Short Story in the Sixties: Reflections of a Changing Society." In *Brazil in the Sixties,* edited by Riordan Roett. Nashville, Tenn., 1972. Pp. 375–396.

Waldman, Berta. *Clarice Lispector.* São Paulo, 1983.

Zagury, Elaine. *A Palavra e os Ecos.* Petrópolis, Brazil, 1971.

_____. "O Que Clarice Diz de Clarice." *Cadernos Brasileiros* 10/50:69–79 (1968).

Egon Wolff

(1926–   )

Elena Castedo-Ellerman

Egon Wolff, the son of German immigrants, was born in Santiago, Chile, on 13 April 1926. In spite of the scientific emphasis of his formal education (he holds a degree in chemical engineering), he showed very early a strong attraction to the humanities. He became well schooled in the classics, in part because of the delicate health of his early years, which afforded him extensive opportunity to read. Imbued by family tradition with the ethics of hard work, devotion to family, and social responsibility, Wolff shunned the artistic circles' gregarious and bohemian style of life. Parallel to his creative work, he pursued a successful career in the manufacture and sale of chemical products.

In 1984 the Chilean Language Academy elected Wolff a member. Outside of Chile, his work has been staged in twenty-nine countries, translated into nineteen languages, and produced as films in Mexico and England. He has received numerous fellowships and invitations from all over the world to attend the premieres of his plays.

Wolff emerged as a playwright in the late 1950's, a time of great cultural ferment in Chile. This ferment became channeled in a search for national identity, and Wolff's unaffected, candid probing into human relationships found a natural place within it. The Chilean stage was no longer willing to satisfy a middle-class theatergoing public's taste for risqué foreign comedies, rehashed melodramas, and, to a minor extent, dramas of rural or slum life ridden with clichés and easy sentimentality. The new demand for quality theater, which also flourished in universities, schools, factories, political groups, and ad hoc artistic groups, produced a theater that has been hailed by critics of international reputation and has been profusely staged in Europe.

From the beginning of this renaissance, Wolff was a key figure, both in Chile and in Latin America. In 1957 two of his plays received first prize in the Experimental Theater's contest at the University of Chile. For the next two decades, every play he wrote received a first prize.

Wolff's plays were enthusiastically received by theatergoers of all political persuasions. He touched an intimate fiber in the public and critics of the middle class. The challenge he set himself was to preserve the format of the fourth-wall theater (that is, the use of the proscenium arch to represent a "fourth wall" to the audience) as well as the style of social and psychological realism, and at the same time to satisfy the public's need for self-identification within a context of modernity.

His first work, *Mansión de lechuzas* (Mansion of Owls, premiered in 1958), is the most poetic of his plays. A coherent lyric symbolism is developed around a garden in an old mansion, a hothouse for flowers and dreams that either preserves ties to the past or breaks them. Poetry is conveyed not through the dialogue but through other dramatic resources: colored lights to indicate social ambiences and stages of family development; ornate and religious objects in a state of decay, representing a rich but anachronistic preservation of tradition; and a cheerful and crudely sensual neighbor as a contrast to the main characters and their aristocratic reveries.

Discípulos del miedo (Disciples of Fear, premiered in 1958) concerns the confrontation of two attitudes symptomatic of class values: blind ambition *vs.* the acceptance of the good and simple things in life. These two positions, when actively opposed, affect every member of the family and their relationships. Eventually the conflict causes a tragedy as well as each character's realization of his true value system. As usual in Wolff's work, the oppositions are symbolized: ambition by the factory, the basic goodness of life by the contented canaries.

Parejas de trapo (From Rags to People, premiered in 1959) has been, after *Paper Flowers*, Wolff's most commercially successful play. Two social classes are engaged in conflict; the arrogant and self-absorbed aristocracy and the *siuticos*, middle-class social climbers. The author views the latter with compassion, as victims of an archaic social system. A third social group—immigrant craftsmen equipped with the ethic of honesty and hard work—is presented as offering an alternative and more satisfactory modus vivendi. As objects that are useful and hide nothing from view, the glass knickknacks manufactured by the craftsmen symbolize their ethical makeup.

Wolff also uses movement as a symbol. In *Parejas de trapo* the constant activity of the aristocrats indicates their existential drift, in contrast to the immigrants' immobility, which mirrors the solidity of their values.

Niñamadre (A Touch of Blue, premiered in English in 1960, in Spanish in 1962), which displays clear influences from the movies, centers around one archetypal character. Unlike previous plays, the poetic is not conveyed through language or objects but through the luminous and gentle spirit of Polla. Her naïveté and internal purity are alternatives to mid-

twentieth-century moral and aesthetic cynicism and modern man's angst.

Los invasores (The Invaders, premiered in 1963) is one of the best-known Latin American plays of this century. Within the forms of a fourth-wall play, Wolff uses techniques of the avant-garde: projections on the walls; phantasmagoric figures that crawl through walls and disappear; and a circular form of composition, by which the play ends the way it starts. While irony and an incisive humor accentuate the tragic and the strange, the main thread that binds the action is ambiguity, which has prompted critics to give it various interpretations: as a rebellion of the masses; a premonition on the metaphysical level; an expressionistic essay; a surrealistic dream; an allegory.

The industrialist Meyer suffers through an internal struggle, torn between guilt, gestures of generosity, and astonished confusion in the face of events. It is never clear whether the slum-dwellers are real, phantoms of guilt and fear, or specters announcing doom. Each character gives his own interpretation, then a subsequent event twists it and throws it into doubt. Perhaps *Los invasores* is an expressionistic thesis of a reality composed of nothing but words, in which everything is said but nothing changes. The play conveys an implicit denunciation of the hardships of poverty in contrast to the lives of the wealthy.

El signo de Caín (The Sign of Cain, premiered in 1969) attempts the difficult task of portraying the elusiveness of reality without breaking the forms of the fourth-wall theater. The conflicts are not so much the struggles between different perceptions of social morality as they are the struggles inherent in dilemmas that are both personal and universal.

The characters, wading through an existential nausea, do not seek abstract truth; rather, they lie to justify their actions to themselves and others. In the process, they attempt to know themselves and each other. Every ignoble gesture has an explanation. Which character carries the sign of Cain? Each one, at one time or another. Although Wolff analyzes them harshly on the surface, in the end he views them compassionately.

The control of dramatic tension and climax, which Wolff characteristically handles well, in *El signo de Caín* is absolute; the play is full of surprises, teasing the spectator into accepting an idea only to unmask it and show it as something else. All the dramatic elements support the theme of the elusiveness of reality.

Flores de papel (*Paper Flowers*, premiered in 1970) continues the exploration of intimate relationships that reflect larger societal trends. To make the focus even more scrutinizing, Wolff presents only two characters, unrelated by family, social class, or profession. One is from the middle class, the other a derelict.

As usual, the stage props faithfully reflect the spirit of the play. The action, although provided with an air of fancy by the whimsical paper and rattan decorations, is still bound by the laws of realism. This realism, which takes an eerie course, breaking the rules of accepted social behavior, never denies the axiom that human beings attempt to communicate because they need each other. The characters attempt to reach some understanding of each other's expectations, which the author constructs out of the obsessive gestures of a particular class at a particular time, such as fashionable clothes. Satire is achieved by transferring these gestures from one social class to another. Through this means, Wolff explores the meaning of freedom and commitment.

Kindergarten (premiered in 1977) takes up again the structure of acts and scenes and the exploration of family relationships. Time and the imprint of childhood are presented with a psychological rather than a philosophical slant, as in *Paper Flowers*. The stage props, as always, reflect the human relationships, in this case hidden in the relics of family and tradition: old family heirlooms, worn out, faded, and useless. Umbrellas are a reminder of protection from the outside, where menacing forces, even criminal ones, put into perspective the petty viciousness of the characters' sibling rivalry.

Espejismos (*Mirages*, premiered in 1978) abandons class conflict and analyzes the nature of the love and other emotions felt by four characters for each other. The form is fourth wall, the tone gently humorous, and the ambience domestic.

Álamos en la azotea (*Poplars in the Terrace*, premiered in 1981) continues the probing of family relationships. The pace is faster, the comedy is gentle, the colorful language is spiced with slang and humor, and the constant judging and accusing take

zany and witty turns. Four characters—a separated couple and their son and daughter-in-law—try to rebuild broken bridges between them, only to see them repeatedly destroyed as soon as they have been crossed. It is a family situation painted with brilliant colors. As in *Kindergarten*, an outside menace—in this case inconsequential—is the catalyst that permits the characters to unite and repair the bridges to a functioning state.

Two other plays—"José," premiered in 1980, and "La balsa de la Medusa" (*Medusa's Barge*), premiered in 1984—were still unpublished at this writing.

All of Wolff's plays have, at the heart, a social conflict organized around the question of how much the characters' pride—often class pride—will affect their relationships and their personal happiness. This theme is clearly defined in his earliest plays, and it becomes more complex with each succeeding work. In some plays, the clash that creates the conflict occurs between the middle and aristocratic classes. In others, the focus is on the striving middle class, suffocated by its climbing ambitions. In *Los invasores* as well as in *Paper Flowers*, there are bizarre confrontations between the well-to-do, or comfortable middle class, and the street- or slum-dwellers. Frequently, characters who belong to the oppressed, and therefore frustrated, class express themselves with sarcasm: the children in *Mansión de lechuzas*, Jaime Mericet in *Parejas de trapo*, Portus in *El signo de Caín* the slum-dwellers in *Los invasores*.

In all these conflicts, individuals are reflections of their social classes, but they are not mere social symbols except in *Los invasores*. Most typically, they are extracts of social types. Some, like Jaime Mericet and Polla, are archetypes.

Female characters dominate Wolff's plays. In his early works, the aristocratic heroine looms largest: cold, haughty, not drawn in great detail. Women from the lower classes are idealized, never unkind. In his later plays, he creates more idiosyncratic characters, such as the spinsterish Eva of *Paper Flowers* and the domestic Maite of *Espejismos*. His male characters, some of whom, like the *siutico*, are analyzed clinically in intimate detail, tend to engage in mutual, savage lashing; such are the cases of the brothers in *Kindergarten* and the father and son in *Álamos en la azotea*.

The internal structure, the timing of climax and subclimax, and the organization of tension and conflict of Wolff's plays are well planned. The conflicting forces are almost always developed in two or three groups of characters which represent different value systems and viewpoints on life. They run parallel, mix, separate, try to compromise or hold on fast, and at the end, one prevails over the others. This is a clear pattern from his first play, *Mansión de lechuzas*, where the three main lines of conflict are Marta's pretensions, her two adolescent boys' yearnings, and their neighbors' impulses. The three clash eventually and Wolff presents this action and its well-resolved conclusion within a veil of mystery and repressed emotions. In succeeding plays, the value systems that prevail have various motives or philosophical bases: for example, that of the youngest son in *Discípulos del miedo*; that of the craftsmen in *Parejas de trapo*; that of the ragged man in *Paper Flowers*; and that of the daughter-in-law in *Álamos en la azotea*.

Sometimes the author's voice, which coincides with the triumphant line, is heard strongly, as in Paulina in *Niñamadre*. In other plays, such as *El signo de Caín* and *Los invasores*, a deliberate ambiguity masks the author's voice; there are no moral victors. Partly for that reason, these works do not project as much optimism as his other plays.

Wolff uses symbols extensively and in several ways. Some concepts are not seen but presented in the dialogue, such as a family's means of livelihood, symbolized by the factory that offers social respectability or umbrellas that protect against a frightening outside world. Other symbols appear half onstage, half offstage, such as the canaries that can be heard but not seen. Wolff sometimes uses visible stage props to symbolize a way of life and a moral stance, such as the glass knickknacks, the paper flowers, and rattan figures.

At times, Wolff's dramatic forms symbolically indicate social values and situations; for instance, the busy stage movement in *Parejas de trapo* represents psychological and emotional instability. The immobility of characters in this and other plays echoes either a psychological and social stagnation or an existential sense of security. The undressing and dressing in *Paper Flowers* indicates a reassessment of the meaning of life.

Physical and social surroundings are keenly observed by Wolff. His settings—the apartment, the office, the park—are well-known places for a middle-class Chilean audience. In most of his plays, there are references to geographic places, resorts, and native dishes and beverages, as well as local jokes. His characters are mirrors of social protoypes which his public can easily identify with and therefore approve or condemn. In the later plays, this identification becomes more humorous and applicable to more specific professions or ambiences.

Egon Wolff falls squarely within the current of the Chilean cultural movement that sought to create an artistic product from national experience. This resulted in his departure from the psychological as well as the experimental drama of the first part of the twentieth century. Wolff created a drama that analyzes family relationships within the context of what his countrymen consider their own cultural heritage, quite apart from current partisan politics, and as a result, he created a drama of universal value.

SELECTED BIBLIOGRAPHY

First Editions

Plays

Parejas de trapo. Santiago, Chile, 1960.
Los invasores. In *El teatro hispanoamericano contemporáneo,* edited by Carlos Solórzano. Mexico City, 1964. Pp. 126–192.
Mansión de lechuzas. In *Teatro chileno actual.* Santiago, Chile, 1966.
Niñamadre. Santiago, Chile, 1966.
Flores de papel. Havana, 1970.
Discípulos del miedo. Santiago, Chile, 1971.
El signo de Caín. Santiago, Chile, 1971.
Kindergarten. In *Teatro de Egon Wolff.* Santiago, Chile, 1978.
Espejismos. In *Revista apuntes 88.* Santiago, Chile, 1981.
Álamos en la azotea. In *Teatro chileno contemporáneo.* Santiago, Chile, 1982.
El sobre azul. In *Caravelle 40.* Toulouse, France, 1983.
Háblame de Laura. Santiago, Chile, 1985.

Translations

Paper Flowers. Translated by Margaret S. Peden. Columbia, Mo., 1971.

Biographical and Critical Studies

Bravo Elizondo, Pedro. "Egon Wolff." In *El teatro hispano-americano de crítica social.* Madrid, 1975.
_____. "Reflexiones de Egon Wolff en torno al estreno de *José.*" *Latin American Theatre Review* 14/2:65–70 (1981).
Castedo-Ellerman, Elena. "Variantes de Egon Wolff: Fórmulas dramática y social." *Hispamérica* 5/15:15–38 (1976).
_____. "Egon Wolff." In *El teatro chileno de mediados del siglo XX.* Santiago, Chile, 1982. Pp. 32–50.
Chrzanowski, Joseph. "Theme, Characterization, and Structure in *Los invasores.*" *Latin American Theatre Review* 11/2:5–10 (1978).
Fernández Rodríguez, Teodosio. "El teatro de Egon Wolff." In *XVII congreso del Instituto Internacional de Literatura Iberoamericana* (1975) 2. Madrid, 1978. Pp. 1247–1257.
_____. *El teatro chileno contemporáneo.* Madrid, 1982.
López, Daniel. "Ambiguity in *Flores de papel.*" *Latin American Theatre Review* 12/1: 43–50 (1978).
Lyday, Leon F. "Egon Wolff's *Los invasores:* A Play within a Dream." *Latin American Theatre Review* 6/1:19–26 (1972).
_____. "Whence Wolff's Canary? A Conjecture on Commonality." *Latin American Theatre Review* 16/2:23–29 (1983).
Mora, Gabriela. "Notas sobre el teatro chileno actual." *Revista interamericana de bibliografía* 18/4:417–421 (1968).
Otano, Rafael. "El teatro de Egon Wolff con motivo del Laurel de Oro concedido a *Flores de papel.*" *Mensaje* 200:313–316 (1971).
_____. "Egon Wolff: Un dramaturgo entre el nacimiento y el suicidio." *Mensaje* 252:443–445 (1976).
Peden, Margaret Sayres. "Three Plays of Egon Wolff." *Latin American Theatre Review* 3/1:29–35 (1969).
_____. "The Theater of Egon Wolff." In *Dramatists in Revolt,* edited by Leon F. Lyday and George W. Woodyard. Austin, Tex., 1976. Pp. 190–201.
_____. "*Kindergarten,* A New Play by Egon Wolff." *Latin American Theatre Review* 10/2:5–10 (1977).
Piña, Juan Andrés. "El teatro de la destrucción y la esperanza." In *Teatro de Egon Wolff.* Santiago, Chile, 1978.
_____. "El retorno de Egon Wolff. *Latin American Theatre Review* 14/2:61–64 (1981).
Rodríguez Sarninas, Orlando. "Art and Antiart in Egon Wolff's *Flores de papel.*" *Latin American Theatre Review* 18/1:65–75 (1984).
Skármeta, Antonio. "La burguesía invadida: I. Egon Wolff." *Revista chilena de literatura* 4:91–102 (1971).
Vidal, Hernán. "*Los invasores:* Egon Wolff y la responsabilidad social del artista católico." *Hispanófila* 55:87–97 (1975).
Wolff, Egon. "Sobre mi teatro." In *Teatro chileno actual.* Santiago, Chile, 1966. P. 164.

Ariano Vilar Suassuna

(1927–)

Maria Teresa Leal

Ariano Vilar Suassuna, poet, playwright, and novelist, was born on 16 June 1927 in João Pessoa, Paraíba, in northeastern Brazil. He was the eighth in a family of nine children. His father, João Suassuna, former governor of the state, was assassinated in 1930. The family had lived in the *sertão* (backlands) since 1928 and was to stay there until 1942. Both circumstances were to be fundamental in Suassuna's work. The *sertão* is a rural area in the northeastern states of Brazil and part of Minas Gerais, strongly characterized by its geological and climatic conditions, its archaic way of life, its rich folklore, its preservation of ethical and religious values. It is the universe seen in such great Brazilian literary works as *Os Sertões* by Euclides da Cunha (*Revolution in the Backlands*, 1902), *Grande Sertão: Veredas* by João Guimarães Rosa (translated into English as *The Devil to Pay in the Backlands*, 1956), some poems by João Cabral de Melo Neto, and all of Ariano Suassuna's work. The years he lived in the *sertão* were, for him, a truly informal education among ballad singers, puppeteers, and storytellers whose themes, world vision, poetic forms, and language would mold his fictional world.

In 1942 the Suassuna family moved to Recife, Pernambuco (the third largest city in the country, with a long cultural tradition) in order to provide a higher education for their children. In 1946 Suassuna enrolled in the school of law. That same year he published his first poems. Suassuna's contemporaries were an exceptionally brilliant and varied group and included poets, novelists, playwrights, and painters who later became famous in Brazilian cultural life, like José Laurênio de Melo, Carlos Pena Filho, Hermilo Borba Filho, Joel Pontes, Osman Lins, and Aloísio Magalhães. Suassuna, together with Laurênio de Melo and Borba Filho, founded the Teatro do Estudante de Pernambuco (TEP). Inspired by Federico García Lorca's theater group, La Barraca (The Tent), TEP's purpose was to bring literature through theater to the working classes. Performances took place in parks, factories, churches, squares, and sometimes with the stages mounted on trucks. The TEP started its activities in 1948 with Suassuna's play *Cantam as Harpas de Sião* (The Harps of Sion are Singing), which was later called *O Desertor de Princesa* (Princesa's Deserter; Princesa being the name of a city). The same year, Suassuna received the prestigious national theater award Prêmio Nicolau Carlo Magno (Nicolau Carlo Magno Prize) for his play *Uma Mulher Vestida de Sol* (A Woman Dressed in Sun), written in 1947 when he was twenty years old.

Another activity of the TEP group was the creation of the Gráfico Amador (Amateur Printer's Press), a manual press that published works by young authors. The local workshop was a landmark in Recife's cultural life and the meeting place for artists, writers, and theater people from all over the country. When Suassuna was asked to provide a text for publication, he wrote *O Auto da Compadecida* (Play of the Merciful Mother, 1957; published in English as *The Rogues' Trial*). Owing to its length it could not be printed manually. With this play the author participated in the Prêmio da Associação Brasileira de Críticos Teatrais (Brazilian Association of Theater Critics Award) and was awarded the gold medal in 1955. No other Brazilian play has become as internationally well known as *The Rogues' Trial*. It was translated into and performed in English, Spanish, French, German, Dutch, Polish, Czech, Hebrew, and Finnish. It was published in English, French, German, and Czech.

The Rogues' Trial was shown in Recife in 1957 by the Teatro Adolescente de Pernambuco, an offspring of the TEP. Acclaimed by the public and the critics, it soon was performed throughout the country. Never did a play cause so much impact in Brazilian literature or on the stage. The novelty did not consist of the introduction of the latest international trends but rather in the revelation of the northeastern Brazilian reality with its problems and cultural values. Suassuna's theater incorporates this reality with the traditions of European, and particularly of Iberian, theater, such as Latin comedy, commedia del l'arte, medieval liturgical theater, and the religious theater of the Golden Age. As the Golden Age theater authors utilized the *romancero español* (Spanish traditional ballads) as a source of subjects, Suassuna is directly inspired by the *romancero popular do nordeste* (northeastern popular ballads), as Suassuna calls the collection of epic, lyric-narrative, and burlesque "ballads," otherwise known as *literatura de cordel*. For Suassuna, the name designates only the way this poetry is sold. Originally popularized in oral form, successful ballads were printed as pamphlets and sold dangling from a *cordel* (string) in the open markets. By preferring the name *romancero popular do nordeste*, Suassuna preserves affiliation of the ballads to Iberian traditional poetry.

Suassuna showed, from his very first works, an extraordinary command of a fast, spontaneous dialogue and a perfect equilibrium between comicality and the exposure of existential and social problems; he also created an extensive and varied gallery of characters. The didactic nature of his works also convey a tone of Christian hope.

Until 1971 Suassuna dedicated himself exclusively to the theater, writing fourteen plays, nine of which were published and five performed but not published. In 1971 he wrote a novel, *Romance d'a Pedra do Reino e o Príncipe do Sangue do Vai-e-Volta* (Story of the Kingdom's Stone and the Prince of the Come-and-Go Blood), which was announced as the first part of volume 1 of a trilogy. The second part of volume 1 appeared in 1977 under the title *História d'o Rei Degolado nas Caatingas do Sertão* (Story of the Decapitated King in the Backland Highlands). Soon thereafter, Suassuna publicly declared that he was abandoning literature and has published nothing since then. Instead, he has gone back to writing poetry and has successfully started painting. He illustrated *A Pedra do Reino* with naive xylographs similar to the ones displayed in the popular-ballad pamphlets. Suassuna attempts to create an integral text, iconographic and literal, in order to offer his poems in a simultaneous reading through letters and images. Suassuna is a professor at the Federal University of Pernambuco; author of many essays on popular northeastern art, music, literature, and sculpture; and a founding member of the National Council of Culture in Brazil.

In 1969 Suassuna launched an artistic movement called *movimento armorial* that gathered painters, musicians, sculptors, novelists, and poets with the purpose of investigating, preserving, and taking advantage of the thematic and expressive elements of the popular-rural art of northeastern Brazil. The principles that motivated this group were an extension of the TEP and the Gráfico Amador programs, both extinct by then. The solemn inauguration of the *movimento armorial* took place in 1970, with a concert titled "Três Séculos de Música Nordestina: Do Barroco ao Armorial" (Three Centuries of Northeastern Music: From Baroque to Armorial), a painting and sculpture exhibit, and a series of lectures on the subject.

The similarity between this inauguration and the 1922 Semana de Arte Moderna (Modern Art Week) is less than their profound differences. Both had the purpose of searching for a Brazilian artistic expression, but the models of the *movimento armorial* were the national tradition in itself, and those of the Semana de Arte Moderna were varied, modern, and international. The *movimento armorial* did not proliferate in "isms"; it was an epiphany rather than a revolution. It exposed popular as well as cultured art forms, whether long existent or recently known, all rooted in a secular tradition. It called the country's attention to a region that had been neglected and ignored by the more developed and cosmopolitan Brazilian south.

Ariano Suassuna defines *armorial* as something related to heraldry—with its fabulous animals painted on metal in bright enamel or carved on stone and its coats of arms surrounded by leaves, suns, moons, fruits, and stars. Also, the ballads, with their epic-lyrical and burlesque stories, are *armoriais* (armorial) in the same manner as the string instruments that accompany these ballads are *armoriais*, with their archaic sounds and harsh, high-pitched notes that recall the harpsichord and the viols of the eighteenth-century Brazilian baroque music. That is to say, *armorial* is the popular northeastern art in all its forms of expression. It is the educated art of Francisco Brennan (painter, sculptor, ceramist), the music of Guerra Peixe, the painting of G. Samico, and the poetry of Janice Jupiassu, to mention a few examples, and, of course, the writing and painting of Ariano Suassuna.

A strong regionalist feeling leads Suassuna to identify Brazilian with northeastern. As a modern exponent of a Brazilian literary trend that searches for a national character and dates back to romanticism, he aligns with Guimarães Rosa and Cabral de Melo Neto. All three share the same traditional sources and the quest for human nature's ultimate truth. For them, this process of universalization is also achieved by reconfirming through regional myths those that are common to various Christian and neo-Latin countries. The expressive resources of these three great Brazilian authors are, nevertheless, quite different. Neither the instrument reinvented by Guimarães Rosa nor the naked preciseness of Cabral de Melo Neto, Suassuna's language seems to reproduce more faithfully that of the *sertão*

man—its archaisms, metaphors, and baroque complexities.

In accordance with this loyalty to his roots, another characteristic of Suassuna's art is his immersion in the Iberian literary tradition. Suassuna combines his extensive knowledge of Brazilian, Portuguese, and Spanish literature with his fascination and interpretation of all forms of popular art of his region.

In his analysis of *The Rogues' Trial*, Martinez-López identifies and studies Suassuna's literary sources, from anonymous popular literature as well as Gonzalo de Berceo, Gil Vicente, Lope de Vega, and Pedro Calderón de la Barca. A reminiscence of the medieval Marian cult and the *auto sacramental* (sacramental play), *The Rogues' Trial* is also nurtured by popular tales and poetry.

The omnipresent didacticism in Suassuna's plays and novels also has double origins: the archaic genres he admires so much and his own religious vision of existence. Providentialism, faith, and hope in divine justice are the beliefs of Suassuna the man, for whom God is the harmonizing center of the universe without whom "everything would be absurd."

Among the popularly rooted expressive techniques Suassuna uses we find the sometimes prolix declaration of intention as found in medieval works, the anticipation of the conflict and its solutions in the lengthy titles and subtitles, and an explicit refusal to be limited by a genre or a tone by previously characterizing his plays or novels as tragic, lyric, pastoral, comic, heroic, or farcical—and sometimes all these at once.

Apparently Suassuna is looking for the simplicity of the rustic forms, rejecting all types of structural elaboration or psychologisms, and presenting unidimensional types in stereotypical dramatic situations. Nevertheless, these types and situations are, in their simple context, universal, and the moral implication of their actions is complex.

Behind the concrete plot in his theater works, the spectator will find what he wants or is capable of finding: the hilarity of a farce or the ontological inquiry of the meaning of man's presence on earth, or both. His characters are related to a Brazilian reality as well as to a western theatrical tradition from Titus Maccius Plautus to Gil Vicente, Miguel de Cervantes, William Shakespeare, Molière, Calderón de la Barca, and Carlo Goldoni, authors whom Suassuna prefers because of their ability to reflect a national theater.

Within the contemporary Brazilian theater, Jorge Andrade, Gianfrancesco Guarnieri, Augusto Boal, and Chico Buarque de Holanda also show Brazilian reality, stressing social problems. Some (Boal, Buarque de Holanda) revindicate the forgotten history to exemplify the persistence of these problems. Their heroes are urban men and women living the drama of the large cities, and they propose political-ideological, anarchic-revolutionary solutions to conflicts. Suassuna's theater turns to moral, religious solutions, to the relationship between guilt and punishment, to the final victory of divine justice, to reward or punishment.

Aside from *The Rogues' Trial*, the plays *O Casamento Suspeitoso* (The Suspicious Marriage), *O Santo e a Porca* (The Holyman and the Piggy Bank), and *A Pena e a Lei* (The Sentence and the Law) were also awarded prizes, both in Brazil and abroad. This strengthened Suassuna's reputation as Brazil's foremost contemporary theatrical author.

The novel *A Pedra do Reino* was enthusiastically received by the critics and acclaimed by such authors as Rachel de Queiroz and Carlos Drummond de Andrade. It is an extremely ambitious work, in which Suassuna, through the quest of the main character, attempts to create a Brazilian superepic based on several preceding examples of real or fictional heroes. The completion of this novel reflected ten years of rigorous investigation of scholarly historic and literary sources, amalgamated with the author's extensive knowledge of traditional popular literature and of northeastern folklore. The novel levels all these references and modifies the models in the creation of a fantastic-heroic fictitious world.

In *A Pedra do Reino* as well as in *O Rei Degolado*, Suassuna remains true to the popular-metaphoric language of his traditional sources and confirms himself as continuator of the Hispanic epic—and the chivalry, picaresque, and Cervantine novels. There exists in his narrative a multiplicity of themes similar to those of the chivalry novel, which seem to repeat themselves by appearing and disappearing in various chapters, but which are intertwined and articulated by time, through passage formulas.

The fantastic element is evident in the transformation of the arid and miserable world of the *sertão* into an epic and sacred kingdom. It expressed the very same search for the myth, for the deepest meaning of life, that is ever present in *sertão* poetry and dramatized in folkloric dances, tournaments, jousts, and stories.

Death and the Hero identified as the Father, always in conflict, are manifestations of Suassuna's personal experience (his own assassinated father-hero), transferred to his fictional world. The presence of human and allegoric figures, of metamorphoses and symbols, of superhuman elements—divine and demoniac—bestow to Suassuna's narrative its epic and fantastic qualities. His work is undoubtedly one of great originality and complexity within Brazilian modern literature.

SELECTED BIBLIOGRAPHY

Editions

Fiction

Romance d'a Pedra do Reino e o Príncipe do Sangue do Vai-e-Volta. Rio de Janeiro, 1971. 3rd ed. 1972.

História d'o Rei Degolado nas Caatingas do Sertão. Rio de Janeiro, 1977.

Plays

O Auto da Compadecida. Rio de Janeiro, 1957.

O Castigo da Soberba. *Revista do Departamento de Extensão Cultural e Artística* (Recife) 2/2 (1960).

O Casamento Suspeitoso. Recife, Brazil, 1961.

Uma Mulher Vestida de Sol. Recife, Brazil, 1964.

A Pena e a Lei. Rio de Janeiro, 1971.

Farsa da Boa Preguiça. Rio de Janeiro, 1974.

O Santo e a Porca and *O Casamento Suspeitoso*. Rio de Janeiro, 1974.

Essays

"Nota Sobre a Poesía Popular Nordestina." *Revista do Departamento de Extensão Cultural e Artística* (Recife) 4/5:15–28 (1962).

"Folktheater in Northeastern Brazil." *Américas* 15:18–23 (1964).

"O 'Cancionero' de Rodrigues de Carvalho." *Cultura* 1/6:23–41 (1967).

"A Arte Popular no Brasil." *Revista Brasileira de Cultura* October–December:37–43 (1969).

"A Compadecida e o Romanceiro Nordestino." In *Literatura Popular em Verso. Estudos 1.* Rio de Janeiro, 1973. Pp. 153–164.

Ferros do Cariri: Uma Heráldica Sertaneja. Recife, Brazil, 1974.

O Movimento Armorial. Recife, Brazil, 1974.

Iniciação à Estética. Recife, Brazil, 1975.

Collected Works

Seleta em Prosa e Verso. Edited by Silviano Santiago. Illustrated by Zélia Suassuna. Rio de Janeiro, 1974.

Translations

The Rogues' Trial. Translated by Dillwyn Ratcliff. Berkeley, Calif., 1963.

Biographical and Critical Studies

Alcada, João Nuno, Elena Clementelli, and Vittorio Minardi, eds. "Topos Medieval do Processo do Paraíso no Auto da Compadecida: Proposta Culta para u en Teatro Popular." In *La Letteratura Latino Americana e la Sua Problematica Europea.* Rome, 1978.

Curran, Mark. "Influências da Literatura de Cordel na Literatura Brasileira." *Revista Brasileira de Folclore* 9/24:111–123 (1969).

Emorine, Jacques. *Lexique et analyse lexicale de "l'Auto da Compadecida."* Porto Alegre, Brazil, 1969.

Figueiredo, Maria do Carmo L. "*O Santo e a Porca. Aulularia:* Um Estudo Comparativo." *Minas Gerais, Suplemento Literário,* 22 July 1972.

Girodon, Jean. "Le testament cynique de l'*Auto da Compadecida.*" *Coloquio* 9:49–51 (1960).

Guerra, José A. "El mundo mágico y poético de Ariano Suassuna." *Revista de cultura brasileña* 35:56–71 (1973).

Houaiss, Antonio. "*Auto da Compadecida.*" In his *Crítica Avulsa.* San Salvador, 1960. Pp. 137–147.

Lind, Georg. "Ariano Suassuna, Romancista." *Coloquio/Letras* 17:29–44 (1974).

———. "*A Pedra do Reino.* Treatment of Folk Literature and Literature in Quotations." *Romatische Forshungen* 91:345–347 (1979).

Lyday, Leon F. "The *Barcas* and the *Compadecida:* Autos Past and Present." *Luso-Brazilian Review* 11/1:84–88 (1974).

Magaldi, Sábato. "Auto da Esperança." Introduction to *A Pena e a Lei.* Rio de Janeiro, 1971.

Martinez-López, Enrique. "Guia para os Leitores Hispánicos do *Auto da Compadecida.*" *Revista do Livro* 24:85–103 (1964).

Mazzara, Richard A. "Poetic Humor and Universality of Ariano Suassuna's *Compadecida.*" *Ball State University Forum* 3:25–30 (1969).

Mertin, Ray-Güde. *Ariano Suassuna: "Romance d'A Pedra do Reino." Zur Verarbeitung von Volks-und Hochliteratur im Zitat.* Geneva, 1979.

Mimoso-Ruiz, Duarte, and Elie Konigson, eds. "Le personnage populaire du malandro dans le theatre luso-brésilien." In *Figures théâtrales du peuple,* Paris, 1985.

Portella, Eduardo. "Folclore e Poesia." In his *Dimensões 1.* Rio de Janeiro, 1958. Pp. 155–162.

Rama, Ángel. "Ariano Suassuna: El teatro y la narrativa popular nacional." *La palabra y el hombre* 13:7–13 (1975).

Ratcliff, Dillwyn. "Folklore and Satire in a Brazilian Comedy." *Hispania* 44/2:282–284 (1961).

Santos, Idelette Muzart da Fonseca. "Uma Epopéia do Sertão." Introduction to Ariano Suassuna's *O Rei Degolado.* Rio de Janeiro, 1977.

———. "La quête romanesque d'Ariano Suassuna: Une lecture du *Romance d'a Pedra do Reino.*" In *Bulletin des études portugaises et brésiliennes.* Paris, 1980–1981. Pp. 179–198.

Slater, Candace A. "Cordel in the Big City." *Studies in Latin American Popular Culture* 5:217–220 (1986).

Wingerter, George. "*El Auto da Compadecida* y los autos de Calderón: Algunos paralelos." *Luso-Brazilian Review* 20/1:150–163 (1983).

Griselda Gambaro

(1928–   )

Evelyn Picon Garfield

Griselda Gambaro, born in Buenos Aires in 1928, is known primarily as one of Latin America's most accomplished dramatists, although she began her literary career with the publication of novellas and short stories. She presently resides in Argentina, where she dedicates her time to both novels and drama. Gambaro has received numerous national awards: in 1963 the National Endowment for the Arts Award (Fondo Nacional de las Artes), which allowed her to publish her first collection of three novellas, *Madrigal en ciudad* (Urban Madrigal, 1963); in 1964 the Emecé Publisher's Prize for the collection of short stories and novellas *El desatino* (The Blunder, premiered in 1966); in 1967 an honorable mention by Sudamericana Publishers for her novel *Una felicidad con menos pena* (Happiness with Less Sorrow, 1968); four first-prize awards in 1968 for the play *El campo* (The Camp, premiered in 1968): from the city of Buenos Aires (Premio Municipal), the magazine *Talía*, the Municipal Radio Station of Buenos Aires (Premio Semanario Teatral del Aire), and the Society of Argentinian Authors (Premio Argentores); and in 1976 the Argentores Prize again for the play *Sucede lo que pasa* (Come What May, premiered in 1976).

Gambaro is the best-known female playwright from Latin America. In 1982, she was a Guggenheim Fellow in the United States, where her plays have been staged by the Spanish Theater Repertory Company of New York and by several university groups. Her drama has also been performed in Italy, France, Germany, Venezuela, Uruguay, and Mexico, and her novels and plays have been translated into English, Italian, Czech, Polish, French, and Swedish for the stage and for radio adaptations.

Largely self-educated, Gambaro attributes her mastery of theatrical techniques to dramatic intuition and to early readings of plays by Luigi Pirandello and Eugene O'Neill. She explains in an interview that her scant theoretical training was due in part to a lack of educational opportunity for people of her class:

My father worked in the post office. I'm from a poor family. Now things are much better but that circumstance marks you forever. I remember how much I wanted to learn English when I was young. But studying was a sacrifice; I went at night to inferior public schools and learned nothing. I ask myself whether or not I might have gone to the best English school, if I'd been born in another class.

> (*Women's Voices from Latin America:*
> *Interviews with Six Contemporary Authors,*
> Evelyn Picon Garfield, pp. 68–69)

Gambaro feels no ties with any specific generation of Argentine writers. Her drama, which emerged in the mid-1960's, during the ascendancy of the realistic school, was attacked for its view of reality. According to Gambaro, the realists err in their belief that there is only one valid level of reality, a photographic one. She prefers to deal with real facts on multiple levels of meaning, some apparent, others latent. Reacting to her mode of expression, various critics have emphasized the influence of the European theater of the absurd and the theater of cruelty in her drama. The term "absurd," however, is ill advised, for unlike European works under that rubric, the anguished or absurd nature of certain scenes in her plays can be explained and even defined in concrete terms. Although gratuitous acts may be pushed to extreme consequences, the character relationships explored are recognizably human ones of power and repression; they do not broach existential questions as in the European theater of the absurd. Cruelty is an omnipresent element in Gambaro's work. Nevertheless, only one of her plays, *The Camp*, exploits cruelty in the sense of a mythic/historic force, as in the works of Antonin Artaud.

Almost all of Gambaro's more than a dozen plays deal with the problems of passivity, impotence, and suffering, concerns Gambaro sees as central to her work.

> One often has a single theme, and I probably have mine, the problem of passivity. It must be due to personal reasons; I am a very cowardly woman. . . . Very cowardly in every way. I'm not brave; I find it difficult to be brave. I am very preoccupied with passivity and the nonassumption of individual responsibility. In society it is that way, and, also, in my plays. Perhaps I have altered that view somewhat now. It is less bitter only on the human level but not on the political one, or the social one.
>
> (*Women's Voices from Latin America*, p. 64)

Most of her characters can be seen as victims or victimizers in relationships of dependence and independence. Arbitrary, sadistic, and authoritarian actions are often mitigated by a smile or a friendly voice, to the extent that the victimizer may even become offended as if he were the victim. On the other hand, when a benevolent character appears to sympathize with and assist the victim, that goodness is firmly rejected by the underdog, who often mistreats his "savior" and then seems even more dependent on his victimizer.

Loss of freedom of movement is the most apparent result of the cruel human relationships in Gambaro's plays. One character is isolated by unknown authorities without explanation in *Las paredes* (The Walls, premiered in 1966); another is immobilized by a large iron artifact clamped to his foot in *El desatino;* and twins are psychologically and unwillingly bound to one another in *Los siameses* (The Siamese Twins, premiered in 1967). In each instance, physical and psychological discomfort is intensified by thwarted and somewhat meek efforts to gain freedom. These victims often seek solace from the very people who have most mistreated them, usually under the guise of protection or familial concern. Thus the victim's frustration increases as his humanity, freedom, and identity wane.

Cruel actions of a physical nature are minimally represented on stage; they are suggested from offstage by noises and odors. The cruelty in Gambaro's drama is based principally on sadistic and even masochistic psychological relationships in which misunderstandings, lack of communication, mercurial personalities, and duplicity play major roles. It is precisely here that Gambaro's dramatic approach coincides with Artaud's use of nonliterary techniques in the theater of cruelty, for they both emphasize sound, facial gestures, movements, lighting, and symbolic props. Unlike Artaud, however, Gambaro does not seek to diminish the importance of language; rather, she plays it off against other, dramatic levels of expression in order to reveal its hypocrisy. The impact of her plays relies heavily on a manipulation of the contradictions between nonverbal stage components and dialogue.

The Camp, Gambaro's most powerful and most accomplished play, was published in 1967 and staged in 1968. There are only three main characters: the authoritarian Franco dressed as an SS officer, the young woman Emma, whose physical appearance is that of a concentration-camp inmate, and the accountant Martín, who tries to help Emma. The title of the play bears a double connotation: a bucolic setting and a military camp. The SS uniform, the whip, and the offstage screams and smells of burning flesh suggest the latter, specifically a Nazi death camp. The songs of peasants returning from the fields and of children playing offstage suggest the former. This duplicity is masterfully sustained throughout the play. Emma's gestures as a great pianist dressed up to please her adoring public contradict her prison-camp appearance—her shaved head, a coarse frock, a festering sore on her hand. Franco's kind face and his assurances that he is unarmed belie the symbolic nature of his SS uniform and his intermittent, brusquely aggressive acts toward Martín and Emma.

Even the props exemplify hypocrisy. In a particularly painful scene—a play within a play—Emma is forced to give a musical performance to other inmates and guards. Before the concert, Franco presents her with some artificial flowers. Even though she knows they are false, she sniffs them and remarks, "Perfect!" When she sits down to play on a piano that emits no sound whatsoever, she feigns playing it and sings in a weak voice. Since objects deny their reality and utility, the person who tries to use them or react to them is publicly humiliated. Yet during this scene and throughout the entire play, Franco's provocations and cruel jokes alternate with his attitude of concern for Emma. His power over her and her dependence on him are so complete that she views Martín's sympathetic gestures to alleviate her suffering as meddlesome and scandalous.

Although Gambaro often explores the dark subtleties of cruelty and passivity, of power and subjugation, nowhere else does she suggest the all-encompassing nature of man's inhumanity to man better than in this play, where individual cruelty is given, through the symbolic use of language and dramatic device, an historical and even mythical significance. The impact of *The Camp* resides in its metaphoric quality as a symbol of a horrific insanity—the Nazi atrocity, an inexplicable collective force of mythic proportions.

It is not until the later plays that Gambaro allows her victims more than an expression of pain or a rare burst of anger. In plays as diverse as *La malasangre* (*Bitter Blood*, premiered in 1982) and *Del sol naciente* (*The Rising Sun*, not yet performed), female protagonists emerge as strong, self-affirming characters despite the tragedies that mark their lives. The former

play is set in the Argentina of the 1840's and the latter in a Japanese town; in both, terror and fear lie in wait as a backdrop. Yet Gambaro insists that some of her plays are humorous. There are a few comic effects and some slapstick scenes, but in general, her humor remains well within the tradition of the grotesque in Argentine theater. Moreover, the horrors she seeks to communicate result in black humor.

A similar grotesquely comic element prevails in Gambaro's prose fiction, where her imagination finds free rein. Among her many novellas and novels, two stand out in this respect: *Dios no nos quiere contentos* (God Doesn't Want Us to Be Content, 1979), and *Lo impenetrable* (The Impenetrable, 1984; published in English as *The Impenetrable Madame X*). The former, somewhat Kafkaesque narrative shares certain characteristics with *The Camp*: pathetic, suffering characters in bizarre situations; oneiric episodes; and cruel, inhumane relationships. The sense of fatality that prevails in the novel is achieved by the use of a narrative cast in a minor key. An almost detached, matter-of-fact voice describes the action, displaying an attitude of abnegation and ascribing a similar attitude to the characters, as seen in the following passage about María:

> She carried her pain like a burden, an internal hunchback never exposed to others, her road was different. Sticky and persistent, the pain adhered to her heart but she would not dignify it, would not call it anguish, melancholy or nostalgia, no great name for sadness, not even sadness. That it would be there, inside, inevitable, because human beings and the world produced it like bees honey, flowers pollen, but she would never play the game of feeding it with her own compassion.
>
> (p. 104)

The characters are few in *Dios no nos quiere contentos*, and dialogue barely exists. Silence seems to bear witness to the lives of three characters who live together: a young orphan boy, Tristan; the Écuyerè, a female contortionist and trapeze artist; and the babe found by them on a crowded bus. The boy experiences sexual adventures with his friend María in a whorehouse; the Écuyerè becomes infatuated with a vagrant who ties her up and robs her; and the babe grows up to support them all. The entire novel has a carnival air about it, a strange fusion of fleeting diversion and grotesque masquerade, with macabre characterizations and nightmarish scenes. The energetic protagonist, the Écuyerè, although victimized—the owner of the circus continually mistreats her and moves the circus on, leaving her behind—is active and even philosophical. From her trapeze, high above the crowd, she affirms her identity and perfects her talents, exacting recognition of her right to exist. In the final pages of the novel, fully aware of the hypocrisy and sadness of life and man, she lifts Tristan into the air with her, where he finally realizes his sole desire in life—to sing, "freeing words from their subjugation to triviality and earth" (p. 63).

The narrator often reflects on the loneliness of these characters, adrift in a hostile atmosphere. Gambaro inserts statements of a proverbial nature into the narrative, philosophizing about dreams, reality, happiness, love, perfection, solitude, human interactions, and forgetfulness. One poignant pronouncement describes the general sense of the characters' situations: "No other destiny unites better than a shared expulsion from the same paradise: solitude fractured" (p. 126).

In much of Gambaro's works, there are lewd insinuations about sex and the body. In two novels in particular, the role of sex is of central concern. It is most abusive, degrading, and violent in physical and psychic forms in the novel *Ganarse la muerte* (To Earn Death, 1976), a book whose distribution was prohibited in Argentina the year it was published. In a much lighter vein, Gambaro's *The Impenetrable Madame X*, an erotic tour de force of desire set in nineteenth-century Spain, appeared in Buenos Aires in 1984. It had been written in Barcelona before 1980, for a contest on the erotic novel announced by a Spanish publishing house, and had been born of Gambaro's need to emerge from the dense atmosphere of her previous work. Gambaro pokes fun at the conventions of the erotic novel and at the same time explores certain themes she had previously dealt with in a more serious manner.

The title refers to the nature of the erotic desire portrayed in the novel, a desire never consummated by Madame X and her lover Jonathan; on the occasion of their final and only intimate meeting, he is unable to penetrate her: "It doesn't matter," he says. "The impenetrable is the source of all pleasures, because there is no pleasure without the unknown." A certain anticlimax prevails, since early in the novel, the hilariously exaggerated reports of Jonathan's sexual capacities promise greater adventures. He was often stimulated by the mere mention of Madame X in a letter, and on one occasion his sexual acrobatics lay him waste when, at the sight of a lock of her hair, he has ninety-nine orgasms in the street below her balcony: he has to be hospitalized for exhaustion. During this marvelously atypical erotic novel, heterosexual and homosexual acts abound, especially the latter, between Madame X and her maid, Marie.

The parody of the genre is also explicit in the epigraphs about eroticism and erotic literature, written by the author, that head each chapter. The initial epigraph sets the humorous tone for the entire volume: "The great disadvantage of the erotic novel is the difficulty with which it reaches a literary climax" (p. 7).

This novel is perhaps the only one of Gambaro's works where sadism, masochism, and cruelty are not of central importance. Sexual freedom, androgyny, and the questions of perversion and innocence, hypocrisy, repressed desire, and the pleasures of the soul and body that affect how one deals with one's surroundings—these are very likely the themes that infused her previous works with such violence and humiliation. Even at the end of *The Impenetrable Madame X*, when Madame X is much older and frustrated by Jonathan's impotence, she prepares herself for another unknown suitor who has appeared below her window. Latent desires are played out, not in cruel victimizations of women by men as in most erotic novels but in "a battle without blood," as the narrator explains, where the booty is shared and the contenders alternate as victors without cruelty and vanquished without humiliation. *The Impenetrable Madame X* is a unique novel, in which a joyous romp from the ridiculous to the exaggeratedly hilarious takes center stage, as can be seen in this brief excerpt from a court scene. A witness has just described in great detail how Jonathan masturbates.

A new interruption, a call to order, and before the witness continued, several accidents happened. An elegantly clad lady, stimulated by the vivid description and the crude language, sat down on top of her companion and was quietly copulating. The act had been noticed and had spread throughout the last row of benches, whose occupants had only capriciously altered position. The groans were soft and contained, but all the same, hindered the judicial process, and the judge banged on the dais warning that he'd empty the chambers. There were many *coitus interruptus,* but the elegant lady, who held an advantage of some minutes over the others, was able to reach a climax. She tidied herself up and with disdain looked haughtily at the frustrated imitators.

(p. 100)

SELECTED BIBLIOGRAPHY

First Editions

Plays

El desatino. Buenos Aires, 1965.

Los siameses. Buenos Aires, 1967. And in *Nueve dramaturgos hispanoamericanos 2,* edited by Frank Dauster et al. Ottawa, 1979. Pp. 93–143.

El campo. Buenos Aires, 1967.

"La gracia." *El Urogallo* 17 (1972).

"Sólo un aspecto." *La palabra y el hombre* 8:52–72 (1973).

"El nombre." *El Cronista,* Suplemento Cultural (6 September 1975).

"Decir sí." *Hispamérica* 7/21:75–82 (1978). And in *Teatro: Las paredes. El desatino. Los siameses.* Barcelona, 1979.

Teatro abierto 1981: Antología. Buenos Aires, 1981. Pp. 93–100.

"El despojamiento." *Tramoya* 21–22 (1981).

Teatro: Nada que ver. Sucede lo que pasa. Ottawa, 1983.

Teatro I. Real envido. La malasangre. De sol naciente. Buenos Aires, 1984.

Teatro II. Dar la vuelta. Información para extranjeros. Puesta en claro. Sucede lo que pasa. Buenos Aires, 1987.

Prose Narratives

Madrigal en ciudad. Buenos Aires, 1963.

"El nacimiento postergado." *Ficción* 41–42 (1963).

El desatino: Cuentos. Buenos Aires, 1965.

Una felicidad con menos pena. Buenos Aires, 1968.

"El trastocamiento." *Análisis* 389 (1968).

"Nosferatu." *Mantrana* 1:5 (1970).

Nada que ver con otra historia. Buenos Aires, 1972.

"El derecho." *La Opinión,* Suplemento Cultural (1975).

La cola mágica Buenos Aires, 1976. Stories for children.

Ganarse la muerte. Buenos Aires, 1976.

Dios no nos quiere contentos. Buenos Aires, 1979.

Lo impenetrable. Buenos Aires, 1984.

Other Works and Articles by Gambaro

"Teatro de vanguardia en la Argentina de hoy." *Revista de la Universidad Nacional del Litoral* 81:301–333 (1970).

"Por qué y para quién hacer teatro." *Revista talia* 39/40:4–6 (1972).

Conversaciones con chicos: Sobre la sociedad, los padres, los afectos, la cultura. Buenos Aires, 1977.

"Disyuntivas de un autor teatral que se convierte en novelista." *La Opinión* (1977).

"¿Es posible y deseable una dramaturgia específicamente femenina?" *Latin American Theatre Review* 13/2 (supplement):17–22 (1980).

"Reflexiones sobre el exilio." *Revista vigencia* (1981).

Translations

Bitter Blood. In *Women's Fiction from Latin America: Selections from Twelve Contemporary Authors,* edited and translated by Evelyn Picon Garfield. Detroit, 1988.

The Camp. In *Voices of Change in the Spanish American Theater,* edited and translated by William I. Oliver. Austin, Tex., and London, 1971. Pp. 47–103.

The Impenetrable Madame X. Translated by Evelyn Picon Garfield. Detroit, 1989.

Biographical and Critical Studies

Arlt, Mirta. "Griselda Gambaro: La verdad tiene cara de absurdo." *Revista lyra* 231–233 (1976).

Azcona Cranwell, Elizabeth. "Griselda Gambaro: *Una felicidad con menos pena.*" *Sur* 315:92–94 (1968).

Boorman, Joan Rea. "Contemporary Latin American Woman Dramatists." *Rice University Studies* 64/1:69–80 (1978).

Carballido, Emilio. "Griselda Gambaro o modos de hacernos pensar en la manzana." *Revista iberoamericana* 36/73:629–634 (1970).

Cypess, Sandra Messinger. "Physical Imagery in the Works of Griselda Gambaro." *Modern Drama* 18/4:357–364 (1975).

———. "The Plays of Griselda Gambaro." In *Dramatists in Revolt: The New Latin American Theater,* edited by George W. Woodyard and Leon F. Lyday. Austin, Tex., 1976. Pp. 95–109.

De Moor, Magda Castellvi. "El vanguardismo en Gambaro." *Escritura* 4/8:241–257 (1979).

——. "The Texture of Dramatic Action in the Plays of Griselda Gambaro." *Hispanic Journal* 1/2:57–66 (1980).

Foster, Virginia Ramos. "The Buenos Aires Theater, 1966–67." *Latin American Theatre Review* 1/2:54–61 (1968).

——. "Mario Trejo and Griselda Gambaro: Two Voices of the Argentine Experimental Theatre." *Books Abroad* 42/4:534–535 (1968).

Garfield, Evelyn Picon. "Una dulce bondad que atempera las crueldades: *El campo* de Griselda Gambaro." *Latin American Theatre Review* 13/2(supplement):95–102 (1980).

——. *Women's Voices from Latin America: Interviews with Six Contemporary Authors.* Detroit, 1985.

Gerdes, Dick. "Recent Argentine Vanguard Theatre: Gambaro's *Información para extranjeros.*" *Latin American Theatre Review* 11/2:11–16 (1978).

Goldsmith, Margaret. "Griselda Gambaro. *El campo.* Bs. As.: Edic. Insurrexit, 1967." *Latin American Theatre Review* 4/1:85–86 (1970).

Holzapfel, Tamara. "Griselda Gambaro's Theatre of the Absurd." *Latin American Theatre Review* 4/1:5–11 (1970).

——. "Evolutionary Tendencies in Spanish American Absurd Theatre." *Latin American Theatre Review* 13/2 (supplement):37–42 (1980).

Kiss, Marilyn Frances. "The Labyrinth of Cruelty: A Study of Selected Works of Griselda Gambaro." Ph.D. diss., Rutgers University, 1982.

McAleer, Janice K. "*El campo,* de Griselda Gambaro: una contradicción de mensajes." *Revista canadiense de estudios hispánicos* 7/1:159–171 (1982).

Martínez, Martha. "Seis estrenos del teatro argentino en 1976." *Latin American Theatre Review* 11/2:95–96 (1978).

Moretta, Eugene L. "Spanish-American Theatre of the 50's and 60's: Critical Perspectives on Role-Playing." *Latin American Theatre Review* 13/2:5–30 (1980).

——. "Reflexiones sobre la tiranía: Tres obras del teatro argentino contemporáneo." *Revista canadiense de estudios hispánicos* 7/1:141–147 (1982).

Muxó, David. "La violencia del doble: *Los siameses* de Griselda Gambaro." *Prismal/Cabral* 2:24–33 (1978).

Paolantonio, José M. "Una obra que dará que hablar." *Teatro XX* 1/6:15 (1964).

Podol, Peter L. "Reality Perception and Stage Setting in Griselda Gambaro's *Las paredes* and Antonio Buero Vallejo's *La fundación.*" *Modern Drama* 24/1:44–53 (1981).

Postma, Rosalea. "Space and Spectator in the Theatre of Griselda Gambaro: *Información para extranjeros.*" *Latin American Theatre Review* 14/1:35–45 (1980).

Saenz, José Luis. "*El campo* de Griselda Gambaro." *Sur* 315:121–122 (1968).

Schóó, Ernesto. "Teatro, Griselda Gambaro: El creador, un hombre como todos." *Confirmado* (4 April 1972): 42–44.

Woodyard, George W. "The Theatre of the Absurd in Spanish America." *Comparative Drama* 3/3:183–192 (1969).

Zalacaín, Daniel. "Marqués, Díaz, Gambaro: Temas y técnicas absurdistas en el teatro hispanoamericano." Ph.D. diss., University of North Carolina at Chapel Hill, 1976.

——. "El personaje 'fuera del juego' en el teatro de Griselda Gambaro." *Revista de estudios hispánicos* 14/2: 59–71 (1980).

Gabriel García Márquez

(1928–   )

George R. McMurray

In October 1982 readers throughout the world applauded the news from Stockholm that Gabriel García Márquez of Colombia had been awarded the Nobel Prize for literature. Although most of his oeuvre has been acclaimed for its high level of excellence, his undisputed masterpiece, *Cien años de soledad* (*One Hundred Years of Solitude*), remains the most widely read of his works, having been translated into more than thirty languages since its appearance in 1967. Indeed, as Peruvian novelist Mario Vargas Llosa stated, this chronicle of the mythical town of Macondo provoked "a literary earthquake" in Latin America, making its author "almost as famous as a great soccer player or an eminent singer of boleros" (*Review* 70, p. 129 [1971]). *One Hundred Years of Solitude* also marks the peak of the so-called boom in recent Latin American letters, that is, the explosion of first-rate novels published during the 1960's. This phenomenon, which broke with the traditional realism that had characterized Spanish-American letters prior to 1940, reflects the influence of, among others, Jorge Luis Borges of Argentina, Miguel Ángel Asturias of Guatemala, Juan Rulfo of Mexico, and Alejo Carpentier of Cuba. The universal themes and avant-garde styles of these writers inspired the present-day generation, whose leaders, in addition to García Márquez, include Argentina's Julio Cortázar, Mex-

ico's Carlos Fuentes, Chile's José Donoso, Peru's Vargas Llosa, and Cuba's Guillermo Cabrera Infante. García Márquez is also indebted to numerous European and North American authors, the most important of whom are Sophocles, Miguel de Cervantes, Franz Kafka, Virginia Woolf, William Faulkner, and Ernest Hemingway.

While García Márquez has become a literary hero in Colombia, the foreign accolades for his saga of Macondo have been equally profuse. In 1972 the novel won the Rómulo Gallegos Prize in Venezuela; Italian critics awarded its author the Chianciano Prize in 1969; the French named it the best foreign book of the same year; and in the United States it was chosen one of the twelve most outstanding novels of 1970. Thus García Márquez, fundamentally a private person, has been thrust into the international limelight by journalists, critics, and scholars seeking to dissect every aspect of his life and writings; this public attention has sometimes equally focused upon his highly publicized bonds of friendship with heads of state Fidel Castro, Daniel Ortega, Belisario Betancur (Colombia), Felipe González (Spain), and François Mitterrand, who in 1981 awarded him the Legion of Honor.

In addition to *One Hundred Years of Solitude*, several of García Márquez' works are set in Macondo, in reality Aracataca, the small town near Colombia's Caribbean coast where he was born on 6 March 1928. The son of a telegraph operator, Gabriel Eligio García, and Luisa Santiaga Márquez, young Gabriel was reared by his maternal grandparents, who had settled in Aracataca during a bitter civil conflict known as the War of the Thousand Days (1899–1902). As a child García Márquez absorbed the legends and myths told by his grandmother, whose naturalness and spontaneity as a spinner of yarns he considers the key to the tone and translucent style of his masterpiece. From his beloved grandfather, an equally talented storyteller, he learned of the exploits of Colombia's military heroes, including General Rafael Uribe Uribe, the model for Colonel Aureliano Buendía in *One Hundred Years of Solitude*.

In 1946 García Márquez graduated from a private Jesuit high school in Zipaquirá, a town near Bogotá, and the following year he enrolled in the law school of the National University in Bogotá. In 1947 he also published his first short story, "La tercera resignación" ("The Third Resignation"), an eerie account of a man who survives death in a kind of surrealistic limbo. The first of fifteen tales published in *El Espectador* (The Spectator) of Bogotá and *El Heraldo* of Barranquilla (both daily newspapers) between 1947 and 1952, "The Third Resignation" reflects García Márquez' readings of Kafka, especially the latter's emphasis on the invention of another reality, often designed to create the experience of terror. Some of these tales also suggest the influence of Faulkner and Hemingway. In "El negro que hizo esperar a los ángeles" ("Nabo: The Black Man Who Made the Angels Wait," 1951), for example, the author uses temporal involutions and shifting points of view to develop a tale of decadence and madness set in a feudal society reminiscent of Faulkner's Deep South. And "La mujer que llegaba a las seis" ("The Woman Who Arrived at Six O'Clock," 1950) bears a marked resemblance to Hemingway's "The Killers" due to its objective description of visible reality, its café setting, and its oblique allusions to a murder. Although some critics have lauded the flashes of stylistic genius and the delineation of psychological tension in these early tales, most detect in them an adolescent striving for experimental technique and,

perhaps for this very reason, a tendency toward abstractness and incoherence.

On 9 April 1948, while García Márquez was studying law at the National University in Bogotá, a popular left-wing politician named Jorge Eliécer Gaitán was assassinated, triggering the *bogotazo*, a bloody upheaval that raged for almost a week in the capital city. This date also marks the beginning of what has become known as *la violencia*, a brutal civil war between conservatives and liberals that lasted into the 1960's, causing the deaths of several hundred thousand Colombians. Soon after the *bogotazo* García Márquez returned to the Caribbean coast, where he continued his law studies at the University of Cartagena. He then moved to the nearby city of Barranquilla to work for *El Heraldo*, during which time he joined a group of aspiring young writers (*el grupo de Barranquilla*) with whom he read and discussed the novels of, among others, Faulkner, Woolf, John Dos Passos, and Hemingway.

In 1954 García Márquez accepted a position as reporter for the Bogotá daily, *El Espectador*, and within a year after his return to the capital published his well-known short story "Isabel viendo llover en Macondo" ("Monologue of Isabel Watching It Rain in Macondo," 1955) and his first novel, *La hojarasca* (*Leaf Storm*, 1955). In 1955 he also wrote a fourteen-installment story, *Relato de un náufrago* (*The Story of a Shipwrecked Sailor*, published in book form in 1970), for *El Espectador*; this was the product of a series of interviews with a young Colombian sailor who spent ten days adrift in the Caribbean after being swept overboard during turbulent weather. The dramatic account of the youth's confrontation with death and his miraculous survival greatly increased *El Espectador*'s circulation, but several months later the government closed the newspaper because the story had revealed that the ship, a Colombian naval vessel, was carrying a badly stowed cargo of illegal goods from the United States. Meanwhile, *El Espectador* had sent García Márquez on assignment to Europe. Finding himself suddenly unemployed and practically penniless, he stayed in Paris long enough to write his now highly acclaimed novelette, *El coronel no tiene quien le escriba* (*No One Writes to the Colonel*, 1961).

Upon his return from Europe in 1957, García Márquez worked in Caracas as a journalist for approximately two years. After the triumph of Fidel Castro's revolution in 1959, he joined the Cuban government's news agency, Prensa Latina. He opened a Prensa Latina office in Bogotá, then worked for the agency in Havana, and finally in New York. In 1961 he resigned this position and, with his wife and son, moved to Mexico City where, within a year of his arrival, he published three books: the above-mentioned *No One Writes to the Colonel*, *La mala hora* (*In Evil Hour*, 1962), and *Los funerales de la Mamá Grande* (*Big Mama's Funeral*, 1962). A period of frustrating sterility ensued, until one day in January 1965, while driving from Mexico City to Acapulco, García Márquez envisioned the magical history of Macondo that had been fermenting in his imagination for more than a decade. The following year and a half of frenzied creativity produced his masterpiece, *One Hundred Years of Solitude*, which brought financial independence and enabled him to move to Barcelona.

During his eight years in Spain (1967–1975) García Márquez published a collection of fantastic short stories entitled *La increíble y triste historia de la cándida Eréndira y de su abuela desalmada* (*The Incredible and Sad Tale of Innocent Eréndira and Her Heartless Grandmother*, 1972); and *El otoño del patriarca* (*The Autumn of the Patriarch*, 1975), an ingenious portrait of an aging dictator. Although he vowed in 1975 not to write any more fiction until the overthrow of General Augusto Pinochet, Chile's right-wing chief of state, two important novels have appeared during the 1980's: *Crónica de una muerte anunciada* (*Chronicle of a Death Foretold*, 1981) and *El amor en los tiempos del cólera* (*Love in the Time of Cholera*, 1985).

Shortly before his departure from Spain, García Márquez resumed his journalistic activities, founding a left-wing news magazine, *Alternativa*, in Bogotá as a vehicle for fomenting radical social change in Latin America. Since the late 1970's his newspaper columns, often dealing with controversial political issues, have been read with great enthusiasm throughout much of the Hispanic world. His continued interest in journalism is perhaps best illustrated by his documentary, *La aventura de Miguel Littín clandestino en Chile* (*Clandestine in Chile. The Adventures of Miguel Littín*, 1986), an exciting account of a Chilean film director's return to his homeland after twelve

years in exile. García Márquez has maintained, since the late 1970's, residences in both Mexico and his native Colombia.

"Monologue of Isabel Watching It Rain in Macondo" represents the first important milestone in the development of García Márquez' fictional world. Instead of the fantastic occurrences and abstract spaces of the early stories, it depicts for the first time a clearly defined geographical setting (Macondo), where the sensitive young protagonist is gradually engulfed by the monotonous rhythms of a torrential tropical storm. Her physical deterioration and mental paralysis—which are conveyed by repetitive phrasing, metaphoric imagery, and the adroit manipulation of the point of view, from Isabel's first-person perspective to the perspective she shares with her stepmother—reach a surprising climax when it becomes evident in the final lines that she has died.

The setting of *Leaf Storm* is also Macondo, but the action covers a period of twenty-five years, from 1903 until 1928, during which time the town experiences a banana boom (an era of economic prosperity brought by companies from the United States exploiting the banana industry) and, subsequently, a devastating depression. The plot evolves through a series of four narrators, with the first collective "we" setting the moral tone of the novel. The other three narrators, all attending a wake, are a highly respected, retired colonel; his daughter Isabel, a reserved woman abandoned by her husband several years ago; and Isabel's ten-year-old son. The deceased is an unnamed doctor of questionable moral character who arrived in Macondo in 1903, and, ten years prior to his death, having refused to treat the casualties of an election dispute, became a recluse in order to avoid the wrath of the townspeople. The main source of dramatic tension is the colonel's determination to carry out his promise to bury the man who once saved his life, despite the opposition of his fellow citizens, whose anger has turned into a chronic disease. Although the colonel ultimately gets the coffin out of the house, the denouement is left to the reader's imagination.

A metaphor of social rot, the leaf storm of the title refers to the swarm of newcomers swept into Macondo during the brief period of prosperity, leaving in their wake bitterness and economic stagnation. The themes of solitude and moral decay, both conveyed by the doctor, pervade the alternating monologues—with recollections of Macondo's recent boom-and-bust cycle—of the passive, introspective narrators. The boy tells his own story, necessarily of limited dimensions; his mother reveals information concerning the family's past; and the colonel narrates the history of the town while alluding to his confrontation with the local authorities over the right to bury the deceased.

Two major influences on *Leaf Storm* are Faulkner's *As I Lay Dying* (1930) and Sophocles' *Antigone*. Like Faulkner, García Márquez utilizes a recent death to bring his characters together and elicit their monologues; both *Leaf Storm* and *As I Lay Dying* dramatize the urgency of interring the corpse; and the stylistic complexity and structural organization of García Márquez' first novel evoke Faulkner's twisted syntax and abrupt temporal dislocations. In view of the quotation from *Antigone* appearing at the beginning of the novel, it comes as no surprise that the moral dilemma in Sophocles' tragedy—the conflict between the individual conscience and the injunctions of men—provides the structural underpinnings for *Leaf Storm*: Creon's decree to leave Polynices' body to the vultures is reflected by the determination of the town citizens to leave the doctor's corpse in his house to rot, and Antigone's resolve to bury her brother parallels the colonel's determination to bury the doctor.

García Márquez' first novel elicited mixed responses from the critics. Some found it static and flat; others described it as more literary device than true art; still others praised its artistic treatment of psychic time and its pervasive sense of the ominous.

If Faulkner is a major influence on *Leaf Storm*, *No One Writes to the Colonel* reflects the direct, pared-to-the bone style of Hemingway; psychological insights are offered through a graphic portrayal of scene, rather than omniscient exploration of characters' pasts or their interior lives; the result is a dynamic and lucid delineation of visual reality. The protagonist is a poverty-stricken retired colonel who fought in the War of the Thousand Days (1899–1902) and now lives in a hot, rain-soaked Colombian village. Almost childlike in his constant good humor and naive optimism, the colonel contrasts sharply with his embittered, asthmatic wife, a confirmed realist. A pillar of probity in the community, he is also the opposite of his friend Don Sabas, whose shady business and political deals have made him the town's most affluent citizen. Other boldly sketched figures include Father Ángel, whose principal occupation consists of enforcing movie censorship; an indolent lawyer hired by the colonel to expedite payment of his pension; and the local doctor, a friend of the colonel and a fellow member of the underground resistance engaged in circulating political propaganda.

Two symbols of hope in the protagonist's drab existence are his long-awaited pension check, which he always expects will arrive on the mail boat he meets every Friday, and his fighting cock, a legacy of his dead son Agustín, which he feels certain will win a major bout and thus enable him to pay the mounting grocery bills and repair the leaky roof. The colonel's fundamental optimism is reaffirmed metaphorically when he comes across an old, moth-eaten umbrella his wife won in a raffle many years before. In contrast to her grumbling remark that everything, themselves included, is rotting alive, he opens the umbrella and, gazing upward through the network of metal rods, observes that the only thing it is good for now is for counting the stars.

Because the fighting cock belonged to Agustín, who died a rebel (the action takes place in 1956, during *la violencia*), and because the whole town plans to bet on it in the forthcoming contest, the colonel resists his wife's pleas to sell it to Don Sabas. Soon thereafter the cock's victory in an exciting trial bout unites the town against the dictatorial regime and strengthens the colonel's resolve to keep the bird. And in the unforgettable final scene he emerges as an absurd hero, physically fragile but mentally tough, who, like Sisyphus, finds existential meaning in the uphill struggle against adversity.

No One Writes to the Colonel has been called a political novel, and indeed its subtle allusions to *la violencia*—the nightly curfew, the underground newsletter, the press censorship—do create an atmosphere charged with political tension. However, the unanimous critical acclaim accorded this intuitively conceived novelette seems above all to acknowledge García Márquez' masterful, aesthetically balanced portraiture of the endearing protagonist, whose wit and dogged determination to survive brighten an otherwise bleak literary canvas. The vividness with which the colonel is drawn is perhaps due to the fact that the character is patterned after García Márquez' beloved grandfather. But equally important are the conditions under which this slim volume was written, that is, while the author himself was living in a Parisian garret and, like the colonel, barely surviving on a shoestring budget.

In Evil Hour has much in common with *No One Writes to the Colonel*, but it is also very different. Both novels reflect the stylistic concision of Hemingway, both deal with *la violencia*, and both are set in the same unnamed pueblo, probably Sucre, where García Márquez' parents lived for a time when he was a boy. Unlike its lineally structured predecessor, however, *In Evil Hour* presents a disjointed montage of episodes, spatializing time and creating an overall sense of simultaneity. Instead of a single unifying protagonist comparable to the colonel, it portrays an entire town. And, in contrast to the wry humor enlivening García Márquez' masterful novelette, *In Evil Hour* interlaces absurd and grotesque passages with horrifying acts of violence.

The plot is based on an episode that actually occurred in Sucre during *la violencia*: the mysterious appearance on house doors of anonymous, scandal-mongering lampoons accusing individuals, usually the wealthy and powerful, of various misdeeds. These broadsides provoked bitter fights, feuds, and even killings, forcing entire families to abandon the community. The action of *In Evil Hour* is set in motion when César Montero, a member of the local oligarchy, finds a lampoon on his door accusing his wife of having an affair with a young clarinet player, Pastor. Showing no emotion whatsoever, Montero heads immediately for Pastor's home and methodically empties his shotgun into the youth. During the next seventeen days lampoons appear with increasing frequency, sending shock waves throughout the community. Eventually, in a desperate move to put an end to the explosive situation, the police murder a young boy caught distributing subversive pamphlets at a cockfight. In the final lines of the novel the mayor's boast of having suppressed the violence is belied by the departure of dissidents to join the guerrillas in the mountains and by the appearance of more lampoons.

The single most important character of *In Evil Hour*, though hardly the protagonist, is the mayor, a corrupt, solitary figure symbolizing authority and, as such, a precursor of Aureliano Buendía in *One Hundred Years of Solitude* and of the Patriarch in *The Autumn of the Patriarch*. His solitude is underscored by his suffering from an abscessed tooth, which the vengeful local dentist, a member of the underground, extracts without anesthesia. In contrast to the mayor, the priest emerges as a weak, tormented individual, all too willing to accept the arbitrary measures taken against the town citizens. The social decomposition resulting from the clashes between the bitterly divided factions reflects in microcosm the tragedy of an entire nation caught in the grip of a civil war.

Because the lampoons are directed against the rich and powerful, and because art is often viewed as a weapon for challenging the status quo, critics have suggested that the lampoons are a metaphor of social-protest literature, and that this novel stands as a parable of the victory of art (imagination) over political oppression (reality). This interpretation is reinforced by the ailing Don Sabas' remark to his physician that he doesn't want to die before finding out how "this novel" (the unraveling events triggered by the lampoons) ends. Although the identity of the town prankster is never revealed, the critic Wolfgang Luchting has pointed his finger at the author, whose novel could be viewed as the most cleverly disguised, complex, and sophisticated lampoon of all (*Books Abroad* 47/3:477).

Big Mama's Funeral, García Márquez' first collection of short stories, consists of eight tales written between 1954 and 1961. Most of these suggest a Chekhovian approach to the genre, the emphasis being on the realistic delineation of characters or situations described by a neutral, omniscient observer. The major stylistic influence, once again, is Hemingway, but several of the pieces, especially "Big Mama's Funeral," display what Frank Dauster called "a crack in the wall of reality," marking them as precursors of *One Hundred Years of Solitude* (*Books Abroad* 47:3/468). "Rosas artificiales" ("Artificial Flowers") depicts the clash between a love-struck girl and her blind grandmother, who guesses her every move. Situational irony informs "En éste pueblo no hay ladrones" ("There Are No Thieves in This Town"), about a youth who gets caught red-handed while trying to return the three billiard balls he has stolen. "La viuda de Montiel" ("Montiel's Widow") also depends on irony to portray its protagonist, a naive widow who never finds out what a scoundrel her husband was. The collection's most baffling piece, "Un día después del sábado" ("One Day After Saturday"), uses biblical symbolism, a senile priest, and dying birds to dramatize an apocalyptic vision of a small town.

Perhaps this volume's best example of objective, Hemingwayesque realism is "La siesta del martes" ("Tuesday Siesta"), in which a mother and her young daughter travel by train to a steamy, tropical town, perhaps Macondo, the purpose of their journey being to lay a bouquet of wilted flowers on the grave of the woman's son, recently shot for attempted robbery. Despite evidence of the woman's extreme poverty, her demeanor is depicted from the opening lines as one of dignity and strength. Her antagonists are the sleepy town priest—it is the siesta hour—a supporter of the status quo who gives her the key to the cemetery, and the curious townspeople, who stare in a hostile manner at the two strangers as they stoically set out for the cemetery in the searing midday heat. The story's open ending dramatizes the dichotomy between classes in a rigidly structured, unjust society that condemns the poor to a life of suffering, symbolized by the wilted flowers.

Another straightforward depiction of Colombian reality, in this case an episode of *la violencia*, is "Un día de estos" ("One of These Days"). Here the antagonists, counterparts of similar characters in *In Evil Hour*, are a dentist and the town mayor, a victim of an abscessed tooth. An exercise in understatement, this tale captures the tensions of a nation at war with itself when the deliberate, laconic dentist avenges the death of scores of rebels by extracting the mayor's tooth without anesthesia. However, when he asks his patient where he should send the bill, to the municipal government or to him, the mayor reestablishes his macho image with his answer, "It's the same damn thing."

The artist's role in society emerges as the major theme of "La prodigiosa tarde de Baltazar" ("Bal-

thazar's Marvelous Afternoon"), perhaps García Márquez' most popular tale and certainly one of his best. A thirty-year-old carpenter, Balthazar, makes an elaborate bird cage for the son of José Montiel, the town's wealthiest citizen. When Montiel refuses to pay for the cage, Balthazar gives it to a squalling child as a gift, but he tells his friends that Montiel has paid him handsomely for his labor. The ensuing celebration in the local pool hall brings the story to its meaningful denouement. As the central motif, the cage represents art and, at the same time, illuminates the clash between the ideal world of imagination and the world of concrete reality. Balthazar typifies the artist whose generous, childlike nature differs markedly from the selfish, disagreeable Montiel. The realms of imagination and reality also come into conflict when Balthazar, inebriated and penniless, is shown stretched out on the street, vaguely aware that he is being robbed of his shoes, but blissfully immersed in his dreams.

In Marxist terms, Montiel symbolizes the capitalist striving only for wealth, whereas the other town citizens, resentful of his power, would seem to represent the proletariat. Also suggested is the Marxist view that in a capitalistic society art becomes a commodity, an alien, antagonistic force devoid of its previous sacred status. Balthazar obviously does not see his cage in this light, nor do the townspeople who flock to his home to admire it. But Montiel's remark that Balthazar should sell his "trinket" to anyone willing to buy it illustrates the bourgeois attitude toward art that Marx deplores. And finally, in the pool hall, Balthazar's friends show no interest in his artistry; they see the cage only in terms of the money it has enabled him to extract from his bourgeois adversary.

"Big Mama's Funeral," the funniest and most fanciful story of the collection, is a satire not only of Colombia's antiquated institutions, but also of the inflated rhetoric characteristic of the national press of the 1950's. The protagonist is the obese virgin-matriarch of Macondo, whose legendary life and fabulous burial are narrated with hyperbolic humor, magical flights of fantasy, and absurd and grotesque details. For example, as Big Mama is dying, the doddering priest—who has to be carried up the stairway to her chamber—cannot apply the oils to her palms because she clenches her fists to prevent him from removing her rings. Soon thereafter she begins to dictate her will, an undertaking that requires several hours because of the size of her estate, but before she can finish her ludicrous enumerations, she emits a resounding burp and expires. The absurdities following her demise include the pope's journey to Macondo by canoe through mosquito-infested bogs, the appearance at the ceremony of numerous beauty queens and boisterous mourners, and the dismantling, brick by brick, of the matriarch's mansion by her greedy heirs once the funeral cortege gets under way. García Márquez elicits the reader's mirth with pompous and flippant language, but at the same time his tone conveys his vehement opposition to a government in collusion with the church and the reactionary landed oligarchy. The magical and humorous elements of this tale characterize much of the author's subsequent work.

Two decades after its publication, *One Hundred Years of Solitude* still stands out as García Márquez' most widely acclaimed work. This tragicomic saga of the fictional town of Macondo, from its founding by José Arcadio Buendía and his wife, Úrsula, to its destruction by a hurricane approximately one hundred years later, owes its universal success to several factors. Its plot is both fascinating and accessible to the average reader; its style is lucid, poetic, and rapidly paced; and, as in Faulkner's Yoknapatawpha County, in Macondo all basic human emotions and experiences are dramatized with extraordinary vividness. García Márquez himself has insisted that *One Hundred Years of Solitude* is a family chronicle devoid of all seriousness; but, as demonstrated below, the riveting history of Macondo can also be read as a metaphor for Western civilization.

Because José Arcadio Buendía and Úrsula are cousins, they and their descendants—the clan lasts for seven generations—are haunted by the fear of begetting a child with a pig's tail; their apprehension stems from the fact that such a child was indeed born to Úrsula's aunt and José Arcadio Buendía's uncle. A metaphor of original sin, this incestuous relationship reverberates throughout the novel until, in the final pages, the torrid love affair between Aureliano Babilonia and his aunt Amaranta Úrsula produces the long-dreaded result.

The fictional world of Macondo is a place where reality is all-encompassing, a world in which everyday events, fantastic phenomena, stark tragedy, and madcap humor seemingly coexist as actual facts, and are narrated in an utterly convincing, authoritative voice. García Márquez' treatment of time also creates the impression of totality; the novel's lineal, historically based structure is modified by brief glimpses into the future and swings back to the present—creating a series of spiral configurations—and by a mythopoetic aura of cyclical recurrences and archetypical images, giving universal meaning to everyday experience. A prominent example of temporal circularity is the repetition of names and traits among the Buendías, the José Arcadios displaying impulsive behavior and individual initiative, and the Aurelianos, lucidity and a tendency toward introversion. Thus, as the aging Úrsula observes generation after generation of her descendants, she is moved to exclaim on various occasions that time is not passing but turning in a circle.

An examination of the plot's structural underpinnings reveals a combination of biblical myth and fundamental elements of history, which define the isolated world of Macondo from its Edenic beginning to its apocalyptic end. The novel's twenty unnumbered chapters can be divided into three parts, the first of which (chapters 1 and 2) describes the founding of Macondo, an earthly paradise visited first by roving bands of gypsies and later by merchants and artisans, harbingers of modern civilization. The third chapter represents a transition between parts 1 and 2, the principal event here being a plague of insomnia. In addition to preventing sleep, the illness causes the loss of memory, inducing José Arcadio Buendía to label numerous objects and then to embark on the creation of a "memory machine," a giant dictionary on an axis, that a person could spin in order to review the words. He has written almost fourteen thousand entries for his project when José Arcadio Buendía's old gypsy friend, Melquíades, returns for one of his frequent visits to Macondo with a miraculous cure for the illness. This episode, involving the destruction of memory and efforts to retain human knowledge via the written word, expresses metaphorically the trauma of a primitive, prehistoric society being transformed into a society aware of its historic past. Thus, a prehistoric society is characterized by circular time, in which everything is repeated and events are shrouded in myth or reenacted periodically through ritual. Once a society enters irreversible, lineal time, however, its past becomes history, which is difficult to remember and so must be preserved in writing.

The passages of the novel most closely paralleling Colombian history are found in part 2 (the fourth through the fifteenth chapters), which deals at considerable length with the civil wars of the late nineteenth and early twentieth centuries and with the banana boom created by the gringo imperialists just prior to World War I. Until its decline (which in reality was soon after World War I), the banana market brings progress and prosperity to Macondo, but it also brings rampant corruption. The banana workers' strike and the massacre of striking workers by army troops in the fifteenth chapter are based on events that occurred in Ciénaga, a town near Aracataca, in 1928.

The sixteenth chapter, a transitional link between parts 2 and 3, describes a tropical storm lasting four years, eleven months, and two days, all but destroying the town. On the positive side, however, the storm has a purifying effect reminiscent of the biblical flood: it hastens the departure of the gringos, puts an end to the decadent materialism they brought, and restores close family ties. In part 3 (the sixteenth through the twentieth chapters), despite efforts to revive the vitality of the past, the deterioration of Macondo continues, culminating in its obliteration.

García Márquez' genius in narrative art, especially noteworthy in *One Hundred Years of Solitude*, is his brilliant commingling of the fantastic with the realistic, a technique known as magical realism which, as mentioned above, contributes to the totalizing vision of the novel. Thus, Father Nicanor Reyna's levitation to prove the existence of God (in the fifth chapter) is made more believable because he insists on drinking a cup of hot chocolate the moment before he performs the miracle; in the twelfth chapter, Remedios the Beauty is carried heavenward while she tries to fold a pair of bed sheets flapping in the wind; and early in the novel, the inhabitants of the still-primitive Macondo accept flying carpets, brought by the gypsies, as a means of transportation. In the seventh chapter, José Arcadio's incredible

death and its utterly fantastic aftermath (his blood flows neatly—and at precise angles—from his home, through the streets of Macondo, and finally into the kitchen where his mother is making bread) is told in such exact terms and surrounded by so many everyday details that the event seems almost real. On the other hand, the arrival in Macondo of the first train and the first movies is presented as something bordering on the supernatural, the former causing great excitement and the latter disbelief and outrage. Similarly José Arcadio Buendía's discovery of ice at the end of the first chapter is surrounded by such a wealth of exotic details and emotion-packed language that an ordinary object (ice) is transformed into "the great invention of our time." García Márquez seems to say that reality depends less on what one sees than on the manner in which, or the perspective from which, one sees it.

Although *One Hundred Years of Solitude* confronts the horrors of war, the evils of imperialism, and the depressing effects of alienation and solitude, it is also replete with humor and irony. Hyperbole and the absurd often come into play, as, for example, when Aureliano Segundo's daughter Meme unexpectedly arrives home from boarding school with sixty-eight schoolmates and four nuns, throwing the household into chaos and necessitating the purchase of seventy-two chamber pots. In a somewhat similar vein, Aureliano Segundo's animals proliferate fabulously in response to the mere presence of his mistress Petra Cotes on his breeding grounds, while Remedios the Beauty's exaggerated physical attractions include not only her comely face and body, but also her "breath of perturbation," or "fatal emanation," that members of the opposite sex find so disturbing when she wanders about au naturel. Hyperbole turns grotesque in the case of an eating contest between Aureliano Segundo and "The Elephant," a perfectly groomed, cultured lady who slowly and methodically consumes the juice of forty oranges, eight quarts of coffee, thirty raw eggs, two pigs, a bunch of bananas, and four cases of champagne. The best example of black humor involves the legendary father of Aureliano Segundo Buendía's beautiful wife, Fernanda: the Buendía children finally come face-to-face with their idealized grandfather, Don Fernando del Carpio, when he arrives unexpectedly one December day in a huge lead container, "dressed in black and with a crucifix on his chest, his skin broken out in pestilential sores and cooking slowly in a frothy stew with bubbles like live pearls."

Úrsula, the novel's most endearing character, is also a victim of its irony. As a young woman she refuses to be photographed in order not to survive as the laughingstock for her grandchildren. But in her old age, senile and shrunken to less than half her original size, she becomes the favorite plaything, a big broken-down doll, for her great-great grandchildren, who paint her cheeks, carry her about the house, and even hide her in the pantry where she is almost eaten by rats. The aristocratic, straitlaced Fernanda is also a source of irony and grotesque humor because she is so completely out of place in the carefree, uninhibited atmosphere of Macondo. She arrives from the highlands with her golden chamber pot bearing the family crest and with a calendar marked by her spiritual adviser, designating all but forty-two days out of the year as dates of "venereal abstinence." In her later years she develops a uterine disorder but, too modest to visit a physician in person, she initiates a lengthy correspondence with her "invisible doctors," who (in the fourteenth chapter) prescribe a telepathic operation. Thus, at the specified day and hour she falls asleep in her room with her head pointed north and upon awakening several hours later discovers a "barbarous stitch in the shape of an arc" from her groin to her sternum.

Although critics have often alluded to the similarities between Macondo and Faulkner's Yoknapatawpha County, perhaps not enough has been said about the Colombian novelist's affinity to the writing of Jorge Luis Borges, an author García Márquez acknowledges having read again and again. *One Hundred Years of Solitude* abounds in literary figures and motifs reminiscent of the Argentine master, especially the oxymoron, the mirror, and the labyrinth; an especially striking parallel between the two authors can be seen through a comparison of Borges' "The Aleph" (1949) with García Márquez' novel. In his fantastic tale Borges comes to grips with an aesthetic problem when he tries in vain to describe a rotating disk-shaped object (the Aleph), which represents a magical, simultaneous vision of the world, in the successive, linear medium of language. Unable to capture in writing the simultaneity of the visual image, Borges resorts to sketching a multifaceted portrait of his protagonist Beatriz, who in the mind of the reader ultimately emerges not only as a metaphor of literature, but also as a metaphor of the world Borges is unable to depict in his story.

García Márquez is faced with a problem somewhat similar to that of Borges, namely, how to condense into a single piece of fiction an all-encompassing, nonlinear metaphor of Western civilization. As mentioned above, lineal time is undermined by cyclical repetitions and spiral configurations in the sequence of events; the line between reality and fantasy is erased by the author's ingenious use of language, thereby creating the impression of an all-pervasive reality. In its founding, development, and decline, Macondo can be seen as a microcosm not only of a nation, but indeed of a continent and of the entire Western world.

It is in the final pages of *One Hundred Years of Solitude*, however, that a comparison to Borges' art adds the greatest dimension toward understanding. Here Aureliano Babilonia barricades himself in Melquíades' room and begins to decipher the Buendía family chronicle that the old gypsy has recorded in Sanskrit on his oft-mentioned parchments. The Aleph is evoked when Aureliano Babilonia discovers that Melquíades has not put events in linear succession, but rather has concentrated a century of daily episodes in such a way that they, like the entire world condensed in the rotating Aleph, coexist in one magical time and place: we discover not only that Melquíades, a major character, is the narrator, but that the old gypsy's mysterious manuscripts and the novel are one and the same. Through this technical device, the fictional universe appears to engender itself from within, eliminating all elements of the real world, including the supposed omniscient or real author.

As a biblical hurricane filled with voices of the past buffets the house, Aureliano Babilonia deciphers his encounter with his aunt Amaranta Úrsula, the final involution in a Borgesian "labyrinth of blood," the result of which is the child with a pig's tail destined to bring the family line to an end. Finally, on the last page of the parchments, and of the novel, Aureliano Babilonia witnesses the climactic moment he is living as if he were looking into a speaking mirror, another of Borges' motifs. And like Aureliano Babilonia, the symbolic reader of fiction, we readers of the novel find ourselves wrenched from the realm of imagination once we finish the last page.

Melquíades' use of Sanskrit, one of the oldest Indo-European languages, would seem to be the ideal medium for recording a compendium of Western civilization. The hurricane filled with voices of the past embodies the destructive forces of history, which are described by the torrent of words—again the compendium of history—Aureliano Babilonia is translating. And the speaking mirror into which he gazes upon deciphering the parchments illustrates the perfect communication between Aureliano Babilonia, the ideal reader, and Melquíades, who represents García Márquez' muse and the creator of fiction par excellence. Indeed, it is entirely possible that the mysterious old gypsy, erudite in the most arcane areas of human endeavor, was modeled after the venerable Argentine.

Though based on the realities of Caribbean life, the seven stories of García Márquez' next book, a collection called *La increíble y triste historia de la cándida Eréndira y de abuela desalmada*, are enlivened by fantastic elements reminiscent of "Big Mama's Funeral" and *One Hundred Years of Solitude*. (Three pieces from this collection are translated in *Innocent Eréndira and Other Stories*, and four appear in English in *Leaf Storm*.) In "El mar del tiempo perdido" ("The Sea of Lost Time"), for example, a seaside villager and his gringo exploiter embark on a turtle hunt to the bottom of the sea, where they meet both the living and the dead. "Muerte constante más allá del amor" ("Death Constant Beyond Love") portrays a corrupt, ailing politician whose more human side is symbolized by a paper butterfly that assumes the characteristics of a beautiful painting when it is fused into the plaster of a wall. Hyperbole, grotesque humor, and fantasy are major ingredients in "Blacamán el bueno, vendedor de los milagros" ("Blacamán the Good, Vendor of Miracles"), describing the hilarious antics of a present-day charlatan and one-time embalmer of viceroys who instilled in their faces such austere authority that they governed better posthumously than when they were alive. "El último viaje del buque fantasma" ("The Last Voyage of the Ghost Ship") is a surrealistic fantasy of vengeance

(an ocean liner runs aground and destroys a village) generated by the mind of a mad narrator, all in a single rambling sentence. "Un señor muy viejo con unas alas enormes" ("A Very Old Man with Enormous Wings"), written especially for children, is a delightful tale of a winged creature who descends onto the patio of a greedy couple and, after being exploited for personal gain, manages to take flight and disappear over the horizon.

A tragicomedy of exploitation and revenge first written as a film script, the title story of this collection portrays a young girl (Eréndira) whose grandmother makes her turn to prostitution in order to recoup the old woman's losses after her granddaughter unintentionally sets fire to her mansion. The girl eventually gains her freedom when her lover, a naive youth named Ulises, murders the grandmother (perhaps symbolic of the capitalist exploiter) and Eréndira flees with the profits she has accumulated during her years of bondage. The three principal characters of this tale can be seen as ironic inversions of mythical archetypes, the grandmother emerging as the Terrible Mother, Eréndira as the Captive Princess, and Ulises as the Young Knight committed to slaying the monster (the grandmother) and liberating the princess. However, Ulises' grotesquely bungled attempts to murder the grandmother (he gives her a strong dose of arsenic, dynamites her piano while she plays it, and finally stabs her until she dies in a pool of oily green blood) only elicit Eréndira's scorn, precipitating her flight along a deserted beach.

The action of "El ahogado más hermoso del mundo" ("The Handsomest Drowned Man in the World"), perhaps the most popular story of this collection, takes place in a drab seaside village, where the corpse of an enormous youth is washed ashore. While preparing his body for burial, the women of the village become enthralled with his good looks, imagining that he is alive and christening him Esteban. The elaborate funeral they prepare for him not only establishes a common bond among all the villagers but also convinces them that Esteban's appearance in their midst will effect a dramatic renovation of their lives. The themes of purification and rebirth are clearly suggested by the dead man's gift of beauty, hope, and solidarity to an economically depressed, lethargic community. The tale is enriched, too, by resonances of myth and allusions to literary masterpieces, making the protagonist a composite figure. Like a classical hero, Esteban arrives mysteriously and, like Odysseus, who also traversed the seas, he assumes superhuman proportions; the wailing women at Esteban's funeral and the sailor tied to the mast of a passing vessel evoke Odysseus' endeavors to resist the song of the sirens upon his return to Ithaca. Esteban also reveals similarities to Quetzalcoatl, the enlightened god who, according to legend, predicted his return to Mexico via the sea; and the impact of Esteban's gigantic stature on the villagers brings to mind Gulliver's adventures among the Lilliputians.

The Autumn of the Patriarch is García Márquez' most political and most stylistically sophisticated novel to date. The plot of this richly textured portrait of a dictator (the Patriarch) consists of episodes from the protagonist's incredibly long life, a time frame, we are told, of somewhere between 107 and 232 years. Because he represents a composite of despots worldwide, the Patriarch personifies all the evils of absolute power, but his salient characteristic is his extreme solitude, stemming from his abuse of authority and paranoic fear of revolution. The setting is a Caribbean nation, perhaps Colombia or one of the islands, a nation plagued by poverty, political violence, and imperialism.

García Márquez' multifaceted portrait of tyranny, an apt description of the novel, contains six sections, each consisting of one long paragraph, the last of which comprises a single fifty-three-page sentence. The complex, rambling style serves, among other things, to highlight the author's ingenious use of shifting point of view, which ranges from the first-person singular and plural to the second- and third-person perspectives. The narrative voices, then, include not only those of the Patriarch and his associates, but also those of his subjects.

The overall structure of *The Autumn of the Patriarch* can best be described as circular, its beginning and end both describing the protagonist's demise. The initial lines of each unit also deal with this central event, the speakers in these passages being nameless citizens who stand in awe of their dead leader, gaze at his decaying palace, and speculate on the future course of the nation. Random episodes of the Patri-

arch's life ensue, with each unit ending at some climactic point during his long reign. The effect of these repetitions and temporal overlappings is the impression that linear time has been brought to a halt and replaced by spatial juxtaposition, often to convey a concept or theme. A case in point is the account of what happens on a certain Friday in October when the Patriarch awakens to find everybody in the palace wearing a red hat. It seems that a party of foreigners has landed, jabbering in a strange tongue and exchanging beads and red hats for local products. Looking out the palace window, the Patriarch discovers three fifteenth-century Spanish caravels anchored near a rusty battleship abandoned by United States marines. Set side by side, these images of Columbus' arrival in the New World and present-day gringo domination denounce imperialism, a problem that has plagued Latin America for almost five centuries. The entire passage, moreover, undermines a popular myth by taking a satirical look at the great moment in 1492 that Columbus recorded in his diary.

The novel's numerous monologues consisting of contradictions, rumors, and outright lies never come to grips with the truth, but rather create a mazelike atmosphere of myth that replicates the adverse psychological conditions of life under a ruthless dictator. Thus for the ordinary citizens who speak to the reader in anonymous voices, the Patriarch becomes a kind of god with the power to prevent earthquakes, cause eclipses, and even determine the time of day. He also furnishes paternal and political guidance without which his subjects find themselves, at least momentarily, incapable of coping with their sudden loss. But never having seen him in person and unable to identify with certainty the incredibly wasted corpse before them, they gradually re-create his myth by evoking his legendary past and bedecking him with flowers.

One of the more memorable mythmaking episodes deals with the Patriarch's double, Patricio Aragonés, who makes it possible for the Patriarch to perform the miracle of appearing in two places at the same time. When Patricio Aragonés is assassinated and his body is torn to shreds by a rampaging mob, the Patriarch slaughters his unmasked enemies, and thus strengthens the popular belief in his immortality. Still other episodes, often bordering on the absurd, serve to undermine his authority, making him seem almost helpless or childlike. His mother, for example, whom he visits daily, exerts much influence over him despite her ridiculous antics: an unpretentious, plebeian woman, Bendición Alvarado drapes her laundry over the balcony used by her son for his public addresses, proclaims at official functions that she would like to see a coup d'état because she is tired of living in the limelight, and announces in the presence of foreign diplomats that had she known her son would become head of state, she would have enrolled him in school.

The Patriarch's buxom wife, Leticia Nazareno, also challenges his authority while providing a source of comic relief. A former nun who becomes rapaciously corrupt and domineering, she spends every afternoon from two until four o'clock teaching her husband to read and write, singing the lessons with him and keeping time with a metronome. He becomes so taken with the preposterous ditties that he begins to sing them during state visits, on one occasion just in time to avoid the discussion of a debt owed to the Dutch government. Soon after the birth of their child, which occurs during the wedding ceremony, the infant is given the rank of general and shortly thereafter appears in a baby carriage presiding over official functions. The Patriarch is powerless, too, in the face of foreign imperialism, an example of which is the demand by a series of United States ambassadors that he surrender the Caribbean Sea as surety for the interest payments due on his government's huge foreign debt. He finally gives in and permits the hated gringos to transport the vast volume of water to Arizona, leaving him with a gnawing nostalgia for the seascape—now described as a barren lunar landscape—he loved to gaze upon from his palace window.

Occasionally the novel's absurdities take on the characteristics of black humor. For example, over a period of years a total of two thousand children disappear, after having helped to rig the national lottery by drawing from a container of balls the only cold one. Eventually, when the parents of the missing children become increasingly inquisitive, the Patriarch orders three officers to transport the two thousand prisoners far out to sea and sink the boat with charges of dynamite. He then promotes the officers, pins medals on their chests, and has them executed.

Even more grotesque is an incident involving the Patriarch's "lifelong friend," General Rodrigo de Aguilar, who, the Patriarch suspects, will lead a barracks revolt on a certain Tuesday, when de Aguilar is slated to offer the main toast at a banquet honoring the palace guard. On the designated evening, as enticing odors filter into the hall from the kitchen, the guests restlessly await the general's arrival. Finally, at the stroke of midnight General Rodrigo de Aguilar makes his entrance, stretched out on a silver platter, decorated with cauliflower and laurel branches, marinated in spices and browned in the oven, ready to be served to his ravenous subordinates.

Critics have speculated that the comic tone of *The Autumn of the Patriarch* reflects a concerted effort to exorcise a dynamic and dangerous myth—that of the godlike *caudillo*, or political strongman, which, though fading from the Latin American consciousness, refuses to die. The litany of grotesque horrors and absurdities narrated here imposes on the reader a hopeless sense of circularity that only the tyrant's demise can bring to a conclusion. Thus, in the final pages of the novel the Patriarch is awakened in the privacy of his heavily guarded quarters by the ghostly image of death hovering over him. Helpless and terrified, he falls victim to the solitude of power—the major theme—which is underscored when his liberated subjects take to the streets and spontaneously celebrate the end of their long nightmare.

In 1981, García Márquez published *Chronicle of a Death Foretold*, which investigates the murder of Santiago Nasar, a youth accused of seducing Ángela Vicario prior to her marriage to another. When Ángela's husband, Bayardo San Román, discovers on their wedding night that his wife is not a virgin, he takes her back to her parents. The following morning her twin brothers commit the heinous crime on the doorstep of the victim's home.

Based on an incident reported in a Colombian newspaper in 1951, the plot is an ingenious mélange of journalism and detective story. The chronicle of events is described by a first-person narrator (the author himself) who returns to the town twenty-seven years later to reconstruct the incidents leading up to the crime. Like a sensational newspaper account, the first sentence of the novel is designed to arouse the reader's curiosity: "On the day they were going to kill him, Santiago Nasar got up at five-thirty in the morning to wait for the boat the bishop was coming on." Although the outcome is clear from the beginning, the author's skill as a storyteller is demonstrated by the reader's unflagging interest in exactly how, why, and under what circumstances the accused seducer will die.

The novel's overriding irony and one of its themes derives from the fact that despite the author's painstaking efforts to record information related to the murder (he interviews more than thirty town citizens) his investigation raises more questions than it answers. Thus, Santiago Nasar, whose guilt is never proved, may have been a mere victim of fate, while Ángela Vicario's and Bayardo San Román's behavior remains at times enigmatic and at other times incomprehensible. The contradictions of the witnesses after so many years have passed and the allusions to unexplained dreams, nightmares, and premonitions also contribute to the pervasive atmosphere of ambiguity.

García Márquez condemns the primitive code of honor prevalent in the community by demonstrating that the town citizens did nothing to prevent the killing because they considered such vengeance justified. The double sexual standard also comes under indictment, as the cult of virginity imposed on females by the church is juxtaposed with the mores represented by the local "house of mercies," whose owner, María Alejandrina Cervantes, has reportedly done away with the virginity of a whole generation. The kindly, likeable brothel owner, however, stands out in contrast to the town priest and the bishop, the former having neglected his duty to prevent the murder and the latter having barely acknowledged the crowd of worshipers that came to meet his boat. The book's numerous religious symbols also cast the mission of Christianity in a negative light. For example, several circumstances surrounding Santiago Nasar would suggest that despite his probable innocence of any crime, he was created as a Christ figure and sacrificed to save the town's collective honor: his family name recalls Nazareth, where Christ resided as a boy; his best friend and alter ego bears the name Cristo (Christ) Bedoya; and the public nature of his "sacrifice" evokes Christ's crucifixion, as does the act

of "nailing" him to the door of his house during the brutal crime.

Chronicle of a Death Foretold can also be read as a parody of romantic fiction, in which young star-crossed lovers are irresistibly drawn together only to die under tragic circumstances. Unlike such protagonists, Ángela Vicario and Bayardo San Román did not feel strongly attracted to one another in their youth, and when, after many years of separation, Bayardo San Román finally returns to his wife with her two thousand unopened love letters, theirs is the grotesque reconciliation of a middle-aged couple responsible for a tragedy that never should have occurred.

A tale about intimate relationships between men and women of all ages, *Love in the Time of Cholera* is indeed laced with allusions to cholera epidemics, but its true meaning lies in the search for love and happiness despite the ravages of time and the constant threat of death. The setting is an unnamed city—more than likely Cartagena—on the Caribbean coast of the author's homeland. Although Colombia itself is never mentioned, references are made to at least six of the nation's presidents, and the capital city of Santa Fe in the novel suggests the original name of Colombia's present-day capital, Santa Fe de Bogotá.

The principal characters are Juvenal Urbino, a native son who studies medicine in France and returns to become one of the city's most prominent citizens; Fermina Daza, Dr. Urbino's strong-willed wife; and Florentino Ariza, a successful businessman who in his youth had a platonic affair with Fermina Daza before she married Dr. Urbino. The three major threads of the plot delineate the relationship between Fermina Daza and Dr. Urbino; Florentino Ariza's numerous love affairs, which he hopes will make him forget Fermina Daza; and, after Dr. Urbino's death, Florentino Ariza's persistent courtship of Fermina Daza.

The structure of *Love in the Time of Cholera* can be compared to that of *The Autumn of the Patriarch*, each novel consisting of six sections and each dramatizing, or alluding to, the demise of a major figure—Dr. Urbino and the Patriarch—in the first and last units. Time is also treated similarly in both works: chronological progression is disrupted and seemingly brought to a standstill by repetitions, flashbacks, and occasional leaps into the future. The temporal landscape of the more recent novel is, nevertheless, not without identifiable landmarks that frame the action between the late 1870's and the early 1930's: Juvenal Urbino is a student in Paris shortly before Victor Hugo's death in 1885; the novel encompasses the War of the Thousand Days (1899–1902) and World War I; characters take a balloon trip to celebrate the turn of the century; the publication of Anatole France's *Penguin Island* (1908) is noted; and also noted is the 1928 labor strike in Ciénaga so vividly described in *One Hundred Years of Solitude*. We are told that on the day of Dr. Urbino's death at the age of eighty-one, the liberals are celebrating their first victory in several decades, probably a reference to the election of 1930, wherein liberals took office after forty-four years of conservative government. The novel ends approximately two years after Dr. Urbino's death.

Although elements of magical realism reminiscent of *One Hundred Years of Solitude* occur occasionally in *Love in the Time of Cholera* (a doll outgrows its skirt and crows emit an odor of perfume), García Márquez' most recent novel emerges as a wistful re-creation of the past, interwoven with traces of romanticism and poetic realism. The love-smitten nineteenth-century hero is evoked by Florentino Ariza's consuming passion for Fermina Daza, while the detailed descriptions of daily life in a city clinging to its colonial past are supplemented by descriptions of the unspoiled Magdalena River prior to its despoliation by technology. The novel's ending likewise strikes a nostalgic note, as a rekindled love affair becomes a form of liberation amidst the destructive forces of old age, disease, war, and ecological disaster.

Fraught with subtle shades of meaning and keen observations of human behavior, the poignant and elegantly stylized *Love in the Time of Cholera* is in some respects García Márquez' most mature creative endeavor. Meanwhile, over the past two decades, he has joined a group of distinguished twentieth-century writers—modernists and postmodernists—who have expanded or set new parameters for the novel. About the time *One Hundred Years of Solitude* was translated into English (1970) the critic Leslie Fiedler made his pronouncement that the novel was dead, and indeed at that moment it had fallen on hard times in France, the United States, the Soviet Union, and other parts of the West. But what Fiedler and many other readers of English could not know, due to the dearth of translations, was that in Latin America the decade of the boom (the 1960's) had reached its peak with the unprecedented popular and critical success of García Márquez' masterpiece.

As mentioned above, the Colombian author's single most important contribution to literature is his commingling of realism and fantasy, resulting in the creation of a total fictional universe in which the fantastic is made real and the real fantastic. Not that García Márquez is the first to depict the magical elements in Latin American life; Miguel Ángel Asturias, Alejo Carpentier, Juan Rulfo, Julio Cortázar, and, especially, Jorge Luis Borges looked beyond the objective and the everyday before their Colombian colleague's rise to fame. But it is the utterly convincing tone of *One Hundred Years of Solitude* that has brought fantasy into the mainstream of world literature and deftly illustrated its author's assertion that reality is not restricted to the price of tomatoes and eggs.

A self-proclaimed leftist who would like to see the world ruled by socialist regimes, García Márquez nevertheless refuses to use his art as a platform for political propaganda. With his broad literary canvases he has rescued the novel from the narrow byways in which it had become mired and, in so doing, has attracted a worldwide audience. To readers who speak of fantasy in his works, García Márquez insists that they accurately reflect the Caribbean ambience he knew as a child, an ambience steeped in folklore and myth but never fantastic. Still, one of the major virtues of works such as *One Hundred Years of Solitude*, *The Autumn of the Patriarch*, and "The Handsomest Drowned Man in the World," to name but a few, is their extraordinary power to liberate the contemporary imagination fettered by the rigid laws of logic.

To other readers García Márquez' oeuvre may suggest a pessimism concerning the fate of contemporary man. He may seem to believe that man has sealed his own destiny because of his consuming quest for power and material gain and his resulting incapacity to sustain a society based on love and solidarity with his fellow beings. Nevertheless, García Márquez provides ample evidence of eternal virtues in such characters as the woman in "Tuesday Siesta," whose strength and dignity dominate every episode; in the courageous and idealistic colonel of *Leaf Storm*; in Úrsula, the archetype of feminine wisdom and stability in *One Hundred Years of Solitude*; and in Úrsula's husband, José Arcadio Buendía, who, though flighty and irrational, embodies man's search for progress and truth.

Presently García Márquez is Latin America's most widely acclaimed living writer. The stark realities of that part of the world have been expanded and universalized in his fiction by the humanistic elements of myth, imagination, and aesthetic perception. His highly original, comprehensive vision of the human experience has made him a worthy recipient of the Nobel Prize.

SELECTED BIBLIOGRAPHY

First Editions

Prose Narratives

La hojarasca. Bogotá, 1955.
El coronel no tiene quien le escriba. Medellín, Colombia, 1961.
Los funerales de la Mamá Grande. Xalapa, Mexico, 1962.
La mala hora. Madrid, 1962.
Cien años de soledad. Buenos Aires, 1967.
Isabel viendo llover en Macondo. Buenos Aires, 1967.
La increíble y triste historia de la cándida Eréndira y de su abuela desalmada. Barcelona, 1972.
El negro que hizo esperar a los ángeles. Montevideo, 1972.
Ojos de perro azul. Rosario, Argentina, 1972.
Cuatro cuentos. Mexico City, 1974.
El otoño del patriarca. Barcelona, 1975.
Todos los cuentos de Gabriel García Márquez (1947–1972). Barcelona, 1975.
Crónica de una muerte anunciada. Bogotá, 1981.
El amor en los tiempos del cólera. Barcelona, 1985.

Miscellaneous

La novela en América Latina: Diálogo. With Mario Vargas Llosa. Lima, 1968.
Relato de un náufrago. Barcelona, 1970.
Cuando era feliz e indocumentado. Caracas, 1973.
Chile, el golpe y los gringos. Bogotá, 1974.

Crónicas y reportajes. Bogotá, 1975.
Operación Carlota. Lima, 1977.
Periodismo militante. Bogotá, 1978.
El secuestro. Salamanca, Spain, 1983. Film script.
Obra periodística. Bogotá. 1–2: *Textos costeños* (1981). 3–4: *Entre cachacos* (1982). 5–6: *De Europa y América (1955–1960)* (1984).

Translations

The Autumn of the Patriarch. Translated by Gregory Rabassa. New York, 1976.
Chronicle of a Death Foretold. Translated by Gregory Rabassa. New York, 1982.
Clandestine in Chile. The Adventures of Miguel Littín. Translated by Asa Zatz. New York, 1987.
In Evil Hour. Translated by Gregory Rabassa. New York, 1979.
Innocent Eréndira and Other Stories. Translated by Gregory Rabassa. New York, 1978.
Leaf Storm and Other Stories. Translated by Gregory Rabassa. New York, 1972. Includes "The Handsomest Drowned Man in the World" and "Monologue of Isabel Watching It Rain in Macondo."
Love in the Time of Cholera. Translated by Edith Grossman. New York, 1988.
No One Writes to the Colonel and Other Stories. Translated by J. S. Bernstein. New York, 1968. Includes all eight stories from *Big Mama's Funeral.*
One Hundred Years of Solitude. Translated by Gregory Rabassa. New York, 1970.
The Story of a Shipwrecked Sailor. Translated by Randolph Hogan. New York, 1986.

Biographical and Critical Studies

Alstrum, James J. "Los arquetipos en *La increíble y triste historia de la cándida Eréndira y de su abuela desalmada* de Gabriel García Márquez." *Proceedings of the Pacific Northwest Conference on Foreign Languages* 21/1:140–142 (1978).
Arenas, Reinaldo. "In the Town of Mirages." *Review* (Center for Inter-American Relations) 70:101–108 (1971).
Bell-Villada, Gene H. "Names and Narrative Pattern in *One Hundred Years of Solitude*." *Latin American Literary Review* 9/18:37–46 (1981).
———. "García Márquez and the Novel." *Latin American Literary Review* [Special issue on García Márquez] 13/25:15–23 (1985).

Benson, John. "Disyunción en los cuentos de García Márquez." *Chasqui* 8/1:8–22 (1978).

Brushwood, John S. "Reality and Imagination in the Novels of García Márquez." *Latin American Literary Review* 13/25:9–14 (1985).

Ciplijauskaité, Birute. "Foreshadowing as a Technique and Theme in *One Hundred Years of Solitude*." *Books Abroad* 47/3:479–484 (1973).

Dauster, Frank. "The Short Stories of García Márquez." *Books Abroad* 47/3:466–470 (1973).

———. "Ambiguity and Indeterminacy in *La hojarasca*." *Latin American Literary Review* 13/25:24–28 (1985).

Davis, Mary E. "The Voyage Beyond the Map: 'El ahogado más hermoso del mundo.'" *Kentucky Romance Quarterly* 26/1:25–33 (1979).

Dreifus, Claudia. "Playboy Interview: Gabriel García Márquez." *Playboy* 30/2:65–77, 172–178 (1983).

Fau, Margaret Eustalia. *Gabriel García Márquez: An Annotated Bibliography, 1947–1979*. Westport, Conn., 1980.

———, and Nelly Sfeir de Gonzalez. *Bibliographic Guide to Gabriel García Márquez, 1979–1985*. Westport, Conn., 1986.

Foster, David William. "The Double Inscription of the Narrataire in 'Los funerales de la Mamá Grande.'" In *Studies in the Contemporary Spanish-American Short Story*. Columbia, Mo., 1979. Pp. 51–62.

———. "García Márquez and the *Écriture* of Complicity: 'La prodigiosa tarde de Baltazar.'" In *Studies in the Contemporary Spanish-American Short Story*. Columbia, Mo., 1979. Pp. 39–50.

Franco, Jean. "The Limits of the Liberal Imagination: *One Hundred Years of Solitude* and *Nostromo*." *Punto de contacto/Point of Contact* 1/1:4–16 (1975).

Fuentes, Carlos. "Macondo, Seat of Time." *Review* (Center for Inter-American Relations) 70:119–121 (1971).

Gallagher, David P. "Gabriel García Márquez." In *Modern Latin American Literature*. London, 1973. Pp. 144–163.

Giacoman, Helmy F., ed. *Homenaje a Gabriel García Márquez*. New York, 1972.

Goetzinger, Judith A. "The Emergence of a Folk Myth in *Los funerales de la Mamá Grande*." *Revista de estudios hispánicos* 6/2:237–248 (1972).

Guibert, Rita. "Gabriel García Márquez." In *Seven Voices: Seven Latin American Writers Talk*. New York, 1973. Pp. 303–337.

Hancock, Joel. "Gabriel García Márquez's *Eréndira* and the Brothers Grimm." *Studies in Twentieth Century Literature* 3/1:45–52 (1978).

Harss, Luis, and Barbara Dohmann. "Gabriel García Márquez, or the Lost Chord." In *Into the Mainstream*. New York, 1967. Pp. 310–341.

Hedeen, Paul M. "Gabriel García Márquez's Dialectic of Solitude." *Southwest Review* 68/4:350–364 (1983).

Janes, Regina. *Gabriel García Márquez: Revolutions in Wonderland*. Columbia, Mo., 1981.

Kadir, Djelal. "The Architectonic Principle of *Cien años de soledad* and the Vichian Theory of History." *Kentucky Romance Quarterly* 24/3:251–261 (1977).

Kennedy, William. "The Yellow Trolley Car in Barcelona and Other Visions: A Profile of Gabriel García Márquez." *Atlantic Monthly* 231/1:50–59 (January 1973).

Kercher, Dona M. "García Márquez's *Crónica de una muerte anunciada* [*Chronicle of a Death Foretold*]: Notes on Parody and the Artist." *Latin American Literary Review* [Special issue on García Márquez] 13/25:90–103 (1985).

Levy, Kurt L. "Planes of Reality in *El otoño del patriarca*." In *Studies in Honor of Gerald E. Wade*, edited by Sylvia Bowman et al. Madrid, 1979. Pp. 133–141.

Luchting, Wolfgang A. "Gabriel García Márquez: The Boom and the Whimper." *Books Abroad* 44/1:26–30 (1970).

———. "Lampooning Literature: *La mala hora*." *Books Abroad* 47/3:471–478 (1973).

McGowan, John P. "À la recherche du temps perdu in *One Hundred Years of Solitude*." *Modern Fiction Studies* 28/4:557–567 (1982–1983).

McGuirk, Bernard, and Richard Cardwell. *Gabriel García Márquez: New Readings*. Cambridge, England, 1987.

McMurray, George R. *Gabriel García Márquez*. New York, 1977.

Mendoza, Plinio Apuleyo. *The Fragance of the Guava: Plinio Apuleyo Mendoza in Conversation with Gabriel García Márquez*. London, 1983.

Merrel, Floyd. "José Arcadio Buendía's Scientific Paradigms: Man in Search of Himself." *Latin American Literary Review* 2/4:59–70 (1974).

Minta, Stephen. *García Márquez: Writer of Colombia*. New York, 1987.

Müller-Bergh, Klaus. "*Relato de un náufrago*: García Márquez's Tale of Shipwreck and Survival at Sea." *Books Abroad* 47/3:460–466 (1973).

Oberhelman, Harley D. *The Presence of Faulkner in the Writings of García Márquez*. Lubbock, Tex., 1980.

Ortega, Julio. "*One Hundred Years of Solitude* and *The Autumn of the Patriarch*: Text and Culture." In *Poetics of Change: The New Spanish-American Narrative*. Austin, Tex., 1984. Pp. 85–95; 96–119.

Peel, Roger M. "The Short Stories of Gabriel García Márquez." *Studies in Short Fiction* 8/1:159–168 (1971).

Penuel, Arnold M. "Death and the Maiden: Demythologization of Virginity in García Márquez's *Cien años de soledad.*" *Hispania* 66/4:552–560 (1983).

———. "The Sleep of Vital Reason in García Márquez's *Crónica de una muerte anunciada.*" *Hispania* 68/4:753–766 (1985).

Rodríguez Monegal, Émir. *"One Hundred Years of Solitude: The Last Three Pages." Books Abroad* 47/3:485–489 (1973).

Simons, Marlise. "A Talk With Gabriel García Márquez." *New York Times Book Review,* 5 December 1982. Pp. 7, 60–61.

Sims, Robert Lewis. "The Banana Massacre in *Cien años de soledad:* A Micro-structural Example of Myth, History and Bricolage." *Chasqui* 8/3:3–23 (1979).

———. "Theme, Narrative, Bricolage and Myth in García Márquez." *Journal of Spanish Studies: Twentieth Century* 8/1–2:143–159 (1980).

Tobin, Patricia. "The Autumn of the Signifier: The Deconstructionist Moment of García Márquez." *Latin American Literary Review* 13/25:65–78 (1985).

Vargas Llosa, Mario. *Gabriel García Márquez: Historia de un deicidio.* Barcelona, 1971.

———. "García Márquez: From Aracataca to Macondo." *Review* (Center for Inter-American Relations) 70:129–142 (1971).

Williams, Raymond L. "The Dynamic Structure of García Márquez's *El otoño del patriarca.*" *Symposium* 32/1:56–75 (1978).

———. *Gabriel García Márquez.* Boston, 1984.

———. "An Introduction to the Early Journalism of García Márquez: 1948–1958." *Latin American Literary Review* 13/25:117–132 (1985).

Woods, Richard D. "Time and Futility in the Novel *El coronel no tiene quien le escriba.*" *Kentucky Romance Quarterly* 17/4:287–295 (1970).

Zamora, Lois Parkinson. "The Myth of Apocalypse and Human Temporality in García Márquez's *Cien años de soledad* and *El otoño del patriarca.*" *Symposium* 32/4:341–355 (1978).

———. "The End of Innocence: Myth and Narrative Structure in Faulkner's *Absalom, Absalom!* and García Márquez's *Cien años de soledad.*" *Hispanic Journal* 4/1:23–40 (1982).

———. "Ends and Endings in García Márquez's *Crónica de una muerte anunciada* [Chronicle of a Death Foretold]." *Latin American Literary Review* 13/25:104–116 (1985).

Luis Alberto Heiremans

(1928–1964)

Grinor Rojo

Born the wealthy son of Chilean aristocrats, educated at the best schools in Santiago, graduated in medicine at age twenty-six, elegantly dressed, handsome, courteous, loved by all who knew him, Luis Alberto Heiremans was a prolific writer who in his brief life completed three collections of short stories, a novel, and fourteen plays. Heiremans was born on 14 July 1928 in the capital of Chile and died in the same city in 1964, barely thirty-six years old, the victim of lymphatic cancer. As one famous journalist described him in a requiem article: "He was somewhat like a postcard, like a drawing by Ingres. . . . He did not walk through the streets of Paris or New York. He flew. . . ." Perhaps that verb, to fly, is the one that suits him best. Everything about Heiremans was light: his life, his relationships, his dealings with people and things, his literature, his theater.

Heiremans published his first book in 1950, and his first play opened a year later, while he was a medical student at the Catholic University of Santiago. The book, entitled *Los niños extraños* (Strange Children), consists of eight short stories in which Heiremans studies, in almost clinical detail, the afflicted personalities of imaginative and sensitive adolescents. These are stories that avoid specific temporal and geographic identification, and that therefore move away from realism, as if describing reality were a reprehensible display of bad manners. Heiremans thus pays tribute to the antirealist and antiregionalist campaign of his Chilean contemporaries, the writers of the Generation of '50, whose peculiar way of being provincial consisted of believing themselves to be universal. On the one hand, those writers were weary of the superficial realism of their predecessors, and on the other, they were living in an age of grave political strife. In 1949, one year before Heiremans published *Los niños extraños*, Pablo Neruda, on horseback and disguised as a muleteer, fled the Chilean police with the manuscript of *Canto general* (General Song, 1950) under his arm. In the United States, conditions were equally troublesome, and the entire world was awaiting the moment when the cold war would turn into a hot one, with the definitive horror that an event of that nature was bound to entail after the bombings of Hiroshima and Nagasaki. These were not the best circumstances for the writing of realist and potentially critical literature, a situation of which the Chilean authors of the Generation of '50 were keenly aware.

Heiremans' esoteric tendencies seem to have had less to do with an avoidance of history than did those of other members of his generation. If they did not arise from a profound spirituality, there is no doubt that they came from a genuine sensitivity. A second collection of short stories, entitled *Los demás* (The Others), appeared two years after the publication of *Los niños extraños*. In the excessively literary style that he would cultivate until his death, Heiremans dealt in this book with a number of contemporary international themes, among them, the dichotomy between the necessity and the impossibility of knowing one's fellow man, existential solitude, the curse of freedom. In *Los demás*, Heiremans achieved a firmer grounding of his subject matter, involving a sincere concern for the common people, those who travel by bus and work in department stores—although not without implicitly deploring the terrible ordinariness that cripples them. The book revolves around the central conflict of Heiremans' narrative and dramatic production, namely the clash between the perfection of the ideal and the misery of the real.

Heiremans' third collection of stories, *Seres de un día* (One-day Beings), appeared first in the United States in 1960 and was republished posthumously in Chile in 1965. Strictly speaking, this book contains, rather than short stories, four novellas, all set in Paris, that focus on the adventures of different "trasplantados," to use the word coined by Alberto Blest Gana to refer to Latin American expatriates living in Europe. It is interesting to see Heiremans yield to a theme that was employed in the novel of the nineteenth and early twentieth centuries: the satirizing of the anxieties of New World millionaires who, with the purpose of acquiring nobility for their offspring, took up residence in European capitals. But this is not a major concern for the author of *Seres de un día*. Without completely ignoring the social dimensions of his theme, Heiremans prefers to linger on the philosophical and psychological implications of the transhumant destinies of his characters. The opposition between a spent and corrupt Europe and a young and pure America, an opposition of a long and enduring tradition in Latin American literature (and not only in Latin American literature, since Henry James also made it one of his favorite subjects), springs up here and there in this book. Nevertheless, the dramas of conscience are the ones that receive the author's preferential attention.

Heiremans' narrative career culminates with the novel *Puerta de salida* (This Way Out), written in Paris between 1961 and 1963, and published in German and Spanish in 1964. "I am interested in describing the concealed rather than the actual reality of individuals," he declared in an interview granted upon the publication of this book, and he added, "I believe that people and things have auras and these auras are the transcendent." The antithesis between the superficial and the profound, between the evident and the occult, remains prominent in the last and most valuable of his narrations. Even its structure reflects it, since *Puerta de salida* is a novel that deliberately juxtaposes two kinds of reality: one prospective, swift, objective, and direct, and the other retrospective, dilatory, subjective, and poetic. As for the story that Heiremans tells, that of a Chilean painter, Andrés, and his unhappy love for a French girl, Sybille, it would not be a memorable one but for the presumably autobiographical elements that it contains and its depiction of the novelist's ambivalent attitude toward European culture and society.

More significant than Heiremans' narrative is his theater. Although his first plays do not differ greatly from his narratives of the same period, in the last four years of his dramatic production he made a notable attempt to overcome the limitations of his earlier work. Critics usually divide Heiremans' theater into two periods: an initial one, from 1951 to 1960, which he himself considered exploratory, and the period of his artistic and intellectual maturity, from 1960 to 1964. The plays that reached the stage between 1951 and 1962 are *Noche de equinoccio* (Night of Equinox, premiered in 1951), *La hora robada* (Stolen Hour, premiered in 1952), *La eterna trampa* (The Eternal Trap, premiered in 1953), *La jaula en el árbol* (Cage in the Treetops, premiered in 1957), *Moscas sobre el mármol* (Flies upon Marble, premiered in 1958), *Esta señorita Trini* (Señorita Trini, premiered in 1958), *Es de contarlo y no creerlo* (Who Would Believe It?, premiered in 1959), and *El palomar a oscuras* (Pigeon-house in the Dark, premiered in 1962). The conflict in these plays, as in Heiremans' short stories, is almost always based on the discrepancy between reality and dreams. In different settings and in different ways, he ponders the weakness of the ideal and the necessary failure of the dreamer who dares to confront the cold obstinacy of facts. When the tone is that of comedy, the efforts of the idealist become grotesque rather than pitiful. When it is that of tragedy, the same kind of chimerical enterprise leads to the melodramatic destruction of the character. The French dramatists Jean Anouilh and Jean Giraudoux, as well as the Latin American Conrado Nalé Roxlo, provide good examples of this type of theater. The Chilean author relies upon such models, most specifically upon the French.

In classifying Heiremans' dramatic work of the 1950's, it is best to divide it into four categories. First, there are the fantastic and drawing room comedies that combine the influence of Anouilh and Noel Coward (*Noche de equinoccio, La hora robada, Es de contarlo y no creerlo*); second, a piece inspired by Luigi Pirandello (*La eterna trampa*); third, two psychological dramas reminiscent of Tennessee Williams' early theater (*Moscas sobre el mármol* and *El palomar a oscuras*); and, finally, two routine comedies, one *La jaula en el árbol*, cast in a style that is somewhat *costumbrista* (depicting local customs and types) and the other a musical (*Esta señorita Trini*). With respect to the musical, although some critics deem it unworthy of Heiremans' overall achievement, we are tempted to say that it is one of his better plays. At least it is an autochthonous musical comedy and therefore preferable to the Broadway productions that, at that time, had already begun to ravage Chilean theater.

Moscas sobre el mármol and *El palomar a oscuras* are the most ambitious plays of the first period of Heiremans' theater and are so intimately related that upon reading the latter, one is overcome by the curious sensation of rereading the former. This is not because the plots are repetitive, although there are points of contact between the two, but because the picture of human relationships that the dramatist has developed in them has essentially the same structure. In both plays we find a central character who is vacillating between antagonistic loyalties: an internal, familial loyalty and an external, amorous one. Every attempt to reach an equilibrium is doomed to failure because these characters are utterly unable to perceive the difference between loving and possessing. In other words, familial love, that of the mother in *Moscas sobre el mármol* and that of the sick brother in *El palomar a oscuras*, is a barrier that isolates one from

the vicissitudes of social life. If the protagonist cannot manage to establish a harmonious relationship with "the others," it is because the people of his own blood prevent him from doing so.

If Heiremans deserves an important place in the history of Latin American drama, it is not because of the works he wrote during the 1950's, but those he completed between 1960 and 1964. At the outset of the 1960's, people in Chile were opting for change: economic, social, political, and cultural change. Just as one could not be president of the Republic of Chile at that time without a program of profound social and political reform, one could not be a significant writer without an advanced aesthetic perspective. As might be expected, proposals for renovation abounded. Among them was one that attempted to combine the early Christian concept of community with modern aspirations for social justice. This program was related to the theses of Jacques Maritain and Pierre Teilhard de Chardin, as well as to the progressive preaching of Pope John XXIII, and found expression in the policies of the Christian Democratic Party and later in the government of President Eduardo Frei. It was not the only option for renewal available, but it was the one that satisfied the most people. The key to its success was that it proclaimed the unity between Christianity and social justice and, not infrequently, at least among the more adventurous, the unity between Christianity and socialism.

Heiremans was a devoted Christian. Furthermore, he was an individual who, for some time, had been trying to find a satisfactory solution to the problem of the relationship between the private and public spheres. Keeping this in mind, one may reread the titles of his works from the 1950's: *Los demás, La eterna trampa, La jaula en el árbol*—all are either direct mentions or oblique metaphors that allude to a state of confinement from which the dramatist feels an increasing need to free himself. The isolation theme in *Moscas sobre el mármol* and *El palomar a oscuras* perhaps acquires the full measure of its meaning when placed in this frame of reference.

Between 1960 and 1964, Heiremans produced *Buenaventura* (Good Fortune, premiered in 1962), a group of one-act plays that are more strongly related to his past than to his future works, and a trilogy of major plays that consists of *Versos de ciego* (Songs of a

Blindman, premiered in 1961), *El abanderado* (The Man with the White Kerchief, premiered in 1962) and *El tony chico* (The Littlest Clown, premiered in 1964). This trilogy is the culmination of his dramatic endeavors and its unity is due less to the maintenance of a single story line throughout the three pieces (the stories vary from one to the next, although there are certain elements that persist) than to their philosophical and technical innovations. Moreover, not only does Heiremans identify in these more mature works with a Christian conception of the world, but he very consciously attempts to endow it with appropriate theatrical vehicles.

New influences may be detected in his writing as a result of this change. One is that of the European Catholic dramatists: Paul Claudel, Gabriel Marcel, Henri Ghéon, Georges Bernanos. More important, however, is Heiremans' interest in the Chilean folkloric tradition, which he studied with a dedication and respect that it is doubtful he would have had a few years before. For most of the numerous Chilean intellectuals and artists at that time who shared this interest, folklore was not only a repertory of ready-made plots, but also a legacy of powerful intuitions about human destiny and history, a register in which the wisdom of the people records its millenary experience of the self. Folklore was therefore a privileged focus that Heiremans and others selected in order to rediscover the reality of their country during the 1960's. After the evasive strategy favored by the Generation of '50, the urgency of knowing one's own reality was once again making itself felt.

Even so, it would be unjust to say that Heiremans changed only as the world around him changed. The truth is that an alternative to solipsism already existed embryonically in two dramatic drafts that he wrote toward the end of the 1950's and that later became *Versos de ciego*. They are *Los güenos versos* (The Best Poems) and *Sigue la estrella* (Follow the Star), both written and produced in 1958. In these drafts one can perceive certain elements that became standard features in his later plays and that were already articulating something akin to a theatrical poetics. Outstanding among them are the interweaving of materials taken from the New Testament with others from the Chilean folkloric tradition, the structure of the search and/or pilgrimage as the connecting thread in the development of the plot, and the stylized popularization of language and characters. Thus, in the drafts of 1958, Heiremans was already opening the path that would lead him to the best of his theater.

Sigue la estrella, the first of the short works from 1958, was a Christmas *auto*, a liturgical drama in the medieval manner. *Los güenos versos* is closer to what were known in medieval French theater as *moralités*, religious pieces that were ethical rather than biblical and that were written in order to represent the vices and virtues of man. As for *Versos de ciego*, the play Heiremans produced in 1961, although it preserves the form of the Christmas *auto*, it also has the characters depart from a village square that clearly symbolizes the world. The Blind Man, Heiremans' Brechtian narrator, emphasizes this fact, stating that "this world is like a square, with four entries and one direction which is not easy to find." Thus, in *Versos de ciego*, the Wise Men advance in pursuit of the only right direction, that of the Star of Bethlehem. They are portrayed as a group of traveling musicians, who, on their way, are joined by various characters who form a faithful catalog of Heiremans' ethical preferences: first Juana Buey, a peasant girl who is the archetype of popular goodness; then Angélica, the Angel of the Anunciation; later Perico Burro, the incarnation of childlike innocence; and, finally, an elementary school teacher, Oliverio Pastor, and a redeemed prostitute, María Chica. They also leave behind the characters of impure heart, those who prefer to attend the funeral of a criminal rather than follow the direction of the star. Within the latter group, Fanor stands out especially as the unscrupulous peddler, who, for that reason, becomes the prototype (although a somewhat naive one) of the bourgeois.

While *Versos de ciego* makes use of one end of the Gospel, that of the birth of Christ, *El abanderado* makes use of the other, that of his death. The play deals, in fact, with the apprehension and transfer of a legendary bandit, Juan Araneda López, alias El Abanderado, to the site where he will be executed. In recounting his *vía crucis*, Heiremans mixes the biblical material with the events of a popular Chilean celebration, that of the Christ of May. The doubles of the Virgin, Judas, Pilate, Caiaphas, and Mary Magdalene are all present. As for El Abanderado himself, he is far from a symbol of goodness. Nor is he someone who would sacrifice his life for his fellow man. He is a highway robber, an individual who has led a despicable career and who recognizes that everything in his criminal record is true and that "there is even more." His adventure, then, is not that of Christ as God, trusting and at the point of being reunited with the Father, but rather that of the other Christ, the guilty and fearful man on the threshold of disintegration. The biblical story authorizes this point of view, and the Spanish writer Miguel de Unamuno has referred to it in his *San Manuel Bueno, mártir* (1933), while emphasizing the strange humanness of the Christian myth. Heiremans' perspective is the same, although more important than the perspective itself are its aesthetic consequences. Contrary to what occurs in *Versos de ciego*, in *El abanderado* the unfolding of the action often induces in the reader and/or spectator a state of intense emotional involvement. For example, the last scene of the first part, the one in which the protagonist is brought face to face with his mother, the madam of a house of prostitution, who is nicknamed La Pepa de Oro (Golden Nugget), is one of the most dramatic in the history of Chilean theater. It is not, therefore, for its recycling of the Bible nor for its accumulation of a few abstract symbols that this play has become a classic. Rather it is because of the depth with which it treats real conflicts, situations laden with the strong pathos of a weak and suffering humanity.

Heiremans died on 25 October 1964. *El tony chico*, his last play, opened on 30 October, only five days after his death. It is believed that Heiremans had written it while in the Untied States, in the middle of the previous year, a fact that would rule out an analysis that attaches too much importance to the ill-fated circumstances of his last months. But the association is inevitable. The confessional tone, the retrospective examination of an existence that is nearing its end, is something that immediately holds one's attention in reading or seeing this last of his works. The setting is that of the circus. Without excluding an interpretation that would make it a new metaphor for the world, similar to the square in *Versos de ciego*, the circus can also be understood as an allusion to the theatrical atmosphere in which Heiremans spent half of his life.

Like El Abanderado, the protagonist of *El tony chico*, Landa, is a character who evaluates himself obsessively with an eye on his impending end. "Hope is nostalgia," he repeats on various occasions. He cares little for what he is and nothing for what he will be; all that matters to him is what he has been. Thus, in his alcoholic hallucinations, the world of his past becomes identified with the whiteness and luminosity of paradise. However, the informed reader or spectator should not find it difficult to discover behind that image the peaceful Chilean landscape of the author's childhood.

Are there links between Heiremans' mature works and the dynamics of Chilean and Latin American history at the beginning of the 1960's? Do *Versos de ciego*, *El abanderado*, and *El tony chico* establish a radical break with the author's production from the previous decade, and do they address the new concerns that from 1960 on burst like a hurricane into the history of Chile and Latin America? The response to these questions is yes, but only a qualified yes. If it is undeniable that Heiremans' mature theater opened itself to the currents of history as neither his narrations nor his earlier theater did, it is also undeniable that such an opening was hampered by individual as well as collective constraints. Heiremans carried with him a burden of personal conflicts, which he tried to overcome without being entirely successful, and in the public sphere, the success of his message is also partial. That his Christianity was sincere and his love for the "poor of spirit" noble and disinterested is beyond suspicion. However, the question remains as to whether this was really what history was asking from him at a such a difficult time.

SELECTED BIBLIOGRAPHY

First Editions

Novel

Puerta de salida. Santiago, Chile, 1964.

Short Stories

Los niños extraños. Santiago, Chile, 1950.
Los demás. Santiago, Chile, 1952.
Seres de un día. Godfrey, Ill., 1960.

LUIS ALBERTO HEIREMANS

Plays

Moscas sobre el mármol. Santiago, Chile, 1958.
La jaula en el árbol. Santiago, Chile, 1959.
La hora robada. Santiago, Chile, 1959.
Es de contarlo y no creerlo. Santiago, Chile, 1959.
El abanderado. Santiago, Chile, 1962.
Versos de ciego. Santiago, Chile, 1962.
Buenaventura. Santiago, Chile, 1965.
La eterna trampa. Santiago, Chile, 1965.
El tony chico. Santiago, Chile, 1965.

Collected Works

Los mejores cuentos de Luis Alberto Heiremans. Santiago, Chile, 1966.

Biographical and Critical Studies

Cajiao Salas, Teresa. *Temas y símbolos en la obra de Luis Alberto Heiremans.* Santiago, Chile, 1970.

Dittborn, Eugenio. "Constantes en la trilogía dramática de Luis Alberto Heiremans." *Boletín de la Universidad de Chile* 56:70–80 (1965).

Estellé, Patricio. "Apuntes a la obra de Luis Alberto Heiremans." In *Memoria del Décimosegundo Congreso del Instituto de Literatura Iberoamericana.* Mexico City, 1966. Pp. 73–84.

Peden, Margaret Sayers. "The Theater of Luis Alberto Heiremans: 1928–1964." In *Dramatists in Revolt: The New Latin American Theater,* edited by Leon F. Lyday and George W. Woodyard. Austin, Tex., and London, 1976. Pp. 120–132.

Carlos Fuentes

(1928–   )

Lanin A. Gyurko

The Mexican writer Carlos Fuentes has through both his fiction and nonfiction made an outstanding contribution to world literature and to humanistic thought. A brilliant novelist, short story writer, playwright, literary critic, and journalist, an accomplished diplomat, and an educator who has lectured at many universities in Mexico and the United States, Fuentes has brought about a renovation in contemporary Hispanic American letters. Several of his novels, such as *La muerte de Artemio Cruz* (*The Death of Artemio Cruz*, 1962) and his magnum opus, *Terra nostra* (1975), are landmarks of Latin American fiction, and the English translation of his recent work, *Gringo viejo* (*The Old Gringo*, 1985), has been a best seller in the United States. Fuentes is a humanist in the classic sense of the word, masterfully combining influences from world literature, philosophy, history, anthropology, and painting in his narrative and dramatic art, and achieving an aesthetic vision that is both profoundly Mexican and universal.

Born in Panama City on 11 November 1928, the son of Rafael Fuentes Boettiger and Berta Macías Rivas, he attended primary school in Washington, D.C., and secondary schools in Buenos Aires and Santiago, Chile. He studied at the Institut des Hautes Études Internationales in Geneva and received a law degree from the National University of Mexico. Following in the footsteps of his father, a career diplomat and Mexican ambassador to Holland, Panama, Portugal, and Italy, Fuentes served for some time as secretary to the Mexican member of the International Law Commission of the United Nations in Geneva (1950) and as press secretary of the United Nations Information Center (1950). In 1956, he and Emmanuel Carballo founded and edited the *Revista mexicana de literatura*. From 1956 until 1959, Fuentes was director of international cultural relations for Mexico's Ministry of Foreign Affairs and from 1974 to 1977 he served as his country's ambassador to France. Fuentes' novel *Cambio de piel* (*A Change of Skin*) received the Biblioteca Breve prize in Barcelona upon its publication in 1967. In 1975 Fuentes received the Javier Villaurrutia prize in Mexico City and in 1977 the Rómulo Gallegos prize in Venezuela for his novel *Terra nostra* (translated into English and published as *Terra Nostra* in 1980). In 1984 he was awarded the National Prize for Literature in Mexico.

In his book of literary criticism *La nueva novela hispanoamericana* (*The New Latin American Novel*, 1969) Fuentes has been instrumental in presenting and defining the complex art of an internationally renowned generation of Hispanic American authors, including Julio Cortázar, Gabriel García Márquez, Mario Vargas Llosa, and José Donoso, who along with Fuentes have reshaped Latin American and world fiction. And Fuentes has given guidance and inspiration to a whole new generation of Mexican and Latin American writers. His thematic, structural, and linguistic innovations, his creation of a new, vital, and exuberant language for the novel, his bold and fascinating experiments in character creation, time, space, and point of view, his masterful fusion of social, historical, and political concerns with the worlds of myth and dream and the supernatural, have markedly expanded and enriched the art of the narrative.

Throughout his work, Fuentes has been preoccupied, as has Octavio Paz, with the theme of the quest for a Mexican national identity. Fuentes' extensive and profound exploration of *la mexicanidad* leads to his portrayal of Old World–New World relationships in *Terra Nostra* and *Una familia lejana* (*Distant Relations*, 1980) and to the examination of United States–Mexican relations in *Orquídeas a la luz de la luna* (*Orchids in the Moonlight*, premiered in 1982) and *The Old Gringo*.

The quest for origins, both individual and national, is one of the basic themes of *La región más transparente* (*Where the Air Is Clear*, 1958), a vast, dynamic narrative of Mexico that fuses historical epochs from pre-Columbian times to the present. The novel provides a panoramic analysis of all social classes in modern Mexico and captures multiple languages: the frivolous language of the jet set, interspersed with gallicisms and anglicisms; the rough and slangy idiom of the *cantina*; the pompous conversation of a group of pretentious aesthetes who recite poetry as they lounge in Second Empire chairs; the self-laudatory rhetoric of entrepreneurs like Federico Robles who celebrate the economic transformation of Mexico as due almost entirely to their own Herculean efforts. Social norms, political ideologies, and personal foibles in the Mexico of the economic boom of the 1950's are all subject to trenchant satire. Fuentes attacks the rigidity and snobbery of the remnants of the Porfirian aristocracy (the elite who had prospered under the rule of Porfirio Díaz) through his portrayal of the de Ovando family: Pimpinela, who ceaselessly attempts to restore the family fortune; the ossified

Doña Lorenza, who takes refuge in memory; and her debilitated grandson Benjamín, who now must work for a living. Fuentes also uses the novel to scorn the meretriciousness and greed of the nouveaux riches who have emerged after the Revolution and who willingly cater to the Porfirian elite, rather than shunning them, in a frenetic desire to trade money for social distinction. Fuentes further lambastes the decadence, hypocrisy, and paralysis of the intelligentsia, who avow sympathy for the masses in their writings but are in reality selling out; Fuentes portrays these people as content to be party ornaments for the pseudosophisticated international set.

In this nervous, kaleidoscopic work, which incessantly shifts from one social class to the next in its desire to encompass the whole of Mexican reality, the ancient Aztec gods serve as Fuentes' vehicle of critical commentary. These gods return to twentieth-century Mexico for a dual purpose. The Indian Ixca Cienfuegos, the narrator and the dominant character in the novel, is the incarnation of Huitzilopochtli, the ancient Aztec god of war. His role is to strip the masks of ostentation, smugness, and self-righteousness from the nouveaux riches, the dominant social class in contemporary Mexico. Ixca shrewdly dissects the character of his victims to discover what temptation he can use to destroy them—fame, wealth, social status, power, or erotic pleasure. He acts to gain their confidence and then suddenly betrays them. With the sexually frustrated Norma Larragoiti, trapped in a marriage of convenience with the banker Federico Robles, a man whom she loathes, Ixca plays the role of lover, luring Norma out to sea and then attempting to drown her. Like Lucifer, Ixca claims the soul if he cannot take the body. Failing to convince Rodrigo Pola to commit suicide to emulate what he falsely holds up as the martyrdom of Pola's father in the Mexican Revolution, Ixca crushes Rodrigo spiritually by introducing the artist to a slick group of film producers for whom Pola prostitutes his considerable creative talent in return for instant wealth and social status.

The ancient god also represents the collective consciousness of the indigenous Mexican, the true *pueblo*, which Fuentes refers to by the ancient Aztec word *macehualli*. This Indian Mexico has been neglected or suppressed throughout the history of the nation, whose ruling classes Fuentes sees as insistently seeking to emulate continental European—particularly Spanish and French—then English and North American social values and economic systems. But Fuentes portrays the indigenous spirit as taking its vengeance through its insatiable demand, from ancient times to the present, for blood sacrifice. In *Where the Air Is Clear*, which begins with a stunning, surrealistic, stream-of-consciousness monologue by Ixca Cienfuegos wherein he seems to summon up the dread spirits of the ancient past, the wrath of the gods falls upon those Mexicans who despise and negate their Indian origins.

Direct antecedents of this novel, and particularly of the dual, paradoxical function of Ixca Cienfuegos, can be found in three short stories from Fuentes' first major work, a collection entitled *Los días enmascarados* (The Masked Days, 1954). The title of this collection is an allusion to the *nemontani*, the last five days of the Aztec year, unnamed and uncounted, a time when all activity ceased. If these ill-fated days passed without calamity, blood sacrifice would be rendered to the gods for having preserved the universe. Fuentes' allusion to this time indicates the fatalistic nature of his stories, in three of which—"Chac Mool" ("Chac-Mool"), "Por boca de los dioses" (Through the Mouth of the Gods), and "Tlactocatzine, del jardín de Flandes" ("In a Flemish Garden")—time becomes cyclical and modern-day protagonists become the victims of ancient blood rites. In these shorter narratives as in *Where the Air Is Clear*, however, the gods are evoked as both negative and positive forces. On the one hand, they awaken to demand the death of humans who have aroused their ire through a violation—either of their resting place, their artistic representation, the rituals in their honor, or the indigenous tradition that they symbolize. On the more positive side, the ancient gods in "Por boca de los dioses" represent a historical consciousness and a voice of social criticism that attempts to make the upper classes confront the truth of Mexico and of themselves, and to assume a moral responsibility for the national welfare.

In these highly original works, which skillfully combine the ancient past and the present, reality and the supernatural, aesthetic innovations and social protest, Fuentes satirizes even the gods themselves.

Their very human failings—irritability, jealousy, wrath, even corruptibility by the luxuries of modern society, as occurs with the idol of the Mayan rain god, Chac Mool, which comes to life and abandons the ancient ways—are emphasized. Instead of using their fearsome power to protect or aid man, these parasitic gods destroy him in order to sustain themselves, just as the ancient gods demanded the hearts of human victims in order to nourish themselves so that the sun would continue to light the earth.

Only in Fuentes' drama *Todos los gatos son pardos* (All Cats Are Gray) is an ancient deity presented in a strongly positive sense. In this epic drama of the Conquest of Mexico, of the clash between Cortés and Moctezuma that is portrayed as a reflection of the incessant battles among the gods, Quetzalcóatl is evoked as the god of life, love, and justice. As a life principle, he opposes the bellicose Huitzilopochtli, a death god venerated by the Aztecs through their continual and massive blood sacrifices. Moctezuma, evoked as a *tlatoani* (emperor) riddled with guilt for the way in which he has misgoverned his empire, believes that Cortés is Quetzalcóatl, returning from exile to demand an accounting of the tyrannical manner in which his kingdom has been governed during his long absence; ironically, however, the Spanish *conquistador*, in his wholesale destruction of the Aztec civilization, demonstrates that he is actually the incarnation of Huitzilopochtli. Thus, instead of being Moctezuma's antagonist and the usurper of his power, Cortés is represented as a perpetuator of the tyrannical cruelty of the Aztec emperor. Indeed, right before his death, Moctezuma (the only victor in this drama of fatalistic, cyclical time, so characteristic of the works of Fuentes) rejoices in the triumph of Cortés, whom he sees as his alter ego, as the conqueror who possesses the boldness and strength of will that the weak and vacillating emperor lacks. *Todos los gatos son pardos* ends with a stunning flash-forward to twentieth-century Mexico (which is always Fuentes' chief concern): the same characters appear, although now in modern guise, as Fuentes portrays a nation still plagued by violence and bloodshed and still awaiting the return of the life-giving redeemer. The plaza of Nonoalco-Tlatelolco—the sixteenth-century scene of the last, fierce battle between the Aztecs and the *conquistadores*, where thousands of the Indian defenders died—has in the twentieth century again become the tragic site of blood sacrifice. Fuentes alludes to the massacre of students there in 1968 through his depiction of a youth pursued and shot down by soldiers—a youth played by the same character who had appeared as a victim of sacrifice in ancient Cholula. The force of creation and of benevolence symbolized by Quetzalcóatl is, at best, only a problematic one: rather, it is the spirit of Huitzilopochtli, in ancient times as in the present, that remains triumphant—as it does in *Where the Air Is Clear*, where Fuentes chose as his ubiquitous narrator (the only force that unites all of the myriad classes and characters in that titanic novel) an agent of Huitzilopochtli instead of the ever-absent Quetzalcóatl.

Fuentes' second full-length novel, one that like *Where the Air Is Clear* dissects postrevolutionary Mexican society and underscores how the revolutionary promise has not been fulfilled in a Mexico where one group of exploiters has been replaced by a new one, is his corrosive *The Death of Artemio Cruz*, a novel generally considered to be his most important work. The enigmatic Cruz is a composite figure, one of the most complex characters in all of Latin American fiction, and in Fuentes' novel we explore Cruz' paradoxical life by following his thoughts through the twelve hours before his death. Like Federico Robles, Cruz is a revolutionary fighter turned opportunist and plutocrat. Again like Robles, who for much of his life isolated himself from his origins and had little but disdain for his own people, Cruz after the Revolution abandons his dream of becoming a small farmer and living a peaceful life and instead marries Catalina Bernal, whom he claims as if she were a prize of war from her accommodating father, Don Gamaliel. Gamaliel sees in Cruz what the defeated Moctezuma of *Todos los gatos son pardos* sees in Cortés—the bold and brutal successor to his power.

At the end of *Where the Air Is Clear*, Federico Robles achieves a spiritual victory; he renounces the power game and leaves Mexico City, marrying his blind Indian mistress, Hortensia Chacón, who is depicted as a benevolent earth goddess, a twentieth-century equivalent of the Aztec goddess Tonantzín. Unlike Robles' sterile marriage with Norma, which is childless, his union with Hortensia produces new life—a son. The fate of Cruz is far more tragic; he dies alienated from his family, catered to only by those who seek his wealth.

In contrast to *Where the Air Is Clear*, a vast, sprawling narrative, similar to Mexico City itself (which is its central theme), *The Death of Artemio Cruz* is a tightly organized novel, consisting of an invariable first-, second-, third-person patterning that serves to underscore the entrapment of Cruz both in his rapidly disintegrating body and in his stricken consciousness. This *yo-tú-él* triadic structure is a favorite of Fuentes; he uses it again in *Zona sagrada* (*Holy Place*, 1967), and in the tripartite *Terra Nostra*, in which there is a whole section devoted to the phenomenon of triality. One of Fuentes' prime goals in *The Death of Artemio Cruz* is to create a single character powerful and complex enough to be convincing, not only as an individual but as a national symbol. Fuentes' creation of Artemio Cruz was also decisively influenced by the ambivalent figure of Charles Foster Kane, the protagonist of Orson Welles' landmark film *Citizen Kane*. Generous and opportunistic; the idealistic builder of a business empire and a sometimes ruthless destroyer of lives; relentlessly energetic yet nearly ossified toward the end of his life, Kane is an explosive and gargantuan character who can be seen as a cinematic antecedent of Cruz. Both film and novel represent tremendous labors of synthesis.

Concepts that Paz elaborates in *El laberinto de la soledad* (*The Labyrinth of Solitude*, 1950), such as *machismo*, solipsism, *malinchismo* (enchantment with the culture of the conquerors), and the mask and the cult of death, are brilliantly fictionalized by Fuentes in *The Death of Artemio Cruz*. The novel presents multiple and constantly shifting views of the protagonist, as it treats Cruz' life not as a chronological progression from birth to death but rather as a series of fragments that shift rapidly in time, from Cruz' old age to his early career, from the postrevolutionary epoch of powermongering back to his childhood, in response to the associational flux of his stricken, moribund consciousness. Death is not intellectualized, but stunningly dramatized, through the thirteen segments of first-person, direct interior monologue, the voice of the pain-wracked, incoherent, dying self, which soon becomes frozen in sterile repetition as Cruz' mind spins off into delirium—a voice that grants immediacy, great intensity, and pathos to the narrative.

Narrative structure projects Cruz' character not only as a multiplicity of selves but also as a series of incompatible selves unable to achieve a self-transcendent or redemptive unity. Only in death do the three voices of the narrative coalesce. Instead, there is a continual antagonism between the first-person narrative—Cruz' self-exalting yo—and the second-person monologue that is both part of him and yet outside of him, as it encompasses other persons such as his son Lorenzo—a voice that relentlessly probes the unfulfilled aspects of the protagonist's nature, his unrealized heroic potential, his incapacity to love. This tú narrative is itself an awesome paradox, both superego and representative of Cruz' physiological self—the self that for the first time in Cruz' life denies his own will, conquering him from within—both individual and collective, condemning Cruz for his moral failings yet seeking to penetrate his motives, and holding out to him, even during the last hours of his life, the possibilities of alternative existences. Obsessed with the recapitulation of Cruz' past, this voice nevertheless addresses him in the future tense, "Ayer volarás" ("Yesterday you will fly"), as if self-renewal and salvation were still possible to him, as if he could construct a future, a new life, out of the fragments of the past.

Not only on his deathbed but throughout his life, Cruz is incapable of integrating ego and conscience, self-serving ambition and sense of social responsibility. Instead, he is constantly torn between the preservation and assertion of his will—of the facade of his machismo—and attainment of spiritual union and communion with others that would require the demolishing of the ego. Ironically, the only time the self-effacing nosotros, or "we," narrative is employed is when Cruz attempts to recall his past adventures at Cocuya with the most precious person in his life, his son Lorenzo. In the first-person narrative, Cruz asserts that his only love has always been the material, and indeed, the final images that penetrate his mind are those of his innumerable possessions. Yet the third-person segments—which provide flashbacks to his past as revolutionary fighter and then oppressive

hacendado (plantation owner), as national defender but secret malinchista—reveal his deep love for both Regina and Laura, who represent the spiritual side of his character that he continually stifles. When called upon by Laura to commit himself totally to their relationship and divorce his wife, who epitomizes Cruz' materialism, Cruz abandons Laura, not out of love for Catalina but because he fears the scandal that would ensue and the consequent loss of social prestige and political power. On a deeper level, commitment to Laura would involve sacrifice of self, and Cruz fears the surrender of his precious selfhood. The obsession with self that characterizes him on his deathbed is but the final, pathetic moment of a whole lifetime of self-absorption and self-aggrandizement.

Cruz loves genuinely only once—in his relationship with Regina, which is severed by her untimely and brutal death. So great is the loss of Regina, whose lyric image haunts Cruz the rest of his life—just as that of Susana San Juan mesmerizes the brutal cacique (political boss) in Juan Rulfo's novel of Eros and Thanatos, Pedro Páramo (1955)—that Cruz will never again risk exposing his inner self to the possibility of hurt, humiliation, or defeat in love. Thus, although he wants to love Catalina, he will never confess to her his guilt over her brother's death, fearing that his proud wife will interpret any show of humility on his part as a sign of weakness that will only arouse her contempt. Even at the end of his life Cruz opts for a loveless relationship with a woman he has bought, Lilia, because he need only command and Lilia, although resentful, will obey him; thus he lives with the delusion that he can create and sustain a world of his own, as he waits out his life in the old monastery of Coyoacán, which he has had restored and where he can reign like an Aztec emperor over his dutiful subjects, the one hundred guests that he annually summons to celebrate the New Year, who pay homage to him and perform on cue for him.

The theme of the fall from paradise—and the desperate, often pathetic attempts, ultimately frustrated, by Cruz throughout his life to regain that lost paradise—is key to the novel. Early in his life Cruz suffers the warping of his idealism and of his capacity to love. Over and over again, he is "expelled": from the natural paradise that is the world of his youth at Cocuya, Veracruz, when his friend and protector,

Lunero, is suddenly killed; from the romantic para-dise within the hell-world of war that he shares but briefly with Regina before her death; and from the illusion of redemptive unity that he seeks with Catalina. His primary response to protect his fragile inner self against the threat of further hurt and loss is to retreat into a self-made and self-sustained world in which he can feel secure. For the spiritual paradise of love that he has been denied, Cruz substitutes a material paradise that seems to proclaim his invinci-bility. Yet he succeeds in preserving only a mummi-fied self, one that is secretly mocked by his guests. He remains trapped in the past, inwardly devoted to his lost son, Lorenzo, but compelled to confront surro-gate sons, offspring of his own relentless ambition and lust for power, like the aggressive Jaime Ceballos, who seeks to become Cruz' successor.

Idealism—and the repeated betrayal of ideals—is another important theme in this challenging and incisive novel. The double who functions as a con-science figure is important in the life of Cruz and at the moment of his death. At key points in his career, Cruz is forced to confront a figure who both resembles him physically and incarnates the moral qualities—courage, strength of conviction, honor, capacity to love—that Cruz has betrayed. The green-eyed soldier on the battlefield, who strangely resembles Cruz and who dies in his place as the cowardly Cruz deserts his men; Gonzalo Bernal, the son of a *porfirista*, who out of idealism and the desire to rebel against his father joins the Revolution but who quickly becomes disil-lusioned with its leaders; Cruz' only son, Lorenzo, evoked as a ghostly presence through the last letter that he writes to his father before his death, whose martyrdom in the Spanish civil war symbolically expiates Cruz' past cowardice: all are spiritual doubles of Cruz. The deaths of these idealists symbolize Cruz' lifelong suppression of his own idealistic potential, which he has supplanted with a cynical, rhetorical facade of revolutionary commitment designed to curry the favor and garner the votes of the *campe-sinos*, the laborers on whose behalf the Revolution was supposedly fought; secretly, Cruz is selling their lands to purchase building lots for himself in Mex-ico City. Like Charles Foster Kane, Cruz becomes extremely skillful at manipulating the media, and the newspaper that he owns will, even after his death, promulgate the false image of him as revolu-tionary hero and national architect. Cruz' behind-the-scenes dealing with foreign investors, bargaining away Mexico's natural resources, exemplifies what Mariano Azuela has referred to as *el complejo de la Malinche*—the Mexican's surrendering of his identity to foreigners before whom he remains awed—repeat-ing the pattern of La Malinche and the other Indian women who voluntarily offered themselves to the *conquistadores*, whom they perceived as gods.

Despite Cruz' persistent attempts to gain immor-tality (similar to so many of Fuentes' character creations, including the egomaniacal Consuelo in *Aura* [1962], the solipsistic Siger de Brabant in *Cumpleaños* [Birthday, 1969], the diabolical André Heredia in *Distant Relations*, and the powerful but highly insecure Claudia Nervo in *Holy Place*), the irremediable finiteness of human existence thwarts the self-exalting and even self-deifying efforts of the protagonist to conquer other men, time, and even death itself. Not only in the final, tormented hours of his existence, surrounded by people he despises, but throughout his life, Cruz has struggled to preserve the self in the face of death, which has always hovered close to him. For seventy years he has been success-ful. At the very moment of his birth Cruz was threatened with extinction by his own father, Ata-nasio, who wanted to have the illegitimate child killed. Violent death is an ever-present danger for Cruz the soldier in the Mexican Revolution, and later, when the war is over, the threat of assassination is a constant hazard of the private war for self-aggrandizement that Cruz wages both against the remnants of the *hacendados*, the feudal Mexican aristocracy, and against the opportunists who, like him, seek to become the new overlords, filling the vacuum of power created by the collapse of the old structures. Once his economic power and political position have been consolidated, however, Cruz is impregnable against social ruin and even believes that he is impervious to death. He has destroyed or rendered ineffective all of his enemies except time, the nemesis of so many of Fuentes' characters.

The extremely fragmented structure of this novel conveys Cruz' permanent isolation, alienation, and physical and psychological disintegration. The trajec-tory of his personal life is toward increasing rigidity, total lack of communication with others, and incarceration within the walls of self. But more positively, the creation of multiple selves constitutes an attempt by the failing and desperate yet still imaginative Cruz to revivify himself and thereby to score a victory over death. Through the first-person monologue, Cruz valiantly attempts to deny the severity of his attack and to thwart death by struggling to separate his commanding and powerful self of the past from his helpless, moribund self of the present. Cruz struggles to convince himself that it is not his true self who is dying but a false, putrefying double that must be exorcized. Grammatical shifts correspond to Cruz' attempt, ultimately frustrated as all of the grammatical persons fuse into one, to create an alternate self or selves to be held up as a shield against death.

Fuentes' *Las buenas conciencias* (*The Good Conscience*, 1959) is a brief novel that focuses on a single city, Guanajuato, and on the history of a single family, the bourgeois Ceballos. Guanajuato is evoked by Fuentes as a self-contained world, proudly isolated from external influences, suspended in tradition. The members of the Ceballos family, who pride themselves on their social distinction, in reality lead hollow, stunted lives in which ritual, ceremony, and the rote application of moral maxims to family crises substitute for genuine relationships founded on the desire to understand and to love. Within this family there is a constant suppression of sexual desire, of emotions, and of truth.

The dominant force in the family is Jorge Balcárcel del Moral. His tyrannical and sententious personality matches his name. Although he attempts to justify his authoritarianism by citing the moral imperative of converting his rebellious nephew Jaime, the protagonist of the novel, into a bourgeois gentleman, the hypocritical Balcárcel really wishes to exploit the boy by using him as a buffer between himself and his wife, Asunción. As long as Jaime remains under the tight control of the Balcárcels, Asunción's maternal desires, frustrated by the sterility of Jorge, can be satisfied vicariously. Asunción tyrannizes Jaime's weak father, Rodolfo, and craftily destroys his marriage. She isolates him both from his wife, Adelana, whom she drives from the house, and from his only child, Jaime, whom she appropriates for herself, seeking to bind him to herself as a perpetual infant.

The protagonist briefly emerges from the stifling confines of the Ceballos' domain. The novel traces Jaime's adolescent sexual awakenings, his intellectual development, and the growth of his social conscience. The youth is for a time enthusiastic about the possibilities latent within him to change both self and world. Yet this idealistic but insecure and cowardly boy fails in his attempts to establish an independent self. In the end, he returns to the state of passivity, dependency, and complete union of self and family that marked his early childhood. Acknowledging his defeat, he reenters the family mansion, which seems to open up like a huge maw to swallow him.

As in many of the markedly pessimistic works of Fuentes, the fatalism of *The Good Conscience* is expressed structurally. At the very beginning, in a brief italicized section that chronologically falls at the end of the narrative, the protagonist appears alone, after he has made the most important decision of his life and suppressed his true conscience in order permanently to adopt the false, easy conscience of Balcárcel. Thus the life of Jaime is not depicted as one genuinely open to change and to positive moral development but rather as a flashback that traces the process leading to his final decision to renounce all social and individual responsibility.

That Jaime's decision to turn his back on the world of the underprivileged is irreversible is confirmed by an examination of Jaime's role in two other novels by Fuentes, *Where the Air Is Clear* and *The Death of Artemio Cruz*, in both of which Jaime appears as a minor character. In *Where the Air Is Clear* he is seen at a later stage in his life, involved in a romance with Betina Régules, the spoiled, pretentious daughter of the nouveau riche entrepreneur Régules, the rival of Federico Robles. Jaime is depicted as a sensitive youth with creative talent who, after only minor protest, abandons his legal studies and succumbs to social pressure as he becomes a minion in Régules' financial empire.

In *The Death of Artemio Cruz*, Ceballos is shown to be thoroughly corrupted. He has become the continuation of the wily, exploitative Balcárcel. Jaime's ambition and greed are apparent as he confronts the wizened magnate Cruz and attempts through a combination of boldness and fawning to insinuate himself into Cruz' favor. In *The Good Conscience* and *Where the Air Is Clear*, Jaime is evoked as a vascillating youth who makes a decision to capitulate only after a struggle between self-integrity and self-interest. In *Artemio Cruz*, however, Jaime does not have even a glimmer of his former idealism. The ideal, rather than being represented as a potential within Jaime, or even as embodied in a close friend who has influenced the youth's development as occurs in *The Good Conscience*, is now symbolized by a remote person—Cruz' son Lorenzo, whom Jaime never knows. A hero who died to protect the lives of others in the Spanish civil war, Lorenzo is now evoked only as a memory within Cruz' own agonized conscience. Thus the heroic self that Jaime Ceballos had once cherished, made pretentious attempts to actualize, reduced to a mere nostalgic memory, and then suppressed altogether, finally appears only in the phantasmal turn of a memory lived by someone else.

Like *The Death of Artemio Cruz*, *Aura* also chronicles the obsessive attempts of the dessicated and dying individual to gain immortality. One of Fuentes' most fascinating works, *Aura* is a brief, powerful, carefully and tightly structured work that provides a fusion of present and remote past, debilitated self and fantasy Other, beauty and horror, waking state and nightmare, sacred and demonic.

The original identity of the passive and vacillating protagonist, Felipe Montero, is usurped and destroyed as he becomes the victim of a supernatural power. What he initially perceives as a vision of paradise offered to himself alone—the enchanting girl Aura, who appears as a succubus to tempt him—turns out to be a demonic presence. *Aura* skillfully fuses quotidian reality with the supernatural; historical or chronological with psychic and mythic time. The 109-year-old Consuelo represents the historical Carlotta, the Belgian princess who married Archduke Maximilian of Austria and later became empress of Mexico. Carlotta, as a result of the disastrous Mexican Intervention that ended with the execution of her husband, succumbed to insanity at an early age and spent more than fifty years as a recluse in her castle at Bouchot, Belgium. She died in 1927. Maximilian was executed in 1867—the fateful year in which the fictional Consuelo marries Llorente, a general in the emperor's army. Like Maximilian with the young, vivacious,

and exceedingly ambitious Carlotta, whom he married when she was seventeen, Llorente is entranced and totally devoted to his fifteen-year-old bride, Consuelo. Even the sterility of Llorente finds a historical parallel in the childless marriage of Maximilian and Carlotta. Extremely frustrated because she cannot perpetuate her great beauty through children, Consuelo resorts to necromancy in an obsessive and deluded attempt to perpetuate herself through parthenogenesis. In her crazed mind, she believes that she has given birth to her own self—by placing into reality the phantom of her own youth, Aura.

Aura is a story of all-consuming love and of physical and spiritual death. The unsuspecting protagonist, Felipe, from the first time he sees her is bewitched by Aura, the alluring wraith used by the wizened Consuelo to trick him into surrendering his soul to her and to her demonic master. By the end of the novel, Felipe has been reduced to a mere vehicle through whom the spirit of Llorente is reincarnated and reunited with his beloved Consuelo. Thus love seems to have triumphed through a bizarre transcendence of both time and death. Yet this weird consummation of love is possible only through the destruction of the original, fragile identity of Felipe.

Throughout *Aura*, the interplay of light and darkness symbolizes not only the struggle between the forces of divine salvation and satanic damnation, but also the battle between ignorance and illumination. Stunned and bewildered, Felipe Montero struggles to understand the strange, dark world in which he has become submerged, a realm of uncanny presences that suddenly appear and then vanish, of mysterious rituals and blood sacrifices. Identity is multiple and unstable, as are time and space. Indeed, the spirit of Llorente, who died sixty years earlier, seems to have been dormant within Felipe even before his contact with Consuelo. Thus his traumatic experiences in her house may serve merely to catalyze or bring to consciousness an identity that was but waiting for the propitious moment to emerge. Felipe's scholarly investigation and his editing of the papers of the dead General turn out to be an ontological exploration as well. The trunk of moldering memoirs that Consuelo keeps under lock and key is not only historical knowledge but, far more importantly for Felipe, knowledge of his true self. The memoirs of Llorente are unfinished not merely because they were interrupted by the General's death, but because Llorente's identity is intrinsically incomplete; it must be fulfilled by Felipe, who not only will study the General's life and learn to imitate his style, as Consuelo commands, but will finally be transformed, utterly, into Llorente.

In *Aura*, both style and point of view emphasize the central theme of bewitchment. The use of second-person narration, which is often in the unreal tense of the future, creates a spellbinding effect. A hypnotist often employs the second person as he addresses an individual who is being placed in a trance in order to suggest to him, or to his subconscious, the behavior that he should carry out. By using the second-person voice, Fuentes also conveys from the very start of the novella the split personality of the protagonist. At the end, this *tú*, which all along has seemed to apply to Felipe Montero, is revealed in its true significance—as specifically designating Llorente, who has returned from the dead to make love to the withered form of his wife. Felipe cannot narrate his story in the first person because he has no autobiographical or existential "I"—the indicator of a single, unique identity and of an independent self. As a personality, Felipe is a perfect candidate for Consuelo's sorcery: he is an extremely weak-willed character who has no ties to either family or friends. Everything about him is unfinished, including his doctoral thesis on a topic that is impossibly grandiose—the whole history of the Spanish Conquest of the New World. Alienated from his profession as a secondary-school teacher, stalled in his dissertation, the directionless Felipe seems almost to require an alternate identity in order to be a complete person.

Felipe is never described in physical detail. This impreciseness is but another indication that he is existentially vague—that his true features are yet to be discovered. Like Llorente, Felipe fashions himself a heroic conqueror, who will battle Consuelo in order to attain his dream princess, Aura. But like Llorente, the ambitions of Felipe forever remain at the dream stage—when tempted by Aura to leave Consuelo's domain, the timid Felipe demurs. Felipe is not only a historian but, when forced to become Llorente, history incarnate. The memoirs of Llorente's career, which Felipe finds banal, are the *datos inútiles*, the

useless facts, of his alternate identity, and thus they mirror the inconsequentiality of Felipe's own professional career and private life. The reason Consuelo seeks to publish her husband's memoirs now, more than a half century after his death, is because they pay tribute to *her*; they have no other value, just as Llorente has meaning only as her worshiper. Ironically, however, Felipe first experiences his alternate self as a self-*completion*; the limbo of his existence seems suddenly infused with purpose. Yet Felipe's alternate identity from beyond the tomb finally becomes like Mr. Hyde for Dr. Jekyll—a monstrous Other that rapidly erodes and finally devours the original self.

There are many indications that Consuelo's home, in Mexico City's old, historic district, is a realm of the demonic. In classical mythology the entrance to Hades is guarded by the dog Cerberus. The copper knocker on the door of Consuelo's tomblike house is grotesquely shaped like the head of a dog, and it seems to possess a demonic quality as it grins at Felipe. Before entering the strange house, in which (as in *Where the Air Is Clear*) all times are fused, Felipe looks back on the outside world, not suspecting that it will be for the last time. His inability to retain even a single image of the external world indicates that his separation from it will be complete and irreversible. The ease with which the door to the mysterious house opens alludes to another of *Aura*'s themes: *facilis descensus Averno* (the descent to hell is easy). Yet, although the approach to evil is easy enough, the hell that Felipe is entering will be inescapable.

Another puzzling presence in *Aura* is that of the rabbit, the most complex animal symbol in this narrative in which the bestial presence—scurrying rats, writhing cats, a goat symbolic of Satan—forms a grotesque and often grisly backdrop. With its glowing red eyes, Consuelo's rabbit symbolizes the demonic. The pet is also a fertility symbol: it represents Consuelo's obsession with rebirth, and also her recourse to demon worship in order to attain her desire. The rabbit also has a third, metaphysical function. Its name is Saga, and in its appearance and disappearance it represents the elusiveness of knowledge—a knowledge that the deluded and benighted Felipe, who clings to the darkness, will never attain and perhaps never wants to obtain.

Felipe never succeeds in understanding the relationship between Aura and Consuelo. He never realizes that it is he, not Aura, who is being kept in a stranglehold by the old woman. He thus insists on believing that Consuelo and Aura are two distinct beings, and constantly struggles to keep distinct identities that are really inseparable. He mistakenly believes that Aura is tyrannized and kept imprisoned by Consuelo when, on the contrary, the elusive girl is sustained by the fanatic strength and indomitable will of the aged sorceress.

The chronological time of *Aura* is only a few days. Yet within Consuelo's mystifying realm linear time becomes meaningless. When Felipe first encounters Aura, she is a young girl. A day later she is a woman of forty, and two days later she is indistinguishable from the aged Consuelo. At the end, an unperceiving, totally mesmerized Felipe is left with only Consuelo, who offers him consolation for the surrender of his soul by promising him the return of Aura. The galaxy of votive lamps kept blazing by the old woman has now been extinguished. Aura, the spectral light of salvation for both Felipe and Consuelo, has now disappeared and the house is left in darkness. There is only the bewitching light of the moon, a light that symbolizes the triumph of the demonic. The cadaverous Consuelo is a vampiric power, who derives new energy and strength through her capturing of a series of young males—Felipe being only the latest—whom she claims as both lovers and sacrificial victims.

Consuelo thus parallels the supernatural figure of Siger de Brabant, the thirteenth-century theologian in *Cumpleaños* who also lives as a recluse in a labyrinthine house and perpetuates himself through the centuries by invading and destroying the identities of individuals, like the twentieth-century English architect George, who are sacrificed to ensure his immortality. Consuelo also foreshadows the mysterious and demonic André Heredia in the third novella of this trilogy, *Distant Relations*. On the supernatural level, *Distant Relations* refers to the entire Heredia family, across the centuries, and in particular to the nineteenth-century Francisco Heredia, his French wife Mademoiselle Lange, and their son André, all of whose spirits invade the present and control the identities of the twentieth-century manifestations of this weird family.

In addition to his great achievements in the genres of the novel and the short story, Fuentes is also the author of three remarkable plays, *Todos los gatos son pardos, El tuerto es rey* (The One-Eyed Man Is King, 1970), and *Orchids in the Moonlight.* In all of these plays, as in the theater of the Spanish playwright Federico García Lorca, women play the most important roles. In his famous study of the Mexican national identity, *The Labyrinth of Solitude,* Octavio Paz presents La Malinche, the Indian woman who became mistress, guide, and interpreter to the *conquistador* Cortés, as a symbol of national betrayal. Paz emphasizes the contrast between the valor and the heroism of the young Cuauhtémoc, the last of the Aztec emperors who fiercely resisted the Spanish invaders, and the self-abasement of La Malinche, whose collaboration with the Spanish facilitated the Conquest of Mexico and resulted in the destruction of her own civilization and the enslavement of her people. Cortés' mistress, according to Paz, is the Mexican Eve, and he stresses that the repudiation of *malinchismo* is necessary in order for Mexico to achieve an independent identity; only thus will the country be freed of the curse of the past, of the terrible humiliation that was the conquest. Yet Fuentes, who in his early works had been significantly influenced by Paz' ideas, takes an opposite tack in his highly original interpretation of the figure of La Malinche in *Todos los gatos son pardos.* Here Fuentes elevates the fallen Malinche from a mere agent of Cortés, dutifully carrying out his orders, into a social conscience and finally into a positive national consciousness. Fuentes consecrates Malinche as the creator of a new people—the synthesis of Aztec and Spanish—and the person who heralds the birth of a new nation. In a work that seeks to vindicate La Malinche, Fuentes depicts her not only as the symbol of the Mexico that will arise from the chaos and destruction of the conquest, but further as the bold and fiery prophetess of the new nation that will be born out of the revolution of 1910, which will be fought by her descendants of mixed European and Aztec blood, by *mestizo* Mexico.

From the beginning to the end of *Todos los gatos son pardos,* La Malinche plays a role that far exceeds her historical significance. She constantly appears as a guiding spiritual presence, a figure of high moral idealism who speaks in extensive and eloquent monologues. The lyrical intensity of her declamations underscores the spiritual depth of her vision: La Malinche is depicted not as a traitor, but as a strong protector and defender of her own people. She is presented as a shrewd woman who utilizes her privileged position as confidant of Cortés in order to sway the Spanish *conquistador* toward assuming a moral responsibility for the Aztecs. She constantly exhorts Cortés to assume the role of Quetzalcóatl, the god of creation, love, and social justice, which is how the Indian people perceive him. And in order to redeem La Malinche, Fuentes places her on an equal if not superior level to the two central antagonists—Moctezuma and Cortés.

Throughout Fuentes' work, which he characterizes as "symbolic realism," fantasy is blended with history. Thus it is important to compare and contrast the manner in which Fuentes portrays La Malinche with the way in which she has been described by chroniclers and historians. Bernal Díaz, who served under Cortés, refers to her respectfully as Doña Marina in his *Historia verdadera de la conquista de la Nueva España* (1632; published in a modern English edition in 1963 as *History of the Conquest of New Spain*); he and other historians emphasize her role as a mediator between two highly disparate civilizations, Aztec and Spanish. Yet in Fuentes' drama, La Malinche is portrayed as an island—estranged from both cultures and therefore in a position to represent a break from both—to symbolize a new nation. Instead of the passive Indian girl mesmerized by the fair-skinned conquerors that is the image of La Malinche projected in Paz' extensive essay, Fuentes' Marina is a mature, pensive, highly skeptical person—critical of Moctezuma and of the cult of blood sacrifice practiced by the Aztecs, which she sees not as offering redemption but as a monstrous destruction and waste of life. Marina emerges as a vindictive person, hating not only her own people for having deprived her of her royal birthright and sold her into slavery, but also the *conquistadores* for their brutality toward her people. Although initially devoted to Cortés, the Marina created by Fuentes finally rebels against him. And her motive for allying herself with Cortés is not love, as the historical record indicates, but hate. In her obsessive desire for vengeance against the tyrannical

Moctezuma, Fuentes' Marina can be seen as a symbol of states such as Cempoala and Tlaxcala, which were repeatedly devastated by the Aztecs and forced to pay human tribute to Moctezuma—captives for blood sacrifice—and whose unrelenting hatred of the despotic Aztecs and desire to regain their autonomy impelled them to ally themselves with Cortés as a means of destroying the Aztec hegemony.

In *Todos los gatos son pardos*, Marina is exculpated for her alliance with Cortés. Instead, Fuentes places most of the blame for the downfall of the Aztec civilization upon the confused and spineless emperor Moctezuma. More so even than Cortés, whom Fuentes portrays unsympathetically, Moctezuma is the object of devastating caricature. He is initially encountered in darkness, on his hands and knees, killing ants in his palace. He appears as a wretched figure, consumed by guilt and paranoia, incapable of governing even himself and totally unconcerned about the welfare of his people. Thus the greatest traitor, the true *malinchista* of this drama, is the Aztec *tlatoani* who instead of defying the invaders prostrated himself before them, treating them as gods and sacrificing his kingdom to them.

Historically, La Malinche was of crucial importance to Cortés at several points in the Conquest of Mexico. But after the fall of the Aztec capital, Tenochtitlán (now Mexico City), her historical importance declines, and she becomes assimilated into Hispanic society. Yet Fuentes—who in this drama as in his epic novel *Terra Nostra* takes historical figures and uses literary license to re-create them imaginatively—portrays Malinche as a person whose stature vastly increases after the conquest. La Malinche, who for most of her life has been a slave, first to the Indian people and then to Cortés, finally gains an independent identity. In Fuentes' stirring drama, she is depicted as a more complex personality than either Moctezuma or Cortés, both of whom remain imprisoned by deterministic forces, external as well as internal, and both of whom are finally reduced to pariahs by their native cultures. Both men are forced to play out their respective roles of emperor and conqueror without being able either to renounce that role, as Moctezuma desperately wishes to do, consumed by a Thanatos impulse from the very start, or to transcend it, as Cortés seeks.

Marina's key significance in *Todos los gatos son pardos* is not as the narrator of the cataclysmic struggle that was the Conquest of Mexico but, surprisingly, as the creator of this historic event. Thus, from the very beginning, La Malinche is presented not as a mere victim of historical forces beyond her control but as a dominant political and even mythic or cosmic power. She sees herself as fulfilling three main roles in the conquest—lover, mother, and goddess. It is significant that from the outset she identifies with her namesake, Malinalxochitl, the sister of Huitzilopochtli. Thus she too achieves the divine status accorded to Moctezuma as emperor/god and to Cortés as the incarnation of Quetzalcóatl. Marina emerges as a highly ambitious person, one whose desire for power not only coincides with but at times even surpasses that of Cortés himself. Marina is motivated by an intense desire both to regain the royal status that she has been denied by her parents and to avenge the downfall of her namesake goddess. Fuentes' Marina, rather than readily acclimating herself to the Spanish culture and converting to the Christian religion, is revealed as continuing to maintain her Indian identity and to worship the old gods, from whom she derives secret power.

Allowing herself to be exploited by Cortés, Marina in turn seeks to exploit him. She seeks to imbue him with a new identity, to re-create him as a god, so that she in turn can be re-created as a goddess. The type of love symbolized by Marina's namesake Malinalxochitl is not compassionate and altruistic but is rather a bizarre, tyrannical love. Love for Marina is but a means of dominating Cortés, in the same fashion that Malinalxochitl enchants the wild beasts. Marina skillfully employs her privileged position as lover, confidant, and confessor to Cortés in an endeavor to control him. She almost succeeds. This is the new and powerful dimension that is granted by Fuentes to the character of La Malinche.

Marina exemplifies the awesome power of the word as both a destructive and creative force. She herself is a creature of the word; her adverse fate was determined upon her birth by a prophecy, by the birth sign of Ce Malinalli, the sign of ill fortune, bloodshed, and perpetual strife. Throughout her life Marina will suffer as the consequence of this dread sign. The

overwhelming belief that her superstitious parents have in the malefic power of that sign impels them to impose upon their royal daughter the name and identity of a dead slave girl, thus seeking to nullify the disastrous effects of the birth sign. Yet, ironically, their actions serve only to bring down upon their offspring—and upon the whole of the Indian civilization—the dire consequences of that sign, as Marina eventually seeks a means of reclaiming her royal birthright and encounters it in the bellicose Cortés.

Cortés is developed as a paradoxical personality. Throughout much of *Todos los gatos son pardos*, Cortés appears as a man of action—resolute in his determination to conquer and convert, ruthless in his treatment of the Indian populace. But his relationship with Marina reveals another side of his character: Cortés as a wistful and melancholy person; Cortés lost in dream, who upon awakening states that everything happened in words. Another of the many roles that Marina plays is that of moral conscience. As she speaks to the dreaming Cortés, her lyric voice seems to merge with the subconsciousness of the *conquistador*, to make him aware that the history of the Aztec people is not economic, social, or political but intensely spiritual. She stresses the beauty and the fragility of the world that Cortés holds in his power, either to redeem or to destroy. And she makes an attempt to divest Cortés of his prejudices against the Aztec civilization, his disgust at the worship of what are to him strange and monstrous gods, the blood sacrifices, and the cannibalism. Marina emphasizes other qualities of the Aztec people, such as their idealism, their profound religious convictions, and their creative aspirations and achievements.

In the final act, Marina, Cortés, and Moctezuma appear in three different circles: an indication both of their dramatic equality and of their irremediable isolation. It is significant that Marina occupies the center circle. She is both vilified and glorified, both accursed and yet heroic. She symbolizes both will and fate. At the outset of the drama, hers is a voice of doom, as she describes the indigenous world as a land of death, as one immense tomb. Yet, in an ironic transposition, at the end of the play Marina is linked with new life, with a renascent Mexico: as the Aztec civilization is in its death throes, with the ruins smoldering in the background, Marina, who dominates the stage, is shown giving birth. Now she is a proud, defiant figure, recalling the phoenix as she rises from the ashes of her disillusionment and degradation, having gained an independent identity, free of Cortés and free of theocratic and cultural determinism. Here again, Marina's role as synthesizer is underscored. She is associated not just with the goddess Malinalxochitl; now she fuses both Aztec and Spanish conceptions of the mother goddess. In her role as comforter and consoler of a defeated people and nurturer of a child orphaned by its father, Marina's image is that of the benevolent Aztec goddess of motherhood, Tonantzín, but she also evokes the Christian Virgin of Sorrows. At the beginning of this powerful drama, the augur-gods surrounded Moctezuma. Now, however, with the emperor dead and Cuauhtémoc defeated and captured, they cluster around Marina as the new center of the indigenous consciousness.

Todos los gatos son pardos is a drama of religious, social, and political forces and times that initially appear as distinct or in opposition but then become fatalistically fused: emperor and usurper, Aztec domination and Spanish tyranny, ancient and contemporary Mexico. Only La Malinche stands out as an individual. Marina is the only character in the drama who develops psychologically. Throughout the play, she displays a marvelous versatility and is capable of repeated self-renewal. This is in marked contrast to the rigid Moctezuma and the compulsive Cortés, neither of whom can modify his initial orientations in order to adapt to and be able to master vastly changing circumstances. Both Cortés and Moctezuma are fated figures. Moctezuma never finds the courage and stamina to protect his people, to transcend his lack of will and become the bold, decisive leader necessary to confront, outwit, and defeat the shrewd, aggressive Cortés. Moctezuma is defeated not only by the Spanish *conquistador* but by his own will toward death, his propensity to become a sacrificial victim in order to gain the peacefulness of oblivion. Cortés, ironically, succeeds in his mastery of the New World but lacks the adroitness to preserve his conquests when his opponents are no longer the Aztecs but the deputies and ministers of his own society. Most importantly, Cortés, like his adversary Mocte-

zuma, fails at his attempts at self-mastery. Instead of being able to divest himself of his military role, as he has promised Marina, Cortés is impelled even after the Conquest of Mexico to continue to aggrandize his dominions and his power. His own excessive pride and ambition lead to his downfall.

Moctezuma, Cuauhtémoc, and Cortés, like Ixca Cienfuegos in *Where the Air Is Clear*, are all linked with the past, with the terrible yet seemingly inevitable cycle of domination, destruction, and incessant blood sacrifice. Only Marina represents a break in this cycle. At the end of the drama, in a sudden flash forward to the twentieth century, all of the characters appear again—in modern guise, to indicate that little has changed in Mexico. Moctezuma appears as the president of Mexico, and Cortés, in the guise of a North American general, is at his side. The fatalistic, cyclical time that operates so often in the world of Fuentes seems to have triumphed again. Marina, in twentieth-century Mexico as in the period of the conquest, is still on the margins of Mexican society, as a *fichadora de cabaret*—a clerk in a nightclub—despite her fiery prophecy of future victory for herself and her offspring. Significantly, however, only Marina has the courage to go up to the wounded student (an allusion by Fuentes to the 1968 student massacre in the Plaza of the Three Cultures) and to comfort him as he is dying. It is Marina who at the end experiences a vision of salvation—a vision of the return of the longed-for Quetzalcóatl to Mexico. The ending of Fuentes' drama, like the endings to so many of his works—*Aura, A Change of Skin, Distant Relations, La cabeza de la hidra (The Hydra Head,* 1978)— is highly ambiguous. The vision is accompanied by a shower of dead vultures, birds that signify the function of Quetzalcóatl as a purifier of corruption, just as the vulture gets rid of putrefying carrion. Does the appearance of the Plumed Serpent to Marina indicate that this god, who has previously appeared as a faceless deity, has finally returned to Mexico? Or is this but a vision of Marina alone, an indication that the spirit of Quetzalcóatl is not an external entity but an inner force, present in every individual act of courage, compassion, and self-sacrifice, and can only be awakened and sustained by these valorous actions?

Mystery, paradox, and ambiguity are also characteristic of Fuentes' third drama, *Orchids in the Moon-*

light, which provides a fascinating portrayal of two lonely *chicanas,* Dolores and María, living in a grim, penitentiarylike apartment in Venice, California, far from their homeland and from the radiant illusion of the Hollywood Dream Factory that functions metaphorically on several levels: the individual and the national, the self and the cinematic Other, the real and the fantastic, the historical and the mythic. Fuentes demonstrates how illusions, in this case powerful cinematic fantasies such as the roles that María Félix has played—as *Doña Bárbara* and *Doña Diabla*; as *Enamorada* and *Juana Gallo*—and the many roles in which Dolores Del Río has starred—as victimized Indian girl in *María Candelaria*; self-sacrificing *revolucionaria* in *Flor silvestre*; as glamorous and sophisticated Brazilian socialite in *Flying Down To Rio*; as the *tigresa* in *The Loves of Carmen*; and as the elegant and scandalous *Madame Du Barry*—have completely permeated the drab and alienated lives of the two *chicanas.* Having failed at establishing cinematic careers in Mexico, the undaunted women fail again in their attempts to enter the El Dorado of Hollywood; nevertheless, within their delusion-enshrouded minds, they convert the seediness of Venice into the romantic Italian Venice—exactly as it would be portrayed in a Hollywood film such as *Top Hat.* An immense wardrobe, containing all of the elaborate costumes worn by María Félix and Dolores Del Río in their many films made in Hollywood, Mexico, Spain, and France, dominates the stage, symbolizing the awesome power of cinematic fantasy to subvert reality, and which for the *chicanas* Dolores and María compensates for their anonymity and impoverishment in real life.

In this masterful play-within-a-play, the lives of the two *chicanas* are dedicated to re-creating scenes and dialogues from the films of their cinematic idols; they are acting both for the audience of *Orchids* and for each other, holding off insanity and death by the incessant assertion of their imaginations, as they dance together the haunting tango "Orchids in the Moonlight," from one of Del Río's most escapist and romantic films, the 1933 RKO production *Flying Down to Rio.* Like the solitude-prone Alonso Quijano, who submerges himself in the readings of the *novelas de caballería* (chivalry novels) and eventually is so enmeshed in his delusions that he sallies forth as a knight errant, Don Quijote, the two women in *Orchids* cut themselves off almost totally from external reality. Once more, as in *Aura* and *A Change of Skin,* illusions triumph over actuality.

Although from the start the agitated Dolores remains disappointed that the audience of *Orchids,* itself a character in the drama, has failed to recognize her as Dolores Del Río, her deepest wishes are suddenly fulfilled when the Fan, presented as a surrealistic combination of Harold Lloyd and James Cagney, of the comic and the sinister roles played respectively by these two Hollywood actors, arrives to confirm her identity as the screen goddess. But just as the two *chicanas* are mere simulacra, so also is the Fan an eloquent impostor: he has come not to pay adoration to them but to blackmail María with a copy of a pornographic film she made in her youth, and to demand possession of Dolores. The Fan, who writes the obituary column for a Los Angeles newspaper, is an emanation of death—a concretization of the Thanatos urge that afflicts María from start to finish of the drama. The desperate Dolores first leaves with the Fan, apparently submitting to his control, but then unexpectedly and brutally slays him by slashing his throat with the very wine bottle with which he has confidently been toasting his conquest of her.

Dolores' victory over the exploitative Fan comes too late to save her soulmate. Engrossed in her cinematic illusions, María can respond to Dolores only in terms of the roles that Dolores Del Río portrayed in films such as *Bird of Paradise.* Thus María believes that Dolores is abandoning her forever in order to remain faithful to the role of victimized or self-sacrificing *campesina* that Del Río so often played; in her paranoia, María fails to understand that Dolores leaves with the Fan not to become his wife but to exact vengeance upon him. Unable to live alone, despite her ambivalent, love-hate relationship with Dolores, María commits suicide. Throughout the drama, with her brashness, irrepressible spirit, and pluck, María has seemingly represented an exuberant life force, but her final role is that of La Calavera Catrina in Diego Rivera's famous mural *Sueño de una tarde dominical en La Alameda* (Sunday Afternoon Dream in the Alameda)—the lavishly dressed skeleton who promenades through the park grasping the young Diego Rivera himself by the hand.

The strangest of the characters in *Orchids* is the mysterious and sinister Mother, who never appears on stage and yet whose impact on the two *chicanas*, who live in constant fear of her, is almost tangible. The Mother's very invisibility seems to augment her power. The ominous Mother, who suppresses the identities of her children, who wants to keep them forever young and virginal, is imbued with a goddess-like quality—not the beautiful and alluring screen goddesses with whom Dolores and María so tenaciously identify, but rather reminiscent of the terrifying deities of the Aztec pantheon that appear throughout the somber fictional universe of Fuentes. In particular she represents another of Fuentes' favorite archetypes—Coatlicue, mother of the fiery sun god Huitzilopochtli and a death-cult figure who appears, for instance, as Ixca Cienfuegos' mother in *Where the Air Is Clear*. The weird Mother pores over the obituary columns for news of those who have died who are younger than herself so she can gloat at having survived them. This is why Dolores herself buries the body of María at the end—to deprive Coatlicue of her triumph.

The supreme irony of Fuentes' drama is that the final understanding, by Dolores of María—the person who is her alter ego—the reconciliation and even unity between the often quarreling actresses who both fortify and tear apart each other's dream worlds, comes only after María's death. While both were living, they could not unite to defy either the Fan or the *mater terribilis* (terrible mother). Ironic too is that in both life and death the basis for their unity is not reality but myth—powerfully signified at the end by Dolores' running together of the film clips from the movies of Del Río and Félix. Now Dolores worships the icon of the movie camera as the salvation of them both—the camera that symbolizes the cinematic process of capturing and immortalizing the image, so that they both will remain forever young and forever beautiful, and through which they will transcend time and gain rebirth.

Like *Orchids*, Fuentes' novel *Holy Place* concentrates on cinematic myth, on the international film star and femme fatale Claudia Nervo, the persona of María Félix. Claudia, like Consuelo in *Aura*, is depicted as a superhuman force. She is a dazzling and captivating cinematic goddess who single-handedly transforms her off-screen life into an extension of her lavish screen existence by maintaining a bizarre court of models, all of whom are ordered to fashion themselves into her likeness and who exist only to perpetuate the illusion of Claudia's eternal youth and beauty—in much the same way Felipe and Aura exist for the tyrannical and defiant Consuelo. Yet Claudia is also portrayed as a victim, not only of a *machista* Mexican society that works to keep women forever entrapped in the traditional and constricting roles of dutiful wife, self-sacrificing mother, and society matron, but also of self, of the devastating effects of her own relentless ambition, of having to destroy her old self in order to construct the image of the legendary Claudia. She has in effect trapped herself in myth, an incarceration grotesquely symbolized by an object that she keeps hidden—a glass cylinder with a mouse caught inside, which the anguished Claudia incessently contemplates and which seems to represent a bizarre mirror of herself.

Throughout his work, Fuentes is drawn toward the *cambio de piel* situation, the "change of skin" that suddenly reverses roles and expectations, that converts victor into victim, *conquistador* into *conquistado*, self into double. Thus, for example, the arrogant protagonist of *The Death of Artemio Cruz*, who fashions himself a terrestrial god in the immense power he wields over the hundreds of workers in his mines and factories, who even attempts to bargain with God—promising to believe in God in exchange for being granted immortality on earth—is suddenly and permanently leveled from twentieth-century *conquistador* to an inert and helpless victim. In *Distant Relations*, the supercilious and violent youth Víctor Heredia is also initially developed in terms of a *conquistador contemporáneo*, as he beats his Indian servants and wantonly destroys the priceless ancient Indian artifact that his father, an eminent Mexican archaeologist, so reveres. Yet Víctor is finally leveled to the status of a sacrificial victim, degraded and destroyed by his relationship with the vampiric André Heredia, who violates him physically and then takes supernatural possession of the youth in order to perpetuate himself. In *A Change of Skin*, one of the most protean of all Fuentes' narratives, the elusive and sinister narrator, Freddy Lambert—who has seemed to be an omniscient power controlling the fate of his character creations—is suddenly revealed as subordinate to the very characters whom he has imaginatively sustained all along, as the Monks rebel against him and demand the death of Franz. (The Monks—a group of rock musicians who are children of victims of Nazi concentration camps—have been traveling through Mexico in pursuit of Franz, an architect who constructed concentration camps during World War II.) Meanwhile the solemn and tormented main characters—Javier and Elizabeth, Isabel and Franz, all of whom are seeking a liberating *cambio de piel,* either a return to the happiness of the time of their honeymoon, as is Elizabeth, or an expiation of guilt, as is Franz—experience only a reductive *cambio de piel,* as their identities are assumed and burlesqued by the irreverent Monks.

One of Fuentes' most significant creations and a stunning testimony to his seemingly inexhaustible capacity for self-transcendence and self-renewal is the vast, epic novel *Terra Nostra.* A strong case can be made that this narrative summa of Fuentes was the most important novel published in Latin America in the 1970's. Like *Where the Air Is Clear, The Death of Artemio Cruz,* and *A Change of Skin* before it, and *Cristóbal nonato* (Christopher Unborn, 1987) after it, *Terra Nostra* breaks new ground, immeasurably expanding the frontiers of the novel as it ranges over and synthesizes thousands of years of civilization, from the Rome of Tiberius to the Spain of the Hapsburgs, from the pre-Columbian myths of creation of the New World to the apocalypse that Fuentes portrays as befalling it in the year 2000. Even among experimental novels, *Terra Nostra* is unique, because so many of these concentrate on developing new techniques in but one or two areas—innovations in multiple points of view, in the use of time, in the variation of narrative sequence, in the creation of new forms of language. Fuentes, in his characteristically pyrotechnic manner, experiments with all of these narrative features, in a work that also stands as a traditional novel—a masterful, compelling adventure story. Indeed, according to Fuentes, it can be seen as the synthesis of the two novels that he believes define the narrative ideal, James Joyce's *Ulysses* and Alexandre Dumas' *The Count of Monte Cristo* (Hispania 63:415 [1980]).

The very title of the work provides an example of Fuentes' complex use of language; it has at least three levels of significance. First, and perhaps most literally, *Terra Nostra* (Our World) has a negative meaning—it refers to Spain's imperial perception of the New World and its indigenous cultures as a realm to be dominated and exploited, so that Hapsburg Spain becomes the continuation in the sixteenth century of the Roman Empire, which regarded the Mediterranean Sea as its *mare nostrum.* Secondly, *Terra Nostra* refers to the New World as finally taking possession of itself; Fuentes in this novel as in *Todos los gatos son pardos* sees a land struggling to achieve an independent consciousness from the very moment of its conquest, from the time of Cuauhtémoc's fierce resistance of the soldiers of Cortés. Thirdly, and perhaps most importantly, the title alludes to an imaginative territory—to the space of the novel, the territory that has marvelously expanded not only in this work but as the result of the masterful accomplishments of all of the Latin American novelists of the 1960's boom, Fuentes and Cortázar, García Márquez and Vargas Llosa. In the companion volume to *Terra Nostra, Cervantes; o, La crítica de la lectura* (1976; published in English as *Don Quixote, or the Critique of Reading*), an essay titled in homage to the master of the Spanish novel, Fuentes sees the one territory, the one possession that all people hold in common, as the *terra nostra* of language.

Terra Nostra is a novel of constant challenge to the reader, who must plunge through almost eight hundred pages of text, grapple with a hydra-headed structure and a narrator who is constantly metamorphosing, and follow the labyrinthine movements of characters who are themselves undergoing myriad transformations of identity. This giant novel envelopes all of Fuentes' previous preoccupations: the theme of the double; the transmigration of souls; the relationship between individual and national identity, between Spain and the New World, between freedom and fate; the intense portrayal of the Aztec past as a living and formidable present and, in *Terra nostra,* even a future for Mexico (which Fuentes depicts as a land in which the sacrificial pyramids will again be put to use); and the experimentation with many different narrative tempos, styles, and tones. It also constitutes a compendium of the major concerns of all the boom novelists and, indeed, concludes with a reunion in Paris, the consecrated city of the boom authors, of many of the characters of these novels—Horacio Oliveira from Cortázar's *Rayuela* (*Hopscotch*, 1963), Esteban and Sofía from Alejo Carpentier's *El siglo de las luces* (*Explosion in a Cathedral*, 1962), and Aureliano Buendía from García Márquez' *Cien años de soledad* (*One Hundred Years of Solitude*, 1967).

The most traditional part of this elaborate narrative, with its dizzying array of historical, literary, and mythic characters and its incessant shiftings in time and space, is part 2, "The New World," which maintains a stable point of view—an autobiographical first-person singular—and for the most part a causal plot, with sequence of exposition, rising action, culminating moment, and denouement. Part 2 traces the voyage to the New World from Spain of the unnamed *peregrino* (pilgrim) and his laborious ascent from the lush coastal regions of Mexico, evoked as a New World paradise, to the high plateau of Aztec Mexico/Tenochtitlan. This journey adumbrates the fateful route of Hernán Cortés; it is a type of counter-conquest in which Fuentes imaginatively explores the *what if* possibilities of history: What if Quetzalcóatl had really returned to the New World during the reign of Moctezuma, rather than the mere mask of Quetzalcóatl, the false god who was Hernán Cortés? Would the conquest have been halted, would the innate altruism of the god, whom Fuentes depicts as flinging away the treasures that are rendered to him, behavior that is exactly opposite that of the avaricious *conquistadores*, have prevailed?

From start to finish, the all-encompassing *Terra Nostra* deals with the themes of tyranny and liberation. Significantly, the work begins on Bastille Day, 14 July 1999, a day of national freedom, and ends on 31 December 1999, a day that ends the millenium and heralds the birth of a new world, free of the tyrannies of the past. Part 1 of the narrative concentrates on the monarch Felipe, a combination of several Hapsburg kings, portrayed as a brooding symbol of absolutism, of stifling authority, and, finally, of living death. The one person successfully to defy the tyranny of Felipe is an artist, the court painter Don Julián, who eloquently summons all the colors and textures of his painting back to him in a confrontation charged with supernatural power,

thereby affirming the autonomy of his art. The suffocating rule of Felipe is also vanquished through a supernatural process: instead of obtaining the final oblivion for which he so desperately longs, the tyrant Felipe is reincarnated as a lowly dog. His master, appropriately, is now Mihail ben-Sama, a man whom Felipe in his past role, as absolute monarch, had executed. *Terra Nostra* thus shows the final defeat of despotic authority, of the repressive spirit evoked as acting in the Old World to crush the revolt of the *comuneros* (the collective landholders) and simultaneously in the New World to destroy the indigenous civilizations. At the end, in the joyous union of the characters Celestina and Polo Febo in Paris, the forces of freedom likewise prevail. Indeed, *Terra Nostra* is one of Fuentes' most optimistic works.

Terra Nostra is a total novel: total in that there is a constant interplay among the individual, the national, and the universal; total in that its movement, as in *One Hundred Years of Solitude*, is from creation to apocalypse; total in that it fuses history and myth, religion and philosophy, orthodoxy and heterodoxy, waking consciousness and dreams and hallucinations, Old World and New World. Ambiguity, irony, paradox, and indeterminacy all are hallmarks of the "new novel" in Latin America, and all are characteristic of *Terra Nostra*. As in Fuentes' novels *Holy Place*, *A Change of Skin*, *Aura*, and *Distant Relations*, metamorphosis is both a thematic constant and a structural principle. Almost all of the characters have multiple—and some, like Isabel and Celestina, protean—identities that are constantly shifting. As the result of this metamorphosis, seemingly insignificant characters such as the sandwich-board man, Polo Febo, turn out to be central: he metamorphoses into the god Quetzalcóatl. Celestina is a re-creation of Fernando de Rojas' immortal, necromancing *alcahueta* (procuress) in his *La Celestina*; in the New World, furthermore, she metamorphoses into the goddess of carnal love, the deity to whom prostitutes were sacrificed, Tlazoltéotl. She later changes into the historical personage of La Malinche, and finally, at the end of the work, becomes linked with Eve, as Fuentes posits a new genesis after the apocalypse destroys everyone except Celestina and Polo Febo.

One of the most striking features of *Terra Nostra* is that it continues the quest for a utopia that characterizes so many of the great novels of the boom—Horacio Oliveira's quest for the absolute, for a center, for nirvana in *Hopscotch*; the feverish quest for a New World paradise of emancipation and creative self-fulfillment by the beleaguered and world-weary protagonist of Carpentier's *Los pasos perdidos* (*The Lost Steps*, 1953); the short-lived paradise of the Macondo settlement founded by José Arcadio Buendía in *One Hundred Years of Solitude*, initially a realm of innocence and felicity. Stretching to the maximum the preoccupations of the boom authors, *Terra Nostra* reiterates the utopian quest first in philosophical terms—in terms of the dreams and visions of Pedro, Celestina, Simón, and Ludovico of a perfect world, free of disease and death, characterized by peace, happiness, and love—and then in terms of the fateful voyage in search of that utopia made by Pedro and the *peregrino*, which demonstrates the impossibility of that quest; the violence and carnage that the idealists encounter transform the New World into a mere reflection of the horrors of the Old.

Although the theme of the double is significant in many of Fuentes' novels and plays, doubling becomes an obsessive phenomenon in *The Hydra Head*. The symbol of the monstrous Hydra—the multiheaded beast encountered by Hercules, which grew two heads in the place of every one that the hero severed—is a symbol of endless proliferation, one that establishes the patterning of incessant doubling that occurs throughout this tale of espionage and subversion. Almost all of the primary characters have dual, and some even triple and quadruple, identities. In addition to the doubling of characters there are almost exact reenactments of scenes and dialogues and even a doubling of the very structure of the work, as the reader is presented with two possible outcomes—one imagined by the narrator, who, failing to take emotional possession of the character Félix Maldonado, claims him authorially, and the other, unknown ending, the one actually experienced by the protagonist.

In the life of the insecure and imaginative protagonist, Félix, the desire for otherness—for a masterful, creative, exotic identity to compensate for his colorless and frustrating existence as a government bureaucrat—is fulfilled in a horribly ironic way, when he is compelled by his captors to assume an alternate

identity and is even forced to undergo facial surgery. Throughout *The Hydra Head*, the positive, transcendental doubles of the protagonist—persons including his love, Sara Klein, and the father figure Captain Harding, who incarnate the political and social ideals that Félix himself seeks to actualize—are destroyed, thus presaging the protagonist's own fate, as at the end he succumbs to his captors and to madness.

The many explicit doublings found in this narrative include a series of paintings that Félix contemplates—each one of which constitutes either a reflection of his present state of limbo, as does the painting of the huge, idollike but phantasmal Indians in the vision of Ricardo Martínez, or of his future fate as pawn and victim—as well as cinematic roles that either exaggerate, mythify, or debunk the roles played by the characters in Fuentes' narrative. Yet the most powerful and the most ominous duplication in this spy thriller is a hidden one. The shadowy narrator, who assumes the name Timon but whose true identity is never revealed, starts out as the seemingly altruistic, positive double of Félix, as his "twin brother" in social concern and heroic resolve, but eventually he seems more to be the mirror image of Maldonado's captor and oppressor, another anonymous person, the shadowy Director General. Timon, in exploiting Félix, whom he regards as his puppet, constantly plays on Félix's idealism, on the need of the protagonist to vindicate his Mexican father's humiliation at the hands of foreign employers who denied him a face, who would turn their backs on him whenever they addressed him. From the very start, Félix himself has two "faces"—his explicit role as punctual and dutiful bureaucrat and his secret career in the employ of the mysterious Timon.

Among other emphases on duality in *The Hydra Head*, the protagonist has two loves—Sara Klein and Mary Benjamin, the first representing the ideal, untouchable woman whom he venerates and the latter the aggressive and sensual one whom Félix exploits; he has two mother figures—his own mother, whose funeral he refuses to attend because he resents her having died and abandoned him, and his wife Ruth, whom he marries as a mother surrogate; and two father figures—one Mexican and the other North American. Two Mexican presidents play an important part in the novel—the anonymous president at the time when the narrative occurs, and the figure from the past whose exalted image falls over the life of the protagonist as an ego ideal, that of Lázaro Cárdenas.

Another level of doubling is given intricate expression in *The Hydra Head,* and that is Félix as symbol of Mexico. One of the most positive and idealistic protagonists ever to appear in the world of Fuentes, Félix is developed as a symbol of Mexican honor, integrity, and independence. Like Cuauhtémoc, Nicolás Bravo, Benito Juárez, and Pancho Villa, historical doubles of the protagonist, Félix represents fierce and stubborn resistance to oppression.

A new identity and a new name, that of Diego Velázquez, will be forcibly imposed upon the protagonist by the Director General, who seeks to implicate Félix in his plot to assassinate the president and finally obliterates his true identity as Félix Maldonado. The imposition of the name Diego Velázquez, an allusion both to the famous Spanish painter of the seventeenth century and to the governor of Cuba during the time of Cortés' expedition to Mexico, symbolizes the working out of a fatalistic cyclical process. It constitutes an allusion to the conquest, which Fuentes regards as the most important event in the entire history of Mexico because it changed the face of the nation forever. As the result of the conquest, a Spanish cultural, linguistic, political, economic, and theological identity was violently and indelibly imposed over that of indigenous Mexico/Tenochtitlan, which for three hundred years after that bore the name Nueva España. The plastic surgery that is inflicted on the hapless protagonist, whose name Maldonado ("ill-given") turns out to be prophetic of his fate, is a horrible replication of the alien identity stamped upon the subjugated Indian people of Mexico by the *conquistadores.* The whole subsequent course of the narrative traces the desperate attempts by Félix to resist this monstrous doubling and to regain his original identity.

The one positive doubling in *The Hydra Head* is an inner one—the development of a new, socially conscious and socially responsible self within Félix Maldonado. Although he himself has benefited immensely from the reforms instituted by Cárdenas, esteemed historically as the protector of indigenous Mexico, Félix at first is evoked as a snobbish dreamer now that he has risen into the upper middle class; he seems out of touch with the grim reality of the Mexican masses—the abject poverty, disease, and suffering—much as were the tycoons Federico Robles and Artemio Cruz in earlier Fuentes novels. Living in a sanitized, hermetic environment, Félix shuns the harsh reality of lower-class Mexico. Although he is willing to appreciate the Indian as an aesthetic phenomenon—as he does when contemplating the painting by Martínez in the house of the aristocrat Rossetti—Félix squeamishly avoids contact with the living Indians all around him, who still travel on foot as they did in the days of pre-Columbian Mexico. But a new, morally responsive Félix will be awakened as the result of his capture, disfigurement, and repeated torture, as his captors attempt to extract information from him concerning the exact size and location of all of Mexico's petroleum resources (information that his employer Timon has amassed through a private espionage system). Félix becomes the twentieth-century equivalent of the valiant Cuauhtémoc, who also resisted his captors, refusing even though tortured to confess to them where the Aztec gold was hidden. The initially aloof Félix will not only be brought to an understanding and empathy with *los de abajo* (represented in this novel by the "underdogs" Licha and Memo) but will himself attempt—and succeed—at protecting them.

The most intricate development as this narrative unfolds is the conscious doubling of Timon and Félix, a relationship that is both positive and negative, that reaches its spiritual height as it parallels the self-sacrificing relationship between the brothers Castor and Pollux (the latter of whom brought his brother back to life by sharing his own gift of immortality with him), but that finally degenerates into a negative counterpart—the fratricidal relationship between Cain and Abel. Throughout his work, Fuentes has linked doubling with duplicity. *Where the Air Is Clear* depicts the one-time soulmates and idealists Federico Robles and Librado Ibarra, whose relationship subsequently erodes into one of deceit and betrayal, as Ibarra after the revolution is abandoned by the avaricious Robles and finally becomes another of the many victims of Robles' rapid and ruthless rise to economic supremacy: he is maimed by defective machinery while working in one of Robles' sweatshops. In *The Death of Artemio Cruz*, *cainismo* functions as a generational curse over the family of Cruz, beginning with the betrayal of Cruz' father, the *hacendado* Atanasio Menchaca, by his own brother Pedro; Pedro, although he is carrying a rifle, deserts Atanasio, leaving him to die at the hands of his enemies. Indeed, throughout his life the ambitious and mercenary Cruz continually betrays—comrades, lovers, wife, even his own son Lorenzo. He deliberately takes Lorenzo back to the land of his youth and there instills in him a thirst for adventure and an idealism that will lead to Lorenzo's heroic sacrifice—and that will expiate Cruz' own lingering sense of guilt and inadequacy. In *Holy Place*, the fratricidal relationship of the twins Romulus and Remus serves as the mythic archetype that vitiates the initially positive relationship between the two "brothers" Guillermo and Giancarlo, as the latter betrays Guillermo by becoming the lover of Claudia. And in *Distant Relations*, Count Branly, the father figure whom Fuentes, himself a character in the novel, regards as a confessor and loyal friend, betrays him by drawing him into the fatalistic world of the Heredias and making him the ultimate custodian of the story that will finally entrap and deprive him of his independent identity.

The most alluring and, along with Timon, enigmatic doubling of Félix Maldonado is found in the person of Sara Klein, the beautiful but remote and impossible love of Félix. Like the identity of the protagonist, the image of Sara Klein is doubled and redoubled throughout the narrative, and indicates the Hydralike grasp she exerts—both in life and even after her grisly death—over Félix. Sara Klein represents the true idealist, who in the pessimistic world of Fuentes is always sacrificed. Even in one of Fuentes' most recent works, *The Old Gringo*, the idealistic revolutionary Tomás Arroyo, a general of Pancho Villa, is at one point defined in terms of the Mirandas—the very family of *terratenientes*, or landed gentry, he is fighting against. When at the end he finally resolves to continue his battle to restore the land to the people, he is slain by his own commander, Villa.

A best seller in the United States in English translation, *The Old Gringo* demonstrates Fuentes' versatility as a novelist—a capacity to write direct, taut novels of action and adventure that appeal to a wide popular audience and complement his mammoth, intricate, more hermetic and metaphysical works such as *A Change of Skin* and *Terra Nostra*. *The Old Gringo* portrays the adventures in Mexico of Ambrose Bierce, the iconoclastic American author of *The Devil's Dictionary* and of the short stories about the Civil War in which Bierce himself fought on the Union side, narratives such as "A Horseman in the Sky" and "Occurrence at Owl Creek Bridge," which are alluded to in Fuentes' novel. How the real Bierce died remains a mystery and thus provides a space of ambiguity for Fuentes' fantasy-making.

What is known for certain is that when he was seventy-one, Bierce crossed the border from El Paso to Ciudad Juárez and wrote a letter to a relative from which Fuentes quotes in his novel: "To be a Gringo in Mexico—ah, that is euthanasia!" The historical Bierce joined the revolutionary army of Francisco "Pancho" Villa and apparently died in the battle at Ojinaga. Fuentes' Bierce suffers a different fate. He is portrayed as a highly complex, enigmatic person, curmudgeon and revolutionary hero, possessed by a Thanatos impulse and yet finding new life in the Mexican desert, a misanthrope who falls in love with a young woman, Harriet Winslow, who is also discontent with her existence in the United States and has come to Mexico as a governess on the Miranda estate. Estranged from his wife, haunted by the memory of one son who committed suicide and another son who died of alcoholism, Bierce finds a surrogate family in Mexico, as he comes to regard the young general Tomás Arroyo, whose forces Bierce joins, as a surrogate son. Yet in both the fictional world created by the historical Ambrose Bierce (for instance in his violent short story "A Horseman in the Sky") and in Fuentes' fictional re-creation, sons fire upon and kill their fathers, and Bierce's desire to die in Mexico is ultimately fulfilled, as he is slain not by the federal troops against whom he shows a desperate courage but by the fiery-tempered Arroyo. Bierce provokes Arroyo into shooting him in the back by deliberately destroying Arroyo's last precious possession—the papers that he has so jealously guarded, the land grant signed by the Spanish crown that legitimizes Arroyo's claim to the vast estate of the Mirandas.

As in so many of Fuentes' novels, it is a female presence who controls the identities of the male protagonists. *The Old Gringo* is narrated from the point of view of Harriet, who conjures up the ghosts of her lover Arroyo and of her surrogate father Bierce. She is similar to many of Fuentes' reclusive female characters, women who are seemingly passive but in reality are strong, mythic beings, with the power of life or death over the male characters whose destinies they determine. Harriet is indirectly responsible for the death of Arroyo, yet it is she who resuscitates him and his story in this poetic, hallucinatory narrative.

Cristóbal nonato, Fuentes' most recent novel, extends the concept of the *novela totalizante*, the all-encompassing novel, to focus on the future—Mexico in the year 1992, the five-hundredth anniversary of Columbus' discovery of the New World. In a major sense, this latest work, a baroque epic, complements *The Death of Artemio Cruz*: instead of a dying narrator, Christopher is a fetal one; instead of a narrative structure reflecting the twelve anguished hours preceding the protagonist's death, there are nine major sections corresponding to the nine months of gestation of Columbus' namesake. In contrast to the tone of marked disillusionment and pessimism concerning the betrayal of the ideals of the Mexican Revolution that saturates *The Death of Artemio Cruz*, *Cristóbal nonato* ends with an exuberant affirmation of new life. Continuing Fuentes' preoccupation with defining the complex components of the Mexican national identity, this novel also constitutes a fascinating experiment in intertextuality. It constantly intercalates lines from the famous patriotic poem by Ramón López Velarde, "Suave patria" ("Gentle Homeland"), and even transforms into narrative episode and amorous encounter the brief poem "Mi prima Agueda" ("My Cousin Agueda") as it re-creates the enigmatic Agueda as the lover of Ángel, the libertine father of Christopher and a main character in *Cristóbal nonato*.

Fuentes' most recent novel is also his most humorous: it combines farcical adventures with satire on Mexican politics and on the absurdly pretentious customs of its social elite; it is saturated with word play, neologisms, and puns. *Cristóbal nonato* also complements Fuentes' three novels of the Mexican revolution of 1910—*Where the Air Is Clear*, *The Death of Artemio Cruz*, and *The Old Gringo*—in that it portrays a future Mexico wracked by rebellion: the uprising of the impoverished inhabitants of Acapulco, the rebellion in Mexico City by the followers of the incendiary Matamoras Concentration, or the enormous problems faced by Mexico City—referred to in the novel as "Makesicko City," just as Acapulco is renamed "Kafkapulco" and "Acapulcalipsis"—the population explosion and the scarcity of food, the air pollution and the incessant acid rain—underscores the intense seriousness that underlies much of the comic surface of this work and further emphasizes Fuentes' role as incisive national conscience.

SELECTED BIBLIOGRAPHY

First Editions

Novels

La región más transparente. Mexico City, 1958.
Las buenas conciencias. Mexico City, 1959.
Aura. Mexico City, 1962.
La muerte de Artemio Cruz. Mexico City, 1962.
Cambio de piel. Mexico City, 1967.
Zona sagrada. Mexico City, 1967.
Cumpleaños. Mexico City, 1969.
Terra nostra. Barcelona, 1975.
La cabeza de la hidra. Barcelona, 1978.
Una familia lejana. Mexico City, 1980.
Gringo viejo. Mexico City, 1985.
Cristóbal nonato. Mexico City, 1987.

Short Stories

Los días enmascarados. Mexico City, 1954.
Cantar de ciegos. Mexico City, 1964.
Agua quemada. Mexico City, 1981.

Plays

Todos los gatos son pardos. Mexico City, 1970.
El tuerto es rey. Mexico City, 1970.
Orquídeas a la luz de la luna. Barcelona, 1978.

Essays

París: La revolución de Mayo. Mexico City, 1968.
El mundo de José Luis Cuevas. Mexico City, 1969.

La nueva novela hispanoamericana. Mexico City, 1969.
Casa con dos puertas. Mexico City, 1970.
Tiempo mexicano. Mexico City, 1971.
Cervantes; o, La crítica de la lectura. Mexico City, 1976.

Collected Works

Obras completas 1: Novelas. With a prologue by Fernando Benítez. Mexico City, 1974.

Translations

Aura. Translated by Lysander Kemp. New York, 1965.
Burnt Water. Translated by Margaret Sayers Peden. New York, 1980. Contains selections from all three volumes of short stories.
A Change of Skin. Translated by Sam Hileman. New York, 1968.
The Death of Artemio Cruz. Translated by Sam Hileman. New York, 1964.
Distant Relations. Translated by Margaret Sayers Peden. New York, 1982.
Don Quixote, or the Critique of Reading. Austin, Tex., 1976.
The Good Conscience. Translated by Sam Hileman. New York, 1961.
Holy Place. Translated by Suzanne Jill Levine. In *Triple Cross.* New York, 1972.
The Hydra Head. Translated by Margaret Sayers Peden. New York, 1978.
The Old Gringo. Translated by Margaret Sayers Peden and Carlos Fuentes. New York, 1985.
Orchids in the Moonlight. Translated by Carlos Fuentes. In *Drama Contemporary: Latin America,* edited by George W. Woodyard and Marion Peter. New York, 1986.
Terra Nostra. Translated by Margaret Sayers Peden. New York, 1976.
Where the Air Is Clear. Translated by Sam Hileman. New York, 1960.

Biographical and Critical Studies

Befumo Boschi, Liliana, and Elisa Calabrese. *Nostalgia del futuro en la obra de Carlos Fuentes.* Buenos Aires, 1974.
Brody, Robert, and Charles Rossman, eds. *Carlos Fuentes: A Critical View.* Austin, Tex., 1982.
Brushwood, John S. "Sobre el referente y la transformación narrativa en las novelas de Carlos Fuentes y Gustavo Sainz." *Revista iberoamericana* 47/166–167:49–54 (1981).

Carballo, Emmanuel. "Carlos Fuentes." In *Diecinueve protagonistas de la literatura mexicana del siglo XX.* Mexico City, 1965. Pp. 424–448.
Durán, Gloria. *La magia y las brujas en la obra de Carlos Fuentes.* Mexico City, 1976.
_____. *The Archetypes of Carlos Fuentes: From Witch to Androgyne.* Hamden, Conn., 1980.
Durán, Manuel. "Carlos Fuentes." In *Tríptico mexicano: Juan Rulfo, Carlos Fuentes, Salvador Elizondo.* Mexico City, 1973. Pp. 51–133.
Faris, Wendy B. *Carlos Fuentes.* New York, 1983.
Foster, David W. "*La región más transparente* and the Limits of Prophetic Art." *Hispania* 56:35–42 (1973).
García Gutiérrez, Georgina. *Los disfraces: La obra mestiza de Carlos Fuentes.* Mexico City, 1981.
Giacoman, Helmy F., ed. *Homenaje a Carlos Fuentes: Variaciones interpretativas en torno a su obra.* New York, 1971.
Goytisolo, Juan. "*Terra nostra,* Our Old New World." *Review* (Center for Inter American Relations) 19:5–24 (1976).
Grossman, Edith. "Myth and Madness in Carlos Fuentes' *A Change of Skin.*" *Latin American Literary Review* 3/1:99–112 (1974).
Guzmán, Daniel de. *Carlos Fuentes.* New York, 1972.
Gyurko, Lanin A. "The Sacred and the Profane in Fuentes' *Zona sagrada.*" *Revista hispánica moderna* 37:188–209 (1972–1973).
_____. "Identity and the Demonic in Two Narratives by Fuentes." [*Aura,* "Tlactocatzine, del jardín de Flandes"] *Revista de letras* 6/21:87–118 (1974).
_____. "The Myths of Ulysses in Fuentes' *Zona sagrada.*" *Modern Language Review* 69/2:316–324 (1974).
_____. "Self, Double, and Mask in Fuentes' *La muerte de Artemio Cruz.*" *Texas Studies in Literature and Language* 16/2:363–384 (1974).
_____. "Social Satire and the Ancient Mexican Gods in the Narrative of Fuentes." *Ibero-Amerikanisches Archiv* 1/2:113–150 (1975).
_____. "The Artist *Manqué* in Fuentes' *Cambio de piel.*" *Symposium* 31:125–150 (1977).
_____. "The Vindication of La Malinche in Fuentes' *Todos los gatos son pardos.*" *Ibero-Amerikanisches Archiv* 3/3:689–709 (1977).
_____. *Freedom and Fate in Fuentes' "Cambio de piel."* Supplement to *Revista/Review Interamericana* 7/4 (1977–1978).
_____. "Autonomous Characters and the Victimized Narrator in *Cambio de piel.*" *Iberoromania* 5:158–188 (1980).

_____. "Structure and Theme in Fuentes' *La muerte de Artemio Cruz.*" *Symposium* 34:29–41 (1980).

_____. "Cinematic Image and National Identity in Fuentes' *Orquídeas a la luz de la luna.*" *Latin American Theatre Review* 17/2:3–24 (1984).

_____. "Fuentes' *Aura* and Wilder's *Sunset Boulevard*: A Comparative Analysis." *Ibero-Amerikanisches Archiv* 10/1:45–86 (1984).

Harss, Luis, and Barbara Dohmann. "Carlos Fuentes, or the New Heresy." In *Into the Mainstream: Conversations with Latin American Writers.* New York, 1967. Pp. 276–309.

Larson, Ross. "Archetypal Patterns in Carlos Fuentes' 'La muñeca reina.'" *Mester* 2/1:41–46 (1982).

Loveluck, Juan. "Intención y forma en *La muerte de Artemio Cruz.*" *Nueva narrativa latinoamericana* 1/1:105–116 (1971).

_____, and Isaac Levy, eds. *Simposio Carlos Fuentes: Actas.* In *University of South Carolina Hispanic Studies* 2 (1980).

Reeve, Richard. "An Annotated Bibliography on Carlos Fuentes, 1949–1969." *Hispania* 53/4:595–652 (1970).

_____. "Carlos Fuentes and the New Short Story in Mexico." *Studies in Short Fiction* 8:169–179 (1971).

Seale-Vásquez, Mary. "Character Development in Fuentes' *A Change of Skin.*" *Latin American Literary Review* 6/12:68–85 (1978).

Sommers, Joseph. "The Field of Choice: Carlos Fuentes." In *After the Storm: Landmarks of the Modern Mexican Novel.* Albuquerque, N. Mex., 1968. Pp. 133–164.

Valdés, M. L. "Myth and History in *Cien años de soledad* and *La muerte de Artemio Cruz.*" *Reflexión* 2/3–4: 243–255 (1974–1975).

Wood, Michael. "The New World and the Old Novel." *INTI* 5–6:109–112 (1977).

Osvaldo Dragún

(1929–   )

George Woodyard

The twentieth century ushered in a period of unprecedented development and expansion in the theater of Argentina and the River Plate region. The Golden Decade (1900–1910) produced such authors as Florencio Sánchez and Gregorio de Laferrère, who combined the disparate values of provincial and urban settings to create an original theater inspired by the realism of Henrik Ibsen and André Antoine. Despite a strong beginning, the theater deteriorated into facile, costumbristic comedies, light plays often with accents of vaudeville or mystery that depended more on showy techniques than on character development, by such authors as Enrique García Velloso or the *sainetero* Alberto Vacarezza. Around 1930 an independent movement under the impetus of Léonidas Barletta and the Teatro del Pueblo (People's Theater) began to develop socially and artistically committed alternative forms of theater. This group and others that followed adapted vanguard European techniques of directing, acting, and stagecraft in order to revitalize a decadent movement. In 1949 the transition of Carlos Gorostiza's *El puente* (The Bridge) from the independent theater to the commercial stage marked a new era of serious theater accessible to the larger public. In this arena Osvaldo Dragún and his contemporaries became the leaders of a new generation of playwrights.

Dragún was born in Paraná, capital of Entre Ríos, Argentina, in 1929, and moved to Buenos Aires in 1944. Lacking formal training in the dramatic arts, he acquired his early experience by acting, directing, and writing for community theater groups. His one-act plays staged during this period have been lost. During a brief stint (1955–1956) with the IFT (Asociación Israelita Argentina Pro Arte) he adapted Alejandro Berrutti's *Madre Tierra* (Mother Earth). He discovered and admired greatly the plays of Eugene O'Neill, William Shakespeare, and Ramón María del Valle-Inclán. Dragún considered that his true theatrical initiation came when he affiliated with the Teatro Popular Independiente Fray Mocho (Popular Independent Theater Fray Mocho) in 1956. The Fray Mocho functioned as an experimental group in Buenos Aires and went on tour throughout Argentina and South America with a repertoire that included classical and modern, foreign and national playwrights.

Fray Mocho's artistic director, Oscar Ferrigno, launched Dragún's career with two historical plays that represent the value of individual and political freedom. *La peste viene de Melos* (The Plague Comes from Melos, 1956) is a three-act play inspired by the involvement of the United States in the fall of the Arbenz government in Guatemala in 1954. The

Athenian siege against the small colony of Melos in 416 B.C. serves to extol the virtues of resistance against imperialism. Although the Melians are finally defeated by their own greed, their example inspires others to revolt. *Tupac Amarú* (1957) exalts the Incan chief from the Peruvian highlands who led an uprising in 1780 against the Spanish empire, anticipating by some thirty years the independence movement in the South American colonies. With a combination of historical heroism and twentieth-century existentialism, the play presents two worlds in conflict, in which the vanquished is paradoxically the long-term victor.

The short plays that brought Dragún international fame also date from 1957. Departing from traditional critical realism, Dragún and his generation—especially Ricardo Halac, Roberto Cossa and Carlos Gorostiza—developed a "new realism" in an effort to find fundamental and coherent elements within the unstable Argentine political reality. They opposed the Peronista regime, but when Juan Perón's government fell in 1955, the ensuing political anarchy of the Frondizi years was even more disconcerting. Dragún's sense of disorientation manifested itself in the aesthetics of the grotesque, an extreme form of dehumanization of the individual. He observed that "the comic and even optimistic element of incommunication produced the Argentine *sainete* [short farce], and the tragic and ridiculous element of that imagination produces the grotesque." *Las historias para ser contadas* (Stories to be Told, 1957) were one-act plays with a Brechtian flavor, written with a commedia dell'arte style and structure. The dichotomy between reality and nonreality had been a common motif in Argentine literature and theater since the days of Armando Discépolo and Roberto Arlt, and Dragún played with this disjuncture in these popular and dynamic vignettes. Almost devoid of plot, they rely on imagery, free association, satire, and evocative, expressionistic language. Written for the Fray Mocho Company, the pieces enjoyed the freedom of an empty stage and established quick rapport with audiences through the actor/audience interaction and the use of popular music. Masterfully ingenuous yet complex, they illustrated graphically Dragún's commitment to sociopolitical issues.

The plays are *Historia de un flemón, una mujer, y dos hombres* (Story of an Abcess, a Woman, and Two Men), the story of a pathetic vendor who dies, caught between the need for medical attention and insufficient resources; *Historia de cómo nuestro amigo Panchito González se sintió responsable de la epidemia de peste bubónica en Africa del Sur* (The Story of How Our Friend Panchito González Felt Guilty about the Epidemic of Bubonic Plague in South Africa), in which a man exports rat meat in order to make money to support his family; and *La historia del hombre que se convirtió en perro* (The Story of the Man Who Turned into a Dog), the dehumanizing story of a man who accepts a position as watchdog. The common denominator of this series is the desperation of people willing to work but thwarted by social injustice and lack of opportunity.

Subsequent to the original three, Dragún continued to exercise the *historia* as a dramatic form. *Los de la mesa diez* (The Couple at Table Ten, 1957) presents a young couple from different socioeconomic backgrounds, very much in love but grappling with family and fiscal pressures that undermine their chances for happiness. Subtitled *Otra historia para ser contada* (Another Story to be Told), the play continues the Brechtian style with the songs, music, and realistic language of the Italian immigrant. The *Historia de mi esquina* (Story of My Corner, 1959) varies the pattern: written in two acts, it gives greater attention to character development. An apparently ahistorical neighborhood corner reveals, on close examination, the anxieties of people dealing with their economic and existential problems. *La historia del mono que se convirtió en hombre* (The Story of the Monkey That Became a Man, added in 1979), resembles the original *historias*, but with reverse dehumanization, and focuses on the empty lives of those who never challenge authority and are oblivious to the social implications of their work efforts.

After a brief incursion into musical drama with *Desde el 80* (Since 80, 1958), written in collaboration with Andrés Lizárraga, Dragún wrote *El jardín del infierno* (Garden of Hell, 1961), a play set in a Buenos Aires slum ("villa miseria") punctuated by poverty, misery, and deprivation. The wretched environment shatters hopes and illusions; a gang rape leading to murder is but one manifestation of the endemic violence in a society where civil prosecution is enforced according to a double standard.

During the period 1961–1963 Dragún lived in Havana, Cuba, invited by the revolutionary government to organize and direct seminars on dramaturgy. He participated with heterogeneous groups involved in developing a theater responsive to the Cuban reality. During that time he finished *Milagro en el Mercado Viejo* (Miracle in the Old Market, premiered 1964) using the *historia* technique to unveil a story of crime and betrayal enacted by vagabonds at night in the marketplace. Music again emphasizes two lines of intercalated action in this long one-act play. Prefaced by a quotation from Antoine de Saint-Exupéry, the play calls for active, not passive, participation in life.

Dragún interrupted the writing of the previous play to write *Y nos dijeron que éramos inmortales* (And They Told Us We Were Immortal, 1963), a work that illustrates how parents and society create illusions for generations of alienated youth. The conflict between two value systems relating to concepts of love, duty, family, sex, and marriage oblige the central figure, a disillusioned war veteran, to look to his own abilities and self-determination. His protective mother and alcoholic father had poorly conditioned him to face a world of changing values.

Amoretta (Little Love, 1964) is a love story in the Argentine *sainete* tradition, in which a man pursues a widow who sells flowers in the market stall next to his. In contrast with Dragún's previous plays, *Amoretta* is tender and sentimental, and the potential violence is averted by a happy ending. The widow, after years of sexual abstinence, represents a feminine liberation that argues against inhibitions and moralistic repression. The protagonist, Giuliana, inspired the main figure in Dragún's next play, *Heroica de Buenos Aires* (Epic of Buenos Aires, 1966), a work that Dragún considers his masterpiece. Family conflicts arise between María's humble origins and the bourgeois values to which she aspires for her children. Underscoring the domestic action is a military conflict that leads to arbitrary violence. Tanks in the streets of Buenos Aires are nearly as common as taxis, Dragún claims hyperbolically, and with this play he attempted to represent the disillusion and frustration that plagued those of his generation who had hoped for a liberated Argentina capable of dealing sensibly

with its political and economic problems. The seasonal changes from spring to winter indicated in the seven scenes parallel the process of change from hope to despair, from promise to desolation.

After *Una mujer por encomienda* (A Kept Woman, 1966), unsuccessful with the critics, *Dos en la ciudad* (Two in the City, 1967) was performed in Spain under the title *¡Un maldito domingo!* (One Damned Sunday!, 1967), and later revised as *El amasijo* (The Hodgepodge, 1968). Combining the stylization of the *historias* with an absurdist language, José and María (Dragún's prototypical characters, as in *Los de la mesa diez* and *Milagro en el Mercado Viejo*) suffer the solitude of lonely beings trying to communicate. A third individual adopts various identities in the past and future that relate to their amorous affair. Humor tempers the hostility, but their paranoid despair is symptomatic of the underlying sickness within the society.

During the five-year period from 1967 to 1972 Dragún lived in Spain, wrote for television, and made movies. His next play, *Pedrito el Grande* (Little Peter the Great, 1972), was presented in Mexico under the title *Juguemos en el bosque* (Let's Play in the Woods, 1972) and recounts childhood experiences. Greatly different in tone is *Historias con cárcel* (Stories with Jail, 1972), in which the central metaphor is the jail cell, representing the loss of freedom in an Argentina subjected to capitalism, military rule, and press censorship. This series of loosely connected vignettes begs for civil disobedience against all oppression, and the "constitutional cantata" at the end of the work extols individual inalienable rights. The earthy language matches the violence, including graphic scenes of torture, in this hyperbolic *historia* that, predictably, incorporates songs and music.

El Che Quijote, as yet unperformed, shows Ernesto (Che) Guevara as a modern Don Quijote in Buenos Aires, living out a fantasy of his impossible dream of replacing guilt and frustration with love and idealism for the future. The credible fusion of the real and the unreal pulls in his entire family, but after his death only his daughter retains the magic and the hope for redemption of the world from selfish behavior.

Hoy se comen al flaco (Today They Eat the Thin Man, 1977) is the result of a collaborative project commissioned by UNESCO and involving Dragún,

Emilio Carballido (Mexico), Enrique Buenaventura (Colombia), and César Rengifo (Venezuela). Dragún's play continues the critique of a political machinery that obliges the oppressed to exploit their fellow men in the struggle for survival. Circus tones and motifs, laced with song and dance, underscore the philosophical issues of freedom that surround Juan Noreira, the much-maligned nineteenth-century gaucho protagonist in this work, who transcends his time period as a talking statue in the town square.

Dragún continued to use the freedom of the empty stage in *Al violador* (To the Rapist, 1980), which depicts a vitriolic dichotomy between philosophical and telluric issues. A rapist, suffering primal instincts without understanding them, is a political metaphor of the effects of censorship and the inability to communicate within the society.

In 1981 Dragún, along with some of Argentina's most active theater artists, conceived a bold new experiment, the Teatro Abierto (Open Theater), to counteract the stagnant condition of the current theater, to attract a new audience for theater-as-art, and to work together collaboratively and joyfully. Disclaiming any relationship with Joseph Chaikin's similarly titled experiment of 1963, the project nevertheless had similar objectives. The first cycle consisted of twenty-one plays, with as many directors, to be performed in a seven-night cycle of three plays each. Their theater building, the Teatro Picadero, burned mysteriously at the end of the first week, but the project soon reopened to even greater public enthusiasm in the Teatro Tabarís. The freedom exercised during a particularly difficult period in Argentina history was an inspiration to performers and public alike.

Dragún continued his involvement with the Open Theater in subsequent cycles. The 1982 promotion was artistically less successful and was somewhat overshadowed by the Argentine-British war of the Malvinas (the Falkland Islands War). The 1983 cycle, coinciding with the euphoria over democratic elections, was organized thematically around projects rather than plays. In 1984 and 1985 the Open Theater directed its efforts toward projects of freedom, followed by seminars and neighborhood theater-development projects.

For the 1981 cycle Dragún wrote *Mi obelisco y yo* (My Obelisk and I), using the expressionistic format of the *historias* to recount the provincial ingenuousness of new arrivals to Buenos Aires. This allegory of life and death, emphasizing the discrepancies between static urban conditions and a dynamic external vitality, requires a youthful liar to break the pattern. For the 1982 cycle Dragún wrote *Al vencedor* (To the Victor), a work that examines through an army general in the early part of the century the dichotomy that exists in Argentina between Latin-American roots and the European tradition. The same year he had premiered *Al perdedor* (To the Loser) in the Teatro Estudio IFT. In this play, a defeated boxer accepts his loss because he can exercise his freedom of choice, over and above the pressures of political, religious, and family systems that attempt to control his behavior. The expressionistic style continues the *historia* tradition in another play that manifests Dragún's commitment to individual liberty. In 1987 Dragún premiered a play he had begun long before. Published as *Hijos del terremoto* (Sons of the Earthquake) and premiered in 1987 as *Arriba Corazón*, a title that plays with protagonist's name, Corazón (Up, Corazón! or Up with Your Heart!), the play's three acts comprise an autobiographical interpretation of childhood, adolescence, and maturity.

Dragún's reputation as Argentina's best contemporary playwright springs from the success of the *historias*, which, along with his other plays, have been performed throughout the Americas and Europe. Impelled by Fray Mocho's economic necessities, he used an empty stage to transform reality, which in turn helped to transform the Argentine theater. His strong sociopolitical commitment often brought censorship from authorities at the same time that he was earning national and international recognition for the artistic quality of his work. When Dragún portrays the Buenos Aires atmosphere he knows so intimately either through popular figures of the *sainete* or the stylized caricatures of the grotesque, it is clear that his basic concerns are the ethics and morality of human behavior. The popular songs and music he uses are an essential part of the rich legacy of Argentine tradition. His originality combines with an extraordinary ability for synthesis in works that make the public laugh at the same time that they take stock of a serious social message. The ubiquitous struggle for freedom pervades his works, now translated and published in many languages. In addition, his several movies and series written for Argentine and Spanish television illustrate his mastery of another medium.

Argentina has been ravaged by political and economic turmoil in the recent past. A crushing external debt, rampant inflation at times approaching one thousand percent per year, the disastrous war of the Malvinas, a repressive military regime responsible for terrorism, torture, and countless "disappeared ones"—all have contributed to the shattered image of a civilized nation unable to govern itself. In the midst of this apparent chaos, Dragún and his contemporaries—their names are legion, but any list must include Griselda Gambaro—have drawn on the rich traditions of Argentine folklore, circus, music (especially the tango), and the linguistic overlays of a heterogeneous population. By combining them with the European influences of Luigi Pirandello, the theater of the absurd and the grotesque, as well as Bertolt Brecht and the political theater, they have created a theater that is one of the richest and most forceful in all of Latin America. Dragún has been a leader in this movement and his plays attest to his personal concern and commitment, his originality, and his innate sense of artistic creativity.

SELECTED BIBLIOGRAPHY

Plays

La peste viene de Melos. Buenos Aires, 1956.
Tupac Amarú. Buenos Aires, 1957.
Amoretta. Buenos Aires, 1965.
El jardín del infierno. Buenos Aires, 1966.
Heroica de Buenos Aires. Buenos Aires, 1967.
Teatro (Historia de mi esquina, Los de la mesa 10, Historias para ser contadas). Buenos Aires, 1967.
El amasijo. Buenos Aires, 1968.
¡Un maldito domingo! Y nos dijeron que éramos inmortales. Milagro en el Mercado Viejo. Madrid, 1968.
Historias con cárcel. Havana, 1973.
Teatro: Hoy se comen al flaco; Al violador. Ottawa, Canada, 1981.

Historias para ser contadas; Al perdedor. Rosario, Argentina, 1982.
Historias para ser contadas. Ottawa, Canada, 1982. Includes *La historia del mono que se convirtió en hombre.*
Mi obelisco y yo. In *7 dramaturgos argentinos,* edited by Miguel Ángel Giella, Peter Roster, and Leandro Urbina. Ottawa, Canada, 1983.
Los hijos del terremoto. Gestos 2: 159–213 (November 1986).

Translations

And They Told Us We Were Immortal. In *The Modern Stage in Latin America: Six Plays,* edited by George W. Woodyard. New York, 1971.
The Story of the Man Who Turned into a Dog. In *The Orgy; Modern One-Act Plays from Latin America,* edited by Gerardo Luzuriaga and Robert S. Rudder. Los Angeles, 1974.

Interviews and Commentaries

Campa, Román V. de la. "Entrevista con el dramaturgo argentino Osvaldo Dragún." *Latin American Theatre Review* 11/1:84–90 (1977).
"Entrevista." In Osvaldo Dragún, *Teatro,* edited by Miguel Ángel Giella and Peter Roster. Ottawa, Canada, 1981. Pp. 7–71. The interview is in two parts: "Teatro, creación y realidad latinoamericana," and "La honesta desnudez."
Dragún, Osvaldo. "Nuevos rumbos en el teatro latinoamericano." *Latin American Theatre Review* 13/2 Supplement:11–16 (1980).

Critical Studies

Dauster, Frank. "Brecht y Dragún: Teoría y práctica." In his *Ensayos sobre Teatro hispanoamericano.* Mexico City, 1975. Pp. 189–197.
Galich, Manuel. "De *Amoretta* a *Historias con cárcel.*" *Conjunto* 16:82–86 (1973).
Leonard, Candyce Crew. "Dragún's Distancing Techniques in *Historias para ser contadas* and *El amasijo.*" *Latin American Theatre Review* 16/2:37–42 (1983).
Lutz, Robyn R. "The Stylization of Theme in Dragún's *Historias para ser contadas.*" *Latin American Literary Review* 7/13:29–37 (1978).
Monleón, Jose. "Dragún, el de las historias." In Osvaldo Dragún, *Teatro.* Madrid, 1968. Pp. 18–40.
Ortega, Julio, "Una nota a las *Historias* de Dragún." *Latin American Theatre Review* 13/2:73–75 (1980).

Pross, Edith E., "Open Theatre Revisited: An Argentine Experiment." *Latin American Theatre Review* 18/1:83–94 (1984).

Reynolds, Bonnie E. "Time and Responsibility in Dragún's *Tupac Amarú.*" *Latin American Theatre Review* 13/1:47–53 (1979).

Schmidt, Donald L. "El teatro de Osvaldo Dragún." *Latin American Theatre Review* 2/2:3–20 (1969).

———. "The Theater of Osvaldo Dragún." In *Dramatists in Revolt: The New Latin American Theater,* edited by Leon F. Lyday and George W. Woodyard. Austin, Tex., and London, 1976. Pp. 77–94.

Woodyard, George W. "Imágenes teatrales de *Tupac Amarú:* Génesis de un mito." *Conjunto* 37:62–68 (1978).

Guillermo Cabrera Infante

(1929–   )

Alfred J. MacAdam

Intellectuals, including those, like Guillermo Cabrera Infante, who had enthusiastically supported the Cuban Revolution and had worked to bring it to a successful conclusion, later found themselves estranged from it. In the years between 1959 and 1962, Fidel Castro managed to gain and then to lose the support of many Cuban intellectuals and artists: they realized that in the name of national solidarity they would now be obliged to espouse an orthodoxy that included politics, economics, and all aspects of cultural life. There would be no room for dissent. It is impossible to understand Cabrera Infante's career without taking into account the Cuban Revolution, especially the years from 1959 to 1965 (the year Cabrera Infante definitively left Cuba). While the revolution is not the actual subject of his writings and does not provide a secret "key" to them, it is the conditioning factor of both his life and his work.

Cabrera Infante seemed fated to participate in radical politics. He was born on 22 April 1929 to Guillermo Cabrera and Zoila Infante, who founded the local cell of the Communist party in the small city of Gibara, on the northern coast of Cuba. In 1932 he witnessed the bombing of Gibara—the first aerial bombardment of any New World city—by Gen. Gerardo Machado's planes. They helped to crush a local uprising against the dictator, in which Cabrera Infante's uncle and father participated on the rebel side. In 1936, with Cuba now under Fulgencio Batista's control, he saw his mother and father arrested and imprisoned because they were communists. Their political persecution continued after their release from prison. Guillermo Cabrera was blacklisted, and in 1941 he was obliged to move his family to Havana in order to find work. Because of their political commitment, the Cabrera Infantes would live for decades in grinding poverty.

The family's migration to the capital in 1941 not only marked a change of setting for Cabrera Infante, it also began the metamorphosis of a poor but happy country boy into a poor and unhappy urban adolescent. The experience of coming of age in Havana is the basis for his autobiographical novel, *La Habana para un infante difunto* (*Infante's Inferno*, 1979). That text provides a model for understanding all of Cabrera Infante's fiction: there is no real separation between life and art, because any reflection made on life involves a verbal formulation of it, and any formulation entails stylization—the subordination of one detail to another—which renders the final product an artificial structure. Life is art because it can be comprehended only by means of an act of interpretation, that is, of fiction making.

This concept of life as a species of writing would

seem to locate Cabrera Infante at a distance from participation in everyday affairs, at a safe, aesthetic distance in the style of Stéphane Mallarmé (one of the poets he most frequently quotes). But this is not the case, because Cabrera Infante does not seek to represent experience in any language other than the "words of the tribe" that Mallarmé sought to purify. Even as he is turning experience into words he is seeking to bring words and experience into close proximity by using all the available forms of the spoken and written language.

One of the main tensions in Cabrera Infante's writing is between the silent permanence of writing and the clamorous but ephemeral spoken word. This tension probably pushed him toward his second love: movies. There the work of art speaks and is seen at the same time. Both language and nonverbal communication are at the disposal of the invisible director, the role Cabrera Infante brings into literature. Thus, while he actively pursues the spoken word in all its manifestations in his writing, Cabrera Infante maintains control over his text, either by delegating narrative authority to one of his characters, as he does with Silvestre in his first novel, *Tres tristes tigres* (*Three Trapped Tigers*, 1967), or by inserting himself directly into the fiction, as he does in *Infante's Inferno.*

A significant ramification of this game of verbal alter egos is his work as a film critic. Convicted in 1952 of having published, in the large-circulation Cuban weekly magazine *Bohemia,* a story containing English obscenities, he was proscribed from publishing under his own name. So he invented an ironically prophetic pseudonym, G. Caín—from Cabrera Infante—which he used when he began to write film reviews for another large-circulation Cuban magazine, *Carteles,* in 1954. In 1962, already in bad political odor in Havana for having been the editor of the literary supplement *Lunes* (Monday) of the non-communist but semiofficial newspaper *Revolución* and for simply continuing to be an independent intellectual, he was banished to Brussels as cultural attaché. While there, Cabrera Infante prepared *Un oficio del siglo veinte* (A Twentieth-Century Profession), which appeared in Cuba in 1963. This was a collection of his film reviews, that is, the film reviews G. Caín published in *Carteles* and *Revolución* between 1954

and 1960, edited and with a prologue by Guillermo Cabrera Infante. When asked in a 1983 *Paris Review* interview how he understood the book, Cabrera Infante answered:

> As a novel. The Prologue, the Intermission, and the Epilogue are biographical comments on G. Caín, the critic. The reviews, his criticism, are the corpus—that is, his body. The whole book is a rite of passage conducted over his dead body. That's what a novel is, don't you think?
>
> (p. 167)

Un oficio del siglo veinte may or may not be a novel, but the point is that Cabrera Infante thinks of himself in the same way he thinks of life and language—that he, too, is literary raw material, that to incorporate himself into language, to write, in this case, about himself as Caín, is to create a character.

It is significant that Cabrera Infante's first discovery of literature should have been an unexpurgated Spanish translation of Petronius Arbiter's *Satyricon,* which he found among his father's books on a vacation trip to Gibara in 1942. This ancient text spoke so directly to his sensibility that it was a decisive influence on *Three Trapped Tigers.* The *Satyricon* has meant various things to him at different stages in his life, but for the writer Cabrera Infante it has mirrored the complex relationship between writer and tradition.

Cabrera Infante published his first work when he was nineteen. Unlike most Latin American writers, he did not begin his career as a poet, but rather as a scriptwriter, although none of these unpublished texts has survived. Fascinated with mass culture from the time he was a child—he claims he learned how to read by deciphering the words in the balloons above comic-strip characters—he became involved with radio. He dramatized lives of the saints for a Catholic association and wrote a radio play based on an American comic strip popular in Cuba, "The Spirit." But the well-timed rejection of his adaptation for radio of Sir Arthur Conan Doyle's "The Speckled Band" obliged him to turn his attention to writing prose.

In 1947, after reading Miguel Ángel Asturias' naturalist-expressionist novel of social criticism, *El señor presidente* (*The President*, 1946), Cabrera Infante decided that if he could do no better, he could certainly do no worse. The result was the short story "Aguas de recuerdo" (Waters of Memory), which, to the astonishment of the nineteen-year-old author, was published by *Bohemia* on 13 June 1948. While the story is not of great literary interest, it does reflect one aspect of the Spanish-American literary environment of the 1940's. On one side, there was the muted voice of Jorge Luis Borges and those like him who wrote a refined, art-for-art's-sake literature concerned with philosophical or aesthetic questions that did not address the problems of everyday life. On the other side were writers who developed directly out of the naturalist-realist tradition of the nineteenth century, whose writing was intended as an indictment of Latin American reality. This tendency in Latin American literature was also characterized by a rediscovery of those elements of Latin American culture—the black, the Indian—that had been repressed or simply thought unfit as literary topics. In Cuba itself, there grew up during the 1920's and 1930's the *poesía negra* (black poetry) school, whose most prominent member is Nicolás Guillén.

"Aguas de recuerdo" is inscribed in this literary line. It is set in a small town not unlike Cabrera Infante's native Gibara and deals with the life of the poor. Its protagonist is a solitary old woman half-crazed with hunger. All she possesses are the memories of her family, her husband and sons, fishermen who were lost at sea under mysterious circumstances. The story tries to show how poverty and hunger reduce people to the level of animals. The stilted, artificial prose and melodrama are totally uncharacteristic of Cabrera Infante's mature style, but they show how the adolescent author attempted to capture the style then current in Cuban and Spanish-American literature. Here Cabrera Infante is writing within the stylistic parameters of other authors, as yet unprepared to attack that style through parody in order to find his own literary space.

That Cabrera Infante wrote in this realist-naturalist vein, and not in the Borgesean fantastic-metaphysical vein, reflects his literary sensibility during the late 1940's and early 1950's. He may have been too skeptical to follow in his parents' footsteps and become a party member, but it was inevitable

that his environment would influence him in some way. His father wrote and set type for the Communist-party newspaper *Hoy* (Today), and Carlos Franqui, an important leader of Fidel Castro's 26 July Movement, who would be editor of the highly influential newspaper *Revolución* during the early 1960's, lived for a time with the Cabrera Infantes. Franqui, who had been expelled from the Communist party but who remained a revolutionary socialist, collaborated with Cabrera Infante on several literary projects and in 1959 named him editor of *Lunes*. The Cabrera Infantes' Havana tenement room, the Zulueta 408 described in *Infante's Inferno*, was a meeting place for writers and artists—most of whom were on the left.

The most significant literary product of this combination of the style of Jean-Paul Sartre and socially critical literature is the short-story cycle *Así en la paz como en la guerra* (As in Peace, So in War), which includes material from the late 1940's but which was published only in 1960. Asked about the book in 1983, Cabrera Infante commented:

> There's juvenilia in that book but also some senilia. It was mostly written when I started writing movie criticism in the mid-fifties. I have nothing against the stories. In fact, half a dozen or so may be salvageable. But it's the book itself I object to. . . . Because it's a book not written but collected under the perverse influence of Sartre and his idea that a writer must not only write about a moment in History (like Marx he always capitalized the word), but also comment on his writing as well. Sartre also demands that the writer include *all* of society. It's esthetically hideous, a kind of social realism with a human face or a species of naturalism with a socialist conscience. Believe me, that book was collated with evil glue.
>
> (*Paris Review*, pp. 163–164)

Cabrera Infante's vehemence is clearly political as well as aesthetic. He expressly rejects those of his literary productions that would link him to the aesthetics of the radical left. But the very term "radical left" has a meaning in today's Cuba that it did not have during the 1940's and 1950's.

On 5 October 1952, Cabrera Infante published yet another of his socially committed short stories in *Bohemia*. With "Resaca" (Undertow), Cabrera Infante captured the attention of readers beyond the editorial offices of *Bohemia*, and he himself seems to have regarded the story as a satisfactory performance because he includes it in *Así en la paz como en la guerra*. The tale, like his first filled with pathos and action, concerns two men fleeing after setting fire to a sugarcane field. In a way reminiscent of John Steinbeck's *Of Mice and Men* (1937), Cabrera Infante presents two protagonists: Cheo, a large man, wounded and dying, and García, a small man, who distracts Cheo from his pain with his description of an "attainable Paradise."

García seeks to alleviate Cheo's anguish, but at the same time, he gives the reader a lesson in politics: "We'll all be equal. The Haitians will be equal to the owners. And we will be equal to the Chinese. There will be no unemployment or dead time. . . . There will be justice for all. Social justice. Yes, it will be a Paradise, a real Paradise." Here Cabrera Infante brings up the central issue in Cuban economic life: sugar production. The annual harvesting of sugar cane (the *safra*) was not done by Cuban workers alone; workers were brought in from other Caribbean nations, including Haiti. But by its nature, sugar production only requires this large supply of workers during the harvest, which means that for half the year the workers are virtually unemployed. This is the "dead time" to which García alludes.

Two weeks after "Resaca" appeared in *Bohemia*, the magazine published another story signed by Guillermo C. Infante: "Balada de plomo y yerro" (Ballad of Lead and Error), which Cabrera Infante also includes in *Así en la paz como en la guerra*. The title contains a pun: *yerro*, ("error," or in slang "small change") sounds like *hierro*, "iron." "Balada de plomo y yerro" has all the makings of a gangster yarn, and it is precisely the gangster world of Cuba during the 1950's, where political assassination and gangland murders were carried out by the same people, that Cabrera Infante seeks to evoke. The "error" in the title refers to the fact that the story's assassins kill the wrong man and work, as one of them puts it, "just for the fun of it."

The story is an exercise in black humor, but Batista's censors were not even mildly amused. Over the course of the tale, a drunken American sings an obscene song in English, and on the ground that his foul language was an "affront to common decency"

(preface to *Así en paz como en la guerra*), Cabrera Infante was jailed, fined, and obliged to leave journalism school for two years. (Cabrera Infante recounts the entire episode in the vignette "Obsceno," included in his 1975 book O.) To survive, he would have to write under the pseudonym G. Caín, a perfectly appropriate name for an outcast.

Así en la paz como en la guerra appeared in 1960, including both "Resaca" and "Balada de plomo y yerro." Its publication marks a moment of transition in Cabrera Infante's career. The book, which the author has repudiated, is in many ways a Janus: it looks backward to his days as a socially committed, realist-naturalist writer and forward to his explorations of literature as an end in itself. *Así en la paz* is itself caught between those two worlds. It divides into two independent sections: fifteen numbered vignettes, brief scenes of revolt and oppression in Batista's Cuba, and fourteen short stories that begin as politically oriented tales— "Resaca" and "Balada de plomo y yerro" are examples—in which ideas take precedence over character and end as short stories about specific characters. Cabrera Infante modeled *Así en la paz* on Ernest Hemingway's early book *In Our Time* (1924). The most striking of Hemingway's characters is Nick Adams, Hemingway's self-portrait, both an actor and a witness to action in these tales. Cabrera Infante's parallel in *Así en la paz* is a character named Silvestre, who reappears in *Three Trapped Tigers* as the book's controlling authority, the author-surrogate who redacts what the other characters say, who "translates" the spoken word into writing. The similarity between the stories in which Silvestre appears in *Así en la paz* and some of the scenes in *Three Trapped Tigers* is so striking that it is impossible to think they are not the same character.

By the same token, the vignettes interspersed in *Así en la paz* strongly resemble those originally written for inclusion in an early manuscript version of *Three Trapped Tigers* that carried the working title *Vista del amanecer en el trópico* (*View of Dawn in the Tropics*); that manuscript won the 1964 Biblioteca Breve Prize in Barcelona. (Those vignettes were taken out of the novel that became *Three Trapped Tigers* and were published in 1974 as *View of Dawn in the Tropics*.) This suggests that Cabrera Infante, from the late 1940's until the early 1960's, was writing in two distinct styles. *Así en la paz* is more a work in progress than a definitive text. In it, we find Cabrera Infante writing objective, reporterlike prose about the violence of the Batista era and subjective, psychological prose about his personal experiences, if we take Silvestre to be a reflection of Cabrera Infante. Thus *Así en la paz* is a prototype of what the original *View of Dawn* would have been if politics had not intervened in the author's life: a book in which vignettes from Cuban history dealing with repression and revolt were interspersed with scenes from the lives of characters living in Havana in 1958.

Así en la paz is a "timely" text, one that reflects a reality the author is now happy to consign to oblivion. The "view of dawn" in the title of the later book also alludes to the Cuban Revolution. Naturally, that title became ironic as the Revolution turned dark for Cabrera Infante, and he began to rewrite the book in 1965, during a time he was obliged to remain in Cuba after his mother's funeral. What *Three Trapped Tigers*, the rewritten version of *View of Dawn*, would seek to do would be the exact opposite of what happens in *Así en la paz*: to preserve the memory of a lost time rather than forget it. The triumphal song becomes an elegy.

It is clear after reading *Un oficio del siglo veinte* that Cabrera Infante is just as much a pen name as Caín. That is, Cabrera Infante had discovered in writing film reviews what Borges had discovered in writing book reviews, namely, that writing blurs the boundary between the real and the unreal, that to write means that the person becomes an author, which means he becomes a fiction. A writer is known by his writing: in a sense, he *becomes* that writing. Caín dies in this book because he ceases to write; thus, writing and living are identical.

But this behind-the-scenes struggle between the author and his alter-ego in no way diminishes the importance of Caín's film reviews. These articles, along with the lectures originally given in Havana in 1962 on Orson Welles, Alfred Hitchcock, Howard Hawks, John Huston, and Vincente Minnelli and published as *Arcadia todas las noches* (Arcadia Every Night, 1978), establish Cabrera Infante as a major film critic.

Caín's film reviews are vastly different from those that appear in our daily newspapers. His reviews usually ran to two thousand words (some much shorter, some much longer), so he had more space than the average reviewer. He could go into considerable depth—discuss technical matters (camera work, color processes, editing) as well as direction and secondary characters—in addition to evaluating the film. This extra information lent an erudite quality to these essays that makes them more like articles in a journal of film criticism than ordinary film reviews. This high level of sophistication recalls Borges' literary reviews in the magazine *Home* during the 1930's: both authors introduce intellectual concerns into a mass-market milieu and thus provide a link between so-called high and mass culture.

Cabrera Infante had founded, with friends, the Cinemateca de Cuba (Cuban Film Society) in 1951 and had helped to build that institution by establishing links with the Museum of Modern Art in New York, but in 1956, he tried to turn it into an anti-Batista organism. The idea failed, and the Batista regime took over the Cinemateca, which quickly died. But Cabrera Infante went on fighting Batista by writing for the underground newspaper *Revolución* (edited by Carlos Franqui) and serving, in 1958, as a liaison between the Communist party and the noncommunist urban guerrillas in the Directorio Revolucionario, for whom he had procured arms.

Batista's departure put Cabrera Infante in a position of some prominence. Not only was he editor of the Monday literary supplement to the now aboveground *Revolución*, but he was also chairman of both the National Cultural Council and the new film institute. He accompanied Fidel Castro on Castro's grand tour of the New World, visiting the United States, Canada, and several Latin-American republics. This was the Cuban Revolution's "open" phase, from January 1959 until the Bay of Pigs in 1961. Political differences were overlooked (Cabrera Infante, again, distrusted the Communist party and displayed decidedly Trotskyist sympathies: he mentions Isaac Deutscher's biography when he lists some of the books in Caín's library, and the parodic chapters on the death of Trotsky in *Three Trapped Tigers* reveal these sympathies), and Cuban intellectuals were sent everywhere to make propaganda for the new-style revolution being carried out in Cuba.

After the Bay of Pigs, orthodoxy and Communist-party control of the Revolution became facts of Cuban life. *Lunes* had extended its activities to include television (there were more television sets in Cuba in 1959 than there were in Italy). In 1960 Cabrera Infante's younger brother, Sabá, made a short film about Havana nightlife, *P.M.*, for *Lunes*, and it was shown on television. In 1961 the film was confiscated by the film institute and condemned as decadent. *Lunes* protested, but with disastrous results: *Lunes* was closed and Cabrera Infante fired from all his various positions.

Technically unemployed—he was nominally vice-president of the writers union, an honorary position that was something of a joke—he began to write "Ella cantaba boleros" a section of the manuscript that would become first *View of Dawn in the Tropics* and then *Three Trapped Tigers*. At the same time, he pieced together *Un oficio del siglo veinte*, whose subversive quality was as powerful under Castro as it had been under Batista. To get him out of the way without causing any scandal, the Castro government, in 1962, named him cultural attaché to Belgium. The translation of *Así en la paz* into French, Italian, and Polish in 1963 gained Cabrera Infante some European fame, and when the manuscript of *View of Dawn* won the Biblioteca Breve Prize in 1964, his international career was launched. The Castro government rewarded him that same year by naming him Cuban chargé d'affaires for Belgium and Luxembourg.

In June 1965, Cabrera Infante returned to Havana for his mother's funeral. Already embittered because he felt she might have lived had she been given better medical treatment, he became totally disillusioned with Castro's Cuba when he saw how Havana had changed since his departure in 1962. He felt the city had been turned into a tropical version of the grim Eastern European capitals he had visited in 1960 and that his former Cuban friends had been turned into political automatons. He was finally allowed to return to Brussels toward the end of 1965. He took with him his two young daughters by his first marriage. (He was divorced in 1960 and married the actress Miriam Gómez in 1961.)

Unlike his brother, Sabá, who sought political asylum in the United States, Cabrera Infante simply left Brussels with his family and moved to Madrid, taking up residence in a Spain still controlled by General Franco, a place where he might have expected Cuban influence would not reach. He was mistaken: first the manuscript of *View of Dawn in the Tropics* was rejected by the Spanish censor, and then, in 1966, he was himself ejected by the Spanish government for having written anti-Franco articles in *Lunes* and elsewhere. In point of fact, relations between the fascist Franco and the communist Castro were quite cordial—Cuba was buying buses from Spain—and the Spaniards were eager to prove that enemies of Castro would not be welcome in Spain.

Experiencing extreme economic difficulty, Cabrera Infante moved his family in late 1966 to London, where he attempted to make a living writing screenplays. Purged of its political content, completely rewritten in self-exile, *Three Trapped Tigers* appeared early in 1967.

In 1968 in the Argentine weekly magazine *Primera Plana* (First Page), Cabrera Infante denounced the Castro regime publicly. (He would redouble his criticism in the extensive interview he granted to Rita Guibert in October 1970, published in *Seven Voices*.) The political storm was incredibly violent. Within Cuba, he was declared a traitor; supporters of the Castro regime outside Cuba echoed that condemnation. This meant that Cabrera Infante was a man doubly without a country: he was decidedly persona non grata in Cuba and was also expelled from the "invisible church" of the Latin-American intelligentsia supporting the Cuban Revolution. These pressures took their toll. Despite his success with the screenplay for *Vanishing Point*, a Guggenheim Fellowship (1970), and an invitation from Joseph Losey to write a script for Malcolm Lowry's *Under the Volcano* (the screenplay was completed in 1972 but never filmed), his mental health deteriorated. He suffered a collapse in the summer of 1972 and had to be hospitalized. His slow recovery meant that he would not publish anything until 1974, when the vignettes of *View of Dawn in the Tropics* appeared.

Slowly rebuilding his life and career in London, Cabrera Infante managed to publish two books of literary essays, *O* in 1975 and *Exorcismos de esti(l)o* (Exorcisms of Style) in 1976. *O*—the title refers to the letter "o"—is a seemingly miscellaneous collection of essays. It covers such disparate topics as the demise of "swinging London" in 1968, Cabrera Infante's Siamese cat Offenbach, an ironic essay on the popular Spanish novelist Corín Tellado, a meditation on Lewis Carroll, and reflections on Cuban popular songs.

In the 1983 *Paris Review* interview, Cabrera Infante describes *Exorcismos de esti(l)o* in this way:

> The title is obviously an homage to Raymond Queneau and, at the same time, an advertisement for itself because of its complicated asymmetry. It means many things: the exorcizing of style, exercises in summertime, even the lure of the pen—all in a send-up of *Exercises de Style*. This is one of my favorites among my own books and it closes the cycle begun in my collected movie reviews, *Un oficio del siglo veinte* (1962). In *Exorcismos*, I expanded my experience (not experiment, a word I loathe when I see it applied to art instead of science) with Havanese, the idiom of *habaneros*, who might perhaps be called *hablaneros* or total talkers. Most of it was written while I was a cultural attaché at the Cuban embassy in Brussels (1962)—and it shows. It contains many messages from an Edmundo Dantés, who read his own name as Inmundo Dantesco, the prisoner of Ifs, waiting for some Abbé Faria and passing time scratching graffiti on the filthy walls of his cell. One of the writings on the wall is a piece on Brillat-Savarin (1765–1826), the gourmet and amateur musician trapped by the French Revolution. I also like a short (one page) biography of Stalin's embalmer, a man the tyrant exiled to Siberia. I can still feel the embalmer's ghoulish glee as he ripped open the belly of the beast. For a moment I was the embalmer and Stalin had a Spanish name.
>
> (pp. 166–167)

Cabrera Infante's reputation as a writer is not based on either *O* or *Exorcismos* because these are relatively unknown, very personal books. His international fame derives from his two major works, *Three Trapped Tigers* and *Infante's Inferno*. It is possible to delineate two phases in Cabrera Infante's literary career: a period of literary social criticism—the early stories included in *Así en la paz* and the vignettes that formed part of the original manuscript of *Three Trapped Tigers* and a period of autobiographical writing that transformed the linguistic realism of the first phase into an attempt to capture the spoken language of a period. The latter phase includes the latest stories in *Así en la paz, Un oficio del siglo veinte, Three Trapped Tigers,* and *Infante's Inferno*.

At the same time that this conflict between literature as a tool for social criticism and literature as a disinterested aesthetic activity is going on within his works, one presence unifies them all. This is the controlling voice or directorial presence that first appears in *Así en la paz* when the character Silvestre appears. Silvestre is a surrogate for the author himself and reappears in *Three Trapped Tigers* as the assembler-redactor of the text in which he appears as a character. His function is not unlike that of Cabrera Infante himself vis-à-vis Caín in *Un oficio del siglo veinte*, but the difference appears in Silvestre's conflict-of-interest dilemma, his having to deform the spoken word by writing it down, and his betrayal of the other characters by inevitably twisting their words for his own purposes.

Written—or rewritten, since the published version differs so radically from the original manuscript, which had been distorted first by the Spanish censor—by a man who felt he had been betrayed by the Cuban Revolution, *Three Trapped Tigers* is itself about betrayal: "But after all, betrayal is the name of the game in *TTT*: betrayal of life through language and literature. The ultimate betrayal is in translation, of literature and of language, of life" (*Paris Review*, p. 171).

Infante's Inferno, as its name implies, is a putting to rest of the character who gives unity to almost all of Cabrera Infante's writings—himself through his avatars. That dead self, that "infante difunto" who punningly replaces the dead princess in Maurice Ravel's "Pavane pour une infante defunte" appears on the cover of Cabrera Infante's text. Or rather, he appears as a point of view—the objective lens of a camera. The original cover of the novel is a photograph by Jesse Fernández taken in 1948: it shows a street photographer sitting in Havana's Parque Central, the purveyor of souvenirs (memories, after all) turned himself into a souvenir.

Infante's Inferno follows the traditional pattern of confessional narrative, especially that subspecies of confessional writing known as the consolation, after Boethius' *Consolation of Philosophy*. These texts proceed in a fairly fixed fashion. At the beginning, the narrator finds himself confused, lost, in a state of spiritual distress. He suffers an "identity crisis" and is not sure who he really is. He wants help but does not know how to find it. Then, either through outside intervention (divine grace, for example) or through a plunge into his inner self, he begins to sort out his personal possibilities: he finds out who he is not and who it is he might be. Finally, he succeeds in discovering or recovering his identity, and his narrative ends.

In 1979, in addition to publishing *Infante's Inferno*, Cabrera Infante became a British subject. While his primary mode of expression is still Cuban Spanish, he has been writing more and more directly in English. Two texts, totally different in nature, reflect this linguistic drift. "Bites from the Bearded Crocodile" (the title playfully alludes to the Cuban version, *El Caimán Barbudo* [The Bearded Crocodile], of the Soviet humor publication *Crocodile*) is a denunciation of the cultural renascence the Castro regime proudly declares to be one of its major accomplishments. The article appeared in the *London Review of Books*. *Holy Smoke*, a long essay on the relationship between cigars and cinema, is a continuation of Cabrera Infante's lifelong interest in cinema by other means. He seizes on the cigar—one of his own personal vices—as a movie prop and gives a humorous history of its use in virtually all movie genres, from gangster movies to horror films.

Cabrera Infante insists that "Cuerpos Divinos" (Divine Bodies), his work in progress, is neither a political nor a historical novel, that its main subject is language, the Cuban Spanish of a still-free Havana. The novel continues the process begun in *Infante's Inferno*, the dispersion of the authority figure, the author surrogate, in Cabrera Infante's works. Here literary discourse is conceived of as free speech, language unfettered, free of authoritarian control— and this may explain why the manuscript has grown so huge that even the author despairs of publishing it.

Guillermo Cabrera Infante debunks the image of the mature writer who assumes a senatorial posture in order to pontificate on life and art. His outlook remains fresh, his approach to writing as innovative as it has ever been. He may be embittered by the disastrous intervention of politics in his life, but without the experience of exile, he might still be editing magazines in Havana instead of writing novels abroad. Personal happiness and literary success do not necessarily go hand in hand; the consolation here is

that out of the crucible of hideous experience have emerged glorious works of art.

SELECTED BIBLIOGRAPHY

Editions

"Aguas de recuerdo." *Bohemia* 40/24: 20–21, 64–66 (13 June 1948).

Así en la paz como en la guerra. Havana, 1960.

Un oficio del siglo veinte. Havana, 1963.

Tres tristes tigres. Barcelona, 1967.

"Delito por bailar el chachachá." In *Guillermo Cabrera Infante*. Madrid, 1974. Pp. 217–253. (A fragment of "Cuerpos Divinos.")

Vista del amanecer en el trópico. Barcelona, 1974.

O. Barcelona, 1975.

Exorcismos de esti(l)o. Barcelona, 1976.

Arcadia todas las noches. Barcelona, 1978.

La Habana para un infante difunto. Barcelona, 1979.

"Bites from the Bearded Crocodile." *London Review of Books* 3/10: 3–8 (June 1981).

Holy Smoke. London, 1985.

Translations

Infante's Inferno. Translated by Suzanne Jill Levine. New York, 1984.

Three Trapped Tigers. Translated by Donald Gardner and Suzanne Jill Levine in collaboration with the author. New York, 1971.

View of Dawn in the Tropics. Translated by Suzanne Jill Levine. New York, 1978.

Biographical And Critical Studies

Cabrera Infante, Guillermo. "The Art of Fiction LXXV." *Paris Review* 87:154–195 (1983).

Guibert, Rita. *Seven Voices: Seven Latin American Writers Talk to Rita Guibert*. Translated by Frances Partridge. With an introduction by Emir Rodríguez Monegal. New York, 1973.

Levine, Suzanne Jill. "Three Trapped Tigers and a Cobra." *Modern Language Notes* 90/2: 265–277 (1975).

Ludmer, Josefina. "*Tres tristes tigres*: Órdenes literarios y jerarquías sociales." *Revista iberoamericana* 108–109: 493–512 (1979).

MacAdam, Alfred J. "Guillermo Cabrera Infante: The Vast Fragment." In his *Modern Latin American Narratives: The Dreams of Reason*. Chicago, 1977. Pp. 61–68.

Merrim, Stephanie. *Logos and the Word: The Novel of Language and Linguistic Motivation in "Grande Sertão: Veredas" and "Tres tristes tigres."* New York, 1983.

Nelson, Ardis. *"Tres tristes tigres* y el cine." *J. M. Hill Monograph Series* 3 (1976).

Ortega, Julio, et al. *Guillermo Cabrera Infante.* Madrid, 1974.

Siemens, William L. "*Heilsgeschichte* and the Structure of *Tres tristes tigres.*" *Kentucky Romance Quarterly* 22/1:77–90 (1975).

_____. "Guillermo Cabrera Infante: Man of Three Islands." *Review: Latin-American Literature and Art.* January–April, 1981. Pp. 8–11.

World Literature Today 61/4 (1987). Contains papers on Cabrera Infante's work delivered at the Eleventh Puterbaugh Conference on Writers of the French-Speaking and Hispanic World as well as lectures given by Cabrera Infante. Also includes a bibliography of works by and about Cabrera Infante.

Jorge Díaz

(1930–   )

George Woodyard

The renovation of the modern Chilean theater began in 1941 when a combination of positive political, economic, and intellectual factors coincided to produce the Experimental Theater of the University of Chile. A similar impetus two years later in the Catholic University helped to professionalize the movement, leading away from the commercialism that had characterized the Chilean theater toward the best of world theater staged with modern techniques. A new generation of Chilean directors and authors (Egon Wolff, Alejandro Sieveking, Luis Alberto Heiremans, and others) guided the theater into psychological realism and sociopolitical compromise.

Jorge Díaz, one of Chile's premier playwrights, was from the beginning both a product of and a rebel in the movement. His later plays transcended an early identification with the theater of the absurd as his search for a language adequate to dramatize the incongruities and frustrations of life in a bourgeois world led him through different stages of development. His basic themes are the difficulties of communication, the dehumanizing effects of society, and the need for relief for the oppressed. An irrepressible humor, often with a corrosive tone, suffuses his work, and his originality is evident in the constant linguistic play and the structural device of the game. Ambiguity and shifting realities with subtle nuances

of cyclical time are trademarks, as much as his attention to details of integrating lighting, music, costuming, and set design.

Díaz was born in 1930 to Spanish parents in Rosario, Argentina. He arrived in Chile in 1934, attended San Pedro Nolasco, earned good grades, and remembers shunning parties and meetings even as a child. With a degree in architecture from the Catholic University in Santiago, he entered professional practice for a short time after graduation in 1955. Attracted to the theater, he studied for two years at the Theater Academy of the Catholic University of Chile, and joined Ictus, a professional company, in 1959. With natural talents in poetry and painting, he moved easily into acting and set design.

Two one-act plays presented as a double bill by Ictus in May of 1961 marked Díaz as a vanguard dramatist, a pioneer in linguistic structure and form. (Two earlier plays, considered "juvenile" by Díaz, have been suppressed.) In *Un hombre llamado Isla* (A Man Called Island) the monologue style (actually a solipsistic dialogue) captured the solitude and anguish of a petty bureaucrat who suffers through a loathsome job and subsequent frustrating retirement. The play that shared the program—*El cepillo de dientes* (The Toothbrush), rewritten in 1966 as a full-length play—was more developed and has become a modern classic. The two characters, an essentially anonymous He and She, engage in a daily ritual of bizarre games to overcome the boredom of their bourgeois existence. With a three-tiered play-within-a-play technique combined with character doubling, the play reminded critics of Eugene Ionesco's *Bald Soprano* and Harold Pinter's *The Caretaker*, both of which had played earlier in Santiago. Díaz achieved originality through his language: the clichéd phrases, slogans, and commercials typified the decadence of these two characters searching desperately for a means of communication, while the confusion produced by misplaced antecedents and nonsequiturs created nonsense, and therefore humor. The character/actor interaction with the public broke conventional styles. At the same time the inherent violence anticipated a dominant motif, not only in Díaz' theater, but in theater throughout the world. Díaz had made his mark in the theater of the absurd.

In rapid succession Díaz premiered five other plays with Ictus. The common denominators throughout were the linguistic and game play, cyclical time, black humor, musical motifs, and an insistence that communication difficulties and bourgeois societies thwart the development of human potential. *Réquiem por un girasol* (Requiem for a Sunflower, 1961)* and *El lugar donde mueren los mamíferos* (*The Place Where the Mammals Die*, 1963) both emphasized the ghoulish nature of bourgeois values that exploit the weak. In *Mammals* the charitable institution that becomes an instrument of aggression echoes, in a slightly different way, the greater concern shown for dead animals than for living people in *Réquiem*. *El velero en la botella* (The Sailboat in the Bottle, 1962) continued Díaz' concern with communication—the power of the word—through the plaintive cry of a youth, metaphorically mute, estranged within the hostile world of his relatives. *Variaciones para muertos de percusión* (Variations for the Percussive Dead, 1964) emphasized, as did *El cepillo de dientes*, the excessive commercialization of modern lives. And *El nudo ciego* (The Blind Knot, 1965) proved to be the most experimental technologically as the subliminal messages transmitted through individual earphones-

*Date in parentheses reflects play's premiere; date in bibliography reflects play's publication.

brought new perspectives to the investigation of a homicide in Chile's coal-mining region.

Early in 1965, Díaz left Ictus and his administrative duties as president, seeking in Spain the solitude necessary for his writing. Since that time he has been living, unmarried, in Madrid, a somewhat reclusive and spartan existence.

Disdainful of the theater public's penchant for easy laughter without real commitment, Díaz entered a new phase. His plays written in Spain between 1965 and 1969 acquire hyperbolic dimensions in both theme and technique. In *Topografía de un desnudo* (Topography of a Nude, 1967) inspired by the massacre of Brazilian slum-dwellers, the central character inexplicably returns from the dead to help investigate his own murder. The documentary base is mitigated by the imaginative nonsequential time and plot structure as well as the integration of slides and film to heighten the emotional impact on the audience. The humor of the earlier plays is gone. Couched in techniques of total theater, the appalling message is that greed and insensitivity permit unrestrained violence against other humans, especially the marginal classes. Equally chilling is *La víspera del degüello* (The Eve of the Decapitation, 1970), earlier titled *El génesis fue mañana* (The Genesis Was Tomorrow), an enigmatic title for a one-act apocalyptic piece based on the three survivors of a nuclear explosion. In a search for "Paradise," they create grotesque images that obliterate their slim chance of re-creating a world.

The next three plays are equally aggressive and flagrant in theme and technique. With a not-so-subtle documentary style, *Introducción al elefante y otras zoologías* (Introduction to the Elephant and Other Zoologies, 1968) chides Latin Americans for passively accepting North American imperialism. *Liturgia para cornudos* (Liturgy for Cuckolds, 1970) protests virtually everything—religion, sex, humor, and protest itself. *La orgástula* (1973), a pseudo-erotic piece involving homicide written with Spanish syntax but invented words, caps off the period and the obsessive urge to communicate. With this play (its title is untranslatable), Díaz considered that he had achieved an amusing and suggestive game, but one he could not replicate.

In 1970, Díaz expanded his role in the theater,

acting for the first time in his own works. With the Chilean actress Magdalena Aguirre he formed an independent group, Teatro del Nuevo Mundo (New World Theater), to present plays in Spanish schools, cultural institutes, and later on tour throughout the world, in the United States and Australia, among other countries. The group performed primarily works of political protest, plus some children's theater. *La pancarta, o Está estrictamente prohibido todo lo que no es obligatorio* (The Political Placard, or Everything That Is Not Obligatory Is Strictly Forbidden, 1971), deals with class struggle and the certain venality of the oppressed who rise to power. When the play was later rewritten as *Amaos los unos vs. los otros* (Love the Ones vs. the Others, 1971), Díaz returned to his traditional humor and linguistic play, as he did also with *Americaliente* (HotAmerica, 1971). A bombastic and polemical collage of sketches about atrocities, genocide, repression, and alienation, the play cries out against the painful presence of the United States in political and economic affairs throughout Latin America.

During this period Díaz collaborated on several plays with a Spaniard living in Stockholm, Francisco Javier Uriz. *Mear contra el viento* (Piss into the Wind; broadcast premiere in 1974, stage premiere in 1976), written for Swedish television, is a rabid denunciation of the involvement of International Telephone and Telegraph in Chilean domestic matters (based on reports published by Jack Anderson) and the subsequent participation of the United States in the fall of the government of Salvador Allende in 1973. The title symbolizes the futility, according to a leftist leader, of trying to stop the popular revolutionary movement. Two other collaborative plays, *Los alacranes* (The Scorpions) and *Las hormigas* (The Ants, both 1973), also deal violently with aspects of exploitation, discrimination, and corruption. In the first play the scorpions infest a drought-plagued area controlled by a merciless landowner; in the second play, set in New York, red and black ants connote racial prejudices and the imperialistic struggle for control.

Díaz' vitriolic pen did not, however, reflect his personal behavior. Painfully shy in public earlier, he overcame his timidity but continued to defend his right to choose his own friends, to live without pretense, and to control his own time. In short, he insisted on living apart from society because only solitude allowed him the freedom to make choices that were essential to his artistic creativity.

In 1975 the death of Francisco Franco, Spain's longtime dictator, brought a new sense of freedom to the Spanish theater and coincided with an end to Díaz' New World Theater. He began to participate more in his environment, took out dual citizenship (Chile and Spain), and wrote plays that fall into distinct categories: some with Spanish syntax and vocabulary, others more Chilean; some focusing on sociopolitical issues, others more personal, domestic, and intimate. *Mata a tu prójimo como a ti mismo* (Kill Thy Neighbor as Thyself, 1976) is an obvious distortion of the biblical commandment. Reality is unstable, just as it was in *El nudo ciego*. Two sisters, interchangeable in their black and white motifs, re-create the past through games of creative delusion with a young man, echoing the sadomasochistic eroticism of *La orgástula*. Díaz remarked once that he wrote "about death and sex, not knowing other themes, because to do so is to write about life." *Ceremonia ortopédica* (Orthopedic Ceremony, 1976), a revision of *Liturgia para cornudos*, continues the ceremonial and ritual aspects of violence, sex, and death between parents, immersed in artificial values, and their only son, who abandons them. "Orthopedic" connotes both artificiality (Díaz does not create fully developed characters) as well as "proper child-rearing" from its Greek etymology. *Contrapunto para dos voces cansadas, o El locutorio* (Counterpoint for Two Tired Voices, or The Locutory, 1979) again uses game play to present the solitude, frustration, and anguish of two old people confined to an institution. Later rewritten as "Entre las voces, una" (Among the Voices, One, as yet unproduced), the same setting allows for new dimensions of fantasy. Unlike the earlier version, the enigmatic quality disappears, replaced by sentimentality and a happy ending that are unusual, if not otherwise unknown, in a Díaz play.

Following were two plays written in popular language that deal with the fringe elements in Madrid society. *La puñeta* (Up Shit Creek, 1977), is based on poems by the Chilean poet Nicanor Parra. *Un día es un día, o Los sobrevivientes* (A Day Is a Day, or the

Survivors, 1978) deals with variations on the oppressor/oppressed syndrome. In *La manifestación* (The Demonstration, 1979), the narrow line between life and death parallels the vagueness and confusion in political positions.

During the 1980's Díaz continued to be prolific and committed to social change. Although not allied with any political position, he advocated freedom from all oppression. The most ambitious work of this period is *Desde la sangre y el silencio, o Fulgor y muerte de Pablo Neruda* (From Blood and Silence, or Splendor and Death of Pablo Neruda, 1984), a work commissioned by the Oxford Playhouse Theatre that re-creates the last four months in the life of Pablo Neruda. Framed within scenes from Neruda's own play about the infamous bandit Joaquín Murieta, the play captures both the joy and pain of Neruda's last days as his death by cancer coincides with the fall of the Allende regime in 1973. Time is expanded through imaginative flashback and flash-forward sequences that personalize the larger-than-life Chilean Nobel laureate. Two other plays mirror aspects of the 1973 military coup: *Canto subterráneo para blindar una paloma* (Subterranean Chant to Shield a Dove) is a spine-chilling revision of *Toda ésta larga noche* (This Whole Long Night, 1981; produced in England as "My Song Is Free") in which a jail cell is a microcosm of terror for four women, "disappeared" political prisoners, who are tortured for their involvement in subversive activities; *Ligeros de equipaje* (Traveling Light, 1982) echoes the insecurities of an actress, a survivor of the Spanish Civil War and the Chilean coup, in her dressing-room monologue on an opening night.

Between 1970, the year of *Liturgia para cornudos*, and 1982, Díaz premiered his new plays in Madrid. In July 1982 *Piel contra piel* (Skin Against Skin) opened in Santiago, Chile. The play is, in a sense, *Cepillo de dientes* come of age—staged twenty-one years later and enacted by the original cast. Suffering the anguish of the "gray syndrome" (midlife crisis), the two characters seek an escape from the emptiness of their despondent, unfulfilled lives as they play roles in a new search for happiness with each other. In 1984 a revised version of *Mata a tu prójimo*, titled *Esplendor carnal de la ceniza* (Carnal Radiance of the Ashes), opened in Santiago. Still hermetic, it synthesized Díaz' prefer-

ence for the dynamics of life (movement, sex, change) over death (passivity and self-destruction), even though the choice leads to violence.

Díaz' obsession with misguided politics does not reduce his concern for people in other social settings. Three recent plays, as yet unperformed, reflect the vicissitudes of a society plagued by drugs, television, and the loss of values. *Andrea* dramatizes the pathos of a runaway adolescent whose life is sacrificed on the altar of a "progressive" society where sex and drugs are more easily accessible than values, goals, and a sense of self-worth. *El extraterrestre* (The Extraterrestrial) echoes the theme through a despicable television-addicted child whose parents are involved in divorce. *Todas las fiestas del mañana* (All Tomorrow's Parties), with its title from a Lou Reed song, creates a punk-rock atmosphere in which death by overdose is the norm.

Some elements of *El extraterrestre* were incorporated into a full-length play about domestic tension in a post-Franco society; under the title *Las cicatrices de la memoria* (Scars of Memories, 1987), the play won the Tirso de Molina prize for 1985 and has since been retitled *Ayer, sin ir mas lejos* (Yesterday, Without Going Further). A play with the original title *Instrucciones para hacer una donación voluntaria* (Instructions on Voluntary Donations) was published and performed under the title *Muero, luego existo* (I Die, Therefore I Exist, 1988), and captures the desperation of a mercenary blood donor engaged in a futile search for escape from grinding poverty and despair. Díaz continues to write, publish, and premiere plays with an astounding regularity, always focusing on the issues that are foremost, from his perspective, within the society. As of this writing, another eight or ten plays have either been recently produced or are awaiting production and publication.

In addition, Díaz also writes children's theater. Since the early years in Chile, at times in collaboration with Mónica Echeverría and others, he has written some twenty-five pieces that contrast with the skeptical, disenchanted work he writes for adults. His fascination with children's theater is rooted in two features: a nostalgia for infancy and the desire to play; and the theatrical convention of the happy ending. The plays are lively, often predicated on a central folkloric or classical figure presented in understandable terms, and captivating for a young, or young-at-heart, audience. Since the dissolution of New World Theater, a group called Trabalenguas (Tongue Twisters) has presented his children's plays. Paradoxically, Díaz normally shuns the theater and rarely attends productions of his own plays, with the exception of the children's theater, which he totally enjoys.

Jorge Díaz is a prolific playwright whose works have been translated into other languages and performed throughout the world. Many of his plays have won prestigious prizes and awards in national and international competitions. Each period of Díaz' career has proved him to be an inveterate experimenter willing to challenge the conventions both of society and of theater craft in dealing with the most fundamental aspects of human existence—life, love, sex, violence, and death. More than any of his contemporaries, he has brought a new language to the Chilean theater.

SELECTED BIBLIOGRAPHY

Editions

Plays

Variaciones para muertos en [de] percusión. Conjunto 1 (1964).

Teatro: La víspera del degüello, El cepillo de dientes, Réquiem por un girasol. Madrid, 1967.

Topografía de un desnudo. Santiago, Chile, 1967.

La orgástula. Latin American Theatre Review 4/1:79–83 (1970).

El lugar donde mueren los mamíferos. Madrid, 1972.

El velero en la botella; El cepillo de dientes. Santiago, Chile, 1973.

Mear contra el viento. With Francisco Uriz. *Conjunto* 21 (1974).

Teatro. Ceremonias de la soledad: El locutorio, Mata a tu prójimo como a ti mismo, Ceremonia ortopédica. Santiago, Chile, 1978.

Ecuación. Estreno 9/2:17–23 (1983).

Las cicatrices de la memoria (Finale: Allegro ma non troppo). Madrid, 1986.

Commentaries

Díaz, Jorge. "A manera de algo que no sé lo que es." In *Teatro.* Madrid, 1967. Pp. 55–57.

———. "Dos comunicaciones" ("Itinerario" and "La ero-

sión del lenguaje"). *Latin American Theatre Review* 4/1:73–78 (1970).

———. "Lucha cuerpo a cuerpo conmigo mismo." *Estreno* 9/2:3–6 (1983).

Translations

The Place Where the Mammals Die. Translated by Naomi Nelson. In *The Modern Stage in Latin America: Six Plays,* edited by George W. Woodyard. New York, 1971.

Biographical and Critical Studies

Burgess, Ronald D. "*El cepillo de dientes*: Empty Words. Empty Games?" *Estreno* 9/2:29–31 (1983).

Castedo-Ellerman, Elena. In *El teatro chileno de mediados del siglo XX.* Santiago, Chile, 1982. Pp. 124–141.

Fernández, Teodosio. In *El teatro chileno contemporáneo (1941–1973).* Madrid, 1982. Pp. 153–167.

Holzapfel, Tamara. "Jorge Díaz y la dinámica del absurdo teatral." *Estreno* 9/2:32–35 (1983).

Ivelić K., Radoslav. "El teatro y su verbo, en torno a la dramaturgia de Jorge Díaz." In *Anales.* Santiago, Chile, 1969. Pp. 17–28.

Kronik, John. Guest editor of special issue of *Estreno* 9/2 (1983) dedicated to theater of Jorge Díaz.

Molina-Lipsky, Liliam. "La incomunicación en dos dramas de Jorge Díaz." *Estreno* 9/2:15–16 (1983).

Monleón, José. "Jorge Díaz, una versión de Latinoamérica." In Jorge Díaz, *Teatro.* Madrid, 1967. Pp. 11–36.

Nigro, Kirsten F. "Stage and Audience: Jorge Díaz's *El lugar donde mueren los mamíferos* and *Topografía de un desnudo.*" *Estreno* 9/2:36–40 (1983).

Piña, Juan Andrés. "Jorge Díaz: La vanguardia teatral chilena." In Jorge Díaz, *Teatro: Ceremonias de la soledad.* Santiago, Chile, 1978. Pp. 7–49.

Quackenbush, L. Howard. "Jorge Díaz, la desmitificación religiosa y el culto a la vida." *Estreno* 9/2:9–12 (1983).

Villegas, Juan. "Teatro y público: El teatro de Jorge Díaz." *Estreno* 9/2:7–9 (1983).

Woodyard, George W. "Jorge Díaz and the Liturgy of Violence." In *Dramatists in Revolt: The New Latin American Theater,* edited by Leon F. Lyday and George W. Woodyard. Austin, Tex. and London, 1976. Pp. 59–76.

———. "Ritual as Reality in Díaz's *Mata a tu prójimo como a ti mismo.*" *Estreno* 9/2:13–15 (1983).

Jorge Edwards

(1931–   )

Miriam Balboa Echeverría

A somewhat controversial figure in the recent decades of Spanish-American prose, Jorge Edwards is best known for his work *Persona non grata* (published in English with the same title, 1973), which narrates his experience as the Chilean chargé de affaires in Fidel Castro's Cuba. He is well known in his country as a creative writer, journalist, diplomat, and literary critic. His published work includes prose fiction, political commentary, journalistic articles and literary studies. A person of strong opinions, Edwards is never afraid of controversy in defending his literary and political views. He is not formally associated with any political party, but he declares himself to be part of the democratic left. Because of the scandal that ensued in Latin America after the publication of his book *Persona Non Grata*, Mario Vargas Llosa, the Peruvian novelist, declared, "He broke the sacred taboo among intellectuals: the untouchability of the Cuban Revolution."

Jorge Edwards was born on 29 July 1931 in Santiago, Chile. These were the final years of General Carlos Ibáñez del Campo's dictatorship, and the beginning of the constitutional year that lasted until September 1973. Edwards attended secondary school at the Colegio de San Ignacio de Santiago, and began his law and philosophy studies at the University of Chile. During those years, he came in contact with a number of young writers and poets who welcomed him enthusiastically. At this time, he published his first collection of short stories in an audacious volume entitled *El patio* (The Backyard) in 1952.

After he received his law degree in 1958, Edwards became a member of the Chilean diplomatic corps. He was in charge of Common Market affairs and also served as legal adviser to the government. In 1959 Edwards traveled to the United States on an assignment from the Chilean government to study political science at Princeton University. While he and his wife were living in the United States, he wrote *Gente de la ciudad* (People of the City), which was published in 1961. While in Paris as secretary of the Chilean embassy and representative for European affairs, he wrote three books, *El peso de la noche* (Night's Burden, 1961), *Las máscaras* (The Masks, 1967), and *Temas y variaciones* (Themes and Variations, 1969).

Back in Chile in 1967, Edwards played an important role in negotiating Chile's diplomatic relations with socialist countries as chairman of the department of Eastern affairs. In December 1970, while working as attaché to the Chilean embassy in Lima, Peru, he was sent to Havana as the first diplomatic representative of Salvador Allende's socialist government. He had the particularly delicate mission of reinstating relations between Chile and Cuba. *Per-*

sona Non Grata is the passionate and polemical account of this experience. The book did not appear until 1973, after the military coup in Chile. It chronicles Edwards' personal experiences and point of view about Cuban political and cultural values. Edwards' clear criticism of what he saw as cultural repression produced a scandal among the militant writers of the left. The battle that ensued earned Edwards a reputation as a writer with essentially bourgeois concerns. His polemical nature has always attracted both suspicion and hostility because of his ongoing collaboration with the leading newspaper, *El Mercurio,* which is owned by a wealthy branch of the Edwardses, one of Chile's most powerful families.

Because of his unsympathetic views of the Cuban Revolution, Edwards was asked to leave Havana and the country in 1971. Upon his forced departure he was sent to Paris to assist the Chilean ambassador, Nobel Prize–winner Pablo Neruda, who was very ill at the time. In October 1973 Edwards was expelled from the diplomatic corps by General Augusto Pinochet Ugarte, the Chilean dictator. Since then he has resided both in Spain and in Chile, where he continues writing. Three more recent works give his novelistic world a more definite shape: *Los convidados de piedra* (The Guests Made of Stone, 1978), *El museo de cera* (Wax Museum, 1981), and *La mujer imaginaria* (The Unreal Woman, 1985).

Edwards' political ideas are today expressed through the Committee for Freedom of Expression of the Chilean Commission on Human Rights, on which he currently serves as president. His support for the dissident forces in Chile was clearly stated in an interview with the *Christian Science Monitor* in 1983: "Chile is no longer afraid and we are emerging from the barbarity of the dictatorship."

In spite of his political notoriety, Edwards is first of all a writer. His intense and condensed works should be given a central place in the complex totality of Chilean literature. He started his career as a modestly successful writer of short stories, yet his first collection, *El patio,* was poles apart from the literary tradition then in fashion. The best-known writers of the 1940's were interested in the rural dimension of Chilean life. Consequently, they had developed an artistic form of expression called *criollismo* (a narrative form of new-folklorism). Edwards broke away

from that tradition by introducing in his first collection autobiographical themes and a poetic mood. He stressed that his reading of James Joyce, William Faulkner, and Marcel Proust served him as an antidote to *criollismo.* The short stories narrate moments in the life of a young man of the bourgeoisie who feels alienated from his own world. Edwards scrutinizes the middle class from its marginal perspectives, showing its social disintegration and decadence and not its better-known aspects of opulence and success.

In *Gente de la ciudad* Edwards' view is perhaps more intensely critical and dispassionate. Here the central theme is the world of the bureaucracy. The clerks, municipal employees, and underworld characters who populate the world of the book are shown as wasted and dehumanized by an oppressive bureaucracy.

The third collection, *Las máscaras,* is a turning point in Edwards' development as a short-story writer. He breaks away from social realism and experiments with the perception of time and simultaneity. He plays with new narrative techniques, and poses the question of the limits between reality and fantasy.

A further elaboration of this theme can be seen in the next collection, *Temas y variaciones.* The stories center on familiar subjects in Edwards' works: self-destruction, isolation, anguish, and the desire for utopia. Edwards' vision is richer in experience, and he shows a better command of literary techniques than in his earlier work. In the story "Orden familiar" (Family Order), he explores the theme of incestuous love by manipulating time, probing the intertwining of memory and history, presenting the narrator's search for "time lost," in the Proustean sense. The characters are impoverished young men from the middle class who are vegetating in the realms of the bureaucracy, dissident teenagers who always go back to the protection of their families. Oppression and anguish are the dominant moods of the stories.

Edwards has written four novels. The first, *El peso de la noche,* connects thematically with the world of the short stories. The novel's two principal dimensions are an intense concentration on the middle-class family structure and its slow disintegration, and an inquiry into the influence of social class upon the bureaucratic social system. In short, this book depicts Chilean society as an authoritarian structure with very rigid norms, imposing sanctions on any kind of personal rebellion. Edwards' first attempt at a full-length novel was less successful in artistic achievement than his previous short stories.

Edwards departed from his usual themes and narrative modes with the appearance of the chronicle *Persona Non Grata*. The mode is autobiographical, yet the life and voice of the narrator are so intertwined with public figures and international events that the book is really a provocative exposé of a historical nature. John H. Turner considers it a historical novel, although it is more a historical chronicle that allows Edwards to make use of his personal and thorough knowledge of the intricacies of Cuban politics. In this manner the author displays his command of the subtleties of diplomatic discourse. The work is full of anecdotes about important figures such as Fidel Castro, his brother Raúl, Ernesto "Che" Guevara, and Salvador Allende. Carlos Fuentes, Vargas Llosa and Neruda are among the many literary figures mentioned.

The structure is episodic, almost like that of the picaresque novel. Events and anecdotes are narrated from notes, diaries, letters, and recollections. One of the main anecdotes has to do with the visit of the Chilean tall ship *Esmeralda* in 1971. During this visit, the first military envoy from the Chilean socialist government, the protocol was very often a source of painful embarrassment. For instance, upon Castro's asking whether there was anything he could do to make the visit more pleasant, the aristocratic Chilean skipper mentioned a round of golf. After a moment of awkward silence, Castro responded that he would be delighted to arrange it, and did.

Besides the anecdotes, the book is a constant criticism of Cuban socialism and Castro's regime. Edwards endlessly complains about the shortage of consumer goods, a situation existing only for the masses, as he clearly points out. The relentless account includes the failure of the volunteer field-work brigade, the malfunctioning air conditioner in his apartment, the failure of the sugar-cane quotas, the harassment of writers, the imprisonment of intellectuals, and the stifling atmosphere. Everything is a failure except the government secret police, whose surveillance works like a well-oiled machine. Edwards is more concerned with the future of the writer in a socialist regime than with the future of the masses, as

Charles Param indicates in his review of *Persona Non Grata*. Edwards aspires to a different type of socialism in Chile. Yet he seems to fear a counterrevolution from the right for he believes that left-wing extremists might be preparing to take control of Allende's government. Since Edwards' criticism was infiltrating Castro's personal circles, he was asked to leave by the premier himself. Edwards was called to a nighttime meeting in which Castro took him to task for his intellectual bourgeois criticism of the revolutionary government. But, despite Edwards' resentment of Castro, he couldn't completely escape the leader's fascinating personality, and the book contains evidence that Edwards admired Castro as well.

The book ends with the section entitled "Epilogo Parisini" (Parisian Epilogue), which includes the life of Neruda in Paris as an ambassador and his receiving the Nobel Prize. Some say Edwards included this episode to save face by linking his name to the impeccable reputation of Neruda among Chilean intellectuals. *Persona Non Grata* portrays Edwards' personal need to liberate himself from the heavy burden of having witnessed the process of the Cuban Revolution, a controversial episode in the history of Latin America. The last part of the book includes reflections on Chilean politics, socialism, and related topics. This section presents a small opening to a new attitude on the part of Edwards. In the latest edition of the book (1985), he defines it as an act of confession and contrition. Political indignation to the book has been especially acute. As Ariel Dorfman points out, this type of writing and its criticism affect world opinion about the Chilean resistance, the popular organizations, and the efforts of Amnesty International to mobilize forces against Pinochet.

Edwards' novelistic works represent the next segment of his prose writings. *Los convidados de piedra* and *El museo de cera* were inspired by Chilean re-creations of Spanish legends and events. Edwards feels that Spanish history and literature survive in Latin American reality and restrain its historical evolution. Edwards creates a literary reality whose main characteristic is its own fictionality.

Los convidados de piedra was inspired by a Chilean re-creation of Tirso de Molina's "Los convidados de piedra," but it is a montage of events leading up to the 1973 military coup. The starting point is a birthday party that takes place in an old mansion toward the end of 1973. A group of friends celebrates the forty-fourth anniversary of Sebastián Agüero, a member of the Chilean oligarchy. It is even more euphoric than the celebration they had when the military coup ended Allende's government. While they drink and laugh, they can hear the shooting outside. Because of the curfew, the party goes on for hours.

One of the characters is the narrator. He serves as the memorialist of the group. His observations suggest that the military coup is the end of an era started in 1891 with the downfall of President Balmaceda, as a consequence of another military coup instigated by the Chilean oligarchy and British imperialism. The old friends remember their golden youth and the bitterness of the recent past. All the characters seem to have lived stultified lives, although they belong to the dominant classes. More important is the insistence on remembering friends who have abandoned the group, but are present at the banquet without having been invited. In addition to the portrayal of hollow characters and their decadence, the book contains many historical references and much political gossip. The literary quality of the novel, as Federico Schopf indicates, resides in the complex use of dialogue, stream of consciousness, erotic descriptions, erudite references, and the use of the Chilean oral discourse, which, in a way, prevents communication. In the Spanish version the protagonist goes to the banquet and dies. In the Chilean version there is an absence of a moral authority to sanction the acts of the characters. The reader can only reflect on the nature of the punishment.

El museo de cera presents as protagonist an anachronistic marquis, whose life and works have been centered on defending the old system against what he calls modern vulgarity and alacrity. The story of the marquis is told by a collective narrator: his associates at the club. Upon retiring, the marquis marries a sensuous young woman. One day he enters the music room of his mansion and finds his wife on top of the piano in the arms of her Italian piano teacher. The old marquis reacts by commissioning a local sculptor to re-create, in life-size wax figures, the exact scene of the music room, including the marquis standing at the door. As the sculptures are finished, he locks up the mansion; by so doing, he freezes the event

forever, imprisoning time. He builds another mansion that is a replica of the old one, and resides there, erasing a fragment of time and history.

If one reflects on contemporary Chile the allegorical relationship to the novel becomes clear. Chile is a country frozen in time, ignoring its recent past. The insistence on erasing the recent past denies history and reality becomes a dream. The marquis and his actions are the signs of an anachronistic dominant class that will not accept change but seeks to impose its own order. The novel underlines the unreal nature of Chilean society transformed into a wax museum by a general, Pinochet, who keeps saying "All is peaceful, ask the people."

If in his first three novels Edwards depicts masculine protagonists, his fourth novel, *La mujer imaginaria*, portrays Inés Vargas Elizalde, a woman, as the protagonist. She is an upper-class woman who abandons her duties as the wife of a politician and starts a career as a painter. Inés, at age forty, has been inspired by a bohemian uncle who escaped from the repressive atmosphere of Santiago to the Latin Quarter in Paris. Inés' first exhibition is a success, but soon after that her paintings begin to convey feelings of horror and indignation toward the cruel reprisals taken against the leftists in 1973. Inés' role as an artist seems to symbolize not only her own liberation, but also the anticipation of her country's freedom.

Aside from the extensive bibliography dedicated to *Persona Non Grata*, Jorge Edwards' political views and his writings have yet to receive the extent of critical assessment that they deserve. From *El patio* to *La mujer imaginaria*, Edwards' works have undergone continual evolution. He delves deeply into the Chilean bourgeoisie, exploring its private and social decadence, and he gives a provocative interpretation of Chilean reality. Edwards' ideas might frequently be disagreeable, but he is very much present in the shaping of today's Latin American novel.

SELECTED BIBLIOGRAPHY

Editions

Short Stories

El patio. Santiago, Chile, 1952. 2nd ed. 1980
Gente de la ciudad. Santiago, Chile, 1961.

Las máscaras. Santiago, Chile, 1967.

Temas y variaciones. Antología de relatos. Santiago, Chile, 1969.

Novels

El peso de la noche. Santiago, Chile, 1961.
Los convidados de piedra. Barcelona, 1978.
El museo de cera. Barcelona, 1981.
La mujer imaginaria. Barcelona, 1985.

Chronicles

Persona non grata. Barcelona, 1973.

Translations

Persona Non Grata: An Envoy in Castro's Cuba. Translated by Colin Harding. London, 1977.

Biographical and Critical Studies

Alegría, Fernando. "Jorge Edwards." In *Nueva historia de la novela hispanoamericana.* Hanover, N.H., 1986. Pp. 385–390.

Basignal Dobal, Beatriz. "El sentido de la máscara en el cuento de Jorge Edwards, a propósito de 'Adiós Luisa. . . .'" *Revista signos de Valparaíso* 4/2:133–140 (1970).

Batalló, José. "En torno a *El peso de la noche.*" *Cuadernos hispanoamericanos* (Madrid) 186:569–574 (1965).

Bello, Enrique. "*El peso de la noche* de Jorge Edwards, una novela tipo." *Boletín de la universidad de Chile* 58:46–47 (1965).

Dorfman, Ariel. "¿Volar?: Un estudio en la narrativa de Skármeta y Edwards." *Revista chilena de literatura* 1:59–78 (1970). Also in *Ensayos quemados en Chile.* . . . Barcelona, 1974. Pp. 133–154.

———. "Jorge Edwards: Máscara non grata." *Plural* 6/76: 76–80 (1978).

Lihn, Enrique. "La aventura y el orden en la narrativa chilena." In Edwards' *Temas y variaciones,* edited by Lihn. Santiago, Chile, 1969. Pp. 9–21.

Luchting, Wolfgang A. "¿Como arrepentirse? Radiografía de una novela." *Nueva narrativa hispanoamericana* 3/2: 191–210 (1973).

McMurray, George R. "Review of *La mujer imaginaria* by Jorge Edwards." *World Literature Today* 61/1 (1987).

Mesa-Lago, Carmelo. "Review of *Persona Non Grata* by Jorge Edwards." *Cuban Studies/Estudios cubanos* 5/1: 36–37 (1975).

Monserrat, Marcelo. "Review of *Persona Non Grata* by Jorge Edwards." *Criterio* 48/1717:318 (1975).

Moody, Michael. "Jorge Edwards, Chile, and *El museo de cera.*" *Chasqui* 14/2–3:37–42 (1985).

Param, Charles. "Review of *Persona Non Grata* by Jorge Edwards." *Books Abroad* 49/1:91–92 (1975).

Santander, Carlos. "*El peso de la noche,* de Jorge Edwards." *Estudios filológicos* 5:41–67 (1972).

———. "*El peso de la noche.*" *Nueva narrativa hispanoamericana* 5:159–178 (1975).

Schopf, Federico. "Dos novelas chilenas." *Eco* 35/216: 653–668 (1979).

Turner, John H. "Review of *Persona Non Grata* by Jorge Edwards." *Chasqui* 4/1:84–85 (1974).

Vallejo, Rafael. "Jorge Edwards: ¿Persona 'non grata'?" *Estafeta literaria* (Madrid) 534:1631–1632 (1974).

Vargas Llosa, Mario. "Un francotirador tranquilo." In *Contra viento y marea (1962–1982).* Barcelona, 1984. Pp. 201–212.

Manuel Puig

(1932–   )

Elizabeth Otero Krauthamner

The Argentine writer Manuel Puig stands out among contemporary novelists for his skill in representing, by means of colloquial language, the characteristics of the society in which he lives. His works show his interest in and concern for the political and social aspects shaping that society, as well as the consequential psychological and emotional impact of this society on its members. Puig uses language typical of the Argentine people to develop characters who illustrate Puig's view of a culture whose values he by no means shares, values of oppression, discrimination, and sexism. Using this popular speech to create an atmosphere in which the protagonists can express their most intimate internal conflicts, he at the same time delineates the characteristics of a specific sociopolitical milieu: one of growing social alienation.

Manual Puig was born on 28 December 1932 in General Villegas, in the province of Buenos Aires. On finishing elementary school at age thirteen, he moved to the capital in 1946 to attend high school and university. From this early stage in his life, Puig dreamed of finding in the big city the marvelous world of Hollywood movies, which had fascinated him and formed his reality since he was five years old.

In a talk at the University of Pittsburgh in 1983, Puig discussed his vivid recollections of those times (Puig and McDuffie, 1983). He clearly relates the beginning of the creative process with his native home on the Argentine pampa, stating in his lecture that the influence of his birthplace has been such an intense part of his development that he cannot separate it from his life as a writer. In fact, he claims that he was actually writing his first novel long before being aware of what he was doing and without ever having planned to do it.

Puig describes the pampa as a place where there is neither color nor musical sound and where there is a total absence of landscape: words such as "mountains," "sea," "ocean," and "lakes" were unknown and never used in ordinary conversation. In the tiny town of General Villegas, square in the middle of the country, the possibility of getting cultural enrichment or of obtaining a larger view of the world was an impossible dream. Puig adds that the sexist and repressive system imposed its political, social, and religious values on all the townspeople, which made life in this part of Argentina even more stultifying than elsewhere in the country.

The only way to escape that rustic reality was by way of the celluloid universe of color and music afforded by the movies. Hollywood seemed to point the way out for Puig. As a teenager, he was convinced that leaving his hometown would enable him to find a life like that portrayed on the screen, but these hopes were dashed when he left General Villegas to begin high school studies in Buenos Aires. There, once again, he faced problems of authority, repression, and violence, and felt the conflict between the reality he rejected and the reality he found in films. This disappointment convinced Puig that his sought-after reality could only lie outside Argentina.

Puig's marked fondness for films had a tremendous influence on him. He began his university studies in 1951, and in 1956 he traveled to Rome with a scholarship to study at the Centro Sperimentale di Cinematografia (Experimental Film Center), where he majored in directing and worked as an assistant director on several films. Puig arrived in Italy at the age of twenty-three, after having studied philosophy in Argentina, as well as English, French, and Italian—the languages he considered to be the languages of filmmaking. Once again, however, he was to undergo disappointments, even in the luminous world of films about which he had dreamed for so long.

In an interview with Saúl Sosnowski, Puig stated his displeasure with work on the set in no uncertain terms. He had imagined the experience to be greatly different, and his frustration had as much to do with the film people with whom he worked as with the work itself. In an attempt to overcome this further disillusionment, Puig set out to become a screenwriter, but the results were lacking, due in no small part to the author's ineptitude with written English:

> It turned out that I didn't like the work on the set. It was the opposite of everything I had imagined it to be, . . . a real disappointment. . . . To compensate for how bad things were on the set, I tried to write, albeit without preparation. That is, I attacked films from the script side. I wrote in English. I knew English pretty well, but not well enough to write it. . . . I realized that it was all a great mistake. What I really wanted was to prolong the hours of being a kid at the movies.
>
> (Sosnowski, 1973, p. 73)

Some friends advised Puig to start writing in Spanish, and he took the first steps toward becoming a novelist. Once he faced up to his inability to succeed in filmmaking, Puig discovered the world of literature, in which he could express himself intellectually, psychologically, and emotionally without hav-

ing to play by the rules of a society that had always worried and displeased him.

Puig's concern for the social, political, religious, and sexual conflicts that have affected Argentine society for years can be seen throughout his works. In all his writings, one finds an insistence on bringing to the surface the psychosexual conflicts of his characters. These conflicts, which have branded the personalities of the characters from their childhood, are the ghosts that have haunted Puig himself since his early days in General Villegas. The pages of his first two novels, especially, are filled with voices echoing in the gallery of memory: the voices of his aunts and other relatives, which flow so quickly through his mind that he can write thirty pages without stopping (Sosnowski, p. 71). Puig himself has said that his first novel began as stream of consciousness. Then, bit by bit, he separated these voices and brought to his first works such subliterary elements as letters, private diaries, school compositions, lyrics of tangos and boleros, texts from fashion magazines, monologous telephone conversations, and bits from movies, which together give to his narrative a strange, unique touch.

Having begun his first novel, Puig moved in 1963 to New York, where he got a job that gave him enough free time to write. He finished the novel in three and a half years but had to wait another three and a half years before finding a publisher. In 1968, *La traición de Rita Hayworth* (*Betrayed by Rita Hayworth*) was published in Buenos Aires and was hailed as one of the best books of the year. Despite the long, difficult process leading to the publication of *Betrayed by Rita Hayworth*, Puig enjoyed this period immensely, because for the first time in his life he had found something that meant more to him than movies. The main character of the novel, as Puig affirms, is autobiographical, and Puig thinks that, to a certain degree, composing the novel was a way to fight his own conflicts with his native town.

In 1967, Puig returned to Argentina from New York, and once again he had to face an environment he found stifling. He says (in the interview with Nora Catelli, p. 23) that he has always had difficulty relating to Argentine men because of their overweening self-confidence, while his dealings with Argentine women have been much more pleasant. His first encounter with Argentine literary critics was a major difficulty facing him on his return: a complete break-down in communication between them ensued, al-though in time this was mended. Puig felt that newspaper critics were too harsh: "They object to novelty. When you try to do something different, they really don't like it" (Puig and McDuffie, 1983). Recently, Puig has recognized the legitimacy of the role played by academic critics, and he has even expressed a desire to see this kind of analytic criticism reach a wider readership.

Once he had again settled in Argentina, Puig began work on his second novel, *Boquitas pintadas* (Painted Little Mouths, 1969; translated as *Heart-break Tango*). Again, the gallery of family voices is present, as is Puig's use of mass media communication. In his third novel, *The Buenos Aires Affair* (written in Spanish with an English title, 1973; translated as *The Buenos Aires Affair*), however, Puig explores new territory: using psychoanalysis, he tries to shed light on the unconscious of his characters, whom he unmasks for the reader. Puig thinks that the major changes in contemporary literature have a great deal to do with Sigmund Freud and the discov-ery of the human unconscious. In Puig's subsequent novels, one finds an increasing use of devices bor-rowed from Freudian psychology as well as elements of the psychoanalytical theories of Jacques Lacan and Carl Jung. In addition to these devices, he has added elements of detective fiction, fantastic literature, and parapsychology.

Whether Manuel Puig belongs to or participates in the program of a specific political party is an open question; what is known about him—since he himself has addressed the issue in several interviews and speeches—is that he left his homeland in 1973 because of his profound disgust over the political situation in Argentina at that time. His characters' lives show the political, social, and religious repres-sion that alienates them and causes them to seek different forms of psychological escape. In an inter-view with Nora Catelli, the author reaffirmed his political opposition to the Perón government:

> When they got rid of Campora and proposed the Perón-Perón [Juan Perón and his third wife, Isabel Perón] ticket and it was accepted, I told myself: I can't go along with this. No way. Things were going so well.

> When Cámpora first resigned, there was talk of a Perón-Balbín ticket. That would let a person have some hope still, but when everybody went along with the Perón-Isabel ticket, I just felt like an outsider.
>
> (p. 23)

After spending about two years in Mexico, Puig returned to New York in 1976, where a year later he happened to meet a young American who turned out to be the inspiration for the character Larry in *Maldición eterna a quien lea estas páginas* (*Eternal Curse on the Reader of These Pages*, 1980), which takes place in Greenwich Village. Puig's experience in New York was not so happy as he might have wished, given his fond memories of his first visit there. Finally, in the early 1980's, he moved to Rio de Janeiro, Brazil, where, as of this writing, he still lives.

Puig's novels have been translated into some four-teen languages, including English. He is one of the youngest members of the so-called Latin American boom, and stands out among boom writers not only for the excellent quality of his literary work, but also for bringing a renovated popular language to prose fiction. By means of breaking language down, Puig symbolically breaks with repression in general and then reconstructs the language in order to open the way for free human expression.

Keith McDuffie considers Puig one of the most important innovators in present-day Latin American literature, especially in terms of his use of popular culture, and, more specifically, because of his use of popular myth. Puig develops myths we all know and share (even though the levels of acceptance of these myths vary). According to McDuffie, Puig avoids judging or condemning the mass cultural myths while at the same time making them the objects of a radical criticism (Puig and McDuffie, 1983).

Novels

Besides those already mentioned, Puig has, to date, published the following novels: *El beso de la mujer araña* (*The Kiss of the Spider Woman*, 1976), *Pubis angelical* (*Pubis Angelical*, 1979), and *Sangre de amor correspondido* (*Blood of Requited Love*, 1982).

Puig's first novel, *Betrayed by Rita Hayworth*, takes place in an imaginary town, Coronel Vallejos, in the province of Buenos Aires, where life goes on in a mediocre way and at a monotonous pace. The work begins with a series of speeches in which the characters introduce themselves, thus emphasizing the absence of a narrator. The reader is left alone to untangle the web of questions and answers with which the novel begins, an act that requires the reader's cooperation. The story begins in 1933, continues to 1948, and then returns to 1933 by means of an unsent letter. The reader slowly and indirectly comes to understand the story by means of dialogues, interior monologues, letters, a notebook of thoughts, a diary, a telephone conversation between one of the characters and an unidentified party, descriptions of dreams, and a primary school composition. The unifying element in all this is the character of the protagonist, Toto Casals.

The alienation of the characters who make up the novelistic nucleus of Coronel Vallejos is the dominant aspect in the book. This emotional and psychological alienation, especially in the case of Toto, has been seen by some critics, and by Puig himself, as a changing or inverting of the order of realities. To escape the monotony of the town, the protagonist goes to the movies with his mother every day, turning the film world into his own reality. Marta Morello-Frosch, referring to the movie-going of the alienated characters in Puig's work, says that one can see "the presence of films as the last vestige of a form of communication that becomes alienating, since this type of language is exterior and totally alien to the man's experiences" (Morello-Frosch, 1970, pp. 77–78). An example of this can be seen in Toto's monologue at the beginning of the novel:

> I'm going to think about the movie I liked the best because momma told me to think about movies so as not to get bored during siesta time. Romeo and Juliet is about love, ends badly since they die and it's sad: one of the ones I liked the best.
>
> (p. 37)

As in Puig's other novels, certain recurrent themes appear in Betrayed by Rita Hayworth: the characters' conflicts about sexual identity, male and female stereotypes, betrayal, illness, isolation, death, Argentine national politics, manifestations of mass popular culture, and the use of movie plots, whether to form

the narrative or to reveal the stream of consciousness that occurs in characters' dreams.

The protagonist's psychosexual ambivalence embodies the theme of sexual identity in Betrayed by Rita Hayworth. Toto's latent homosexuality is masked by the psychological projections that allow him to experience his repressed sexuality:

> I don't want him to get married, he's much better looking than she is, but he was chopping wood without a shirt and you could see his arms and that strong boxer's chest. . . . How great it would be for us to go live together in a cabin . . .
>
> (p. 85)

The homosexual character will appear again, this time openly, in The Kiss of the Spider Woman, discussed below.

In Heartbreak Tango, his second novel, Puig is still psychologically linked to Coronel Vallejos. In this work, he shows the frustrations and failures of people who are apparently successful. According to Puig, male chauvinism, the system on which they have all relied, has failed them, and under their masks lies a profound disillusion. Some critics have interpreted this novel as a parody. In response to this, Puig has said,

> I went to the dictionary and it said "mocking version of something." I did not like the word "mocking," because I was not mocking anybody. There were some parodical elements in themselves, in the characters, especially because they were trying to portray characters that they were not. I wanted to work with this game of masks.
>
> (Puig and McDuffie, 1983)

In Heartbreak Tango, Puig incorporates pulp novels into his narrative, and for the first time he uses an objective, third-person point of view. The novel is presented to the reader by means of "offerings" made up of semiliterary sources, such as the lyrics of tangos, letters, medical and police reports, "lonely hearts" letters, funeral notices, and clippings from the society pages. His intention is to create a form of popular literature while at the same time exposing and unmasking the mass communications media that are responsible for his characters' alienation.

The novel begins with a funeral announcement

telling of the death of Juan Carlos Etchepare in 1947. The story is a reconstruction, in retroactive time, of the dreams, falsehoods, intrigues, and frustrations that crowd the memories of Nené, whose impossible love for Juan Carlos stays with her until the day of her death in 1968.

In his detective novel, *The Buenos Aires Affair*, Puig begins his incursion into psychoanalysis. Sexual violence, both homosexual and heterosexual, figures importantly in this novel and the deep conflicts that stem from the childhoods of the main characters, Gladys and Leo, are the novel's psychological center. The story revolves around these two people whose psychological frustrations are projected in the form of aggressive, distorted sexuality. Elements from the cinema are also incorporated into the novel. Each of the chapters begins with a bit of dialogue taken from a movie. For example, the book begins with a fragment from *Camille* and ends with another fragment from *Gilda*.

The characteristics of ideological discourse are seen for the first time in Puig's narrative in *The Kiss of the Spider Woman*. The work deals with the encounter between Valentín, a revolutionary, and Molina, a homosexual, in a cell in a Buenos Aires prison. The storyline, which develops by means of the dialogue between these two characters, is intercut with accounts of dreams and movies, police communiques, letters, telephone conversations, and the notes from psychoanalytic appointments. The representatives of two oppressed but opposite groups are brought together in the small cell: Valentín, a guerrilla, is ruled by the laws of *machismo*, while the homosexual Molina has adapted his life to fit the norms of traditional, passive femininity. As the narrative unfolds, notes about different aspects of homosexuality are introduced, here and there, into the text, and one notices the attempt to make the reader a part of the process of liberation being described in the book. By means of this process of liberation, Valentín and Molina begin to overcome the stereotypical roles assigned them by traditional society: toward the end of the novel, both have experienced a psychological transformation that brings them together physically and emotionally. Just how close they have become is shown in chapter 14, when the two friends say goodbye:

—Valentín, you and my mom are the two people that I've loved most in the world.

— . . .

—And you, are you really going to remember me?
—I learned a lot from you, Molina . . .

(Thomas Colchie, trans., p. 261)

In his fifth novel, *Pubis Angelical*, Puig explores a variety of techniques—the diary form, interior monologues, dialogues, elements of film, Freudian and Lacanian concepts, and parapsychological elements—to develop a number of interwoven concerns. The novel revolves around Ana, an Argentine woman hospitalized in a clinic in Mexico City. Through Ana, Puig presents the image of "woman" projected on two parallel and complementary levels. One of the levels is the conscious/objective plane, the other the unconscious/oneiric level. On the first level, one sees Ana's conflicts as the result of her having received a traditional education in a sexist society. On the deeper level, those conflicts are veiled and yet reveal Ana's internal process of self-liberation as "woman." The degree to which sexual stereotypes, repressed sexuality, the depersonalization of the human being, and the use and exploitation of women by men are emphasized in this book is illustrated by the following quotation:

How great it is to be a woman, so many alternatives, . . . to give way towards one side . . . or the other. The wild man who falls asleep after having his thrills, and the noble, self-sacrificing woman who falls asleep with the satisfaction of knowing she has been useful, even if she hasn't felt a goddamn thing.

(p. 194)

It can be said that *Pubis Angelical* is the only novel of Puig's in which a process of self-liberation is developed and perfected on an unconscious level while being projected onto the protagonist's conscious/objective plane. Ana, the protagonist, is able to solve some of her problems as a repressed individual through her dreams. When she dreams she becomes transformed into different characters who deal symbolically with similar conflicts. As these characters overcome their difficulties, Ana is unconsciously guided toward a resolution of her own repressions.

In Puig's sixth novel, *Eternal Curse on the Reader of These Pages*, as in the rest of his work, the writer proves his ability to highlight the causes of his characters' internal conflicts through his language and his use of the elements of psychoanalysis. The story builds around the dialogue of two cultured male characters, whose discourses draw back the veil that hides each one's past, allowing the reader to find out bits and pieces of their lives. Larry, a thirty-six-year-old divorced American, has been hired to take care of Señor Ramirez, an exiled Argentine invalid, aged seventy-four. Ramirez' novelistic discourses clash with Larry's cold, harsh speech, and then turn into an old man's hallucinatory monologues. Again, the majority of the themes developed in this novel are those one finds in Puig's earlier work: repressed sexuality, the use of women as sexual objects, and the problems that result from frustrated, Oedipal relationships between parents and children. The influence of Freud and Lacan can be traced throughout the characters' speeches, as seen in the following quotes taken from the second part of the book:

> I was a torpid adolescent. The girl attracted me very much, I wanted to slide my hand under her blouse. . . . One day I got the courage to invite her to go out. She accepted. We went to the movies. The film was mediocre . . . I was very tense that afternoon, rigid, without spontaneity. It was a torture for me. I was happy when it ended. . . . The situation produces a terrible excitement . . . it is the first time that the sexuality, repressed, in relation to the mother, becomes liberated once and for all from those connotations, and it is applied to a new object.
>
> (pp. 177–178)

As in his other novels, Puig in *Eternal Curse* shows a profound understanding of human nature. Lacan's concept of the "mirror phase" is seen in the following:

> —Believe me, advice is not important. Words are not important. Intelligence is not important.
> —Then what is important?
> —The sensation that the child receives. That he has pleased his parents. Everything they feel for him and for themselves is intuited by the son, who gets confused, and thinks that this is his own image, that which he is seeing when leaning over the stinking water of the sewer

. . .

> —The boy sees himself reflected in the stinking sewer water?
> —It is with those lights and shadows that he should construct his soul. Not with some shitty advice.
>
> (p. 161)

Blood of Requited Love, Puig's latest novel as of this writing, is a book in which adolescent love and passion intermingle with the cruel reality that destroys and frustrates them. Puig returns to a depiction of the kind of sexual violence one finds in the earlier *Buenos Aires Affair.* The other topics that characterize Puig's novels can likewise be found. *Blood of Requited Love* confronts the reader with the consequences of the imposition of those social and religious values that repress and alienate human beings. Elias Miguel Muñoz (1987) makes a pithy comparison between this novel and the two previous works, *Angelical Pubis* and *The Kiss of the Spider Woman:*

> If these two novels could be read as the materialization of the author's ideology about sexuality and what sex should be, *Blood of Requited Love* would be an antitheory of this ideology and Josemar, the protagonist, an antihero. In this last novel Puig draws upon myth and patriarchal, male chauvinist discourse to tell us what sexuality should not be.
>
> (p. 128)

Theater

In 1983, Puig published two pieces for the theater; *Bajo un manto de estrellas (Under a Mantle of Stars)* and *El beso de la mujer araña* ("The Kiss of the Spider Woman," an adaptation of the novel by the same name). Both are published in a single volume.

Puig's theatrical adaptation of *Kiss of the Spider Woman* was staged for the first time in 1981. The success of its premier performance was repeated in performances across Latin America and Europe. (Before Puig adapted the novel for the stage, Luis Felipe Ormeno had staged a version of his own in 1979 in Lima, Peru.)

Under a Mantle of Stars is the only work, thus far, that Puig has written exclusively for the theater. It has not, as of this writing, been produced. In it one finds again the themes of sexual repression and the conflictive, Freudian relationship between parents and their children. The story revolves around a fifty-year-old couple who fluctuate between fantasy and reality. What is real and what is imagined blends together to satisfy the characters' unrealized desires and to ease the agony of their loneliness.

Film Scripts

Two film scripts by Puig, *La cara del villano* (The Face of the Villain) and *Recuerdo de Tijuana* (Souvenir of Tijuana), appeared, in a single volume, in 1985. These scripts maintain the literary quality of the author's novels and theatrical pieces. *La cara del villano* reproduces the hallucinatory fantasy world characteristic of Puig's earlier works. The real and the imaginary, desire and fear, and the conscious and unconscious realms intertwine in this work, in which the barriers that normally separate these opposites are broken down. *Recuerdo de Tijuana* shows once more the author's skill in giving life and color to his work through colloquial speech, thus transforming language into a demythologizing instrument. Both of these scripts provide the reader an entertaining experience, even without being transformed into their filmed versions.

Among his other contributions to film, and prior to the publication of these two scripts, Puig in 1973 wrote an adaptation of *Heartbreak Tango* for the Argentine director Leopoldo Torre Nilsson. In 1977 Puig adapted José Donoso's short novel, *El lugar sin límites* (The Place Without Limits), for the Mexican director Arturo Ripstein.

Such was his enthusiasm about working with Ripstein (because of a mutual understanding) that Puig proposed an adaptation of "El impostor" (The Impostor), a short story by the Argentine writer Silvina Ocampo. Puig's intention was to see the film shot by a production company directed by Manuel Barbachano Ponce. Changes in the Mexican government caused the cancellation of funds for the film production. In 1984, the filming of "El impostor" was undertaken again, and the film was released under the title of *Otro* (Another). Actually, the *Otro* script is the basis for *La carra del villano*, which elaborates and

completes the earlier work. In an informative prologue, Puig writes, "Now the reader can judge my work directly, a new opportunity for communication that merits a new title, the third and final one as far as I am concerned, *La carra del villano.*"

Recuerdo de Tijuana was also commissioned by Barbachano Ponce in 1978. Though it has not yet been produced, Puig indicates that from time to time there is talk about the possibility of making this film.

In August 1982, the film adaptation of *Pubis Angelical* opened in Buenos Aires. The film version is inferior to the novel, probably because of the impossibility of conveying in filmic terms the different objective and subjective levels that structure the novel. The film *The Kiss of the Spider Woman*, directed by Hector Babenco in 1986, became a great success and won awards in the United States and at Cannes.

Throughout his works Manuel Puig shows his concern about all the types of repression afflicting humankind. David William Foster has written that "Manuel Puig comes immediately to mind as an internationally recognized writer identified with the need to portray the degradation of modern city life" (Foster, 1985, pp. 558–559).

Everyday Buenos Aires speech is transformed by Puig into a demythologizing and desacralizing technique. Cedomil Goic writes that Puig "destroys the traditional conventions and already fixed forms of previous generations, achieving a notable attempt at popular literature" (Goic, 1972, p. 270–271). By contrasting his own writing, which represents the speech of the people, with the more typical, cultured language of the Argentine elite, Puig confronts, in a revolutionary and symbolic way, a society that he believes oppresses and twists its members, both psychologically and emotionally.

SELECTED BIBLIOGRAPHY

Editions

Novels

La traición de Rita Hayworth. Buenos Aires, 1968.
Boquitas pintadas. Buenos Aires, 1969.

The Buenos Aires Affair. Buenos Aires, 1973.
El beso de la mujer araña. Barcelona, Spain, 1976.
Pubis angelical. Barcelona, Spain, 1979.
Maldición eterna a quien lea estas páginas. Barcelona, Spain, 1980.
Sangre de amor correspondido. Barcelona, Spain, 1982.

Plays

Bajo un manto de estrellas. El beso de la mujer araña. Barcelona, Spain, 1983.

Film Scripts

La cara del villano. Recuerdo de Tijuana. Barcelona, Spain, 1985.

Translations

Betrayed by Rita Hayworth. Translated by Suzanne Jill Levine. New York, 1971.
Blood of Requited Love. Translated by Jan L. Grayson. New York, 1984.
The Buenos Aires Affair: A Detective Novel. No translator. New York, 1982.
Heartbreak Tango: A Serial. Translated by Suzanne Jill Levine. New York, 1973.
Kiss of the Spider Woman. Translated by Thomas Colchie. New York, 1979.
"The Kiss of the Spider Woman." Play. Translated and revised by Michael Feingold. In *Latin America: Plays,* edited by George W. Woodyard and Marion Peter Holt. New York, 1986. Pp. 19–61.
Pubis Angelical. Translated by Elena Brunet. New York, 1986.
Under a Mantle of Stars: A Play in Two Acts. Translated by Ronald Christ. New York, 1985.

Biographical and Critical Studies

Alter, Robert. "Mimesis and the Motive for Fiction." *Tri-Quarterly* 42:228–249 (1978).
Andreu, Alicia G. "El folletín: de Galdós a Manuel Puig." *Revista iberoamericana* 49:541–546 (1983).
Bernal, Alejandro A. "Super-hombre versus super-mujer: Tiranía y sexo en *Pubis angelical,* de Manuel Puig." *Revista iberoamericana* 52:991–997 (1986).
Borinsky, Alicia. "Castration: Artifices; Notes on the Writing of Manuel Puig." *Georgia Review* 29:95–114 (1975).
Bouman, Katherine A. "Manuel Puig at the University of

Missouri-Columbia." *The American Hispanist* 2/17:11–12 (1977).
Campos, Jorge. "Dos novelas recientes." *Insula* 37/428–429:18 (1982).
Campos, René A. *Espejos: La textura cinemática en "La traición de Rita Hayworth."* Madrid, 1985.
———. "Las 'películas de mujeres' y *La traición de Rita Hayworth.*" In *Literature and Popular Culture in the Hispanic World: A Symposium,* edited by Rose S. Minc. Gaithersburg, Md., 1981. Pp. 59–67.
Catelli, Nora. "Entrevista con Manuel Puig, Una narrativa de lo melifluo." *Quimera* 18:22–25 (1982).
Christ, Ronald. "Fact and Fiction." *Review* 73:49–54 (1973).
———. "An Interview with Manuel Puig." *Partisan Review* 44:52–61 (1977).
Coddou, Marcelo. "Seis preguntas a Manuel Puig sobre su última novela: *El beso de la mujer araña.*" *The American Hispanist* 2/18:12–13 (1977).
———. "Complejidad estructural de *El beso de la mujer araña* de Manuel Puig." *Inti (Revista de literatura hispánica)* 7:15–27 (1978).
———. Review of *El beso de la mujer araña. Revista iberoamericana* 44:251–253 (1978).
Corbatta, Jorgelina F. "Encuentros con Manuel Puig." *Revista iberoamericana* 49:591–620 (1983).
Echavarren, Roberto, and Enrique Giordano. *Manuel Puig: Montaje y alteridad del sujeto.* Santiago, Chile, 1986.
Foster, David William. "Manuel Puig and the Uses of Nostalgia." *Latin American Literary Review* 1/1:79–81 (1972).
———. In *Currents in the Contemporary Argentine Novel.* Columbia, Mo., 1975. Pp. 144–148.
———. "Varieties of Urban Colloquiality in the Contemporary Latin American and American Novel." *World Literature Today* 59:556–560 (1985).
García Ramos, J. M. *La narrativa de Manuel Puig.* Santa Cruz de Tenerife, Canary Islands, 1982.
Goic, Cedomil. In *Historia de la novela hispanoamericana.* Valparaíso, Chile, 1972. Pp. 270–271.
Josef, Bella. "Manuel Puig: Reflexión al nivel de la enunciación." *Nueva narrativa hispanoamericana* 4:111–115 (1974).
Kerr, Lucille. *Suspended Fictions: Reading Novels by Manuel Puig.* Urbana, Ill., 1987.
Lázaro, Jesús. "La inquisición sobre la soledad de Manuel Puig." *Quimera* 4:28–31 (1981).
Lindstrom, Naomi. "The Problem of Pop Culture in the Novels of Manuel Puig." *The American Hispanist* 4/30–31:28–31 (1978).
MacAdam, Alfred J. "Manuel Puig's Chronicles of Provin-

cial Life." *Revista hispánica moderna* 36:50–65 (1970–1971).

Maldonado, Armando. *Manuel Puig: The Aesthetics of Cinematic and Psychological Fiction.* Ph.D. diss., University of Oklahoma, 1977. Available through University Microfilms, Ann Arbor, Mich.

Marcos, Juan Manuel. "Puig, Plutarco, Goethe: La dramaticidad cronotópica de *El beso de la mujer araña.*" *Latin American Theatre Review* 20/1:5–10 (1986).

McCraken, Ellen. "Manuel Puig's *Heartbreak Tango:* Women and Mass Culture." *Latin American Literary Review* 18:27–35 (1981).

Merrim, Stephanie. "For a New (Psychological) Novel in the Works of Manuel Puig." *Novel* 17/2:141–157 (1984).

Morales, Miguel Ángel. "The Puig Affair." *Revista de la Universidad de México* 33/7:22–24 (1979).

Morello-Frosch, Marta. "*La traición de Rita Hayworth,* o el nuevo arte de narrar películas." *Sin nombre* 4/1:77–82 (1970).

———. "The New Art of Narrating Films." *Review* 4–5:52–55 (1971–1972).

———. "La sexualidad opresiva en las obras de Manuel Puig." *Nueva narrativa hispanoamericana* 5:151–157 (1975).

———. "Usos y abusos de la cultura popular: *Pubis angelical* de Manuel Puig." In *Literature and Popular Culture in the Hispanic World: A Symposium,* edited by Rose S. Minc. Gaithersburg, Md., 1981. Pp. 31–42.

Muñoz, Elías Miguel. "*Sangre de amor correspondido* y el discurso del poder judeocristiano." *Revista iberoamericana* 51:73–88 (1985).

———. *El discurso utópico de la sexualidad en Manuel Puig.* Madrid, 1987.

Piglia, Ricardo. "Clase media: Cuerpo y destino (Una lectura de *La traición de Rita Hayworth* de Manuel Puig)." In *Nueva novela latinoamericana,* edited by Jorge Lafforgue. Buenos Aires, 1972. Pp. 350–362.

Pittarello, Elide. "Manuel Puig, *Sangre de amor correspondido.*" *Rassegna iberistica* 14:81–84 (1982).

Puig, Manuel. "Síntesis y análisis: Cine y literatura." *Revista de la Universidad de México* 37/8:2–4 (1981).

———, and Keith McDuffie. "New Directions in Narrative Form: The Novel and Its Productions." Lecture, University of Pittsburgh, 4 March 1983.

Rodríguez Monegal, Emir. "El folletín rescatado." *Revista de la Universidad de México* 27/2:15–33 (1972).

———. "Los sueños de Evita (a propósito de la última novela de Manual Puig." *Plural* 22:34–36 (1973).

———. Review of *Maldición eterna a quien lea estas páginas.* *Vuelta* 54:36–37 (1981).

———. Review of *Sangre de amor correspondido.* *Vuelta* 72:34–35 (1982).

Roffé, Reina. "Manuel Puig: Del 'Kitsch' a Lacan." In *Espejos de escritores.* Hanover, N.H., 1985. Pp. 131–145.

Ruffinelli, Jorge. *Crítica en marcha.* Mexico City, 1979. Pp. 192–195.

Sarduy, Severo. "Notas a las notas a las notas . . . A propósito de Manuel Puig." *Revista iberoamericana* 37:555–567 (1971).

Sarlo, Beatriz. "Cortázar, Sábato, Puig: ¿Parodia o reportaje?" *Los libros* 36:32–33 (1974).

Schiminovich, Flora H. "El juego narcisista y ficcional en *Sangre de amor correspondido.*" *Discurso literario* 1/2:295–301 (1984).

Shaw, Donald L. *Nueva narrativa hispanoamericana.* 2nd ed. Madrid, 1983.

Sosnowski, Saúl. "Entrevista." *Hispamérica* 3:69–80 (1973).

Torres Fierro, Danubio. "Conversación con Manuel Puig: La redención de la cursilería." *Eco* 28:507–515 (1975).

Weiss, Judith. "Dynamic Correlations in *Heartbreak Tango.*" *Latin American Literary Review* 3/5:137–141 (1974).

Zamora, Lois Parkinson. "Cliches and Defamiliarization in the Fiction of Manual Puig and Luis Rafael Sánchez." *The Journal of Aesthetics and Art Criticism* 41:421–436 (1983).

José Triana

(1933–   )

Frank Dauster

The theater of José Triana is a product of the Cuban Revolution, and he is a member of the group of youthful dramatists who created an exciting, if brief, theatrical renaissance in Havana after 1959. Triana was born in Camagüey in 1933, and lived in a series of provincial cities, first Hatuey and later for fourteen years in Bayamo, where he attended school, and in Havana. He earned his living as a teacher and employee of the telephone company. From 1955 to 1959, the latter years of the dictatorship of Fulgencio Batista, Triana, like many other Cuban writers, lived in Madrid, where he published a volume of poetry and wrote his earliest plays. His first performed works were done under the auspices of the revolutionary government's imaginative program to stimulate the arts, and in 1965 he achieved international fame with *La noche de los asesinos* (*The Criminals*). Oddly, this work is also his last published and performed piece. Since then Triana has been still as a dramatist, quite possibly due to the hostility of some influential Cuban critics who felt that his work continued to deal with prerevolutionary society rather than showing the progress under the new system. Ironically, others have been critical because the setting of the works was not clearly prerevolutionary, so that the play is sometimes interpreted as an attack on revolutionary society. In any case, Triana left Cuba in 1980 and has since resided primarily in Paris.

Triana's theater focuses on the irrational and the incoherent in human behavior, and on the violence that he sees at the core of Cuban psychology. He examines the deeper realities that lie beneath apparent everyday existence. His characters come from an urban world, and especially from its infrastructures, the world of vagrants, beggars, prostitutes, and the ever-present political boss. As he made clear in a series of interviews, Triana looks within himself and others, he examines humankind at its most critical moments. He considers his theater to be essentially tragic, in that it examines human beings at the moment of critical choice. He rejects conventional realism; Triana's theater attempts to raise reality to a more poetic level, without in any way prettifying it or ignoring its most devastating implications.

At the same time, Triana's work is rooted in a critical sense of Cuban reality, the same critical sense that had led him to abandon the social and political corruption of his nation before 1958. His characters are rooted in the precariousness of Cuban reality. The social structures shown in his plays are controlled by disorder, by lack of organic sense, by a cosmos that is beyond human control. In one direction, this related him to the theater of the absurd, but where the

European authors working in this tradition tended to accept the absurdity of existence, Triana is more judgmental and rejects the inhumanity of such absurdity. Triana has a clear and negative vision of the society in which he lived and of its failures, and his works are distinctly critical of these shortcomings.

Triana's first two plays were one-acts written in 1957 while he was living in Madrid. "El incidente cotidiano" (The Daily Incident) was never published or staged, and its author refers to it as a diversion. *El mayor general hablará de teogonía* (The Major General Will Speak of Theogony) was premiered in 1960. It takes place in 1929 in an unidentified Latin American city. The characters are two sisters, Elisiria and Petronila, and the latter's husband, Higinio. They have taken refuge in the general's home after an obscure incident, perhaps an accident, perhaps an attempt at murder, twenty-five years earlier, a fall that caused the death of Petronila's unborn daughter. The three are chained together by obsessive guilt and fear. They present two versions of the absent general; Elisiria paints an unstable tyrant capable of murdering them all, while Petronila sees a benevolent patriarch. Ultimately, all three plan to murder him in order to free themselves from his domination and cleanse themselves of guilt for the earlier death. But when the general finally appears, the conspirators are paralyzed by fear while he berates them mildly and expresses his fatigue and disgust with the whole nonsense of origins, gods, and cosmic purposes.

The general's identity is hardly a secret; although the play is also, in another sense, an examination of psychological oppression, it has a clear biblical subtext. Elisiria dreams of a vaguely Edenic earlier life, Petronila keeps the body of her dead child as a "relic" of love. Everyone, including the general himself, refers to his sermons; Petronila calls the public knowledge of the family secret the flood, and confesses that in moments of private passion she calls Higinio the Apostle. The preparations for their feast allude to the mass, and the wine and hors d'oeuvres parody the communion. The sound of a distant bell is followed by Petronila's noisy parody of the joy of the Epiphany and Elisiria's savage elation at the prospect of the murder. The entire sequence is a bitter mockery of the perversion of the significance of Christ's sacrifice. There is a curious inversion of roles

between the General-God and Higinio-Judas, since the former betrayed the latter in the home of the Olivo family. But this general wishes no one ill; he is simply bored and tired. Human existence hangs on the thread of his goodwill, and he is not sure that it is all worth the bother.

Triana's attack is directed not at the concept of God but at those of his worshippers who are too lacking in moral fiber to make decisions for themselves. They are trapped in the jail of their imagination; they need only to exercise their will and they will be free. But a life without their general to worship would be intolerable, and they would simply have to invent another. This ironic concept of a divine genealogy, whose existence is owing to mankind's inability or unwillingness to live without divine aid, suggests an exercise in the construction of myths that leads directly to Triana's later works.

Medea en el espejo (Medea in the Mirror) was written in 1959 and first produced the following year. Basing his play on the classical myth of the woman who, betrayed by her lover, murders their children in a fit of passion, Triana follows Euripides closely in his conversion of the classical work into an urban tragedy, although he was probably inspired by another Cuban version of the myth, Virgilio Piñera's *Electra Garrigó*. The chief difference lies in the slow discovery of Julián's treachery, while the Greek model establishes it at the beginning. Medea is María, Jason is Julián, the nurse becomes Amparo. Medea's nurse becomes the old servant Erundina, and she has a much larger role; Creon is Perico Piedra Fina. María is mulatto. Julián, her blond lover, is a dubious individual who hopes to marry advantageously the daughter of the police chief. Like the Greek Jason, he seeks to blame María for her misfortunes, rather than confess his own treachery. Less important dramatically than Jason, he is equally egotistical. Morally, they are of a kind. The minor characters of *Medea en el espejo* are almost a catalog of urban types, and the old black servant Erundina is straight from Cuban folklore: practically a member of the family, her speech is a catalog of popular sayings with the spice of African cults. This search for meaning in the social infrastructure has fascinated other Cuban playwrights beside Triana; they are seeking something of permanent value in a sordid social reality.

María is the character closest to Euripides' model. Her passion is totally destructive; the murders of Perico and his daughter, and of her own children, matter nothing to her. It is clear by the play's end that she has slowly lost control and is now mad. She does have, however, two marked individual characteristics: her highly individualized speech and her obsession with mirrors. She oscillates between rhetorical grandiloquence and ordinary language. The mirrors represent her search for authenticity, for real identity. But mirrors are all surface, without depth, and she is finally driven to the ultimate mirror, the blade of her knife.

Medea en el espejo is an effort to subvert the established order of crass mediocrity through the search for identity of a passionate tragic figure; Triana wished to endow the ordinary with extraordinary significance. His *Medea* demonstrates that as the classical tragic figures are of flesh and blood, so characters of the twentieth century are capable of tragic grandeur. His people are Cuban to the core, even to the violent burlesquing of their reactions.

In 1962 Triana staged two plays, "La casa ardiendo" (The Burning House) and *El Parque de la Fraternidad* (Brotherhood Park). The former is a monodrama of the frustrations of a prostitute; like "La visita del angel" (The Angel's Visit), performed the following year, it is unpublished and unavailable. *El Parque de la Fraternidad* takes place in the Havana park of the same name; its two principal characters recall well-known figures of Cuban street life, but the play is also a parody of the Christian Trinity and the bankruptcy of the prerevolutionary social system.

With *La muerte del ñeque* (The Death of the Boogieman, 1963), Triana took a considerable step forward in his obsessive recreation of the myths of Cuban life. Again, the setting is the underworld; the title character, the mulatto Hilario, is a corrupt and powerful chief of police. His white mistress, Blanca Estela, is involved with the son of an old enemy; his own son, Pablo, has ambiguous feelings, sexual and racial, toward the mulatto Berta, a childhood friend. The cast is completed by the black maid and three thugs, Pepe, Juan, and Ñico, who both comment on the action after the fashion of the classical chorus and participate in it actively. The plot is relatively simple: the intrigues against Hilario and his overthrow and murder, with the subplot of Pablo's ambiguous feelings toward both Berta and Blanca Estela.

The story is not complex, but Triana makes use of ritual to raise to another level this tale of a brutal chieftain and his doomed house. Hilario is as destined to a violent end as any barbaric king, and his fall follows the pattern of the classical tragedy in its handling of his overweening pride, the stunning reversal of fortune, and his ritual destruction at the hands of the three murderers. Mankind is ruled by pure chance; by luck Hilario has risen, and now by luck he falls. The underpinnings of this elaborate tale of murder, lechery, hatred, and revenge are the three murderers. Besides intervening directly and playing the role of the Fates who measure out human life, they are also the chorus, commenting sardonically on the action about them. It is not by chance that they are a white, a black, and a mulatto; they represent the spectrum of the Cuban world. But even more, they are the mythos of evil. It is their actions, expressed in the form of ritualized games, that prepare the atmosphere, maintain the tension, and lead finally to Hilario's death.

Triana's last published and produced play is *The Criminals*, written in 1964 and winner of the 1965 Casa de las Américas drama award. First performed in Havana in 1966 and later in major cities and university campuses in Europe and America, it has been translated into a number of languages. The play has awakened widely differing interpretations, but it has been uniformly successful. There is no sequential action; rather, it uses a juxtaposition of different times and a fluid shifting of roles, so that the audience is drawn into the play in an effort to give meaning to its complexity. The action takes place in a cellar or attic room furnished with discarded objects; the characters are two sisters, Beba and Cuca, and their brother, Lalo. They appear to be in late adolescence, but there are also hints that one or more are in their early twenties or even older. This ambiguity characterizes the entire play, which is the acting out of the murder of their parents and the events leading up to it. Further, it is an acting out that is neither new nor unusual, but rather something they have done repeatedly. The savage game is a parody of the mediocrity of the adult world, its family instability, and the obsession of aging human beings with the slow decomposition of their bodies. But this terrible game becomes increasingly more serious as each of the three takes the roles of parents, family friends, and even each other. Cuca and Beba see it as a sort of purging of their emotions toward their parents; Cuca even defends them and participates reluctantly, while Beba oscillates between the rancor and meanness offered by the world outside and the alternative offered by Lalo: accept totally or rebel totally, accept the crassness or overthrow it through violence.

But the game becomes even more complicated as we hear neighbors' comments on the savagery of the murder and a reliving of the infidelity, mediocrity, and violence that has led the family to this terrible stage. The three sometimes step outside the play and shift roles rapidly. The first act ends as Lalo drives the knife into the table top. The audience still does not know whether this is a bloody dress rehearsal or a dreadful game invented by bored and angry adolescents. The parents are seen as uniformly cruel and thoughtless, Lalo is violent, Cuca is at first reluctant and then increasingly willing to participate, Beba becomes almost ill. In act 2 much of this is reversed: the sisters pretend that the parents are already dead and prepare their alibi, but Lalo is almost incapable of functioning, and when he attempts to distance himself from the crime, he is prevented by the new avenging angel, Cuca.

The major part of the second act is taken up by the police investigation, represented by the sisters. But the violent symbolism sought by the criminals becomes lost in the legalistic, cold-blooded world of the police, so that Lalo, horrified by the reduction of his rebellion to simply another act of human barbarism, refuses to sign the confession. Finally the questions of Cuca reduce him to collapse and delirium. But the intensity of these scenes is followed by a totally different vision of the parents; behind their cruelty lies the despair and hopelessness of an existence into which they have been betrayed. The mother is undone by the anguish of approaching old age, the loss of love, the husband's mediocrity and infidelities. But he in turn has his moment: his adventures outside the house and the marriage are a response to the constant complaints of a nagging wife. Abruptly, the game within a game is ended, and

the sisters speak calmly. They emerge from their trial hardened; only Lalo is weak. The game has ended, but inevitably it must begin again.

In this dazzling sequence of plays within a play, Triana has created a work that lends itself to a variety of interpretations. Many have wished to see the play as a document of the terrible generational conflict that threatens to destroy society. Certainly, it is a desolate vision of generational relationships, of the anguish of approaching age or of repressed adolescence. Lalo, Cuca, and Beba, like María of *Medea en el espejo*, are in search of their own reality. They wish to make their own world; at its heart, their obsessive shifting of furniture can lead nowhere. Removing the old without replacing it with something else leads only to chaos. Other critics see in the family the structures of a decaying bourgeois world that was overthrown by the Revolution, so that *The Criminals* becomes a sort of parable of revolution. Once again, this family is obviously in collapse, characterized by cruelty, ferocity, and corruption, its authority undermined or close to nonexistent. But to see in this dance of mirrors with its shifting realities only an orthodox vision of social problems is simplistic. The doublings of characters and structural parellelisms, the shifting levels of reality make the work a complex meditation on the very nature of theater.

Once again in *The Criminals* Triana is constructing the myth of violent irrationality, and again, he uses the structure of a murderous game. It is a ceremonial rite, the chanting of apparent nonsense phrases a litany, and the shifting of furniture the placing of ceremonial objects. The whole performance is a ritual that has been performed in the past and that will take place again. But this rite is not a substitute for something else. It is a ritual purgation in preparation for its counterpart. It is a rite before the act, rather than after, and so even more sinister.

Triana is not a social critic in the normal sense of the words. In his obsessive presentation of the myth of violence and the irrational in Cuban life, there is no direct approach to social, economic, or political problems. The object of his attack is the stagnation that led to the need for a revolution, the blind religiosity, the political corruption, and the decadence of the family, subjects also portrayed in the work of other Cuban dramatists of the period.

JOSÉ TRIANA

SELECTED BIBLIOGRAPHY

Editions

El Parque de la Fraternidad. Havana, 1962. Also includes *El mayor general hablará de teogonía* and *Medea en el espejo.*
La muerte del ñeque. Havana, 1964.
La noche de los asesinos. Havana, 1965.

Translations

The Criminals. In *The Modern Stage in Latin America: Six Plays,* edited by George Woodyard. New York, 1971. Also in *The Drama Review* 14/2:105–129 (1970).

Biographical and Critical Studies

Arrufat, Antón. "An Interview on the Theater in Cuba and in Latin America." Translated by Duard MacInnes. *Odyssey Review* 2/4:248–263 (1962).
Brownell, Virginia. "The Eucharistic Image as a Symbol of the Downfall of Modern Man." *Latin American Theatre Review* 10/1:37–43 (1976).
Dauster, Frank. "The Game of Chance: The Theatre of José Triana." *Latin American Theatre Review* 3/1:3–8 (1969).
_____. "José Triana: El juego violento." In *Ensayos sobre teatro hispanoamericano.* Mexico City, 1975. Pp. 9–36.
De la Campa, Román V. *José Triana: Ritualización de la sociedad cubana.* Institute for the Study of Ideologies and Literature. Minneapolis, Minn., 1979.
Estorino, Abelardo. "Destruir los fantasmas: Los mitos de las relaciones familiares." *Conjunto* 2/4:6–14 (1967).
Green, Joan Rea. "The Hero in Contemporary Spanish American Theatre: A Case of Diminishing Returns." *Latin American Theatre Review* 5/2:19–27 (1972).

Meléndez, Priscilla. "El espacio dramático como signo." *Latin American Theatre Review* 17/1:25–35 (1983).
Miranda, Julio. "José Triana o el conflicto." *Cuadernos hispanoamericanos* 230:439–444 (1969).
_____. "Sobre el nuevo teatro cubano." In *Nueva literatura cubana.* Madrid, 1971. Pp. 105–115.
Montes Huidobro, Matías. "Máscara familiar: Esquizofrenia mágica." In *Persona, vida y máscara en el teatro cubano.* Miami, 1973. Pp. 413–427.
Moretta, Eugene. "Spanish American Theatre of the 50's and 60's: Critical Perspectives." *Latin American Theatre Review* 13/2:5–30 (1980).
Murch, Anne C. "Genet-Triana-Kopit: Ritual as 'Danse macabre.'" *Modern Drama* 15/4:369–381 (1973).
Neglia, Erminio. "El asedio a la casa: Un estudio del decorado en *La noche de los asesinos.*" *Revista iberoamericana* 46/110–111:139–149 (1980).
Nigro, Kirsten. "*La noche de los asesinos:* Playscript and Stage Enactment." *Latin American Theatre Review* 11/1:45–57 (1977).
Ortega, Julio. "La noche de los asesinos." *Cuadernos americanos* 164/3:262–267 (1969).
_____. *Figuración de la persona.* Madrid, 1970.
Palls, Terry L. "The Theatre of the Absurd in Cuba After 1959." *Latin American Theatre Review* 4/7:67–72 (1975).
Skinner, Eugene. "Research Guide to Post-Revolutionary Cuban Drama." *Latin American Theatre Review* 7/2:59–68 (1974).
Woodyard, George. "Perspectives on Cuban Theatre." *Revista/Review Interamericana* 9/1:42–49 (1979).
_____, and Leon Lyday, eds. *Dramatists in Revolt: The New Latin American Theater.* Austin, Tex., 1976.
_____, Leon Lyday, and Frank Dauster, eds. *9 Dramaturgos hispanoamericanos* 1. Ottawa, Canada, 1979. Contains *La noche de los asesinos.*

Mario Vargas Llosa

(1936–   )

Sara Castro-Klarén

Before the publication of *La ciudad y los perros* (The City and the Dogs; published in English as *The Time of the Hero*, 1963), the realm of Peruvian letters was dominated by the towering twentieth-century figures of José Carlos Mariátegui, Cesár Vallejo, and José María Arguedas. Mariátegui had laid the foundation for a debate about the constitution of Peru as a modern national state. In doing so, he established the idea that Peru's indigenous masses are the crucial factor for understanding not only Peru's history but also the possibility of a future national literature.

Vallejo, a contemporary of Mariátegui, did not achieve a position of influence among Peruvian and Latin American intellectuals during his lifetime, as Mariátegui did with the publication of his review *Amauta* (Inca Wiseman) and his watershed book *Siete ensayos de interpretación de la realidad peruana* (*Seven Interpretive Essays on Peruvian Reality*, 1928). Considered one of the greatest poets of the Spanish language, Vallejo's presence grew in intensity and prestige after his premature and dramatic death in 1938. His poetry, prose, and theater were fundamentally iconoclastic and deeply innovative. His work is an aesthetic and political statement of commitment to an inviolable human solidarity. Vallejo's work became a point of reference for all future writing in Peru.

Arguedas continued, philosophically and politically, in the footsteps of the two great men who preceded him. His best novel, *Los ríos profundos* (*Deep Rivers*, 1958), established Arguedas as the major Peruvian novelist. His fictional world gradually expanded from incisive recollections of life in Andean villages to a portrayal of the contradictions of the large urban centers in coastal Peru. Arguedas rendered, in a tender and moving realism, the vision of the world of the Quechua people.

It is within this context of national literature that Mario Vargas Llosa began his literary career in 1952 with the staging of his play "La huída del inca" (The Flight of the Inca), in Piura. He briefly resided in this small northern Peruvian town during his high school years. Vargas Llosa was born on 28 March 1936 in Arequipa in southern Peru, to a relatively well-to-do family of old aristocratic name and connections. His mother and father separated at about the time of his birth, and he spent his early childhood as a spoiled grandchild in his maternal grandfather's household. Following his grandfather's appointments to diplomatic and other government posts, Vargas Llosa's early schooling took place in Cochabamba, Bolivia, from 1937 to 1941. Later his grandfather moved to Piura, and there Vargas Llosa attended a religious private school.

In 1950 Vargas Llosa's parents reconciled, and the reunited family moved to Lima. The fourteen-year-old boy was sent to the Leoncio Prado Military Academy, in his father's view to correct the spoiled and unmanly brat his wife's family had raised. This period probably marks Vargas Llosa's first acquaintance with pain, violence, and death. The young man who was to become the author of brutal tales discovered, in these troubled years, the complicity of evil and experience, and suffered a profound alienation. The spirit of a rebel was formed.

Like Mariátegui and many other Latin American writers, the young man, aspiring to be an intellectual, began to feel an acute need to leave his native country and search for wider horizons in Europe. As soon as he finished his college degree with a major in literature at the University of San Marcos in Lima, he secured a grant to continue his doctoral studies in Spain. According to him and to the accounts of his first wife, Julia Urquidi, in *Lo que Varguitas no dijo* (What Varguitas Didn't Say, 1983), he spent most of his time reading as well as writing and rewriting the manuscript of what was to become his first novel. The novel attempted to capture his recollections of the two years that he had spent in the Leoncio Prado Military Academy in Lima as an adolescent. When the scholarship ended, he did not feel ready to return to Peru. His goal had always been to spend an extended period of time in Paris, and so without much money he and his wife settled there in 1959.

During his college years in Lima, Vargas Llosa had helped support himself and his wife—he had married when he was nineteen years old—by holding a variety of part-time jobs. He worked for a television network as a newscaster and also was a local reporter for several Lima newspapers. This journalistic experience held him in good stead in Paris, and he was able to find work as a radio journalist at the Radio Television Française. Throughout his career as a novelist, he has continued to work as a special reporter for many major newspapers and magazines in Latin America, the United States, and Europe.

His early experience with the military as an institution and ideology, as well as his experiences as a journalist and broadcaster can, in retrospect, be seen as major sources for Vargas Llosa's novelistic world and social thought. Army men, journalists, soap

operas, war, and organized violence appear in all his major novels, including *The Time of the Hero*, *La casa verde* (*The Green House*, 1966), *Conversación en La Catedral* (*Conversation in The Cathedral*, 1969), *Pantaleón y las visitadoras* (*Captain Pantoja and the Special Service*, 1973), *La tía Julia y el escribidor* (*Aunt Julia and the Scriptwriter*, 1977), and his two historical novels, *La guerra del fin del mundo* (*The War of the End of the World*, 1981) and *Historia de Mayta* (*The Real Life of Alejandro Mayta*, 1984).

During the time that he worked full-time in journalism and broadcasting, the café life was a temptation that Vargas Llosa avoided assiduously. He had a plan: to devour the French classics and advance, rewrite, and polish the manuscript of his novel, provisionally entitled "Los impostores" (The Imposters). Though he was still a young and unknown writer, he had already received minor rewards and recognition for his work. In 1958 he had won a short trip to Paris as the first-place prize for one of his short stories in a contest sponsored in Peru by the *Revue française*. A year later he had won the Leopoldo Alas Prize, one of many Spanish literary prizes, for his first collection of short stories, *Los jefes* (The Leaders, 1959; some of which were published in English in *The Cubs and Other Stories*).

The young writer struggled with a manuscript that continued to grow bigger and become more technically demanding. Vargas Llosa was not sure what steps to take to see it published, for he was aware of its technical complexity as well as the scandalous and neopornographic experiences of his characters. A chance meeting with Carlos Barral, one of the owners of the influential Catalan publishing house Seix-Barral, decided the fate of the manuscript, no longer called "Los impostores," but retitled "La morada del héroe" (The Home of the Hero). Soon after submission, it was not only accepted for publication, but it also won, by a rare unanimous vote, the annual Spanish Biblioteca Breve Prize. Unlike the Leopoldo Alas Prize, this was a very important award in the Spanish-speaking world, and it had never before been awarded to a Latin American writer.

The novel, published in 1963 with the title *La ciudad y los perros*, quickly moved to the foreground of the crest of the "new" Latin American novels that were gaining international prominence. Vargas Llosa was the youngest of the handful of writers to be associated with the boom of Latin American literature. The early 1960's also saw the publication of Julio Cortázar's *Rayuela* (*Hopscotch*, 1963), Carlos Fuentes' *La muerte de Artemio Cruz* (*The Death of Artemio Cruz*, 1962), and Gabriel García Márquez' *Cien años de soledad* (*One Hundred Years of Solitude*, 1967).

When *The Time of the Hero* was read in Lima, it was regarded as more than a literary novelty or success. Unwittingly responding to Vargas Llosa's adoption of the Sartrian concept of literature as fire, or a kind of permanent state of insurrection against the established order, the military viewed the novel as an affront to its prestige and burned a large number of copies in the patios of the Leoncio Prado Military Academy. News of the scandal spread through different sectors of the reading public, and ironically, sales of the book became quite brisk. At the critical level, *The Time of the Hero* was immediately recognized as a very important novel. The wealth of technical innovations that it incorporated made it a dazzling text and established it as a challenge to any reader. The story it told was gripping. It appealed to a very basic reason for reading literature: the desire to experience, in the realm of the imagination, a human drama in which we can become deeply involved for philosophical, political, emotional, or aesthetic reasons.

In retrospect, it is evident that *The Time of the Hero* constitutes the thematic as well as the rhetorical touchstone of Vargas Llosa's narrative oeuvre. In his later novels he would repeat, change, enhance, add, drop, and alter aspects of the narrative structure of his first novel; but the skeleton of that book would always be visible as the basic structure of his narrative imagination. With regard to the established tradition—a realism respectful of the categories of linear time, consistent and continuous point of view, identifiable omniscient or first-person narration, unity in the story, round and/or flat characters—*The Time of the Hero* can be seen as an exploration, even a flaunting, of a variety of avant-garde narrative rhetorical devices associated with James Joyce and William Faulkner. Most of these techniques affect the nature of the point of view and identity of the narrator.

In *The Time of the Hero*, the novelist mixes at will, and without warning, interior monologue, omniscient narration, memories recounted in conversation, flashback, and straight reporting. Sudden shifts in point of view and the withholding of the identity of the character-narrator combine to produce a first impression of narrative chaos. Not only are the identities of many narrators withheld until later in the novel, but information about plot elements is denied to the reader, who thus finds his task of linear reading transformed into that of puzzle working. The storytelling of Vargas Llosa is not centered on the question "What happened?" or even "Why did it happen?" but rather on "How did it happen?" Thus the reader is much more in charge of the production of meaning than he would be in a traditional text in which the author has marked most of the points of connection.

The story line of *The Time of the Hero* is actually very simple. At the command of the leader (Jaguar) of a gang, a cadet (Cava) in a military academy steals the questions for an examination. Though he is seen by another cadet (El Esclavo), the crime is not discovered by school officials until much later. The "honor" code operating among the cadets keeps them silent. Finally El Esclavo reports the theft. An investigation follows, uncovering much more than the stealing of an examination. Later, while on maneuvers, Jaguar kills the informer. Though the murderer is fingered by another cadet (Alberto), the military authorities decide that, in view of what has been uncovered, the best thing is to pretend that nothing irregular has happened. This declaration has an indelible and irreversible effect on the lives of the cadets who are thus, after their last year, returned to society.

The combination of a simple story line with a complex narrative rhetoric may appear paradoxical. However, the narrative dwells exhaustively on the portrayal of a violent society, the military academy, and Jaguar's gang. The fears of the boys, faced with the saturating violence in the academy, are portrayed from several angles and from differing distances. Their violent and cynical responses are revealed by a juxtaposition of scenes, whose effect is reminiscent of the speed and illusion of authenticity of the *cinéma vérité*. In the orgiastic scene of the rape of the hen, for example, the statements of different voices succeed each other with such speed and detailed precision that the reader is forced to forget the need to know who is narrating or who is doing what to whom, as he feels himself assaulted and overwhelmed by the "facts" that compose the repulsive scene in which the boys engage. The complications in the novelistic form embedded in the narrative are constantly bulldozed under by the relentless action in the novel. In *The Time of the Hero,* as well as in Vargas Llosa's other novels, something urgent and insufficiently portrayed is always happening, either in the inner world of a character or in the external world.

The Time of the Hero tells the story of six adolescent boys, sent by their parents to finish high school in a military academy named for a young hero in Peruvian history: Leoncio Prado. The parents' choice of a military academy is predicated on the need for the boys to become men or to become educated. People from different geographical, class, and racial sectors of Peru suddenly find themselves together, but separate, in the halls and patios of the military academy. Because of Vargas Llosa's own statements about his admiration for Jean-Paul Sartre's existentialism, this novel has often been read as an existentialist account of young men acting in rebellion against the corrupt established order, in order to gain some freedom and dignity. Within this reading, it has also been necessary to accept that none of the boys, not even Alberto, gain any freedom, for they all succumb to and learn to exploit the rules of organized violence and fratricidal war as an essential part of survival.

What the social organization at the military academy—a mirror image of family life in the city—predicates is that the hierarchical authority embodied in the rules of *machismo* (an exaggerated masculinity) prevails even to the point of a denial of concrete reality. In this world, the strong dominate. All members of society take their place in the pecking order, with Jaguar at the top and El Esclavo at the bottom. An individual must accept and endure violence done to his person. He must steal an examination under orders, or drink urine, or perform rape under orders, or lick another's boots, or torture and rape animals. He must, in turn, in order to keep his place in the hierarchy, dole out pain and humiliation to those below him. This behavior ensures the

individual the "protection" of the system that thus allows his survival.

If the system's justification is survival, murder would seem an intolerable transgression of its rules. Yet the epilogue of the novel shows that in spite of Alberto's hypocritical heroic stance in fingering Jaguar as the killer of El Esclavo and revealing many other ghastly deeds, the system will use any means at its disposal to uphold the illusion that the order it sustains resembles justice or education. Therefore, for the convenience of those involved in the status quo—and this includes Alberto's "good" family—all parties agree to pretend that nothing that violates the rules of justice has happened. Lieutenant Gamboa, the only person who insists on the recognition of the truth, is banished. Thus the breached circle closes, having made "imposters" of all the cadets. The possibility of truth is denied to all by a system that pretends to uphold values of dignity and justice.

The brutal and numbing reality that Vargas Llosa depicts in *The Time of the Hero* is physically organized around two spatial centers—the city and the academy—between which the past and present of the lives and needs of the adolescents become articulated. In *The Green House,* his second novel, Vargas Llosa attempts to bridge even wider spatial, temporal, and social gaps. The action of the novel takes place in a distant part of the yet-unsettled Peruvian jungle and the desert coastal town of Piura. It spans three generations and includes more than thirty-four characters.

Just as his experience at the military academy became an unforgettable period in Vargas Llosa's life and affected his sense of the world, his personal discovery of the Peruvian jungle also marked his novelistic world indelibly. When he began working on *The Green House,* Vargas Llosa tells in *La historia secreta de una novela* (A Novel's Secret Story, 1971), he was attempting to fashion into narrative form his obsessive memories of a legendary whorehouse on the outskirts of Piura. But as his imagination elaborated this site of the forbidden, the memories of stories he had heard about a Japanese bandit and rubber trader in the Amazon jungle kept disturbing his narrative of the desert. The need to write about the jungle became pressing. However, Vargas Llosa was aware that his firsthand acquaintance with the jungle was brief and that Latin American letters already boasted a long and rich tradition of works set in the Amazonian basin. He thus set out to read everything possible, including decidedly third-rate stories and novels, set in the South American tropics.

The result was a two-strand composite of five major stories bridged at most times by the lives of two characters. Sergeant Lituma and Bonifacia move, in inverse directions, from Piura in the desert to Santa María de Nieva in the Amazon jungle. The narrative begins at a river near Santa María de Nieva. A group of Spanish nuns, supported by a detachment of soldiers, are attempting to kidnap native girls in order to take them to their school and integrate them into Christian civilization. From this point, the narrative begins a movement backward, chronicling the rape of the blind girl Antonia by the musician Anselmo in Piura, the sale of the adolescent Lalita into concubinage with the Japanese outlaw Fushía, the flight of Bonifacia from the nuns' convent into matrimonial servitude with Sergeant Lituma, Fushía's death in a leprosarium, and Bonifacia's final destination—the Piura whorehouse known as La Casa Verde.

In this novel Vargas Llosa attempts the impossible: to bring together many disparate fragments of the lives of people who live in a territory cartographically known as Peru. Three institutions—the army, the church, and the family, or the whorehouse—become the vehicles by which the lives of these characters establish relations of mutual exploitation and violence. It would seem that the final meaning of life, as seen by the author of *The Green House*, is that it is an ever-changing adventure in pain, humiliation, and general abjection that people never understand.

More so than in *The Time of the Hero*, in *The Green House* Vargas Llosa exercises his passion for the telling of the adventure, a legacy of his early reading of the works of Alexandre Dumas. Although Bonifacia and Sergeant Lituma hold the novel together inasmuch as they, directly or indirectly, maintain relations with all the other characters, the adventures of Fushía and Anselmo have proved more captivating to the imaginations of some readers.

No matter what the ambitions or desires of the characters, they all end their lives miserably. The women, who in Vargas Llosa's novels are stereotypical of the vision of women in patriarchal societies, hope only to attach themselves to men who will not be too cruel in exchange for all the services a female can provide within or outside the household. For the men, the higher their aim—for money or power—the greater their fall.

Even simplified the story is not easy to summarize. Bonifacia has been kidnapped by the nuns and raised in their school. When a fresh group of captured girls arrives, Bonifacia, now a young woman, cannot collaborate in their imprisonment and lets the girls go, against the commands of the nuns. For this she is berated and expelled from the convent. Having nowhere to go, she funds asylum in the home of Lalita, who takes her in as a sort of servant. Lalita is at this point living with Nieves, a sergeant in the Peruvian army.

When Lalita was an adolescent, her mother had practically sold her to the rubber king Fushía. The ambitious Japanese took the pubescent girl for his lover. In those days, Fushía controlled an island and had an army with which he would raid the native villages to steal their rubber and women. Lalita is now fat and content, for living with Nieves is a great deal easier than being the object of Fushía's orgies and sadism. Lalita introduces Bonifacia to Nieves' friend Sergeant Lituma and blesses their marriage. Bonifacia moves to Piura when Lituma's period of service in the army comes to an end. There she is called Selvática (Wildflower) by Lituma's old drinking buddies, the "unconquerables." She soon has to support them all by working at La Casa Verde, where she meets Chunga, the present owner of the whorehouse and daughter of the mysterious Anselmo and the orphan girl Antonia. The story ends with the revelation that Fushía had contracted leprosy while still on the island and subsequently lost his hold over his army of Huambisas. He is finally seen floating down the river in the kind company of Aquilino, who is taking him to a leprosarium.

To narrate this complex group of stories, each replete with adventures, Vargas Llosa had to use the plethora of narrative devices he so innovatively deployed in *The Time of the Hero*, as well as additional innovations. He once again exploited the device of starting to tell the story after the major and critical event had taken place. From this position his narrator could move forward with a present-tense narrative or backward to recall the events that led up to the point when the narrative began. In *The Green House*, Vargas Llosa introduced what would later be called "telescopic conversations." This narrative device places two characters in conversation about past events. However, each time a person speaks, the statement he or she makes is picked up by a character participating in yet another conversational situation. The result is a double-helical structure in the narrative. In this manner Vargas Llosa superimposes one distant set of events over another.

Vargas Llosa also superimposes one point of view over another, one temporal sequence over another, one social or geographical space over another. Once again the reader finds himself in the presence of a series of fragments or puzzle pieces that he must fit together in order to gain a sense of linear sequence or spatial correspondences by which all the events can make sense, if not as a unit, at least as a totality. This was indeed a daring but necessary strategy for dealing with the diversity of historical elements included in *The Green House*. The characters are almost never presented in solitary introspection. It is in conversation, in relation to another person, that they attempt, in the telling of "what happened," to understand, though without much success, the sequence of events that have come to constitute their lives.

Yet *The Green House* stands as an achievement precisely because Vargas Llosa has succeeded in interweaving all these competing, and at times disparate, narrative traditions and realities. He creates something new that stands above the sum of its fragments. In the speed of the shifts, similar to the speed of film, the distances and limits separating the parts become imperceptible. Once the reader has adjusted the focus of his vision, once the reader's resistance to reading on without knowing certain pieces of information has been worn down, the narrative moves like an avalanche. In this movement, the discrete separation of the book's elements—narration, description, dialogue, reflection, flashback, omniscient narrator, first-person narrator—takes second place to the story or stories emerging from the text of the novel.

In spite of the sense of fragmentation and the torrential movement of the story, a close scrutiny of the novel shows that the author has taken care to organize his material with scrupulous rigor. The novel is divided into four books and an epilogue. Each book in turn contains a prologue and three or four chapters, and each chapter is further divided into five sequences in the first two books and four in the last two books. In contrast to the arrangement in *The Time of the Hero*, the lengths of the chapters and number of sequences in *The Green House* is carefully regulated.

The critical reception of this novel was characterized by almost sheer acclaim. By this time Vargas Llosa had visited Cuba and participated as judge in several of the prizes awarded by Casa de las Américas, the major publishing house in Cuba. *The Green House*, along with his previous novel, was quickly translated into some twenty European languages, and in 1967 it was selected for the Rómulo Gallegos Prize.

Between the publication of his next novel, *Conversation in The Cathedral*, and *The Green House*, he refurbished an older manuscript and published *Los cachorros* (*The Cubs*, 1967; published in English in *The Cubs and Other Stories*) as a novella. With this truculent story about a young man who loses his sexual organ when bitten by a dog, Vargas Llosa returns to the theme of adolescents growing up in a *machista* society. Here again, the young men simply adjust or collapse. Any possible heroic stance is wasted in the *machista* rituals that the initiation into manhood requires of the luckier upper-class boys who did not have to attend the brutal military academy.

With *Conversation in The Cathedral*, originally published in two volumes, Vargas Llosa returns to Lima, the part of Peru that he knows best, and to his own experiences in that city. This novel, like *The Time of the Hero*, is indeed autobiographical. Once again we see the portrayal of a young man facing choices that will define his life irreversibly. In this case Vargas Llosa returns to the problem of authenticity, outlining a depressingly mediocre life. He describes the places and social pockets that he knows intimately because of his upper-middle-class origins, as well as his stints as broadcaster for Radio Panamericana, reporter for *La Crónica* (The Chronicle), and librarian at the exclusive and aristocratic Club Nacional. He also attempts to chronicle the political atmosphere during the dictatorship of General Manuel Odría from 1948 to 1956. Once again he researched the period thoroughly, with a care for documentary sources that began with *The Green House.*

Conversation in The Cathedral takes place, on one narrative level, during a four-hour conversation between Santiago Zavala and his father's former servant Ambrosio, held at a miserable and fetid little bar in Lima. This conversation will serve as the outer case for many other conversations between other characters in the novel. The days of the Odría regime are evoked from many points of view and points in time, in an effort to identify the moment or reason why Santiago Zavala has become Zavalita, a failed rebel, a failed writer, and a stillborn hero.

Once again Vargas Llosa minimizes the presence of the omniscient narrator to an almost imperceptible level. The narrative task is given to the characters, who often narrate without proper self-identification, creating many opportunities for confusion. It is often difficult to tell, for example, when Ambrosio is talking to Santiago—whom he addresses as Niño—and when he is talking to his master and lover Don Fermín. The conversational structure in *Conversation in The Cathedral* works in the manner of ·stacked Russian dolls or Chinese boxes, for the outer casing of the conversation between Santiago and Ambrosio at times contains as many as six other conversations. These conversations within conversations, located at different times and involving different people, engage in a united polyphonic performance. Each time a character speaks, often not in response to the statements made by the person he or she is physically addressing, a bit more of the "how" of the story becomes clear to the reader.

Santiago accidentally runs into Ambrosio, his father's former chauffeur. While drinking at the bar called The Cathedral, Santiago probes Ambrosio's recollections in order to confirm his suspicion that Ambrosio is in fact the murderer of La Musa, a local whore. As the past is evoked, the voices of the other participants in the plot begin to tell their part in the story. Don Fermín Zavala, a well-to-do aristocratic industrialist, has become a "senator" in the parliament of the dictator. Though as a member of his class he despises the lower-class military and its front man Odría, he collaborates with them in order to main-

tain certain very important privileges for his business enterprises.

Santiago, his favorite son, has been growing uncomfortable with the socioeconomic structure of the country and especially with the compromising role his family and class play in the sociopolitical process. In the subsequent rejection of his class and especially his father, Santiago decides to attend San Marcos, a public university in which the rebellious lower classes enroll and attempt to gain political power. There he considers the idea of joining the critics of the status quo, whose dissatisfaction he fully shares. These young men and women see no alternative to the political process but to become active Marxists and communists. This is a step that Santiago can never take, according to him, for lack of faith in any ideology.

Nevertheless, Santiago plays along as a member of a secret cell whose existence is discovered by the dictator's secret police, precisely because his father's own home and telephone are being watched. Santiago is detained along with all the other members of the clandestine cell, but because of his father's connections with the regime, he is freed in less than twenty-four hours. The other students are processed and punished. Santiago once again feels that his father has robbed him of an opportunity for heroism, and rather than feeling grateful, he grows more enraged by his father and what he represents. He moves out of the paternal household and finds a job as a reporter for the criminal page of *La Crónica.* In this occupation he learns even more about the life of degradation and violence common to many Peruvians and begins to dwell more and more hopelessly on his own failure.

Through Ambrosio's narrative we, along with Santiago, learn that Cayo Bermúdez, the minister of the interior, is the man whose political alliance with Don Fermín required that his men tap the telephone of the aristocrat. Cayo Bermúdez has maintained a simulation of a home, where he keeps two whores for his amusement and the amusement (and later blackmail) of the upper-class men who support or benefit from the dictator's regime. The two whores La Musa and Queta have a lesbian liaison, which Cayo Bermúdez enjoys as a voyeur. Don Fermín not only accepts invitations to Don Cayo's parties but one day rides off with Don Cayo's childhood friend and now chauffeur, Ambrosio. This huge and humble black man becomes, in spite of his heterosexual habits and preferences, Don Fermín's lover. The fact that Don Fermín's homosexuality is publically known in the world of pimps and whores is learned by Santiago when he searches for the truth about La Musa's murder. He hears Queta tell the editor of the criminal page of *La Crónica* that Ambrosio killed La Musa in order to protect Don Fermín (also known as Bola de Oro [Golden Balls]) from La Musa's blackmail.

Once again Vargas Llosa brings together a veritable human multitide to populate his novel. As in *The Green House*, most of the characters—and therefore most of the flavor, tenor, and vision of the world that marks their speech—come from the urban lower classes. The linguistic practices that mark this type of discourse had thus far been represented in literature only sporadically and had almost never been treated as a source of literary language. While it is true that this Peruvian novelist is not a linguistic innovator, as Vallejo was in both prose and poetry, Vargas Llosa has nevertheless made a new and important contribution in employing popular linguistic practices in his novels.

This novel tells a sordid and scatological tale at a galloping rhythm. One shocking discovery follows another equally pornographic or violent scene. It is indeed difficult to say in which of Vargas Llosa's novels the reader's revulsion—and curiosity—are most intensely and deftly engaged. In *Conversation in The Cathedral*, however, the central character, Santiago Zavala, is a character with whose needs and goals the reader can comfortably identify. Unlike the boys in *The Time of the Hero*, adolescents foundering in a sea of pain and cynicism, and unlike the violent and ambitious Fushía, Santiago is engaged in a worthwhile enterprise. He aims to bring about the possibility of progressive change in Peruvian society and history. Santiago is a character positioned at the crux of the most important question before Latin American nations: Is progress with a human face possible?

Conversation in The Cathedral is the only one of Vargas Llosa's novels in which the possibility of a heroic character is provided. Further, the novel openly presents itself, formally and historically, as an autobiography. For these and other reasons that have to do with the fact that we indeed recognize the fictional world as Peru itself, the failed search of Santiago Zavala and his transformation into the gray Zavalita, who turns out to be a very unsympathetic character, touches the reader's sense of empathy more intensely than the stories of other equally alienated characters of Vargas Llosa.

In this novel, in which the characters are immersed in evil, everything contributes to the infernal atmosphere. Nothing, not even "love," such as that of Ana for Santiago, mitigates the fallen state. Quite to the contrary, everything divides, everyone is suspicious. Perhaps the only two people close to innocence or, better yet, ignorance of the world, Amalia (La Musa's servant) and La Musa herself, know truly, though fleetingly, some unspoiled excitement and joy. Race separates, politics divide, kinship disconnects, money keeps people apart, social position isolates. The relation of victim to oppressor is the only one possible, and this relation, as in *The Time of the Hero*, is mediated by violence. *Conversation in The Cathedral* is perhaps Vargas Llosa's bitterest and most pessimistic novel before he turned to literary criticism and the cultivation of parody.

Between 1969 and 1975, Vargas Llosa published a number of critical texts. Aside from numerous interviews and essays in which he speaks of his narrative art, Vargas Llosa's first influential piece of literary criticism appeared in 1969 as a prologue to the first modern Spanish edition of the Catalan chivalric novel *Tirant lo blanc* (first Spanish edition, 1511). In previous essays and interviews, he had made the point that Joanot Martorell's novel, like Vargas Llosa's own work, attempts to capture reality on more than one plane. He is also impressed by Martorell because this fifteenth-century writer stressed storytelling and adventure as the essential ingredients of the novel. Though Vargas Llosa lived and breathed the development of the French *nouveau roman* (new novel) in Paris, he never had much in common with this French experiment, whose stated goal was to write novels denying characters or action or both. In his book on Gustave Flaubert, *La orgía perpetua: Flaubert y "Madame Bovary"* (The Perpetual Orgy: Flaubert and *Madame Bovary*, 1975), the author of *The Green House* states, "Even though almost all of them [Alain Robbe-Grillet, Michel Butor, and Claude Simon] bored me, with the exception of Beckett . . . who also bored me but somehow I felt the boredom justified, I always liked them because they openly proclaimed the importance of Flaubert for the modern novel" (p. 49).

Vargos Llosa's literary criticism focuses on writers whose work he admires because it has had a profound influence on his own. He has written not only about *Tirant lo blanc* but also about the work of Gabriel García Márquez (*García Márquez: Historia de un deicidio* [Gabriel García Marquez: The Story of a Deicide], 1971), Flaubert (*La orgía perpetua*), and Sartre and Camus in a collection of essays entitled *Entre Sartre y Camus* (Between Sartre and Camus, 1981). In his prolific output as novelist, journalist, and critic, Vargas Llosa has also coauthored books, such as one with Oscar Collazos and Julio Cortázar, *Literatura en la revolución y revolución en la literatura* (Literature in Revolution and Revolution in Literature, 1970), another with Martín de Riquer, *El combate imaginario: Las cartas de batalla de Joanot Martorell* (The Imaginary Combat: The Challenge Letters of Joanot Martorell, 1972), and a third with Ángel Rama, *García Márquez y la problemática de la novela* (García Márquez and the Theory of the Novel, 1973).

A close reading of his literary criticism in conjunction with what he has said about his own work in numerous interviews (such as the one with Elena Poniatonska published in *Antología mínima de M. Vargas Llosa* [Minimal Anthology of Vargas Llosa, 1969] or the collection of interviews published by R. Cano Gaviria as *El buitre y el ave fénix: Conversaciones con Vargas Llosa* [The Vulture and the Phoenix: Conversations with Vargas Llosa, 1972]), show a close coincidence of interest and critical concepts between what Vargas Llosa says of his own novelistic practice and the work of the writers he admires so passionately. Vargas Llosa regards the novel—and he gives Flaubert as a good example of this theory—as a genre that feeds on rotting flesh, that cannibalizes all objects and experiences that come to the novelist. He also believes that the challenge of the novel is to represent life in its fullest sense. He calls this the "totalizing vocation" of the novel and sees Flaubert's *Madame Bovary* (1857) and García Márquez' *One Hundred Years of Solitude* as prime examples of this idea.

With respect to ideological or propagandist ends, Vargas Llosa feels that the novel is or ought to be truly disinterested, representing all aspects of life with equal passion and verisimilitude. This quality, he argues, is present in Martorell's saucy chivalric tale. When he was writing *The Time of the Hero* and *The Green House,* he was very much taken with Sartre's existentialism and especially with the influential literary theory he advanced in *Qu'est-ce que la littérature? (What Is Literature?,* 1947). Those were the days when Vargas Llosa thought of "literature as fire," as a constant critique of the status quo, as a "permanent state of insurrection." Ten years later in his book on Flaubert, however, he finds himself closer to the nineteenth-century master and agrees with him in viewing literature and writing as a sort of revenge. "For Flaubert, who throughout his life repeated that he wrote in order to take *revenge* on reality, it was his negative experiences that in the end proved to be more stimulating artistically" (p. 105).

The scholarship that originally took him in the late 1950's to Spain to earn his doctoral degree in literature finally came to fruition when Vargas Llosa presented his manuscript on García Márquez to the University of Madrid as his doctoral thesis. In this book he develops the concept of the personal obsession or demons of the novelist. Often without the novelist's knowledge, these demons mark the path for his selection of themes and problems. In this context, all novels are autobiographical. Adhering to this thesis in his book on García Márquez, as well as in his later book on Flaubert, Vargas Llosa carefully traces the relation of materials in the novelistic text to events—psychological, physical, or intellectual—in the writer's life.

In the case of García Márquez, Vargas Llosa draws heavily on his close friendship with the Colombian writer, and in the case of Flaubert, he quotes amply from the thirteen volumes of Flaubert's correspondence. It is interesting to see that Vargas Llosa's criticism in his analysis of Flaubert retains a number of the concepts he had advanced for the reading of García Márquez' "total" novel, narrated by means of "mutations in the narrator" and deployed within a combination of "planes of reality," as well as a combination of "times." These concepts, along with the notion that modern novelists, that is, the true heirs to Flaubert, erect themselves in their fictional texts into a sort of god, have their source in Flaubert himself.

It is as if with his critical work Vargas Llosa wanted to clear the air and open the possibility of a new departure for his fictional work. After the book on García Márquez and before the revealing book on Flaubert, Vargas Llosa published his first parodic work, *Captain Pantoja and the Special Service*, in which he returned to three themes from his previous work: the military, the whorehouse, and the Peruvian jungle. The reality depicted is as scatological as in his other books. This time, however, the humor that he so carefully analyzed in García Márquez is evident in Pantaleón Pantoja's efforts to determine the number of orgasms necessary to satisfy the army troops stationed in the Amazon basin. The humor is definitely raunchy. It relies on two principles: exaggeration and the exploitation of the perception of class differences.

Much of what Pantaleón does is funny because he is a *cholo* (an acculturated Quechuan), a *huachafo* (a person of the lower class imitating the life-style of the upper class) who misreads in more than one way the instructions of his "superiors." If he had known better, as an upper-class person would, he would not have accepted the mission given to him. Pantaleón is the grotesque counterpart of Lieutenant Gamboa in *The Time of the Hero*. Gamboa also took the army seriously, but he knew a possibly dignifying mission from one calculated to ridicule his abilities as a manager.

The story unfolds by means of all types of writing except the narrative of an omniscient narrator. Dialogues, letters, radio news, commentaries, official memoranda, and scientific and statistical studies chronicle the adventures of Pantaleón as he tries to accomplish his mission: to provide a satisfactory sexual service for the troops stationed in the jungle.

Pantaleón is happily married to Pochita when he is promoted to captain and receives his orders for a most unusual duty. He is told that he must pose as a civilian but always think as a military man. He was chosen for this delicate mission because of his proven capacity as an organizer. It is in the exaggerated excess of his managerial capacity that Pantaleón finds his undoing. Having calculated the number of prostitutes, the number of soldiers, and the number of "lendings" that each man requires to satisfy his sexual needs, he proceeds to organize his service. Pantaleón and his crew arrive at each army post by boat or plane, secretly but punctually. There he has the men queue up, so that each may receive equal benefit from his service.

Eventually Pantaleón, in his scientific zeal, decides that he ought to try out his own product. In doing so he falls prey to the jungle aphrodisiacs, as well as to the charms of La Brasileña. His indefatigable zeal keeps him going, in spite of such challenges to his dutiful conscience. Eventually the news of his work leaks, and people in the neighboring villages demand or denounce his services, according to how they are affected. A strange cult, given to infanticide and other excesses, also causes problems for Pantaleón. His final undoing comes when a radio broadcaster named Sinchi denounces Pantaleón's services to an outraged and hypocritical middle class. The army brass disowns him, demotes him, and sends him, like Gamboa, to a remote post in the Andes.

There is no question that with this novel Vargas Llosa attempted something new, both in literary technique and in tenor. However, a critical controversy arose over whether Vargas Llosa, at the peak of success, had abandoned his earlier view of literature as social criticism. It has also been argued that through the parodic mode he continues to criticize an obviously distorted and unjust society.

Captain Pantoja and the Special Service unabashedly embraces the *huachafo*: the corny linguistic and social modalities of the Peruvian middle classes. Pocha's letters, Sinchi's radio communiqués, the preaching of the cult's leader, the army communiqués—all are unintentional parodic copies of some invisible but "correct" model of letter writing or news broadcasting, as the case may be. As in his previous novels, Vargas Llosa finds in *Captain Pantoja and the Special Service* an opportunity to utilize these *huachafo* forms in highbrow literature. He does so by dispensing completely with any type of narrator who might be in charge of organizing the different segments of the narrative. Yet we know, of course, that Pocha's letter and La Brasileña's obituary are indeed his writing, his stylizing of the *huachafo*.

With *Aunt Julia and the Scriptwriter*, Vargas Llosa once again attempts an autobiography. This time, he tells the story of the eighteen-year-old Marito, who works as a newscaster in a radio station at the same time that he falls in love with and marries his thirty-two-year-old aunt. This story of incestuous love is told in chapters that alternate with the story of Pedro Camacho, a Bolivian soap-opera writer who brings the women and retirees of Lima to their knees in empathy with his plots. While Camacho the scriptwriter is cast as a veritable writing machine, Marito feels that Camacho is actually dictating from some invisible master text. The aspiring writer tears apart his failed short stories and manages to earn a living by recasting the writing of others for his news bulletins.

In the end the Bolivian goes mad because he cannot keep the plots of his nine soap operas separate. Characters who died in one story reappear in another, marriages that should have been consummated evaporate, and Marito is asked to come in and take the place of the scriptwriter; from the point of view of the owners of the radio station, Marito and Camacho are involved in the same task. Though the story does not end conclusively, the last vision given to us is the return of Marito from Paris. He is now a consecrated writer, just as Camacho was a few years earlier, and the radio station prepares to celebrate the emergence of a new king.

Vargas Llosa establishes a counterpoint between the autobiography and the soap opera as two types of fiction that imitate one another. The aunt herself says that their love affair could easily fit in Camacho's serials. Though we read the autobiographical chapters under the illusion that they are part of the novel and we read Camacho's tales of infanticide, incest, castration, patricide, prostitution, and genocide as the product of an imagination bordering on madness, we cannot fail to realize that the two narrative modes belong to the same author. Marito and Pedro Camacho, are, of course, the products of one man's imagination. What is more, the themes that Camacho touches and the characters that he creates (Lalita/Sarita Huanca, Lituma/Lituma, Negro Salvaje/ Ambrosio, evangelical convert/brother) are not far removed from what Vargas Llosa had explored in his previous work, for example, nymphets, sexual per-

verts preaching under the aegis of newly minted religions, and the myth of the giant black penis.

In *Aunt Julia and the Scriptwriter* Vargas Llosa faced yet another challenge. For the first time he dealt with historical events and characters, no matter how mediocre, presenting them directly, without pretending to fictionalize them. He referred to his family and everyone connected with his side of the story with their "real" names. What flows from Pedro Camacho's side, including his name, is fictional. Precisely because Vargas Llosa deals with his family in this historical manner, Julia Urquidi (Aunt Julia) was outraged by the publication of the novel. Feeling used and unfairly portrayed, she published her own memoirs, giving a lengthy account of how the marriage came to be and how it foundered in Paris, soon after the success of *The Time of the Hero*.

In many of his interviews and through the activities of characters such as Ambrosio, Amalia, Aunt Julia, Ana, and Marito, Vargas Llosa shows that he is addicted to movies of all kinds. In 1973 he was asked by the Brazilian cinematographer Rui Guerra to adapt for the screen the great Brazilian historical account *Os Sertões* (*Rebellion in the Backlands*, 1902). In his masterpiece Euclides da Cunha indelibly described the rebellion of António Conselheiro and the people of Brazil's northeast backland. Vargas Llosa went to Brazil and traveled to the backlands of Bahia to familiarize himself with the territory, as he had done previously in the Peruvian jungle. The movie, however, was not made.

With the direct presentation of his family affair in *Aunt Julia and the Scriptwriter*, Vargas Llosa had made a first incursion into the realm of the historical novel. He had learned how to fictionalize and still remain faithful to the peculiarities of sequences of events and characters not totally devised by his novelistic imagination. After an enormous documentary effort that included the study of da Cunha's diary and nineteenth-century newspapers, Vargas Llosa wrote a gripping adventure tale in *The War of the End of the World*. He delves, in a realism bordering on naturalism, into the subjects of religious fanaticism, corrupt and misguided politics, faltering and inadequate ideological systems, ridiculous yellow journalism, sexual excesses of various sorts, mutilation, murder, starvation, and a blundering military. The forty or so lives that he develops are cut short in the inexorable historical apocalypse of the last days of the siege of Canudos by the Brazilian army.

While Vargas Llosa has added a good number of characters to da Cunha's original account, the thrust of the story remains faithful to that of the Brazilian master. As usual, he develops the story in a pair of locales, with two sets of characters and stories. As he deploys them, they begin to intersect. The events in the *sertão* (backlands), chronicled by da Cunha, have been balanced in *The War of the End of the World* with another set of events in Bahia, the capital city of the state. Galileo Gall, a phrenologist, is the most completely fictional character. The Barão (Baron) may have been based on the Barão de Gerembao. Goncalvez Viana was indeed a local politician. The myopic journalist seems to lack an historical counterpart.

The War of the End of the World—though modeled on the double helix Bahia/*sertão*—is, rhetorically speaking, one of the most traditional novels of Vargas Llosa. Each character's antecedents are carefully and sequentially given until the point when he or she meets the religious mystic António Conselheiro and decides to follow him. As in da Cunha's account, the Conselheiro is followed by all sorts of outcasts, from the innocent faithful to former bandits. The central figure of the Conselheiro remains, as in da Cunha's version, shrouded in mystery.

António Conselheiro is a lay brother who travels around the miserable villages and towns of the backlands of Bahia, repairing abandoned cemeteries and churches. He lives exclusively on alms. As time goes on, he begins preaching repentance. He announces that the end of the world is near. In the backlands and in the Conselheiro's conception of the world, this means that the end of suffering is near and that the chance for a peaceful rest in the embrace of Jesus is a real possibility. Others, who also wander in the backlands, begin to keep him company. Some pious women join the traveling band. They continue to live on alms as well as the repair of run-down sacred places. As the group grows, the preaching of the Conselheiro increases. As one thing leads to another, the authorities realize that they face a social challenge, for many people would rather heed the Conselheiro than customary wisdom or the new laws of recently inaugurated Brazilian republic.

The Conselheiro wants to preach in churches. Some priests see no harm in this, for at least he attracts the unfaithful parishioners. Other priests, who see this as a dangerous challenge to their authority and means of livelihood, oppose his wishes and close their churches to him. Slowly, hostilities between the Church and the Conselheiro grow. Those who represent civilian power also grow suspicious of the mysterious man and the almost divine way in which he is revered by his followers, as well as the townspeople. In Bahia, it is felt that his power and influence should be curbed; a detachment of soldiers is asked to apprehend him. His people, who have sympathizers everywhere, soon learn of this plan and decide to take the initiative. The first battle between the Conselheiro and the army takes place, and though they suffer many losses, the Conselheiro's people, by this time including many former bandits, win.

The news spreads like wildfire in Bahia. The "army" of the Conselheiro is thought to be enormous and well furnished. Time passes, and the Conselheiro, together with an ever-swelling number of followers, settles in the abandoned lands of the Canudos ranch by the banks of the Vassa Barris, one of the few permanent streams in the backlands. In Canudos his lieutenants—former merchants, bandits, carpenters, and midwives—build a miserable but orderly and solidaristic society. It is at this point that the Brazilian army lays siege to Canudos. It takes four separate butchering assaults by thousands of Brazilian soldiers to defeat Canudos after more than a year and a half of vicious war. In the end Canudos and the people who had assembled there are totally destroyed, in one of the many genocides in the history of Latin America.

Vargas Llosa displays his power as a narrator of action in *The War of the End of the World*. The account of the war of Canudos is comparable in excitement to the feats of *The Three Musketeers* by Alexandre Dumas, or *War and Peace*, by Leo Tolstoy. Even if one has previously read *Rebellion in the Backlands* and therefore knows the end, one keeps hoping, for example, that Pajeu, the one-eyed bandit, will return safely from his mission or that one more catastrophe will befall the Brazilian army, so that the adventure of Canudos will last just a little longer.

The War of the End of the World is a powerful narrative that opens yet another vast field for Vargas Llosa: the historical novel. The Peruvian author's interest in history, especially in the making of revolts and revolutionaries, was no doubt one of the factors that led him to reinscribe the story of António Conselheiro, a chapter in Brazilian history, in a text of his own. This capital passion, it would seem, was in no way satisfied by Vargas Llosa's inquiry into the happenings of Canudos. On the contrary, his obsession with revolution appears to have been only whetted by *The War of the End of the World*. He has repeatedly taken up the subject of rebellion and revolution in his journalistic phase. He has written, for instance, for the *New York Times Magazine* on both the Nicaraguan Sandinista revolution and the Maoist guerrilla group Sendero Luminoso (Shining Path), now operating in Peru. *The Real Life of Alejandro Mayta*, one of his recent novels, deals entirely with the making of a revolutionary and the possibility of revolution in Peru.

In *La señorita de Tacna* (The Spinster from Tacna, 1981) and *Kathie y el hipopótamo* (Kathie and the Hippopotamus, 1983), two recent plays, Vargas Llosa centers part of the action on characters who are either writers or would-be writers. In *La señorita de Tacna*, Belisario writes with the conviction that writing is the only tool capable of rescuing the past from the debris of oblivion. The narrator of this play takes every opportunity to experiment with and meditate on the possible ways of telling his story—dramatization being only one. The opposite is true in *Kathie y el hipopótamo*, for Kathie Kennedy, the idle wife of a rich man, has no memories to save or even to live by. However, she has the desire to have memories, so she fantasizes. Kathie does not have the slightest idea of how to write, that is, how to re-present, by means of words arranged in a specific order and according to certain conventions, the fantasies that animate her. Thus she hires Santiago Zavala to write her fabulistic travel "memoirs" of an imaginary trip to Africa. *Kathie y el hipopótamo*, like the story of Marito and his Aunt Julia, or even *The Real Life of Alejandro Mayta*, has more in common with soap operas and various elements of plot production than with any deep experimentation into the nature of the linguistic sign or signification.

In *The Real Life of Alejandro Mayta*, this prolific writer pushed further some experiments already essayed in his plays and novels. This work is an almost essayistic inquiry into the relation between writing—a means of re-presentation—and reality itself. In this novel the question of writing and its complex and paradoxical relation to fiction and history becomes paramount. It is within the framework of his larger topic, writing, that the novel's preoccupation with ideology—be it Christianity or Marxism—must be considered. While the writer in the novel asserts in chapter 4 that his desire is to learn "what is the connection . . . the secret thread that ties together . . . the Catholic Church . . . and the obscure revolutionary," the same writer keeps telling everyone that what he wants to write is a novel that would draw its "power of suggestion and invention, its color and dramatic force," from the "veracity of many testimonies" but that it "would nevertheless be an unrecognizable version of what happened."

These problematic relations between happenings and elaborated "facts," between testimony and reporting, between reporting and elaborating history or fiction, between the truth and a version of the events, are posited by the story itself. Mayta's story, the story of a strange, sad, caring, and searching person—hardly a revolutionary—is reconstituted by a character presented as the writer. This character, the writer, speaks directly to the reader, thus breaking one of the most cherished conventions of realism, the indirect narrative mode in which the bulk of the story is told. This "writer" also meets directly and speaks with most of the characters in the novel.

Presumably this "writer" is Vargas Llosa himself, for, like him, this man is a famous and respected writer, lives in Lima, runs every day on the Barranco beach, is influential enough to be received by anyone he needs to interview, and speaks to the reader with the understanding that he is indeed a writer of novels concerned with fundamental historical questions. The novel is clearly the story of a generation in the same way that *Conversation in The Cathedral* marks the path of Vargas Llosa's generation. In the course of the novel, the "writer" does write a story about Mayta, along with a meditation on the question—including the chances, wisdom, possibilities, and ideologies—of revolutionary change in Peru.

With his most recent novel, *¿Quien mató a Palomino Molero?* (*Who Killed Palomino Molero?*, 1986), Vargas Llosa returns to the coastal setting of *The Green House*. Lituma reappears in this novel of suspense and false clues as the Dr. Watson in the investigation of the brutal murder of an innocent young man, Palomino Molero. The novel begins after the fact. The first scene conveys, in conversation, the details of the murder. The rest of the narrative moves both forward and backward in search of motive and the identity of the murderers. Vargas Llosa displays an almost conscious refinement of his previously dazzling narrative techniques in the service of sheer suspense. In this regard, *Who Killed Palomino Molero?* is reminiscent of García Márquez' *Crónica de una muerte anunciada* (*Chronicle of a Death Foretold*, 1981).

Vargas Llosa's career as a novelist and journalist describes the trajectory of an indefatigable man of letters. Both his production and his themes have remained remarkably steady, and he constantly places his characters at the limits of human experience.

SELECTED BIBLIOGRAPHY

Editions

Los jefes. Barcelona, 1959.
La ciudad y los perros. Barcelona, 1963.
La casa verde. Barcelona, 1966.
Los cachorros. Barcelona, 1967.
Conversación en La Catedral. 2 vols. Barcelona, 1969.
La historia secreta de una novela. Barcelona, 1971.
García Márquez: Historia de un deicidio. Barcelona, 1971.
Pantaleón y las visitadoras. Barcelona, 1973.
La orgía perpetua: Flaubert y "Madame Bovary." Barcelona, 1975.
La tía Julia y el escribidor. Barcelona, 1977.
La guerra del fin del mundo. Barcelona, 1981.
Entre Sartre y Camus. Barcelona, 1981.
La señorita de Tacna. Barcelona, 1981.
Kathie y el hipopótamo. Barcelona, 1983.
Historia de Mayta. Barcelona, 1984.
¿Quien mató a Palomino Molero? Barcelona, 1986.

Translations

Aunt Julia and the Scriptwriter. Translated by Helen R. Lane. New York, 1982.
Captain Pantoja and the Special Service. Translated by Gregory Kolovakos and Ronald Christ. New York, 1978.
Conversation in The Cathedral. Translated by Gregory Rabassa. New York, 1975.
The Cubs and Other Stories. Translated by Gregory Kolovakos and Ronald Christ. New York, 1979.
The Green House. Translated by Gregory Rabassa. New York, 1968.
The Real Life of Alejandro Mayta. Translated by Alfred Mac Adam. New York, 1986.
The Time of the Hero. Translated by Lysander Kemp. New York, 1966.
The War of the End of the World. Translated by Helen R. Lane. New York, 1984.
Who Killed Palomino Molero? Translated by Alfred Mac Adam. New York, 1987.

Biographical and Critical Studies

Benedetti, Mario. "Vargas Llosa y su fértil escándalo." In *Homenaje a Mario Vargas Llosa*, edited by Helmy F. Giacoman and José Miguel Oviedo. Madrid, 1972. Pp. 245–262.
———. "Ni cínicos ni oportunistas." In *El desexilio y otras conjeturas.* Buenos Aires, 1985. Pp. 173–177.
Brotherston, Gordon. "Social Structure: Mario Vargas Llosa." In *The Emergence of the Latin American Novel.* Cambridge, England, 1977. Pp. 110–121.
Castro-Klarén, Sara. "Fragmentation and Alienation in *La casa verde.*" *Modern Language Notes* 87/2:286–299 (1972).
———. "Humor and Class in *Pantaleón y las visitadoras.*" *Latin American Literary Review* 7/13:64–79 (1978).
———. "Locura y dolor: La elaboración de la historia en *Os Sertões* y *La guerra del fin del mundo.*" *Revista de crítica literaria latinoamericana* (Lima) 10/20:207–230 (1984).
———. "Santos and Cangaceiros: Inscription without Discourse in *Os Sertões* and *La guerra del fin del mundo.*" *Modern Language Notes* 101/2:366–388 (1986).
Christ, Ronald. "Talk with Mario Vargas Llosa." *New York Times Book Review*, 9 April 1978. Pp. 11, 32, 33.
Cornejo Polar, Antonio. "La historia como apocalipsis." *Qué hacer* (Lima) 33 (1985).
Davis, Mary E. "*Dress Gray* y *La ciudad y los perros*: El laberinto del honor." *Revista iberoamericana* 47/116–117:117–126 (1981).
Dauster, Frank. "Vargas Llosa and the End of Chivalry." *Books Abroad* 44/1:41–45 (1970).
Diez, Luis Alfonso. *Mario Vargas Llosa's Pursuit of the Total Novel.* Cuernavaca, Mexico, 1970.
Fenwick, M. J. *Dependency Theory and Literary Analysis:*

Reflections on Vargas Llosa's "The Green House." Minneapolis, Minn., 1981.

Fernández, Casto M. *Aproximación formal a la novelística de Vargas Llosa.* Madrid, 1977.

Gerdes, Dick. *Mario Vargas Llosa.* Boston, 1985.

Harss, Luis, and Barbara Dohmann. *Into the Mainstream.* New York, 1967.

Jones, Julie. "The Search for Paradise in *Captain Pantoja and the Special Service.*" *Latin American Literary Review* 9/19:41–46 (1981).

Machen, Stephen M. "'Pornoviolence' and Point of View in Mario Vargas Llosa's *La tía Julia y el escribidor.*" *Latin American Literary Review* 9/17:9–16 (1980).

Moody, Michael. "Paisajes de los condenados: El escenario natural de *La casa verde.*" *Revista iberoamericana* 47/116–117:127–136 (1981).

Morello-Frosch, Marta. "Of Heroes and Martyrs: The Grotesque in *Pantaleón y las visitadoras.*" *Latin American Literary Review* 7/14:40–44 (1979).

Ortega, Julio. *La contemplación y la fiesta.* Lima, 1968. Pp. 123–133.

Osorio Tejeda, Nelson. "La expresión de los niveles de realidad en la narrativa de Vargas Llosa." In *Asedios a Vargas Llosa.* Santiago, Chile, 1972. Pp. 67–88.

Oviedo, José Miguel. *Mario Vargas Llosa: La invención de una realidad.* Barcelona, 1970. 3rd ed. 1982.

———, ed. *Mario Vargas Llosa: El escritor y la crítica.* Madrid, 1981.

———, et al. "Focus: *Conversation in The Cathedral.*" *Review 75:* Center for Inter-American Relations. (Spring 1975). Pp. 5–37.

Pacheco, José Emilio. "El contagio de la culpa." In *Asedios a Vargas Llosa.* Santiago, Chile, 1972. Pp. 11–36.

Prieto, René. "The Two Narrative Voices in Mario Vargas Llosa's *Aunt Julia and the Scriptwriter.*" *Latin American Literary Review* 11/22:15–25 (1983).

Rama, Ángel, and Mario Vargas Llosa. *García Márquez y la problemática de la novela.* Buenos Aires, 1974.

Rossman, Charles, and Alan Friedman, eds. *Mario Vargas Llosa: A Collection of Critical Essays.* Austin, Tex., and London, 1978.

Sommers, Joseph. "Literatura e ideología: La evaluación novelística del militarismo en Vargas Llosa." *Hispamérica* 4/1:83–117 (1975).

Standish, Peter. *Vargas Llosa: La ciudad y los perros.* London, 1982.

World Literature Today. Mario Vargas Llosa issue 52/1 (1978).

Severo Sarduy

(1936–   )

Roberto González Echevarría

Severo Sarduy was born in Camagüey, in the eastern part of Cuba, on 25 February 1936. He is of proletarian background, and of Spanish, African, and Chinese heritage. A brilliant student in both arts and sciences at the local secondary schools, he began publishing verse in the town's newspapers while in his teens. Though a provincial town, Camagüey has a long literary tradition. The first poem known to have been written in Cuba, *Espejo de paciencia* (Mirror of Patience, 1608), was authored by Silvestre de Balboa in Camagüey. Among the writers born in the town are Gertrudis Gómez de Avellaneda, an important romantic poet of the nineteenth century, and Nicolás Guillén, the leading Afro-Cuban poet, still active. Camagüey nurtured Sarduy's literary interests. In the 1940's the town still had a very active cultural life, with regular gatherings of writers at the carfés, as in the nineteenth century.

By the mid-1950's, Sarduy was in Havana, studying medicine at the university and working in an advertising agency. Sarduy had long been a devoted reader of José Lezama Lima and his collaborators, such as José Rodríguez Feo, who published *Orígenes*, one of the greatest journals in the history of Latin America, in Havana from 1944 to 1956. In the capital, Sarduy began to publish in *Ciclón*, the magazine edited by Rodríguez Feo after the demise of *Orígenes*, and in *Carteles*, a weekly with a national circulation, whose literary editor was Guillermo Cabrera Infante, famous today for his novel *Tres tristes tigres* (*Three Trapped Tigers*, 1967). Sarduy's medical studies did not progress very far because of the turmoil brought on by the struggle against dictator Fulgencio Batista, which often closed the university. With Cabrera Infante, Sarduy was among the very few writers involved in that fight, and with the victory of the revolutionary forces, he was vaulted, at a young age, into a fairly visible role as a writer and editor. He published often in *Lunes de revolución*, the weekly cultural tabloid run by Cabrera Infante and his group. The weekly was the cultural supplement of the newspaper *Revolución*, the official organ of Fidel Castro's Twenty-sixth of July movement, whose editor was Carlos Franqui, autl.or of *Retrato de familia con Fidel* (Family Portrait with Fidel, 1981). (Both Franqui and Cabrera Infante, important writers in their own right, later went into exile.) Sarduy also edited a page on culture in *Diario libre*. In December 1960 he left for Paris, with a scholarship from the revolutionary government to study art criticism at the École du Louvre.

When the scholarship expired in 1961, Sarduy did not return to Cuba. By this time the government was showing signs that it would become a totalitarian state. *Lunes de revolución* had been closed down, and all publishing was controlled by the government. Sarduy, in his mid-twenties, had begun to make a future for himself in Paris. He had joined the structuralist *Tel quel* group and become a close associate of François Wahl and Roland Barthes, two of its main theoreticians. The *Tel quel* group, named after the journal they published, became the center of critical and theoretical activity in the West. Sarduy also began to publish novels that had an immediate impact on the Spanish-speaking world, during the so-called boom of the Latin American narrative, whose main figures were Julio Cortázar, Gabriel García Márquez, Mario Vargas Llosa, Carlos Fuentes, and Cabrera Infante. These writers won several international prizes, and their works were translated into many languages. Their work appeared regularly in *Mundo nuevo*, a literary journal published in Paris under the editorship of Emir Rodríguez Monegal, an Uruguayan critic who was instrumental in the promotion of the new Latin American novel. They became a very visible and talked-about group, traveling all over the world and giving lectures at the most prestigious universities. Sarduy shared in some of this renown and published often in *Mundo nuevo*.

It was a good moment for young Latin American novelists, and Sarduy made the most of it. *Gestos* (Gestures) appeared in 1963, *De donde son los cantantes* (translated as *From Cuba with a Song*) in 1967, and *Cobra (Cobra)* in 1972. These books did not have the success of those by Cortázar, Vargas Llosa, García Márquez, Fuentes, and Cabrera Infante, but they sold well and were translated into several languages. It was generally agreed that to really understand the boom novelists one had to grapple with Sarduy, who was the only Latin American writer capable of understanding Claude Lévi-Strauss, Barthes, and Jacques Lacan, that is to say, the leading French intellectuals of the moment, on whose work a great deal of criticism and literature was based. Sarduy participated in the two booms: that of the Latin American novel and that of literary theory. His work appeared in both *Mundo nuevo* and *Tel quel*. Most of the main figures involved in both movements resided in Paris.

Sarduy's prestige and power were enhanced when in the late 1960's he was named head of the Latin American collection of Éditions du Seuil, the house that published the structuralists and the journal *Tel quel*. From that position he launched García Márquez' *Cien años de soledad* (*One Hundred Years of Solitude*, 1967) in French, along with short stories by Jorge Luis Borges, Lezama Lima's *Paradiso* (translated as *Paradiso*, 1966) and more recently works by Cabrera Infante and Reinaldo Arenas. Sarduy's book of essays *Escrito sobre un cuerpo* (Written on a Body, 1969) remains the most authoritative and imaginative application of a structuralist style of criticism in Spanish. Although Sarduy does use some of the semiotic terminology dear to structuralism, his fictional characters occasionally appear, making irreverent comments and dispelling the scientific solemnity. Another book of essays, *Barroco* (Baroque, 1974), put forth a theory of Latin American art drawn from the work of Lezama Lima and French linguistic and psychoanalytic theory. The book displayed Sarduy's mastery of art history and his ability to relate the history of architecture, sculpture, and painting to that of literature. This book has had a wide-ranging impact because it has helped readers understand two great Cuban writers who have had an immense influence on Sarduy: Lezama Lima and Alejo Carpentier. In the aftermath of the boom, Sarduy published two novels, *Maitreya* (Maitreya [a deity], 1978) and *Colibrí* (Hummingbird, 1984), as well as another collection of essays, *La simulación* (Simulation, 1982).

Sarduy has for many years hosted a program on literature for Radio France Internationale, which is broadcast to Spain and Latin America, published literary and art criticism in the most prestigious Parisian newspapers, and written and produced a number of plays for both the stage and the radio. In 1985, the Latin American Literary Review Press in Pittsburgh published translations of the plays in a volume called *For Voice* (in Spanish, the plays are collected in *Para la voz*, 1978), which shares much with Sarduy's fiction and can give the uninitiated clues on how to read the novels. These pieces are as innovative as the fiction but have had a smaller impact because Sarduy lacks a country, that is to say, an audience in his own language to support his work. The radio plays, which belong to a genre that is virtually extinct outside of Europe, have met with considerable success in French and Italian translation.

Several poetry collections have also appeared, including *Overdose* (1972), which combines the experimentation of Stéphane Mallarmé with poetic form, big bang theory, and hallucinogenic experiences, and *Daiquirí* (1980), a book of sonnets on erotic topics, evoking Cuba at times (hence the title, after the Cuban drink made with rum). Another book of poems, *Un testigo fugaz y disfruzado* (A Fleeting and Disguised Witness), was published in Spain in 1985. This most recent work uses baroque prosody, figures of speech, and the themes of bodily decay and death (Francisco Gómez de Quevedo and Luis de Góngora are the sources) to describe homosexual love in explicit, yet far from vulgar, terms. Submission to the highly regulated verbal gymnastics of Spanish baroque poetry is part and parcel of the theme of the book, which stresses the subjection of corruptible bodies to the exertions of a very demanding erotic discipline. There is nothing else published in Spanish along these lines. It is significant that in this book Sarduy frequently uses the *décima*, a ten-line, highly complex and demanding stanza that was a favorite of the Spanish poets of the sixteenth and seventeenth centuries, and that is, as well, the poetic form of folk music in Cuba. These poems are based on a startling contrast: heterodox themes cast in a classical or folkloric poetic form. In spite of his many years abroad, Sarduy retains great mastery over the Spanish language, both in prose and in verse.

Sarduy has also published a number of what could be called *livres-objets*, that is to say books whose physical makeup is part of their meaning and intended impact. He has usually produced these in conjunction with a plastic artist, like Léonor Fini, Marta Kuhn Weber, or Ramón Díaz Alejandro. With the latter, Sarduy published *Big Bang* (1973), a book with Alejandro's characteristic drawings of detached machines floating in space, and Sarduy's texts about or echoing the big bang theory of the origin of the cosmos. With Marta Kuhn Weber, Sarduy published *Poupées* (Dolls, 1973), a boxed collection of photographs of her hideous dolls, accompanied by poems. These rag dolls are the models of characters in Sarduy's most recent novels. Since only a limited edition of this "book" was published, it is nearly impossible to obtain.

Since his university years, Sarduy has dabbled in painting. In the 1970's and 1980's this activity has increased, and he has exhibited his work in a number of important museums in Europe. His most recent work, heavily influenced by oriental painting, consists of very detailed, repetitive patterns of colored points, making up large chromatic patterns, as in an Indian fabric. This highly detailed, minute work is very much in line with Sarduy's prose descriptions, in which every word, every syllable, is a potential unit of meaning that can subdivide into others, forming independent clusters of signification. Sarduy's paintings have appeared in several handsome catalogs and continue to gain recognition.

But Sarduy's most visible impact so far has been on the novel, where he has a recognizable style, has already created a familiar host of characters, and is known for a number of very personal themes. As a novelist, Sarduy is reputed to be the most experimental and difficult writer in contemporary Latin American fiction. Sarduy is to the Latin American novel what Hieronymus Bosch was to the great Renaissance painters or what Pablo Picasso was to the impressionists, in that all three artists render their predecessors intelligible by revealing the conventional nature of their art. Bosch and Picasso painted figures before they became art. Sarduy writes in a language that antedates literature, that unveils, as it were, that which ideology and craft tame. Sarduy's narrative is the subconscious of Latin American fiction, thus his repression by some writers and critics.

Gestos was a surprisingly mature first novel, dealing with a mulatto cabaret singer who blows up the main power station in Havana to please her white boyfriend, an urban guerrilla. The action takes place during Batista's dictatorship in Cuba. The style is that of the *nouveau roman*, or objective novel; that is to say, there are very minute, impersonal descriptions of the settings. These, in fact, are not actual places, but often descriptions of paintings, mostly Victor Vasarely's. *Gestos* was very well received by critics all over Latin America and Spain, and the novel was translated into several languages. Containing a good deal of quite direct social criticism, *Gestos* is by far the most conventional of Sarduy's novels and is very much in line with the fiction written in the early years of the Revolution in Cuba. Although Sarduy broke early with the Revolution, he owes to the original thrust of that radical political experiment his tendency to reassess the Latin American tradition from the ground up. *Gestos* did not exhibit this tendency as fully as did Sarduy's next novelistic adventure.

Sarduy's first truly experimental work was *From Cuba with a Song*, considered among the most difficult avant-garde texts produced in Latin America. This novel, much talked about but little read and less understood by the public at large, has had a great deal of influence on Latin American writers. The book is divided into three sections or stories, each corresponding to one of the ethnic groups that make up Cuban culture (and Sarduy's own background): Spanish, African, and Chinese. The Chinese section takes place in The Shanghai, a notoriously vulgar burlesque theater in prerevolutionary Havana, totally transformed in the novel (it is also described in Graham Greene's *Our Man in Havana*, 1958). Lotus Flower, a Chinese transvestite, is pursued by a lecherous Spanish general, who kills her/him when he realizes that he will never be able to have her/him. In the African segment, Dolores Rondón, a black woman from Camagüey, comes to Havana after marrying Mortal Pérez, an ambitious local politician, who becomes a senator in Batista's congress. She dies after Mortal falls from grace, a victim of tragic pride—she and Mortal forget to make offerings to the Afro-Cuban pantheon in their moment of glory. This section is based on the epitaph on Dolores' tomb at the Camagüey cemetery, which is written as a *décima*. The story is told following each of the lines of the poem, not in chronological order. In the Spanish section two transvestites called Auxilio (Help) and Socorro (Mercy) retrace all of Cuban history in their long voyage from Arabic Spain to an ultramodern Havana. When they reach the capital, the city is covered with snow. On the last leg of their trip, Auxilio and Socorro carry in a procession from Santiago (Cuba) to Havana a rapidly decaying wooden Christ. They call themselves the "Cristo's Fans." There are reminiscences here of Castro's triumphant march across Cuba after the fall of Batista. The white, or European, component in Cuban culture is the historical one, leading up to violence and nothingness (symbolized by the white snow that covers all, white being associated with death in Afro-Cuban lore) in its quest for fulfillment.

It is clear that *From Cuba with a Song* deals with the issue of Cuban national identity. The original title is a line from a popular song that literally means "where the singers are from" or "where are the singers from?" In other words, the title refers elliptically to Cuba. "Singers" could mean the many voices of the characters. However, rather than provide a synthesis of Cuban identity, *From Cuba with a Song* shows a dynamic picture of the disparate elements at work in the makeup of Cuban, and, by implication, Latin American culture in general. Culture appears in the novel as the result of a series of violent displacements and errors. Columbus, whose texts are quoted in the last section, which treats of the origins of Cuban history, thinks that the Caribbean islands are part of India and Japan. The Spaniard in the first part chases a transvestite whom he takes for a gorgeous Chinese cabaret dancer. Transvestitism is the common denominator in this view of culture and identity, the most visible parts of which are physical transformations and disfigurements produced by desire. To desire is to disfigure, to kill. The Spaniard kills Lotus Flower, Auxilio and Socorro make themselves up to cover their original (natural?) sex. The three stories wind up in violence and death. Cuban, Latin American culture, *machismo*—everything, including art, is the product of this contradictory process, beginning with sexual roles. It is in this cauldron of contradictory drives that Sarduy locates and displays the subconscious of the Latin American narrative. Among these bizarre figures of dubious sexuality, we encounter the origins of the epic, bemedaled dictators who populate the continent and its novelistic tradition, of García Márquez's macho characters, of the brooding protagonists of Cortázar's fiction, of the religious fanatics in Vargas Llosa's *La guerra del fin del mundo* (*The War of the End of the World*, 1982), and of the tattooed Celestina in Fuentes' *Terra nostra* (translated as *Terra Nostra*, 1975).

Cobra, Sarduy's next novel, goes further. Sarduy presents as the protagonist a transvestite, Cobra, who undergoes a painful sex-change operation. She/he is the star of a plush whorehouse/transvestite theater, where she/he is surrounded by doubles, rivals, and a host of weird figures that includes a body painter after whom she/he hankers. He is an Oriental who tries to escape from Cobra's grasp by returning home. The story also involves a motorcycle gang of tattooed drug pushers allied to a sect of exiled Tibetan monks who provide the raw stuff for the business. The forming of protoreligious groups among the radical young is linked here to the splintering of a great religion, smashed by the same modernity from which the members of the gang flee. The monks yearn to go back to their homeland, occupied by the Communist Chinese. The gang searches for utopia in the sacred Himalayas. As if this were not enough, there are in the last sections of the novel—called "Indian Diary"—quotations (again) from Columbis' diary of the first voyage. Columbus' first trip east appears as the first Western flight in search of a mythic, utopic East in which all the contradictions of Western civilization will be resolved. Columbus looks for the fleeting isle of spices. But he errs, creating in his writings a fake East in America. The same happens in *Cobra*, where the characters wind up on the frontier between Tibet and China, unable to find the real East, irrevocably destroyed by the West. All they can find is the fake Orient created by the West, a contrivance as false (yet historically real) as Cobra's sexuality.

Cobra's rival, la Cadillac, also has a sex change, but in reverse (she has a penis grafted on), and goes around brandishing a big cigar and speaking in the tough manner of a prosperous Latin pimp. In *Cobra*, all the characters are deformed, either by sex operations or by elaborate makeup practices that involve doing violence to any and all parts of the body. At a historical level—and Sarduy's novels are, all appearances to the contrary, quite historical—these deformations stand for those that result from the West's desire for the East (Mortal's for Lotus), an East that is really a projection of the West's own mystification. At a psychoanalytic level, these deformations obey the death wish inscribed within the very urge to live. Culture is the product of such disfigurement, of such elaborate and violent faking. At another level, these disfigurements in the characters are reflections of rhetorical figures. Thus the tropological makeup of language (we speak in figures of speech that deform a mythically innocent discourse devoid of rhetoric) is reflected in the deformation of the characters. In Sarduy's work, the metaphor for all this is more often

than not the "art" of tattooing, on which he is an expert.

Sarduy refuses to put forth in his fiction characters that stand as representations of individuals, for he sees such representations as false and conventional. Each individual in Sarduy's novels is a host of various, often conflicting elements that interact with others. Characters are usually given in sets of two: they are twins, correlative opposites, distorted reflections of each other, scaled-down models, rivals disguised as one another. Cobra is as she interacts with Pup, her dwarf double, or la Cadillac, her rival and correlative opposite. In stasis and isolated, Cobra is a void, an absence. To describe such a character with a lesser literary skill might be to depict a representation of a representation, to appeal to the conventionalisms of the craft of fiction. Instead, Sarduy has his characters' appearances drawn from paintings; James Ensor's dancing skeletons, Diego Velázquez' dwarves, Wilfredo Lam's elongated Afro-Cuban figures, Fernando Botero's plump and placid bourgeois.

Sarduy's insistence on theater as the setting of his novels underscores this conception of the characters, who are always acting; only in faking and pretending are they really being themselves. Hence they tend to express themselves with lines drawn from popular music, bits of poetry, commonplaces of literature, and popular culture, including advertising. These, in a way, form their "script," which they recite in a manner that sets off the utterance to show its artificiality. Like the elaborate makeup of which the characters are composed, their speech does not belong to them yet is their mode of being. In the play *La playa* (*The Beach*, premiered in 1977), this effect is achieved by having the characters lip-synch recordings of voices made prior to the performance.

Sarduy's most recent novels, *Maitreya* and *Colibrí*, have continued the same line of experimentation, but their plots are easier to follow. *Maitreya* tells the story of Luis Leng, a Cuban Chinese cook mentioned in passing in Lezama Lima's monumental *Paradiso*. Leng is, according to Sarduy, one of the reincarnations of Buddha. This novel begins with the Chinese invasion of Tibet (a foreshadowing of the Cuban Revolution), continues in Sagua la Grande, Cuba (where there is a large Cuban-Chinese colony), moves to the Miami of Cuban exiles, from there goes to New York (where Leng sets up a restaurant, like many other Cuban Chinese), and winds up in Iran. The novel is rich in political and historical suggestions: beginning with the destruction of a religious society by troops wielding a Western, progressive ideology, it ends with a religious revolution that seeks to purge the East of Western doctrines and practices. Leng's genealogy, as those in other of Sarduy's novels, is not conventional, because of the changing sexual roles of the characters. Family ties, the family as a unit of narrative, as a storehouse of memories, meets its demise in Sarduy's work. No proliferation of Buendía children all looking like the Colonel, no Úrsula to keep the house together and bind historical time to family history, as in *One Hundred Years of Solitude*. Leng's family, like others created by Sarduy, reproduces as in a theogony, with miraculous births, obscure paternities, the birth of dioscuric twins, and serendipitous inclusions in the family romance. In Sarduy's work, there is no house of spirits wherein dwell the memories of a patriarchal or matriarchal clan, as in Isabel Allende's work and that of other followers of García Márquez. Sarduy has changed the very nature of the house of fiction.

As the biography of Luis Leng, *Maitreya* is also in a sense a fragment of Lezama's dense and voluminous *Paradiso*, one of the major texts in modern Latin American literature. In fact, the time of Maitreya, when this important deity returns, is for Buddhists a paradisiacal one, so the title of the novel also means "paradise"; *Maitreya* is, in a sense, *Paradiso*. This does not mean that Sarduy pretends that his characters come to utopia at the end, but that his book is blessed insofar as it is a rewriting of that of the master. Of course, it is a very liberal rewriting. In Lezama's work, there is a longing for the attainment of a poetic knowledge that is divine and that includes a communion with the motherland, with Cuba. Sarduy's version is less optimistic. The paradisiacal is found only in the textual play, in the laughter, in the displacements of identities that are never found by his peripatetic characters. In many ways *Maitreya* is a novel about Sarduy's exile, as well as the exile of many other Cubans. Hence the long voyages of the characters, their yearning to return to a motherland that beckons with a view of paradise. Like a Buddhist monk, like a cabalist, Sarduy has taken a textual fragment from the master's work and expanded it, not copied it.

If *From Cuba with a Song* and *Cobra* defined Sarduy's kind of character, *Maitreya* shows more development in his description of setting. Some of the descriptions are pieces of bravura that purposely stop the flow of the narration to send off myriad suggestions of meanings. There is, for instance, in *Maitreya*, a minute description of the boudoir of Iluminada Leng, a hooker, that is conveyed as the reflection of the whole room on a drop of semen. There is an implicit joke in the disseminatory nature of the drop, its ability to reflect and thus multiply. Passages like this abound in Sarduy's text, to the exasperation of fast readers interested only in the action.

By abolishing the chronology of the family as the unit of narrative time, Sarduy has dismantled Henry James' house of fiction. He replaces it with the Big House in *Colibrí*, his latest novel. The Big House is a brothel in the jungle in which the Whales, businessmen rich with petrodollars, satisfy their sadomasochistic whims. The Señora, an aging, plump transvestite who runs the place with an iron hand, stages wrestling matches between beautiful young men and evil figures, such as the Fat Jap, for the pleasure of her clients, who are thus stimulated and allowed to view the merchandise in action. Colibrí (Hummingbird) is the most beautiful of these ephebes, so much so that the Señora wants him for herself and has him pursued through the jungle by her agents. The Señora goes after Colibrí as if after an ideal of beauty that she must own in order to deform. Colibrí goes to the deepest part of the jungle in search of a place where he can be at rest, free from evil and deviant desire. But in the middle of the jungle, in what the reader would expect to be the utopian origin, he finds the Señora's agents ready to snatch him back. Finally, Colibrí returns to the Big House, which has been turned, in the absence of the Señora, into an insane asylum. Colibrí burns it down and has it rebuilt as it was before. He takes the place of the Señora, arranging new matches for the clientele. There is a clear circularity in the novel: Colibrí will be the señora, and a new ephebe will appear to take his place.

Colibrí is both a parody of the novel of the jungle

in Latin American fiction (compare José Eustasio Rivera's *La vorágine [The Vortex,* 1924], Vargas Llosa's *La casa verde, [The Green House,* 1965], Carpentier's *Los pasos perdidos [The Lost Steps,* 1953]) and a vast allegory of Latin American society. In the novel of the jungle, novelists sought to find, in the description of wild American nature, the essence of the New World, that which made it different and new. In Sarduy's work, nature appears as the realm of constant transformations, of persistent faking, of unwillingness to yield any truth or essence, save its changing and deceiving character. Nature is not pure or innocent but made up of contradictory forces. Latin America appears as the realm of the tyrannical Señora, propped up by her powerful and perverse clients (among whom are decorated generals as well as entrepeneurs), as a world of violent faking and repression, or as an insane asylum.

Maitreya and *Colibrí* are among the most compelling products of contemporary Latin American fiction, as finished and original as Cortázar's *Rayuela* (*Hopscotch,* 1963) or *One Hundred Years of Solitude* when they first appeared. Yet there is nothing ponderous or solemn about *Maitreya* and *Colibrí,* in spite of all the theorizing and the heavy intellectual background of French psychoanalysis and semiotics. They are funny, kitschy, irreverent, and willing to poke fun; they subject to a severe critique the most hallowed theme in Latin American fiction: the quest for identity. Laughter releases the real demons, carefully closeted in the boom novels.

Made up of transvestites, gays, pushers, sadomasochists, perverse doctors specializing in sex operations, and dwarfed and otherwise deformed monsters, Sarduy's fictional world is at first glance not a very pleasant one. It is much less pleasant if one considers that, in presenting such an underworld, he is offering a view of the prime movers of Latin American culture, the purveyors of the much-sought Latin American identity. Yet there is a tragicomic beauty to this world of brilliant, clashing colors, of feisty midgets who scream at the author to challenge what he is doing, of aging transvestites bent on a Faustian preservation of beauty and youth at the expense even of life. There is also, in the dismantling of the ideological apparatus of Latin American fictions of the self, a promised liberation, an implicit release.

This is ultimately the feeling that emerges when, in the end, Colibrí asks for new boys "to liven up the place" and resume the feast, even if, like the wrestling, it is all a fake.

Sarduy's work is the secret and repressed source of many of the efforts at self-renewal made in recent years by Fuentes, Vargas Llosa, and perhaps García Márquez. Sarduy's presence is felt even in the ultra-baroque Carpentier of *Concierto barroco* (Baroque Concert, 1974) and *El recurso del métado* (*Reasons of State,* 1974). Sarduy is the main influence on Fuentes' *Terra nostra* and to a lesser extent on Vargas Llosa's *La tía Julia y el escribidor* (*Aunt Julia and the Scriptwriter,* 1977). Sarduy has appeared as a character in Luis Rafael Sánchez' *La guaracha del macho Camacho* (*Macho Camacho's Beat,* 1976), where the psychoanalyst is called Severo Severino. Sánchez has seen clearly that the one component in Sarduy's intellectual and artistic equipment totally missing in Spanish-language literary discourse is Sigmund Freud. Lezama, a Catholic, says somewhere that Freudians take a stage in human development for a system, and Borges' prudish aversion to Freud's insistence on sex is notorious. Sarduy's Freud, given its Lacanian veneer, is a very literary one. Yet because of Freud Sarduy is able to dismantle Latin America's cultural fictions—this is his master story, as it were, the other Latin American novel.

SELECTED BIBLIOGRAPHY

First Editions

Novels

Gestos. Barcelona, 1963.
De donde son los cantantes. Mexico City, 1967.
Cobra. Buenos Aires, 1972.
Maitreya. Barcelona, 1978.
Colibrí. Barcelona, 1984.

Essays

Escrito sobre un cuerpo: Ensayos de crítica. Buenos Aires, 1969.
Barroco. Buenos Aires, 1974.
La simulación. Caracas, 1982.

Poetry

Flamenco. With illustrations by Grabados de Ehrhardt. Stuttgart, 1969.

Mood indigo. With illustrations by Grabados de Ehrhardt. Stuttgart, 1970.

Merveilles de la nature. With illustrations by Leonor Fini. Paris. 1971.

Overdose. Las Palmas de Gran Canaria, Spain, 1972.

Big Bang: Para situar en órbita cinco máquinas de Ramón Alejandro. Montpellier, France, 1973.

Daiquirí. Santa Cruz de Tenerife, Spain, 1980.

Un testigo fugaz y disfruzado. Barcelona, 1985.

Plays

Para la voz (La playa, La caída, Relato, Los matadores de hormigas). Madrid, 1978.

Translations

Cobra. Translated by Suzanne Jill Levine. New York, 1975.

For Voice (The Beach, Fall, Re-cite, The Ant-Killers). Translated by Philip Barnard. Pittsburgh, Pa., 1985.

From Cuba with a Song. Translated by Suzanne Jill Levine and Hallie D. Taylor. In *Triple Cross: Novellas by Carlos Fuentes, José Donoso, Severo Sarduy.* New York, 1972. Pp. 231–329.

Biographical and Critical Studies

Barrenechea, Ana María. "Severo Sarduy o la aventura textual." In *Textos hispanoamericanos de Sarmiento a Sarduy.* Caracas, 1978. Pp. 221–234.

Barthes, Roland. "Sarduy: La faz barroca." *Mundo nuevo* 14:70–71 (1967).

Bush, Andrew. "Literature, History, and Literary History: A Cuban Family Romance." *Latin American Literary Review* 8/16:161–172 (1980).

González, Eduardo. "Baroque Endings: Carpentier, Sarduy and Some Textual Contingencies." *Modern Language Notes* 92/2:269–295 (1977).

González Echevarría, Roberto. "Severo Sarduy: Interview." *Diacritics* 2/2:41–45 (1972).

———. "Para una bibliografía de y sobre Severo Sarduy." *Revista iberoamericana* 79:333–343 (1972).

———. "In Search of the Lost Center." *Review* 72 (1972). Pp. 28–30. Partially reprinted in *Modern Latin American Literature* 2, edited by David William Foster and Virginia Ramos Foster. New York, 1975. P. 345.

———. *La ruta de Servero Sarduy.* Hanover, N.H., 1986.

Goytisolo, Juan. "El lenguaje del cuerpo (Sobre Octavio Paz y Severo Sarduy)." In *Disidencias.* Barcelona, 1977. Pp. 171–192.

Méndez Rodenas, Adriana. *Severo Sarduy: El neobarroco de la transgresión.* Mexico City, 1983.

Pellón, Gustavo. "Severo Sarduy's Strategy of Irony." *Latin American Literary Review* 12/23:7–14 (1983).

Review 74: Focus on "Cobra." Seven essays on Sarduy's novel. Winter issue, 1974.

Ríos, Julián, ed. *Severo Sarduy.* Barcelona, 1976. A collection of essays by various authors.

Santí, Enrico Mario. "Textual Politics." *Latin American Literary Review* 8/16:152–160 (1980).

Ulloa, Justo C., and Leonor A. de Ulloa. "Proyecciones y ramificaciones del deseo en 'Junto al río de cenizas de rosa.'" *Revista iberoamericana* 41/92–93:569–578 (1975).

Luisa Valenzuela

(1938–   )

Evelyn Picon Garfield

Luisa Valenzuela, born on 26 November 1938 in Buenos Aires, has become the best-known and most-translated contemporary woman author from Latin America. Of her four novels and five collections of short stories and novellas, six have been translated into English and published in the United States. In her native Argentina she was a contributor to various magazines, a journalist for the newspapers *La Nación* and *El Mundo,* and a writer for radio programs. She has traveled widely, frequently living in Paris, New York, and Mexico. She participated in the International Writers Program at the University of Iowa in 1969, received a grant from the National Arts Foundation of Argentina to research North American literature in 1972, and settled in New York City in 1978, where she conducts creative-writing workshops at Columbia University and New York University. Valenzuela was named a Fellow of the Institute for the Humanities in 1981, a Distinguished Writer in Residence at New York University in 1985, and a Guggenheim Fellow in 1982.

Valenzuela's prose is critical and revolutionary. As such, it is well within the Latin American "tradition" of the best contemporary prose fiction of such writers as Gabriel García Márquez and Julio Cortázar. In its critical stance it parodies the conventions of bourgeois society and the fatuous nature of the writerly art

itself. Her fiction is, in fact, revolutionary in two seemingly antithetical ways. First, it ruptures ties with traditions in its future orientation and emphasis on constant change. In this regard, Valenzuela asserts, "If we are to walk, let's walk on the edge of a precipice knowing that something else lies beyond" (Evelyn Picon Garfield, *Women's Voices from Latin America: Interviews with Six Contemporary Authors,* p. 155). In addition, it is revolutionary in the sense of cyclical return, as of a planet on its axis, a return to timeless mythical roots. "Right now," she confesses, "I'm interested in myths, that is, how myths originate, and I sense that literature may be a form of anthropological exploration" (p. 149). Both revolutionary tendencies—violent change and cyclical return—encompass searches of all kinds, which for Valenzuela are ultimately the pursuit of knowledge about the self and the other. These searches are portrayed with irony and humor in imaginative metaphors that transform themes that would be too painful for her to explore otherwise.

Valenzuela's critical barbs are aimed at diverse segments of society, its institutions, customs, and taboos—social structures that permit poverty, hunger, and humiliation; Gallup polls, high culture (semiotics), and pop culture (soap operas); religion; *machismo* (an exaggerated masculinity), marriage,

1445

and virginity. For example, in the novel *El gato eficaz* (Cat-O-Nine-Deaths, 1972), Valenzuela pokes fun at the adage "absence makes the heart grow fonder" and at the same time at the literary tradition of "courtly love." In one chapter a couple finds that they must be far apart in order to make love to each other. This odd circumstance often has serious consequences, for he may begin to gyrate in a movie theater, seeking physical contact with his faraway lover, while those about him join in until they achieve a true universal love. Some even find a mystical experience in this lovemaking at a distance and decide to found a sect of "telecoitus." "Everything livable can be laughable," Valenzuela explains in chapter 10 of the same novel, where eroticism and death play hide-and-seek among marginal characters who are typical of her fiction in general—prostitutes, homosexuals, peeping toms, and assassins.

That humor is evident in another erotic adventure, from chapter 17 of *El gato eficaz*, in which capitalist exploitation is satirized:

> She, on the other hand, was green like a Lorca poem and combed the vines of her body coursing with sap. Sap with chlorophyll, photosynthesis, a vegetable world decomposing until it becomes oil. And since there is never a scarcity of vampires—I repeat—she, too, met hers in spite of her metamorphoses.
>
> He was a rich Texan with a mighty fine ten-gallon hat who planted his rig deep down and sucked up the heaviest oils instead of irrigating her. A drill, that Texan, a real craftsman of wells even inside her. That's how he managed to extract a high percentage of combustible gases, a little bit of solvent. He could wrench from her a love that also burns, lose himself in petroputrid caresses.

Although almost surrealistic at times, with its dreamlike sequences and its transformational realities, Valenzuela's fiction is often based on the very tangible Latin American political realities of authoritarian power, repression, torture, and disappearances. In "Los mejores calzados" ("The Best Shod"), a beggar finds shoes in a vacant lot among the dismembered limbs of those who have disappeared; in "De noche soy tu caballo" ("I'm Your Horse in the Night"), a woman is interrogated and tortured to reveal the whereabouts of a lover who may have spent

the night with her, bodily or in her dreams; in "Cambio de armas" ("Other Weapons"), Laura is sequestered and repeatedly violated sexually in a spectacle witnessed by the bodyguards of her keeper, the man she and her companion tried to kill; and in the novel *Cola de lagartija* (*The Lizard's Tail*, 1983) the Sorcerer hallucinates with images of those he has tortured.

> And the monsters who break away from the cloth to harass me take advantage of my new sensibility. And they're all creatures of my own harvest. I identify them one by one. I had that one's fingernails pulled out and then I had his hands cut off and now he's threatening me with the stumps as if they were fists. I myself put a mouse in that one's vagina so it would slowly gnaw at her and now there's that huge black hollow like a mouth that wants to devour me. I don't shout, I don't twist, I contemplate, recognize, and challenge them.*
>
> (p. 265)

In Valenzuela's fiction, violence and death are often linked to metamorphosis, eroticism, ritual, or myth. All that does not change is fatuous. From dispersion, destruction, and cataclysm issue forth fertility and primordial vitality. This protean becoming is particularly apparent in her novelistic characters who assume disguises in *Como en la guerra* (*He Who Searches*, 1977) and undergo physical mutations in *El gato eficaz* and *The Lizard's Tail*. Transsexuality and androgyny are common in her short stories and novels, for Valenzuela believes that "every human being is transsexual and the idea of a perfect, true sex is false. We all harbor both sexes; just as we have many masks, so we are both sexes only because there is no further choice" (Garfield, *Women's Voices*, . . . p. 157).

Even in the narrative discourse, these choices and changes are an integral part of a prose style whose dynamic quality is also the result of a fragmented episodic structure and a multiplicity of narrative perspectives. For instance, in *He Who Searches*, masculine and feminine, first-person-singular and plural voices alternate as narrators, while in *The*

*Excerpts from *The Lizard's Tail* are translated by Gregory Rabassa, from the edition published by Farrar, Straus and Giroux (New York, 1983).

Lizard's Tail, Valenzuela as a character in the novel narrates part of the story in the first person. In this way the author emphasizes the relativity of perspectives and the spurious nature of omniscience.

Valenzuela's kaleidoscopic prose modifies reality and is modified to reflect the polysemous nature of its subject matter. For example, in the eighteen chapters of the structurally fractured novel *El gato eficaz,* we follow the female protagonist, an accomplice of the cats-of-death, in her adventurous search for somatic/semantic bliss, an eroticism of body and language in constant flux. The novel concludes:

> Everything that tries to hold us back and detains us for a while is fatuous. The inalterable is fatuous with pretensions of eternity and not I who am not me myself I am transforming into colors on my retina, I gasify my shapes and keep on calling myself I, me, mine, not because of some old routine but rather for lack of something better and in the hope of a new comrade like you who may discover the keys to this game, line up the pieces—the white dogs-lives, the black cats-of-death—and renew the cycle. Checkmate again, may he smite me from afar. Smite me, imiteme, imitateme: my only hope lies in a rebirth.
>
> (p. 119)

In this self-reflexive prose, both characters and language seek otherness, distancing. Language, in doing so, relies on puns and games that invent and, at the same time, demythify the serious role of language, as communicator of truths. Instead, writing is seen as a paper trap that, nevertheless, is possibly the only salvation. Such is the sentiment expressed by Valenzuela-as-character in *The Lizard's Tail,* where words seem like a weak ploy when one is faced with the horrors of torture and disappearances: "I move, I keep on writing, with growing disillusionment and with a certain disgust. Disgust even with myself, for believing that literature can save us, for doubting that literature can save us, all that bullshit" (p. 181).

There have been many Spanish-American authors who have written fiction to denounce political repression. Among them, Argentines have been particularly prolific: Julio Cortázar, Griselda Gambaro, Elvira Orphée, and Marta Traba, to name but a few. Valenzuela, however, is among the most imaginative in the counterattack that produced the witchdoc, or

Sorcerer, of her latest novel, *The Lizard's Tail.* Her protagonist is based on José López Rega, the controversial minister of social welfare and personal secretary to former President Isabel Perón. He serves as a great metaphor for the megalomaniac character of power and cruelty. In this novel, Valenzuela creates her own biography from history and centers it on the personality of that self-acclaimed astrologer, known in Argentina as a sorcerer of black-magic rites, the mastermind of the right-wing terrorist group The Triple A (Anti-Communist Association of Argentina), and the adviser and confidant to Perón. In Valenzuela's portrayal, the witchdoc embodies *machismo* at its fullest, for he not only "has balls," as the saying goes, referring to virility, but furthermore he is born with a "trinity in the crotch," three testicles, one of which he calls his "sister Estrella," the Star. Even more ironically, most of his sexual prowess centers around homosexual activities with his eunuch aide, the Egret, in the marshlands where the Sorcerer holds forth, plotting his return to power and domination of the world. Central to this plan is the prolonged ritual during which he unites the semen of his masculinity with his feminine counterpart, his sister Estrella, whom he has developed by means of hormones. Atop a white pyramid, he sets about conceiving of himself a son, without woman's intervention.

> I am the fathermother neuron, the being in the White Pyramid repeats, and although s/he no longer says Mirror am I, look into me, the transparency will be found in my image which is in the purity of one who suspects and is. . . . I will be motherfatherchild and then no one will be able to come and take my place. There will be no more presidents, no more generals, isn't that just what so many people want? There will be me, only me and I, and I don't know whether I shall allow my son to be separated from me or whether I shall retain I himself forever in my innards.
>
> (pp. 256–257)

By means of this great cosmic orgasm, this "theocopulation," Valenzuela has described in mythic terms the gestation of power, its evil self-sufficiency. For it is during this unholy "immaculate conception," as Estrella grows, that the Sorcerer thinks of those he has tortured and of the happiness he feels when destroying others.

Although the biography of the Sorcerer is rooted in fact and the novel is placed in a historical/political setting where the military, dissident groups, Peronists, and rural and urban inhabitants are depicted, the protagonist's bizarre adventures, his gallery of strange accomplices—the old shaman Machi, 730-Wrinkles, Sixfingers—and their rituals permeate the novel. Alongside the magical realism of ethnic-based religious rites such as those of the Umbanda cult of Afro-Brazilian origin, Valenzuela invents her own myths, equally infused with that magical realism that is born only of a collective belief in the supernatural. Valenzuela maintains that

the separation between what we usually call reality and fiction is more tenuous than we can imagine. And there are people or historic moments that serve as pivots, bridges or shifters. José López Rega, and the whole period of Peronism in which he was a major figure, is situated in that difficult limit that almost mediates with hell, above all with the infernos of Argentine superstition that we refuse to recognize. López Rega was really called the Sorcerer in Argentina, and rightfully so. Perón used him more as an advisor in occult sciences and astrology than as a minister. Many of the scenes in my book are true, even his attempt to resurrect Perón when he died. And that's not to mention his contacts with Brazilian "macumba" or his book on talismans.

(Evelyn Picon Garfield, "Interview with Luisa Valenzuela," *The Review of Contemporary Fiction* 6/3:25 [1986])

Valenzuela's rites poke fun at power and ultimately control its fictionalized representative, at least for a while. For example, by means of absurd exaggerations about the preposterous Altar to the Sacred Finger, Valenzuela parodies the equally exaggerated Argentine cult to the memory of Eva Perón. And at the end of the novel, which coincides with the elaborate ritual/gestation period that the Sorcerer undergoes, his emissary sees an omen, a fireball of copulating vipers that announce misfortune. Egret arrives just as the Sorcerer explodes, puffed up with the fruit of his own semen and "womb," as blood streams from him down the sacrificial pyramid like vipers heading south to the capital to announce the twenty years of peace, promised by the prophecy at the start of the novel. Ironically, this omen is contradicted by the two

people (one of whom is the curly-headed Valenzuela herself) in the plaza, who, upon seeing the rivulets of blood, comment that one tyranny will most surely replace another.

Perhaps Susan Sontag best sums up the unique qualities of Valenzuela's prose fiction in a comment that appears on the dust jacket of the English version of *The Lizard's Tail*: "Luisa Valenzuela has written a wonderfully free, ingenious novel about sensuality and power, history and death, the 'I' and literature. Only a Latin American could have written *The Lizard's Tail*, but there is nothing like it in contemporary Latin American literature." This eminently Latin American focus, which exposes non-European continental roots and political cults that hold sway over a supposedly sophisticated people, is of primary importance to Luisa Valenzuela. As a "porteña," an inhabitant of Buenos Aires, the most cosmopolitan, "Europeanized" capital in Latin America, she asserts that "the only thing that I am consciously proposing is that we recognize to what extent we are Latin Americans, we Argentines who always pretend we are so 'European'" (Garfield, "Interview," p. 28).

SELECTED BIBLIOGRAPHY

Editions

Novels

Hay que sonreír. Buenos Aires, 1966.
El gato eficaz. Mexico City, 1972.
Como en la guerra. Buenos Aires, 1977.
Cola de lagartija. Buenos Aires, 1983. First published as *The Lizard's Tail*, translated by Gregory Rabassa. New York, 1983.

Short Stories and Novellas

Los heréticos. Buenos Aires, 1967.
Aquí pasan cosas raras. Buenos Aires, 1975.
Libro que no muerde. Mexico City, 1980.
Cambio de armas. Hanover, N.H., 1982.
Donde viven las águilas. Buenos Aires, 1983.

Translations

Clara: Thirteen Short Stories and a Novel. Translated by Hortense Carpentier and J. Jorge Castello. New York and London, 1976. Includes the novel *Hay que sonreír* and the short stories from *Los heréticos.*

The Lizard's Tail. Translated by Gregory Rabassa. New York, 1983.

Open Door. Translated by Hortense Carpenter et al. Berkley, Calif., 1988.

Other Weapons. Translated by Deborah Bonner. Hanover, N.H., 1985.

Strange Things Happen Here. Translated by Helen Lane. New York and London, 1979. Includes the novel *Como en la querra* (as *He Who Searches*) and the short stories from *Aquí pasan cosas raras.*

"The Censors" and "Papito's Story." Translated by David Unger. *City* 8 1/8:8–10, 66–68 (1980).

"The Efficient Cat," from *El gato eficaz.* Translated by Evelyn Picon Garfield. *The River Styx* 14:87–89 (1984).

"The First Feline Vision," from *El gato eficaz.* Translated by Evelyn Picon Garfield. *Antaeus* 48:75–78 (1983).

"Generous Impediments Float Down the River." Translated by Clementine Rabassa. In *Contemporary Women Authors of Latin America 2,* edited by Doris Meyer and Margarite Fernández Olmos. New York, 1983. Pp. 245–249.

"My Extraordinary Ph.D.," from *El gato eficaz.* Translated by Evelyn Picon Garfield. *The Review of Contemporary Fiction* 6/3:7–8 (1986).

"Springtime," from *El gato eficaz.* Translated by Evelyn Picon Garfield. *Formations* 3/1:1–3 (1986).

"The Word, That Milk Cow." In *Contemporary Women Authors of Latin America 1,* edited by Doris Meyer and Margarite Fernández Olmos. New York, 1983. Pp. 96–97.

Biographical and Critical Studies

Case, Barbara. "On Writing, Magic, and Eva Perón: An Interview with Argentina's Luisa Valenzuela." *Ms.* 12/4:18–20 (1983).

Cook, Carole. "*Strange Things Happen Here:* Twenty-six Short Stories and a Novel." *Saturday Review* (23 June 1979): 80.

Cortázar, Julio. "Luisa Valenzuela." *Review 24. Latin American Literature and Arts.* Center for Inter-American Relations. 24:44 (1979).

———. "*El gato eficaz.*" *Bellas artes,* 21 January 1981.

De Feo, Ronald. "Two from Argentina." *The Nation* 237/16:505–508 (1983).

Forché, Carolyn. "Grasping the Gruesome." *Esquire* 100/3:239–242 (1983).

Garfield, Evelyn Picon. *Women's Voices from Latin America: Interviews with Six Contemporary Authors.* Detroit, Mich., 1985. Pp. 141–165.

———. "Muerte—Metamorfosis—Modernidad: *El gato eficaz* de Luisa Valenzuela." *Insula* 35/400–401:17, 23 (1980).

———. "Interview with Luisa Valenzuela." *The Review of Contemporary Fiction* 6/3:25–30 (1986).

Grossman, Edith. "To Speak the Unspeakable." *Review 32. Latin American Literature and Arts.* Center for Inter-American Relations. 32:33–34 (1984).

Hernández, Ana María. "Luisa Valenzuela's *The Lizard's Tail.*" *World Literature Today* 58/2:247 (1984).

Herron, Carol Olivia. "*The Lizard's Tail.*" *Womanews* 8/1–2:239–240.

Ibargon, Saúl. "Todo libro debe morder: Luisa Valenzuela intenta moverle el piso al lector." *Excelsior,* 12 August 1980.

Josephs, Allen. "Sorcerers and Despots." *New York Times Book Review,* 2 October 1983. Pp. 15, 26.

Katz, Jane. "I Was Always a Bit of a Rebel." In *Artists in Exile.* New York, 1983. Pp. 59–70.

Lauzen, Sarah E. "*Strange Things Happen Here.*" *Review 28. Latin American Literature and Arts.* Center for Inter-American Relations 28:81–82 (1981).

Magnarelli, Sharon. "Gatos, lenguaje y mujeres en *El gato eficaz* de Luisa Valenzuela." *Revista iberoamericana* 45/108–109:603–611 (1979).

———. "Juego y fuego del *gato eficaz.*" *Los universitarios* 187:21 (1981).

———. "Juego/fuego de la esperanza (En torno a *El gato eficaz* de Luisa Valenzuela)." *Cuadernos americanos* 247/2:199–208 (1983).

———. "Censorship and the Female Writer: An Interview/Dialogue with Luisa Valenzuela." *Letras femeninas* 10/1:55–64 (1984).

———. "Luisa Valenzuela: From *Hay que sonreír* to *Cambio de armas.*" *World Literature Today* 58/1:9–13 (1984).

Martínez, Zulma Nelly. "*El gato eficaz* de Luisa Valenzuela: La productividad del texto." *Revista canadiense de estudios hispánicos* 4/1:73–80 (1979).

Resnick, Margery. "*Other Weapons.*" *New York Times Book Review,* 6 October 1985. P. 38.

Tanner, Stephen L. "Reality by the Tail." *Chronicles of Culture* 8/12:10–13 (1984).

Tobin, Patricia. "Voices in the Silence." *Review 76.* Center for Inter-American Relations 18:78–80 (1976).

Reinaldo Arenas

(1943–   )

Dolores M. Koch

Reinaldo Arenas is perhaps the only writer of international stature that Cuba has produced since the revolution of 1959. His works have been published in English, Italian, German, Dutch, Japanese, Polish, Portuguese, and French, with the latter often the first language into which his works have been translated. Only his novel *Celestino antes del alba* (Celestino Before Dawn) has been published in Cuba, where he lived until 1980.

Born in a small town near Holguín, in the Cuban province of Oriente, on 16 July 1943, Reinaldo Arenas was only fifteen years old at the triumph of the revolution. In 1962, after winning a scholarship, he moved to Havana and enrolled in the university. The next year he entered a contest in which he had to tell a famous children's story in five minutes. He could not find any he really liked, so he told one of his own. The jury was very impressed, particularly the poet Eliseo Diego, head of the children's department at the Biblioteca Nacional José Martí (the National Library). Arenas' job at the library was a turning point in his career. While working there he wrote a few short stories and a novel about adolescence, *Celestino antes del alba*, which received second place in a 1965 literary contest and in 1967 was published by UNEAC, the Unión Nacional de Escritores y Artistas Cubanos (National Union of Cuban Writers

and Artists). While doing research at the library on the Mexican writer Juan Rulfo, he found an autobiography of Friar Servando Teresa de Mier (1765–1827), a revolutionary Mexican friar who spent most of his life traveling through Europe, fleeing from intellectual persecution. Arenas identified completely with this almost mythical figure.

Adopting the friar's personality and giving free rein to his imagination, Arenas rewrote the biography as *El mundo alucinante* (This Hallucinatory World, 1969; published in English as *The Ill-Fated Peregrinations of Fray Servando*, 1987). It received an honorary mention from UNEAC, but the authorities decided not to publish it. Since there was no private enterprise in Cuba, the only recourse was to have the manuscript published outside the country. When it appeared in Mexico, it was so well received that Arenas became a writer of renown, though only outside of Cuba. The novel has been translated into many languages and is considered his best work to date.

Celestino antes del alba and *El mundo alucinante*, both written before Arenas was twenty-three years old, show two of his most notable characteristics: the ability to reimagine the awakening of adolescence and the ability to recreate a historical event on many levels of reality, including fantasy.

Arenas sees the power of imagination and that of

language as man's only salvation. His musical, poetic prose and ear for dialogue are combined with a sense of humor sometimes verging on the grotesque and a fantasy somewhat akin to magical realism, a movement that flourished in Latin America during the late 1960's.

During this time in Cuba, many intellectuals and writers suspected of being dissidents were silenced by the revolutionary authorities. Having books published outside the country was considered counterrevolutionary, and in 1970 Arenas, together with other writers, was sent to a sugarcane plantation for forced labor. There Arenas wrote a long poem, *El central* (*El Central: A Cuban Sugar Mill*, 1981); a few years later, he managed to get the manuscript secretly delivered to Spain for publication. While his works were being published and translated into other languages, Arenas was being invited to attend conferences abroad. He never got permission from the Cuban government to leave the country, nor could he receive any royalties for his works.

Arenas became a clandestine writer, secretly preparing his next novel, *El palacio de las blanquísimas mofetas* (The Palace of the Pure White Skunks, 1980), a sequel to the novel Celestino, with the main character now an adolescent. After this, he began *Otra vez el mar* (*Farewell to the Sea*, 1982). The first version disappeared in Havana in 1969, the second version was confiscated in 1971, and the present, or third, version was smuggled out of Havana in 1974 and published in 1982. Incidentally, in one of those rare instances in which life copies art, Arenas was jailed in the same prison that held Friar Servando while he was in Cuba. When Arenas was released in 1976, he was forbidden to write. Not until 1980, when more than ten thousand people crowded into the gardens of the Peruvian embassy, hoping to flee the country, did Arenas manage to leave from the port of Mariel and come to the United States. After ten years of silence, he published the third version of *Farewell to the Sea*, revised other works, and started a monthly publication entitled *Mariel*.

Celestino antes del alba displays the same basic concerns that permeate all of Arenas' works: the struggle between the liberating experience of writing and the violent forces that try to suppress it. Arenas' characters do not accept the world as given. They aspire to a liberation almost beyond human means, always subverting not only the established social order but also the conventions of time, and of literary discourse as well. For the poet there are no barriers between reality and fantasy. Just as in the work of Jorge Luis Borges, Arenas' central theme is literary creation.

Arenas intends to complete a semiautobiographical series of five novels, which he calls a "pentagonía" (five agonies). The main character, who changes names from novel to novel and who dies several times to be reborn, first appears in *Celestino* when he is about ten years old. His vocation as a writer is well established. This child feels such an urge to write that he inscribes poems on leaves and tree trunks. This behavior has no place in the rural environment in which he lives, a small town in the Oriente province of Cuba during the 1950's. His family, particularly his grandfather, react violently: they go after him with an enormous ax and fell the trees in a futile effort to eradicate his writing. At total odds with the world, he assuages his loneliness by creating an imaginary companion for himself, Celestino. This is his great victory. The power of the word and of the imagination make irrevocable his decision to be a writer. The foregoing is not expressed in these terms but rather is transferred as a vital experience to the reader.

Celestino's image unfolds and multiplies. Voices proliferate. From the perspective of a child, images reflect eternally in a set of mirrors; voices become communal and polyphonic, and sustain the protagonist amid violence and hostility. But these reflections return him to his own image, completing the cycle of his inextricable loneliness.

The antagonism and cruelty the boy faces are created by ignorance and stupidity rather than by evil. The image of the mother is ambivalent—she is sometimes loving, sometimes castrating. Images fade and recur as if reflected in the water of a well in which the surface is disturbed by falling stones. The image of the well becomes more prominent in the title the author selected for the revised edition of 1982, *Cantando en el pozo* (*Singing from the Well*).

The protagonist and his imaginary friend decide to stay inside the hole in a tree trunk, and they remain there for a thousand years. Celestino nurtures the child by pulling apart his own arm to feed him. The boy is able to restore Celestino through the power of his imagination, and he becomes more real than the protagonist himself: "Me down here, seeing my reflection up there" (1967 ed., p. 13).

Arenas' second novel, *El mundo alucinante*, presents constantly shifting voices. Chapter 1, for example, appears in three versions, each called chapter 1, and the same happens with chapter 2. The individual voice asserts itself only after being a participant in the chorus, of being one with the others. This serves not as a literary device but as an ideological principle. This time the narrator identifies with a Mexican friar who escapes from a kind of inquisition in Nueva España (Mexico) by traveling on foot all over Europe.

El mundo alucinante could be considered a neobaroque picaresque novel. It offers as a pre-text a letter addressed to Friar Servando stating how the narrator knew about his incredible life and realized that "you and I are the same person." Like *Celestino*, this novel is structured in such a way that there is a double narrative voice in dialogue with itself, a personality that inhabits another like a hermit crab. The events and the setting are very different. The language is not that of rural Cuba, but of the Golden Age of Spanish literature. This is by far the most successful and best known of Arenas' novels.

Arenas' main theme is the quest for liberation. To combat stupidity and cruelty he offers fantasy and humor. The only possible way to achieve liberation is through language itself.

In chapter 24, the episode of the imprisonment of the friar at Los Toribios (the jail) speaks for itself:

Something made that prison always imperfect, something clashed against that network of chains and rendered them poor and useless. *Incapable of imprisoning....* The reason was that the friar's thoughts were free. And breaking the chains, his thoughts escaped, light and unencumbered, outside the walls, without stopping for a moment to imagine new escapes.... And if it were not for those hated chains that tightened the corners of his mouth, entering through the spaces between his teeth and tying his tongue, one could have seen inside that frame, like a fantastic bird, Servando's smile, peaceful, animated by a kind of imperturbable tenderness.

The attractiveness of this character for Arenas comes from the obvious associations with the re-

stricted society in which he was living toward the end of the first decade of the Cuban revolution. The limited edition of Arenas' first novel was out of print, and *El mundo alucinante* was not published in Cuba for political reasons, even though it had received an honorable mention from UNEAC in a contest in 1968. The manuscript left Cuba secretly and was first published in France as *Le monde hallucinant* in 1968. Many editions in Spanish and many translations in different languages appeared during the next decade, but the Cuban authorities considered this a subversive act. Arenas received no royalties and lived in extreme poverty. He was unknown as a writer in his own country, but this did not deter him from writing.

His next novel, *El palacio de las blanquísimas mofetas* also appeared first in French, in 1975, as *Le palais de trè blanches mouffettes*. He had managed to get the manuscript out of Cuba through an acquaintance with diplomatic connections. It is the second novel of the "pentagonía." The protagonist is now an adolescent named Fortunato. Arenas plays again with the choral voices, from the living and from the dead. The narrator becomes, in a way, the voice of history of the island. The narrative *yo* becomes several voices: *yo, tú, él* (I, you, he). There are reports from the government forces and from the rebel forces. Every discourse seems to contradict the others. The "palace" in the title refers ironically to Fortunato's humble home, and the "skunks" to the "bestial adults." It is interesting to note that Arenas and his character Fortunato were fifteen years old when Fidel Castro's revolution came to power.

In 1972 Arenas published a volume of short stories, *Con los ojos cerrados* (With Eyes Closed), that he had written before *El mundo alucinante*. This volume about adolescence includes some of his best writing, particularly the title story, which is a masterpiece. "La vieja Rosa" (Old Rosie), a novelette of great dramatic power contained in this volume, was later published separately. It shows Arenas to be a consummate narrator.

"Comienza el desfile" (The Beginning of the Parade), the story that opens the volume, tells of the failed attempt of a young boy to join the rebel army, and of the parade that celebrated the triumph of the Cuban revolution, reminiscent of the world of *El palacio*. A few years later, Arenas added another story, "Termina el desfile" (The End of the Parade), and the volume was again published in Barcelona under that title in 1981. The story is a Dantesque mural of another historic moment, when the huge crowd thronged the gardens of the Peruvian embassy in Havana with the hope of leaving the country after twenty years of revolutionary life.

Arenas' style is never testimonial, political, or realistic. ("Testimonial" is a genre developed in Cuba for highly political accounts of heroic deeds for the sake of the revolution.) His imagination sometimes knows no boundaries, but he is always a poet. As if to prove the point, he published *El Central: A Cuban Sugar Mill* in 1981. It is a long poem, with segments in poetic prose, written during his stay at a labor camp in 1970. The volume centers on three different instances in the history of Cuba when different ethnic groups had to suffer slavery: Indians in colonial times, blacks in the eighteenth and nineteenth centuries, and dissidents in labor camps during the Castro government. Arenas' strong poetic sensibility brings this experience to a universal level. This book received in France the prize for the best translation of the year (1983).

In 1982 Arenas published the third novel of his "pentagonía," *Farewell to the Sea*. In the first part, the female narrator is nameless. In the second, a long poem in six cantos, the reader hears the same story from Héctor's point of view. The woman is apparently Héctor's wife. At the end of the story, it is possible to understand that there is in fact only one character. The main character now an adult, has created for himself a companion, this time a very different one from the Celestino of his childhood.

This novel took Arenas sixteen years to finish. The main characters are on the return trip from a six-day vacation by the sea. These six days parallel Genesis, the six days of Creation, or the search for the other half of the self, an ideal companion, which once found, is destroyed. Their lives are under the surveillance of the revolutionary authorities. The sea represents their yearning for freedom.

Arturo, la estrella más brillante (Arthur, The Most Brilliant Star, 1984) is a short novel, with a style somewhat reminiscent of Jean Genet, that continues the story of Old Rosie's son as he grows older. In 1986 Arenas published two works: *Necesidad de libertad*,

which bears the subtitle *Mariel: Testimonios de un intelectual disidente* (Need for Freedom. Mariel: Testimony from a Dissident Intellectual); and *Persecución* (Persecution), experimental theater pieces on the theme of repression, some of them set in a future world in which writing is not possible and which is, therefore, the worst of all possible worlds for Arenas.

Fascinated by the countess of Merlin's account of life in Havana during the nineteenth century and by Cirilio Villaverde's antislavery novel, *Cecilia Valdés* (1839, 1882), Arenas wrote a short novel based on Villaverde's characters. Arenas became so enthralled with the possibilities the setting and the characters offered that he wrote a much longer, "heretic" version of *Cecilia Valdés*, titled *La loma del Ángel* (Hill of the Angel, 1987), published in English as *The Graveyard of the Angels*, in 1987.

Still a young writer, Arenas is one of the most vigorous voices in Latin American literature today. He has received numerous awards, including that of best foreign novelist in France in 1969 and a Guggenheim Fellowship in 1982. His other honors include Writer in Residence at the Center for Inter-American Relations (1982) and a Woodrow Wilson Center Fellowship (1987). He was a Visiting Professor at Florida International University (1980, 1983, and 1987) and at Cornell University (1985). He has also lectured at Harvard, Yale, Stockholm, and the Sorbonne. His manuscripts have been deposited at Princeton University.

SELECTED BIBLIOGRAPHY

Editions

Prose Narratives

Celestino antes del alba. Havana, 1967. Caracas, 1980. Rev. ed. published under the title *Cantando en el pozo*. Barcelona, 1982.

El mundo alucinante. Una novela de aventuras. 1st Spanish ed. Mexico City, 1969; 2nd ed. 1973; 3rd ed. 1978. Published originally in French as *Le monde hallucinant*. Paris, 1968.

El palacio de las blanquísimas mofetas. 1st Spanish ed. Caracas, 1980. Rev. ed. Barcelona, 1983. Published

originally in French as *Le palais de tres blanches mouffettes*. Paris, 1975.
La vieja Rosa. Caracas, 1980.
Cantando en el pozo. Barcelona, 1982.
Otra vez el mar. Barcelona, 1982.
Arturo, la estrella más brillante. Barcelona, 1984.
La loma del Ángel. New York, 1987.

Short Stories

Con los ojos cerrados. Montevideo, 1972. Published as *Termina el desfile*, with the addition of the title story. Barcelona, 1981.

Poetry

El central. Barcelona, 1981.

Essays

Necesidad de libertad. Mariel: Testimonios de un intelectual disidente. Mexico City, 1986.

Plays

Persecución: Cinco piezas de teatro experimental. Miami, Fla., 1986.

Translations

El central: A Cuban Sugar Mill. Translated by Anthony Kerrigan. New York, 1984.
Farewell to the Sea. Translated by Andrew Hurley. New York, 1986.
The Graveyard of the Angels. Translated by Alfred J. MacAdam. New York, 1987.
Hallucinations: Being an Account of the Life and Adventures of Friar Servado Teresa de Mier. Translated by Gordon Brotherston. London and New York, 1971.
The Ill-Fated Peregrinations of Fray Servando. Translated by Andrew Hurley. New York, 1987. Arenas supervised this translation of *El mundo alucinante*.
Singing from the Well. Translated by Andrew Hurley. New York, 1987.

Biographical and Critical Studies

Borinsky, Alicia. "Re-escribir y escribir: Arenas, Ménard, Borges, Cervantes, Fray Servando." *Revista iberoamericana* 41/92–93:605–616 (1975). Published in English as "Rewritings and Writings." *Diacritics* (Ithaca, N.Y.) 4/4:22–28 (1974).

Bovi-Guerra, Pedro. "El mundo alucinante: Ecos de Orlando y otros ecos." *Románica* (New York) 15:97–107 (1979).
Cabrera Infante, Guillermo. "Bites from the Bearded Crocodile." *London Review of Books* 3/10:2–8 (1981).
Diego, Eliseo. Review of *Celestino antes del alba*. *Casa de las Américas* 7/45:162–166 (1967).
Edwards, Jorge. "Una historia de nuestra época." *Noticias de arte* (Sept.–Oct. 1984):11.
Fell, Claude. "Un neobarroco del desequilibrio: El mundo alucinante de Reinaldo Arenas. In *El barroco en América* 1. Madrid, 1978. Pp. 725–731.
González, Eduardo G. "A razón de Santo: Ultimos lances de Fray Servando." *Revista iberoamericana* 41/92–93:593–603 (1967).
González, Flora. "Repetición y escritura en la obra de Reinaldo Arenas." In *Historia y ficción en la narrativa hispanoamericana*, edited by Roberto González Echevarría. Caracas, 1984. Pp. 395–408.
Gordon, Ambrose, Jr. "Rippling Ribaldry and Pouncing Puns: The Two Lives of Fray Servando." *Review* (Center for Inter-American Relations) 73:40–44 (1973).
Guzmán, Cristina. "Apéndice." In *La vieja Rosa*, by Reinaldo Arenas. Caracas, 1980. Pp. 103–114.
Jára, René. "Aspectos de intertextualidad en *El mundo alucinante*." *Texto crítico* 5/13:219–235 (1979).
Jiménez Emán, Gabriel. "La transgresión imaginaria." *Quimera* 9–10:70–74 (1981).
Koch, Dolores M. Review of *Termina el desfile*. *Explicación de textos literarios* 12/1:88–90 (1983–1984).
MacAdam, Alfred. "La vocación literaria de Arenas." *Linden Lane* 1/4:9–10 (1982).
Mastandrea Albitre, Ariel. Review of *El palacio de las blanquísimas mofetas*. *Zona franca* 3/21–22:59–61 (1980–1981).
Méndez Rodena, Adriana. "*El palacio de las blanquísimas mofetas*: ¿Narración historiográfica o narración imaginaria?" *Revista de la Universidad de México* 27:14–21 (1983).
Menton, Seymour. *Prose Fiction of the Cuban Revolution*. Austin, Tex., and London, 1975. Pp. 43, 100–104, 173, 196, 273–275.
Miaja, María Teresa. "Lo verosímil y lo inverosímil en *El mundo alucinante*." Ph.D., diss. El Colegio de México, 1977.
Molinero, Rita V. "Donde no hay furia y desgarro no hay literatura." *Quimera* 17:19–23 (1982).
Morley, Mónica, and Enrico M. Santí. "Reinaldo Arenas y su mundo alucinante: Una entrevista." *Hispania* 66/1:114–118 (1983).

Nieves Colón, Mirna. "Un acercamiento a *El mundo alucinante.*" *Lugar sin límites* 1/1:40–45 (1978).

Ortega, Julio. "The Dazzling World of Friar Servando." *Review* (Center for Inter-American Relations) 73:45–48 (1973).

———. "*El mundo alucinante* de Reinaldo Arenas." In *Relato de la utopía: Notas sobre la narrativa cubana de la revolución.* Barcelona, 1973. Pp. 217–226.

Rodríguez Monegal, Emir. "The Labyrinthine World of R. Arenas." *Latin American Literary Review* 8/16:126–131 (1980).

Rodríguez Ortiz, Oscar. *Sobre narradores y héroes: A propósito de Arenas, Scorza y Adoum.* Caracas, 1980.

———. "Reinaldo Arenas después del alba." *Escandalar* 4/1:74–75 (1981).

———. "Reinaldo Arenas: La textualidad del yo." *Zona franca* 3/12:27–28 (1979).

Rozencvaig, Perla. "Entrevista: Reinaldo Arenas." *Hispamérica* 10/28:41–48 (1981).

———. *Reinaldo Arenas: Narrativa de transgresión.* Mexico City, 1986.

———. Review of *El palacio de las blanquísimas mofetas.* *Revista iberoamericana* 48/118–119:453–454 (1982).

Sánchez-Grey, Alba Ester. "Un acercamiento a *Celestino antes del alba.*" *Círculo: Revista de cultura* 10:15–24 (1982).

Santí, Enrico M. "Entrevista con Reinaldo Arenas." *Vuelta* 4/47:18–25 (1980).

Tifft, Susan. "Working Hard Against an Image." *Time,* 12 September 1983. Pp. 24–25.

Vesterman, William. "Going No Place with Arenas." *Review* (Center for Inter-American Relations) 73:49–51 (1973).

Waller, Claudia J. "Reinaldo Arenas' *El mundo alucinante:* Aesthetic and Thematic Focal Points." *Kentucky Romance Quarterly* 19/1:41–50 (1972).

Wood, Michael. Review of *Farewell to the Sea. The New York Review of Books,* 27 March 1986. Pp. 34–38.

Zaldívar, Gladys. "La metáfora de la historia en *El mundo alucinante.*" In *Novelística cubana de los años sesenta.* Miami, Fla., 1977. Pp. 41–71.

INDEX

INDEX

INDEX

Lima Barreto, Alfonso Henriques de, **565–572**
Lins do Rego, José, **909–912**
Lispector, Clarice, **1303–1307**
Machado de Assis, Joaquim Maria, **253–265**
Mattos, Gregório de, **65–68**
Meireles, Cecília, **915–920**
Queiroz, Rachel de, **1119–1122**
Ramos, Graciliano, **745–752**
Silveira de Queiroz, Dinah, **1145–1149**
Suassuna, Ariano Vilar, **1317–1320**
Veríssimo, Érico, **1043–1046**
Brazilian Tenement, A (O Cortiço) (Azevedo), 333, 336, 338–339
Brecht, Bertolt, influence on Dragún, 1378, 1381
Brenda (Acevedo Díaz), 300, 302
Bride of Messina, The (Schiller), Portuguese translation by Gonçalves Dias, 189
Brief Life, A (La vida breve) (Onetti), 1090, 1091–1092, 1095
Broad and Alien is the World (El mundo es ancho y ajeno) (Alegría), 1099, 1100, 1101–1102
Brother Ass (El hermano asno) (Barrios), 611, 614–615, 617
Brull, Mariano, 1082
Bruzandangas, Os (Lima Barreto), 566, 567, 569
Bueno, Cosme, influence on Carrió de la Vandera, 109
Buenos Aires Affair, The (Puig), 1407, 1409, 1410
Burning Plain, The (El llano en llamas), Rulfo, 1215, 1218, 1219
Bustos y rimas (Casal), 368, 369
Byron, Lord (George Gordon)
 influence on Alberdi, 155
 influence on Echeverría, 141
 influence on Gómez de Avellaneda, 175, 177
 influence on Heredia, 136
 influence on Mármol, 182

C

Cabeza de Vaca, Alvar Núñez, influence on Garcilaso, 43
Cabot Prize, Arciniegas, 800
Cabral de Melo Neto, João, **1247–1252**
 awards and honors, 1248
 concretist elements, 1248, 1319
 cordel poems, 1247
 critical assessment, 1251

Generation of '45 in Brazil, 1247
 influenced by Moore, 1251
 influences on, 1248
 poetic techniques, 1249
 poetry as construction, 1248, 1250
Cabrera Infante, Guillermo, **1383–1390**
 awards and honors, 1386, 1388
 Cuban Revolution, 1383, 1387, 1388, 1389
 film criticism, 1384, 1387, 1390
 imprisoned by Batista regime, 1386
 influenced by Hemingway, 1386
 influences on, 1384
 relationship with and denunciation of Castro, 1387, 1388, 1389
 social criticism, 1385, 1389
Cacau, Amado, 1153, 1154, 1157
Cachoeira de Paulo Alfonso, A (Castro Alves), 291, 295–296
Cacique de Turmeque, El (Gómez de Avellaneda), 179
Cacique (political boss), Rulfo's writings on, 1220–1221, 1222
Cadalso y Vazquez, José de, influence on Fernández de Lizardi, 125
Caetés (Ramos), 747, 748
Cain, G., *see* Cabrera Infante, Guillermo
Calderón de la Barca, Fanny, diaries of, 1297
Calderón de la Barca, Pedro, influence on Juana Inés de la Cruz, 93
Calendario manual y guía universal de forasteros de Venezuela, El (Bello), 130
Callado, Antônio, 783
Câmara, Eugênia, 290–291
Cambaceres, Eugenio, **269–276**
 admiration for Zola, 269
 development of Spanish-American novel, 269, 274
 Generation of 1880, 269
 naturalism, 269, 271, 272–273, 275
Camino de las horas (Prado), 644
Camoes, Luiz Vaz de, influence on Mattos, 66
Camp, The (El Campo) (Gambaro), 1323, 1324–1325
Campesinos, Rulfo's depiction of, 1218
Campo, Estanislao del, **229–233**
 critical assessment, 232–233
 gaucho poetry, 230–233
 influenced by Ascasubi, 230
 influenced by Hidalgo, 230
Campoamor, Ramón de, 543
Camus, Albert, influence of, 1280

Canaíma (Gallegos), 607–608
"Cançao do Exílio" (Gonçalves Dias), 186
"Cançao do Tamoio, A" (Gonçalves Dias), 187, 190
Cancionero del amor infeliz (Blanco Fombona), 507–508
Canillita (Sánchez), 532–533, 534
Cansinos-Asséns, Rafael, influence on Borges, 847
Cantaclaro (Gallegos), 607
Cántaro fresco, El (Ibarbourou), 804
Canto a la primavera y otros poemas (Villaurrutia), 977
Canto errante, El (Darío), 406–407
Canto General (Neruda), 688, 1004, 1005, 1009–1010, 1012, 1347
Cantos, Gonçalves Dias, 188
Cantos de la prisión y del destierro (Blanco Fombona), 505
Cantos del Pacífico, Los (Chocano), 543–544
Cantos del peregrino (Mármol), 182–183
Cantos de vida y esperanza (Darío), 402–405, 541
Canudos, War of the, *see* War of the Canudos
Captain Pantoja and the Special Service (Pantaleón y las visitadoras) (Vargas Llosa), 1422, 1430
Captain's Verses, The (Los versos del capitán) (Neruda), 1005
Carballido, Emilio, **1289–1292**
 depiction of nineteenth-century Mexican history, 1292
 fantastical realism, 1290–1291
 influences on, 1292
 one-act plays, 1292
 portrayal of large provincial families, 1290
 revitalization of Mexican national theater, 1289–1290
 themes and subjects, 1290, 1292
 traditional comedies, 1291
Carikea, La (Semper), 26
Carlyle, Thomas, 503
Carnaval afuera, carnaval adentro (Marqués), 1243
Caro, Miguel Antonio, **277–281**
 articles on Latin studies, 280
 articles on linguistics, 280
 author of Colombian constitution, 278
 philosophical influences on, 279
 president of Colombia, 278
 protest over Herrán-Hay Treaty, 279, 280

Volume One 1–446; Volume Two 447–974; Volume Three 975–1497

1463

prose, 929–930
themes, 928–929
Gracián, Baltasar, influence on Juana Inés
de la Cruz, 90
Gracias por el fuego, Benedetti, 1258–1259
*Gramática de la lengua castellana destinada
al uso de los americanos* (Bello),
132
Gramática de la lengua latina, Caro and
Cuervo, 277
Grandes escritores de América (Blanco
Fombona), 507
Grandeza (Carrasquilla), 344, 346
Grandeza Mexicana (Balbuena), 55–56
Gran señor y rajadiablos (Barrios), 611,
616, 617
"Graus de Cultura" (Amoroso Lima), 786
*Graveyard of the Angels, The (La loma del
Angel)* (Arenas), 1454
Great Zoo, The (El gran zoo) (Guillén),
952, 953
Green House, The (La casa verde) (Vargas
Llosa), 1422, 1424–1426, 1428,
1429
*Gregório de Mattos e Guerra: Uma Revisao
Biográfica* (Rocha Peres), 65
"Grimorio, El" (Anderson Imbert), 1106,
1108–1109
Gringa, La (Sánchez), 533, 534
Grito de gloria (Acevedo Díaz), 299, 301
Group of *Sur*, see *Sur*
Guajiro, El (Villaverde), 170
Guanabara (journal), 187
Guapo del 900, Un (Eichelbaum), 798, 799
Guarani, O (Alencar), 196, 197, 198,
336, 746
Guatemala
Asturias, Miguel Ángel, **865–872**
Gómez Carrillo, Enrique, **465–468**
Guerra dos Mascates, A (Alencar), 197,
198, 199
Guerra gaucha, La (Lugones), 498–499
Guevera, Ernesto (Che), 1379
Guillén, Nicolás, **947–954**
Afro-Antillean movement, 948, 949,
1385
Afro-Cuban poetry, 1084, 1385
awards and honors, 947, 952
influenced by Spengler, 948
Marxism, 947
reaction to Negritude movement,
947–948
son-poems, 948
Guimarães Rosa, João, **1069–1079**
awards and honors, 1069, 1070

Brazilian *modernismo*, 1070, 1072
conception of art, 1078–1079
critical assessment, 1073
departure from traditional regionalism,
1071, 1073, 1319
depiction of *jagunço*, 1075, 1076
fusion of prose and poetic elements,
1075
linguistic innovations, 1070–1071,
1072, 1075, 1078
synthesis of opposites, 1072–1073,
1078–1079
themes, 1076, 1077
use of myth and fantasy, 1072
Güiraldes, Ricardo, **619–626**, 1111
association with Arlt, 882
critical assessment, 625–626
gaucho literature, 473, 560, 883, 888
Generation of 1922, 620, 810
influence on Laguerre, 1050
poetry, 624–625
Guitara, La (Echeverría), 143–144
Gutiérrez, Joaquín Posada, 280
Gutiérrez Nájera, Manuel, **351–355**
critical assessment, 352–353
crónicas, 352, 354
French influence, 351, 354
influence on Rojas, 594
pen names, 352
poetry, 352–353, 354–355
short stories, 353
Guzmán, Martín Luis, **655–661**
Mexican Revolution novels, 655
relationship with Villa, 655–659
Guzmán, Ruy Díaz de, 1209, 1210

H

Haiku form, Tablada's use of, **444**, 445
Hand and the Glove, The (A Mão e a Luva)
(Machado de Assis), 254, 262
Heartbreak Tango (Boquitas pintadas)
(Puig), 1407, 1408–1409
"Heights of Macchu Picchu" ("Alturas de
Macchu Picchu") (Neruda), 1001,
1004, 1010
Heiremans, Luis Alberto, **1347–1351**
Christian conception of world, 1349,
1350, 1351
critical assessment, 1351
discrepancy between reality and dreams,
1348
dramatic works, 1348–1351
Generation of '50, 1347

influences on, 1349, 1350
themes, 1348
Hemingway, Ernest
influence on Cabrera Infante, 1386
influence on García Márquez, 1329,
1332, 1333, 1334
Henríquez Ureña, Pedro, **597–600**
influence on Gorostiza, 930
philosophical influences, 598–599
Heptamerón (Marechal), 890
Herculano, Alexandre, influence on
Alencar, 198
Heredia, José María, **135–139**
aesthetic theory, 139
critical assessment, 138–139
Hispanic romanticism, 135–136
historical works, 139
influence on Gómez de Avellaneda,
175, 176
influences on, 136
literary essays, 139
"Hermana agua, La" (Nervo), 427
Hernández, José, 150, 160, **235–244**
biography by Gálvez, 588
critical assessment, 236, 242–244
director of *El Rio de La Plata*, 239
Lugones' lectures on *Martín Fierro*, 494,
500
Martínez Estrada's interpretation of
Martín Fierro, 812
Martín Fierro compared with other
gauchesque works, 230, 233, 241
philosophical influences, 237
Hernández Girón, Francis, 24
Hernán Cortés: Creador de la nacionalidad
(Vasconcelos), 579–580
Heroínas mexicanas (Fernández de Lizardi),
125
Herrán-Hay Treaty, 279–280
Herrera y Reissig, Julio, **519–528**, 547
critical assessment, 525, 528
friendship with Carreras, 520, 521
modernismo, 520, 522, 523
Hesse, Herman, 1304
Hidalgo, Alberto, 484, 488
Hidalgo, Bartolomé, 147, 150, 230
Hierba del cielo (Denevi), 1267
Hima-Sumac (Matto de Turner), 306
*His Excellency the Ambassador (O Senhor
Embaixador)* (Veríssimo), 1046
Historia de la literatura hispanoamericana
(Anderson Imbert), 1105
Historia de la noche (Borges), 847, 849, 850
*Historia de las ideas contemporáneas en
Centro-América* (Valle), 724

Neruda, Pablo (*continued*)
  use of spiraling pattern, 1011
Nervo, Amado, **425–428,** 442
  critical assessment, 428
  influences on, 426, 428
  prose, 428
  spiritualism, 427–428
  themes, 427
Neto, Coelho, 782
New novel, Brazilian (1920's–1930's), 340
New novel, Latin American
  Asturias, 867
  Macedonio Fernández, 483, 485–490
New Short Stories (Contos Novos)
    (Andrade), 773
New World
  Carrió de la Vandera, Alonso, **107–110**
  Díaz del Castillo, Bernal, **17–20**
  Ercilla y Zúñiga, Don Alonso de, **23–31**
  Fernández de Oviedo y Valdés, Gonzalo,
    11–14
  first epic poem about, 62
  Garcilaso de la Vega, El Inca, **39–45**
  González de Eslava, Fernán, **33–36**
  Guillén on blacks' role in, 947
  Heredia as transition writer, 139
  Las Casas, Bartolomé, **1–7**
  novelistic form reflecting, 460
  Oña, Pedro de, **59–62**
"Niágara," Heredia, 137–138
Nicaragua
  Darío, Rubén, **397–410**
Nietzsche, Friedrich
  influence on Barrios, 614
  influence on Cambaceres, 503
  influence on Chocano, 545–546
  influence on Rodó, 451
Nieve (Casal), 367, 368
Night (Noite) (Veríssimo), 1046
Nine Guardians, The (Balún-Canán)
    (Castellanos), 1295
Niño que enloqueció de amor, El (Barrios),
    611, 613
Niño y la niebla, El (Usigli), 1035, 1037
Nobel Prize for literature
  Asturias, 865
  García Márquez, 1329
  Mistral, 677, 680
  Neruda, 1001, 1006
"Noche entró . . . , La" (Agustini), 651
Noches tristes y día alegre (Fernández de
    Lizardi), 121, 125
"Nocturno" (Silva), 378, 381, 382, 383
Norris, Frank, 336
Norther, The (El norte) (Carballido), 1292

Nostalgia de la muerte (Villaurrutia),
    976–977
Novel
  first in Spanish America, 109, 119, 122
  historical, 587–588
  introspective, 1303, 1304
  novelita (novelette), 1278, 1279, 1286
  of the 1930's in Northeast, 1119, 1122
  of the land, 1059
  open, 1092
  picaresque, 109, 459, 711, 1222
  poetic, 1106, 1107
  within-a-novel, 1091
  see also names of specific works; New
    novel
Novela Totalizante (Fuentes), 1373
Novos Poemas (Drummond de Andrade),
    967
"Nudo, El" (Agustini), 652
Nuestra Señora del Mar (Ballagas), 1085,
    1086
Nuestros hijos (Sánchez), 535
"Nuestros indios" (González Prada), 285
Nueva burguesía (Azuela), 461
Nueva novela hispanoamericana, La
    (Fuentes), 153–154
Numa e a Ninfa (Lima Barreto), 566, 568
Núñez de Arce, Gaspar, influence on
    Isaacs, 249

O

Obligado, Rafael, influenced by
    Echeverría, 143
Obras (Costa), 114
Obras (Villaurrutia), 976
Obras completas (Güiraldes), 621–622
Obras completas (Reyes), 696, 698,
    699–700, 701
Obras Poéticas (Cruz e Sousa), 360
Obras poéticas (Juana Inés de la Cruz), 91
Obregón, Alvaro, 581
*Obscene Bird of the Night, The (El obsceno
    pájarode la noche)* (Donoso), 1091,
    1278, 1281–1284, 1286
Ocampo, Victoria, **705–708**
  first female member of Argentine
    Academy of Letters, 707
  founder of *Sur*, 706, 707, 1112
  relationship with Bioy Casares, 1202
  relationships with other intellectuals,
    706
  themes, 707
Odas elementales (Neruda), 688

Odas para el hombre y la mujer (Marechal),
    889
Odas seculares (Lugones), 497
Odes, Neruda's four volumes, 1010–1012
Oedipus Aegyptiacus (Kircher), 96
Oficio del siglo veinte, Un (Cabrera
    Infante), 1384, 1387, 1388, 1389
Oficio de tinieblas (Castellanos), 1299
Ojerosa y pintada (Yáñez), 996, 997
Old Gringo, The (Gringo viejo) (Fuentes),
    657, 1353, 1372–1373
Omniscient narrator
  Cortázar, 1183
  Queiroz, 1120
Oña, Pedro de, **59–62**
  critical assessment, 62
  influences on, 59, 60, 61, 62
  relationship with Hurtado de Mendoza,
    59
Onda (Sinán), 941
O'Neill, Eugene, influence on Gambaro,
    1323
*One Hundred Years of Solitude (Cien años de
    soledad)* (García Márquez), 1219,
    1329, 1330, 1331, 1333,
    1335–1338, 1342, 1343, 1370
Onetti, Juan Carlos, **1089–1095,** 1279
  awards and honors, 1089
  critical assessment, 1092, 1095
  influenced by Faulkner, 1093
  influence on Benedetti, 1256
  influence on Donoso, 1280
  influence on Generation of '45 writers,
    1256
  novel-within-novel, 1091
  open novel, 1092
  superimposition of several realities,
    1090, 1091
  themes, 1090
  use of ambiguity, 1092–1093, 1094
  use of parody, 1094
*On Heroes and Tombs (Sobre héros y
    tumbas)* (Sábato), 1139, 1141–1142
Only a Rose (No más que una rosa)
    (Prado), 644
*On the Literature of the South of Europe (De
    la littérature du midi de L'Europe)*
    (Simonde de Sismondi), 132
Open theater, Dragún, 1380
Oráculos de Talia (Gómez de Avellaneda),
    177
*Orchids in the Moonlight (Orquídeas a la luz
    de la luna)* (Fuentes), 1354,
    1365–1367
Order of Preachers, *see* Dominican Order

Orgástula, La (Díaz), 1394, 1395
Origeneists group, Lezama Lima, 1125, 1126
Originalidad de Rubén Darío (Anderson Imbert), 1105
Orillas del Ebro (Larreta), 474
Orlando Furioso (Ariosto), 26
Ortega, Daniel, 1329
Ortiz, Scalabrini, influenced by Macedonio Fernández, 486
Ortología y métrica (Bello), 133
Ossian, influence on Heredia, 136
Os Subterrâneos da Liberdade (Amado), 1155
Os Timbiras (Gonçalves Dias), 188
Other Inquisitons (Otras inquisiciones) (Borges), 853
Other Side of the Mirror, The (El grimorio) (Anderson Imbert), 1108–1109
Otoño del patriarca, El (García Márquez), 878
"Otra vez Sor Juana" (Castellanos), 1296–1297
Otro, el mismo, El (Borges), 850
Outsider, The (El túnel) (Sábato), 1139, 1140–1141, 1142
Ovid, influence on Oña, 62
Oxcart, The (La carreta) (Marqués), 1238, 1243
O'Yarkandal (Salarrué), 867, 877

P

Padilla, Herberto, 1279–1280
Padre Casafús, El (Carrasquilla), 343, 345
Padre Horán, El (Aréstegui), 305
Páginas desconocidas (Montalvo), 218
Pago Chico (Payró) 414, 415–416
Pago de las deudas, El (Blest Gana), 206
País de la cola de paja, El (Benedetti), 1257, 1259
Pájinas libres (González Prada), 284
Palés Matos, Luis, **821–829**
  caricatures of blacks, 828
  critical assessment, 823
  diepalismo (Puerto Rican avant-garde movement), 823
  influenced by Spengler, 826, 827
  influence on other Puerto Rican writers, 829
  modernista and *postmodernista* influences, 825, 826
  negrismo, 821, 823, 824, 826, 827
  relationships with other writers, 822

  themes, 822, 826
  ultraismo, 822
Palindroma (Arreola), 1229, 1233, 1234
Palma, Ramon de, influence on Villaverde, 170
Palma, Ricardo, **221–227**, 551
  critical assessment, 226
  influence on Matto de Turner, 305, 306
  tradiciones, 222–227
Palomar a oscuras, El (Heiremans), 1348, 1349
Paloma de vuelo popular, La (Guillén), 951, 952
Panama
  Sinán, Rogelio, **941–945**
Pando, José Antonio, criticized by Carrió de la Vandera, 108
Panegírico con que la mue noble e imperial ciudad de México aplaudió . . . al Marqués de la Laguna (Sigüenza de Góngora), 72
Pantheism, Borges, 855, 856
Papaioannou, Kostas, association with Paz, 1168
Papéis Avulsos (Machado de Assis), 255
Papeles de recienvenido (Fernández), 484, 485, 487–489
Paper Flowers (Flores de papel) (Wolff), 1313
Paradiso (Lezama Lima), 1125, 1126, 1128–1129
Paraguay
  Roa Bastos, Augusto, **1209–1212**
Paraguayan Revolution (1811), 1210
Paraguayan War (1865–1870), Gálvez's fictional trilogy, 587
Parnaso Obsequioso, O, (Costa), 114, 116
Parnassianism, 917
Parody technique, Onetti, 1094
Parra, Nicanor, **1195–1200**, 1395
  antipoems, 1197–1198
  awards and honors, 1195
  critical assessment, 1197
  ecopoems, 1199
  environmentalism, 1199
  themes, 1196, 1198
Parra Sanojo, Ana Teresa de la, **717–720**
  critical assessment, 718
  depiction of Caracas, 718, 719
  feminism, 717, 720
  letters, 719, 720
  materials on Bolívar, 718–719
  relationship with Zea Uribe, 719
Pascal, Blaise, influence on Machado de Assis, 260

"Pata, La" (Mistral), 686
Patio, El (Edwards), 1399, 1400
Patkull (Gonçalves Dias), 186
Paul and Virginia (Paul et Virginie) (Saint-Pierre), 249
"Pax animae" (Gutiérrez Nájera), 355
Payador, El (Lugones), 500
Payró, Roberto Jorge, **413–417**
  critical assessment, 416
  dramatic works, 414
  portrayals of sociopolitical conditions, 414
Paz, Octavio, **1163--1173**
  association with Papaioannou, 1168
  associations with Spanish and Spanish-American writers, 1165
  avant-garde influence, 1168
  awards and honors, 1173
  critical assessment, 1165
  editor of *Taller*, 1163, 1166, 1167
  influenced by Eliot and Pound, 1166
  influenced by Mistral, 688
  influenced by Tablada, 1167, 1169
  influences on, 1164
  literary criticism and essays, 1170, 1171
  love and eroticism as themes, 1165
  modern city as theme, 1166
  on Gorostiza's *Death Without End*, 929
  other influences on, 1164
  relationship between history and poetry, 1168–1169, 1170, 1362
  surrealism, 1168, 1169
  translations by, 1171–1172
Pedro Arnáz (Marín Cañas), 993–994
Pedro Páramo (Rulfo), 463, 1215, 1216, 1219–1221, 1223, 1224
Pela América do Norte (Amoroso Lima), 784
Pellicer, Carlos
  influence on Gorostiza, 930
  influence on Paz, 1164, 1165
Peña blanca, La (Villaverde), 169
Penitente, El (Villaverde), 170
Perdido, Un (Barrios), 611, 614
Perdido en su roche (Gálvez), 586
Peregrina, o El pozo encantado (Díaz Rodríguez), 437
Peregrinación de Luz del Día, o Viaje y aventuras de la Verdad en el Neuvo Mundo (Alberdi), 156–157
Peregrinaje de Gualpo, El (Echeverría), 144
Peregrinos de piedra, Los (Herrera y Reissig), 523–527
Perjurio, El (Villaverde), 169
Perón, Juan, 587–588, 706, 888, 1407

Rodó, José Enrique (*continued*)
  influences on, 451, 453
  modernismo, 448, 449–450
Rogues Trial, The (O Auto da Compadecida)
  (Suassuna), 1318, 1319, 1320
Rojas, Fernando de, influence on González
  de Eslava, 35
Rojas, Manuel, **815–819**
  anarchism, 815, 816
  awards and honors, 816
  critical assessment, 819
  influences on, 817–818
  mondoviste influence, 817, 818
  reaction against *criollismo*, 817
  theme of working men, 817–818
Rojas, Ricardo, **591–594**
  critical assessment, 594
  influences on, 593, 594
Roldán, Amadeo, association with
  Carpentier, 1021
*Romance d'a Pedra do Reino e o Príncipe do
  Sangue do Vai-e-Volta* (Suassuna),
  1318, 1320
Romancero (Lugones), 497–498
Roman Catholic Church
  Amoroso Lima's literary defense of, 783,
    784, 786
  Arceniegas' criticism of role in Spanish
    conquest, 900
  censorship by, 33, 45, 307
  dramatization of Christian tradition, 36
  Galvez's literary defense of, 585–586
  Indians' rights advocates, 1–7, 13, 14
  Jesuit Order, 47, 60, 71, 72, 73, 113
  Meireles' writings, 918
  Tradicionista, El, 277, 279
Romanticism
  Alencar, 195–201
  Chocano, 543–544
  Gonçalves Dias, 185–192
  Heredia, 135–136
  Isaacs, 247, 249–250
  Latin American, 650
  Machado de Assis, 256
  Mármol, 181, 183, 184
  Matto de Turner's *tradiciones*, 305, 306,
    307
Romero, José Rubén, **711–714**
  awards and honors, 713
  critical assessment, 714
  picaresque novel, 711
  revolutionary activities and themes, 712,
    713
Romero, Silvio, influence on Amoroso
  Lima, 783, 784–785

"Ronda de espadas, La" (Eguren),
  515–516
Ronde du sabbat, La (Hugo), 142
Rosa do Povo, A, Drummond, 957,
  965–967
Rosa profunda, La (Borges) 847, 848
Rosas, Juan Manuel de, 147–149,
  161–162, 229, 230
  Gálvez's depiction of, 587, 588
  Mármol's opposition to, 181–182
Rosa de los vientos, La (Ibarbourou) 805
Rosa at Ten o'Clock (Rosaura a las diez)
  (Denevi), 1265, 1266
Rosaura (Güiraldes) 622–623
Rousseau, Jean-Jacques
  influence on Alberdi, 153
  influence on Gonçalves Dias, 190
*Royal Commentaries of the Incas, see
  Commentaries*
Rulfo, Juan, **1215–1224,** 1279
  awards and honors, 1215
  compared with Arguedas, 1134
  depiction of *cacique* (political boss),
    1220–1221, 1222
  depiction of *campesinos*, 1218
  influenced by Azuela, 463
  influenced by Bierce, 1222
  influenced by Faulkner, 1218, 1224
  influences on, 1217
  literary criticism, 1222
  magical realism, 878, 1220, 1223, 1342
  technique of freezing character, 1222
  themes, 1216, 1217
  use of political satire, 1221
  views on American and European
    authors, 1224
  views on novelists of Mexican
    Revolution, 1222–1223
  writings in context of Mexican novel
    tradition, 1222–1223
Russell, Bertrand, on fantastic fiction, 853,
  858

S

Sab (Gómez de Avellaneda), 175, 177–178
Sábato, Ernesto, **1139–1142**
  critical assessment, 1140, 1141, 1142
  psychoanalytic method, 1140
  themes, 1139, 1141
Sabor eterno (Ballagas), 1081, 1084, 1085
Saco, José Antonio, 171
*Sad End of Policarpo Quaresma, The (Triste
  Fim de Policarpo Quaresma)* (Lima
  Barreto), 565, 566, 567, 568

Sagarana (Guimarães Rosa), 1069, 1070,
  1073–1074, 1075, 1076
Saint-Pierre, Jacques Henri Bernardin de
  influence on Alencar, 198
  influence on Isaacs, 249
Salarrué, *see* Salazar Arrué, Salvador
Salazar Arrué, Salvador (Salarrué),
  875–878
  awards and honors, 876
  criollista (nativist) short stories, 877
  critical assessment, 876, 878
  depiction of peasant life, 876, 877–878
  theosophy, 876
Salazar y Torres, Agustin, influence on
  Juana Inés de la Cruz, 90
"Salve, Regina" (Carrasquilla), 348
Sánchez, Florencio, 519, **531–537**
  critical assessment, 533, 537
  depiction of *criollo*-immigrant
    antagonism, 537
Sand, George, influence on Gómez de
  Avellaneda, 175
Sangre devota, La (López Velarde), 665,
  666–667, 668
Sangre patricia (Díaz Rodríguez), 433,
  434–436
Sannazaro, Jacopo, influence on Balbuena,
  54
"San Antonio y el Centauro" (Valencia),
  479–480
"San Cirilo de Alejandria" (Caro), 279
Santa (Gamboa), 372–373
Santayana, George, influence on
  Henríquez Ureña, 599
Santos Vega, o Los mellizos de la Flor
  (Ascasubi), 150
Sao Bernardo (Ramos), 747, 748–749,
  751, 752
Sarduy, Severo, **1437–1443**
  avant-garde movement, 1440
  Cuban national identity theme, 1440
  Cuban Revolution, 1437
  influence on other Latin American
    writers, 1443
  livre-objets, 1439
Sarmiento, Domingo Faustino, 148,
  159–166, 415, 471
  association with Rosas, 161
  compared with Martínez Estrada, 811
  critical biography by Gálvez, 588
  founder of El Progresso, 162
  gaucho literature, 159–166, 229, 811,
    961
  influenced by Echeverría, 143
  influence on Gallegos, 604, 605

Suassuna, Ariano Vilar (*continued*)
awards, and honors, 1317, 1318
compared with other Brazilian writers, 1319, 1320
critical assessment, 1319
founder of *movimento armorial*, 1318–1319
founder of Teatro do Estudante de Pernambuco (TEP), 1317–1318
influences on, 1318, 1319
portrayal of *sertao* (backlands), 1317, 1319, 1320
Subterrâneos da Liberdade, Os (Amado), 1155, 1157
Sueños de mala muerte (Donoso), 1286
Sueños son vida, Los (Jaimes Freyre), 419
Sugar Cane Cycle (Lins do Rego), 909–911
Sumario de la natural historia de las Indias (Oviedo y Valdés), 5–6, 12
Suprema ley (Gamboa), 373–374
Sur (literary magazine and group), 982, 1202
Surrealism
Asturias, 867
Carpentier, 1022
Cortázar, 1178, 1179, 1182
Fagundes Telles, 1271
Lima, 766
Paz, 1168, 1169
Uslar Pietri, 1060
Suspension punctuation, Meireles, 917
Suspiros poéticos e saudades (Gonçalves de Magalhaes), 195
Swift, Jonathan, influence on Lima Barreto, 566, 569
Symbolic realism, Fuentes, 1363
Symbolism
Cruz e Sousa's poetry, 359–362
Gallegos, 604
Goméz Carrillo's advocacy, 467
Machado de Assis's impressionism, 257
Meireles, 917
poet-Christ image, 685
Valencia's poetry, 480, 481
Wolff, 1312, 1314

T

Tabaré (Zorrilla), 328, 329–331
Tablada, José Juan, **441–445**
French influences, 442, 444
influence on Paz, 1167, 1169
Japanese influence, 443–444

modernismo, 442
vanguardismo, 443–444
Tahuantinsuyu, *see* Incan Empire
Tala (Mistral), 680, 681–682, 684
Taller (magazine), 1163, 1166, 1167
Tamarugal (Barrios), 611, 612, 615
Teatro de virtudes políticas que constituyen a un príncipe (Sigüenza Góngora), 72
Teatro do Estudante de Pernambuco (TEP), Suassuna, 1317–1318
Telescopic conversations (narrative device), Vargas Llosa, 1426
Temas y variaciones (Edwards), 1399, 1400
Temblor de cielo (Huidobro), 759
Temblor de Lima, año de 1609 (Oña), 60
Tempo e Eternidade (Lima and Mendes), 767, 769
Tengo (Guillén), 952
Tent of Miracles (*Tenda dos Milagres*) (Amado), 1158–1159
Tercera llamada itercera o empezamos sin usted (Arreola), 1229, 1233–1234
Tereza Batista, Home from the Wars (*Tereza Batista, Cansalda de Guerra*) (Amado), 1159
Ternura (Mistral), 680, 681
Terra Nostra (*Terra nostra*) (Fuentes), 1353, 1368–1370
Testimonios (Ocampo), 707–708
"They Gave Us the Land" ("Nos han dado la tierra") (Rulfo), 1217, 1218
Third Bank of the River and Other Stories (*Primeiras Estórias*) (Guimarães Rosa), 1070, 1076–1078
Three Trapped Tigers (*Tres tristes tigres*) (Cabrera Infante) 1384, 1386, 1387, 1388, 1389
Tierra bajo los pies, La (Gallegos), 608–609
Tierra pródiga, La (Yáñez), 996–997
Tieta, the Goat Girl (*Tieta do Agreste, Pastora de Cabras*) (Amado), 1159
Til (Alencar), 199
Timbiras, Os (Gonçalves Dias), 187, 188
Time and the Wind (*O Tempo e o Vento*) (Veríssimo), 1044, 1046
Time of the Hero, The (*La ciudad y los perros*) (Vargas Llosa), 1421, 1422–1424, 1425, 1428, 1429, 1431
Tirsis, habitador del tajo umbrío (Bello), 130
Tocaia Grande: A Face Obscura (Amado), 1159–1160
Todos los gatos son pardos (Fuentes), 1355–1356, 1362, 1363, 1364–1365, 1368
Tolstoy, Leo, 372

Torres, Carlos Arturo, relationship with Ródo, 449
Torres Bodet, Jaime, **933–938**
awards and honors, 938
campaign against illiteracy, 934
Contemporáneos, 933–936
influences on, 933, 936
literary criticism, 937
themes, 935
UNESCO director general, 934
Torres Lara, José, 1100
Torri, Julio, influence on Arreola, 1230
To the Ship (*A la nave*) (Bello), 130
To the Victory of Bailén (*A la victoria de Bailén*) (Bello), 130
Tradiciones cuzqueñas (Matto de Turner), 306
Tradiciones genre
Matto de Turner, 305–306, 307
Palma, 222–227
Tradicionista, El (publication), 277, 279
Traducciones poéticas (Caro), 278
Tragedia de un hombre fuerte, La (Gálvez), 587
Tránsito Guzmán (Gálvez), 587–588
Trasmallo (Salarrué), 878
Trasplantados, Los (Blest Gana), 206, 210
Tratado del participio (Caro), 277
"Tree, The" ("El árbol") (Bombal), 1112, 1116
Trepadora, La, (Gallegos), 604, 605
Tres de cuatro soles (Asturias), 866, 871
Tres gauchos orientales: Coloquio entre los paisanos, Los (Lussich), 150
Tres inmensas novelas (Huidobro), 761–762
Triana, José, **1415–1418**
awards and honors, 1417
focus on human behavior, 1415, 1418
recreation of Cuban myths, 1417
Trilce (Vallejo), 729–730, 923
Trillo y Figueroa, influence on Juana Inés de la Cruz, 90
Triunfo parténico (Sigüenza y Góngora), 72
Trobos de Paulino Lucero, o Coleccíon de poesías campestres desde 1833 hasta el presente (Ascasubi), 148
Trofeo de la justicia española (Sigüenza y Góngora), 73
Tronco do ipê, O (Alencar), 199
Trovas y lamentos de Donato Jurado, soldado argentino, a la muerte de la infeliz Da. Camila O'Gorman (Ascasubi), 148
Truce, The (*La tregua*) (Benedetti), 1257, 1259

INDEX

social protest novels, 996–997
theme of civilization vs. primitivism, 997
urban novels, 997
Young, Edward, influence on Fernández de Lizardi, 125

Z

Zapata, Emiliano, 1223
Zarco, El (Carrasquilla), 344, 346

Zea Uribe, Luis, relationship with Parra, 719
Zeno Gandía, Manuel, **321–325**
  compared with Laguerre, 1050
  influenced by Lucretius, 323–324
  naturalism, 323–325
  Puerto Rican independence advocacy, 322
Zogoibi (Larreta), 473–474
Zola, Émile
  compared with Zeno Gandía, 324

influence on Azuela, 458
influence on Cambaceres, 269, 275
influence on Gálvez, 586
influence on Gamboa, 372, 373
naturalism, 323, 324, 336, 339
Zorrilla de San Martín, Juan, 327–331
  influences on, 329
Zorro de arriba ye el zorro de abajo, El (Arguedas), 1136–1137
Zozobra (López Velarde), 665, 667

LIST OF SUBJECTS BY COUNTRY

The following list indicates the native countries of Latin American writers treated in this book. Subjects dating from the colonial period, or subjects who were born in the Old World, have been grouped beneath the modern nation with which they are commonly associated.

ARGENTINA

Esteban Echeverría (1805–1851)
Hilario Ascasubi (1807–1875)
Juan Bautista Alberdi (1810–1884)
Domingo Faustino Sarmiento (1811–1888)
José Mármol (1817–1871)
Estanislao del Campo (1834–1880)
José Hernández (1834–1886)
Eugenio Cambaceres (1843–1889)
Roberto Jorge Payró (1867–1928)
Enrique Larreta (1873–1961)
Macedonio Fernández (1874–1952)
Leopoldo Lugones (1874–1938)
Benito Lynch (1880–1951)
Manuel Gálvez (1882–1962)
Ricardo Rojas (1882–1957)
Ricardo Güiraldes (1886–1927)
Victoria Ocampo (1890–1979)
Alfonsina Storni (1892–1938)
Samuel Eichelbaum (1894–1967)
Ezequiel Martínez Estrada (1895–1964)
Ricardo E. Molinari (1898–   )
Jorge Luis Borges (1899–1986)
Roberto Arlt (1900–1942)
Leopoldo Marechal (1900–1970)
Eduardo Mallea (1903–1982)
Enrique Anderson Imbert (1910–   )
Ernesto Sábato (1911–   )
Adolfo Bioy Casares (1914–   )
Julio Cortázar (1914–1984)
Marco Denevi (1922–   )
Griselda Gambaro (1928–   )
Osvaldo Dragún (1929–   )
Manuel Puig (1932–   )
Luisa Valenzuela (1938–   )

BOLIVIA

Ricardo Jaimes Freyre (1868–1933)

BRAZIL

Gregório de Mattos (1636–1695)
Cláudio Manuel da Costa (1729–1789)
Antônio Gonçalves Dias (1823–1864)
José de Alencar (1829–1877)
Joaquim Maria Machado de Assis (1839–1908)
Antônio de Castro Alves (1847–1871)
Aluísio Azevedo (1857–1913)
João da Cruz e Sousa (1861–1898)
Euclides da Cunha (1866–1909)
Afonso Henriques de Lima Barreto (1881–1922)
Manuel Bandeira (1886–1968)
Graciliano Ramos (1892–1953)
Alceu Amoroso Lima (1893–1983)
Jorge de Lima (1893–1953)
Mário de Andrade (1893–1945)
José Lins do Rego (1901–1957)
Cecília Meireles (1901–1964)
Carlos Drummond de Andrade (1902–1987)
Érico Veríssimo (1905–1975)
João Guimarães Rosa (1908–1967)
Rachel de Queiroz (1910–   )
Dinah Silveira de Queiroz (1911–1982)
Jorge Amado (1912–   )
João Cabral de Melo Neto (1920–   )
Lygia Fagundes Telles (1923–   )
Clarice Lispector (1925–1977)
Ariano Vilar Suassuna (1927–   )

CHILE

Don Alonso de Ercilla y Zúñiga (1533–1594)
Pedro de Oña (1570–1643?)
Alberto Blest Gana (1830–1920)
Eduardo Barrios (1884–1963)
Pedro Prado (1886–1952)
Gabriela Mistral (1889–1957)
Vicente Huidobro (1893–1948)
Manuel Rojas (1896–1973)
Pablo Neruda (1904–1973)
María Luisa Bombal (1910–1980)
Nicanor Parra (1914–   )
José Donoso (1924–   )
Egon Wolff (1926–   )
Luis Alberto Heiremans (1928–1964)
Jorge Díaz (1930–   )
Jorge Edwards (1931–   )

COLOMBIA

Jorge Isaacs (1837–1895)
Miguel Antonio Caro (1843–1909)
Tomás Carrasquilla (1858–1940)
José Asunción Silva (1865–1896)
Guillermo Valencia (1873–1943)
José Eustacio Rivera (1888–1928)
Germán Arciniegas (1900–   )
Gabriel García Márquez (1928–   )

COSTA RICA

José Marín Cañas (1904–1980)

CUBA

Gonzalo Fernández de Oviedo y Valdés
   (1478–1557)
José María Heredia (1803–1839)
Cirilo Villaverde (1812–1894)
Gertrudis Gomez de Avellaneda (1814–1873)
José Martí (1853–1895)
Julián del Casal (1863–1893)
Jorge Mañach Robato (1898–1961)
Nicolás Guillén (1902–   )
Alejo Carpentier (1904–1980)
Emilio Ballagas (1908–1954)
José Lezama Lima (1910–1976)
Guillermo Cabrera Infante (1929–   )
Severo Sarduy (1936–   )
José Triana (1933–   )
Reinaldo Arenas (1943–   )

DOMINICAN REPUBLIC

Bartolomé de las Casas (1474–1566)
Pedro Henríquez Ureña (1884–1946)

ECUADOR

Juan Montalvo (1832–1889)
Jorge Icaza (1906–1978)

EL SALVADOR

Salvador (Salarrué) Salazar Arrué (1899–1975)

GUATEMALA

Enrique Gómez Carrillo (1873–1927)
Miguel Ángel Asturias (1899–1974)

HONDURAS

Juan Ramón Molina (1875–1908)
Rafael Heliodoro Valle (1891–1959)

MEXICO

Bernal Díaz del Castillo (ca. 1496–1584)
Fernán González de Eslava (1534–1601?)
Bernardo de Balbuena (1561?–1627)
Carlos de Sigüenza y Góngora (1645–1700)
Sor Juana Inés de la Cruz (1651–1695)
José Joaquín Fernández de Lizardi (1776–1827)
Manuel Gutiérrez Nájera (1859–1895)
Federico Gamboa (1864–1939)
Amado Nervo (1870–1919)
José Juan Tablada (1871–1945)
Mariano Azuela (1873–1952)
José Vasconcelos (1882–1959)
Martín Luis Guzmán (1887–1976)
Ramón López Velarde (1888–1921)
Alfonso Reyes (1889–1959)
José Rubén Romero (1890–1952)
José Gorostiza (1901–1979)
Jaime Torres Bodet (1902–1974)
Xavier Villaurrutia (1903–1950)
Agustín Yáñez (1904–1980)
Rodolfo Usigli (1905–1979)
Octavio Paz (1914–   )
Juan José Arreola (1918–   )
Juan Rulfo (1918–1986)
Rosario Castellanos (1925–1974)
Emilio Carballido (1925–   )
Carlos Fuentes (1928–   )

NICARAGUA

Rubén Darío (1867–1916)

PANAMA

Rogelio Sinán (1902–   )

PARAGUAY

Augusto Roa Bastos (1917–   )

PERU

El Inca Garcilaso de la Vega (1539–1616)
Father Joseph de Acosta (1540–1600)

Juan del Valle y Caviedes (1645?–1697?)
Alonso Carrió de la Vandera (ca. 1715–1783)
Ricardo Palma (1833–1919)
Manuel González Prada (1844–1918)
Clorinda Matto de Turner (1852–1909)
José María Eguren (1874–1942)
José Santos Chocano (1875–1934)
César Vallejo (1892–1938)
José Carlos Mariátegui (1894–1930)
Ciro Alegría (1909–1967)
José María Arguedas (1911–1969)
Mario Vargas Llosa (1936–   )

PUERTO RICO

Manuel Zeno Gandía (1855–1930)
Luis Palés Matos (1898–1959)
Enrique A. Laguerre (1906–   )
René Marqués (1919–1979)

URUGUAY

Eduardo Acevedo Díaz (1851–1921)
Juan Zorrilla de San Martín (1855–1931)
José Enrique Rodó (1871–1917)
Julio Herrera y Reissig (1875–1910)
Florencio Sánchez (1875–1910)
Horacio Quiroga (1878–1937)
Delmira Agustini (1886–1914)
Juana de Ibarbourou (1895–1979)
Juan Carlos Onetti (1909–   )
Mario Benedetti (1920–   )

VENEZUELA

Andrés Bello (1781–1865)
Manuel Díaz Rodríguez (1871–1927)
Rufino Blanco Fombona (1874–1944)
Rómulo Gallegos (1884–1969)
Ana Teresa de la Parra Sanojo (1890–1936)
Mariano Picón Salas (1901–1965)
Arturo Uslar Pietri (1906–   )

ALPHABETICAL LISTING
OF *SUBJECTS*

Ibarbourou, Juana de (1895–1979)
Icaza, Jorge (1906–1978)
Isaacs, Jorge (1837–1895)

Jaimes Freyre, Ricardo (1868–1933)
Juana Inés de la Cruz, Sor (1651–1695)

Laguerre, Enrique A. (1906–   )
Larreta, Enrique (1873–1961)
Las Casas, Bartolomé de (1474–1566)
Lezama Lima, José (1910–1976)
Lima, Jorge de (1893–1953)
Lima Barreto, Afonso Henriques de (1881–1922)
Lins do Rego, José (1901–1957)
Lispector, Clarice (1925–1977)
López Velarde, Ramón (1888–1921)
Lugones, Leopoldo (1874–1938)
Lynch, Benito (1880–1951)

Machado de Assis, Joaquim Maria (1839–1908)
Mallea, Eduardo (1903–1982)
Mañach Robato, Jorge (1898–1961)
Marechal, Leopoldo (1900–1970)
Mariátegui, José Carlos (1894–1930)
Marín Cañas, José (1904–1980)
Mármol, José (1817–1871)
Marqués, René (1919–1979)
Martí, José (1853–1895)
Martínez Estrada, Ezequiel (1895–1964)
Matto de Turner, Clorinda (1852–1909)
Mattos, Gregório de (1636–1695)
Meireles, Cecília (1901–1964)
Mistral, Gabriela (1889–1957)
Molina, Juan Ramón (1875–1908)
Molinari, Ricardo E. (1898–   )
Montalvo, Juan (1832–1889)

Neruda, Pablo (1904–1973)
Nervo, Amado (1870–1919)

Ocampo, Victoria (1890–1979)
Oña, Pedro de (1570–1643?)
Onetti, Juan Carlos (1909–   )

Palés Matos, Luis (1898–1959)
Palma, Ricardo (1833–1919)
Parra, Nicanor (1914–   )
Parra Sanojo, Ana Teresa de la (1890–1936)
Payró, Roberto Jorge (1867–1928)
Paz, Octavio (1914–   )
Picón Salas, Mariano (1901–1965)

Prado, Pedro (1886–1952)
Puig, Manuel (1932–   )

Queiroz, Rachel de (1910–   )
Quiroga, Horacio (1878–1937)

Ramos, Graciliano (1892–1953)
Reyes, Alfonso (1889–1959)
Rivera, José Eustasio (1888–1928)
Roa Bastos, Augusto (1917–   )
Rodó, José Enrique (1871–1917)
Rojas, Manuel (1896–1973)
Rojas, Ricardo (1882–1957)
Romero, José Rubén (1890–1952)
Rulfo, Juan (1918–1986)

Sábato, Ernesto (1911–   )
Salazar Arrué, Salvador (Salarrué) (1899–1975)
Sánchez, Florencio (1875–1910)
Sarduy, Severo (1936–   )
Sarmiento, Domingo Faustino (1811–1888)
Sigüenza y Góngora, Carlos de (1645–1700)
Silva, José Asunción (1865–1896)
Silveira de Queiroz, Dinah (1911–1982)
Sinán, Rogelio (1902–   )
Storni, Alfonsina (1892–1938)
Suassuna, Ariano Vilar (1927–   )

Tablada, José Juan (1871–1945)
Torres Bodet, Jaime (1902–1974)
Triana, José (1933–   )

Usigli, Rodolfo (1905–1979)
Uslar Pietri, Arturo (1906–   )

Valencia, Guillermo (1873–1943)
Valenzuela, Luisa (1938–   )
Valle, Rafael Heliodoro (1891–1959)
Valle y Caviedes, Juan del (1645?–1697?)
Vallejo, César (1892–1938)
Vargas Llosa, Mario (1936–   )
Vasconcelos, José (1882–1959)
Veríssimo, Érico (1905–1975)
Villaurrutia, Xavier (1903–1950)
Villaverde, Cirilo (1812–1894)

Wolff, Egon (1926–   )

Yáñez, Agustín (1904–1980)

Zeno Gandía, Manuel (1855–1930)
Zorrilla de San Martín, Juan (1855–1931)

LIST OF CONTRIBUTORS

Maria Isabel Abreu
Georgetown University
GRACILIANO RAMOS (1892–1953)

Ramón L. Acevedo
Universidad de Puerto Rico, Río
Piedras
JOSÉ MARÍN CAÑAS (1904–1980)
JUAN RAMÓN MOLINA
(1875–1908)
SALVADOR (SALARRUÉ) SALAZAR
ARRUÉ (1899–1975)

Hugo Achugar
Northwestern University
MANUEL DÍAZ RODRÍGUEZ
(1871–1927)
JULIO HERRERA Y REISSIG
(1875–1910)

Marjorie Agosin
Wellesley College
JUANA DE IBARBOUROU
(1895–1979)
ALFONSINA STORNI (1892–1938)

Maureen Ahern
Arizona State University
ROSARIO CASTELLANOS
(1925–1974)

Jaime Alazraki
Columbia University
JORGE LUIS BORGES (1899–1986)

Fernando Alegría
Stanford University
MARÍA LUISA BOMBAL
(1910–1980)
PEDRO PRADO (1886–1952)

Manuel Alvar
Real Academia Española de la
Lengua
DELMIRA AGUSTINI (1886–1914)

Nicolás Álvarez
Denison University
JORGE MAÑACH ROBATO
(1898–1961)

Enrique Anderson Imbert
Harvard University
RUBÉN DARÍO (1867–1916)
PEDRO HENRÍQUEZ UREÑA
(1884–1946)

Luis A. Arocena
University of Texas at Austin
FATHER JOSEPH DE ACOSTA
(1540–1600)
BERNAL DÍAZ DEL CASTILLO (CA.
1496–1584)
GONZALO FERNÁNDEZ DE OVIEDO
Y VALDÉS (1478–1557)

Francisco de Assis Barbosa
Academia Brasileira de Letras
AFONSO HENRIQUES DE LIMA
BARRETO (1881–1922)

Miriam Balboa Echeverría
Southwest Texas State University
JORGE EDWARDS (1931–   )

María Luisa Bastos
The Graduate Center, CUNY
VICTORIA OCAMPO (1890–1979)

Gabriella de Beer
City College, CUNY
JOSÉ VASCONCELOS (1882–1959)

Rubén Benítez
University of California, Los
Angeles
JUAN ZORRILLA DE SAN MARTÍN
(1855–1931)

Leopoldo M. Bernucci
Yale University
EUCLIDES DA CUNHA (1866–1909)

Almir C. Bruneti
Tulane University
ANTÔNIO GONÇALVES DIAS
(1823–1864)

Mireya Camurati
State University of New York at
Buffalo
ADOLFO BIOY CASARES
(1914–   )

Raúl H. Castagnino
Academia Argentina de Letras
RICARDO GÜIRALDES (1886–1927)

Elena Castedo-Ellerman
Writer and Critic
EGON WOLFF (1926–   )

José Aderaldo Castello
Universidade de São Paulo
JOSÉ DE ALENCAR (1829–1877)

Dário M. de Castro Alves
Ambassador, Brazilian Mission to
the OAS
DINAH SILVEIRA DE QUEIROZ
(1911–1982)

Sara Castro-Klarén
Johns Hopkins University
MARIO VARGAS LLOSA
(1936–   )

Bobby J. Chamberlain
University of Pittsburgh
JOSÉ LINS DO REGO (1901–1957)

Eugenio Chang-Rodríguez
Queens College, CUNY
MANUEL GONZÁLEZ PRADA
(1844–1918)
JOSÉ CARLOS MARIÁTEGUI
(1894–1930)

Raquel Chang-Rodríguez
City College and Graduate School
and University Center, CUNY

ALONSO CARRIÓ DE LA VANDERA
(CA. 1715–1783)
CARLOS DE SIGÜENZA Y GÓNGORA
(1645–1700)
PEDRO DE OÑA (1570–1643?)

Irlemar Chiampi
Universidade de São Paulo
JOSÉ LEZAMA LIMA (1910–1976)

Stella T. Clark
California State University, San
Bernadino
AGUSTÍN YÁÑEZ (1904–1980)

Russell M. Cluff
L. Howard Quackenbush
Brigham Young University
JUAN JOSÉ ARREOLA (1918–)

Howard R. Cohen
James Madison University
ERNESTO SÁBATO (1911–)

Manuel Corrales Pascual
Pontificia Universidad Católica
del Ecuador
JORGE ICAZA (1906–1978)

Darío A. Cortés
Johns Hopkins University
RICARDO JAIMES FREYRE
(1868–1933)

Luiz Costa Lima
Pontifícia Universidade Católica
do Río de Janeiro
CARLOS DRUMMOND DE ANDRADE
(1902–1987)

Afrânio Coutinho
Universidade Federal do Río de
Janeiro
JOAQUIM MARIA MACHADO DE
ASSIS (1839–1908)

Eduardo F. Coutinho
Universidade Federal do Río de
Janeiro
JOÃO GUIMARÃES ROSA
(1908–1967)

Frank Dauster
Rutgers—The State University of
New Jersey
AMADO NERVO (1870–1919)
JOSÉ TRIANA (1933–)

Georgette M. Dorn
Georgetown University and
Library of Congress
HILARIO ASCASUBI (1807–1875)
FLORENCIO SÁNCHEZ (1875–1910)
RAFAEL HELIODORO VALLE
(1891–1959)

Peter G. Earle
University of Pennsylvania
JOSÉ ENRIQUE RODÓ (1871–1917)
DOMINGO FAUSTINO SARMIENTO
(1811–1888)

Fred P. Ellison
University of Texas at Austin
RACHEL DE QUEIROZ (1910–)

Peter Elmore
University of Texas at Austin
JOSÉ MARÍA EGUREN (1874–1942)

Jacqueline Eyring Bixler
Virginia Polytechnic Institute
EMILIO CARBALLIDO (1925–)

Rosario Ferré
Writer and Critic
ENRIQUE A. LAGUERRE
(1906–)

Merlin H. Forster
Brigham Young University
VICENTE HUIDOBRO (1893–1948)
LEOPOLDO LUGONES (1874–1938)
XAVIER VILLAURRUTIA
(1903–1950)

David William Foster
Arizona State University
BENITO LYNCH (1880–1951)

Jean Franco
Columbia University
MIGUEL ÁNGEL ASTURIAS
(1899–1974)

Delfín Leocadio Garasa
Universidad Nacional de Buenos
Aires
JUAN BAUTISTA ALBERDI
(1810–1884)
JOSÉ MÁRMOL (1817–1871)
EZEQUIEL MARTÍNEZ ESTRADA
(1895–1964)

Ismael García
Academia Panameña de la Lengua
ROGELIO SINÁN (1902–)

Adriana García de Aldridge
City College, CUNY
JOSÉ JUAN TABLADA (1871–1945)

John F. Garganigo
Washington University
ESTANISLAO DEL CAMPO
(1834–1880)
ROBERTO JORGE PAYRÓ
(1867–1928)

Ester Gimbernat González
University of Northern Colorado
ESTEBAN ECHEVERRÍA
(1805–1851)

Robert Jay Glickman
University of Toronto
JULIÁN DEL CASAL (1863–1893)

Cedomil Goic
University of Michigan
JOSÉ DONOSO (1924–)
GABRIELA MISTRAL (1889–1957)
MANUEL ROJAS (1896–1973)

Roberto González Echevarría
Yale University
SEVERO SARDUY (1936–)

Aníbal González-Pérez
University of Texas at Austin
LUIS PALÉS MATOS (1898–1959)
MANUEL ZENO GANDÍA
(1855–1930)

Pedro Grases
Fundación Casa Bello, Caracas
ANDRÉS BELLO (1781–1865)

Lanin A. Gyurko
University of Arizona
CARLOS FUENTES (1928–   )
MARTÍN LUIS GUZMÁN
(1887–1976)

David T. Haberly
University of Virginia
ALUÍSIO AZEVEDO (1857–1913)
ANTÔNIO DE CASTRO ALVES
(1847–1871)

Aden W. Hayes
St. Lawrence University
ROBERTO ARLT (1900–1942)

Bonnie Hildebrand Reynolds
University of Louisville
RENÉ MARQUÉS (1919–1979)

Claude L. Hulet
University of California, Los
Angeles
ÉRICO VERÍSSIMO (1905–1975)

Regina Igel
University of Maryland, College
Park
CECÍLIA MEIRELES (1901–1964)

Julie Greer Johnson
University of Georgia, Athens
FERNÁN GONZÁLEZ DE ESLAVA
(1534–1601?)

Sonja P. Karsen
Skidmore College
JAIME TORRES BODET (1902–1974)
GUILLERMO VALENCIA
(1873–1943)

Dolores M. Koch
Herbert H. Lehman College,
CUNY
REINALDO ARENAS (1943–   )

Efraín Kristal
Harvard University

CLORINDA MATTO DE TURNER
(1852–1909)

John W. Kronik
Cornell University
ENRIQUE GÓMEZ CARRILLO
(1873–1927)

Vera M. Kutzinski
Yale University
NICOLÁS GUILLÉN (1902–   )

Ramón Layera
Miami University
RODOLFO USIGLI (1905–1979)

Luis Leal
University of California at Santa
Barbara
MARIANO AZUELA (1873–1952)
JOSÉ RUBÉN ROMERO (1890–1952)
JUAN RULFO (1918–1986)

Maria Teresa Leal
Rice University
ARIANO VILAR SUASSUNA
(1927–   )

Isaías Lerner
Herbert H. Lehman College,
CUNY
DON ALONSO DE ERCILLA Y
ZÚÑIGA (1533–1594)

Kurt L. Levy
University of Toronto
TOMÁS CARRASQUILLA
(1858–1940)

Myron I. Lichtblau
Syracuse University
MANUEL GÁLVEZ (1882–1962)
EDUARDO MALLEA (1903–1982)

Naomi Lindstrom
University of Texas at Austin
MACEDONIO FERNÁNDEZ
(1874–1952)

Lily Litvak
University of Texas at Austin

JOSÉ ASUNCIÓN SILVA
(1865–1896)

Fábio Lucas
Writer and Critic
LYGIA FAGUNDES TELLES
(1923–   )

William Luis
Dartmouth College
CIRILO VILLAVERDE (1812–1894)

Adelia Lupi
Universita di Perugia
ENRIQUE LARRETA (1873–1961)

Alfred J. MacAdam
Barnard College and Columbia
University
GUILLERMO CABRERA INFANTE
(1929–   )

Javier Malagón
Embassy of Spain, Washington,
D.C.
BARTOLOMÉ DE LAS CASAS
(1474–1566)

Juan Manuel Marcos
Oklahoma State University
AUGUSTO ROA BASTOS
(1917–   )

Heitor Martins
Indiana University
CLÁUDIO MANUEL DA COSTA
(1729–1789)

Elba Mata-Kolster
Independent Scholar
GERTRUDIS GÓMEZ DE
AVELLANEDA (1814–1873)
ANA TERESA DE LA PARRA SANOJO
(1890–1936)

Graciela Maturo
Universidad Nacional de
Buenos Aires
LEOPOLDO MARECHAL
(1900–1970)

George R. McMurray
Colorado State University
GABRIEL GARCÍA MÁRQUEZ
(1928–   )

Gilberto Mendonça Teles
Pontifícia Universidade Católica
do Río de Janeiro
MANUEL BANDEIRA (1886–1968)

Seymour Menton
University of California at Irvine
FEDERICO GAMBOA (1864–1939)

Massaud Moisés
Universidade de São Paulo
MÁRIO DE ANDRADE (1893–1945)

Klaus Müller-Bergh
University of Illinois at Chicago
ALEJO CARPENTIER (1904–1980)

Cassiano Nunes
Universidade Federal de Brasília
JORGE DE LIMA (1893–1953)

María Rosa Olivera Williams
University of Notre Dame
MARIO BENEDETTI (1920–   )

Julio Ortega
Brandeis University
JOSÉ MARÍA ARGUEDAS
(1911–1969)
CÉSAR VALLEJO (1892–1938)

Elizabeth Otero Krauthamner
Southwest Texas State University
MANUEL PUIG (1932–   )

José Miguel Oviedo
University of California, Los
Angeles
RICARDO PALMA (1833–1919)

J. E. Pacheco
Universidad Nacional Autónoma
de México
JOSÉ GOROSTIZA (1901–1979)

Antonio Pagés Larraya
Universidad Nacional de Buenos
Aires
JOSÉ HERNÁNDEZ (1834–1886)
RICARDO ROJAS (1882–1957)

Alfredo Pareja Diezcanseco
Writer, Historian, and Critic
JUAN MONTALVO (1832–1889)

Fernando da Rocha Peres
Universidade Federal da Bahia
GREGÓRIO DE MATTOS
(1636–1695)

Allen W. Phillips
University of California at Santa
Barbara
RAMÓN LÓPEZ VELARDE
(1888–1921)

Evelyn Picon Garfield
University of Illinois at
Urbana-Champaign
JULIO CORTÁZAR (1914–1984)
GRISELDA GAMBARO (1928–   )
LUISA VALENZUELA (1938–   )

Argyll Pryor Rice
Connecticut College
EMILIO BALLAGAS (1908–1954)

Enrique Pupo-Walker
Vanderbilt University
EL INCA GARCILASO DE LA VEGA
(1539–1616)
JORGE ISAACS (1837–1895)

L. Howard Quackenbush
Brigham Young University
SAMUEL EICHELBAUM
(1894–1967)

José Rabasa
University of Maryland, College
Park
BERNARDO DE BALBUENA
(1561?–1627)

Daniel R. Reedy
University of Kentucky
JUAN DEL VALLE Y CAVIEDES
(1645?–1697?)

James Willis Robb
George Washington University
ALFONSO REYES (1889–1959)

Alfredo A. Roggiano
University of Pittsburgh
JOSÉ MARÍA HEREDIA
(1803–1839)
RICARDO E. MOLINARI
(1898–   )

Grinor Rojo
Ohio State University
LUIS ALBERTO HEIREMANS
(1928–1964)

Fernando Rosemberg
Universidad Nacional de Buenos
Aires
ENRIQUE ANDERSON IMBERT
(1910–   )

Jorge Ruffinelli
Stanford University
EDUARDO ACEVEDO DÍAZ
(1851–1921)
RÓMULO GALLEGOS (1884–1969)

Alberto Ruy-Sánchez
Artes de México
OCTAVIO PAZ (1914–   )

Georgina Sabat-Rivers
State University of New York,
Stony Brook
SOR JUANA INÉS DE LA CRUZ
(1651–1695)

Raymond S. Sayers
Queens College, CUNY
JOÃO DA CRUZ E SOUSA
(1861–1898)

George D. Schade
University of Texas at Austin
ALBERTO BLEST GANA
(1830–1920)
EUGENIO CAMBACERES
(1843–1889)
PABLO NERUDA (1904–1973)
HORACIO QUIROGA (1878–1937)

Ivan A. Schulman
University of Illinois at
Urbana-Champaign
MANUEL GUTIÉRREZ NÁJERA
(1859–1895)
JOSÉ MARTÍ (1853–1895)

Guillermo Servando Pérez
Universidad Simón Bolívar,
Caracas
RUFINO BLANCO FOMBONA
(1874–1944)

Alexandrino Severino
Vanderbilt University
CLARICE LISPECTOR (1925–1977)

Antonio Skármeta
Writer and Critic
NICANOR PARRA (1914–   )

Martin S. Stabb
Pennsylvania State University

ARTURO USLAR PIETRI
(1906–   )

Guillermo Sucre
Biblioteca Ayacucho, Caracas
MARIANO PICÓN SALAS
(1901–1965)

J. David Suarez-Torres
Georgetown University
GERMÁN ARCINIEGAS
(1900–   )
JOSÉ EUSTASIO RIVERA
(1888–1928)

Augusto Tamayo y Vargas
Academia Peruana de la Lengua
JOSÉ SANTOS CHOCANO
(1875–1934)

Vera Regina Teixeira
Northwestern University
ALCEU AMOROSO LIMA
(1893–1983)

Antonio Urrello
University of British Columbia
CIRO ALEGRÍA (1909–1967)

Carlos Valderrama Andrade
Instituto Caro y Cuervo, Bogotá
MIGUEL ANTONIO CARO
(1843–1909)

Hugo J. Verani
University of California at Davis
JUAN CARLOS ONETTI
(1909–   )

Jon S. Vincent
University of Kansas at Lawrence
JORGE AMADO (1912–   )

Nancy Vogeley
University of San Francisco
JOSÉ JOAQUÍN FERNÁNDEZ DE
LIZARDI (1776–1827)

John Walker
Queens University, Canada
EDUARDO BARRIOS (1884–1963)

George Woodyard
University of Kansas at Lawrence
JORGE DÍAZ (1930–   )
OSVALDO DRAGÚN (1929–   )

Donald A. Yates
Michigan State University
MARCO DENEVI (1922–   )

Richard Zenith
Independent Scholar
JOÃO CABRAL DE MELO NETO
(1920–   )